The Golf
Course Guide
2012

AA Lifestyle Guides

D1384233

Please contact:
Advertising Sales Department: advertisingsales@theAA.com
Editorial Department: lifestyleguides@theAA.com
AA Hotel Scheme Enquiries: 01256 844455

The Automobile Association would like to thank the following photographers, companies and picture libraries for their assistance in the preparation of this book.

Abbreviations for the picture credits are as follows – (t) top; (b) bottom; (c) centre; (l) left; (r) right; (AA) AA World Travel Library.

Front Cover (t) Abbey Hotel Golf & Country Club; (bl) Getty Images/MedioImages: (br) Carnoustie Golf Links; Back Cover (l) Getty Images/MedioImages; (c) Fulwell Golf Club: (r) Mallow Golf Club

1 Forest of Dean Golf Club & Bells Hotel; 3bl Malin Court; 3br AA/Jonathan Smith; 4tl Corbis; 4b Menzies Welcombe Hotel Spa & Golf Club; 5t Cooden Beach Golf Club; 5b Leighton Buzzard Golf Club; 6tl Corbis; 6c Crews Hill Golf Club; 9 New Wilmington Hotel; 8tl Corbis; 10tl Corbis; 12tl Corbis; 14/15 Dale Hill Golf Club; 308/309 AA/Jim Henderson; 384/385 AA/Chris Warren; 415 AA/Karl Blackwell; 429 AA/Chris Hill.

Every effort has been made to trace the copyright holders, and we apologise in advance for any unintentional omissions or errors. We would be pleased to apply any corrections in a following edition of this publication.

Typeset/repro by Servis Filmsetting Ltd, Manchester
Printed and bound in Italy by Printer Trento S.r.l

A CIP catalogue record for this book is available from the British Library

ISBN 978-0-7495-7070-5
A04609

Maps prepared by the
Mapping Services Department
of AA Publishing.
© AA Media Limited 2011.

Contains Ordnance Survey data
© Crown copyright and database right 2011

Land &
Property
Services.
This is based upon Crown Copyright and is reproduced with the permission of Land & Property Services under delegated authority from the Controller of Her Majesty's Stationery Office.
© Crown copyright and database rights 2011
Licence number 100,363. Permit number 110023

Ordnance
Survey
Ireland
Ireland's National Mapping Agency
Republic of Ireland mapping based on
© Ordnance Survey Ireland/Government of Ireland
Copyright Permit number MP000611

Contents

Welcome

Welcome to the AA Golf Course Guide 2012. The guide includes revised and updated information for over 2,500 courses. Whether you want to know about courses near your home that you haven't played, or what your holiday might offer you in the way of new challenges, you should find plenty of choice here.

Golf is one of the most democratic of sports. Unlike football or rugby, amateur players always have the opportunity of following in the actual footsteps of the some of the most famous names in the game.

On pages 10 and 12 you'll find the Championship Course finder which will give you at-a-glance information about the top courses (feature pages and extensive descriptions can be found within the main gazetteer). Throughout the guide, courses of particular merit or interest are highlighted.

This guide also contains AA-recommended Hotels and Guest Accommodation establishments. After most entries you'll find details of local hotels or B&Bs, complete with their ratings. See pages 6-9 for more details on how to use this information.

The expanded index section means there are several ways to find a course to play. To browse by place name see page 497, or if you know a specific course you could try the Course Name Index on page 507. Alternatively, if you just want to practice

your swing, there's the Driving Range index on page 487.

So, if you are interested in reliving the glories of a well-known golfing moment, looking to organise a golfing trip with friends or just feel like playing a few holes down the back nine of your local municipal course, you'll be able to find a place to play and stay in the AA Golf Course Guide 2012.

To recommend a new course for the guide, please write to:
The Editor, AA Golf Course Guide,
Fanum House, Basingstoke,
Hampshire RG21 4EA

How to Use the Guide

The golf courses in the AA Golf Course Guide are selected by the AA and their entry is free of charge. The guide is updated every year for new courses, changes, closures and new features, and AA recommended accommodation follows most entries. To avoid disappointment we recommend that you phone before visiting a golf course; please mention the guide when you make an enquiry. The country directories are arranged alphabetically by county, then by town or village name. The town or village locations are shown on the atlas and listed in the index. A sample entry is explained below.

1 Town name and map reference
The atlas at the end of the guide (page 470) shows the locations of the courses.
The map reference includes the atlas page number and the National Grid reference. The grid references for the Republic of Ireland are unique to this atlas.

2 Club name and contact details
Where the club name appears in *italics* we have been unable to verify current course details with the club. If a club or course has not responded to our invitation to amend their details for two or more years, we show reduced details for them. You should check any details with the club before your visit.

3 Description The description highlights the significant features of the course or courses.

4 Course statistics The number of holes, distance, par, Standard Scratch Score, Course Record, and the number of club members.

5 Visitor information Playing days, booking requirements or restrictions are noted.
A small number of courses in the guide are not open to visitors and we have included their details for information only.

6 Society information Booking requirements or restrictions for societies.

7 Green fees The most up-to-date green fees are given, including any variations or restrictions. Where green fees are not confirmed you should contact the club for current rates.

8 Professional The name of the club professional(s).

1 **CHELMSFORD** **Map 5 TL70**

2 **Channels Golf Club** Belstead Farm Ln, Little Waltham CM3 3PT
☎ 01245 440005 01245 442032
e-mail: info@channelsgolf.co.uk
web: www.channelsgolf.co.uk

3 The Channels course is built on land from reclaimed gravel pits, 18 very exciting holes with plenty of lakes providing an excellent test of golf. Belsteads, a nine-hole course, is mainly flat but has three holes where water has to be negotiated.

4 *Channels Course: 18 Holes, 6413yds, Par 71, SSS 71, Course record 65.*
Belsteads: 9 Holes, 2467yds, Par 34, SSS 32.
Club membership 800.

5 **Visitors** Mon-Fri except BHs. Booking required. **Societies** booking 6
7 required. **Green Fees** phone **Course Designer** Cotton & Swan **Prof** Ian 8
Sinclair **Facilities** 9
Leisure fishing, 9 hole pitch & putt course. **Conf** facs Corporate 10
Hospitality Days **Location** 2m NE on A130 11
12 **Hotel** ★★★ 80% HL County Hotel, 29 Rainsford Road, CHELMSFORD ☎ 01245 455700 01245 492762 50 en suite

9 Facilities See the key to symbols on page 7.

10 Conference facilities The available conference facilities are noted, and corporate hospitality days.

⑪ Location The location of the club is given in relation to the nearest town or motorway junction. Many golf courses are in rural locations and we do not provide detailed directions in the guide. You should contact the club for further details, or use the AA Route Planner at theAA.com.

⑫ Accommodation An AA rated hotel is provided for most entries. This does not imply that the hotel offers special terms for the golf club, though in some cases the golf course is in the grounds of the hotel. The Star rating, and Merit (%) score appear as applicable. Contact details and the number of rooms are given. Where there is no nearby AA recognised hotel, an AA guest accommodation is recommended. See pages 8-9 for details of AA ratings. Where golf courses offer club accommodation the bed symbol appears under Facilities. Unless the club accommodation has an AA Star classification, the only AA recognised accommodation is the hotel or guest house that follows the entry.

Golf courses and hotels in the guide can illustrate their entry with a photograph or an advertisement.

Championship courses

Major championship courses have a full-page entry in the guide with an extensive description. A list of championship courses can be found on pages 10-11.

Selected courses

Courses considered to be of particular merit or interest are highlighted with a green box. These may include historic clubs, particularly testing or enjoyable courses, or those in holiday areas popular with visiting golfers. The selection is not exhaustive nor totally objective, but it is independent - courses cannot pay to have an entry in the guide, nor can they pay to have a highlighted entry. Highlighted courses do not represent any formal category on quality or other grounds.

Key to symbols

☎	Phone number
🖹	Fax number
€	Euro (Republic of Ireland)
ⓘ	Lunch
🍽	Dinner
🍺	Bar snacks
☕	Tea/coffee
🍷	Bar open midday and evenings
◇	Accommodation at club
⌲	Changing rooms
🏬	Well stocked shop
🏌	Clubs for hire
🛒	Motorized cart/trolley for hire
🚙	Buggies for hire
🛒	Trolley for hire
🏌	Driving range
★	AA star rating
Ⓤ	Hotel not yet rated by the AA
⚊	Credit cards not accepted

Links to other sections of the book

AA Hotel & Guest Accommodation

The AA inspects and rates establishments under two different accommodation schemes. Guest houses, B&Bs, farmhouses and inns are rated under the Guest Accommodation Scheme and hotels are rated under the Hotel Scheme. Establishments recognised by the AA pay an annual fee according to the rating and the number of bedrooms.

Star Quality

Stars shown in the guide indicate where the accommodation has been rated by the AA under a common standard rating agreed between the AA, VisitBritain, VisitScotland and Visit Wales. Under the common standards, guests can be confident that, for example, a guest house anywhere in the UK and Ireland will offer consistent quality and facilities. The system also uses a brief description or designator to classify the establishment (abbreviations for these designators are described in the box opposite).

The Inspection Process

Establishments applying for AA recognition are visited by a qualified AA accommodation inspectors as a mystery guest. Inspectors stay overnight to make a thorough test of the accommodation, food, and hospitality. After paying the bill the following morning, they identify themselves and ask to be shown around the premises. The inspector completes a full report, resulting in a recommendation for the appropriate star rating. After this first visit, the establishment will receive an annual visit to check that standards are maintained. If it changes hands, the new owners must re-apply for rating, as standards can change.

AA Hotel Classification

★ In a one-Star hotel you should expect relatively informal yet competent service and an adequate range of facilities, including a television in the lounge or bedroom, and a reasonable choice of hot and cold dishes. The majority of bedrooms are en suite with a bath or shower room always available.

★★ Run by professionally presented staff and offers at least one restaurant or dining room for breakfast and dinner.

★★★ Three-Star hotels have direct-dial phones, a wide selection of drinks in the bar, and last orders for dinner no earlier than 8pm.

★★★★ A four-Star hotel is characterised by uniformed, well-trained staff, additional services, a night porter and a serious approach to cuisine.

★★★★★ Finally, and most luxurious of all, five-Star hotels offer many extra facilities, attentive staff, top-quality rooms and a full concierge service. A wide selection of drinks, including cocktails, are available in the bar, and the impressive menu reflects the hotel's own style of cooking.

% The Merit score appears after the Star rating for hotels in this guide. This is an additional assessment made by AA hotel inspectors, covering everything the hotel has to offer, including hospitality. The score allows a quick comparison between hotels with the same Star rating: the higher the score the better the hotel.

★ Red stars highlight the very best hotels in Britain and Ireland across all ratings. Such hotels offer outstanding levels of quality, comfort, cleanliness and customer care, and serve food of at least one-Rosette standard. No Merit score is shown for hotels with red Stars.

AA Guest Accommodation Classification

Guests can expect to find the following minimum standards at all levels:

- Pleasant and helpful welcome and service, and sound standards of housekeeping and maintenance
- Comfortable accommodation equipped to modern standards

- Bedding and towels changed for each new guest, and at least weekly if the room is taken for a long stay
- Adequate storage, heating, lighting and comfortable seating
- A sufficient hot water supply at reasonable times
- A full cooked breakfast. (If this is not provided, the fact must be advertised and a substantial continental breakfast must be offered.)

There are additional requirements for an establishment to achieve three, four or five Stars:

- Three Stars and above - access to both sides of all beds for double occupancy.
- Three Stars and above – bathrooms/shower rooms cannot be shared by the proprietor.
- Three Stars and above – a washbasin in every guest bedroom (either in the bedroom or the en suite/ private facility).
- Four Stars – half of the bedrooms must be en suite or have private facilities.

- Five Stars – all bedrooms must be en suite or have private facilities.

★ Yellow stars highlight the top 10% of establishments within the 3, 4 and 5 star ratings.

Designators

B&B	Private house managed by owner
GH	Guest house, a larger B&B
GA	Guest Accommodation
INN	Traditional inn with pub atmosphere
FH	B&B on working farm
HL	Hotel
SHL	Small hotel managed by owner
RR	Restaurant with rooms
THH	Town House Hotel
CHH	Country House Hotel
MH	Metro Hotel
BUD	Budget Hotel

Championship Courses

Name	Location	Course(s)	Map Ref	Page
Sunningdale	Sunningdale, Berkshire	Old Course: 18 holes, 6063yds, Par 70 New Course: 18 holes, 6083yds, Par 70	Map 04 SU96	25
Woburn	Little Brickhill, Buckinghamshire	Duke's Course: 18 holes, 6976yds, Par 72 Duchess Course: 18 holes, 6651yds, Par 72 Marquess Course: 18 holes, 7214yds, Par 72	Map 04 SP93	31
St Mellion International Resort	St Mellion, Cornwall	Nicklaus Signature Course: 18 holes, 7010yds, Par 72 Kernow Course: 18 holes, 5606yds, Par 69	Map 04 SX36	51
Rockcliffe Hall	Darlington, Co, Durham	18 holes, 7879yds, Par 72	Map 08 NZ21	79
Old Thorns Golf & Country Estate	Liphook, Hampshire	18 holes, 6461yds, Par 72	Map 04 SU83	121
Marriott Hanbury Manor Golf & Country Club	Ware, Hertfordshire	18 holes, 6124yds, Par 72	Map 05 TL31	133
Royal St George's	Sandwich, Kent	18 holes, 7204, Par 70	Map 05 TR35	143
Royal Lytham & St Annes	Lytham St Annes, Lancashire	18 holes, 6882yds, Par 71	Map 07 SD32	153
The National Golf Centre	Woodhall Spa, Lincolnshire	The Hotchkin: 18 holes, 7080yds, Par 71 The Bracken: 18 holes, 6719yds, Par 72	Map 08 TF16	169
Royal Liverpool	Hoylake, Merseyside	18 holes, 6452yds, Par 72	Map 07 SJ28	177
Royal Birkdale	Southport, Merseyside	18 holes, 6381yds, Par 72	Map 07 SD31	181
Wentworth	Virginia Water, Surrey	West Course: 18 holes, 7308yds, Par 72 East Course: 18 holes, 6201yds, Par 68 Edinburgh Course: 18 holes, 7004yds, Par 72	Map 04 TQ06	239
Walton Heath	Walton-on-the-Hill, Surrey	Old Course: 18 holes, 7406yds, Par 72 New Course: 18 holes, 7175yds, Par 72	Map 04 TQ25	241
East Sussex National Golf Resort & Spa	Uckfield, East Sussex	East Course: 18 holes, 7138yds, Par 72 West Course: 18 holes, 7154yds, Par 72	Map 05 TQ42	247
The Belfry	Wishaw, Warwickshire	The Brabazon: 18 holes, 7160yds, Par 72 PGA National: 18 holes, 7053yds, Par 72 The Derby: 18 holes, 6057yds, Par 69	Map 07 SP19	259
Marriott Forest of Arden Hotel & Country Club	Meriden, West Midlands	Arden Course: 18 holes, 7213yds, Par 72 Aylesford Course: 18 holes, 5801, Par 69	Map 04 SP28	265
Carnoustie Golf Links	Carnoustie, Angus	Championship: 18 holes, 6941yds, Par 72 Burnside: 18 holes, 6028, Par 68 Buddon Links: 18 holes, 5420yds, Par 66	Map 12 NO53	317

10

continued on page 12

why not spend less and relax more on UK breaks?

Make AA Travel your first destination and you're on the way to a more relaxing golf break or holiday.

AA Members and customers can get great deals on accommodation, from B&Bs to farmhouses, inns and hotels.

You can also save up to 10% at cottages4you, enjoy a 5% discount with Hoseasons, and up to 60% off the very best West End shows.

Thinking of going further afield?

Check out our attractive discounts on car hire, airport parking, ferry bookings, travel insurance and much more.

Then simply relax.

These are just some of our well-known partners:

Visit theAA.com/travel

Name	Location	Course(s)	Map Ref	Page
Muirfield: The Honourable Company of Edinburgh Golfers	Gullane, East Lothian	Murfield Course: 18 holes, 6673yds, Par 70	Map 12 NT68	331
Marriott Dalmahoy Hotel, Golf & Country Club	Edinburgh	East Course: 18 holes, 6814yds, Par 73 West Course: 18 holes, 5051yds, Par 68	Map 11 NT27	335
St Andrews Links	St Andrews, Fife	Old Course: 18 holes, 6721yds, Par 72 New Course: 18 holes, 6625yds, Par 71 Jubilee Course: 18 holes, 6742yds, Par 72 Eden Course: 18 holes, 6112yds, Par 70 Strathtyrum Course:18 holes, 5094yds, Par 69 Castle Course: 18 holes, 7200yds, Par 72 Balgove Course: 9 holes, 1530yds, Par 30	Map 12 NO51	345
Royal Dornoch	Dornoch, Highland	Championship Course: 18 holes, 6595yds, Par 70 Struie Course: 18 holes, 6192yds, Par 71	Map 14 NH78	349
Gleneagles Hotel	Auchterarder, Perth and Kinross	King's Course: 18 holes, 6471yds, Par 70 Queen's Course: 18 holes, 5965yds, Par 68 PGA Centenary Course: 18 holes, 6815yds, Par 73	Map 11 NN91	363
Royal Troon	Troon, South Ayrshire	Old Course: 18 holes, 6641yds, Par 71 Portland: 18 holes, 6289yds, Par 71 Craigend: 9 holes, 1539yds, Par 29	Map 10 NS33	371
Turnberry Resort	Turnberry, South Ayrshire	Ailsa Course: 18 holes, 7211yds, Par 70 Kintyre Course: 18 holes, 6921yds, Par 72 Arran Course: 9 holes, 1996, Par 31	Map 10 NS20	373
Aberdovey	Aberdyfi, Gwynedd	18 holes, 6615yds, Par 71	Map 06 SN69	399
Marriott St Pierre Hotel Country Club	Chepstow, Monmouthshire	Old Course: 18 holes, 7023yds, Par 72 Mathern Course: 18 holes, 5800, Par 68	Map 03 ST59	401
Celtic Manor Resort	Celtic Manor Resort, Newport	Roman Road: 18 holes, 6039yds, Par 70 Montgomerich: 18 holes, 5863yds, Par 69 Twenty Ten: 18 holes, 6570yds, Par 71	Map 03 ST38	405
Vale Resort	Hensol, Vale of Glamorgan	Lake Course: 18 holes, 6436yds, Par 72 Wales National: 18 holes. 7433yds, Par 73	Map 03 ST07	411
Royal Portrush	Co Antrim	Dunluce: 18 holes, 7143yds, Par 72 Valley: 18 holes, 6304yds, Par 70	Map 01 C6	419
Royal County Down	Newcastle, Co Down	Championship Course: 18 holes, 7181yds, Par 71 Annesley: 18 holes, 4681yds, Par 66	Map 01 D5	425
Fota Island Resort	Cork, Co Cork	Deerpark 18 holes, 6334 mtrs, Par 71 Belvelly 18 holes, 6511 mtrs, Par 72 Barryscourt 18 holes, 6732 mtrs, Par 73	Map 01 B2	433
Portmarnock	Portmarnock, Co Dublin	Red & Yellow Course: 18 holes, 7259yds, Par 73 Red & Blue Course: 18 holes, 7382yds, Par 73 Yellow & Blue Course: 18 holes, 7045yds, Par 73	Map 01 D4	443
Ballybunion	Ballybunion, Co Kerry	Old Course: 18 holes, 6236 mtrs, Par 71 Cashen: 18 holes, 5766 mtrs, Par 72	Map 01 A3	449
The K Club	Straffan, Co Kildare	Palmer Course: 18 holes, 6709 mtrs, Par 74 Smurfit Course: 18 holes, 6608 mtrs, Par 72	Map 01 D4	451
Mount Juliet Hotel	Thomastown, Co Kilkenny	18 holes, 6639metres, Par 72	Map 01 C3	453
Heritage Spa & Golf Resort	Killenard, Co Laois	18 holes, 6889yds, Par 72	Map 01 C3	455
Druids Glen Golf Club	Kilcoole, Co Wicklow	Druids Glen: 18 holes, 5998mtrs, Par 71 Druids Heath: 18 holes, 6062mtrs, Par 71	Map 01 D3	469

England

Dale Hill Golf Club, Ticehurst, East Sussex

BEDFORDSHIRE

ASPLEY GUISE
Map 4 SP93

Aspley Guise & Woburn Sands Golf Club West Hill MK17 8DX
☎ 01908 583596 📠 01908 288140 (Secretary)
e-mail: info@aspleyguisegolfclub.co.uk
web: www.aspleyguisegolfclub.co.uk

A fine undulating course in expansive heathland interspersed with many attractive clumps of gorse, broom and bracken. Some well-established silver birch is a feature. The really tough 7th, 8th and 9th holes complete the first half. Accuracy is the premium and a good putting touch will be required to score well. Built on sandy foundations, the course plays well all year.

18 Holes, 6079yds, Par 71, SSS 70, Course record 65.
Club membership 590.

Visitors Mon-Sun & BHs. Booking required. Handicap certificate. Dress code. Societies booking required. Green Fees £34 per round weekdays (£50 weekends) Course Designer Sandy Herd Prof Colin Clingan Facilities ⑪ ⑩ ⒧ ⬜ ⬚ ⬩ ⬛ ⬥ ⬦
Conf Corporate Hospitality Days Location M1 junct 13, 2m W
Hotel ★★★ 77% HL Best Western Moore Place, The Square, ASPLEY GUISE ☎ 01908 282000 📠 01908 281888 62 en suite

BEDFORD
Map 4 TL04

Bedford & County Golf Club Green Ln, Clapham MK41 6ET
☎ 01234 352617 📠 01234 357195
e-mail: office@bandcgc.co.uk
web: www.bandcgc.co.uk

A mature, undulating parkland course established in 1912, with views over Bedford and surrounding countryside. Beware of the brook that discreetly meanders through the 7th, 10th, 11th and 15th holes. The testing par 4 15th is one of the most challenging holes in the area.

18 Holes, 6420yds, Par 70, SSS 70, Course record 63.
Club membership 600.

Visitors dress code. Societies booking required. Green Fees £42 per day, £34 per round Prof R Tattersall Facilities ⑪ ⑩ ⒧ ⬜ ⬚ ⬩ ⬛ ⬦ Conf facs Corporate Hospitality Days Location 2m N of Bedford, off A6 in Clapham village
Hotel ★★★★ 73% HL The Barns Hotel, Cardington Road, BEDFORD ☎ 0844 855 9101 📠 01234 273102 49 en suite

The Bedford Golf Club Great Denham Golf Village, Carnoustie Dr, Biddenham MK40 4FF
☎ 01234 320022 📠 01234 320023
e-mail: info@thebedfordgc.com
web: www.thebedfordgc.com

American-style course with 89 bunkers, eight large water features and large contoured USPGA specification greens. Built on sand and gravel the course is open all year round and provides a good test of golf for both the beginner and the seasoned player.

18 Holes, 6471yds, Par 72, SSS 72, Course record 63.
Club membership 500.

Visitors contact for details Societies booking required. Green Fees £25 per 18 holes (£35 weekends) Course Designer David Pottage Prof Mark Litton Facilities ⑪ ⑩ ⒧ ⬜ ⬚ ⬩ ⬛

⬚ ⬩ ⬛ ⬦ ⬥ ⬛ ⬦ ⬥ Conf facs Corporate Hospitality Days
Location 2.5m W of Bedford off A428
Hotel ★★★ 70% HL Park Inn Bedford, 2 St Marys Street, BEDFORD ☎ 01234 799988 & 799900 📠 01234 799902 120 en suite

Bedfordshire Golf Club Spring Ln, Stagsden MK43 8SR
☎ 01234 822555 📠 01234 825052
e-mail: info@bedfordshiregolf.com
web: www.bedfordshiregolf.com

A challenging 18-hole course on undulating terrain with established trees and woods and water hazards. Magnificent views over surrounding countryside. The 9 hole academy course is ideal for those with less time, those learning the game or to work on your short game.

18 Holes, 6565yds, Par 70, SSS 71, Course record 65.
Academy Course: 9 Holes, 1354yds, Par 28.
Club membership 600.

Visitors Mon-Fri. Weekends & BHs pm. Dress code on 18 hole course. Societies booking required. Green Fees £32 per 18 holes (£40 weekends). 9 hole course £6.50 (£7.50 weekends) Course Designer Cameron Sinclair Prof Geraint Dixon Facilities ⑪ ⑩ by prior arrangement ⒧ ⬜ ⬚ ⬩ ⬛ ⬦ ⬥ ⬛ ⬦ ⬥
Conf facs Corporate Hospitality Days Location 3m W of Bedford on A422 at Stagsden
Hotel ★★★ 68% HL Woodland Manor Hotel, Green Lane, Clapham, BEDFORD ☎ 01234 363281 📠 01234 272390 34 en suite

Mowsbury Golf Club Cleat Hill, Kimbolton Rd, Ravensden MK41 8BJ
☎ 01234 772700 📠 01234 772700

Parkland municipal course in rural surroundings. Long and testing 13-bay driving range.

18 Holes, 6182yds, Par 72, SSS 69. Club membership 360.

Visitors Mon-Sun & BHs. Dress code. Societies booking required. Green Fees not confirmed Course Designer Hawtree Prof Malcolm Summers Facilities ⑪ ⑩ by prior arrangement ⒧ ⬜ ⬚ ⬩ ⬛ ⬦ ⬥ ⬛ ⬦ ⬥ Leisure squash Location 2m N of town centre on B660
Hotel ★★★ 68% HL Woodland Manor Hotel, Green Lane, Clapham, BEDFORD ☎ 01234 363281 📠 01234 272390 34 en suite

CHALGRAVE
Map 4 TL02

Chalgrave Manor Golf Club Dunstable Rd LU5 6JN
☎ 01525 876556 & 876554
e-mail: steve@chalgravegolf.co.uk
web: www.chalgravegolf.co.uk

Undulating parkland course set in 150 acres of Bedfordshire countryside. No two consecutive holes play in the same direction. Four holes have water hazards including the signature 10th hole, playing 130yds across water to a sloping green. The par 5 9th, at 621yds, is one of the longest holes in the country.

18 Holes, 6398yds, Par 72, SSS 70, Course record 69.
Club membership 550.

Visitors Mon-Fri. Weekends & BHs after 11.30am. Booking required weekends & BHs. Dress code. Societies booking required. Green Fees £23 per round (£35 weekends & BHs) Course Designer M Palmer Prof Simon Wagstaff Facilities ⑪ ⑩ by prior arrangement ⒧ ⬜ ⬚ ⬩ ⬛ ⬦ ⬥ Conf facs Corporate Hospitality Days Location M1 junct 12, A5120 through Toddington, signed 1m
Hotel ★★★★ 73% CHH Menzies Flitwick Manor, Church Road, FLITWICK ☎ 01525 712242 📠 01525 718753 18 en suite

COLMWORTH   Map 4 TL15

Colmworth & North Bedfordshire Golf Course New Rd
MK44 2NN
☎ 01234 378181 📄 01234 376678
e-mail: info@colmworthgolf club.co.uk
web: www.colmworthgolfclub.co.uk
An easy walking course with well-bunkered greens, opened in 1991.
The course is often windy and plays longer than the yardage suggests.
Water comes into play on three holes.
18 Holes, 6434yds, Par 72, SSS 71, Course record 67.
Club membership 250.
Visitors Mon-Sun & BHs. Booking required Fri-Sun & BHs.
Societies booking required. **Green Fees** £15 per 18 holes, £12 per
12 holes, £9 per 9 holes (£25/£17/£14 weekends & BHs) **Course
Designer** John Glasgow **Prof** Graham Bithrey **Facilities** ⊕ ⓧ
by prior arrangement ▨ ▱ ▰ ⚲ ▤ ▱ ◇ ▨ ✦ ⚡
Leisure fishing, par 3 course **Conf** facs Corporate Hospitality Days
Location off A1 between Bedford & St Neots
Hotel ★★★★ 73% HL The Barns Hotel, Cardington Road,
BEDFORD ☎ 0844 855 9101 📄 01234 273102 49 en suite

DUNSTABLE   Map 4 TL02

Caddington Golf Club Chaul End Rd, Caddington LU1 4AX
☎ 01582 415573 📄 01582 415314
e-mail: info@caddingtongolfclub.co.uk
web: www.caddingtongolfclub.co.uk
A challenging 18-hole parkland course with ponds and lakes on top
of Blows Downs.
18 Holes, 6226yds, Par 71, SSS 70, Course record 65.
Club membership 400.
Visitors Mon-Sun & BHs. Dress code. **Societies** booking required.
Green Fees £20 per round (£35 weekends) **Prof** Daren Turner
Facilities ⊕ ⓧ by prior arrangement ▨ ▱ ▰ ⚲ ▤ ▰
✦ ⚡**Leisure** indoor tuition studio **Conf** Corporate Hospitality Days
Location M1 junct 11 towards Dunstable, after 0.5m exit left at Tesco
rdbt, towards Luton
Hotel ★★★ INN The Highwayman, London Road, DUNSTABLE
☎ 01582 601122 📄 01582 603812 52 rooms

Dunstable Downs Golf Club Whipsnade Rd LU6 2NB
☎ 01582 604472 📄 01582 478700
e-mail: dunstabledownsgc@btconnect.com
web: www.dunstabledownsgolf.co.uk
A fine downland course set on two levels with far-reaching views
and frequent sightings of graceful gliders. The 9th hole is one of the
best short holes in the country.
18 Holes, 6303yds, Par 70, SSS 69, Course record 64.
Club membership 600.
Visitors Mon-Fri, Sun & BHs. Dress code. **Societies** booking
required. **Green Fees** £50 per day, £35 per round ▣ **Course
Designer** James Braid **Prof** Darren Charlton **Facilities** ⊕ ⓧ ▰
▱ ⓧ ⚲ ▤ ⚡ **Conf** facs Corporate Hospitality Days
Location 2m S off B4541
Hotel ★★★ INN The Highwayman, London Road, DUNSTABLE
☎ 01582 601122 📄 01582 603812 52 rooms

LEIGHTON BUZZARD   Map 4 SP92

Leighton Buzzard Golf Club Plantation Rd LU7 3JF
☎ 01525 244800 (Office) 📄 01525 244801
e-mail: lbgc.secretary1@btopenworld.com
web: www.leightonbuzzardgolf.net
Mature parkland and heathland with easy walking. The 17th and 18th
holes are challenging tree-lined finishing holes with tight fairways.
The par 3 11th is the signature hole.
18 Holes, 6101yds, Par 71, SSS 69. Club membership 700.
Visitors Mon, Wed-Fri except BHs. Dress code. **Societies** booking
required. **Green Fees** phone **Prof** Maurice Campbell **Facilities** ⊕ ⓧ
▨ ▱ ⓧ ⚲ ▤ ✦ ▰ ✦ **Conf** facs Corporate Hospitality
Days **Location** 1.5m N of town centre off A4146
Hotel ★★★ 80% HL The Inn at Woburn, George Street, WOBURN
☎ 01525 290441 📄 01525 290432 55 en suite

LOWER STONDON   Map 4 TL13

Mount Pleasant Golf Course Station Rd SG16 6JL
☎ 01462 850999
e-mail: tarasimkins@mountpleasantgolfclub.co.uk
web: www.mountpleasantgolfclub.co.uk
Undulating meadowland course with three ponds in play and many
tree plantations. A deep ditch, sometimes with water, runs through
the middle of the course and is crossed four times per nine holes.
The main feature of the course is its presentation and superb greens.
The course is seldom closed by bad weather. Stunning new clubhouse
opened in July 2010.
9 Holes, 6185yds, Par 70, SSS 70, Course record 67.
Club membership 300.
Visitors Mon-Sun & BHs. Booking required. Dress code.
Societies booking required. **Green Fees** £19 per 18 holes, £11 per
9 holes (£23/£13 weekends & BHs) **Course Designer** Derek Young
Prof Glen Kemble **Facilities** ⊕ ⓧ by prior arrangement ▨ ▱
ⓧ ⚲ ▤ ▰ ▰ ✦ **Leisure** undercover driving nets **Conf** facs
Corporate Hospitality Days **Location** 0.75m W of A600, 4m N of Hitchin
Hotel ★★★ 71% SHL Redcoats Farmhouse Hotel, Redcoats Green,
HITCHIN ☎ 01438 729500 📄 01438 723322 13 en suite

LUTON
Map 4 TL02

Luton Hoo Hotel, Golf & Spa The Mansion House LU1 3TQ
☎ 01582 698856
e-mail: golf@lutonhoo.com
web: www.elitehotels.co.uk

The front nine is quite open and has an inland links feel, the back nine meanders through mature parkland. An old 9 hole course was sited on 6 holes off the back nine. Water comes into play in 6 holes on the front nine. A serious test for all levels of golf with a choice of four different tees to play from.

*Luton Hoo: 18 Holes, 7107yds, Par 73, SSS 73,
Course record 67.*

Visitors Contact Hotel for details. **Societies** booking required. **Green Fees** £35 (£45 weekends & BHs). Twilight £25/£35 **Prof** Paul Simpson **Facilities** ⊕ ⚑ ᝰ ☕ 🍴 ♨ 🏌 🛒 ♿ ⛳ 🚗 ♿ **Leisure** hard and grass tennis courts, heated indoor swimming pool, sauna, gymnasium, bike hire, spa **Conf** facs Corporate Hospitality Days **Location** M1 junct 10A, 3rd exit to A1081 towards Harpenden/St Albans. Hotel less then a mile on left
Hotel ★★★★★ 89% HL Luton Hoo Hotel, Golf and Spa, The Mansion House, LUTON ☎ 01582 734437 & 698888 🖹 01582 485438 228 en suite

South Beds Golf Club Warden Hill Rd LU2 7AE
☎ 01582 591500 🖹 01582 495381
e-mail: office@southbedsgolfclub.co.uk
web: www.southbedsgolfclub.co.uk
18-hole and nine-hole chalk downland courses, slightly undulating.

*Galley Hill Course: 18 Holes, 6401yds, Par 71, SSS 71,
Course record 64.*
Warden Hill Course: 9 Holes, 4794yds, Par 64, SSS 63.
Club membership 1000.

Visitors Mon-Sun & BHs. Handicap certificate required for Galley Hill course. Dress code. **Societies** booking required. **Green Fees** phone **Prof** Michael Davis **Facilities** ⊕ ᝰ ☕ 🍴 🏌 🛒 ♿ ⛳ **Conf** Corporate Hospitality Days **Location** 3m N of Luton on A6
Hotel BUD Ibis London Luton Airport, Spittlesea Road, LUTON ☎ 01582 424488 🖹 01582 455511 162 en suite

Stockwood Park Golf Centre London Rd LU1 4LX
☎ 01582 413704 (pro shop)
18 Holes, 6049yds, Par 69, SSS 69, Course record 67.
Course Designer Charles Lawrie **Location** 1m S
Telephone for further details
Hotel ★★★★★ 89% HL Luton Hoo Hotel, Golf and Spa, The Mansion House, LUTON ☎ 01582 734437 & 698888 🖹 01582 485438 228 en suite

MILLBROOK
Map 4 TL03

The Millbrook Golf Club Millbrook Village MK45 2JB
☎ 01525 840252 & 402269 (booking) 🖹 01525 406249
e-mail: info@themillbrook.com
web: www.themillbrook.com
Long parkland course on rolling countryside high above the Bedfordshire plains. Laid out on well-drained sandy soil with many fairways lined with silver birch, pine and larch. The course provides a continuous test of the tee where length and accuracy pay a huge premium.

18 Holes, 6966yds, Par 73, SSS 73, Course record 68.
Club membership 560.

Visitors Mon-Fri. Weekends & BHs pm only. Dress code.
Societies booking required. **Green Fees** £30 per 18 holes Tue-Fri (£20 Mon) **Course Designer** William Sutherland **Prof** Robert Brightman **Facilities** ⊕ ᝰ ☕ 🍴 🏌 🛒 ♿ ⛳ 🚗 ♿ **Conf** facs Corporate Hospitality Days **Location** M1 junct 12/13, A507 Woburn-Ampthill road
Hotel ★★★ 77% HL Best Western Moore Place, The Square, ASPLEY GUISE ☎ 01908 282000 🖹 01908 281888 62 en suite

PAVENHAM
Map 4 SP95

Pavenham Park Golf Club High St MK43 7PE
☎ 01234 822202
e-mail: pavenhampark@o2.co.uk
web: www.pavenhampark.com
Mature, undulating parkland with fast contoured greens.

18 Holes, 6351yds, Par 72, SSS 71, Course record 65.
Club membership 790.

Visitors Mon-Sun & BHs. Booking required. Dress code.
Societies booking required. **Green Fees** not confirmed **Course Designer** Zac Thompson **Prof** Zac Thompson **Facilities** ⊕ ᝰ ☕ 🍴 🏌 🛒 ♿ ⛳ **Leisure** 100 yd short game zone **Conf** facs Corporate Hospitality Days **Location** 1.5m from A6, N of Bedford
Hotel ★★★ 68% HL Woodland Manor Hotel, Green Lane, Clapham, BEDFORD ☎ 01234 363281 🖹 01234 272390 34 en suite

SANDY
Map 4 TL14

John O'Gaunt Golf Club Sutton Park SG19 2LY
☎ 01767 260360 🖹 01767 262834
e-mail: admin@johnogauntgolfclub.co.uk
web: www.johnogauntgolfclub.co.uk
Two magnificent parkland courses - John O'Gaunt and Carthagena - covering a gently undulating and tree-lined terrain. The John O'Gaunt course makes the most of numerous natural features, notably a river which crosses the fairways of four holes. The Carthagena course has larger greens, longer tees and from the back tees is a challenging course.

*John O'Gaunt Course: 18 Holes, 6513yds, Par 71, SSS 71,
Course record 64.*
Carthagena Course: 18 Holes, 5869yds, Par 69, SSS 69.
Club membership 1500.

Visitors Mon-Sun & BHs. Booking required. Handicap certificate required. Dress code. **Societies** booking required. **Green Fees** not confirmed **Course Designer** Hawtree **Prof** Lee Scarbrow **Facilities** ⊕ ᝰ ☕ 🍴 🏌 ♿ ⛳ **Conf** Corporate Hospitality Days **Location** 3m NE of Biggleswade on B1040
Hotel ★★★★ 73% HL The Barns Hotel, Cardington Road, BEDFORD ☎ 0844 855 9101 🖹 01234 273102 49 en suite

SHEFFORD   Map 4 TL13

Beadlow Manor Hotel & Golf & Country Club SG17 5PH
☎ 01525 860800   📠 01525 861345
e-mail: office@beadlowmanor.co.uk
web: www.beadlowmanor.co.uk

A 36-hole golf and leisure complex. The Baroness Manhattan and the Baron Manhattan courses are undulating with water hazards on numerous holes. These are good challenging courses for both the beginner and low handicap player.

Baroness Course: 18 Holes, 5792yds, Par 71, SSS 68.
Baron Course: 18 Holes, 6341yds, Par 73, SSS 70.
Club membership 500.

Visitors Mon-Sun & BHs. Dress code. **Societies** booking required.
Green Fees not confirmed **Facilities** 🏦 🍴 🛍 🖤 🏌 🏊
🏠 🏇 ♦ ♂ 🛒 ♂ 🏇 **Conf** facs Corporate Hospitality Days
Location on A507
Hotel ★★★★ 73% CHH Menzies Flitwick Manor, Church Road,
FLITWICK ☎ 01525 712242 📠 01525 718753 18 en suite

TILSWORTH   Map 4 SP92

Tilsworth Golf Centre Dunstable Rd LU7 9PU
☎ 01525 210721/2   📠 01525 210465
e-mail: nick@tilsworthgolf.co.uk
web: www.tilsworthgolf.co.uk

The course is in first-class condition and, although not a long course, is particularly demanding and challenging where the key is straight driving. The course has its own Amen Corner between the 14th and 16th holes, which will challenge all golfers. Panoramic views of three counties from the 6th tee.

18 Holes, 5306yds, Par 69, SSS 67, Course record 64.
Club membership 400.

Visitors Mon-Sun & BHs. Dress code. **Societies** booking required.
Green Fees £19 for 18 holes (£21 weekends & BHs) **Prof** Nick Webb
Facilities 🏦 🍴 🛍 🖤 🏌 🏊 🏠 🏇 ♦ ♂ 🛒 ♂ 🏇
Conf facs Corporate Hospitality Days **Location** 0.5m NE off A5, N of
Dunstable
Hotel ★★★ INN The Highwayman, London Road, DUNSTABLE
☎ 01582 601122 📠 01582 603812 52 rooms

WYBOSTON   Map 4 TL15

Wyboston Lakes Great North Rd MK44 3AL
☎ 01480 212625   📠 01480 223000
e-mail: golf@wybostonlakes.co.uk
web: www.wybostonlakes.co.uk

Parkland with narrow fairways and small greens, set around four lakes and a river, which provide the biggest challenge on this very scenic course.

18 Holes, 6000yds, Par 70, SSS 68, Course record 63.
Club membership 375.

Visitors Mon-Sun & BHs. Booking required weekends & BHs.
Societies booking required. **Green Fees** phone **Course Designer** N
Oakden **Prof** Paul Ashwell **Facilities** 🏦 🍴 🛍 🖤 🏌 🏊
🏠 🏇 ♂ 🛒 ♂ 🏇 **Leisure** heated indoor swimming
pool, fishing, sauna, gymnasium, watersports **Conf** facs Corporate
Hospitality Days **Location** 1m S of St Neots off A1/A428
Hotel ★★★ 73% HL Wyboston Lakes Hotel, Wyboston Lakes,
Great North Road, WYBOSTON ☎ 01480 212625 & 479300
📠 01480 223000 103 en suite

BERKSHIRE

ASCOT   Map 4 SU96

The Berkshire Golf Club Swinley Rd SL5 8AY
☎ 01344 621495   📠 01344 623328
e-mail: secretary@theberkshire.co.uk
web: www.theberkshire.co.uk

Two classic heathland courses, with splendid tree-lined fairways, that have remained the same since they were constructed in 1928. The Red Course, on slightly higher ground, is a little longer than the Blue. It has an unusual assortment of holes, six par 3s, six par 4s and six par 5s, the short holes, particularly the 10th and 16th, being the most intimidating. The Blue Course starts with a par 3 and shares with the 16th the reputation of being the finest holes of the 18. Both courses are in the Top 100 in Europe and the Red Course is in the Top 50 in the world.

Red Course: 18 Holes, 6452yds, Par 72, SSS 71.
Blue Course: 18 Holes, 6398yds, Par 71, SSS 71.
Club membership 1000.

Visitors Mon-Fri except BHs. Sun pm only. Booking required. Dress
code. **Societies** booking required. **Green Fees** £150 per day, £120 per
round (£150 weekends) **Course Designer** H Fowler **Prof** P Anderson
Facilities 🏦 🛍 🖤 🏌 🏊 🏠 🏇 ♂ 🛒 ♂ 🏇 **Conf** facs
Corporate Hospitality Days **Location** M3 junct 3, 2.5m NW on A332
Hotel ★★★★ 78% HL Macdonald Berystede Hotel &
Spa, Bagshot Road, Sunninghill, ASCOT ☎ 0844 879 9104
📠 01344 872301 126 en suite

Lavender Park Golf Centre Swinley Rd SL5 8BD
☎ 01344 893344
e-mail: lavenderpark@yahoo.com
web: www.lavenderparkgolf.co.uk
Public parkland course, ideal for the short game featuring challenging narrow fairways. Driving range with nine-hole par 3 course, floodlit until 10pm.

9 Holes, 1102yds, Par 27, SSS 28.

Visitors Mon-Sun & BHs. **Societies** welcome. **Green Fees** phone **Prof** David Johnson **Facilities** ⬜ 🍴 🏠 ⛳ ✏ 🏌
Leisure snooker **Location** 1.5m W of Ascot, off the A329 on the B3017
Hotel ★★★★ 78% HL Macdonald Berystede Hotel & Spa, Bagshot Road, Sunninghill, ASCOT ☎ 0844 879 9104 📄 01344 872301 126 en suite

Mill Ride Golf & Country Club Mill Ride SL5 8LT
☎ 01344 886777 (tee times) & 01344 891494
📄 01344 886820
e-mail: f.greenwood@mill-ride.com
web: www.mill-ride.com
Formerly a prestigious polo club and stud of King George V, this 18-hole course combines links and parkland styles. The manicured and cross cut fairways intermingle with lakes and the mounding and hollows which gives the course a unique parkland design coupled with an inland links feel to the starting and closing holes.

18 Holes, 6885yds, Par 72, SSS 73. Club membership 350.

Visitors Mon-Fri. Weekends & BHs after noon. Booking required. Dress code. **Societies** booking required. **Green Fees** not confirmed **Course Designer** Donald Steel **Prof** Terry Wild **Facilities** ⓘ 🍴 🏠 ⬜ 🍴 🏠 ⛳ 🏌 **Leisure** sauna, gymnasium **Conf** facs Corporate Hospitality Days **Location** 2m W of Ascot
Hotel ★★★★ 78% HL Macdonald Berystede Hotel & Spa, Bagshot Road, Sunninghill, ASCOT ☎ 0844 879 9104 📄 01344 872301 126 en suite

Royal Ascot Golf Club Winkfield Rd SL5 7LJ
☎ 01344 625175 📄 01344 872330
e-mail: admin@royalascotgolfclub.co.uk
web: www.royalascotgolfclub.co.uk

Situated in a former medieval deer park, east of Ascot Racecourse. A challenging parkland course bounded by the mature woodland setting of Windsor Forest. The attractive undulating and mature course has been designed to the latest international golfing standards, with tees and greens meeting USGA specifications.

18 Holes, 5836yds, Par 70, SSS 69. Club membership 600.

Visitors Mon-Sun & BHs. Handicap certificate. Dress code. **Societies** booking required. **Green Fees** £40 per day (£55 weekends)

Course Designer Jonathan Tucker **Prof** Alistair White **Facilities** ⓘ 🍴 🏠 ⬜ 🍴 🏠 ⛳ 🏠 🏌 **Conf** Corporate Hospitality Days **Location** 0.5m N on A330
Hotel ★★★★ 78% HL Macdonald Berystede Hotel & Spa, Bagshot Road, Sunninghill, ASCOT ☎ 0844 879 9104 📄 01344 872301 126 en suite

See advert on opposite page

Swinley Forest Golf Club Coronation Rd SL5 9LE
☎ 01344 295283 (Secretary) & 620197 (clubhouse)
📄 01344 874733
e-mail: office@swinleyfgc.co.uk
An attractive and immaculate course of heather and pine situated in the heart of Swinley Forest. The 17th is as good a short hole as can be found, with a bunkered plateau green, and the 12th is one of the most challenging par 4s.

18 Holes, 6019yds, Par 68, SSS 70.
Club membership 350.

Visitors Mon-Fri except BHs. Booking required. Handicap certificate. Dress code. **Societies** booking required. **Green Fees** not confirmed **Course Designer** Harry Colt **Prof** Stuart Hill **Facilities** ⓘ 🏠 ⬜ 🍴 🏠 ⛳ 🏠 🏌 **Conf** Corporate Hospitality Days **Location** 2m S of Ascot, off A30
Hotel ★★★★ 78% HL Macdonald Berystede Hotel & Spa, Bagshot Road, Sunninghill, ASCOT ☎ 0844 879 9104 📄 01344 872301 126 en suite

BINFIELD   Map 4 SU87

Blue Mountain Golf Centre Wood Ln RG42 4EX
☎ 01344 300200 📄 01344 360960
web: www.bluemountaingolf.co.uk
18 Holes, 6097yds, Par 70, SSS 70, Course record 63.
Location From M4 junct 10, take A329(M) signed Bracknell. 1st exit signed B3408 Binfield. Straight over rdbt and lights to next rdb. 2nd exit, 1st left into Wood Lane
Telephone for further details
Hotel ★★★★ 75% HL Coppid Beech, John Nike Way, BRACKNELL ☎ 01344 303333 📄 01344 301200 205 en suite

CAVERSHAM   Map 4 SU77

Caversham Heath Golf Club Chazey Heath RG4 7UT
☎ 0118 947 8600 📄 0118 947 8700
web: www.cavershamgolf.co.uk
18 Holes, 7151yds, Par 73, SSS 73, Course record 66.
Course Designer David Williams **Location** 2m NE of Caversham on A4074 towards Oxford
Telephone for further details
Hotel ★★★★ 78% HL Novotel Reading Centre, 25b Friar Street, READING ☎ 0118 952 2600 📄 0118 952 2610 178 en suite

CHADDLEWORTH   Map 4 SU47

West Berkshire Golf Course RG20 7DU
☎ 01488 638574 🖩 01488 638781
e-mail: info@thewbgc.co.uk
web: www.thewbgc.co.uk
Challenging and interesting downland course with views of the Berkshire Downs. The course is bordered by ancient woodland and golfers will find manicured fairways with well-constructed greens and strategically placed hazards. The testing 627yd 5th hole is one of the longest par 5s in southern England. Bunkers are well placed from tees and around the greens to catch any wayward shots.

18 Holes, 7022yds, Par 73, SSS 74. Club membership 450.
Visitors Mon-Fri & BHs. Weekends pm. Booking required weekends & BHs. Dress code. **Societies** booking required. **Green Fees** not confirmed **Prof** Paul Simpson **Facilities** ⊕ 🖪 ⊑ 🖫 ⚑ 🖾 🖾 ⚏ 🏴 **Conf** Corporate Hospitality Days **Location** 1m S of village off A338
Hotel ★★★★ 71% HL Ramada Newbury Elcot Park, ELCOT
☎ 01488 658100 & 0844 815 9060 🖩 01488 658288 73 en suite

COOKHAM   Map 4 SU88

Winter Hill Golf Club Grange Ln SL6 9RP
☎ 01628 527613 🖩 01628 527479
e-mail: winterhill_administration@johnlewis.co.uk
web: www.winterhillgolfclub.net
Peaceful parkland course owned by the John Lewis partnership and set in a curve of the Thames with wonderful views across the river to Cliveden.

18 Holes, 6397yds, Par 72, SSS 71, Course record 63. Club membership 770.
Visitors Mon-Fri except BHs. Dress code. **Societies** booking required. **Green Fees** not confirmed **Course Designer** Charles Lawrie **Prof** Julian Goodman **Facilities** ⊕ 🖤 by prior arrangement 🖪 ⊑ 🖫 ⚑ 🖾 ⚏ 🖾 🏴 **Conf** facs Corporate Hospitality Days **Location** 1m NW off B4447
Hotel ★★★★ HL Macdonald Compleat Angler, Marlow Bridge, MARLOW ☎ 0844 879 9128 🖩 01628 486388 64 en suite

CROWTHORNE   Map 4 SU86

East Berkshire Golf Club Ravenswood Ave RG45 6BD
☎ 01344 772041 🖩 01344 777378
e-mail: thesecretary@eastberkshiregolfclub.com
web: www.eastberkshiregolfclub.com
An attractive heathland course with an abundance of heather and pine trees. Walking is easy and the greens are exceptionally good. Some fairways become tight where the heather encroaches on the line of play. The course is testing and demands great accuracy.

18 Holes, 6236yds, Par 69, SSS 70, Course record 63. Club membership 766.
Visitors Mon, Wed-Fri except BHs. Dress code **Societies** welcome. **Green Fees** £60 per day, £40 per round **Course Designer** P Paxton **Prof** Jason Brant **Facilities** ⊕ 🖤 🖪 ⊑ 🖫 ⚑ 🖾 ⚏ **Conf** Corporate Hospitality Days **Location** W side of town centre off B3348, approx 0.25m from railway station
Hotel ★★★★★ CHH Pennyhill Park Hotel & The Spa, London Road, BAGSHOT ☎ 01276 471774 🖩 01276 473217 123 en suite

DATCHET   Map 4 SU97

Datchet Golf Club Buccleuch Rd SL3 9BP
☎ 01753 543887 🖩 01753 541872
e-mail: secretary@datchetgolfclub.co.uk
web: www.datchetgolfclub.co.uk
Meadowland course, easy walking.

9 Holes, 6087yds, Par 70, SSS 69. Club membership 430.
Visitors Mon-Fri & BHs. Weekends pm. Booking required weekends & BHs. **Societies** booking required. **Green Fees** £25 per 18 holes (£30 weekends & BHs) ⊛ **Course Designer** J H Taylor **Prof** Paul Cook **Facilities** ⊕ 🖤 🖪 ⊑ 🖫 ⚑ 🖾 🖳 ⚏ 🏴 **Location** NW side of Datchet off B470
Hotel ★★★★ 77% HL Mercure Castle, 18 High Street, WINDSOR ☎ 01753 851577 🖩 01753 856930 108 en suite

MAIDENHEAD
Map 4 SU88

Bird Hills Golf Centre Drift Rd, Hawthorn Hill SL6 3ST
☎ 01628 771030 📄 01628 631023
e-mail: info@birdhills.co.uk
web: www.birdhills.co.uk

A gently undulating course with easy walking and several water hazards. Challenging holes include the par 5 6th dog-leg, par 3 9th surrounded by water and bunkers, and the 16th which is a long uphill par 4 with a two-tier green. Bent grass green and grass teeing areas.

18 Holes, 6176yds, Par 72, SSS 69, Course record 65.
Club membership 400.

Visitors Mon-Sun & BHs. Booking required. Dress code
Societies booking required. **Green Fees** not confirmed **Prof** N Slimming/C Connell **Facilities** ⓉⒺ 🍴 ᵇₑ ☕ 🍷 ♨ ᐃ 🏠 ♈
🚚 ⚙ ⚑ **Leisure** pool tables. **Conf** facs Corporate Hospitality Days **Location** M4 junct 8/9, 4m S on A330
Hotel ★★★ 80% HL Stirrups Country House, Maidens Green, BRACKNELL ☎ 01344 882284 📄 01344 882300 30 en suite

Maidenhead Golf Club Shoppenhangers Rd SL6 2PZ
☎ 01628 624693 📄 01628 780758
e-mail: manager@maidenheadgolf.co.uk
web: www.maidenheadgolf.co.uk

Pleasant parkland with excellent greens and some challenging holes. The long par 4 4th and short par 3 13th are only two of the many outstanding aspects of this course.

18 Holes, 6338yds, Par 70, SSS 70, Course record 65.
Club membership 650.

Visitors Mon-Thu except BHs. Booking required. Handicap certificate required. Dress code. **Societies** booking required. **Green Fees** not confirmed **Course Designer** Alex Simpson **Prof** Steve Geary **Facilities** ⓉⒺ 🍴 ᵇₑ ☕ ᐃ 🏠 ♈ **Conf** facs Corporate Hospitality Days **Location** S side of town centre off A308
Hotel ★★★★ HL Fredrick's Hotel Restaurant Spa, Shoppenhangers Road, MAIDENHEAD ☎ 01628 581000
📄 01628 771054 34 en suite

Temple Golf Club Henley Rd, Hurley SL6 5LH
☎ 01628 824795 📄 01628 828119
e-mail: secretary@templegolfclub.co.uk
web: www.templegolfclub.co.uk

Chalk downland with extensive views over the Thames Valley. Firm, relatively fast greens, natural slopes and subtle contours provide a challenging test to golfers of all abilities. Excellent drainage assures play during inclement weather.

18 Holes, 6210yds, Par 70, SSS 71, Course record 63.
Club membership 480.

Visitors Mon-Sun & BHs. Booking required. Handicap certificate preferred. Dress code. **Societies** booking required. **Green Fees** not confirmed **Course Designer** Willie Park (Jnr) **Prof** James Whiteley **Facilities** ⓉⒺ 🍴 by prior arrangement ᵇₑ ☕ 🍷 ᐃ 🏠 ♈
⚙ ⚙ **Conf** Corporate Hospitality Days **Location** M4 junct 8/9, A404(M) then A4130, signed Henley
Hotel ★★★★ HL Macdonald Compleat Angler, Marlow Bridge, MARLOW ☎ 0844 879 9128 📄 01628 486388 64 en suite

MORTIMER
Map 4 SU66

Wokefield Park Golf Club Wokefield Park RG7 3AE
☎ 0118 933 4072 📄 0118 933 4031
web: www.deverevenues.co.uk

18 Holes, 6579yds, Par 72, SSS 72, Course record 65.

Course Designer Jonathan Gaunt **Location** M4 junct 11, A33 towards Basingstoke. 1st rdbt, 3rd exit towards Grazeley. After 2.5m right bend, club on right
Telephone for further details
Hotel ★★★★ 74% HL Copthorne Hotel Reading, Pingewood, READING ☎ 0118 950 0885 📄 0118 939 1996 81 en suite

NEWBURY
Map 4 SU46

Donnington Valley Golf Club Snelsmore House, Snelsmore Common RG14 3BG
☎ 01635 568144
e-mail: golf@donningtonvalley.co.uk
web: www.donningtonvalleygolfclub.co.uk

Undulating, testing course with mature trees and elevated greens, some protected by water. The closing four holes present a real challenge to all levels of golfer.

18 Holes, 6296yds, Par 71, SSS 71. Club membership 330.

Visitors Mon-Sun & BHs. Dress code. **Societies** booking required. **Green Fees** £27 per 18 holes (£36 weekends) **Course Designer** Mike Smith **Prof** Martin Balfour **Facilities** ⓉⒺ 🍴 by prior arrangement ᵇₑ ☕ 🍷 ᐃ 🏠 ♈ ◇ 🚚 ⚙ **Leisure** heated indoor swimming pool, sauna, gymnasium **Conf** facs Corporate Hospitality Days **Location** from M4 junct 13 take A34 for Newbury. Left at sign for Donnington/Services. At next rdbt 2nd exit signed Donnington and at following rdbt turn left for 2m, club on right
Hotel ★★★★ 84% HL Donnington Valley Hotel & Spa, Old Oxford Road, Donnington, NEWBURY ☎ 01635 551199 📄 01635 551123
111 en suite

Save on Hotels. Book at **theAA.com/hotel**

BERKSHIRE

ENGLAND

Newbury & Crookham Golf Club Bury's Bank Rd, Greenham RG19 8BZ
☎ 01635 40035
e-mail: ed.richardson@newburygolf.co.uk
web: www.newburygolf.co.uk

A traditional English parkland course, whose tree-lined fairways and small fast greens provide a challenge of consistency and accuracy.

18 Holes, 5961yds, Par 69, SSS 69, Course record 64. Club membership 600.

Visitors Mon-Fri except BHs. Dress code. **Societies** booking required. **Green Fees** not confirmed **Course Designer** J H Taylor **Prof** Martin Balfour **Facilities** ⓣ ⑩ ▮ ☴ ⑲ ⚬ 亼 ⚐ 🛍 ⚍ ❀ Conf Corporate Hospitality Days **Location** 4m S of M4 off A339
Hotel ★★★★ 71% HL Ramada Newbury Elcot Park, ELCOT
☎ 01488 658100 & 0844 815 9060 ▤ 01488 658288 73 en suite

READING   Map 4 SU77

Calcot Park Golf Club Bath Rd, Calcot RG31 7RN
☎ 0118 942 7124 ▤ 0118 945 3373
e-mail: info@calcotpark.com
web: www.calcotpark.com

A delightfully picturesque, slightly undulating parkland course just outside the town. The subtle borrows on the greens challenge all categories of golfer. Hazards include streams, a lake and many trees. The 6th is a 503yd par 5, with the tee-shot hit downhill over cross-bunkers to a green well-guarded by a ditch meandering across the fairway; the 7th (156yds) is played over the lake to an elevated green and the 13th (also 156yds) requires a carry across a valley to a plateau green.

18 Holes, 6300yds, Par 70, SSS 71, Course record 62. Club membership 730.

Visitors Mon-Fri except BHs (Sun pm if available). Booking required. Handicap certificate. Dress code. **Societies** booking required. **Green Fees** £50 per day/round, £40 after 2pm **Course Designer** H S Colt **Prof** Mark Grieve **Facilities** ⓣ ⑩ ▮ ☴ ⑲ 亼 ⚐ 🛍 ⚬ **Leisure** fishing **Conf** facs Corporate Hospitality Days **Location** 1.5m from M4 junct 12 on A4 towards Reading
Hotel ★★★ 72% HL Best Western Calcot Hotel, 98 Bath Road, Calcot, READING ☎ 0118 941 6423 ▤ 0118 945 1223 78 en suite

The Club at Mapledurham Chazey Heath, Mapledurham RG4 7UD
☎ 0118 946 3353 ▤ 0118 946 3363
e-mail: t.williams@theclubcompany.com
web: www.theclubcompany.com

An 18-hole parkland and woodland course designed by Bob Sandow. Flanked by hedgerows and mature woods, it is testing for players of all levels.

Chazey Heath: 18 Holes, 5689yds, Par 69, SSS 67, Course record 64. Club membership 700.

Visitors Mon-Sun & BHs. Booking required. Dress code. **Societies** booking required. **Green Fees** £25 per round (£30 weekends) **Course Designer** Robert Sandow **Prof** David Boyce **Facilities** ⓣ ⑩ ▮ ☴ ⑲ 亼 ⚐ 🛍 ⚬ **Leisure** sauna, gymnasium, 3 studios, creche **Conf** facs Corporate Hospitality Days **Location** on A4074 to Oxford
Hotel ★★★ 83% HL The French Horn, SONNING ON THAMES
☎ 0118 969 2204 ▤ 0118 944 2210 22 en suite

Hennerton Golf Club Crazies Hill Rd, Wargrave RG10 8LT
☎ 0118 940 1000 & 0118 940 4778 ▤ 0118 940 1042
e-mail: info@hennertongolfclub.co.uk
web: www.hennertongolfclub.co.uk

Overlooking the Thames Valley, this course has many existing natural features and a good number of hazards such as bunkers, mature trees and two small lakes.

18 Holes, 4187yds, Par 65, SSS 62, Course record 62. Club membership 450.

Visitors Mon-Sun & BHs. Dress code. **Societies** booking required. **Green Fees** £22 per 18 holes, £16 per 9 holes (£28/£19 weekends and BHs) **Course Designer** Col D Beard **Prof** Glenn Johnson **Facilities** ⓣ ▮ ☴ ⑲ 亼 ⚐ ⑰ ⚬ 🛍 ⚬ ❀ Conf Corporate Hospitality Days **Location** signed from A321 Wargrave High St
Hotel ★★★★ 76% TH Hotel du Vin Henley-on-Thames, New Street, HENLEY-ON-THAMES ☎ 01491 848400 ▤ 01491 848401 43 en suite

Reading Golf Club 17 Kidmore End Rd, Emmer Green RG4 8SG
☎ 0118 947 2909 (Secretary) ▤ 0118 946 4468
e-mail: secretary@readinggolfclub.com
web: www.readinggolfclub.com

Pleasant parkland, part hilly and part flat with interesting views and several challenging par 3s. After the opening holes the course moves across the valley. The par 4 5th is played from an elevated tee and although relatively short, the well-placed bunkers and trees come into play. The 470yd par 4 12th is a great hole. It has a slight dog-leg and requires an accurate second shot to hit a well-guarded green. The finishing hole requires two great shots to have any chance of reaching par.

18 Holes, 6224yds, Par 70, SSS 70, Course record 64. Club membership 600.

Visitors Mon-Fri except BHs. Dress code. **Societies** booking required. **Green Fees** £40 per day **Course Designer** James Braid **Prof** Will Alsop **Facilities** ⓣ ⑩ ▮ ☴ ⑲ 亼 ⚐ ⚬ 🛍 ⚬ **Leisure** indoor nets **Conf** Corporate Hospitality Days **Location** 2m N off B481
Hotel ★★★ 83% HL The French Horn, SONNING ON THAMES
☎ 0118 969 2204 ▤ 0118 944 2210 22 en suite

SINDLESHAM   Map 4 SU76

Bearwood Golf Club Mole Rd RG41 5DB
☎ 0118 976 0060
e-mail: barrytustin@btconnect.com

Flat parkland with one water hazard, the 40-acre lake that features on the challenging 6th and 7th holes.

9 Holes, 5610yds, Par 70, SSS 68, Course record 66. Club membership 500.

Visitors Mon-Fri. Weekends & BH pm only. Booking required weekends & BHs. Handicap certificate. Dress code. **Societies** booking required. **Green Fees** not confirmed **Course Designer** Barry Tustin **Prof** Bayley Tustin **Facilities** ⓣ ▮ ☴ ⑲ 亼 ⚐ 🛍 ⚬ ❀ Conf Corporate Hospitality Days **Location** 1m SW on B3030
Hotel ★★★★ 79% HL Millennium Madejski Hotel Reading, Madejski Stadium, READING ☎ 0118 925 3500 ▤ 0118 925 3501 201 en suite

SONNING
Map 4 SU77

Sonning Golf Club Duffield Rd RG4 6GJ
☎ 0118 969 3332
e-mail: secretary@sonning-golf-club.co.uk
web: www.sonning-golf-club.co.uk

A quality parkland course and the scene of many county championships. Wide fairways, not over-bunkered, and very good greens. Holes of changing character through wooded belts. Four challenging par 4s over 450yds. An excellent test of golf for all levels of player.

18 Holes, 6366yds, Par 70, SSS 70.
Club membership 750.

Visitors Mon-Sun except BHs. Booking required. Dress code. **Societies** booking required. **Green Fees** £50 (£60 weekends) **Course Designer** J H Taylor & H Colt **Prof** J Dunn **Facilities** ⑪ ⑂ ⬛ ➘ ⛳ ⬛ ⚲ ✦ **Conf** facs Corporate Hospitality Days **Location** 1m S off A4
Hotel ★★★ 83% HL The French Horn, SONNING ON THAMES ☎ 0118 969 2204 📠 0118 944 2210 22 en suite

STREATLEY
Map 4 SU58

Goring & Streatley Golf Club RG8 9QA
☎ 01491 873229 📠 01491 875224
e-mail: secretary@goringgolf.co.uk
web: www.goringgolf.co.uk

A parkland and moorland course that requires negotiating. Four well-known holes lead up to the heights of the 5th tee, to which there is a 300ft climb. Wide fairways, not over-bunkered, with nice rewards on the way home down the last few holes. A delightful course that commands magnificent views of the Ridgeway and the River Thames.

18 Holes, 6355yds, Par 71, SSS 70, Course record 65.
Club membership 740.

Visitors Mon-Fri except BHs. Booking required. Dress code. **Societies** booking required. **Green Fees** not confirmed **Course Designer** Tom Morris **Prof** Jason Hadland **Facilities** ⑪ ⑂ ⬛ ➘ ⛳ ⬛ ⚲ **Location** N of village off A417
Hotel ★★★★ 73% HL The Swan at Streatley, High Street, STREATLEY ☎ 01491 878800 📠 01491 872554 45 en suite

SUNNINGDALE
Map 4 SU96

Sunningdale see page 25
Ridgemount Rd SL5 9RR
☎ 01344 621681 📠 01344 624154
e-mail: info@sunningdalegolfclub.co.uk
web: www.sunningdale-golfclub.co.uk

Sunningdale Ladies Golf Club Cross Rd SL5 9RX
☎ 01344 620507
e-mail: secretary@sunningdaleladies.co.uk
web: www.sunningdaleladies.co.uk

A short but challenging 18-hole course with a typical Surrey heathland layout. A very tight course and the heather can be punishing. Excellent test for all levels of golfer.

18 Holes, 3705yds, Par 61, SSS 61, Course record 54.
Club membership 400.

Visitors Contact club for details. **Societies** booking required. **Green**

Fees £30 per round (£35 weekends & BHs) ⊛ **Course Designer** H Colt **Facilities** ⑪ ⬛ ➘ ⛳ ➘ **Leisure** practice net **Conf** Corporate Hospitality Days **Location** 400 yds S of A30, 0.5 W of Sunningdale village
Hotel ★★★★ 78% HL Macdonald Berystede Hotel & Spa, Bagshot Road, Sunninghill, ASCOT ☎ 0844 879 9104 📠 01344 872301 126 en suite

THEALE
Map 4 SU67

Theale Golf Club North St RG7 5EX
☎ 0118 930 5331
e-mail: info@thealegolf.com
web: www.thealegolf.com

Challenging parkland course set in the heart of the Berkshire countryside, with mature trees and a number of water hazards.

18 Holes, 6600yds, Par 71, SSS 69, Course record 68.
Club membership 300.

Visitors Mon-Sun & BHs. Booking required weekends & BHs. Dress code. **Societies** booking required. **Green Fees** £35 per day, £20 per 18 holes, £14 per 9 holes. (£45/£27/£18 weekends & BHs) **Course Designer** Mike Lowe **Prof** Michael Lowe **Facilities** ⑪ ⬛ ➘ ⛳ ➘ ⚲ ⚲ ⬛ ⚲ ✦ **Conf** facs Corporate Hospitality Days **Location** Off M4 junct 12
Hotel ★★★ 72% HL Best Western Calcot Hotel, 98 Bath Road, Calcot, READING ☎ 0118 941 6423 📠 0118 945 1223 78 en suite

WOKINGHAM
Map 4 SU86

Downshire Golf Complex Easthampstead Park RG40 3DH
☎ 01344 302030 📠 01344 301020
e-mail: downshiregc@bracknell-forest.gov.uk
web: www.bracknell-forest.gov.uk/be

Beautiful municipal parkland course with mature trees. Water hazards come into play on the 14th and 18th holes, and especially on the short 7th, a testing downhill 169yds over the lake. Pleasant easy walking. Challenging holes: 7th (par 4), 15th (par 4), 16th (par 3). Rated as one of the finest municipal courses in the country.

18 Holes, 6371yds, Par 72, SSS 71. Club membership 1000.

Visitors Mon-Sun & BHs. Booking required. Dress code. **Societies** booking required. **Green Fees** not confirmed **Prof** W Owers/R Iolo/M Billies **Facilities** ⑪ ⬛ ➘ ⛳ ➘ ⚲ ⚲ ⚲ ⬛ ⚲ ✦ **Leisure** 9 hole pitch & putt, power tees **Conf** facs Corporate Hospitality Days **Location** 3m SW of Bracknell. M4 junct 10, signs for Crowthorne
Hotel ★★★★ 75% HL Coppid Beech, John Nike Way, BRACKNELL ☎ 01344 303333 📠 01344 301200 205 en suite

SUNNINGDALE

BERKSHIRE - SUNNINGDALE - MAP 4 SU96

The club has two championship courses, laid out on the most glorious piece of heathland and both courses have their own individual characteristics. The Old Course, founded in 1900, was designed by Willie Park. It is a classic course with gorse and pines, silver birch, heather and immaculate turf. The New Course was created by H S Colt in 1922. It is a mixture of wood and open heath with long carries and tight fairways.

Ridgemount Rd SL5 9RR ☎ 01344 621681 ▤ 01344 624154
e-mail: info@sunningdalegolfclub.co.uk web: www.sunningdale-golfclub.co.uk
Old Course: 18 Holes, 6063yds, Par 70, SSS 69.
New Course: 18 Holes, 6083yds, Par 70, SSS 70. Club membership 1000.
Visitors Mon-Thu except BHs. Booking required. Handicap certificate. Dress code. **Societies** booking required.
Green Fees not confirmed **Course Designer** W Park (Old) H Colt (New) **Prof** Keith Maxwell **Facilities** ⑪ ⓛ ☕
🏐 ⚒ 🛋 ⛳ ✗ ⚑ **Conf** Corporate Hospitality Days **Location** 1m S off A30
Hotel ★★★★★ CHH Pennyhill Park Hotel & The Spa, London Road, BAGSHOT ☎ 01276 471774
▤ 01276 473217 123 en suite

Sand Martins Golf Club Finchampstead Rd RG40 3RQ
☎ 0118 979 2711 📠 0118 977 0282
web: www.sandmartins.com

18 Holes, 6212yds, Par 70, SSS 70, Course record 64.
Course Designer Edward Fox **Location** 1m S of Wokingham
Telephone for further details
Hotel ★★★★ 75% HL Coppid Beech, John Nike Way, BRACKNELL
☎ 01344 303333 📠 01344 301200 205 en suite

BRISTOL

BRISTOL   Map 3 ST57

Bristol and Clifton Golf Club Beggar Bush Ln, Failand
BS8 3TH
☎ 01275 393474 📠 01275 394611
e-mail: mansec@bristolgolf.co.uk
web: www.bristolgolf.co.uk

Utilising the aesthetics and hazards of a former quarry, a valley,
stone walls and spinneys of trees, the course is a stern challenge
but one always in tip top condition, due in summer to the irrigation
and in winter to the natural draining land upon which it is situated.
Par 3s from 120 to 220yds, dog-legs which range from the gentle to
the brutal and a collection of natural obstacles and hazards add to
the charm of the layout.
18 Holes, 6387yds, Par 70, SSS 71, Course record 63.
Club membership 850.
Visitors handicap certificate. Dress code. **Societies** welcome.
Green Fees £50.50 per day (£60.50 weekends) **Prof** Paul Mitchell
Facilities Ⓣ 🍴 🛍 🖥 🍺 🎿 🏠 ⛳ 🏌 🚌 ⛳
Leisure chipping green, practice bunkers **Conf** facs Corporate
Hospitality Days **Location** M5 junct 19, A369 for 4m, onto B3129,
club 1m on right
Hotel ★★★ 74% HL The Avon Gorge, Sion Hill, Clifton, BRISTOL
☎ 0117 973 8955 📠 0117 923 8125 75 en suite

Filton Golf Club Golf Course Ln, Filton BS34 7QS
☎ 0117 969 4169 📠 0117 931 4359
e-mail: thesecretary@filtongolfclub.co.uk
web: www.filtongolfclub.co.uk
Interesting and challenging mature parkland course situated on high
ground north of the city. Extensive views can be enjoyed from the
course to the Concorde and Severn bridges.
18 Holes, 6000yds, Par 70, SSS 70, Course record 64.
Club membership 650.
Visitors Mon-Fri. Weekends & BHs pm only. Dress code
Societies booking required. **Green Fees** £36 per round **Prof** D Kelley
Facilities Ⓣ 🍴 🛍 🖥 🍺 🎿 🏠 ⛳ 🏌 🚌 ⛳ **Conf**
Corporate Hospitality Days **Location** M5 junct 15, off A38
Hotel ★★★★ 80% HL Aztec Hotel & Spa, Aztec West Business
Park, Almondsbury, BRISTOL ☎ 01454 201090 📠 01454 201593
128 en suite

Henbury Golf Club Henbury Rd, Westbury-on-Trym
BS10 7QB
☎ 0117 950 0044 & 950 2121 (Pro) 📠 0117 959 1928
e-mail: thesecretary@henburygolfclub.co.uk
web: www.henburygolfclub.co.uk
A parkland course in mature woodland bordering the Blaise Castle
Estate. The course provides a number of different challenges
including the par 3 7th over the River Trym and the par 4 8th which
follows the river along the valley. A test for golfers of all abilities.
18 Holes, 6007yds, Par 69, SSS 69, Course record 62.
Club membership 640.
Visitors Mon-Sun & BHs. Dress code. **Societies** booking required.
Green Fees £40 per day/round **Prof** Nick Riley **Facilities** Ⓣ 🍴
by prior arrangement 🛍 🖥 🍺 🎿 🏠 ⛳ 🏌 🚌 ⛳
Conf facs Corporate Hospitality Days **Location** M5 junct 17, take
A4018 S, right at 1st lights, on left at top of hill (Henbury Rd)
Hotel ★★★ 77% HL Best Western Henbury Lodge Hotel, Station
Road, Henbury, BRISTOL ☎ 0117 950 2615 📠 0117 950 9532
20 en suite

Knowle Golf Club Fairway BS4 5DF
☎ 0117 977 0660 📠 0117 972 0615
web: www.knowlegolfclub.co.uk
18 Holes, 6061yds, Par 69, SSS 69, Course record 61.
Course Designer Hawtree/J H Taylor **Location** 3m SE of city centre
off A37
Telephone for further details
Hotel ★★★★★ 85% HL The Royal Crescent, 16 Royal
Crescent, BATH ☎ 01225 823333 📠 01225 339401 45 en suite

Shirehampton Park Golf Club Park Hill, Shirehampton
BS11 0UL
☎ 0117 982 2083
e-mail: info@shirehamptonparkgolfclub.co.uk
web: www.shirehamptonparkgolfclub.co.uk
Lovely parkland course with views across the Avon Gorge.
18 Holes, 5502yds, Par 67, SSS 67. Club membership 530.
Visitors Mon-Sun & BHs. Booking required weekends & BHs. Handicap
certificate preferred. Dress code. **Societies** booking required.
Green Fees £36 per day, £30 per round (£35 per round weekends).
Twilight rates available **Prof** Jon Palmer **Facilities** Ⓣ 🍴 by prior

continued

arrangement 🛇 🖵 ▦ ⚒ 🖿 ⚑ ✦ **Conf** facs Corporate Hospitality Days **Location** M5 junct 18, 2m E on B4054
Hotel ★★★ 77% HL Best Western Henbury Lodge Hotel, Station Road, Henbury, BRISTOL ☎ 0117 950 2615 📄 0117 950 9532 20 en suite

Shortwood Lodge Golf Club Carsons Rd, Mangotsfield BS16 9LW
☎ 0117 956 5501 📄 0117 957 3640
e-mail: info@shortwoodlodge.com
web: www.shortwoodlodge.com
An easy walking parkland course with well-placed bunkers.

18 Holes, 5295yds, Par 68, SSS 66. Club membership 200.
Visitors Mon-Sun & BHs. **Societies** booking required. **Green Fees** £12 (£14 weekends & BHs) **Course Designer** John Day **Facilities** ⓦ
🍴 🛇 🖵 ▦ ⚒ 🖿 ⚑ ✦ 🚗 ✦ **Conf** facs Corporate Hospitality Days **Location** 6m NE of city centre off B4465
Hotel ★★★ 74% HL Arnos Manor Hotel, 470 Bath Road, Arno's Vale, BRISTOL ☎ 0117 971 1461 📄 0117 971 5507 73 en suite

Woodlands Golf & Country Club Trench Ln, Almondsbury BS32 4JZ
☎ 01454 619319 📄 01454 619397
e-mail: info@woodlands-golf.com
web: www.woodlands-golf.com
Situated on the edge of the Severn Valley, bordered by Hortham Brook and Shepherds Wood, this course has been designed to the highest standards with USGA greens. Both courses have 10 holes where water comes into play, most notably on the 17th hole (Island Green) of the Signature course.

The Masters: 18 Holes, 6111yds, Par 71, SSS 70.
The Signature: 18 Holes, 5541yds, Par 70, SSS 70.
Club membership 100.
Visitors Contact club for details. **Societies** booking required.
Green Fees £14 per round (£16 weekends & BHs) **Prof** L Riddiford **Facilities** ⓦ 🍴 🛇 🖵 ▦ ⚒ 🖿 ⚑ ✦
Leisure fishing, fishing lake **Conf** facs Corporate Hospitality Days
Location M5 junct 16, A38 towards Bradley Stoke
Hotel ★★★★ 73% CHH Grange, Northwoods, Winterbourne, BRISTOL ☎ 0844 8159063 📄 01454 777447 68 en suite

BUCKINGHAMSHIRE

AYLESBURY   Map 4 SP81

Aylesbury Golf Centre Hulcott Ln, Bierton HP22 5GA
☎ 01296 393644
web: www.aylesburygolfclub.co.uk
Parkland with magnificent views to the Chiltern Hills. A good test of golf with out of bounds coming into play on nine of the holes, plus a number of water hazards and bunkers.

Aylesbury Golf Club: 18 Holes, 5965yds, Par 71, SSS 69.
Visitors Mon-Sun & BHs. Booking required weekends & BHs. Dress code. **Societies** booking required. **Green Fees** phone **Course Designer** T S Benwell **Prof** D Macdonald **Facilities** ⓦ 🍴 🛇
🖵 ▦ ⚒ 🖿 ⚑ ✦ 🏃 **Conf** Corporate Hospitality Days
Location 1m N of Aylesbury on A418
Hotel ★★★★ HL Hartwell House Hotel, Restaurant & Spa, Oxford Road, AYLESBURY ☎ 01296 747444 📄 01296 747450 46 en suite

Aylesbury Park Golf Club Andrews Way, Off Coldharbour Way, Oxford Rd HP17 8QQ
☎ 01296 399196
e-mail: info@aylesburyparkgolf.com
web: www.aylesburyparkgolf.com
Parkland with mature trees, located very close to Aylesbury.

18 Holes, 6166yds, Par 70, SSS 69, Course record 66.
Club membership 300.
Visitors Mon-Sun & BHs. Bookinhg required. Dress code.
Societies booking required. **Green Fees** £20 per round (£25 weekends) **Course Designer** M Hawtree **Prof** John Major **Facilities** ⓦ
🛇 🖵 ▦ ⚒ 🖿 ⚑ ✦ **Leisure** 9 hole par 3 course
Location 0.5m SW of Aylesbury, on the A418
Hotel ★★★★ HL Hartwell House Hotel, Restaurant & Spa, Oxford Road, AYLESBURY ☎ 01296 747444 📄 01296 747450 46 en suite

Chiltern Forest Golf Club Aston Hill, Halton HP22 5NQ
☎ 01296 631267 📄 01296 632709
e-mail: secretary@chilternforest.co.uk
web: www.chilternforest.co.uk
The course nestles in the Chiltern Hills above Aylesbury with stunning views of the surrounding countryside and meanders around challenging wooded terrain. Although not a long course the tightly wooded holes and smallish greens present a challenge to all standards of golfer.

18 Holes, 5765yds, Par 70, SSS 69, Course record 65.
Club membership 650.
Visitors Mon-Sun & BHs. Handicap certificate. Dress code.
Societies welcome. **Green Fees** £46 per 36 holes Mon-Fri. £36 per 18 holes Mon-Thu, £40 Fri-Sun **Prof** Simon Perks **Facilities** ⓦ 🍴
🛇 🖵 ▦ ⚒ ✦ ✦ **Conf** Corporate Hospitality Days
Location off A41 between Tring and Aylesbury
Hotel ★★★★ 78% HL Pendley Manor, Cow Lane, TRING ☎ 01442 891891 📄 01442 890687 73 en suite

Ellesborough Golf Club Wendover Rd, Butlers Cross HP17 0TZ
☎ 01296 622114 📄 01296 622114
e-mail: admin@ellesboroughgolf.co.uk
web: www.ellesboroughgolf.co.uk
Once part of the property of Chequers, and under the shadow of the famous Coombe monument at the Wendover end of the Chilterns. A downland course, it is rather hilly with most holes enhanced by far-ranging views over the Aylesbury countryside.

18 Holes, 6384yds, Par 71, SSS 72.
Club membership 700.
Visitors Mon-Fri except BHs. Handicap certificate. Dress code.
Societies booking required. **Green Fees** £60 per day, £40 per round
🍴 **Course Designer** James Braid **Prof** Mark Squire **Facilities** ⓦ
🍴 by prior arrangement 🛇 🖵 ▦ ⚒ 🖿 ✦ **Conf**
Corporate Hospitality Days **Location** 1m W of Wendover on B4010 towards Princes Risborough
Hotel ★★★ 78% HL Holiday Inn Aylesbury, Aston Clinton Road, AYLESBURY ☎ 01296 734000 📄 01296 392211 139 en suite

BEACONSFIELD
Map 4 SU99

Beaconsfield Golf Club Seer Green HP9 2UR
☎ 01494 676545 📄 01494 681148
e-mail: secretary@beaconsfieldgolfclub.co.uk
web: www.beaconsfieldgolfclub.co.uk
An interesting and, at times, testing tree-lined and parkland course which frequently plays longer than appears on the card. Each hole differs to a considerable degree and here lies the charm. Walking is easy, except perhaps to the 6th and 8th. Well bunkered.
18 Holes, 6506yds, Par 72, SSS 71, Course record 63.
Club membership 900.
Visitors contact club for details. **Societies** welcome. **Green Fees** not confirmed **Course Designer** H S Colt **Prof** Michael Brothers **Facilities** 🏤 🍴 ⚑ 🏌 🛄 🛋 🏕 ⚐ 🚗 🏌 **Conf** Corporate Hospitality Days **Location** M40 junct 2, next to Seer Green railway station
Hotel ★★★ 78% HL Chequers Inn, Kiln Lane, Wooburn, WOOBURN COMMON ☎ 01628 529575 📄 01628 850124 17 en suite

BLETCHLEY
Map 4 SP83

Windmill Hill Golf Centre Tattenhoe Ln MK3 7RB
☎ 01908 631113
18 Holes, 6720yds, Par 73, SSS 72, Course record 68.
Course Designer Henry Cotton **Location** W side of town centre on A421
Telephone for further details
Hotel BUD Campanile Milton Keynes, 40 Penn Road (off Watling St), Fenny Stratford, Bletchley, MILTON KEYNES ☎ 01908 649819 📄 01908 649818 80 en suite

BUCKINGHAM
Map 4 SP63

Buckingham Golf Club Tingewick Rd MK18 4AE
☎ 01280 815566 📄 01280 821812
e-mail: admin@buckinghamgolfclub.co.uk
web: www.buckinghamgolfclub.co.uk
Undulating parkland with a stream and river affecting eight holes.
18 Holes, 6162yds, Par 71, SSS 70, Course record 66.
Club membership 740.
Visitors Mon-Fri except BHs. Handicap certificate preferred. Dress code. **Societies** booking required. **Green Fees** £40 per 18 holes **Course Designer** Peter Jones **Prof** Greg Hannah **Facilities** 🏤 🍴 🍺 ⚑ 🏌 🛄 🛋 ⚐ 🚗 ⚐ 🏌 **Leisure** snooker room **Conf** facs Corporate Hospitality Days **Location** 1.5m W on A421
Hotel ★★★ 77% HL Best Western Buckingham Hotel, Buckingham Ring Road, BUCKINGHAM ☎ 01280 822622 📄 01280 823074 70 en suite

BURNHAM
Map 4 SU98

Burnham Beeches Golf Club Green Ln SL1 8EG
☎ 01628 661448 📄 01628 668968
e-mail: enquiries@bbgc.co.uk
web: www.bbgc.co.uk
Wooded parkland on the edge of the historic Burnham Beeches Forest, with a good variety of holes.
18 Holes, 6449yds, Par 70, SSS 71.
Club membership 670.
Visitors Mon-Fri except BHs. Booking required. Dress code. **Societies** booking required. **Green Fees** £50 per round (£31 Country cards) **Course Designer** J H Taylor **Prof** Ronnie Bolton **Facilities** 🏤 🍴 🍺 ⚑ 🏌 🛄 🛋 ⚐ 🚗 ⚐ 🏌 **Conf** Corporate Hospitality Days **Location** 0.5m NE of Burnham
Hotel ★★★★ 74% HL Burnham Beeches Hotel, Grove Road, BURNHAM ☎ 0844 736 8603 📄 01628 603994 82 en suite

Huntswood Golf Club Taplow Common Rd SL1 8LS
☎ 01628 667144 📄 01628 663145
e-mail: huntswoodgc@btconnect.com
web: www.huntswoodgolf.com
Well presented course, which opened in 1996 and has now matured into one of the most popular courses in the county. Sweeping fairways set in the heart of a picturesque valley and small greens guarded by numerous bunkers, making a good second shot a must.
18 Holes, 5286yds, Par 68, SSS 66, Course record 66.
Club membership 365.
Visitors Mon-Sun & BHs. Dress code. **Societies** booking required. **Green Fees** £24 per 18 holes, £14 per 9 holes (£27/£16.50 weekends) **Prof** Graham Benyon **Facilities** 🏤 🍴 🍺 ⚑ 🏌 🛄 🛋 ⚐ 🚗 ⚐ **Conf** facs Corporate Hospitality Days **Location** M4 junct 7, take 1st exit at rdbt, at next rdbt take 3rd exit into Taplow Common Rd. Under rail bridge and over mini-rdbt with petrol station on right. Straight across next mini-rdbt into Taplow Common Rd, golf club on left
Hotel ★★★★ 76% HL Grovefield House Hotel, Taplow Common Road, BURNHAM ☎ 01628 603131 📄 01628 668078 40 en suite

The Lambourne Golf Club Dropmore Rd SL1 8NF
☎ 01628 666755 📄 01628 663301
e-mail: info@lambourneclub.co.uk
web: www.lambourneclub.co.uk
Parkland course of undulating terrain with many trees and several lakes, notably on the tricky 7th hole which has a tightly guarded green reached via a shot over a lake. Seven par 4s over 400yds with six picturesque lakes, excellent drainage and full irrigation.
18 Holes, 6798yds, Par 72, SSS 73. Club membership 600.
Visitors Mon-Fri except BHs. Booking required. Dress code. **Societies** booking required. **Green Fees** £60 per round **Course Designer** Donald Steel **Prof** David Hart **Facilities** 🏤 🍴 🍺 ⚑ 🏌 🛄 🛋 ⚐ 🚗 ⚐ 🏌 **Leisure** sauna **Conf** facs Corporate Hospitality Days **Location** M4 junct 7 or M40 junct 2, towards Burnham
Hotel ★★★★ 74% HL Burnham Beeches Hotel, Grove Road, BURNHAM ☎ 0844 736 8603 📄 01628 603994 82 en suite

CHALFONT ST GILES   Map 4 SU99

Harewood Downs Golf Club Cokes Ln HP8 4TA
☎ 01494 762184 📄 01494 766869
e-mail: secretary@hdgc.co.uk
web: www.hdgc.co.uk
A testing undulating parkland course with sloping greens and plenty of trees.

Harewood Downs: 18 Holes, 6036yds, Par 69, SSS 70, Course record 64. Club membership 600.

Visitors Mon-Fri except BHs. Handicap certificate. Dress code. **Societies** booking required. **Green Fees** £40 per round 🏵 **Course Designer** J H Taylor Prof G C Morris **Facilities** ⓣ 🍽 by prior arrangement 🏌 ▱ ⛳ ⚐ 🚡 ⛳ **Conf facs** Corporate Hospitality Days **Location** 2m E of Amersham on A413
Hotel ★★★ 79% HL The Bedford Arms Hotel, CHENIES
☎ 01923 283301 📄 01923 284825 18 en suite

Oakland Park Golf Club Threehouseholds HP8 4LW
☎ 01494 871277 & 877333 (pro) 📄 01494 874692
e-mail: info@oaklandparkgolf.co.uk
web: www.oaklandparkgolf.co.uk
Parkland with mature trees, hedgerows and water features, designed to respect the natural features of the land and lakes while providing a good challenge for players at all levels.

Oakland Park: 18 Holes, 5246yds, Par 67, SSS 66, Course record 66. Club membership 620.

Visitors Mon-Sun & BHs. Booking required. Dress code. **Societies** booking required. **Green Fees** £31 per 18 holes (£36 weekends & BHs) **Course Designer** Jonathan Gaunt **Prof** Dale Moore & Alistair Thatcher **Facilities** ⓣ 🏌 ▱ ⛳ 🍽 ⚐ 🚡 ⛳ **Conf** facs Corporate Hospitality Days **Location** M40 junct 2, 3m N
Hotel ★★★ 79% HL The Bedford Arms Hotel, CHENIES
☎ 01923 283301 📄 01923 284825 18 en suite

CHARTRIDGE   Map 4 SP90

Chartridge Park Golf Club HP5 2TF
☎ 01494 791772 📄 01494 786462
web: www.cpgc.co.uk
18 Holes, 5409yds, Par 68, SSS 67, Course record 65.
Course Designer John Jacobs **Location** 3m NW of Chesham
Telephone for further details
Hotel ★★★ 75% HL The Bobsleigh Hotel, Hempstead Road, Bovingdon, HEMEL HEMPSTEAD ☎ 0844 879 9033 📄 01442 832471 47 en suite

CHESHAM   Map 4 SP90

Chesham & Ley Hill Golf Club Ley Hill Common HP5 1UZ
☎ 01494 784541 📄 01494 785506
web: www.cheshamgolf.co.uk
9 Holes, 5296yds, Par 67, SSS 65, Course record 62.
Location 2m E of Chesham, off A41 on B4504 to Ley Hill
Telephone for further details
Hotel ★★★ 75% HL The Bobsleigh Hotel, Hempstead Road, Bovingdon, HEMEL HEMPSTEAD ☎ 0844 879 9033 📄 01442 832471 47 en suite

DAGNALL   Map 4 SP91

Whipsnade Park Studham Ln HP4 1RH
☎ 01442 842330 📄 01442 842090
e-mail: secretary@whipsnadeparkgolf.co.uk
web: www.whipsnadeparkgolf.co.uk
Parkland on downs adjoining Whipsnade Zoo. Easy walking, good views and great test of golf.

18 Holes, 6704yds, Par 73, SSS 72, Course record 68. Club membership 500.

Visitors Mon-Fri. Sun & BHs. Booking required. Dress code. **Societies** booking required. **Green Fees** £40 per day, £30 per round **Prof** Mark Day **Facilities** ⓣ 🍽 by prior arrangement 🏌 ▱ 🦰 ▱ ⛳ 🚡 ⚐ 🚡 ⛳ ⛳ **Conf** Corporate Hospitality Days **Location** M1 junct 8, follow signs for Whipsnade Zoo to Dagnall. Golf club off B4506
Hotel ★★★ INN The Highwayman, London Road, DUNSTABLE
☎ 01582 601122 📄 01582 603812 52 rooms (52 en suite)

DENHAM   Map 4 TQ08

Buckinghamshire Golf Club Denham Court Dr UB9 5PG
☎ 01895 835777 📄 01895 835210
web: www.buckinghamshiregc.com
18 Holes, 6880yds, Par 72, SSS 73, Course record 62.
Course Designer John Jacobs **Location** M25 junct 16, signed Uxbridge
Telephone for further details
Hotel ★★★ 78% HL Barn Hotel, West End Road, RUISLIP
☎ 01895 636057 📄 01895 638379 73 en suite

Denham Golf Club Tilehouse Ln UB9 5DE
☎ 01895 832022 📄 01895 835340
web: www.denhamgolfclub.co.uk
18 Holes, 6462yds, Par 70, SSS 71, Course record 66.
Course Designer H S Colt **Location** 0.5m N of North Orbital Road, 2m from Uxbridge
Telephone for further details
Hotel ★★★ 78% HL Barn Hotel, West End Road, RUISLIP
☎ 01895 636057 📄 01895 638379 73 en suite

FLACKWELL HEATH   Map 4 SU89

Flackwell Heath Golf Club Treadaway Rd, High Wycombe HP10 9PE
☎ 01628 520929 📄 01628 530040
e-mail: secretary@fhgc.co.uk
web: www.fhgc.co.uk
Open sloping heath and tree-lined course on hills overlooking the Chilterns. Some good challenging par 3s and several testing small greens.

18 Holes, 5839yds, Par 71, SSS 70. Club membership 550.

Visitors Mon-Fri & Sun. Booking required. Dress code. **Societies** booking required **Green Fees** not confirmed **Course Designer** J H Taylor **Prof** Simon Quilliam **Facilities** ⓣ 🍽 🏌 ▱ 🦰 ⛳ ⚐ 🚡 ⛳ **Conf** facs Corporate Hospitality Days **Location** M40 junct 3, SE side of High Wycombe
Hotel ★★★★ 82% HL Crowne Plaza Marlow, Field House Lane, MARLOW ☎ 01628 496800 📄 01628 496959 168 en suite

GERRARDS CROSS　　　　　　　Map 4 TQ08

Gerrards Cross Golf Club Chalfont Park SL9 0QA
☎ 01753 883263 (Sec) & 885300 (Pro)
🖷 01753 883593
e-mail: secretary@gxgolf.co.uk
web: www.gxgolf.co.uk

A mature wooded parkland course originally designed in 1922 and set in the grounds of an ancient estate. The course is challenging for all levels of golfer and is recognised as one of the best par 69 courses in southern England.

18 Holes, 6243yds, Par 69, SSS 70, Course record 64.
Club membership 700.

Visitors Mon-Fri. Handicap certificate. Dress code.
Societies booking required. **Green Fees** £55 per day weekdays, £45 per round. Juniors £10 **Course Designer** Bill Pedlar **Prof** Matthew Barr **Facilities** ⑪ ⬛ 🖵 🍴 ⚲ 🖻 ⚒ 🛒 ⚒ **Location** NE side of town centre off A413
Hotel ★★★★ INN The Falcon Inn, Village Road, DENHAM VILLAGE ☎ 01895 832125　4 rooms (4 en suite)

HIGH WYCOMBE　　　　　　　Map 4 SU89

Hazlemere Golf Club Penn Rd, Hazlemere HP15 7LR
☎ 01494 719300　🖷 01494 713914
e-mail: enquiries@hazlemeregolfclub.co.uk
web: www.hazlemeregolfclub.co.uk

Undulating parkland course located in the Chiltern Hills in an Area of Outstanding Natural Beauty. Deceiving in its yardage and a challenge to golfers of all standards.

18 Holes, 5833yds, Par 70, SSS 69, Course record 61.
Club membership 600.

Visitors Mon-Fri except BHs. Booking required. Dress code.
Societies booking required. **Green Fees** not confirmed **Course Designer** Terry Murray **Prof** G Cousins/C Carsberg **Facilities** ⑪ ⬛ 🖵 🍴 ⚲ ⚒ 🛒 ⚒ **Conf** facs **Location** on B474, 2m NE of High Wycombe
Hotel ★★★★★ GA Crazy Bear Beaconsfield, 75 Wycombe End, Old Town, BEACONSFIELD ☎ 01494 673086 🖷 01494 730183 10 rooms

IVER　　　　　　　　　　　　Map 4 TQ08

Richings Park Golf & Country Club North Park SL0 9DL
☎ 01753 655370 & 655352 (pro shop)　🖷 01753 655409
web: www.richingspark.co.uk

18 Holes, 6144yds, Par 70, SSS 69, Course record 63.

Course Designer Alan Higgins **Location** M4 junct 5, A4 towards Colnbrook, left at lights, Sutton Lane, right at next lights North Park
Telephone for further details
Hotel ★★★★ 75% HL Heathrow/Windsor Marriott, Ditton Road, Langley, SLOUGH ☎ 01753 544244 🖷 01753 540240　382 en suite

Thorney Park Golf Club Thorney Mill Rd SL0 9AL
☎ 01895 422095　🖷 01895 431307
web: www.thorneypark.com

18 Holes, 5765yds, Par 69, SSS 68, Course record 69.

Course Designer David Walker **Location** M4 junct 5, left onto A4, left onto Sutton Ln, right for Thorney Mill Rd

Telephone for further details
Hotel ★★★★ 75% HL Heathrow/Windsor Marriott, Ditton Road, Langley, SLOUGH ☎ 01753 544244 🖷 01753 540240　382 en suite

LITTLE BRICKHILL　　　　　　Map 4 SP93

Woburn Golf & Country Club **see page 31**
MK17 9LJ
☎ 01908 370756　🖷 01908 378436
e-mail: golf.enquiries@woburn.co.uk
web: www.woburn.co.uk/golf

LOUDWATER　　　　　　　　Map 4 SU89

Wycombe Heights Golf Centre Rayners Ave HP10 9SZ
☎ 01494 816686　🖷 01494 816728
e-mail: sales@wycombeheightsgc.co.uk
web: www.wycombeheightsgc.co.uk

An impressive tree-lined parkland course with panoramic views of the Chilterns. The final four holes are particularly challenging. A delightful 18 hole par 3 course and floodlit driving range complement the High Course.

High Course: 18 Holes, 6062yds, Par 69, SSS 69,
Course record 62. Club membership 600.

Visitors Mon-Sun & BHs. Dress code. **Societies** booking required.
Green Fees £20 per round (£27 weekends & BHs) **Course Designer** John Jacobs **Prof** Chris Reeves **Facilities** ⑪ 🍴 ⬛ 🖵 🍴 ⚲ 🖻 ⚒ ⚒ 🌳 **Leisure** par 3 course **Conf** facs Corporate Hospitality Days **Location** M40 junct 3, A40 towards High Wycombe. 0.5m right onto Rayners Ave at lights
Hotel ★★★★★ GA Crazy Bear Beaconsfield, 75 Wycombe End, Old Town, BEACONSFIELD ☎ 01494 673086 🖷 01494 730183 10 rooms

MARLOW　　　　　　　　　　Map 4 SU88

Harleyford Golf Club Harleyford Estate, Henley Rd SL7 2SP
☎ 01628 816161　🖷 01628 816160
e-mail: manager@harleyfordgolf.co.uk
web: www.harleyfordgolf.co.uk

Set in 160 acres, this Donald Steel designed course, founded in 1996, makes the most of the natural rolling contours of the beautiful parkland of the historic Harleyford Estate. A challenging course to golfers of all handicaps. Stunning views of the Thames Valley.

18 Holes, 6708yds, Par 72, SSS 72, Course record 67.
Club membership 750.

Visitors Mon-Sun & BHs. Booking required. Dress code.
Societies booking required. **Green Fees** not confirmed **Course Designer** Donald Steel **Prof** Graham Finch **Facilities** ⑪ 🍴 ⬛ 🖵 🍴 ⚲ 🖻 ⚒ ⚒ 🛒 ⚒ 🌳 **Conf** facs Corporate Hospitality Days **Location** S side A4156 Marlow-Henley road
Hotel ★★★★ 81% HL Danesfield House Hotel & Spa, Henley Road, MARLOW-ON-THAMES ☎ 01628 891010 🖷 01628 890408 84 en suite

WOBURN GOLF & COUNTRY CLUB
BUCKINGHAMSHIRE - LITTLE BRICKHILL - MAP 4 SP93

Easily accessible from the M1, Woburn is famed not only for its golf courses but also for the magnificent stately home and wildlife park, which are both well worth a visit. Charles Lawrie of Cotton Pennink designed two great courses here among trees and beautiful countryside. From the back tees they are rather long for the weekend amateur golfer. The Duke's Course is a tough challenge for golfers at all levels. The Duchess Course, although relatively easier, still demands a high level of skills to negotiate the fairways guarded by towering pines. A third course, the Marquess, opened in June 2000 and has already staged the British Masters twice. The town of Woburn and the abbey are in Bedfordshire, while the golf club is over the border in Buckinghamshire.

MK17 9LJ ☎ 01908 370756 ▤ 01908 378436
e-mail: golf.enquiries@woburn.co.uk web: www.woburn.co.uk/golf
Duke's Course: 18 Holes, 6976yds, Par 72, SSS 74, Course record 62.
Duchess Course: 18 Holes, 6651yds, Par 72, SSS 72.
Marquess Course: 18 Holes, 7214yards, Par 72, SSS 74.
Visitors Mon-Fri except BHs. Booking required. Handicap certificate. Dress code. **Societies** booking required.
Green Fees phone **Course Designer** Charles Lawrie/Peter Alliss & others **Prof** Luther Blacklock **Facilities** ⑪ ▯
🍴 ⛳ 🏪 ⛳ ✦ 🏌 ⛳ 🏌 **Conf** Corporate Hospitality Days **Location** M1 junct 13, 4m W off A5130
Hotel ★★★ 80% HL The Inn at Woburn, George Street, WOBURN ☎ 01525 290441
▤ 01525 290432 55 en suite

MENTMORE   Map 4 SP91

Mentmore Golf & Country Club LU7 0UA
☎ 01296 662020 📄 01296 662592
e-mail: enquiries@mentmorecountryclub.co.uk
web: www.mentmorecountryclub.co.uk

Two 18-hole courses - Rosebery and Rothschild - set within the wooded estate grounds of Mentmore Towers. Gently rolling parkland course with mature trees and lakes and two interesting feature holes; the long par 5 (606 yds) 9th on the Rosebery course with fine views of the Chilterns and the par 4 (340yd) 14th on the Rothschild course, in front of the Towers.

The Rosebery: 18 Holes, 6827yds, Par 72.
The Rothschild: 18 Holes, 6777yds, Par 72.
Club membership 1100.

Visitors Mon-Sun except BHs. Dress code. Societies booking required. Green Fees Winter £35 Mon-Thu, £45 Fri (£50 weekends) Course Designer Bob Sandow Prof Alister Halliday Facilities ⊕ ⊺⊙⊺ ᗐ ⊑ ⊓ ⊔ ᗐ ⊏ ⊓ᵗ ᵍ ⊨ ᵍ ᵍ Leisure hard tennis courts, heated indoor swimming pool, sauna, gymnasium Conf facs Corporate Hospitality Days Location 4m S of Leighton Buzzard
Hotel ★★★ 78% HL Holiday Inn Aylesbury, Aston Clinton Road, AYLESBURY ☎ 01296 734000 📄 01296 392211 139 en suite

MILTON KEYNES   Map 4 SP83

Abbey Hill Golf Centre Monks Way MK8 8AA
☎ 01908 563845

18 Holes, 6122yds, Par 71, SSS 69, Course record 66.

Course Designer Howard Swann Location 2m W of town centre off A5 Telephone for further details
Hotel ★★★ 73% HL Novotel Milton Keynes, Saxon Street, Layburn Court, Heelands, MILTON KEYNES ☎ 01908 322212 📄 01908 322235 124 en suite

Three Locks Golf Club Great Brickhill MK17 9BH
☎ 01525 270050 📄 01525 270470
e-mail: info@threelocksgolfclub.co.uk
web: www.threelocksgolfclub.co.uk

Parkland course offering a challenge to beginners and experienced golfers, with water coming into play on ten holes. Magnificent views. Good winter course with trolleys allowed.

18 Holes, 6036yds, Par 70, SSS 69, Course record 60.
Club membership 300.

Visitors contact club for details. Societies welcome. Green Fees not confirmed Course Designer MRM Sandown Facilities ⊕ ⊺⊙⊺ ᗐ ⊑ ⊓ ⊔ ᗐ ⊏ ⊓ᵗ ᵍ ᵍ Leisure fishing Conf facs Corporate Hospitality Days Location A4146 between Leighton Buzzard & Bletchley
Hotel BUD Campanile Milton Keynes, 40 Penn Road (off Watling St), Fenny Stratford, Bletchley, MILTON KEYNES ☎ 01908 649819 📄 01908 649818 80 en suite

PRINCES RISBOROUGH   Map 4 SP80

Whiteleaf Golf Club Upper Icknield Way, Whiteleaf HP27 0LY
☎ 01844 274058 📄 01844 275551
e-mail: whiteleafgc@tiscali.co.uk
web: www.whiteleafgolfclub.co.uk

A picturesque course on the edge of the Chilterns. Good views over the Vale of Aylesbury. A short challenging course requiring great accuracy.

9 Holes, 5391yds, Par 66, SSS 66, Course record 63.
Club membership 280.

Visitors Mon-Fri, after midday Sat-Sun & BHs. Societies booking required. Green Fees £35 per day, £25 per 18 holes, £15 per 9 holes Prof Ken Ward Facilities ⊕ ⊺⊙⊺ ᗐ ⊑ ⊓ ⊔ ᗐ ⊏ ᵍ Conf Corporate Hospitality Days Location 1m NE off A4010
Hotel ★★★★ HL Hartwell House Hotel, Restaurant & Spa, Oxford Road, AYLESBURY ☎ 01296 747444 📄 01296 747450 46 en suite

STOKE POGES   Map 4 SU98

Farnham Park Golf Course Park Rd SL2 4PJ
☎ 01753 643332 📄 01753 646617
e-mail: nigel.whitton@southbucks.gov.uk
web: www.farnhamparkgolfcourse.co.uk

Fine public course set in 130 acres of attractive mature wooded parkland. The Colt/Hawtree design is both challenging and rewarding in equal measure with several good birdie opportunities and a selection of memorable holes in the 6th, 10th, 11th, 13th and 16th.

18 Holes, 6119yds, Par 70, SSS 69. Club membership 300.

Visitors Mon-Sun & BHs. Booking required. Societies booking required. Green Fees not confirmed Course Designer Colt/Hawtree Prof Nigel Whitton Facilities ⊕ ⊺⊙⊺ ᗐ ⊑ ⊓ ⊔ ᗐ ⊏ ⊓ᵗ ᵍ ᵍ Conf Corporate Hospitality Days Location 1m along Park Road, E of A355 at Farnham Royal
Hotel ★★★★ 75% HL Heathrow/Windsor Marriott, Ditton Road, Langley, SLOUGH ☎ 01753 544244 📄 01753 540240 382 en suite

Save on Hotels. Book at **theAA.com/hotel**

BUCKINGHAMSHIRE

Top 100 Golf Courses in the World.'

olf World

'lay one of Harry Colt's
Classic Courses...

ounded 1908.

nly 35 minutes from London,
nd 7 miles from Heathrow.

asual Green Fees welcome.

ww.stokepark.com

Please contact the Pro Shop
on **01753 71 71 84**
Stoke Park . Park Road . Stoke Poges . Bucks . SL2 4PG

Stoke Park Stoke Park, Park Rd SL2 4PG
☎ 01753 717171 📄 01753 717181
e-mail: info@stokepark.com
web: www.stokepark.com

Judgement of the distance from the tee is all important on this classic parkland course made up of three 9 hole courses, Colt, Alison and Lane Jackson. Fairways are wide and the challenge seemingly innocuous - testing par 4s, superb bunkering and fast putting surfaces. The 7th hole is the model for the well-known 12th hole at Augusta. Recent improvements have seen a complete reconstruction of the 15th hole with new bunkers and a new tee and on the 16th hole a new championship tee has been built.

Colt: 9 Holes, 3509yds, Par 36.
Alison: 9 Holes, 3242yds, Par 35.
Lane: 9 Holes, 3060yds, Par 36. Club membership 2500.

Visitors Subject to availability 14 days in advance. Booking required. **Societies** booking required. **Green Fees** Winter (Nov-Mar) £85 (£145 weekends), Junior £40. Summer (Apr-Oct) £145 (£205 weekends), Junior £40 **Course Designer** Harry Shapland Colt **Prof** Stuart Collier **Facilities** ⓣ ⅃ 🍴 🛅 ⬛ 🏌 ◇ ✐ 🛒 ✎ 🏌 **Leisure** hard and grass tennis courts, heated indoor swimming pool, fishing, sauna, gymnasium, indoor tennis courts, treatment room spa **Conf** facs Corporate Hospitality Days **Location** off A4 at Slough onto B416 Stoke Poges Ln, club 1.5m on left

Hotel ★★★★★ 85% HL Stoke Park, Park Road, STOKE POGES
☎ 01753 717171 📄 01753 717181 49 en suite

See advert on page 33

See advert on page 33

STOWE Map 4 SP63

Silverstone Golf Course Silverstone Rd MK18 5LH
☎ 01280 850005 📄 01280 850156
e-mail: enquiries@silverstonegolfclub.co.uk
web: www.silverstonegolfclub.co.uk

A challenging parkland course situated opposite the Grand Prix circuit. Suitable for both high and low handicap players but care must be taken with the water hazards that are a distinctive feature of the course.

18 Holes, 6224yds, Par 72, SSS 69.
Club membership 500.

Visitors Mon-Sun & BHs. Booking required. Dress code **Societies** booking required. **Green Fees** phone **Course Designer** David Snell **Prof** Rodney Holt **Facilities** ⓣ 🍴 🛅 ⬛ 🏌 ⅃ 🛒 ✐ 🛒 ✎ 🏌 **Conf** facs Corporate Hospitality Days **Location** from Silverstone signs to Grand Prix track. Club 1m past entrance on right

Hotel ★★★★ 72% HL Villiers, 3 Castle Street, BUCKINGHAM
☎ 01280 822444 📄 01280 822113 49 en suite

WAVENDON Map 4 SP93

Wavendon Golf Centre Lower End Rd MK17 8DA
☎ 01908 281811 📄 01908 281257
e-mail: wavendon@jack-barker.co.uk
web: www.jack-barker.co.uk

Pleasant parkland course set within mature oak and lime trees and incorporating several small lakes as water hazards. Easy walking.

Wavedon: 18 Holes, 5462yds, Par 69, SSS 67.
Club membership 300.

Visitors Mon-Sun & BHs. Booking required weekends & BHs. **Societies** welcome. **Green Fees** Per 18 holes - Mon £10, Tue-Thu £16.50, Sat-Sun & BHs £22 **Course Designer** J Drake/N Elmer **Prof** Greg Iron **Facilities** ⓣ 🍴 🛅 ⬛ 🏌 ⅃ 🛒 ✎ 🏌 **Leisure** 9 hole par 3 course, pitch & putt 9 hole course **Conf** facs **Location** M1 junct 13, off A421

Hotel ★★★ 77% HL Best Western Moore Place, The Square, ASPLEY GUISE ☎ 01908 282000 📄 01908 281888 62 en suite

---

WESTON TURVILLE Map 4 SP81

Weston Turville Golf Club New Rd HP22 5QT
☎ 01296 424084 📄 01296 395376
web: www.westonturvillegolfclub.co.uk

18 Holes, 6008yds, Par 69, SSS 69, Course record 68.

Location 2m SE of Aylesbury, off A41
Telephone for further details
Hotel ★★★ 78% HL Holiday Inn Aylesbury, Aston Clinton Road, AYLESBURY ☎ 01296 734000 📄 01296 392211 139 en suite

WEXHAM STREET　　　　　　　　　Map 4 SU98

Wexham Park Golf Club SL3 6ND
☎ 01753 663271 📄 01753 663318
e-mail: info@wexhamparkgolfcentre.co.uk
web: www.wexhamparkgolfcentre.co.uk

Gently undulating parkland. Three courses, an 18 hole, a challenging nine hole, and another nine hole suitable for beginners.

Blue: 18 Holes, 5346yds, Par 68, SSS 66.
Red: 9 Holes, 2822yds, Par 34.
Green: 9 Holes, 2233yds, Par 32. Club membership 950.

Visitors Mon-Sun & BHs. Booking required. **Societies** booking required. **Green Fees** £17 for 18 holes, £9.50 for 9 holes (£23/£12.75 weekends) **Course Designer** E Lawrence/D Morgan **Prof** John Kennedy **Facilities** ⓘ ⓑ ⓛ ⓟ ⓣ ⓐ 🏠 ⓟ 🍴 ⓔ 🏌 **Conf** Corporate Hospitality Days **Location** 0.5m S of Wexham

Hotel ★★★★ 75% HL Heathrow/Windsor Marriott, Ditton Road, Langley, SLOUGH ☎ 01753 544244 📄 01753 540240 382 en suite

WING　　　　　　　　　　　　　Map 4 SP82

Aylesbury Vale Golf Club Stewkley Rd LU7 0UJ
☎ 01525 240196 📄 01525 240848
e-mail: info@avgc.co.uk
web: www.avgc.co.uk

This gently undulating course is set amid tranquil countryside. There are five ponds to pose the golfer problems, notably on the par 4 420yd 13th - unlucky for some - where the second shot is all downhill with an inviting pond spanning the approach to the green. Fairways are treelined but wide enough to give a fair chance for all levels of golfer.

18 Holes, 6612yds, Par 72, SSS 72, Course record 67.
Club membership 515.

Visitors Mon-Sun & BHs. Booking required weekends & BHs. Dress code. **Societies** booking required. **Green Fees** not confirmed **Course Designer** D Wright **Prof** Terry Bunyan **Facilities** ⓘ 🍴 ⓑ ⓟ ⓣ ⓐ 🏠 ⓟ ⓔ 🏠 ⓔ 🏌 **Conf** facs Corporate Hospitality Days **Location** 2m NW of Leighton Buzzard on unclassified Stewkley road, between Wing & Stewkley

Hotel ★★★ 78% HL Holiday Inn Aylesbury, Aston Clinton Road, AYLESBURY ☎ 01296 734000 📄 01296 392211 139 en suite

CAMBRIDGESHIRE

ENGLAND

BAR HILL　　　　　　　　　　　　Map 5 TL36

Menzies Cambridgeshire Golf Club Bar Hill CB23 8EU
☎ 01954 780098 📄 01954 780010
e-mail: cambridge.golfpro@menzieshotels.co.uk
web: www.menzieshotels.co.uk

Mature undulating parkland course with tree-lined fairways, easy walking. Challenging opening and closing holes with water on the right and out of bounds on the left of both.

18 Holes, 6750yds, Par 72, SSS 73, Course record 66.
Club membership 500.

Visitors Mon-Sun & BHs. Booking required. Dress code. **Societies** booking required. **Green Fees** £30 per round (£40 weekends & BHs). Winter £25/£30 **Prof** Mike Clemons **Facilities** ⓘ 🍴 ⓑ ⓟ ⓣ ⓐ 🏠 ⓟ ◇ ⓔ 🏠 ⓔ **Leisure** hard tennis courts, heated indoor swimming pool, sauna, gymnasium, 2 practice grounds **Conf** facs Corporate Hospitality Days **Location** M11/A14, then B1050 (Bar Hill)

Hotel ★★★★ 77% HL Menzies Cambridge Hotel & Golf Club, Bar Hill, CAMBRIDGE ☎ 01954 249988 📄 01954 780010 136 en suite

BOURN　　　　　　　　　　　　　Map 5 TL35

Bourn Golf Course Toft Rd CB3 7TT
☎ 01954 718958 📄 01954 718908
e-mail: info@bourngolfandleisure.co.uk
web: www.bourngolfandleisure.co.uk

Set in a rural location yet only 8 miles from Cambridge. 18 holes of challenging parkland course with rolling hills and many large mature trees combined with 3 lakes and a brook running through the course.

18 Holes, 6229yards, Par 72, SSS 72, Course record 63.
Club membership 640.

Visitors may play Mon-Sun & BHs. Dress code. **Societies** booking required. **Green Fees** £22 per 18 holes (£30 weekends) **Course Designer** P Crow **Prof** Mark Sturgess **Facilities** ⓘ 🍴 ⓑ ⓟ ⓣ ⓐ 🏠 ⓟ ⓔ 🏠 ⓔ **Leisure** heated indoor swimming pool, sauna, gymnasium **Conf** facs Corporate Hospitality Days **Location** M11 junct 12, A603 towards Sandy. Right onto B1046, through Barton, Comberton and Toft. On leaving Toft, course is 0.5m on right.

Hotel ★★★★ 79% HL The Cambridge Belfry, Back Street, CAMBOURNE ☎ 01954 714600 📄 01954 714610 120 en suite

BRAMPTON

Map 4 TL27

Brampton Park Golf Club Buckden Rd PE28 4NF
☎ 01480 434700 & 434705 (pro shop) 🖷 01480 411145
e-mail: admin@bramptonparkgc.co.uk
web: www.bramptonparkgc.co.uk
Set in truly attractive countryside, bounded by the River Great Ouse
and bisected by the River Lane. Great variety with mature trees, lakes
and water hazards. One of the most difficult holes is the 4th, a par 3
island green, 175yds in length.

18 Holes, 6300yds, Par 71, SSS 72, Course record 62.
Club membership 650.
Visitors Mon-Sun except BHs. Booking required Wed and weekends.
Dress code. **Societies** welcome. **Green Fees** £37 per day, £27 per
round (£46 per round weekends) **Course Designer** Simon Gidman
Prof Alisdair Currie **Facilities** 🕀 🍴 🖢 ☕ 🍴 🏖 🏠 ◇ ✔
🍺 ◇ 🟊 **Conf** facs Corporate Hospitality Days **Location** signs from
A1 or A14 to RAF Brampton
Hotel ★★★★ 77% HL Huntingdon Marriott Hotel, Kingfisher
Way, Hinchingbrooke Business Park, HUNTINGDON ☎ 01480 446000
🖷 01480 451111 150 en suite

CAMBRIDGE

Map 5 TL45

The Gog Magog Golf Club Shelford Bottom CB22 3AB
☎ 01223 247626 🖷 01223 414990
e-mail: secretary@gogmagog.co.uk
web: www.gogmagog.co.uk
Gog Magog, established in 1901, is situated just outside the centre
of the university town. The chalk downland courses are on high
ground, and it is said that if you stand on the highest point and
could see far enough to the east the next highest ground would be
the Ural Mountains. The courses are open but there are enough trees
and other hazards to provide plenty of problems. Views from the
high parts are superb. The nature of the ground ensures good winter
golf. The area has been designated a Site of Special Scientific
Interest.

Old Course: 18 Holes, 6398yds, Par 70, SSS 71,
Course record 60.
Wandlebury: 18 Holes, 6735yds, Par 72, SSS 73,
Course record 65. Club membership 1400.
Visitors Mon, Tue, Thu, Fri, Sun & BHs. Wed & Sun booking required.
Handicap certificate. Dress code. **Societies** welcome. **Green**
Fees £64 per day, £47 per round (£67 per round Sun & BHs) **Course**
Designer Hawtree Ltd **Prof** Ian Bamborough **Facilities** 🕀 🍴
🖢 ☕ 🍴 🏖 🏠 ◇ ✔ 🍺 ◇ 🟊 **Conf** facs Corporate
Hospitality Days **Location** 3m SE on A1307
Hotel ★★★ 77% HL Duxford Lodge, Ickleton Road, DUXFORD
☎ 01223 836444 🖷 01223 832271 15 en suite

ELY

Map 5 TL58

Ely City Golf Club 107 Cambridge Rd CB7 4HX
☎ 01353 662751 (Office) 🖷 01353 668636
e-mail: info@elygolf.co.uk
web: www.elygolf.co.uk.
Slightly undulating parkland with water hazards formed by lakes
and natural dykes. Demanding par 4 5th hole (467yds), often into
a headwind, and a testing par 3 2nd hole (160yds) played over two
ponds. Magnificent views of the cathedral.

18 Holes, 6627yds, Par 72, SSS 72, Course record 65.
Club membership 700.
Visitors Mon-Sun & BHs. Dress code. **Societies** welcome. **Green**
Fees £36 per day (£42 weekends) **Course Designer** Sir Henry Cotton
Prof Andrew George **Facilities** 🕀 🍴 🖢 ☕ 🍴 🏖 🏠 ◇ ✔
🍺 ◇ **Conf** Corporate Hospitality Days **Location** S of city on A10
Hotel ★★★★ GA The Nyton, 7 Barton Road, ELY
☎ 01353 662459 🖷 01353 666217 9 rooms (9 en suite)

GIRTON

Map 5 TL46

Girton Golf Club Dodford Ln CB3 0QE
☎ 01223 276169 🖷 01223 277150
e-mail: info@girtongolf.co.uk
web: www.girtongolf.co.uk
Mature, easy walking parkland course.

18 Holes, 6012yds, Par 69, SSS 69.
Club membership 800.
Visitors Mon-Fri. Booking required weekends & BHs.
Societies booking required. **Green Fees** £25 per 18 holes (from
£30 weekends) **Course Designer** Allan Gow **Prof** Scott Thomson
Facilities 🕀 🍴 🖢 ☕ 🍴 🏖 🏠 ◇ ✔ **Conf** facs
Corporate Hospitality Days **Location** 3m from Cambridge, off A14
junct 31
Hotel ★★★★ 82% HL Hotel Felix, Whitehouse Lane,
CAMBRIDGE ☎ 01223 277977 🖷 01223 277973 52 en suite

LONGSTANTON

Map 5 TL36

Cambridge Golf Club Station Rd CB24 5DS
☎ 01954 789388
e-mail: cambridgegolfclub@tiscali.co.uk
web: www.cambridgegolfclub.net
Undulating parkland with bunkers and ponds.

18 Holes, 6818yds, Par 72, SSS 74. Club membership 350.
Visitors Mon-Sun & BHs. Booking required weekends & BHs. Dress
code. **Societies** welcome. **Green Fees** £14 per 18 holes (£18
weekends). £10 winter specials **Prof** Adrienne Engelman **Facilities** 🕀
🍴 🖢 ☕ 🍴 🏖 🏠 ◇ ✔ 🍺 ◇ 🟊 **Leisure** fishing,
hot air balloons, fishing **Conf** facs Corporate Hospitality Days
Location A14, junct 29 onto B1050 towards Willingham. Straight over
1st rdbt, turn right at 2nd and 3rd rdbt. Club entrance on left
Hotel ★★★★ 77% HL Menzies Cambridge Hotel & Golf Club, Bar
Hill, CAMBRIDGE ☎ 01954 249988 🖷 01954 780010 136 en suite

MARCH

Map 5 TL49

March Golf Club Frogs Abbey, Grange Rd PE15 0YH
☎ 01354 652364
e-mail: secretary@marchgolfclub.co.uk
web: www.marchgolfclub.co.uk
Parkland course with a particularly challenging par 3 9th hole, with
out of bounds on the right and high hedges to the left.

9 Holes, 6204yds, Par 70, SSS 70, Course record 65.
Club membership 315.
Visitors Mon-Sun & BHs. Dress code. **Societies** booking required.
Green Fees phone **Prof** Alex Oldham **Facilities** 🕀 🖢 ☕ 🍴 🏖
🏠 🍺 ◇ **Conf** facs Corporate Hospitality Days **Location** 0.5m off
A141, March bypass
Hotel ★★★ 83% HL Crown Lodge, Downham Road, Outwell,
WISBECH ☎ 01945 773391 & 772206 🖷 01945 772668 10 en suite

MELDRETH   Map 5 TL34

New Malton Golf Course Malton Rd SG8 6PE
☎ 01763 262200
e-mail: info@newmaltongolf.co.uk
web: www.newmaltongolf.co.uk

Set among 230 acres of beautiful undulating countryside teeming with wildlife. The River Cam bisects part of this peaceful course which is surrounded by woodlands and wetlands. Flat course and water comes into play on several holes. Full greens and tees used all year round. To date this is the UK's only 100% chemical free organic golf course.

18 Holes, 6635yds, Par 71, SSS 71. Club membership 150.

Visitors Mon-Sun & BHs. Booking required. Etiquette code. **Societies** booking required. **Green Fees** £16 per 18 holes (£26 weekends & BHs) **Course Designer** Bruce Critchley/John Jacobs **Prof** Brian Mudge **Facilities** ⑪ ⑩ ⅃ ⌹ ⅌ ⅃ ⌂ ⅋ ⅋ ⅋ **Leisure** fishing **Conf** Corporate Hospitality Days **Location** off A10, between Orwell & Meldreth.
Hotel ★★★ 77% HL Duxford Lodge, Ickleton Road, DUXFORD ☎ 01223 836444 ⅌ 01223 832271 15 en suite

PETERBOROUGH   Map 4 TL19

Elton Furze Golf Club Bullock Rd, Haddon PE7 3TT
☎ 01832 280189 & 280614 (Pro shop) ⅌ 01832 280299
e-mail: info@efgc.co.uk
web: www.efgc.co.uk

Elton Furze Golf Club is set in the picturesque surroundings of the Cambridgeshire countryside. The course has been designed in and around mature woodland with ponds and slopes, which provides an interesting and enjoyable round of golf.

18 Holes, 6279yds, Par 70, SSS 71, Course record 63.
Club membership 620.

Visitors Mon-Sun & BHs. Booking preferred. **Societies** booking required. **Green Fees** £48 per day, £35 per round (£55/£39 weekends) **Course Designer** Roger Fitton **Prof** Glyn Krause **Facilities** ⑪ ⑩ by prior arrangement ⅃ ⌹ ⅌ ⅃ ⌂ ⅋ ⅋ **Conf** facs Corporate Hospitality Days **Location** 4m SW of Peterborough, off A605/A1
Hotel ★★★★ 77% HL Peterborough Marriott, Peterborough Business Park, Lynchwood, PETERBOROUGH ☎ 01733 371111 ⅌ 01733 236725 163 en suite

Orton Meadows Golf Centre Ham Ln, Orton Waterville PE2 5UU
☎ 01733 237478 ⅌ 01733 332774
e-mail: enquiries@ortonmeadowsgolfcourse.co.uk
web: www.ortonmeadowsgolfcourse.co.uk

Picturesque course with trees, lakes and an abundance of water fowl, providing some challenges with water featuring on 10 holes.

18 Holes, 5269yds, Par 67, SSS 68, Course record 64.
Club membership 650.

Visitors contact club for details. **Societies** welcome. **Green Fees** not confirmed **Course Designer** D & R Fitton **Prof** Stuart Brown **Facilities** ⑪ ⑩ ⅃ ⌹ ⅌ ⅃ ⌂ ⅋ ◇ ⅋ **Leisure** 12 hole pitch & putt **Location** 3m W of town on A605
Hotel ★★★ 81% HL Best Western Orton Hall, Orton Longueville, PETERBOROUGH ☎ 01733 391111 ⅌ 01733 231912 73 en suite

Peterborough Milton Golf Club Milton Ferry PE6 7AG
☎ 01733 380489 ⅌ 01733 380489
e-mail: secretary@pmgc.org.uk
web: www.pmgc.org.uk

Designed by James Braid, this well-bunkered parkland course is set in the grounds of the Milton Estate, many of the holes being played in full view of Milton Hall. Challenging holes are the difficult dog-leg 10th and 15th. Easy walking.

Milton: 18 Holes, 6516yds, Par 71, SSS 72.
Club membership 800.

Visitors Mon-Sun & BHs. Booking required weekends & BHs. Handicap certificate. Dress code. **Societies** booking required. **Green Fees** £40 per 36 holes (£50 weekends & BHs) **Course Designer** James Braid **Prof** Jasen Barker/Matt Thorpe **Facilities** ⑪ ⑩ ⅃ ⌹ ⅌ ⅃ ⌂ ⅋ ⅋ ⅋ ⅋ **Conf** facs Corporate Hospitality Days **Location** 2m W of Peterborough on A47
Hotel ★★★★ 74% HL Holiday Inn Peterborough West, Thorpe Wood, PETERBOROUGH ☎ 0871 942 9186 & 01733 289988 ⅌ 01733 262737 133 en suite

Thorpe Wood Golf Course Thorpe Wood, Nene Parkway PE3 6SE
☎ 01733 267701 ⅌ 01733 332774
e-mail: enquiries@thorpewoodgolfcourse.co.uk
web: www.thorpewoodgolfcourse.co.uk

Gently undulating, parkland course designed by Peter Alliss and Dave Thomas. Challenging holes include the 5th, the longest hole, usually played with prevailing wind, and the 14th, which has a difficult approach shot over water to a two-tier green.

18 Holes, 7086yds, Par 73, SSS 74, Course record 68.
Club membership 750.

Visitors Dress code. **Societies** booking required. **Green Fees** £16 per round (£22 weekends & BHs). £10 seniors midweek **Course Designer** Peter Alliss/Dave Thomas **Prof** Simon Fitton **Facilities** ⑪ ⑩ ⅃ ⌹ ⅌ ⅃ ⌂ ⅋ ⅋ ⅋ **Location** 3m W of city centre on A47
Hotel ★★★ 81% HL Best Western Orton Hall, Orton Longueville, PETERBOROUGH ☎ 01733 391111 ⅌ 01733 231912 73 en suite

PIDLEY   Map 5 TL37

Lakeside Lodge Golf Club Fen Rd PE28 3DF
☎ 01487 740540 ⅌ 01487 740852
e-mail: info@lakeside-lodge.co.uk
web: www.lakeside-lodge.co.uk

The Lodge is a well-designed, spacious course incorporating eight lakes, 12,000 trees and a modern clubhouse. The 9th and 18th holes both finish dramatically alongside a lake in front of the clubhouse. The Manor provides an interesting contrast with its undulating fairways and angular greens. In 2001 work was completed on 6 new holes adjacent to the Manor, forming another option, the Church course. Also nine-hole par 3, and 25-bay driving range.

Lodge Course: 18 Holes, 6885yds, Par 72, SSS 73.
The Manor: 9 Holes, 2601yds, Par 34, SSS 33.
The Church: 12 Holes, 3290yds, Par 44.
Club membership 800.

Visitors Mon-Sun & BHs. **Societies** welcome. **Green Fees** not confirmed **Course Designer** A W Headley **Prof** Scott Waterman **Facilities** ⑪ ⑩ ⅃ ⌹ ⅌ ⅃ ⌂ ⅋ ◇ ⅋ ⅋ ⅋ **Leisure** gymnasium, ten pin bowling **Conf** facs Corporate Hospitality Days **Location** A141 from Huntingdon, then B1040
Hotel ★★★ 74% HL Olivers Lodge, Needingworth Road, ST IVES ☎ 01480 463252 ⅌ 01480 461150 17 en suite

ENGLAND

RAMSEY
Map 4 TL28

Ramsey Golf & Bowls Club 4 Abbey Ter PE26 1DD
☎ 01487 812600 📠 01487 815746
e-mail: admin@ramseyclub.co.uk
web: www.ramseyclub.co.uk

Flat parkland with water hazards and well-irrigated greens, mature tees and fairways - a good surface whatever the conditions. The impression of wide-open spaces will soon punish the wayward shot.

18 Holes, 5998yds, Par 70, SSS 69, Course record 63. Club membership 600.

Visitors Mon-Sun & BHs. Booking required Fri-Sun & BHs. Dress code. **Societies** booking required. **Green Fees** £25 per 18 holes **Course Designer** J Hamilton Stutt **Prof** Stuart Scott **Facilities** 🕙 🍔 ☕ 🍴 ⚔ 🏠 ⛳ 🚞 ⚔ **Leisure** snooker tables, bowls rinks **Location** 12m SE of Peterborough on B1040
Hotel ★★★ 86% HL The Old Bridge Hotel, 1 High Street, HUNTINGDON ☎ 01480 424300 📠 01480 411017 24 en suite

ST IVES
Map 4 TL37

St Ives Golf Club Needingworth Rd PE27 4NB
☎ 01480 499920 📠 01480 301489
e-mail: manager@stivesgolfclub.co.uk
web: www.stivesgolfclub.co.uk

Inland links style course opened 1st May 2010.

18 Holes, 6566yds, Par 72, SSS 70, Course record 68. Club membership 550.

Visitors Mon-Fri except BHs. Handicap certificate. Dress code. **Societies** booking required. **Green Fees** £40 **Course Designer** Cameron Sinclair **Prof** Mark Pond **Facilities** 🕙 🍽 🍔 ☕ 🍴 ⚔ 🏠 🚞 ⚔ 🏁 **Location** NW side of town centre off A1123
Hotel ★★★ 70% HL The Dolphin Hotel, London Road, ST IVES ☎ 01480 466966 📠 01480 495597 67 en suite

ST NEOTS
Map 4 TL16

Abbotsley Golf & Squash Club Eynesbury Hardwicke PE19 6XN
☎ 01480 474000 📠 01480 403280

Abbotsley Course: 18 Holes, 6311yds, Par 73, SSS 72, Course record 69.
Cromwell Course: 18 Holes, 6134yds, Par 70, SSS 69, Course record 66.

Course Designer D Young/V Saunders **Location** off A1 & A428 **Telephone for further details**
Hotel ★★★ 87% HL The George Hotel & Brasserie, High Street, Buckden, ST NEOTS ☎ 01480 812300 📠 01480 813920 12 en suite

St Neots Golf Club Crosshall Rd PE19 7GE
☎ 01480 472363 📠 01480 472363
e-mail: office@stneotsgolfclub.co.uk
web: www.stneotsgolfclub.co.uk

Set in picturesque rolling parkland and divided by the River Kym, the course offers a challenge to all standards of golfer with tree-lined fairways, water hazards and outstanding greens. Fine views of the Ouse on several holes.

18 Holes, 6087yds, Par 70, SSS 70, Course record 65. Club membership 575.

Visitors Mon-Fri except BHs. Booking required. Dress code. **Societies** booking required. **Green Fees** £45 per day, £35 per round **Course Designer** H Vardon **Prof** Paul Toyer **Facilities** 🕙 🍽 🍔 ☕ 🍴 🏠 ⚔ 🚞 ⚔ **Conf** Corporate Hospitality Days **Location** A1 onto B1048 into St Neots
Hotel ★★★ 87% HL The George Hotel & Brasserie, High Street, Buckden, ST NEOTS ☎ 01480 812300 📠 01480 813920 12 en suite

THORNEY
Map 4 TF20

Thorney Golf Centre English Drove, Thorney PE6 0TJ
☎ 01733 270570 📠 01733 270842
e-mail: info@thorneygolfcentre.com
web: www.thorneygolfcentre.com

The 18-hole Fen course is ideal for the beginner, while the Lakes Course has a challenging links-style layout with eight holes around water.

Fen Course: 18 Holes, 6104yds, Par 70, SSS 69, Course record 66.
Lakes Course: 18 Holes, 6441yds, Par 71, SSS 71, Course record 69. Club membership 500.

Visitors Mon-Sun & BHs. Booking required weekends & BHs. Dress code. **Societies** booking required. **Green Fees** phone **Course Designer** A Dow **Prof** Mark Templeman **Facilities** 🕙 🍽 🍔 ☕ 🍴 🏠 ⚔ 🚞 ⚔ **Leisure** par 3 course **Location** off A47, 7m NE of Peterborough
Hotel ★★★★ 75% HL Bull, Westgate, PETERBOROUGH ☎ 01733 561364 📠 01733 557304 118 en suite

TOFT
Map 5 TL35

Cambridge Meridian Golf Course Comberton Rd CB23 2RY
☎ 01223 264700 & 264702 📠 01223 264701
e-mail: meridian@golfsocieties.com
web: www.cambridgemeridiangolf.co.uk

Set in 207 acres to a Peter Alliss and Clive Clark design, with sweeping fairways, lakes and well-bunkered greens. The 4th hole has bunker complexes, a sharp dog-leg and a river with the green heavily guarded by bunkers. The 9th and 10th holes challenge the golfer with river crossings.

18 Holes, 6651yds, Par 73, SSS 72, Course record 72. Club membership 450.

Visitors Mon-Sun & BHs. Dress code. **Societies** welcome. **Green Fees** not confirmed **Course Designer** Peter Alliss/Clive Clark **Prof** Craig Watson **Facilities** 🕙 🍽 by prior arrangement 🍔 ☕ 🍴 🏠 ⚔ 🚞 ⚔ **Leisure** indoor golf simulator **Conf** facs Corporate Hospitality Days **Location** 3m W of Cambridge, on B1046
Hotel ★★★★ 79% HL The Cambridge Belfry, Back Street, CAMBOURNE ☎ 01954 714600 📠 01954 714610 120 en suite

TYDD ST GILES
Map 9 TF41

Tydd St Giles Golf & Leisure Estate Kirkgate PE13 5NZ
☎ 01945 871007
e-mail: enquiries@tyddgolf.co.uk
web: www.tyddgolf.co.uk

This is a comparatively new course. All the greens are around 50 yards long so pin positions in the summer months will add approximately 400 yards to the course making the length around 6,700 yards. Even in its early years, it is a challenge for even the most talented of golfers and with a few more years of maturity, this course should become one of the finest in the area.

18 Holes, 6103yds, Par 70, SSS 70, Course record 64.
Club membership 1000.

Visitors Mon-Sun & BHs. Booking required. **Societies** booking required. **Green Fees** £21 per day (£24 weekends & BHs). Twilight £14 every day from 1pm **Course Designer** Adrian Hurst **Facilities** ⓉⒾ ⓁⒹⓇⒶ🍴 🚹 ⛳ ♦ ♂ ✦ **Leisure** fishing **Conf** facs Corporate Hospitality Days **Location** A1101 N of Wisbech to Long Sutton, turn left into Hannath Rd at Tydd Gate/River
Hotel ★★★ 70% HL Elme Hall, Elm High Road, WISBECH ☎ 01945 475566 📠 01945 475666   8 en suite

CHESHIRE

ALDERLEY EDGE
Map 7 SJ87

Alderley Edge Golf Club Brook Ln SK9 7RU
☎ 01625 586200
e-mail: office@aegc.co.uk
web: www.aegc.co.uk

Well-wooded, undulating pastureland course. A stream crosses seven of the nine holes. A challenging course even for the low handicap player.

9 Holes, 5586yds, Par 68, SSS 67, Course record 60.
Club membership 400.

Visitors Mon, Wed-Fri, Sun & BHs. Booking required. Handicap certificate. Dress code. **Societies** booking required. **Green Fees** £25 per 18 holes (£30 weekends & BHs). £15 per 9 holes (£20 weekends & BHs) **Facilities** Ⓣ Ⓘ ⓁⒹⓇⒶ 🚹 ✦ **Conf** facs Corporate Hospitality Days **Location** 1m NW on B5085
Hotel ★★★ 86% HL Alderley Edge Hotel, Macclesfield Road, ALDERLEY EDGE ☎ 01625 583033 📠 01625 586343   50 en suite

ALDERSEY GREEN
Map 7 SJ45

Aldersey Green Golf Club CH3 9EH
☎ 01829 782157
e-mail: bradburygolf@aol.com
web: www.alderseygreengolfclub.co.uk

An exciting, tricky, beautiful parkland course set in 200 acres of countryside, with tree-lined fairways and 14 lakes.

18 Holes, 6165yds, Par 71, SSS 70, Course record 68.
Club membership 350.

Visitors Mon-Sun & BHs. Dress code. **Societies** booking required. **Green Fees** not confirmed **Prof** Stephen Bradbury **Facilities** Ⓣ Ⓘ ⓁⒹⓇⒶ 🚹 ✦ **Conf** Corporate Hospitality Days **Location** On A41 Whitchurch Rd, 6m S of Chester
Hotel ★★★★ 81% HL De Vere Carden Park, Carden Park, BROXTON ☎ 01829 731000 📠 01829 731599   196 en suite

ANTROBUS
Map 7 SJ68

Antrobus Golf Club Foggs Ln CW9 6JQ
☎ 01925 730890
e-mail: antrobusgolfclub@gmail.com
web: www.antrobusgolfclub.co.uk

A challenging parkland course where water is the main feature with streams and ponds in play on most holes. Large undulating greens.

18 Holes, 6220yards, Par 71, SSS 71, Course record 65.
Club membership 400.

Visitors Mon-Wed, Fri, Sun & BHs. Booking required. Dress code. **Societies** booking required. **Green Fees** £28 per day (£30 Sun and BHs) **Course Designer** Mike Slater **Prof** Paul Farrance **Facilities** Ⓣ Ⓘ ⓁⒹⓇⒶ 🚹 ♦ ♂ ✦ **Leisure** fishing **Conf** facs Corporate Hospitality Days **Location** M56 junct 10, A559 towards Northwich, 2nd left after Birch pub onto Knutsford Rd, 1st left into Foggs Ln
Hotel ★★★★ 78% HL The Park Royal, Stretton Road, Stretton, WARRINGTON ☎ 01925 730706 📠 01925 730740   146 en suite

BROXTON
Map 7 SJ45

Carden Park Hotel, Golf Resort and Spa Carden Park CH3 9DQ
☎ 01829 731000 📠 01829 731032
e-mail: reservations.carden@devere-hotels.com
web: www.cardenpark.co.uk

A superb golf resort set in 900 acres of beautiful Cheshire countryside. Facilities include the mature parkland Cheshire Course, the Nicklaus Course, the Golf School and a luxurious clubhouse.

The Cheshire: 18 Holes, 6824yds, Par 72.
The Nicklaus: 18 Holes, 7045yds, Par 72.
Club membership 200.

Visitors Dress code. **Societies** booking required. **Green Fees** phone **Course Designer** Jack Nicklaus (Nicklaus course) **Prof** Steve Priest **Facilities** Ⓣ Ⓘ ⓁⒹⓇⒶ 🚹 ♦ ♂ ✦ **Leisure** hard tennis courts, heated indoor swimming pool, sauna, gymnasium, residential golf school, crazy golf, archery, quad biking **Conf** facs Corporate Hospitality Days **Location** S of City on A41, right at Broxton rdbt onto A534 signed Wrexham. Situated 1.5m on left
Hotel ★★★★ 81% HL De Vere Carden Park, Carden Park, BROXTON ☎ 01829 731000 📠 01829 731599   196 en suite

CHESTER
Map 7 SJ46

Chester Golf Club Curzon Park CH4 8AR
☎ 01244 677760 📠 01244 676667
e-mail: secretary@chestergolfclub.co.uk
web: www.chestergolfclub.co.uk

Parkland course on two levels contained within a loop of the River Dee. The car park overlooks the racecourse across the river.

18 Holes, 6461yds, Par 71, SSS 72, Course record 64.
Club membership 820.

Visitors Sun-Mon & BHs. Booking required. Dress code. **Societies** booking required. **Green Fees** not confirmed **Prof** Scott Booth **Facilities** Ⓣ Ⓘ ⓁⒹⓇⒶ 🚹 ♦ **Conf** facs Corporate Hospitality Days **Location** 1m W of city centre
Hotel ★★★★ 74% HL Grosvenor Pulford Hotel & Spa, Wrexham Road, Pulford, CHESTER ☎ 01244 570560 📠 01244 570809 73 en suite

Eaton Golf Club Guy Ln, Waverton CH3 7PH
☎ 01244 335885 📄 01244 335782
e-mail: office@eatongolfclub.co.uk
web: www.eatongolfclub.co.uk

Parkland with challenging cultured greens which are fast, firm and true, situated beside the Shropshire Union Canal. Course features many mature oaks, a brook and several ponds which add to the golfing challenge and provide a habitat for a variety of wildlife.

18 Holes, 6580yds, Par 72, SSS 71. Club membership 550.

Visitors Mon, Tue, Thu-Sun & BHs. Booking required. Dress code. **Societies** booking required. **Green Fees** not confirmed 🅿 **Course Designer** Donald Steel **Prof** William Tye **Facilities** ⑪ ⑩ 🏐 ☕ 🍴 🛒 🏧 ✔ 🏌 **Conf** Corporate Hospitality Days **Location** 3m SE of Chester off A41

Hotel ★★★★★ HL The Chester Grosvenor & Spa, Eastgate, CHESTER ☎ 01244 324024 📄 01244 313246 80 en suite

Upton-by-Chester Golf Club Upton Ln, Upton-by-Chester CH2 1EE
☎ 01244 381183 📄 01244 376955
e-mail: secretary@uptongolf.co.uk
web: www.uptonbychestergolfclub.co.uk

A challenging parkland course with fantastic full USGA specified greens. Not a physically demanding course, but tight and fully tests golfers of all abilities. Not easy for low-handicap players to score well. Testing holes are 2nd (par 4), 14th (par 4) and 15th (par 3).

18 Holes, 5807yds, Par 69, SSS 68, Course record 63. Club membership 750.

Visitors Mon-Sun & BHs. Dress code. **Societies** booking required. **Green Fees** £40 per day, £30 per round **Course Designer** Bill Davies **Prof** Stephen Dewhurst **Facilities** ⑪ ⑩ 🏐 ☕ 🍴 🛒 🏧 ✔ 🏧 🏌 **Conf** Corporate Hospitality Days **Hotel** ★★★★ GH Green Gables, 11 Eversley Park, CHESTER ☎ 01244 372243 📄 01244 376352 2 rooms

Vicars Cross Golf Club Tarvin Rd, Great Barrow CH3 7HN
☎ 01244 335595 📄 01244 335686
e-mail: manager@vicarscrossgolf.co.uk
web: www.vicarscrossgc.co.uk

Tree-lined parkland course, in rural surroundings.

18 Holes, 6443yds, Par 72, SSS 71, Course record 64. Club membership 750.

Visitors Mon-Sun & BHs except competition days. Dress code. **Societies** booking required. **Green Fees** £35 per day (£40 weekends & BHs). £25 per round after 3pm **Course Designer** J Richardson **Prof** Gavin Beddow **Facilities** ⑪ ⑩ 🏐 ☕ 🍴 🛒 🏧 ✔ 🏧 ✔ 🏌 **Conf** facs Corporate Hospitality Days **Location** 4m E on A51

Hotel ★★★★ 81% HL Rowton Hall Country House Hotel & Spa, Whitchurch Road, Rowton, CHESTER ☎ 01244 335262 📄 01244 335464 37 en suite

CONGLETON
Map 7 SJ86

Astbury Golf Club Peel Ln CW12 4RE
☎ 01260 272772 📄 01260 276420
web: www.astburygolfclub.com

18 Holes, 6296yds, Par 71, SSS 70, Course record 61.

Location 1.5m S of Congleton on A34, turn into Peel Lane by Astbury Church for 1m

Telephone for further details

Hotel ★★★★ INN Egerton Arms Country Inn, Astbury Village, CONGLETON ☎ 01260 273946 📄 01260 277273 6 rooms

Congleton Golf Club Biddulph Rd CW12 3LZ
☎ 01260 273540 📄 01256 290902
e-mail: congletongolfclub@btconnect.com
web: www.congletongolfclub.co.uk

Superbly-manicured parkland course with views over three counties from the balcony of the clubhouse.

9 Holes, 5103yds, Par 68, SSS 65, Course record 59. Club membership 400.

Visitors Mon-Sun & BHs. Booking required. Dress code. **Societies** booking required. **Green Fees** Mon-Fri £24 per round (£40 weekends) 🅿 **Course Designer** Frank Wingate **Prof** Andrew Preston **Facilities** ⑪ ⑩ 🏐 ☕ 🍴 🏧 🏧 ✔ **Conf** Corporate Hospitality Days **Location** 1.5m SE on A527

Hotel ★★★★ INN Egerton Arms Country Inn, Astbury Village, CONGLETON ☎ 01260 273946 📄 01260 277273 6 rooms (6 en suite)

CREWE
Map 7 SJ75

Crewe Golf Club Fields Rd, Haslington CW1 5TB
☎ 01270 584099 📄 01270 256482
e-mail: secretary@crewegolfclub.co.uk
web: www.crewegolfclub.co.uk

Undulating parkland.

18 Holes, 6414yds, Par 71, SSS 71, Course record 63. Club membership 611.

Visitors Dress code. **Societies** booking required. **Green Fees** £30 per day **Course Designer** James Braid **Prof** David Wheeler **Facilities** ⑪ ⑩ 🏐 ☕ 🍴 🏧 ✔ **Location** 2.25m NE off A534

Hotel ★★★ 78% HL Hunters Lodge, Sydney Road, Sydney, CREWE ☎ 01270 539100 📄 01270 500553 57 en suite

Wychwood Park Golf Club Wychwood Park CW2 5GP
☎ 01270 829247 (manager) & 829248 (pro)
📄 01270 829201
web: www.deverevenues.co.uk

18 Holes, 6736yds, Par 72, SSS 73.

Course Designer Hawtree & Co **Location** M6 junct 16, A500 for Nantwich, A531 for Keele

Telephone for further details

Hotel ★★★ 71% HL The Crewe Arms Hotel, Nantwich Road, CREWE ☎ 01270 213204 📄 01270 588615 61 en suite

Save on Hotels. Book at **theAA.com/hotel**

CHESHIRE

ENGLAND

DELAMERE
Map 7 SJ56

Delamere Forest Golf Club Station Rd CW8 2JE
☎ 01606 883800 📠 01606 889444
e-mail: info@delameregolf.co.uk
web: www.delameregolf.co.uk

Played mostly on undulating open heath there is great charm in the way this course drops down into the occasional pine sheltered valley. Six of the first testing nine holes are from 420 to 455yds in length.

18 Holes, 6348yds, Par 72, SSS 72, Course record 65.
Club membership 500.

Visitors Mon-Sun & BHs. Dress code **Societies** booking required.
Green Fees £70 per day, £50 per round (£70 per round weekends)
Course Designer H Fowler **Prof** Martin Brown **Facilities** ⊕ ⦿ by prior arrangement 🏌 🖥 🍽 🏌 📷 ✎ 🏌 ✎ 🏌 **Conf**
Corporate Hospitality Days **Location** 1.5m NE, off B5152
Hotel ★★★★ CHH Nunsmere Hall Hotel, Tarporley Road, SANDIWAY ☎ 01606 889100 📠 01606 889055 36 en suite

DISLEY
Map 7 SJ98

Disley Golf Club Stanley Hall Ln SK12 2JX
☎ 01663 764001 📠 01663 762678
e-mail: secretary@disleygolfclub.co.uk
web: www.disleygolfclub.co.uk

This parkland and moorland course offers panoramic views of the Cheshire countryside and a great test of golf. Tree-lined fairways call for an accurate game, as do the tricky slopes on the well manicured greens. Testing holes are the long 3rd and the demanding 17th.

18 Holes, 5942yds, Par 70, SSS 69, Course record 64.
Club membership 500.

Visitors Mon-Wed, Fri-Sun & BHs. Booking required. Dress code.
Societies booking required. **Green Fees** £30 per day (£40 weekends)
Course Designer James Braid **Prof** Scott Jackson **Facilities** ⊕
⦿ 🏌 🖥 🍽 🏌 📷 🍽 ✎ 🏌 ✎ **Conf** facs Corporate
Hospitality Days **Location** NW side of village off A6
Hotel ★★★ 73% HL Best Western Moorside Grange Hotel & Spa, Mudhurst Lane, Higher Disley, DISLEY ☎ 01663 764151
📠 01663 762794 98 en suite

FRODSHAM
Map 7 SJ57

Frodsham Golf Club Simons Ln WA6 6HE
☎ 01928 732159 📠 01928 734070
web: www.frodshamgolfclub.co.uk

18 Holes, 6328yds, Par 70, SSS 70, Course record 63.

Course Designer John Day **Location** M56 junct 12, 1.5m SW, signs for Forest Hills Hotel, golf club 1st left on Simons Ln
Telephone for further details
Hotel ★★★ 72% HL Holiday Inn Runcorn, Wood Lane, Beechwood, RUNCORN ☎ 0871 942 9070 📠 01928 714611 153 en suite

HELSBY
Map 7 SJ47

Helsby Golf Club Towers Ln WA6 0JB
☎ 01928 722021 📠 01928 726816
e-mail: secretary@helsbygolfclub.org
web: www.helsbygolfclub.org

This gentle but challenging parkland course was originally designed by James Braid. With a wide variety of trees and natural water hazards interspersed throughout the course, it is an excellent test of golfing ability. The last six holes are reputed to be perhaps among the most difficult home stretch in Cheshire, with the last being a par 3 of 205yds to a narrow green guarded by bunkers. A wide variety of wildlife lives around the several ponds which are features to be noted (and hopefully avoided).

18 Holes, 6260yds, Par 70, SSS 70, Course record 66.
Club membership 600.

Visitors Mon-Fri except BHs. Dress code. **Societies** booking required.
Green Fees £37 per day, £27.50 per round **Course Designer** James
Braid (part) **Prof** Matthew Jones **Facilities** ⊕ ⦿ 🏌 🖥 🍽
🏌 📷 🍽 ✎ 🏌 **Conf** Corporate Hospitality Days **Location** M56
junct 14, 1m. (6m from Chester)
Hotel ★★★★★ HL The Chester Grosvenor & Spa, Eastgate, CHESTER ☎ 01244 324024 📠 01244 313246 80 en suite

KNUTSFORD
Map 7 SJ77

Heyrose Golf Club Budworth Rd, Tabley WA16 0HZ
☎ 01565 733664 📠 01565 734578
e-mail: info@heyrosegolfclub.com
web: www.heyrosegolfclub.com

Course in wooded and gently undulating terrain. The par 3 16th (237yds), bounded by a small river in a wooded valley, is an interesting and testing hole - one of the toughest par 3s in Cheshire. Several water hazards. Both the course and the comfortable clubhouse have attractive views.

18 Holes, 6499yds, Par 73, SSS 71, Course record 64.
Club membership 600.

Visitors Mon-Sun & BHs. Booking required. Dress code.
Societies booking required. **Green Fees** £26 per round weekdays
and BHs (£31 weekends) **Course Designer** E & C N Bridge/B Schons
Prof Philip Bills **Facilities** ⊕ ⦿ 🏌 🖥 🍽 🏌 📷 🍽 ✎
🍽 ✎ 🏌 **Leisure** practice bunker, practice nets **Conf** facs Corporate
Hospitality Days **Location** M6 junct 19, 1m, follow tourist signs
Hotel ★★★★ 78% HL Cottons Hotel & Spa, Manchester Road, KNUTSFORD ☎ 01565 650333 📠 01565 755351 109 en suite

ENGLAND

High Legh Park Country Club Warrington Rd WA16 0WA
☎ 01565 830012 (office) & 830888 (pro shop)
🖨 01565 830999
web: www.highleghpark.com
Championship: 18 Holes, 6715yds, Par 72.
South: 18 Holes, 6281yds, Par 70.
North: 18 Holes, 6472yds, Par 70.
Location M6 junct 20, A50 to High Legh
Telephone for further details
Hotel ★★★★ 78% HL Cottons Hotel & Spa, Manchester Road,
KNUTSFORD ☎ 01565 650333 🖨 01565 755351 109 en suite

Knutsford Golf Club Mereheath Ln WA16 6HS
☎ 01565 633355
e-mail: secretary@knutsfordgolf.com
web: www.knutsfordgolf.com
Parkland course set in a beautiful old deer park. It demands some
precise iron play.
9 Holes, 6200yds, Par 70, SSS 70, Course record 67.
Club membership 365.
Visitors Mon, Tue, Thu, Fri, Sun & BHs. Booking required Sun & BHs.
Handicap certificate required. Dress code. **Societies** booking required.
Green Fees £28 Mon-Fri (£35 Sun & BHs) 🅰 **Prof** Tim Maxwell
Facilities 🏌 🍴 🏌 🖥 🍽 ⚐ 🚗 ⛳ **Location** N side of town
centre off A50, close to Tatton Park (town entrance)
Hotel ★★★★ 78% HL Cottons Hotel & Spa, Manchester Road,
KNUTSFORD ☎ 01565 650333 🖨 01565 755351 109 en suite

Mere Golf & Country Club Chester Rd WA16 6LJ
☎ 01565 830155 🖨 01565 830713
web: www.meregolf.co.uk
18 Holes, 6817yds, Par 71, SSS 73, Course record 64.
Course Designer James Braid/George Duncan **Location** M6
junct 19, 1m E. M56 junct 7, 1m W
Telephone for further details
Hotel ★★★★ 78% HL Cottons Hotel & Spa, Manchester Road,
KNUTSFORD ☎ 01565 650333 🖨 01565 755351 109 en suite

Peover Golf Club Plumley Moor Rd WA16 9SE
☎ 01565 723337 🖨 01565 723311
web: www.peovergolfclub.co.uk
18 Holes, 6702yds, Par 72, SSS 72, Course record 69.
Course Designer P A Naylor **Location** M6 junct 19, A556 onto Plumley
Moor Rd
Telephone for further details
Hotel ★★ 81% HL The Longview Hotel & Stuffed Olive
Restaurant, 55 Manchester Road, KNUTSFORD ☎ 01565 632119
🖨 01565 652402 32 en suite

LITTLE SUTTON — Map 7 SJ47

Ellesmere Port Golf Centre Chester Rd CH66 1QF
☎ 0151 339 7689
web: www.active8leisure.ltd.uk
18 Holes, 6296yds, Par 71, SSS 70.
Course Designer Cotton, Pennick & Lawrie **Location** NW side of town
centre. M53 junct 5, A41 for Chester, club 2m on left
Telephone for further details
Hotel ★★★ 74% HL Brook Meadow, Health Lane, CHILDER
THORNTON ☎ 0151 339 9350 🖨 0151 347 4221 25 en suite

LYMM — Map 7 SJ68

Lymm Golf Club Whitbarrow Rd WA13 9AN
☎ 01925 755020 🖨 01925 755020
e-mail: lymmgolfclub@btconnect.com
web: www.lymm-golf-club.co.uk
First ten holes are gently undulating with the Manchester Ship Canal
running alongside the 6th hole. The remaining holes are comparatively
flat.
18 Holes, 6341yds, Par 71, SSS 70. Club membership 800.
Visitors Mon-Sun & BHs. Booking weekends & BHs. Dress code.
Societies booking required. **Green Fees** £40 per round weekday (£50
weekends) **Prof** Steve McCarthy **Facilities** 🏌 🍴 🏌 🖥 🍽 ⚐
🎥 🚗 ⛳ **Location** 0.5m N off A6144
Hotel ★★★ 73% HL The Lymm Hotel, Whitbarrow Road, LYMM
☎ 01925 752233 🖨 01925 756035 62 en suite

MACCLESFIELD — Map 7 SJ97

Barceló Shrigley Hall Hotel, Golf & Country Club
Shrigley Park SK10 5SB
☎ 01625 575626 🖨 01625 575437
web: www.barcelo-hotels.co.uk
18 Holes, 6281yds, Par 71, SSS 71, Course record 68.
Course Designer Donald Steel **Location** off A523 Macclesfield-
Stockport road
Telephone for further details
Hotel ★★★★ 76% HL Barceló Shrigley Hall Hotel, Golf & Country
Club, Shrigley Park, Pott Shrigley, MACCLESFIELD ☎ 01625 575757
🖨 01625 573323 148 en suite

Macclesfield Golf Club The Hollins SK11 7EA
☎ 01625 423227 🖨 01625 260061
e-mail: secretary@maccgolfclub.co.uk
web: www.maccgolfclub.co.uk
Hillside heathland course situated on the edge of the Pennines with
excellent views across the Cheshire Plain. The signature hole is the
410yd 3rd, which drops majestically to a plateau green situated above
a babbling brook. The temptation is to over-club, thus bringing the
out of bounds behind into play. The 7th hole is aptly named Seven
Shires as seven counties can be seen on a clear day, as well as the
mountains.
18 Holes, 5727yds, Par 70, SSS 68.
Visitors Mon-Tue, Fri & Sun except BHs. Booking required. Dress
code. **Societies** booking required. **Green Fees** not confirmed **Course
Designer** Hawtree & Son **Prof** Tony Taylor **Facilities** 🏌 🍴 🏌
🖥 🍽 ⚐ 🎥 🚗 ⛳ **Conf** facs Corporate Hospitality Days
Location SE side of town centre off A523
Hotel ★★★★ 76% HL Barceló Shrigley Hall Hotel, Golf & Country
Club, Shrigley Park, Pott Shrigley, MACCLESFIELD ☎ 01625 575757
🖨 01625 573323 148 en suite

The Tytherington Club Dorchester Way SK10 2JP
☎ 01625 506000 📠 01625 506040
web: www.theclubcompany.com/clubs/Tytherington/
18 Holes, 6765yds, Par 72, SSS 74.
Course Designer Dave Thomas/Patrick Dawson **Location** 1m N of Macclesfield off A523
Telephone for further details
Hotel ★★★★ 76% HL Barceló Shrigley Hall Hotel, Golf & Country Club, Shrigley Park, Pott Shrigley, MACCLESFIELD
☎ 01625 575757 📠 01625 573323 148 en suite

NANTWICH
Map 7 SJ65

Reaseheath Golf Club Reaseheath College CW5 6DF
☎ 01270 625131 📠 01270 625665
e-mail: chrisb@reaseheath.ac.uk
web: www.reaseheath.ac.uk

The course here is attached to Reaseheath College, which is one of the major centres of green-keeper training in the UK. It is a short nine-hole parkland course with challenging narrow fairways, bunkers and a water hazard, all of which make accuracy essential.

9 Holes, 3682yds, Par 62, SSS 58, Course record 52. Club membership 520.

Visitors Mon-Sun & BHs. Booking required. Handicap certificate. Dress code. **Societies** booking required. **Green Fees** not confirmed 😊 **Course Designer** D Mortram **Prof** Andrew Pointon **Facilities** ⫽ ⚘ **Conf** facs **Location** 1.5m NE of Nantwich, off A51
Hotel ★★★★ 84% HL Rookery Hall Hotel and Spa, Main Road, Worleston, NANTWICH ☎ 01270 610016 & 0845 072 7533 📠 01270 615617 70 en suite

OSCROFT
Map 7 SJ56

Pryors Hayes Golf Club Willington Rd CH3 8NL
☎ 01829 741250 & 740140 📠 01829 749077
e-mail: info@pryors-hayes.co.uk
web: www.pryorshayes.com

A picturesque 18-hole parkland course set in the heart of Cheshire. Gently undulating fairways demand accurate drives, and numerous trees and water hazards make the course a challenging test of golf.

18 Holes, 6054yds, Par 69, SSS 69, Course record 65. Club membership 530.

Visitors Mon-Sun & BHs. Dress code. **Societies** booking required. **Green Fees** £30 per round (£40 weekends) **Course Designer** John Day **Prof** Martin Redrup **Facilities** ⫽ ⊓ ⚘ ⌂ 🕏 **Conf** facs Corporate Hospitality Days **Location** between A51 & A54, 6m E of Chester
Hotel ★★★★ CHH Nunsmere Hall Hotel, Tarporley Road, SANDIWAY ☎ 01606 889100 📠 01606 889055 36 en suite

POYNTON
Map 7 SJ98

Davenport Golf Club Worth Hall, Middlewood Rd SK12 1TS
☎ 01625 876951 📠 01625 877489
e-mail: elaine@davenportgolf.co.uk
web: www.davenportgolf.co.uk

Gently undulating parkland. Extensive view over the Cheshire plain from elevated 18th tee. Testing 1st hole, par 4. Several long par 3s, water hazards and tree-lined fairways make this a challenging test of golf.

18 Holes, 6034yds, Par 69, SSS 69. Club membership 700.
Visitors Mon-Tue, Thu-Fri, Sun & BHs. Booking required. Dress code. **Societies** booking required. **Green Fees** £30-£35 per 18 holes (£35-£45 Sun) **Prof** Tony Stevens **Facilities** ⫽ by prior arrangement 🍽 by prior arrangement ⌂ ⊓ ⚘ ⌂ 🕏 **Leisure** snooker **Conf** facs Corporate Hospitality Days **Location** 1m E off A523
Hotel ★★★ 73% HL Best Western Moorside Grange Hotel & Spa, Mudhurst Lane, Higher Disley, DISLEY ☎ 01663 764151 📠 01663 762794 98 en suite

PRESTBURY
Map 7 SJ97

Prestbury Golf Club Macclesfield Rd SK10 4BJ
☎ 01625 828241 📠 01625 828241
e-mail: office@prestburygolfclub.com
web: www.prestburygolfclub.com

Undulating parkland with many plateau greens. The 9th hole has a challenging uphill three-tier green and the 17th is over a valley. Host to county and inter-county championships, including having hosted Open qualifying events

18 Holes, 6371yds, Par 71, SSS 71, Course record 64. Club membership 730.
Visitors Mon, Thu-Fri except BHs. Booking required. Dress code. **Societies** booking required **Green Fees** not confirmed **Course Designer** Harry S Colt **Prof** Nick Summerfield **Facilities** ⫽ 🍽 ⌂ ⊓ ⚘ ⌂ 🕏 **Conf** Corporate Hospitality Days **Location** S side of village off A538
Hotel ★★★★ 79% HL De Vere Mottram Hall, Wilmslow Road, MOTTRAM ST ANDREW ☎ 01625 828135 📠 01625 828950 131 en suite

RUNCORN
Map 7 SJ58

Runcorn Golf Club Clifton Rd WA7 4SU
☎ 01928 574214 📠 01928 574214
e-mail: secretary@runcorngolfclub.ltd.uk
web: www.runcorngolfclub.

Easy walking parkland with tree-lined fairways. Fine views over Mersey and Weaver valleys. Testing holes: 7th par 5; 14th par 5; 17th par 4.

18 Holes, 5877yds, Par 69, SSS 69, Course record 63. Club membership 570.
Visitors Mon, Wed-Fri & Sun except BHs. Booking required. **Societies** booking required. **Green Fees** not confirmed 😊 **Prof** Kevin Hartley **Facilities** ⫽ 🍽 by prior arrangement ⌂ ⊓ ⚘ ⌂ **Location** 1.25m S of Runcorn Station
Hotel ★★★ 72% HL Holiday Inn Runcorn, Wood Lane, Beechwood, RUNCORN ☎ 0871 942 9070 📠 01928 714611 153 en suite

SANDBACH
Map 7 SJ76

Malkins Bank Golf Course Betchton Rd, Malkins Bank
CW11 4XN
☎ 01270 765931 📠 01270 764730
web: www.cheshireeast.gov.uk

This parkland course has a different challenge around every corner.
The four par 3s on the course are all a challenge, especially the
signature hole 14th. Trees in all directions make the short par 3 a
really exciting hole. In fact, holes 12, 13 and 14 are the Amen Corner
of Malkins Bank. Three very tricky holes, yet for straight hitters low
scores are possible.

18 Holes, 6005yds, Par 70, SSS 69, Course record 65.
Club membership 500.

Visitors Mon-Sun & BHs. Booking required weekend & BHs.
Societies booking required. **Green Fees** £13.70 per 18 holes, £10.50
per 9 holes (£16.30/£12 weekends) **Course Designer** Hawtree
Prof D Hackney **Facilities** ⑪ ⑪ ⅃ ❑ ❑ 옙 ⚲ 🏠 ᴾ ✦
Location 1.5m SE off A533
Hotel ★★★ 78% HL Hunters Lodge, Sydney Road, Sydney, CREWE
☎ 01270 539100 📠 01270 500553   57 en suite

SANDIWAY
Map 7 SJ67

Sandiway Golf Club Chester Rd CW8 2DJ
☎ 01606 883247 (Secretary) 📠 01606 888548
e-mail: information@sandiwaygolf.co.uk
web: www.sandiwaygolf.co.uk

Delightful undulating wood and heathland course with long hills
up to the 8th, 16th and 17th holes. Many dog-leg and tree-lined
holes give opportunities for the deliberate fade or draw. True
championship test and one of the finest inland courses in north-
west England.

18 Holes, 6404yds, Par 70, SSS 72, Course record 65.
Club membership 750.

Visitors Mon-Sun & BHs. Booking required. Dress code.
Societies booking required. **Green Fees** £60 per day, £50 per round
(£65 per round weekends) **Course Designer** Ted Ray **Prof** William
Laird **Facilities** ⑪ ⑪ ⅃ ❑ ❑ 옙 ⚲ 🏠 ✦ **Conf** facs
Corporate Hospitality Days **Location** 2m W of Northwich on A556
Hotel ★★★★ CHH Nunsmere Hall Hotel, Tarporley Road,
SANDIWAY ☎ 01606 889100 📠 01606 889055   36 en suite

SUTTON WEAVER
Map 7 SJ57

Sutton Hall Golf Course Aston Ln WA7 3ED
☎ 01928 790747 📠 01928 759174
e-mail: info@suttonhallgolf.co.uk
web: www.suttonhallgolf.co.uk

Undulating parkland on south-facing slopes of the Weaver Valley. A
challenge to all levels of play.

18 Holes, 6618yards, Par 72, Course record 68.
Club membership 600.

Visitors Mon-Sun & BHs. Booking required. Dress code.
Societies welcome. **Green Fees** not confirmed **Course Designer** Ace
Golf Associates **Prof** Jamie Hope **Facilities** ⑪ ⑪ ⅃ ❑ ❑ 옙 ⚲
🏠 🛏 ✦ **Location** M56 junct 12, follow signs for A56 to Warrington,
on entering Sutton Weaver take 1st turn right
Hotel ★★★ 72% HL Holiday Inn Runcorn, Wood Lane, Beechwood,
RUNCORN ☎ 0871 942 9070 📠 01928 714611   153 en suite

TARPORLEY
Map 7 SJ56

Macdonald Portal Hotel Golf & Spa Cobbler's Cross Ln
CW6 0DJ
☎ 01829 734160 📠 01829 733928
web: www.macdonaldhotels.co.uk

Championship Course: 18 Holes, 6577yds, Par 73, SSS 72.
Premier Course: 18 Holes, 6293yds, Par 71, SSS 70.
Arderne Course: 9 Holes, 1724yds.

Course Designer Donald Steel **Location** off A49
Telephone for further details
Hotel ★★★★ 78% HL Macdonald Portal, Cobblers Cross Lane,
TARPORLEY ☎ 0844 879 9082   83 en suite

WARRINGTON
Map 7 SJ68

Birchwood Golf Club Kelvin Close, Science Park North,
Birchwood WA3 7PB
☎ 01925 818819 (Club) & 825216 (Pro)
📠 01925 822403
e-mail: enquiries@birchwoodgolfclub.co.uk
web: www.birchwoodgolfclub.co.uk

Very testing parkland course with many natural water hazards and
the prevailing wind creating a problem on each hole. The 11th hole is
particularly challenging.

18 Holes, 6596yds, Par 71, SSS 72, Course record 64.
Club membership 745.

Visitors Mon-Sat & BHs. Booking required. Dress code.
Societies booking required. **Green Fees** £26 (£31 weekends).
£20 twilight. **Course Designer** T J A Macauley **Prof** Carl Edwards
Facilities ⑪ ⑪ ⅃ ❑ ❑ 옙 ⚲ 🏠 ᴾ 🛏 ✦ **Conf** facs
Corporate Hospitality Days **Location** M62 junct 11, signs for Science
Park North, course 2m
Hotel ★★★ 78% HL The Rhinewood Country House Hotel,
Glazebrook Lane, Glazebrook, WARRINGTON ☎ 0161 775 5555
📠 0161 775 7965   32 en suite

Leigh Golf Club Kenyon Hall, Broseley Ln, Culcheth
WA3 4BG
☎ 01925 762943 (Secretary) 📠 01925 765097
e-mail: golf@leighgolf.fsnet.co.uk
web: www.leighgolf.co.uk

This compact parkland course has benefited in recent years from
intensive tree planting and extra drainage and the rebuilding of 12
greens. An interesting course to play with narrow fairways making
accuracy from the tees essential.

18 Holes, 5904yds, Par 69, SSS 69, Course record 63.
Club membership 770.

Visitors Mon-Tue, Fri, Sun & BHs. Booking required. Handicap
certificate. Dress code. **Societies** booking required. **Green Fees** not
confirmed 🅟 **Course Designer** Harold Hilton **Prof** Andrew Baguley
Facilities ⑪ ⑪ ⅃ ❑ ❑ 옙 ⚲ 🏠 ᴾ ✦ **Conf** facs
Corporate Hospitality Days **Location** 5m NE off A579
Hotel ★★★ 78% HL Best Western Fir Grove, Knutsford Old Road,
WARRINGTON ☎ 01925 267471 📠 01925 601092   52 en suite

Poulton Park Golf Club Dig Ln WA2 0SH
☎ 01925 822802 & 825220 (pro) 📠 01925 822802
web: www.poultonparkgolfclub.co.uk

9 Holes, 5650yds, Par 68, SSS 67, Course record 66.

Course Designer Mike Millington **Location** M6 junct 12, follow
Woolston Grange Av parallel to motorway across 6 rdbts onto Crab
Lane. Cross mini-rdbt and car park on right.
Telephone for further details
Hotel ★★★ 78% HL Best Western Fir Grove, Knutsford Old Road,
WARRINGTON ☎ 01925 267471 📠 01925 601092 52 en suite

Walton Hall Golf Course Warrington Rd WA4 5LU
☎ 01925 263061 (bookings) 📠 01925 263061

18 Holes, 6647yds, Par 72, SSS 73, Course record 70.

Course Designer Peter Alliss/Dave Thomas **Location** M56 junct 11,
2m
Telephone for further details
Hotel ★★★★ 78% HL The Park Royal, Stretton Road, Stretton,
WARRINGTON ☎ 01925 730706 📠 01925 730740 146 en suite

Warrington Golf Club Hill Warren WA4 5HR
☎ 01925 261775 (Secretary) 📠 01925 265933
web: www.warringtongolfclub.co.uk

18 Holes, 6211yds, Par 71, SSS 71, Course record 63.

Course Designer James Braid **Location** M56 junct 10, 1.5m N on A49
Telephone for further details
Hotel ★★★★ 78% HL The Park Royal, Stretton Road, Stretton,
WARRINGTON ☎ 01925 730706 📠 01925 730740 146 en suite

WIDNES   Map 7 SJ58

Mersey Valley Golf & Country Club Warrington Rd,
Bold Heath WA8 3XL
☎ 0151 4246060 📠 0151 2579097
e-mail: chrismgerrard@yahoo.co.uk
web: www.merseyvalleygolfclub.co.uk

Parkland with very easy walking, designed to play as a links type
course.

18 Holes, 6511yards, Par 72, SSS 71.
Club membership 500.

Visitors Mon-Sun & BHs. Booking required. **Societies** booking
required. **Green Fees** £30 per day, £20 per round (£40/£25 weekends
and BHs) **Course Designer** R Bush **Prof** Andy Stevenson **Facilities** ⑨
†⊚¶ by prior arrangement 🌆 ⬛ ¶ 🍴 ☷ ♿ 🛒 ♿
Leisure fishing **Conf** facs Corporate Hospitality Days **Location** M62
junct 7, A57 towards Warrington, club 2m on left
Hotel ★★ 63% HL Villaggio, 5-9 Folly Lane, WARRINGTON
☎ 01925 630106 📠 01925 631377 19 en suite

Widnes Golf Club Highfield Rd WA8 7DT
☎ 0151 424 2440 & 424 2995 📠 0151 495 2849
e-mail: office@widnesgolfclub.co.uk
web: www.widnesgolfclub.co.uk

An easy walking parkland course, challenging in parts.

18 Holes, 5726yds, Par 69. Club membership 500.

Visitors Mon, Wed-Fri & Sun except BHs. Booking required. Handicap
certificate. Dress code. **Societies** booking required. **Green Fees** £20
per 18 holes **Prof** J O'Brien **Facilities** ⑨ †⊚¶ by prior arrangement
🌆 ⬛ ¶ 🍴 ☷ 🖼 **Conf** Corporate Hospitality Days **Location** M62
junct 7, A57 to Warrington, right at lights onto Wilmere Ln, right at
T-junct. 1st left at rdbt onto Birchfield Rd, right after 3rd pelican
crossing onto Highfield Rd, right before lights
Hotel ★★★ 72% HL Holiday Inn Runcorn, Wood Lane, Beechwood,
RUNCORN ☎ 0871 942 9070 📠 01928 714611 153 en suite

WILMSLOW   Map 7 SJ88

De Vere Mottram Hall Wilmslow Rd, Mottram St Andrew
SK10 4QT
☎ 01625 828135 📠 01625 829312
e-mail: dmhgolf@devere-hotels.com
web: www.deveregolf.co.uk

Championship-standard course - flat meadowland on the front nine
and undulating woodland on the back nine, with well-guarded greens.
The course is unusual as each half opens and closes with par 5s. Good
test for both professional and novice golfers alike. Excellent drainage.

Mottram Hall: 18 Holes, 7006yds, Par 72, SSS 75,
Course record 63. Club membership 275.

Visitors Mon-Sun & BHs. Booking required. Dress code.
Societies booking required. **Green Fees** £60 per round summer,
£40 per round winter **Course Designer** Dave Thomas **Prof** Matthew
Turnock **Facilities** ⑨ †⊚¶ 🌆 ⬛ ¶ 🍴 ☷ 🖼 🏌 ♿ ♿ 🛒
♿ ⚐ **Leisure** hard tennis courts, heated indoor swimming pool,
squash, sauna, gymnasium, bag store & drying room **Conf** facs
Corporate Hospitality Days **Location** on A538 between Wilmslow and
Prestbury
Hotel ★★★★ 79% HL De Vere Mottram Hall, Wilmslow Road,
MOTTRAM ST ANDREW ☎ 01625 828135 📠 01625 828950
131 en suite

Styal Golf Club Station Rd, Styal SK9 4JN
☎ 01625 531359 📠 01625 416373
e-mail: gtraynor@styalgolf.co.uk
web: www.styalgolf.co.uk

Well-designed flat parkland course with USGA specification greens.
Challenging and enjoyable test for all standards of golfer. The par
3 course is widely regarded as one of the finest short courses in the
country.

18 Holes, 6238yds, Par 70, SSS 70, Course record 61.
Academy: 9 Holes, 1203yds, Par 27, SSS 27,
Course record 24. Club membership 800.

Visitors Mon-Sun & BHs. Booking required. Dress code.
Societies booking required. **Green Fees** £25 per round (£30
weekends). Par 3 course £8 per 9 holes, £12 per 18 holes **Course
Designer** Tony Holmes **Prof** Simon Forrest **Facilities** ⑨ †⊚¶ 🌆 ⬛
¶ 🍴 ☷ 🖼 🏌 ♿ ♿ ♿ **Leisure** par 3 nine hole course.
Conf facs Corporate Hospitality Days **Location** M56 junct 5, 5 mins
from Wilmslow/Manchester Airport
Hotel ★★★★ 79% HL Stanneylands, Stanneylands Road,
WILMSLOW ☎ 01625 525225 📠 01625 537282 56 en suite

Wilmslow Golf Club Great Warford, Mobberley WA16 7AY
☎ 01565 872148 📄 01565 872172
e-mail: admin@wilmslowgolfclub.co.uk
web: www.wilmslowgolfclub.co.uk
Peaceful parkland in the heart of the Cheshire countryside offering golf for all levels.
18 Holes, 6635yds, Par 72, SSS 72, Course record 62. Club membership 790.
Visitors Mon, Tue, Thu-Sun & BHs. Wed after 2.30pm. Booking required. Dress code. **Societies** booking required. **Green Fees** £60 per day, £50 per round (£65/£55 weekends & BHs) **Prof** Matthew Gillingham **Facilities** ⊕ ⫟◎⫟ ⊫ ⬜ ⬛⫟ ⊿ 🖻 🛏 ✔ **Conf** Corporate Hospitality Days **Location** 2m SW off B5058
Hotel ★★★ 86% HL Alderley Edge Hotel, Macclesfield Road, ALDERLEY EDGE ☎ 01625 583033 📄 01625 586343 50 en suite

WINSFORD   Map 7 SJ66

Knights Grange Golf Course Grange Ln CW7 2PT
☎ 01606 552780
Course set in beautiful Cheshire countryside on the town outskirts. The front nine is mainly flat but players have to negotiate water, ditches and other hazards along the way. The back nine takes the player deep into the countryside, with many of the tees offering panoramic views. A lake known as the Ocean is a feature of many holes - a particular hazard for slicers of the ball. There are also many mature woodland areas to catch the wayward drive.
18 Holes, 5921yds, Par 70, SSS 68.
Visitors Mon-Sun & BHs. Booking required. **Societies** booking required. **Green Fees** not confirmed **Course Designer** Steve Dawson **Facilities** ⬜ ⊿ ⬛⫟ ✔ **Leisure** hard and grass tennis courts, football pitches **Location** N side of town off A54
Hotel ★★★★ CHH Nunsmere Hall Hotel, Tarporley Road, SANDIWAY ☎ 01606 889100 📄 01606 889055 36 en suite

WINWICK   Map 7 SJ69

Alder Root Golf Club Alder Root Ln WA2 8R2
☎ 01925 291919 📄 01925 291961
e-mail: office@alderrootgolfclub.com
web: www.alderroot.com
A woodland course, flat in nature but with many undulations. Several holes have water hazards. One of the most testing short courses in the north-west.
10 Holes, 6152yds, Par 71, SSS 70, Course record 67. Club membership 400.
Visitors dress code. **Societies** booking required. **Green Fees** Mon-Fri £15 per 18 holes (weekends £20) **Course Designer** Mr Lander/Mr Millington **Prof** C McKevitt **Facilities** ⊕ ⊫ ⬜ ⬛⫟ ⊿ 🖻 ✔ 🛏 ✔ **Location** M62 junct 9, A49 N for 800yds, left at lights right into Alder Root Ln
Hotel ★★ 74% HL Paddington House, 514 Old Manchester Road, WARRINGTON ☎ 01925 816767 📄 01925 816651 37 en suite

CORNWALL & ISLES OF SCILLY

BODMIN   Map 2 SX06

Lanhydrock Hotel & Golf Club Lostwithiel Rd PL30 5AQ
☎ 01208 262570 📄 01208 262579
e-mail: info@lanhydrockhotel.com
web: www.lanhydrockhotel.com
An acclaimed parkland course adjacent to the National Trust property of Lanhydrock House. Nestling in a picturesque wooded valley of oak and birch, this undulating course provides an exciting and enjoyable challenge.
Lanhydrock: 18 Holes, 6078yds, Par 70, SSS 70, Course record 64. Club membership 300.
Visitors Mon-Sun. Dress code. **Societies** booking required. **Green Fees** £30-£45 per day, £22.50-£35 per round **Course Designer** Hamilton Stutt **Prof** Richard O'Hanlon **Facilities** ⊕ ⫟◎⫟ ⊫ ⬜ ⬛⫟ ⊿ 🖻 ⬛⫟ ◇ 🛏 ✔ 🏌 **Conf** facs Corporate Hospitality Days **Location** 1m S of Bodmin off B3268
Hotel ★★★ 75% HL Best Western Restormel Lodge, Castle Hill, LOSTWITHIEL ☎ 01208 872223 📄 01208 873568 36 en suite

BUDE   Map 2 SS20

Bude & North Cornwall Golf Club Burn View EX23 8DA
☎ 01288 352006 📄 01288 356855
e-mail: secretary@budegolf.co.uk
web: www.budegolf.co.uk
A traditional links course established in 1891. Situated in the centre of Bude with magnificent views to the sea. A challenging course with super greens and excellent drainage enables the course to be playable throughout the year off regular tees and greens.
18 Holes, 6006yds, Par 71, SSS 70. Club membership 800.
Visitors Mon-Sun & BHs. Booking required. Handicap certificate preferred. Dress code. **Societies** welcome. **Green Fees** £48 per day, £32 per round **Course Designer** Tom Dunn **Prof** Mark Yeo **Facilities** ⊕ ⫟◎⫟ ⊫ ⬜ ⬛⫟ ⊿ 🖻 ⬛⫟ 🛏 ✔ **Leisure** snooker room **Conf** facs Corporate Hospitality Days **Location** N side of town
Hotel ★★★ 75% HL Camelot, Downs View, BUDE
☎ 01288 352361 📄 01288 355470 24 en suite

Save on Hotels. Book at **theAA.com/hotel**

CORNWALL & ISLES OF SCILLY

ENGLAND

BUDOCK VEAN
Map 2 SW73

Budock Vean - The Hotel on the River Mawnan Smith, Helford Passage TR11 5LG
☎ 01326 252102 (shop) 🖹 01326 250892
e-mail: relax@budockvean.co.uk
web: www.budockvean.co.uk

Set in 65 acres of mature grounds with a private foreshore to the Helford River, this 18-tee undulating parkland course has a tough par 4 5th hole (456yds) which dog-legs at halfway around an oak tree. The 16th hole measures 572yds, par 5.

9 Holes, 5115yds, Par 68, SSS 66. Club membership 150.

Visitors Mon-Sun & BHs. Booking required. Dress code.
Societies booking required. **Green Fees** £23 per day (£27 weekends & BHs) **Course Designer** James Braid **Prof** David Short **Facilities** 🏧 🍴 by prior arrangement 🦽 ⛳ 🍺 🎿 🏖 🏯 ◇ 🏌 🚂 🏇 **Leisure** hard tennis courts, heated indoor swimming pool, fishing, sauna, boating facilities, health spa, outdoor hot tub **Conf** facs Corporate Hospitality Days **Location** 1.5m SW of Mawnan Smith
Hotel ★★★★ 79% CHH Budock Vean-The Hotel on the River, MAWNAN SMITH ☎ 01326 252100 & 0800 833927 🖹 01326 250892 57 en suite

CAMBORNE
Map 2 SW64

Tehidy Park Golf Club TR14 0HH
☎ 01209 842208 🖹 01209 842208
e-mail: secretary-manager@tehidyparkgolfclub.co.uk
web: www.tehidyparkgolfclub.co.uk

A well-maintained parkland course providing good holiday golf and a challenge for golfers of all abilities.

18 Holes, 6098yds, Par 71, SSS 71, Course record 68. Club membership 700.

Visitors Mon-Sun & BHs. Handicap certificate. Dress code
Societies booking required. **Green Fees** £30.50 per day (£40.50

weekends & BHs) **Course Designer** C K Cotton **Prof** Jonathan Lamb **Facilities** 🏧 🍴 🦽 ⛳ 🍺 🎿 🏖 🏯 🏇 🚂 🏇 **Leisure** snooker/pool **Conf** facs Corporate Hospitality Days **Location** on Portreath-Pool road, 2m S of Camborne
Hotel ★★★ 79% HL Penventon Park, REDRUTH ☎ 01209 203000 🖹 01209 203001 64 en suite

CAMELFORD
Map 2 SX18

Bowood Park Hotel & Golf Course Lanteglos PL32 9RF
☎ 01840 213017 🖹 01840 212622
e-mail: golf@bowood-park.co.uk
web: www.bowood-park.co.uk
A rolling parkland course set in 230 acres of ancient deer park once owned by the Black Prince. 27 lakes and ponds test the golfer and serve as a haven for wildlife.

Bowood Park: 18 Holes, 6692yds, Par 72, SSS 72, Course record 68. Club membership 300.

Visitors Mon-Sun & BHs. Booking required. Dress code.
Societies booking required. **Green Fees** £35 per 18 holes. Winter £25 **Course Designer** Sandow **Prof** Chris Kaminski **Facilities** 🏧 🍴 🦽 ⛳ 🍺 🎿 🏖 🏯 🏇 ◇ 🏌 🚂 🏇 **Conf** facs Corporate Hospitality Days **Location** through Camelford, 0.5m turn right Tintagel/Boscastle B3266, 1st left after garage, 300yds on left
Hotel ★★ 76% SHL Atlantic View Hotel, Treknow, TINTAGEL ☎ 01840 770221 🖹 01840 770995 9 en suite

CARLYON BAY
See St Austell

CONSTANTINE BAY
Map 2 SW87

Trevose Golf Club PL28 8JB
☎ 01841 520208 🖹 01841 521057
e-mail: info@trevose-gc.co.uk
web: www.trevose-gc.co.uk
Well-known links course with early holes close to the sea on excellent springy turf. A championship course affording varying degrees of difficulty appealing to both the professional and higher handicap player. It is a good test with well-positioned bunkers, and a meandering stream, and the wind playing a decisive role in preventing low scoring.

Championship Course: 18 Holes, 7068yds, Par 72, SSS 74.
Headland Course: 9 Holes, 3031yds, Par 35.
Short Course: 9 Holes, 1360yds, Par 29.
Club membership 1650.

Visitors Mon-Sun & BHs. Booking required. Dress code.
Societies welcome. **Green Fees** not confirmed **Course Designer** H S Colt **Prof** Gary Lenaghan **Facilities** 🏧 🍴 🦽 ⛳ 🍺 🎿 🏖 🏯 ◇ 🏌 🚂 🏇 **Leisure** hard tennis courts, heated outdoor swimming pool **Conf** facs Corporate Hospitality Days **Location** 4m W of Padstow on B3276, to St Merryn, 500yds past x-rds turn, signed
Hotel ★★ 75% HL The Old Ship Hotel, Mill Square, PADSTOW ☎ 01841 532357 🖹 01841 533211 14 en suite

FALMOUTH
Map 2 SW83

Falmouth Golf Club Swanpool Rd TR11 5BQ
☎ 01326 314296 & 311262   📠 01326 317783
e-mail: steve@falmouthgolfclub.com
web: www.falmouthgolfclub.com

Dating from 1894, Falmouth is one of the oldest courses in the county situated in a picturesque setting with fine sea and coastal views. Excellent greens.

18 Holes, 5903yds, Par 71, SSS 70, Course record 66. Club membership 630.

Visitors Mon-Sun & BHs. Booking required. Dress code.
Societies booking required. **Green Fees** £38 per day, £32 per round **Prof** Nick Rogers **Facilities** ⑪ ⑩ 🍴 ⚑ ⟟ 🍴 ⚿ 🛋 🎖 ⚡ 🐟 ⚡ 🦮 **Conf** Corporate Hospitality Days **Location** SW of town centre
Hotel ★★★★ 79% HL Royal Duchy, Cliff Road, FALMOUTH
☎ 01326 313042 & 214001 📠 01326 319420 43 en suite

HOLYWELL BAY
Map 2 SW75

Holywell Bay Golf Park TR8 5PW
☎ 01637 832916   📠 01637 831000
e-mail: golf@trevornick.co.uk
web: www.holywellbay.co.uk/golf

Situated beside a family fun park with many amenities. The course is an 18-hole short course with excellent sea views. Fresh Atlantic winds make the course hard to play and there are several tricky holes, particularly the 18th over the trout pond. The site also has an excellent 18-hole Pitch and Putt course for the whole family.

18 Holes, 2407yds, Par 54, Course record 52. Club membership 200.

Visitors Mon-Sun & BHs. **Societies** booking required. **Green Fees** not confirmed **Course Designer** Hartley **Facilities** ⑪ ⑩ 🍴 ⚑ 🍴 🛋 🎖 ⚡ **Leisure** heated outdoor swimming pool, fishing, 18 hole pitch & putt course, touring & camping facilities **Conf** Corporate Hospitality Days **Location** off A3075 Newquay-Perranporth road
Hotel ★★★ 75% HL Crantock Bay, West Pentire, CRANTOCK
☎ 01637 830229 📠 01637 831111 31 en suite

LAUNCESTON
Map 2 SX38

Launceston Golf Club St Stephens PL15 8HF
☎ 01566 773442 & 775359   📠 01566 777506
e-mail: secretary@launcestongolfclub.co.uk
web: www.launcestongolfclub.co.uk

Highly rated course with magnificent views over the historic town and moors. Noted for superb greens and lush fairways.

18 Holes, 6385yds, Par 70, SSS 71. Club membership 500.
Visitors Mon-Sun & BHs. Booking required. Dress code.
Societies booking advised. **Green Fees** £40 per day, £30 per round **Course Designer** Hamilton Stutt **Prof** John Tozer **Facilities** ⑪ 🍴 ⚑ 🍴 🛋 🎖 ⚡ 🦮 **Leisure** practice nets **Conf** facs Corporate Hospitality Days **Location** NW of town centre on B3254
Hotel ★★ 74% SHL Eagle House, Castle Street, LAUNCESTON
☎ 01566 772036 & 774488 📠 01566 772036 14 en suite

Trethorne Golf Club Kennards House PL15 8QE
☎ 01566 86903   📠 01566 880925
e-mail: reservations@trethornegolfclub.com
web: www.trethornegolfclub.com

A challenging and scenic par 71 parkland layout, with numerous water hazards and tree-lined fairways. The greens are built to USGA specification making them free draining and playable all year round.

18 Holes, 6301yds, Par 71, SSS 71, Course record 65. Club membership 280.

Visitors Mon-Sun & BHs. Booking required. Dress code.
Societies booking required. **Green Fees** £25 per round (£36 weekends) **Course Designer** Frank Frayne **Prof** Wayne Basford **Facilities** ⑪ ⑩ 🍴 ⚑ 🍴 🛋 🎖 ⚡ 🦮 ⚡ **Leisure** leisure farm and tenpin bowling. **Conf** facs Corporate Hospitality Days **Location** off junct A30, 3m W of Launceston
Hotel ★★ 74% SHL Eagle House, Castle Street, LAUNCESTON
☎ 01566 772036 & 774488 📠 01566 772036 14 en suite

LELANT
Map 2 SW53

West Cornwall Golf Club TR26 3DZ
☎ 01736 753401
e-mail: secretary@westcornwallgolfclub.co.uk
web: www.westcornwallgolfclub.co.uk

Established in 1889, a seaside links with sandhills and lovely turf adjacent to the Hayle estuary and St Ives Bay. A real test of the player's skill, especially Calamity Corner starting at the 5th on the lower land by the River Hayle.

West Cornwall: 18 Holes, 5984yds, Par 69, SSS 69, Course record 63. Club membership 703.

Visitors Mon-Sun & BHs. Handicap certificate. Dress code.
Societies booking required. **Green Fees** £37 per day (£42 Wed, Sat & BHs) **Course Designer** Reverend Tyacke **Prof** Jason Broadway **Facilities** ⑪ ⑩ 🍴 ⚑ 🍴 🛋 🎖 ⚡ **Conf** Corporate Hospitality Days **Location** N side of village off A3074
Hotel ★★★ 80% HL Carbis Bay, Carbis Bay, ST IVES
☎ 01736 795311 📠 01736 797677 40 en suite

LOOE
Map 2 SX25

Looe Golf Club Bindown PL13 1PX
☎ 01503 240239   📠 01503 240864
e-mail: enquiries@looegolfclub.co.uk
web: www.looegolfclub.co.uk

Designed by Harry Vardon in 1935, this downland and parkland course commands panoramic views over south-east Cornwall and the coast. Easy walking.

18 Holes, 5940yds, Par 70, SSS 69, Course record 64. Club membership 420.

Visitors Mon-Sun & BHs. Booking required. Dress code.
Societies booking required. **Green Fees** £28 per 18 holes **Course**

continued

Save on Hotels. Book at **theAA.com/hotel**   **CORNWALL & ISLES OF SCILLY**

ENGLAND

Designer Harry Vardon **Prof** Barrie Evans/Edward Goodaire
Facilities ⑪ ⓑ ⌷ ⒆ ⌄ 🍴 ⒤ ⌑ ✔ 🏌 ✔ **Conf** Corporate
Hospitality Days **Location** 3.5m NE off B3253
Hotel ★★★ 71% HL Hannafore Point, Marine Drive, West Looe,
LOOE ☎ 01503 263273 📠 01503 263272 37 en suite

LOSTWITHIEL   Map 2 SX15

Lostwithiel Hotel, Golf & Country Club Lower Polscoe
PL22 0HQ
☎ 01208 873550   📠 01208 873479
e-mail: reception@golf-hotel.co.uk
web: www.golf-hotel.co.uk

This 18-hole course is one of the most varied in the county, designed
to take full advantage of the natural features of the landscape,
combining two distinct areas of hillside and valley. The challenging
front nine has magnificent views of the surrounding countryside, while
the picturesque back nine runs through parkland flanked by the River
Fowey.

18 Holes, 5907yds, Par 72, SSS 71, Course record 63.
Club membership 300.

Visitors Mon-Sun & BHs. Booking required. Handicap certificate. Dress
code. **Societies** booking required. **Green Fees** £34 per round (£40
weekends). Reductions during winter months **Course Designer** S Wood
Prof Andrew Hooper **Facilities** ⑪ 🍴 ⓑ ⌷ ⒆ ⌄ ⌑ ⒤ ⌑
✔ 🏌 ✔ 🏌 **Leisure** hard tennis courts, heated indoor swimming
pool, fishing, gymnasium, indoor golf simulator **Conf** facs Corporate
Hospitality Days **Location** 1m from Lostwithiel off A390
Hotel ★★★ 68% HL Lostwithiel Hotel Golf & Country Club,
Lower Polscoe, LOSTWITHIEL ☎ 01208 873550 📠 01208 873479
27 en suite

MAWGAN PORTH   Map 2 SW86

Merlin Golf Course TR8 4DN
☎ 01841 540222   📠 01841 541031
e-mail: play@merlingolfcourse.co.uk
web: www.merlingolfcourse.co.uk
A heathland course with fine views of the coast and countryside. Fairly
easy walking. The most challenging hole is the par 4 18th with out of
bounds on the left and ponds on either side of the green.

18 Holes, 6181yds, Par 71, SSS 70, Course record 68.
Club membership 350.

Visitors Mon-Sun & BHs. Dress code. **Societies** welcome. **Green
Fees** £35 per day, £25 per round **Course Designer** Ross Oliver
Prof John Rule **Facilities** ⑪ 🍴 ⓑ ⌷ ⒆ ⌄ ⌑ ⒤ ⌑ ◇
✔ 🏌 ✔ 🏌 **Conf** facs Corporate Hospitality Days **Location** on
Newquay-Padstow coast road. After Mawgan Porth signs for St Eval,
course on right
Hotel ★★★★ 76% HL Bedruthan Steps Hotel, MAWGAN PORTH
☎ 01637 860555 & 860860 📠 01637 860714 101 en suite

MULLION   Map 2 SW61

Mullion Golf Club Cury TR12 7BP
☎ 01326 240685 (sec) & 241176 (pro)
📠 01326 241527
e-mail: secretary@mulliongolfclub.plus.com
web: www.mulliongolfclub.co.uk
Founded in 1895, a clifftop and links course with panoramic views
over Mount's Bay. A steep downhill slope on the 6th and the 10th
descends to the beach with a deep ravine alongside the green. The
most southerly course in England.

18 Holes, 6053yds, Par 70, SSS 70, Course record 63.
Club membership 700.

Visitors Mon-Sun & BHs. Handicap certificate. Dress code.
Societies booking required. **Green Fees** £35 per day **Course
Designer** W Sich **Prof** Ian Harris **Facilities** ⑪ 🍴 ⓑ ⌷ ⒆
⌑ ⒤ ⌑ ✔ 🏌 ✔ **Leisure** indoor computerised teaching
academy **Location** 1.5m NW of Mullion, off A3083
Hotel ★★★ 77% HL Polurrian, MULLION ☎ 01326 240421
📠 01326 240083 39 en suite

NEWQUAY   Map 2 SW86

Newquay Golf Club Tower Rd TR7 1LT
☎ 01637 874354   📠 01637 874066
e-mail: newquaygolf@btconnect.com
web: www.newquaygolfclub.co.uk
One of Cornwall's finest seaside links with magnificent views over
Fistral Beach and the Atlantic Ocean. Open to the unpredictable
nature of the elements and possessing some very demanding
greenside bunkers, the prerequisite for good scoring at Newquay is
accuracy.

18 Holes, 6141yds, Par 69, SSS 69, Course record 63.
Club membership 550.

Visitors Mon-Sun & BHs. Booking required weekends & BHs. Handicap
certificate. Dress code. **Societies** booking required. **Green Fees** £31
per round (£36 per round weekends and BHs). **Course Designer** H Colt
Prof Joel Cant **Facilities** ⑪ 🍴 ⓑ ⌷ ⒆ ⌄ ⌑ ⒤ ⌑ ✔ 🏌
✔ **Conf** Corporate Hospitality Days **Location** from W side of town take
Gannel bypass and follow signs for Fistral Beach. At top of by-pass
take 2nd exit off rdbt, club signed
Hotel ★★★ 77% HL Best Western Hotel Bristol, Narrowcliff,
NEWQUAY ☎ 01637 875181 📠 01637 879347 74 en suite

PADSTOW

See Constantine Bay

PERRANPORTH
Map 2 SW75

Perranporth Golf Club Budnic Hill TR6 0AB
☎ 01872 572454
e-mail: secretary@perranporthgolfclub.co.uk
web: www.perranporthgolfclub.com

There are three testing par 5 holes on the links course (2nd, 5th, 11th). This seaside links course has magnificent views of the North Cornwall coastline, and excellent greens. The drainage of the course, being sand-based, is also exceptional.

18 Holes, 6292yds, Par 72, SSS 72, Course record 65. Club membership 650.

Visitors Mon-Sun & BHs. Booking required. Dress code. **Societies** booking required. **Green Fees** £36 per round (£42 weekends & BHs). Additional £5 for extra holes **Course Designer** James Braid **Prof** D Michell **Facilities** ⓣ ⑩ ▮ 亾 ♐ ♜ 亾 ⚑ ♂ 🛒 **Conf** Corporate Hospitality Days **Location** 0.75m NE on B3285 **Hotel** ★★★ 70% HL Rosemundy House, Rosemundy Hill, ST AGNES ☎ 01872 552101 📄 01872 554000 46 en suite

PORTWRINKLE
Map 2 SX45

Whitsand Bay Hotel & Golf Club PL11 3BU
☎ 01503 230276 📄 01503 230329
e-mail: whitsandbayhotel@btconnect.com
web: www.whitsandbayhotel.co.uk

Testing seaside course laid out on cliffs overlooking Whitsand Bay. Easy walking after first hole. The par 3 3rd hole is acknowledged as one of the most attractive holes in Cornwall.

Whitsand Bay: 18 Holes, 5776yds, Par 70, SSS 68, Course record 65. Club membership 300.

Visitors Mon-Sun & BHs. Booking required. Dress code. **Societies** booking required. **Green Fees** £25 per 18 holes (£30 weekends) **Course Designer** Fernie **Prof** Andy Welch **Facilities** ⓣ ⑩ ▮ 亾 ♐ 亾 亾 ⚑ ♂ 🛒 ♂ 🛒 **Leisure** heated indoor swimming pool, sauna, gymnasium, spa centre **Conf** Corporate Hospitality Days **Location** from Tamar Bridge, left at Trerulefoot rdbt for Polbathic. Right after 2m to Crafthole then Portwrinkle. Golf course on right
Hotel ★★★ 74% HL Whitsand Bay Hotel & Golf Club, PORTWRINKLE ☎ 01503 230276 📄 01503 230329 32 en suite

PRAA SANDS
Map 2 SW52

Praa Sands Golf Club & Country Club Germoe Cross Roads TR20 9TQ
☎ 01736 763445
web: www.haulfryn.co.uk/leisure/praa-sands-golf

9 Holes, 4122yds, Par 62, SSS 62, Course record 58.

Location A394 between Penzance & Helston
Telephone for further details
Hotel ★★★ 84% HL Mount Haven Hotel & St Michaels Restaurant, Turnpike Road, MARAZION ☎ 01736 710249 📄 01736 711658 18 en suite

ROCK
Map 2 SW97

St Enodoc Golf Club PL27 6LD
☎ 01208 863216 📄 01208 862976
e-mail: enquiries@st-enodoc.co.uk
web: www.st-enodoc.co.uk

Classic links course with huge sand hills and rolling fairways. James Braid laid out the original 18 holes in 1907 and changes were made in 1922 and 1935. On the Church, the 10th is the toughest par 4 on the course and on the 6th is a truly enormous sand hill known as the Himalayas. The Holywell is not as exacting as the Church; it is less demanding on stamina but still a real test of skill for golfers of any handicap.

Church Course: 18 Holes, 6547yds, Par 69, SSS 71, Course record 65.
Holywell Course: 18 Holes, 4802yds, Par 63, SSS 61. Club membership 1400.

Visitors Mon-Fri, Sun & BHs. Sat late pm. Booking required for Church Course. Handicap certificate. Dress code. **Societies** booking required. **Green Fees** Church Course £93 per day, £67 per round (£77 per round Sun & BHs). Holywell Course: £32 per day, £22 per round **Course Designer** James Braid **Prof** Nick Williams **Facilities** ⓣ ▮ 亾 ♐ 亾 亾 ⚑ ♂ 🛒 ♂ 🛒 **Location** W side of village
Hotel ★★★★ 73% HL The Metropole, Station Road, PADSTOW ☎ 01841 532486 📄 01841 532867 58 en suite

ST MELLION INTERNATIONAL RESORT

CORNWALL - ST MELLION - MAP 2 SX36

Set among 450 acres of glorious Cornish countryside, St Mellion with its two outstanding courses is heralded as the premier golf and country club in the south-west. The Kernow Course is perfect for golfers of all abilities. Complete with well-sited bunkers, strategically tiered greens and difficult water features, this is definitely not a course to be overlooked. But if you really want to test your game, then head to the renowned Nicklaus Course, designed by the great man himself. On its opening in 1998 Jack declared, 'St Mellion is potentially the finest golf course in Europe'. The spectacularly sculptured fairways and carpet greens of the Nicklaus Course are a challenge and an inspiration to all golfers.

PL12 6SD ☎ 01579 351351 📠 01579 350537
e-mail: stmellion@crown-golf.co.uk **web:** www.st-mellion.co.uk
Nicklaus Signature Course: 18 Holes, 6284yds, Par 72, SSS 71, Course record 63.
Kernow Course: 18 Holes, 5606yds, Par 70, SSS 70, Course record 67. Club membership 1000.
Visitors Playing guidelines apply. Dress code. **Societies** booking required. **Green Fees** Nicklaus Course Mon-Wed £75 per 18 holes, Thu-Fri £85, weekends £95. Kernow Course Mon-Wed £40, Thu-Fri £45, weekends £50
Course Designer Kernow Course H J Stutt/Jack Nicklaus **Prof** David Moon **Facilities** ⑨ ⑩ 🏌 ⌁ 🍴 ⚒ 🏠 ⛳
◇ 🏌 🚜 🏌 🏌 **Leisure** hard tennis courts, heated indoor swimming pool, sauna, gymnasium, bowling green
Conf facs Corporate Hospitality Days **Location** A38 to Saltash, onto A388 to Callington
Hotel ★★★ 85% HL Horn of Plenty, Gulworthy, TAVISTOCK ☎ 01822 832528 📠 01822 834390 10 en suite

ENGLAND

ST AUSTELL
Map 2 SX05

Carlyon Bay Hotel Spa & Golf Beach Rd, Carlyon Bay
PL25 3RD
☎ 01726 814228 📄 01726 814250
e-mail: golf@carlyonbay.com
web: www.carlyonbay.com

A championship-length, clifftop parkland course, running east to west and back again - uphill and down. The fairways stay in excellent condition all year as they have since the course was laid down in 1925. Magnificent views from the course across St Austell Bay; particularly from the 9th green, where an approach shot remotely to the right will plummet over the cliff edge.

18 Holes, 6597yds, Par 72, SSS 71, Course record 63. Club membership 500.

Visitors Mon-Sun & BHs. Booking required. Dress code.
Societies booking required. **Green Fees** from £28-£48 per round depending on season. £10 for extra round **Course Designer** Hamilton Stutt **Prof** Mark Rowe **Facilities** ⊕ ⑩ ⓑ ⓓ 🍴 ⓧ 🎣 ⓧ ⓧ 🛒 ⓧ **Leisure** hard tennis courts, outdoor and indoor heated swimming pool, sauna, gymnasium, 9 hole par 3 course **Conf** facs Corporate Hospitality Days **Location** 3m SE of St Austell off A390
Hotel ★★★★ 77% HL The Carlyon Bay Hotel, Sea Road, Carlyon Bay, ST AUSTELL ☎ 01726 812304 & 811006 📄 01726 814938 86 en suite

Porthpean Golf Club Porthpean PL26 6AY
☎ 01726 64613 📄 01726 64613
e-mail: porthpeangolfclub@hotmail.co.uk
web: www.porthpeangolfclub.co.uk
A picturesque 18-hole course, the outward holes are in a pleasant parkland setting while the return holes command spectacular views over St Austell Bay.
18 Holes, 5175yds, Par 67, SSS 68. Club membership 550.
Visitors Mon-Sun & BHs. **Societies** booking required. **Green Fees** £22 per round, £14 per 9 holes **Facilities** ⊕ ⓑ ⓓ 🍴 ⓧ ⓓ 🛒 **Conf** facs Corporate Hospitality Days **Location** 1.5m from St Austell bypass, A390. Signed
Hotel ★★★ 73% HL Pier House, Harbour Front, Charlestown, ST AUSTELL ☎ 01726 67955 📄 01726 69246 28 en suite

St Austell Golf Club Tregongeeves Ln PL26 7DS
☎ 01726 74756 📄 01726 71978
e-mail: office@staustellgolf.co.uk
web: www.staustellgolf.co.uk
Challenging inland parkland course designed by James Braid and offering glorious views of the surrounding countryside. Undulating,

well-covered with tree plantations and well-bunkered. Notable holes are 8th (par 4) and 16th (par 3).
18 Holes, 6042yds, Par 69, SSS 69. Club membership 600.
Visitors Mon-Fri & BHs. Booking required Tue & Thu. Dress code.
Societies booking required. **Green Fees** £30 per round **Course Designer** James Braid **Prof** Tony Pitts **Facilities** ⊕ ⑩ ⓑ ⓓ 🍴 ⓧ 🍴 ⓧ 🎣 **Conf** facs Corporate Hospitality Days
Location 1m W of St Austell on A390
Hotel ★★★ 73% HL Pier House, Harbour Front, Charlestown, ST AUSTELL ☎ 01726 67955 📄 01726 69246 28 en suite

ST IVES
Map 2 SW54

Tregenna Castle Hotel TR26 2DE
☎ 01736 797381 📄 01736 796066
web: www.tregenna-castle.co.uk
14 Holes, 1846yds, Par 42, SSS 42.
Course Designer Abercrombie **Location** off A30 past Hayle onto A3074
Telephone for further details
Hotel ★★★ 73% HL Tregenna Castle Hotel, ST IVES
☎ 01736 795254 📄 01736 796066 81 en suite

ST JUST (NEAR LAND'S END)
Map 2 SW33

Cape Cornwall Golf & Leisure Resort Cape Cornwall
TR19 7NL
☎ 01736 788611 📄 01736 786366
e-mail: golf@capecornwall.com
web: www.capecornwall.com
Coastal parkland, walled course. The walls are an integral part of its design. Britain's first and last 18-hole, course overlooking the only Cape in England, with views of the north Cornwall coast and old fishing coves. Features a flat front nine followed by a challenging back nine. Extremely scenic wild coastal views.
18 Holes, 5529yds, Par 69, SSS 68, Course record 66. Club membership 350.
Visitors Mon-Sun & BHs. **Societies** welcome. **Green Fees** £25 per round (£30 Fri-Sun) **Course Designer** Bob Hamilton **Prof** Scott Richards **Facilities** ⊕ ⑩ ⓑ ⓓ 🍴 ⓧ ⓓ 🛒 ⓧ ⓧ **Leisure** heated indoor swimming pool, sauna, gymnasium **Conf** facs Corporate Hospitality Days **Location** 1m W of St Just, follow brown signs for Cape Cornwall
Hotel ★★★ 71% HL The Land's End Hotel, LANDS END
☎ 01736 871844 📄 01736 871599 32 en suite

ST MELLION
Map 2 SX36

St Mellion International Resort see page 51
PL12 6SD
☎ 01579 351351 📄 01579 350537
e-mail: stmellion@crown-golf.co.uk
web: www.st-mellion.co.uk

SALTASH Map 2 SX45

China Fleet Country Club PL12 6LJ
☎ 01752 848668 📄 01752 848456
e-mail: golf@china-fleet.co.uk
web: www.china-fleet.co.uk
Parkland with river views. The 14th tee shot has to carry a lake of some 150yds.

China Fleet: 18 Holes, 6551yds, Par 72, SSS 72.
Club membership 600.

Visitors Mon-Sun & BHs. Booking required. Dress code.
Societies booking required. **Green Fees** £30 (£35 weekends) **Course Designer** Hawtree **Prof** Dominic Rehaag **Facilities** ⑪ ↑◎ ⓛ ☐ ⌐ 🖎 🕳 🏊 🏌 ♦ ❄ 🚶 ♦ 🏆 **Leisure** hard tennis courts, heated indoor swimming pool, squash, sauna, gymnasium, golf simulator **Conf** facs Corporate Hospitality Days **Location** 1m from the Tamar Bridge
Hotel ★★★ 77% HL China Fleet Country Club, SALTASH
☎ 01752 854664 & 854661 📄 01752 848456 40 en suite

TRURO Map 2 SW84

Killiow Golf Club Kea TR3 6AG
☎ 01872 270246 📄 01872 240915
e-mail: sec@killiow.co.uk
web: www.killiowgolf.co.uk
A picturesque and testing parkland course in the grounds of Killiow Estate, with mature trees, water hazards, small greens and tight fairways making this a challenge for golfers of all abilities. Five holes are played across or around water. Floodlit, all-weather driving range and practice facilities.

18 Holes, 6115yds, Par 72, SSS 71, Course record 70.
Club membership 500.

Visitors Mon-Sun & BHs. Booking preferred. **Societies** booking required. **Green Fees** not confirmed **Prof** Richard Sadler **Facilities** ⑪ ↑◎ ⓛ ☐ 🖎 🏊 ♦ 🏆 **Leisure** 3 hole academy course **Conf** Corporate Hospitality Days **Location** 3m SW of Truro, off A39
Hotel ★★★ 78% HL Alverton Manor, Tregolls Road, TRURO
☎ 01872 276633 📄 01872 222989 33 en suite

Truro Golf Club Treliske TR1 3LG
☎ 01872 278684 (manager) 📄 01872 225972
e-mail: trurogolfclub@tiscali.co.uk
web: www.trurogolfclub.co.uk
A picturesque and gently undulating parkland course with lovely views of the cathedral city of Truro and the surrounding countryside. The course offers a great challenge to golfers of all standards and ages. The many trees and shrubs offer open invitations for wayward balls, and with many fairways boasting out of bounds markers, play needs to be safe and sensible. Fairways are tight and the greens small and full of character, making it difficult to play to one's handicap.

18 Holes, 5306yds, Par 66, SSS 66, Course record 59.
Club membership 500.

Visitors Mon-Sun & BHs. Booking required. **Societies** booking required. **Green Fees** £25 per day (£30 weekends & BHs) 🚭 **Course Designer** Colt, Alison & Morrison **Prof** Nigel Bicknell **Facilities** ⑪ ↑◎ ⓛ ☐ 🖎 🏊 🏌 🚶 ❄ **Conf** Corporate Hospitality Days **Location** 1.5m W on A390 towards Redruth, adjacent to Treliske Hospital
Hotel ★★★ 78% HL Alverton Manor, Tregolls Road, TRURO
☎ 01872 276633 📄 01872 222989 33 en suite

WADEBRIDGE Map 2 SW97

St Kew Golf Course St Kew Highway PL30 3EF
☎ 01208 841500 📄 01208 841500
web: www.thisisnorthcornwall.com
9 Holes, 4550yds, Par 64, SSS 62, Course record 63.

Course Designer David Derry **Location** 2m N of Wadebridge main A39
Telephone for further details
Hotel ★★★ 74% SHL Trehellas House Hotel & Restaurant, Washaway, BODMIN ☎ 01208 72700 📄 01208 73336 12 en suite

CUMBRIA

ALSTON Map 12 NY74

Alston Moor Golf Club The Hermitage, Middleton in Teesdale Rd CA9 3DB
☎ 01434 381675 📄 01434 381675
e-mail: secretary@alstonmoorgolfclub.org.uk
web: www.alstonmoorgolfclub.org.uk
Parkland and Fell, in process of upgrading to full 18 holes, stunning views of the North Pennines.

10 Holes, 5518yds, Par 68, SSS 66, Course record 67.
Club membership 170.

Visitors Mon-Sun & BHs. Dress code. **Societies** booking required. **Green Fees** £15 per day 🚭 **Facilities** ☐ 🖎 🏊 **Location** 1 S of Alston on B6277
Hotel ★★★★ RR Alston House, Townfoot, ALSTON
☎ 01434 382200 📄 01434 382493 7 rooms

APPLEBY-IN-WESTMORLAND Map 12 NY62

Appleby Golf Club Brackenber Moor CA16 6LP
☎ 017683 51432 📄 017683 52773
e-mail: enquiries@applebygolfclub.co.uk
web: www.applebygolfclub.co.uk
This remotely situated heather and moorland course offers interesting golf with the rewarding bonus of several long par 4 holes that will be remembered, and challenging par 3s. There are superb views of the Pennines and the Lakeland hills. Renowned for the excellent greens and very good drainage.

18 Holes, 5993yds, Par 68, SSS 69, Course record 61.
Club membership 800.

Visitors Mon-Sun & BHs. Booking recommended. Casual dress code. **Societies** booking required. **Green Fees** £32 per day, £25 per round (£38/£31 weekends & BHs) **Course Designer** Willie Fernie **Prof** Gaele Tapper **Facilities** ⑪ ↑◎ ⓛ ☐ 🖎 🏊 🕳 🏌 ❄ 🚶 **Leisure** buggy for disabled use **Conf** Corporate Hospitality Days **Location** 2m E of Appleby 0.5m off A66
Hotel ★★★★ 76% CHH Appleby Manor Country House Hotel, Roman Road, APPLEBY-IN-WESTMORLAND ☎ 017683 51571 📄 017683 52888 30 en suite

ASKAM-IN-FURNESS Map 7 SD27

Dunnerholme Golf Club Duddon Rd LA16 7AW
☎ 01229 462675 & 467421 📠 01229 462675
e-mail: dunnerholmegolfclub@btinternet.com
web: thedunnerholmegolfclub.co.uk

Unique 10-hole (18-tee) links course with view of the Cumbrian mountains and Morecambe Bay. Two streams run through and around the course, providing water hazards on the 1st, 2nd, 3rd and 9th holes. The par 3 6th is the feature hole on the course, playing to an elevated green on Dunnerholme Rock, an imposing limestone outcrop jutting out into the estuary.

10 Holes, 6122yds, Par 72, SSS 72. Club membership 320.

Visitors Mon-Sat & BHs. Dress code. **Societies** welcome. **Green Fees** £15 per day **Facilities** **Location** 1m N on A595
Hotel ★★★★ 72% HL Clarence House Country Hotel & Restaurant, Skelgate, DALTON-IN-FURNESS ☎ 01229 462508 📠 01229 467177 19 en suite

BARROW-IN-FURNESS Map 7 SD26

Barrow Golf Club Rakesmoor Ln LA14 4QB
☎ 01229 825444

18 Holes, 6010yds, Par 71, SSS 70, Course record 65.

Course Designer A M Duncan **Location** M6 junct 35, A590 towards Barrow. 2m to K Papermill, left to top of hill
Telephone for further details
Hotel ★★★★ 72% HL Clarence House Country Hotel & Restaurant, Skelgate, DALTON-IN-FURNESS ☎ 01229 462508 📠 01229 467177 19 en suite

Furness Golf Club Central Dr LA14 3LN
☎ 01229 471232 📠 01229 475100
e-mail: furnessgolfclub@chessbroadband.co.uk
web: www.furnessgolfclub.co.uk

Links golf with 6 outward holes, 6 inward holes and 6 alternating in each direction. Slopes and undulations in equal quantities. Beautiful views of the Lakes and the sea.

18 Holes, 6304yds, Par 71, SSS 70, Course record 65. Club membership 500.

Visitors Mon-Sun & BHs. Booking required. Dress code. **Societies** booking required. **Green Fees** £45 per day, £35 per round (£45/£40 weekends) **Facilities** **Conf** facs Corporate Hospitality Days **Location** 1.75 W of town centre off A590 to Walney Island
Hotel ★★★ 77% HL Abbey House Hotel, Abbey Road, BARROW-IN-FURNESS ☎ 01229 838282 📠 01229 820403 57 en suite

BOWNESS-ON-WINDERMERE Map 7 SD49

Windermere Golf Club Cleabarrow LA23 3NB
☎ 015394 43123 📠 015394 46370
e-mail: office@windermeregolfclub.co.uk
web: www.windermeregolfclub.co.uk

Located in the heart of the Lake District, just 2m from Windermere. The course offers some of the finest views in the country. Not a long course but makes up for its lack of distance with heather and tight undulating fairways. The 6th hole has a nerve wracking but exhilarating blind shot - 160yds over a rocky face to a humpy fairway with a lake to avoid on the second shot.

18 Holes, 5151yds, Par 67, SSS 65, Course record 58. Club membership 890.

Visitors Mon-Sun & BHs. Dress code. **Societies** welcome. **Green Fees** £40 per round (£45 weekends & BHs) **Course Designer** G Lowe **Prof** Simon Edwards **Facilities** **Leisure** snooker **Conf** Corporate Hospitality Days **Location** B5284 1.5m from Bowness
Hotel ★★★★ INN The Queen's Head, Main Street, HAWKSHEAD ☎ 015394 36271 📠 015394 36722 13 rooms (12 en suite)

BRAMPTON Map 12 NY56

Brampton Golf Club Tarn Rd CA8 1HN
☎ 016977 2255 📠 016977 41487
e-mail: secretary@bramptongolfclub.com
web: www.bramptongolfclub.com

Undulating heathland course set in rolling fell country. A number of particularly fine holes, the pick of which may arguably be the lengthy 3rd and 11th. The challenging nature of the course is complemented by unspoilt panoramic views of the Lake District, Pennines and southern Scotland.

18 Holes, 6408yds, Par 72, SSS 71, Course record 60. Club membership 750.

Visitors Mon-Sun & BHs. Booking required weekends & BHs. Handicap certificate. Dress code. **Societies** booking required. **Green Fees** not confirmed **Course Designer** James Braid **Prof** Stewart Wilkinson **Facilities** **Conf** facs Corporate Hospitality Days **Location** 1.5m SE of Brampton on B6413
Hotel ★★★ HL Farlam Hall, BRAMPTON ☎ 016977 46234 📠 016977 46683 12 en suite

CARLISLE Map 11 NY35

Carlisle Golf Club Aglionby CA4 8AG
☎ 01228 513029 (secretary) 📠 01228 513303
e-mail: secretary@carlislegolfclub.org
web: www.carlislegolfclub.org

Majestic, long-established parkland course with great appeal, providing a secure habitat for red squirrels and deer. A complete but not too severe test of golf, with fine turf, natural hazards, streams and many beautiful trees; no two holes are similar.

18 Holes, 6263yds, Par 71, SSS 70, Course record 65. Club membership 700.

Visitors Mon, Wed-Fri & BHs. Dress code. **Societies** booking required. **Green Fees** £60 per day, £40 per round **Course Designer** Mackenzie Ross **Prof** Graeme Lisle **Facilities**

continued

Save on Hotels. Book at **theAA.com/hotel**

CUMBRIA

ENGLAND

🖵 🍴 ⛱ 🏠 ⛳ 🚘 ❀ 🏌 **Conf facs** Corporate Hospitality
Days **Location** M6 junct 43, 0.5m E on A69
Hotel ★★★ 81% HL Crown, Station Road, Wetheral, CARLISLE
☎ 01228 561888 📄 01228 561637 51 en suite

COCKERMOUTH
Map 11 NY13

Cockermouth Golf Club, Embleton CA13 9SG
☎ 017687 76223 & 76941 📄 017687 76941
e-mail: secretary@cockermouthgolf.co.uk
web: www.cockermouthgolf.co.uk

Fell course, fenced, with exceptional views of Lakeland hills and
valleys and the Solway Firth. A hard climb on the 3rd and 11th holes.
Testing holes: 10th and 16th (rearranged by James Braid).

18 Holes, 5410yds, Par 69, SSS 66, Course record 62.
Club membership 400.

Visitors Mon-Sun & BHs. Booking required weekends & BHs.
Societies booking required. **Green Fees** £25 per day (£30 weekends
and BHs). Winter £16/£20 per round 🅿 **Course Designer** J Braid
Facilities 🍴 🖵 ⛱ 🚘 ❀ **Leisure** snooker table **Conf**
Corporate Hospitality Days **Location** 3m E of Cockermouth to N of A66
Hotel ★★★★ 77% HL The Trout Hotel, Crown Street,
COCKERMOUTH ☎ 01900 823591 📄 01900 827514 49 en suite

CROSBY-ON-EDEN
Map 12 NY45

Eden Golf Course CA6 4RA
☎ 01228 573003 📄 01228 818435
e-mail: info@edengolf.co.uk
web: www.edengolf.co.uk

Open, championship-length parkland course following the River Eden.
Tight tree-lined fairways and numerous natural water hazards mark
this course out as a great test of golf. The nine hole Hadrian's course
is set in natural undulating surroundings and has a contrasting style
to the main 18.

Eden: 18 Holes, 6432yds, Par 72, SSS 71, Course record 64.
Hadrian's: 9 Holes, 3262yds, Par 36, SSS 36.
Club membership 500.

Visitors Mon-Sun & BHs. Booking required. Dress code.
Societies booking required. **Green Fees** Eden Course £30 (£40
weekends & BHs). Hadrian's £12/£15 **Course Designer** A G M Wannop
Prof Steve Harrison **Facilities** 🍴 🖵 ⛱ 🚘 ❀
🚘 ❀ 🏌 **Leisure** marquee & garden site for functions **Conf** facs
Corporate Hospitality Days **Location** M6 junct 44, 5m on A689 towards
Brampton
Hotel ★★★ 81% HL Crown, Station Road, Wetheral, CARLISLE
☎ 01228 561888 📄 01228 561637 51 en suite

GRANGE-OVER-SANDS
Map 7 SD47

Grange Fell Golf Club Fell Rd LA11 6HB
☎ 015395 32536

A fell course with no excessive climbing and dependant on how
straight you hit the ball. Fine views in all directions.

9 Holes, 5380yds, Par 70, SSS 66, Course record 65.
Club membership 300.

Visitors Mon, Wed-Sat except BHs. Dress code. **Green Fees** £20
per day 🅿 **Course Designer** A B Davy **Facilities** 🖵 🍴 ⛱
Location 1m W on Grange-Over-Sands towards Cartmel
Hotel ★★★ 80% HL Netherwood, Lindale Road, GRANGE-
SANDS ☎ 015395 32552 📄 015395 34121 34 en suite

Grange-over-Sands Golf Club Meathop Rd LA11 6QX
☎ 015395 33180
e-mail: office@grangegolfclub.co.uk
web: www.grangegolfclub.co.uk

Interesting parkland course with well-sited tree plantations, ditches
and water features, which has recently been drained and extended.
The five par 3s are considered to be some of the best in the area.

18 Holes, 6065yds, Par 70, SSS 69. Club membership 375.

Visitors Contact club for details **Societies** booking required. **Green
Fees** £45 per day, £34 per round. Special twilight, 3 round & weekly
rates **Course Designer** Dr A MacKenzie **Prof** Nick Lowe **Facilities** 🍴
🔩 🖵 ⛱ 🚘 ❀ 🏌 **Leisure** Hi-tech swing studio
Conf facs Corporate Hospitality Days **Location** NE of town centre off
B5277
Hotel ★★★ 68% HL Graythwaite Manor, Fernhill Road, GRANGE-
OVER-SANDS ☎ 015395 32001 & 33755 📄 015395 35549
24 en suite

KENDAL
Map 7 SD59

Carus Green Golf Course & Driving Range Burneside Rd
LA9 6EB
☎ 01539 721097 📄 01539 721097
e-mail: info@carusgreen.co.uk
web: www.carusgreen.co.uk

Very picturesque flat course surrounded by the rivers Kent and Mint
with an open view of the Kentmere and Howgill fells. The course is a
mixture of relatively easy and difficult holes. These rivers come into
play on five holes and there are also a number of ponds and bunkers.

Carus Green: 18 Holes, 6000yds, Par 70, SSS 68,
Course record 64. Club membership 600.

Visitors Mon-Sun & BHs. Booking required. Dress code,
Societies booking required. **Green Fees** £20 per round (£22 weekends
& BHs). 🅿 **Course Designer** W Adamson **Prof** D Turner/A Pickering
Facilities 🍴 🔩 🖵 🍴 ⛱ 🏠 ⛳ ❀ 🚘 ❀ 🏌
Conf Corporate Hospitality Days **Location** 1m from Kendal centre on
Burneside Road
Hotel ★★★ 82% HL Best Western Castle Green Hotel in Kendal,
KENDAL ☎ 01539 734000 📄 01539 735522 99 en suite

Kendal Golf Club The Heights LA9 4PQ
☎ 01539 723499 (pro)
e-mail: secretary@kendalgolfclub.co.uk
web: www.kendalgolfclub.co.uk

Elevated parkland and fell course with breathtaking views of Lakeland fells and the surrounding district.

18 Holes, 5773yds, Par 69, SSS 69, Course record 65.
Club membership 450.

Visitors Mon-Fri, Sun & BHs. Booking required Sun & BHs. Dress code. **Societies** booking required. **Green Fees** £32 per day, £25 per round (£40/£30 Sun) **Prof** Ben Waller **Facilities** ⑪ ⑨ 📭 ◻ ☜️
⅄ 📦 🖈 🖋 🚜 🖋 **Leisure** golf clinic with computer analysis
Location 1m W of town centre, turn left at town hall and follow signs
Hotel ★★★ 77% HL Riverside Hotel Kendal, Beezon Road, Stramongate Bridge, KENDAL ☎ 01539 734861 🖹 01539 734863
50 en suite

KESWICK   Map 11 NY22

Keswick Golf Club Threlkeld Hall, Threlkeld CA12 4SX
☎ 017687 79324 🖹 017687 79861
e-mail: secretary@keswickgolfclub.com
web: www.keswickgolfclub.com

A challenging parkland course. Not very long but a good test for golfers of all abilities.

18 Holes, 6225yds, Par 71, SSS 70. Club membership 400.

Visitors Mon-Sun & BHs. Booking recommended. **Societies** booking required. **Green Fees** contact club **Course Designer** Eric Brown **Prof** Gary Watson **Facilities** ⑪ ⑨ 📭 ◻ ☜️ ⅄ 📦 🖈
🖋 🚜 🖋 **Leisure** driving net **Conf** Corporate Hospitality Days
Location 4m E of Keswick, off A66
Hotel ★★★★ 79% HL Wordsworth Hotel & Spa, GRASMERE
☎ 015394 35592 🖹 015394 35765 36 en suite

KIRKBY LONSDALE   Map 7 SD67

Kirkby Lonsdale Golf Club Scaleber Ln, Barbon LA6 2LJ
☎ 015242 76365 & 76366   🖹 015242 76503
e-mail: klgolf@dial.pipex.com
web: www.kirkbylonsdalegolf.co.uk

Parkland on the east bank of the River Lune and crossed by Barbon Beck. Mainly following the lie of the land, the gently undulating course uses the beck to provide water hazards.

18 Holes, 6542yds, Par 72, SSS 72, Course record 64.
Club membership 500.

Visitors booking required. Handicap certificate. Dress code. **Societies** booking required. **Green Fees** £40 per day **Course Designer** Bill Squires **Prof** Paul Brunt **Facilities** ⑪ ⑨ 📭 ◻ ☜️ ⅄ 📦 🖈 🖋 **Conf** Corporate Hospitality Days **Location** 3m NE of Kirkby Lonsdale on A683
Hotel ★★ 76% HL The Whoop Hall, Burrow with Burrow, KIRKBY LONSDALE ☎ 015242 71284 🖹 015242 72154 24 en suite

MARYPORT   Map 11 NY03

Maryport Golf Club Bankend CA15 6PA
☎ 01900 812605 🖹 01900 815626
e-mail: maryportgolfclub@tiscali.co.uk

A tight seaside links course exposed to Solway breezes. Fine views across Solway Firth. Course comprises nine links holes and nine

parkland holes, and small streams can be hazardous on several holes. The first three holes have the seashore on their left and an errant tee shot can land in the water. Holes 6-14 are parkland in quality, gently undulating and quite open. Holes 15-18 revert to links.

18 Holes, 5982yds, Par 70, SSS 69, Course record 65.
Club membership 486.

Visitors Mon-Sun except BHs. Booking required Wed, Thu, weekends & BHs. Dress code. **Societies** booking required. **Green Fees** £25 per 18 holes (£30 weekends). £35 all day **Facilities** ⑪ ⑨ 📭 ◻ ☜️ ⅄ 🖈 📦 🖋 **Location** 1m N on B5300
Hotel ★★★★ 74% HL Washington Central Hotel, Washington Street, WORKINGTON ☎ 01900 65772 🖹 01900 68770 46 en suite

PENRITH   Map 12 NY53

Penrith Golf Club Salkeld Rd CA11 8SG
☎ 01768 891919   🖹 01768 891919
e-mail: secretary@penrithgolfclub.co.uk
web: www.penrithgolfclub.co.uk

A beautiful and well-balanced course, always changing direction, and demanding good length from the tee. It is set on rolling moorland with occasional pine trees and some fine views.

18 Holes, 6072yds, Par 69, SSS 70, Course record 63.
Club membership 800.

Visitors Mon-Sun & BHs. Booking required Fri-Sun & BHs. Handicap certificate. Dress code. **Societies** booking required. **Green Fees** £37 per day, £32 per round (£45/£40 weekends). **Prof** Garry Key **Facilities** ⑪ ⑨ 📭 ◻ ☜️ ⅄ 📦 🖈 🖋 🚜 🖋 **Conf facs** Corporate Hospitality Days **Location** M6 junct 41, A6 to Penrith, left after 30mph sign
Hotel ★★★ 77% HL George, Devonshire Street, PENRITH
☎ 01768 862696 & 0800 840 1242 🖹 01768 868223 35 en suite

ST BEES   Map 11 NX91

St Bees Golf Club Peckmill CA27 0EJ
☎ 01946 824300

9 Holes, 5306yds, Par 66, SSS 66, Course record 64.
Location 0.5m W of village off B5345
Telephone for further details
Hotel ★★★ 74% HL Ennerdale Country House, CLEATOR
☎ 01946 813907 🖹 01946 815260 30 en suite

SEASCALE   Map 6 NY00

Seascale Golf Club The Banks CA20 1QL
☎ 019467 28202   🖹 019467 28042
web: www.seascalegolfclub.co.uk

18 Holes, 6416yds, Par 71, SSS 72, Course record 64.
Course Designer Willie Campbell **Location** NW side of village off B5344
Telephone for further details
Hotel ★★★ INN The Lutwidge Arms, HOLMROOK
☎ 019467 24230 🖹 019467 24100 16 rooms (16 en suite)

SEDBERGH   Map 7 SD69

Sedbergh Golf Club Dent Rd LA10 5SS
☎ 015396 21551 📠 015396 21551
e-mail: info@sedberghgolfclub.com
web: www.sedberghgolfclub.com

A tree-lined parkland course with superb scenery in the Yorkshire Dales National Park. Undulating fairways cross or are adjacent to the Dee and Rawthey rivers. Well guarded greens and many water features make the course a test for golfers of all abilities.

10 Holes, 5834yds, Par 70, SSS 68, Course record 66. Club membership 200.

Visitors Mon-Sun & BHs. Booking required Mon, Thu-Sun & BHs. **Societies** booking required. **Green Fees** £20 per 18 holes, £14 per 9 holes 🅿 **Course Designer** W G Squires **Facilities** ⊕ ⅃ 🖵 🏶 🧍 🏠 ⚑ ✦ 🚜 ✦ **Leisure** fishing **Conf** facs Corporate Hospitality Days **Location** 1m S off A683
Hotel ★★★ 82% HL Best Western Castle Green Hotel in Kendal, KENDAL ☎ 01539 734000 📠 01539 735522   99 en suite

SILECROFT   Map 6 SD18

Silecroft Golf Club Silecroft, Millom LA18 4NX
☎ 01229 770467
e-mail: sgcsecretary@hotmail.co.uk
web: www.silecroftgolfclub.co.uk

Seaside links course parallel to the coast of the Irish Sea with spectacular views inland of Lakeland hills. Looks deceptively easy but an ever present sea breeze ensures a sporting challenge.

9 Holes, 5695yds, Par 68, SSS 67. Club membership 200.

Visitors Mon-Sun & BHs. Dress code. **Societies** booking required. **Green Fees** £20 per day (£25 weekends & BHs). 🅿 **Facilities** 🧍 **Location** 3m W of Millom
Hotel ★★★ 77% HL Abbey House Hotel, Abbey Road, BARROW-IN-FURNESS ☎ 01229 838282 📠 01229 820403   57 en suite

SILLOTH   Map 11 NY15

Silloth on Solway Golf Club The Clubhouse CA7 4BL
☎ 016973 31304 📠 016973 31782
e-mail: office@sillothgolfclub.co.uk
web: www.sillothgolfclub.co.uk

Championship links course with stunning views to the lake district and across the Solway to Scotland. Billowing dunes, narrow fairways, heather and gorse and the constant subtle problems of tactics and judgement make these superb links on the Solway an exhilarating and searching test. The 13th is a good long hole.

18 Holes, 6641yds, Par 72, SSS 72. Club membership 600.

Visitors handicap certificate. Dress code. **Societies** booking required. **Green Fees** £45 per round (£56 weekends) **Course Designer** David Grant/Willie Park Jnr **Prof** J Graham **Facilities** ⊕ 🍽 ⅃ 🖵 🏶 🧍 🏠 🚜 ✦ **Conf** facs Corporate Hospitality Days **Location** S side of village off B5300. Clubhouse & carpark beside harbour
Hotel ★★ 71% HL Golf Hotel, Criffel Street, SILLOTH ☎ 016973 31438 📠 016973 32582   22 en suite

ULVERSTON   Map 7 SD27

Ulverston Golf Club Bardsea Park LA12 9QJ
☎ 01229 582824 📠 01229 588910
e-mail: enquiries@ulverstongolf.co.uk
web: www.ulverstongolf.co.uk

Undulating parkland course overlooking Morecambe Bay with extensive views to the Lakeland Fells.

18 Holes, 6261yds, Par 71, SSS 71, Course record 63. Club membership 828.

Visitors Mon-Sun & BHs. Booking required. Handicap certificate. Dress code. **Societies** welcome. **Green Fees** Mar-Oct £40 per day, £36 per round (£45/£40 weekends). Nov-Feb £28/£26 (£30/£28 weekends) **Course Designer** A Herd/H S Colt **Prof** P A Stoller **Facilities** ⊕ 🍽 🏶 🖵 🏶 🧍 🏠 ⚑ ✦ **Leisure** practice ball dispensing machine **Conf** facs Corporate Hospitality Days **Location** 2m S off A5087
Hotel ★★★★ 75% HL Whitewater Hotel, The Lakeland Village, NEWBY BRIDGE ☎ 015395 31133 📠 015395 31881   38 en suite

WINDERMERE

See Bowness-on-Windermere

WORKINGTON   Map 11 NY02

Workington Golf Club Branthwaite Rd CA14 4SS
☎ 01900 603460 📠 01900 607123
e-mail: secretary@workingtongolfclub.com
web: www.workingtongolfclub.com

Meadowland course, undulating, with natural hazards created by stream and trees. Good views of Solway Firth and Lakeland Hills. 10th, 13th and 15th holes are particularly testing.

18 Holes, 6203yds, Par 72, SSS 70. Club membership 850.

Visitors Mon-Sun & BHs. Booking required. Dress code. **Societies** booking required **Green Fees** not confirmed 🅿 **Course Designer** James Braid **Prof** Andrew Wells **Facilities** ⊕ 🍽 🏶 🖵 🏶 🧍 🏠 🚜 ✦ **Leisure** snooker table **Conf** facs Corporate Hospitality Days **Location** 1.75m E off A596
Hotel ★★★★ 74% HL Washington Central Hotel, Washington Street, WORKINGTON ☎ 01900 65772 📠 01900 68770   46 en suite

DERBYSHIRE

ALFRETON
Map 8 SK45

Alfreton Golf Club Wingfield Rd, Oakerthorpe DE55 7LH
☎ 01773 832070
e-mail: bradleyalton@aol.com
web: www.alfretongolfclub.co.uk
A small, well-established parkland course with tight fairways and many natural hazards.

11 Holes, 5408yds, Par 67, SSS 66, Course record 64. Club membership 350.

Visitors Mon-Fri & BHs. Booking required. Handicap certificate. Dress code. **Societies** booking required, **Green Fees** not confirmed **Prof** Neville Hallam **Facilities** ⑪ by prior arrangement ⑪ by prior arrangement ⓑ ⌲ ⑪ ⚲ 🏠 ✔ **Conf** facs Corporate Hospitality Days **Location** 1m W on A615
Hotel ★★★ 79% HL Santo's Higham Farm Hotel, Main Road, HIGHAM ☎ 01773 833812 🖹 01773 520525 28 en suite

ASHBOURNE
Map 7 SK14

Ashbourne Golf Club Wyaston Rd DE6 1NB
☎ 01335 347960 (pro shop)
e-mail: ashbourne.golf.club@gmail.com
web: www.ashbournegolfclub.co.uk
With fine views over surrounding countryside, the course uses natural contours and water features.

18 Holes, 6306yds, Par 71, SSS 70, Course record 65. Club membership 550.

Visitors Mon-Fri except BHs. Booking required. Dress code. **Societies** booking required. **Green Fees** £22 per 18 holes **Course Designer** D Hemstock **Prof** Andrew Smith **Facilities** ⑪ ⑪ ⓑ ⌲ ⑪ ⚲ 🏠 ✔ **Leisure** snooker table **Conf** facs Corporate Hospitality Days **Location** off Wyaston Rd, club signed
Hotel ★★★ 82% HL Callow Hall, Mappleton Road, ASHBOURNE ☎ 01335 300900 🖹 01335 300512 16 en suite

BAKEWELL
Map 8 SK26

Bakewell Golf Club Station Rd DE45 1GB
☎ 01629 812307
e-mail: administrator@bakewellgolfclub.co.uk
web: www.bakewellgolfclub.org.uk
Hilly parkland course with plenty of natural hazards to test the golfer. Magnificent views across the Wye Valley.

9 Holes, 5122yds, Par 68, SSS 66, Course record 65. Club membership 340.

Visitors contact club for details. **Societies** booking required. **Green Fees** £20 per day (£25 Sun & BHs) 🌐 **Facilities** ⑪ ⑪ ⓑ ⌲ ⑪ ⚲ **Conf** Corporate Hospitality Days **Location** from A619 (bridge over River Wye) right up hill (Station Rd) past industrial estate, club 200yds on left
Hotel ★★★ 88% HL Riverside House, Fennel Street, ASHFORD-IN-THE-WATER ☎ 01629 814275 🖹 01629 812873 14 en suite

BAMFORD
Map 8 SK28

Sickleholme Golf Club Saltergate Ln S33 0BN
☎ 01433 651306 🖹 01433 659498
e-mail: sickleholme.gc@btconnect.com
web: www.sickleholme.co.uk
Undulating downland course in the lovely Peak District, with rivers and ravines and spectacular scenery.

18 Holes, 6064yds, Par 69, SSS 69, Course record 62. Club membership 700.

Visitors Mon-Sun & BHs. Booking required. Handicap certificate. Dress code. **Societies** booking required. **Green Fees** £29 per round/day (£34 weekends) **Prof** P H Taylor **Facilities** ⑪ ⑪ ⓑ ⌲ ⑪ ⚲ 🏠 ✔ 🛒 ✔ **Conf** Corporate Hospitality Days **Location** 0.75m S on A6013
Hotel ★★★ 81% HL George Hotel, Main Road, HATHERSAGE ☎ 01433 650436 🖹 01433 650099 22 en suite

BREADSALL
Map 8 SK33

Breadsall Priory, A Marriott Hotel & Country Club
Moor Rd, Morley DE7 6DL
☎ 01332 836016 🖹 01332 836089
e-mail: ian.knox@marriotthotels.com
web: www.breadsallpriorygolf.com
Set in 200 acres of mature undulating parkland, the Priory Course is built on the site of a 13th-century priory. Full use has been made of natural features and fine old trees. A degree of accuracy is required to play small protected greens along tree-lined fairways. Signature hole is the 16th. In contrast the Moorland Course is a sand based course allowing all year round play to full greens. Slighter wider fairways allow for more attacking tee shots but beware of well-placed bunkers, trees and rough. At the 13th the tee shot is narrow with trees and bushes lining the fairway.

Priory Course: 18 Holes, 6054yds, Par 70, SSS 70, Course record 63.
Moorland Course: 18 Holes, 6028yds, Par 70, SSS 69. Club membership 700.

Visitors Mon-Sun & BHs. Booking required. Dress code. **Societies** booking required. **Green Fees** from £53 **Course Designer** D Steel **Prof** Darren Steels **Facilities** ⑪ ⑪ ⓑ ⌲ ⑪ ⚲ 🏠 ⚓ ◇ 🛒 ✔ 🏌 **Leisure** hard tennis courts, heated indoor swimming pool, sauna, gymnasium **Conf** facs Corporate Hospitality Days **Location** From S, M1 junct 28, filter left towards Derby at 1st rdbt, left at 2nd rdbt into Breadsall Village, left into Rectory Lane. Follow road right then left into Moor Rd, hotel on left
Hotel ★★★★ 75% CHH Breadsall Priory, A Marriott Hotel & Country Club, Moor Road, MORLEY ☎ 01332 832235 🖹 01332 833509 112 en suite

BUXTON
Map 7 SK07

Buxton & High Peak Golf Club SK17 7EN
☎ 01298 26263 🖹 01298 26333
e-mail: admin@bhpgc.co.uk
web: www.bhpgc.co.uk
Bracing, well-drained meadowland course, the highest in Derbyshire. Challenging course where wind direction is a major factor on some holes; others require blind shots to sloping greens.

18 Holes, 5966yds, Par 69, SSS 69. Club membership 650.

Visitors handicap certificate. Dress code. **Societies** booking required.
continued

Green Fees £30 per day, £24 per round (£36/£30 weekends & BHs) **Course Designer** J Morris **Prof** Nick Berry **Facilities** ⓣ ⓘⓞⓘ by prior arrangement ⓑ ⯒ 🖥️ ⯒ 🏠 ⯒ ⯒ 🛒 ⯒ **Conf** facs Corporate Hospitality Days **Location** 1m NE off A6
Hotel ★★★★ 72% HL Barceló Buxton Palace Hotel, Palace Road, BUXTON ☎ 01298 22001 📄 01298 72131 122 en suite

Cavendish Golf Club Gadley Ln SK17 6XD
☎ 01298 79708 📄 01298 79708
web: www.cavendishgolfcourse.com
18 Holes, 5721yds, Par 68, SSS 68, Course record 61.
Course Designer Dr MacKenzie **Location** 0.75m W of town centre off A53
Telephone for further details
Hotel ★★★ 81% HL Best Western Lee Wood, The Park, BUXTON
☎ 01298 23002 📄 01298 23228 39 en suite

CHAPEL-EN-LE-FRITH   Map 7 SK08

Chapel-en-le-Frith Golf Club The Cockyard, Manchester Rd SK23 9UH
☎ 01298 812118 & 813943   📄 01298 814990
e-mail: admin@chapelgolf.co.uk
web: www.chapelgolf.co.uk
Scenic parkland course surrounded by hills and bordering the picturesque Combs Reservoir. A tough but fair test for golfers at all levels.
18 Holes, 6400yds, Par 72, SSS 71, Course record 66.
Club membership 570.
Visitors Mon-Sun & BHs. Booking required Wed, Thu, weekends & BHs. **Societies** booking required. **Green Fees** £24 per day for 18 holes (£30 weekends) **Course Designer** David Williams **Prof** Jonny Pearce **Facilities** ⓣ ⓘⓞⓘ ⓑ ⯒ 🖥️ ⯒ 🏠 🛒 ⯒ **Leisure** snooker room **Conf** facs Corporate Hospitality Days **Location** A623 to Chapel. Club on B5470
Hotel ★★★ 81% HL Best Western Lee Wood, The Park, BUXTON
☎ 01298 23002 📄 01298 23228 39 en suite

CHESTERFIELD   Map 8 SK37

Chesterfield Golf Club Walton S42 7LA
☎ 01246 279256 📄 01246 276622
e-mail: secretary@chesterfieldgolfclub.co.uk
web: www.chesterfieldgolfclub.co.uk
A varied and interesting, undulating parkland course with trees picturesquely adding to the holes and the outlook alike. Stream hazard on the back nine.
18 Holes, 6075yds, Par 71, SSS 69, Course record 64.
Club membership 600.
Visitors Mon-Fri except BHs. Booking required. Handicap certificate. Dress code. **Societies** booking required. **Green Fees** £40 per round 🅿 **Prof** Mike McLean **Facilities** ⓣ ⓘⓞⓘ ⓑ ⯒ 🖥️ ⯒ 🏠 🛒 ⯒ **Leisure** snooker **Location** 2m SW off A632
Hotel ★★★ 67% HL Sandpiper, Sheffield Road, Sheepbridge, CHESTERFIELD ☎ 01246 450550 📄 01246 452805 46 en suite

Grassmoor Golf Centre North Wingfield Rd, Grassmoor S42 5EA
☎ 01246 856044 📄 01246 853486
e-mail: enquiries@grassmoorgolf.co.uk
web: www.grassmoorgolf.co.uk
An 18-hole heathland course with interesting and challenging water features, testing greens and testing par 3s.
18 Holes, 5875yds, Par 69, SSS 68, Course record 64.
Club membership 450.
Visitors Booking required. Dress code. **Societies** booking required. **Green Fees** £12 per 18 holes (£15 weekends & BHs) **Course Designer** Hawtree **Prof** Gary Hagues **Facilities** ⓣ ⓘⓞⓘ ⓑ ⯒ 🖥️ ⯒ 🏠 ⯒ ⯒ 🛒 ⯒ ⯒ **Conf** facs Corporate Hospitality Days **Location** M1 junct 29, 4m off B6038 between Chesterfield & Grassmoor
Hotel ★★★ 67% HL Sandpiper, Sheffield Road, Sheepbridge, CHESTERFIELD ☎ 01246 450550 📄 01246 452805 46 en suite

Stanedge Golf Club Walton Hay Farm, Stonedge, Ashover S45 0LW
☎ 01246 566156
e-mail: chrisshaw56@tiscali.co.uk
web: www.stanedgegolfclub.co.uk
Moorland course in hilly situation open to strong winds. Some tricky short holes with narrow fairways, so accuracy is paramount. Magnificent views over four counties.
10 Holes, 5801yds, Par 69, SSS 68, Course record 69.
Club membership 210.
Visitors Mon-Fri before 4pm, Sat-Sun after 3pm. Booking required weekends. Dress code. **Societies** booking required. **Green Fees** £15 per round 🅿 **Facilities** ⓑ ⯒ 🖥️ ⯒ 🏠 **Conf** Corporate Hospitality Days **Location** 5m SW of Chesterfield, off B5057 near Famous Red Lion pub
Hotel ★★ 85% SHL The Red House Country Hotel, Old Road, Darley Dale, MATLOCK ☎ 01629 734854 9 en suite

Tapton Park Golf Club Tapton Park, Tapton S41 0EQ
☎ 01246 239500 & 273887
web: www.taptonparkgolfcourse.co.uk
Municipal parkland course with some fairly hard walking. The 625yd (par 5) 5th is a testing hole.
Tapton Main: 18 Holes, 6104yds, Par 72, SSS 70.
Dobbin Clough: 9 Holes, 2613yds, Par 34.
Club membership 322.
Visitors Mon-Sun & BHs. Booking required. Dress code. **Societies** booking required. **Green Fees** Mon-Thu £13.50 per 18 holes, £7.50 per 9 holes (£16.50/£8.50 Fri-Sun) **Prof** Andrew Carnall/ Craig Pollard **Facilities** ⓣ ⓘⓞⓘ ⓑ ⯒ 🖥️ ⯒ 🏠 ⯒ ⯒ 🛒 ⯒ **Leisure** 9 hole Academy course & 6 hole pitch & putt course **Conf** facs Corporate Hospitality Days **Location** 0.5m E of Chesterfield station
Hotel ★★★ 67% HL Sandpiper, Sheffield Road, Sheepbridge, CHESTERFIELD ☎ 01246 450550 📄 01246 452805 46 en suite

CODNOR
Map 8 SK44

Ormonde Fields Golf & Country Club, Nottingham Rd DE5 9RG
☎ 01773 570043 (Secretary) 🖥 01773 742987
e-mail: info@ormondefieldsgolfclub.co.uk
web: www.ormondefieldsgolfclub.co.uk
Parkland course with undulating fairways and natural hazards. There is a practice area.

18 Holes, 6520yds, Par 72, SSS 72, Course record 63.
Club membership 500.

Visitors Mon-Sun & BHs. Booking required. Dress code.
Societies booking required. **Green Fees** £16 per 18 holes (£30 weekend & BHs) 🏌 **Course Designer** John Fearn **Prof** Richard White
Facilities 🍴 🅿 🏆 ⚑ 🏌 △ 🏠 ◇ 🛒 ♂ **Conf** facs
Corporate Hospitality Days **Location** 1m SE on A610
Hotel ★★★★ 73% HL Makeney Hall Hotel, Makeney, Milford, BELPER ☎ 0845 609 9966 🖥 01332 842777 46 en suite

DERBY
Map 8 SK33

Allestree Park Golf Course Allestree Hall, Duffield Rd, Allestree DE22 2EU
☎ 01332 550616 🖥 01332 541195
Public course, picturesque and undulating, set in 300-acre park with views across Derbyshire.

18 Holes, 5728yds, Par 68, SSS 68, Course record 61.
Club membership 220.

Visitors Mon-Sun & BHs. **Societies** welcome. **Green Fees** £13.50 per round **Prof** Leigh Woodward **Facilities** 🍴 🏌 🅿 🏆 △ 🏠
🏌 ♂ **Leisure** fishing, pool table **Conf** Corporate Hospitality Days
Location N of Derby, A38 onto A6 N, course 1.5m on left
Hotel ★★★★ 75% CHH Breadsall Priory, A Marriott Hotel & Country Club, Moor Road, MORLEY ☎ 01332 832235
🖥 01332 833509 112 en suite

Mickleover Golf Club Uttoxeter Rd DE3 9AD
☎ 01332 518662 (pro) 🖥 01332 516011
18 Holes, 5727yds, Par 68, SSS 67, Course record 64.
Course Designer J Pennink **Location** 3m W of Derby on A516/B5020
Telephone for further details
Hotel ★★★★ 73% HL Menzies Mickleover Court, Etwall Road, Mickleover, DERBY ☎ 01332 521234 🖥 01332 521238 99 en suite

Sinfin Golf Course Wilmore Rd DE24 9HD
☎ 01332 766462 🖥 01332 769004
web: www.sinfingolfcourse.co.uk
18 Holes, 6163yds, Par 70, SSS 70, Course record 65.
Location 2.5m S of city centre
Telephone for further details
Hotel ★★★★ 79% HL Hallmark Derby, Midland Road, DERBY
☎ 01332 345894 🖥 01332 293522 100 en suite

DRONFIELD
Map 8 SK37

Hallowes Golf Club Hallowes Ln S18 1UR
☎ 01246 413734 🖥 01246 413753
e-mail: secretary@hallowesgolfclub.org
web: www.hallowesgolfclub.org
Attractive moorland and parkland course in the Derbyshire hills. Several testing par 4s and splendid views.

18 Holes, 6300yds, Par 71, SSS 71, Course record 60.
Club membership 630.

Visitors Mon-Sun except BHs. Booking required weekends. Handicap certificate. Dress code. **Societies** welcome. **Green Fees** £35 per day, £32.50 per round (£40/£37.50 weekends) **Course Designer** George Lowe **Prof** John Oates **Facilities** 🍴 🅿 🏆 ⚑ △ 🏠 🛒
♂ **Leisure** snooker **Conf** Corporate Hospitality Days **Location** S side of town, off B6057 onto Cemetery Rd and Hallowes Rise/Drive
Hotel ★★★ 67% HL Sandpiper, Sheffield Road, Sheepbridge, CHESTERFIELD ☎ 01246 450550 🖥 01246 452805 46 en suite

DUFFIELD
Map 8 SK34

Chevin Golf Club Golf Ln DE56 4EE
☎ 01332 841864 🖥 01332 844028
e-mail: secretary@chevingolf.co.uk
web: www.chevingolf.co.uk
A mixture of parkland and moorland, this course is rather hilly which makes for some hard walking, but with most rewarding views of the surrounding countryside. The 8th hole, aptly named Tribulation, requires an accurate tee shot, and is one of the most difficult holes in the county.

18 Holes, 6057yds, Par 69, SSS 69, Course record 64.
Club membership 750.

Visitors dress code. **Societies** booking required. **Green Fees** not confirmed **Course Designer** J Braid **Prof** Willie Bird **Facilities** 🍴 🍴
🏌 🅿 △ 🏠 ⚑ ♂ **Conf** facs Corporate Hospitality Days
Location N side of town off A6
Hotel ★★★★ 73% HL Makeney Hall Hotel, Makeney, Milford, BELPER ☎ 0845 609 9966 🖥 01332 842777 46 en suite

GLOSSOP
Map 7 SK09

Glossop and District Golf Club Hurst Rd, off Sheffield Rd SK13 7PU
☎ 01457 865247 (club house) & 853117 (pro)
🖥 01457 864003
e-mail: glossopgolfclub@talktalk.net
web: www.glossopgolfclub.co.uk
Moorland course in good position, excellent natural hazards. Difficult closing hole (9th & 18th).

9 Holes, 5759yds, Par 68, SSS 68, Course record 64.
Club membership 350.

Visitors Mon-Fri, Sun & BHs. Dress code. **Societies** booking required.
Green Fees phone 🏌 **Prof** Mike Williams **Facilities** 🍴 🅿 🏆 🅿
⚑ △ 🏠 ⚑ ♂ **Conf** Corporate Hospitality Days **Location** 1m E off A57 from town centre
Hotel ★★ 83% HL Wind in the Willows Hotel, Derbyshire Level, GLOSSOP ☎ 01457 868001 🖥 01457 853354 12 en suite

Save on Hotels. Book at **theAA.com/hotel**　　　　　　　　　　　**DERBYSHIRE**

ENGLAND

HORSLEY　　　　　　　　　　　Map 8 SK34

Horsley Lodge Golf Club Smalley Mill Rd DE21 5BL
☎ 01332 780838 🖹 01332 781118
e-mail: enquiries@horsleylodge.co.uk.
web: www.horsleylodge.co.uk.

Parkland course set in 180 acres of Derbyshire countryside, has some very challenging holes. Also floodlit driving range. Big undulating greens designed by former World Champion Peter McEvoy providing the golfer with a great test of ability.

18 Holes, 6600yds, Par 71, SSS 71, Course record 65.
Club membership 650.

Visitors Mon-Sun & BHs. Booking required Fri-Sun & BHs.
Societies booking required. **Green Fees** £30 per 18 holes (£35 weekends) **Course Designer** Bill White/Peter McEvoy **Prof** Mark Whithorn **Facilities** ⓣ 🍴 ⅃ ☕ 🏌 🏐 ⌲ ☂ ♢ ✦
🔥 ✦ ✦ **Leisure** fishing **Conf** facs Corporate Hospitality Days
Location 4m NE of Derby, off A38 at Denby, follow tourist signs
Hotel ★★★ 79% HL Horsley Lodge Hotel & Golf Club, Smalley Mill Road, HORSLEY ☎ 01332 780838 🖹 01332 781118　11 en suite

KEDLESTON　　　　　　　　　　Map 8 SK34

Kedleston Park Golf Club DE22 5JD
☎ 01332 840035 🖹 01332 840035
e-mail: secretary@kedlestonparkgolfclub.co.uk
web: www.kedlestonparkgolfclub.co.uk

The course is laid out in flat mature parkland with fine trees and background views of historic Kedleston Hall (National Trust). Many testing holes are included in each nine and there is an excellent modern clubhouse.

18 Holes, 6713yds, Par 72, SSS 72, Course record 65.
Club membership 681.

Visitors Mon-Fri, Sun & BHs. Booking required. Dress code.
Societies booking required. **Green Fees** £40 per round (£45 per round Sun & BHs) **Course Designer** James Braid **Prof** Paul Wesselingh **Facilities** ⓣ 🍴 ⅃ ☕ 🏐 ⌲ ☂ 🏐
🔥 🍴 ✦ **Leisure** sauna **Conf** Corporate Hospitality Days
Location signposted Kedleston Hall from A38
Hotel ★★★★★ FH Park View Farm, WESTON UNDERWOOD
☎ 01335 360352 & 07771 573057 🖹 01335 360352　3 rooms

LONG EATON　　　　　　　　　Map 8 SK43

Trent Lock Golf Centre Lock Ln, Sawley NG10 2FY
☎ 0115 946 4398 🖹 0115 946 1183
e-mail: trentlockgolf@aol.com
web: www.trentlock.co.uk

Main course has two par 5, five par 3 and eleven par 4 holes, plus water features and three holes adjacent to the river. A challenging test of golf. A 22-bay floodlit golf range is available.

Riverside Course: 18 Holes, 5883yds, Par 69, SSS 69.
Academy: 9 Holes, 2911yds, Par 36, SSS 36.
Club membership 500.

Visitors Mon-Sun & BHs. Booking required on Riverside course.
Societies booking required. **Green Fees** 18 hole course £18.50 per round (£23.50 weekends). 9 hole course £6.50 per round (£8 per round weekends) **Course Designer** E McCausland **Prof** M Taylor **Facilities** ⓣ 🍴 ⅃ ☕ 🏐 ⌲ ☂ 🏐 ✦ **Leisure** club fitting centre **Conf** facs Corporate Hospitality Days **Location** 5 mins from M1 junct 24/25
Hotel ★★★ 67% HL Novotel Nottingham East Midlands, Bostock Lane, LONG EATON ☎ 0115 946 5111 🖹 0115 946 5900
108 en suite

MATLOCK　　　　　　　　　　Map 8 SK36

Matlock Golf Club Chesterfield Rd, Matlock Moor DE4 5LZ
☎ 01629 582191 🖹 01629 582135
e-mail: secretary@matlockgolfclub.co.uk
web: www.matlockgolfclub.co.uk

Moorland course with fine views of the beautiful Peak District.

18 Holes, 5804yds, Par 70, SSS 68, Course record 63.
Club membership 700.

Visitors Mon-Sun except BHs. Booking required. Handicap certificate. Dress code. **Societies** booking required. **Green Fees** £35 per day, £35 per round **Course Designer** Tom Williamson **Prof** Christian Goodman **Facilities** ⓣ 🍴 ⅃ ☕ 🏐 ⌲ ☂ 🏐 ✦ **Conf** facs Corporate Hospitality Days **Location** 1.5m NE of Matlock on A632
Hotel ★★ 85% SHL The Red House Country Hotel, Old Road, Darley Dale, MATLOCK ☎ 01629 734854　9 en suite

MORLEY
Map 8 SK34

Morley Hayes Golf Course Main Rd DE7 6DG
☎ 01332 780480 & 782000 (shop) 🖷 01332 781094
e-mail: golf@morleyhayes.com
web: www.morleyhayes.com

Peaceful pay-and-play course set in a splendid valley and incorporating charming water features and woodland. Floodlit driving range. Challenging nine-hole short course (Tower Course).

Manor Course: 18 Holes, 6477yds, Par 72, SSS 72, Course record 63.
Tower Course: 9 Holes, 1614yds, Par 30.

Visitors Mon-Sun & BHs. Booking required. Dress code.
Societies booking required. **Green Fees** not confirmed **Prof** James Whatley **Facilities** ⊕ ⍑ ▥ ⌺ ⬚ ⬚ ⬚ ⬚ ⬚
⬚ **Conf** facs Corporate Hospitality Days **Location** on A608 4m N of Derby
Hotel ★★★★ 77% HL The Morley Hayes Hotel, Main Road, MORLEY ☎ 01332 780480 🖷 01332 781094 32 en suite

NEW MILLS
Map 7 SK08

New Mills Golf Club Shaw Marsh SK22 4QE
☎ 01663 743485 🖷 01663 743485
web: www.newmillsgolfclub.com
Moorland course with panoramic views and first-class greens.

18 Holes, 5604yds, Par 69, SSS 67, Course record 62. Club membership 483.

Visitors Mon-Sun & BHs. Booking required weekends. Dress code.
Societies welcome. **Green Fees** phone ☻ **Course Designer** Williams **Prof** Carl Cross **Facilities** ⊕ ⍑ ▥ ⌺ ⬚ ⬚ ⬚ ⬚ ⬚
⬚ ⬚ **Conf** Corporate Hospitality Days **Location** 0.5m N off B6101
Hotel ★★★ 73% HL Best Western Moorside Grange Hotel & Spa, Mudhurst Lane, Higher Disley, DISLEY ☎ 01663 764151
🖷 01663 762794 98 en suite

RENISHAW
Map 8 SK47

Renishaw Park Golf Club Club House S21 3UZ
☎ 01246 432044 & 435484 🖷 01246 432116
web: www.renishawparkgolf.co.uk
18 Holes, 6107yds, Par 71, SSS 70, Course record 64.
Course Designer Sir George Sitwell **Location** M1 junct 30, 1.5m W
Telephone for further details
Hotel ★★★ 70% HL Sitwell Arms Hotel, Station Road, RENISHAW
☎ 01246 641263 & 435226 🖷 01246 433915 31 en suite

RISLEY
Map 8 SK43

Maywood Golf Course Rushy Ln DE72 3SW
☎ 0115 939 2306 & 949 0043 (pro)
web: www.maywoodgolfclub.com

18 Holes, 6424yds, Par 72, SSS 71, Course record 70.

Course Designer P Moon **Location** M1 junct 25
Telephone for further details
Hotel BUD Days Inn Donington - A50, Welcome Break Services, A50 Westbound, SHARDLOW ☎ 01332 799666 🖷 01332 794166
47 en suite

SHIRLAND
Map 8 SK45

Shirland Golf Club Lower Delves DE55 6AU
☎ 01773 834935
web: www.shirlandgolfclub.co.uk
18 Holes, 6072yds, Par 71, SSS 70, Course record 65.
Location S side of village off A61
Telephone for further details
Hotel ★★★ 79% HL Santo's Higham Farm Hotel, Main Road, HIGHAM ☎ 01773 833812 🖷 01773 520525 28 en suite

STANTON BY DALE
Map 8 SK43

Erewash Valley DE7 4QR
☎ 0115 932 3258 🖷 0115 944 0061
e-mail: secretary@erewashvalley.co.uk
web: www.erewashvalley.co.uk
Challenging parkland course with many specimen trees. Greens meet USGA specification and there is the unique feature of two holes played into and within an old Victorian sandstone quarry.

18 Holes, 6434yds, Par 72, SSS 71. Club membership 750.
Visitors Mon-Sun except BHs. Dress code. **Societies** booking required. **Green Fees** not confirmed ☻ **Course Designer** Hawtree **Prof** Darren Bartlett **Facilities** ⊕ ⍑ ▥ ⌺ ⬚ ⬚ ⬚ ⬚ ⬚ ⬚
Conf facs Corporate Hospitality Days **Location** 1m W. M1 junct 25, 2m
Hotel ★★★ 73% HL Holiday Inn Derby/Nottingham, Bostocks Lane, SANDIACRE ☎ 0871 942 9062 🖷 0115 949 0469 92 en suite

UNSTONE
Map 8 SK37

Birch Hall Golf Course Sheffield Rd S18 4DB
☎ 01246 291979 🖷 01246 412912
18 Holes, 6379yds, Par 73, SSS 71, Course record 72.
Course Designer D Tucker **Location** off A61 between Sheffield & Chesterfield, outskirts of Unstone
Telephone for further details
Hotel ★★★ 67% HL Sandpiper, Sheffield Road, Sheepbridge, CHESTERFIELD ☎ 01246 450550 🖷 01246 452805 46 en suite

DEVON

AXMOUTH
Map 3 SY29

Axe Cliff Golf Club Squires Ln EX12 4AB
☎ 01297 21754 ▤ 01297 24371
e-mail: d.quinn@axecliff.co.uk
web: www.axecliff.co.uk

One of the oldest courses in Devon, established in 1894. An undulating links course with spectacular coastal views over the Jurassic coastline of Lyme Bay. Good natural drainage gives excellent winter play. A challenge to golfers of all levels.

18 Holes, 6000yds, Par 70, SSS 70, Course record 64.
Club membership 300.

Visitors Mon-Sun & BHs. Booking required Mon, Wed, Fri-Sun & BHs. **Societies** booking required. **Green Fees** £20 per round (£25 weekends & BHs). Twilight after 4pm £10. Reduced winter rates. **Course Designer** James Braid **Prof** Duncan Driver **Facilities** ⓣ ⓞ ▤ ⬚ ▥ ⬕ ⛫ ⬚ ⬚ ⚑ ✦ ⚙ ⚵ ✦ **Conf** Corporate Hospitality Days **Location** 0.75m S on B3172
Hotel ★★ 82% HL Swallows Eaves, Swan Hill Road, COLYFORD
☎ 01297 553184 ▤ 01297 553574 8 en suite

BIGBURY-ON-SEA
Map 3 SX64

Bigbury Golf Club TQ7 4BB
☎ 01548 810557
e-mail: enquiries@bigburygolfclub.co.uk
web: www.bigburygolfclub.com

A challenging but forgiving cliff top course with stunning views and great greens.

18 Holes, 6035yds, Par 70, SSS 70, Course record 63.
Club membership 850.

Visitors dress code. **Societies** booking required. **Green Fees** not confirmed **Course Designer** J H Taylor **Prof** Nigel Blenkarne **Facilities** ⓣ ⓞ by prior arrangement ▤ ⬚ ▥ ⬕ ⬚ ⚑ ✦ ⚙ ⚵ ✦ **Conf** Corporate Hospitality Days **Location** 1m S on B3392 between Bigbury village and Bigbury-on-Sea
Hotel ★★★★ 83% HL Thurlestone Hotel, THURLESTONE
☎ 01548 560382 ▤ 01548 561069 66 en suite

BLACKAWTON
Map 3 SX85

Dartmouth Golf & Country Club TQ9 7DE
☎ 01803 712686 ▤ 01803 712628
e-mail: info@dgcc.co.uk
web: www.dgcc.co.uk

Both courses are worth a visit and not just for the beautiful views. The Championship course is one of the most challenging courses in the West Country with 12 water hazards and a daunting par 5 4th hole that visitors will always remember. The spectacular final hole, looking downhill and over a water hazard to the green, can be difficult to judge and has been described as one of the most picturesque finishing holes in the country.

18 Holes, 6663yds, Par 72.
Dartmouth Course: 9 Holes, 2252yds, Par 33.
Club membership 600.

Visitors Mon-Sun & BHs. Booking advised. Dress code. **Societies** booking required. **Green Fees** not confirmed **Course Designer** Jeremy Pern **Prof** Rob Glazier/Stuart Barnett **Facilities** ⓣ

ⓞ ▤ ⬚ ▥ ⬕ ⬚ ⚑ ✦ ⚙ ⚵ ✦ ⛳ **Leisure** heated indoor swimming pool, sauna, gymnasium, massage & beauty treatments **Conf** facs Corporate Hospitality Days **Location** A38 from Buckfastleigh. Follow brown signs for Woodlands Leisure Park. 800yds beyond park turn left into club
Hotel ★★★ 73% HL Stoke Lodge, Stoke Fleming, DARTMOUTH
☎ 01803 770523 ▤ 01803 770851 25 en suite

BUDLEIGH SALTERTON
Map 3 SY08

East Devon Golf Club Links Rd EX9 6DG
☎ 01395 443370 ▤ 01395 445547
e-mail: secretary@edgc.co.uk
web: www.edgc.co.uk

An interesting course with downland turf, much heather and gorse, and superb views over the bay. Laid out on cliffs 250 to 400 feet above sea level, the early holes climb to the cliff edge. The downhill 17th has a heather section in the fairway, leaving a good second to the green. In addition to rare orchids, the course is home to an abundance of wildlife including deer and peregrine falcons.

18 Holes, 6231yds, Par 70, SSS 71, Course record 61.
Club membership 850.

Visitors Mon-Fri after noon. Weekends & BHs after 10.30am. Handicap certificate. Dress code. **Societies** booking required. **Green Fees** £70 per 27/36 holes, £44 per 18 holes **Prof** Trevor Underwood **Facilities** ⓣ ⓞ ▤ ⬚ ▥ ⬕ ⬚ ⚑ ✦ **Conf** Corporate Hospitality Days **Location** W side of town centre
Hotel ★★ 68% HL Bulstone, High Bulstone, BRANSCOMBE
☎ 01297 680446 ▤ 01297 680000 7 en suite

CHITTLEHAMHOLT
Map 3 SS62

Highbullen Hotel Golf & Country Club EX37 9HD
☎ 01769 540561 ▤ 01769 540492
web: www.highbullen.co.uk
18 Holes, 5755yds, Par 68, SSS 67.
Course Designer M Neil/ J Hamilton **Location** 0.5m S of village
Telephone for further details
Hotel ★★★ CHH Northcote Manor, BURRINGTON ☎ 01769 560501
▤ 01769 560770 11 en suite

CHRISTOW
Map 3 SX88

Teign Valley Golf & Hotel EX6 7PA
☎ 01647 253026 ▤ 01647 253026
web: www.teignvalleygolf.co.uk
18 Holes, 5913yds, Par 70, SSS 69.
Course Designer P Nicholson **Location** A38 Teign Valley exit, Exeter/ Plymouth Expressway signs on B3193
Telephone for further details
Hotel ★★★ 74% HL Best Western Lord Haldon Country Hotel, Dunchideock, EXETER ☎ 01392 832483 ▤ 01392 833765
23 en suite

ENGLAND

CHULMLEIGH
Map 3 SS61

Chulmleigh Golf Club Leigh Rd EX18 7BL
☎ 01769 580519 📠 01769 580519
e-mail: chulmleighgolf@aol.com
web: www.chulmleighgolf.co.uk

Situated in a scenic area with views to distant Dartmoor, this undulating meadowland course offers a good test for the most experienced golfer and is enjoyable for newcomers to the game. Short 18-hole summer course with a tricky 1st hole; in winter the course is changed to nine holes and made longer for players to extend their game.

Summer Chulmleigh: 18 Holes, 1419yds, Par 54.
Club membership 100.

Visitors contact club for details. **Societies** booking required. **Green Fees** £9.50 per 18 holes, £8.50 before 10am **Course Designer** John Goodban **Facilities** 🍴 ⬛ 🖥 ⚒ 🚶 🏠 ⛳ ◇ ⛳ **Location** SW side of village just off A377
Hotel ★★★ CHH Northcote Manor, BURRINGTON ☎ 01769 560501 📠 01769 560770 11 en suite

CHURSTON FERRERS
Map 3 SX95

Churston Golf Club Dartmouth Rd TQ5 0LA
☎ 01803 842751 & 842218 📠 01803 845738
web: www.churstongolf.com
18 Holes, 6219yds, Par 70, SSS 70, Course record 64.
Location NW side of village on A379
Telephone for further details
Hotel ★★★ 72% HL Berry Head Hotel, Berry Head Road, BRIXHAM ☎ 01803 853225 📠 01803 882084 32 en suite

CREDITON
Map 3 SS80

Downes Crediton Golf Club Hookway EX17 3PT
☎ 01363 773025 & 774464 📠 01363 775060
e-mail: golf@downescreditongc.co.uk
web: www.downescreditongc.co.uk

Parkland. Tight, flat front nine. Undulating, more open back nine with three ponds. Signature par 3s - 13th and 15th.

18 Holes, 5962yds, Par 70, SSS 70, Course record 65.
Club membership 650.

Visitors Contact club for details. **Societies** booking required. **Green Fees** Apr-Oct £40 per day (£50 weekends). Nov-Mar £28/£32.
Prof Barry Austin **Facilities** 🍴 🍴 ⬛ ⬛ 🖥 ⚒ 🚶 🏠 ⚒ ⛳
Conf Corporate Hospitality Days **Location** 1.5m SE off A377
Hotel ★★★ 71% HL Barton Cross Hotel & Restaurant, Huxham, Stoke Canon, EXETER ☎ 01392 841245 📠 01392 841942 9 en suite

CULLOMPTON
Map 3 ST00

Padbrook Park Golf Club EX15 1RU
☎ 01884 836100 📠 01884 836101
e-mail: events@padbrook.co.uk
web: www.padbrookpark.co.uk

Course extended to 18 holes in 2009 with all tees and greens to USPGA standards. Feature holes are the 3rd (par 4) and the 14th (par 5). 2 Loops of 9 holes returning to club house. Classic design, 4 par 5s, 4 par 3s, 10 par 4s.

Padbrook Park: 18 Holes, 6500yds, Par 72, SSS 72,
Course record 66. Club membership 250.

Visitors Mon-Sun & BHs. **Societies** booking required. **Green Fees** £25 per 18 holes **Course Designer** Bob Sandow/Trevor Spurway **Prof** Stuart Disney **Facilities** 🍴 🍴 ⬛ ⬛ 🖥 ⚒ 🚶 🏠 ⚒ ◇ ⛳ 🚗 ⛳ ⚒ **Leisure** fishing, gymnasium, indoor bowling centre **Conf** facs Corporate Hospitality Days **Location** M5 junct 28, 1m on S edge of town
Hotel ★★★ 77% HL Padbrook Park, CULLOMPTON ☎ 01884 836100 📠 01884 836101 40 en suite

DAWLISH WARREN
Map 3 SX97

Warren Golf Club EX7 0NF
☎ 01626 862255
e-mail: golf@dwgc.co.uk
web: www.dwgc.co.uk

The only links course in South Devon, this typical flat course lies on a spit between the sea and the Exe estuary. Picturesque scenery, a few trees but much gorse. Testing in windy conditions. The 7th hole provides the opportunity to go for the green across a bay on the estuary.

18 Holes, 5935yds, Par 69, SSS 70, Course record 64.
Club membership 600.

Visitors Mon-Sun & BHs. Dress code. **Societies** booking required. **Green Fees** not confirmed **Course Designer** James Braid **Prof** Darren Prowse **Facilities** 🍴 🍴 ⬛ ⬛ 🖥 ⚒ 🚶 🏠 ⚒ ⛳ **Conf** facs Corporate Hospitality Days **Location**
Hotel ★★★ 78% HL Langstone Cliff, Dawlish Warren, DAWLISH ☎ 01626 868000 📠 01626 868006 66 en suite

DOWN ST MARY
Map 3 SS70

Waterbridge Golf Course EX17 5LG
☎ 01363 85111
web: www.waterbridgegc.co.uk

A testing course of nine holes set in a gently sloping valley. The par of 32 will not be easily gained, with one par 5, three par 4s and five par 3s, although the course record holder has par 29. The 3rd hole which is a raised green is surrounded by water and the 4th (439yds) is demanding for beginners.

9 Holes, 3889yds, Par 64, SSS 64. Club membership 120.
Visitors Mon-Sun & BHs. **Societies** welcome. **Green Fees** £14.50 per 18 holes, £9 per 9 holes (£16/£10 weekends & BHs) **Course Designer** D Taylor **Facilities** 🍴 ⬛ ⬛ 🖥 ⚒ 🚶 🏠 ⚒ ⛳ **Conf** Corporate Hospitality Days **Location** A377 from Exeter towards Barnstaple, 1m past Copplestone
Hotel ★★★ CHH Northcote Manor, BURRINGTON ☎ 01769 560501 📠 01769 560770 11 en suite

EXETER
Map 3 SX99

Exeter Golf & Country Club Topsham Rd, Countess Wear EX2 7AE
☎ 01392 874639 📠 01392 874914
e-mail: golf@exetergcc.co.uk
web: www.exetergcc.co.uk

Sheltered parkland with very mature tree-lined fairways. An easy walking course set in the grounds of a fine mansion, which is now the clubhouse. The 15th-18th finishing stretch is one of the toughest in South West England. Small well guarded greens in excellent condition all year round.

continued

Save on Hotels. Book at **theAA.com/hotel**   DEVON

ENGLAND

18 Holes, 6023yds, Par 69, SSS 70. Club membership 800.
Visitors Mon, Wed-Fri, Sun & BHs. Booking required. Handicap certificate. Dress code. **Societies** booking required. **Green Fees** not confirmed **Course Designer** J Braid **Prof** Gary Milne **Facilities** ⓣ ⒶⓁ ⓛⒷ 🏌 ⏃ 🏠 🎯 **Leisure** hard tennis courts, outdoor and indoor heated swimming pool, squash, sauna, gymnasium, short game area **Conf** facs Corporate Hospitality Days **Location** M5 junct 30 towards Topsham, SE side of city centre off A379
Hotel ★★★★ 71% HL Buckerell Lodge Hotel, Topsham Road, EXETER ☎ 0844 855 9112 🖹 01392 424333 54 en suite

Woodbury Park Hotel and Golf Club Woodbury Castle EX5 1JJ
☎ 01395 233500 🖹 01395 233384
web: www.woodburypark.co.uk

Oaks: 18 Holes, 6578yds, Par 72, SSS 72, Course record 66.
Acorn: 9 Holes, 2297yds, Par 32, SSS 32.
Course Designer J Hamilton-Stutt **Location** M5 junct 30, A3052
Telephone for further details
Hotel ★★★★ 74% HL Woodbury Park Hotel and Golf Club, Woodbury Castle, WOODBURY ☎ 01395 233382 🖹 01395 234701 60 en suite

See advert on opposite page

HIGH BICKINGTON — Map 2 SS52

Libbaton Golf Club EX37 9BS
☎ 01769 560269 & 560167 🖹 01769 560342
web: www.libbatongc.com
18 Holes, 6481yds, Par 73, SSS 71, Course record 72.
Course Designer Col Badham **Location** B3217 1m fromf High Bickington, off A377
Telephone for further details
Hotel ★★★ CHH Northcote Manor, BURRINGTON ☎ 01769 560501 🖹 01769 560770 11 en suite

HOLSWORTHY — Map 2 SS30

Holsworthy Golf Club Killatree EX22 6LP
☎ 01409 255390 (pro shop) & 253177 🖹 01409 255393
e-mail: info@holsworthygolfclub.co.uk
web: www.holsworthygolfclub.co.uk
Pleasant parkland with gentle slopes, numerous trees and a few strategic bunkers. Small greens offer a good test for players of all abilities.
18 Holes, 6045yds, SSS 70, Course record 64.
Club membership 400.

Visitors Mon-Sun & BHs. Dress code. **Societies** booking required.
Green Fees £28 per day & per round **Prof** Dan Wood **Facilities** ⓣ ⒶⓁ ⓛⒷ 🏌 ⏃ 🏠 🎯 🍴 🎣 🎯 **Conf** facs Corporate Hospitality Days **Location** 1.5m W on A3072 towards Bude
Hotel ★★★ 79% HL Falcon, Breakwater Road, BUDE ☎ 01288 352005 🖹 01288 356359 29 en suite

HONITON — Map 3 ST10

Honiton Golf Club Middlehills EX14 9TR
☎ 01404 44422 & 42943 🖹 01404 46383
e-mail: secretary@honitongolfclub.fsnet.co.uk
web: www.honitongolfclub.fsnet.co.uk
Founded in 1896, this level parkland course is situated on a plateau 850ft above sea level. Easy walking and good views. The 4th hole is a testing par 3. The 17th and 18th provide a challenging finish. A premium is placed on accuracy especially from the tee.
18 Holes, 5892yds, Par 69, SSS 69, Course record 63.
Club membership 800.
Visitors Mon-Sun & BHs. Booking required. Handicap certificate.
Dress code. **Societies** booking required. **Green Fees** not confirmed
Prof Adrian Cave **Facilities** ⓣ ⒶⓁ ⓛⒷ 🏌 ⏃ 🏠 🎯 🎣 **Leisure** hardstanding for touring caravans with services **Conf** Corporate Hospitality Days **Location** 1.25m SE of Honiton, turn towards Farway at Tower Cross on A35
Hotel ★★ 75% SHL Home Farm Hotel & Restaurant, Wilmington, HONITON ☎ 01404 831278 🖹 01404 831411 12 en suite

ILFRACOMBE — Map 2 SS54

Ilfracombe Golf Club Hele Bay EX34 9RT
☎ 01271 862176 🖹 01271 867731
e-mail: ilfracombegolfclub@btinternet.com
web: www.ilfracombegolfclub.com
A challenging coastal parkland course with views over the Bristol Channel and South Wales from every hole.
18 Holes, 5596yds, Par 69, SSS 67. Club membership 400.
Visitors Mon-Sun & BHs. Booking required. Dress code.
Societies booking required. **Green Fees** £27.50 per round (£33 weekends & BHs) **Course Designer** T K Weir **Prof** Mark Davies
Facilities ⓣ ⒶⓁ ⓛⒷ 🏌 ⏃ 🏠 🎯 🎣 🍴 🎯
Location 1.5m E of Ilfracombe, off A399
Hotel ★★★ 87% HL Watersmeet Hotel, Mortehoe, WOOLACOMBE ☎ 01271 870333 🖹 01271 870890 25 en suite

IPPLEPEN — Map 3 SX86

Dainton Park Golf Club Totnes Rd TQ12 5TN
☎ 01803 815000
e-mail: info@daintonparkgolf.co.uk
web: www.daintonparkgolf.co.uk
A spectacular 18 hole golf course set in 125 acres of rolling South Devon parkland, with magnificent views over Dartmoor National Park and the South Hams.
18 Holes, 6400yds, Par 71, SSS 72, Course record 67.
Club membership 550.
Visitors Mon-Sun & BHs. Booking required. Dress code.
Societies booking required. **Green Fees** not confirmed **Course Designer** Adrian Stiff **Prof** Michael Cayless **Facilities** ⓣ ⒶⓁ ⓛⒷ 🏌 ⏃ 🏠 🎯 🎣 🎯 🎯 **Leisure** gymnasium, fitness gym

continued

Save on Hotels. Book at **theAA.com/hotel**

DEVON

ENGLAND

Conf Corporate Hospitality Days **Location** 2m S of Newton Abbot on A381
Hotel ★★★ 70% MET Best Western Queens Hotel, Queen Street, NEWTON ABBOT ☎ 01626 363133 📠 01626 354106 26 en suite

IVYBRIDGE
Map 2 SX65

Dinnaton Golf Club Blachford Rd PL21 9HU
☎ 01752 892512
e-mail: info@mccaulays.com
web: www.mccaulays.com
Challenging nine-hole moorland course overlooking the South Hams. With five par 4 and four par 3 holes, three lakes and tight fairways; excellent for improving the short game. Floodlit practice area.
9 Holes, 4089yds, Par 64, SSS 63, Course record 60.
Club membership 130.

Visitors Mon-Sun & BHs. Dress code. **Societies** booking required.
Green Fees not confirmed **Course Designer** Cotton & Pink **Prof** Paul Hendriksen **Facilities** ⑪ ⑩ ⅃ ▭ ⅄ ⑨⁺ ♂ **Leisure** hard tennis courts, heated indoor swimming pool, squash, sauna, gymnasium, steam room, jacuzzi, aerobic studio **Conf** facs Corporate Hospitality Days **Location** off A38 at Ivybridge junct towards town centre, 1st rdbt brown signs for club 1m
Hotel ★★ 78% HL Glazebrook House Hotel, SOUTH BRENT
☎ 01364 73322 📠 01364 72350 10 en suite

MORETONHAMPSTEAD
Map 3 SX78

Bovey Castle TQ13 8RE
☎ 01647 445009 📠 01647 440961
web: www.boveycastle.com
18 Holes, 6303yds, Par 70, SSS 70, Course record 63.
Course Designer J Abercrombie **Location** 2m W of Moretonhampstead, off B3212
Telephone for further details
Hotel ★★★ 81% HL Best Western The White Hart Hotel, The Square, MORETONHAMPSTEAD ☎ 01647 441340 📠 01647 441341 28 en suite

MORTEHOE
Map 2 SS44

Mortehoe & Woolacombe Golf Club Easewell EX34 7EH
☎ 01271 870566 & 870745
web: www.woolacombegolf.co.uk
Easewell: 9 Holes, 4729yds, Par 66, SSS 63, Course record 66.
Course Designer D Hoare **Location** 0.25m before Mortehoe on station road
Telephone for further details
Hotel ★★★ 87% HL Watersmeet Hotel, Mortehoe, WOOLACOMBE
☎ 01271 870333 📠 01271 870890 25 en suite

NEWTON ABBOT
Map 3 SX87

Hele Park Golf Centre Ashburton Rd TQ12 6JN
☎ 01626 336060
e-mail: info@heleparkgolf.co.uk
web: www.heleparkgolf.co.uk
Gently undulating parkland course with views stretching to Dartmoor. A fair test of golf with water in play on 3 holes.

9 Holes, 5228yds, Par 68, SSS 66, Course record 63.
Club membership 400.

Visitors Mon-Sun & BHs. Booking required. Dress code.
Societies welcome. **Green Fees** £20 per 18 holes, £11.50 per 9 holes. (£22/£12.50 weekends & BHs) **Course Designer** M Craig **Prof** Duncan Arnold **Facilities** ⑪ ⅃ ▭ ⑨⁺ ⅄ 🏠 ⑨⁺ ♂ 🛒 ♂ ♟ **Conf** Corporate Hospitality Days **Location** W of town off A383 Newton Abbot to Ashburton road.
Hotel ★★★ 73% HL Passage House, Hackney Lane, Kingsteignton, NEWTON ABBOT ☎ 01626 355515 📠 01626 363336 90 en suite

Stover Golf Club Bovey Rd TQ12 6QQ
☎ 01626 352460 (Secretary) 📠 01626 330210
e-mail: info@stovergolfclub.co.uk
web: www.stovergolfclub.co.uk
Mature wooded parkland with water coming into play on eight holes.
18 Holes, 5952yds, Par 69, SSS 70, Course record 65.
Club membership 700.

Visitors Mon-Sun & BHs. Booking required. Handicap certificate. Dress code. **Societies** booking required. **Green Fees** £32.30 per round **Course Designer** James Braid **Prof** James Langmead **Facilities** ⑪ ⑩ ⅃ ▭ ⅄ 🏠 ♂ **Conf** facs Corporate Hospitality Days **Location** 3m N of Newton Abbot on A382. Bovey Tracey exit on A38
Hotel ★★★ 70% MET Best Western Queens Hotel, Queen Street, NEWTON ABBOT ☎ 01626 363133 📠 01626 354106 26 en suite

OKEHAMPTON · Map 2 SX59

Ashbury Golf Hotel Higher Maddaford EX20 4NL
☎ 01837 55453 📄 01837 55468
web: www.ashburygolfhotel.co.uk

A combination of courses occupying a lightly wooded parkland setting in rolling Devon countryside on the foothills of Dartmoor National Park. Extra hazards have been added to the natural ones already present, with over 100 bunkers and 18 lakes. The courses are open throughout the year with either larger main greens or purpose built alternate ones.

Oakwood: 18 Holes, 5400yds, Par 67, SSS 66.
Pines: 18 Holes, 6400yds, Par 72.
Beeches: 18 Holes, 5765yds, Par 69, SSS 66.
Kigbeare: 18 Holes, 6464yds, Par 72.
Ashbury: 18 Holes, 5804yds, Par 69.
Forest: 18 Holes, 6140yds, Par 71. Club membership 170.

Visitors Mon-Sun & BHs. Booking required. Dress code.
Societies booking required. **Green Fees** not confirmed **Course Designer** David Fensom **Facilities** ⑪ ⅃ ▭ ▯⅃ ⅃ 🏠 ⑭ ◇ 🛏 ⅌ ↟ **Leisure** hard tennis courts, fishing, sauna, par 3 course, indoor bowls, snooker. **Conf** facs Corporate Hospitality Days **Location** off A3079 Okehampton-Holsworthy
Hotel ★★ 74% HL Ashbury Hotel, Higher Maddaford, Southcott, OKEHAMPTON ☎ 01837 55453 📄 01837 55468 184 en suite

See advert on page 67

Okehampton Golf Club Tors Rd EX20 1EF
☎ 01837 52113 📄 01837 53541
e-mail: secretary@okehamptongolfclub.co.uk
web: www.okehamptongolfclub.co.uk

A good combination of moorland, woodland and river makes this one of the prettiest, yet testing courses in Devon. Built into an ancient deer park, with mature oak woodlands and the West Okement river running along its northern border.

18 Holes, 5090yds, Par 69, SSS 67, Course record 62.
Club membership 500.

Visitors Mon-Sun & BHs. Booking required. Dress code.
Societies booking required. **Green Fees** £35 per day, £30 per round (£15 Sun) **Course Designer** J H Taylor **Prof** Ashley Moon **Facilities** ⑪ ⑩ ⅃ ▭ ▯⅃ ⅃ 🏠 ⑭ ↟ **Conf** Corporate Hospitality Days **Location** 1m S off A30, signed from town centre
Hotel ★★ 72% HL White Hart Hotel, Fore Street, OKEHAMPTON ☎ 01837 52730 & 54514 📄 01837 53979 19 en suite

PLYMOUTH · Map 2 SX45

Elfordleigh Hotel, Golf & Country Club Colebrook, Plympton PL7 5EB
☎ 01752 336428 (hotel) & 348425 (golf shop)
📄 01752 344581
e-mail: reception@elfordleigh.co.uk
web: www.elfordleigh.co.uk

Undulating, scenic parkland course set deep in the secluded Plym Valley and offering a true challenge to all levels of player. The 11th hole, par 3 is one of the best in the South West area.

18 Holes, 5664yds, Par 69, SSS 67, Course record 66.
Club membership 500.

Visitors may play Mon-Sun & BHs. Dress code. **Societies** booking required. **Green Fees** phone **Course Designer** J H Taylor **Prof** Nick Cook **Facilities** ⑪ ⑩ ⅃ ▭ ▯⅃ ⅃ 🏠 ⑭ ◇ ⅌ 🛏 ↟ **Leisure** hard tennis courts, heated indoor swimming pool, squash, sauna, gymnasium, golf tuition breaks. **Conf** facs Corporate Hospitality Days **Location** 2m NE off A374, follow signs from Plympton town centre
Hotel ★★★ 74% HL Elfordleigh Hotel, Golf & Country Club, Colebrook, Plympton, PLYMOUTH ☎ 01752 336428 📄 01752 344581 34 en suite

Staddon Heights Golf Club Plymstock PL9 9SP
☎ 01752 402475 📄 01752 401998
e-mail: golf@shgc.uk.net
web: www.staddonheightsgolf.co.uk

Cliff top course affording spectacular views across Plymouth Sound, Dartmoor and Bodmin Moor.

18 Holes, 6164yds, Par 70, SSS 71, Course record 66.
Club membership 900.

Visitors Mon-Sun & BHs. Booking required. Handicap certificate. Dress code. **Societies** booking required. **Green Fees** £28 (£32 weekends & BHs) **Course Designer** Hamilton Stutt **Prof** Nick Horrocks **Facilities** ⑪ ⑩ ⅃ ▭ ▯⅃ ⅃ 🏠 ⑭ ⅌ **Leisure** Short game practice area. **Conf** facs Corporate Hospitality Days **Location** from city centre follow signs for Kingsbridge, Turnchapel and Staddon Heights
Hotel ★★★ 77% HL Langdon Court Hotel & Restaurant, Langdon, Wembury, PLYMOUTH ☎ 01752 862358 📄 01752 863428 18 en suite

SAUNTON · Map 2 SS43

Saunton Golf Club EX33 1LG
☎ 01271 812436 📄 01271 814241
web: www.sauntongolf.co.uk

Two traditional championship links courses. The opening 4 holes of the East course total over one mile in length. The par 3 5th and 13th holes are short but testing with undulating features and the 16th is notable. On the West course club selection is paramount as positioning the ball is the key to success. The loop on the back nine, comprising the 12th, 13th and 14th is as testing as it is pleasing to the eye.

East Course: 18 Holes, 6427yds, Par 71, SSS 73.
West Course: 18 Holes, 6138yds, Par 71, SSS 70.
Club membership 1250.

Visitors Mon-Sun & BHs. Booking required. Handicap certificate preferred. Dress code. **Societies** booking required. **Green Fees** £94 per 36 holes, £74 per 18 holes (£105/£79 weekends) **Course Designer** F Pennick/W H Fowler **Prof** Albert MacKenzie **Facilities** ⑪

continued

Save on Hotels. Book at **theAA.com/hotel**

DEVON

ENGLAND

🖦 🖵 🖥 🛋 🖼 ⛳ ✤ 🛒 ✦ ✦ **Conf** Corporate
Hospitality Days **Location** S side of village off B3231
Hotel ★★★★ 79% HL Saunton Sands, SAUNTON
☎ 01271 890212 & 892001 🗎 01271 890145 92 en suite

SIDMOUTH
Map 3 SY18

Sidmouth Golf Club Cotmaton Rd EX10 8SX
☎ 01395 513451 🗎 01395 514661
e-mail: secretary@sidmouthgolfclub.co.uk
web: www.sidmouthgolfclub.co.uk
Situated on the side of Peak Hill, offering beautiful coastal views of
Lyme Bay and Sidmouth. Sheltered, undulating fairways and superb
greens.
18 Holes, 5088yds, Par 66, SSS 67, Course record 59.
Club membership 600.
Visitors Mon-Sun & BHs. Dress code. **Societies** booking required.
Green Fees £40 per round **Course Designer** J H Taylor **Prof** Chris
Haigh **Facilities** 🏧 🍴 🖦 🖵 🖥 🛋 🖼 ✤ ✦
Location W side of town centre
Hotel ★★★★ 83% HL Victoria, The Esplanade, SIDMOUTH
☎ 01395 512651 🗎 01395 579154 65 en suite

SOUTH BRENT
Map 3 SX66

Wrangaton (S Devon) Golf Club Golf Links Rd, Wrangaton
TQ10 9HJ
☎ 01364 73229 🗎 01364 73229
e-mail: wrangatongolf@btconnect.com
web: www.wrangatongolfclub.co.uk
Unique 18-hole course with nine holes on moorland and nine holes on
parkland. The course lies within Dartmoor National Park. Spectacular
views towards sea and rugged terrain. Natural fairways and hazards
include bracken, sheep and ponies.
18 Holes, 6065yds, Par 70, SSS 70, Course record 59.
Club membership 600.
Visitors Mon-Sun & BHs. Dress code. **Societies** booking required.
Green Fees not confirmed **Course Designer** D M A Steel **Prof** Glenn
Richards **Facilities** 🏧 🍴 by prior arrangement 🖦 🖵 🖥 🛋
🖼 🛒 ✦ **Location** 2.25m SW off A38, between South Brent and
Ivybridge
Hotel ★★ 78% HL Glazebrook House Hotel, SOUTH BRENT
☎ 01364 73322 🗎 01364 72350 10 en suite

TAVISTOCK
Map 2 SX47

Hurdwick Golf Club Tavistock Hamlets PL19 0LL
☎ 01822 612746
e-mail: info@hurdwickgolf.com
web: www.hurdwickgolf.com
An executive parkland course with many bunkers and fine views.
Executive golf originated in America and the concept is that a round
should take no longer than 3 hours while offering a solid challenge.
18 Holes, 5300yds, Par 69, SSS 67, Course record 67.
Club membership 100.
Visitors Contact club for details. **Societies** booking required. **Green
Fees** £10 weekdays (£14 weekends & BHs) per 18 holes ⓔ **Course
Designer** Hawtree **Facilities** 🏧 🖦 🖵 🖥 🛋 🖼 ✦
Location 1m N of Tavistock on the Brentor Road
Hotel ★★★ 76% HL Bedford Hotel, 1 Plymouth Road, TAVISTOCK
☎ 01822 613221 🗎 01822 618034 31 en suite

Tavistock Golf Club Down Rd PL19 9AQ
☎ 01822 612344 🗎 01822 612344
e-mail: info@tavistockgolfclub.org.uk
web: www.tavistockgolfclub.org.uk
Set on Whitchurch Down in south-west Dartmoor with easy walking
and magnificent views over rolling countryside into Cornwall.
Downland turf with some heather, and interesting holes on
undulating ground.
18 Holes, 6144yds, Par 71, SSS 70, Course record 60.
Club membership 700.
Visitors Mon-Sun & BHs. Booking required. Handicap certificate.
Dress code **Societies** booking required. **Green Fees** £40 per day/
round **Course Designer** H Fowler **Prof** S Steel **Facilities** 🏧 🍴 🖦
🖵 🖥 🛋 🖼 ✦ **Conf** Corporate Hospitality Days **Location** 1m
SE of town centre, on Whitchurch Down
Hotel ★★★ 76% HL Bedford Hotel, 1 Plymouth Road, TAVISTOCK
☎ 01822 613221 🗎 01822 618034 31 en suite

TEDBURN ST MARY
Map 3 SX89

Fingle Glen Golf Hotel EX6 6AF
☎ 01647 61817 🗎 01647 61135
web: www.fingleglen.com
18 Holes, 5878yds, Par 70, SSS 68, Course record 63.
Course Designer Bill Pile **Location** 5m W of Exeter, off A30
Telephone for further details
Hotel ★★★ 75% HL St Olaves Hotel, Mary Arches Street, EXETER
☎ 01392 217736 🗎 01392 413054 18 en suite

TEIGNMOUTH
Map 3 SX97

Teignmouth Golf Club Haldon Moor TQ14 9NY
☎ 01626 777070 🗎 01626 777304
e-mail: tgc@btconnect.com
web: www.teignmouthgolfclub.co.uk
This fairly flat heathland course is high up with fine panoramic
views of sea, moors and river valley. Good springy turf with some
heather and an interesting layout makes for very enjoyable holiday
golf. Designed by Dr A MacKenzie, the world famous architect who
also designed Augusta GC USA.
18 Holes, 6082yds, Par 69, SSS 70, Course record 64.
Club membership 900.
Visitors Mon, Tue, Thu, Fri & BHs. Booking required. Dress code.
Societies booking required. **Green Fees** £40 per day **Course
Designer** Dr Alister MacKenzie **Prof** Rob Selley **Facilities** 🏧 🍴
🖦 🖵 🖥 🛋 🖼 ✤ 🛒 ✦ **Conf** facs Corporate Hospitality
Days **Location** 2m NW off B3192
Hotel ★★ 71% HL Cockhaven Manor Hotel, Cockhaven Road,
BISHOPSTEIGNTON ☎ 01626 775252 🗎 01626 775572 12 en suite

ENGLAND

THURLESTONE
Map 3 SX64

Thurlestone Golf Club TQ7 3NZ
☎ 01548 560405 📠 01548 562149
e-mail: secretary@thurlestonegolfclub.co.uk
web: www.thurlestonegolfclub.co.uk
Situated on the edge of the cliffs with downland turf and good greens. The course, after an interesting opening hole, rises to higher land with fine sea views, and finishes with an excellent 502yd downhill hole to the clubhouse.
18 Holes, 6340yds, Par 71, SSS 70, Course record 65. Club membership 820.
Visitors Mon-Sun & BHs. Booking required. Handicap certificate. Dress code. **Green Fees** £42 per day/round, £35 after 1 pm **Course Designer** Harry S Colt **Prof** Peter Laugher **Facilities** ⑪ ⑨ by prior arrangement ⓑ ⏤ 🕿 ⚐ ⚑ 🏌 **Leisure** hard and grass tennis courts **Location** S side of village
Hotel ★★★★ 83% HL Thurlestone Hotel, THURLESTONE
☎ 01548 560382 📠 01548 561069 66 en suite

TIVERTON
Map 3 SS91

Tiverton Golf Club Post Hill EX16 4NE
☎ 01884 252187
e-mail: tivertongolfclub@lineone.net
web: www.tivertongolfclub.co.uk
Parkland with many different species of tree, and lush pastures that ensure some of the finest fairways in the south-west. The undulating ground provides plenty of variety and there are a number of interesting holes which visitors will find a real challenge.
18 Holes, 6346yds, Par 71, SSS 71, Course record 65. Club membership 750.
Visitors Mon-Sun & BHs. Booking required. Dress code. **Societies** booking required. **Green Fees** £36 per 18 holes **Course Designer** Braid **Prof** Michael Hawton **Facilities** ⑪ ⑨ ⓑ ⏤ 🕿 ⚐ 🏌 **Conf** Corporate Hospitality Days **Location** 3m E of Tiverton. M5 junct 27, through Sampford Peverell & Halberton
Hotel ★★★ 77% HL Padbrook Park, CULLOMPTON
☎ 01884 836100 📠 01884 836101 40 en suite

TORQUAY
Map 3 SX96

Torquay Golf Club 30 Petitor Rd, St Marychurch TQ1 4QF
☎ 01803 314591 📠 01803 316116
e-mail: info@torquaygolfclub.co.uk
web: www.torquaygolfclub.co.uk
Unusual combination of cliff and parkland golf, with wonderful views over the sea and Dartmoor.
18 Holes, 6159yds, Par 69, SSS 70, Course record 64. Club membership 725.
Visitors Mon-Sun & BHs. Handicap certificate. Dress code. **Societies** booking required. **Green Fees** £40 per day, £30 per round (£45/£35 weekends) **Prof** Martin Ruth **Facilities** ⑪ ⑨ ⓑ ⏤ 🕿 ⚐ ⚑ 🏌 🕿 🏌 **Conf** Corporate Hospitality Days **Location** 1.25m N
Hotel ★★★ 87% HL Orestone Manor Hotel & Restaurant, Rockhouse Lane, Maidencombe, TORQUAY ☎ 01803 328098
📠 01803 328336 12 en suite

TORRINGTON (GREAT)
Map 2 SS41

Great Torrington Golf Club Weare Trees EX38 7EZ
☎ 01805 622229 & 623878 📠 01805 623878
e-mail: torringtongolfclub@btconnect.com
web: www.torringtongolfclub.co.uk
Attractive and challenging nine-hole course. Free draining to allow play all year round. Excellent greens and outstanding views.
9 Holes, 4440yds, Par 64, SSS 62. Club membership 380.
Visitors Mon, Thu & Fri. Tue, Wed, weekends & BHs pm only. Booking required. Dress code. **Societies** booking required. **Green Fees** £23 per day, £18 per round **Facilities** ⑪ ⓑ ⏤ 🕿 ⚑ 🏌 **Location** 1m W of Torrington
Hotel ★★★ 74% HL Royal, Barnstaple Street, BIDEFORD
☎ 01237 472005 📠 01237 478957 32 en suite

WESTWARD HO!
Map 2 SS42

Royal North Devon Golf Club Golf Links Rd EX39 1HD
☎ 01237 473817 📠 01237 423456
e-mail: info@royalnorthdevongolfclub.co.uk
web: www.royalnorthdevongolfclub.co.uk
Oldest links course in England with traditional links features and a museum in the clubhouse.
18 Holes, 6682yds, Par 72, SSS 73, Course record 64. Club membership 1150.
Visitors Mon-Sun & BHs. Dress code. **Societies** booking required. **Green Fees** not confirmed **Course Designer** Old Tom Morris **Prof** Iain Parker **Facilities** ⑪ ⑨ ⓑ ⏤ 🕿 ⚐ 🕿 ⚑ 🏌 **Leisure** Museum of Golf Memorabilia, snooker **Conf** facs Corporate Hospitality Days **Location** N side of village off B3236
Hotel ★★★ 74% SHL Yeoldon Country House, Durrant Lane, Northam, BIDEFORD ☎ 01237 474400 📠 01237 476618
10 en suite

WOOLFARDISWORTHY
Map 2 SS80

Hartland Forest Golf Club EX39 5RA
☎ 01237 431777
e-mail: hfgbookings@googlemail.com
web: www.hartlandforestgolf.co.uk
Exceptionally varied course with water hazards and gentle slopes.
18 Holes, 5902yds, Par 70, SSS 68. Club membership 100.
Visitors Contact club for details. **Societies** booking required. **Green Fees** £15 per 9/18 holes **Course Designer** A Cartwright **Facilities** ⓑ ⏤ 🕿 ⚐ 🕿 ⚑ ◇ 🛏 🏌 **Leisure** fishing **Conf** Corporate Hospitality Days **Location** 4m S of Clovelly Cross, 1.7m E of A39
Hotel ★★★ 72% HL The Hoops Inn & Country Hotel, The Hoops, HORNS CROSS ☎ 01237 451222 📠 01237 451247 13 en suite

Save on Hotels. Book at **theAA.com/hotel**   DEVON – DORSET

ENGLAND

YELVERTON   Map 2 SX56

Yelverton Golf Club Golf Links Rd PL20 6BN
☎ 01822 852824 📄 01822 854869
e-mail: secretary@yelvertongolfclub.co.uk
web: www.yelvertongolfclub.co.uk

An excellent course on Dartmoor with plenty of gorse and heather. Tight lies in the fairways, fast greens and challenging hazards with outstanding views.

18 Holes, 6353yds, Par 71, SSS 71, Course record 63. Club membership 650.

Visitors Mon-Fri, Sun & BHs. Booking required BHs. Handicap certificate. Dress code. **Societies** booking required. **Green Fees** not confirmed **Course Designer** Herbert Fowler **Prof** Tim McSherry **Facilities** ⑪ ⑩ ⓛ ⌑ ⟰ ⌓ ⌂ ⬆ 🥢 **Leisure** indoor golf academy. **Conf** facs Corporate Hospitality Days **Location** 1m S of Yelverton, off A386
Hotel ★★★ 77% HL Moorland Links, YELVERTON
☎ 01822 852245 📄 01822 855004 44 en suite

DORSET

ASHLEY HEATH   Map 4 SU10

Moors Valley Golf Course Horton Rd BH24 2ET
☎ 01425 479776
e-mail: golf@moorsvalleygolf.co.uk
web: www.moors-valley.co.uk/golf

Skilfully designed by Hawtree, this mature heathland and woodland course is scenically set within a wildlife conservation area, exuding peace and tranquillity. Each hole has its own character, the back seven being in particular very special. The course is renowned for its greens.

The Park Course: 18 Holes, 6337yds, Par 72, SSS 70.

Visitors Mon-Sun & BHs. Booking required. Dress code. **Societies** booking required. **Green Fees** £26 per round **Course Designer** Hawtree & Son **Facilities** ⑪ ⑩ by prior arrangement ⓛ ⌑ ⟰ ⌓ ⌂ 🥢 ⬆ 🥢 **Leisure** fishing, 4 hole game improvement course, bike hire, aerial assault course **Conf** facs Corporate Hospitality Days **Location** 1.5m from A331/A338 rdbt, signed
Hotel ★★★ 71% SHL Tyrrells Ford Country House Hotel, Avon, RINGWOOD ☎ 01425 672646 📄 01425 672262 14 en suite

BEAMINSTER   Map 3 ST40

Chedington Court Golf Club South Perrott DT8 3HU
☎ 01935 891413 📄 01935 891217
e-mail: info@chedingtoncourtgolfclub.com
web: www.chedingtongolfclub.co.uk

This beautiful 18-hole parkland course is set on the Dorset-Somerset borders, with mature trees and interesting water hazards. A challenge from the first hole, par 5, blind drive to the elevated tee on the 15th, and the closing holes can be tricky.

18 Holes, 6002yds, Par 70, SSS 72, Course record 70. Club membership 449.

Visitors Mon-Sun & BHs. Booking required. Dress code. **Societies** booking required. **Green Fees** not confirmed **Course Designer** David Hemstock/Donald Steel **Prof** Steve Ritchie **Facilities** ⑪ ⑩ ⓛ ⌑ ⟰ ⌓ ⌂ ⬆ 🥢

Leisure gymnasium, par 3 nine hole course **Conf** facs Corporate Hospitality Days **Location** 5m NE of Beaminster on A356 Dorchester-Crewkerne
Hotel ★★★ 81% HL BridgeHouse, 3 Prout Bridge, BEAMINSTER
☎ 01308 862200 📄 01308 863700 13 en suite

BERE REGIS   Map 3 SY89

The Dorset Golf & Country Club BH20 7NT
☎ 01929 472244 📄 01929 471294
e-mail: admin@dorsetgolfresort.com
web: www.dorsetgolfresort.com

Lakeland/Parkland is the longest course in Dorset. Designed by Martin Hawtree with numerous interconnected water features, carefully planned bunkers and sculptured greens. A player who completes a round within handicap has every reason to celebrate. The Woodland course, although shorter, is equally outstanding with rhododendron and tree-lined fairways. All holes built to USGA specification.

Lakeland/Parkland Course: 18 Holes, 7027yds, Par 72, SSS 72, Course record 69.
Lakeland/Woodland Course: 18 Holes, 5901yards, Par 69, SSS 68.
Parkland/Woodland: 18 Holesyds, Par 69, SSS 68.
Club membership 600.

Visitors Mon-Sun & BHs. Booking required. **Societies** booking required. **Green Fees** £40 (£44 weekend & BHs) **Course Designer** Martin Hawtree **Prof** Scott Porter **Facilities** ⑪ ⑩ ⓛ ⌑ ⟰ ⌓ ⌂ ⬆ ◇ 🥢 🛒 🥢 ⟟ **Leisure** fishing, sauna, gymnasium, longmat bowling centre **Conf** facs Corporate Hospitality Days **Location** 5m from Bere Regis on Wool Road
Hotel ★★ 75% HL Cromwell House, Lulworth Cove, WEST LULWORTH ☎ 01929 400253 & 400332 📄 01929 400566 18 en suite

BLANDFORD FORUM   Map 3 ST80

The Ashley Wood Golf Club Wimborne Rd DT11 9HN
☎ 01258 452253 📄 01258 450590
e-mail: generalmanager@ashleywoodgolfclub.com
web: www.ashleywoodgolfclub.com

The course is one of the oldest in the county. The first record of play on Keyneston Down was in 1896, and part of the course is played over Buzbury Rings, a prehistoric hill fort with magnificent views over the Stour and Tarrant valleys. Constructed on downland, the fairways are undulating and, apart from the 3rd hole with a short sharp hill, all holes are easy walking. Four holes are played within the ancient woodland of Ashley Woods. The natural chalk provides excellent drainage.

18 Holes, 6308yds, Par 70, SSS 70, Course record 66. Club membership 670.

Visitors Mon-Fri after 10am. Weekends & BHs pm. Booking advised. Handicap certificate. Dress code. **Societies** booking required. **Green Fees** £44 per day, £30 per 18 holes (£36 per 18 holes weekends) **Course Designer** P Tallack **Prof** Jon Shimmons **Facilities** ⑪ ⑩ by prior arrangement ⓛ ⌑ ⟰ ⌓ ⌂ ⬆ 🥢 🛒 🥢 **Conf** facs Corporate Hospitality Days **Location** 2m E on B3082
Hotel ★★★ BB The Old Bakery, Church Road, Pimperne, BLANDFORD FORUM ☎ 01258 455173 & 07799 853784 3 rooms

BOURNEMOUTH · Map 4 SZ09

The Club at Meyrick Park · Central Dr, Meyrick Park BH2 6LH

☎ 01202 786000 📠 01202 786020
e-mail: meyrickpark.lodge@theclubcompany.com
web: www.theclubcompany.com
Picturesque municipal parkland course founded in 1890.

18 Holes, 5540yds, Par 69, SSS 68, Course record 63.
Visitors Mon-Sun & BHs. Booking required. **Societies** booking required. **Green Fees** not confirmed **Course Designer** Tom Dunn **Prof** Marcus Urbye **Facilities** ⓣ ⓘ ⓛ ⏛ ⏱ 🏌 ⓐ 🏴 ◇ ◇ 🛒 🏌 **Leisure** sauna, gymnasium, spa and steam room **Conf** Corporate Hospitality Days **Location**
Hotel ★★★ 61% HL Burley Court, Bath Road, BOURNEMOUTH
☎ 01202 552824 & 556704 📠 01202 298514 38 en suite

Knighton Heath Golf Club · Francis Av BH11 8NX

☎ 01202 572633 📠 01202 590774
e-mail: manager@knightonheathgolfclub.co.uk
web: www.knightonheathgolfclub.co.uk
Undulating heathland course on high ground inland from Poole.

Knighton Heath: 18 Holes, 6065yds, Par 70, SSS 70, Course record 64. Club membership 550.
Visitors Mon-Fri except BHs. Handicap certificate. Dress code.
Societies booking required. **Green Fees** £30 per day, £23 per round
Prof David Miles **Facilities** ⓣ ⓘ ⓛ ⏛ ⏱ 🏌 ⓐ ◇ **Conf** Corporate Hospitality Days **Location** N side of Poole, off junct A348/A3049, signed at rdbt
Hotel ★★★★ GA Ashton Lodge, 10 Oakley Hill, WIMBORNE
☎ 01202 883423 📠 01202 883423 5 rooms (2 en suite)

Playgolf Bournemouth · Riverside Av, off Castle Lane East BH7 7ES

☎ 01202 436436 📠 01202 436444
e-mail: enquiries.bournemouth@playgolfworld.com
web: www.playgolfbournemouth.com
A well drained meadowland course beside the River Stour with many mature trees and lakes on five holes. Enjoyable for intermediates and beginners off white tees and a test for any golfer off the back blue tees. Greens are superb and need careful reading.

Bridge Course: 18 Holes, 6200yds, Par 72, SSS 70, Course record 67.
Stour Course: 9 Holes, 964yds, Par 27.
Club membership 400.
Visitors Mon-Sun & BHs. Booking required. Dress code.
Societies booking required. **Green Fees** £20 per 18 holes, £12 per 9 holes. £6 par 3 course **Course Designer** John Jacobs Golf Associates **Prof** Tim Allen **Facilities** ⓣ ⓘ ⓛ ⏛ ⏱ 🏌 ⓐ 🏴 ◇ 🏌 **Leisure** 9 hole par 3 course **Conf** facs Corporate Hospitality Days **Location** off A338 onto A3060 for Christchurch, past Tesco, left onto Riverside Av
Hotel ★★★★ 81% HL Captain's Club Hotel and Spa, Wick Ferry, Wick Lane, CHRISTCHURCH ☎ 01202 475111 📠 01202 490111 29 en suite

Queen's Park Golf Course · Queens Park Drive West BH8 9BY

☎ 01202 451675 📠 01202 304678
e-mail: queenspark@bournemouth.gov.uk
web: www.queensparkgolfcourse.com
Mature parkland with undulating tree-lined fairways. A demanding test of golf, with each hole having a unique character.

18 Holes, 6132yds, Par 71. Club membership 190.
Visitors Mon-Sun & BHs. Booking required. Dress code.
Societies booking required. **Green Fees** £19 per round (£25 weekends & BHs). Reduced winter rates. **Facilities** ⓣ ⓘ ⓛ ⏛ ⏱ ⓐ 🏴 🛒 ◇ **Conf** facs Corporate Hospitality Days **Location** 2m NE of Bournemouth town centre off A338
Hotel ★★★ 78% HL Queens, Meyrick Rd, East Cliff, BOURNEMOUTH ☎ 01202 554415 📠 01202 294810 109 en suite

Solent Meads Golf Centre · Rolls Dr, Hengistbury Head BH6 4NA

☎ 01202 420795
e-mail: solentmeads@yahoo.co.uk
web: www.solentmeads.com
An 18-hole par 3 links course overlooking Hengistbury Head with fine views of Christchurch Harbour and the Isle of Wight. Expect a sea breeze. One of the driest courses in the county with no temporary greens.

Solent Meads: 18 Holes, 2189yds, Par 54, SSS 54, Course record 52.
Visitors Mon-Sun & BHs. **Societies** welcome. **Green Fees** £8 per 18 holes ⓔ **Prof** Warren Butcher **Facilities** ⓣ ⓛ ⏛ ⓐ 🏴 ◇ 🏌 **Leisure** 9 hole fun golf, driving range **Conf** Corporate Hospitality Days **Location** from A35 take B3509 (signed Tuckton/Southbourne). Straight on at 2nd rdbt then 1st left (Broadway). Left after 0.75m into Rolls Drive
Hotel ★★★★ 82% HL Christchurch Harbour Hotel, 95 Mudeford, CHRISTCHURCH ☎ 01202 483434 📠 01202 479004 64 en suite

BRIDPORT · Map 3 SY49

Bridport & West Dorset Golf Club · The Clubhouse, Burton Rd DT6 4PS

☎ 01308 421491 & 421095
e-mail: secretary@bridportgolfclub.org.uk
web: www.bridportgolfclub.org.uk
Seaside links course on the top of the east cliff, with fine views over Lyme Bay and surrounding countryside. The signature 6th hole, known as Port Coombe, is only 133yds but dropping from the top of the cliff to a green almost at sea level far below. Fine sea views along the Chesil Bank to Portland Bill and across Lyme Bay.

18 Holes, 6213yds, Par 70, SSS 68. Club membership 700.
Visitors contact club for details **Societies** booking required.
Green Fees not confirmed **Course Designer** Hawtree **Prof** David Parsons **Facilities** ⓣ ⓘ ⓛ ⏛ ⏱ 🏌 ⓐ ◇ 🛒 ◇ 🏌 **Leisure** pitch & putt (holiday season) **Conf** Corporate Hospitality Days **Location** 1m E of Bridport on B3157
Hotel ★★★ 67% HL Haddon House, West Bay, BRIDPORT ☎ 01308 423626 & 425323 📠 01308 427348 12 en suite

Save on Hotels. Book at **theAA.com/hotel**   **DORSET**

ENGLAND

BROADSTONE   Map 3 SZ09

Broadstone (Dorset) Golf Club Wentworth Dr BH18 8DQ
☎ 01202 692595 📄 01202 642520
e-mail: admin@broadstonegolfclub.com
web: www.broadstonegolfclub.com

Undulating and demanding heathland course with the 2nd, 7th, 13th and 16th being particularly challenging holes.

18 Holes, 6419yds, Par 70, SSS 71, Course record 62. Club membership 620.

Visitors Mon-Wed, Fri & Sun except BHs. Thu pm. Booking required. Handicap certificate. Dress code. **Societies** booking required. **Green Fees** not confirmed **Course Designer** Colt/Dunn **Prof** Mathew Wilson **Facilities** ⓣ ⑩ 🏌 ⌸ 🍴 ⚘ 🏠 🍺 ⚑ ⚫ ⚫ **Conf** Corporate Hospitality Days **Location** N side of village off B3074
Hotel ★★★★ GA Ashton Lodge, 10 Oakley Hill, WIMBORNE ☎ 01202 883423 📄 01202 883423 5 rooms (2 en suite)

CHRISTCHURCH   Map 4 SZ19

Dudmoor Farm Golf Course Dudmoor Farm Rd, Off Fairmile Rd BH23 6AQ
☎ 01202 473826 📄 01202 480207
e-mail: peter@dudmoorfarm.co.uk
web: www.dudmoorfarm.co.uk

A testing par 3 and 4 wooded heathland course.

9 Holes, 1575yds, Par 31.

Visitors contact course for details. **Societies** booking required. **Green Fees** £10 per 18 holes (£11 weekends & BHs) 🈺 **Facilities** ⌸ ⚑ 🏠 ⚫ **Leisure** adjoining riding stables **Location** private road off B3073 Christchurch-Hurn road
Hotel ★★★ 78% HL Best Western Waterford Lodge, 87 Bure Lane, Friars Cliff, CHRISTCHURCH ☎ 01425 282100 & 282101 📄 01425 278396 18 en suite

DORCHESTER   Map 3 SY69

Came Down Golf Club DT2 8NR
☎ 01305 813494 (manager) 📄 01305 815122
e-mail: manager@camedowngolfclub.co.uk
web: www.camedowngolfclub.co.uk

Scene of the West of England championships on several occasions, this fine course lies on a high plateau commanding glorious views over Portland. Three par 5 holes add interest to a round. The turf is of the springy, downland type. Connected with Samuel Ryder and the beginnings of the Ryder Cup.

18 Holes, 6255yds, Par 70, SSS 70, Course record 63. Club membership 650.

Visitors Mon-Sun & BHs. Booking required. Dress code. **Societies** welcome. **Green Fees** £40 per day (£44 weekends) **Course Designer** J H Taylor/H S Colt **Prof** Nick Rodgers **Facilities** ⓣ ⑩ 🏌 ⌸ 🍴 ⚘ 🏠 ⚫ 🍺 ⚫ **Location** 2m off A354 between Dorchester & Weymouth
Hotel ★★★ 73% HL The Wessex Royale, High West Street, DORCHESTER ☎ 01305 262660 📄 01305 251941 27 en suite

FERNDOWN   Map 4 SU00

Dudsbury Golf Club 64 Christchurch Rd BH22 8ST
☎ 01202 593499 📄 01202 594555
e-mail: info@dudsburygolfclub.co.uk
web: www.dudsburygolfclub.co.uk

Set in 160 acres of beautiful Dorset countryside rolling down to the River Stour. Wide variety of interesting and challenging hazards, notably water which comes into play on 14 holes. The well-drained greens are protected by large bunkers and water hazards. A feature hole is the 16th where the green is over two lakes; the more aggressive the drive, the greater the reward.

Championship Course: 18 Holes, 6904yds, Par 71, SSS 73, Course record 64. Club membership 715.

Visitors Mon-Sun & BHs. Dress code. **Societies** booking required. **Green Fees** £50 per 36 holes, £40 per 18 holes (£60/£50 weekend and BHs) **Course Designer** Donald Steel **Prof** Steve Pockneall **Facilities** ⓣ ⑩ 🏌 ⌸ 🍴 ⚘ 🏠 ◇ ⚫ 🍺 ⚫ **Leisure** fishing, sauna, gymnasium, 6 hole par 3 short game academy course **Conf** facs Corporate Hospitality Days **Location** 3m N of Bournemouth on B3073
Hotel ★★★★ 72% HL Norfolk Royale, Richmond Hill, BOURNEMOUTH ☎ 01202 551521 📄 01202 299729 95 en suite

Ferndown Forest Golf Club Forest Links Rd BH22 9PH
☎ 01202 876096 📄 01202 894095
e-mail: golf@ferndownforestgolf.co.uk
web: www.ferndownforestgolf.co.uk

Flat parkland dotted with mature oaks, several interesting water features, and some tight fairways.

18 Holes, 5100yds, Par 68, SSS 67, Course record 61. Club membership 400.

Visitors Mon-Sun & BHs. Booking required weekends & BHs. **Societies** booking required. **Green Fees** not confirmed **Course Designer** Guy Hunt/Richard Graham **Prof** Graham Howell **Facilities** ⓣ ⑩ 🏌 ⌸ 🍴 ⚘ 🏠 🍺 ⚫ 🍺 ⚫ 🏑 **Conf** Corporate Hospitality Days **Location** off A31 N of Ferndown, follow signs to Dorset Police Headquarters
Hotel ★★★ 71% SHL Tyrrells Ford Country House Hotel, Avon, RINGWOOD ☎ 01425 672646 📄 01425 672262 14 en suite

Ferndown Golf Club 119 Golf Links Rd BH22 8BU
☎ 01202 653950 🖹 01202 653960
e-mail: golf@ferndowngolfclub.co.uk
web: www.ferndowngolfclub.co.uk
Fairways are gently undulating among heather, gorse and pine trees, giving the course a most attractive appearance. There are a number of dog-leg holes.
Old Course: 18 Holes, 6556yds, Par 71, SSS 72, Course record 63.
Presidents Course: 18 Holes, 5475yds, Par 70, SSS 66. Club membership 600.
Visitors Mon-Fri. Weekends & BHs Presidents course only. Handicap certificate. Dress code. Societies Booking required. Green Fees not confirmed Course Designer Harold Hilton Prof Neil Plke Facilities ⑪ ⑩ ᴸ ⛻ 🍴 ⅄ 🏠 🛏 ⚷ ⚑ Conf Corporate Hospitality Days Location S side of town centre off A347. Follow brown signs.
Hotel ★★★ 71% SHL Tyrrells Ford Country House Hotel, Avon, RINGWOOD ☎ 01425 672646 🖹 01425 672262 14 en suite

HIGHCLIFFE   Map 4 SZ29

Highcliffe Castle Golf Club 107 Lymington Rd BH23 4LA
☎ 01425 272210 🖹 01425 272953
e-mail: secretary@highcliffecastlegolfclub.co.uk
web: www.highcliffecastlegolfclub.co.uk
Picturesque parkland with easy walking.
18 Holes, 4798yds, Par 64, SSS 63, Course record 58. Club membership 450.
Visitors Mon-Sun & BHs. Handicap certificate. Dress code. Societies booking required. Green Fees £27.50 per round (£30 weekends) ⊛ Facilities ⑪ ⑩ by prior arrangement ᴸ ⛻ 🍴 ⅄ Conf Corporate Hospitality Days Location SW side of town on A337
Hotel ★★★ 78% HL Best Western Waterford Lodge, 87 Bure Lane, Friars Cliff, CHRISTCHURCH ☎ 01425 282100 & 282101 🖹 01425 278396 18 en suite

HURN   Map 4 SZ19

Parley Golf Course Parley Green lane BH23 6BB
☎ 01202 591600 🖹 01202 579043
web: www.parleygolf.co.uk
9 Holes, 4938yds, Par 68, SSS 64, Course record 69.
Course Designer P Goodfellow Location on B3073 opp Bournemouth airport
Telephone for further details
Hotel ★★★ 80% HL Elstead, Knyveton Road, BOURNEMOUTH ☎ 01202 293071 🖹 01202 293827 50 en suite

LYME REGIS   Map 3 SY39

Lyme Regis Golf Club Timber Hill DT7 3HQ
☎ 01297 442963 🖹 01297 444368
e-mail: secretary@lrgc.eclipse.co.uk
web: www.lymeregisgolfclub.co.uk
Undulating cliff-top course with magnificent views of Golden Cap and Lyme Bay.
18 Holes, 6264yds, Par 71, SSS 71. Club membership 575.
Visitors Mon-Sun & BHs. Dress code. Societies booking required. Green Fees not confirmed Course Designer Donald Steel Prof Duncan Driver Facilities ⑪ ⑩ ᴸ ⛻ 🍴 ⅄ 🏠 ⚷ 🛏 ⚷ ⚑ Conf Corporate Hospitality Days Location W end of Charmouth bypass (A35), take A3052 to Lyme Regis. 1.5m from A3052/A35 rdbt
Hotel ★★ 76% HL Royal Lion, Broad Street, LYME REGIS ☎ 01297 445622 🖹 01297 445859 33 en suite

LYTCHETT MATRAVERS   Map 3 SY99

Bulbury Woods Golf Club Bulbury Ln BH16 6HR
☎ 01929 459574 🖹 01929 459000
web: www.bulbury-woods.co.uk
Parkland with a mixture of American and traditional style greens and extensive views over the Purbecks and Poole harbour. A comprehensive programme of tree planting coupled with ancient woodland ensures a round that is picturesque as well as providing interest and challenge.
18 Holes, 6002yds, Par 71, SSS 69. Club membership 450.
Visitors Mon-Sun & BHs. Booking required. Societies booking required. Green Fees not confirmed Facilities ⑪ ⑩ ᴸ ⛻ 🍴 ⅄ 🏠 ⚷ 🛏 ⚷ Conf facs Corporate Hospitality Days Location A35 Poole-Dorchester, 3m from Poole centre
Hotel ★★★★ 78% HL Hotel du Vin Poole, Thames Street, POOLE ☎ 01202 758570 🖹 01202 758571 38 en suite

POOLE   Map 4 SZ09

Parkstone Golf Club Links Rd, Parkstone BH14 9QS
☎ 01202 707138 🖹 01202 706027
e-mail: admin@parkstonegolfclub.co.uk
web: www.parkstonegolfclub.co.uk
Very scenic heathland course with views of Poole Bay. Designed in 1909 by Willie Park Jnr and enlarged in 1932 by James Braid. The result of this highly imaginative reconstruction was an intriguing and varied test of golf set among pines and heather fringed fairways where every hole presents a different challenge.
18 Holes, 6282yds, Par 72, SSS 71, Course record 64. Club membership 840.
Visitors Mon-Sun & BHs. Booking required. Handicap certificate. Dress code. Societies booking required. Green Fees £95 per day, £65 per round (£95/£75 BHs) Course Designer Willie Park Jnr Prof Martyn Thompson Facilities ⑪ ⑩ ᴸ ⛻ 🍴 ⅄ 🏠 ⚷ ⚷ Conf Corporate Hospitality Days Location E side of town centre off A35
Hotel ★★★ 70% HL Arndale Court Hotel, 62/66 Wimborne Road, POOLE ☎ 01202 683746 🖹 01202 668838 39 en suite

SHERBORNE   Map 3 ST61

Sherborne Golf Club Higher Clatcombe DT9 4RN
☎ 01935 814431 🖺 01935 814218
e-mail: office@sherbornegolfclub.co.uk
web: www.sherbornegolfclub.co.uk

Beautiful established parkland course with three memorable par 3 holes. Situated on the Dorset/Somerset border in a peaceful location with stunning views.

18 Holes, 6415yds, Par 72, SSS 71, Course record 62.
Club membership 700.

Visitors Mon-Sun & BHs. Booking required. Dress code.
Societies booking required. **Green Fees** £50 per day, £40 per round **Course Designer** James Braid (part) **Prof** Alistair Tresidder **Facilities** ⊕ ⍥ ⊫ ⊑ ⊌ ⟰ ⌂ ⋔ 🛒 ✂ ✦ Conf Corporate Hospitality Days **Location** 2m N off B3145
Hotel ★★★ 78% HL Eastbury, Long Street, SHERBORNE
☎ 01935 813131 🖺 01935 817296   23 en suite

STURMINSTER MARSHALL   Map 3 ST90

Sturminster Marshall Golf Course Moor Ln BH21 4AH
☎ 01258 858444
e-mail: mike@smgc.eu
web: www.smgc.eu

Privately owned club with pay-and-play facilities set in beautiful Dorset countryside. Played off 18 different tees the course is ideal for golfers of all standards.

9 Holes, 3850yds, Par 64, SSS 59, Course record 64.
Club membership 200.

Visitors dress code. **Societies** booking required. **Green Fees** £15 per 18 holes, £10 per 9 holes (£17/£10 weekends) **Course Designer** John Sharkey/David Holdsworth **Prof** Mike Dodd **Facilities** ⊕ ⍥ ⊫ ⊑ ⊌ ⟰ ⌂ ⋔ 🛒 ✂ ✦ **Leisure** children's golf school, ladies academy **Conf** facs Corporate Hospitality Days **Location** on A350, signed from village
Hotel ★★★ BB Kenways, 90a Wareham Road, CORFE MULLEN
☎ 01202 694655   3 rooms (3 pri facs)

SWANAGE   Map 4 SZ07

Isle of Purbeck Golf Club BH19 3AB
☎ 01929 450361 & 450354 🖺 01929 450501
e-mail: iop@purbeckgolf.co.uk
web: www.purbeckgolf.co.uk

A heathland course sited on the Purbeck Hills with grand views across Poole Harbour. Holes of note include the 5th, 8th, 14th, 15th, and 16th where trees, gorse and heather assert themselves. The very attractive clubhouse is built of local stone.

Purbeck Course: 18 Holes, 6295yds, Par 70, SSS 71,
Course record 63.
Dene Course: 9 Holes, 2007yds, Par 30.
Club membership 500.

Visitors Mon-Sun & BHs. Booking required. Dress code.
Societies booking required. **Green Fees** phone **Course Designer** H Colt **Prof** Philippe Bonfanti **Facilities** ⊕ ⍥ by prior arrangement ⊫ ⊑ ⊌ ⟰ ⌂ ⋔ 🛒 ✂ Conf Corporate Hospitality Days **Location** 2.5m N on B3351
Hotel ★★★ 70% HL Grand, Burlington Road, SWANAGE
☎ 01929 423353 🖺 01929 427068   30 en suite

VERWOOD   Map 4 SU00

Crane Valley Golf Club The Club House BH31 7LE
☎ 01202 814088 🖺 01202 813407
e-mail: general@crane-valley.co.uk
web: www.crane-valley.co.uk

Two secluded parkland courses set amid rolling Dorset countryside and mature woodland. The 6th nestles in the bend of the River Crane and there are four long par 5s ranging from 499 to 545yds.

Valley: 18 Holes, 6412yds, Par 72, SSS 71,
Course record 65.
Woodland: 9 Holes, 2060yds, Par 33, SSS 30.
Club membership 560.

Visitors Mon-Sun & BHs. Booking required. **Societies** booking required. **Green Fees** Valley £25 per round (£30 weekends and BHs). Woodland £12 for 18 holes, £8.50 for 9 holes (£14/£9.50 weekends) **Course Designer** Donald Steel **Prof** Darrel Ranson **Facilities** ⊕ ⍥ ⊫ ⊑ ⊌ ⟰ ⌂ ⋔ 🛒 ✂ ✦ Conf facs Corporate Hospitality Days **Location** 6m W of Ringwood on B3081
Hotel ★★★ 71% SHL Tyrrells Ford Country House Hotel, Avon, RINGWOOD ☎ 01425 672646 🖺 01425 672262   14 en suite

WAREHAM   Map 3 SY98

Wareham Golf Club Sandford Rd BH20 4DH
☎ 01929 554147 🖺 01929 557993
e-mail: secretary@warehamgolfclub.com
web: www.warehamgolfclub.com

At the entrance to the Purbeck Hills with splendid views over Poole Harbour and Wareham Forest. A mixture of undulating parkland and heathland fairways. A challenge for all abilities.

18 Holes, 5432yds`, Par 69, SSS 67. Club membership 400.

Visitors Mon-Fri from 9.30am. Weekends & BHs from 1pm. Dress code. **Societies** booking required. **Green Fees** £30 per day, £20 per round **Facilities** ⊕ ⍥ ⊫ ⊑ ⊌ ⟰ ⌂ ✂ 🛒 ✂ Conf Corporate Hospitality Days **Location** 0.5m N of Wareham on A351
Hotel ★★★ 86% HL Mortons House Hotel, 49 East Street, CORFE CASTLE ☎ 01929 480988 🖺 01929 480820   21 en suite

ENGLAND

WEYMOUTH Map 3 SY67

Weymouth Golf Club Links Rd DT4 0PF
☎ 01305 750831 (Manager) & 01305 773997 (Pro)
🖹 01305 788029
e-mail: weymouthgolfclub@gmail.com
web: www.weymouthgolfclub.co.uk

A seaside parkland course situated in the heart of the town with views over the Dorset coast and countryside. Recent developments have seen the building and completion of 18 new tees and the club celebrated its centenary in 2009. The course was designed and built by James Braid, a multiple Open Winner and respected course designer.

18 Holes, 6044yds, Par 70, SSS 70, Course record 63. Club membership 1300.

Visitors Mon-Sun & BHs. Booking required. Handicap certificate. Dress code. **Societies** booking required. **Green Fees** £45 per day, £34 per round (£40 weekends) **Course Designer** James Braid **Prof** Des Lochrie **Facilities** ⑪ ⑩ ⛳ ♣ ⬛ 🍴 ⚐ ⚑ 🏌 ⬛ ∠ 🏠 ⚐ ✦ 🏌 ⚬ 🏇 ⚬ ✦ **Conf** Corporate Hospitality Days **Location** N side of town centre off B3157 **Hotel** ★★★ 71% HL Hotel Rex, 29 The Esplanade, WEYMOUTH ☎ 01305 760400 🖹 01305 760500 31 en suite

WIMBORNE Map 3 SZ09

Canford Magna Golf Club Knighton Ln BH21 3AS
☎ 01202 592552 🖹 01202 592550
e-mail: admin@canfordmagnagc.co.uk
web: www.canfordmagnagc.co.uk

Lying in 350 acres of Dorset countryside, the Canford Magna Golf Club provides 45 holes of challenging golf for the discerning player. The 18-hole Parkland and Riverside courses are quite different and the new nine-hole Knighton course demands the same level of playing skill. For those wishing to improve their handicap, the Golf Academy offers a covered driving range, pitching greens, a chipping green and bunkers, together with a 6-hole par 3 academy course.

Parkland: 18 Holes, 6560yds, Par 71, SSS 71, Course record 63.
Riverside: 18 Holes, 6173yds, Par 70, SSS 69, Course record 63. Club membership 1000.

Visitors Mon-Sun & BHs. Booking required. Dress code. **Societies** booking required. **Green Fees** Parkland £25.50 per round (£29 weekends). Riverside £21.50/£24.50. Knighton £8/£9 **Course Designer** Howard Swan **Prof** David Cooper **Facilities** ⑪ ⑩ ⛳ ♣ ⬛ 🍴 ∠ 🏠 ⚐ ✦ 🏇 ⚬ ✦ **Leisure** par 3 nine hole Knighton course **Conf** facs Corporate Hospitality Days **Location** on A341 **Hotel** ★★★★ GA Ashton Lodge, 10 Oakley Hill, WIMBORNE ☎ 01202 883423 🖹 01202 883423 5 rooms (2 en suite)

CO DURHAM

BARNARD CASTLE Map 12 NZ01

Barnard Castle Golf Club Harmire Rd DL12 8QN
☎ 01833 638355 🖹 01833 695551
e-mail: secbc@btconnect.com
web: www.barnardcastlegolfclub.org.uk

Flat parkland in open countryside. Plantations and natural water add colour and interest to this classic course.

18 Holes, 6406yds, Par 73, SSS 71, Course record 64. Club membership 650.

Visitors Mon-Sun & BHs. Booking required weekends & BHs. Dress code. **Societies** welcome. **Green Fees** £27 per round (£30 weekends & BHs) ⚐ **Course Designer** A Watson **Prof** Darren Pearce **Facilities** ⑪ ⑩ ⛳ ♣ ⬛ 🍴 ∠ 🏠 ⚐ 🏇 ⚬ ✦ **Conf** Corporate Hospitality Days **Location** 1m N of town centre on B6278 **Hotel** ★★★ 86% HL Rose & Crown, ROMALDKIRK ☎ 01833 650213 🖹 01833 650828 12 en suite

BEAMISH Map 12 NZ25

Beamish Park Golf Club DH9 0RH
☎ 0191 370 1382 🖹 0191 370 2937
e-mail: beamishgolf@btconnect.com
web: www.beamishgolf.co.uk

Attractivel parkland course with varied and interesting holes. Good greens and stunning views. Well drained course providing all year play.

18 Holes, 6183yds, Par 71, SSS 70, Course record 64. Club membership 630.

Visitors Mon-Sun & BHs. Booking required. **Societies** booking required. **Green Fees** £25 per day, £22 per round **Course Designer** H Cotton / W. Woodend **Prof** Chris Cole **Facilities** ⑪ ⑩ ⛳ 🍴 ∠ 🏠 ✦ 🏇 ⚬ ✦ **Conf** Corporate Hospitality Days **Location** 1m NW off A693 towards Stanley. **Hotel** ★★★ 82% HL Beamish Park Hotel, Beamish Burn Road, Marley Hill, BEAMISH ☎ 01207 230666 🖹 01207 281260 42 en suite

Save on Hotels. Book at **theAA.com/hotel**

CO DURHAM

ENGLAND

BILLINGHAM
Map 8 NZ42

Billingham Golf Club Sandy Ln TS22 5NA
☎ 01642 533816 & 557060 (Pro) 📠 01642 533816
web: www.billinghamgolfclub.com
18 Holes, 6346yds, Par 71, SSS 70, Course record 62.
Course Designer F Pennick **Location** 1m W of town centre
Telephone for further details
Hotel ★★★ 79% HL Best Western Parkmore Hotel & Leisure Club,
636 Yarm Road, Eaglescliffe, STOCKTON-ON-TEES ☎ 01642 786815
📠 01642 790485 55 en suite

Wynyard Golf Club Wellington Dr TS22 5QJ
☎ 01740 644399 📠 01740 644599
Wellington: 18 Holes, 7063yds, Par 72, SSS 73,
Course record 63.
Course Designer Hawtree **Location** off A689 between A19 & A1
Telephone for further details
Hotel ★★★★ 73% HL Thistle Hotel Middlesbrough, Fry
Street, MIDDLESBROUGH ☎ 0871 376 9028 & 01642 232000
📠 0871 376 9128 132 en suite

BISHOP AUCKLAND
Map 8 NZ22

Bishop Auckland Golf Club High Plains DL14 8DL
☎ 01388 661618 📠 01388 607005
web: www.bagc.co.uk
18 Holes, 6504yds, Par 72, SSS 71, Course record 63.
Course Designer James Kay **Location** 1m NE on A689
Telephone for further details
Hotel ★★★ 79% HL Best Western Whitworth Hall Hotel,
Whitworth Hall Country Park, SPENNYMOOR ☎ 01388 811772
📠 01388 818669 29 en suite

BURNOPFIELD
Map 12 NZ15

Hobson Golf Club Hobson NE16 6BZ
☎ 01207 270941 📠 01207 271069
18 Holes, 6403yds, Par 69, SSS 68, Course record 65.
Location 0.75m S on A692
Telephone for further details
Hotel ★★★ 82% HL Beamish Park Hotel, Beamish Burn Road,
Marley Hill, BEAMISH ☎ 01207 230666 📠 01207 281260 42 en suite

CHESTER-LE-STREET
Map 12 NZ25

Chester-le-Street Golf Club Lumley Park DH3 4NS
☎ 0191 388 3218 (Secretary)
e-mail: clsgcoffice@tiscali.co.uk
web: www.clsgolfclub.co.uk
Parkland course in castle grounds, good views, easy walking.
18 Holes, 6479yds, Par 71, SSS 71, Course record 67.
Club membership 650.
Visitors Mon-Sun & BHs. Booking required. Dress code.
Societies booking required. **Green Fees** £30 per day, £25 per round
(£35/£30 weekends) 🅫 **Course Designer** J H Taylor **Prof** David
Fletcher **Facilities** 🛈 🍴 🛒 🖥 🍴 🧍 🏠 📺 ☕ 🛍 ⚑
Leisure snooker room **Conf** Corporate Hospitality Days **Location** 0.5m
E off B1284
Hotel ★★★★ 73% HL Ramside Hall, Carrville, DURHAM
☎ 0191 386 5282 📠 0191 386 0399 80 en suite

Roseberry Grange Golf Course Grange Villa DH2 3NF
☎ 0191 370 0670 📠 0191 370 0224
e-mail: grahamstephenson@chester-le-street.gov.uk
web: www.chester-le-street.gov.uk
Parkland course providing a good test of golf for all abilities. Fine
panoramic views of County Durham.
18 Holes, 6152yds, Par 71, SSS 69, Course record 67.
Club membership 500.
Visitors contact course for details. **Societies** booking required. **Green
Fees** £15 per round (£20 weekends) **Course Designer** Durham County
Council **Prof** Chris Jones **Facilities** 🛈 🍴 🛒 🖥 🍴 🧍 🏠
⚑ 🚩 **Location** 5m W of Chester-le-Street. Off A694 into West Pelton,
signed
Hotel ★★★ 81% HL Mercure Newcastle George Washington Hotel,
Stone Cellar Road, High Usworth, WASHINGTON ☎ 0191 402 9988
📠 0191 415 1166 103 en suite

CONSETT
Map 12 NZ15

Consett & District Golf Club Elmfield Rd DH8 5NN
☎ 01207 505060 (secretary) 📠 01207 505060
e-mail: consettgolfclub@btconnect.com
web: www.consettgolfclub.com
Undulating parkland and moorland course with views across the
Derwent Valley to the Cheviot Hills.
18 Holes, 6041yds, Par 71, SSS 69, Course record 64.
Club membership 600.
Visitors Mon-Sun & BHs. Booking required. Handicap certificate.
Dress code. **Societies** booking required. **Green Fees** £22 per day (£26
weekends) **Course Designer** Harry Vardon **Facilities** 🛈 🍴 🛒 🖥
🍴 🧍 🏠 🚢 **Leisure** pool room **Conf** facs Corporate Hospitality
Days **Location** N side of town on A691
Hotel ★★★ 75% HL Best Western Derwent Manor, Allensford,
CONSETT ☎ 01207 592000 📠 01207 502472 48 en suite

CROOK
Map 12 NZ13

Crook Golf Club Low Jobs Hill DL15 9AA
☎ 01388 762429 📠 01388 762137
e-mail: secretary@crookgolfclub.co.uk
web: www.crookgolfclub.co.uk
Meadowland and parkland on an elevated position with natural
hazards and varied holes. Panoramic views over Durham and the
Cleveland Hills.
18 Holes, 6096yds, Par 70, SSS 69, Course record 64.
Club membership 550.
Visitors Mon-Sun & BHs. Booking required weekends. Dress code.
Societies welcome. **Green Fees** phone **Prof** Lee Findley **Facilities** 🛈
🍴 🛒 🖥 🍴 🧍 🏠 ☕ ⚑ 🛍 ⚑ **Conf** facs Corporate
Hospitality Days **Location** 0.5m E off A690
Hotel ★★★ 79% HL Best Western Whitworth Hall Hotel, Whitworth
Hall Country Park, SPENNYMOOR ☎ 01388 811772 📠 01388 818669
29 en suite

DARLINGTON
Map 8 NZ21

Blackwell Grange Golf Club Briar Close DL3 8QX
☎ 01325 464458 📠 01325 464458
web: www.blackwellgrangegolf.com

18 Holes, 5621yds, Par 68, SSS 67, Course record 63.

Course Designer F Pennink **Location** 1.5m SW off A66 into Blackwell, signed
Telephone for further details
Hotel ★★★ 79% HL The Blackwell Grange Hotel, Blackwell Grange, DARLINGTON ☎ 0870 609 6121 & 01325 509955 📠 01325 380899 108 en suite

Darlington Golf Club Haughton Grange DL1 3JD
☎ 01325 355324 📠 01325 366086
web: www.darlington-gc.co.uk

18 Holes, 6181yds, Par 70, SSS 69, Course record 65.

Course Designer Dr Alistair McKenzie **Location** N side of town centre off A1150
Telephone for further details
Hotel ★★★★ 75% HL Headlam Hall, Headlam, Gainford, DARLINGTON ☎ 01325 730238 📠 01325 730790 40 en suite

Hall Garth Hotel, Golf & Country Club Coatham Mundeville DL1 3LU
☎ 01325 379710 📠 01325 310083
web: www.foliohotels.com/hallgarth

9 Holes, 6621yds, Par 72, SSS 72.

Course Designer Brian Moore **Location** 0.5m from A1(M), junct 59 off A167
Telephone for further details
Hotel ★★★ 75% HL Hall Garth Hotel, Golf and Country Club, Coatham Mundeville, DARLINGTON ☎ 0844 855 9110 📠 01325 310083 52 en suite

Headlam Hall Hotel Headlam, Gainford DL2 3HA
☎ 01325 730238 📠 01325 730790
e-mail: admin@headlamhall.co.uk
web: www.headlamhall.co.uk

Course set over the mature rolling pastureland of Headlam Hall. Abundance of natural features including woodland, streams and ponds, making the course both challenging to the player and pleasing to the eye. Each hole has its own character but the 7th Pond Hole is particularly special with a stepped green protruding into a picturesque pond with woodland lining the back.

9 Holes, 2074yards, Par 31. Club membership 200.

Visitors Mon-Fri except BHs. Dress Code. **Societies** booking required. **Green Fees** £18 per 18 holes, £12 per 9 holes. Winter: £15/£10 **Course Designer** Ralph Givens **Prof** Steven Carpenter **Facilities** ⊕ ⦿ 🍴 🗓 🖥 🍽 ᨂ 🏠 ⛳ ✦ ⚡ 🏌 **Leisure** fishing, sauna, gymnasium **Conf** facs Corporate Hospitality Days **Location** 8m W of Darlington, off A67
Hotel ★★★★ 75% HL Headlam Hall, Headlam, Gainford, DARLINGTON ☎ 01325 730238 📠 01325 730790 40 en suite

Rockcliffe Hall see page 79
Rockliffe Park, Hurworth on Tees DL2 2DU
☎ 01325 729999 📠 01325 722792
e-mail: enquiries@rockliffehall.com
web: www.rockliffehall.com

Stressholme Golf Club Snipe Ln DL2 2SA
☎ 01325 461002 📠 01325 461002
web: www.darlington.gov.uk

Picturesque municipal parkland course, long but wide, with 98 bunkers and a par 3 hole played over a river.

18 Holes, 6431yds, Par 71, SSS 71, Course record 68.
Club membership 450.

Visitors Mon-Sun & BHs. Booking required. **Societies** booking required. **Green Fees** not confirmed **Prof** Ralph Givens **Facilities** ⊕ ⦿ 🗓 🖥 🍽 ᨂ 🏠 🍽 ✦ ⛳ **Conf** facs Corporate Hospitality Days **Location** SW of town centre on A67
Hotel ★★★ 79% HL The Blackwell Grange Hotel, Blackwell Grange, DARLINGTON ☎ 0870 609 6121 & 01325 509955 📠 01325 380899 108 en suite

DURHAM
Map 12 NZ24

Brancepeth Castle Golf Club Brancepeth Village DH7 8EA
☎ 0191 378 0075 📠 0191 378 3835
e-mail: enquiries@brancepeth-castle-golf.co.uk
web: www.brancepeth-castle-golf.co.uk

The course was established in 1924 to the design of Harry S. Colt. The castle is a dominant feature on almost half of the holes and the ravines which intersect the course make for a series of challenging shots. The signature hole is the 9th, the Garden Hole, a par 3 of 200 yds which is played to a narrow green below the castle with a cedar tree to negotiate to reach the green. The 5 par 3 holes are the secret to making a good score but they are tricky to play.

18 Holes, 6400yds, Par 70, SSS 70, Course record 64.
Club membership 780.

Visitors Mon-Sun & BHs. Booking recommended. **Societies** booking required. **Green Fees** Winter £18, Summer £36 (£27/£42 weekends) **Course Designer** H S Colt **Facilities** ⊕ ⦿ 🗓 🖥 🍽 ᨂ 🏠 🛺 ⛳ **Conf** Corporate Hospitality Days **Location** 4m from Durham A690 towards Crook, left at x-rds in Brancepeth, left at Castle Gates, 400yds
Hotel ★★★★ 78% HL Durham Marriott Hotel, Royal County, Old Elvet, DURHAM ☎ 0191 386 6821 📠 0191 386 0704 150 en suite

Durham City Golf Club Littleburn, Langley Moor DH7 8HL
☎ 0191 378 0069 📠 0191 378 4265
e-mail: enquiries@durhamcitygolf.co.uk
web: www.durhamcitygolf.co.uk

Parkland course bordered on several holes by the River Browney.

18 Holes, 6349yds, Par 71, SSS 70, Course record 65.
Club membership 750.

Visitors Mon-Sun & BHs. Booking required weekends. Handicap certificate preferred. Dress code. **Societies** booking required. **Green Fees** £30 (£40 weekends & BHs) 🅿 **Course Designer** C Stanton **Prof** Steve Corbally **Facilities** ⊕ ⦿ 🗓 🖥 🍽 ᨂ 🏠 ⛳ ⚡ **Conf** Corporate Hospitality Days **Location** 2m W of Durham City, turn left off A690 into Littleburn Ind Est
Hotel ★★★★ 78% HL Durham Marriott Hotel, Royal County, Old Elvet, DURHAM ☎ 0191 386 6821 📠 0191 386 0704 150 en suite

ROCKCLIFFE HALL

CO DURHAM - DARLINGTON - MAP 8 NZ21

Designed by Marc Westenborg, this 350-acre course is located on the banks of the River Tees, and features lakes, wetland and woodland. There are five different tee positions, so any player, whether a beginner or a professional, can enjoy the course's challenge.

Rockliffe Park, Hurworth on Tees DL2 2DU ☎ 01325 729999 ▤ 01325 722792
e-mail: enquiries@rockliffehall.com **web:** www.rockliffehall.com
Rockliffe Hall: 18 Holes, 7879yds, Par 72, SSS 72, Course record 68.
Visitors Dress code. **Societies** booking required. **Green Fees** £95 per 18 holes high season (£50 low season)
Course Designer Hawtree/Marc Westonborg **Prof** Tom Godwin **Facilities** ⑪ ⑩ ⬛ ▱ ⬛ ⬛ ⬛ ⬛ ◇ ✎ ⬛
✎ ✦ **Leisure** heated indoor swimming pool, fishing, sauna, gymnasium, Nordic walking, fitness suite **Conf** facs
Corporate Hospitality Days **Location** A1(M) junct 57, A66 (M), A66 towards Darlington, A167, through Hurworth-on-Tees. In Croft-on-Tees left into Hurworth Rd, follow signs
Hotel ★★★★★ **86%** HL Rockliffe Hall, Rockliffe Park, Hurworth on Tees, DARLINGTON ☎ 01325 729999
▤ 01325 720464 61 en suite

Mount Oswald Manor & Golf Course South Rd DH1 3TQ
☎ 0191 386 7527 📄 0191 386 0975
e-mail: information@mountoswald.co.uk
web: www.mountoswald.co.uk

Picturesque parkland that gently undulates through the Durham countryside. The easy walking course attracts golfers of all levels and abilities.

18 Holes, 5991yds, Par 71, SSS 70, Course record 67. Club membership 124.

Visitors Mon-Sun & BHs. Booking required weekends & BHs. **Societies** booking required. **Green Fees** £16 per round (£19.50 weekends & BHs). Reduced winter rates **Prof** Chris Calder **Facilities** ⓣ 🍽 🍺 ☐ 🏌 🛆 🏠 ⛳ ✦ **Conf** facs Corporate Hospitality Days **Location** on A177, 1m SW of city centre **Hotel** ★★★★ 73% HL Ramside Hall, Carrville, DURHAM ☎ 0191 386 5282 📄 0191 386 0399 80 en suite

Ramside Hall Golf Club Carrville DH1 1TD
☎ 0191 386 9514 📄 0191 386 9519
e-mail: robin.smith@ramsidehallhotel.co.uk
web: www.ramsidehallhotel.co.uk

Parkland course consisting of three loops of nine holes, Princes, Bishops, and Cathedral - with 14 lakes and panoramic views surrounding an impressive hotel. Excellent golf academy and driving range on site.

Princes: 9 Holes, 3319yds, Par 36, SSS 36.
Bishops: 9 Holes, 3532yds, Par 36, SSS 36.
Cathedral: 9 Holes, 2898yds, Par 34, SSS 34.
Club membership 450.

Visitors Mon-Sun & BHs. Booking required. Dress code. **Societies** booking required. **Green Fees** £35 per 18 holes (£40 weekends) **Course Designer** Jonathan Gaunt **Prof** Kevin Jackson **Facilities** ⓣ 🍽 🍺 ☐ 🏌 🛆 🏠 ✦ **Leisure** sauna, steam room **Conf** facs Corporate Hospitality Days **Location** 500yds from junct 62 A1/M towards Sunderland **Hotel** ★★★★ 73% HL Ramside Hall, Carrville, DURHAM ☎ 0191 386 5282 📄 0191 386 0399 80 en suite

EAGLESCLIFFE   Map 8 NZ41

Eaglescliffe and District Golf Club Yarm Rd TS16 0DQ
☎ 01642 780238 (office) 📄 01642 781128
web: www.eaglescliffegolfclub.co.uk
18 Holes, 6275yds, Par 72, SSS 70, Course record 64.
Course Designer J Braid/H Cotton **Location** on E side of A135 **Telephone for further details**
Hotel ★★★ 79% HL Best Western Parkmore Hotel & Leisure Club, 636 Yarm Road, Eaglescliffe, STOCKTON-ON-TEES ☎ 01642 786815 📄 01642 790485 55 en suite

HARTLEPOOL   Map 8 NZ53

Castle Eden Golf Club Castle Eden TS27 4SS
☎ 01429 836510 📄 01429 836510
web: www.castleedengolfclub.co.uk

Beautiful parkland course alongside a nature reserve. Hard walking but trees provide wind shelter.

18 Holes, 6272yds, Par 70, SSS 70, Course record 63. Club membership 750.

Visitors Contact club for details. **Societies** booking required. **Green**

Fees £30 (£38 weekends & BHs) ⊕ **Course Designer** Henry Cotton **Prof** Peter Jackson **Facilities** ⓣ 🍽 🍺 ☐ 🏌 🛆 🏠 ✦ **Leisure** snooker **Location** 2m S of Peterlee on B1281 off A19 **Hotel** ★★★ 77% HL Best Western Grand, Swainson Street, HARTLEPOOL ☎ 01429 266345 📄 01429 265217 48 en suite

Hartlepool Golf Club Hart Warren TS24 9QF
☎ 01429 274398 📄 01429 274129
e-mail: hartlepoolgolf@btconnect.com
web: www.hartlepoolgolfclub.co.uk

A seaside course, half links, overlooking the North Sea. A good test and equally enjoyable to all handicap players. The 10th, par 4, demands a precise second shot over a ridge and between sand dunes to a green down near the edge of the beach, alongside which several holes are played.

18 Holes, 5991yds, Par 70, SSS 69, Course record 63. Club membership 650.

Visitors Mon-Sat & BHs. Booking required. Handicap certificate. Dress code. **Societies** booking required. **Green Fees** £30 per day (£40 Sat) **Course Designer** J Braid (partly) **Prof** Graham Laidlaw **Facilities** ⓣ 🍽 🍺 ☐ 🏌 🛆 🏠 ✦ **Conf** Corporate Hospitality Days **Location** N of Hartlepool, off A1086 **Hotel** ★★★ 77% HL Best Western Grand, Swainson Street, HARTLEPOOL ☎ 01429 266345 📄 01429 265217 48 en suite

MIDDLETON ST GEORGE   Map 8 NZ31

Dinsdale Spa Golf Club Neasham Rd DL2 1DW
☎ 01325 332297
e-mail: dinsdalespagolf@btconnect.com
web: www.dinsdalespagolfclub.co.uk

With views of the Cleveland Hills, this gentle undulating parkland course provides a challenge to all categories of golfers. Water hazards in front of the 15th tee and green; the prevailing west wind affects the later holes.

18 Holes, 6107yds, Par 72, SSS 69, Course record 65. Club membership 700.

Visitors Mon, Wed-Fri & BHs. Booking required. Dress code. **Societies** booking required. **Green Fees** £35 per day ⊕ **Prof** Martyn Stubbings **Facilities** ⓣ 🍽 🍺 ☐ 🏌 🛆 🏠 ✦ **Conf** Corporate Hospitality Days **Location** 1.5m SW of Darlington Railway Station **Hotel** ★★★★★ 86% HL Rockliffe Hall, Rockliffe Park, Hurworth on Tees, DARLINGTON ☎ 01325 729999 📄 01325 720464 61 en suite

NEWTON AYCLIFFE   Map 8 NZ22

Oakleaf Golf Complex School Aycliffe Ln DL5 6QZ
☎ 01325 310820 📄 01325 318918
18 Holes, 5568yds, Par 70, SSS 67, Course record 67.
Location 6m N of Darlington, off A6072
Telephone for further details
Hotel ★★★★ 77% CHH Barceló Redworth Hall Hotel, REDWORTH ☎ 01388 770600 📄 01388 770654 143 en suite

Save on Hotels. Book at **theAA.com/hotel**

CO DURHAM

ENGLAND

SEAHAM
Map 12 NZ44

Seaham Golf Club Dawdon SR7 7RD
☎ 0191 513 0837 & 581 1268
e-mail: seahamgolfclub@btconnect.com
web: www.seahamgolfclub.co.uk
Heathland links course with 5 par 3 and 3 par 5 holes.
Seaham: 18 Holes, 6009yds, Par 69, SSS 68,
Course record 62. Club membership 600.
Visitors Mon-Fri & BHs. Dress code. **Societies** booking required.
Green Fees not confirmed **Prof** Andrew Blunt **Facilities** ⊕ ⊙
⌸ ⊡ ⊓ ⊼ ⊟ ⊓ ⌷ ⌁ **Conf** Corporate Hospitality Days
Location 3m E of A19, exit for Seaham and Murton
Hotel ★★★★ 73% HL Sunderland Marriott, Queen's Parade,
Seaburn, SUNDERLAND ☎ 0191 529 2041 ⊟ 0191 529 4227
82 en suite

SEATON CAREW
Map 8 NZ52

Seaton Carew Golf Club Tees Rd TS25 1DE
☎ 01429 266249 ⊟ 01429 267952
web: www.seatoncarewgolfclub.co.uk
The Old Course: 18 Holes, 6633yds, Par 72, SSS 72.
Brabazon Course: 18 Holes, 6857yds, Par 73, SSS 72.
Course Designer McKenzie **Location** SE side of village off A178
Telephone for further details
Hotel ★★★ 77% HL Best Western Grand, Swainson Street,
HARTLEPOOL ☎ 01429 266345 ⊟ 01429 265217 48 en suite

SEDGEFIELD
Map 8 NZ32

Knotty Hill Golf Centre TS21 2BB
☎ 01740 620320 ⊟ 01740 622227
e-mail: knottyhill@btconnect.com
web: www.knottyhill.com
The 18-hole Princes and Bishops Courses are situated in mature
parkland with strategically placed water hazards and bunkers, along
with tree-lined fairways, making accuracy a premium and the courses
rewarding for all standards of play. The recently completed Academy
Course is ideal for aspiring golfers and those seeking more leisurely
play.
Princes Course: 18 Holes, 6433yds, Par 72, SSS 71.
Bishops Course: 18 Holes, 6053yds, Par 70.
Academy Course: 9 Holes, 2494yds, Par 32.
Visitors Tue-Sun & BHs. **Societies** booking required. **Green Fees** £14
per round (£16 weekends) **Course Designer** C Stanton **Facilities** ⊕
⊙ ⌸ ⊡ ⊼ ⊟ ⊓ ⌁ ⌿ **Leisure** tuition range.
Conf facs Corporate Hospitality Days **Location** A1(M) junct 60, 1m N
of Sedgefield on A177
Hotel ★★★★ 79% HL Best Western Hardwick Hall, SEDGEFIELD
☎ 01740 620253 ⊟ 01740 622771 51 en suite

STANLEY
Map 12 NZ15

South Moor Golf Club The Middles, Craghead DH9 6AG
☎ 01207 232848 ⊟ 01207 284616
e-mail: secretary@southmoorgc.co.uk
web: www.southmoorgc.co.uk
Moorland course with natural hazards, designed by Dr A MacKenzie
in 1926 and still one of the most challenging of its type in north
east England. Out of bounds features on 11 holes from the tee, and
the testing par 5 12th hole is uphill and usually against a strong
headwind.
18 Holes, 6293yds, Par 72, SSS 71, Course record 66.
Club membership 500.
Visitors Mon-Sun except BHs. Booking required weekends. Dress
code. **Societies** booking required. **Green Fees** £23 per day (£30
weekends & BHs) **Course Designer** Dr Alister MacKenzie **Prof** Shaun
Cowell **Facilities** ⊕ ⊙ ⌸ ⊡ ⊓ ⊼ ⊟ ⊓ ⌁ ⌷ ⌁
Leisure snooker table **Conf** Corporate Hospitality Days **Location** 1.5m
SE on B6313
Hotel ★★★ 82% HL Beamish Park Hotel, Beamish Burn Road,
Marley Hill, BEAMISH ☎ 01207 230666 ⊟ 01207 281260 42 en suite

STOCKTON-ON-TEES
Map 8 NZ41

Norton Golf Course Blakeston Ln TS20 3LQ
☎ 01642 676385 ⊟ 01642 607854
18 Holes, 5855yds, Par 70.
Course Designer T Harper **Location** in Norton 2m N off A19
Telephone for further details
Hotel ★★★ 79% HL Best Western Parkmore Hotel & Leisure Club,
636 Yarm Road, Eaglescliffe, STOCKTON-ON-TEES ☎ 01642 786815
⊟ 01642 790485 55 en suite

Teesside Golf Club Acklam Rd, Thornaby TS17 7JS
☎ 01642 616516 & 673822 (pro) ⊟ 01642 676252
e-mail: teessidegolfclub@btconnect.com
web: www.teessidegolfclub.co.uk

Flat, easy walking parkland.
18 Holes, 6535yds, Par 72, SSS 71, Course record 64.
Club membership 700.
Visitors Mon-Fri & BHs. Booking required. Dress code.
Societies booking required. **Green Fees** £30 per day (£34 per round
BHs) ⊛ **Prof** Stewart Pilgrim **Facilities** ⊕ ⊙ ⌸ ⊡ ⊓ ⊼
⊟ ⌁ ⌷ ⌁ **Conf** facs Corporate Hospitality Days **Location** 1.5m
SE on A1130, off A19 at Mandale interchange
Hotel ★★★ 79% HL Best Western Parkmore Hotel & Leisure Club,
636 Yarm Road, Eaglescliffe, STOCKTON-ON-TEES ☎ 01642 786815
⊟ 01642 790485 55 en suite

ESSEX

ABRIDGE
Map 5 TQ49

Abridge Golf and Country Club Epping Ln, Stapleford Tawney RM4 1ST
☎ 01708 688396
e-mail: info@abridgegolf.com
web: www.abridgegolf.com
Easy walking parkland. The quick drying course is a challenge for all levels. This has been the venue of several professional tournaments. Abridge is a golf and country club and has all the attendant facilities. Open Championship regional qualifying course 2009-2013.

18 Holes, 6439yds, Par 72, SSS 72, Course record 67. Club membership 600.

Visitors contact club for details. **Societies** booking required. **Green Fees** not confirmed **Course Designer** Henry Cotton **Prof** Steve Tyson **Facilities** ⊕ ⓘ ┗ ❑ ❍ ⚑ 亼 ┌ ◢ ╡ ◢ ╽ **Leisure** 2 snooker tables **Conf** facs Corporate Hospitality Days **Location** 1.75m NE of Abridge

Hotel 63% ⓤ The Bell Hotel Epping, High Road, Bell Common, EPPING ☎ 01992 573138 ◲ 01992 560402 79 en suite

BENFLEET
Map 5 TQ78

Boyce Hill Golf Club Vicarage Hill, South Benfleet SS7 1PD
☎ 01268 793625 & 752565 ◲ 01268 750497
e-mail: secretary@boycehillgolfclub.co.uk
web: www.boycehillgolfclub.co.uk
Hilly parkland with good views.

18 Holes, 6003yds, Par 68, SSS 69, Course record 63. Club membership 700.

Visitors Mon-Fri except BHs. Booking required. Dress code **Societies** ⊛ booking required. **Green Fees** £45 per 27/36 holes, £35 per 18 holes ⊛ **Course Designer** James Braid **Prof** Graham Burroughs **Facilities** ⊕ ⓘ ┗ ❑ ❍ 亼 ┌ ◢ ╽ ◢ **Conf** Corporate Hospitality Days **Location** 0.75m NE of Benfleet Station **Hotel** ★★★ 77% HL Chichester, Old London Road, Wickford, BASILDON ☎ 01268 560555 ◲ 01268 560580 35 en suite

BILLERICAY
Map 5 TQ69

The Burstead Golf Club Tye Common Rd, Little Burstead CM12 9SS
☎ 01277 631171 ◲ 01277 632766
e-mail: info@thebursteadgolfclub.com
web: www.thebursteadgolfclub.com
The Burstead is an attractive parkland course set amidst some of the loveliest countryside in south Essex. It is an excellent test of golf to players of all standards with the greens showing maturity beyond their years. Good management of shots is necessary throughout play and the narrow fairways, ditches and water hazards prove a good test of golf.

18 Holes, 6275yds, Par 71, SSS 70, Course record 69. Club membership 850.

Visitors Mon-Fri. Weekends & BHs after 11am. Dress code. **Societies** booking required. **Green Fees** phone **Course Designer** Patrick Tallack **Prof** Keith Bridges/Dean Bullock

Facilities ⊕ ⓘ ┗ ❑ ❍ 亼 ┌ ◢ ╽ ◢ **Conf** facs
Corporate Hospitality Days **Location** M25 onto A127, E to exit for A176
Hotel ★★★ 77% HL Chichester, Old London Road, Wickford, BASILDON ☎ 01268 560555 ◲ 01268 560580 35 en suite

Stock Brook Golf & Country Club Queens Park Av, Stock CM12 0SP
☎ 01277 653616 & 650400 ◲ 01277 633063
e-mail: events@stockbrook.com
web: www.stockbrook.com
Set in 250 acres of picturesque countryside the 27 holes comprise three undulating nines, offering the challenge of water on a large number of holes. Any combination can be played, but the Stock and Brook courses make the 18-hole championship course. There are extensive clubhouse facilities.

Stock: 9 Holes, 3387yds, Par 36.
Brook: 9 Holes, 3205yds, Par 36.
Manor Course: 9 Holes, 2919yds, Par 35.

Visitors Mon-Fri.Weekends & BHs pm only. Booking required. Dress code. **Societies** booking required. **Green Fees** £25 (£35 weekends) **Course Designer** Martin Gillet **Prof** Craig Laurence **Facilities** ⊕ ⓘ ┗ ❑ ❍ 亼 ┌ ◢╻ ◢ ╽ ◢ ╽ **Leisure** hard tennis courts, heated indoor swimming pool, sauna, gymnasium, bowls **Conf** facs Corporate Hospitality Days **Location** off B1007 **Hotel** ★★★★ 75% HL Marygreen Manor, London Road, BRENTWOOD ☎ 01277 225252 ◲ 01277 262809 44 en suite

BRAINTREE
Map 5 TL72

Braintree Golf Club Kings Ln, Stisted CM77 8DD
☎ 01376 346079 ◲ 01376 348677
e-mail: manager@braintreegolfclub.co.uk
web: www.braintreegolfclub.co.uk
Parkland with many rare mature trees. Good par 3s with the 14th - Devils Lair - regarded as one of the best in the county.

18 Holes, 6228yds, Par 70, SSS 69, Course record 64. Club membership 750.

Visitors Mon-Sun & BHs. Dress code. **Societies** booking required. **Green Fees** £50 per day, £35 per round (visitors after 2pm £50 weekends) **Course Designer** Hawtree **Prof** Duncan Woolger **Facilities** ⊕ ⓘ ┗ ❑ ❍ 亼 ┌ ◢ ╽ ◢ ╽ ◢ **Conf** Corporate Hospitality Days **Location** 1m E, off A120 **Hotel** ★★★ 73% HL White Hart Hotel, Market End, COGGESHALL ☎ 01376 561654 ◲ 01376 561789 18 en suite

Towerlands Park Golf Club Panfield Rd CM7 5BJ
☎ 01376 326802 ◲ 01376 552487
e-mail: info@towerlandspark.com
web: www.towerlandspark.com
Undulating, grassland course, nine holes with 18 tees.

9 Holes, 5559yds, Par 68, SSS 67, Course record 66. Club membership 135.

Visitors Mon-Sun & BHs. Booking required Wed & Sun. Dress code. **Societies** booking required. **Green Fees** phone ⊛ **Course Designer** G Shiels **Facilities** ❑ ❍ 亼 **Conf** facs **Location** on B1053 **Hotel** ★★★ 73% HL White Hart Hotel, Market End, COGGESHALL ☎ 01376 561654 ◲ 01376 561789 18 en suite

Save on Hotels. Book at **theAA.com/hotel**

ESSEX

BRENTWOOD
Map 5 TQ59

Bentley Golf Club Ongar Rd CM15 9SS
☎ 01277 373179 📄 01277 375097
e-mail: info@bentleygolfclub.com
web: www.bentleygolfclub.com
Mature parkland course with water hazards.
18 Holes, 6703yds, Par 72, SSS 72. Club membership 580.
Visitors contact club for details **Societies** welcome. **Green Fees** not
confirmed **Course Designer** Howard Swann **Prof** Nick Garrett
Facilities ⑪ ⑩ ⓛ ▯ ▯ ♨ ⚐ ⚑ **Conf** Corporate
Hospitality Days **Location** 3m NW on A128
Hotel ★★★★ 75% HL Marygreen Manor, London Road,
BRENTWOOD ☎ 01277 225252 📄 01277 262809 44 en suite

Hartswood Golf Club King George's Playing Fields, Ingrave
Rd CM14 5AE
☎ 01277 214830 📄 01277 214830
Municipal mature parkland course with easy walking.
18 Holes, 6200yds, Par 70, Course record 60.
Club membership 250.
Visitors Mon-Sun & BHs. Booking required. Dress code.
Societies booking required. **Green Fees** not confirmed ⓔ **Course
Designer** H Cotton **Prof** Stephen Cole **Facilities** ♨ 📷 ⚐
Location 0.75m SE of Brentwood town centre on A128 from A127
Hotel ★★★★ 75% HL Marygreen Manor, London Road,
BRENTWOOD ☎ 01277 225252 📄 01277 262809 44 en suite

Warley Park Golf Club Magpie Ln, Little Warley CM13 3DX
☎ 01277 224891 📄 01277 200679
e-mail: enquiries@warleyparkgc.co.uk
web: www.warleyparkgc.co.uk
Parkland with panoramic views of Essex and the Kent countryside.
Numerous water hazards.
1st & 2nd: 18 Holes, 5985yds, Par 69, SSS 67,
Course record 66.
1st & 3rd: 18 Holes, 5925yds, Par 71, SSS 69,
Course record 65.
2nd & 3rd: 18 Holes, 5917yds, Par 70, SSS 69,
Course record 65. Club membership 800.
Visitors dress code **Societies** welcome. **Green Fees** not confirmed
Course Designer Reg Plumbridge **Prof** Kevin Smith **Facilities** ⑪
⑩ by prior arrangement ⓛ ▯ ▯ ♨ ⚐ ⚑ ☕ ⚑
Conf facs Corporate Hospitality Days **Location** M25 junct 29, A127 E
onto B186, 0.5m N
Hotel ★★★★ 74% HL De Rougemont Manor, Great Warley
Street, BRENTWOOD ☎ 01277 226418 & 220483 📄 01277 239020
79 en suite

Weald Park Hotel, Golf & Country Club Coxtie Green Rd
CM14 5RJ
☎ 01277 375101 📄 01277 374888
web: www.bw-wealdparkhotel.co.uk
18 Holes, 6285yds, Par 71, SSS 70, Course record 65.
Course Designer Reg Plumbridge **Location** 3m from M25
Telephone for further details
Hotel ★★★ 80% HL Holiday Inn Brentwood, Brook Street,
BRENTWOOD ☎ 0871 942 9012 📄 01277 264264 149 en suite

BULPHAN
Map 5 TQ68

Langdon Hills Golf Club Lower Dunton Rd RM14 3TY
☎ 01268 548444 📄 01268 490084
web: www.golflangdon.co.uk
Langdon & Bulphan Course: 18 Holes, 6760yds, Par 72,
SSS 72, Course record 67.
Bulphan & Horndon Course: 18 Holes, 6537yds, Par 73,
SSS 72.
Horndon & Langdon Course: 18 Holes, 6279yds, Par 71,
SSS 71.
Course Designer Howard Swan **Location** off A13 onto B1007
Telephone for further details
Hotel ★★★★ 75% HL Marygreen Manor, London Road,
BRENTWOOD ☎ 01277 225252 📄 01277 262809 44 en suite

BURNHAM-ON-CROUCH
Map 5 TQ99

Burnham-on-Crouch Golf Club Ferry Rd, Creeksea
CM0 8PQ
☎ 01621 782282 📄 01621 784489
e-mail: burnhamgolf@hotmail.com
web: www.burnhamgolfclub.co.uk
Undulating meadowland riverside course, easy walking and stunning
views. Challenging for all standards of player.
18 Holes, 6056yds, Par 70, SSS 69, Course record 66.
Club membership 520.
Visitors booking required. Dress code. **Societies** booking required.
Green Fees £40 per 18 holes (£44 weekends) **Course Designer** Swan
Prof Steve Parkin/Ken Light **Facilities** ⑪ ⑩ ⓛ ▯ ▯ ♨
📷 ⚐ ☕ ⚑ **Conf** Corporate Hospitality Days **Location** 1.25m W
off B1010

CANEWDON
Map 5 TQ99

Ballards Gore Golf Club Gore Rd SS4 2DA
☎ 01702 258917 📄 01702 258571
web: www.ballardsgore.com
18 Holes, 6874yds, Par 73, SSS 73, Course record 69.
Course Designer Arthur Elvin **Location** 2m NE of Rochford
Telephone for further details
Hotel ★★★★ GA Ilfracombe House, 9-13 Wilson Road,
SOUTHEND-ON-SEA ☎ 01702 351000 📄 01702 393989 20 rooms

CANVEY ISLAND
Map 5 TQ78

Castle Point Golf Club Somnes Av SS8 9FG
☎ 01268 510830 & 511149 📄 01268 511758
web: www.glendale-golf.co.uk
18 Holes, 6176yds, Par 71, SSS 69, Course record 66.
Location SE of Basildon, A130 to Canvey Island
Telephone for further details
Hotel ★★★ 77% HL Chichester, Old London Road, Wickford,
BASILDON ☎ 01268 560555 📄 01268 560580 35 en suite

CHELMSFORD Map 5 TL70

Channels Golf Club Belstead Farm Ln, Little Waltham
CM3 3PT
☎ 01245 440005 📠 01245 442032
e-mail: info@channelsgolf.co.uk
web: www.channelsgolf.co.uk

The Channels course is built on land from reclaimed gravel pits, 18 very exciting holes with plenty of lakes providing an excellent test of golf. Belsteads, a nine-hole course, is mainly flat but has three holes where water has to be negotiated.

Channels Course: 18 Holes, 6413yds, Par 71, SSS 71, Course record 65.
Belsteads: 9 Holes, 2467yds, Par 34, SSS 32.
Club membership 800.

Visitors Mon-Fri except BHs. Booking required. **Societies** booking required. **Green Fees** phone **Course Designer** Cotton & Swan **Prof** Ian Sinclair **Facilities** ⊕ †◎ ⅃ ☐ ☜ ☐ ♨ ◇ ⚬ **Leisure** fishing, 9 hole pitch & putt course. **Conf** facs Corporate Hospitality Days **Location** 2m NE on A130
Hotel ★★★ 80% HL County Hotel, 29 Rainsford Road, CHELMSFORD ☎ 01245 455700 📠 01245 492762 50 en suite

Chelmsford Golf Club Widford Rd CM2 9AP
☎ 01245 256483 📠 01245 256483
e-mail: office@chelmsfordgc.co.uk
web: www.chelmsfordgc.co.uk

An undulating parkland course, hilly in parts, with three holes in woods and four difficult par 4s. From the clubhouse there are fine views over the course and the wooded hills beyond.

18 Holes, 5996yds, Par 68, SSS 69, Course record 63.
Club membership 650.

Visitors Mon-Fri except BHs. Booking required. Dress code. **Societies** booking required. **Green Fees** £40 per round **Course Designer** Tom Dunn **Prof** Mark Welch **Facilities** ⊕ ⅃ ☐ ☜ ☐ ⚬ **Conf** Corporate Hospitality Days **Location** 1.5m S of town centre off A12
Hotel ★★★ 80% HL County Hotel, 29 Rainsford Road, CHELMSFORD ☎ 01245 455700 📠 01245 492762 50 en suite

Regiment Way Golf Centre Back Ln, Little Waltham
CM3 3PR
☎ 01245 361100 📠 01245 442032
e-mail: info@channelsgolf.co.uk
web: www.regimentway.co.uk

A nine-hole course with alternate tee positions, offering an 18-hole course. Fully automatic tee and green irrigation plus excellent drainage ensure play at most times of the year. The course is challenging but at the same time can be forgiving.

9 Holes, 4887yds, Par 65, SSS 64. Club membership 265.

Visitors Mon-Sun & BHs. **Societies** welcome. **Green Fees** £15 per 18 holes, £11 per 9 holes **Course Designer** R Stubbings/R Clark **Prof** David March **Facilities** ⊕ †◎ ⅃ ☐ ☜ ☐ ⚬ ◇ ☐ ⚬ **Conf** facs Corporate Hospitality Days **Location** off A130 N of Chelmsford
Hotel ★★★ 77% HL Best Western Atlantic Hotel, New Street, CHELMSFORD ☎ 01245 268168 📠 01245 268169 59 en suite

CHIGWELL Map 5 TQ49

Chigwell Golf Club High Rd IG7 5BH
☎ 020 8500 2059 📠 020 8501 3410
e-mail: info@chigwellgolfclub.co.uk
web: www.chigwellgolfclub.co.uk

A course of high quality, mixing meadowland with parkland. For those who believe 'all Essex is flat' the undulating nature of Chigwell will be a refreshing surprise. The greens are excellent and the fairways tight with mature trees.

18 Holes, 6296yds, Par 71, SSS 70, Course record 66.
Club membership 800.

Visitors Mon & Wed-Fri except BHs. Booking required. Handicap certificate. Dress code. **Societies** booking required. **Green Fees** not confirmed ⊕ **Course Designer** Hawtree/Taylor **Prof** James Fuller **Facilities** ⊕ †◎ ⅃ ☐ ☜ ☐ ⚬ **Conf** facs Corporate Hospitality Days **Location** 0.5m S on A113
Hotel ★★★★ 72% HL Menzies Prince Regent, Manor Road, WOODFORD BRIDGE ☎ 020 8505 9966 📠 020 8506 0807 61 en suite

CHIGWELL ROW   Map 5 TQ49

Hainault Forest Golf Complex Romford Rd IG7 4QW
☎ 020 8500 2131 📠 020 8501 5196
web: www.hainaultforestgolf.co.uk

No 1 Course: 18 Holes, 5687yds, Par 70, SSS 67,
Course record 65.
No 2 Course: 18 Holes, 6238yds, Par 71, SSS 71.

Course Designer Taylor & Hawtree **Location** 0.5m S on A1112
Telephone for further details
Hotel ★★★★ 72% HL Menzies Prince Regent, Manor Road,
WOODFORD BRIDGE ☎ 020 8505 9966 📠 020 8506 0807 61 en suite

CLACTON-ON-SEA   Map 5 TM11

Clacton Golf Club West Rd CO15 1AJ
☎ 01255 421919 📠 01255 424602
e-mail: secretary@clactongolfclub.com
web: www.clactongolfclub.com

The course covers 110 acres and runs alongside the sea wall and
then inland. Easy walking layout, part open and part woodland. The
course is well bunkered and a unique feature is the fleets, ditches
and streams that cross and border many of the fairways, demanding
accuracy and good striking.

18 Holes, 6448yds, Par 71, SSS 69, Course record 65.
Club membership 650.

Visitors Mon-Sun & BHs. Handicap certificate. Dress code.
Societies welcome. **Green Fees** £35 per day, £25 per round (£45/£30
weekends and BHs) **Course Designer** Jack White **Prof** S J Levermore
Facilities ⏱ ⍨ 🍴 🛒 🖥 ⚐ 🏠 🛏 ✦ **Leisure** practice
nets available **Conf** facs Corporate Hospitality Days **Location** 1.25m
SW of town centre
Hotel ★★ 65% HL Esplanade Hotel, 27-29 Marine Parade East,
CLACTON-ON-SEA ☎ 01255 220450 📠 01255 221800 29 en suite

COLCHESTER   Map 5 TL92

Birch Grove Golf Club Layer Rd, Kingsford CO2 0HS
☎ 01206 734276
e-mail: maureen@birchgrove.fsbusiness.co.uk
web: www.birchgrovegolfclub.co.uk

A pretty, undulating course surrounded by woodland - small but
challenging with excellent greens. Challenging 6th hole cut through
woodland with water hazards and out of bounds.

9 Holes, 4532yds, Par 66, SSS 63, Course record 66.
Club membership 250.

Visitors Mon, Wed-Sat & BHs. Tue & Sun pm. Dress code
Societies booking required. **Green Fees** £17 for 18 holes, £12 for 9
holes ⏱ **Course Designer** L A Marston **Facilities** ⏱ 🍴 🛒 ⍨
🖥 🏠 ✦ **Conf** facs Corporate Hospitality Days **Location** 2.5m
S on B1026
Hotel ★★★ 80% HL Best Western The Rose & Crown, East Street,
COLCHESTER ☎ 01206 866677 📠 01206 866616 39 en suite

Colchester Golf Club Braiswick CO4 5AU
☎ 01206 853396 📠 01206 852698
web: www.colchestergolfclub.com

18 Holes, 6357yds, Par 70, SSS 70, Course record 63.

Course Designer James Braid **Location** 1.5m NW of town centre on
B1508 (West Bergholt Rd)
Telephone for further details
Hotel ★★★ 80% HL Best Western The Rose & Crown, East Street,
COLCHESTER ☎ 01206 866677 📠 01206 866616 39 en suite

Lexden Wood Golf Club Bakers Ln CO3 4AU
☎ 01206 843333 📠 01206 854775
e-mail: info@lexdenwood.com
web: www.lexdenwood.com

A challenging parkland course with 80 bunkers and water in play on
5 holes. USGA tees and greens mean that it is playable all year round.
There is also a 9 hole pitch and putt and 24 bay driving range on site.

18 Holes, 6000yds, Par 70, SSS 69, Course record 65.
Club membership 500.

Visitors Mon-Sun & BHs. Dress code. **Societies** booking required.
Green Fees £22 (£30 weekends and BHs, £25 after 11am) **Course
Designer** Jonathan Gaunt **Prof** leighton Oakey **Facilities** ⏱ 🍴 🛒
⍨ 🖥 🏠 ⚐ ✦ 🛏 ✦ **Leisure** 9 hole par 3 **Conf** facs
Corporate Hospitality Days **Location** A12 towards Colchester Central,
follow tourist signs
Hotel ★★★ 80% HL Best Western The Rose & Crown, East Street,
COLCHESTER ☎ 01206 866677 📠 01206 866616 39 en suite

Stoke by Nayland Golf Club Keeper's Ln, Leavenheath
CO6 4PZ
☎ 01206 262836 📠 01206 265840
e-mail: sales@stokebynayland.com
web: www.stokebynaylandclub.co.uk

Two 18-hole Championship courses, The Gainsborough and The
Constable. Created in the 1970s, both courses are well established
and feature mature woodland, undulating fairways and picturesque
water features which include four large natural lakes. The 18th hole
on both courses presents a challenging and spectacular finish with
tee-offs over the largest of the lakes to a green resting in front of the
clubhouse. The venue is a regular host to PGA and European events.

Gainsborough: 18 Holes, 6561yds, Par 72, SSS 72,
Course record 63.
Constable: 18 Holes, 6544yds, Par 72, SSS 72,
Course record 67. Club membership 1200.

Visitors Mon-Sun & BHs. Booking required. Dress code.
Societies booking required. **Green Fees** not confirmed **Course
Designer** Howard Swan **Prof** Roly Hitchcock **Facilities** ⏱ 🍴 🛒
⍨ 🖥 🏠 ⚐ ◇ ✦ 🛏 ✦ **Leisure** heated indoor
swimming pool, squash, fishing, sauna, gymnasium, halfway hut,
snooker, spa treatments **Conf** facs Corporate Hospitality Days
Location 1.5m NW of Stoke by Nayland on B1068
Hotel ★★★ 82% HL Stoke by Nayland Hotel, Golf & Spa, Keepers
Lane, Leavenheath, COLCHESTER ☎ 01206 262836 📠 01206 265840
80 en suite

EARLS COLNE
Map 5 TL82

Colne Valley Golf Club Station Rd CO6 2LT
☎ 01787 224343 📄 01787 224126
e-mail: info@colnevalleygolfclub.co.uk
web: www.colnevalleygolfclub.co.uk

Opened in 1991, this surprisingly mature parkland course belies its tender years. Natural water hazards, and well-defined bunkers, along with USGA standard greens offer year round playability, and a stimulating test for all abilities.

18 Holes, 6295yds, Par 70, SSS 71, Course record 69. Club membership 400.

Visitors Mon-Sun & BHs. Booking required. Dress code. Societies welcome. **Green Fees** £40 per day, £30 per 18 holes (£35 per 18 holes weekends). **Course Designer** Howard Swan **Prof** Jamie Lowe (PGA) Facilities ⚑ 🍽 🛒 ▭ 🍴 ⛏ 🏠 ⛳ 🚗 ✦ **Leisure** fishing **Conf** facs Corporate Hospitality Days **Location** off A1124

Hotel ★★★ 73% HL White Hart Hotel, Market End, COGGESHALL ☎ 01376 561654 📄 01376 561789 18 en suite

Essex Golf & Country Club CO6 2NS
☎ 01787 224466 📄 01787 224410
e-mail: l.cocker@theclubcompany.com
web: www.the clubcompany.com

Created on the site of a World War II airfield, this challenging course contains 10 lakes and strategically placed bunkering. Also a nine-hole course and a variety of leisure facilities.

County Course: 18 Holes, 7019yds, Par 73, SSS 73, Course record 67.
Garden Course: 9 Holes, 2190yds, Par 34, SSS 34. Club membership 700.

Visitors may play Mon-Sun & BHs. Advance booking required. Dress code. **Societies** booking required. **Green Fees** not confirmed **Course Designer** Reg Plumbridge **Prof** Lee Cocker/Paul Grotier Facilities ⚑ 🍽 🛒 ▭ 🍴 ⛏ 🏠 ⛳ ◇ ✦ 🚗 ✦ 🏌 **Leisure** hard tennis courts, fishing, sauna, gymnasium, video golf tuition studio **Conf** facs Corporate Hospitality Days **Location** signed off A120 onto B1024

Hotel ★★★ 73% HL White Hart Hotel, Market End, COGGESHALL ☎ 01376 561654 📄 01376 561789 18 en suite

EPPING
Map 5 TL40

Blakes Golf Club Epping Rd, North Weald CM16 6RZ
☎ 01992 525151
e-mail: info@blakesgolfclub.com
web: www.blakesgolfclub.com

An inland links course originally designed by Howard Swan in the 1990s. No temporary greens or tees are used and allows for all weather play. The course is a memorable one, tough, challenging, yet fair to a wide range of golfers.

Blakes: 18 Holes, 6631yds, Par 71. Club membership 900.

Visitors Dress code. **Societies** booking required. **Green Fees** £15 per round Mon-Thu, £18 Fri, £20 weekends **Course Designer** Howard Swan Facilities 🛒 ▭ 🍴 ⛏ 🏠 🚗 ✦ 🏌 **Conf** facs Corporate Hospitality Days **Location** M11 junct 7/A414. At Talbot rdbt straight over & club 400 yds on right

Hotel 63% Ⓤ The Bell Hotel Epping, High Road, Bell Common, EPPING ☎ 01992 573138 📄 01992 560402 79 en suite

The Epping Golf Course Fluxs Ln CM16 7PE
☎ 01992 572282 📄 01992 575512
e-mail: info@eppinggolfcourse.org.uk
web: www.eppinggolfcourse.org.uk

Undulating parkland with extensive views over Essex countryside and excellent fairways. Incorporates many water features designed to use every club in the bag. Some driveable par 4s, and the spectacular 18th, Happy Valley, is rarely birdied.

Epping: 18 Holes, 5400yds, Par 68, SSS 65, Course record 62. Club membership 350.

Visitors Mon-Sun & BHs. Dress code. **Societies** booking required. **Green Fees** £21 per day, £14 per round (£33/£21 weekends & BHs) 🐌 **Course Designer** Sjoberg **Prof** Warren Sargeant Facilities ⚑ 🛒 ▭ 🍴 ⛏ 🏠 ⛳ ✦ 🚗 ✦ 🏌 **Conf** facs Corporate Hospitality Days **Location** M11 junct 7, 2.5m on B1393, left in Epping High Rd towards station

Hotel ★★★★ 73% HL Waltham Abbey Marriott Hotel, Old Shire Lane, WALTHAM ABBEY ☎ 01992 717170 📄 01992 711841 162 en suite

Nazeing Golf Club Middle St, Nazeing EN9 2LW
☎ 01992 893798 📄 01992 893882
e-mail: golfdays@nazeinggolfclub.co.uk
web: www.nazeinggolfclub.co.uk

Parkland course built with American sand-based greens and tees and five strategically placed lakes. One of the most notable holes is the difficult par 3 13th with out of bounds and a large lake coming into play.

18 Holes, 6617yds, Par 72, SSS 72, Course record 64. Club membership 400.

Visitors Mon-Sun & BHs. Dress code. **Societies** welcome. **Green Fees** £22 per round (£28 weekends & BHs) **Course Designer** M Gillete **Prof** Robert Green Facilities ⚑ 🍽 🛒 ▭ 🍴 ⛏ 🏠 ✦ 🚗 ✦ 🏌 **Conf** facs Corporate Hospitality Days **Location** M25 junct 26, near Waltham Abbey

Hotel ★★★★ 73% HL Waltham Abbey Marriott Hotel, Old Shire Lane, WALTHAM ABBEY ☎ 01992 717170 📄 01992 711841 162 en suite

FRINTON-ON-SEA
Map 5 TM22

Frinton Golf Club 1 The Esplanade CO13 9EP
☎ 01255 674618 📄 01255 682450
e-mail: thesecretary@frintongolfclub.com
web: www.frintongolfclub.com

Deceptive, flat seaside links course providing fast, firm and undulating greens that will test the best putters, and tidal ditches that cross many of the fairways, requiring careful placement of shots. Its open character means that every shot has to be evaluated with both wind strength and direction in mind. Easy walking.

Havers: 18 Holes, 6265yds, Par 71, SSS 70.
Kirkby: 9 Holes, 1417yds, Par 30. Club membership 850.

Visitors Mon-Sun & BHs. Booking required. Dress code. Societies booking required. **Green Fees** not confirmed **Course Designer** Willy Park Jnr/Harry Colt **Prof** Peter Taggart Facilities ⚑ by prior arrangement 🛒 ▭ 🍴 ⛏ 🏠 ⛳ ✦ 🚗 ✦ **Leisure** indoor practice nets **Conf** facs Corporate Hospitality Days **Location** SW of town centre

Hotel ★★ 65% HL Esplanade Hotel, 27-29 Marine Parade East, CLACTON-ON-SEA ☎ 01255 220450 📄 01255 221800 29 en suite

Save on Hotels. Book at **theAA.com/hotel**

ESSEX

ENGLAND

GOSFIELD — Map 5 TL72

Gosfield Lake Golf Club The Manor House, Hall Dr
CO9 1SE
☎ 01787 474747 📠 01787 476044
e-mail: gosfieldlakegc@btconnect.com
web: www.gosfield-lake-golf-club.co.uk
Parkland with bunkers, lakes and water hazards. Designed by Sir
Henry Cotton and Howard Swan. Also a nine-hole course; ideal for
beginners and improvers.
Lakes Course: 18 Holes, 6615yds, Par 72, SSS 72,
Course record 68.
Meadows Course: 9 Holes, 4990yds, Par 66, SSS 64.
Club membership 650.
Visitors Mon-Sun & BHs. **Societies** welcome. **Green Fees** Lakes
£35 per round, Meadows £17 per round. Twilight £20/£10 **Course
Designer** Henry Cotton/Howard Swan **Prof** Richard Wheeler
Facilities ⊕ ⊙ 📶 ⏹ 🐚 ⚲ 🏠 ✦ 🛏 ✦ **Conf**
Corporate Hospitality Days **Location** 1m W of Gosfield off B1017
Hotel ★★★ 73% HL White Hart Hotel, Market End, COGGESHALL
☎ 01376 561654 📠 01376 561789 18 en suite

HARLOW — Map 5 TL41

Canons Brook Golf Club Elizabeth Way CM19 5BE
☎ 01279 421482 📠 01279 626393
e-mail: manager@canonsbrook.com
web: www.canonsbrook.com
Challenging parkland course designed by Henry Cotton. Accuracy is
the key requiring straight driving from the tees, especially on the par
5 11th to fly a gap with out of bounds left and right before setting up
the shot to the green.
18 Holes, 6771yds, Par 73, SSS 73, Course record 69.
Club membership 650.
Visitors Mon-Fri except BHs. **Societies** welcome. **Green Fees** not
confirmed **Course Designer** Henry Cotton **Prof** Alan McGinn
Facilities ⊕ ⊙ 🐚 ⏹ 📶 ⚲ 🏠 ✦ **Conf** facs
Location M11 junct 7, 3m NW
Hotel ★★★ 74% HL Manor of Groves Hotel, Golf & Country Club,
High Wych, SAWBRIDGEWORTH ☎ 01279 600777 & 0870 410 8833
📠 01279 600374 80 en suite

North Weald Golf Club Rayley Ln, North Weald CM16 6AR
☎ 01992 522118 📠 01992 522881
e-mail: info@northwealdgolfclub.co.uk
web: www.northwealdgolfclub.co.uk
This well established 18 hole course has undergone extensive
modifications during recent years, including drainage and additional
tees. The sand-based tees and greens, all built to USGA specifications
allow the course to be played all year.
18 Holes, 6377yds, Par 71, SSS 71. Club membership 300.
Visitors Mon-Sun & BHs. Booking required. Dress code
Societies welcome. **Green Fees** not confirmed **Course Designer** David
Williams **Prof** Paul Sullivan **Facilities** ⊕ 🐚 ⏹ 📶 ⚲ 🏠
✦ 🛏 ✦ ✦ **Leisure** fishing, gymnasium **Conf** facs Corporate
Hospitality Days **Location** M11 exit 7, A414 2m towards Chipping
Ongar
Hotel ★★★ 64% HL Park Inn by Radisson Harlow, Southern Way,
HARLOW ☎ 01279 829988 📠 01279 829906 119 en suite

HARWICH — Map 5 TM23

Harwich & Dovercourt Golf Club Station Rd, Parkeston
CO12 4NZ
☎ 01255 503616 📠 01255 503323
e-mail: secretary@harwichanddovercourtgolfclub.com
web: www.harwichanddovercourtgolfclub.com
Flat parkland with easy walking. The 243yd par 3 9th hole to an
invisible green is a real experience.
9 Holes, 5906yds, Par 70, SSS 69, Course record 64.
Club membership 410.
Visitors dress code. **Societies** booking required. **Green Fees** £24 per
18 holes, £13 per 9 holes **Facilities** ⊕ ⊙ by prior arrangement
🐚 ⏹ 📶 ⚲ 🏠 🛏 ✦ **Conf** Corporate Hospitality Days
Location off A120 near Ferry Terminal
Hotel ★★★ 87% HL The Pier at Harwich, The Quay, HARWICH
☎ 01255 241212 📠 01255 551922 14 en suite

INGRAVE — Map 5 TQ69

Thorndon Park Golf Club CM13 3RH
☎ 01277 810345 📠 01277 810645
e-mail: office@thorndonpark.com
web: www.thorndonparkgolfclub.com
Course is playable even at the wettest times of the year. Holes
stand on their own surrounded by mature oaks, some of which
are more than 500 years old. The lake in the centre of the course
provides both a challenge and a sense of peace and tranquillity.
The Palladian Thorndon Hall, site of the old clubhouse, is the
magnificent backdrop to the closing hole.
18 Holes, 6511yds, Par 71, SSS 71, Course record 64.
Club membership 670.
Visitors Mon-Fri except BHs. Booking required. Dress code.
Societies booking required. **Green Fees** £70 per day, £55 per 18
holes **Course Designer** Colt **Prof** Brian White **Facilities** ⊕ ⊙
by prior arrangement 🐚 ⏹ 📶 ⚲ 🏠 🛏 ✦ **Conf**
Corporate Hospitality Days **Location** W side of village off A128
Hotel ★★★★ 74% HL De Rougemont Manor, Great Warley
Street, BRENTWOOD ☎ 01277 226418 & 220483 📠 01277 239020
79 en suite

LOUGHTON — Map 5 TQ49

Loughton Golf Club Clays Ln IG10 2RZ
☎ 020 8502 2923
9 Holes, 4652yds, Par 66, SSS 63, Course record 69.
Location 1.5m SE of Theydon Bois
Telephone for further details
Hotel ★★★★ 73% HL Waltham Abbey Marriott Hotel, Old
Shire Lane, WALTHAM ABBEY ☎ 01992 717170 📠 01992 711841
162 en suite

MALDON
Map 5 TL80

Forrester Park Golf Club Beckingham Rd, Great Totham CM9 8EA
☎ 01621 891406 🖹 01621 891406
e-mail: info@forresterparkltd.com
web: www.forresterparkltd.com

Set in undulating parkland in the Essex countryside and commanding some beautiful views across the River Blackwater. Accuracy is more important than distance and judgement more important than strength on this traditional club course. There is a separate 10-acre practice ground.

Forrester Park: 18 Holes, 6073yds, Par 71, SSS 69, Course record 63. Club membership 700.

Visitors Mon-Sun & BHs. Booking required. **Societies** booking required. **Green Fees** £15-£25 depending on time/day **Course Designer** T R Forrester-Muir **Prof** Gary Pike/Craig Lockwood **Facilities** ⓘ 🍴 🖳 ♥️ 🍴 ⚖️ ✔ 🛍 ✔ ❄ **Leisure** hard tennis courts, heated indoor swimming pool **Conf** facs Corporate Hospitality Days **Location** 3m NE of Maldon off B1022
Hotel ★★★ 80% HL Rivenhall, Rivenhall End, WITHAM ☎ 01376 516969 🖹 01376 513674 55 en suite

Maldon Golf Club Beeleigh CM9 6LL
☎ 01621 853212 🖹 01621 855232
web: www.maldon-golf.co.uk

9 Holes, 6253yds, Par 71, SSS 70, Course record 66.

Course Designer Thompson of Felixstowe **Location** 1m NW off B1019
Telephone for further details
Hotel ★★★ 77% HL Pontlands Park Country Hotel, West Hanningfield Road, Great Baddow, CHELMSFORD ☎ 01245 476444 🖹 01245 478393 35 en suite

ORSETT
Map 5 TQ68

Orsett Golf Club Brentwood Rd RM16 3DS
☎ 01375 891352 🖹 01375 892471
e-mail: enquiries@orsettgolfclub.co.uk
web: www.orsettgolfclub.co.uk

A very good test of golf - this heathland course with its sandy soil is quick drying and provides easy walking. Close to the Thames estuary it is seldom calm and the main hazards are the prevailing wind and thick gorse. Any slight deviation can be exaggerated by the wind and result in a ball lost in the gorse. Host for regional qualifying for the Open Championship on eleven occasions.

18 Holes, 6682yds, Par 72, SSS 73, Course record 63. Club membership 650.

Visitors Mon-Fri except BHs. Booking required. Dress code. **Societies** booking required. **Green Fees** £45 per day, £35 per 18 holes **Course Designer** James Braid **Prof** Richard Herring **Facilities** ⓘ 🍴 🖳 ♥️ 🍴 ⚖️ 🛍 ✔ ✔ **Leisure** coaching **Conf** facs Corporate Hospitality Days **Location** junct of A13/A128, then S on A128 towards Chadwell St Mary for 0.5m. Entrance on left.
Hotel ★★★ 70% HL Park Inn Thurrock, High Road, North Stifford, GRAYS ☎ 01708 719988 🖹 01708 719980 97 en suite

PURLEIGH
Map 5 TL80

Three Rivers Golf & Country Club Stow Rd CM3 6RR
☎ 01621 828631 🖹 01621 828060
web: www.threeriversclub.com

Kings Course: 18 Holes, 6403yds, Par 72, SSS 71, Course record 66.
Jubilee Course: 18 Holes, 4501yds, Par 64, SSS 62.

Course Designer Hawtree **Location** 2.5m from South Woodham Ferrers
Telephone for further details
Hotel ★★★ 77% HL Chichester, Old London Road, Wickford, BASILDON ☎ 01268 560555 🖹 01268 560580 35 en suite

ROCHFORD
Map 5 TQ89

Rochford Hundred Golf Club Hall Rd SS4 1NW
☎ 01702 544302 🖹 01702 541343
e-mail: admin@rochfordhundredgolfclub.co.uk
web: www.rochfordhundredgolfclub.co.uk

This traditional James Braid parkland course is one of the oldest in the south east. The club house, a former home of Anne Boleyn of Henry VIII fame, was built around 1480 and still retains its historic charm. The course features picturesque water gardens, par 3s and 'risk and reward' par 4s and 5s.

18 Holes, 6221yds, Par 71, SSS 71, Course record 64. Club membership 800.

Visitors Mon-Fri except BHs. Booking required. Handicap certificate required. Dress code. **Societies** booking required. **Green Fees** £40 per day/round **Course Designer** James Braid **Prof** Graham Hill **Facilities** ⓘ 🍴 🖳 🖳 🍴 ⚖️ 🛍 🛍 ✔ **Conf** facs Corporate Hospitality Days **Location** W on B1013
Hotel ★★★★ GA Ilfracombe House, 9-13 Wilson Road, SOUTHEND-ON-SEA ☎ 01702 351000 🖹 01702 393989 20 rooms

SAFFRON WALDEN
Map 5 TL53

Saffron Walden Golf Club Windmill Hill CB10 1BX
☎ 01799 522786 🖹 01799 520313
e-mail: office@swgc.com
web: www.swgc.com

Undulating parkland in the former deer park of Audley End House. Fine views over rolling countryside. Two par 3 signature holes, the 5th and 18th.

18 Holes, 6632yds, Par 72, SSS 72, Course record 66. Club membership 900.

Visitors Mon-Fri, Sun & BHs. Booking required. Dress code. **Societies** booking required. **Green Fees** £54 (£60 Sun), £44 per 18 holes **Course Designer** Howard Swan **Prof** Philip Davis **Facilities** ⓘ 🍴 🖳 🖳 🍴 ⚖️ 🛍 ✔ 🛍 ✔ ❄ **Conf** facs Corporate Hospitality Days **Location** N side of town centre off B184
Hotel ★★★ 72% HL The Crown House, GREAT CHESTERFORD ☎ 01799 530515 🖹 01799 530683 18 en suite

SOUTHEND-ON-SEA   Map 5 TQ88

Belfairs Golf Course Eastwood Road North SS9 4LR
☎ 01702 525345 & 520202
web: www.southend.gov.uk
18 Holes, 5840yds, Par 70, SSS 68, Course record 68.
Course Designer H S Colt **Location** off A127/A13
Telephone for further details
Hotel ★★★ GA The Trinity, 3 Trinity Avenue, WESTCLIFF-ON-SEA
☎ 01702 342282 7 rooms

Thorpe Hall Golf Club Thorpe Hall Av, Thorpe Bay SS1 3AT
☎ 01702 582205 📠 01702 584498
e-mail: sec@thorpehallgc.co.uk
web: www.thorpehallgc.co.uk
Tree-lined parkland with narrow fairways, where placement rather than length is essential.
18 Holes, 6290yds, SSS 70. Club membership 995.
Visitors Mon-Fri except BHs. Handicap certificate. Dress code.
Societies booking required. **Green Fees** not confirmed **Course Designer** Various **Prof** J Fryatt **Facilities** ⓣ ✝◎⌇ by prior arrangement 🏌 ☕ 🏐 ⚐ 🍴 ⚒ ⚒ **Leisure** squash, sauna, snooker room **Conf** facs Corporate Hospitality Days **Location** 2m E off A13
Hotel ★★★ 79% HL Roslin Beach Hotel, Thorpe Esplanade, THORPE BAY ☎ 01702 586375 📠 01702 586663 57 en suite

STAPLEFORD ABBOTTS   Map 5 TQ59

Stapleford Abbotts Golf Club Horsemanside RM4 1JU
☎ 01708 381108 📠 01708 386345
web: www.staplefordabbottsgolf.co.uk
Abbotts Course: 18 Holes, 6501yds, Par 72, SSS 71.
Priors Course: 18 Holes, 5735yds, Par 70, SSS 69.
Course Designer Henry Cotton/Howard Swan **Location** 1m E of Stapleford Abbotts, off B175
Telephone for further details
Hotel ★★★★ 75% HL Marygreen Manor, London Road, BRENTWOOD ☎ 01277 225252 📠 01277 262809 44 en suite

STOCK   Map 5 TQ69

Crondon Park Golf Club Stock Rd CM4 9DP
☎ 01277 843027 📠 01277 841356
e-mail: paul@crondon.com
web: www.crondon.com
Undulating parkland with many water hazards, set in the Crondon Valley.
18 Holes, 6627yds, Par 72, SSS 73, Course record 71.
Club membership 750.
Visitors Mon-Fri after 10am. Weekends after 3pm. Booking required. Handicap certificate. Dress code. **Societies** booking required. **Green Fees** £30 per 18 holes (£50 weekends) **Course Designer** Mr M Gillet **Prof** Chris Wood **Facilities** ⓣ ◎⌇ 🏌 ☕ 🏐 🏌 🏐 ⚒ ⚒ ⚒ **Conf** facs Corporate Hospitality Days **Location** on B1007, between Stock and A12 junct16
Hotel ★★★★ 75% HL Greenwoods Hotel Spa & Retreat, Stock Road, STOCK ☎ 01277 829990 & 829205 📠 01277 829899 39 en suite

THEYDON BOIS   Map 5 TQ49

Theydon Bois Golf Club Theydon Rd CM16 4EH
☎ 01992 812460 (pro) & 813054 (office)
📠 01992 815602
web: www.theydongolf.co.uk
18 Holes, 5490yds, Par 68, SSS 67, Course record 64.
Course Designer James Braid **Location** M25 junct 26, 2m
Telephone for further details
Hotel ★★★★ 73% HL Waltham Abbey Marriott Hotel, Old Shire Lane, WALTHAM ABBEY ☎ 01992 717170 📠 01992 711841 162 en suite

TOLLESHUNT KNIGHTS   Map 5 TL91

Five Lakes Hotel, Golf, Country Club & Spa
Colchester Rd CM9 8HX
☎ 01621 868888 & 862426 📠 01621 869696
e-mail: golfoffice@fivelakes.co.uk
web: www.fivelakes.co.uk
Set in 320 acres, the two 18-hole courses both offer their own particular challenges. Water is the predominant feature of the Lakes Course, coming into play on nine holes. Generous fairways, large greens and water hazards provide a great test for golfers and ensure every club in the bag is used. The Links course presents a very different challenge, testing precision with narrow fairways and strategically placed water hazards, sand-bunkers and well guarded greens. Accuracy is the key to success on this course.
Links Course: 18 Holes, 6181yds, Par 71, SSS 70, Course record 64.
Lakes Course: 18 Holes, 6767yds, Par 72, SSS 73, Course record 63. Club membership 430.
Visitors Mon-Sun & BHs. Booking required. Dress code.
Societies booking required. **Green Fees** not confirmed **Course Designer** Neil Coles **Prof** Gary Carter **Facilities** ⓣ ◎⌇ 🏌 ☕ 🏐 🏌 🏐 🏌 ⚐ 🍴 ⚒ 🏐 ⚒ 🏐 **Leisure** hard tennis courts, heated indoor swimming pool, squash, sauna, gymnasium, snooker, badminton, fitness studio **Conf** facs Corporate Hospitality Days **Location** 1.75m NE on B1026, 15 mins from A12 Kelvedon exit. Brown tourist signs
Hotel ★★★★ 77% HL Five Lakes Hotel, Golf, Country Club & Spa, Colchester Road, TOLLESHUNT KNIGHTS ☎ 01621 868888 📠 01621 869696 194 en suite

TOOT HILL   Map 5 TL50

Toot Hill Golf Club School Rd CM5 9PU
☎ 01277 365523 📠 01277 364509
e-mail: office@toothillgolfclub.co.uk
Pleasant course with several water hazards and sand greens.
18 Holes, 6053yds, Par 70, SSS 69, Course record 65.
Club membership 400.
Visitors contact club for details. **Societies** booking required. **Green Fees** £30 per 18 holes weekdays **Course Designer** Martin Gillett **Prof** Mark Bishop **Facilities** ⓣ ◎⌇ 🏌 ☕ 🏐 🏌 🏐 ⚐ 🍴 ⚒ 🏐 ⚒ **Conf** facs **Location** 7m SE of Harlow off A414
Hotel ★★★ 80% HL Holiday Inn Brentwood, Brook Street, BRENTWOOD ☎ 0871 942 9012 📠 01277 264264 149 en suite

ENGLAND

WITHAM
Map 5 TL81

Benton Hall Golf & Country Club Wickham Hill CM8 3LH
☎ 01376 502454 📄 01376 521050
e-mail: bentonhall.retail@theclubcompany.com
web: www.theclubcompany.com
Set in rolling countryside surrounded by dense woodland, this challenging course provides a severe test even to the best golfers. The River Blackwater dominates the front nine and natural lakes come into play on five other holes. The clubhouse incorporates health and fitness facilities.
18 Holes, 6417yds, Par 71, SSS 71, Course record 64.
Club membership 600.
Visitors Mon-Sun except BHs. Dress code **Societies** welcome. **Green Fees** not confirmed **Course Designer** Alan Walker/Charles Cox **Prof** Shane Diles **Facilities** ⊕ 🍴 📭 🖵 🎣 ⚑ 🏌 ✔
🛒 ✔ **Leisure** heated indoor swimming pool, sauna, gymnasium, 9 hole par 3 course **Conf** facs Corporate Hospitality Days **Location** off A12 at Witham, signed
Hotel ★★★ 80% HL Rivenhall, Rivenhall End, WITHAM
☎ 01376 516969 📄 01376 513674 55 en suite

WOODHAM WALTER
Map 5 TL80

Bunsay Downs Golf Club Little Baddow Rd CM9 6RU
☎ 01245 222648 📄 01245 223989
Bunsay Downs: 9 Holes, 2932yds, Par 70, SSS 68.
Badgers: 9 Holes, 1319yds, Par 54.
Course Designer John Durham **Location** 2m from Danbury on A414, signed
Telephone for further details
Hotel ★★★ 80% HL County Hotel, 29 Rainsford Road, CHELMSFORD ☎ 01245 455700 📄 01245 492762 50 en suite

Warren Golf Club CM9 6RW
☎ 01245 223258 📄 01245 223989
e-mail: enquiries@warrengolfclub.co.uk
web: www.warrengolfclub.co.uk
Attractive parkland with natural hazards and good views.
The Warren: 18 Holes, 6263yds, Par 70, SSS 70,
Course record 62. Club membership 500.
Visitors Mon-Fri & Sun except BHs. Booking required Mon-Fri. Dress code. **Societies** booking required. **Green Fees** phone **Prof** David Brooks **Facilities** ⊕ 📭 🖵 🎣 🛒 ⚑ 🏌 ✔ **Conf** Corporate Hospitality Days **Location** 0.5m SW
Hotel ★★★ 80% HL County Hotel, 29 Rainsford Road, CHELMSFORD ☎ 01245 455700 📄 01245 492762 50 en suite

GLOUCESTERSHIRE

ALMONDSBURY
Map 3 ST68

Bristol Golf Club St Swithins Park, Blackhorse Hill
BS10 7TP
☎ 01454 620000 📄 01454 202700
e-mail: bristol@crown-golf.co.uk
web: www.crown-golf.co.uk
An undulating course set in 200 acres of parkland with magnificent views of the Severn estuary and surrounding countryside.
18 Holes, 6124yds, Par 70, SSS 69, Course record 63.
Club membership 850.
Visitors Mon-Fri. Weekends & BHs after 1pm. Booking required. Dress code. **Societies** booking required. **Green Fees** not confirmed **Course Designer** Pierson **Prof** Andrew Etherington **Facilities** ⊕ 🍴 📭 🖵 🎣 🏌 ✔ 🛒 ✔ **Leisure** par 3 academy course **Conf** facs Corporate Hospitality Days **Location** M5 junct 17, 100yds
Hotel ★★★ 77% HL Best Western Henbury Lodge Hotel, Station Road, Henbury, BRISTOL ☎ 0117 950 2615 📄 0117 950 9532
20 en suite

CHELTENHAM
Map 3 SO92

Cotswold Hills Golf Club Ullenwood GL53 9QT
☎ 01242 515264 📄 01242 515317
e-mail: contact.us@cotswoldhills-golfclub.com
web: www.cotswoldhills-golfclub.com
A beautiful free draining, gently undulating parkland course situated high on the Cotswolds with stunning panoramic views of the surrounding countryside. Playable all year, Cotswold Hills is a course that visitors of all abilities will enjoy.
18 Holes, 6555yds, Par 72, SSS 72, Course record 66.
Club membership 750.
Visitors Mon-Sun & BHs. Handicap certificate. Dress code. **Societies** booking required. **Green Fees** £37 per 18 holes (£43 weekends & BHs) **Course Designer** M D Little **Prof** James Latham **Facilities** ⊕ 🍴 📭 🖵 🎣 🏌 🛒 ✔ 🛒 ✔ **Conf** Corporate Hospitality Days **Location** 3m from M5 junct 11a between A436 & B4070
Hotel ★★★★ 73% HL Barceló Cheltenham Park Hotel, Cirencester Road, Charlton Kings, CHELTENHAM ☎ 01242 222021 📄 01242 254880 152 en suite

Lilley Brook Golf Club Cirencester Rd, Charlton Kings
GL53 8EG
☎ 01242 526785 📄 01242 256880
e-mail: caroline@lilleybrook.co.uk
web: www.lilleybrook.co.uk
Challenging parkland/downland course on the lower slopes of Leckhampton Hill with outstanding views of Cheltenham, the Malverns and the Black Mountains.
18 Holes, 6212yds, Par 69, SSS 70, Course record 61.
Club membership 900.
Visitors Mon-Sun & BHs. Handicap certificate. Dress code. **Societies** booking required. **Green Fees** £37 per 18 holes (£42 weekends & BHs) **Course Designer** Dr Alister Mackenzie **Prof** Simon Harrison **Facilities** ⊕ 🍴 📭 🖵 🎣 🏌 🛒 ✔ 🛒 ✔ 🏌 **Conf** facs Corporate Hospitality Days **Location** 2m S of Cheltenham on A435
Hotel ★★★★ 80% HL Hotel du Vin Cheltenham, Parabola Road, CHELTENHAM ☎ 01242 588450 📄 01242 588455 49 en suite

Save on Hotels. Book at **theAA.com/hotel**   **GLOUCESTERSHIRE**

ENGLAND

Shipton Golf Course Shipton Oliffe GL54 4HT
☎ 01242 890237
web: www.shiptongolf.co.uk
9 Holes, 2516yds, Par 35, SSS 63, Course record 33.
Location on A436, S of A40 junct
Telephone for further details
Hotel ★★★ 74% SHL Charlton Kings, London Road, Charlton Kings, CHELTENHAM ☎ 01242 231061 📄 01242 241900 14 en suite

CHIPPING SODBURY   Map 3 ST78

Chipping Sodbury Golf Club Trinity Ln BS37 6PU
☎ 01454 319042 📄 01454 320052
e-mail: info@chippingsodburygolfclub.co.uk
web: www.chippingsodburygolfclub.co.uk
Founded in 1905, a parkland course of championship proportions on the edge of the Cotswolds. The easy walking terrain, delicately interrupted by a medley of waterways and lakes, is complimented by a stylish clubhouse.
Beaufort Course: 18 Holes, 6995yds, Par 72, SSS 74.
Club membership 800.
Visitors Mon-Fri except BHs. Booking preferred. Dress code.
Societies booking required. **Green Fees** phone. **Course Designer** Hawtree Prof Mike Watts **Facilities** ⑪ ⑩ ⓘ 📶 ⌷ 🍴
⚘ 🏠 ⛐ ✐ 🛒 ✦ **Leisure** 6 hole academy course **Conf** facs Corporate Hospitality Days **Location** 0.5m N off of St Johns Way
Hotel ★★ 72% HL Rangeworthy Court, Church Lane, Wotton Road, RANGEWORTHY ☎ 01454 228347 📄 01454 65089
13 en suite

CIRENCESTER   Map 4 SP00

Cirencester Golf Club Cheltenham Rd, Bagendon GL7 7BH
☎ 01285 652465 📄 01285 650665
e-mail: info@cirencestergolfclub.co.uk
web: www.cirencestergolfclub.co.uk
Undulating open Cotswold course with excellent views.
18 Holes, 6030yds4, Par 70, SSS 69, Course record 64.
Club membership 800.
Visitors Mon-Sun & BHs. Dress code. **Societies** booking required.
Green Fees £35 per round/day (£40 weekends) **Course Designer** J Braid **Prof** Ed Goodwin **Facilities** ⑪ ⑩ ⓘ 📶 ⌷ 🍴 ⚘ 🏠 ✐
🛒 ✦ **Leisure** 6 hole par 3 academy course. **Conf** facs Corporate Hospitality Days **Location** 2m N of Cirencester on A435
Hotel ★★★ 77% HL Best Western Stratton House, Gloucester Road, CIRENCESTER ☎ 01285 651761 📄 01285 640024 39 en suite

South Cerney Golf Course & Driving Range
Northmoor Ln, South Cerney GL7 5QD
☎ 01285 861001 📄 01285 861012
e-mail: info@southcerneygolfcourse.co.uk
web: www.southcerneygolfcourse.co.uk
Parkland course situated within the Cotswold Water Park on the outskirts of Cirencester. The course offers a challenge for all golfing abilities.
18 Holes, 5987yds, Par 70, SSS 69. Club membership 400.
Visitors Mon-Sun & BHs. Booking required weekends & BHs. Dress code. **Societies** booking required. **Green Fees** £17 per 18 holes, £12 per 9 holes (weekends & BHs £20/£14) **Facilities** ⑪ ⑩ 📶 ⌷
🍴 ⚘ 🏠 ⛐ ✐ ✦ **Conf** facs Corporate Hospitality Days
Location M4 junct 15/A419
Hotel ★★★ 73% HL The Crown of Crucis, Ampney Crucis, CIRENCESTER ☎ 01285 851806 📄 01285 851735 25 en suite

CLEEVE HILL   Map 3 SO92

Cleeve Hill Golf Club GL52 3PW
☎ 01242 672025 📄 01242 67444
e-mail: hugh.fitzsimons@btconnect.com
web: www.cleevehillgolfcourse.com
Undulating and open heathland course affected by crosswinds. Situated on the highest point of the Cotswolds with fine views over Cheltenham racecourse, the Malvern Hills and the Bristol Channel. An ideal setting to enjoy a challenging round of golf.
18 Holes, 6448yds, Par 72, SSS 71, Course record 66.
Club membership 600.
Visitors Mon-Sun & BHs. Booking required. **Societies** booking required. **Green Fees** not confirmed **Prof** Dave Finch **Facilities** ⑪
⑩ 📶 ⌷ ⚘ 🏠 ⛐ ✐ **Conf** facs Corporate Hospitality Days
Location 1m NE on B4632
Hotel ★★★ 81% HL George Hotel, St Georges Road, CHELTENHAM ☎ 01242 235751 📄 01242 224359 31 en suite

COALPIT HEATH   Map 3 ST68

The Kendleshire Golf Course Henfield Rd BS36 2TG
☎ 0117 956 7007 📄 0117 957 3433
e-mail: info@kendleshire.com
web: www.kendleshire.com
Opened in 1997, the course has 27 holes with water coming into play on 18 holes. Notable holes are the 11th, the 16th and the 27th. The 11th is a short hole with an island green set in a 3-acre lake and the 16th has a second shot played over water. The course is never short of interest and the greens have been built to USGA specification.
Hollows & Ruffet: 18 Holes, 6567, Par 71, SSS 72, Course record 63.
Badminton & Hollows: 18 Holes, 6249, Par 70.
Ruffet & Badminton: 18 Holes, 6376, Par 69.
Club membership 900.
Visitors Mon-Fri, Sun & BHs. Booking required except Mon-Tue. Dress code. **Societies** booking required. **Green Fees** Mon £25 per round, Tue-Thu £37, Fri-Sun £43 **Course Designer** A Stiff/P McEvoy **Prof** Tony Mealing **Facilities** ⑪ ⑩ ⓘ 📶 ⌷ 🍴 ⚘ 🏠 ⛐
✐ 🛒 ✐ ✦ **Conf** facs Corporate Hospitality Days **Location** M32 junct 1, on Avon Ring Road
Hotel ★★★★ 73% CHH Grange, Northwoods, Winterbourne, BRISTOL ☎ 0844 8159063 📄 01454 777447 68 en suite

CODRINGTON
Map 3 ST78

The Players Golf Club BS37 6RZ
☎ 01454 313029 📄 01454 323446
e-mail: enquiries@theplayersgolfclub.com
web: www.theplayersgolfclub.com

Three courses, two eighteen hole and a par 3 built to the highest specifications. One of the striking features is its maturity with woodland, lakes, trees and gorse coming into play

*Codrington: 18 Holes, 6575yards, Par 72, SSS 73,
Course record 63.*
Stranahan: 18 Holes, 5540yds, Par 68.
Club membership 2000.

Visitors dress code. **Societies** booking required. **Green Fees** not confirmed **Course Designer** Adrian Stiff **Prof** Mark Brookes
Facilities Ⓣ ⍩⃝ ⍳ ⌧ ⍩⃝ ⍾ ⌂ ⌖ ⍾ ⌖
Leisure fishing, 9 hole par 3 course **Conf** facs Corporate Hospitality Days **Location** M4 junct 18, 1m on B4465
Hotel ★★★★ 73% CHH Grange, Northwoods, Winterbourne, BRISTOL ☎ 0844 8159063 📄 01454 777447 68 en suite

COLEFORD
Map 3 SO51

Forest Hills Golf Club Mile End Rd GL16 7QD
☎ 01594 810620 📄 01594 810823
e-mail: enquiries@foresthillsgolfclub.co.uk
web: www.foresthillsgolfclub.co.uk

Parkland on a plateau with panoramic views of Coleford and Forest of Dean. Some testing holes with the par 5 13th hole sitting tight on a water hazard, and the challenging 18th with second shot over large pond to a green protected by another pond and bunker - all in front of the clubhouse.

18 Holes, 6385yds, Par 72, SSS 70. Club membership 470.
Visitors Mon-Sun & BHs. Booking required. Dress code.
Societies booking required. **Green Fees** £22 per 18 holes (£25 weekends). Twilight £15/£20. Winter £15 **Course Designer** A Stiff
Prof Stuart Archibald **Facilities** Ⓣ ⍩⃝ ⍳ ⌧ ⍩⃝ ⍾ ⌂ ⍾
⍾ ⌖ ⍾ **Conf** facs Corporate Hospitality Days **Location**
Hotel ★★★ 79% HL Tudor Farmhouse Hotel & Restaurant, High Street, CLEARWELL ☎ 01594 833046 📄 01594 837093 20 en suite

Forest of Dean Golf Club & Bells Hotel Lords Hill GL16 8BE
☎ 01594 832583 📄 01594 832584
e-mail: enquiries@bells-hotel.co.uk
web: www.bells-hotel.co.uk

Established in 1973 and now matured into an extremely pleasant parkland course. Well bunkered with light rough, a few blind tee shots and water in play on several holes. Easy course to walk.
18 Holes, 5925yds, Par 69. Club membership 375.

Visitors Mon-Sun & BHs. Booking required. Dress code.
Societies booking required. **Green Fees** £15 per 18 holes (£30 weekends) **Course Designer** John Day **Prof** Stuart Jenkins
Facilities Ⓣ ⍩⃝ ⍳ ⌧ ⍩⃝ ⍾ ⌂ ⌖ ◇ ⍾ ⍾ ⌖
Leisure hard tennis courts, bowling green, indoor short mat bowling
Conf facs Corporate Hospitality Days **Location** 0.25m from Coleford town centre on B4431 Coleford-Parkend road
Hotel ★★ 72% HL Bells Hotel & The Forest of Dean Golf Club, Lords Hill, COLEFORD ☎ 01594 832583 📄 01594 832584 53 en suite

See advert on opposite page

DURSLEY
Map 3 ST79

Stinchcombe Hill Golf Club Stinchcombe Hill GL11 6AQ
☎ 01453 542015 📄 01453 549545
web: www.stinchcombehillgolfclub.com

18 Holes, 5734yds, Par 68, SSS 68, Course record 61.
Course Designer Arthur Hoare **Location** 1m W off A4135
Telephone for further details
Hotel ★★★★ 74% HL Tortworth Court Four Pillars, Tortworth, WOTTON-UNDER-EDGE ☎ 0800 374 692 & 01454 263000 📄 01454 263001 190 en suite

GLOUCESTER
Map 3 SO81

Brickhampton Court Golf Complex Cheltenham Rd, Churchdown GL2 9QF
☎ 01452 859444 📄 01452 859333
e-mail: info@brickhampton.co.uk
web: www.brickhampton.co.uk

Rolling parkland featuring lakes, streams and plantations - but no steep hills.

Spa: 18 Holes, 6449yds, Par 71, SSS 71, Course record 64.
Glevum: 9 Holes, 1859yds, Par 31. Club membership 860.
Visitors Mon-Sun & BHs (Sat mornings members only). Booking required. Dress code. **Societies** booking required. **Green Fees** not confirmed **Course Designer** Simon Gidman **Prof** Bruce Wilson
Facilities Ⓣ ⍩⃝ ⍳ ⌧ ⍩⃝ ⍾ ⌂ ⌖ ⍾ ⍾ ⌖ **Conf** facs
Corporate Hospitality Days **Location** M5 junct 11, A40 towards Gloucester, at Elmbridge Court rdbt B4063 signed Churchdown, 2m
Hotel ★★★ 78% HL Hatherley Manor, Down Hatherley Lane, GLOUCESTER ☎ 01452 730217 📄 01452 731032 50 en suite

Ramada Gloucester Golf Club Matson Ln, Robinswood Hill GL4 6EA
☎ 01452 525653 📄 01452 307212
e-mail: golfclub.gloucester@ramadajarvis.co.uk
web: www.gloucestergolf.com

Undulating, wooded course, built around a hill with superb views over Gloucester and the Cotswolds. The 12th is a drive straight up a hill, nicknamed 'Coronary Hill'.

18 Holes, 6444yds, SSS 71, Course record 66.
Club membership 600.

Visitors Mon-Sun & BHs. Booking required. Handicap certificate. Dress code. **Societies** booking required. **Green Fees** not confirmed
Prof Keith Wood **Facilities** Ⓣ ⍩⃝ ⍳ ⌧ ⍩⃝ ⍾ ⌂ ⌖
◇ ⍾ ⍾ ⌖ **Leisure** hard tennis courts, heated indoor swimming pool, squash, sauna, gymnasium, 9 hole par 3 course
Conf facs Corporate Hospitality Days **Location** 2.5m SE of Gloucester, off B4073
Hotel ★★★ 75% HL Hatton Court, Upton Hill, Upton St Leonards, GLOUCESTER ☎ 01452 617412 📄 01452 612945 45 en suite

Bells Hotel
Forest of Dean Golf Club

Lords Hill, Coleford, Gloucestershire GL16 8BE
Tel: 01594 832583   **Fax:** 01594 832584
Website: www.bells-hotel.co.uk   **Email:** enquiries@bells-hotel.co.uk

AA
★★
Hotel

Situated on its own golf course, featuring lakes, streams and woodland, Bells Hotel is the ideal place for your golf break. With 53 en-suite rooms, including two with wheelchair access, the hotel can cater for the individual as well as groups of varying sizes. The Clubhouse offers a warm welcome and friendly atmosphere, where drinks and homemade food are served throughout the day.

Golf Breaks at Bells include games on our golf course which is easily playable yet offers a challenge to the more experienced golfer. There is a practice chipping and putting green and a well stocked golf shop on site.

Our bowling green is available free of charge to Hotel guests. A four mat short mat bowling venue is a new addition to *The Forest of Dean Golf Club.*

In addition to the amenities on site, Bells Hotel is in an ideal location from which to explore the Forest of Dean and The Wye Valley. This area of outstanding natural beauty offers the chance to take part in many activities as well as being a place to relax and enjoy the scenery.

Rodway Hill Golf Course Newent Rd, Highnam GL2 8DN
☎ 01452 384222 📄 01452 313814
e-mail: info@rodway-hill-golf-course.co.uk
web: www.rodway-hill-golf-course.co.uk
A challenging 18-hole course with superb panoramic views. Testing front five holes and the par 5 13th and par 3 16th affected by strong crosswinds off the River Severn.

18 Holes, 6040yds, Par 70, SSS 69, Course record 63.
Club membership 400.

Visitors Mon-Sun & BHs. Dress code. **Societies** welcome. **Green Fees** £15 per 18 holes, £9 per 9 holes (£17-£18/£9-£10 weekends) **Course Designer** John Gabb **Prof** Chris Murphy **Facilities** ⊕ ⊧©⊣ 📧 ⊑ ⊩⊔ ⊼ 📦 ⊶ ⊘ 🚜 ⊘ ⊬ **Conf** facs Corporate Hospitality Days **Location** 2m outside Gloucester on B4215
Hotel ★★★ 78% HL Hatherley Manor, Down Hatherley Lane, GLOUCESTER ☎ 01452 730217 📄 01452 731032 50 en suite

LYDNEY   Map 3 SO60

Lydney Golf Club Lakeside Av GL15 5QA
☎ 01594 841186
web: www.lydneygolfclub.org.uk
Flat parkland and meadowland course with prevailing wind along fairways.

9 Holes, 5298yds, Par 66, SSS 68, Course record 64.
Club membership 190.

Visitors Mon-Sat except BHs. Sun pm. Booking required Thu & weekends. **Societies** booking required. **Green Fees** not confirmed 🖾 **Facilities** ⊕ ⊧©⊣ 📧 ⊑ ⊩⊔ ⊼ **Location** SE side of town centre
Hotel ★★★ 79% HL Tudor Farmhouse Hotel & Restaurant, High Street, CLEARWELL ☎ 01594 833046 📄 01594 837093 20 en suite

MINCHINHAMPTON   Map 3 SO80

Minchinhampton (New Course) New Course GL6 9BE
☎ 01453 833866 📄 01453 837360
e-mail: alan@mgcnew.co.uk
web: www.minchinhamptongolfclub.co.uk
Set high on the Cotswolds, both courses offer scenic countryside and outstanding tests of golf. The Cherington is a testing inland links course and was an Open Qualifying venue from 2002-2007. The Avening is a parkland course offering a different but no less challenging experience.

Avening: 18 Holes, 6308yds, Par 70, SSS 71.
Cherington: 18 Holes, 6459yds, Par 71, SSS 71.
Club membership 1200.

Visitors Mon-Sun & BHs. Booking recommended. Dress code. **Societies** booking required. **Green Fees** £40 per day/round (£50 weekends) **Course Designer** Hawtree & Son **Prof** Chris Steele **Facilities** ⊕ ⊧©⊣ 📧 ⊑ ⊩⊔ ⊼ 📦 ⊶ 🚜 ⊘ ⊬ **Conf** Corporate Hospitality Days **Location** B4014 from Nailsworth into Avening, left at Cross pub towards Minchinhampton, club 0.25m on right
Hotel ★★★ 79% HL Burleigh Court, Burleigh, Minchinhampton, STROUD ☎ 01453 883804 📄 01453 886870 18 en suite

Minchinhampton (Old Course) Old Course GL6 9AQ
☎ 01453 832642 & 836382 📄 01453 832642
e-mail: alan@mgcold.co.uk
web: www.old.minchinhamptongolfclub.co.uk
An open grassland course 600 feet above sea level, best described as an inland links course with no water or sand bunkers. The numerous humps and hollows around the greens test the golfer's ability to play a variety of shots - often in difficult windy conditions. Panoramic Cotswold views. Two of the par 3s, the 8th and the 16th, often require an accurate long iron or wood depending on the strength and direction of the wind.

18 Holes, 6088yds, Par 71, SSS 70. Club membership 550.

Visitors Mon & Sun. Booking required. Dress code.
Societies booking preferable. **Green Fees** £18 per day (£22 weekends and BHs) **Prof** Peter Dangerfield **Facilities** ⊕ ⊧©⊣ 📧 ⊑ ⊩⊔ ⊼ 📦 ⊶ ⊘ **Location** 1m NW
Hotel ★★★ 79% HL Burleigh Court, Burleigh, Minchinhampton, STROUD ☎ 01453 883804 📄 01453 886870 18 en suite

NAUNTON   Map 4 SP12

Naunton Downs Golf Club GL54 3AE
☎ 01451 850090 📄 01451 850091
e-mail: admin@nauntondowns.co.uk
web: www.nauntondowns.co.uk
Naunton Downs course plays over beautiful Cotswold countryside. A valley running through the course is one of the main features, creating one par 3 hole that crosses over it. The prevailing wind adds extra challenge to the par 5s (which play into the wind), combined with small undulating greens.

18 Holes, 6186yds, Par 71, SSS 71. Club membership 750.

Visitors Mon-Fri. Weekends & BHs after 11am. Booking required. Dress code. **Societies** booking required. **Green Fees** Mon £20 per round, Tue-Thu £27 (£30 Fri, weekends and BHs) **Course Designer** J Pott **Prof** Nick Ellis **Facilities** ⊕ ⊧©⊣ 📧 ⊑ ⊩⊔ ⊼ 📦 ⊶ 🚜 ⊘ ⊬ **Leisure** hard tennis courts **Conf** facs Corporate Hospitality Days **Location** off B4068
Hotel ★★★★ CHH Lords of the Manor, UPPER SLAUGHTER ☎ 01451 820243 📄 01451 820696 26 en suite

PAINSWICK   Map 3 SO80

Painswick Golf Club GL6 6TL
☎ 01452 812180
web: www.painswickgolf.com
18 Holes, 4895yds, Par 67, SSS 63, Course record 61.
Location 1m N of Painswick, off A46 to Cheltenham
Telephone for further details
Hotel ★★★ 75% HL Hatton Court, Upton Hill, Upton St Leonards, GLOUCESTER ☎ 01452 617412 📄 01452 612945 45 en suite

ENGLAND

TEWKESBURY   Map 3 SO83

Hilton Puckrup Hall Puckrup GL20 6EL
☎ 01684 271591
web: www.hilton.co.uk/tewkesbury
Set in 140 acres of undulating parkland, Puckrup Hall has fast
matured into one of the county's finest courses. A strong and testing
course that belies its relatively modest yardage, it demands excellent
course management and accurate striking in a lay-out that manages
to entertain golfers of all abilities.
18 Holes, 6219yds, Par 70, SSS 70, Course record 63.
Club membership 380.
Visitors Mon-Sun & BHs. Booking required. Dress code.
Societies booking required. **Green Fees** not confirmed **Course
Designer** Simon Gidman **Prof** Edward Litchfield **Facilities** ⑪ ⑩
🍽 ☐ 🐴 👤 🏠 🏌 ◇ 🏌 🛒 🏌 **Leisure** heated indoor
swimming pool, sauna, gymnasium **Conf facs** Corporate Hospitality
Days **Location** 4m N of Tewkesbury on A38
Hotel ★★★ GA Willow Cottages, Shuthonger Common,
TEWKESBURY ☎ 01684 298599 ▤ 01684 298599 3 rooms

Tewkesbury Park Hotel Golf & Country Club Lincoln
Green Ln GL20 7DN
☎ 01684 295405 ▤ 01684 292386
web: www.brook-hotels.co.uk
18 Holes, 6533yds, Par 73, SSS 71, Course record 66.
Course Designer Frank Pennick **Location** M5 junct 9, take A438 into
town centre, 1st exit at rdbt passing abbey on left, 3rd right into
Lincoln Green Lane
Telephone for further details
Hotel ★★★★ INN The Bell, 52 Church Street, TEWKESBURY
☎ 01684 293293 ▤ 01684 295938 24 rooms

THORNBURY   Map 3 ST69

Thornbury Golf Centre Bristol Rd BS35 3XL
☎ 01454 281144 ▤ 01454 281177
web: www.thornburygc.co.uk
High Course: 18 Holes, 6308yds, Par 71, SSS 69.
Low Course: 18 Holes, 2195yds, Par 54.
Course Designer Hawtree **Location** M5 junct 16, off A38 towards
Gloucester
Telephone for further details
Hotel ★★★ 81% HL Alveston House Hotel, Davids Lane, Alveston,
BRISTOL ☎ 01454 415050 ▤ 01454 415425 30 en suite

WESTONBIRT   Map 3 ST88

Westonbirt Golf Course Westonbirt School GL8 8QG
☎ 01666 881404
e-mail: sportscentre@westonbirtleisure.com
web: www.westonbirtleisure.com
Picturesque and challenging 9 hole course confined within a woodland
environment.
9 Holes, 2202yds, Par 32. Club membership 287.
Visitors may play Mon-Sun & BHs. Dress code. **Societies** booking
required. **Green Fees** £10 per person weekdays (£12.50 per person
weekends & BHs) ⑭ **Facilities** ⑪ ☐ 👤 🏌 **Leisure** hard
tennis courts, heated indoor swimming pool, gymnasium **Conf** facs
Location E side of village off A433
Hotel ★★★★ 78% HL Hare & Hounds, Westonbirt, TETBURY
☎ 01666 880233 & 881000 ▤ 01666 880241 42 en suite

95

WICK Map 3 ST77

Tracy Park Golf & Country Club Tracy Park Estate, Bath Rd BS30 5RN
☎ 0117 937 1800 ▤ 0117 937 1813
e-mail: info@tracypark.co.uk
web: www.tracypark.co.uk

The two 18-hole championship courses set in the 240-acre estate of this golf and country club are on the south-western escarpment of the Cotswolds, affording fine views. Both courses present a challenge to all levels of player, with water playing a part on a number of occasions. The elegant clubhouse dates from 1600.

The Crown Course: 18 Holes, 5082yds, Par 69, SSS 70, Course record 64.
The Cromwell Course: 18 Holes, 5094yds, Par 71, SSS 70, Course record 59. Club membership 350.

Visitors Contact club for details. **Societies** booking required. **Green Fees** £34 weekdays (£40 weekends) **Prof** James Tuck **Facilities** ⓣ ⦿ 🍴 ▤ ♺ 🏌 ⚐ ☇ 🛒 ◇ 🏌 ⚐ ♟ **Conf** facs Corporate Hospitality Days **Location** M4 junct 18, then follow A46 towards Bath followed by A420. Course off A420 E of village of Wick
Hotel ★★★ HL Queensberry, Russel Street, BATH
☎ 01225 447928 ▤ 01225 446065   29 en suite

See advert on page 95

WOTTON-UNDER-EDGE Map 3 ST79

Cotswold Edge Golf Club Upper Rushmire GL12 7PT
☎ 01453 844167 ▤ 01453 845120
e-mail: nnewman@cotswoldedgegolfclub.org.uk
web: www.cotswoldedgegolfclub.org.uk
Meadowland course situated in a quiet Cotswold valley with magnificent views. First half flat and open, second half more varied.
18 Holes, 6170yds, Par 71, SSS 71. Club membership 800.
Visitors booking required. Dress code. **Societies** booking required. **Green Fees** not confirmed **Prof** Rod Hibbitt **Facilities** ⓣ ▤ ♺ 🍴 🏌 ⚐ ☇ 🛒 ⚐ **Location** N of town on B4058 Wotton-Tetbury road
Hotel ★★★★ HL Calcot Manor, Calcot, TETBURY
☎ 01666 890391 ▤ 01666 890394   35 en suite

GREATER LONDON

ADDINGTON Map 5 TQ36

Addington Court Golf Centre Featherbed Ln CR0 9AA
☎ 020 8657 0281 (booking) & 8651 5270 (admin)
▤ 020 8651 0282
e-mail: addington@crown-golf.co.uk
web: www.addingtoncourt-golfclub.co.uk
Challenging, well-drained courses designed by F. Hawtree. Two 18-hole courses and a 9-hole course.
Championship Course: 18 Holes, 5599yds, Par 68, SSS 67, Course record 60.
Falconwood: 18 Holes, 5472yds, Par 68, SSS 67.
9 Holes, 1804yds, Par 31. Club membership 363.
Visitors Mon-Sun & BHs. Dress code. **Societies** booking required. **Green Fees** not confirmed **Course Designer** Hawtree Snr **Prof** Paul Oliver **Facilities** ⓣ ⦿ ▤ ♺ 🍴 🏌 🛒 ⚐ ☇ 🛒 ⚐ **Conf** facs Corporate Hospitality Days **Location** 1m S off A2022
Hotel ★★★ 73% HL South Park Hotel, 3-5 South Park Hill Road, South Croydon, CROYDON ☎ 020 8688 5644 ▤ 020 8760 0861 30 en suite

The Addington Golf Club 205 Shirley Church Rd CR0 5AB
☎ 020 8777 1055 ▤ 020 8777 6661
e-mail: info@addingtongolf.com
web: www.addingtongolf.com

This heather and woodland course is considered to be one of the best laid out courses in Southern England with the world famous 13th, par 3 at 230yds. A good test of golfing ability with no two holes the same.

18 Holes, 6284yds, Par 69, SSS 71.
Visitors Mon-Sun & BHs. Booking required. Dress code **Societies** booking required. **Green Fees** phone **Course Designer** J F Abercromby **Prof** M Churchill **Facilities** ⓣ ⦿ ▤ ♺ 🍴 🏌 🛒 ⚐ ☇ 🛒 ⚐ ♟ **Conf** Corporate Hospitality Days **Location** M25 junct 7, 3m from Croydon
Hotel ★★★ 73% HL South Park Hotel, 3-5 South Park Hill Road, South Croydon, CROYDON ☎ 020 8688 5644 ▤ 020 8760 0861 30 en suite

Save on Hotels. Book at **theAA.com/hotel**

GREATER LONDON

Addington Palace Golf Club Addington Park, Gravel Hill CR0 5BB
☎ 020 8654 3061 🖹 020 8655 3632
e-mail: info@addingtonpalacegolf.co.uk
web: www.addingtonpalacegolf.co.uk
Set in the grounds of Addington Palace, which was once the home of the Archbishops of Canterbury. There are a number of tree-lined fairways and the 17th hole follows one of the original roads into the Palace and has a fine array of horse chestnut trees. The course winds its way through tree-lined fairways for the first nine holes. The second nine holes opens out and needs full concentration to achieve a good score. The 12th hole is one to remember, over a fountain and onto a green bunkered on all sides.
18 Holes, 6404yds, Par 71. Club membership 700.
Visitors Mon-Fri except BHs. Booking required. Dress code.
Societies booking required. **Green Fees** £50 per day, £45 per round
Course Designer J H Taylor **Prof** Roger Williams **Facilities** ⊕
🍴 by prior arrangement 🍺 ⬚ 🏌 ⬚ 🏋 ✦ 🏌 ✦
Leisure snooker **Conf** facs Corporate Hospitality Days **Location** 2m SE of Croydon station on A212
Hotel ★★★ 73% HL South Park Hotel, 3-5 South Park Hill Road, South Croydon, CROYDON ☎ 020 8688 5644 🖹 020 8760 0861 30 en suite

---

BARNEHURST Map 5 TQ57

Barnehurst Golf Course Mayplace Road East DA7 6JU
☎ 01322 523746 🖹 01322 523860
9 Holes, 4796yds, Par 70, SSS 67.
Course Designer James Braid **Location** 0.75m NW of Crayford off A2000
Telephone for further details
Hotel ★★★★ 76% HL Bexleyheath Marriott Hotel, 1 Broadway, BEXLEYHEATH ☎ 020 8298 1000 🖹 020 8298 1234 142 en suite

---

BARNET Map 4 TQ29

Arkley Golf Club Rowley Green Rd EN5 3HL
☎ 020 8449 0394 🖹 020 8440 5214
e-mail: secretary@arkley.demon
web: www.arkleygolfclub.co.uk
Wooded parkland on high ground with fine views.
9 Holes, 6046yds, Par 69, SSS 69. Club membership 400.
Visitors Mon-Sun & BHs. Dress code. **Societies** booking required.
Green Fees £32 per day, £25 per round. £15 twilight after 4pm except Thu **Course Designer** Braid **Prof** Andrew Hurley **Facilities** ⊕
🍴 🍺 ⬚ 🏌 ⬚ 🏋 ✦ **Conf** facs Corporate Hospitality Days
Location off A1 at Arkley sign
Hotel ★★★★ 73% HL Holiday Inn London - Elstree, Barnet Bypass, BOREHAMWOOD ☎ 0871 942 9071 & 020 8214 9988 🖹 020 8207 6817 135 en suite

Old Fold Manor Golf Club Old Fold Ln EN5 4QN
☎ 020 8440 9185 🖹 020 8441 4863
web: www.oldfoldmanor.co.uk
18 Holes, 6447yds, Par 71, SSS 71, Course record 66.
Course Designer H S Colt **Location** off A1000 between Barnet & Potters Bar
Telephone for further details
Hotel ★★★★ 80% HL West Lodge Park, Cockfosters Road, HADLEY WOOD ☎ 020 8216 3900 & 8216 3903 🖹 020 8216 3937 59 en suite

The Shire London St Albans Rd EN5 4RE
☎ 020 8441 7649 🖹 020 8440 2757
e-mail: golf@theshirelondon.com
web: www.theshirelondon.com
A 27-hole golf complex, opened in May 2007 and designed by Seve Ballesteros, his first full golf course in the UK. The 18-hole Seve Masters course is a championship style layout with six par 3s, six par 4s and six par 5s. The 9-hole Seve Challenge course is a mix of par 4s and 3s on a smaller scale, ideal for juniors, beginners and as a warm-up nine. The complex is also home to the Shire Academy incorporating up to date golf teaching facilities and a short game centre of excellence.
Seve Masters: 18 Holes, 7100yds, Par 72, SSS 73, Course record 69.
Seve Challenge: 9 Holes, 3000yds, Par 30.
Club membership 400.
Visitors Mon-Fri. Weekends & BHs pm. Booking required. Dress code. **Societies** booking required. **Green Fees** £55 per 18 holes (£70 weekends) **Course Designer** Severiano Ballesteros **Prof** Cox/Whitelegg/Menai-Davis **Facilities** ⊕ 🍴 🍺 ⬚ 🏌 ⬚ 🏋 🏋 ✦ **Leisure** sauna, gymnasium, The Shire Academy **Conf** facs Corporate Hospitality Days **Location** M25 junct 23 (A1/M25 interchange), take A1081 towards Barnet, Course on right
Hotel ★★★★ 73% HL Holiday Inn London - Elstree, Barnet Bypass, BOREHAMWOOD ☎ 0871 942 9071 & 020 8214 9988 🖹 020 8207 6817 135 en suite

---

BECKENHAM Map 5 TQ36

Langley Park Golf Club Barnfield Wood Rd BR3 6SZ
☎ 020 8658 6849 🖹 020 8658 6310
web: www.langleyparkgolf.co.uk
18 Holes, 6453yds, Par 69, SSS 71, Course record 65.
Course Designer J H Taylor **Location** 0.5 N of Beckenham on B2015
Telephone for further details
Hotel ★★★ 77% HL Best Western Bromley Court, Bromley Hill, BROMLEY ☎ 020 8461 8600 🖹 020 8460 0899 114 en suite

---

BEXLEYHEATH Map 5 TQ47

Bexleyheath Golf Club Mount Rd DA6 8JS
☎ 020 8303 6951
9 Holes, 5162yds, Par 66, SSS 66, Course record 65.
Location 1m SW
Telephone for further details
Hotel ★★★★ 76% HL Bexleyheath Marriott Hotel, 1 Broadway, BEXLEYHEATH ☎ 020 8298 1000 🖹 020 8298 1234 142 en suite

ENGLAND

BIGGIN HILL
Map 5 TQ45

Cherry Lodge Golf Club Jail Ln TN16 3AX
☎ 01959 572250 📠 01959 540672
e-mail: info@cherrylodgegc.co.uk
web: www.cherrylodgegc.co.uk

Undulating parkland 600ft above sea level with panoramic views of the surrounding countryside and fully open all year. An enjoyable test of golf for all standards.

18 Holes, 6593yds, Par 72, SSS 72, Course record 62.
Club membership 1500.

Visitors Mon-Sun & BHs. Phone for availability. Dress code. **Societies** booking required. **Green Fees** not confirmed **Course Designer** John Day **Prof** Craig Sutherland **Facilities** ⚫ 🍴 🛒 🛒 🍸 👤 🏠 🛒 🗡 🐟 **Conf** Corporate Hospitality Days **Location** 1m E of Biggin Hill Airport
Hotel ★★★★ GA Corner Cottage, Toys Hill, WESTERHAM ☎ 01732 750362 📠 01732 750754 1 room

BROMLEY
Map 5 TQ46

Sundridge Park Golf Club Garden Rd BR1 3NE
☎ 020 8460 0278 📠 020 8289 3050
e-mail: info@spgc.co.uk
web: www.spgc.co.uk

The East Course is longer than the West but many think the shorter of the two courses is the more difficult. The East is surrounded by trees while the West is more hilly, with good views. Both are certainly a good test of golf. An Open qualifying course with year round irrigation of fairways.

East Course: 18 Holes, 6494yds, Par 71, SSS 71.
West Course: 18 Holes, 5999yds, Par 69, SSS 69.
Club membership 1200.

Visitors Mon-Wed & Fri except BHs. Booking required. Dress code. **Societies** welcome. **Green Fees** not confirmed **Course Designer** Willie Park **Prof** Stuart Dowsett **Facilities** ⚫ 🍴 🛒 🛒 👤 🏠 🛒 🗡 **Conf** facs Corporate Hospitality Days **Location** N side of town centre off A2212
Hotel ★★★ 77% HL Best Western Bromley Court, Bromley Hill, BROMLEY ☎ 020 8461 8600 📠 020 8460 0899 114 en suite

CARSHALTON
Map 4 TQ26

Oaks Sports Centre Woodmansterne Rd SM5 4AN
☎ 020 8643 8363 📠 020 8661 7880
e-mail: info@theoaksgolf.co.uk
web: www.theoaksgolf.co.uk

Public parkland course with floodlit, covered driving range.

18 Holes, 6026yds, Par 70, SSS 69.
9 Holes, 1497yds, Par 28. Club membership 250.

Visitors Mon-Sun & BHs. Booking required. Dress code. **Societies** booking required. **Green Fees** not confirmed **Prof** Mitchell/Pilkington/Mulcahy **Facilities** ⚫ 🍴 🛒 🛒 🍸 🏠 🛒 🗡 🐟 **Leisure** gymnasium **Conf** facs Corporate Hospitality Days **Location** 0.5m S on B278
Hotel ★★★★ 80% CHH Cannizaro House, West Side, Wimbledon Common, LONDON ☎ 020 8879 1464 📠 020 8879 7338 46 en suite

CHESSINGTON
Map 4 TQ16

Chessington Golf Centre Garrison Ln KT9 2LW
☎ 020 8391 0948 📠 020 8397 2068
e-mail: info@chessingtongolf.co.uk
web: www.chessingtongolf.co.uk

Tree-lined parkland course designed by Patrick Tallack, with panoramic views over the Surrey countryside.

Chessington: 9 Holes, 1741yds, Par 30, SSS 55.
Club membership 90.

Visitors Contact centre for details. **Societies** booking required. **Green Fees** £10 per round (£12.50 weekends and BHs) **Course Designer** Patrick Tallack **Prof** Mark Janes **Facilities** ⚫ 🛒 🛒 🍸 🏠 🛒 🗡 🐟 **Leisure** automated ball teeing facility on driving range **Conf** facs Corporate Hospitality Days **Location** M25 junct 9, 3m N on A243, 0.5m from Chessington World of Adventure
Hotel ★★★★ 71% HL Holiday Inn London-Chessington, Leatherhead Road, CHESSINGTON ☎ 01372 734600 📠 01372 734698 150 en suite

CHISLEHURST
Map 5 TQ47

Chislehurst Golf Club Camden Park Rd BR7 5HJ
☎ 020 8467 2782 📠 020 8295 0874
web: www.chislehurstgolfclub.co.uk

18 Holes, 5120yds, Par 66, SSS 66, Course record 61.

Course Designer Park **Location**
Telephone for further details
Hotel ★★★ 77% HL Best Western Bromley Court, Bromley Hill, BROMLEY ☎ 020 8461 8600 📠 020 8460 0899 114 en suite

COULSDON
Map 4 TQ25

Coulsdon Manor Hotel & Golf Course Coulsdon Court Rd CR5 2LL
☎ 0844 414 6530 📠 0844 414 6529
e-mail: reservations.coulsdon@ohiml.com
web: www.oxfordhotelsandinns.com

Designed by Harry S Colt and set in its own 140 acres of landscaped parkland.

Coulsdon Court: 18 Holes, 6073yds, Par 70, SSS 68, Course record 62. Club membership 150.

Visitors Mon-Sun & BHs. Booking required weekends & BHs. Dress code. **Societies** booking required. **Green Fees** £23 per round (£29.50 weekends and BHs) **Course Designer** Harry Colt **Prof** Matt Asbury **Facilities** ⚫ 🍴 🛒 🛒 🍸 👤 🏠 🛒 🗡 🐟 **Leisure** hard tennis courts, squash, sauna, gymnasium **Conf** facs Corporate Hospitality Days **Location** 0.75m E off A23 on B2030
Hotel ★★★★ 70% HL Coulsdon Manor, Coulsdon Court Road, Coulsdon, CROYDON ☎ 020 8668 0414 📠 020 8668 3118 37 en suite

Save on Hotels. Book at **theAA.com/hotel**

GREATER LONDON

ENGLAND

Woodcote Park Golf Club Meadow Hill, Bridle Way CR5 2QQ

☎ 020 8668 2788 📠 020 8660 0918

e-mail: info@woodcotepgc.com

web: www.woodcotepgc.com

Slightly undulating parkland.

18 Holes, 6720yds, Par 71, SSS 73, Course record 67. Club membership 700.

Visitors Mon-Fri except BHs. Booking required. Handicap certificate. Dress code. **Societies** booking required. **Green Fees** £50 per day/ round **Course Designer** H S Colt **Prof** Wraith Grant **Facilities** ⊕ 🍴 🛥 ⬛ 🏌 ⚲ 🖬 🏐 🏌 ⚿ 🏳 **Conf** facs Corporate Hospitality Days **Location** 1m N of town centre off A237

Hotel ★★★★ 70% HL Coulsdon Manor, Coulsdon Court Road, Coulsdon, CROYDON ☎ 020 8668 0414 📄 020 8668 3118 37 en suite

CROYDON   Map 4 TQ36

Croham Hurst Golf Club Croham Rd CR2 7HJ

☎ 020 8657 5581 📠 020 8657 3229

e-mail: secretary@chgc.co.uk

web: www.chgc.co.uk

Easy walking parkland with tree-lined fairways and bounded by wooded hills. Very dry course with play available all year long.

18 Holes, 6305yds, Par 70, SSS 70, Course record 62. Club membership 800.

Visitors Mon-Sun & BHs. Booking required. Dress code. **Societies** booking required. **Green Fees** £50 per day, £40 per 18 holes after noon (£55 per 18 holes after noon weekends) **Course Designer** Hawtree/Braid **Prof** David Green **Facilities** ⊕ 🍴 🛥 ⬛ 🏌 ⚲ 🖬 🏐 🏌 ⚿ 🏳 **Conf** facs Corporate Hospitality Days **Location** 1.5m SE of Croydon on B269

Hotel ★★★ 73% HL South Park Hotel, 3-5 South Park Hill Road, South Croydon, CROYDON ☎ 020 8688 5644 📄 020 8760 0861 30 en suite

Selsdon Park Hotel & Golf Club, Addington Rd, Sanderstead CR2 8YA

☎ 020 8768 3113 📠 020 657 3401

e-mail: caroline.screene@principal-hayley.com

web: www.principal-hayley.com

Parkland course in 250 acres of rolling woodland only 12 miles from the centre of London.

18 Holes, 6473yds, Par 73, SSS 71.

Visitors Mon-Sun & BHs. Dress code. **Societies** booking required. **Green Fees** £25 (£35 weekends & BHs) **Course Designer** J H Taylor **Prof** Stewart Corstorphine **Facilities** ⊕ 🍴 🛥 ⬛ 🏌 ⚲ 🖬 🏐 ⚿ 🏳 **Leisure** hard and grass tennis courts, outdoor and indoor heated swimming pool, squash, sauna, gymnasium **Conf** facs Corporate Hospitality Days **Location** 3m S on A2022

Hotel ★★★★ 70% HL Selsdon Park Hotel & Golf Club, Addington Road, Sanderstead, CROYDON ☎ 020 8657 8811 📄 020 8651 6171 199 en suite

Shirley Park Golf Club 194 Addiscombe Rd CR0 7LB

☎ 020 8654 1143 📠 020 8654 6733

e-mail: secretary@shirleyparkgolfclub.co.uk

web: www.shirleyparkgolfclub.co.uk

The parkland course lies amid fine woodland with good views of Shirley Hills. The more testing holes come in the middle section of the course. The remarkable 7th hole calls for a 187yd iron or wood shot diagonally across a narrow valley to a shelved green set right-handed into a ridge. The 13th hole, 160yds, is considered to be one of the finest short holes in the county.

18 Holes, 6180yds, Par 71, SSS 69. Club membership 600.

Visitors Mon-Fri, Sun & BHs. Booking required Sun. Dress code. **Societies** booking required. **Green Fees** £35 per 18 holes **Course Designer** Tom Simpson/Herbert Fowler **Prof** Michael Taylor **Facilities** ⊕ 🍴 🛥 ⬛ 🏌 ⚲ 🖬 🏐 🏌 ⚿ **Leisure** snooker, indoor tuition centre **Conf** facs Corporate Hospitality Days **Location** E of town centre on A232

Hotel ★★★ 73% HL South Park Hotel, 3-5 South Park Hill Road, South Croydon, CROYDON ☎ 020 8688 5644 📄 020 8760 0861 30 en suite

DOWNE   Map 5 TQ46

West Kent Golf Club Milking Ln BR6 7LD

☎ 01689 851323 📠 01689 858693

e-mail: golf@wkgc.co.uk

web: www.wkgc.co.uk

Undulating woodland course close to south London but providing a quiet rural setting in three valleys.

18 Holes, 6417yds, Par 71, SSS 71, Course record 63. Club membership 700.

Visitors Mon-Fri except BHs. Booking required. Handicap certificate. Dress code. **Societies** booking required. **Green Fees** £60 per day, £45 per round **Course Designer** H S Colt **Prof** Chris Forsyth **Facilities** ⊕ 🍴 🛥 ⬛ 🏌 ⚲ 🖬 🏐 🏌 ⚿ 🏳 **Conf** Corporate Hospitality Days **Location** M25 junct 4, A21 towards Bromley, left signed Downe, through village on Luxted road 0.5m, West Hill on right

Hotel ★★★ 77% HL Best Western Bromley Court, Bromley Hill, BROMLEY ☎ 020 8461 8600 📄 020 8460 0899 114 en suite

ENFIELD   Map 4 TQ39

Crews Hill Golf Club Cattlegate Rd, Crews Hill EN2 8AZ

☎ 020 8363 6674

e-mail: info@crewshillgolfclub.com

web: www.crewshillgolfclub.com

A beautiful parkland course designed by Harry Colt and a good test of golf for all levels.

18 Holes, 6281yds, Par 70, SSS 70. Club membership 600.

Visitors Mon-Fri except BHs. Booking required. Dress code. **Societies** booking required. **Green Fees** phone **Course Designer** Harry Colt **Prof** Carl Parker **Facilities** ⊕ 🍴 by prior arrangement 🛥 ⬛ 🏌 ⚲ 🖬 🏐 ⚿ **Conf** facs Corporate Hospitality Days **Location** M25 junct 24, A1005 for Enfield, signed Crews Hill

Hotel ★★★★ 75% HL Royal Chace, The Ridgeway, ENFIELD ☎ 020 8884 8181 📄 020 8884 8150 92 en suite

Enfield Golf Club Old Park Road South EN2 7DA
☎ 020 8363 3970 🖹 020 8342 0381
e-mail: secretary@enfieldgolfclub.co.uk
web: www.enfieldgolfclub.co.uk

Parkland with tree-lined fairways and a meandering brook that comes into play on nine holes. There are no hidden or unfair hazards and, although not easy, the course is highly playable and always attractive.

18 Holes, 6154yds, Par 72, SSS 70, Course record 61. Club membership 600.

Visitors Mon-Sun & BHs. Booking required. Dress code.
Societies booking required. **Green Fees** Mon £20, Tue-Fri £28, weekends & BHs £36 **Course Designer** James Braid **Prof** Martin Porter **Facilities** ⊕ ✝◎✝ ⑂ ⌷ ☢◎ ⚲ 🖻 ✔ 🛒 ✔ **Conf** facs Corporate Hospitality Days **Location** M25 junct 24, A1005 to Enfield to rdbt with church on left, right down Slades Hill, 1st left to end
Hotel ★★★★ 75% HL Royal Chace, The Ridgeway, ENFIELD ☎ 020 8884 8181 🖹 020 8884 8150 92 en suite

Whitewebbs Park Golf Course Whitewebbs Ln EN2 9HH
☎ 020 8363 4454 🖹 020 8366 2257
web: www.enfield.gov.uk

This challenging parkland course was first opened for play in 1932 and is set in over 140 acres of attractive rolling countryside with mature woodland and the meandering Cuffley brook that comes into play on four holes.

18 Holes, 5822yds, Par 68, SSS 67, Course record 59. Club membership 350.

Visitors Dress code. **Societies** welcome. **Green Fees** £26 per day, £15 per round (£31/£19 weekends) **Prof** Gary Sherriff **Facilities** ⊕ ✝◎✝ ⑂ ⌷ ☢◎ ⚲ ✔ **Conf** Corporate Hospitality Days **Location** 5 mins from M25 junct 25, N of town centre
Hotel ★★★★ 75% HL Royal Chace, The Ridgeway, ENFIELD ☎ 020 8884 8181 🖹 020 8884 8150 92 en suite

GREENFORD   Map 4 TQ18

C & L Golf & Country Club Westend Rd UB5 6RD
☎ 020 8845 5662 🖹 020 8841 5515

18 Holes, 4458yds, Par 67, SSS 62, Course record 58.
Course Designer Patrick Tallack **Location** junct Westend Rd
Telephone for further details
Hotel ★★★ 78% HL Barn Hotel, West End Road, RUISLIP ☎ 01895 636057 🖹 01895 638379 73 en suite

Ealing Golf Club Perivale Ln UB6 8SS
☎ 020 8997 0937 🖹 020 8998 0756
web: www.ealinggolfclub.com

18 Holes, 6191yds, Par 70, SSS 70, Course record 62.
Course Designer H S Colt **Location** exit at the Perivale turn-off on the A40
Telephone for further details
Hotel ★★★★ 77% HL Crowne Plaza London-Ealing, Western Avenue, Hanger Lane, Ealing, LONDON ☎ 0871 942 9114 & 020 8233 3200 🖹 020 8233 3201 131 en suite

Horsenden Hill Golf Club Woodland Rise UB6 0RD
☎ 020 8902 4555 🖹 020 8902 4555

9 Holes, 1632yds, Par 28, SSS 28.

Location 3m NE on A4090
Telephone for further details
Hotel ★★★ 71% HL Quality Hotel Wembley, Empire Way, WEMBLEY ☎ 020 8733 9000 🖹 020 8733 9001 165 en suite

Perivale Park Golf Course Stockdove Way UB6 8TJ
☎ 020 8575 7116

Parkland beside the River Brent.

9 Holes, 2620yds, Par 68, SSS 67. Club membership 100.
Visitors Mon-Sun & BHs. Booking required weekends am.
Societies booking required. **Green Fees** £9 per 9 holes (£10 weekends & BHs) **Prof** Peter Bryant/Craig Hawkes **Facilities** ⊕ ⑂ ⌷ ⚲ 🖻 ⊣ ✔ **Location** E side of town centre, off A40
Hotel ★★★ 72% MET Best Western Cumberland Hotel, 1 St Johns Road, HARROW ☎ 020 8863 4111 🖹 020 8861 5668 84 en suite

HADLEY WOOD   Map 4 TQ29

Hadley Wood Golf Club Beech Hill EN4 0JJ
☎ 020 8449 4328 & 8449 4486   🖹 020 8364 8633
e-mail: gm@hadleywoodgc.com
web: www.hadleywoodgc.com

Parkland on the north-west edge of London. The gently undulating fairways have a friendly width inviting the player to open the shoulders, though the thick rough can be very punishing to the unwary. The course is pleasantly wooded and there are some admirable views.

18 Holes, 6514yds, Par 72, SSS 71, Course record 67. Club membership 650.

Visitors dress code. **Societies** booking required. **Green Fees** not confirmed **Course Designer** Alister MacKenzie **Prof** Peter Jones **Facilities** ⊕ ✝◎✝ ⑂ ⌷ ☢◎ ⚲ 🖻 ⊣ ✔ 🛒 ✔ **Conf** facs Corporate Hospitality Days **Location** M25 junct 24, take A111 to Cockforsters, 2m to 3rd turning right
Hotel ★★★★ 80% HL West Lodge Park, Cockfosters Road, HADLEY WOOD ☎ 020 8216 3900 & 8216 3903 🖹 020 8216 3937 59 en suite

HAMPTON   Map 4 TQ17

Fulwell Golf Club Wellington Rd TW12 1JY
☎ 020 8977 3844 🖹 020 8977 7732
web: www.fulwellgolfclub.co.uk

18 Holes, 6544yds, Par 71, SSS 71.
Course Designer John Morrison **Location** off M3/M25 junct, 1.5m N on A311
Telephone for further details
Hotel ★★★★ 79% HL London Marriott Hotel Twickenham, 198 Whitton Road, TWICKENHAM ☎ 020 8891 8200 🖹 020 8891 8201 156 en suite

HAMPTON WICK   Map 4 TQ16

Hampton Court Palace Golf Club Home Park KT1 4AD
☎ 020 8977 2423 📄 020 8614 4747
e-mail: hamptoncourtpalace@crown-golf.co.uk
web: www.hamptoncourtgolf.co.uk

Flat course with easy walking situated in the grounds of Hampton
Court Palace. Unique blend of parkland and inland links built on a
base of sand and gravel, making it one of the finest winter courses in
the country.

18 Holes, 6514yds, Par 71, SSS 71, Course record 64.
Club membership 750.

Visitors Mon-Sun & BHs. Booking required. **Societies** booking
required. **Green Fees** Mon-Thu £42 per 18 holes, £46 Fri, £46
weekends after noon. £29 twilight Mon-Thu, £31.50 Fri-Sun **Course
Designer** James Braid/Willie Park **Prof** Karl Wesson **Facilities** ⊕
†⊙¹ ㋫ ☐ ㋡ ㋐ ㋓ ㋕ 🚗 ㋑ ㋐ **Conf** facs Corporate
Hospitality Days **Location** Off A308 on W side of Kingston Bridge
Hotel ★★★★ 75% HL Holiday Inn London - Kingston South,
Kingston Tower, Portsmouth Road, SURBITON ☎ 020 8786 6565 &
8786 6500 📄 020 8786 6575   116 en suite

HARROW   Map 4 TQ18

Playgolf Northwick Park Watford Rd HA1 3TZ
☎ 020 8864 2020 📄 020 8864 4040
web: www.northwickpark.com

Majors Course: 9 Holes, 1804yds, Par 29, SSS 29.

Course Designer Peter McEvoy **Location** SE of Harrow on A404
Watford road. Follow directions to Northwick Park Hospital, course
adjacent
Telephone for further details
Hotel ★★★ 72% MET Best Western Cumberland Hotel, 1 St Johns
Road, HARROW ☎ 020 8863 4111 📄 020 8861 5668   84 en suite

HOUNSLOW   Map 4 TQ17

Airlinks Golf Club Southall Ln TW5 9PE
☎ 020 8561 1418 📄 020 8813 6284

Meadowland and parkland with four water holes.

18 Holes, 5813yds, Par 71, SSS 68, Course record 65.
Club membership 200.

Visitors Mon-Sun & BHs. Dress code. **Societies** booking required.
Green Fees not confirmed **Course Designer** P Alliss/D Thomas
Prof Adam Stacey **Facilities** ⊕ †⊙¹ ㋫ ☐ ㋡ ㋐ ㋑ ㋐ ㋓
㋕ **Conf** facs Corporate Hospitality Days **Location** M4 junct 3, W of
Hounslow
Hotel ★★★★ 73% HL Ramada London Heathrow, Bath Road,
Cranford, HOUNSLOW ☎ 0844 815 9041 📄 020 8897 7014
200 en suite

ILFORD   Map 5 TQ48

Ilford Golf Club Wanstead Park Rd IG1 3TR
☎ 020 8554 2930 📄 020 8554 0822
e-mail: info@ilfordgolfclub.com
web: www.ilfordgolfclub.com

Fairly flat parkland on the River Roding. The river borders four holes,
and is crossed by three holes. While not a particularly long course,
the small greens, and many holes requiring brains rather than brawn,
provide a challenging test to all.

*Ilford Golf Club: 18 Holes, 5299yds, Par 67, SSS 66,
Course record 61. Club membership 500.*

Visitors Mon-Sun & BHs. Booking required. Dress code.
Societies booking required. **Green Fees** £15 (£20 weekends) **Course
Designer** Whitehead **Prof** G Cant **Facilities** ⊕ †⊙¹ ㋫ ☐ ㋡
㋐ ㋑ ㋓ **Conf** facs Corporate Hospitality Days **Location** NW of
town centre off A12
Hotel ★★★★ 72% HL Menzies Prince Regent, Manor Road,
WOODFORD BRIDGE ☎ 020 8505 9966 📄 020 8506 0807   61 en suite

ISLEWORTH   Map 4 TQ17

Wyke Green Golf Club Syon Ln TW7 5PT
☎ 020 8847 0685 (Pro) & 8560 8777 (Sec)
📄 020 8569 8392
web: www.wykegreengolfclub.co.uk

18 Holes, 6182yds, Par 69, SSS 70, Course record 64.

Course Designer Hawtree **Location** 0.5m N on B454, off A4 at Gillette
Corner
Telephone for further details
Hotel ★★★★ 74% HL The Continental Hotel, 29-31 Lampton
Road, HOUNSLOW ☎ 020 8572 3131 📄 020 8572 3334   71 en suite

KINGSTON UPON THAMES   Map 4 TQ16

Coombe Hill Golf Club Golf Club Dr, Coombe Lane West
KT2 7DF
☎ 020 8336 7600 📄 020 8336 7601
e-mail: office@chgc.net
web: www.coombehillgolfclub.com

Charming heathland course featuring a fine display of
rhododendrons during May and June. The course presents a
challenge to golfers of all standards offering superb greens, quality
short holes and a number of testing long holes requiring approach
shots to elevated greens.

18 Holes, 6028yds, Par 71, SSS 71, Course record 67.
Club membership 520.

Visitors Mon, Tue, Thu & Fri. Other days pm only. Booking required.
Handicap certificate. Dress code. **Societies** booking required. **Green
Fees** not confirmed **Course Designer** J F Abercromby **Prof** Mark
Lawrence **Facilities** ⊕ ㋫ ☐ ㋡ ㋐ ㋑ ㋐ ㋓ ㋕
Leisure sauna, halfway house **Conf** facs Corporate Hospitality Days
Location 1.75m E on A238
Hotel ★★★★ 80% CHH Cannizaro House, West Side,
Wimbledon Common, LONDON ☎ 020 8879 1464 📄 020 8879 7338
46 en suite

ENGLAND

Coombe Wood Golf Club George Rd, Kingston Hill
KT2 7NS
☎ 020 8942 0388 📄 020 8942 5665
e-mail: geoff.seed@coombewoodgolf.com
web: www.coombewoodgolf.com

Mature parkland featuring challenging par 3s complemented by
tree-lined par 4s with blind tee shots and green heavily protected
by bunkers. Despite not being considered long by today's standards,
these features make it a tract to be reckoned with.

18 Holes, 5111yds, Par 66. Club membership 700.
Visitors Mon, Wed & Thu. Tue pm only. Other times by arrangement.
Dress code. Societies welcome. **Green Fees** not confirmed **Course
Designer** Tom Williamson **Prof** Phil Wright **Facilities** ⑪ ⑧ ⓛ
⚑ ⑪ ⚐ 🍴 ⚑ ⚘ **Conf** facs Corporate Hospitality Days
Location 1.25m NE on A308
Hotel ★★★★ 80% CHH Cannizaro House, West Side, Wimbledon
Common, LONDON ☎ 020 8879 1464 📄 020 8879 7338 46 en suite

MITCHAM   Map 4 TQ26

Mitcham Golf Club Carshalton Rd, Mitcham Junction
CR4 4HN
☎ 020 8640 4280 📄 020 8647 4197
e-mail: mitchamgc@hotmail.co.uk
web: www.mitchamgolfclub.co.uk
A wooded heathland course on a gravel base, playing as an inland
links course.

*18 Holes, 6022yds, Par 69, SSS 69, Course record 63.
Club membership 500.*
Visitors Mon-Sun & BHs. Booking required. **Dress code.
Societies** booking required. **Green Fees** £20 per 18 holes (£27
weekends & BHs) **Course Designer** T Scott/T Morris **Prof** Paul Burton
Facilities ⑪ ⑧ ⓛ ⚑ ⑪ ⚐ 🍴 ⚐ ⚘ **Conf** Corporate
Hospitality Days **Location** adjacent Mitcham Junction railway station
Hotel ★★★ 79% HL Holiday Inn London-Sutton, Gibson Road,
SUTTON ☎ 020 8234 1100 & 8234 1104 📄 020 8770 1539
119 en suite

NEW MALDEN   Map 4 TQ26

Malden Golf Club Traps Ln KT3 4RS
☎ 020 8942 0654 📄 020 8336 2219
web: www.maldengolfclub.com
18 Holes, 6252yds, Par 71, SSS 70.
Location N of town centre off B283
Telephone for further details
Hotel ★★★★ 80% CHH Cannizaro House, West Side, Wimbledon
Common, LONDON ☎ 020 8879 1464 📄 020 8879 7338 46 en suite

NORTHWOOD   Map 4 TQ09

Haste Hill Golf Club The Drive HA6 1HN
☎ 01923 825224
18 Holes, 5787yds, Par 68, SSS 68, Course record 63.
Location 0.5m S off A404
Telephone for further details
Hotel ★★★ 82% HL Grim's Dyke Hotel, Old Redding, HARROW
WEALD ☎ 020 8385 3100 & 020 8954 4227 📄 020 8954 4560
46 en suite

Northwood Golf Club Rickmansworth Rd HA6 2QW
☎ 01923 821384 📄 01923 840150
web: www.northwoodgolf.co.uk
18 Holes, 6514yds, Par 71, SSS 71, Course record 67.
Course Designer James Braid **Location** on A404
Telephone for further details
Hotel ★★★ 82% HL Grim's Dyke Hotel, Old Redding, HARROW
WEALD ☎ 020 8385 3100 & 020 8954 4227 📄 020 8954 4560
46 en suite

Sandy Lodge Golf Club Sandy Lodge Ln HA6 2JD
☎ 01923 825429 📄 01923 824319
e-mail: info@sandylodge.co.uk
web: www.sandylodge.co.uk
A links-type, very sandy, heathland course. Excellent drainage
giving good all year playing conditions.

*18 Holes, 6466yds, Par 70, SSS 71, Course record 64.
Club membership 780.*
Visitors Mon-Fri except BHs. Booking required. Handicap certificate.
Dress code. Societies booking required. **Green Fees** £50 per round
Course Designer H Vardon **Prof** Jeff Pinsent **Facilities** ⑪ ⑧ ⓛ
⚑ ⑪ ⚐ ⚘ 🍴 ⚘ ⚑ **Conf** facs Corporate Hospitality
Days **Location** N of town centre off A4125
Hotel ★★★ 73% HL Best Western White House, Upton Road,
WATFORD ☎ 01923 237316 📄 01923 233109 57 en suite

ORPINGTON   Map 5 TQ46

Chelsfield Lakes Golf Centre Court Rd BR6 9BX
☎ 01689 896266 📄 01689 824577
web: www.chelsfieldlakesgolf.co.uk
18 Holes, 6077yds, Par 71, SSS 69, Course record 64.
Course Designer M Sandow **Location** M25 junct 4, on A224
Telephone for further details
Hotel ★★★ 77% HL Best Western Bromley Court, Bromley Hill,
BROMLEY ☎ 020 8461 8600 📄 020 8460 0899 114 en suite

Orpington Golf Centre Sandy Ln BR5 3HY
☎ 01689 839677 📄 01689 891428
web: www.orpingtongolf.co.uk
*Cray Valley 18: 18 Holes, 5669yds, Par 70, SSS 67.
Ruxley Park: 18 Holes, 5703yds, Par 70, SSS 68,
Course record 63.
Cray Valley 9: 9 Holes, 2140yds, Par 32.*
Location 1m off A20, Crittals Corner junction
Telephone for further details
Hotel ★★★ 77% HL Best Western Bromley Court, Bromley Hill,
BROMLEY ☎ 020 8461 8600 📄 020 8460 0899 114 en suite

PINNER   Map 4 TQ18

Grims Dyke Golf Club Oxhey Ln, Hatch End HA5 4AL
☎ 020 8428 4539 📄 020 8421 5494
e-mail: info@grimsdyke.co.uk
web: www.club-noticeboard.co.uk/grimsdyke
Pleasant, undulating parkland.

18 Holes, 5647yds, Par 69, SSS 67, Course record 63.
Club membership 440.

Visitors dress code. **Societies** booking required. **Green Fees** £36 per round (£40 weekends) **Course Designer** James Baird **Prof** Lee Curling **Facilities** ⊕ 🏌 ⊑ 🍴 人 🏠 ✆ 🛒 ✆ **Conf** facs Corporate Hospitality Days **Location** 3m N of Harrow on A4008
Hotel ★★★ 72% MET Best Western Cumberland Hotel, 1 St Johns Road, HARROW ☎ 020 8863 4111 📄 020 8861 5668   84 en suite

Pinner Hill Golf Club Southview Rd, Pinner Hill HA5 3YA
☎ 020 8866 0963 📄 020 8868 4817
e-mail: phgc@pinnerhillgc.com
web: www.pinnerhillgc.com
On the top of Pinner Hill surrounded by rolling parkland and mature woods, this peaceful atmosphere will make you feel a million miles from North West London's suburbia. Two nine-hole loops of mature fairways and undulating greens will lift and challenge your game.

18 Holes, 6393yds, Par 71, SSS 71. Club membership 611.

Visitors Mon-Sun except BHs. Booking required Mon, Tue, Fri-Sun. Handicap certificate. Dress code. **Societies** booking required. **Green Fees** £42 per day (£47 weekends). Wed & Thu £19.50 per round. **Course Designer** J H Taylor **Prof** Greg Smith **Facilities** ⊕ 🍴 🏌 ⊑ 🍴 人 🏠 ✆ **Leisure** snooker room **Conf** facs **Location** 2m NW off A404
Hotel ★★★ 82% HL Grim's Dyke Hotel, Old Redding, HARROW WEALD ☎ 020 8385 3100 & 020 8954 4227 📄 020 8954 4560 46 en suite

PURLEY   Map 5 TQ36

Purley Downs Golf Club 106 Purley Downs Rd CR2 0RB
☎ 020 8657 8347 📄 020 8651 5044
e-mail: info@purleydowns.co.uk
web: www.purleydownsgolfclub.co.uk
Hilly downland course which is a good test for golfers and is in play all year round.

18 Holes, 6077yds, Par 70, SSS 69, Course record 64.
Club membership 750.

Visitors Mon-Fri except BHs. Dress code. **Societies** welcome. **Green Fees** phone **Course Designer** J Taylor/H S Colt **Prof** Scott Graham **Facilities** ⊕ 🍴 🏌 ⊑ 🍴 人 🏠 🛒 ✆ **Conf** facs
Location E of town centre off A235
Hotel ★★★ 73% HL South Park Hotel, 3-5 South Park Hill Road, South Croydon, CROYDON ☎ 020 8688 5644 📄 020 8760 0861 30 en suite

RICHMOND (UPON THAMES)   Map 4 TQ17

The Richmond Golf Club Sudbrook Park TW10 7AS
☎ 020 8940 4351 (office) & 8940 7792 (shop)
📄 020 8940 8332/7914
web: www.the richmondgolfclub.com

18 Holes, 6100yds, Par 70, SSS 70, Course record 65.
Course Designer Tom Dunn **Location** 1.5m S off A307 between Kingston & Richmond
Telephone for further details
Hotel ★★★★ 74% HL The Richmond Gate Hotel, 152-158 Richmond Hill, RICHMOND-UPON-THAMES ☎ 0845 906 9966 📄 020 8332 0354   68 en suite

Royal Mid-Surrey Golf Club Old Deer Park, Twickenham Rd TW9 2SB
☎ 020 8940 1894 📄 020 8939 0150
e-mail: secretary@rmsgc.co.uk
web: www.rmsgc.co.uk
A long playing historic parkland course. The flat fairways are cleverly bunkered. The first hole at 245yds from the medal tees is a tough par 3 opening hole. The 18th provides an exceptionally good par 4 finish with a huge bunker before the green to catch the not quite perfect long second. The Pam Barton Course, while shorter than the J H Taylor, offers a fair challenge to all golfers. Again the 18th offers a strong par 4 finish with bunkers threatening from the tee. A long second to a sloping, well-bunkered green will reward the accurate player.

J H Taylor Course: 18 Holes, 6402yds, Par 69, SSS 71.
Pam Barton Course: 18 Holes, 5544yds, Par 68, SSS 67.
Club membership 1250.

Visitors Mon-Fri except BHs. Handicap certificate. Dress code. **Societies** booking required. **Green Fees** J H Taylor Course £75, Pam Barton Course £65 **Course Designer** J H Taylor **Prof** Matthew Paget **Facilities** ⊕ 🏌 ⊑ 🍴 人 🏠 🍴 ✆ 🛒 ✆ 🏴 **Leisure** snooker **Conf** facs Corporate Hospitality Days **Location** 0.5m N of Richmond off A316
Hotel ★★★ 81% TH Bingham, 61-63 Petersham Road, RICHMOND UPON THAMES ☎ 020 8940 0902 📄 020 8948 8737 15 en suite

ROMFORD   Map 5 TQ58

Maylands Golf Club Colchester Rd, Harold Park RM3 0AZ
☎ 01708 341777 📄 01708 343777
e-mail: maylands@maylandsgolf.com
web: www.maylandsgolf.com
Picturesque undulating parkland course.

18 Holes, 6361yds, Par 71, SSS 70, Course record 62.
Club membership 550.

Visitors Mon-Sun & BHs. Booking required. Dress code. **Societies** booking required. **Green Fees** from £25 per round **Course Designer** H S Colt **Prof** Darren Parker **Facilities** ⊕ 🍴 🏌 ⊑ 🍴 人 🏠 ✆ 🛒 ✆ 🏴 **Conf** Corporate Hospitality Days **Location** M25 junct 28, A12, 0.5m towards London, club on right
Hotel ★★★★ 75% HL Marygreen Manor, London Road, BRENTWOOD ☎ 01277 225252 📄 01277 262809   44 en suite

Risebridge Golf Centre Risebridge Chase, Lower Bedfords Rd RM1 4DG
☎ 01708 741429 📄 01708 741429
e-mail: risebridge@btconnect.com
web: www.jackbarker.com

A well matured parkland golf course, with many challenging holes especially the long 12th, the par 4 13th and par 5 14th with water and a two tiered green.

18 Holes, 5900yds, Par 71, SSS 70, Course record 66. Club membership 300.

Visitors Mon-Sun & BHs. **Societies** welcome. **Green Fees** not confirmed **Course Designer** Hawtree **Prof** Paul Jennings
Facilities ⑪ ⑩ 🏌 ⬚ 🍴 🏌 ⬚ 🏌 Conf facs
Location between Collier Row and Harold Hill
Hotel ★★★ 80% HL Holiday Inn Brentwood, Brook Street, BRENTWOOD ☎ 0871 942 9012 📄 01277 264264 149 en suite

---

Romford Golf Club Heath Dr, Gidea Park RM2 5QB
☎ 01708 740986 📄 01708 752157
e-mail: info@romfordgolfclub.co.uk
web: www.romfordgolfclub.co.uk

A many-bunkered parkland course with easy walking. It is said there are as many bunkers as there are days in the year. The ground is quick drying making a good course for winter play when other courses might be too wet.

18 Holes, 6408yds, Par 71, SSS 71, Course record 64. Club membership 650.

Visitors Mon, Tue, Thu & Fri except BHs. Booking required. Dress code. **Societies** booking required. **Green Fees** £45 per 36 holes, £35 per 18 holes **Course Designer** H Colt/J Braid **Prof** Chris Goddard
Facilities ⑪ ⑩ 🏌 ⬚ 🍴 ⬚ 🏌 **Location** 1m NE on A118
Hotel ★★★ 80% HL Holiday Inn Brentwood, Brook Street, BRENTWOOD ☎ 0871 942 9012 📄 01277 264264 149 en suite

---

RUISLIP   Map 4 TQ08

Ruislip Golf Club Ickenham Rd HA4 7DQ
☎ 01895 638835 & 623980 📄 01895 635780
e-mail: ruislipgolf@ymail.com
web: www.mackgolf.co.uk

Municipal parkland course. Flat with easy walking. Greens are fairly small placing a premium on accuracy.

18 Holes, 5571yds, Par 69, SSS 67. Club membership 300.

Visitors Mon-Sun & BHs. **Societies** booking required. **Green Fees** £17 (£23 weekends & BHs) **Course Designer** Sand Herd **Prof** Paul Glozier
Facilities ⑪ ⑩ 🏌 ⬚ 🍴 ⬚ 🏌 🏌
Conf facs **Location** from A40, 0.5m SW on B466 opposite West Ruislip underground station
Hotel ★★★ 78% HL Barn Hotel, West End Road, RUISLIP ☎ 01895 636057 📄 01895 638379 73 en suite

---

SIDCUP   Map 5 TQ47

Sidcup Golf Club Rear of Hurstmere School, Hurst Rd DA15 9AW
☎ 020 8300 2150 📄 020 8300 2150
e-mail: sidcupgolfclub@googlemail.com
web: www.sidcupgolfclub.co.uk

Challenging but easy walking parkland with two lakes and the River Shuttle running through. Water hazards on six of the 9 holes.

9 Holes, 5571yds, Par 68, SSS 68. Club membership 330.

Visitors Mon-Fri except BHs. Booking required. Handicap certificate. Dress code. **Green Fees** not confirmed **Course Designer** James Braid
Facilities ⑪ 🏌 ⬚ 🍴 ⬚ **Location** N of town centre off A222
Hotel ★★★★ 76% HL Bexleyheath Marriott Hotel, 1 Broadway, BEXLEYHEATH ☎ 020 8298 1000 📄 020 8298 1234 142 en suite

---

SOUTHALL   Map 4 TQ17

West Middlesex Golf Club Greenford Rd UB1 3EE
☎ 020 8574 3450 📄 020 8574 2383
e-mail: westmid.gc@virgin.net
web: www.westmiddxgolfclub.co.uk

Gently undulating parkland course founded in 1891, the oldest private course in Middlesex, designed by James Braid.

18 Holes, 6119yds, Par 69, SSS 69, Course record 64. Club membership 250.

Visitors Mon-Sun & BHs. Booking required. Handicap certificate. Dress code. **Societies** booking required. **Green Fees** £20 per round (£30 weekends & BHs) **Course Designer** James Braid **Prof** T Talbot
Facilities ⑪ ⑩ 🏌 ⬚ 🍴 ⬚ 🏌 **Leisure** fishing, snooker **Conf** facs Corporate Hospitality Days **Location** W of town centre on A4127
Hotel ★★ BB Hanwell Bed and Breakfast, 110A Grove Avenue, Hanwell, LONDON W7 ☎ 020 8567 5015 & 020 8840 8555 2 rooms (1 en suite)

STANMORE   Map 4 TQ19

Stanmore Golf Club 29 Gordon Av HA7 2RL
☎ 020 8954 2599 📄 020 8954 2599
web: www.stanmoregolfclub.co.uk

18 Holes, 5885yds, Par 68, SSS 68, Course record 61.

Course Designer Dr A MacKenzie **Location** S of town centre between Stanmore & Belmont
Telephone for further details
Hotel ★★★ 82% HL Grim's Dyke Hotel, Old Redding, HARROW WEALD ☎ 020 8385 3100 & 020 8954 4227 📄 020 8954 4560 46 en suite

Save on Hotels. Book at theAA.com/hotel

GREATER LONDON

SURBITON
Map 4 TQ16

Surbiton Golf Club Woodstock Ln KT9 1UG
☎ 020 8398 3101 (Sec) 📠 020 8339 0992
web: www.surbitongolfclub.com

18 Holes, 6055yds, Par 70, SSS 69, Course record 63.
Course Designer Tom Dunn **Location** A3 Hook junct, A309 S 2m, left onto Woodstock Ln
Telephone for further details
Hotel ★★★★ 71% HL The Carlton Mitre, Hampton Court Road, HAMPTON COURT ☎ 020 8979 9988 & 8783 3505 📠 020 8979 9777 36 en suite

TWICKENHAM
Map 4 TQ17

David Lloyd Hampton Golf Staines Rd TW2 5JD
☎ 020 8783 1698 📠 020 8783 9475
e-mail: golf.hampton@davidlloyd.co.uk
web: www.davidlloyd.co.uk
A nine-hole pay-and-play course situated within 70 acres of mature parkland with a water feature coming into play on the 2nd and 3rd holes. The course is mature but has undergone extensive improvement work, including new tees and greens and the installation of an automated irrigation system.

9 Holes, 2720yds, Par 35, SSS 34, Course record 30.
Club membership 100.
Visitors Mon-Sun & BHs. Booking required. Dress code.
Societies booking required. **Green Fees** not confirmed **Prof** Jamie Skinner **Facilities** ⑨ ⑩ ⬛ ⬛ ⬛ ⬛ ⬛ ⬛ ⬛
Leisure hard tennis courts, heated indoor swimming pool, squash, sauna, gymnasium, indoor virtual golf **Conf** facs Corporate Hospitality Days **Location** 2m W on a305
Hotel ★★★★ 79% HL London Marriott Hotel Twickenham, 198 Whitton Road, TWICKENHAM ☎ 020 8891 8200 📠 020 8891 8201 156 en suite

Strawberry Hill Golf Club Wellesley Rd, Strawberry Hill TW2 5SD
☎ 020 8894 0165 & 8898 2082
e-mail: secretary@shgc.net
web: www.shgc.net
Parkland with easy walking.

9 Holes, 4625yds, Par 64, SSS 63, Course record 59.
Club membership 300.
Visitors Mon-Fri except BHs. Booking required weekends & BHs.
Dress code. **Societies** booking required **Green Fees** £35/£25 per day, £25/£15 per 18 holes (£28/£20 per 18 holes weekends) **Course Designer** J H Taylor **Prof** Peter Buchan **Facilities** ⑨ ⑩ by prior arrangement ⬛ ⬛ ⬛ ⬛ ⬛ ⬛ **Location** S of town centre off A316, next to Strawberry Hill railway station
Hotel ★★★★ 79% HL London Marriott Hotel Twickenham, 198 Whitton Road, TWICKENHAM ☎ 020 8891 8200 📠 020 8891 8201 156 en suite

UPMINSTER
Map 5 TQ58

Upminster Golf Club 114 Hall Ln RM14 1AU
☎ 01708 222788 (Secretary) 📠 01708 222484
e-mail: secretary@upminstergolfclub.co.uk
web: www.upminstergolfclub.co.uk
The meandering River Ingrebourne features on several holes of this partly undulating parkland course, situated on one side of the river valley. It provides a challenge for golfers of all abilities. The clubhouse is a beautiful Grade II listed building.

18 Holes, 6021yds, Par 69, SSS 69, Course record 62.
Club membership 900.
Visitors Mon-Fri except BHs. Dress code. **Societies** booking required.
Green Fees phone ❷ **Course Designer** W G Key **Prof** Jodie Dartford
Facilities ⑨ ⑩ ⬛ ⬛ ⬛ ⬛ ⬛ ⬛ ⬛ **Leisure** bowling, snooker **Conf** facs Corporate Hospitality Days **Location** M25 junct 29, take A127 W towards Romford for 1m to Hall Lane slip road signed Upminster/Cranham. Proceed S on Hall Lane for 0.5m, entrance past park on left
Hotel ★★★★ 74% HL De Rougemont Manor, Great Warley Street, BRENTWOOD ☎ 01277 226418 & 220483 📠 01277 239020 79 en suite

UXBRIDGE
Map 4 TQ08

Stockley Park Golf Club Stockley Park UB11 1AQ
☎ 020 8813 5700 📠 020 8813 5655
web: www.stockleyparkgolf.com

18 Holes, 6754yds, Par 72, SSS 71.
Course Designer Robert Trent Jones Snr **Location** M4 junct 4, 1m N off A408
Telephone for further details
Hotel ★★★★ 72% HL Novotel London Heathrow, Cherry Lane, WEST DRAYTON ☎ 01895 431431 📠 01895 431221 178 en suite

Uxbridge Golf Course The Drive UB10 8AQ
☎ 01895 272457 📠 01895 813539
web: www.uxbridgegolfclub.co.uk
18 Holes, 5677yds, Par 68, SSS 68, Course record 64.
Location 2m N off B467
Telephone for further details
Hotel ★★★ 78% HL Barn Hotel, West End Road, RUISLIP ☎ 01895 636057 📠 01895 638379 73 en suite

WEMBLEY
Map 4 TQ18

Sudbury Golf Club Bridgewater Rd HA0 1AL
☎ 020 8902 3713 📠 020 8902 3713
e-mail: enquiries@sudburygolfclubltd.co.uk
web: www.sudburygolfclubltd.co.uk
Undulating parkland near the centre of London providing an excellent test of golf.

18 Holes, 6297yds, Par 69, SSS 70, Course record 63.
Club membership 650.
Visitors Mon-Fri except BHs. Handicap certificate. Dress code.
Societies booking required. **Green Fees** £35 per 18 holes weekdays (£20 Mon) **Course Designer** Harry Colt **Prof** Neil Jordan **Facilities** ⑨ ⑩ ⬛ ⬛ ⬛ ⬛ ⬛ ⬛ ⬛ **Conf** facs **Location** SW of town centre on A4090
Hotel ★★★ 71% HL Quality Hotel Wembley, Empire Way, WEMBLEY ☎ 020 8733 9000 📠 020 8733 9001 165 en suite

WOODFORD GREEN

Map 5 TQ49

Woodford Golf Club Sunset Av IG8 0ST
☎ 020 8504 3330 & 8504 0553 📠 020 8559 0504
e-mail: office@woodfordgolf.co.uk
web: www.woodfordgolf.co.uk

Forest course on the edge of Epping Forest. Views over the Lea Valley to the London skyline. When played as 18 holes from dual tees, the course is comprised of four par 3s, two par 5s and twelve par 4s. Although fairly short, the tree-lined fairways and subtle undulations provide an excellent test of golfing skill. Noted for its fine greens.

9 Holes, 5878yds, Par 70, SSS 69, Course record 68. Club membership 310.

Visitors Contact club for details. **Societies** booking required. **Green Fees** £18 per 18 holes, £12 per 9 holes (£20/£14 weekends) 🚫 **Course Designer** Tom Dunn **Prof** Adam Baker **Facilities** ⊕ ⦿ by prior arrangement ⬜ 🍴 ⬠ 🏌 🎯 **Conf** Corporate Hospitality Days **Location** NW of town centre off A104

Hotel ★★★★ 72% HL Menzies Prince Regent, Manor Road, WOODFORD BRIDGE ☎ 020 8505 9966 📠 020 8506 0807 61 en suite

---

GREATER MANCHESTER

ALTRINCHAM

Map 7 SJ78

Altrincham Golf Club Stockport Rd WA15 7LP
☎ 0161 928 0761 📠 0161 928 8542
web: www.altringhamgolfclub.org.uk

18 Holes, 6385yds, Par 71, SSS 69.
Location 0.75m E of town ventre on A560
Telephone for further details
Hotel ★★★ 73% HL Mercure Altrincham Bowden Hotel, Langham Road, Bowdon, ALTRINCHAM ☎ 0161 928 7121 & 941 1866 📠 0161 927 7560 87 en suite

Dunham Forest Golf & Country Club Oldfield Ln WA14 4TY
☎ 0161 928 2605 📠 0161 929 8975
e-mail: enquiries@dunhamforest.com
web: www.dunhamforest.com

An attractive parkland course cut through magnificent beech woods.

Dunham Forest: 18 Holes, 6600yds, Par 72, SSS 72, Course record 63. Club membership 600.

Visitors Mon-Sun & BHs. Booking required. Handicap certificate. Dress code. **Societies** booking required. **Green Fees** £58 per 18 holes (£60 weekends) **Course Designer** Dave Thomas **Prof** Ian Wrigley **Facilities** ⊕ ⦿ by prior arrangement ⬠ ⬜ 🍴 ⬠ 🏌 🎯 🛒 🎯 🏌 **Conf** facs Corporate Hospitality Days **Location** 1.5m W off A56

Hotel ★★★ 73% HL Mercure Altrincham Bowden Hotel, Langham Road, Bowdon, ALTRINCHAM ☎ 0161 928 7121 & 941 1866 📠 0161 927 7560 87 en suite

Ringway Golf Club Hale Mount, Hale Barns WA15 8SW
☎ 0161 980 2630 📠 0161 980 4414
e-mail: fiona@ringwaygolfclub.co.uk
web: www.ringwaygolfclub.co.uk

Parkland with interesting natural hazards. Easy walking and good views of the Pennines and the Peak District.

18 Holes, 6235yds, Par 71, SSS 71. Club membership 800.

Visitors Mon-Thu, weekends & BHs. Booking required. Handicap certificate. Dress code. **Societies** booking required. **Green Fees** not confirmed **Course Designer** Colt Prof Nick Ryan **Facilities** ⊕ ⦿ ⬠ ⬜ ⬠ 🏌 🎯 🛒 🎯 **Conf** Corporate Hospitality Days **Location** M56 junct 6, A538 for 1m signed Hale, right onto Shay Ln

Hotel ★★★ 73% HL Mercure Altrincham Bowden Hotel, Langham Road, Bowdon, ALTRINCHAM ☎ 0161 928 7121 & 941 1866 📠 0161 927 7560 87 en suite

ASHTON-IN-MAKERFIELD

Map 7 SJ59

Ashton-in-Makerfield Golf Club Garswood Park, Liverpool Rd WN4 0YT
☎ 01942 719330 📠 01942 719330
e-mail: secretary@ashton-in-makerfieldgolfclub.co.uk
web: www.ashton-in-makerfieldgolfclub.co.uk

Well-wooded parkland course. Easy walking.

Ashton: 20 Holes, 6200yds, Par 70, SSS 70, Course record 63. Club membership 700.

Visitors Mon-Fri, Sun & BHs. Booking required Sun & BHs. **Societies** booking required **Green Fees** £32 per day **Prof** Peter Allan **Facilities** ⊕ ⦿ ⬠ ⬜ 🍴 ⬠ 🏌 🎯 **Conf** facs Corporate Hospitality Days **Location** M6 junct 24, 5m W on A580

Hotel ★★★★ 76% HL Thistle Haydock, Penny Lane, HAYDOCK ☎ 0871 376 9044 📠 0871 376 9144 137 en suite

ASHTON-UNDER-LYNE

Map 7 SJ99

Ashton-under-Lyne Golf Club Gorsey Way, Higher Hurst OL6 9HT
☎ 0161 330 1537 📠 0161 330 6673
e-mail: info@ashtongolfclub.co.uk
web: www.ashtongolfclub.co.uk

A testing, varied moorland course, with large greens. Easy walking.

18 Holes, 6209yds, Par 70, SSS 70, Course record 63. Club membership 760.

Visitors Mon-Fri except BHs. Booking required Tue-Fri. Dress code. **Societies** booking required **Green Fees** not confirmed **Prof** Colin Boyle **Facilities** ⊕ ⦿ ⬠ ⬜ 🍴 ⬠ 🎯 **Conf** facs Corporate Hospitality Days **Location** N off B6194

Hotel ★★★ 80% HL Best Western Hotel Smokies Park, Ashton Road, Bardsley, OLDHAM ☎ 0161 785 5000 📠 0161 785 5010 73 en suite

Dukinfield Golf Club Lyne Edge SK16 5DB
☎ 0161 338 2340 📄 0161 303 0205
web: www.dukinfieldgolfclub.co.uk
18 Holes, 5338yds, Par 67, SSS 66.
Location S off B6175
Telephone for further details
Hotel ★★★ 75% HL Holiday Inn Manchester Airport, Altrincham
Road, WILMSLOW ☎ 0871 942 9096 📄 01625 531876 126 en suite

BOLTON   Map 7 SD70

Bolton Golf Club Lostock Park, Chorley New Rd BL6 4AJ
☎ 01204 843067 & 843278 📄 01204 843067
e-mail: secretary@boltongolfclub.co.uk
This well-maintained heathland course is always a pleasure to visit.
The 12th hole should be treated with respect and so too should the
final four holes which have ruined many a card.
18 Holes, 6213yds, Par 70, SSS 71, Course record 65.
Club membership 510.
Visitors Mon, Wed-Fri & BHs. Booking required. Dress code.
Societies booking required **Green Fees** £46 per day, £36 per round
Prof D. Fitzgerald **Facilities** ⓣ ⭐ 📓 ⭕ 🍴 ⚘ ✦
Conf Corporate Hospitality Days **Location** 3m W of Bolton on A673
Hotel ★★★★ 74% HL De Vere Whites, De Havilland Way,
HORWICH ☎ 01204 667788 📄 01204 474663 125 en suite

Breightmet Golf Club Red Bridge, Ainsworth BL2 5PA
☎ 01204 527381
Long parkland course with spectacular views over the Welsh
mountains.
18 Holes, 6405yds, Par 72, SSS 71, Course record 67.
Club membership 400.
Visitors Mon, Tue, Thu, Fri except BHs. Dress code. Societies Booking
required. **Green Fees** £20 per round (£25 weekends & BHs) 🥤 **Course
Designer** D Griffiths **Facilities** ⓣ ⭐ 📓 ⭕ 🍴 ⚘ **Conf**
Corporate Hospitality Days **Location** E of town centre off A58
Hotel ★★★★ 70% HL Holiday Inn Bolton Centre, 1 Higher Bridge
Street, BOLTON ☎ 0871 9429 050 & 01204 879988 📄 01204 879983
132 en suite

Deane Golf Club Broadford Rd, Deane BL3 4NS
☎ 01204 61944 (Pro) & 651808 (Sec) 📄 01204 652047
e-mail: secretary@deanegolfclub.com
web: www.deanegolfclub.co.uk
Undulating parkland with small ravines on the approach to some
holes.
18 Holes, 5652yds, Par 68, SSS 68, Course record 64.
Club membership 470.
Visitors Mon-Fri & BHs. Booking required. Dress code.
Societies booking required. **Green Fees** not confirmed **Prof** David
Martindale **Facilities** ⓣ ⭐ 📓 ⭕ 🍴 ⚘ ✦ **Conf** facs
Location M61 junct 5, 1m towards Bolton
Hotel ★★★★ 70% HL Holiday Inn Bolton Centre, 1 Higher Bridge
Street, BOLTON ☎ 0871 9429 050 & 01204 879988 📄 01204 879983
132 en suite

Dunscar Golf Club Longworth Ln, Bromley Cross BL7 9QY
☎ 01204 303321 📄 01204 303321
e-mail: dunscargolfclub@uk2.net
web: www.dunscargolfclub.co.uk
A scenic moorland course with panoramic views. .
18 Holes, 6024yds, Par 71, SSS 69, Course record 63.
Club membership 500.
Visitors Mon, Wed-Fri & Sun. Booking required. Handicap certificate.
Dress code. Societies booking required. **Green Fees** £22.50 for 18
holes **Course Designer** Mr G Lowe **Prof** Andy Green **Facilities** ⓣ
⭐ 📓 ⭕ 🍴 ⚘ ✦ **Conf** facs Corporate Hospitality Days
Location 2m N off A666
Hotel ★★★ 81% HL Egerton House, Blackburn Road, Egerton,
BOLTON ☎ 01204 307171 📄 01204 593030 29 en suite

Great Lever & Farnworth Golf Club Plodder Ln, Farnworth
BL4 0LQ
☎ 01204 656137 📄 01204 656137
e-mail: greatlever@btconnect.com
web: www.greatleverfarnworthgolfclub.co.uk
Downland course with easy walking.
18 Holes, 5745yds, Par 69, SSS 68, Course record 63.
Club membership 379.
Visitors Mon-Sun & BHs. Booking required. Handicap certificate. Dress
code. Societies booking required. **Green Fees** £12.50 (£15 weekends)
🥤 **Prof** Andrew Green **Facilities** ⓣ ⭐ 📓 ⭕ 🍴 ⚘ ⊟
✦ **Leisure** snooker, darts **Conf** facs Corporate Hospitality Days
Location M61 junct 4, 1m
Hotel ★★★★ 70% HL Holiday Inn Bolton Centre, 1 Higher Bridge
Street, BOLTON ☎ 0871 9429 050 & 01204 879988 📄 01204 879983
132 en suite

Harwood Golf Club (Bolton) Roading Brook Rd, Harwood
BL2 4JD
☎ 01204 522878
e-mail: secretary@harwoodgolfclub.co.uk
web: www.harwoodgolfclub.com
Contrasting course, first nine undulating, second half flat on parkland
with several water features.
18 Holes, 5915yds, Par 70, SSS 70, Course record 65.
Club membership 691.
Visitors Mon-Fri except BHs. Booking required. Handicap certificate.
Dress code. Societies booking required. **Green Fees** £25 per round 🥤
Course Designer G Shuttleworth **Prof** Clive Loydall **Facilities** ⓣ ⭐
📓 ⭕ 🍴 ⚘ ⊟ ✦ 🛵 ✦ **Conf** Corporate Hospitality Days
Location 2.5m NE off B6196
Hotel ★★★ 77% HL Mercure Last Drop Village Hotel & Spa,
Hospital Road, Bromley Cross, BOLTON ☎ 01204 591131
📄 01204 304122 128 en suite

Old Links Golf Club Chorley Old Rd, Montserrat BL1 5SU

☎ 01204 842307 📄 01204 497549
e-mail: mail@boltonoldlinksgolfclub.co.uk
web: www.boltonoldlinksgolfclub.co.uk
Championship moorland course.

18 Holes, 6479yds, SSS 72. Club membership 600.
Visitors Mon, Wed-Fri except BHs. Dress code. **Societies** booking required. **Green Fees** £35 per day (Mon & Thu £20). £45 weekends & BHs) **Course Designer** Dr Alister MacKenzie **Prof** Paul Horridge **Facilities** ⓣ ⑩ 🍴 ▐ ▭ 🔊 🍺 ✎ **Conf** facs Corporate Hospitality Days **Location** NW of town centre on B6226
Hotel ★★★★ 74% HL De Vere Whites, De Havilland Way, HORWICH ☎ 01204 667788 📄 01204 474663 125 en suite

Regent Park Golf Course Links Rd, Chorley New Rd BL6 4AF

☎ 01204 495421 📄 01204 844620
Parkland course with exceptional moorland views.

18 Holes, 6067yds, Par 71, SSS 70, Course record 65.
Club membership 200.
Visitors Mon-Sun & BHs. Booking required. Dress code. **Societies** booking required. **Green Fees** not confirmed **Course Designer** James Braid **Prof** Neil Brazell **Facilities** ⓣ ⑩ ▐ ▭ 🍴 🔊 🍺 ⚑ ✎ **Conf** facs Corporate Hospitality Days **Location** M61 junct 6, 1m E off A673
Hotel ★★★★ 74% HL De Vere Whites, De Havilland Way, HORWICH ☎ 01204 667788 📄 01204 474663 125 en suite

Turton Golf Club Wood End Farm, Hospital Rd, Bromley Cross BL7 9QD

☎ 01204 852235 📄 01204 856921
e-mail: info@turtongolfclub.com
web: www.turtongolfclub.com
Moorland/parkland course with panoramic views. A wide variety of holes which challenge any golfer's technique.

18 Holes, 6124yds, Par 70, SSS 69, Course record 68.
Club membership 550.
Visitors Mon-Fri, Sun & BHs. Booking required Tue, Wed & Sun. Dress code. **Societies** booking required. **Green Fees** not confirmed **Course Designer** Alex Herd **Prof** Sean Owen **Facilities** ⓣ ⑩ ▐ ▭ 🍴 🔊 ✎ 🍺 **Leisure** indoor computer system **Location** 3m N off A666, follow signs for 'Last Drop Village'
Hotel ★★★ 81% HL Egerton House, Blackburn Road, Egerton, BOLTON ☎ 01204 307171 📄 01204 593030 29 en suite

---

BRAMHALL   Map 7 SJ88

Bramall Park Golf Club 20 Manor Rd SK7 3LY

☎ 0161 485 7101 📄 0161 485 7101
web: www.bramallparkgolfclub.co.uk
18 Holes, 6247yds, Par 70, SSS 70, Course record 63.
Course Designer James Braid **Location** NW of town centre off B5149
Telephone for further details
Hotel ★★★ 74% HL Alma Lodge Hotel, 149 Buxton Road, STOCKPORT ☎ 0161 483 4431 📄 0161 483 1983 52 en suite

Bramhall Golf Club Ladythorn Rd SK7 2EY

☎ 0161 439 6092 📄 0161 439 6092
e-mail: office@bramhallgolfclub.com
web: www.bramhallgolfclub.co.uk
Undulating parkland with easy walking and USGA greens. Excellent practice facilities. Indoor golf improvement centre.

18 Holes, 6347yds, Par 70, SSS 70, Course record 64.
Club membership 840.
Visitors Mon-Wed, Fri & Sun except BHs. Booking required. Handicap certificate. Dress code. **Societies** booking required. **Green Fees** £44 per 18 holes. Reduced winter rates ⊛ **Course Designer** Alex Herd **Prof** Richard Green **Facilities** ⓣ ⑩ by prior arrangement ▐ ▭ 🍴 🔊 🍺 ✎ **Conf** Corporate Hospitality Days **Location** E of town centre off A5102
Hotel ★★★ 74% HL Alma Lodge Hotel, 149 Buxton Road, STOCKPORT ☎ 0161 483 4431 📄 0161 483 1983 52 en suite

---

BURY   Map 7 SD81

Bury Golf Club Unsworth Hall, Blackford Bridge, Manchester Rd BL9 9TJ

☎ 0161 766 4897 📄 0161 796 3480
e-mail: secretary@burygolfclub.com
web: www.burygolfclub.com
Moorland course, difficult in part. Tight and good test of golf.

18 Holes, 5961yds, Par 69, SSS 69, Course record 61.
Club membership 650.
Visitors contact club for details. **Societies** welcome. **Green Fees** £18 per round (£22 weekends) **Course Designer** MacKenzie **Prof** G Coope **Facilities** ⓣ ⑩ ▐ ▭ 🍴 🔊 ✎ **Conf** facs Corporate Hospitality Days **Location** 2m N of M60 junct 17 on A56
Hotel ★★★★ 77% HL Mercure Norton Grange Hotel & Spa, Manchester Road, Castleton, ROCHDALE ☎ 0870 1942119 & 01706 630788 📄 01706 649313 81 en suite

Lowes Park Golf Club Hilltop, Lowes Rd BL9 6SU

☎ 0161 764 1231
e-mail: lowesparkgc@btconnect.com
web: www.lowesparkgc.co.uk
Moorland with easy walking. Exposed outlook with good views.

9 Holes, 6006yds, Par 70, SSS 69, Course record 63.
Club membership 250.
Visitors Mon-Fri except BHs. Booking required. Dress code. **Societies** booking required. **Green Fees** £20 per 18 holes ⊛ **Facilities** ⓣ ⑩ ▐ ▭ 🍴 🔊 ✎ **Conf** facs Corporate Hospitality Days **Location** N side of town centre off A56
Hotel ★★★★ 77% HL Mercure Norton Grange Hotel & Spa, Manchester Road, Castleton, ROCHDALE ☎ 0870 1942119 & 01706 630788 📄 01706 649313 81 en suite

Pike Fold Golf Club Pike Fold, Hills Ln, Unsworth BL9 8QP

☎ 0161 766 3561
e-mail: secretary@pikefold.co.uk
web: www.pikefold.co.uk
Inland course that plays like a links with a number of water hazards that come into play. USGA standard greens. Ideal, easy walking for all ages.

18 Holes, 6252yds, Par 71, SSS 70, Course record 64.
Club membership 478.
Visitors Mon-Sat & BHs. Booking required. Dress code.

continued

Save on Hotels. Book at **theAA.com/hotel**

GREATER MANCHESTER

ENGLAND

Societies booking required. **Green Fees** £30 per 18 holes 🏌 **Course Designer** Steve Marnoch **Prof** Grant Hamerton **Facilities** ⓉⒾ 🅷 🖥 ♨ 🎒 🔫 ♂ **Leisure** indoor swing room **Conf** facs Corporate Hospitality Days **Location** 4m N of city centre off Rochdale Rd
Hotel ★★★★ 77% HL Mercure Norton Grange Hotel & Spa, Manchester Road, Castleton, ROCHDALE ☎ 0870 1942119 & 01706 630788 📠 01706 649313 81 en suite

Walmersley Golf Club Garretts Close, Walmersley BL9 6TE
☎ 0161 764 1429 & 0161 764 7770 📠 0161 764 7770
e-mail: wgcsecretary@btconnect.com
web: www.walmersleygc.co.uk
Moorland hillside course, with wide fairways, large greens and extensive views. Testing holes: 2nd (484 yds) par 5 and the 13th par 4 with severe dog-leg and various hazards.
18 Holes, 6054yds, Par 71, SSS 70. Club membership 475.
Visitors Mon, Wed-Fri & BHs. Sun pm. Booking required. Dress code. **Societies** booking required. **Green Fees** not confirmed 🏌 **Course Designer** S Marnoch **Prof** M. Eubank **Facilities** Ⓣ by prior arrangement Ⓘ by prior arrangement 🅷 🖥 ♨ 🎒 🔫 ♂ **Conf** Corporate Hospitality Days **Location** 2m N off A56
Hotel ★★★★ 77% HL Mercure Norton Grange Hotel & Spa, Manchester Road, Castleton, ROCHDALE ☎ 0870 1942119 & 01706 630788 📠 01706 649313 81 en suite

CHEADLE   Map 7 SJ88

Cheadle Golf Club Cheadle Rd SK8 1HW
☎ 0161 491 4452
e-mail: cheadlegolfclub@msn.com
web: www.cheadlegolfclub.com
Parkland with hazards on every hole, from sand bunkers and copses to a stream across six of the fairways.
9 Holes, 4712yds, Par 64, SSS 65. Club membership 280.
Visitors Mon-Sun & BHs. Booking required. Dress code. **Societies** booking required. **Green Fees** not confirmed **Course Designer** T Renouf **Prof** Anthony Millar **Facilities** Ⓣ Ⓘ 🅷 🖥 ♨ 🎒 🔫 ♂ **Conf** facs Corporate Hospitality Days **Location** S of village off A5149
Hotel ★★★ 73% HL The Wycliffe Hotel, 74 Edgeley Road, Edgeley, STOCKPORT ☎ 0161 477 5395 📠 0161 476 3219 20 en suite

DENTON   Map 7 SJ99

Denton Golf Club Manchester Rd M34 2GG
☎ 0161 336 3218 📠 0161 336 4751
web: www.dentongolfclub.com
Easy walking parkland course with brook running through. One notable hole is called Death and Glory.
18 Holes, 6461yds, Par 71, SSS 71. Club membership 865.
Visitors Mon-Fri & BHs. Dress code. **Societies** booking required. **Green Fees** not confirmed **Prof** M Hollingworth **Facilities** Ⓣ Ⓘ by prior arrangement 🅷 🖥 ♨ 🎒 🔫 ♂ **Leisure** indoor teaching facility **Conf** facs **Location** M60 junct 24, 1.5m W on A57
Hotel ★★★ 70% HL Chancellors Hotel & Conference Centre, Moseley Road, Fallowfield, MANCHESTER ☎ 0161 9077414 69 en suite

FAILSWORTH   Map 7 SD80

Brookdale Golf Club Medlock Rd M35 9WQ
☎ 0161 681 4534 📠 0161 688 6872
e-mail: brookdalegolf@btconnect.com
web: www.brookdalegolf.co.uk
Challenging parkland course in the Medlock Valley with great Pennine views, although only 5m from the centre of Manchester. The River Medlock meanders through the course and features on six of the holes.
18 Holes, 5864yds, Par 68, SSS 68. Club membership 700.
Visitors Mon-Fri except BHs. Booking required Fri. Dress code. **Societies** booking required. **Green Fees** not confirmed **Prof** Tony Cuppello **Facilities** Ⓣ Ⓘ 🅷 🖥 🔫 ♨ 🎒 🔫 ♂ ♂ **Conf** facs Corporate Hospitality Days **Location** M60/A62 Oldham exit, towards Manchester, left at Nat West bank, left at road end. Right at minirdbt, 0.5m on left
Hotel ★★★ 80% HL Best Western Hotel Smokies Park, Ashton Road, Bardsley, OLDHAM ☎ 0161 785 5000 📠 0161 785 5010 73 en suite

FLIXTON   Map 7 SJ79

William Wroe Municipal Golf Course Pennybridge Ln M41 5DX
☎ 0161 748 8680 📠 0161 748 8680
web: www.traffordleisure.co.uk/golf.htm
18 Holes, 4368yds, Par 64.
Location E of village off B5158, 3m from Manchester centre
Telephone for further details
Hotel ★★★★ GA The Ascott, 6 Half Edge Lane, Ellesmere Park, Eccles, MANCHESTER ☎ 0161 950 2453 📠 0161 661 7063 14 rooms

GATLEY   Map 7 SJ88

Gatley Golf Club Waterfall Farm, Styal Rd, Heald Green SK8 3TW
☎ 0161 437 2091
e-mail: enquiries@gatleygolfclub.com
web: www.gatleygolfclub.com
Moderately testing parkland course with a tough finish.
9 Holes, 5934yds, Par 68, SSS 68, Course record 67. Club membership 300.
Visitors may play Mon, Wed-Fri, Sun & BHs. Dress code. **Societies** welcome. **Green Fees** not confirmed **Prof** Tom Bolton **Facilities** Ⓣ 🅷 🖥 🔫 ♨ 🎒 ♂ **Conf** Corporate Hospitality Days **Location** S of village off B5166
Hotel ★★★★ 72% HL Crowne Plaza Manchester Airport, Ringway Road, MANCHESTER ☎ 0871 942 9055 📠 0161 436 2340 294 en suite

HAZEL GROVE
Map 7 SJ98

Hazel Grove Golf Club Buxton Rd SK7 6LU
☎ 0161 483 3978 📠 0161 483 3978
e-mail: secretary@hazelgrovegolfclub.com
web: www.hazelgrovegolfclub.com
Testing parkland course with tricky greens and water hazards coming into play on several holes. Year round play on the greens and fairways.
18 Holes, 6234yds, Par 71, SSS 70. Club membership 630.
Visitors contact club for details. **Societies** booking required.
Green Fees £40.50 per day, £35.50 per 18 holes (£45.50 per 18 holes weekends & BHs) **Course Designer** McKenzie **Prof** J Hopley **Facilities** ⊕ †⊙ ⅃ ᒥ ᒧ 🎱 ⅄ 🖾 ⅂ ✔ **Leisure** golf electronic teaching system (GASP) **Conf** facs Corporate Hospitality Days **Location** 1m E off A6
Hotel ★★★ 74% HL Alma Lodge Hotel, 149 Buxton Road, STOCKPORT ☎ 0161 483 4431 📠 0161 483 1983 52 en suite

HYDE
Map 7 SJ99

Werneth Low Golf Club Werneth Low Rd, Gee Cross SK14 3AF
☎ 0161 368 2503 & 367 9376 (sec) 📠 0161 367 9376
e-mail: admin@wernethlowgolf.co.uk
web: www.wernethlowgolf.co.uk
Hard walking but good views of six counties from this undulating moorland course, which is played in a 7-4-7 loop. Exposed to wind with small greens. A good test of golfing skill.
18 Holes, 6184yds, Par 70, SSS 70, Course record 64. Club membership 375.
Visitors Mon, Wed, Fri & Sat. Thu am only. Booking required BHs. Handicap certificate. Dress code. **Societies** welcome. **Green Fees** £25 weekdays (£30 Sat). £15 per 11 holes **Prof** Tony Bacchus **Facilities** ⊕ †⊙ ᒥ ᒧ 🎱 ⅄ 🖾 🚆 ✔ **Conf** Corporate Hospitality Days **Location** 2m S of town centre
Hotel ★★ 83% HL Wind in the Willows Hotel, Derbyshire Level, GLOSSOP ☎ 01457 868001 📠 01457 853354 12 en suite

LITTLEBOROUGH
Map 7 SD91

Whittaker Golf Club Whittaker Ln OL15 0LH
☎ 01706 378310
e-mail: whittaker_golf@yahoo.co.uk
web: www.whittakergolfclub.co.uk
Moorland course with outstanding views of Hollingworth Lake Countryside Park and the Pennine Hills.
9 Holes, 2845yds, Par 68, SSS 67, Course record 65. Club membership 200.
Visitors Mon-Sun & BHs. Dress code. **Societies** booking required. **Green Fees** £15 per 18 holes (£20 Sat). Reduced winter rates. ☺ **Facilities** ᒧ ⅄ **Location** 1.5m from Littleborough off A58
Hotel ★★★★ 77% HL Mercure Norton Grange Hotel & Spa, Manchester Road, Castleton, ROCHDALE ☎ 0870 1942119 & 01706 630788 📠 01706 649313 81 en suite

MANCHESTER
Map 7 SJ89

Blackley Golf Club Victoria Ave East, Blackley M9 7HW
☎ 0161 643 2980 & 654 7770 📠 0161 653 8300
e-mail: office@blackleygolfclub.com
web: www.blackleygolfclub.com
Parkland course crossed by a footpath. The course has been redesigned giving greater challenge and interest including water features.
18 Holes, 6168yds, Par 70, SSS 71. Club membership 800.
Visitors Mon-Fri except BHs. Booking required Thu. Dress code. **Societies** booking required. **Green Fees** phone **Course Designer** Gaunt & Marnoch **Prof** Craig Gould **Facilities** ⊕ †⊙ by prior arrangement ᒥ ᒧ 🎱 ⅄ 🖾 ✔ 🚆 ✔ **Conf** facs Corporate Hospitality Days **Location** 4m N of city centre
Hotel ★★★ 88% HL Malmaison Manchester, Piccadilly, MANCHESTER ☎ 0161 278 1000 📠 0161 278 1002 167 en suite

Chorlton-cum-Hardy Golf Club Barlow Hall, Barlow Hall Rd, Chorlton-cum-Hardy M21 7JJ
☎ 0161 881 5830 📠 0161 881 4532
e-mail: chorltongolf@hotmail.com
web: www.chorltoncumhardygolfclub.co.uk
Set in the grounds of Barlow Hall, this challenging parkland course winds its way around the banks of the Mersey. The testing opening holes lead up to the stroke 1 7th, an impressive 474yd par 4, with its elevated green. The course then meanders through parkland culminating at the par 4 18th.
18 Holes, 5994yds, Par 70, SSS 69, Course record 62. Club membership 550.
Visitors Mon-Sun & BHs. Booking required except Mon. Dress code. **Societies** booking advisable. **Green Fees** £15 (£20 weekends & BHs) **Prof** James Curtis **Facilities** ⊕ †⊙ ᒥ ᒧ 🎱 ⅄ 🖾 ✔ **Leisure** snooker **Conf** facs Corporate Hospitality Days **Location** 4m S of Manchester, A5103/A5145
Hotel ★★★ 79% HL Best Western Willow Bank, 340-342 Wilmslow Road, Fallowfield, MANCHESTER ☎ 0161 224 0461 📠 0161 257 2561 116 en suite

Didsbury Golf Club Ford Ln, Northenden M22 4NQ
☎ 0161 998 9278 📠 0161 902 3060
e-mail: golf@didsburygolfclub.com
web: www.didsburygolfclub.com
Attractive and easy walking 18 hole parkland course located alongside the River Mersey. Founded in 1891.
18 Holes, 6212yds, Par 70, SSS 70. Club membership 750.
Visitors contact club for details. **Societies** booking required. **Green Fees** £29 per round (£33 weekends & BHs) **Course Designer** Alister MacKenzie/Peter Alliss/Dave Thomas **Prof** Peter Barber **Facilities** ⊕ †⊙ ᒥ ᒧ 🎱 ⅄ 🖾 ✔ 🚆 ✔ **Conf** facs Corporate Hospitality Days **Location** 6m S of city centre off A5145
Hotel ★★★★ 71% HL Etrop Grange Hotel, Thorley Lane, MANCHESTER AIRPORT ☎ 0844 855 9118 📠 0161 499 0790 64 en suite

Save on Hotels. Book at **theAA.com/hotel**

GREATER MANCHESTER

ENGLAND

Fairfield Golf and Sailing Club 'Boothdale', Booth Rd, Audenshaw M34 5QA
☎ 0161 301 4528 ▤ 0161 301 4254
e-mail: manager@fairfieldgolfclub.co.uk
web: www.fairfieldgolfclub.co.uk
Parkland course set around a reservoir. Course demands particularly accurate placing of shots.
18 Holes, 6006yds, Par 70, SSS 69, Course record 62. Club membership 450.
Visitors Mon, Tue, Fri & BHs. Booking required. **Societies** booking required. **Green Fees** £26 per round **Course Designer** Andrew Murray **Prof** Stephen Pownell **Facilities** ⊕ ⊚ ⓛ ⌺ ⊡ ⌻ ⚐ 🍴 ⚐
🍴 ⚘ **Location** 5m E of Manchester off A635
Hotel ★★★ 80% HL Best Western Hotel Smokies Park, Ashton Road, Bardsley, OLDHAM ☎ 0161 785 5000 ▤ 0161 785 5010 73 en suite

Marriott Worsley Park Hotel & Country Club Worsley Park M28 2QT
☎ 0161 975 2043 ▤ 0161 975 2058
web: www.marriott.co.uk/golf
18 Holes, 6611yds, Par 71, SSS 72, Course record 61.
Course Designer Ross McMurray **Location** M60 junct 13, A585, course 0.5m on left
Telephone for further details
Hotel ★★★★ 80% HL Worsley Park, A Marriott Hotel & Country Club, Worsley Park, Worsley, MANCHESTER ☎ 0161 975 2000 ▤ 0161 799 6341 158 en suite

Northenden Golf Club Palatine Rd, Northenden M22 4FR
☎ 0161 998 4738 ▤ 0161 945 5592
e-mail: manager@northendengolfclub.com
web: www.northendengolfclub.com
Parkland course surrounded by the River Mersey with 18 USGA specification greens.
18 Holes, 6460yds, Par 72, SSS 71, Course record 64. Club membership 700.
Visitors Mon-Wed, Fri & Sun & BHs. Booking required. Handicap certificate. Dress code. **Societies** booking required. **Green Fees** £32 per day (£35 Sun & BHs) **Course Designer** Renouf/S Gidman **Prof** Grant Doyle **Facilities** ⊕ ⊚ ⓛ ⌺ ⊡ ⌻ ⚐
Leisure chipping area, bunker practice area, putting area. **Conf** facs Corporate Hospitality Days **Location** M60 junct 5, 6.5m S of city centre on B1567
Hotel ★★★ 79% HL Best Western Willow Bank, 340-342 Wilmslow Road, Fallowfield, MANCHESTER ☎ 0161 224 0461 ▤ 0161 257 2561 116 en suite

Withington Golf Club 243 Palatine Rd, West Didsbury M20 2UE
☎ 0161 445 9544 ▤ 0161 445 5210
e-mail: secretary@withingtongolfclub.co.uk
web: www.withingtongolfclub.co.uk
Flat parkland course bordering the River Mersey and only four miles from the city centre. Famed for its tree-lined fairways and manicured greens.
18 Holes, 6388yds, Par 71, SSS 70. Club membership 600.
Visitors Mon-Fri, Sun & BHs. Booking required. Dress code. **Societies** booking required. **Green Fees** £35 per round (Fri & Sun £45) **Prof** S Marr **Facilities** ⊕ ⊚ ⓛ ⌺ ⊡ ⌻ ⚐ 🍴 ⚐

🍴 ⚐ **Conf** facs Corporate Hospitality Days **Location** 4m SW of city centre off B5167
Hotel ★★★ 79% HL Best Western Willow Bank, 340-342 Wilmslow Road, Fallowfield, MANCHESTER ☎ 0161 224 0461 ▤ 0161 257 2561 116 en suite

Worsley Golf Club Stableford Av, Worsley M30 8AP
☎ 0161 789 4202 ▤ 0161 789 3200
e-mail: secretary@worsleygolfclub.co.uk
web: www.worsleygolfclub.co.uk
Well-wooded parkland course.
18 Holes, 6252yds, Par 71, SSS 70, Course record 65. Club membership 600.
Visitors Mon-Fri, Sun & BHs. Handicap certificate. Dress code. **Societies** welcome. **Green Fees** phone **Course Designer** James Braid **Prof** Andrew Cory **Facilities** ⊕ ⊚ ⓛ ⌺ ⊡ ⌻ ⚐
Location 6.5m NW of city centre off A572
Hotel ★★★ 72% HL Novotel Manchester West, Worsley Brow, WORSLEY ☎ 0161 799 3535 ▤ 0161 703 8207 119 en suite

MELLOR
Map 7 SJ98

Mellor & Townscliffe Golf Club Gibb Ln, Tarden SK6 5NA
☎ 0161 427 2208 (secretary)
web: www.mellorgolf.co.uk
Scenic parkland and moorland course, undulating with some hard walking. Good views. Testing 200yd 9th hole, par 3.
18 Holes, 5936yds, Par 70, SSS 69, Course record 63. Club membership 550.
Visitors Mon-Fri, Sun & BHs. Booking required Mon, Wed, Fri, Sun & BHs. Dress code. **Societies** booking required. **Green Fees** not confirmed **Prof** Gary R Broadley **Facilities** ⊕ ⊚ ⓛ ⌺ ⊡ ⌻ ⚐
⚐ ⚘ **Location** 7m SE of Stockport off A626
Hotel ★★★ 81% HL Bredbury Hall Hotel & Country Club, Goyt Valley, BREDBURY ☎ 0161 430 7421 ▤ 0161 430 5079 150 en suite

MIDDLETON
Map 7 SD80

The Manchester Golf Club Hopwood Cottage, Rochdale Rd M24 6QP
☎ 0161 643 3202 ▤ 0161 643 9174
e-mail: secretary@mangc.co.uk
web: www.mangc.co.uk
Moorland golf of unique character over a spaciously laid out course with generous fairways sweeping along to large greens. A wide variety of holes will challenge the golfer's technique, particularly the testing last four holes.
18 Holes, 6491yds, Par 72, SSS 72, Course record 63. Club membership 650.
Visitors Mon-Fri, Sun & BHs. Booking required. Handicap certificate. Dress code. **Societies** booking required. **Green Fees** £70 per day, £60 per round (£75/£65 Sun & BHs) **Course Designer** Shapland Colt **Prof** Brian Connor **Facilities** ⊕ ⊚ ⓛ ⌺ ⊡ ⌻ ⚐ 🍴
⚐ 🍴 ⚘ **Leisure** snooker **Conf** facs Corporate Hospitality Days **Location** 1m S of M62 junct 20 on A664
Hotel ★★★★ 77% HL Mercure Norton Grange Hotel & Spa, Manchester Road, Castleton, ROCHDALE ☎ 0870 1942119 & 01706 630788 ▤ 01706 649313 81 en suite

New North Manchester Golf Club Rhodes House, Manchester Old Rd M24 4PE
☎ 0161 643 9033 ▤ 0161 643 7775
e-mail: tee@nmgc.co.uk
web: www.northmanchestergolfclub.co.uk
Delightful moorland and parkland with several water features. Challenging but fair for the accomplished golfer.
18 Holes, 6443yds, Par 71, SSS 71, Course record 65. Club membership 480.
Visitors Mon-Fri, Sun & BHs. Booking required. Dress code. **Societies** booking required. **Green Fees** £36 (£40 Sun). Reduced winter rates **Course Designer** J Braid **Prof** Jason Peel **Facilities** ⊕ ⊙ ▤ ⬚ ⬚ ⬚ ⬚ ⬚ ⬚ **Leisure** 2 full size snooker tables **Conf** facs Corporate Hospitality Days **Location** M60 junct 19, W of town centre off A576
Hotel ★★★★ 77% HL Mercure Norton Grange Hotel & Spa, Manchester Road, Castleton, ROCHDALE ☎ 0870 1942119 & 01706 630788 ▤ 01706 649313 81 en suite

MILNROW   Map 7 SD91

Tunshill Golf Club Kiln Ln OL16 3TS
☎ 01706 342095
e-mail: tunshillgolfclub@btinternet.com
web: www.tunshillgolfclub.co.uk
Testing moorland course with two demanding par 5s and out of bounds features on eight of the nine holes.
9 Holes, 5800yds, Par 70, SSS 68. Club membership 300.
Visitors Mon-Fri except BHs. Dress code. **Societies** booking required. **Green Fees** £16 per day ⬚ **Facilities** ⊕ by prior arrangement ⊙ by prior arrangement ▤ ⬚ ⬚ ⬚ **Conf** facs Corporate Hospitality Days **Location** 1m NE M62 exit junct 21 off B6225
Hotel ★★★★ 77% HL Mercure Norton Grange Hotel & Spa, Manchester Road, Castleton, ROCHDALE ☎ 0870 1942119 & 01706 630788 ▤ 01706 649313 81 en suite

OLDHAM   Map 7 SD90

Crompton & Royton Golf Club Highbarn, Royton OL2 6RW
☎ 0161 624 0986 ▤ 0161 652 4711
e-mail: secretary@cromptonandroytongolfclub.co.uk
web: www.cromptonandroytongolfclub.co.uk
Heathland/parkland course.
18 Holes, 6186yds, Par 70, SSS 70, Course record 62. Club membership 700.
Visitors Mon-Fri, Sun & BHs. Booking required. Dress code. **Societies** booking required. **Green Fees** £20 per round (£25 weekends & BHs) ⬚ **Course Designer** George Lowe **Prof** Martin Beatty **Facilities** ⊕ ⊙ ▤ ⬚ ⬚ ⬚ ⬚ **Leisure** practice nets **Conf** facs Corporate Hospitality Days **Location** 0.5m NE of Royton
Hotel ★★★★ 77% HL Mercure Norton Grange Hotel & Spa, Manchester Road, Castleton, ROCHDALE ☎ 0870 1942119 & 01706 630788 ▤ 01706 649313 81 en suite

Werneth Golf Club Green Ln, Garden Suburb OL8 3AZ
☎ 0161 624 1190
e-mail: secretary@wernethgolfclub.co.uk
web: www.wernethgolfclub.co.uk
Semi-moorland course, with a deep gully and stream crossing eight fairways. Testing hole: 3rd (par 3).

18 Holes, 5365yds, Par 68, SSS 66, Course record 61. Club membership 400.
Visitors Contact club for details. **Societies** booking required. **Green Fees** £18 per day ⬚ **Course Designer** Sandy Herd **Prof** James Matterson **Facilities** ⊕ ⊙ ▤ ⬚ ⬚ ⬚ **Conf** Corporate Hospitality Days **Location** S of town centre off A627
Hotel ★★★ 80% HL Best Western Hotel Smokies Park, Ashton Road, Bardsley, OLDHAM ☎ 0161 785 5000 ▤ 0161 785 5010 73 en suite

PRESTWICH   Map 7 SD80

Heaton Park Golf Centre Heaton Park, Middleton Rd M25 2SW
☎ 0161 654 9899 ▤ 0161 653 2003
e-mail: heatonpark@btconnect.com
web: www.mackgolf.co.uk
An award winning municipal parkland-style course in historic Heaton Park, with rolling hills and lakes, designed by five times Open Champion, J H Taylor. It has some spectacular holes and is a good test of skill for golfers of all abilities.
Championship: 18 Holes, 5755yds, Par 70, SSS 68, Course record 64. Club membership 140.
Visitors Mon-Sun & BHs. Booking required. Dress code. **Societies** booking required. **Green Fees** not confirmed **Course Designer** J H Taylor **Prof** Gary Dermott **Facilities** ⊕ ⊙ ▤ ⬚ ⬚ ⬚ ⬚ ⬚ ⬚ **Leisure** fishing, 18 hole par 3 course. **Conf** facs Corporate Hospitality Days **Location** N of Manchester near M60 junct 19
Hotel ★★★★ 78% HL Marriott Manchester Victoria & Albert Hotel, Water Street, MANCHESTER ☎ 0161 832 1188 ▤ 0161 834 2484 148 en suite

ROCHDALE   Map 7 SD81

Castle Hawk Golf Club Chadwick Ln, Castleton OL11 3BY
☎ 01706 640841 ▤ 01706 860587
e-mail: castlehawkbookings@hotmail.co.uk
web: www.castlehawk.co.uk
Two parkland courses that are an ideal place to start for beginners whilst still offering a stern test for the better golfer. The 18 hole course consists of 17 par 3s and one par 4. The 9 hole course is a more traditional test of golf with seven par 4s and two par 3s, each offering a test of skill be it length, accuracy or both.
New Course: 9 Holes, 2756yds, Par 34, SSS 33, Course record 32.
Old Course: 18 Holes, 3189yds, Par 55, SSS 57, Course record 55. Club membership 160.
Visitors Mon-Fri, Sun & BHs. 18 hole course only on Sat. Booking required. **Societies** welcome. **Green Fees** not confirmed **Course Designer** T Wilson **Prof** Ryan Crumbridge/Dave Hutton **Facilities** ⊕ ⊙ ▤ ⬚ ⬚ ⬚ ⬚ ⬚ ⬚ **Conf** Corporate Hospitality Days **Location** M62 junct 20, S of Rochdale
Hotel ★★★★ 77% HL Mercure Norton Grange Hotel & Spa, Manchester Road, Castleton, ROCHDALE ☎ 0870 1942119 & 01706 630788 ▤ 01706 649313 81 en suite

Save on Hotels. Book at **theAA.com/hotel**

GREATER MANCHESTER

ENGLAND

Rochdale Golf Club Edenfield Rd OL11 5YR
☎ 01706 643818 🖹 01706 861113
e-mail: manager@rochdalegolfclub.co.uk
web: www.rochdalegolfclub.co.uk
Easy walking parkland for enjoyable golf.

18 Holes, 5731yds, Par 71, SSS 68, Course record 63.
Club membership 750.

Visitors Mon, Wed, Fri, Sun & BHs. Booking required. Dress code.
Societies booking required. **Green Fees** not confirmed **Course
Designer** George Lowe **Prof** Andrew Laverty **Facilities** ⊕ ⊺⊙⊺
🗲 ⊒ 🕱 ⊿ 🖻 🗡 **Conf** facs Corporate Hospitality Days
Location 1.75m W on A680
Hotel ★★★★ 77% HL Mercure Norton Grange Hotel & Spa,
Manchester Road, Castleton, ROCHDALE ☎ 0870 1942119 & 01706
630788 🖹 01706 649313 81 en suite

ROMILEY   Map 7 SJ99

Romiley Golf Club Goose House Green SK6 4LJ
☎ 0161 430 2392 🖹 0161 430 7258
e-mail: office@romileygolfclub.org
web: www.romileygolfclub.org

Semi-parkland course on the edge of the Derbyshire Hills, providing a
good test of golf with a number of outstanding holes, notably the 6th,
9th, 14th and 16th. The latter enjoys magnificent views from the tee.
18 Holes, 6412yds, Par 71, SSS 71. Club membership 700.
Visitors contact club for details. **Societies** booking required. **Green
Fees** phone **Prof** Matthew Ellis **Facilities** ⊕ ⊺⊙⊺ 🗲 ⊒ 🕱 ⊿
🖻 🗡 **Location** E of town centre off B6104
Hotel ★★★ 73% HL The Wycliffe Hotel, 74 Edgeley Road, Edgeley,
STOCKPORT ☎ 0161 477 5395 🖹 0161 476 3219 20 en suite

SALE   Map 7 SJ79

Ashton on Mersey Golf Club Church Ln M33 5QQ
☎ 0161 976 4390 & 962 3727   🖹 0161 976 4390
web: www.aomgc.co.uk
9 Holes, 6146yds, Par 71, SSS 69, Course record 66.
Location M60 junct 7, 1m W off Glebelands Rd
Telephone for further details
Hotel ★★★★ GA The Belmore, 143 Brooklands Road, SALE
☎ 0161 973 2538 🖹 0161 973 2665 20 rooms

Sale Golf Club Golf Rd M33 2XU
☎ 0161 973 1638 (Office) & 973 1730 (Pro)
🖹 0161 962 4217
e-mail: mail@salegolfclub.com
web: www.salegolfclub.com

Tree-lined parkland course. Feature holes are the 13th - Watery Gap -
and the par 3 3rd hole of 210yds over water.

18 Holes, 6301yds, Par 70, SSS 70, Course record 64.
Club membership 700.

Visitors Mon-Sun & BHs. Booking required Thu, weekends & BHs.
Dress code. **Societies** booking required. **Green Fees** not confirmed 🖘
Prof Mike Stewart **Facilities** ⊕ ⊺⊙⊺ 🗲 ⊒ 🕱 ⊿ 🖻 🗡 🖛
🗡 **Conf** Corporate Hospitality Days **Location** M60 junct 6, 0.5m NW of
town centre off A6144
Hotel ★★★★ GA The Belmore, 143 Brooklands Road, SALE
☎ 0161 973 2538 🖹 0161 973 2665 20 rooms (20 en suite)

SHEVINGTON   Map 7 SD50

Gathurst Golf Club 62 Miles Ln WN6 8EW
☎ 01257 255235 (Secretary) 🖹 01257 255953
e-mail: secretary@gathurstgolfclub.co.uk
web: www.gathurst-golf-club.co.uk
A testing parkland course. Slightly hilly.

18 Holes, 6063yds, Par 70, SSS 69, Course record 63.
Club membership 630.

Visitors Mon, Tue, Thu & Fri except BHs. Handicap certificate. Dress
code. **Societies** booking required. **Green Fees** £30 per round **Course
Designer** N Pearson **Prof** David Clarke **Facilities** ⊕ ⊺⊙⊺ 🗲 ⊒
🕱 ⊿ 🖻 🗡 **Conf** Corporate Hospitality Days **Location** M6
junct 27, 1m SW of village on B5375
Hotel ★★★★ 73% HL Macdonald Kilhey Court, Chorley Road,
Standish, WIGAN ☎ 0870 1942122 🖹 01257 422401 62 en suite

STALYBRIDGE   Map 7 SJ99

Stamford Golf Club Oakfield House, Huddersfield Rd
SK15 3PY
☎ 01457 832126
e-mail: admin@stamfordgolfclub.co.uk
web: www.stamfordgolfclub.co.uk
Part parkland, part moorland course with gentle sloping hills. Tree-
lined fairways with some heather lined rough.

18 Holes, 5701yds, Par 70, SSS 68, Course record 62.
Club membership 600.

Visitors Mon-Fri & Sun except BHs. Booking required Sun. Dress code.
Societies booking required. **Green Fees** not confirmed **Prof** Mark
Smith **Facilities** ⊕ ⊺⊙⊺ 🗲 ⊒ 🕱 ⊿ 🖻 🗡 **Conf** facs
Corporate Hospitality Days **Location** 2m NE off A635
Hotel ★★★ 80% HL Best Western Hotel Smokies Park, Ashton
Road, Bardsley, OLDHAM ☎ 0161 785 5000 🖹 0161 785 5010
73 en suite

STANDISH Map 7 SD51

Standish Court Golf Club Rectory Ln WN6 0XD
☎ 01257 425777 🖹 01257 425777
web: www.standishgolf.co.uk

18 Holes, 4860yds, Par 68, SSS 64, Course record 63.
Course Designer P Dawson **Location** E of town centre on B5239
Telephone for further details
Hotel ★★★★ 73% HL Macdonald Kilhey Court, Chorley Road,
Standish, WIGAN ☎ 0870 1942122 🖹 01257 422401 62 en suite

STOCKPORT Map 7 SJ89

Heaton Moor Golf Club Mauldeth Rd, Heaton Mersey SK4 3NX
☎ 0161 432 2134 🖹 0161 432 2134
e-mail: heatonmoorgolfclub@yahoo.co.uk
web: www.heatonmoorgolfclub.co.uk

Gently undulating parkland with two separate nine holes starting from
the clubhouse. The narrow fairways are challenging.
18 Holes, 5970yds, Par 70, SSS 69. Club membership 700.
Visitors Contact club for details regarding booking. Dress code.
Societies booking required. **Green Fees** £32 per day, £27 per round
(£40/£35 weekends) **Prof** Simon Marsh **Facilities** ⓣ ⑩ ⓑ ⎚
⎚ 🍴 👤 📷 ⛱ ⚑ **Location** M60, junct 1, N of town centre off
B5169
Hotel ★★★ 81% HL Bredbury Hall Hotel & Country Club, Goyt
Valley, BREDBURY ☎ 0161 430 7421 🖹 0161 430 5079 150 en suite

Houldsworth Golf Club Houldsworth Park, Reddish SK5 6BN
☎ 0161 442 1714 🖹 0161 947 9678
e-mail: houldsworthsecretary@hotmail.co.uk
web: www.houldsworthgolfclub.co.uk

Flat, tree-lined parkland course with water hazards. Testing holes
11th (par 4) and 13th (par 5).
18 Holes, 6209yds, Par 70, SSS 70, Course record 67.
Club membership 400.
Visitors Mon-Sun & BHs. Booking required. Dress code.
Societies booking required. **Green Fees** £18 to £36 **Course
Designer** Dave Thomas **Prof** Daniel Marsh **Facilities** ⓣ ⑩ ⓑ
⎚ 🍴 👤 📷 ⛱ ⚑ **Conf** facs Corporate Hospitality Days
Location 4m SE of city centre off A6
Hotel ★★★ 79% HL Best Western Willow Bank, 340-342 Wilmslow
Road, Fallowfield, MANCHESTER ☎ 0161 224 0461 🖹 0161 257 2561
116 en suite

Marple Golf Club Barnsfold Rd, Hawk Green, Marple SK6 7EL
☎ 0161 427 2311 & 427 1195 (pro) 🖹 0161 427 2311
e-mail: secretary@marple-golf-club.co.uk
web: www.marplegolfclub.co.uk

Parkland with several ponds or other water hazards. Gentle slopes
overlook the Cheshire plains.
18 Holes, 5554yds, Par 68, SSS 67. Club membership 600.
Visitors booking required Tue & Thu. Dress code. **Societies** welcome.
Green Fees not confirmed **Prof** David Myers **Facilities** ⓣ ⑩ ⓑ
⎚ 🍴 👤 📷 ⚑ **Leisure** snooker **Conf** Corporate Hospitality
Days **Location** S of Marple town centre
Hotel ★★★ 81% HL Bredbury Hall Hotel & Country Club, Goyt
Valley, BREDBURY ☎ 0161 430 7421 🖹 0161 430 5079 150 en suite

Reddish Vale Golf Club Southcliffe Rd, Reddish SK5 7EE
☎ 0161 480 2359 🖹 0161 480 2359
e-mail: admin@rvgc.co.uk
web: www.rvgc.co.uk

Undulating heathland course designed by Dr A MacKenzie and
situated in the Tame Valley.
18 Holes, 6086yds, Par 69, SSS 70, Course record 63.
Club membership 550.
Visitors Mon-Fri, Sun except BHs. Booking required Tue-Thu & Sun.
Dress code. **Societies** booking required. **Green Fees** £34-£40 per day,
£21-£29 per round **Course Designer** Dr A MacKenzie **Prof** Andrew
Myers **Facilities** ⓣ ⑩ ⓑ ⎚ 🍴 👤 📷 ⛱ ⚑ ⚑
Conf facs Corporate Hospitality Days **Location** Off Reddish Road, M6
junct 27
Hotel ★★★ 73% HL The Wycliffe Hotel, 74 Edgeley Road, Edgeley,
STOCKPORT ☎ 0161 477 5395 🖹 0161 476 3219 20 en suite

Stockport Golf Club Offerton Rd, Offerton SK2 5HL
☎ 0161 427 8369 🖹 0161 427 8369
e-mail: info@stockportgolf.co.uk
web: www.stockportgolf.co.uk

A beautifully situated course in wide open countryside with views of
the Cheshire and Derbyshire hills. It is not too long but requires that
the player plays all the shots to excellent greens. Demanding holes
include the dog-leg 3rd, 12th and 18th and the 460yd opening hole
is among the toughest in Cheshire. Regional qualifying course for
Open Championship.
18 Holes, 6392yds, Par 71, SSS 69, Course record 63.
Club membership 500.
Visitors Mon, Wed-Fri, Sun & BHs. Booking required Wed, Thu,
Sun & BHs. **Societies** booking required. **Green Fees** not confirmed
Course Designer P Barrie/A Herd **Prof** Gary Norcott **Facilities** ⓣ
⑩ ⓑ ⎚ 🍴 👤 📷 ⛱ ⚑ **Conf** Corporate Hospitality
Days **Location** 4m SE on A627
Hotel ★★★ 81% HL Bredbury Hall Hotel & Country Club,
Goyt Valley, BREDBURY ☎ 0161 430 7421 🖹 0161 430 5079
150 en suite

Save on Hotels. Book at **theAA.com/hotel**

GREATER MANCHESTER

ENGLAND

SWINTON
Map 7 SD70

Swinton Park Golf Club East Lancashire Rd M27 5LX
☎ 0161 794 0861 📠 0161 281 0698
web: www.spgolf.co.uk
18 Holes, 6472yds, Par 73, SSS 71.
Course Designer James Braid **Location** Entrance off A580
Telephone for further details
Hotel ★★★ 72% HL Novotel Manchester West, Worsley Brow,
WORSLEY ☎ 0161 799 3535 📠 0161 703 8207 119 en suite

UPPERMILL
Map 7 SD90

Saddleworth Golf Club Mountain Ash OL3 6LT
☎ 01457 873653 📠 01457 820647
e-mail: secretary@saddleworthgolfclub.org.uk
web: www.saddleworthgolfclub.co.uk
Moorland course, with superb views of Pennines.
18 Holes, 6196yds, Par 71, SSS 70, Course record 62.
Club membership 700.
Visitors Mon-Fri & BHs. Handicap certificate. Dress code.
Societies booking required. **Green Fees** not confirmed **Course
Designer** George Lowe/Dr McKenzie **Prof** Robert Johnson **Facilities** ⑪
🍽 🛍 ⌁ 🖥 ⚑ ⚷ 🍴 ⚷ **Location** E of town centre
off A670
Hotel ★★★ 80% HL Best Western Hotel Smokies Park, Ashton
Road, Bardsley, OLDHAM ☎ 0161 785 5000 📠 0161 785 5010
73 en suite

URMSTON
Map 7 SJ79

Flixton Golf Club Church Rd, Flixton M41 6EP
☎ 0161 748 2116 📠 0161 748 2116
e-mail: flixtongolfclub@mail.com
web: www.flixtongolfclub.co.uk
Meadowland course bounded by the River Mersey.
9 Holes, 6185yds, Par 71, SSS 71, Course record 66.
Club membership 430.
Visitors Mon, Tue, Thu, Fri, Sun & BHs. Dress code. **Societies** booking
required. **Green Fees** £15 (£25 Sun) ⓹ **Prof** Mike Williams
Facilities ⑪ 🍽 🛍 ⌁ 🖥 🝖 🛍 **Conf** facs Corporate
Hospitality Days **Location** S of town centre on B5213
Hotel ★★★★ 76% HL Copthorne Hotel Manchester,
Clippers Quay, Salford Quays, MANCHESTER ☎ 0161 873 7321
📠 0161 877 8112 166 en suite

WALKDEN
Map 7 SD70

Brackley Municipal Golf Club M38 9TR
☎ 0161 790 6076
9 Holes, 3003yds, Par 35, SSS 69, Course record 68.
Location 2m NW on A6
Telephone for further details
Hotel ★★★ 72% HL Novotel Manchester West, Worsley Brow,
WORSLEY ☎ 0161 799 3535 📠 0161 703 8207 119 en suite

WESTHOUGHTON
Map 7 SD60

Hart Common Golf Club Wigan Rd BL5 2BX
☎ 01942 813195
18 Holes, 5719yards, Par 71, SSS 68.
Course Designer Mike Shattock **Location** on A58 between Bolton and
Wigan
Telephone for further details
Hotel ★★★★ 74% HL De Vere Whites, De Havilland Way,
HORWICH ☎ 01204 667788 📠 01204 474663 125 en suite

Westhoughton Golf Club Long Island, School St BL5 2BR
☎ 01942 811085 & 608958 📠 01942 811085
e-mail: honsec.wgc@btconnect.com
web: www.westhoughtongolfclub.co.uk
Compact downland course.
18 Holes, 5918yds, Par 70, SSS 71. Club membership 370.
Visitors Mon, Wed-Fri except BHs. **Societies** booking required.
Green Fees not confirmed ⓹ **Course Designer** Jeff Shuttleworth
Facilities ⑪ 🍽 🛍 ⌁ 🖥 ⚷ **Leisure** snooker **Conf** Corporate
Hospitality Days **Location** 0.5m NW off A58
Hotel ★★★★ 74% HL De Vere Whites, De Havilland Way,
HORWICH ☎ 01204 667788 📠 01204 474663 125 en suite

WHITEFIELD
Map 7 SD80

Stand Golf Club The Dales, Ashbourne Grove M45 7NL
☎ 0161 766 3197 📠 0161 796 3234
e-mail: secretary@standgolfclub.co.uk
web: www.standgolfclub.co.uk
A semi-parkland course with five moorland holes. Undulating
fairways with views of five counties. A fine test of golf over varied and
characterful holes.
18 Holes, 5695yds, Par 72, Course record 64.
Club membership 500.
Visitors Mon-Fri & BHs. Booking required. Handicap certificate. Dress
code. **Societies** booking required. **Green Fees** £35 **Course Designer** G
Lowe/A Herd **Prof** Mark Dance **Facilities** ⑪ 🍽 🛍 ⌁ 🖥 ⌁
🛍 🝖 ⚷ ⚷ **Leisure** snooker **Conf** Corporate Hospitality Days
Location M60 junct 17, follow A56/A667
Hotel ★★★★ 77% HL Mercure Norton Grange Hotel & Spa,
Manchester Road, Castleton, ROCHDALE ☎ 0870 1942119 & 01706
630788 📠 01706 649313 81 en suite

Whitefield Golf Club Higher Ln M45 7EZ
☎ 0161 351 2700 📠 0161 351 2712
e-mail: enquiries@whitefieldgolfclub.com
web: www.whitefieldgolfclub.co.uk
Picturesque parkland course with stunning views and well-watered
greens. Considered to have some of the best par 3 holes in the North
West.
18 Holes, 5992yds, Par 69, SSS 69, Course record 60.
Club membership 540.
Visitors Mon-Sun & BHs. Booking required. Dress code.
Societies booking required. **Green Fees** phone **Facilities** ⑪ 🍽 🛍
⌁ 🖥 ⌁ 🛍 ⚷ 🝖 ⚷ **Leisure** indoor swing analysis centre
Conf facs Corporate Hospitality Days **Location** M60 junct 17, N of town
centre on A665
Hotel ★★★ 88% HL Malmaison Manchester, Piccadilly,
MANCHESTER ☎ 0161 278 1000 📠 0161 278 1002 167 en suite

ENGLAND

WIGAN — Map 7 SD50

Haigh Hall Golf Complex Copperas Ln WN2 1PE
☎ 01942 831107 ▤ 01942 831417
web: www.haighhall.net

Balcarres Course: 18 Holes, 6300yards, Par 70, SSS 71.
Crawford Course: 9 Holes, 1446yards, Par 28.

Course Designer Steve Marnoch **Location** M6 junct 27/M61 junct 5 or 6, signed Haigh Hall
Telephone for further details
Hotel ★★★★ 73% HL Macdonald Kilhey Court, Chorley Road, Standish, WIGAN ☎ 0870 1942122 ▤ 01257 422401   62 en suite

Wigan Golf Club Arley Hall, Haigh WN1 2UH
☎ 01257 421360 ▤ 01257 426500
e-mail: info@wigangolfclub.co.uk
web: www.wigangolfclub.co.uk

Fairly level parkland with outstanding views and magnificent trees. The fine old clubhouse is the original Arley Hall, and is surrounded by a medieval moat.

18 Holes, 6008yds, Par 70, SSS 69, Course record 62.
Club membership 300.

Visitors Mon. Wed-Fri, Sun & BHs. Booking required. Dress code. **Societies** booking required. **Green Fees** £30 per round **Course Designer** Gaunt & Marnoch **Facilities** ⓕ ⎇ ⮾ ⌨ ⌦ ⌖ ⤫ **Conf** facs Corporate Hospitality Days **Location** M6 junct 27, 3m NE off B5238
Hotel ★★★★ 73% HL Macdonald Kilhey Court, Chorley Road, Standish, WIGAN ☎ 0870 1942122 ▤ 01257 422401   62 en suite

WORSLEY — Map 7 SD70

Ellesmere Golf Club Old Clough Ln M28 7HZ
☎ 0161 790 2122 ▤ 0161 790 2122
e-mail: honsec@ellesmeregolfclub.co.uk
web: www.ellesmeregolfclub.co.uk

Parkland with natural hazards and hard walking. Trees and two streams running through the course make shot strategy an important aspect of the round. Testing holes: 3rd (par 5), 9th (par 3), 15th (par 5).

18 Holes, 6264yds, Par 70, SSS 70. Club membership 700.
Visitors Mon-Fri, Sun & BHs. Booking required. Dress code. **Societies** booking required. **Green Fees** not confirmed **Prof** Simon Wakefield **Facilities** ⓕ ⎇ ⮾ ⌨ ⌦ ⌖ ⤫ **Conf** Corporate Hospitality Days **Location** N of village off A580
Hotel ★★★ 72% HL Novotel Manchester West, Worsley Brow, WORSLEY ☎ 0161 799 3535 ▤ 0161 703 8207   119 en suite

ALDERSHOT — Map 4 SU85

Army Golf Club Laffans Rd GU11 2HF
☎ 01252 337272 ▤ 01252 337562
web: www.armygolfclub.co.uk

18 Holes, 6550yds, Par 71, SSS 71, Course record 66.

Course Designer Frank Pennine/Mackenzie Ebert **Location** 1.5m N of town centre off A323/A325
Telephone for further details
Hotel ★★★ 68% HL Potters International, 1 Fleet Road, ALDERSHOT ☎ 01252 344000 ▤ 01252 311611   103 en suite

ALTON — Map 4 SU73

Worldham Golf Course Cakers Ln, East Worldham GU34 3BF
☎ 01420 543151 ▤ 01420 544606
e-mail: manager@worldhamgolfclub.co.uk
web: www.worldhamgolfclub.co.uk

The course is in a picturesque parkland setting with an abundance of challenging holes (dog-legs, water and sand). Suitable for all golfing standards.

18 Holes, 6257yds, Par 72, SSS 70. Club membership 400.

Visitors Mon-Sun & BHs. **Societies** booking required **Green Fees** £18 per 18 holes Mon-Thu, £20 Fri (£22 weekends and BHs) **Course Designer** F J Whidborne **Prof** Adam Harnett **Facilities** ⓕ ⎇ by prior arrangement ⮾ ⌨ ⌦ ⌖ ⤫ ⌖ **Conf** Corporate Hospitality Days **Location** A31, on B3004
Hotel ★★★ INN The Swan, High Street, ALTON ☎ 01420 83777 ▤ 01420 87975   37 rooms)

AMPFIELD — Map 4 SU42

Ampfield Golf Club Winchester Rd SO51 9BQ
☎ 01794 368480
e-mail: clubhouse@ampfieldgolf.com
web: www.ampfieldgolf.com

Pretty parkland course designed by Henry Cotton in 1963. Well-bunkered greens.

18 Holes, 2478yds, Par 54, SSS 53, Course record 49.
Club membership 230.

Visitors Mon-Sun & BHs. Dress code. **Societies** booking required. **Green Fees** not confirmed **Course Designer** Henry Cotton **Prof** Jon Barnes **Facilities** ⓕ ⎇ ⮾ ⌨ ⌦ ⌖ ⤫ **Conf** facs Corporate Hospitality Days **Location** 4m NE of Romsey on A31
Hotel ★★★ 79% HL Best Western Chilworth Manor, CHILWORTH ☎ 023 8076 7333 ▤ 023 8070 1743   95 en suite

Save on Hotels. Book at **theAA.com/hotel**

HAMPSHIRE

ANDOVER

Map 4 SU34

Andover Golf Club 51 Winchester Rd SP10 2EF
☎ 01264 358040 🗐 01264 358040
e-mail: secretary@andovergolfclub.co.uk
web: www.andovergolfclub.co.uk

Undulating downland course combining a good test of golf for all abilities with breathtaking views across Hampshire countryside. Well-guarded greens and a notable par 3 9th (225yds) with the tee perched on top of a hill, 100ft above the green. Excellent drainage on the chalk base.

18 Holes, 6096yds, Par 70, SSS 69, Course record 64. Club membership 225.

Visitors Mon-Sun & BHs. Booking required. Dress code.
Societies booking required. **Green Fees** not confirmed **Course Designer** J H Taylor **Facilities** ⊕ ⦿ 🍴 🍺 ♨ 🏌 ✆ **Conf** facs Corporate Hospitality Days **Location** 0.5m S on A3057
Hotel ★★★ 62% HL Quality Hotel Andover, Micheldever Road, ANDOVER ☎ 01264 369111 🗐 01264 369000 49 en suite

Hampshire Golf Club Winchester Rd SP11 7TB

☎ 01264 357555 (pro shop) & 356462 (office)
🗐 01264 356606
e-mail: enquiry@thehampshiregolfclub.co.uk
web: www.thehampshiregolfclub.co.uk

Pleasant undulating parkland with fine views and a backdrop of 35,000 young trees and shrubs. The challenging Manor course has two lakes to catch the unwary. Based on chalk which provides very good drainage, with a superb finishing hole.

The Manor: 18 Holes, 6393yds, Par 72, SSS 71, Course record 67. Club membership 500.

Visitors Mon-Sun & BHs. Booking required weekends & BHs. Dress code. **Societies** booking required. **Green Fees** £22 per 18 holes (£29 weekends & BHs) **Course Designer** T C Fiducia **Prof** Tim Baker **Facilities** ⊕ 🍺 ♨ 🏌 ✆ **Leisure** 9 hole par 3 course **Conf** facs Corporate Hospitality Days **Location** 1.5m S of Andover on A3057
Hotel ★★★ 62% HL Quality Hotel Andover, Micheldever Road, ANDOVER ☎ 01264 369111 🗐 01264 369000 49 en suite

BARTON-ON-SEA

Map 4 SZ29

Barton-on-Sea Golf Club Milford Rd BH25 5PP
☎ 01425 615308 🗐 01425 621457
e-mail: admin@barton-on-sea-golf.co.uk
web: www.barton-on-sea-golf.co.uk

A cliff top course with 3 loops of nine giving a great variety and challenge to golfers of all handicaps. Fine views over the Solent and to the Isle of Wight and the Needles.

Becton: 9 Holes, 3182yds, Par 36.
Needles: 9 Holes, 3339yds, Par 36.
Stroller: 9 Holes, 3125yds, Par 36. Club membership 750.

Visitors Mon-Sun & BHs. Booking required Tue, Sun & BHs. Dress code. **Societies** booking required. **Green Fees** £44 per day (£55 weekends & BHs) **Course Designer** Vardon/Colt/Stutt **Prof** Peter Rodgers **Facilities** ⊕ ⦿ by prior arrangement 🍺 ♨ 🏌 🍴 🏌 ✆ 🏌 **Leisure** snooker tables **Conf** Corporate Hospitality Days **Location** B3058 SE of town
Hotel ★★★★ CHH Chewton Glen Hotel & Spa, Christchurch Road, NEW MILTON ☎ 01425 275341 🗐 01425 272310 58 en suite

BASINGSTOKE

Map 4 SU65

See also **Rotherwick**

Basingstoke Golf Club Kempshott Park RG23 7LL
☎ 01256 465990 🗐 01256 331793
e-mail: office@basingstokegolfclub.co.uk
web: www.basingstokegolfclub.co.uk

A well-maintained parkland course. Excellent bunkering requires good course management from the tee and all clubs will be required with many long testing par 4s. A true test of golf, yet fair and playable for the less experienced golfer.

18 Holes, 6289yds, Par 70, SSS 70, Course record 63. Club membership 700.

Visitors Mon-Fri except BHs. Dress code. **Societies** booking required. **Green Fees** £52 per day, £42 per round. Reduced winter fees **Course Designer** James Braid **Prof** Daniel Fisher **Facilities** ⊕ ⦿ 🍺 ♨ 🏌 🍴 🏌 ✆ 🚗 🏌 **Conf** facs Corporate Hospitality Days **Location** M3 junct 7, 1m SW on A30
Hotel ★★★★ 72% HL Apollo Hotel, Aldermaston Roundabout, BASINGSTOKE ☎ 01256 796700 🗐 01256 796701 125 en suite

Dummer Golf Club Dummer RG25 2AD
☎ 01256 397888 (office) & 397950 (pro)
🗐 01256 397889
e-mail: enquiries@dummergolfclub.com
web: www.dummergolfclub.com

Designed by Peter Alliss, this course is set in 165 acres of fine Hampshire countryside with panoramic views. The course meanders around lakes, mature trees and hedgerows. The course combines large, level teeing areas, undulating fairways, fast true greens and cleverly positioned bunkers to provide a challenging golf experience.

18 Holes, 6500yds, Par 72, SSS 71. Club membership 500.

Visitors Mon-Sun & BHs. **Societies** booking required. **Green Fees** not confirmed **Course Designer** Pete Alliss **Prof** Andrew Fannon/Darren Lovegrove **Facilities** ⊕ ⦿ 🍺 ♨ 🏌 🍴 🏌 ✆ 🚗 🏌 **Conf** facs Corporate Hospitality Days **Location** M3 junct 7, towards Dummer, club 0.25m on left
Hotel ★★★★ 74% HL Audleys Wood, Alton Road, BASINGSTOKE ☎ 01256 817555 🗐 01256 817500 72 en suite

Weybrook Park Golf Club Rooksdown Ln RG24 9NT

☎ 01256 320347 🗐 01256 812973
e-mail: info@weybrookpark.co.uk
web: www.weybrookpark.co.uk

An all year course designed to be enjoyable for all standards of player. Easy walking with fabulous views. Extensive practice facility and a further 9 holes opened in 2010.

18 Holes, 6468yds, Par 71, SSS 71. Club membership 600.

Visitors Mon-Fri. Booking required. Handicap certificate. Dress code. **Societies** booking required. **Green Fees** phone **Prof** Anthony Dillon **Facilities** ⊕ ⦿ 🍺 ♨ 🏌 🍴 🏌 ✆ 🚗 🏌 🏌 **Conf** facs Corporate Hospitality Days **Location** 2m W of town centre via A339
Hotel ★★★★ 72% HL Apollo Hotel, Aldermaston Roundabout, BASINGSTOKE ☎ 01256 796700 🗐 01256 796701 125 en suite

BORDON
Map 4 SU73

Blackmoor Golf Club Firgrove Rd, Whitehill GU35 9EH
☎ 01420 472775 📄 01420 487666
e-mail: admin@blackmoorgolf.co.uk
web: www.blackmoorgolf.co.uk

A first-class moorland course with a great variety of holes. Fine greens and wide pine tree-lined fairways are a distinguishing feature. The ground is mainly flat and walking easy.

18 Holes, 6164yds, Par 69, SSS 70, Course record 63.
Club membership 650.

Visitors Mon-Fri except BHs. Handicap certificate. Dress code.
Societies booking required. Green Fees not confirmed Course Designer H S Colt Prof Stephen Clay Facilities ⑪ ⑭ by prior arrangement 🏌 ⛳ 🍴 🏹 🏠 ✂ Conf Corporate Hospitality Days Location 6m S from Farnham on A325, through Whitehill, right at rdbt
Hotel ★★★★ 71% HL Old Thorns Hotel Golf & Country Estate, Griggs Green, LIPHOOK ☎ 01428 724555 📄 01428 725036 150 en suite

BOTLEY
Map 4 SU51

Macdonald Botley Park Hotel, Golf & Spa Winchester Rd, Boorley Green SO32 2UA
☎ 01489 778451 📄 01489 789242
e-mail: golfbotley@macdonald-hotels.co.uk
web: www.macdonaldhotels.co.uk

Pleasantly undulating course with water hazards. Driving range and country club facilities.

Macdonald Botley Park: 18 Holes, 6389yds, Par 70, SSS 70, Course record 63. Club membership 450.

Visitors Mon-Sun & BHs. Booking required. Dress code.
Societies booking required. Green Fees £36 per 18 holes (£42 weekends) Course Designer Ewan Murray Prof Simon Blanshard Facilities ⑪ ⑭ 🏌 ⛳ 🍴 🏹 🏠 🍺 ♨ 🏠 ✂ 🏌
Leisure hard tennis courts, heated indoor swimming pool, squash, sauna, gymnasium, health and beauty spa Conf facs Corporate Hospitality Days Location 1m NW of Botley off B3354
Hotel ★★★★ 76% CHH Macdonald Botley Park, Golf & Country Club, Winchester Road, Boorley Green, BOTLEY ☎ 01489 780 888 & 0870 194 2132 📄 01489 789 242 130 en suite

BROCKENHURST
Map 4 SU20

Brokenhurst Manor Golf Club Sway Rd SO42 7SG
☎ 01590 623332 (Secretary) 📄 01590 624691
e-mail: secretary@brokenhurst-manor.org.uk
web: www.brokenhurst-manor.org.uk

An attractive forest course set in the New Forest, with the unusual feature of three loops of six holes each to complete the round. Fascinating holes include the short 5th and 12th, and the 4th and 17th, both dog-legs. A stream also features on seven of the holes.

18 Holes, 6222yds, Par 70, SSS 70.
Club membership 800.

Visitors Mon-Sun & BHs (weekends after 1.30pm). Booking required. Dress code. Societies booking required. Green Fees £60 per day (£70 weekends & BHs) Course Designer H S Colt Facilities ⑪ ⑭ 🏌 ⛳ 🍴 🏹 🏠 ✂ 🏌 Conf facs Corporate Hospitality Days Location 1m S on B3055

Hotel ★★★★ 74% HL Balmer Lawn, Lyndhurst Road, BROCKENHURST ☎ 01590 623116 📄 01590 623864 54 en suite

BURLEY
Map 4 SU20

Burley Golf Club Cott Ln BH24 4BB
☎ 01425 402431 & 403737 📄 01425 404168
web: www.burleygolfclub.co.uk

9 Holes, 6151yds, Par 71, SSS 70, Course record 62.
Location E of village
Telephone for further details
Hotel ★★★ 78% CHH Moorhill House, BURLEY ☎ 01425 403285 📄 01425 403715 31 en suite

CORHAMPTON
Map 4 SU62

Corhampton Golf Club Shepherds Farm Ln SO32 3GZ
☎ 01489 877279 📄 01489 877680
e-mail: secretary@corhamptongc.co.uk
web: www.corhamptongc.co.uk

Free draining downland course situated in the heart of the picturesque Meon Valley.

18 Holes, 6398yds, Par 71, SSS 71, Course record 65.
Club membership 800.

Visitors Mon-Fri except BHs. Booking required. Dress code.
Societies booking required. Green Fees £48 per 36 holes, £32 per 18 holes Prof Ian Roper Facilities ⑪ ⑭ 🏌 ⛳ 🍴 🏹 🏠 ✂ 🍺 ✂ Conf facs Corporate Hospitality Days Location 1m W of Corhampton off B3035
Hotel ★★★ 80% HL Old House Hotel & Restaurant, The Square, WICKHAM ☎ 01329 833049 📄 01329 833672 12 en suite

CRONDALL
Map 4 SU74

Oak Park Golf Club Heath Ln GU10 5PB
☎ 01252 850850 📄 01252 850851
web: www.oakparkgolf.co.uk

Woodland: 18 Holes, 6352yds, Par 70, SSS 70, Course record 69.
Village: 9 Holes, 3279yds, Par 36.

Course Designer Patrick Dawson Location 0.5m E of village off A287 Farnham-Odiham
Telephone for further details
Hotel ★★★ 77% HL Mercure Bush Hotel, The Borough, FARNHAM ☎ 01252 715237 📄 01252 719297 94 en suite

DENMEAD
Map 4 SU61

Furzeley Golf Course Furzeley Rd PO7 6TX
☎ 023 9223 1180 📄 023 9223 0921

18 Holes, 4488yds, Par 62, SSS 61, Course record 56.
Course Designer Mark Sale/Robert Brown Location from Waterlooville NW onto Hambledon road, signed
Telephone for further details
Hotel ★★★★ 79% HL Portsmouth Marriott Hotel, Southampton Road, PORTSMOUTH ☎ 0870 400 7285 📄 0870 400 7385 174 en suite

Save on Hotels. Book at **theAA.com/hotel**

HAMPSHIRE

EASTLEIGH
Map 4 SU41

East Horton Golf Centre Mortimers Ln, Fair Oak SO50 7EA
☎ 023 8060 2111 📠 023 8069 6280
e-mail: info@easthorton.com
web: www.easthorton.com

Courses set out over 260 acres of glorious Hampshire countryside. Three beautifully kept courses offering a range of challenges, outstanding practice facilities and a 19th hole in the 16th century tithe barn.
Greenwood: 18 Holes, 6186yds, Par 72, SSS 70.
Parkland: 18 Holes, 5672yds, Par 69, SSS 70.
Club membership 700.
Visitors Mon-Sun & BHs. Booking recommended. Dress code.
Societies booking required. **Green Fees** not confirmed **Course Designer** Guy Hunt **Prof** Miles Harding/Conrad Claxton **Facilities** ⓘ ⑩ 🍴 🛢 ⬜ 🏌 ◇ 🏐 🛒 🚽 🏊 **Leisure** sauna, gymnasium, 9 hole par 3 Marwell course **Conf** facs Corporate Hospitality Days **Location** off B3037
Hotel ★★★ 73% HL Marwell, Thompsons Lane, Colden Common, Marwell, WINCHESTER ☎ 01962 777681 📠 01962 777160 66 en suite

Fleming Park Golf Club Passfield Av SO50 9NL
☎ 023 8061 2797 📠 023 8065 1686

18 Holes, 4524yds, Par 65, SSS 62, Course record 62.
Course Designer David Miller **Location** E of town centre
Telephone for further details
Hotel ★★★ 79% HL Holiday Inn Southampton-Eastleigh M3 Jct 13, Leigh Road, EASTLEIGH ☎ 0871 942 9075 📠 023 8064 3945 129 en suite

FAREHAM
Map 4 SU50

Cams Hall Estate Golf Club Cams Hall Estate PO16 8UP
☎ 01329 827222 📠 01329 827111
e-mail: camshall@crown-golf.co.uk
web: www.camshallgolf.co.uk

Two Peter Alliss/Clive Clark designed golf courses. The Creek Course is coastal and has salt and fresh water lakes and the fairways are lined with undulating hills. The Park Course is designed in the grounds of Cams Hall.
Creek Course: 18 Holes, 6201yds, Par 71, SSS 70, Course record 62.
Park Course: 9 Holes, 3202yds, Par 36.
Club membership 1100.
Visitors Mon-Sun & BHs. Creek weekends after noon. Booking required. Dress code. **Societies** booking required. **Green Fees** not confirmed **Course Designer** Peter Alliss **Prof** Sam Pleshette **Facilities** ⓘ ⑩ 🛢 ⬜ 🏌 🏊 🏐 🚽 🛒 🚽 **Leisure** sauna **Conf** facs Corporate Hospitality Days **Location** M27 junct 11, A27
Hotel ★★★ 73% HL Lysses House, 51 High Street, FAREHAM ☎ 01329 822622 📠 01329 822762 21 en suite

FARNBOROUGH
Map 4 SU85

Southwood Golf Course Ively Rd, Cove GU14 0LJ
☎ 01252 548700 📠 01252 549091
e-mail: enquiries@southwoodgolfcourse.co.uk
web: www.southwoodgolfcourse.co.uk
Municipal parkland golf course.
18 Holes, 5669yds, Par 69, SSS 68, Course record 64.
Club membership 400.
Visitors Mon-Sun & BHs. Booking advisable. **Societies** booking required. **Green Fees** £19 per 18 holes Mon-Thu (£22 Fri-Sun). 9 holes £11/£13 **Course Designer** Hawtree & Son **Prof** Chris Hudson **Facilities** ⓘ ⑩ 🛢 ⬜ 🏌 🏊 🏐 🚽 🛒 🚽 **Conf** facs Corporate Hospitality Days **Location** 0.5m W
Hotel ★★★ 81% HL Holiday Inn Farnborough, Lynchford Road, FARNBOROUGH ☎ 0871 942 9029 & 01252 894300 📠 01252 523166 142 en suite

FLEET
Map 4 SU85

North Hants Golf Club Minley Rd GU51 1RF
☎ 01252 616443 📠 01252 811627
e-mail: secretary@north-hants-fleetgc.co.uk
web: www.northhantsgolf.co.uk

Picturesque tree-lined course with much heather and gorse close to the fairways. The club is currently completing a woodland management scheme which will give new views and incorporate a review of fairway and greenside bunkering. A testing first hole to the course is a 214yd followed by many other testing holes around the course. The ground is rather undulating and, though not tiring, does offer some excellent blind shots, and more than a few surprises in judging distance.
18 Holes, 6472yds, Par 70, SSS 72, Course record 65.
Club membership 600.
Visitors Mon-Sun & BHs. Booking required Tue & Wed. Handicap certificate. Dress code. **Societies** Booking required. **Green Fees** not confirmed **Course Designer** James Braid **Prof** Steve Porter **Facilities** ⓘ ⑩ 🛢 ⬜ 🏌 🏊 🏐 ◇ 🚽 **Conf** facs Corporate Hospitality Days **Location** 0.25m N of Fleet station on B3013
Hotel ★★★ 70% HL The Ely, London Road (A30), Blackwater, CAMBERLEY ☎ 01252 860444 📠 01252 878265 35 en suite

GOSPORT
Map 4 SZ69

Gosport & Stokes Bay Golf Club Off Fort Rd, Haslar
PO12 2AT
☎ 023 9252 7941
e-mail: secretary@gosportandstokesbaygolfclub.co.uk
web: www.gosportandstokesbaygolfclub.co.uk
A testing links course overlooking the Solent, with plenty of gorse and short rough. Changing winds.
9 Holes, 6189yds, Par 71, SSS 69, Course record 65.
Club membership 400.
Visitors Mon-Sat except BHs. Dress code Societies booking required.
Green Fees £18 per 18 holes, £9 per 9 holes. ⊛ Facilities ⑪ ⚑
⫿ ⛴ ⚒ 🏠 🛒 ✦ Location A32 S from Fareham, E onto Fort Rd
to Haslar
Hotel ★★★ 73% HL Lysses House, 51 High Street, FAREHAM
☎ 01329 822622 📄 01329 822762 21 en suite

HARTLEY WINTNEY
Map 4 SU75

Hartley Wintney Golf Club London Rd RG27 8PT
☎ 01252 844211 (Sec/Gen Mgr) 📄 01252 844211
e-mail: office@hartleywintneygolfclub.com
web: www.hartleywintneygolfclub.com
Easy walking parkland and partly wooded course in pleasant countryside. Provides a challenging test for golfers of all abilities with many mature trees and water hazards.
18 Holes, 6240yds, Par 71, SSS 71. Club membership 650.
Visitors Mon-Sun & BHs. Booking required. Dress code.
Societies booking required. Green Fees £50 per day, £38 per 18 holes
(£45 per 18 holes weekends) Prof Martin Smith Facilities ⑪ ⚑
⫿ ⛴ ⚒ 🏠 🛒 ✦ Leisure indoor teaching studio Conf facs
Corporate Hospitality Days Location NE of village on A30
Hotel ★★★ 79% HL The Elvetham Hotel, HARTLEY WINTNEY
☎ 01252 844871 📄 01252 844161 72 en suite

HAYLING ISLAND
Map 4 SU70

Hayling Golf Club Links Ln PO11 0BX
☎ 023 9246 4446
e-mail: members@haylinggolf.co.uk
web: www.haylinggolf.co.uk
A quality links course offering fine seascapes and views of the Isle of Wight. Varying sea breezes and sometimes strong winds ensure that the course seldom plays the same two days running. The course builds and improves from the opening par 3.
18 Holes, 6531yds, Par 71, SSS 71, Course record 63.
Club membership 1000.
Visitors Mon-Fri, Sun & BHs. Booking required Sun & BHs. Dress code. Societies booking required. Green Fees £70 per day, £56 per round (weekends £80/£70) Course Designer Taylor 1905, Simpson 1933 Prof Mark Treleaven Facilities ⑪ ⑪ ⚑ ⫿ ⛴ ⚒ 🏠
🛒 ✦ Conf facs Corporate Hospitality Days Location SW side
of island at West Town
Hotel ★★★ 80% HL Brookfield, Havant Road, EMSWORTH
☎ 01243 373363 📄 01243 376342 39 en suite

KINGSCLERE
Map 4 SU55

Sandford Springs Golf Club RG26 5RT
☎ 01635 296800 & 296808 (Pro Shop)
📄 01635 296801
e-mail: info@sandfordspringsgolf.co.uk
web: www.sandfordsprings.co.uk
The course has unique variety in beautiful surroundings and offers three distinctive loops of nine holes. There are water hazards, woodlands and gradients to negotiate, providing a challenge for all playing categories.
The Park: 9 Holes, 2978yds, Par 34, SSS 34.
The Lakes: 9 Holes, 3127yds, Par 35, SSS 35.
The Woods: 9 Holes, 3148yds, Par 36, SSS 36.
Club membership 600.
Visitors Mon-Fri. Weekends & BHs after 1pm. Booking required.
Dress code. Societies booking required. Green Fees Mon-Thu
£35 per 18 holes, Fri-Sun £40 (4 for 3 offer daily) Course
Designer Hawtree & Son Prof Neal Granville Facilities ⑪ ⑪
⚑ ⫿ ⛴ ⚒ 🏠 🛒 ⚐ ✦ ✦ Conf facs Corporate
Hospitality Days Location on A339 between Basingstoke & Newbury
Hotel ★★★★ 72% HL Apollo Hotel, Aldermaston Roundabout,
BASINGSTOKE ☎ 01256 796700 📄 01256 796701 125 en suite

KINGSLEY
Map 4 SU73

Dean Farm Golf Club GU35 9NG
☎ 01420 489478
web: www.deanfarmgolf.co.uk
9 Holes, 1600yds, Par 31.
Location W of village off B3004
Telephone for further details
Hotel ★★★ 79% HL Best Western Frensham Pond Hotel, Bacon
Lane, CHURT ☎ 01252 795161 📄 01252 792631 51 en suite

LEE-ON-THE-SOLENT
Map 4 SU50

Lee-on-the-Solent Golf Club Brune Ln PO13 9PB
☎ 023 9255 1170 📄 023 9255 4233
e-mail: enquiries@leeonthesolentgolfclub.co.uk
web: www.leegolf.co.uk
Predominantly heath and oak woodland. While not long in length, still a good test of golf requiring accuracy off the tee to score well. Excellent greens and five very challenging par 3s.
18 Holes, 5962yds, SSS 68, Course record 62.
Club membership 725.
Visitors Mon-Sun & BHs. Booking required. Dress code
Societies welcome. Green Fees not confirmed Prof Rob Edwards
Facilities ⑪ ⑪ ⚑ ⫿ ⛴ ⚒ 🏠 ✦ ✦ Conf facs
Corporate Hospitality Days Location 3m S of Fareham
Hotel ★★★ 73% HL Lysses House, 51 High Street, FAREHAM
☎ 01329 822622 📄 01329 822762 21 en suite

OLD THORNS GOLF & COUNTRY ESTATE

HAMPSHIRE - LIPHOOK - MAP 4 SU83

The wonderful location of this demanding 18 hole championship course makes it a delight for golfers of all standards. Set in a country estate of 400 acres, the course winds its way through rolling hills past natural springs and lakes and offers spectacular views across the beautiful Hampshire countryside. Designed in 1976 by Commander John Harris, the construction was overseen by former golfer and broadcaster Peter Alliss, and opened in 1982. The 10th is a particularly tricky hole, while the 16th has a sign reading 'if your tee shot does not come to rest on the green could you please put a pound in the charity box on the bar'. It is a challenging course and one with many rewards.

Griggs Green GU30 7PE ☎ 01428 724555 📠 01428 725036
e-mail: sales@oldthorns.com **web:** www.oldthorns.com
18 Holes, 6461yds, Par 72, SSS 72. Club membership 200.
Visitors Mon-Sun & BHs. Booking required BHs. Dress code. **Societies** booking required. **Green Fees** £40 (£50 weekends & BHs). £65 per day (£80) **Course Designer** Peter Alliss **Prof** Peter Chapman **Facilities** 🍴 🍽 🍔 ☕ 🍷 🧥 🏠 ⛳ 📘 🚗 🛒 🏌 **Leisure** hard tennis courts, heated indoor swimming pool, fishing, sauna, gymnasium **Conf** facs Corporate Hospitality Days **Location** off A3 at Griggs Green, S of Liphook, signed Old Thorns
Hotel ★★★★ 71% HL Old Thorns Hotel Golf & Country Estate, Griggs Green, LIPHOOK ☎ 01428 724555 📠 01428 725036 150 en suite

LIPHOOK
Map 4 SU83

Liphook Golf Club Wheatsheaf Enclosure GU30 7EH
☎ 01428 723271 & 723785 📄 01428 724853
e-mail: secretary@liphookgolfclub.com
web: www.liphookgolfclub.com
Heathland course with easy walking and fine views.
*18 Holes, 6295yds, Par 70, SSS 70, Course record 67.
Club membership 800.*
Visitors Mon-Sat. Sun & BHs pm. Booking required Wed-Fri.
Handicap certificate. Dress code. **Societies** booking required. **Green
Fees** £74 per day, £58 per round (£80/£74 Sat) **Course Designer** A
C Croome **Prof** Ian Mowbray **Facilities** ⊕ ⓘ 🏌 ⚐ ⊡ ⚑ ⚘ 𝄞
⚑ ✎ ⚑ ✎ ⚑ **Conf** Corporate Hospitality Days **Location** 1m
S on B2070
Hotel ★★★★ 74% HL Lythe Hill Hotel and Spa, Petworth Road,
HASLEMERE ☎ 01428 651251 📄 01428 644131 41 en suite

Old Thorns Golf & Country Estate see page 121
Griggs Green GU30 7PE
☎ 01428 724555 📄 01428 725036
e-mail: sales@oldthorns.com
web: www.oldthorns.com

LYNDHURST
Map 4 SU20

Bramshaw Golf Club Brook SO43 7HE
☎ 023 8081 3433 📄 023 8081 3460
web: www.bramshaw.co.uk
*Manor Course: 18 Holes, 6527yds, Par 71, SSS 71,
Course record 65.
Forest Course: 18 Holes, 5774yds, Par 69, SSS 68,
Course record 65.*
Location M27 junct 1, 1m W on B3079
Telephone for further details
Hotel ★★★ 83% HL Bell Inn, BROOK ☎ 023 8081 2214
📄 023 8081 3958 27 en suite

New Forest Golf Club Southampton Rd SO43 7BU
☎ 023 8028 2484 & 8028 3094 📄 023 8028 4030
e-mail: secretarynfgc@aol.com
web: www.newforestgolfclub.co.uk
One of the oldest courses in Hampshire, established 1888, situated
in the heart of the New Forest in an Area of Outstanding Natural
Beauty with some of the most scenic holes in Hampshire. An easy
walking course but with some testing holes giving the feel of
playing golf as it was originally intended.
*18 Holes, 5536yds, Par 69, SSS 67, Course record 64.
Club membership 500.*
Visitors Mon-Sat & BHs. Sun pm only. Booking required. Handicap
certificate. Dress code. **Societies** booking required. **Green
Fees** phone **Prof** Chris Tyrrell **Facilities** ⊕ ⓘ 🏌 ⚐ ⊡ ⚑ ⚘
⚑ ⚑ ✎ **Conf** Corporate Hospitality Days **Location** 0.5m NE
off A35
Hotel ★★★ 75% HL Best Western Crown, High Street,
LYNDHURST ☎ 023 8028 2922 📄 023 8028 2751 38 en suite

NEW ALRESFORD
Map 4 SU53

Alresford Golf Club Cheriton Rd, Tichborne Down
SO24 0PN
☎ 01962 733746 & 733998 (pro shop) 📄 01962 736040
e-mail: secretary@alresfordgolf.co.uk
web: www.alresfordgolf.co.uk
A rolling downland course on well-drained chalk. The five difficult par
3s, tree-lined fairways and well-guarded fast greens ensure that the
course offers a true test of skill, even for the most experienced golfer.
Regular venue for county tournaments.
*18 Holes, 5984yds, Par 69, SSS 69, Course record 64.
Club membership 600.*
Visitors Mon-Sun & BHs. Dress code. **Societies** booking required.
Green Fees summer £32 per 18 holes (£40 weekends). Winter
£24/£30 **Course Designer** Scott, Webb & Young **Prof** Malcolm Scott
Facilities ⊕ ⓘ by prior arrangement 🏌 ⚐ ⊡ ⚑ ⚘ ✎
⚑ ⚘ ✎ **Conf** Corporate Hospitality Days **Location** 1m S
of Alresford on the B3046 with easy access from the A31 and M3
Hotel ★★ 68% HL Swan, 11 West Street, ALRESFORD
☎ 01962 732302 & 734427 📄 01962 735274 23 en suite

OVERTON
Map 4 SU54

Test Valley Golf Club Micheldever Rd RG25 3DS
☎ 01256 771737 📄 01256 771285
e-mail: pro@testvalleygolf.com
web: www.testvalleygolf.com
A downland course with excellent drainage, fine year-round greens
and prominent water and bunker features. On undulating terrain with
lovely views over the Hampshire countryside.
*18 Holes, 6605yds, Par 72, SSS 71, Course record 63.
Club membership 500.*
Visitors Mon-Sun & BHs. Booking required. **Societies** booking
required. **Green Fees** not confirmed **Course Designer** Don Wright
Prof Alastair Briggs/Claire Duffy **Facilities** ⊕ ⓘ 🏌 ⚐ ⊡ ⚑
⚘ ⚑ ⚑ ✎ ⚑ ✎ **Conf** facs Corporate Hospitality Days
Location M3 junct 8 southbound, from A303 take junct signed Overton
and follow brown signs. M3 junct 9 northbound, take A34 to A303
signed Basingstoke, leave at junct signed Overton and follow brown
signs
Hotel ★★★★ 76% HL Norton Park, SUTTON SCOTNEY
☎ 0845 074 0055 & 01962 763000 📄 01962 760860 175 en suite

OWER
Map 4 SU31

Paultons Golf Centre Old Salisbury Rd SO51 6AN
☎ 023 8081 3992 📄 023 8081 3993
web: www.paultonsgolf.co.uk
18 Holes, 6238yds, Par 71, SSS 70, Course record 67.
Course Designer J R Smith **Location** M27 junct 2, A36 towards
Salisbury, 1st rdbt 1st exit, 1st right at Vine pub
Telephone for further details
Hotel ★★★ 80% HL Bartley Lodge Hotel, Lyndhurst Road, CADNAM
☎ 023 8081 2248 📄 023 8081 2075 40 en suite

Save on Hotels. Book at **theAA.com/hotel**

HAMPSHIRE

ENGLAND

PETERSFIELD
Map 4 SU72

Petersfield Golf Club Tankerdale Ln, Liss GU33 7QY
☎ 01730 895165 (office)
e-mail: manager@pgc1892.net
web: www.petersfieldgolfclub.co.uk
Gently undulating course of downland and parkland with mature trees and hedgerows. Very free drainage in an Area of Outstanding Natural Beauty.
18 Holes, 6450yds, Par 72, SSS 71, Course record 66.
Club membership 800.
Visitors Booking required. Dress code. **Societies** booking required.
Green Fees £42 per day per 18 holes, £32 per round (£50/£40 weekends & BHs) **Course Designer** M Hawtree **Prof** Greg Hughes
Facilities ⓘ ⓞ ⓑ ⓒ ⓕ ⓛ ⓐ ⓔ ⓔ ⓕ **Location** off the A3(M), between the Liss/Petersfield exits southbound
Hotel ★★★ 75% HL Langrish House, Langrish, PETERSFIELD
☎ 01730 266941 ☒ 01730 260543 13 en suite

PORTSMOUTH
Map 4 SU60

Great Salterns Public Course Burrfields Rd PO3 5HH
☎ 023 9266 4549 ☒ 023 9265 0525
e-mail: enquiries@portsmouthgolfcentre.co.uk
web: www.portsmouthgolfcentre.co.uk
Easy walking, seaside course with open fairways and testing shots onto well-guarded, small greens. Testing 13th hole, par 4, requiring 130yd shot across a lake.
18 Holes, 5426yds, Par 69, SSS 67. Club membership 700.
Visitors Mon-Sun & BHs. Booking required. **Societies** booking required. **Green Fees** not confirmed **Prof** Terry Healy **Facilities** ⓘ ⓞ ⓑ ⓕ ⓐ ⓓ ◇ ⓕ **Conf** facs **Location** NE of town centre on A2030
Hotel ★★★★ 79% HL Portsmouth Marriott Hotel, Southampton Road, PORTSMOUTH ☎ 0870 400 7285 ☒ 0870 400 7385 174 en suite

ROMSEY
Map 4 SU32

Dunwood Manor Golf Club Danes Rd SO51 0GF
☎ 01794 340549 ☒ 01794 341215
web: www.dunwood-golf.co.uk
18 Holes, 5655yds, Par 69, SSS 68, Course record 65.
Location 4m NW of Romsey off A27
Telephone for further details
Hotel ★★★ 83% HL Bell Inn, BROOK ☎ 023 8081 2214
☒ 023 8081 3958 27 en suite

Romsey Golf Club Romsey Rd, Nursling SO16 0XW
☎ 023 8073 4637 ☒ 023 8074 1036
e-mail: secretary@romseygolfclub.co.uk
web: www.romseygolfclub.com
Parkland and woodland course with narrow tree-lined fairways. Six holes are undulating, the rest are sloping. Excellent test of golf for all standards.
18 Holes, 5718yds, Par 69, SSS 68, Course record 64.
Club membership 800.
Visitors Mon-Fri except BHs. **Societies** booking required. **Green Fees** £38 per day, £32 per round **Prof** Ben Stambrough **Facilities** ⓘ ⓞ ⓑ ⓒ ⓕ ⓐ ⓔ ⓕ ⓔ ⓕ **Leisure** refreshments at 11th

tee **Conf** facs Corporate Hospitality Days **Location** 1m N M27 junct 3 on A3057
Hotel ★★★ 79% HL Best Western Chilworth Manor, CHILWORTH
☎ 023 8076 7333 ☒ 023 8070 1743 95 en suite

Wellow Golf Course Ryedown Ln, East Wellow SO51 6BD
☎ 01794 323833 & 322872 ☒ 01794 323832
web: www.wellowgolfclub.co.uk
Three nine-hole courses set in 217 acres of parkland surrounding Embley Park, former home of Florence Nightingale.
Ryedown: 18 Holes, 5955yds, Par 70, SSS 68.
Embley: 18 Holes, 5955yds, Par 70, SSS 68.
Blackwater: 18 Holes, 6305yds, Par 72, SSS 70.
Club membership 600.
Visitors Mon-Sun & BHs. Booking required. **Societies** booking required. **Green Fees** £23 per 18 holes (£28 weekends & BHs).
Special offers afternoon ⓐ **Course Designer** W Wiltshire
Prof Neil Bratley **Facilities** ⓘ ⓞ ⓑ ⓒ ⓕ ⓐ ⓔ ⓕ
ⓔ ⓕ **Leisure** gymnasium **Conf** facs Corporate Hospitality Days
Location M27 junct 2, A36 towards Salisbury, 1m right to Whinwhistle Rd
Hotel ★★★ 79% HL Best Western Chilworth Manor, CHILWORTH
☎ 023 8076 7333 ☒ 023 8070 1743 95 en suite

ROTHERWICK
Map 4 SU75

Tylney Park Golf Club RG27 9AY
☎ 01256 762079 ☒ 01256 763079
web: www.tylneypark.co.uk
18 Holes, 7017yds, Par 72, SSS 74, Course record 68.
Course Designer D Steel/T Mackenzie **Location** M3 junct 5, 2m NW of Hook. 9m S of M4 junct 11 via A33.
Telephone for further details
Hotel ★★★★ HL Tylney Hall Hotel, ROTHERWICK
☎ 01256 764881 ☒ 01256 768141 112 en suite

ROWLAND'S CASTLE
Map 4 SU71

Rowlands Castle Golf Club 31 Links Ln PO9 6AE
☎ 023 9241 2784 ☒ 023 9241 3649
e-mail: manager@rowlandscastlegolfclub.co.uk
web: www.rowlandscastlegolfclub.co.uk
Reasonably dry in winter, the flat parkland course is a testing one with a number of tricky dog-legs and bunkers much in evidence. The par 4 13th is a signature hole necessitating a drive to a narrow fairway and a second shot to a two-tiered green. The 7th, at 522yds, is the longest hole on the course and leads to a well-guarded armchair green.
18 Holes, 6642yds, Par 72, SSS 72, Course record 67.
Club membership 800.
Visitors Mon-Fri, Sun & BHs. Dress code. **Societies** booking required. **Green Fees** £40 per day (£45 Sun) **Course Designer** Colt
Prof Peter Klepacz **Facilities** ⓘ ⓞ ⓑ ⓒ ⓕ ⓐ ⓔ ⓕ
ⓔ ⓕ **Conf** Corporate Hospitality Days **Location** W of village off B2149
Hotel ★★★ 80% HL Brookfield, Havant Road, EMSWORTH
☎ 01243 373363 ☒ 01243 376342 39 en suite

SHEDFIELD
Map 4 SU51

Meon Valley, A Marriott Hotel & Country Club Sandy Ln SO32 2HQ
☎ 01329 833455 🖹 01329 834411

It has been said that a golf-course architect is as good as the ground on which he has to work. Here Hamilton Stutt had magnificent terrain at his disposal and a very good and lovely parkland course is the result. There are three holes over water.

Meon Course: 18 Holes, 6520yds, Par 71, SSS 71, Course record 66.
Valley Course: 9 Holes, 2879yds, Par 35, SSS 34.
Club membership 560.

Visitors Mon-Sun & BHs. Booking required. **Societies** booking required. **Green Fees** not confirmed **Course Designer** Hamilton Stutt **Prof** Neal Grist **Facilities** ⑪ ⑪ ⬛ ⬜ 卪 ⌿ 🖫 ◇ ⚒ 🍴 ⚒ 🏌 **Leisure** hard tennis courts, heated indoor swimming pool, sauna, gymnasium **Conf** facs Corporate Hospitality Days **Location** M27 junct 7, off A334 between Botley & Wickham
Hotel ★★★★ 80% HL Meon Valley, A Marriott Hotel & Country Club, Sandy Lane, SHEDFIELD ☎ 01329 833455 🖹 01329 834411 113 en suite

SOUTHAMPTON
Map 4 SU41

Chilworth Golf Club Main Rd SO16 7JP
☎ 023 8074 0544 🖹 023 8073 3166

Manor Golf Course: 18 Holes, 5915yds, Par 69, SSS 69, Course record 68.

Course Designer J Garner **Location** A27 between Chilworth & Romsey
Telephone for further details
Hotel ★★★ 79% HL Best Western Chilworth Manor, CHILWORTH ☎ 023 8076 7333 🖹 023 8070 1743 95 en suite

Stoneham Golf Club Monks Wood Close, Bassett SO16 3TT
☎ 023 8076 9272 🖹 023 8076 6320
e-mail: richard@stonehamgolfclub.org.uk
web: www.stonehamgolfclub.org.uk

Undulating through an attractive parkland and heathland setting with views over the Itchen Valley towards Winchester, this course rewards brains over brawn. It is unusual in having five par 5s and five par 3s and no two holes alike. The quality of the course means that temporary greens are never used and the course is rarely closed.

18 Holes, 6392yds, Par 72, SSS 71, Course record 63.
Club membership 710.

Visitors Mon-Sun & BHs. Booking required. Handicap certificate.

Dress code. **Societies** booking required. **Green Fees** £57 per day, £50 per round (£67/£57 weekends & BHs) **Course Designer** Willie Park Jnr **Prof** Ian Young **Facilities** ⑪ ⑪ ⬛ ⬜ 卪 ⌿ 🖫 ⚒ ◢ **Conf** facs Corporate Hospitality Days **Location** end of M3, 4m N of city centre off A27
Hotel ★★★ 79% HL Best Western Chilworth Manor, CHILWORTH ☎ 023 8076 7333 🖹 023 8070 1743 95 en suite

SOUTHWICK
Map 4 SU60

Southwick Park Golf Club Pinsley Dr PO17 6EL
☎ 023 923 80131 🖹 0871 8559809
web: www.southwickparkgolfclub.co.uk

18 Holes, 5884yds, Par 69, SSS 69, Course record 64.

Course Designer C Lawrie **Location** 0.5m SE off B2177
Telephone for further details
Hotel ★★★ 80% HL Old House Hotel & Restaurant, The Square, WICKHAM ☎ 01329 833049 🖹 01329 833672 12 en suite

TADLEY
Map 4 SU66

Bishopswood Golf Course Bishopswood Ln RG26 4AT
☎ 0118 940 8600
e-mail: kpickett@bishopswoodgc.co.uk
web: www.bishopswoodgc.co.uk

Wooded parkland with numerous water hazards. Considered to be one of the best nine-hole courses in the UK and venue of the National 9s regional finals.

9 Holes, 6474yds, Par 72, SSS 71. Club membership 400.

Visitors Advance booking required. Dress code. **Societies** booking required. **Green Fees** £23 per 18 holes (£30 weekends), £14 per 9 holes **Course Designer** M W Phillips/G Blake **Prof** Steve Ward **Facilities** ⑪ ⑪ ⬛ ⬜ 卪 ⌿ 🖫 ⚒ 🍴 ◢ **Conf** facs Corporate Hospitality Days **Location** 6m N of Basingstoke off A340
Hotel ★★★★ 73% HL Best Western West Grange, Cox's Lane, Bath Road, Midgham, NEWBURY ☎ 01635 273074 🖹 01635 862351 68 en suite

WATERLOOVILLE
Map 4 SU60

Portsmouth Golf Course Crookhorn Ln, Purbrook PO7 5QL
☎ 023 9237 2210 🖹 023 9220 0766
e-mail: info@portsmouthgc.com
web: www.portsmouthgc.com

Hilly, challenging course with good views of Portsmouth Harbour. Rarely free from the wind and the picturesque 6th, 17th and 18th holes can test the best.

18 Holes, 5641yds, Par 69, SSS 68, Course record 64.
Club membership 600.

Visitors Mon-Sun & BHs. Booking required weekends & BHs. Dress code. **Societies** booking required. **Green Fees** £18 per 18 holes (weekends £21) **Course Designer** Hawtree **Prof** James Green **Facilities** ⑪ ⑪ ⬛ ⬜ 卪 ⌿ 🖫 ⚒ 🍴 ⚒ ◢ **Conf** facs Corporate Hospitality Days **Location** 2m S off A3
Hotel ★★★★ 79% HL Portsmouth Marriott Hotel, Southampton Road, PORTSMOUTH ☎ 0870 400 7285 🖹 0870 400 7385 174 en suite

Save on Hotels. Book at theAA.com/hotel

HAMPSHIRE – HEREFORDSHIRE

ENGLAND

Waterlooville Golf Club Cherry Tree Av, Cowplain PO8 8AP
☎ 023 9226 3388 📠 023 9224 2980
e-mail: secretary@waterloovillegolfclub.co.uk
web: www.waterloovillegolfclub.co.uk

Easy walking but challenging parkland course, with five par 5s over 500yds and featuring four ponds and a stream running through. The 13th hole, at 556yds, has a carry over a pond for a drive and a stream crossing the fairway and ending in a very small green.

18 Holes, 6550yds, Par 72, SSS 71, Course record 63.
Club membership 800.

Visitors Mon-Fri except BHs (Sat-Sun phone ahead). Booking required. Handicap certificate. Dress code. **Societies** booking required. **Green Fees** £40 per day/round **Course Designer** Henry Cotton **Prof** John Hay **Facilities** ⓘ ▢◎▢ by prior arrangement �& ▢ ▯◎ ▢ ▵ ▭ ▣ ▰
✦ **Conf** Corporate Hospitality Days **Location** NE of town centre off A3
Hotel ★★★ 80% HL Brookfield, Havant Road, EMSWORTH
☎ 01243 373363 📠 01243 376342 39 en suite

WICKHAM   Map 4 SU51

Wickham Park Titchfield Ln PO17 5PJ
☎ 01329 833342 & 836356 📠 01329 834798
e-mail: wickhampark-memberships@crown-golf.co.uk
web: www.crown-golf.co.uk

An attractive 18-hole parkland course set in the Meon Valley. Ideal for beginners and established golfers alike. The course is not overly demanding but is challenging enough to provide an enjoyable round of golf.

18 Holes, 5898yards, Par 69, SSS 68, Course record 65.
Club membership 600.

Visitors Dress code. **Societies** booking required. **Green Fees** £18 per 18 holes (£22 weekends) **Prof** Scott Edwards **Facilities** ⓘ ▢◎▢ ▵
▢ ▵ ▭ ▣ ✦ ▰ ✦ **Leisure** chipping area **Conf** facs Corporate Hospitality Days **Location** M27 junct 9/10
Hotel ★★★ 80% HL Old House Hotel & Restaurant, The Square, WICKHAM ☎ 01329 833049 📠 01329 833672 12 en suite

---

WINCHESTER   Map 4 SU42

Hockley Golf Club Twyford SO21 1PL
☎ 01962 713165 📠 01962 713612
e-mail: secretary@hockleygolfclub.com
web: www.hockleygolfclub.com

A James Braid designed course set in 250 acres of historical chalk downland overlooking Winchester.

18 Holes, 6420yds, Par 71, SSS 72, Course record 64.
Club membership 750.

Visitors Mon-Sun & BHs. Dress code. **Societies** booking required.
Green Fees £50 per day, £40 per round (£50 weekends) **Course Designer** James Braid **Prof** Gary Stubbington **Facilities** ⓘ ▢◎▢ ▵
▢ ▵ ▭ ▣ ✦ ▰ ✦ ✦ **Conf** Corporate Hospitality Days
Location M3 junct 11, signed to Twyford
Hotel ★★★★ 69% HL Mercure Wessex, Paternoster Row, WINCHESTER ☎ 01962 861611 📠 01962 841503 94 en suite

Royal Winchester Golf Club Sarum Rd SO22 5QE
☎ 01962 852462 📠 01962 865048
e-mail: manager@royalwinchestergolfclub.com
web: www.royalwinchestergolfclub.com

The Royal Winchester course is a sporting downland course centred on a rolling valley, so the course is hilly in places with fine views over the surrounding countryside. Built on chalk downs, the course drains extremely well and offers an excellent playing surface.

18 Holes, 6387yds, Par 72, SSS 72, Course record 68.
Club membership 800.

Visitors Mon-Sun except BHs. Handicap certificate. Dress code.
Societies booking required. **Green Fees** phone **Course Designer** J H Taylor **Prof** Steven Hunter **Facilities** ⓘ ▢◎▢ by prior arrangement
▢ ▵ ▭ ▣ ✦ ▰ ✦ **Conf** Corporate Hospitality Days
Location 1.5m W off A3090
Hotel ★★★★ CHH Lainston House, Sparsholt, WINCHESTER
☎ 01962 776088 📠 01962 776672 49 en suite

South Winchester Golf Club Romsey Rd SO22 5QX
☎ 01962 877800 📠 01962 877900
e-mail: swgc@crown-golf.co.uk
web: www.crown-golf.co.uk/southwinchester

This links style course in two loops of nine holes provides all golfers with a fair challenge. The course undulates between grassy slopes and beside several lakes offering easy walking and excellent views. Excellent drainage on the chalk based surface.

18 Holes, 7086yds, Par 72, SSS 72, Course record 63.
Club membership 800.

Visitors Mon-Sun & BHs. Booking required. Dress code.
Societies booking required. **Green Fees** not confirmed **Course Designer** Dave Thomas/Peter Alliss **Prof** Richard Adams **Facilities** ⓘ
▢◎▢ ▵ ▢ ▵ ▭ ▣ ✦ ▰ ✦ ✦ **Conf** facs Corporate Hospitality Days **Location** M3 junct 11, on A3090 Romsey road
Hotel ★★★ 78% HL The Winchester Royal Hotel, St Peter Street, WINCHESTER ☎ 01962 840840 📠 01962 841582 75 en suite

---

HEREFORDSHIRE

BODENHAM   Map 3 SO55

Brockington Hall Golf Club & Country House HR1 3HX
☎ 01568 797877 📠 01568 797877
web: www.brockingtonhall.co.uk

9 Holes, 2344yds, Par 66, SSS 63, Course record 32.

Course Designer Derek Powell **Location** On A417 on outskirts of Bodenham village between Leominster and Hereford.
Telephone for further details
Hotel ★★★ 75% HL Best Western Talbot, West Street, LEOMINSTER
☎ 01568 616347 📠 01568 614880 28 en suite

CLIFFORD   Map 3 SO24

Summerhill Golf Course HR3 5EW
☎ 01497 820451 📠 01497 820451
web: www.summerhillgolfcourse.co.uk

9 Holes, 2872yds, Par 70, SSS 67, Course record 71.

Course Designer Bob Sandow **Location** 0.5m N from Hay on B4350, on right
Telephone for further details
Hotel ★★★★★ RR The Talkhouse, Pontdolgoch, CAERSWS
☎ 01686 688919 & 07876 086183 3 rooms (3 en suite)

HEREFORD
Map 3 SO53

Belmont Lodge & Golf Belmont HR2 9SA
☎ 01432 352666 📄 01432 358090
web: www.belmont-hereford.co.uk

18 Holes, 6369yds, Par 72, SSS 71, Course record 66.

Course Designer Bob Sandow **Location** 2m S off A465
Telephone for further details
Hotel ★★★ 75% HL Three Counties Hotel, Belmont Road,
HEREFORD ☎ 01432 299955 📄 01432 275114 60 en suite

Burghill Valley Golf Club Tillington Rd, Burghill HR4 7RW
☎ 01432 760456 📄 01432 761654
e-mail: info@bvgc.co.uk
web: www.bvgc.co.uk

The course is situated in typically beautiful Herefordshire countryside.
The walking is easy on gently rolling fairways with a background of
hills and woods and in the distance, the Welsh mountains. Some holes
are played through mature cider orchards and there are two lakes to
negotiate. A fair but interesting test for players of all abilities.

18 Holes, 6224yds, Par 71, SSS 70. Club membership 700.

Visitors Mon-Sun & BHs. Booking required. **Societies** booking
required. **Green Fees** phone **Course Designer** M Barnett **Prof** Keith
Preece/Andy Cameron **Facilities** ⊕ ⏨ ⓛ ⬜ 🛒 🖎 📷 ✎
🖎 ✎ **Leisure** chipping practice area. **Location** 4m NW of Hereford
Hotel ★★★ 86% HL Castle House, Castle Street, HEREFORD
☎ 01432 356321 📄 01432 365909 15 en suite

Hereford Municipal Golf Course Hereford Leisure Centre HR4 9UD
☎ 01432 344376 📄 01432 266281

9 Holes, 3060yds, Par 35, SSS 68.

Course Designer J Leek **Location** within racecourse on A49 Hereford-
Leominster road
Telephone for further details
Hotel ★★★ 86% HL Castle House, Castle Street, HEREFORD
☎ 01432 356321 📄 01432 365909 15 en suite

KINGTON
Map 3 SO25

Kington Golf Club Bradnor Hill HR5 3RE
☎ 01544 230340 (club) & 231320 (pro shop)
📄 01544 230340 /231320 (pro)
e-mail: kingtongolf@ukonline.co.uk
web: www.kingtongolf.co.uk

The highest 18-hole course in England, with magnificent views over
seven counties. A natural heathland course with easy walking on
mountain turf cropped by sheep. There is bracken to catch any really
bad shots but no sand traps. The greens play true and fast and are
generally acknowledged as some of the best in the west Midlands.

18 Holes, 5980yds, Par 70, SSS 69, Course record 63.
Club membership 510.

Visitors contact club for details. **Societies** welcome. **Green
Fees** £26 per day (£32 weekends & BHs) **Course Designer** Major C
K Hutchison **Prof** Dan Jarman **Facilities** ⊕ ⏨ ⓛ ⬜ 🛒 🖎
📷 🍴 ✎ 🚗 ✎ 🌲 **Location** 0.5m N of Kington off B4355
Hotel ★★★ 74% HL Burton, Mill Street, KINGTON
☎ 01544 230323 📄 01544 239023 16 en suite

LEOMINSTER
Map 3 SO45

Leominster Golf Club Ford Bridge HR6 0LE
☎ 01568 610055 📄 01568 610055
e-mail: contact@leominstergolfclub.co.uk
web: www.leominstergolfclub.co.uk

On undulating parkland with the lower holes running alongside the
River Lugg and others on the higher part of the course affording fine
panoramic views over the surrounding countryside.

18 Holes, 6011yds, SSS 70. Club membership 500.

Visitors Mon-Sun & BHs. Booking required. Dress code.
Societies booking required. **Green Fees** £25 per day, £20 per 18
holes (£30/£24 weekends & BHs) **Course Designer** Bob Sandow
Prof Nigel Clarke **Facilities** ⊕ ⏨ ⓛ ⬜ 🛒 🖎 📷 🚗 ✎
Leisure fishing **Conf** facs Corporate Hospitality Days **Location** 3m S of
Leominster on A49, signed
Hotel ★★★ 75% HL Best Western Talbot, West Street, LEOMINSTER
☎ 01568 616347 📄 01568 614880 28 en suite

ROSS-ON-WYE
Map 3 SO62

Ross-on-Wye Golf Club Two Park HR9 7UT
☎ 01989 720267 📄 01989 720212
web: www.therossonwyegolfclub.co.uk

18 Holes, 6451yds, Par 72, SSS 71, Course record 68.

Course Designer Mr C K Cotton **Location** M50 junct 3, on B4221 N
Telephone for further details
Hotel ★★★ 68% HL King's Head, 8 High Street, ROSS-ON-WYE
☎ 01989 763174 📄 01989 769578 15 en suite

South Herefordshire Golf Club Twin Lakes HR9 7UA
☎ 01989 780535 📄 01989 780535
e-mail: info@herefordshiregolf.co.uk
web: www.herefordshiregolf.co.uk

Impressive parkland course fast maturing into one of Herefordshire's
finest. Magnificent panoramic views of the Welsh mountains and
countryside. Drains well and is playable in any weather. The landscape
has enabled the architect to design 18 individual and varied holes.

Twin Lakes: 18 Holes, 6672yds, Par 72, SSS 71,
Course record 69. Club membership 595.

Visitors Mon-Sun & BHs. Booking required. Dress code.
Societies welcome. **Green Fees** not confirmed **Course Designer** John
Day **Prof** Lewis Hanney **Facilities** ⊕ ⓛ ⬜ 🖎 📷 🍴 ✎ 🚗
✎ 🌲 **Leisure** par 3 academy course **Conf** Corporate Hospitality
Days **Location** M50 junct 4, to Upton Bishop, right onto B4224, 1m left
Hotel ★★★★ GA Brookfield House, Over Ross Street, ROSS-ON-
WYE ☎ 01989 562188 3 rooms

UPPER SAPEY
Map 3 SO66

Sapey Golf Club WR6 6XT
☎ 01886 853288 & 853567 📄 01886 853485
e-mail: anybody@sapeygolf.co.uk
web: www.sapeygolf.co.uk

Easy walking parkland with views of the Malvern Hills. The mixture
of long or short holes, including trees, lakes and water hazards, is a
demanding challenge for all golfers.

The Rowan: 18 Holes, 5939yds, Par 69, SSS 68,
Course record 64.

continued

Save on Hotels. Book at **theAA.com/hotel**

HEREFORDSHIRE – HERTFORDSHIRE

ENGLAND

The Oaks: 9 Holes, 1203yds, Par 27, SSS 27, Course record 24. Club membership 330.

Visitors Mon-Sun & BHs. Booking required. Dress code. **Societies** booking required. **Green Fees** Rowan £28 per round (£33 weekends). Oaks £8 (£10 weekends) **Course Designer** R McMurray **Prof** Chris Knowles **Facilities** 🏌 ⛳ by prior arrangement 🛍 ⛳ 🍴 🔋 🏪 🚩 🎣 🏌 **Leisure** 9 hole par 3 Oaks Course **Conf** Corporate Hospitality Days **Location** B4203 Bromyard-Stourport road **Hotel** ★★★ 75% HL Best Western Talbot, West Street, LEOMINSTER ☎ 01568 616347 📠 01568 614880 28 en suite

WORMSLEY
Map 3 SO44

The Herefordshire Golf Club Ravens Causeway HR4 8LY
☎ 01432 830219 & 830465 (pro)
e-mail: herefordshire.golf@breathe.com
web: www.herefordshiregolfclub.co.uk

Undulating parkland with expansive views of the Clee Hills to the east and the Black Mountains to the west. Peaceful and relaxing situation.

18 Holes, 6055yds, Par 70, SSS 70, Course record 61. Club membership 750.

Visitors Mon-Sun & BHs. Booking required. Dress code **Societies** booking required. **Green Fees** £35 per day £30per 18 holes. (£40/£45 weekends & BHs) **Course Designer** James Braid **Prof** Julian Parry **Facilities** 🏌 ⛳ 🛍 ⛳ 🍴 🔋 🏪 🚩 🎣 🏪 🎣 **Conf** Corporate Hospitality Days **Location** 7m NW of Hereford on B road to Weobley
Hotel ★★★ 75% HL Three Counties Hotel, Belmont Road, HEREFORD ☎ 01432 299955 📠 01432 275114 60 en suite

HERTFORDSHIRE

ALDENHAM
Map 4 TQ19

Aldenham Golf and Country Club Church Ln WD25 8NN
☎ 01923 853929 📠 01923 858472
e-mail: info@aldenhamgolfclub.co.uk
web: www.aldenhamgolfclub.co.uk

Gently undulating parkland with woods, water hazards and ditches. Many specimen trees and beautiful views across the countryside.

Church Course: 18 Holes, 6409yds, Par 70, SSS 71, Course record 64.
Berry Grove Course: 9 Holes, 2350yds, Par 33, SSS 32. Club membership 400.

Visitors Mon-Fri & BHs. Weekends pm. Booking required. **Societies** booking required. **Green Fees** Church £35 per round (£45 weekends & BHs). Berry Grove £12 (£15 weekends & BHs) **Prof** Tim Dunstan **Facilities** 🏌 ⛳ 🛍 ⛳ 🍴 🔋 🏪 🚩 🎣 **Conf** facs Corporate Hospitality Days **Location** M1 junct 5, 0.5m to W of village
Hotel ★★★ 73% HL Best Western White House, Upton Road, WATFORD ☎ 01923 237316 📠 01923 233109 57 en suite

BERKHAMSTED
Map 4 SP90

Berkhamsted Golf Club The Common HP4 2QB
☎ 01442 865832 📠 01442 863730
e-mail: admin@berkhamstedgc.co.uk
web: www.berkhamstedgolfclub.co.uk

There are no sand bunkers on this championship heathland course but this does not make it any easier to play. The natural hazards will test the skill of the most able players. Fine greens, long carries and heather and gorse

18 Holes, 6605yds, Par 71, SSS 72. Club membership 700.

Visitors Mon-Sun & BHs. Booking required. Handicap certificate. Dress code. **Societies** booking required. **Green Fees** phone **Course Designer** Colt/Braid **Prof** John Clarke **Facilities** 🏌 🛍 ⛳ 🍴 🔋 🏪 🚩 🎣 **Conf** Corporate Hospitality Days **Location** 1.5m NE of Berkhamsted
Hotel ★★★★ 78% HL Pendley Manor, Cow Lane, TRING ☎ 01442 891891 📠 01442 890687 73 en suite

BISHOP'S STORTFORD
Map 5 TL42

Bishop's Stortford Golf Club Dunmow Rd CM23 5HP
☎ 01279 654715 📠 01279 655215
e-mail: office@bsgc.co.uk
web: www.bsgc.co.uk

Well-established parkland course, fairly flat, but undulating, with easy walking.

18 Holes, 6415yds, Par 71, SSS 71. Club membership 900.

Visitors Mon-Fri except BHs. Handicap certificate. Dress code. **Societies** booking required. **Green Fees** £50 per day (27 or 36 holes), £40 per round per 18 holes **Course Designer** James Braid **Prof** Simon Sheppard **Facilities** 🏌 ⛳ 🛍 ⛳ 🍴 🔋 🏪 🚩 🎣 🏪 🎣 **Leisure** snooker tables **Conf** facs Corporate Hospitality Days **Location** M11 junct 8, 0.5m W on A1250
Hotel BUD Days Inn Bishop's Stortford - M11, BIRCHANGER GREEN ☎ 01279 656477 📠 01279 656590 60 en suite

Great Hadham Golf & Country Club Great Hadham Rd, Much Hadham SG10 6JE
☎ 01279 843558 📠 01279 842122
e-mail: info@ghgcc.co.uk
web: www.ghgcc.co.uk

An undulating meadowland and links course offering excellent country views and a challenge with its ever present breeze.

18 Holes, 6854yds, Par 72, SSS 72, Course record 69. Club membership 800.

Visitors Mon-Fri. Weekends & BHs pm. Booking required. Dress code. **Societies** booking required. **Green Fees** not confirmed **Course Designer** Iain Roberts **Prof** Kevin Lunt **Facilities** 🏌 ⛳ by prior arrangement 🛍 ⛳ 🍴 🔋 🏪 🚩 🎣 🏪 🎣 🏌 **Leisure** sauna, gymnasium **Conf** facs Corporate Hospitality Days **Location** on the B1004, 3m SW of Bishop's Stortford
Hotel ★★★★ 75% HL Down Hall Country House, Hatfield Heath, BISHOPS STORTFORD ☎ 01279 731441 📠 01279 730416 99 en suite

BRICKENDON
Map 5 TL30

Brickendon Grange Golf Club Pembridge Ln SG13 8PD
☎ 01992 511258 📠 01992 511411
e-mail: play@bggc.org.uk
web: www.bggc.org.uk

Undulating parkland with some fine par 4s. The 17th hole reputed to
be one of the best in the county.

18 Holes, 6458yds, Par 71, SSS 71, Course record 67.
Club membership 680.

Visitors Mon-Fri except BHs. Weekends pm. Booking required. Dress
code. Societies booking required. Green Fees not confirmed Course
Designer C K Cotton Prof Andy Clapp Facilities ⊕ ⍩ ⓑ ⌷ ⍟
⌂ 🖻 🚌 ⟋ Conf facs Corporate Hospitality Days Location W
of village
Hotel ★★★★ 71% HL Ponsbourne Park Hotel, Newgate Street
Village, POTTERS BAR ☎ 01707 876191 & 879277 📠 01707 875190
50 en suite

BROOKMANS PARK
Map 4 TL20

Brookmans Park Golf Club Golf Club Rd AL9 7AT
☎ 01707 652487 📠 01707 661851
web: www.bpgc.co.uk

18 Holes, 6249yds, Par 71, SSS 71, Course record 65.
Course Designer Hawtree/Taylor Location N of village off A1000
Telephone for further details
Hotel ★★★★ 71% HL Ponsbourne Park Hotel, Newgate
Street Village, POTTERS BAR ☎ 01707 876191 & 879277
📠 01707 875190 50 en suite

BROXBOURNE
Map 5 TL30

Hertfordshire Golf & Country Club Broxbournebury
Mansion EN10 7PY
☎ 01992 466666 & 441268 (pro shop)
📠 01992 470326
web: www.crowngolf.co.uk

18 Holes, 6388yds, Par 70, SSS 70, Course record 62.
Course Designer Jack Nicklaus II Location off A10 for Broxbourne,
signs for Paradise Wildlife Park, left at Bell Ln over A10, on right
Telephone for further details
Hotel ★★★★ 76% HL Cheshunt Marriott, Halfhide Lane,
Turnford, BROXBOURNE ☎ 01992 451245 📠 01992 440120
143 en suite

BUNTINGFORD
Map 5 TL32

East Herts Golf Club Hamels Park SG9 9NA
☎ 01920 821978 (office) & 821922 (pro)
📠 01920 823700
e-mail: secretary@easthertsgolfclub.co.uk
web: www.easthertsgolfclub.co.uk

Mature, attractive, undulating parkland course with magnificent
specimen trees.

18 Holes, 6451yds, Par 71, SSS 71, Course record 65.
Club membership 800.

Visitors Mon-Fri except BHs. Dress code. Societies booking required.
Green Fees not confirmed Prof D Field Facilities ⊕ ⍩ ⓑ ⌷

🍴 ⌂ 🖻 ⍟ ⟋ 🚌 ⟋ Conf Corporate Hospitality Days
Location 1m N of Puckeridge off A10, opposite Pearce's Farm Shop
Hotel ★★★ 78% HL Novotel Stevenage, Knebworth Park,
STEVENAGE ☎ 01438 346100 📠 01438 723872 101 en suite

BUSHEY
Map 4 TQ19

Bushey Golf & Country Club High St WD23 1TT
☎ 020 8950 2215(pro shop) & 8950 2283 (club)
📠 020 8386 1181
e-mail: info@busheycountryclub.com
web: www.busheycountryclub.com

Undulating parkland with challenging 2nd and 9th holes. The
latter has a sweeping dog-leg left, playing to a green in front of the
clubhouse. For the rather too enthusiastic golfer, Bushey offers its own
physiotherapist.

9 Holes, 6120yds, Par 70, SSS 69, Course record 67.
Club membership 325.

Visitors Mon, Tue & Fri. Thu, weekends & BHs pm. Booking required.
Dress code. Societies welcome. Green Fees not confirmed Course
Designer Donald Steele Prof Martin Siggins Facilities ⊕ ⍩ ⓑ
⌷ ⍟ 🖻 ⟋ 🚌 ⟋ Leisure sauna, gymnasium, health &
fitness club Conf facs Corporate Hospitality Days Location M1 junct 5
Hotel ★★★ 82% HL Grim's Dyke Hotel, Old Redding, HARROW
WEALD ☎ 020 8385 3100 & 020 8954 4227 📠 020 8954 4560
46 en suite

Bushey Hall Golf Club Bushey Hall Dr WD23 2EP
☎ 01923 222253 📠 01923 229759
e-mail: gordon@golfclubuk.co.uk
web: www.busheyhallgolfclub.co.uk

A tree-lined parkland course, the oldest established course in
Hertfordshire.

18 Holes, 6055yds, Par 69, SSS 69, Course record 63.
Club membership 500.

Visitors Mon-Sun & BHs. Booking required. Dress code.
Societies booking required. Green Fees not confirmed Course
Designer J Braid Prof Robert Edwards Facilities ⊕ ⓑ ⌷ ⍟
⌂ 🖻 ⍟ ⟋ 🚌 ⟋ Leisure practice nets Conf facs Corporate
Hospitality Days Location M1 junct 5, A41 Harrow to Bushey, 4th exit
at rdbt, club 150yds on left
Hotel ★★★ 73% HL Best Western White House, Upton Road,
WATFORD ☎ 01923 237316 📠 01923 233109 57 en suite

CHESHUNT
Map 5 TL30

Cheshunt Park Golf Centre Cheshunt Park, Park Ln
EN7 6QD
☎ 01992 624009 📠 01992 637551
e-mail: golf.leisure@broxbourne.gov.uk
web: www.broxbourne.gov.uk/golf

Municipal parkland course, well bunkered with ponds, easy walking.

18 Holes, 6635yds, Par 71, SSS 72, Course record 63.
Club membership 400.

Visitors Mon-Sun & BHs. Booking required. Societies booking
required. Green Fees £18.50 per 18 holes (£24 weekends & BHs)
Course Designer P Wawtry Facilities ⊕ ⍩ ⓑ ⌷ ⍟ ⌂ 🖻
⍟ 🚌 ⟋ Leisure club repair service Conf facs Corporate Hospitality
Days Location 1.5m NW off B156. M25 junct 25, 3m N
Hotel ★★★★ 76% HL Cheshunt Marriott, Halfhide Lane, Turnford,
BROXBOURNE ☎ 01992 451245 📠 01992 440120 143 en suite

Save on Hotels. Book at **theAA.com/hotel**   **HERTFORDSHIRE**

ENGLAND

CHORLEYWOOD
Map 4 TQ09

Chorleywood Golf Club Common Rd WD3 5LN
☎ 01923 282009 🖹 01923 286739
e-mail: secretary@chorleywoodgolfclub.co.uk
web: www.chorleywoodgolfclub.co.uk
Very attractive mix of woodland and heathland with natural hazards and good views.

9 Holes, 5686yds, Par 68, SSS 67, Course record 62.
Club membership 270.

Visitors Mon-Sun & BHs. Booking required Tue, Wed, weekends & BHs. Dress code. **Societies** booking required. **Green Fees** £20 per round, £15 for 9 holes (£25/20 weekends) **Prof** J Little **Facilities** ⑪ 🏐 ☕
🍴 ⚲ ♂ **Location** M25 junct 18, E of village off A404
Hotel ★★★ 79% HL The Bedford Arms Hotel, CHENIES
☎ 01923 283301 🖹 01923 284825 18 en suite

ELSTREE
Map 4 TQ19

Elstree Golf and Country Club Watling St WD6 3AA
☎ 020 8953 6115 & 8238 6941 🖹 020 8207 6390
e-mail: admin@elstree-golf.co.uk
web: www.elstree-golfclub.co.uk
Parkland course incorporating ponds and streams and challenging doglegs.

18 Holes, 6556yds, Par 73, SSS 72. Club membership 400.

Visitors Mon-Sun & BHs. Booking required weekends & BHs. Dress code. **Societies** booking required. **Green Fees** not confirmed **Course Designer** Donald Steel **Prof** Marc Warwick **Facilities** ⑪ 🍽 🏐 ☕
🍴 ⚲ 🏠 🍴 ♂ 🍴 ♂ 🏸 **Leisure** snooker, golf academy
Conf facs Corporate Hospitality Days **Location** A5183 between Radlett and Elstree, next to Wagon & Horses pub
Hotel ★★★★ 73% HL Holiday Inn London - Elstree, Barnet Bypass, BOREHAMWOOD ☎ 0871 942 9071 & 020 8214 9988
🖹 020 8207 6817 135 en suite

ESSENDON
Map 4 TL20

Hatfield London Country Club Bedwell Park AL9 6HN
☎ 01707 260360 🖹 01707 278475
e-mail: info@hatfieldlondon.co.uk
web: www.hatfieldlondon.co.uk
Parkland course with many varied hazards, including ponds, a stream and a ditch.

Old Course: 18 Holes, 6808yds, Par 72, SSS 72.
New Course: 18 Holes, 6938yds, Par 72, SSS 73.
Club membership 350.

Visitors Mon-Sun & BHs. Booking required. Dress code.
Societies booking required. **Green Fees** Old Course £29 (£42 weekends & BHs). New Course £39 (£54 weekends & BHs) **Course Designer** Fred Hawtree **Prof** Jamie Little **Facilities** ⑪ 🍽 🏐 ☕
🍴 ⚲ 🏠 🍴 ♂ **Leisure** sauna, 9 hole pitch and putt, Japanese bath **Conf** facs Corporate Hospitality Days **Location** 1m S on B158
Hotel ★★★★ 71% HL Ponsbourne Park Hotel, Newgate Street Village, POTTERS BAR ☎ 01707 876191 & 879277 🖹 01707 875190
50 en suite

GRAVELEY
Map 4 TL22

Chesfield Downs Golf & Country Club Jack's Hill SG4 7EQ
☎ 01462 482929 🖹 01462 482930
web: www.crown-golf.co.uk
18 Holes, 6648yds, Par 71, SSS 72, Course record 65.
Course Designer J Gaunt **Location** A1 junct 8, B197 to Graveley
Telephone for further details
Hotel BUD Ibis Stevenage Centre, Danestrete, STEVENAGE
☎ 01438 779955 🖹 01438 741880 98 en suite

HARPENDEN
Map 4 TL11

Aldwickbury Park Golf Club Piggottshill Ln AL5 1AB
☎ 01582 760112 🖹 01582 760113
web: www.aldwickburyparkgolfclub.com
Park Course: 18 Holes, 6368yds, Par 71, SSS 71,
Course record 66.

Course Designer Ken Brown/Martin Gillett **Location** M1 junct 9, off Wheathampstead Rd between Harpenden & Wheathampstead
Telephone for further details
Hotel ★★★★ 72% HL Harpenden House Hotel, 18 Southdown Road, HARPENDEN ☎ 01582 855 9113 🖹 01582 760511 76 en suite

Harpenden Common Golf Club Cravells Rd, East Common AL5 1BL
☎ 01582 711328 (pro shop) & 01582 460655
🖹 01582 711321
e-mail: manager@hcgc.co.uk
web: www.harpendencommongolfcourse.co.uk
Flat, easy walking, parkland with good greens. Golf has been played on the common for well over 100 years.

18 Holes, 6214yds, Par 70, SSS 70, Course record 63.
Club membership 710.

Visitors Mon-Sat & BHs. Booking required. Dress code.
Societies booking required. **Green Fees** £45 per day, £35 per round. £25 per round winter 🍴 **Course Designer** K Brown **Prof** Danny Fitzsimmons **Facilities** ⑪ 🍽 🏐 ☕ 🍴 ⚲ 🏠 🍴 ♂
Location on A1081 0.5m S of Harpenden
Hotel ★★★★ 72% HL Harpenden House Hotel, 18 Southdown Road, HARPENDEN ☎ 01582 855 9113 🖹 01582 760511 76 en suite

Harpenden Golf Club Hammonds End, Redbourn Ln AL5 2AX
☎ 01582 712580 🖹 01582 712725
e-mail: office@harpendengolfclub.co.uk
web: www.harpendengolfclub.co.uk
Gently undulating parkland, easy walking.

18 Holes, 6377yds, Par 70, SSS 71, Course record 64.
Club membership 800.

Visitors Mon-Wed, Fri-Sun & BHs. Booking required Mon, weekends & BHs. Dress code. **Societies** booking required. **Green Fees** £50 per day, £40 per round (£45 per round weekends & BHs) **Course Designer** Hawtree & Taylor **Prof** Peter Lane **Facilities** ⑪ 🍽 by prior arrangement 🏐 ☕ 🍴 ⚲ 🏠 🍴 ♂ 🏸 **Conf** Corporate Hospitality Days **Location** 1m S on B487
Hotel ★★★★ 72% HL Harpenden House Hotel, 18 Southdown Road, HARPENDEN ☎ 01582 855 9113 🖹 01582 760511 76 en suite

HEMEL HEMPSTEAD
Map 4 TL00

Boxmoor Golf Club 18 Box Ln HP3 0DJ
☎ 01442 242434
web: www.boxmoorgolfclub.co.uk
9 Holes, 4812yds, Par 64, SSS 63, Course record 62.
Location 2m SW on B4505
Telephone for further details
Hotel ★★★ 74% HL Best Western The Watermill, London Road,
Bourne End, HEMEL HEMPSTEAD ☎ 01442 349955 ▤ 01442 866130
71 en suite

Little Hay Golf Complex Box Ln HP3 0DQ
☎ 01442 833798 ▤ 01442 831399
web: www.littlehavgolfclub.co.uk
18 Holes, 6300yds, Par 72, SSS 72.
Course Designer Hawtree **Location** 1.5m SW off A41 onto B4505
Telephone for further details
Hotel ★★★ 75% HL The Bobsleigh Hotel, Hempstead Road,
Bovingdon, HEMEL HEMPSTEAD ☎ 0844 879 9033 ▤ 01442 832471
47 en suite

Shendish Manor Hotel & Golf Course London Rd, Apsley
HP3 0AA
☎ 01442 251806 ▤ 01442 230683
e-mail: golfmanager@shendish-manor.com
web: www.shendish-manor.com
A hilly course which is set with challenges through both parkland and
woodland copses and provides a test of golfing ability regardless of
handicap.
Shendish Manor: 18 Holes, 5660yds, Par 70.
Club membership 200.
Visitors Mon-Sun & BHs. Booking required. Dress code.
Societies booking required. **Green Fees** phone for details **Course
Designer** D Steel **Facilities** ⑪ ⑩ by prior arrangement ⚑ ⬜
🍴 ⚐ 🏢 ☂ ♢ 🚍 ✎ **Conf** facs Corporate Hospitality Days
Location off A4251
Hotel ★★★★ 78% HL Pendley Manor, Cow Lane, TRING
☎ 01442 891891 ▤ 01442 890687 73 en suite

KNEBWORTH
Map 4 TL22

Knebworth Golf Club Deards End Ln SG3 6NL
☎ 01438 812752 ▤ 01438 815216
e-mail: admin@knebworthgolfclub.com
web: www.knebworthgolfclub.com
Easy walking parkland.
18 Holes, 6518yds, Par 71, SSS 71, Course record 66.
Club membership 900.
Visitors dress code. **Societies** booking required. **Green Fees** not
confirmed **Course Designer** W Park (Jun) **Prof** Garry Parker
Facilities ⑪ ⑩ ⚑ ⬜ 🍴 ⚐ 🏢 ✎ **Conf** facs
Corporate Hospitality Days **Location** N of village off B197
Hotel ★★★ 71% HL Best Western Roebuck Inn, London Road,
Broadwater, STEVENAGE ☎ 01438 365445 ▤ 01438 741308
26 en suite

LETCHWORTH
Map 4 TL23

Letchworth Golf Club Letchworth Ln SG6 3NQ
☎ 01462 683203 ▤ 01462 484567
e-mail: secretary@letchworthgolfclub.com
web: www.letchworthgolfclub.com
Planned more than 100 years ago by Harry Vardon, this is an
adventurous parkland course. To its variety of natural and artificial
hazards is added an unpredictable wind.
18 Holes, 6459yds, Par 71, SSS 71, Course record 64.
Club membership 950.
Visitors Mon-Fri except BHs. Dress code. **Societies** booking
required. **Green Fees** £45 per round Tue-Fri (£22 Mon). £3.50 par
3 short course **Course Designer** Harry Vardon **Prof** Karl Teschner
Facilities ⑪ ⑩ ⚑ ⬜ 🍴 ☂ 🏢 ☂ ♢ 🚍 ✎ ✿
Leisure 9 hole par 3 course. **Conf** facs Corporate Hospitality Days
Location S side of town centre off A505
Hotel ★★★ 71% SHL Redcoats Farmhouse Hotel, Redcoats
Green, HITCHIN ☎ 01438 729500 ▤ 01438 723322 13 en suite

LITTLE GADDESDEN
Map 4 SP91

Ashridge Golf Club HP4 1LY
☎ 01442 842244 ▤ 01442 843770
e-mail: info@ashridgegolfclub.ltd.uk
web: www.ashridgegolfclub.ltd.uk
Classic wooded parkland in Area of Outstanding Natural Beauty.
18 Holes, 6625yds, Par 72, SSS 71, Course record 63.
Club membership 720.
Visitors Mon-Fri except BHs. Booking required. Dress code.
Societies booking required. **Green Fees** phone **Course Designer** Sir
G Campbell/C Hutchinson/N V Hotchkin **Prof** Peter Cherry
Facilities ⑪ ⑩ ⚑ ⬜ 🍴 ☂ 🏢 ☂ ♢ ♢ 🚍 ✎ **Conf**
Corporate Hospitality Days **Location** 5m N of Berkhamsted on B4506
Hotel ★★★★ 72% HL Harpenden House Hotel, 18 Southdown
Road, HARPENDEN ☎ 01582 855 9113 ▤ 01582 760511
76 en suite

MUCH HADHAM
Map 5 TL41

Ash Valley Golf Club Little Hadham Rd SG10 6HD
☎ 01279 843253 ▤ 01279 842389
web: www.ashvalley.co.uk
Naturally undulating course with good views extending to Canary
Wharf in London on a clear day. Tough enough for lower handicapped
players but forgiving for the beginner and higher handicapped player.
18 Holes, 6586yds, Par 71, SSS 71, Course record 64.
Club membership 100.
Visitors Mon-Sun & BHs. Booking required weekends & BHs. Dress
code. **Societies** booking required. **Green Fees** not confirmed **Course
Designer** Martin Gillett **Facilities** ⑪ ⚑ ⬜ 🍴 ☂ 🚍 ✎
Leisure par 3 pitch and putt **Location** 1.5m S of A120 Little Hadham
lights
Hotel ★★★ 72% HL Roebuck, Baldock Street, WARE
☎ 01920 409955 ▤ 01920 468016 47 en suite

Save on Hotels. Book at **theAA.com/hotel**

HERTFORDSHIRE

ENGLAND

POTTERS BAR
Map 4 TL20

Potters Bar Golf Club Darkes Ln EN6 1DE
☎ 01707 652020 📠 01707 655051
web: www.pottersbargolfclub.com
18 Holes, 6279yds, Par 71, SSS 70.
Course Designer James Braid **Location** M25 junct 24, 1m N
Telephone for further details
Hotel BUD Days Inn South Mimms - M25, Bignells Corner, POTTERS
BAR ☎ 01707 665440 📠 01707 660189 74 en suite

RADLETT
Map 4 TL10

Porters Park Golf Club Shenley Hill WD7 7AZ
☎ 01923 854127 📠 01923 855475
e-mail: enquiries@porterspark.com
web: www.porterspark.com
A splendid, undulating parkland course with fine trees and lush
grass. The holes are all different and interesting - on many,
accuracy of shot to the green is of paramount importance.
18 Holes, 6313yds, Par 70, SSS 70, Course record 64.
Club membership 700.
Visitors Mon-Fri except BHs. Dress code. **Societies** booking required.
Green Fees not confirmed **Course Designer** Braid **Prof** David
Gleeson **Facilities** 🟉 🍴 🍺 🖵 🏌️ 🏌 🚶 **Conf**
Corporate Hospitality Days **Location** NE of village off A5183
Hotel ★★★★ 73% HL Holiday Inn London - Elstree, Barnet
Bypass, BOREHAMWOOD ☎ 0871 942 9071 & 020 8214 9988
📠 020 8207 6817 135 en suite

REDBOURN
Map 4 TL11

Redbourn Golf Club Kinsbourne Green Ln AL3 7QA
☎ 01582 793493 📠 01582 794362
e-mail: info@redbourngc.co.uk
web: www.redbourngolfclub.com
A mature parkland course offering a fair test of golf to all standards.
Water comes into play on a number of holes.
Ver Course: 18 Holes, 6486yds, Par 70, SSS 71.
Kinsbourne Course: 9 Holes, 2722yds, Par 27.
Club membership 890.
Visitors Weekends & BHs pm. Booking required. Dress code.
Societies booking required. **Green Fees** £30 per 18 holes Mon-Thu,
£35 Fri-Sun **Prof** Stephen Hunter **Facilities** 🟉 🍺 🖵 🏌️ 🚶 🏡
🚜 🏌 **Leisure** 9 hole par 3 course **Conf** Corporate Hospitality
Days **Location** M1 junct 9, 1m N off A5183
Hotel ★★★★ 72% HL Harpenden House Hotel, 18 Southdown
Road, HARPENDEN ☎ 01582 855 9113 📠 01582 760511 76 en suite

RICKMANSWORTH
Map 4 TQ09

The Grove Chandler's Cross WD3 4TG
☎ 01923 294266 📠 01923 294268
e-mail: golf@thegrove.co.uk
web: www.thegrove.co.uk
A course built to USGA specifications but following the slopes, ridges
and mounds that occur naturally within the landscape. The fairway
grass encourages crisp ball striking and the greens have firm, fast
putting surfaces. Continuous cart path around all holes.
18 Holes, 7152yds, Par 72, SSS 74.

Visitors Mon-Sun & BHs. Booking required. **Societies** booking
required. **Green Fees** not confirmed **Course Designer** Kyle Phillips
Prof Anna Darnell **Facilities** 🟉 🍴 🍺 🖵 🏌️ 🚶 🏡 🏌 ◇
🚜 🏎 🏌 🏌 **Leisure** hard tennis courts, outdoor and indoor heated
swimming pool, sauna, gymnasium **Conf** facs Corporate Hospitality
Days **Location** M25 junct 19/20, follow signs to Watford. At 1st large
rdbt take exit for A411. Proceed for 0.5m, entrance on right
Hotel ★★★★★ 87% HL The Grove, Chandler's Cross,
RICKMANSWORTH ☎ 01923 807807 📠 01923 221008 227 en suite

Moor Park Golf Club WD3 1QN
☎ 01923 773146 📠 01923 777109
e-mail: enquiries@moorparkgc.co.uk
web: www.moorparkgc.co.uk

Two parkland courses with rolling fairways - High Course is
challenging and will test the best golfer and West Course demands
a high degree of accuracy. The clubhouse is a Grade I listed
mansion.
High Golf Course: 18 Holes, 6717yds, Par 72, SSS 73,
Course record 63.
West Golf Course: 18 Holes, 5833yds, Par 69, SSS 68,
Course record 63. Club membership 1480.
Visitors Mon-Sun & BHs. Booking required. Handicap certificate.
Dress code. **Societies** booking required. **Green Fees** High £85
per round, West £55 per round (£125/£85 weekends) **Course
Designer** H S Colt **Prof** Rob Darwin **Facilities** 🟉 🍴 🍺 🖵 🏌️
🚶 🏡 🏌 🏌 🏌 **Leisure** hard and grass tennis courts,
chipping green, snooker room, video golf studio **Conf** facs Corporate
Hospitality Days **Location** M25 junct 17/18, off A404 to Northwood
Hotel ★★★ 79% HL The Bedford Arms Hotel, CHENIES
☎ 01923 283301 📠 01923 284825 18 en suite

Rickmansworth Public Golf Course Moor Ln WD3 1QL
☎ 01923 775278
web: www.rickmansworthgolfcourse.co.uk
Undulating, municipal parkland course, short but tests skills to the
full.
18 Holes, 4446yds, Par 65, SSS 63, Course record 63.
Club membership 240.
Visitors Mon-Sun & BHs. Booking required. Handicap certificate. Dress
code. **Societies** booking required. **Green Fees** not confirmed **Course
Designer** Colt **Prof** Darren Hodgson **Facilities** 🟉 🍴 🍺 🖵 🏌️
🚶 🏡 🏌 🏌 🏎 🏌 **Leisure** Little Ricky par 3 course **Conf** facs
Corporate Hospitality Days **Location** 2m S of town off A4145
Hotel ★★★ 79% HL The Bedford Arms Hotel, CHENIES
☎ 01923 283301 📠 01923 284825 18 en suite

ROYSTON — Map 5 TL34

Barkway Park Golf Club Nuthampstead Rd, Barkway SG8 8EN

☎ 01763 849070

e-mail: gc@barkwaypark.fsnet.co.uk

web: www.barkwayparkgolfclub.co.uk

An undulating course criss-crossed by ditches which come into play on several holes. The challenging par 3 7th features a long, narrow green with out of bounds close to the right edge of the green.

18 Holes, 6926yds, Par 74, SSS 74, Course record 70.
Club membership 380.

Visitors Mon-Sun & BHs. Booking required weekends & BHs. **Societies** welcome **Green Fees** not confirmed **Course Designer** Vivien Saunders **Prof** Jamie Bates **Facilities** ⊕ ⏵ ⍩ ⎕ ⛻ ⌂ ⎈ ⌖ **Location** A10 onto B1368

Hotel ★★★ 77% HL Duxford Lodge, Ickleton Road, DUXFORD ☎ 01223 836444 ▤ 01223 832271 15 en suite

Heydon Grange Golf & Country Club, Heydon SG8 7NS

☎ 01763 208988 ▤ 01763 208926

e-mail: enquiries@heydon-grange.co.uk

web: www.heydongrange.co.uk

Three nine-hole parkland courses - the Essex, Cambridgeshire and Hertfordshire - situated in gently rolling countryside. Courses are playable all year round.

Essex: 9 Holes, 2891yds, Par 36, SSS 36.
Cambridgeshire: 9 Holes, 3057yds, Par 36, SSS 36.
Hertfordshire: 9 Holes, 2937yds, Par 36, SSS 36.
Club membership 250.

Visitors Mon-Sun & BHs. Booking required weekends & BHs. Dress code. **Societies** welcome. **Green Fees** not confirmed **Course Designer** Cameron Sinclair **Prof** Stuart Smith **Facilities** ⊕ ⏵ ⍩ ⎕ ⛻ ⌂ ⎈ ⌖ **Conf** facs Corporate Hospitality Days **Location** M11 junct 10, A505 between Royston and Newmarket

Hotel ★★★ 77% HL Duxford Lodge, Ickleton Road, DUXFORD ☎ 01223 836444 ▤ 01223 832271 15 en suite

Kingsway Golf Centre Cambridge Rd SG8 6EY

☎ 01763 262943 ▤ 01763 263038

Melbourn Course: 9 Holes, 2455yds, Par 33, SSS 32.

Location off A10
Telephone for further details

Hotel ★★★ 77% HL Duxford Lodge, Ickleton Road, DUXFORD ☎ 01223 836444 ▤ 01223 832271 15 en suite

Royston Golf Club Baldock Rd SG8 5BG

☎ 01763 243476 & 242696 ▤ 01763 246910

e-mail: roystongolf@btconnect.com

web: www.roystongolfclub.co.uk

Heathland course on undulating terrain and fine fairways. The 8th, 10th and 15th are the most notable holes on this all weather course.

18 Holes, 6046yds, Par 70, SSS 70, Course record 63.
Club membership 750.

Visitors Mon-Sun & BHs. Dress code. **Societies** booking required. **Green Fees** from £15 **Course Designer** Harry Vardon **Prof** Sean Clark **Facilities** ⊕ ⏵ ⍩ ⎕ ⛻ ⌂ ⎈ ⌖ **Conf** facs Corporate Hospitality Days **Location** 0.5m W of town centre

Hotel ★★★ 77% HL Duxford Lodge, Ickleton Road, DUXFORD ☎ 01223 836444 ▤ 01223 832271 15 en suite

ST ALBANS — Map 4 TL10

Abbey View Golf Course Westminster Lodge Leisure Ctr AL1 2DL

☎ 01727 868227 ▤ 01727 848468

web: www.abbeyviewgolf.com

9 Holes, 1411yds, Par 29, Course record 27.

Location city centre, off Holywell Hill in Verulamium Park
Telephone for further details

Hotel ★★★★ 77% HL St Michael's Manor, Fishpool Street, ST ALBANS ☎ 01727 864444 ▤ 01727 848909 30 en suite

Verulam Golf Club London Rd AL1 1JG

☎ 01727 853327 ▤ 01727 812201

e-mail: gm@verulamgolf.com

web: www.verulamgolf.co.uk

Easy walking parkland with fast undulating greens. Frequent out of bounds and water affects the 12th, 13th and 14th holes. Samuel Ryder was captain here in 1927 when he began the now celebrated Ryder Cup competition.

18 Holes, 6429yds, Par 72, SSS 72, Course record 67.
Club membership 650.

Visitors Mon-Fri except BHs. Booking required. Handicap certificate. Dress code. **Societies** booking advised. **Green Fees** Mon £25 per round, Tue-Fri £35 **Course Designer** James Braid **Prof** Nick Burch **Facilities** ⊕ ⏵ by prior arrangement ⍩ ⎕ ⛻ ⌂ ⎈ ⌖ **Conf** facs Corporate Hospitality Days **Location** 0.5m from St Albans centre on A1081 London Rd, signed by railway bridge

Hotel ★★★ 71% HL Quality Hotel St Albans, 232-236 London Road, ST ALBANS ☎ 01727 857858 ▤ 01727 855666 81 en suite

SAWBRIDGEWORTH — Map 5 TL41

Manor of Groves Hotel, Golf & Country Club High Wych CM21 0JU

☎ 01279 603539 & 0870 410 8833 ▤ 01279 726972

e-mail: golf@manorofgroves.co.uk

web: www.manorofgroves.com

The course is set out over 150 acres of established parkland and rolling countryside and is a challenge to golfers at all levels.

18 Holes, 6237yds, Par 71, SSS 70. Club membership 550.

Visitors Mon-Sun & BHs. Booking required. Dress code. **Societies** booking required. **Green Fees** £30 per 18 holes (£34 weekends and BHs) **Course Designer** S Sharer **Prof** Ben Goodey **Facilities** ⊕ ⏵ ⍩ ⎕ ⛻ ⌂ ⎈ ⌖ **Leisure** heated indoor swimming pool, sauna, gymnasium **Conf** facs Corporate Hospitality Days **Location** 1.5m west of town centre

Hotel ★★★ 74% HL Manor of Groves Hotel, Golf & Country Club, High Wych, SAWBRIDGEWORTH ☎ 01279 600777 & 0870 410 8833 ▤ 01279 600374 80 en suite

HANBURY MANOR, A MARRIOTT HOTEL & COUNTRY CLUB
HERTFORDSHIRE - WARE - MAP 5 TL31

There can be few golf venues that combine so successfully the old and the new. The old is the site itself, dominated since the 19th century by Hanbury Manor, a Jacobean-style mansion; the wonderful grounds included a nine-hole parkland course designed by the legendary Harry Vardon. The new is the conversion of the estate into the golf and country club; the manor now offers a five-star country house hotel, while Jack Nicklaus II redesigned the grounds for an 18-hole course. The American-style design took the best of Vardon's original and added meadowland to produce a course that looks beautiful and plays superbly. Hanbury Manor has hosted a number of professional events.

SG12 0SD ☎ 01920 885000 📄 01920 487692
web: www.marriotthanburymanor.co.uk
18 Holes, 6124yds, Par 72, SSS 70, Course record 61. Club membership 674.
Visitors handicap certificate. Dress code. Must be hotel resident or minimum of 12 golfers. **Societies** booking required. **Green Fees** phone **Course Designer** Jack Nicklaus II **Facilities** ⑨ ⑩ 🍴 ᴸ ▱ ⑨ 🏌 🏡 ⑨ ◇ 🚜
🏌 🏹 **Leisure** hard tennis courts, heated indoor swimming pool, sauna, gymnasium, health spa **Conf** facs Corporate Hospitality Days **Location** M25 junct 25, 12m N on A10
Hotel ★★★★★ 81% CHH Hanbury Manor, A Marriott Hotel & Country Club, WARE ☎ 01920 487722 & 0870 400 7222 📄 01920 487692 161 en suite

ENGLAND

STANSTEAD ABBOTTS
Map 5 TL31

Briggens Park Golf Club Briggens Park, Stanstead Rd SG12 8LD
☎ 01279 793867 📠 01279 793867
e-mail: briggensparkgolf@aol.co.uk

An attractive nine-hole course set in the grounds of what was once a stately house in 80 acres of parkland.

9 Holes, 2581yds, Par 70, SSS 67, Course record 67.
Club membership 200.

Visitors Mon-Sun & BHs. Booking required weekends & BHs. Dress code. **Societies** booking required. **Green Fees** £15 per 18 holes, £10 per 9 holes (£18/£12 weekends & BHs). Concessions for seniors & juniors **Facilities** ⛳ 🍴 👤 🏠 ⚑ 🏌 🚕 🏌 **Location** off A414 Stanstead road
Hotel ★★★ 72% HL Roebuck, Baldock Street, WARE
☎ 01920 409955 📠 01920 468016 47 en suite

STEVENAGE
Map 4 TL22

Stevenage Golf Centre 6 Aston Ln SG2 7EL
☎ 01438 880223 & 880424 (pro shop) 📠 01438 880040
Bragbury Course: 18 Holes, 6451yds, Par 72, SSS 71,
Course record 63.
Aston Course: 9 Holes, 880yds, Par 27, SSS 27.
Course Designer John Jacobs **Location** 4m SE off B5169
Telephone for further details
Hotel ★★★ 71% HL Best Western Roebuck Inn, London Road, Broadwater, STEVENAGE ☎ 01438 365445 📠 01438 741308
26 en suite

WARE
Map 5 TL31

Hanbury Manor, A Marriott Hotel & Country Club
see page 133
SG12 0SD
☎ 01920 885000 📠 01920 487692
web: www.marriotthanburymanor.co.uk

Whitehill Golf Dane End SG12 0JS
☎ 01920 438495 📠 01920 438891
e-mail: andrew@whitehillgolf.co.uk
web: www.whitehillgolf.co.uk

Undulating course providing a good test for both the average golfer and the low handicapper. Several lakes in challenging positions.

18 Holes, 6618yds, Par 72, SSS 72. Club membership 400.

Visitors Mon-Sun & BHs. **Societies** booking required. **Green Fees** not confirmed **Prof** Matt Belsham **Facilities** ⛳ 🍴 ⛳ 🍴 👤 🏠 ⚑ 🏌 🚕 🏌 **Leisure** snooker room **Conf** facs Corporate Hospitality Days **Location** M25 junct 25 towards Cambridge (A10). Take turn for Ware A1170 and turn right at rdbt. After 2m turn left, proceed for 2m, course on left
Hotel ★★★ 72% HL Roebuck, Baldock Street, WARE
☎ 01920 409955 📠 01920 468016 47 en suite

WATFORD
Map 4 TQ19

West Herts Golf Club Cassiobury Park WD3 3GG
☎ 01923 236484 📠 01923 222300
e-mail: gm@westhertsgolf.demon.co.uk
web: www.westhertsgolfclub

Set in parkland, the course is close to Watford but its tree-lined setting is beautiful and tranquil. Set out on a plateau the course is exceedingly dry. It also has a very severe finish with the 17th, a hole of 378yds, the toughest on the course. The last hole measures over 480yds.

18 Holes, 6612yds, Par 72, SSS 72, Course record 66.
Club membership 900.

Visitors Mon-Sun & BHs. Booking required. Handicap certificate. Dress code. **Societies** booking required. **Green Fees** not confirmed **Course Designer** Tom Morris **Prof** Charles Gough **Facilities** ⛳ 🍴 ⛳ 🍴 👤 🏠 ⚑ 🏌 🚕 🏌 ⚑ **Leisure** indoor teaching facility **Conf** Corporate Hospitality Days **Location** W of town centre off A412
Hotel ★★★ 73% HL Best Western White House, Upton Road, WATFORD ☎ 01923 237316 📠 01923 233109 57 en suite

WELWYN GARDEN CITY
Map 4 TL21

Mill Green Golf Club Gypsy Ln AL7 4TY
☎ 01707 276900 & 270542 (Pro shop) 📠 01707 276898
e-mail: millgreen@crown-golf.co.uk
web: www.millgreengolf.co.uk

A course of two contrasting 9 hole loops. The front 9 plays over a gently undulating landscape. The back 9 plays over fairways winding through ancient woodland and around large lakes. The par 3 course has small greens guarded by testing bunkers.

Mill Green: 18 Holes, 6615yds, Par 72, SSS 72,
Course record 66.
Romany: 9 Holes, 1058yds, Par 54. Club membership 850.

Visitors Mon-Sun & BHs (visitors after midday at weekends). Booking required. Dress code. **Societies** booking required. **Green Fees** phone **Course Designer** Alliss & Clark **Prof** Ian Parker **Facilities** ⛳ 🍴 ⛳ 🍴 👤 🏠 🚕 🏌 ⚑ **Leisure** 9 hole par 3 course. **Conf** facs Corporate Hospitality Days **Location** exit 4 of A1(M), A414 to Mill Green
Hotel ★★★ 75% HL Best Western Homestead Court Hotel, Homestead Lane, WELWYN GARDEN CITY ☎ 01707 324336
📠 01707 326447 74 en suite

Panshanger Golf & Squash Complex Old Herns Ln AL7 2ED
☎ 01707 333350 📠 01707 390010
web: www.finesseleisure.com
18 Holes, 6347yds, Par 72, SSS 70, Course record 65.
Course Designer Peter Kirkham **Location** 1m N of town centre signed off B1000
Telephone for further details
Hotel ★★★★ 75% HL Tewin Bury Farm Hotel, Hertford Road (B1000), WELWYN GARDEN CITY ☎ 01438 717793 📠 01438 840440
39 en suite

Welwyn Garden City Golf Club Mannicotts, High Oaks Rd
L8 7BP
☎ 01707 325243 📄 01707 393213
-mail: secretary@welwyngardencitygolfclub.co.uk
web: www.welwyngardencitygolfclub.co.uk
ndulating parkland with a ravine. Nick Faldo is a former course
ecord holder.
8 Holes, 6114yds, Par 70, SSS 69, Course record 63.
Club membership 930.
isitors contact for details. **Societies** welcome. **Green Fees** phone
ourse Designer Hawtree Prof Stuart Mason **Facilities** ⒯ ⦿ by
rior arrangement 🏌 ⬛ 🍴 ⚖ 🛏 ✎ 🛒 ✎ **Conf** facs
orporate Hospitality Days **Location** A1 junct 6, W of city
otel ★★★ 75% HL Best Western Homestead Court Hotel,
omestead Lane, WELWYN GARDEN CITY ☎ 01707 324336
📄 01707 326447 74 en suite

WHEATHAMPSTEAD   **Map 4 TL11**

Mid Herts Golf Club Lamer Ln, Gustard Wood AL4 8RS
☎ 01582 832242 📄 01582 834834
-mail: secretary@mid-hertsgolfclub.co.uk
web: www.mid-hertsgolfclub.co.uk
ommonland, wooded with heather and gorse-lined fairways.
8 Holes, 6060yds, Par 69, SSS 69, Course record 61.
Club membership 760.
isitors Mon-Fri except BHs. Dress code. **Societies** booking required.
Green Fees phone. **Course Designer** James Braid **Prof** Barney Puttick
acilities ⒯ 🏌 ⬛ 🍴 ⚖ 🛏 🛒 ✎ **Conf** facs **Location** 1m
on B651
otel ★★★ 72% HL Harpenden House Hotel, 18 Southdown
oad, HARPENDEN ☎ 01582 855 9113 📄 01582 760511 76 en suite

KENT

DDINGTON   **Map 5 TQ65**

West Malling Golf Club London Rd ME19 5AR
☎ 01732 844785 📄 01732 844795
-mail: mike@westmallinggolf.com
web: www.westmallinggolf.com
wo 18-hole parkland courses. Year round play on main greens and
es.
pitfire Course: 18 Holes, 6135yds, Par 70, SSS 70.
urricane Course: 18 Holes, 6281yds, Par 70, SSS 70.
isitors Mon-Sun & BHs. Dress code. **Societies** booking required.
reen Fees phone **Course Designer** Max Falkner **Prof** Duncan
ambert **Facilities** ⒯ 🏌 ⬛ 🍴 ⚖ 🛏 ✎ 🛒 ✎
🍀 **Leisure** sauna, gymnasium, jaccuzi & steam room. **Conf** facs
orporate Hospitality Days **Location** 1m S off A20
otel ★★★★ GA Pretty Maid House B&B, London Road, WROTHAM
EATH ☎ 01732 886445 📄 01732 886439 7 rooms

ASH   **Map 5 TQ66**

The London Golf Club Stansted Ln TN15 7EH
☎ 01474 879899 📄 01474 879912
e-mail: info@londongolf.co.uk
web: www.londongolf.co.uk
The two championship courses were designed by Jack Nicklaus. The
signature Heritage course is a par 72 parkland course which has
hosted the European Open and presents a true golfing challenge with
risky carries over water and sand. It is strictly reserved for members
and their guests. Players of all standards can enjoy the inland links
feel of the International course which is available to visitors. Both
courses feature true fairways and pristine greens and the practice
facilities are among the very best.
Heritage Course: 18 Holes, 7208yds, Par 72, SSS 74,
Course record 63.
International Course: 18 Holes, 7005yds, Par 72, SSS 74,
Course record 68. Club membership 1800.
Visitors Mon-Sun & BHs. Handicap certificate. Dress code.
Societies welcome **Green Fees** not confirmed **Course Designer** Jack
Nicklaus/Ron Kirby **Prof** Paul Stuart **Facilities** ⒯ 🏌 ⬛ 🍴
⚖ 🛏 🍴 ✎ 🛒 ✎ 🏌 **Leisure** on site heli-pad **Conf** facs
Corporate Hospitality Days **Location** off A20, 2m from Brands Hatch
Hotel ★★★★ 79% HL Brandshatch Place Hotel & Spa,
Brands Hatch Road, Fawkham, BRANDS HATCH ☎ 01474 875000
📄 01474 879652 38 en suite

ASHFORD   **Map 5 TR04**

Ashford (Kent) Golf Club Sandyhurst Ln TN25 4NT
☎ 01233 622655 📄 01233 627494
e-mail: secretary@ashfordgolfclub.co.uk
web: www.ashfordgolfclub.co.uk
Parkland with good views and easy walking. Considered to be one of
the best inland courses in the county. Narrow fairways and tightly
bunkered greens ensure a challenging game for all levels of golfer.
18 Holes, 6280yds, Par 71, SSS 70, Course record 67.
Club membership 672.
Visitors Mon-Fri, weekends & BHs pm only. Dress code.
Societies booking required. **Green Fees** not confirmed **Course**
Designer Cotton **Prof** Paul Sherman **Facilities** ⒯ 🏌 ⬛ 🍴
🍴 ⚖ 🛏 ✎ 🛒 ✎ **Conf** facs Corporate Hospitality Days
Location 1m NW M20 junct 9
Hotel ★★★★ 80% HL Ashford International Hotel, Simone Weil
Avenue, ASHFORD ☎ 01233 219988 📄 01233 647743 179 en suite

Homelands Golf Centre Ashford Rd, Kingsnorth TN26 1NJ
☎ 01233 661620
e-mail: info@ashfordgolf.co.uk
web: www.ashfordgolf.co.uk
Challenging nine-hole course designed by Donald Steel to provide a stern test for experienced golfers and for others to develop their game. With three par 3s, five par 4s and one par 5 and different tees for the back 9, it demands accuracy rather than length.
9 Holes, 5053yds, Par 68, SSS 65. Club membership 400.
Visitors Mon-Sun & BHs. Dress code. **Societies** booking required.
Green Fees £17 per 18 holes, £13 per 9 holes (weekends £21/£16)
Course Designer Donald Steel **Prof** Howard Bonaccorsi **Facilities** ⓣ
🏌 ⌷ 🍴 🍽 🕇 ✂ 🏌 **Leisure** teaching facilities **Conf** Corporate Hospitality Days **Location** M20 junct 10, A2070, signed from 2nd rdbt to Kingsnorth. Shared entrance with football club
Hotel ★★★★ 80% HL Ashford International Hotel, Simone Weil Avenue, ASHFORD ☎ 01233 219988 📄 01233 647743 179 en suite

BARHAM
Map 5 TR25

Broome Park Golf Club The Broome Park Estate CT4 6QX
☎ 01227 830728 📄 01227 832591
e-mail: golf@broomepark.co.uk
web: www.broomepark.co.uk
Parkland course set in a valley with a 370 year old mansion clubhouse and with lovely views of the surrounding countryside.
18 Holes, 6580yds, Par 72, SSS 71. Club membership 600.
Visitors Mon-Sun & BHs. Booking required. Handicap certificate. Dress code. **Societies** booking required. **Green Fees** £40 per round (£50 weekends) **Course Designer** Donald Steel **Prof** Tienie Britz **Facilities** ⓣ 🍽 🏌 ⌷ 🍴 🏌 🍽 🕇 ✂ 🍴 ✂ **Leisure** hard tennis courts, heated indoor swimming pool, squash, sauna, gymnasium **Conf** facs Corporate Hospitality Days **Location** 1.5m SE on A260
Hotel ★★★★ BB Heathwood Lodge B&B, Wheelbarrow Town, STELLING MINNIS ☎ 01227 709315 & 07831 347395 📄 01227 709475 3 rooms (3 en suite)

BEARSTED
Map 5 TQ85

Bearsted Golf Club Ware St ME14 4PQ
☎ 01622 738198 📄 01622 735608
e-mail: bearstedgolfclub@tiscali..com
web: www.bearstedgolfclub.co.uk
Parkland with fine views of the North Downs.
18 Holes, 6437yds, Par 72, SSS 71. Club membership 780.
Visitors Mon-Sat except BHs. Booking required. Handicap certificate. Dress code. **Societies** booking required. **Green Fees** not confirmed ⓦ **Prof** Tim Simpson **Facilities** ⓣ 🍽 🏌 ⌷ 🍴 🏌 🍽 ✂ **Location** M20 junct 7, right at rdbt, left at mini rdbt, left at 2nd mini rdbt. Pass Bell pub on right, under bridge, on left
Hotel ★★★★ 78% HL Tudor Park, A Marriott Hotel & Country Club, Ashford Road, Bearsted, MAIDSTONE ☎ 01622 734334 & 632004 📄 01622 735360 120 en suite

BIDDENDEN
Map 5 TQ83

Chart Hills Golf Club Weeks Ln TN27 8JX
☎ 01580 292222 📄 01580 292233
e-mail: info@charthills.co.uk
web: www.charthills.co.uk
Created by Nick Faldo, he has truly left his mark on this course. Signature features include the 200-yard long snake-like Anaconda Bunker (one of 138) on the 5th and the island green at the short 17th
18 Holes, 6530yds, Par 72, SSS 71. Club membership 500.
Visitors Mon-Sun & BHs. Booking required. Dress code. **Societies** booking required. **Green Fees** not confirmed **Course Designer** Nick Faldo **Prof** James Cornish **Facilities** ⓣ 🍽 🏌 ⌷ 🍴 🏌 🍽 🕇 ✂ 🍴 ✂ **Leisure** fishing **Conf** facs Corporate Hospitality Days **Location** 1m N of Biddenden off A274
Hotel ★★★ 73% HL London Beach Country Hotel, Spa & Golf Club, Ashford Road, TENTERDEN ☎ 01580 766279 📄 01580 763884 26 en suite

BOROUGH GREEN
Map 5 TQ65

Wrotham Heath Golf Club Seven Mile Ln TN15 8QZ
☎ 01732 884800 📄 01732 887370
e-mail: wrothamheathgolf@btconnect.com
web: www.wrothamheathgolfclub.co.uk
Heathland woodland course with magnificent views of the North Downs.
18 Holes, 5994yds, Par 70, SSS 69, Course record 65. Club membership 550.
Visitors Mon-Fri except BHs. Booking required. Handicap certificate. Dress code. **Societies** booking required. **Green Fees** not confirmed **Course Designer** Donald Steel (part) **Prof** Harry Dearden **Facilities** ⓣ 🍽 🏌 ✂ **Location** 2.25m E on B2016
Hotel ★★★ 73% HL Hadlow Manor, Goose Green, HADLOW ☎ 01732 851442 📄 01732 851875 29 en suite

BRENCHLEY
Map 5 TQ64

Kent National Golf & Country Club Watermans Ln TN12 6ND
☎ 01892 724400 📄 01892 723300
web: www.kentnational.com
18 Holes, 6693yds, Par 72, SSS 72, Course record 63.
Course Designer T Saito **Location** 3m N of Brenchley off B2160
Telephone for further details
Hotel ★★ 63% MET Russell Hotel, 80 London Road, TUNBRIDGE WELLS ☎ 01892 544833 📄 01892 515846 25 en suite

BROADSTAIRS   Map 5 TR36

North Foreland Golf Club Convent Rd CT10 3PU
☎ 01843 862140   🖷 01843 862663
e-mail: office@northforeland.co.uk
web: www.northforeland.co.uk

A picturesque cliff top course situated where the Thames Estuary widens towards the sea. One of the few courses where the sea can be seen from every hole. Walking is easy and the wind is deceptive. The 8th and 17th, both par 4, are testing holes. There is also an 18-hole approach and putting course.

Main Course: 18 Holes, 6198yds, Par 70, SSS 70,
Course record 65.
Northcliffe Course: 18 Holes, 1752yds, Par 54, SSS 54,
Course record 48. Club membership 1100.

Visitors Mon-Sun & BHs. Booking required weekends & BHs. Dress code. **Societies** booking required. **Green Fees** £55 per day, £40 per round (£40 per round weekends). Par 3 course £8 (£10 weekends) **Course Designer** Fowler & Simpson **Prof** Darren Parris **Facilities** 🎌 🍴 🛍 🖥 🍴 🎿 📷 🍸 ✂ 🏌 ♂ **Leisure** hard tennis courts, 18 hole par 3 course **Conf** facs Corporate Hospitality Days **Location** A256 through St Peter's Village to Beacon Rd which changes to Convent Rd. Club on right
Hotel ★★★ 79% HL The Fayreness, Marine Drive, KINGSGATE
☎ 01843 868641 & 861103 🖷 01843 608750   29 en suite

CANTERBURY   Map 5 TR15

Canterbury Golf Club Scotland Hills, Littlebourne Rd CT1 1TW
☎ 01227 453532   🖷 01227 784277
e-mail: secretary@canterburygolfclub.co.uk

Undulating parkland, densely wooded in places, with elevated tees and challenging drives on several holes.

18 Holes, 6272yds, Par 71, SSS 70, Course record 64.
Club membership 700.

Visitors Mon, Tue, Thu-Sun & BHs. Booking required. Dress code **Societies** booking required. **Green Fees** £48 per 18 holes **Course Designer** Harry Colt **Prof** Paul Everard **Facilities** 🎌 🍴 🛍 🖥 🍴 🎿 📷 🍸 ✂ 🏌 **Conf** facs Corporate Hospitality Days **Location** 1.5m from Canterbury city centre E on A257 (Littlebourne Rd)
Hotel ★★★★ GA Castle House, 28 Castle Street, CANTERBURY
☎ 01227 761897   12 rooms

CRANBROOK   Map 5 TQ73

Hemsted Forest Golf Club Golford Rd TN17 4AL
☎ 01580 712833   🖷 01580 714274
e-mail: golf@hemstedforest.co.uk
web: www.hemstedforest.co.uk

Scenic parkland with easy terrain, backed by Hemsted Forest. The course lies in a beautiful natural setting and offers a tranquil haven. The clubhouse, a converted oast, is the only one of its kind.

18 Holes, 6305yds, Par 70, SSS 71, Course record 64.

Visitors Tue-Sun & BHs. Booking required weekends. Dress code. **Societies** booking required. **Green Fees** £25 per round (£40 weekends) **Course Designer** Commander J Harris **Prof** Henry Law **Facilities** 🎌 🍴 🛍 🖥 🍴 🎿 📷 ✂ **Leisure** practice nets **Conf** facs Corporate Hospitality Days **Location** 2m E
Hotel ★★★ 73% HL London Beach Country Hotel, Spa & Golf Club, Ashford Road, TENTERDEN ☎ 01580 766279 🖷 01580 763884 26 en suite

DARTFORD   Map 5 TQ57

Birchwood Park Golf Centre Birchwood Rd, Wilmington DA2 7HJ
☎ 01322 662038 & 660554   🖷 01322 667283
e-mail: info@birchwoodparkgc.co.uk
web: www.birchwoodparkgc.co.uk

The main course offers highly challenging play and will test golfers of all abilities. Beginners and those requiring a quick game or golfers wishing to improve their short game will appreciate the Orchard course where holes range from 96 to 258yds.

Main Course: 18 Holes, 6364yds, Par 71, SSS 70,
Course record 64.
Orchard Course: 9 Holes, 1145yds, Par 28.
Club membership 600.

Visitors Mon-Sun & BHs. Week advance booking. Dress code. **Societies** booking required. **Green Fees** £25 per 18 holes (£30 weekends) **Course Designer** Howard Swann **Prof** Leon Stenford **Facilities** 🎌 🍴 🛍 🖥 🍴 🎿 📷 🍸 ✂ 🏌 ♂ 🏌 **Leisure** sauna, gymnasium **Conf** facs Corporate Hospitality Days **Location** B258 between Dartford & Swanley
Hotel ★★★★ 76% HL Bexleyheath Marriott Hotel, 1 Broadway, BEXLEYHEATH ☎ 020 8298 1000 🖷 020 8298 1234   142 en suite

Dartford Golf Club Heath Lane (Upper), Dartford Heath DA1 2TN
☎ 01322 226455   🖷 01322 226455
e-mail: dartfordgolf@hotmail.com
web: www.dartfordgolfclub.co.uk

Challenging parkland course with tight fairways and easy walking.

18 Holes, 5909yds, Par 69, SSS 69. Club membership 700.

Visitors dress code. **Societies** booking required. **Green Fees** £37 per 36 holes, £26 per 18 holes **Course Designer** James Braid **Prof** John Gregory **Facilities** 🎌 🍴 🛍 🖥 🍴 🎿 📷 ✂ **Conf** facs Corporate Hospitality Days **Location** 2m from town centre off A2
Hotel ★★★★ 81% HL Rowhill Grange Hotel & Utopia Spa, WILMINGTON ☎ 01322 615136 🖷 01322 615137   38 en suite

DEAL
Map 5 TR35

Royal Cinque Ports Golf Club Golf Rd CT14 6RF
☎ 01304 374007 📄 01304 379530
web: www.royalcinqueports.com

Famous championship seaside links, windy but with easy walking. Outward nine is generally considered the easier, inward nine is longer and includes the renowned 16th, perhaps the most difficult hole. On a fine day there are wonderful views across the Channel.

18 Holes, 6899yds, Par 72, SSS 73.
Club membership 950.

Visitors restricted Wed mornings, weekends & bank holidays. Must contact in advance and have a handicap certificate. Men max 20 handicap; Ladies max 30 handicap. **Societies** must contain in advance. **Green Fees** Winter £60 per round/day (£70 weekends). Summer £125 per round, £150 per day (£150/£180 weekends) **Course Designer** James Braid **Prof** Andrew Reynolds **Facilities** ⊕ ⊚ by prior arrangement ⓑ ⊑ ⊓ ⊿ ⊜ ⊓ᵀ ◇ ⏉ ✧ ✦ **Conf** Corporate Hospitality Days **Location** on seafront at N end of Deal

Hotel ★★★★ 74% HL Wallett's Court Country House Hotel & Spa, West Cliffe, St Margarets-at-Cliffe, DOVER ☎ 01304 852424 & 0800 035 1628 📄 01304 853430 16 en suite

EDENBRIDGE
Map 5 TQ44

Sweetwoods Park Golf Club Cowden TN8 7JN
☎ 01342 850729 (Pro shop) 📄 01342 850866
e-mail: golf@sweetwoodspark.com
web: www.sweetwoodspark.com

An undulating and mature parkland course with very high quality greens, testing water hazards and fine views across the Weald from four holes. A good challenge off the back tees. Signature holes include the 7th, 14th and 17th.

Cowden: 18 Holes, 6515yds, Par 72, SSS 69.
Club membership 600.

Visitors Mon-Sun & BHs. Booking required. Dress code.
Societies booking required. **Green Fees** £40 per round (£48 weekends and BHs) **Prof** Julian Reason **Facilities** ⊕ ⊚ ⓑ ⊑ ⊓ᵀ ⊿ ⊜ ⊓ᵀ ✦ ⏉ ✧ ✦ **Conf** facs Corporate Hospitality Days **Location** 4m E of East Grinstead on A264

Hotel ★★★★ 86% HL Felbridge Hotel & Spa, London Road, EAST GRINSTEAD ☎ 01342 337700 📄 01342 337715 120 en suite

EYNSFORD
Map 5 TQ56

Austin Lodge Golf Club Upper Austin Lodge Rd DA4 0HU
☎ 01322 863000 📄 01322 862406
web: www.pentlandgolf.co.uk

18 Holes, 7026yds, Par 73, SSS 71, Course record 68.
Course Designer P Bevan **Location** 6m S of Dartford
Telephone for further details

Hotel ★★★★ 79% HL Brandshatch Place Hotel & Spa, Brands Hatch Road, Fawkham, BRANDS HATCH ☎ 01474 875000 📄 01474 879652 38 en suite

FAVERSHAM
Map 5 TR06

Boughton Golf Brickfield Ln ME13 9AJ
☎ 01227 752277 📄 01227 752361
web: www.pentlandgolf.co.uk

18 Holes, 6469yds, Par 72, SSS 71, Course record 68.
Course Designer P Sparks **Location** M2 junct 7, Brenley Corner
Telephone for further details

Hotel ★★★★ HL Eastwell Manor, Eastwell Park, Boughton Lees, ASHFORD ☎ 01233 213000 📄 01233 635530 62 en suite

Faversham Golf Club Belmont Park ME13 0HB
☎ 01795 890561 📄 01795 890760
e-mail: themanager@favershamgolf.co.uk
web: www.favershamgolf.co.uk

A beautiful inland course laid out over part of a large estate with pheasants walking the fairways quite tamely. Play follows two heavily wooded valleys but the trees affect only the loose shots going out of bounds. Fine views.

18 Holes, 5978yds, Par 70, SSS 69, Course record 63.
Club membership 800.

Visitors Mon-Fri & BHs. Dress code. **Societies** booking required.
Green Fees £35 per round **Course Designer** J H Taylor/D Steel
Prof Stuart Rokes **Facilities** ⊕ ⊚ ⓑ ⊑ ⊓ᵀ ⊿ ⊜ ✦ **Conf** Corporate Hospitality Days **Location** 3.5m S on Belmont road

Hotel ★★★★ HL Eastwell Manor, Eastwell Park, Boughton Lees, ASHFORD ☎ 01233 213000 📄 01233 635530 62 en suite

FOLKESTONE
Map 5 TR23

Etchinghill Golf Course Canterbury Rd CT18 8FA
☎ 01303 863863 📄 01303 863210
web: www.pentlandgolf.co.uk

27 Holes, 6101yds, Par 70, SSS 69, Course record 67.
Course Designer John Sturdy **Location** M20 junct 11/12
Telephone for further details

Hotel ★★★ 75% HL Best Western Clifton Hotel, The Leas, FOLKESTONE ☎ 01303 851231 📄 01303 223949 80 en suite

Save on Hotels. Book at theAA.com/hotel

KENT

ENGLAND

GILLINGHAM   Map 5 TQ76

Gillingham Golf Club Woodlands Rd ME7 2AP
☎ 01634 853017 (office)
e-mail: golf@gillinghamgolf.idps.co.uk
web: www.gillinghamgolfclub.co.uk
Mature parkland course with views of the estuary.

18 Holes, 5473yds, Par 68, SSS 67. Club membership 700.

Visitors Mon-Sun except BHs. Booking required. Dress code.
Societies booking required. **Green Fees** £45 per day, £25 per round
Course Designer James Braid/Steel **Prof** Martin Daniels **Facilities** ⊕
⬛ ♿ 🍴 🏌 ⚐ 🏚 ⚙ ⚒ **Conf** facs Corporate Hospitality
Days **Location** 1.5m SE off A2
Hotel ★★★★ 74% HL Bridgewood Manor, Bridgewood
Roundabout, Waldslade Woods, CHATHAM ☎ 01634 201333
🖨 01634 201330 100 en suite

GRAVESEND   Map 5 TQ67

Mid Kent Golf Club Singlewell Rd DA11 7RB
☎ 01474 568035 🖨 01474 564218
web: www.mkgc.co.uk
18 Holes, 6106yds, Par 70, SSS 69, Course record 60.
Course Designer Frank Pennick **Location** S of town centre off A227
Telephone for further details

Southern Valley Golf Course Thong Ln DA12 4LF
☎ 01474 568568 🖨 01474 360366
web: www.southernvalley.co.uk
18 Holes, 6200yds, Par 69, SSS 69.
Course Designer Weller/Richardson **Location** A2 junct 4, off slip-road
left onto Thong Ln, continue 1m, follow signs for Inn on the Lake Hotel
Telephone for further details

HALSTEAD   Map 5 TQ46

Broke Hill Golf Club Sevenoaks Rd TN14 7HR
☎ 01959 533225 🖨 01959 532680
web: www.crown-golf.co.uk/brokehill

18 Holes, 6469yds, Par 72, SSS 71, Course record 65.
Course Designer David Williams **Location** M25 junct 4, opp Knockholt
station
Telephone for further details
Hotel ★★★ 73% HL 7 Hotel Diner, London Road, Polhill, HALSTEAD
☎ 01959 535890 25 en suite

HAWKHURST   Map 5 TQ73

Hawkhurst Golf Club High St TN18 4JS
☎ 01580 752396 🖨 01580 754074
web: www.hawkhurstgolfclub.org.uk
9 Holes, 5751yds, Par 70, SSS 68, Course record 69.
Course Designer W A Baldock **Location** W of village off A268
Telephone for further details
Hotel ★★★ 73% HL London Beach Country Hotel, Spa & Golf
Club, Ashford Road, TENTERDEN ☎ 01580 766279 🖨 01580 763884
26 en suite

HEADCORN   Map 5 TQ84

Weald of Kent Golf Course Maidstone Rd TN27 9PT
☎ 01622 890866 🖨 01622 890070
e-mail: proshop@weald-of-kent.co.uk
web: www.weald-of-kent.co.uk
Enjoying delightful views over the Weald, this pay-and-play course
features a range of natural hazards, including lakes, trees, ditches
and undulating fairways. A good test for golfers of every standard.

*18 Holes, 6310yds, Par 70, SSS 70, Course record 63.
Club membership 350.*

Visitors Mon-Sun & BHs. Dress code. **Societies** booking required.
Green Fees not confirmed **Course Designer** John Millen **Prof** Jacques
Gous **Facilities** ⊕ 🍴 ⬛ ♿ 🍴 🏌 🏚 ⚐ ⛳ ⚒
Leisure training academy **Conf** facs Corporate Hospitality Days
Location M20 junct 8, through Leeds village, A274 towards Headcorn,
course on left
Hotel ★★★★ 78% HL Tudor Park, A Marriott Hotel & Country
Club, Ashford Road, Bearsted, MAIDSTONE ☎ 01622 734334 &
632004 🖨 01622 735360 120 en suite

HEVER   Map 5 TQ44

Hever Castle Golf Club, Hever Rd, Edenbridge TN8 7NP
☎ 01732 700771 🖨 01732 700775
e-mail: mail@hevercastlegolfclub.co.uk
web: www.hever.co.uk

Originally part of the Hever Castle estate, set in 250 acres of Kentish
countryside, the Championship course has matured well and, with the
addition of the Princes' nine holes, offers stunning holes to challenge
all golfers. Water plays a prominent part in the design of the course,
particularly around Amen Corner, holes 11 through 13. The golfer is
then met with the lengthy stretch home, especially up the 17th, a
daunting 644yd par 5, one of Europe's longest.

*Championship Course: 18 Holes, 7002yds, Par 72, SSS 74,
Course record 67.* continued

Princes Course: 9 Holes, 5568yds, Par 70, SSS 67.
Club membership 500.

Visitors contact club for details. **Societies** booking required. **Green Fees** Championship Course £40 summer (£50 weekends), £28 winter. Princes 9 Course £11 **Course Designer** Dr Nicholas **Prof** Peter Parks **Facilities** ⓣ ⌯ 🝖 ☕ 🍴 ⚒ 🛎 🗭 ◇ 🛒 🏌 🏹
Leisure hard tennis courts **Conf** facs Corporate Hospitality Days **Location** off B269 between Oxted and Tonbridge, 0.5m from Hever Castle
Hotel ★★★★ 80% HL The Spa, Mount Ephraim, TUNBRIDGE WELLS ☎ 01892 520331 📠 01892 510575 70 en suite

HOO
Map 5 TQ77

Deangate Ridge Golf Club Dux Court Rd ME3 8RZ
☎ 01634 251180 📠 01634 250537
web: www.deangateridge.co.uk
Parkland, municipal course designed by Fred Hawtree. 18-hole pitch and putt.

18 Holes, 6300yds, Par 71, SSS 70, Course record 65.
Club membership 300.

Visitors Mon-Sun & BHs. Booking required. Dress code.
Societies booking required. **Green Fees** £16.50 per 18 holes (£21 weekends) **Course Designer** Hawtree **Prof** Richard Fox **Facilities** ⓣ ⌯ 🝖 ☕ 🍴 ⚒ 🛎 🗭 🛒 🏹 **Leisure** hard tennis courts, gymnasium **Location** 4m NE of Rochester off A228
Hotel ★★★★ 74% HL Bridgewood Manor, Bridgewood Roundabout, Walderslade Woods, CHATHAM ☎ 01634 201333 📠 01634 201330 100 en suite

HYTHE
Map 5 TR13

Mercure Hythe Imperial Princes Pde CT21 6AE
☎ 01303 267441 📠 01303 264610
e-mail: h6862-th@accor.com
web: www.mercure.com
A nine-hole 18-tee links course bounded by the Royal Military Canal and the English Channel. Although the course is relatively flat, its aspect offers an interesting and challenging round to a wide range of golfers.

9 Holes, 5560yds, Par 68, SSS 66, Course record 62.
Club membership 200.

Visitors contact hotel for details. **Societies** booking required. **Green Fees** phone **Prof** Simon Wood **Facilities** ⓣ ⌯ 🝖 ☕ 🍴 ⚒ 🛎 🗭 ◇ 🏹 **Leisure** hard and grass tennis courts, heated indoor swimming pool, squash, sauna, gymnasium, snooker **Conf** facs Corporate Hospitality Days **Location** Exit M20 junct 11. Follow into Hythe towards town centre. Right into Twiss Road. Golf course in grounds of Mercure Hythe Imperial
Hotel ★★★★ 71% HL Mercure Hythe Imperial, Princes Parade, HYTHE ☎ 01303 267441 📠 01303 264610 80 en suite

Sene Valley Golf Club Sene CT18 8BL
☎ 01303 268513 (Manager) 📠 01303 237513
e-mail: senevalleygolf@btconnect.com
web: www.senevalleygolfclub.co.uk
A two-level downland course in excellent condition, standing 350 feet above the town and providing interesting golf over an undulating landscape with sea views. A typical hole that challenges most players, is the par 3, 11th which combines a stunning sea view with a testing tee shot to a green surrounded by bunkers and gorse.

18 Holes, 6271yds, Par 71, SSS 70, Course record 62.
Club membership 700.

Visitors Booking recommended weekends. **Societies** booking required. **Green Fees** £32 weekdays (£40 weekends) **Course Designer** Henry Cotton **Prof** Nick Watson **Facilities** ⓣ ⌯ 🝖 ☕ 🍴 ⚒ 🛎 🗭 🏹 🛒 🏹 **Conf** facs Corporate Hospitality Days **Location** M20 junct 12, A20 towards Ashford for 3m, left at rdbt, Hythe Rd for 1m
Hotel ★★★ 74% HL Best Western Stade Court, Stade Street, West Parade, HYTHE ☎ 01303 268263 📠 01303 261803 42 en suite

KINGSDOWN
Map 5 TR34

Walmer & Kingsdown Golf Club The Leas CT14 8EP
☎ 01304 373256 📠 01304 382336
e-mail: info@kingsdowngolf.co.uk
web: www.kingsdowngolf.co.uk
This beautiful downland site is situated near Deal and, being situated on top of the famous White Cliffs, offers breathtaking views of the Channel from every hole.

18 Holes, 6471yds, Par 72, SSS 71, Course record 64.
Club membership 600.

Visitors Mon-Fri. Summer weekends & BHs pm only. Booking required Mon-Wed & weekends. Handicap certificate. Dress code.
Societies booking required. **Green Fees** £32 per round (£40 per round weekends & BHs) **Course Designer** James Braid **Prof** Jude Read **Facilities** ⓣ ⌯ 🝖 ☕ 🍴 ⚒ 🛎 🗭 🛒 🏹 **Conf** Corporate Hospitality Days **Location** 1.5m E of Ringwould off A258 Dover-Deal road
Hotel ★★★ 80% HL Dunkerleys Hotel & Restaurant, 19 Beach Street, DEAL ☎ 01304 375016 📠 01304 380187 16 en suite

LAMBERHURST
Map 5 TQ63

Lamberhurst Golf Club Church Rd TN3 8DT
☎ 01892 890591 📠 01892 891140
e-mail: secretary@lamberhurstgolfclub.com
web: www.lamberhurstgolfclub.com
Parkland course crossing the river twice. Fine views.

18 Holes, 6423yds, Par 72, SSS 71, Course record 65.
Club membership 650.

Visitors Mon-Sun & BHs. Booking required. Dress code.
Societies booking required. **Green Fees** not confirmed **Prof** Brian Impett **Facilities** ⓣ ⌯ 🝖 ☕ 🍴 ⚒ 🛎 🗭 🏹 🛒 🏹 **Conf** Corporate Hospitality Days **Location** N of village on B2162
Hotel ★★★★ 80% HL The Spa, Mount Ephraim, TUNBRIDGE WELLS ☎ 01892 520331 📠 01892 510575 70 en suite

LITTLESTONE
Map 5 TR02

Littlestone Golf Club St Andrew's Rd TN28 8RB
☎ 01797 363355 📠 01797 362740
e-mail: secretary@littlestonegolfclub.org.uk
web: www.littlestonegolfclub.org.uk
Located in the Romney Marshes, this fairly flat seaside links course calls for every variety of shot. The 8th, 15th, 16th and 17th are regarded as classics by international golfers. Fast running fairways and faster greens.
18 Holes, 6486yds, Par 71, SSS 72.
Club membership 350.
Visitors dress code. **Societies** welcome. **Green Fees** not confirmed **Course Designer** Laidlaw Purves **Prof** Andrew Jones **Facilities** ⓨ 🍴 🛅 🖥 🍴 🏌 🛋 🛺 🏌 🛢 **Leisure** hard tennis courts **Conf** Corporate Hospitality Days **Location** from A259 at New Romney take B2071 (Littlestone road)
Hotel ★★★★ 71% HL Mercure Hythe Imperial, Princes Parade, HYTHE ☎ 01303 267441 📠 01303 264610 80 en suite

Littlestone Warren Golf Club St Andrews Rd TN28 8RB
☎ 01797 362231
web: www.littlestonegolfclub.org.uk
A links-style course, normally very dry. Flat, providing easy walking and play challenged by sea breezes. Although not overly long, narrow fairways and small greens place a premium on shot selection and placement.
18 Holes, 5242yds, Par 67, Course record 64.
Club membership 550.
Visitors Mon-Sun & BHs. Booking required Tue, Thu, weekends & BHs. Dress code. **Societies** booking required. **Green Fees** not confirmed **Course Designer** Evans/Lewis **Prof** Andrew Jones **Facilities** ⓨ 🍴 🛅 🖥 🍴 🏌 🛋 🛺 🏌 🛢 **Conf** Corporate Hospitality Days **Location** from A259 at New Romney take B2071 (Littlestone road)
Hotel ★★★★ 71% HL Mercure Hythe Imperial, Princes Parade, HYTHE ☎ 01303 267441 📠 01303 264610 80 en suite

LYDD
Map 5 TR02

Lydd Golf Club Romney Rd TN29 9LS
☎ 01797 320808 📠 01797 321482
web: www.lyddgolfclub.co.uk
18 Holes, 6529yds, Par 71, SSS 71, Course record 65.
Course Designer Mike Smith **Location** A259 onto B2075 by Lydd Airport
Telephone for further details
Hotel ★★★★ 76% HL George in Rye, 98 High Street, RYE
☎ 01797 222114 📠 01797 224065 34 en suite

MAIDSTONE
Map 5 TQ75

Cobtree Manor Park Golf Course Chatham Rd, Sandling ME14 3AZ
☎ 01622 753276
e-mail: golf.manager@mytimeactive.co.uk
web: www.cobtreemanorgolfcourse.co.uk
Undulating parkland with some water hazards.
18 Holes, 5648yds, Par 69, SSS 69, Course record 62.
Club membership 400.

Visitors dress code. **Societies** booking required. **Green Fees** phone **Course Designer** Lawtree **Prof** Gary Stewart **Facilities** ⓨ 🍴 🛅 🖥 🍴 🏌 🛋 🛺 🏌 🛢 **Conf** facs Corporate Hospitality Days **Location** M20 junct 6, 0.25m N on A229
Hotel ★★★★ 78% HL Tudor Park, A Marriott Hotel & Country Club, Ashford Road, Bearsted, MAIDSTONE ☎ 01622 734334 & 632004 📠 01622 735360 120 en suite

Leeds Castle Golf Course Ashford Rd ME17 1PL
☎ 01622 767828 & 880467 📠 01622 735616
web: www.leedscastlegolf.com

9 Holes, 2681yds, Par 33, SSS 33, Course record 29.
Course Designer Neil Coles **Location** M20 junct 8, 4m E of Maidstone on A20 towards Lenham
Telephone for further details
Hotel ★★★★ 78% HL Tudor Park, A Marriott Hotel & Country Club, Ashford Road, Bearsted, MAIDSTONE ☎ 01622 734334 & 632004 📠 01622 735360 120 en suite

See advert on this page

Tudor Park, A Marriott Hotel & Country Club Ashford Rd, Bearsted ME14 4NQ
☎ 01622 739412 📠 01622 735360
web: www.marriottgolf.co.uk

The course is set in a 220-acre former deer park with the pleasantly undulating Kent countryside as a backdrop. The natural features of the land have been incorporated into this picturesque course to form a challenge for those of both high and intermediate standard. The par 5 14th is particularly interesting. It can alter your score dramatically should you gamble with a drive to a narrow fairway. This hole has to be carefully thought out from tee to green depending on the wind direction.

Milgate Course: 18 Holes, 6049yds, Par 70, SSS 69, Course record 64. Club membership 450.

Visitors Visitors 11am onwards on weekends (no restrictions during week). Booking required. Dress code. **Societies** booking required. **Green Fees** £30 per 18 holes (£40 weekends) **Course Designer** Donald Steel **Prof** Jason Muller **Facilities** ⊕ ⏄ ⬟ ⌂ 🍴 ⚑ ⛳ Leisure hard tennis courts, heated indoor swimming pool, sauna, gymnasium, steam room & spa bath, golf academy **Conf** facs Corporate Hospitality Days **Location** M20 junct 8, 1.25m W on A20
Hotel ★★★★ 78% HL Tudor Park, A Marriott Hotel & Country Club, Ashford Road, Bearsted, MAIDSTONE ☎ 01622 734334 & 632004 📠 01622 735360 120 en suite

---

NEW ASH GREEN
Map 5 TQ66

Redlibbets Golf Club Manor Ln, West Yoke TN15 7HT
☎ 01474 879190 📠 01474 879290
e-mail: info@redlibbets.com
web: www.redlibbets.co.uk
Delightful rolling Kentish course cut through an attractive wooded valley.

18 Holes, 6639yds, Par 72, SSS 72. Club membership 575.

Visitors Mon-Tue & Thu-Fri pm except BHs. Weekends pm. Booking required. Dress code. **Societies** booking required. **Green Fees** £55 **Course Designer** Jonathan Gaunt **Prof** Peter Appleyard/Philip Beever **Facilities** ⊕ 🍴 ⬟ ⌂ ⏄ ⬟ ⌂ ⚑ ⛳ **Conf** facs Corporate Hospitality Days **Location** off A20, close to Brand's Hatch
Hotel ★★★★ 79% HL Brandshatch Place Hotel & Spa, Brands Hatch Road, Fawkham, BRANDS HATCH ☎ 01474 875000 📠 01474 879652 38 en suite

---

RAMSGATE
Map 5 TR36

St Augustine's Golf Club Cottington Rd, Cliffsend CT12 5JN
☎ 01843 590333 📠 01843 590444
e-mail: sagc@ic24.net
web: www.staugustinesgolfclub.co.uk
A comfortably flat course in this famous championship area of Kent. St Augustine's will provide a fair challenge for most golfers. Dykes run across the course.

18 Holes, 5254yds, Par 69, SSS 66.
Club membership 670.

Visitors Mon-Sun & BHs. Booking required. **Societies** booking required. **Green Fees** £24 per 18 holes (£30 weekends) **Course Designer** Tom Vardon **Prof** Derek Scott **Facilities** ⊕ 🍴 ⬟ ⌂ ⏄ ⬟ ⌂ ⚑ ⛳ **Location** off A256 Ramsgate-Sandwich
Hotel ★★★ 77% HL Pegwell Bay, 81 Pegwell Road, Pegwell, RAMSGATE ☎ 01843 599590 📠 01843 599591 42 en suite

Stonelees Golf Centre Ebbsfleet Ln CT12 5DJ
☎ 01843 823133 📠 01843 850569
e-mail: stonelees@stonelees.com
web: www.stonelees.com
Stonelees Golf Centre offers three 9 hole courses, each demanding a different ability level, from the par 3 through the demanding Executive course to the challenging full length Heights course.

Executive: 9 Holes, 1510yds, Par 29.
Heights: 9 Holes, 2908yds, Par 35. Club membership 200.

Visitors Contact centre for details. **Societies** booking required. **Green Fees** From £5.10-£17.50. Junior rates available **Prof** David Bonthron/Joe Jezzard **Facilities** ⊕ 🍴 ⬟ ⌂ ⏄ ⬟ ⌂ ⚑ ⛳ Leisure 9 hole par 3 course, golf simulator **Conf** facs Corporate Hospitality Days **Location** off A256 between Ramsgate and Sandwich
Hotel ★★★ 77% HL Pegwell Bay, 81 Pegwell Road, Pegwell, RAMSGATE ☎ 01843 599590 📠 01843 599591 42 en suite

---

ROCHESTER
Map 5 TQ76

Rochester & Cobham Park Golf Club Park Pale ME2 3UL
☎ 01474 823411 📠 01474 824446
e-mail: rcpgc@talk21.com
web: www.rochesterandcobhamgc.co.uk
A first-rate course of challenging dimensions in undulating parkland. All holes differ and each requires accurate drive placing to derive the best advantage. Open Championship regional qualifying course.

18 Holes, 6597yds, Par 71, SSS 72, Course record 63.
Club membership 730.

Visitors Mon-Fri except BHs. Booking required. Handicap certificate. Dress code. **Societies** booking required. **Green Fees** £40 per round **Course Designer** Donald Steel **Prof** Warren Wood **Facilities** ⊕ 🍴 ⬟ ⌂ ⏄ ⬟ ⌂ ⚑ ⛳ **Conf** Corporate Hospitality Days **Location** A2, exit for Cobham/Shore
Hotel ★★★★ 74% HL Bridgewood Manor, Bridgewood Roundabout, Walderslade Woods, CHATHAM ☎ 01634 201333 📠 01634 201330 100 en suite

ROYAL ST GEORGE'S

KENT - SANDWICH - MAP 5 TR35

Consistently ranked among the leading golf courses in the world, Royal St George's occupies a unique place in the history of golf, playing host in 1894 to the first Open Championship outside Scotland. Set among the dunes of Sandwich Bay, the links provide a severe test for the greatest of golfers. Only three Open winners (Bill Rogers in 1981, Greg Norman in 1993 and Ben Curtis in 2003) have managed to remain under par after 72 holes. The undulating fairways, the borrows on the greens, the strategically placed bunkers, and the prevailing winds that blow on all but the rarest of occasions; these all soon reveal any weakness in the player. There are few over the years who have mastered all the vagaries in one round. It hosted its thirteenth Open Championship in 2003, won dramatically by outsider Ben Curtis and was also the venue in 2011.

CT13 9PB ☎ 01304 613090 🖹 01304 611245
e-mail: secretary@royalstgeorges.com **web:** www.royalstgeorges.com
18 Holes, 7204yds, Par 70, SSS 74, Course record 67. Club membership 750.
Visitors Mon-Fri except BHs. Booking required. Handicap certificate. Dress code. **Societies** booking required.
Green Fees £190 per 36 holes, £150 per 18 holes. Reduced winter rates **Course Designer** Dr Laidlaw Purves
Prof A Brooks **Facilities** ⑪ ♡ ♑ ⚐ 📷 ↑ ◇ ✦ ⚑ **Conf** Corporate Hospitality Days **Location** 1.5m E of
Sandwich. Enter town for golf courses
Hotel ★★★ 77% HL Pegwell Bay, 81 Pegwell Road, Pegwell, RAMSGATE ☎ 01843 599590
🖹 01843 599591 42 en suite

SANDWICH

Map 5 TR35

Prince's Golf Club Prince's Dr CT13 9QB
☎ 01304 611118 📠 01304 612000
web: www.princesgolfclub.co.uk
Dunes: 9 Holes, 3432yds, Par 36, SSS 36.
Himalayas: 9 Holes, 3201yds, Par 35, SSS 35.
Shore: 9 Holes, 3348yds, Par 36, SSS 36.
Course Designer Sir Guy Campbell & J S F Morrison **Location** 2m E via toll road, signs from Sandwich
Telephone for further details
Hotel ★★★ 80% HL Dunkerleys Hotel & Restaurant, 19 Beach Street, DEAL ☎ 01304 375016 📠 01304 380187 16 en suite

Royal St George's Golf Club see page 143
CT13 9PB
☎ 01304 613090 📠 01304 611245
e-mail: secretary@royalstgeorges.com
web: www.royalstgeorges.com

SEVENOAKS

Map 5 TQ55

Knole Park Golf Club Seal Hollow Rd TN15 0HJ
☎ 01732 452150 📠 01732 463159
e-mail: secretary@knoleparkgolfclub.co.uk
web: www.knoleparkgolfclub.co.uk

The course is laid out within the grounds of the Knole Estate and can rightfully be described as a natural layout. The course designer has used the contours of the land to produce a challenging course in all weather conditions and throughout all seasons. While, for most of the year, it may appear benign, in summer, when the bracken is high, Knole Park represents a considerable challenge but always remains a fair test of golf.

18 Holes, 6444yds, Par 70, SSS 71, Course record 65.
Club membership 750.
Visitors Mon-Fri except BHs. Booking required. Handicap certificate. Dress code. **Societies** booking required. **Green Fees** £52 per day, £42 per round **Course Designer** J A Abercromby **Prof** Marisa Newman **Facilities** ⊕ ⚑ ⛳ ⚑ ⛳ ⚑ ⚑ ⚑ ⚑
Leisure squash **Conf** Corporate Hospitality Days **Location** NE of town centre off B2019

Wildernesse Golf Club, Park Ln TN15 0JE
☎ 01732 761199 📠 01732 763809
e-mail: golf@wildernesse.co.uk
web: www.wildernesse.co.uk
A tight inland course, heavily wooded with tree-lined fairways. Straight driving and attention to the well-placed bunkers is essential. With few slopes and easy walking, it is difficult to beat par.
18 Holes, 6532yds, Par 72, SSS 71, Course record 63.
Club membership 720.
Visitors Mon-Fri except BHs. Booking required Mon,Thu & Fri. Handicap certificate. Dress code. **Societies** welcome. **Green Fees** not confirmed **Course Designer** Braid (part) **Prof** Craig Walker **Facilities** ⊕ ⚑ ⛳ ⚑ ⛳ ⚑ ⚑ ⚑ **Conf** Corporate Hospitality Days **Location** take A25 from Sevenoaks to Seal, turn right into Park Lane, club entrance on left.
Hotel ★★★ 79% HL Best Western Donnington Manor, London Road, Dunton Green, SEVENOAKS ☎ 01732 462681 📠 01732 458116 59 en suite

SHEERNESS

Map 5 TQ97

Sheerness Golf Club Power Station Rd ME12 3AE
☎ 01795 662585 📠 01795 668100
e-mail: secretary@sheernessgolfclub.co.uk
web: www.sheernessgolfclub.co.uk
Semi-links, marshland course, few bunkers, but many ditches and water hazards.
18 Holes, 6390yds, Par 71, SSS 71, Course record 64.
Club membership 500.
Visitors Mon-Sun & BHs. Booking required. **Societies** booking required. **Green Fees** £35 per day, £25 per 18 holes **Prof** Daniel Webb **Facilities** ⊕ ⚑ ⛳ ⚑ ⛳ ⚑ ⚑ ⚑ ⚑ **Location** 1.5m E off A249
Hotel ★★★★ 74% HL Bridgewood Manor, Bridgewood Roundabout, Walderslade Woods, CHATHAM ☎ 01634 201333 📠 01634 201330 100 en suite

SHOREHAM

Map 5 TQ56

Darenth Valley Golf Course Station Rd TN14 7SA
☎ 01959 522922 & 522944 📠 01959 525089
e-mail: enquiries@dvgc.co.uk
web: www.dvgc.co.uk

Gently undulating parkland in a beautiful Kent valley, with excellent well-drained greens. The course has matured and developed to become a challenge to both high and low handicap golfers.

continued

Darenth Valley Golf Course

18 Holes, 6193yds, Par 72, SSS 71, Course record 56.
Visitors Mon-Sun & BHs. Dress code. **Societies** booking required.
Green Fees not confirmed **Course Designer** Michael Cross **Prof** Pete
Stopford **Facilities** ⊕ ⑩ 🏋 ▦ 🍴 🎿 🏠 🍴 ✔ 🏌 ✔
Conf facs Corporate Hospitality Days **Location** 3m N of Sevenoaks off
A225 between Otford & Eynsford
Hotel ★★★ 73% HL 7 Hotel Diner, London Road, Polhill, HALSTEAD
☎ 01959 535890 25 en suite

SITTINGBOURNE   Map 5 TQ96

The Oast Golf Centre Church Rd, Tonge ME9 9AR
☎ 01795 473527
e-mail: info@oastgolf.co.uk
web: www.oastgolf.co.uk

A par 3 approach course of nine holes with 18 tees augmented by a
17-bay floodlit driving range and a putting green.

9 Holes, 1664yds, Par 54, SSS 54.
Visitors Mon-Sun & BHs. **Societies** welcome. **Green Fees** £9 for 18
holes, £6.50 for 9 holes. Weekdays £6.50 per am, £9 per pm unlimited
Course Designer D Chambers **Prof** D Chambers **Facilities** 🏋 ▦
🍴 🏠 🍴 ✔ 🏌 **Leisure** power tees **Location** 2m NE, A2 from
Sittingbourne, turn left after Bapchild
Hotel ★★★★ 74% HL Bridgewood Manor, Bridgewood
Roundabout, Walderslade Woods, CHATHAM ☎ 01634 201333
🖹 01634 201330 100 en suite

Sittingbourne & Milton Regis Golf Club Wormdale,
Newington ME9 7PX
☎ 01795 842261
e-mail: sittingbournegc@btconnect.com
web: www.sittingbournegolfclub.com

A downland course with pleasant vistas and renowned for its high
quality greens. The back nine holes are challenging whilst the front
nine require accuracy and precision. Regular host to county and
regional fixtures and finals.

18 Holes, 6295yds, Par 71, SSS 70, Course record 63.
Club membership 715.
Visitors Mon-Fri except BHs. Booking required Wed. Dress code.
Societies booking required. **Green Fees** £32 per day (summer), £20
per day (winter) **Course Designer** Donald Steel **Prof** John Hearn
Facilities ⊕ ⑩ by prior arrangement 🏋 ▦ 🍴 🏠 🍴 ✔
🍴 ✔ **Conf** Corporate Hospitality Days **Location** 0.5m from M2
junct 5, off Chestnut St at Danaway
Hotel ★★★★ 74% HL Bridgewood Manor, Bridgewood
Roundabout, Walderslade Woods, CHATHAM ☎ 01634 201333
🖹 01634 201330 100 en suite

Upchurch River Valley Golf Centre Oak lane ME9 7AY
☎ 01634 379592 🖹 01634 387784
18 Holes, 6237yds, Par 70, SSS 70.
Course Designer David Smart **Location** A2 between Rainham &
Newington
Telephone for further details
Hotel ★★★ 86% HL Hempstead House Country Hotel, London
Road, Bapchild, SITTINGBOURNE ☎ 01795 428020 🖹 01795 436362
34 en suite

SNODLAND   Map 5 TQ76

Oastpark Golf Course Malling Rd ME6 5LG
☎ 01634 242661 🖹 01634 240744
e-mail: oastparkgolfclub@btconnect.com

A challenging parkland course for golfers of all abilities. The course
has water hazards and orchards.

9 Holes, 2170yds, Par 33, SSS 33. Club membership 60.
Visitors Mon-Sun & BHs. Dress code **Societies** welcome. **Green
Fees** not confirmed **Course Designer** J D Banks **Prof** David Porthouse
Facilities 🏋 ▦ 🍴 🏠 🍴 ✔ 🏌 **Location** M20 junct 4
Hotel ★★★★ 74% HL Bridgewood Manor, Bridgewood
Roundabout, Walderslade Woods, CHATHAM ☎ 01634 201333
🖹 01634 201330 100 en suite

TENTERDEN   Map 5 TQ83

London Beach Country Hotel & Golf Club Ashford Rd
TN30 6HX
☎ 01580 766279 🖹 01580 763884
e-mail: enquiries@londonbeach.com
web: www.londonbeach.com

Located in a mature parkland setting in the Weald. A test of golf for
all abilities of golfer with its rolling fairways and undulating greens.
Many of the holes have water features.

9 Holes, 5200yds, Par 70, Course record 64.
Club membership 250.
Visitors Mon-Sun & BHs. Booking required Tue, Wed, weekends & BHs.
Dress code. **Societies** booking required. **Green Fees** not confirmed
Course Designer Golf Landscapes **Prof** Mark Chilcott **Facilities** ⊕
⑩ 🏋 ▦ 🍴 🏠 🍴 ✔ 🔾 ✔ 🍴 ✔ **Leisure** fishing,
pitch & putt, clay pigeon shooting, spa **Conf** facs Corporate Hospitality
Days **Location** M20 junct 9, A28 towards Tenterden, hotel on right 1m
before Tenterden
Hotel ★★★ 73% HL London Beach Country Hotel, Spa & Golf
Club, Ashford Road, TENTERDEN ☎ 01580 766279 🖹 01580 763884
26 en suite

Tenterden Golf Club Woodchurch Rd TN30 7DR
☎ 01580 763987 📄 01580 763430
e-mail: enquiries@tenterdengolfclub.co.uk
web: www.tenterdengolfclub.co.uk
Set in tranquil undulating parkland with beautiful views, the course is challenging with several difficult holes. Open fairways with short rough allows for speedy play. Tree positioning demands accuracy without spoiling enjoyment.

18 Holes, 6001yds, Par 70, SSS 69. Club membership 500.
Visitors Mon-Sun & BHs. Booking required weekends & BHs (weekends after 11.30am). Dress code. Societies booking required. Green Fees £45 per day, £25 per round (£50/£35 weekends & BHs). Winter £20/£25 Prof Richard Silman Facilities ⊞ ⊠ ▯ ▯ ▯ ⊿ 🍴 🚗 🏌 Conf facs Corporate Hospitality Days Location M20 junct 10, take A28 signed Tenterden. Before Tenterden turn left at B2080 signed Appledore/Woodchurch and left at B2067 Woodchurch Rd
Hotel ★★★ 73% HL London Beach Country Hotel, Spa & Golf Club, Ashford Road, TENTERDEN ☎ 01580 766279 📄 01580 763884 26 en suite

TONBRIDGE   Map 5 TQ54

Poult Wood Golf Centre Higham Ln TN11 9QR
☎ 01732 364039 & 366180 📄 01732 354640
e-mail: leisure.services@tmbc.gov.uk
web: www.poultwoodgolf.co.uk
There are two public pay-and-play parkland courses in an idyllic woodland setting. The courses are ecologically designed over predominantly flat land offering challenging hazards and interesting playing conditions for all standards of golfer.

18 Holes, 5524yds, Par 68, SSS 67.
9 Holes, 1281yds, Par 28, SSS 28.
Visitors Mon-Sun & BHs. Dress code. Societies booking required.
Green Fees 18 hole course £17 (£24 weekends & BHs). 9 hole course £6.50/£8.30 Course Designer Hawtree Prof David Copsey Facilities ⊞ ⊠ ▯ ▯ ▯ ⊿ 🍴 🏌 Leisure squash Conf facs Corporate Hospitality Days Location off A227 3m N of Tonbridge
Hotel ★★★ 78% HL Rose & Crown Hotel, 125 High Street, TONBRIDGE ☎ 01732 357966 📄 01732 357194 56 en suite

TUNBRIDGE WELLS (ROYAL)   Map 5 TQ53

Nevill Golf Club Benhall Mill Rd TN2 5JW
☎ 01892 525818 📄 01892 517861
e-mail: manager@nevillgolfclub.co.uk
web: www.nevillgolfclub.co.uk
The Kent-Sussex border forms the northern perimeter of the course. Open undulating ground, well-wooded with some heather and gorse for the first half. The second nine holes slope away from the clubhouse to a valley where a narrow stream hazards two holes.

18 Holes, 6349yds, Par 71, SSS 70, Course record 63. Club membership 800.
Visitors Mon, Wed-Fri & BHs. Booking required. Dress code. Societies booking required. Green Fees £50 per day, £40 per round Course Designer Henry Cotton Prof Nick Duc Facilities ⊞ ⊠ ▯ ▯ ▯ ⊿ 🍴 🏌 Conf facs Corporate Hospitality Days Location S of Tunbridge Wells
Hotel ★★★★ 80% HL The Spa, Mount Ephraim, TUNBRIDGE WELLS ☎ 01892 520331 📄 01892 510575 70 en suite

Tunbridge Wells Golf Club Langton Rd TN4 8XH
☎ 01892 523034
e-mail: tunbridgewelgolf@btconnect.com
web: www.tunbridgewellsgolf.com
Somewhat hilly, well-bunkered parkland course with lake; trees form natural hazards.

9 Holes, 2355yds, Par 65, SSS 62.
Visitors Mon-Sun & BHs. Booking required. Dress code. Societies booking required. Green Fees not confirmed Prof Sharon Hinton Facilities ⊞ ⊠ ▯ ▯ ▯ ⊿ 🍴 🏌 Location 1m W on A264
Hotel ★★★★ 80% HL The Spa, Mount Ephraim, TUNBRIDGE WELLS ☎ 01892 520331 📄 01892 510575 70 en suite

WEST KINGSDOWN   Map 5 TQ56

Woodlands Manor Golf Club Tinkerpot Ln, Otford TN15 6AB
☎ 01959 523806 📄 01959 524398
e-mail: info@woodlandsmanorgolf.co.uk
web: www.woodlandsmanorgolf.co.uk
Two distinct nine-hole layouts with views over an Area of Outstanding Natural Beauty. The course is challenging but fair with varied and memorable holes of which the 7th, 10th and 18th stand out. Good playing conditions all year round.

18 Holes, 6032yds, Par 69, SSS 69, Course record 64. Club membership 600.
Visitors Mon-Sun & BHs. Booking required. Societies booking required. Green Fees £26 per 18 holes (£35 weekends) Course Designer Lyons/Coles Prof Philip Womack Facilities ⊞ ⊠ by prior arrangement ▯ ▯ ▯ ⊿ 🍴 ◇ 🚗 🏌 🏌 Conf facs Corporate Hospitality Days Location A20 through West Kingsdown, right opp Portbello Inn onto School Ln, clubhouse left after 2m
Hotel ★★★★ 76% HL Thistle Brands Hatch, BRANDS HATCH ☎ 0871 376 9008 📄 0871 376 9108 121 en suite

WEST MALLING   Map 5 TQ65

Kings Hill Golf Club Fortune Way, Discovery Dr, Kings Hill ME19 4GF
☎ 01732 875040 📄 01732 875019
e-mail: khatkhgolf@aol.com
web: www.kingshillgolf.co.uk
Set in over 200 acres of undulating terrain and features large areas of protected heath and mature woodland. USGA standard greens and tees.

18 Holes, 6622yards, Par 72, SSS 72. Club membership 530.
Visitors booking required. Societies booking required. Green Fees £35 (£45 weekends & BHs) Course Designer David Williams Partnership Prof David Hudspith Facilities ⊞ ⊠ by prior arrangement ▯ ▯ ▯ ⊿ 🍴 🚗 🏌 🏌 Conf facs Location M20 junct 4, A228 towards Tonbridge
Hotel ★★★ 73% HL Hadlow Manor, Goose Green, HADLOW ☎ 01732 851442 📄 01732 851875 29 en suite

Save on Hotels. Book at **theAA.com/hotel**

KENT

ENGLAND

WESTERHAM

Map 5 TQ45

Park Wood Golf Club Chestnut Av, Tatsfield TN16 2EG
☎ 01959 577744 & 577177 (pro-shop)
📠 01959 577765
e-mail: mail@parkwoodgolf.co.uk
web: www.parkwoodgolf.co.uk

Situated in an Area of Outstanding Natural Beauty, flanked by an ancient woodland with superb views across Kent and Surrey countryside. An undulating course, tree-lined and with some interesting water features. Playable in all weather conditions.

18 Holes, 6835yds, Par 72, SSS 72, Course record 65. Club membership 500.

Visitors Tue, Wed & Fri except BHs. Mon & Thu pm. Weekends in summer after 11am. Booking required. Dress code. **Societies** welcome. **Green Fees** phone for details **Prof** Nick Terry **Facilities** ⓣ 🍴 🏌 ⌧ 🍴 🏌 🍷 🏌 **Conf** facs Corporate Hospitality Days **Location** A25 onto B2024 Croydon Rd, turn right at Church Hill junct onto Chestnut Ave
Hotel ★★★ 73% HL 7 Hotel Diner, London Road, Polhill, HALSTEAD ☎ 01959 535890 25 en suite

Westerham Golf Club Valence Park, Brasted Rd TN16 1LJ
☎ 01959 567100 📠 01959 567101
e-mail: info@westerhamgc.co.uk
web: www.westerhamgc.co.uk

Originally forestry land with thousands of mature pines. The storms of 1987 created natural fairways and the mature landscape makes the course both demanding and spectacular. A clubhouse with first-class facilities and magnificent views.

18 Holes, 6270yds, Par 72, SSS 72. Club membership 550.

Visitors Mon-Sun & BHs. Booking required. Dress code.
Societies booking required. **Green Fees** £38 per round Mon-Thu, £45 Fri, weekends and BHs **Course Designer** D Williams **Prof** J Marshall **Facilities** ⓣ 🏌 ⌧ 🍴 🏌 🍷 🏌 🍷 🏌 🍷

Leisure short game practice area **Conf** facs Corporate Hospitality Days
Location A25 between Westerham & Brasted
Hotel ★★★★ GA Corner Cottage, Toys Hill, WESTERHAM
☎ 01732 750362 📠 01732 750754 1 room

WESTGATE ON SEA

Map 5 TR37

Westgate and Birchington Golf Club 176 Canterbury Rd CT8 8LT
☎ 01843 831115
e-mail: wandbgc@tiscali.co.uk

A fine blend of inland and seaside holes which provide a good test of the golfer despite the apparently simple appearance of the course.

18 Holes, 4926yds, Par 64, SSS 64, Course record 58. Club membership 350.

Visitors Mon-Sun & BHs. Dress code. **Societies** welcome. **Green Fees** £20 per day (£22 weekends & BHs) 🏌 **Prof** Mark Young **Facilities** ⓣ 🍴 🏌 ⌧ 🍴 🏌 🏌 🍷 🏌 **Conf** Corporate Hospitality Days **Location** E of town centre off A28
Hotel ★★★ 77% HL Pegwell Bay, 81 Pegwell Road, Pegwell, RAMSGATE ☎ 01843 599590 📠 01843 599591 42 en suite

WHITSTABLE

Map 5 TR16

Chestfield (Whitstable) Golf Club 103 Chestfield Rd, Chestfield CT5 3LU
☎ 01227 794411 & 792243 📠 01227 794454
e-mail: secretary@chestfield-golfclub.co.uk
web: www.chestfield-golfclub.co.uk

Changes have been made in recent years to this parkland course with undulating fairways and fine views of the sea and countryside. These consist of six new greens and five new tees. The ancient clubhouse, dating back to the 15th century, is reputed to be the oldest building in the world used for this purpose.

18 Holes, 6200yds, Par 70, SSS 70, Course record 66. Club membership 725.

Visitors Dress code. **Societies** booking required. **Green Fees** £44 per day, £36 per round **Course Designer** D Steel/James Braid **Prof** John Brotherton **Facilities** ⓣ 🍴 🏌 ⌧ 🍴 🏌 🏌 🍷 🏌 🍷
Leisure half-way house providing snacks/refreshments **Conf** Corporate Hospitality Days **Location** 0.5m S by Chestfield Railway Station, off A2990

Whitstable & Seasalter Golf Club Collingwood Rd CT5 1EB
☎ 01227 272020 📠 01227 280822

9 Holes, 5357yds, Par 66, SSS 65, Course record 64.
Location W of town centre off B2205
Telephone for further details

LANCASHIRE

ACCRINGTON   Map 7 SD72

Accrington & District Golf Club Devon Av, Oswaldtwistle BB5 4LS
☎ 01254 350110 🖷 01254 350111
e-mail: info@accringtongolfclub.com
web: www.accringtongolfclub.com
Moorland course with pleasant views of the Pennines and surrounding areas. The course is a real test for even the best amateur golfers and has hosted many county matches and championships over its 100 plus years of history.
18 Holes, 6031yds, Par 70, SSS 69. Club membership 600.
Visitors Mon-Sun & BHs. Booking required. Dress code.
Societies booking required. **Green Fees** £25 per round (£35 weekends & BHs) 🅿 **Course Designer** J Braid **Prof** Mark Harling **Facilities** ⑨ by prior arrangement 🍴 by prior arrangement 🍺 ⬜ 🏌 ⛳ 🏠 🚌 ⚡ **Conf** Corporate Hospitality Days **Location** between Accrington & Blackburn
Hotel ★★★★ 74% HL Mercure Dunkenhalgh Hotel & Spa, Blackburn Road, Clayton-le-Moors, ACCRINGTON ☎ 01254 398021 🖷 01254 872230 175 en suite

Baxenden & District Golf Club Top o' th' Meadow, Baxenden BB5 2EA
☎ 01254 234555 🖷 01254 234555
e-mail: baxgolf@hotmail.com
web: www.baxendengolf.co.uk
Moorland course with panoramic views and a long par 3 to start.
9 Holes, 5300yds, Par 70, SSS 68, Course record 65. Club membership 340.
Visitors Mon, Wed-Fri & BHs. Booking required. Dress code
Societies welcome. **Green Fees** £15 per 18 holes (£25 BHs) 🅿
Facilities ⑨ 🍴 🍺 ⬜ 🏌 ⛳ **Conf** facs Corporate Hospitality Days **Location** 1.5m SE off A680
Hotel ★★★★ 74% HL Mercure Dunkenhalgh Hotel & Spa, Blackburn Road, Clayton-le-Moors, ACCRINGTON ☎ 01254 398021 🖷 01254 872230 175 en suite

Green Haworth Golf Club Green Haworth BB5 3SL
☎ 01254 237580 & 382510 🖷 01254 396176
web: www.greenhaworthgolfclub.co.uk
9 Holes, 5522yds, Par 68, SSS 67, Course record 66.
Location 2m S off A680
Telephone for further details
Hotel ★★★★ 74% HL Mercure Dunkenhalgh Hotel & Spa, Blackburn Road, Clayton-le-Moors, ACCRINGTON ☎ 01254 398021 🖷 01254 872230 175 en suite

BACUP   Map 7 SD82

Bacup Golf Club Maden Rd OL13 8HY
☎ 01706 873170
e-mail: secretary_bgc@btconnect.com
Tree-lined moorland course, predominantly flat except climbs to 1st and 10th holes.
9 Holes, 6018yds, Par 70, SSS 69, Course record 60. Club membership 350.
Visitors dress code. **Societies** booking required **Green Fees** not

confirmed 🅿 **Facilities** ⑨ by prior arrangement 🍴 by prior arrangement 🍺 ⬜ 🏌 ⛳ **Conf** Corporate Hospitality Days **Location** W of town off A671
Hotel ★★★ 79% HL Rosehill House, Rosehill Avenue, BURNLEY ☎ 01282 453931 🖷 01282 455628 34 en suite

BARNOLDSWICK   Map 7 SD84

Ghyll Golf Club Skipton Rd BB18 6JH
☎ 01282 842466 & 844359
e-mail: secretary@ghyllgolfclub.co.uk
web: www.ghyllgolfclub.co.uk
Excellent parkland course with outstanding views, especially from the Ingleborough tee where you can see the Three Peaks. Testing Mast hole is an uphill par 3. Eleven holes in total, nine in Yorkshire and two in Lancashire.
Tudor: 9 Holes, 6259yds, Par 70.
York: 9 Holes, 5770yds, Par 68. Club membership 345.
Visitors Mon-Sat & BHs. Dress code. **Societies** booking required.
Green Fees £15 per day 🅿 **Facilities** ⑨ by prior arrangement 🍴 by prior arrangement 🍺 ⬜ 🏌 ⛳ **Conf** Corporate Hospitality Days **Location** NE of town on B6252
Hotel ★★★ 77% HL Herriots Hotel, Broughton Road, SKIPTON ☎ 01756 792781 🖷 01756 793967 23 en suite

BICKERSTAFFE   Map 7 SD40

Mossock Hall Golf Club Liverpool Rd L39 0EE
☎ 01695 421717 🖷 01695 424961
e-mail: jackie@mossockhallgolfclub.co.uk
web: www.mossockhallgolfclub.co.uk
Relatively flat parkland with scenic views. USGA greens and water features on four holes.
18 Holes, 6504yards, Par 71, SSS 71, Course record 68. Club membership 580.
Visitors Mon-Sun & BHs. Booking required. Dress code
Societies booking required. **Green Fees** £27 per 18 holes (£34 weekends & BHs) **Course Designer** Steve Marnoch **Prof** Brad Millar **Facilities** ⑨ 🍴 🍺 ⬜ 🏌 ⛳ 🏠 ⚡ 🚌 ⚡ **Conf** facs Corporate Hospitality Days **Location** M58 junct 3
Hotel ★★★★ 73% HL Suites Hotel Knowsley, Ribblers Lane, KNOWSLEY ☎ 0151 549 2222 🖷 0151 549 1116 101 en suite

BLACKBURN   Map 7 SD62

Blackburn Golf Club Beardwood Brow BB2 7AX
☎ 01254 51122 🖷 01254 665578
e-mail: sec@blackburngolfclub.com
web: www.blackburngolfclub.com
Parkland on a high plateau with stream and hills. Superb views of the Pennine hills and Fylde Coast.
18 Holes, 6144yds, Par 71, SSS 70, Course record 62. Club membership 550.
Visitors Mon-Fri & Sun. BHs by arrangement. Dress code.
Societies booking required. **Green Fees** £32 per day (£38 weekends) **Prof** Alan Rodwell **Facilities** ⑨ 🍴 🍺 ⬜ 🏌 ⛳ 🏠 ⚡ 🚌 ⚡ **Conf** facs Corporate Hospitality Days **Location** 1.25m NW of town centre off A677
Hotel ★★ 85% HL Millstone at Mellor, Church Lane, Mellor, BLACKBURN ☎ 01254 813333 🖷 01254 812628 23 en suite

BLACKPOOL   Map 7 SD33

Blackpool North Shore Golf Club Devonshire Rd FY2 0RD
☎ 01253 352054 📄 01253 591240
e-mail: office@bnsgc.com
web: www.bnsgc.com

Links type course with rolling fairways and good sized greens. Excellent views of the Lake District and Pennine Hills.

18 Holes, 6431yds, Par 71, SSS 71, Course record 64. Club membership 800.

Visitors Mon-Wed, Fri & Sun except BHs. Booking required Fri & Sun. Dress code. **Societies** booking required. **Green Fees** not confirmed **Course Designer** H S Colt **Prof** Andrew Richardson **Facilities** ⊕ ⊖ ⊪ ⊑ ⊓ ⅃ ⚐ ⏚ ℱ **Conf** Corporate Hospitality Days **Location** on A587 N of town centre
Hotel ★★ 72% HL Hotel Sheraton, 54-62 Queens Promenade, BLACKPOOL ☎ 01253 352723 📄 01253 595499 104 en suite

Blackpool Park Golf Club North Park Dr FY3 8LS
☎ 01253 397916 & 478176 (tee times)
📄 01253 397916
e-mail: secretary@blackpoolparkgc.co.uk
web: www.blackpoolparkgc.co.uk

Opened in 1925, this municipal course is situated in Stanley Park. The golf club (Blackpool Park) is private but golfers may use the clubhouse facilities if playing the course. An abundance of grassy pits, ponds and open dykes.

18 Holes, 6048yds, Par 70, SSS 70, Course record 63. Club membership 500.

Visitors Mon-Sun & BHs. Booking required weekends. Dress code. **Societies** booking required. **Green Fees** phone **Course Designer** A. McKenzie **Prof** Brian Purdie **Facilities** ⊕ ⊖ ⊪ ⊑ ⊓ ⅃ ⚐ ⏚ ⟊ ℱ **Conf** Corporate Hospitality Days **Location** 1m E of Blackpool Tower
Hotel ★★★ 77% HL Carousel, 663-671 New South Prom, BLACKPOOL ☎ 01253 402642 📄 01253 341100 92 en suite

Herons' Reach Golf Club De Vere Hotel FY3 8LL
☎ 01253 766156 & 838866   📄 01253 798800
web: www.devere.co.uk

18 Holes, 5848yds, Par 72, SSS 68, Course record 64.

Course Designer Peter Alliss/Clive Clark **Location** M55 junct 4, follow signs for zoo, hotel situated just before
Telephone for further details
Hotel ★★★★ 73% HL Barceló Blackpool Imperial Hotel, North Promenade, BLACKPOOL ☎ 01253 623971 📄 01253 751784 180 en suite

BURNLEY   Map 7 SD83

Burnley Golf Club Glen View BB11 3RW
☎ 01282 455266
e-mail: burnleygolfclub@onthegreen.co.uk
web: www.burnleygolf.sitenet.pl

Challenging moorland course with exceptional views.

Glen View: 18 Holes, 5939yds, Par 69, SSS 69, Course record 62. Club membership 602.

Visitors Mon-Fri, Sun & BHs. Booking required. Dress code. **Societies** booking required. **Green Fees** £25 per day (£30 weekends & BHs) ⊕ **Course Designer** James Braid **Prof** James Webster **Facilities** ⊕ ⊖ ⊪ ⊑ ⊓ ⅃ ⚐ ⏚ ℱ

Leisure snooker table **Conf** facs Corporate Hospitality Days **Location** S of town off A646
Hotel ★★★ 79% HL Rosehill House, Rosehill Avenue, BURNLEY ☎ 01282 453931 📄 01282 455628 34 en suite

Towneley Golf Club Towneley Park, Todmorden Rd BB11 3ED
☎ 01282 438473
web: www.towneleygolfclub.co.uk

Parkland course, with other sporting facilities.

18 Holes, 5834yds, Par 70, SSS 68, Course record 63. Club membership 290.

Visitors Mon-Sun & BHs. **Societies** booking required. **Green Fees** not confirmed **Facilities** ⊕ ⊑ ⊓ ⅃ ⚐ ⏚ ℱ **Conf** Corporate Hospitality Days **Location** 1m SE of town centre on A671
Hotel ★★★ 79% HL Rosehill House, Rosehill Avenue, BURNLEY ☎ 01282 453931 📄 01282 455628 34 en suite

CHORLEY   Map 7 SD51

Charnock Richard Golf Club Preston Rd, Charnock Richard PR7 5LE
☎ 01257 470707 📄 01257 791196
e-mail: mail@crgc.co.uk
web: www.charnockrichardgolfclub.co.uk

Flat parkland course with plenty of American-style water hazards. Signature hole the 6th par 5 with an island green.

18 Holes, 5904yds, Par 70, SSS 69, Course record 65. Club membership 550.

Visitors Mon-Sun & BHs. Booking required. Dress code. **Societies** booking required. **Green Fees** £34 (£42 weekends & BHs). £15 member guest **Course Designer** Martin Turner **Prof** Alan Lunt **Facilities** ⊕ ⊖ ⊪ ⊑ ⊓ ⅃ ⚐ ⏚ ℱ **Conf** facs Corporate Hospitality Days **Location** on A49, 0.25m from Camelot Theme Park
Hotel ★★★★ GA Parr Hall Farm, 8 Parr Lane, ECCLESTON ☎ 01257 451917 📄 01257 453749 10 rooms

Chorley Golf Club Hall o' th' Hill PR6 9HX
☎ 01257 480263 📄 01257 480722
web: www.chorleygolfclub.co.uk
18 Holes, 6269yds, Par 71, SSS 70, Course record 62.
Course Designer J A Steer **Location** 2.5m SE on A673
Telephone for further details
Hotel ★★★ 82% HL Pines, 570 Preston Rd, Clayton-Le-Woods, CHORLEY ☎ 01772 338551 📄 01772 629002 35 en suite

Duxbury Jubilee Park Golf Club Duxbury Hall Rd PR7 4AT
☎ 01257 265380 📄 01257 274500

A municipal parkland course set in parkland and mature woodland. The contours, elevated tees and greens, the bunkers and the water hazards on several holes give constant interest and challenge, particularly around the turn when the woods come into play. The 10th to the 12th offer the hardest challenges with the 17th not far behind.

18 Holes, 6380yds, Par 71, SSS 70. Club membership 160.

Visitors Mon-Sun & BHs. **Societies** booking required. **Green Fees** not confirmed **Course Designer** Hawtree & Sons **Prof** C Lea **Facilities** ⊕ ⊪ ⊑ ⊓ ⅃ ⚐ ⏚ ℱ **Conf** facs Corporate Hospitality Days **Location** 2.5m S off A6
Hotel BUD Days Inn Charnock Richard - M6, Welcome Break Service Area, CHORLEY ☎ 01257 791746 📄 01257 793596 100 en suite

Shaw Hill Hotel Golf & Country Club Preston Rd, Whittle-Le-Woods PR6 7PP
☎ 01257 269221 & 279222 (pro shop)
🖥 01257 261223
e-mail: golf@shaw-hill.co.uk
web: www.shaw-hill.co.uk

A fine heavily wooded parkland course offering a considerable challenge as well as tranquillity and scenic charm. Six holes are protected by water and signature holes are the 8th and the closing 18th played slightly up hill to the imposing club house.

18 Holes, 6283yds, Par 72, SSS 71, Course record 65. Club membership 500.

Visitors Mon-Fri except BHs. Handicap certificate. **Societies** booking required. **Green Fees** Mon-Thu £50 per 18 holes, Fri £60 **Course Designer** Laurence Allamby **Prof** David Clark **Facilities** ⓦ 🍴 🍺 🖥 🍷 ⚲ 🏠 ⚑ ♦ 🚐 🏌 **Leisure** heated indoor swimming pool, sauna, gymnasium, snooker **Conf** facs Corporate Hospitality Days **Location** 1.5m N on A6
Hotel ★★★★ 75% HL Wrightington Hotel & Country Club, Moss Lane, Wrightington, WIGAN ☎ 01257 425803 🖥 01257 425830 73 en suite

CLITHEROE   Map 7 SD74

Clitheroe Golf Club Whalley Rd, Pendleton BB7 1PP
☎ 01200 422292 🖥 01200 422292
e-mail: secretary@clitheroegolfclub.com
web: www.clitheroegolfclub.com

One of the best inland courses in the country. Clitheroe is a parkland-type course with water hazards and good scenic views, particularly towards Longridge and Pendle Hill. An Open Championship regional qualifying course from 2010.

18 Holes, 6504yds, Par 71, SSS 71, Course record 66. Club membership 700.

Visitors Sun-Fri & BHs. Booking required. Handicap certificate. Dress code. **Societies** booking required. **Green Fees** Mon-Thu £48 per day, £38 per 18 holes, Fri & Sun £50/£43 **Course Designer** James Braid **Prof** Paul McEvoy **Facilities** ⓦ 🍴 🍺 🖥 🍷 🏠 ⚑ 🚐 ♦ 🏌 **Conf** facs Corporate Hospitality Days **Location** 2m S of Clitheroe
Hotel ★★★ 77% HL Eaves Hall Country Hotel, Eaves Hall Lane, West Bradford, CLITHEROE ☎ 01200 425271 🖥 01200 425131 34 en suite

COLNE   Map 7 SD84

Colne Golf Club Law Farm, Skipton Old Rd BB8 7EB
☎ 01282 863391 🖥 01282 870547
e-mail: colnegolfclub@hotmail.co.uk
Moorland course with scenic surroundings.

9 Holes, 6053yds, Par 70, SSS 69, Course record 63. Club membership 440.

Visitors Mon-Wed & Fri. Dress code. **Societies** booking required. **Green Fees** not confirmed 🅿 **Facilities** ⓦ 🍴 🍺 🖥 🍷 🏠 **Leisure** snooker **Conf** Corporate Hospitality Days **Location** 1m E off A56

DARWEN   Map 7 SD62

Darwen Golf Club Winter Hill BB3 0LB
☎ 01254 701287 (club) & 704367 (office)
🖥 01254 773833
e-mail: admin@darwengolfclub.com
web: www.darwengolfclub.com

Built on undulating moorland with the front nine having more of a parkland setting. The front nine holes have many water features and are pleasurable but challenging to play. The back nine are more undulating with fine views and challenging holes for all levels of golfer.

18 Holes, 6354yds, Par 71, SSS 71. Club membership 600.

Visitors Mon-Fri, Sun & BHs. Booking required Tue & Sun. Handicap certificate. Dress code. **Societies** welcome. **Green Fees** not confirmed 🅿 **Prof** Wayne Lennon **Facilities** ⓦ 🍴 🍺 🖥 🍷 🏠 🏌 **Conf** facs Corporate Hospitality Days **Location** M65 junct 4, 1m NW of Darwen
Hotel ★★ 85% HL Millstone at Mellor, Church Lane, Mellor, BLACKBURN ☎ 01254 813333 🖥 01254 812628 23 en suite

FLEETWOOD   Map 7 SD34

Fleetwood Golf Club Golf House FY7 8AF
☎ 01253 773573
web: www.fleetwoodgolf.co.uk
18 Holes, 6723yds, Par 72, SSS 72.

Course Designer J A Steer **Location** W of town centre
Telephone for further details
Hotel ★★ 72% HL Hotel Sheraton, 54-62 Queens Promenade, BLACKPOOL ☎ 01253 352723 🖥 01253 595499 104 en suite

GARSTANG   Map 7 SD44

Best Western Garstang Country Hotel & Golf Centre Garstang Rd, Bowgreave PR3 1YE
☎ 01995 600100 🖥 01995 600950
e-mail: enquiries@garstang-golf.com
web: www.garstanghotelandgolf.com

Fairly flat parkland course following the contours of the Rivers Wyre and Calder, some greens being close to the hazards. The good drainage all year and the fine views of the Pennines add to the enjoyment of a challenging game of golf.

18 Holes, 6050yds, Par 68, SSS 68.

Visitors Mon-Sun & BHs. **Societies** booking required. **Green Fees** £16 per 18 holes (£18 weekends) **Course Designer** Richard Bradbeer **Prof** Robert Head **Facilities** ⓦ 🍴 🍺 🖥 🍷 🏠 🏠 ⚑ ♦

continued

Save on Hotels. Book at **theAA.com/hotel**

LANCASHIRE

ENGLAND

🏌 🏌 **Leisure** short course, indoor putting zone, ball/club fitting bay **Conf** facs Corporate Hospitality Days **Location** 1m S of Garstang on B6430
Hotel ★★★ 77% HL Best Western Garstang Country Hotel & Golf Centre, Garstang Road, Bowgreave, GARSTANG ☎ 01995 600100 📠 01995 600950 32 en suite

See advert on this page

GREAT HARWOOD   Map 7 SD73

Great Harwood Golf Club Harwood Bar, Whalley Rd BB6 7TE
☎ 01254 884391
web: www.greatharwoodgolfclub.co.uk
Flat parkland with fine views of the Pendle region.
9 Holes, 6404yds, Par 73, SSS 71. Club membership 400.
Visitors Mon-Fri & BHs. Dress code. **Societies** booking required **Green Fees** £24 (£30 weekends & BHs) 🏌 **Facilities** ⓘ ⓘ 🍴 ⓘ 🍴
⏛ **Location** E of town centre on A680
Hotel ★★★★ 74% HL Mercure Dunkenhalgh Hotel & Spa, Blackburn Road, Clayton-le-Moors, ACCRINGTON ☎ 01254 398021 📠 01254 872230 175 en suite

HASLINGDEN   Map 7 SD72

Rossendale Golf Club Ewood Lane Head BB4 6LH
☎ 01706 831339 (Secretary) & 213616 (Pro)
📠 01706 228669
e-mail: admin@rossendalegolfclub.net
web: www.rossendalegolfclub.net
A surprisingly flat parkland course, situated on a plateau with panoramic views and renowned for excellent greens.
18 Holes, 6293yds, Par 72, SSS 71. Club membership 600.
Visitors Mon-Fri, Sun & BHs. Booking required. Handicap certificate. Dress code. **Societies** booking required. **Green Fees** £40 per day, £30 per round (£45/£35 Sun) **Prof** Stephen Nicholls **Facilities** ⓘ ⓘ 🍴
ⓘ 🍴 ⏛ 🍴 🏌 🏌 **Location** 0.5m S off A56
Hotel ★★ 85% HL Millstone at Mellor, Church Lane, Mellor, BLACKBURN ☎ 01254 813333 📠 01254 812628 23 en suite

HEYSHAM
Map 7 SD46

Heysham Golf Club Trumacar Park, Middleton Rd LA3 3JH
☎ 01524 851011 (Sec) & 852000 (Pro)
🖨 01524 853030
e-mail: secretary@heyshamgolfclub.co.uk
web: www.heyshamgolfclub.co.uk

A parkland course situated at the extreme west of the Morecambe/ Heysham boundary close to the coast. Long holes and open fairways characterise the course together with the introduction of a number of water features to complement the extended 6360 yards par 70. The elevated part of the course has stunning views across Morecambe Bay to the Lakeland Hills in the north and the Pennines to the east.

18 Holes, 6355yds, Par 70, SSS 70. Club membership 850.
Visitors Mon-Fri except BHs. Booking required. Handicap certificate. Dress code. **Societies** welcome. **Green Fees** £35 per day, £30 per round (£40 per round weekends) **Course Designer** Alex Herd **Prof** Ryan Done **Facilities** ⑪ †◎¶ 🛍 ⬚ 🏐 ⬩ 🖼 ♂ 🛒 ♂ **Leisure** snooker **Conf** Corporate Hospitality Days **Location** 0.75m S off A589

Hotel ★★★ 71% HL Clarendon, 76 Marine Road West, West End Promenade, MORECAMBE ☎ 01524 410180 🖨 01524 421616 29 en suite

KNOTT END-ON-SEA
Map 7 SD34

Knott End Golf Club Wyreside FY6 0AA
☎ 01253 810576 🖨 01253 813446
e-mail: louise@knottendgolfclub.com
web: www.knottendgolfclub.com

Scenic links and parkland course next to the Wyre Estuary. The opening five holes run along the river and have spectacular views of the Fylde coast. Although the course is quite short, the prevailing winds can add to one's score. Over-clubbing can be disastrous with trouble behind most of the smallish and well-guarded greens.

18 Holes, 5825yds, Par 69, SSS 68, Course record 63. Club membership 650.
Visitors Mon-Fri, Sun & BHs. Booking required. Dress code. **Societies** booking required. **Green Fees** £35 per day, £33 per round (£45/£41Sun) **Course Designer** Braid **Prof** Paul Walker **Facilities** ⑪ †◎¶ 🛍 ⬚ 🏐 ⬩ 🖼 ♂ 🛒 ♂ **Leisure** practice net **Conf** Corporate Hospitality Days **Location** W of village off B5377

Hotel ★★ 72% HL Hotel Sheraton, 54-62 Queens Promenade, BLACKPOOL ☎ 01253 352723 🖨 01253 595499 104 en suite

LANCASTER
Map 7 SD46

Lancaster Golf Club Ashton Hall, Ashton-with-Stodday LA2 0AJ
☎ 01524 751247
e-mail: office@lancastergc.co.uk
web: www.lancastergc.co.uk

This parkland course is unusual as it is exposed to winds from the Irish Sea. It is situated on the Lune estuary and has some natural hazards and easy walking. There are several fine holes among woods near the old clubhouse. Fine views towards the Lake District.

18 Holes, 6512yds, Par 71, SSS 71, Course record 65. Club membership 900.
Visitors Mon-Fri except BHs. Booking required. Handicap certificate. Dress code. **Societies** booking required. **Green Fees** not confirmed **Course Designer** James Braid **Prof** David Sutcliffe **Facilities** ⑪

†◎¶ 🛍 ⬚ 🏐 ⬩ 🖼 ♂ 🛒 ♂ 🏳 ♂ 🛒 ♂ **Conf** facs Corporate Hospitality Days **Location** 3m S on A588
Hotel ★★★★ 76% HL Lancaster House, Green Lane, Ellel, LANCASTER ☎ 01524 844822 🖨 01524 844766 99 en suite

LANGHO
Map 7 SD73

Mytton Fold Hotel & Golf Complex Whalley Rd BB6 8AB
☎ 01254 245392 🖨 01254 248119
web: www.myttonfold.co.uk

The course has panoramic views across the Ribble Valley and Pendle Hill. Tight fairways and water hazards are designed to make this a challenging course for any golfer.

18 Holes, 5938yds, Par 72, SSS 69. Club membership 450.
Visitors Mon-Sun & BHs. Booking required. Dress code. **Societies** booking required. **Green Fees** not confirmed **Course Designer** Frank Hargreaves **Facilities** ⑪ †◎¶ 🛍 ⬚ 🏐 ⬩ 🖼 ♦ 🛒 ♂ **Conf** facs Corporate Hospitality Days **Location** on A59 between Langho and Billington

Hotel ★★★ 76% HL Mercure Blackburn Foxfields Country Hotel, Whalley Road, Billington, CLITHEROE ☎ 01254 822556 🖨 01254 824613 44 en suite

LEYLAND
Map 7 SD52

Leyland Golf Club Wigan Rd PR25 5UD
☎ 01772 436457 🖨 01772 435605
e-mail: manager@leylandgolfclub.co.uk
web: www.leylandgolfclub.co.uk

Fairly flat parkland course.

18 Holes, 6276yds, Par 70, SSS 70, Course record 65. Club membership 700.
Visitors Mon-Fri except BHs. Booking required. Handicap certificate. Dress code. **Societies** booking required. **Green Fees** £40 per round. Winter £36 **Prof** Colin Burgess **Facilities** ⑪ †◎¶ 🛍 ⬚ 🏐 ⬩ 🖼 ♂ 🛒 ♂ 🏳 **Conf** facs Corporate Hospitality Days **Location** M6 junct 28, right to lights at A49, right again, course 0.5m on left
Hotel ★★★ 82% HL Pines, 570 Preston Rd, Clayton-Le-Woods, CHORLEY ☎ 01772 338551 🖨 01772 629002 35 en suite

LONGRIDGE
Map 7 SD63

Longridge Golf Club Fell Barn, Jeffrey Hill PR3 2TU
☎ 01772 783291 🖨 01772 783022
e-mail: secretary@longridgegolfclub.com
web: www.longridgegolfclub.com

Founded in 1877, Longridge is one of the oldest clubs in England, having celebrated its 125th anniversary in 2002. A moorland course with panoramic views of the Trough of Bowland, the Fylde coast and Welsh mountains. Small, sloping greens, difficult to read and a good test of golf.

18 Holes, 5974yds, Par 70, SSS 69, Course record 61. Club membership 600.
Visitors Mon-Sun & BHs. Booking required weekends & BHs. Dress code. **Societies** booking required. **Green Fees** not confirmed **Prof** Stephen Taylor **Facilities** ⑪ †◎¶ 🛍 ⬚ 🏐 ⬩ 🖼 ♂ 🛒 ♂ 🏳 **Conf** Corporate Hospitality Days **Location** 8m NE of Preston off B6243
Hotel ★★ 85% HL Millstone at Mellor, Church Lane, Mellor, BLACKBURN ☎ 01254 813333 🖨 01254 812628 23 en suite

ROYAL LYTHAM & ST ANNES

LANCASHIRE - LYTHAM ST ANNES - MAP 7 SD32

Founded in 1886, this huge links course can be difficult, especially in windy conditions. Unusually for a championship course, it starts with a par 3, the nearby railway line and red-brick houses creating distractions that add to the challenge. The course has hosted 10 Open Championships with some memorable victories: amateur Bobby Jones famously won the first here in 1926; Bobby Charles of New Zealand became the only left-hander to win the title; in 1969 Tony Jacklin helped to revive British golf with his win; and the most recent in 2001 was won by David Duval.

Links Gate FY8 3LQ ☎ 01253 724206 🗎 01253 780946
e-mail: bookings@royallytham.org **web:** www.royallytham.org
18 Holes, 6882yds, Par 71, SSS 74, Course record 64. Club membership 850.
Visitors Mon-Fri & Sun. Booking required. Handicap certificate. Dress code. **Societies** booking required.
Green Fees £225 per 36 holes, £150 per 18 holes (Sun £150 per 18 holes). All prices including lunch
Course Designer George Lowe **Prof** Eddie Birchenough **Facilities** ⑪ ⑩ 🍺 ⬜ 🍽 ⛱ 🏠 ◇ 🛏 ⚐ ⚑
Conf Corporate Hospitality Days **Location** 0.5m E of St Annes
Hotel ★★★ 77% HL Chadwick, South Promenade, LYTHAM ST ANNES ☎ 01253 720061
🗎 01253 714455 75 en suite

ENGLAND

LYTHAM ST ANNES
Map 7 SD32

Fairhaven Golf Club Oakwood Av FY8 4JU
☎ 01253 736741 (Secretary) 🖷 01253 731461
e-mail: secretary@fairhavengolfclub.co.uk
web: www.fairhavengolfclub.co.uk

A flat, but interesting parkland/links course of good standard. There are natural hazards as well as numerous bunkers, and players need to produce particularly accurate second shots. Excellent natural drainage ensures year round play. An excellent test of golf for all abilities.

18 Holes, 6983yds, Par 73, SSS 73, Course record 64.
Club membership 750.

Visitors Mon-Sun & BHs. Booking required. Handicap certificate. Dress code. **Societies** booking required. **Green Fees** £75 per day, £55 per round (£85/£65 weekends & BHs) **Course Designer** J A Steer & J Braid **Prof** Andrew Lancaster **Facilities** ⊕ ⵏ⊘⧵ ⵏ ⵏ ⵏ ⵏ ⵏ ⵏ **Leisure** snooker **Conf** Corporate Hospitality Days **Location** E of town centre off B5261
Hotel ★★★ 80% HL Bedford Hotel, 307-313 Clifton Drive South, LYTHAM ST ANNES ☎ 01253 724636 🖷 01253 729244 45 en suite

Lytham Green Drive Golf Club Ballam Rd FY8 4LE
☎ 01253 737390 🖷 01253 731350
e-mail: secretary@lythamgreendrive.co.uk
web: www.lythamgreendrive.co.uk

Green Drive provides a stern but fair challenge for even the most accomplished golfer. Tight fairways, strategically placed hazards and small tricky greens are the trademark of this testing course which meanders through pleasant countryside and is flanked by woods, pastures and meadows. The course demands accuracy in spite of the relatively flat terrain.

18 Holes, 6305yds, Par 70, SSS 70, Course record 63.
Club membership 700.

Visitors Mon-Fri, Sun & BHs. Dress code. **Societies** booking required. **Green Fees** £50 per day, £40 per round. Golf packages from £30 per person **Course Designer** Steer **Prof** Andrew Lancaster **Facilities** ⊕ ⵏ⊘⧵ ⵏ ⵏ ⵏ ⵏ ⵏ ⵏ **Conf** Corporate Hospitality Days **Location** E of town centre off B5259
Hotel ★★★ 80% HL Bedford Hotel, 307-313 Clifton Drive South, LYTHAM ST ANNES ☎ 01253 724636 🖷 01253 729244 45 en suite

Royal Lytham & St Annes Golf Club see page 153
Links Gate FY8 3LQ
☎ 01253 724206 🖷 01253 780946
e-mail: bookings@royallytham.org
web: www.royallytham.org

St Annes Old Links Golf Highbury Rd East FY8 2LD
☎ 01253 723597 🖷 01253 781506
e-mail: secretary@stannesoldlinks.com
web: www.stannesoldlinks.com

Seaside links, final qualifying course for Open Championship 2012; compact and of very high standard, particularly greens. Very long 5th, 17th and 18th holes. Famous hole: 9th (171yds), par 3.

18 Holes, 6684yds, Par 72, SSS 73.
Club membership 700.

Visitors Mon-Fri & Sun except BHs. Booking required Sun. Handicap certificate. Dress code. **Societies** welcome. **Green Fees** Mon-Thu £60 per day, £50 am only, £45 pm only, Fri & Sun £65/£55/£50 **Course Designer** George Lowe **Prof** D J Webster **Facilities** ⊕ ⵏ⊘⧵ ⵏ ⵏ ⵏ ⵏ ⵏ ⵏ ⵏ **Leisure** snooker room, golf studio for indoor lessons **Conf** facs Corporate Hospitality Days **Location** N of town centre
Hotel ★★★ 77% HL Chadwick, South Promenade, LYTHAM ST ANNES ☎ 01253 720061 🖷 01253 714455 75 en suite

MORECAMBE
Map 7 SD46

Morecambe Golf Club Marine Road East, Bare LA4 6AJ
☎ 01524 412841 🖷 01524 400088
e-mail: secretary@morecambegolfclub.com
web: www.morecambegolfclub.com

Holiday golf at its most enjoyable. The well-maintained, wind-affected seaside parkland course is not long but full of character. Even so the panoramic views of Morecambe Bay, the Lake District and the Pennines make concentration difficult. The 4th is a testing hole.

18 Holes, 5791yds, Par 67, SSS 69, Course record 69.
Club membership 850.

Visitors Mon-Sun & BHs. Booking required. Dress code. **Societies** booking required. **Green Fees** not confirmed **Course Designer** Dr Alister MacKenzie **Prof** Simon Fletcher **Facilities** ⊕ ⵏ⊘⧵ ⵏ ⵏ ⵏ ⵏ ⵏ ⵏ ⵏ **Leisure** snooker room **Conf** Corporate Hospitality Days **Location** N of town centre on A5105
Hotel ★★★ 71% HL Clarendon, 76 Marine Road West, West End Promenade, MORECAMBE ☎ 01524 410180 🖷 01524 421616 29 en suite

NELSON
Map 7 SD83

Marsden Park Golf Course Townhouse Rd BB9 8DG
☎ 01282 661912 & 661384
e-mail: martin.robinson@pendleleisuretrust.co.uk
web: www.pendleleisuretrust.co.uk

A semi-parkland course offering panoramic views of surrounding countryside, set in the foothills of Pendle Marsden Park, a testing 18 holes for golfers of all abilities.

18 Holes, 5989yds, Par 70, SSS 69, Course record 65.
Club membership 750.

Visitors Mon-Sun & BHs. Booking required. **Societies** booking required **Green Fees** not confirmed **Facilities** ⊕ ⵏ⊘⧵ ⵏ ⵏ ⵏ ⵏ ⵏ ⵏ **Conf** facs Corporate Hospitality Days **Location** take M65 from Blackburn to end, turn right at rdbt, 2nd exit at next rdbt, left at Hour Glass Pub, signed on left

Save on Hotels. Book at **theAA.com/hotel**

LANCASHIRE

Nelson Golf Club King's Causeway, Brierfield BB9 0EU
☎ 01282 611834 📄 01282 611834
e-mail: secretary@nelsongolfclub.com
web: www.nelsongolfclub.com

Moorland course. Dr MacKenzie, who laid out the course, managed a design that does not include any wearisome climbing and created many interesting holes with wonderful panoramic views of the surrounding Pendle area.

18 Holes, 6006yds, Par 70, SSS 69, Course record 61.
Club membership 590.

Visitors Mon-Wed, Fri, Sun & BHs. Booking required. Handicap certificate. Dress code. **Societies** booking required. **Green Fees** £30 per day (£35 Sun & BHs). 🏵 **Course Designer** Dr A MacKenzie **Prof** Simon Eaton **Facilities** ⓣ ⑪ 🛍 🖵 ⑪ 🎿 🏠 ⑪ 🚍
✐ **Conf** Corporate Hospitality Days **Location** M65 junct 12, A682 to Brierfield, left at lights onto Halifax Rd & King's Causeway

ORMSKIRK
Map 7 SD40

Hurlston Hall Golf & Country Club Hurlston Ln, Southport Rd, Scarisbrick L40 8HB
☎ 01704 840400 & 842829 (pro shop) 📄 01704 841404
e-mail: info@hurlstonhall.co.uk
web: www.hurlstonhall.co.uk

Designed by Donald Steel, this gently undulating course offers fine views of the Pennines and Bowland Fells. With generous fairways, large tees and greens, two streams and seven lakes, it provides a good test of golf for players of all standards.

18 Holes, 6540yds, Par 72. Club membership 650.

Visitors Booking required. Dress code. **Societies** booking required. **Green Fees** £42 per 18 holes (£47 weekends). **Course Designer** Donald Steel **Prof** Tim Hastings **Facilities** ⓣ ⑪ 🛍 🖵 ⑪ 🎿 🏠 🛎 ✐ **Leisure** heated indoor swimming pool, fishing, sauna, gymnasium **Conf** facs Corporate Hospitality Days **Location** 2m from Ormskirk on A570
Hotel ★★★★ 75% HL Formby Hall Golf Resort & Spa, Southport Old Road, FORMBY ☎ 01704 875699 📄 01704 832134 62 en suite

Ormskirk Golf Club Cranes Ln, Lathom L40 5UJ
☎ 01695 572227 📄 01695 572227
e-mail: mail@ormskirkgolllfclub.com
web: www.ormskirkgolfclub.com

Pleasantly secluded, fairly flat parkland with much heath and silver birch. Accuracy from the tees will provide an interesting variety of second shots.

18 Holes, 6358yds, Par 70, SSS 71, Course record 63.
Club membership 300.

Visitors Mon-Sun & BHs. Booking required. Dress code.
Societies booking required. **Green Fees** £55 per day, £45 per round (£60/£50 Sun, £60 per round Sat) **Course Designer** Harold Hilton **Prof** Jack Hammond **Facilities** ⓣ ⑪ 🛍 🖵 ⑪ 🎿 🏠 ✐ **Conf** Corporate Hospitality Days **Location** 1.5m NE
Hotel ★★★★ 75% HL Formby Hall Golf Resort & Spa, Southport Old Road, FORMBY ☎ 01704 875699 📄 01704 832134 62 en suite

PLEASINGTON
Map 7 SD62

Pleasington Golf Club BB2 5JF
☎ 01254 202177 📄 01254 201028
e-mail: secretary-manager@pleasington-golf.co.uk
web: www.pleasington-golf.co.uk

Featuring mature parkland and heathland aspects, the course tests judgement of distance through the air to greens of widely differing levels. The 11th and the 4th are testing holes. A regular regional qualifying course for the Open Championship.

18 Holes, 6539yds, Par 71, SSS 72, Course record 65.
Club membership 700.

Visitors Mon-Fri, Sun & BHs. Booking required. Dress code.
Societies booking required. **Green Fees** £50 per day (£55 Sun & BHs) **Course Designer** George Lowe **Prof** Ged Furey **Facilities** ⓣ ⑪ 🛍 🖵 ⑪ 🎿 🏠 ✐ ⑪ **Conf** facs Corporate Hospitality Days **Location** M65 junct 3, signed for Blackburn
Hotel ★★ 85% HL Millstone at Mellor, Church Lane, Mellor, BLACKBURN ☎ 01254 813333 📄 01254 812628 23 en suite

POULTON-LE-FYLDE
Map 7 SD33

Poulton-le-Fylde Golf Club Breck Rd FY6 7HJ
☎ 01253 892444
e-mail: greenwood-golf@hotmail.co.uk
web: www.poultonlefyldegolfclub.co.uk

A pleasant, municipal parkland course suitable for all standards of golfers although emphasis on accuracy is required. Good mix of holes.

9 Holes, 3000yds, Par 35. Club membership 360.

Visitors Mon-Sun & BHs. Booking required Fri-Sun. **Societies** booking required. **Green Fees** not confirmed **Course Designer** H Taylor **Prof** John Greenwood **Facilities** ⓣ ⑪ 🛍 🖵 ⑪ 🎿 🏠 ⑪ ✐ 🛎 ✐ **Leisure** gymnasium, indoor custom fitting centre **Conf** Corporate Hospitality Days **Location** M55 junct 3, A585 signed Fleetwood, 1st exit at River Wyre rdbt, club 500 yds on right signed
Hotel ★★ 72% HL Hotel Sheraton, 54-62 Queens Promenade, BLACKPOOL ☎ 01253 352723 📄 01253 595499 104 en suite

PRESTON
Map 7 SD52

Ashton & Lea Golf Club Tudor Av, Lea PR4 0XA
☎ 01772 735282 📄 01772 735762
e-mail: info@ashtonleagolfclub.co.uk
web: www.ashtonleagolfclub.co.uk

Fairly flat, well-maintained parkland course with natural water hazards, offering pleasant walks and some testing holes for golfers of all standards. Water comes into play on seven of the last nine holes. The course has three challenging par 3s.

18 Holes, 6334yds, Par 71, SSS 70, Course record 65.
Club membership 650.

Visitors Mon-Sun except BHs. Dress code. **Societies** booking required. **Green Fees** £30 per 18 holes (£35 weekends) **Course Designer** J Steer **Prof** M Greenough **Facilities** ⓣ ⑪ 🛍 🖵 ⑪ 🎿 🏠 ✐ 🛎 ✐ **Leisure** snooker table **Conf** facs Corporate Hospitality Days **Location** 3m W of Preston on A5085
Hotel ★★★★ 75% HL Preston Marriott Hotel, Garstang Road, Broughton, PRESTON ☎ 01772 864087 📄 01772 861728 149 en suite

Fishwick Hall Golf Club Glenluce Dr, Farringdon Park PR1 5TD
☎ 01772 798300 📄 01772 704600
e-mail: fishwickhallgolfclub@supanet.com
web: www.fishwickhallgolfclub.co.uk
Meadowland course overlooking River Ribble. Natural hazards.

18 Holes, 6045yds, Par 70, SSS 69, Course record 66. Club membership 650.

Visitors Mon-Sun & BHs. Dress code. **Societies** booking required.
Green Fees £22 per round (£34 weekends) **Prof** Martin Watson
Facilities ⓦ ⓞⓁ ⓛ ⓓ ⓣⓛ ⓧ ⓐ 🔗 **Conf** Corporate
Hospitality Days **Location** M6 junct 31
Hotel ★★★ 75% HL Macdonald Tickled Trout, Preston New
Road, Samlesbury, PRESTON ☎ 0844 8799053 📄 01772 877463
98 en suite

Ingol Golf Club Tanterton Hall Rd PR2 7BY
☎ 01772 734556 📄 01772 729815
web: www.ingolgolfclub.co.uk

18 Holes, 6294yds, Par 72, SSS 70, Course record 68.
Course Designer Henry Cotton **Location** A5085 onto B5411, signs
to Ingol
Telephone for further details
Hotel ★★★ 75% HL Macdonald Tickled Trout, Preston New
Road, Samlesbury, PRESTON ☎ 0844 8799053 📄 01772 877463
98 en suite

Penwortham Golf Club Blundell Ln, Penwortham PR1 0AX
☎ 01772 744630 📄 01772 740172
e-mail: admin@penworthamgc.co.uk
web: www.penworthamgc.co.uk
A progressive golf club set close to the banks of the River Ribble.
The course has tree-lined fairways, excellent greens, and provides
easy walking. Testing holes include the 177 yd, par 3 3rd, the 480
yd, par 5 6th, and the 386 yd par 4 16th.

18 Holes, 5865yds, Par 69, SSS 69, Course record 65. Club membership 1100.

Visitors Mon, Wed-Fri except BHs. Booking required. Dress code.
Societies booking required. **Green Fees** £35 per day, £29 per round.
Course Designer Ken Moodie **Prof** Darren Hopwood **Facilities** ⓦ
ⓞⓁ ⓛ ⓓ ⓣⓛ ⓧ ⓐ 🔗 **Conf** Corporate Hospitality Days
Location 1.5m W of town centre off A59
Hotel ★★★ 75% HL Macdonald Tickled Trout, Preston New
Road, Samlesbury, PRESTON ☎ 0844 8799053 📄 01772 877463
98 en suite

Preston Golf Club Fulwood Hall Ln, Fulwood PR2 8DD
☎ 01772 700011 📄 01772 794234
e-mail: secretary@prestongolfclub.com
web: www.prestongolfclub.com
Pleasant inland golf at this course set in very agreeable parkland.
There is a well-balanced selection of holes, undulating among groups
of trees, and not requiring great length.

18 Holes, 6312yds, Par 71, SSS 71, Course record 68. Club membership 800.

Visitors contact club for details. **Societies** welcome. **Green Fees** £45
per day, £40 per round. **Course Designer** James Braid **Prof** Andrew
Greenbank **Facilities** ⓦ ⓞⓁ ⓛ ⓓ ⓣⓛ ⓧ ⓐ 🔗 🏌
Conf facs Corporate Hospitality Days **Location** 1m N of city centre on

A6, right at lights onto Watling St, left onto Fulwood Hall Ln, course
300yds on left
Hotel ★★★★ 75% HL Preston Marriott Hotel, Garstang Road,
Broughton, PRESTON ☎ 01772 864087 📄 01772 861728 149 en suite

RISHTON   Map 7 SD73

Rishton Golf Club Eachill Links BB1 4HG
☎ 01254 884442 📄 01254 887701
web: www.rishtongolfclub.co.uk

Eachill Links: 10 Holes, 6097yds, Par 70, SSS 69, Course record 68.

Course Designer Peter Alliss/Dave Thomas **Location** M65 junct 6/7,
1m. Signed from Station Rd in Rishton
Telephone for further details
Hotel ★★★★ 74% HL Mercure Dunkenhalgh Hotel & Spa,
Blackburn Road, Clayton-le-Moors, ACCRINGTON ☎ 01254 398021
📄 01254 872230 175 en suite

SILVERDALE   Map 7 SD47

Silverdale Golf Club Redbridge Ln LA5 0SP
☎ 01524 701300 📄 01524 702074
e-mail: info@silverdalegolfclub.co.uk
web: www.silverdalegolfclub.co.uk
Interesting heathland course with rock outcrops, set in an Area of
Outstanding Natural Beauty with spectacular views of the Lake
District hills and Morecambe Bay. It is a course of two halves, being
either open fairways or tight hilly limestone valleys. The 13th hole has
been described as one of Britain's 100 extraordinary golf holes.

18 Holes, 5592yds, Par 70, SSS 67, Course record 66. Club membership 400.

Visitors Mon-Sun & BHs. Booking required. Dress code.
Societies booking required. **Green Fees** £28.50 per round (£36
weekends). Special offer: £14 Mon, £14 students **Prof** Alyn Cousins
Facilities ⓦ ⓞⓁ ⓛ ⓓ ⓣⓛ ⓧ ⓐ ⓟ 🔗 🍴 **Conf** facs
Corporate Hospitality Days **Location** opp Silverdale station & Leighton
Moss RSPB nature reserve
Hotel ★★★ 68% HL Cumbria Grand, GRANGE-OVER-SANDS
☎ 015395 32331 📄 015395 34534 122 en suite

UPHOLLAND   Map 7 SD50

Beacon Park Golf & Country Club Beacon Ln WN8 7RU
☎ 01695 622700 📄 01695 628362
web: www.beaconparkgolf.com

18 Holes, 6151yds, Par 72, SSS 70, Course record 68.

continued

Course Designer Donald Steel **Location** M6 junct 26, follow signs for Upholland & Orrell, then brown Beacon Country Park signs
Telephone for further details
Hotel ★★★★ 75% HL Wrightington Hotel & Country Club, Moss Lane, Wrightington, WIGAN ☎ 01257 425803 📄 01257 425830
73 en suite

See advert on this page

Dean Wood Golf Club Lafford Ln WN8 0QZ
☎ 01695 622219 📄 01695 622245
web: www.deanwoodgolfclub.co.uk
18 Holes, 6148yds, Par 71, SSS 70, Course record 65.
Course Designer James Braid **Location** M6 junct 26, 1m on A577
Telephone for further details
Hotel ★★★★ 75% HL Wrightington Hotel & Country Club, Moss Lane, Wrightington, WIGAN ☎ 01257 425803 📄 01257 425830
73 en suite

WHALLEY   Map 7 SD73

Whalley Golf Club Long Leese Barn, Clerk Hill Rd BB7 9DR
☎ 01254 822236
e-mail: secretary@whalleygolfclub.com
web: www.whalleygolfclub.com
A parkland course near Pendle Hill, overlooking the Ribble Valley. Superb views. Ninth hole over pond.
9 Holes, 6258yds, Par 72, SSS 71, Course record 66.
Club membership 450.

Visitors Mon-Wed, Fri-Sun & BHs. Booking required weekends. Handicap certificate. Dress code. **Societies** booking required. **Green Fees** not confirmed 🅿 **Prof** Jamie Hunt **Facilities** ⑪ ⑩ ⛳ ⛨ ⛴ ⛾ 🏠 ⛿ ⛵ **Conf** Corporate Hospitality Days **Location** 1m SE off A671
Hotel ★★★★ SHL Northcote, Northcote Road, LANGHO ☎ 01254 240555 📄 01254 246568 14 en suite

WHITWORTH   Map 7 SD81

Lobden Golf Club Lobden Moor OL12 8XJ
☎ 01706 343228 & 345598 📄 01706 343228
Moorland course, with hard walking. Windy with superb views of surrounding hills. Excellent greens.
9 Holes, 5697yds, Par 70, SSS 68, Course record 63.
Club membership 250.

Visitors contact club for details. **Societies** welcome. **Green Fees** not confirmed **Facilities** ⛳ **Location** E of town centre off A671
Hotel ★★★★ 77% HL Mercure Norton Grange Hotel & Spa, Manchester Road, Castleton, ROCHDALE ☎ 0870 1942119 & 01706 630788 📄 01706 649313 81 en suite

Beacon Park Golf Club

When Donald Steel and Sir Michael Bonallack played the very first round of golf at *Beacon Park Golf Club* in the summer of 1982 a little piece of history was added to the annals of 'Historic Upholland'. The course was selected as one of the 'The Ten Best' in the UK by the *Independent* in 2006. Societies and Visitors Welcome.

Beacon Lane, Dalton, Lancashire WN8 7RU
Proshop: 01695 622700
Email: info@beaconparkgolf.com
Website: www.beaconparkgolf.com

WILPSHIRE   Map 7 SD63

Wilpshire Golf Club 72 Whalley Rd BB1 9LF
☎ 01254 248260 📄 01254 246745
e-mail: admin@wilpshiregolfclub.co.uk
web: www.wilpshiregolfclub.co.uk
Parkland/moorland course with varied and interesting holes. Magnificent views of Ribble Valley, the coast and the Yorkshire Dales. The course is not long by modern standards but it has two excellent par 5s and five par 3s, none of which are easy.
18 Holes, 5843yds, Par 69, SSS 69, Course record 62.
Club membership 650.

Visitors Mon-Sun & BHs. Booking required Fri-Sun & BHs. Dress code. **Societies** booking required. **Green Fees** Mon-Thu £20 (Fri-Sun & BHs £30). **Course Designer** James Braid **Prof** Walter Slaven **Facilities** ⑪ ⑩ ⛳ ⛨ ⛴ ⛵ 🏠 🛏 ⛿ **Conf** facs Corporate Hospitality Days **Location** M6, junct 31, A59 towards Blackburn, remain on this road at Swallow Hotel towards Clitheroe/Skipton. Right at next lights onto B6245 towards Blackburn, then right at next lights onto A666 towards Clitheroe, club 400yds on right
Hotel ★★★ 76% SHL Sparth House Hotel, Whalley Road, Clayton Le Moors, ACCRINGTON ☎ 01254 872263 📄 01254 872263
16 en suite

LEICESTERSHIRE

ASHBY-DE-LA-ZOUCH
Map 8 SK31

Willesley Park Golf Club Measham Rd LE65 2PF
☎ 01530 414596 📠 01530 564169
web: www.willesleypark.com
18 Holes, 6304yds, Par 70, SSS 70, Course record 63.
Course Designer Cotton/MacKenzie **Location** SW of town centre on B5006
Telephone for further details
Hotel ★★★ 64% HL The Royal Hotel, Station Road, ASHBY-DE-LA-ZOUCH ☎ 01530 412833 📠 01530 564548 34 en suite

BIRSTALL
Map 4 SK50

Birstall Golf Club Station Rd LE4 3BB
☎ 0116 267 4322
e-mail: sue@birstallgolfclub.co.uk
web: www.birstallgolfclub.co.uk
Parkland with trees, shrubs, ponds and ditches, next to the Great Central Railway Steam Train line.
18 Holes, 6239yds, Par 70, SSS 71. Club membership 650.
Visitors Mon, Wed & Fri. Tue pm. Thu am. Weekends & BHs by arrangement. Booking required. **Societies** booking required. **Green Fees** £35 per day, £30 per round (£40 per round weekends) 🏌
Prof David Clark **Facilities** 🏌 🕿 🖿 🖵 🍴 🎿 🛍 🚗
🏌 **Leisure** billiard room **Conf** facs Corporate Hospitality Days
Location 3m N of Leicester on A6
Hotel ★★★★ 73% SHL Hotel Maiyango, 13-21 St Nicholas Place, LEICESTER ☎ 0116 251 8898 📠 0116 242 1339 14 en suite

BOTCHESTON
Map 4 SK40

Forest Hill Golf Club Markfield Ln LE9 9FJ
☎ 01455 824800 📠 01455 828522
e-mail: admin@foresthillgolfclub.co.uk
web: www.foresthillgolfclub.co.uk
Parkland course with many trees, four par 5s, but no steep gradients. Water features on 7 holes.
18 Holes, 6599yds, Par 73, SSS 72, Course record 70. Club membership 700.
Visitors Mon-Sun & BHs. Booking required. Dress code.
Societies booking required. **Green Fees** not confirmed **Course Designer** Gaunt & Marnoch **Prof** Richard Hughes **Facilities** 🏌 🕿
🖿 🖵 🍴 🎿 🛍 🍺 ◇ 🍴 🚗 🏌 **Leisure** 9 hole par 3 academy course **Conf** facs Corporate Hospitality Days **Location** M1 junct 22, take A50 towards Leicester, turn right at 1st rdbt and follow road for 4m, club on left.

COSBY
Map 4 SP59

Cosby Golf Club Chapel Ln, Broughton Rd LE9 1RG
☎ 0116 286 4759 📠 0116 286 4484
e-mail: secretary@cosbygolfclub.co.uk
web: www.cosbygolfclub.co.uk
Undulating parkland course. Challenging holes include the par 4 1st with an unseen meandering brook, the deceptively long par 4 3rd,

the 12th from an elevated tee and the hogs-back par 3 14th, both affected by the prevailing wind. A genuine but enjoyable test of golf for all abilities.
18 Holes, 6474yds, Par 71, SSS 71, Course record 65. Club membership 850.
Visitors Mon-Fri & BHs. Booking required. Handicap certificate. Dress code. **Societies** booking required. **Green Fees** not confirmed **Course Designer** Hawtree **Prof** Gary Coysh **Facilities** 🏌 🕿 🖿 🖵
🍴 🎿 🛍 🍺 ◇ 🚗 ◇ 🏌 **Leisure** snooker table **Conf** facs Corporate Hospitality Days **Location** M1 junct 21, take B4114, turn left at BP service station, signed Cosby
Hotel ★★★★ 81% HL Sketchley Grange, Sketchley Lane, Burbage, HINCKLEY ☎ 01455 251133 📠 01455 631384 94 en suite

EAST GOSCOTE
Map 8 SK61

Beedles Lake Golf Centre 170 Broome Ln LE7 3WQ
☎ 0116 260 6759 📠 0116 269 4127
e-mail: joncoleman@jelson.co.uk
web: www.beedleslake.co.uk
Fairly flat parkland with easy walking situated in the heart of the Wreake Valley with the river meandering through a number of holes. Older trees and thousands of newly planted ones give the course a mature feel. The course is maintained to a high standard and proper tees and greens are used at all times.
18 Holes, 6641yds, Par 72, SSS 72, Course record 68. Club membership 498.
Visitors Mon-Sun & BHs. Booking required weekends & BHs. Dress code. **Societies** booking required. **Green Fees** £18 per 18 holes (£22 weekends) **Course Designer** D Tucker **Prof** Sean Byrne **Facilities** 🏌
🕿 🖿 🖵 🍴 🎿 🛍 🍺 ◇ 🚗 ◇ 🏌 **Leisure** fishing
Conf facs Corporate Hospitality Days **Location** off A607
Hotel ★★★★ 76% HL Quorn Country Hotel, Charnwood House, 66 Leicester Road, QUORN ☎ 01509 415050 & 415061 📠 01509 415557 36 en suite

ENDERBY
Map 4 SP59

Enderby Golf Course Mill Ln LE19 4LX
☎ 0116 284 9388 📠 0116 284 9388
web: www.enderbygolfshopandcourse.co.uk
An attractive gently undulating nine-hole course with various water features. The longest hole is the 1st at 471yds.
9 Holes, 2900yds, Par 72, SSS 71, Course record 71. Club membership 150.
Visitors contact for details. **Societies** welcome. **Green Fees** £9.95 per 18 holes, £8.25 per 9 holes **Course Designer** David Lowe **Prof** Chris D'Araujo **Facilities** 🏌 🕿 🖿 🖵 🍴 🎿 🛍 🍺 ◇ ◇
Leisure heated indoor swimming pool, squash, sauna, gymnasium, indoor bowls snooker badminton **Conf** Corporate Hospitality Days
Location M1 junct 21, 2m S on Narborough road, right at Toby Carvery rdbt, 0.5m on left, signed
Hotel ★★★★ 79% HL Leicester Marriott, Smith Way, Grove Park, Enderby, LEICESTER ☎ 0116 282 0100 📠 0116 282 0101 227 en suite

HINCKLEY   Map 4 SP49

Hinckley Golf Club Leicester Rd LE10 3DR
☎ 01455 615124 & 615014 📄 01455 890841
e-mail: proshop@hinckleygolfclub.com
web: www.hinckleygolfclub.com
Parkland course with a good variety of holes to test all abilities. Water comes into play on a number of holes.
18 Holes, 6467yds, Par 71, SSS 71, Course record 64. Club membership 750.
Visitors Mon-Fri & BHs. Booking required Tue & Thu. Dress code. **Societies** booking required. **Green Fees** not confirmed **Course Designer** Southern Golf Ltd **Prof** Richard Jones **Facilities** 🕙 🍴 🛢 🖥 🍴 ☂ 🖇 🚑 🖇 **Leisure** snooker **Conf** facs Corporate Hospitality Days **Location** 1.5m NE on B4668
Hotel ★★★ 73% HL Best Western Weston Hall, Weston Lane, Bulkington, NUNEATON ☎ 024 7631 2989 📄 024 7664 0846 40 en suite

KIBWORTH BEAUCHAMP   Map 4 SP69

Kibworth Golf Club Weir Rd LE8 0LP
☎ 0116 279 2301 📄 0116 279 6434
e-mail: secretary@kibworthgolfclub.freeserve.co.uk
web: www.kibworthgolfclub.co.uk
Attractive parkland course with two loops of nine holes and easy walking. The fairways are lined with mature trees and a meandering stream crosses eight holes.
18 Holes, 6364yds, Par 71, SSS 71. Club membership 700.
Visitors Booking required weekends & BHs. Dress code
Societies booking required. **Green Fees** £40 per day, £32 per round.
Prof Bryn Morris **Facilities** 🕙 🍴 🛢 🖥 🍴 ☂ 🖇 **Conf** Corporate Hospitality Days **Location** S of village off A6
Hotel ★★★ 77% HL Best Western Three Swans, 21 High Street, MARKET HARBOROUGH ☎ 01858 466644 📄 01858 433101 61 en suite

KIRBY MUXLOE   Map 4 SK50

Kirby Muxloe Golf Club Station Rd LE9 2EP
☎ 0116 239 3457 📄 0116 238 8891
e-mail: kirbymuxloegolf@btconnect.com
web: www.kirbymuxloe-golf.co.uk
Very pleasant parkland that has water features on the 11th and 17th holes. Also ditches on 8 of the holes. Excellent greens all year round.
18 Holes, 6428yds, Par 71, SSS 71, Course record 63. Club membership 870.
Visitors Tue, Sat & Sun am. **Societies** booking required. **Green Fees** £50 per day, £37 per round. Winter £25 per 18 holes & meal.
Prof Bruce Whipham **Facilities** 🕙 🍴 🛢 🖥 🍴 ☂ 🖇 🚑 🖇 **Leisure** two snooker rooms, extra Green for short game **Conf** Corporate Hospitality Days **Location** S of village off B5380
Hotel ★★★★ 79% HL Leicester Marriott, Smith Way, Grove Park, Enderby, LEICESTER ☎ 0116 282 0100 📄 0116 282 0101 227 en suite

LEICESTER   Map 4 SK50

Humberstone Heights Golf Club Gyspy Ln LE5 0TB
☎ 0116 276 3680 & 299 5570 (pro) 📄 0116 299 5569
web: www.humberstoneheightsgc.co.uk
Municipal parkland course with varied layout.
18 Holes, 6216yds, Par 70, SSS 70. Club membership 200.
Visitors Mon-Sun & BHs. Booking required weekends. Dress code.
Societies booking required. **Green Fees** £17.50 per 18 holes **Course Designer** Hawtry & Sons **Prof** Jon Alcock **Facilities** 🕙 🍴 🛢 🖥 🍴 ☂ 🖇 🚑 🖇 **Leisure** 9 hole pitch and putt course. **Conf** Corporate Hospitality Days **Location** 2.5m NE of city centre
Hotel ★★★ 81% HL Belmont Hotel, De Montfort Street, LEICESTER ☎ 0116 254 4773 📄 0116 247 0804 75 en suite

The Leicestershire Golf Club Evington Ln LE5 6DJ
☎ 0116 273 8825 📄 0116 249 8799
e-mail: secretary@theleicestershiregolfclub.co.uk
web: www.theleicestershiregolfclub.co.uk
Mature parkland course providing a challenging test of golf.
18 Holes, 6329yds, Par 68, SSS 71, Course record 62. Club membership 750.
Visitors Mon, Wed-Fri & Sun except BHs. Booking required. Handicap certificate. Dress code. **Societies** booking required. **Green Fees** £45 per day (weekdays only), £35 per 18 holes **Course Designer** Hawtree **Prof** Darren Jones **Facilities** 🕙 🍴 🛢 🖥 🍴 ☂ 🖇 🚑 🖇 **Location** 2m E of city off A6030
Hotel ★★★ 71% HL Regency, 360 London Road, LEICESTER ☎ 0116 270 9634 📄 0116 270 1375 32 en suite

Western Park Golf Club Scudamore Rd LE3 1UQ
☎ 0116 299 5566 📄 0116 299 5568
web: www.westernpkgc.co.uk
18 Holes, 6486yds, Par 72, SSS 71, Course record 66.
Course Designer Hawtree **Location** 1.5m W of city centre off A47 Telephone for further details
Hotel ★★★★ 79% HL Leicester Marriott, Smith Way, Grove Park, Enderby, LEICESTER ☎ 0116 282 0100 📄 0116 282 0101 227 en suite

LOUGHBOROUGH   Map 8 SK51

Longcliffe Golf Club Snell's Nook Ln, Nanpantan LE11 3YA
☎ 01509 239129 📄 01509 231286
e-mail: longcliffegolf@btconnect.com
web: www.longcliffegolf.co.uk
Course of natural heathland, tree-lined fairways with water in play on the 14th and 15th holes. This course is recognised by the English Golf Championship.
18 Holes, 6625yds, Par 72, SSS 73. Club membership 700.
Visitors Mon-Fri except BHs. Booking required. Dress code.
Societies booking required. **Green Fees** £50 per day, £40 per round **Course Designer** Williamson **Prof** David Mee **Facilities** 🕙 🍴 🛢 🖥 🍴 ☂ 🖇 🚑 🖇 **Conf** Corporate Hospitality Days **Location** 1.5m from M1 junct 23 off A512
Hotel ★★★★ 76% HL Quorn Country Hotel, Charnwood House, 66 Leicester Road, QUORN ☎ 01509 415050 & 415061 📄 01509 415557 36 en suite

LUTTERWORTH
Map 4 SP58

Kilworth Springs Golf Club South Kilworth Rd, North Kilworth LE17 6HJ
☎ 01858 575082 ▤ 01858 575078
e-mail: admin@kilworthsprings.co.uk
web: www.kilworthsprings.co.uk

Set in the scenic Avon Valley, a course for all abilities. A links style front nine and a parkland back nine with greens to USGA specification.

18 Holes, 6669yds, Par 72, SSS 72, Course record 65. Club membership 700.

Visitors contact club for details. **Societies** welcome. **Green Fees** £25 per 18 holes (£28 weekends) **Course Designer** Ray Baldwin **Prof** Michael Bent **Facilities** ⑪ ⑱ ⓘ ⓘ ⓘ ⓘ ⓘ ⓘ ⓘ **Leisure** half way house on course **Conf** facs Corporate Hospitality Days **Location** M1 junct 20, 5m E on A4304 towards Market Harborough between villages of North & South Kilworth
Hotel ★★★ 78% HL Best Western Ullesthorpe Court Hotel & Golf Club, Frolesworth Road, ULLESTHORPE ☎ 01455 209023 ▤ 01455 202537 72 en suite

Lutterworth Golf Club Rugby Rd LE17 4HN
☎ 01455 552532 ▤ 01455 553586
e-mail: sec@lutterworthgc.co.uk
web: www.lutterworthgc.co.uk

Hilly course with the River Swift running through.

18 Holes, 6243yds, Par 70, SSS 70. Club membership 650.

Visitors Mon-Fri except BHs. Weekends pm. Booking advised weekends. Dress code. **Societies** booking required. **Green Fees** Summer £30 per day/round. Winter £20 **Prof** Lee Challinor **Facilities** ⑪ ⑱ ⓘ ⓘ ⓘ ⓘ ⓘ ⓘ ⓘ **Location** M1 junct 20, 0.25m
Hotel ★★★ 78% HL Brownsover Hall Hotel, Brownsover Lane, Old Brownsover, RUGBY ☎ 0844 855 9123 ▤ 01788 535367 47 en suite

MARKET HARBOROUGH
Map 4 SP78

Market Harborough Golf Club Oxendon Rd LE16 8NF
☎ 01858 463684 ▤ 01858 432906
e-mail: proshop@mhgolf.co.uk
web: www.mhgolf.co.uk

A parkland course close to the town. Undulating and in parts hilly. There are wide-ranging views over the surrounding countryside. Lakes feature on four holes; challenging last three holes.

18 Holes, 6014yds, Par 70, SSS 69, Course record 61. Club membership 650.

Visitors Mon-Fri except BHs. Handicap certificate. Dress code. **Societies** booking required. **Green Fees** £30 per round. **Course Designer** H Swan **Prof** Frazer Baxter **Facilities** ⑪ ⑱ ⓘ ⓘ ⓘ ⓘ ⓘ **Conf** Corporate Hospitality Days **Location** 1m S on A508
Hotel ★★★ 77% HL Best Western Three Swans, 21 High Street, MARKET HARBOROUGH ☎ 01858 466644 ▤ 01858 433101 61 en suite

Stoke Albany Golf Course Ashley Rd, Stoke Albany LE16 8PL
☎ 01858 535208 ▤ 01858 535505
e-mail: info@stokealbanygolfclub.co.uk
web: www.stokealbanygolfclub.co.uk

A parkland course in the picturesque Welland Valley. Affording good views, the course should appeal to the mid-handicap golfer, and provide an interesting test to the more experienced player. There are several water features and the greens are individually contoured, adding to the golfing challenge.

18 Holes, 6175yds, Par 71, SSS 70. Club membership 500.

Visitors Mon-Sun & BHs. Booking required weekends & BHs. Dress code. **Societies** booking required. **Green Fees** £21 per 18 holes (£23 weekends & BHs) **Course Designer** Hawtree **Prof** Adrian Clifford **Facilities** ⓘ ⓘ ⓘ ⓘ ⓘ ⓘ ⓘ **Conf** facs Corporate Hospitality Days **Location** N off A427 Market Harborough-Corby road, follow Stoke Albany 500yds towards Ashley
Hotel ★★★ 77% HL Best Western Three Swans, 21 High Street, MARKET HARBOROUGH ☎ 01858 466644 ▤ 01858 433101 61 en suite

MELTON MOWBRAY
Map 8 SK71

Melton Mowbray Golf Club Waltham Rd, Thorpe Arnold LE14 4SD
☎ 01664 562118 ▤ 01664 562118
e-mail: meltonmowbraygc@btconnect.com
web: www.mmgc.org

Easy walking heathland course with undulating fairways. Deceptively challenging.

18 Holes, 6279yds, Par 70, SSS 70, Course record 61. Club membership 650.

Visitors Mon-Fri & BHs. Sat after 2pm, Sun after11am. Booking required. Handicap certificate. Dress code. **Societies** booking required. **Green Fees** £40 per day, £29 per round (£34 per round weekends & BHs) **Prof** Neil Curtis **Facilities** ⑪ ⑱ ⓘ ⓘ ⓘ ⓘ ⓘ ⓘ **Conf** facs Corporate Hospitality Days **Location** 2m NE of Melton Mowbray on A607
Hotel ★★★ 78% HL Sysonby Knoll, Asfordby Road, MELTON MOWBRAY ☎ 01664 563563 ▤ 01664 410364 30 en suite

Stapleford Park Golf Club Stapleford LE14 2EF
☎ 01572 787000 & 787044 ▤ 01572 787001
e-mail: clubs@stapleford.co.uk
web: www.staplefordpark.com

Set in 500 acres of parkland, lake and woods. Reminiscent of some Scottish links, the course wraps around the heart of the estate in two extended loops. Never more than two holes wide, the whole course is spacious and tranquil. The beauty of the surrounding countryside is the perfect backdrop.

Stapleford Park: 18 Holes, 6944yds, Par 73, SSS 73, Course record 64. Club membership 310.

Visitors Mon-Sun & BHs. Booking required. Handicap certificate. Dress code. **Societies** booking required. **Green Fees** £75 per day, £50 per 18 holes, £25 per 9 holes **Course Designer** Donald Steel **Prof** Richard Alderson **Facilities** ⑪ ⑱ ⓘ ⓘ ⓘ ⓘ ⓘ ⓘ ⓘ

continued

↣ **Leisure** hard tennis courts, heated indoor swimming pool, fishing, sauna, gymnasium, shooting, falconry, offroading, horseriding, archery **Conf** facs Corporate Hospitality Days **Location** 4m E of Melton Mowbray off B676, follow brown signs
Hotel ★★★★ CHH Stapleford Park, Stapleford, MELTON MOWBRAY ☎ 01572 787000 📄 01572 787651 55 en suite

OADBY   Map 4 SK60

Glen Gorse Golf Club Glen Rd LE2 4RF
☎ 0116 271 4159 📄 0116 271 4159
e-mail: secretary@gggc.org
web: www.gggc.org
Attractive mature parkland course with strategically placed trees encountered on every hole, rewarding the straight hitter. The long approaches and narrow greens require the very best short game. However, a premium is placed on accuracy and length, and no more so than over the closing three holes, considered to be one of the finest finishes in the county.
18 Holes, 6648yds, SSS 72. Club membership 715.
Visitors Mon-Fri except BHs. Booking required. Dress code.
Societies booking required. **Green Fees** phone 🅿 **Prof** Dominic Fitzpatrick **Facilities** 🕐 🍽 🍺 ⬚ ☕🏌 🏊 🛋 🚗 🚌
🏌 **Leisure** snooker room **Conf** facs Corporate Hospitality Days **Location** on A6 between Oadby and Great Glen, 5m S of Leicester
Hotel ★★★ 71% HL Regency, 360 London Road, LEICESTER ☎ 0116 270 9634 📄 0116 270 1375 32 en suite

Oadby Golf Club Leicester Rd LE2 4AJ
☎ 0116 270 9052
web: www.oadbygolfclub.co.uk
18 Holes, 6376yds, Par 72, SSS 71, Course record 69.
Location W of Oadby off A6
Telephone for further details
Hotel ★★★ 71% HL Regency, 360 London Road, LEICESTER ☎ 0116 270 9634 📄 0116 270 1375 32 en suite

ROTHLEY   Map 8 SK51

Rothley Park Golf Club Westfield Ln LE7 7LH
☎ 0116 230 2809 📄 0116 237 4847
e-mail: clubmanager@rothleypark.co.uk
web: www.rothleypark.co.uk
A picturesque parkland course. Challenging but easy walking.
18 Holes, 6501yds, Par 71, SSS 71, Course record 65. Club membership 600.
Visitors Mon, Wed-Sun & BHs. Booking required. Dress code.
Societies welcome. **Green Fees** phone 🅿 **Course Designer** Hawtree & Son Ltd **Prof** K Tebbet **Facilities** 🕐 🍽 🍺 ⬚ ☕🏌 🏊 🛋
🚗 🚌 🏌 **Conf** Corporate Hospitality Days **Location** N of Leicester, W off A6
Hotel ★★★★ 76% HL Quorn Country Hotel, Charnwood House, 66 Leicester Road, QUORN ☎ 01509 415050 & 415061 📄 01509 415557 36 en suite

SCRAPTOFT   Map 4 SK60

Scraptoft Golf Club Beeby Rd LE7 9SJ
☎ 0116 241 9000 📄 0116 241 9000
web: www.scraptoft-golf.co.uk
18 Holes, 6166yds, Par 70, SSS 70.
Location 1m NE
Telephone for further details
Hotel ★★★ 81% HL Belmont Hotel, De Montfort Street, LEICESTER ☎ 0116 254 4773 📄 0116 247 0804 75 en suite

SEAGRAVE   Map 8 SK61

Park Hill Golf Club Park Hill LE12 7NG
☎ 01509 815454 📄 01509 816062
e-mail: mail@parkhillgolf.co.uk
web: www.parkhillgolf.co.uk
Nestled in the heart of Leicestershire, overlooking the Charnwood Forest and beyond, Park Hill Golf Club has an 18-hole championship length course that uses the land's natural features to ensure that no two holes are the same. The combination of water features and precisely positioned bunkers provide for a challenging, yet enjoyable course, with excellent playing conditions all year round. The newly added par 3 Academy Course provides a perfect way to practice the short game.
18 Holes, 7219yds, Par 73, SSS 75, Course record 68. Club membership 500.
Visitors Mon-Sun & BHs. **Societies** welcome. **Green Fees** £27 (£33 weekends & BHs) **Prof** Matthew Ulyett **Facilities** 🕐 🍽 🍺 ⬚ ☕🏌
🏊 🛋 ⛳ 🚗 🚌 🏌 🏌 **Leisure** fishing, par 3 academy course
Conf facs Corporate Hospitality Days **Location** 3m N of Leicester off A46, signs to Seagrave
Hotel ★★★★ 76% HL Quorn Country Hotel, Charnwood House, 66 Leicester Road, QUORN ☎ 01509 415050 & 415061 📄 01509 415557 36 en suite

SIX HILLS   Map 8 SK62

Six Hills Golf Club Six Hills Rd LE14 3PR
☎ 01509 881225 📄 01509 881846
Flat parkland.
18 Holes, 5824yds, Par 71, SSS 68.
Visitors Mon-Sun & BHs. Booking required weekends & BHs.
Societies booking required. **Green Fees** not confirmed **Prof** James Hawley **Facilities** 🕐 🍽 🍺 ⬚ ☕🏌 🏊 🚗 🚌 🏌 🏌 **Location** on B676 between Melton Mowbray & Loughborough
Hotel ★★★ 73% HL Best Western Leicester North, A46 Fosse Way, Station Road, Upper Broughton, GRIMSTON ☎ 01664 823212 📄 01664 823371 75 en suite

ULLESTHORPE
Map 4 SP58

Best Western Ullesthorpe Court Hotel & Golf Club
Frolesworth Rd LE17 5BZ
☎ 01455 209150 📠 01455 202537
e-mail: golf@ullesthorpecourt.co.uk
web: www.bw-ullesthorpecourt.co.uk

Set in 120 acres of parkland surrounding a 17th-century manor house, this championship length course can be very demanding and offers a challenge to both beginners and professionals. Excellent leisure facilities. Water plays a part on four holes.

18 Holes, 6662yds, Par 72, SSS 72, Course record 67.
Club membership 520.

Visitors Mon-Fri except BHs. Booking required. Dress code. Societies booking required. Green Fees £35 per day, £25 per round Prof Jon Salter Facilities ⊕ ⑩ ⓘ ⓛ ⓓ ⓔ ⓛ ⓐ ⓕ ⑨ ⓕ Leisure hard tennis courts, heated indoor swimming pool, sauna, gymnasium, snooker room, beauty treatment rooms Conf facs Corporate Hospitality Days Location M1 junct 20, towards Lutterworth, follow brown signs to B577 (Bitteswell and Ullesthorpe), follow road 3m to Ullesthorpe. Through village, just before exiting, turn right signed Frolesworth and Golf Course
Hotel ★★★★ 78% HL Best Western Ullesthorpe Court Hotel & Golf Club, Frolesworth Road, ULLESTHORPE ☎ 01455 209023 📄 01455 202537 72 en suite

WHETSTONE
Map 4 SP59

Whetstone Golf Club Cambridge Rd, Cosby LE9 1SJ
☎ 0116 286 1424 📄 0116 286 1424
e-mail: sam@whetstonegolfclub.co.uk
web: www.whetstonegolfclub.co.uk

Easy to walk, parkland course where accuracy rather than length is required.

18 Holes, 6182yds, Par 71. Club membership 500.

Visitors contact club for details. Societies welcome. Green Fees £16 Course Designer E Calloway Prof David Raitt Facilities ⊕ ⑩ ⓘ ⓓ ⓔ ⓛ ⓐ ⓕ ⓐ ⓕ Location 1m S of village
Hotel ★★★★ 79% HL Leicester Marriott, Smith Way, Grove Park, Enderby, LEICESTER ☎ 0116 282 0100 📄 0116 282 0101 227 en suite

WOODHOUSE EAVES
Map 8 SK51

Charnwood Forest Golf Club Breakback Rd LE12 8TA
☎ 01509 890259
e-mail: secretary@charnwoodforestgolfclub.com
web: www.charnwoodforestgolfclub.com

Oldest course in the county, founded in 1890. Hilly heathland course with hard walking, but no bunkers. Play is round volcanic rock giving panoramic views over the Charnwood Forest area.

9 Holes, 5972yds, Par 69, SSS 69. Club membership 360.

Visitors Mon-Sun & BHs. Booking recommended. Handicap certificate. Dress code. Societies booking required. Green Fees £30 per 18 holes (£40 weekends & BHs) Course Designer James Braid Facilities ⊕ ⑩ ⓘ ⓓ ⓔ ⓛ ⓐ Location M1 junct 23, take A512 towards Loughborough. After 0.5m turn right into Snells Nook Lane. Club 3m on left.
Hotel ★★★★ 76% HL Quorn Country Hotel, Charnwood House, 66 Leicester Road, QUORN ☎ 01509 415050 & 415061 📄 01509 415557 36 en suite

Lingdale Golf Club Joe Moore's Ln LE12 8TF
☎ 01509 890703
e-mail: secretary@lingdalegolfclub.co.uk
web: www.lingdalegolfclub.co.uk

Parkland in Charnwood Forest with some hard walking at some holes. The par 3 3rd and par 5 8th are testing holes. Several holes have water hazards and the blend of strategic holes requires good club selection.

18 Holes, 6545yds, Par 71, SSS 71, Course record 68.
Club membership 800.

Visitors Mon-Fri except BHs. Dress code. Societies booking required. Green Fees phone 🚗 Course Designer David Tucker Prof Peter Sellears Facilities ⊕ ⑩ ⓘ ⓓ ⓔ ⓛ ⓐ ⓕ Location 1.5m S off B5330
Hotel ★★★★ 76% HL Quorn Country Hotel, Charnwood House, 66 Leicester Road, QUORN ☎ 01509 415050 & 415061 📄 01509 41555 36 en suite

LINCOLNSHIRE

BELTON
Map 8 SK93

De Vere Belton Woods Hotel NG32 2LN
☎ 01476 593200 📄 01476 574547
e-mail: belton.woods@devere-hotels.com
web: www.devere.co.uk

Two challenging 18-hole Championship courses, a nine-hole par 3 and a driving range. The Lakes Course (host of the Midlands PGA Championships) features water on 8 holes and the 9th is one of the longest holes in Europe at 609yds. The Woodside is an inland Links-style course with changes in elevation and many pot bunkers. Resort hotel and extensive leisure facilities.

The Lakes Course: 18 Holes, 6831yds, Par 72, SSS 73, Course record 65.
The Woodside Course: 18 Holes, 6623yds, Par 73, SSS 72, Course record 67. Club membership 600.

Visitors Mon-Sun & BHs. Dress code. Societies booking required. Green Fees Lakes £45 per round (£55 weekends). Woodside £45/£55. Winter (both courses) £20/£25. Academy £6 Prof Ian Fulton Facilities ⊕ ⑩ ⓘ ⓓ ⓔ ⓛ ⓐ ⓕ ⓐ ⓔ ⓕ ⓐ ⓕ Leisure hard tennis courts, heated indoor swimming pool, squash, fishing, sauna, gymnasium, 9 hole par 3 Red Arrows course Conf facs Corporate Hospitality Days Location on A607 2m N of Grantham
Hotel ★★★★ 71% HL De Vere Belton Woods, BELTON ☎ 01476 593200 📄 01476 574547 136 en suite

BLANKNEY
Map 8 TF06

Blankney Golf Club LN4 3AZ
☎ 01526 320202 📄 01526 322521
e-mail: manager@blankneygolfclub.co.uk
web: www.blankneygolfclub.co.uk

Established in 1904, a parkland course in pleasant surroundings, set in the Blankney estate with mature trees and testing greens offering a challenging test of golf.

18 Holes, 6636yds, Par 72, SSS 73, Course record 66.
Club membership 700.

Visitors Mon-Sun & BHs. Booking required. Dress code. Societies booking required. Green Fees £30 weekdays (£36 weekends & BHs) Course Designer C Sinclair Prof Graham Bradley Facilities ⊕

continue►

◔) ┗ ◻ ▯ ⊼ 🏠 ╤ ✆ 🛥 ⚶ **Leisure** snooker
onf facs Corporate Hospitality Days **Location** 10m SW on B1188
otel ★★★ 75% CHH Branston Hall, Branston Park, Branston,
NCOLN ☎ 01522 793305 📄 01522 790734 50 en suite

OSTON   Map 8 TF34

oston Golf Club Cowbridge, Horncastle Rd PE22 7EL
☎ 01205 350589 📄 01205 367526
-mail: steveshaw@bostongc.co.uk
eb: www.bostongc.co.uk
arkland with water coming into play on a number of holes. Renowned
r the quality of the greens.
8 Holes, 6415yds, Par 72, SSS 71, Course record 65.
lub membership 575.
sitors Mon-Sun & BHs. Booking required weekends & BHs.
ocieties booking required. **Green Fees** £33 per day, £25 per round
efore 2.30pm, £16 after 2.30pm (£31 per round weekends & BHs) ⊗
rof Nick Hiom **Facilities** ⊕ |◎| ┗ ◻ ▯ ⊼ 🏠 ╤ ⚶ ✆
onf Corporate Hospitality Days **Location** 2m N of Boston on B1183
otel ★★★ 73% HL Boston West Hotel, Hubberts Bridge, BOSTON
☎ 01205 292969 & 290670 📄 01205 290725 24 en suite

oston West Golf Centre Hubbert's Bridge PE20 3QX
☎ 01205 290670 📄 01205 290725
-mail: info@bostonwestgolfclub.co.uk
eb: www.bostonwestgolfclub.co.uk
well maintained maturing golf course, nestled in the Lincolnshire
ountryside featuring excellent greens, well positioned lakes and
unkers. Good test of golf for all levels of golfer.
8 Holes, 6411yds, Par 72, SSS 71, Course record 64.
lub membership 500.
sitors Mon-Sun & BHs. Booking required. Dress code.
ocieties booking required. **Green Fees** £20 per 18 holes **Course**
esigner Michael Zara **Prof** Sophie Hunter **Facilities** ⊕ |◎| ┗ ◻
▯ ⊼ 🏠 ◇ ⚶ 🛥 ⚶ **Leisure** 6 hole academy course
onf facs Corporate Hospitality Days **Location** 2m W of Boston on
121/B1192 x-rds
otel ★★★ 66% HL Golf Hotel, The Broadway, WOODHALL SPA
☎ 01526 353535 📄 01526 353096 50 en suite

irton Holme Golf Course Holme Rd, Kirton Holme
E20 1SY
☎ 01205 290669
eb: www.kirtonholmegolfclub.com
parkland course designed for mid to high handicappers. It is flat but
as 2500 young trees, two natural water courses plus water hazards.
he 2nd is a challenging, 386yd, par 4 dog-leg. The course offers an
teresting challenge to all levels of golfer.
irton Holme: 9 Holes, 5778yds, Par 70, SSS 67,
ourse record 64. Club membership 320.
sitors Mon-Sun & BHs. Booking required. Dress code.
ocieties booking required. **Green Fees** £12.50 per 18 holes, £8.50
er 9 holes (£13.50/£9.50 weekends & BHs) **Course Designer** D W
elberry **Prof** Alison Johns **Facilities** ⊕ ┗ ◻ ▯ ⊼ ⊓ ⚶
onf Corporate Hospitality Days **Location** 4m W of Boston off A52
otel ★★★ 73% HL Boston West Hotel, Hubberts Bridge, BOSTON
☎ 01205 292969 & 290670 📄 01205 290725 24 en suite

CLEETHORPES   Map 8 TA30

Cleethorpes Golf Club Kings Rd DN35 0PN
☎ 01472 816110
e-mail: secretary@cleethorpesgolfclub.co.uk
web: www.cleethorpesgolfclub.co.uk
A mature coastal course founded in 1894. Slight undulations give
variety but the flat landscape makes for easy walking. Fine putting
surfaces. The course provides a challenge to all levels of player,
especially when the wind blows.
18 Holes, 6272yds, Par 70, SSS 71, Course record 65.
Club membership 650.
Visitors Mon,Tue, Thu, Fri, Sun & BHs. Dress code. **Societies** booking
required. **Green Fees** £35 per day, £25 per round (£40/£30 Sun &
BHs) **Course Designer** Harry Vardon **Prof** Paul Davies **Facilities** ⊕
|◎| ┗ ◻ ▯ ⊼ 🏠 ╤ ⚶ **Location** 2m SE of Cleethorpes
near theme park
Hotel ★★★ 77% HL Kingsway, Kingsway, CLEETHORPES
☎ 01472 601122 📄 0871 236 0671 49 en suite

Tetney Golf Club Station Rd, Tetney DN36 5HY
☎ 01472 211644 📄 01472 211644
An 18-hole parkland course at the foot of the Lincolnshire Wolds,
noted for its challenging water features.
18 Holes, 6151yds, Par 71, SSS 69, Course record 65.
Club membership 300.
Visitors Mon-Sun & BHs. Booking required weekends. Dress code.
Societies booking required. **Green Fees** £12 per 18 holes (£15
weekends & BHs) ⊗ **Course Designer** J S Grant **Prof** Jason Abrams
Facilities ⊕ |◎| ┗ ◻ ▯ ⊼ 🏠 ╤ ⚶ ⚶ 🏌
Conf facs **Location** 1m off A16 Louth-Grimsby road
Hotel ★★★ 77% HL Kingsway, Kingsway, CLEETHORPES
☎ 01472 601122 📄 0871 236 0671 49 en suite

CROWLE   Map 8 SE71

The Lincolnshire Golf Club DN17 4BU
☎ 01724 711619 📄 01724 711619
18 Holes, 6283yds, Par 71, SSS 70.
Course Designer Stubley/Byrne **Location** M180 junct 2, 0.5m on
Crowle road
Telephone for further details
Hotel ★★★★ 79% HL Forest Pines Hotel & Golf Resort, Ermine
Street, Broughton, SCUNTHORPE ☎ 01652 650770 📄 01652 650495
188 en suite

ELSHAM
Map 8 TA01

Elsham Golf Club Barton Rd DN20 0LS
☎ 01652 680291 (Secretary) 🖹 0872 111 3238
e-mail: office@elshamgolfclub.co.uk
web: www.elshamgolfclub.co.uk

Gently undulating quality, part parkland and part heathland course in a rural setting with a variety of wildlife, including many pheasants. Each hole is different and has its own challenge. Very secluded with easy walking, three ponds plus a reservoir to maintain irrigation.

18 Holes, 6426yds, Par 71, SSS 72, Course record 65.
Club membership 650.

Visitors Mon-Fri except BHs. Booking required. Handicap certificate. Dress code. **Societies** booking required. **Green Fees** £42 per 36 holes, £32 per 18 holes **Course Designer** Various **Prof** Stuart Brewer **Facilities** ⓘ 🍴 🏌 ▭ 🎿 🏐 🍽 🏖 🚰 ⚙ **Conf** facs Corporate Hospitality Days **Location** M180 junct 5, through Elsham village, left onto B1206 for 1m & course on left
Hotel ★★★★ 79% HL Forest Pines Hotel & Golf Resort, Ermine Street, Broughton, SCUNTHORPE ☎ 01652 650770 🖹 01652 650495 188 en suite

GAINSBOROUGH
Map 8 SK88

Gainsborough Golf Club Thonock DN21 1PZ
☎ 01427 613088 🖹 01427 810172
e-mail: kate@gainsboroughgc.co.uk
web: www.gainsboroughgc..co.uk

Thonock Park course, founded in 1894 is an attractive parkland course with many deciduous trees. Karsten Lakes course is a championship course designed by Neil Coles. Set in rolling countryside the lakes and well bunkered greens provide a true test of golf. Floodlit driving range.

Thonock Park: 18 Holes, 6266yds, Par 70, SSS 70,
Course record 63.
Karsten Lakes: 18 Holes, 6721yds, Par 72, SSS 72,
Course record 65. Club membership 700.

Visitors Mon-Sun & BHs. Booking required. **Societies** booking required. **Green Fees** not confirmed **Course Designer** Neil Coles **Prof** Stephen Cooper **Facilities** ⓘ 🍴 🏌 ▭ 🎿 🏐 🍽 ◇ ⚙ 🚰 ⚙ 🏁 **Conf** facs Corporate Hospitality Days **Location** 1m N off A159. Signed off A631
Hotel ★★ 68% HL Hickman Hill Hotel, Cox's Hill, GAINSBOROUGH ☎ 01427 613639 🖹 01427 677591 10 en suite

GEDNEY HILL
Map 8 TF31

Gedney Hill Golf Course West Drove PE12 0NT
☎ 01406 330922 🖹 01406 330323
web: www.gedneyhillgolfclub.co.uk

18 Holes, 5493yds, Par 70, SSS 66, Course record 65.
Course Designer Monkwise Ltd **Location** 10m SE of Spalding
Telephone for further details
Hotel ★★★ 70% HL Elme Hall, Elm High Road, WISBECH ☎ 01945 475566 🖹 01945 475666 8 en suite

GRANTHAM
Map 8 SK93

Belton Park Golf Club Belton Ln, Londonthorpe Rd NG31 9SH
☎ 01476 542900 🖹 01476 592078
e-mail: greatgolf@beltonpark.co.uk
web: www.beltonpark.co.uk

Three nine-hole courses set in classic mature parkland of Lord Brownlow's country seat, Belton House. Gently undulating with streams, ponds, plenty of trees and beautiful scenery, including a deer park. Famous holes: 5th, 12th, 16th and 18th. Combine any of the three courses for a testing 18-hole round.

Brownlow: 18 Holes, 6427yds, Par 71, SSS 71.
Ancaster: 18 Holes, 6227yds, Par 70, SSS 70.
Belmont: 18 Holes, 6016yds, Par 70, SSS 70.
Club membership 850.

Visitors Mon, Wed-Fri, Sun & BHs. Booking required. Dress code. **Societies** booking required. **Green Fees** £40 per day, £35 per round (£50/£40 Sun & BHs) 🎿 **Course Designer** Williamson/Alliss **Prof** Simon Williams **Facilities** ⓘ 🍴 🏌 ▭ 🎿 🏐 🍽 🚰 ⚙ **Conf** facs Corporate Hospitality Days **Location** 1.5m NE of Grantham
Hotel ★★★★ 71% HL De Vere Belton Woods, BELTON ☎ 01476 593200 🖹 01476 574547 136 en suite

Sudbrook Moor Golf Club Charity St, Carlton Scroop NG32 3AT
☎ 01400 250796
web: www.sudbrookmoor.co.uk

A testing nine-hole parkland and meadowland course in a picturesque valley setting with easy walking.

9 Holes, 4966yds, Par 66, SSS 64. Club membership 600.

Visitors Mon-Sun & BHs. Phone for availability. Dress code. **Green Fees** £10 per day (£12 weekends and BHs) **Course Designer** Tim Hutton **Prof** Tim Hutton **Facilities** ⓘ 🏌 ▭ 🎿 🏐 🍽 🏖 ⚙ 🏁 **Location** 6m NE of Grantham on A607 in village of Carlton Scroop
Hotel ★★★★★ INN The Brownlow Arms, High Road, HOUGH-ON-THE-HILL ☎ 01400 250234 🖹 01400 271193 5 rooms

GRIMSBY   Map 8 TA21

Grimsby Golf Club Littlecoates Rd DN34 4LU
☎ 01472 342630 📄 01472 342630
e-mail: secretary@grimsbygc.fsnet.co.uk
web: www.grimsbygolfclub.com

Mature undulating parkland course, not particularly long, but demanding and a good test of golf. Unusually, the par 3s are all feature holes. The summer greens are fast and quite small.

18 Holes, 6801yds, Par 71, SSS 71, Course record 66. Club membership 730.

Visitors Mon & Fri except BHs. Booking required. **Societies** booking required. **Green Fees** £30 per round **Course Designer** Harry Colt **Prof** Richard Smith **Facilities** ⓣ 🍴 🍺 ▯ 🍽 △ 🖼 ✔ 🛜 ✔ **Conf** facs Corporate Hospitality Days **Location** 1m from A180. 1m from A46

Hotel ★★★ 73% HL Stallingborough Grange Hotel, Riby Road, STALLINGBOROUGH ☎ 01469 561302 📄 01469 561338 42 en suite

Waltham Windmill Golf Club Cheapside, Waltham DN37 0HT
☎ 01472 824109 📄 01472 828391
e-mail: secretary@walthamwindmillgolfclub.co.uk
web: www.walthamwindmillgolfclub.co.uk

Nestling in 125 acres of Lincolnshire countryside, the natural springs have been used to great effect giving individuality and challenge to every shot. The course has a mixture of long par 5s and water comes into play on nine holes.

18 Holes, 6433yds, Par 71, SSS 71, Course record 64. Club membership 680.

Visitors dress code. **Societies** booking required. **Green Fees** £27 per round (£33 weekends). Reduced winter rates **Course Designer** J Payne **Prof** M Stephenson **Facilities** ⓣ 🍴 🍺 ▯ 🍽 △ 🖼 ✔ 🛜 **Conf** facs Corporate Hospitality Days **Location** 1m off A16

Hotel ★★★ 77% HL Kingsway, Kingsway, CLEETHORPES
☎ 01472 601122 📄 0871 236 0671 49 en suite

HORNCASTLE   Map 8 TF26

Horncastle Golf Club West Ashby LN9 5PP
☎ 01507 526800
web: www.horncastlegolfclub.com

18 Holes, 5717yds, Par 70, SSS 68, Course record 71.
Course Designer E C Wright **Location** off A153/A158 at West Ashby
Telephone for further details
Hotel ★★★ 71% HL Best Western Admiral Rodney Hotel, North Street, HORNCASTLE ☎ 01507 523131 📄 01507 523104 31 en suite

IMMINGHAM   Map 8 TA11

Immingham Golf Club St Andrews Ln DN40 2EU
☎ 01469 575298 📄 01469 577636
web: www.immgc.com

18 Holes, 6215yds, Par 71, SSS 70, Course record 69.

Course Designer Hawtree & Son **Location** 7m NW of Grimsby
Telephone for further details
Hotel ★★★ 73% HL Stallingborough Grange Hotel, Riby Road, STALLINGBOROUGH ☎ 01469 561302 📄 01469 561338 42 en suite

LACEBY   Map 8 TA20

Manor Golf Club Barton St, Laceby Manor DN37 7LD
☎ 01472 873468
e-mail: mackayj@grimsby.ac.uk
web: www.lmgc.co.uk

The first seven holes played as a parkland course lined with mature trees. The second nine are more open fairways with water courses running alongside and through the holes. The 16th hole green is surrounded by water. Holes 17 and 18 are tree-lined like the first seven holes.

18 Holes, 6343yds, Par 72, SSS 71. Club membership 500.

Visitors Mon-Sun & BHs. **Societies** booking required. **Green Fees** £22 per round (£25 weekends and BHs) **Course Designer** Charles Nicholson **Prof** Dayne Hawkins **Facilities** ⓣ 🍴 🍺 ▯ 🍽 △ 🖼 🛜 ✔ **Leisure** fishing **Conf** facs Corporate Hospitality Days **Location** A18 Laceby-Louth

Hotel ★★★ 73% HL Stallingborough Grange Hotel, Riby Road, STALLINGBOROUGH ☎ 01469 561302 📄 01469 561338 42 en suite

LINCOLN   Map 8 SK97

See also **Torksey**

Canwick Park Golf Club Canwick Park, Washingborough Rd LN4 1EF
☎ 01522 542912
e-mail: manager@canwickpark.org
web: www.canwickpark.org

Attractive parkland course with fine views of Lincoln Cathedral. The 5th and 13th holes are particularly testing par 3s.

18 Holes, 6148yds, Par 70, SSS 70. Club membership 412.

Visitors Mon-Fri, Sun & BHs. Sat pm. Booking preferred. **Societies** booking required. **Green Fees** not confirmed **Course Designer** Hawtree & Sons **Facilities** ⓣ 🍴 🍺 ▯ 🍽 △ 🖼 ✔ 🛜 ✔ **Conf** Corporate Hospitality Days **Location** 2m E of city centre on B1190

Hotel ★★★ 78% HL The Lincoln, Eastgate, LINCOLN
☎ 01522 520348 📄 01522 510780 71 en suite

Carholme Golf Club Carholme Rd LN1 1SE
☎ 01522 523725 📄 01522 533733
e-mail: secretary@carholmegolfclub.co.uk
web: www.carholmegolfclub.co.uk
Parkland where prevailing west winds can add interest. Good views.
First hole out of bounds left and right of fairway, pond left of 6th
green, lateral water hazards across several fairways.
18 Holes, 5501yds, Par 68, SSS 67, Course record 63.
Club membership 500.
Visitors Mon-Sun & BHs. Booking required weekends & BHs
Societies booking required. **Green Fees** £24 per day, £20 per round
Course Designer Willie Park Jnr **Facilities** ⊕ ⊮○⎮ ⊫ ⊑ ⊪⎧ ⩫
⭑ **Conf** Corporate Hospitality Days **Location** 1m W of city centre on
A57
Hotel ★★★ 73% HL The White Hart, Bailgate, LINCOLN
☎ 01522 526222 & 563293 📄 01522 531798 50 en suite

LOUTH   Map 8 TF38

Kenwick Park Golf Club Kenwick Park LN11 8NY
☎ 01507 605134 📄 01507 606556
e-mail: secretary@kenwickparkgolf.co.uk
web: www.kenwickparkgolf.co.uk
Situated on the edge of the Lincolnshire Wolds with panoramic
views. Course features a mixture of parkland and woodland holes,
complemented by a network of lakes.
18 Holes, 6715yds, Par 71, SSS 73, Course record 65.
Club membership 520.
Visitors Mon-Fri, Sun & BHs. Booking required. Handicap certificate.
Dress code. **Societies** booking required. **Green Fees** not confirmed
Course Designer Patrick Tallack **Prof** P Spence/M Langford
Facilities ⊕ ⊮○⎮ by prior arrangement ⊫ ⊑ ⊪⎧ ⩫ ⊟ ◇
⛟ ⭑ ⛳ **Leisure** squash, sauna, gymnasium **Conf** Corporate
Hospitality Days **Location** 2m S of Louth on A157 (Louth bypass)
Hotel ★★★ 77% HL Best Western Kenwick Park, Kenwick Park
Estate, LOUTH ☎ 01507 608806 📄 01507 608027 34 en suite

Louth Golf Club Crowtree Ln LN11 9LJ
☎ 01507 603681 📄 01507 608501
web: www.louthgolfclub.com
18 Holes, 6430yds, Par 72, SSS 71, Course record 66.
Location from A157/A16 rdbt take B1521 to Louth, 1st right up Love
Lane to top.
Telephone for further details
Hotel ★★★ 87% HL Brackenborough Hotel, Cordeaux Corner,
Brackenborough, LOUTH ☎ 01507 609169 📄 01507 609413
24 en suite

MARKET RASEN   Map 8 TF18

Market Rasen & District Golf Club Legsby Rd LN8 3DZ
☎ 01673 842319 📄 01673 849245
e-mail: marketrasengolf@onetel.net
web: www.marketrasengolfclub.co.uk

Picturesque, well-wooded heathland course, easy walking, with many
natural hazards.
18 Holes, 6239yds, Par 71, SSS 70, Course record 64.
Club membership 600.
Visitors Mon-Fri except BHs. Booking required. Dress code.
Societies booking required **Green Fees** £39 per day, £29 per round
Course Designer Hawtree Ltd **Prof** A M Chester **Facilities** ⊕ ⊮○⎮
⊫ ⊑ ⊪⎧ ⩫ ⊟ ⛟ ⭑ **Conf** Corporate Hospitality Days
Location 1m E, A46 onto A631
Hotel ★★★★★ RR The Advocate Arms, 2 Queen Street, MARKET
RASEN ☎ 01673 842364 10 rooms

Market Rasen Race Course (Golf Course) Legsby Rd
LN8 3EA
☎ 01673 843434 📄 01673 844532
web: www.marketrasenraces.co.uk
9 Holes, 2532yds, Par 32.
Course Designer Edward Stenton **Location** 1m E of Market Rasen
Telephone for further details
Hotel ★★★★★ RR The Advocate Arms, 2 Queen Street, MARKET
RASEN ☎ 01673 842364 10 rooms

NORMANBY   Map 8 SE81

Normanby Hall Golf Club Normanby Park DN15 9HU
☎ 01724 720226 (Pro shop)
18 Holes, 6547yds, Par 72, SSS 71, Course record 66.
Course Designer Hawtree & Son **Location** 3m N of Scunthorpe on
B1130 next to Normanby Hall
Telephone for further details
Hotel ★★★★★ RR Winteringham Fields, WINTERINGHAM
☎ 01724 733096 📄 01724 733898 11 rooms

CUNTHORPE   Map 8 SE81

shby Decoy Golf Club Burringham Rd DN17 2AB
☎ 01724 866561 📠 01724 271708
-mail: info@ashbydecoygolfclub.co.uk
web: www.ashbydecoy.co.uk
leasant, flat parkland course to satisfy all tastes, yet test the
xperienced golfer.
8 Holes, 6281yds, Par 71, SSS 71, Course record 66.
Club membership 650.
Visitors Mon-Fri except BHs. Booking required. Handicap certificate.
ress code. **Societies** booking required. **Green Fees** £30 per day, £25
er round. **Prof** A Miller **Facilities** ⓘ 🍴 🍺 ⬜ 🍸 🏌 ⤳ 📷 ✦
🔽 ✦ **Conf** facs Corporate Hospitality Days **Location** 2.5m SW on
1450 near Asda store
otel ★★★★ 79% HL Forest Pines Hotel & Golf Resort, Ermine
treet, Broughton, SCUNTHORPE ☎ 01652 650770 📠 01652 650495
88 en suite

Forest Pines Hotel & Golf Resort Ermine St, Broughton
DN20 0AQ
☎ 01652 650756 📠 01652 650495
e-mail: forestpinesproshop@qhotels.co.uk
web: www.qhotels.co.uk
A 27 hole course set in 185 acres, meandering through majestic pines
into open heathland. Forest Pines offers three challenging nine-hole
courses - Forest, Pines and Beeches. Any combination can be played.
Forest/Pines: 18 Holes, 6842yds, Par 73, SSS 74,
Course record 64.
Pines/Beeches: 18 Holes, 6653yds, Par 72, SSS 73.
Beeches/Forest: 18 Holes, 6393yds, Par 71, SSS 71.
Club membership 300.
Visitors Mon-Sun & BHs. Booking required. Dress code.
Societies booking required. **Green Fees** not confirmed **Course
Designer** John Morgan **Prof** Matthew Peacock/Dan Greenwood
Facilities ⓘ 🍴 🍺 ⬜ 🍸 🏌 ⤳ 📷 ◇ ✦ 🔽 ✦ 🏇 ✦
Leisure heated indoor swimming pool, sauna, gymnasium **Conf** facs
Corporate Hospitality Days **Location** M180 junct 4, 1st exit for
cunthorpe. At next rdbt take 2nd exit, hotel on left
otel ★★★★ 79% HL Forest Pines Hotel & Golf Resort, Ermine
treet, Broughton, SCUNTHORPE ☎ 01652 650770 📠 01652 650495
88 en suite

Grange Park Golf Club Butterwick Rd, Messingham
DN17 3PP
☎ 01724 762945 & 01724 762945
e-mail: info@grangepark.com
web: www.grangepark.com
Challenging parkland course with wide tree-lined lush fairways and
well manicured greens. There are many testing water hazards to
negotiate, especially the 4th par 3, known as the 'pond hole' requiring
a tee shot of over 136 yards to clear the pond and stop the ball dead
n the green to have a chance of reaching par.
8 Holes, 6233yds, Par 70, SSS 70, Course record 64.
Club membership 320.
Visitors Mon-Sun & BHs. Dress code. **Societies** booking required.
Green Fees £18 per 18 holes (£20 weekends & BHs) **Course
Designer** R Price **Prof** Jonathan Drury **Facilities** ⓘ 🍴 🍺 ⬜ 🍸
⤳ 📷 ◇ 🔽 ✦ 🏌 **Leisure** hard tennis courts, fishing, 9 hole
ar 3 course **Conf** facs Corporate Hospitality Days **Location** 1.5m W of
Messingham towards East Butterwick

Hotel ★★★★ 79% HL Forest Pines Hotel & Golf Resort, Ermine
Street, Broughton, SCUNTHORPE ☎ 01652 650770 📠 01652 650495
188 en suite

Holme Hall Golf Club Holme Ln, Bottesford DN16 3RF
☎ 01724 862078 📠 01724 862081
e-mail: secretary@holmehallgolf.co.uk
web: www.holmehallgolf.co.uk
Natural heathland course with gorse and heather and sandy subsoil.
Easy walking. Tight driving holes and good greens.
18 Holes, 6413yds, Par 71, SSS 71, Course record 64.
Club membership 650.
Visitors Mon-Fri except BHs. Booking required. Dress code.
Societies welcome. **Green Fees** £40 per day, £35 per 27 holes, £30
per round **Prof** Richard McKiernan **Facilities** ⓘ 🍴 🍺 ⬜ 🍸
⤳ 📷 🔽 ✦ 🏌 **Conf** facs Corporate Hospitality Days
Location M180 junct 4, 4m SE of Scunthorpe
Hotel ★★★★ 79% HL Forest Pines Hotel & Golf Resort, Ermine
Street, Broughton, SCUNTHORPE ☎ 01652 650770 📠 01652 650495
188 en suite

SKEGNESS   Map 9 TF56

North Shore Hotel & Golf Course North Shore Rd
PE25 1DN
☎ 01754 763298 📠 01754 761902
e-mail: info@northshorehotel.co.uk
web: www.northshorehotel.co.uk

Part links, part parkland, with two of the nine holes situated next to
the sea. Drainage ditches create additional challenges even for the
most accomplished golfer.
18 Holes, 6214yds, Par 71. Club membership 370.
Visitors Mon-Sun & BHs. Booking required. Dress code.
Societies booking required. **Green Fees** £41 per day, £31 per 18
holes (£51/£39 weekends) **Course Designer** James Braid **Prof** J
Cornelius **Facilities** ⓘ 🍴 🍺 ⬜ 🍸 🏌 ⤳ 📷 ◇ 🛏 ✦
Leisure snooker **Conf** facs Corporate Hospitality Days **Location** 1m N
of town centre off A52, opp North Shore Holiday Centre
Hotel ★★★ 66% HL North Shore Hotel & Golf Course, North Shore
Road, SKEGNESS ☎ 01754 763298 📠 01754 761902 34 en suite

Seacroft Golf Club Drummond Rd, Seacroft PE25 3AU
☎ 01754 763020 📄 01754 763020
e-mail: enquiries@seacroft-golfclub.co.uk
web: www.seacroft-golfclub.co.uk

A championship seaside links traditionally laid out with tight undulations and hogsback fairways. Adjacent to Gibraltar Point Nature Reserve, overlooking the Wash.

18 Holes, 6492yds, Par 71, SSS 72, Course record 64. Club membership 590.

Visitors Contact club for details. **Societies** booking required. **Green Fees** phone **Course Designer** Tom Dunn/Willie Fernie **Prof** Robin Lawie **Facilities** ⑪ �🍽 ⒧ ☐ 🍴 ⅄ 🏠 ⚑ ⚐ 🛺 ⚑
Conf Corporate Hospitality Days **Location** 1m S of town centre towards Gibralter Point Nature Reserve
Hotel ★★★ GA Sunnyside B&B, 34 Scarborough Av, SKEGNESS
☎ 01754 765119 & 07990 534757   8 rooms

SLEAFORD   Map 8 TF04

Sleaford Golf Club Willoughby Rd, Greylees NG34 8PL
☎ 01529 488273 📄 01529 488644
e-mail: manager@sleafordgolfclub.co.uk
web: www.sleafordgolfclub.co.uk

Inland links-type course, moderately wooded and fairly flat with sandy well-draining soil, which supports a variety of trees and shrubs. While the lowest index hole is the awkward dog-leg 4th, the 2nd hole requires two mighty hits to be reached. The feature hole is the 12th, where the green is totally protected by a copse of pine trees. A stream running through the course provides water hazards on several holes.

18 Holes, 6503yds, Par 72, SSS 71, Course record 64. Club membership 630.

Visitors Mon-Sun & BHs. Handicap certificate may be requested. Dress code. **Societies** booking required. **Green Fees** £35 per day, £28 per round (£36 weekends). Special Mon rate £24 per round 🅿 **Course Designer** T Williamson **Prof** Nigel Pearce **Facilities** ⑪ ⅋🍽 ⒧ ☐
🍴 ⅄ 🏠 🛺 ⚑ **Conf** Corporate Hospitality Days **Location** 2m W of Sleaford off A153
Hotel ★★★ 68% SHL Carre Arms Hotel & Conference Centre, 1 Mareham Lane, SLEAFORD ☎ 01529 303156 📄 01529 303139 13 en suite

SOUTH KYME   Map 8 TF14

South Kyme Golf Club Skinners Ln LN4 4AT
☎ 01526 861113 📄 01526 861113
e-mail: southkymegc@hotmail.com
web: www.skgc.co.uk

A challenging fenland course in a tranquil location, described as an inland links with water hazards, trees and fairway hazards. Renowned par 3 14th hole.

18 Holes, 6556yds, Par 72, SSS 72, Course record 66. Club membership 400.

Visitors Mon-Sun & BHs. Dress code. **Societies** welcome. **Green Fees** £22 per round, £12 per 9 holes (£25/£14 weekends & BHs) **Prof** Peter Chamberlain **Facilities** ⑪ ⅋🍽 ⒧ ☐ 🍴 ⅄ 🏠 ⚑
🛺 ⚑ **Leisure** 6 hole short course. **Conf** Corporate Hospitality Days **Location** off B1395 into South Kyme
Hotel ★★★ 68% SHL Carre Arms Hotel & Conference Centre, 1 Mareham Lane, SLEAFORD ☎ 01529 303156 📄 01529 303139 13 en suite

SPALDING   Map 8 TF22

Spalding Golf Club Surfleet PE11 4EA
☎ 01775 680386 (office) & 680474 (pro)
📄 01775 680988
e-mail: secretary@spaldinggolfclub.co.uk
web: www.spaldinggolfclub.co.uk

A pretty, well-laid out course in a fenland area. The River Glen runs beside the 1st, 2nd and 4th holes, and ponds and lakes are very much in play on the 9th, 10th and 11th holes. Challenging holes include the river dominated 2nd and the 17th where a good drive is needed for the right hand side of the fairway to leave a challenging second shot to a well protected green, bunkered in front and right with out of bounds on the left.

18 Holes, 6527yds, Par 72, SSS 72. Club membership 750.

Visitors Mon-Sun except BHs. Booking required weekends, phone other times for availability. Handicap certificate preferred. Dress code. **Societies** booking required. **Green Fees** £35 per day, £30 per round (£40 per round weekends & BHs) **Course Designer** Price/Spencer/Ware **Prof** John Spencer/Chris Huggins **Facilities** ⑪ ⅋🍽 ⒧ ☐ 🍴
⅄ 🏠 🛺 ⚑ ⚐ **Conf** Corporate Hospitality Days **Location** 4m N of Spalding next to A16
Hotel ★★★★ BB Westgate House & Barn, Little Lane, WHAPLODE ☎ 01406 370546   2 rooms

THE NATIONAL GOLF CENTRE

LINCOLNSHIRE - WOODHALL SPA - MAP 8 TF16

The Championship Course at Woodhall Spa, now known as the Hotchkin, is one of the best inland courses in the UK (voted 19th best in the world by Golf World Magazine). This classic course has cavernous bunkers and heather-lined fairways. Golf has been played here for over a century and the Hotchkin has hosted most of the top national and international amateur events. The English Golf Union acquired Woodhall Spa in 1995 to create a centre of excellence. A second course, the Bracken, has been built, along with extensive practice facilities including one of Europe's finest short-game practice areas. The English Golf Union actively encourages visitors to the National Golf Centre throughout the year, to experience the facilities and to enjoy the unique ambience.

The Broadway LN10 6PU ☎ 01526 352511 🖹 01526 351817
e-mail: booking@englishgolfunion.org **web:** www.woodhallspagolf.com
The Hotchkin: 18 Holes, 6501yds, Par 71.
The Bracken: 18 Holes, 6719yds, Par 72. Club membership 520.
Visitors Mon-Sun & BHs. Booking required. Handicap certificate. Dress code. **Societies** booking required.
Green Fees Hotchkin £110 per day, £71 per round. Bracken £75 per day, £48 round. £102 per day playing both courses **Course Designer** Col S V Hotchkin/Donald Steel (Bracken) **Facilities** ⑪ ⑩ 🖺 ⤷ ⑪ 🦺 🖺 ⚌ 🏌 **Leisure** pitch & putt 9 hole course **Conf** facs Corporate Hospitality Days **Location** Exit A1 just after Colsterworth rdbt onto B6403 to Ancaster. Right onto A153 to Coningsby/Tattershall then left onto B1192
Hotel ★★★ 74% HL Petwood, Stixwould Road, WOODHALL SPA ☎ 01526 352411 🖹 01526 353473 53 en suite

STAMFORD Map 4 TF00

Burghley Park Golf Club St Martins PE9 3JX
☎ 01780 753789 📄 01780 753789
e-mail: secretary@burghleyparkgolfclub.co.uk
web: www.burghleygolf.org.uk

A compact parkland layout. Tree planting, the introduction of sand
and water hazards and the maintenance of fair but punishing rough,
have made the course a real challenge. Free draining fairways and
greens give first class playing all year.

18 Holes, 6296yds, Par 70, SSS 71. Club membership 700.

Visitors may play Mon-Fri. Advance booking required Mon & Fri.
Handicap certificate required. Dress code. **Societies** booking required.
Green Fees £35 per 18 holes Mon-Fri ex BHs **Course Designer** Rev J
D Day **Prof** Andy Lavers **Facilities** ⊕ ⍟ ᓂ ⊑ ꇉ ⽓ ⛁ ⛾
⽼ **Conf** Corporate Hospitality Days **Location** From A1 exit at turnoff
1m S of Stamford
Hotel ★★★ 86% HL The George of Stamford, 71 St Martins,
STAMFORD ☎ 01780 750750 & 750700 (res) 📄 01780 750701
47 en suite

STOKE ROCHFORD Map 8 SK92

Stoke Rochford Golf Club NG33 5EW
☎ 01476 530275 📄 01476 530237
e-mail: srg.mail@btinternet.com
web: www.stokerochfordgolfclub.co.uk

Parkland course designed by C Turnor in 1924 and extended in 1936 to
18 holes by Major Hotchkin.

18 Holes, 6252yds, Par 70, SSS 70, Course record 65.
Club membership 525.

Visitors contact club for details **Societies** booking required. **Green
Fees** £32 per round (£40 weekends) **Course Designer** Major Hotchkin
Prof Angus Dow **Facilities** ⊕ ⍟ ᓂ ⊑ ꇉ ⽓ ⛁ ⽼ ⛾
⽼ **Location** 5m S of Grantham off A1 southbound signed Stoke
Rochford, onto A1 northbound, enter club via BP service station
Hotel ★★★★ 72% HL Ramada Grantham, Swingbridge Road,
GRANTHAM ☎ 01476 593000 📄 01476 592592 89 en suite

SUTTON BRIDGE Map 9 TF42

Sutton Bridge Golf Club New Rd PE12 9RQ
☎ 01406 350323
web: www.club-noticeboard.co.uk/suttonbridge

9 Holes, 5724yds, Par 70, SSS 68, Course record 64.

Location E of village off A17
Telephone for further details
Hotel ★★★ 83% HL Bank House Hotel, King's Staithe Square,
KING'S LYNN ☎ 01553 660492 11 en suite

SUTTON ON SEA Map 9 TF58

Sandilands Golf Club Roman Bank LN12 2RJ
☎ 01507 441432 📄 01507 441617
e-mail: sandilandsgolf@googlemail.com
web: www.sandilandsgolfclub.co.uk

Well-manicured links course next to the sea, renowned for the
standard of its greens. Playable all year and easy walking due to the
subtle undulations. The variety of holes and bunker placement will
require the use of every club in the bag.

18 Holes, 6021yds, Par 70, SSS 69, Course record 64.
Club membership 300.

Visitors Mon-Sun & BHs. Booking required. Dress code.
Societies booking required. **Green Fees** £33.50 per day, £25.50
per round (£39.50/£30.50 weekends & BHs). Reduced winter rates
Prof Simon Sherratt **Facilities** ⊕ ⍟ ᓂ ⊑ ꇉ ⽓ ⛁ ⛾ ⽓
⽼ ⽼ ⛚ ⽼ **Leisure** hard and grass tennis courts, gymnasium
Conf facs Corporate Hospitality Days **Location** 1.5m S off A52
Hotel ★★★ 73% HL The Grange & Links, Sea Lane, Sandilands,
SUTTON-ON-SEA ☎ 01507 441334 📄 01507 443033 23 en suite

TORKSEY Map 8 SK87

Lincoln Golf Club Torksey LN1 2EG
☎ 01427 718721 📄 01427 718721
e-mail: info@lincolngc.co.uk
web: www.lincolngc.co.uk

A mature championship standard course offering a variety of holes,
links style to parkland.

18 Holes, 6438yds, Par 71, SSS 71, Course record 65.
Club membership 750.

Visitors dress code. **Societies** booking required **Green Fees** not
confirmed **Course Designer** J H Taylor **Prof** Ashley Carter **Facilities** ⊕
⍟ ᓂ ⊑ ꇉ ⽓ ⛁ ⛾ ⽼ ⛚ ⽼ **Leisure** 3 hole practice
course **Conf** facs Corporate Hospitality Days **Location** NE of village
off A156
Hotel ★★★ 73% HL The White Hart, Bailgate, LINCOLN
☎ 01522 526222 & 563293 📄 01522 531798 50 en suite

Millfield Golf Complex Laughterton LN1 2LB
☎ 01427 718255 📄 01427 718473

This golf complex offers a range of facilities to suit every golfer. The
Millfield is designed to suit the more experienced golfer and follows
the natural contours of the landscape. The Grenville Green is designed
for more casual golfers and the par 3 is suitable for beginners, family
games or for warm-up and practice play.

The Millfield: 18 Holes, 6004yds, Par 72, SSS 69,
Course record 68.
The Grenville Green: 18 Holes, 4485yds, Par 65.

Visitors contact course for details. **Societies** telephone in advance.
Green Fees not confirmed ⊗ **Course Designer** C W Watson
Prof Brian Cummings **Facilities** ⊕ ᓂ ⊑ ꇉ ⽓ ⛚ ⽼ ⛚ ⽼ ⽓
Leisure grass tennis courts **Location** on A1133 1m N of A57
Hotel ★★★ 73% HL The White Hart, Bailgate, LINCOLN
☎ 01522 526222 & 563293 📄 01522 531798 50 en suite

WOODHALL SPA Map 8 TF16

The National Golf Centre see page 169
The Broadway LN10 6PU
☎ 01526 352511 📄 01526 351817
e-mail: booking@englishgolfunion.org
web: www.woodhallspagolf.com

Save on Hotels. Book at **theAA.com/hotel**

LINCOLNSHIRE – LONDON

ENGLAND

WOODTHORPE

Map 9 TF48

Woodthorpe Hall Golf Club LN13 0DD
☎ 01507 450000 📄 01507 450000
e-mail: secretary@woodthorpehallgolfclub.fsnet.co.uk
web: www.woodthorpehallleisure.co.uk
Parkland course.
18 Holes, 5140yds, Par 67, SSS 65. Club membership 300.
Visitors Mon-Sun & BHs. Dress code. **Societies** booking required
Green Fees not confirmed **Facilities** ⓦ 🍴 ⤴ ♨ 🏐 🛒 ⚲ ◇
🖙 ✐ **Leisure** fishing **Conf** facs **Location** 3m N of Alford on B1373
Hotel ★★★ 73% HL The Grange & Links, Sea Lane, Sandilands,
SUTTON-ON-SEA ☎ 01507 441334 📄 01507 443033 23 en suite

LONDON

E4 CHINGFORD

Royal Epping Forest Golf Club Forest Approach,
Chingford E4 7AZ
☎ 020 8529 2195 📄 020 8559 4664
e-mail: office@refgc.co.uk
web: www.refgc.co.uk
Woodland course. Red garments must be worn.
18 Holes, 6281yds, Par 71, SSS 70, Course record 64.
Club membership 400.
Visitors contact club for details. **Societies** welcome. **Green Fees** £20
(£25 weekends)) **Course Designer** J G Gibson **Prof** A Traynor
Facilities ⓦ by prior arrangement 🍴 by prior arrangement ⤴ ♨
🏐 ⚲ 🛒 🖈 🖙 ✐ **Conf** facs **Location** 300yds E of Chingford
station on Chingford Plain
Hotel ★★★★ 72% HL Menzies Prince Regent, Manor Road,
WOODFORD BRIDGE ☎ 020 8505 9966 📄 020 8506 0807 61 en suite

West Essex Golf Club Bury Rd, Sewardstonebury,
Chingford E4 7QL
☎ 020 8529 7558 📄 020 8524 7870
e-mail: sec@westessexgolfclub.co.uk
web: www.westessexgolfclub.co.uk
Testing parkland course within Epping Forest with spectacular
views over Essex and Middlesex, only ten miles from central London.
Designed by James Braid in 1900 and designed to make full use of
the landscape's natural attributes. The front nine is the shorter of
the two and provides a test of accuracy with tree-lined fairways that
meander through the undulating countryside. The back nine is equally
challenging although slightly longer and requiring more long iron play.
18 Holes, 6262yds, Par 71, SSS 71. Club membership 650.
Visitors Mon-Fri, Sun & BHs. Dress code. **Societies** booking required.
Green Fees £45 **Course Designer** James Braid **Prof** Robert Joyce
Facilities ⓦ 🍴 ⤴ ♨ 🏐 ⚲ 🛒 🖈 ✐ 🖙 ✐
Leisure halfway house **Conf** facs Corporate Hospitality Days
Location M25 junct 26, 1.5m N of Chingford station
Hotel ★★★★ 72% HL Menzies Prince Regent, Manor Road,
WOODFORD BRIDGE ☎ 020 8505 9966 📄 020 8506 0807 61 en suite

E11 LEYTONSTONE & WANSTEAD

Wanstead Golf Club Overton Dr E11 2LW
☎ 020 8989 3938 📄 020 8532 9138
web: www.wansteadgolf.org.uk
18 Holes, 6015yds, Par 69, SSS 69, Course record 62.
Course Designer James Braid **Location** off A12 in Wanstead
Telephone for further details
Hotel ★★★★ 72% HL Menzies Prince Regent, Manor Road,
WOODFORD BRIDGE ☎ 020 8505 9966 📄 020 8506 0807 61 en suite

N2 EAST FINCHLEY

Hampstead Golf Club Winnington Rd N2 0TU
☎ 020 8455 0203 📄 020 8731 6194
e-mail: secretary@hampsteadgolfclub.co.uk
web: www.hampsteadgolfclub.co.uk
Undulating parkland with many mature trees.
9 Holes, 2909yds, Par 68, SSS 68. Club membership 526.
Visitors Mon, Wed-Sun & BHs. Dress code. **Green Fees** £30 per
18 holes (£35 Sun) **Course Designer** Tom Dunn **Prof** Peter Brown
Facilities ⓦ ⤴ ♨ 🏐 ⚲ 🛒 ✐ **Location** off Hampstead Ln
Hotel ★★★★ GA The Langorf, 20 Frognal, Hampstead, LONDON
☎ 020 7794 4483 📄 020 7435 9055 31 rooms

N6 HIGHGATE

Highgate Golf Club Denewood Rd N6 4AH
☎ 020 8340 1906 📄 020 8348 9152
e-mail: nick@highgategc.co.uk
web: www.highgategc.co.uk
Parkland with fine views over London. The nearest 18-hole course north
of the river from Marble Arch. Many interesting holes with a premium
on accuracy. The 15th and 16th holes are very demanding par 4s.
18 Holes, 5721yds, Par 69, SSS 68, Course record 66.
Club membership 700.
Visitors Mon-Fri except BHs. Booking required. Dress code. **Green
Fees** £60 per day, £42 per round, Mon-Fri **Course Designer** Cuthbert
Butchart **Prof** Robin Turner **Facilities** ⓦ ⤴ ♨ 🏐 ⚲ 🛒
🖈 ✐ **Conf** facs Corporate Hospitality Days **Location** off B519
Hampstead Ln
Hotel ★★★★ 75% HL London Marriott Hotel Regents Park, 128
King Henry's Road, LONDON ☎ 020 7722 7711 & 0800 221222
📄 020 7586 5822 304 en suite

N9 LOWER EDMONTON

Lee Valley Leisure Golf Course Lee Valley Leisure
Complex, Meridian Way, Edmonton N9 0AR
☎ 020 8803 3611 📄 020 8884 4975
e-mail: rgarvey@leevalleypark.org.uk
web: www.leevalleypark.org.uk
Testing parkland course with a large lake and the River Lee providing
natural hazards. Good quality greens all year round.
18 Holes, 5204yds, Par 67, SSS 65. Club membership 200.
Visitors Mon-Sun & BHs. Booking required weekends & BHs.
Societies booking required. **Green Fees** not confirmed **Course
Designer** John Jacobs **Prof** R Gerken **Facilities** ⤴ ♨ ⚲ 🛒 🖈
✐ **Location**
Hotel ★★★★ 75% HL Royal Chace, The Ridgeway, ENFIELD
☎ 020 8884 8181 📄 020 8884 8150 92 en suite

N14 SOUTHGATE

Trent Park Golf Club Bramley Rd, Oakwood N14 4UW
☎ 020 8367 4653 📠 020 8366 4581
e-mail: proshop@trentparkgolf.co.uk
web: www.trentparkgolf.co.uk
Parkland course set in 150 acres of green belt area. Seven holes
played across Merryhills brook. Testing holes are 2nd (423 yds) over
brook, 190 yds from the tee, and up to a plateau green; par 4 7th (463
yds) with a dog-leg, over a brook.
18 Holes, 6175yds, Par 70, SSS 70, Course record 64.
Club membership 250.
Visitors Mon-Sun & BHs. Booking required (can be done online).
Societies booking required. **Course Designer** Hugh Stovin **Prof** John Frances
Facilities Ⓣ 🍴 🛏 ⬇ 🍽 🎿 🏠 ⛳ ✦ ⚒ ✦ **Conf** facs
Corporate Hospitality Days **Location** opp Oakwood tube station
Hotel ★★★★ 80% HL West Lodge Park, Cockfosters Road,
HADLEY WOOD ☎ 020 8216 3900 & 8216 3903 📠 020 8216 3937
59 en suite

N20 WHETSTONE

North Middlesex Golf Club The Manor House,
Friern Barnet Ln, Whetstone N20 0NL
☎ 020 8445 1604 & 020 8445 3060 📠 020 8445 5023
e-mail: manager@northmiddlesexgc.co.uk
web: www.northmiddlesexgc.co.uk
Parkland course with many attractive water features and many mature
trees. Renowned for its tricky greens and a spectacular final hole
which is a demanding par 3.
18 Holes, 5594yds, Par 69, SSS 67, Course record 64.
Club membership 520.
Visitors Mon-Fri. Weekends & BHs after 1pm. Dress code.
Societies booking required. **Green Fees** £25 (£30 weekends & BHs).
Winter £20/£27 **Course Designer** Willie Park Jnr **Prof** Freddy George
Facilities Ⓣ 🍴 🛏 ⬇ 🍽 🎿 🏠 ⚒ 🚜 ✦ **Conf** facs
Corporate Hospitality Days **Location** M25 junct 23, 5m S
Hotel ★★★★ 75% HL Hendon Hall, Ashley Lane, Hendon, LONDON
☎ 020 8203 3341 📠 020 8457 2502 57 en suite

> ### South Herts Golf Club Links Dr N20 8QU
> ☎ 020 8445 2035 📠 020 8445 7569
> **web:** www.southhertsgolfclub.co.uk
> *18 Holes, 6432yds, Par 72, SSS 71, Course record 63.*
> **Course Designer** Harry Vardon **Location** 2m E of A1 at Apex Corner
> **Telephone for further details**
> **Hotel** ★★★★ 80% HL West Lodge Park, Cockfosters Road,
> HADLEY WOOD ☎ 020 8216 3900 & 8216 3903 📠 020 8216 3937
> 59 en suite

N21 WINCHMORE HILL

Bush Hill Park Golf Club Bush Hill, Winchmore Hill
N21 2BU
☎ 020 8360 4103 📠 020 8360 5583
e-mail: events@bhpgc.com
web: www.bhpgc.com
Pleasant parkland course in a tranquil setting. The holes set a
challenge due to the vast array of mature trees, which make it an

enjoyable course to play. The premium is on accuracy rather than
length off the tee. The six par threes are all visually stunning and
along with the remodelled 17th contribute to an enjoyable round of
golf for all levels of golfer.
18 Holes, 5776yds, Par 70, SSS 68, Course record 61.
Club membership 700.
Visitors Mon-Fri, Sun & BHs. Booking required. Dress code.
Societies booking required. **Green Fees** £29.50 per round (£35 Sun
& BHs). Twilight £19 **Course Designer** Harry Vardon **Prof** Lee Fickling
Facilities Ⓣ 🍴 🛏 ⬇ 🍽 🎿 🏠 ⛳ ✦ 🚜 ✦ 🏹 **Conf** facs Corporate Hospitality Days **Location** 1m S of Enfield off
A105
Hotel ★★★★ 75% HL Royal Chace, The Ridgeway, ENFIELD
☎ 020 8884 8181 📠 020 8884 8150 92 en suite

N22 WOOD GREEN

Muswell Hill Golf Club Rhodes Av, Wood Green N22 7UT
☎ 020 8888 1764 📠 020 8889 9380
e-mail: manager@muswellhillgolfclub.co.uk
web: www.muswellhillgolfclub.co.uk
Undulating parkland course with a brook running through the centre,
set in 87 acres.
18 Holes, 6431yds, Par 71, SSS 71. Club membership 530.
Visitors Mon-Fri. Weekends & BHs after 2pm. Booking required
weekends & BHs. Dress code. **Societies** welcome. **Green Fees** Mon £30
per day, Tue-Fri £45 per day (£45 per 18 holes weekends). Fees include
a drink. **Course Designer** Braid/Wilson **Prof** David Wilton **Facilities** Ⓣ
🍴 🛏 ⬇ 🍽 🎿 🏠 ⛳ ✦ ✦ **Conf** facs Corporate
Hospitality Days **Location** off N Circular Rd near Bounds Green
Hotel ★★★ 67% HL Days Hotel London North - M1, Welcome
Break Service Area, LONDON ☎ 020 8906 7000 📠 020 8906 7011
200 en suite

NW7 MILL HILL

Finchley Golf Club Nether Court NW7 1PU
☎ 020 8346 2436 📠 020 8343 4205
web: www.finchleygolfclub.com
18 Holes, 6356yds, Par 72, SSS 71.
Course Designer James Braid **Location** near Mill Hill East Tube
Station
Telephone for further details
Hotel ★★★ 67% HL Days Hotel London North - M1, Welcome
Break Service Area, LONDON ☎ 020 8906 7000 📠 020 8906 7011
200 en suite

Hendon Golf Club Ashley Walk, Devonshire Rd, Mill Hill
NW7 1DG
☎ 020 8346 6023 📠 020 8343 1974
e-mail: admin@hendongolfclub.co.uk
web: www.hendongolfclub.co.uk
Easy walking parkland course with a good variety of trees, and
providing testing golf.
18 Holes, 6289yds, Par 70, SSS 70, Course record 65.
Club membership 560.
Visitors Mon-Sun & BHs. Booking required. **Societies** welcome.
Green Fees not confirmed **Course Designer** H S Colt **Prof** Matt Deal
Facilities Ⓣ 🍴 🛏 ⬇ 🍽 🎿 🏠 ⚒ ✦ **Conf** facs
Corporate Hospitality Days **Location** M1 junct 2 southbound
Hotel ★★★★ 75% HL Hendon Hall, Ashley Lane, Hendon, LONDON
☎ 020 8203 3341 📠 020 8457 2502 57 en suite

Save on Hotels. Book at **theAA.com/hotel**   **LONDON**

ENGLAND

Mill Hill Golf Club 100 Barnet Way, Mill Hill NW7 3AL
☎ 020 8959 2339 📄 020 8906 0731
e-mail: cluboffice@millhillgc.co.uk
web: www.millhillgc.co.uk
A mature course set in 145 acres of parkland. The 18 holes are all
individually designed with many bordered by ancient oaks. Lake
features on the 2nd, 9th, 10th and 17th holes.
18 Holes, 6247yds, Par 70, SSS 70, Course record 68.
Club membership 550.
Visitors Mon-Sun except BHs. Dress code. **Societies** booking
required. **Green Fees** £30 per round (£37 weekends). Reduced winter
rates **Course Designer** J F Abercrombie/H S Colt **Prof** David Beal
Facilities ⑪ 🍴 🛏 ☐ 🍸 ⚐ 🏠 ♂ 🛥 ♂ 🏌
Leisure snooker **Conf** facs Corporate Hospitality Days **Location** M1
junct 4, take A41 towards central London. At Apex rdbt turn left and
immediately right onto A5109, 3rd turn left into Hankins Lane. M25
junct 23 onto A1, 2nd exit at Stirling rdbt, A1 on left
Hotel ★★★★ 73% HL Holiday Inn London - Elstree, Barnet
Bypass, BOREHAMWOOD ☎ 0871 942 9071 & 020 8214 9988
📄 020 8207 6817 135 en suite

SE9 ELTHAM

Eltham Warren Golf Club Bexley Rd, Eltham SE9 2PE
☎ 020 8850 4477 📄 020 8850 0522
e-mail: secretary@elthamwarren.idps.co.uk
web: www.elthamwarrengolfclub.co.uk
Parkland course founded in 1890 with narrow tree-lined fairways and
small greens.
9 Holes, 5850yds, Par 69, SSS 68, Course record 64.
Club membership 440.
Visitors Mon-Sun & BHs. Booking required. **Societies** booking
required. **Green Fees** £30 per day **Course Designer** James Braid
Prof Gary Brett **Facilities** ⑪ 🛏 ☐ 🍸 🏠 ♂ 🛥 ♂
Leisure snooker **Location** 0.5m from Eltham station on A210 (Bexley
Rd)
Hotel ★★★ 77% HL Best Western Bromley Court, Bromley Hill,
BROMLEY ☎ 020 8461 8600 📄 020 8460 0899 114 en suite

Royal Blackheath Golf Club Court Rd, Eltham SE9 5AF
☎ 020 8850 1795 📄 020 8859 0150
e-mail: info@rbgc.com
web: www.royalblackheath.com
A pleasant, parkland course of great character, with many great
trees and two ponds. The 18th requires a pitch to the green over a
thick clipped hedge, which also crosses the front of the 1st tee. The
clubhouse dates from the 17th century, and you may wish to visit
the club's fine museum of golf.
18 Holes, 6147yds, Par 70, SSS 70, Course record 63.
Club membership 720.
Visitors Mon-Fri except BHs. Dress code. **Societies** booking required.
Green Fees £75 per day, £55 per round **Course Designer** James
Braid **Prof** Matt Johns **Facilities** ⑪ 🍴 🛏 ☐ 🍸 🏠
🏠 🔧 ♂ 🛥 ♂ **Leisure** golf museum **Conf** facs Corporate
Hospitality Days **Location** M25 junct 3, A20 towards London, 2nd
lights right, club 500yds on right
Hotel ★★★ 77% HL Best Western Bromley Court, Bromley Hill,
BROMLEY ☎ 020 8461 8600 📄 020 8460 0899 114 en suite

SE18 WOOLWICH

Shooters Hill Golf Club Eaglesfield Rd, Shooters Hill
SE18 3DA
☎ 020 8854 6368 📄 020 8854 0469
e-mail: admin@shgc.uk.com
web: www.shgc.uk.com
Hilly and wooded parkland with good views and natural hazards.
18 Holes, 5704yds, Par 69, SSS 68, Course record 63.
Club membership 750.
Visitors Mon-Fri except BHs. Handicap certificate. Dress code.
Societies booking required. **Green Fees** £35 per day, £28 per round
🚸 **Course Designer** Willie Park **Prof** David Brotherton **Facilities** ⑪
🍴 🛏 ☐ 🍸 🏠 🏠 🛥 ♂ **Conf** facs Corporate Hospitality
Days **Location** Shooters Hill road from Blackheath
Hotel ★★★★ 75% HL Novotel London ExCeL, 7 Western Gateway,
Royal Victoria Docks, LONDON ☎ 020 7540 9700 & 0870 850 4560
📄 020 7540 9710 257 en suite

SE21 DULWICH

Dulwich & Sydenham Hill Golf Club Grange Ln,
College Rd SE21 7LH
☎ 020 8693 3961 📄 020 8693 2481
e-mail: info@dulwichgolf.co.uk
web: www.dulwichgolf.co.uk
Parkland course set among mature oaks on the slopes of Sydenham
Hill, overlooking Dulwich College and boasting spectacular views of
London. Demanding par 4s and challenging par 3s are interspersed
with reachable but testing par 5s. Tree-lined fairways off the tees,
hazards and cannily placed bunkers await the approach shot. Having
made the green, the golfer is then faced with small undulating greens.
Dulwich & Sydenham Hill: 18 Holes, 6047yds, Par 69,
SSS 69, Course record 61. Club membership 850.
Visitors Mon-Fri except BHs. Dress code. **Societies** booking required.
Green Fees £60 per day, £45 per round. Winter £30 per round **Course**
Designer H Colt **Prof** David Baillie **Facilities** ⑪ 🍴 🛏 ☐
🍸 🏠 🏠 🔧 ♂ ♂ **Leisure** short game area **Conf** facs
Corporate Hospitality Days **Location** 0.5m from Dulwich College off
A205 (South Circular)
Hotel ★★★ 77% HL Best Western Bromley Court, Bromley Hill,
BROMLEY ☎ 020 8461 8600 📄 020 8460 0899 114 en suite

SE28 WOOLWICH

Thamesview Golf Centre Fairway Dr, Summerton Way,
Thamesmead SE28 8PP
☎ 020 8310 7975 📄 020 8312 0546
e-mail: golf@tvgc.co.uk
web: www.tvgc.co.uk
A delightful but tricky course with a mix of mature trees, new trees
and water hazards. The 6th hole, while only 357 yds, is one of the
toughest par 4's a golfer can play.
9 Holes, 5068yds, Par 70, SSS 66, Course record 74.
Club membership 60.
Visitors Contact centre for details. **Societies** booking required. **Green**
Fees Mon-Fri £10 per 18 holes, £8 per 9 holes (weekends £14/£11)
Course Designer Heffernan **Prof** Stephen Lee **Facilities** ⑪ 🍴
🛏 ☐ 🍸 🏠 🔧 ♂ 🏌 **Conf** facs Corporate Hospitality Days
Location off A2 near Woolwich ferry
Hotel BUD Ibis London East Barking, Highbridge Road, BARKING
☎ 020 8477 4100 📄 020 8477 4101 86 en suite

SW15 PUTNEY

Richmond Park Golf Course Roehampton Gate SW15 5JR

☎ 020 8876 1795 ▯ 020 8878 1354
web: www.glendale-golf.com

Princes Course: 18 Holes, 5868yds, Par 69, SSS 67.
Dukes Course: 18 Holes, 6036yds, Par 69, SSS 68.

Course Designer Fred Hawtree **Location** inside Richmond Park, entrance via Roehampton Gate
Telephone for further details
Hotel ★★★★ 74% HL The Richmond Gate Hotel, 152-158 Richmond Hill, RICHMOND-UPON-THAMES ☎ 0845 906 9966 ▯ 020 8332 0354 68 en suite

SW17 WANDSWORTH

Central London Golf Centre Burntwood Ln SW17 0AT

☎ 020 8871 2468 ▯ 020 8874 7447
web: www.clgc.co.uk

9 Holes, 2277yds, Par 62, SSS 62, Course record 59.

Course Designer Patrick Tallack/Michael Anscomb **Location** between Garatt Ln and Trinity Rd
Telephone for further details
Hotel ★★★★ 80% CHH Cannizaro House, West Side, Wimbledon Common, LONDON ☎ 020 8879 1464 ▯ 020 8879 7338 46 en suite

SW19 WIMBLEDON

London Scottish Golf Club Windmill Enclosure, Wimbledon Common SW19 5NQ

☎ 020 8788 0135 & 8789 1207 ▯ 020 8789 7517
e-mail: secretary.lsgc@btconnect.com
web: www.londonscottishgolfclub.co.uk

Heathland course. The original course was seven holes around the windmill, laid out by 'Old' Willie Dunn of Musselburgh. His son, Tom Dunn, was the first professional to the club and laid out the 18-hole course.

18 Holes, 5458yds, Par 68, SSS 66, Course record 61.
Club membership 300.

Visitors Mon-Fri except BHs. Dress code - red tops must be worn. **Societies** booking required. **Green Fees** Mon £30 per day, £20 per round. Tue-Fri £35/£25 **Course Designer** Tom Dunn **Prof** Steve Barr **Facilities** ⑪ ↑◎↑ ⊾ ⬜ ▧ ⅄ 🖾 ⅋ ✧ **Location**
Hotel ★★★★ 80% CHH Cannizaro House, West Side, Wimbledon Common, LONDON ☎ 020 8879 1464 ▯ 020 8879 7338 46 en suite

Royal Wimbledon Golf Club 29 Camp Rd SW19 4UW

☎ 020 8946 2125 ▯ 020 8944 8652
e-mail: secretary@rwgc.co.uk
web: www.rwgc.co.uk

The third-oldest club in England, established in 1865 and steeped in the history of the game. Mainly heathland with trees and heather, a good test of golf with many fine holes, the 12th being rated as the best.

18 Holes, 6348yds, Par 71, SSS 71, Course record 64.
Club membership 1050.

Visitors Wed & Thu except BHs. Booking required. Handicap certificate. Dress code. **Societies** booking required **Green Fees** not confirmed **Course Designer** H Colt **Prof** David Jones **Facilities** ⑪

⊾ ⬜ ▧ ⅄ 🖾 ⅋ ✧ ⊱ ✧ ⋔ **Conf** Corporate Hospitality Days **Location** 1m from Tibbatt's Corner rdbt on A3 off Wimbledon Parkside before war memorial in village
Hotel ★★★★ 80% CHH Cannizaro House, West Side, Wimbledon Common, LONDON ☎ 020 8879 1464 ▯ 020 8879 7338 46 en suite

Wimbledon Common Golf Club 19 Camp Rd SW19 4UW

☎ 020 8946 0294 (Pro shop) ▯ 020 8947 8697
e-mail: office@wcgc.co.uk
web: www.wcgc.co.uk

Quick-drying course on Wimbledon Common with no temporary greens. Well wooded, with tight fairways, challenging short holes but no bunkers.

18 Holes, 5438yds, Par 68, SSS 66, Course record 62.
Club membership 320.

Visitors Mon-Sat except BHs. Booking required Sat. **Societies** booking required. **Green Fees** £35 per day, £25 per round **Course Designer** Tom & Willie Dunn **Prof** J S Jukes **Facilities** ⑪ ↑◎↑ ⊾ ⬜ ▧ ⅄ 🖾 ⅋ ✧ **Leisure** snooker room. **Conf** facs Corporate Hospitality Days **Location** 0.5m N of Wimbledon Village
Hotel ★★★★ 80% CHH Cannizaro House, West Side, Wimbledon Common, LONDON ☎ 020 8879 1464 ▯ 020 8879 7338 46 en suite

Wimbledon Park Golf Club Home Park Rd SW19 7HR

☎ 020 8946 1250 ▯ 020 8944 8688
web: www.wpgc.co.uk

18 Holes, 5483yds, Par 66, SSS 66, Course record 59.
Course Designer Willie Park Jnr **Location** 400yds from Wimbledon Park station
Telephone for further details
Hotel ★★★★ 80% CHH Cannizaro House, West Side, Wimbledon Common, LONDON ☎ 020 8879 1464 ▯ 020 8879 7338 46 en suite

MERSEYSIDE

BEBINGTON   Map 7 SJ38

Brackenwood Golf Club Brackenwood Golf Course CH63 2LY

☎ 0151 608 5394
web: www.brackenwoodgolf.co.uk

18 Holes, 6285yds, Par 70, SSS 70, Course record 66.
Location M53 junct 4, 0.75m N on B5151
Telephone for further details
Hotel ★★★★ 79% HL Thornton Hall Hotel and Spa, Neston Road, THORNTON HOUGH ☎ 0151 336 3938 & 353 3717 ▯ 0151 336 7864 63 en suite

Save on Hotels. Book at **theAA.com/hotel**

MERSEYSIDE

ENGLAND

BIRKENHEAD   Map 7 SJ38

Prenton Golf Club Golf Links Rd, Prenton CH42 8LW
☎ 0151 609 3426
e-mail: nigel.brown@prentongolfclub.co.uk
web: www.prentongolfclub.co.uk

Parkland with easy walking and views of Welsh hills.

*18 Holes, 6429yds, Par 71, SSS 71, Course record 65.
Club membership 610.*

Visitors Mon-Fri, Sun & BHs. Booking required Sun & BHs. Dress code. **Societies** booking required. **Green Fees** phone 📞 **Course Designer** James Braid **Prof** Robin Thompson **Facilities** 🍴 🍽 🏌 🖥 🛋 🔧 ⚐ 🛒 🎯 **Conf** facs Corporate Hospitality Days **Location** M53 junct 3, off A552 towards Birkenhead
Hotel ★★★ 80% HL The RiverHill Hotel, Talbot Road, Prenton, BIRKENHEAD ☎ 0151 653 3773 📄 0151 653 7162   15 en suite

Wirral Ladies Golf Club 93 Bidston Rd CH43 6TS
☎ 0151 652 1255 📄 0151 651 3775
web: www.wirral-ladies-golf-club.co.uk

18 Holes, 5185yds, Par 68, SSS 65.

Location W of town centre on B5151
Telephone for further details
Hotel ★★★ 80% HL The RiverHill Hotel, Talbot Road, Prenton, BIRKENHEAD ☎ 0151 653 3773 📄 0151 653 7162   15 en suite

BLUNDELLSANDS   Map 7 SJ39

West Lancashire Golf Club Hall Road West L23 8SZ
☎ 0151 924 1076 📄 0151 931 4448
e-mail: golf@westlancashiregolf.co.uk
web: www.westlancashiregolf.co.uk

Challenging, traditional links with sandy subsoil overlooking the Mersey estuary. The course provides excellent golf throughout the year. The four short holes are very fine.

*18 Holes, 6800yds, Par 72, SSS 74, Course record 65.
Club membership 650.*

Visitors Mon, Wed-Fri, Sun & BHs. Booking required. Dress code. **Societies** booking required. **Green Fees** £90 per day, £75 per round (£100/£85 Sun) **Course Designer** C K Cotton **Prof** Gary Edge **Facilities** 🍴 🍽 🏌 🖥 🛋 🔧 ⚐ 🎯 **Conf** Corporate Hospitality Days **Location** N of village, next to Hall Road station
Hotel ★★★ 80% HL Grove House, Grove Road, WALLASEY ☎ 0151 639 3947 & 630 4558 📄 0151 639 0028   14 en suite

BOOTLE   Map 7 SJ39

Bootle Golf Club 2 Dunnings Bridge Rd L30 2PP
☎ 0151 928 1371 📄 0151 949 1815
e-mail: bootlegolfcourse@btconnect.com

Municipal parkland course, with prevailing north-westerly wind. Testing holes: 5th (191 yds) par 3; 7th (431 yds) par 4.

18 Holes, 6242yds, Par 71. Club membership 380.

Visitors Mon-Sun & BHs. Booking required weekends & BHs. **Societies** booking required. **Green Fees** not confirmed **Prof** Alan Bradshaw **Facilities** 🍴 🏌 🖥 🛋 🔧 ⚐ 🎯 **Leisure** fishing **Location** 2m NE on A5036
Hotel ★★★★ 73% HL Suites Hotel Knowsley, Ribblers Lane, KNOWSLEY ☎ 0151 549 2222 📄 0151 549 1116   101 en suite

BROMBOROUGH   Map 7 SJ38

Bromborough Golf Club Raby Hall Rd CH63 0NW
☎ 0151 334 2155 📄 0151 334 7300
e-mail: enquiries@bromboroughgolfclub.org.uk
web: www.bromboroughgolfclub.org.uk

Parkland course.

*18 Holes, 6650yds, Par 72, SSS 72, Course record 65.
Club membership 800.*

Visitors contact for details. **Societies** booking required. **Green Fees** not confirmed **Course Designer** J Hassall/Hawtree & Son **Prof** Geoff Berry **Facilities** 🍴 🍽 🏌 🖥 🛋 🔧 🎯 **Conf** Corporate Hospitality Days **Location** 0.5m W of Station
Hotel ★★★★ 79% HL Thornton Hall Hotel and Spa, Neston Road, THORNTON HOUGH ☎ 0151 336 3938 & 353 3717 📄 0151 336 7864   63 en suite

CALDY   Map 7 SJ28

Caldy Golf Club Links Hey Rd CH48 1NB
☎ 0151 625 5660 📄 0151 625 7394
e-mail: golfcaldygc@btconnect.com
web: www.caldygolfclub.co.uk

A heathland and clifftop links course situated on the estuary of the River Dee with many of the fairways running parallel to the river. Of championship length, the course offers excellent golf all year, but is subject to variable winds that noticeably alter the day-to-day playing of each hole. There are excellent views of the Welsh Hills.

*18 Holes, 6707yds, Par 72, SSS 73, Course record 65.
Club membership 900.*

Visitors Mon, Thu, Fri & Sun except BHs. Booking required. **Societies** booking required. **Green Fees** not confirmed **Course Designer** J Braid **Prof** A Gibbons **Facilities** 🍴 🍽 🏌 🖥 🛋 🔧 🍺 🎯 **Leisure** ball hire & collection **Conf** Corporate Hospitality Days **Location** A540 (Thurstaston to West Kirby), take exit for Caldy at rdbt, club signed
Hotel ★★★★ 79% HL Thornton Hall Hotel and Spa, Neston Road, THORNTON HOUGH ☎ 0151 336 3938 & 353 3717 📄 0151 336 7864   63 en suite

EASTHAM
Map 7 SJ38

Eastham Lodge Golf Club 117 Ferry Rd CH62 0AP
☎ 0151 327 3003 📄 0151 327 7574
e-mail: easthamlodge.g.c@btinternet.com
web: www.easthamlodgegolfclub.co.uk

A parkland course with many mature trees. Most holes have a subtle dog-leg to left or right. The 1st hole requires an accurate drive to open up the green which is guarded on the right by a stand of pine trees.

18 Holes, 5436yds, Par 68, SSS 66, Course record 63. Club membership 800.

Visitors Mon-Sun & BHs. Booking required. Handicap certificate. Dress code. **Societies** booking required. **Green Fees** £30 per round **Course Designer** Hawtree/D Hemstock **Prof** N Sargent **Facilities** ⊕ ⏣ 🍽 ⬚ 🏐 ⚑ 🏠 ⚐ ⚑ **Leisure** snooker **Conf** facs Corporate Hospitality Days **Location** 1.5m N, off A41 to Wirral Metropolitan College Country Park
Hotel ★★★ 74% HL Brook Meadow, Health Lane, CHILDER THORNTON ☎ 0151 339 9350 📄 0151 347 4221 25 en suite

FORMBY
Map 7 SD30

Formby Golf Club Golf Rd L37 1LQ
☎ 01704 872164 📄 01704 833028
e-mail: info@formbygolfclub.co.uk
web: www.formbygolfclub.co.uk

Championship seaside links through sandhills and pine trees. Partly sheltered from the wind by high dunes it features firm, springy turf, fast seaside greens and natural sandy bunkers. Well drained it plays well throughout the year. Host to four Amateur Championships.

18 Holes, 7028yds, Par 72, SSS 74, Course record 66. Club membership 650.

Visitors Mon-Sun & BHs. Booking required. Handicap certificate. Dress code **Societies** booking required. **Green Fees** £110 per day/round (£130 weekends) **Course Designer** Park/Colt **Prof** Andrew Witherup **Facilities** ⊕ 🍽 ⏣ ⬚ 🏐 ⚑ 🏠 ◇ ⚐ ⚑ **Conf** facs Corporate Hospitality Days **Location** N of town next to Freshfield railway station
Hotel ★★★★ 75% HL Formby Hall Golf Resort & Spa, Southport Old Road, FORMBY ☎ 01704 875699 📄 01704 832134 62 en suite

Formby Hall Resort & Spa Southport Old Rd L37 0AB
☎ 01704 875699 📄 01704 832134
e-mail: golf@formbyhallresort.co.uk
web: www.formbyhallresort.co.uk

A spectacular parkland course with links style bunkers. American style design with water on 16 holes. Generous sized fairways with large undulating greens, many of which are protected by water.

Old Course: 18 Holes, 7081yds, Par 72, Course record 64. Club membership 750.

Visitors Mon-Sun & BHs. Booking required. Handicap certificate at peak times. Dress code. **Societies** booking required. **Green Fees** not confirmed **Course Designer** Alan Higgens **Prof** Mark Williams **Facilities** ⊕ 🍽 ⏣ ⬚ 🏐 ⚑ 🏠 ⚐ ◇ ⚐ 🏌 ⚐ ⚑ **Leisure** heated indoor swimming pool, sauna, gymnasium, 9 hole 3 course (27 holes in total), clay pigeon shooting, paintball, archery **Conf** facs Corporate Hospitality Days **Location** 0.5m off A565 Formby bypass, opp RAF Woodvale
Hotel ★★★★ 75% HL Formby Hall Golf Resort & Spa, Southport Old Road, FORMBY ☎ 01704 875699 📄 01704 832134 62 en suite

Formby Ladies Golf Club Golf Rd L37 1YH
☎ 01704 873493 📄 01704 874127
e-mail: secretary@formbyladiesgolfclub.co.uk
web: www.formbyladiesgolfclub.co.uk

Seaside links - one of the few independent ladies' clubs in the country. The course has contrasting hard-hitting holes in flat country and tricky holes in sandhills and woods.

18 Holes, 5374yds, Par 71, SSS 72, Course record 60. Club membership 350.

Visitors Mon-Wed, Fri-Sun except BHs. Dress code. **Societies** booking required. **Green Fees** £52 per day (£60 weekends) **Prof** Andrew Witherup **Facilities** ⊕ ⏣ ⬚ 🏐 ⚑ 🏠 ⚐ 🏌 **Conf** Corporate Hospitality Days **Location** N of town centre
Hotel ★★★★ 75% HL Formby Hall Golf Resort & Spa, Southport Old Road, FORMBY ☎ 01704 875699 📄 01704 832134 62 en suite

HESWALL
Map 7 SJ28

Heswall Golf Club Cottage Ln CH60 8PB
☎ 0151 342 1237 📄 0151 342 6140
web: www.heswallgolfclub.com

18 Holes, 6556yds, Par 72, SSS 72, Course record 62.

Course Designer McKenzie/Ebert **Location** 1m S off A540
Telephone for further details
Hotel ★★★★ 79% HL Thornton Hall Hotel and Spa, Neston Road, THORNTON HOUGH ☎ 0151 336 3938 & 353 3717 📄 0151 336 7864 63 en suite

HOYLAKE
Map 7 SJ28

Hoylake Golf Club Carr Ln, Municipal Links CH47 4BG
☎ 0151 632 2956
web: www.hoylakegolfclub.com

Flat, generally windy semi-links course. Tricky fairways, with some very deep bunkers.

18 Holes, 6313yds, Par 70, SSS 70, Course record 63. Club membership 303.

Visitors Mon-Sun & BHs. Booking required weekends & BHs. Dress code. **Societies** booking required. **Green Fees** £11.50 per round 📱 **Course Designer** James Braid **Prof** Simon Hooton **Facilities** ⬚ 🏐 ⚑ 🏠 ⚐ ⚐ 🚗 ⚑ **Location** SW of town off A540
Hotel ★★★ 78% HL Leasowe Castle, Leasowe Road, MORETON ☎ 0151 606 9191 📄 0151 678 5551 47 en suite

ROYAL LIVERPOOL

MERSEYSIDE - HOYLAKE - MAP 7 SJ28

Built in 1869 on the site of a former racecourse, this world-famous championship course was one of the first seaside courses to be established in England. In 1921 Hoylake was the scene of the first international match between the US and Britain, now known as the Walker Cup. Over the years, golfing enthusiasts have come to Hoylake to witness 18 amateur championships and 11 Open Championships, the latest being in 2006. Visitors playing on this historic course can expect a challenging match, with crosswinds, deep bunkers and hollows, all set against the backdrop of stunning Welsh hills. Watch out for the 8th hole, which saw the great Bobby Jones take an 8 on this par 5 on the way to his famous Grand Slam in 1930. The club will host the 2012 Women's British Open and the 2014 British Open Championship.

Meols Dr CH47 4AL ☎ 0151 632 3101 & 632 3102 🖹 0151 632 6737
e-mail: secretary@royal-liverpool-golf.com **web:** www.royal-liverpool-golf.com
18 Holes, 6452yds, Par 72, SSS 71.
Visitors contact for details. **Societies** booking required. **Green Fees** Contact club for details **Course Designer** R Chambers/G Morris/D Steel/M Hawtree **Prof** John Heggarty **Facilities** ⑪ 🖢 ☑ 🕎 🏊 📤 🔌 🏌
🏴 **Conf** facs Corporate Hospitality Days **Location** SW side of town on A540
Hotel ★★★ 78% HL Leasowe Castle, Leasowe Road, MORETON ☎ 0151 606 9191 🖹 0151 678 5551 47 en suite

Royal Liverpool Golf Club see page 177
Meols Dr CH47 4AL
☎ 0151 632 3101 & 632 3102 📄 0151 632 6737
e-mail: secretary@royal-liverpool-golf.com
web: www.royal-liverpool-golf.com

HUYTON   Map 7 SJ49

Huyton & Prescot Golf Club Hurst Park, Huyton Ln
L36 1UA
☎ 0151 489 3948 📄 0151 489 0797
e-mail: handpgolfclub@btconnect.com
web: www.huytonandprescotgolf.co.uk
The easy walking parkland course provides excellent golf.
18 Holes, 5900yds, Par 68, SSS 68, Course record 62.
Club membership 700.
Visitors Contact professional for details. **Societies** booking required.
Green Fees £35 per day midweek, £40 per round weekends & BHs
Course Designer James Braid **Prof** John Fisher **Facilities** ⑰ 🍴 ⅃
⌷ 🍴 ⚲ 🖿 ✂ **Conf** facs **Location** 1.5m NE off B5199
Hotel ★★★★ 73% HL Suites Hotel Knowsley, Ribblers Lane,
KNOWSLEY ☎ 0151 549 2222 📄 0151 549 1116 101 en suite

LIVERPOOL   Map 7 SJ39

See also **Blundellsands**

Allerton Park Golf Club Allerton Manor Golf Estate,
Allerton Rd L18 3JT
☎ 0151 428 7490 📄 0151 428 7490
Parkland course.
18 Holes, 5494yds, Par 67, SSS 66.
Visitors Mon-Sun & BHs. Booking required. Dress code.
Societies booking required. **Green Fees** £10.50 (£12 weekends & BHs)
Prof Barry Large **Facilities** ⅃ ⌷ 🍴 🖿 ☝ ✂ **Leisure** 9 hole
par 3 course. **Location** 5.5m SE of city centre off A562, 3m from John
Lennon Airport
Hotel ★★★ 78% HL Best Western Alicia Hotel, 3 Aigburth Drive,
Sefton Park, LIVERPOOL ☎ 0151 727 4411 📄 0151 727 6752
41 en suite

The Childwall Golf Club Naylors Rd, Gateacre L27 2YB
☎ 0151 487 0654 📄 0151 487 0654
e-mail: office@childwallgolfclub.co.uk
web: www.childwallgolfclub.co.uk
Parkland golf is played here over a testing course, where accuracy
from the tee is well-rewarded. The course is very popular with
visiting societies for the clubhouse has many amenities. Course
designed by James Braid.
18 Holes, 6597yds, Par 72, SSS 72, Course record 64.
Club membership 650.
Visitors Mon-Fri except BHs. Booking required. Handicap certificate.
Dress code. **Societies** booking required. **Green Fees** not confirmed
Course Designer James Braid **Prof** Nigel M Parr **Facilities** ⑰ 🍴
by prior arrangement ⅃ ⌷ 🍴 ⚲ 🖿 ☝ ✂ **Conf** facs
Corporate Hospitality Days **Location** 7m E of city centre off B5178
Hotel ★★★ 78% HL Best Western Alicia Hotel, 3 Aigburth Drive,
Sefton Park, LIVERPOOL ☎ 0151 727 4411 📄 0151 727 6752
41 en suite

Lee Park Golf Club Childwall Valley Rd L27 3YA
☎ 0151 487 3882 📄 0151 498 4666
e-mail: lee.park@virgin.net
web: www.leepark.co.uk

Award winning, well-presented, easy walking parkland course. A test
for the short game, being in the right position to attack the pins is a
premium.
18 Holes, 5959yds, Par 70, SSS 69, Course record 66.
Club membership 600.
Visitors Mon, Wed-Sat & BHs. **Societies** booking required. **Green
Fees** £40 per day (£45 Sat & BHs) ⊕ **Course Designer** Frank
Pennick **Prof** Chris Crowder **Facilities** ⑰ 🍴 ⅃ ⌷ 🍴 ⚲
✂ **Leisure** snooker room **Conf** facs Corporate Hospitality Days
Location M62 junct 6/M57 junct 1, take A5080 towards Huyton. Turn
left at 2nd set of lights into Wheathill Rd. After 1m turn left at 1st set
of lights into Childwall Valley Rd, club on right
Hotel ★★★ 78% HL Best Western Alicia Hotel, 3 Aigburth Drive,
Sefton Park, LIVERPOOL ☎ 0151 727 4411 📄 0151 727 6752
41 en suite

West Derby Golf Club Yew Tree Ln, West Derby L12 9HQ
☎ 0151 254 1034 📄 0151 259 0505
e-mail: pmilne@westderbygc.freeserve.co.uk
web: www.westderbygc.co.uk
A parkland course always in first-class condition, and flat, giving
easy walking. The fairways are well-wooded. Care must be taken
on the first nine holes to avoid the brook which guards many of the
greens.
18 Holes, 6275yds, Par 72, SSS 70, Course record 65.
Club membership 550.
Visitors Mon, Wed-Fri except BHs. Dress code. **Societies** booking
required. **Green Fees** not confirmed ⊕ **Prof** Stuart Danchin
Facilities ⑰ 🍴 ⅃ ⌷ 🍴 ⚲ 🖿 ✂ **Conf** facs Corporate
Hospitality Days **Location** 4.5m E of city centre off A57
Hotel ★★★★ 73% HL Suites Hotel Knowsley, Ribblers Lane,
KNOWSLEY ☎ 0151 549 2222 📄 0151 549 1116 101 en suite

Save on Hotels. Book at **theAA.com/hotel**

MERSEYSIDE

ENGLAND

Woolton Golf Club Doe Park, Speke Rd, Woolton L25 7TZ
☎ 0151 486 2298 📠 0151 486 1664
e-mail: golf@wooltongolf.co.uk
web: www.wooltongolfclub.com

Parkland course providing a good round of golf for all standards. A members-owned course that includes two par 5s and five par 3s.

18 Holes, 5747yds, Par 69, SSS 68. Club membership 600.

Visitors Mon-Fri. Limited play weekends & BHs. Booking required. Handicap certificate. Dress code. **Societies** booking required. **Green Fees** £30 per 18 holes (£40 weekends) **Prof** Dave Thompson **Facilities** ⊕ ⊙⏐ ⓛ ⌑ ⍨ ⎐ ⌂ ⌀ ⌀ **Leisure** indoor teaching unit **Conf** facs Corporate Hospitality Days **Location** 7m SE of city centre off A562, near Liverpool Airport
Hotel ★★★ 78% HL Best Western Alicia Hotel, 3 Aigburth Drive, Sefton Park, LIVERPOOL ☎ 0151 727 4411 📠 0151 727 6752 41 en suite

---

NEWTON-LE-WILLOWS   Map 7 SJ59

Haydock Park Golf Club Newton Ln WA12 0HX
☎ 01925 228525 📠 01925 224984
e-mail: secretary@haydockparkgc.co.uk
web: www.haydockparkgc.co.uk

A well-wooded parkland course, close to the well-known racecourse, and always in excellent condition. The pleasant undulating fairways offer some very interesting golf and the 6th, 9th, 11th and 13th holes are particularly testing.

18 Holes, 6073yds, Par 70, SSS 69, Course record 65. Club membership 630.

Visitors Mon-Sun except BHs. Booking required. Dress code. **Societies** welcome. **Green Fees** £35 per day, £32 per round **Course Designer** James Braid **Prof** Peter Kenwright **Facilities** ⊕ ⊙⏐ ⓛ ⌑ ⍨ ⎐ ⌂ ⌀ **Conf** Corporate Hospitality Days **Location** 0.75m NE off A49
Hotel ★★★ 78% HL Holiday Inn Haydock M6 Jct 23, Lodge Lane, Newton Le Willows, HAYDOCK ☎ 0871 942 9039 📠 01942 718419 136 en suite

---

RAINHILL   Map 7 SJ49

Eccleston Park Golf Club Rainhill Rd L35 4PG
☎ 0151 493 0033 📠 0151 493 0044
e-mail: ecclestonpark@crown-golf.co.uk
web: www.ecclestonparkgolf.co.uk

A tough parkland course designed to test all golfing abilities. Strategically placed water features, bunkers and mounding enhance the beauty and difficulty of this manicured course.

18 Holes, 6477yds, Par 71, SSS 70. Club membership 800.

Visitors Mon-Sun & BHs. Booking required. Dress code. **Societies** booking required. **Green Fees** not confirmed **Prof** Bryan Joelson-Mulhall **Facilities** ⊕ ⊙⏐ ⓛ ⌑ ⍨ ⎐ ⌂ ⎈ ⌀ **Conf** facs Corporate Hospitality Days **Location** M62 junct 7, A57 to Prescot, at hump bridge right at lights, course 1m on left
Hotel ★★★★ 73% HL Suites Hotel Knowsley, Ribblers Lane, KNOWSLEY ☎ 0151 549 2222 📠 0151 549 1116 101 en suite

---

ST HELENS   Map 7 SJ59

Grange Park Golf Club Prescot Rd WA10 3AD
☎ 01744 26318 📠 01744 26318
e-mail: secretary@grangeparkgolfclub.co.uk
web: www.grangeparkgolfclub.co.uk

Possibly one of the finest tests of inland golf in the northwest, set in 150 acres only a short distance from the centre of town. While not too long, the contours of the fairways, small greens and penal rough demand the best from players. A wide shot-making repertoire is required to gain the best score possible.

18 Holes, 6446yds, Par 72, SSS 71, Course record 65. Club membership 730.

Visitors Mon, Wed-Fri. Limited play at weekends & BHs. Booking required Tue, Sun & BHs. Dress code. **Societies** welcome. **Green Fees** not confirmed **Course Designer** James Braid **Prof** Paul Roberts **Facilities** ⊕ ⊙⏐ ⓛ ⌑ ⍨ ⎐ ⌂ ⌀ **Conf** facs Corporate Hospitality Days **Location** 1.5m SW on A58
Hotel ★★★★ 73% HL Suites Hotel Knowsley, Ribblers Lane, KNOWSLEY ☎ 0151 549 2222 📠 0151 549 1116 101 en suite

Houghwood Golf Billinge Hill, Crank Rd, Crank WA11 8RL
☎ 01744 894444 & 894754 📠 01744 894754
e-mail: houghwoodgolf@btinternet.com
web: www.houghwoodgolfclub.co.uk

From the course's highest point, the 12th tee, there are panoramic views over the Lancashire plain to the Welsh hills. All greens built to USGA specification with a permanent track around the entire course for buggies and trolleys.

18 Holes, 6268yds, Par 70, SSS 70, Course record 64. Club membership 580.

Visitors Mon-Sun & BHs. Booking required weekends. Dress code. **Societies** booking required. **Green Fees** £31 per round (£42 weekends & BHs) **Course Designer** Neville Pearson **Prof** Paul Dickenson **Facilities** ⊕ ⊙⏐ ⓛ ⌑ ⍨ ⎐ ⌂ ⎈ ⌀ **Leisure** snooker table **Conf** facs Corporate Hospitality Days **Location** M6, 3.5m N of St Helens off B5205
Hotel ★★★★ 76% HL Thistle Haydock, Penny Lane, HAYDOCK ☎ 0871 376 9044 📠 0871 376 9144 137 en suite

Sherdley Park Golf Course Sherdley Rd WA9 5DE
☎ 01744 813149 ▤ 01744 817967
e-mail: sherdleyparkgolfcourse@sthelens.gov.uk
web: www.sthelens.gov.uk/goactive
Fairly hilly, challenging, pay-and-play parkland course with ponds in places. Excellent greens.

18 Holes, 5912yds, Par 71, SSS 68.
Visitors Booking advisable. **Societies** booking required. **Green Fees** £15 per 18 holes (£17 weekends & BHs). Twilight £8.50 (£6 seniors & juniors) Mon & Tue after 2pm, Wed-Sun after 5pm **Prof** Alan Gibson **Facilities** ⓣ ▐ ♇ ♑ ♨ ♙ ⌂ ㏗ ♂ ☙ **Conf**
Corporate Hospitality Days **Location** 2m S of St Helens off A570
Hotel ★★★ 78% HL Holiday Inn Haydock M6 Jct 23, Lodge Lane, Newton Le Willows, HAYDOCK ☎ 0871 942 9039 ▤ 01942 718419 136 en suite

SOUTHPORT   Map 7 SD31

The Hesketh Golf Club Cockle Dick's Ln, off Cambridge Rd PR9 9QQ
☎ 01704 536897 ▤ 01704 539250
e-mail: secretary@heskethgolfclub.co.uk
web: www.heskethgolfclub.co.uk
The Hesketh is the oldest of the six clubs in Southport, founded in 1885. Set at the northern end of south-west Lancashire's dune system, the course sets a unique challenge with half of the holes threaded through tall dunes while the other holes border the Ribble estuary. The course is next to a renowned bird reserve and across the estuary are fine views of the mountains of Lancashire, Cumbria and Yorkshire. Used as a final qualifying course for the Open Championship.

18 Holes, 6691yds, Par 72, SSS 73, Course record 66.
Club membership 700.
Visitors Dress code. **Societies** booking required. **Green Fees** £80 per day, £60 per round (£80 per round weekends & BHs) **Course Designer** J F Morris/M Hawtree **Prof** Scott Astin **Facilities** ⓣ ♑
▐ ♇ ♨ ♙ ⌂ ㏗ ♂ ☙ ☙ **Leisure** snooker **Conf**
Corporate Hospitality Days **Location** 1m NE of town centre off A565
Hotel ★★ 74% HL Balmoral Lodge Hotel, 41 Queens Road, SOUTHPORT ☎ 01704 544298 ▤ 01704 501224 15 en suite

Hillside Golf Club Hastings Rd, Hillside PR8 2LU
☎ 01704 567169 ▤ 01704 563192
e-mail: secretary@hillside-golfclub.co.uk
web: www.hillside-golfclub.co.uk
Championship links course with natural hazards open to strong wind. The back nine holes are particularly memorable.

18 Holes, 7029yds, Par 72, SSS 75, Course record 65.
Club membership 700.
Visitors dress code. **Societies** booking required. **Green Fees** not confirmed **Course Designer** Hawtree/Steel **Prof** Brian Seddon
Facilities ⓣ ♑ ▐ ♇ ♨ ♙ ⌂ ㏗ ♂ ☙ ☙ **Conf**
Corporate Hospitality Days **Location** 3m S of town centre on A565
Hotel ★★★ 77% HL Scarisbrick, Lord Street, SOUTHPORT
☎ 01704 543000 ▤ 01704 533335 88 en suite

The Royal Birkdale Golf Club see page 181
Waterloo Rd, Birkdale PR8 2LX
☎ 01704 552020 ▤ 01704 552021
e-mail: secretary@royalbirkdale.com
web: www.royalbirkdale.com

Southport & Ainsdale Golf Club Bradshaws Ln, Ainsdale PR8 3LG
☎ 01704 578000 ▤ 01704 570896
e-mail: secretary@sandagolfclub.co.uk
web: www.sandagolfclub.co.uk
S and A, as it is known in the north, is another of the fine championship courses for which this part of the country is famed. The club has staged many important events and offers golf of the highest order, including two Ryder Cups and Open Final qualifying.

18 Holes, 6768yds, Par 72, SSS 74, Course record 64.
Club membership 815.
Visitors Mon-Wed & Fri except BHs. Thu after noon, Sun after 1pm, Sat after 3.30pm. Booking required. Dress code. **Societies** booking required. **Green Fees** £80 per 18 holes, £105 per 36 holes (£100 per 18 holes weekends) **Course Designer** James Braid **Prof** Jim Payne **Facilities** ⓣ ♑ ▐ ♇ ♨ ♙ ⌂ ㏗ ♨ ♂ ☙
Conf facs Corporate Hospitality Days **Location** 0.5m S off A565
Hotel ★★★ 74% HL Best Western Royal Clifton Hotel & Spa, Promenade, SOUTHPORT ☎ 01704 533771 ▤ 01704 500657 120 en suite

Southport Old Links Golf Club Moss Ln, Churchtown PR9 7QS
☎ 01704 228207 ▤ 01704 505353
e-mail: secretary@southportoldlinksgolfclub.co.uk
web: www.southportoldlinksgolfclub.co.uk
Seaside course with tree-lined fairways and easy walking. One of the oldest courses in Southport.

9 Holes, 6450yds, Par 72, SSS 71, Course record 68.
Club membership 450.
Visitors Mon, Tue, Thu-Sat except BHs. Booking required. Handicap certificate. Dress code. **Societies** booking required. **Green Fees** not confirmed **Course Designer** James Braid **Prof** Gary Copeman
Facilities ♑ ▐ ♇ ♨ ♙ ⌂ ㏗ ♂ **Conf** Corporate Hospitality Days **Location** NW of town centre off A5267
Hotel ★★ 74% HL Balmoral Lodge Hotel, 41 Queens Road, SOUTHPORT ☎ 01704 544298 ▤ 01704 501224 15 en suite

WALLASEY   Map 7 SJ29

Bidston Golf Club Bidston Link Rd CH44 2HR
☎ 0151 638 3412
e-mail: linda@bidstongolf.co.uk
web: www.bidstongolf.co.uk
Flat, easy walking parkland with westerly winds. The course will prove a challenge to the low handicapper, but will not overwhelm the beginner.

18 Holes, 6153yds, Par 70, SSS 70, Course record 60.
Club membership 600.
Visitors Mon-Sun & BHs. Booking required weekends & BHs. Dress code. **Societies** welcome. **Green Fees** not confirmed **Prof** Alan Norwood **Facilities** ⓣ ♑ ▐ ♇ ♨ ♙ ⌂ ㏗ ♂
Location M53 junct 1, 0.5m W off A551
Hotel ★★★ 78% HL Leasowe Castle, Leasowe Road, MORETON
☎ 0151 606 9191 ▤ 0151 678 5551 47 en suite

ROYAL BIRKDALE

MERSEYSIDE - SOUTHPORT - MAP 7 SD31

Founded in 1889, the Royal Birkdale is considered by many to be the ultimate championship venue, having hosted every major event in the game including nine Open Championships, two Ryder Cup matches, the Walker Cup, the Curtis Cup and many amateur events. The 1st hole provides an immediate taste of what is to come, requiring a well-placed drive to avoid a bunker, water hazard and out-of-bounds and leave a reasonably clear view of the green. The 10th, the first of the inward nine is unique in that it is the only hole to display the significant fairway undulations one would expect from a classic links course. The 12th is the most spectacular of the short holes on the course, and is considered by Tom Watson to be one of the best par 3s in the world; tucked away in the sand hills it continues to claim its fair share of disasters. The approach on the final hole is arguably the most recognisable in golf with the distinctive clubhouse designed to appear like an ocean cruise liner rising out of the sand hills. It's a par 5 for mere mortals, and played as a par 4 in the Open, but it will provide a memorable finish to any round of golf.

Waterloo Rd, Birkdale PR8 2LX ☎ 01704 552020 🖷 01704 552021
e-mail: secretary@royalbirkdale.com **web:** www.royalbirkdale.com
18 Holes, 6381yds, Par 72, SSS 73, Course record 63. Club membership 800.
Visitors Mon, Wed & Thu except BHs. Tue pm. Fri & Sun am. Booking required. Handicap certificate. Dress code.
Societies booking required. **Green Fees** Apr-Sep £175 per round (£205 weekends). Winter £125/£160.
Prices include soup and sandwiches **Course Designer** Hawtree **Prof** Brian Hodgkinson **Facilities** ⑪ ⑩
by prior arrangement 🏌 🛒 🍴 ⚖ 🏪 ⛳ ✂ 🏌 **Conf** Corporate Hospitality Days **Location** 1.75m S of town centre on A565
Hotel ★★★ 77% HL Scarisbrick, Lord Street, SOUTHPORT ☎ 01704 543000 🖷 01704 533335 88 en suite

ENGLAND

Leasowe Golf Club Moreton CH46 3RD
☎ 0151 677 5852 📠 0151 641 8519
web: www.leasowegolfclub.co.uk
18 Holes, 6276yds, Par 71, SSS 70.
Course Designer John Ball Jnr **Location** M53 junct 1, 2m W on A551
Telephone for further details
Hotel ★★★ 78% HL Leasowe Castle, Leasowe Road, MORETON
☎ 0151 606 9191 📠 0151 678 5551 47 en suite

Wallasey Golf Club Bayswater Rd CH45 8LA
☎ 0151 691 1024 📠 0151 638 8988
e-mail: wallaseygc@aol.com
web: www.wallaseygolf.com
A well-established links course, adjacent to the Irish Sea. A true test of golf due in part to the prevailing westerly winds and the natural undulating terrain. Spectacular views across Liverpool Bay and the Welsh hills.
18 Holes, 6508yds, Par 72, SSS 73, Course record 66.
Club membership 650.
Visitors Sun-Fri & BHs. Booking required. Dress code. **Societies** booking required. **Green Fees** not confirmed **Course Designer** Tom Morris **Prof** Mike Adams **Facilities** 🏌 🍽 by prior arrangement 🛒 🛋
🍴 🏖 🏚 🏌 **Conf** Corporate Hospitality Days **Location** N of town centre, M53 junct 1, take A554 to New Brighton
Hotel ★★★ 80% HL Grove House, Grove Road, WALLASEY
☎ 0151 639 3947 & 630 4558 📠 0151 639 0028 14 en suite

Warren Golf Club Grove Rd CH45 0JA
☎ 0151 639 8323
web: www.warrengc.freeserve.co.uk
9 Holes, 5854yds, Par 72, SSS 68, Course record 68.
Location N of town centre off A554
Telephone for further details
Hotel ★★★ 78% HL Leasowe Castle, Leasowe Road, MORETON
☎ 0151 606 9191 📠 0151 678 5551 47 en suite

NORFOLK

BARNHAM BROOM
Map 5 TG00

Barnham Broom Hotel, Golf & Spa Honingham Rd NR9 4DD
☎ 01603 757505 & 759393 📠 01603 758224
e-mail: shop@barnham-broom.co.uk
web: www.barnham-broom.co.uk
Parkland courses of contrasting character, with mature trees, meandering through the Yare Valley.
Valley Course: 18 Holes, 6483yds, Par 72, SSS 71.
Hill Course: 18 Holes, 6495yds, Par 71, SSS 71.
Club membership 500.
Visitors Mon-Sun & BHs. Booking required. Dress code. **Societies** welcome. **Green Fees** Valley & Hill £40 (£50 weekends). Twilight & off peak from £15 **Course Designer** Frank Pennink **Prof** Alan Hemsley **Facilities** 🏌 🍽 🛒 🛋 🍴 🏖 🍷
🌿 🏌 🏚 🏌 **Leisure** hard tennis courts, heated indoor swimming pool, squash, sauna, gymnasium, 3 academy holes, golf school, squash tuition **Conf facs** Corporate Hospitality Days **Location** off A47 at Honingham
Hotel ★★★ 74% HL Barnham Broom Hotel, Golf & Restaurant, BARNHAM BROOM ☎ 01603 759393 📠 01603 758224 46 en suite

BAWBURGH
Map 5 TG10

Bawburgh Golf Club Glen Lodge, Marlingford Rd NR9 3LU
☎ 01603 740404 📠 01603 740403
e-mail: info@bawburgh.com
web: www.bawburgh.com
Undulating course, mixture of parkland and heathland. The main feature is a large hollow that meanders down to the River Yare creating many interesting tee and green locations. Excellent 18th hole to finish requiring a long accurate second shot to clear the lake in front of the elevated green. 9 hole course opened in 2010. Very tricky stroke index one, par 6 for ladies.
Bawburgh Course: 18 Holes, 6720yds, Par 72, SSS 72, Course record 67.
Easton Course: 9 Holes, 3129yds, Par 36, SSS 35.
Club membership 600.
Visitors Mon-Sun & BHs. Booking required. **Societies** booking required. **Green Fees** £25 per 18 holes, £10 per 9 holes, £5 juniors **Course Designer** The Barnard Family **Prof** Mark Spooner **Facilities** 🏌 🍽 by prior arrangement 🛒 🛋 🍴 🏖 🏚 🏌 🏌 **Conf** facs Corporate Hospitality Days **Location** S of Royal Norfolk Showground, off A47 to Bawburgh (signed to Park & Ride)
Hotel ★★★★ 76% HL Park Farm Hotel, HETHERSETT
☎ 01603 810264 📠 01603 812104 53 en suite

BRANCASTER
Map 9 TF74

Royal West Norfolk Golf Club PE31 8AX
☎ 01485 210087 📠 01485 210087
e-mail: secretary@rwngc.org
web: www.rwngc.org
A fine links laid out in grand manner characterised by sleepered greens, superb cross bunkers and salt marshes. The tranquil surroundings include a harbour, the sea, farmland and marshland, inhabited by many rare birds. A great part of the year the club is cut off by tidal flooding that restricts the amount of play.
Brancaster: 18 Holes, 6457yds, Par 71, SSS 71.
Club membership 910.
Visitors Mon-Fri except BHs. Booking required. Handicap certificate. **Societies** booking required. **Green Fees** £110 per day singles, £85 per round (£60 per round, £75 per day foursomes) **Course Designer** Holcombe-Ingleby **Prof** S Rayner **Facilities** 🏌 🛒 🛋 🍴 🏖 🏚 🏌 🌿 🏚 🏌 🏌 **Location** off A149 in Brancaster 1m to seafront
Hotel ★★★ 79% HL White Horse, BRANCASTER STAITHE
☎ 01485 210262 📠 01485 210930 15 en suite

CROMER
Map 9 TG24

Royal Cromer Golf Club 145 Overstrand Rd NR27 0JH
☎ 01263 512884 📠 01263 512430
web: www.royalcromergolfclub.com
18 Holes, 6508yds, Par 72, SSS 72, Course record 67.
Course Designer J H Taylor **Location** 1m E on B1159
Telephone for further details
Hotel ★★★ 75% HL The Cliftonville, Seafront, CROMER
☎ 01263 512543 📠 01263 515700 30 en suite

DENVER　　　　　　　　　Map 5 TF60

Ryston Park Golf Club Ely Rd PE38 0HH
☎ 01366 382133 📄 01366 383834
e-mail: rystonparkgc@talktalkbusiness.net
web: www.club-noticeboard.co.uk
Mature parkland course with two challenging par 4s to open. Water comes into play on holes 5, 6 and 7. The course is well wooded with an abundance of wildlife.
Ryston Park: 9 Holes, 6330yds, Par 70, SSS 71, Course record 66. Club membership 330.
Visitors Mon-Fri except BHs. Booking required Wed & Thu. Dress code. **Societies** booking required. **Green Fees** £35 per day, £25 per 18 holes, £15 per 9 holes ⊛ **Course Designer** James Braid **Facilities** ⓦ 🍽 by prior arrangement 🛍 ⌷ 🍴 🏌 ✎ **Conf** facs Corporate Hospitality Days **Location** 0.5m S of Downham Market southern bypass on A10
Hotel ★★★ 73% HL Castle Hotel, High Street, DOWNHAM MARKET ☎ 01366 384311 📄 01366 384311 12 en suite

DEREHAM　　　　　　　　Map 9 TF91

Dereham Golf Club Quebec Rd NR19 2DS
☎ 01362 695900
e-mail: office@derehamgolfclub.com
web: www.derehamgolfclub.com
Friendly club with 9 hole parkland course with 17 different tees.
9 Holes, 6272yds, Par 71, SSS 70, Course record 64. Club membership 400.
Visitors contact club for details. **Societies** booking required. **Green Fees** £35 per day, £20 per round. £12.50 per 9 holes ⊛ **Prof** Neil Allsebrook **Facilities** ⓦ 🍽 🛍 ⌷ 🍴 🏌 🏨 🚌 ✎ **Conf** Corporate Hospitality Days **Location** N of town centre off B1110
Hotel ★★★★ 74% HL Barnham Broom Hotel, Golf & Restaurant, BARNHAM BROOM ☎ 01603 759393 📄 01603 758224 46 en suite

The Norfolk Golf & Country Club Hingham Rd NR9 4QQ
☎ 01362 850297 📄 01362 850614
web: www.the norfolkgolfclub.co.uk
18 Holes, 6609yds, Par 72, SSS 72, Course record 66.
Location off B1135
Telephone for further details
Hotel ★★★★ 74% HL Barnham Broom Hotel, Golf & Restaurant, BARNHAM BROOM ☎ 01603 759393 📄 01603 758224 46 en suite

FRITTON　　　　　　　　　Map 5 TG40

Caldecott Hall Golf & Leisure Caldecott Hall, Beccles Rd NR31 9EY
☎ 01493 488488 📄 01493 488561
web: www.caldecotthall.co.uk

Parkland/links style course with testing dog-leg fairways.
Main Course: 18 Holes, 6685yards, Par 73, SSS 72, Course record 67. Club membership 500.
Visitors Mon-Sun & BHs. Dress code. **Societies** booking required. **Green Fees** £36 per day, £29 per round (£41/£30 weekends) **Prof** Mark Tungate **Facilities** ⓦ 🍽 🛍 ⌷ 🍴 🏌 🏨 ◇ 🚌 ✎ 🏌 **Leisure** heated indoor swimming pool, gymnasium, 18 hole par 3 course, spa **Conf** facs Corporate Hospitality Days **Location** on A143
Hotel ★★★ 79% HL Caldecott Hall Golf & Leisure, Caldecott Hall, Beccles Road, FRITTON ☎ 01493 488488 📄 01493 488561 8 en suite

GORLESTON ON SEA　　　　Map 5 TG50

Gorleston Golf Club Warren Rd NR31 6JT
☎ 01493 661911 📄 01493 661911
e-mail: manager@gorlestongolfclub.co.uk
web: www.gorlestongolfclub.co.uk
Clifftop course, the most easterly in the British Isles. One of the outstanding features of the course is the 7th hole, which was rescued from cliff erosion about 20 years ago. The green, only 8yds from the cliff edge, is at the mercy of the prevailing winds so club selection is critical.
18 Holes, 6341yds, Par 71, SSS 71, Course record 66. Club membership 800.
Visitors Mon-Sun & BHs. Booking required weekends & BHs. Handicap certificate preferable. Dress code. **Societies** booking required. **Green Fees** £43 per day, £32 per 18 holes (£48/£38 weekends & BHs) **Course Designer** J H Taylor **Prof** Nick Brown **Facilities** ⓦ 🍽 by prior arrangement 🛍 ⌷ 🍴 🏌 🏨 ✎ **Conf** Corporate Hospitality Days **Location** between Gt Yarmouth and Lowestoft, signed from A12
Hotel ★★★ 67% HL Burlington Palm Hotel, 11 North Drive, GREAT YARMOUTH ☎ 01493 844568 & 842095 📄 01493 331848 70 en suite

GREAT YARMOUTH Map 5 TG50

Great Yarmouth & Caister Golf Club Beach House, Caister-on-Sea NR30 5TD
☎ 01493 728699 📠 01493 728831
e-mail: office@caistergolf.co.uk
web: www.caistergolf.co.uk

A traditional links-style course played over tight and undulating fairways and partly set amongst sand dunes with gorse and marram grass. Well drained with excellent greens. A challenge for golfers of all abilities.

18 Holes, 6330yds, Par 70, SSS 71, Course record 65. Club membership 600.

Visitors Mon-Sun & BHs. Booking required. Dress code.
Societies booking required. **Green Fees** £30 weekdays. Phone for special rates **Course Designer** H Colt **Prof** Gary Potter **Facilities** ⓘ
🍴 🛍 ♿ 🍺 🏌 🏠 ⛳ 🏌 **Leisure** snooker **Conf**
Corporate Hospitality Days **Location** 0.5m N off A149, at S end of Caister
Hotel ★★★★ 75% HL Imperial, North Drive, GREAT YARMOUTH
☎ 01493 842000 📠 01493 852229 39 en suite

See advert on opposite page

HEACHAM Map 9 TF63

Heacham Manor Golf Club & Hotel Hunstanton Rd PE31 7JX
☎ 01485 536030 📠 01485 533815
e-mail: golf@heacham-manor.co.uk
web: www.heacham-manor.co.uk

This championship length course has been designed to incorporate the natural features of the surrounding landscape. With two rivers and four lakes to negotiate, the course varies between links and parkland styles with views of the Wash. A long course, but with a number of teeing areas on each hole the course is playable for all handicaps. The two rivers are an integral part of several holes and the lakes feature on the 7th hole which demands a long carry of 180 yards straight to the green with water all the way.

Heacham Manor: 18 Holes, 6622yds, Par 72, SSS 72. Club membership 195.

Visitors Mon-Sun & BHs. Booking required. Handicap certificate. Dress code. **Societies** booking required. **Green Fees** £50 per day, £20 per round (£25 per round weekends). Twilight after 3pm weekday £20. Winter £40/£25/£30 **Course Designer** Paul Searle **Prof** Ray Stocker **Facilities** ⓘ 🍴 🛍 ♿ 🍺 🏌 🏠 ⛳ ♢ 🛒 🏌 🏌
Leisure hard tennis courts, fishing, sauna, bowls green **Conf** facs
Corporate Hospitality Days **Location** A149 from King's Lynn by-pass, straight on at lights in Heacham, immediately before approach of hill to Hunstanton left turning signed Heacham, hotel on right
Hotel ★★★ 86% HL Heacham Manor Hotel, Hunstanton Rd, HEACHAM ☎ 01485 536030 & 579800 📠 01485 533815 45 en suite

See advert on opposite page

HUNSTANTON Map 9 TF64

Hunstanton Golf Club Golf Course Rd PE36 6JQ
☎ 01485 532811 📠 01485 532319
e-mail: secretary@hunstantongolfclub.com
web: www.hunstantongolfclub.com

A championship links course set among some of the best natural golfing country in East Anglia. Keep out of the numerous bunkers and master the fast greens to play to your handicap - then you only have the wind to contend with. Good playing conditions all year round.

18 Holes, 6750yds, Par 72, SSS 73, Course record 65. Club membership 675.

Visitors Mon-Sun. Booking required. Handicap certificate. Dress code. **Societies** booking required. **Green Fees** £90 per day, £70 after noon, £60 after 3pm (£95/£75/£60 weekends) **Course Designer** James Braid **Prof** James Dodds **Facilities** ⓘ 🛍 ♿ 🍺 🏌 🏠 ⛳ 🏌 🛒 🏌 🏌 **Location** off A149 in Old Hunstanton, signed

Save on Hotels. Book at **theAA.com/hotel**

NORFOLK

Searles Leisure Resort South Beach Rd PE36 5BB
☎ 01485 536010 📄 01485 533815
e-mail: golf@searles.co.uk
web: www.searles.co.uk/golf-and-country-club.html

This nine-hole par 34 course is designed in a links style and provides generous fairways with good greens. A river runs through the 3rd and 4th holes and the par 5 8th follows the ancient reed bed to finish with the lake-sided par 3 9th in front of the clubhouse. Good views of Hunstanton and the surrounding countryside and a challenge for all standards of golfer.

Searle Resort Course: 9 Holes, 2671yds, Par 34, SSS 33.
Club membership 350.

Visitors Mon-Sun & BHs. Dress code. **Societies** booking required.
Green Fees 18 holes £17, 9 holes £10.50 (£18.50/£11.50 weekends & BHs) **Course Designer** Paul Searle **Prof** Ray Stocker **Facilities** ⊕ 🍴 by prior arrangement 🛍 ☕ 🍽 ♿ 🏪 ⛳ ♦ ♦ 🛺 ♦
🏌 **Leisure** hard tennis courts, outdoor and indoor heated swimming pool, fishing, sauna, gymnasium, bowls green **Conf** facs Corporate Hospitality Days **Location** A149 N to Hunstanton, 2nd left at rdbt, over minirdbt, 1st left signed Sports and Country Club
Hotel ★★★ 82% HL Best Western Le Strange Arms, Golf Course Road, Old Hunstanton, HUNSTANTON ☎ 01485 534411 📄 01485 534724 43 en suite

KING'S LYNN   Map 9 TF62

Eagles Golf Centre 39 School Rd, Tilney All Saints PE34 4RS
☎ 01553 827147 📄 01553 829777
e-mail: shop@eagles-golf-tennis.co.uk
web: www.eagles-golf-tennis.co.uk

Parkland with a variety of trees and shrubs lining the fairways. A large area of water comes into play on several holes.

Main Course: 9 Holes, 4284yds, Par 64, SSS 61.
Club membership 150.

Visitors Mon-Sun & BHs. **Societies** booking required. **Green Fees** 18 holes £15, 9 holes £12. Par 3 18 holes £8.50, 9 holes £5.80 **Course Designer** D W Horn **Prof** Nigel Pickerell **Facilities** ⊕ by prior arrangement 🍴 🛍 ☕ 🍽 ♿ 🏪 ⛳ 🛺 ♦ 🏌
Leisure hard tennis courts, par 3 course **Conf** Corporate Hospitality Days **Location** off A47 at rdbt to Tilney All Saints, between Kings Lynn & Wisbech
Hotel ★★★ 71% HL Stuart House, 35 Goodwins Road, KINGS LYNN ☎ 01553 772169 📄 01553 774788 18 en suite

ENGLAND

King's Lynn Golf Club Castle Rising PE31 6BD
☎ 01553 631654 📄 01553 631036
web: www.club-noticeboard.co.uk

18 Holes, 6609yds, Par 72, SSS 73, Course record 64.
Course Designer Thomas & Alliss **Location** 4m NE off A149
Telephone for further details
Hotel ★★★ 78% HL Best Western Knights Hill, Knights Hill Village, South Wootton, KING'S LYNN ☎ 01553 675566 📄 01553 675568 79 en suite

---

MATTISHALL   Map 9 TG01

Mattishall Golf Course South Green NR20 3JZ
☎ 01362 850111

Mattishall has the distinction of having the longest hole in Norfolk at a very demanding 638 yd par 5.

9 Holes, 6170yds, Par 70. Club membership 120.
Visitors Mon-Sun & BHs. Booking required weekends & BHs.
Societies booking required. **Green Fees** £20 per day, £14 per 18 holes, £10 per 9 holes **Course Designer** B Todd **Facilities** 🍴 🛒
🍴 ⚐ ⚑ ✎ **Location** 0.75m S of Mattishall Church
Hotel ★★★★ 74% HL Barnham Broom Hotel, Golf & Restaurant, BARNHAM BROOM ☎ 01603 759393 📄 01603 758224 46 en suite

---

MIDDLETON   Map 9 TF61

Middleton Hall Golf Club Hall Orchards PE32 1RY
☎ 01553 841800 & 841801   📄 01553 841800
e-mail: enquiries@middletonhallgolfclub.com
web: www.middletonhallgolfclub.com

Natural undulations and mature specimen trees offer a most attractive environment for golf. The architecturally designed course provides a challenge for the competent golfer; there is also a covered floodlit driving range.

18 Holes, 5904yds, Par 71, SSS 69, Course record 71.
Club membership 500.
Visitors Booking advised. Dress code. **Societies** booking required.
Green Fees £40 per day, £25 per round (£40/£30 weekends & BHs)
Course Designer D Scott **Prof** Steve White **Facilities** 🍴 🛒 🛒
🍴 ⚐ 🏠 ⚑ ✎ 🚗 ✎ **Conf** Corporate Hospitality Days
Location 4m from King's Lynn on A47 towards Norwich
Hotel ★★★ 78% HL Best Western Knights Hill, Knights Hill Village, South Wootton, KING'S LYNN ☎ 01553 675566 📄 01553 675568 79 en suite

---

MUNDESLEY   Map 9 TG33

Mundesley Golf Club Links Rd NR11 8ES
☎ 01263 720095   📄 01263 722849
e-mail: manager@mundesleygolfclub.co.uk
web: www.mundesleygolfclub.co.uk

Downland course, undulating with panoramic views. Small fast greens, tight fairways, one mile from the sea.

Mundesley: 9 Holes, 5377yds, Par 68, SSS 66,
Course record 62. Club membership 500.
Visitors Mon-Sun & BHs. Booking required Wed, Sat, Sun & BHs.
Handicap certificate. Dress code. **Societies** booking required. **Green Fees** not confirmed ✉ **Course Designer** Harry Vardon **Prof** Ryan Pudney **Facilities** 🍴 🛒 by prior arrangement 🍴 ⚐ 🍴 ⚑
🏠 ✎ ✎ **Conf** facs Corporate Hospitality Days **Location** W of village off B1159
Hotel ★★★★ GA White House Farm, Knapton, NORTH WALSHAM
☎ 01263 721344 & 07879 475220 3 rooms

NORWICH   Map 5 TG20

Costessey Park Golf Course Old Costessey NR8 5AL
☎ 01603 746333 & 747085   📄 01603 746185
e-mail: cpgc@ljgroup.com
web: www.costesseypark.com

The course lies in the gently contoured Tud Valley, providing players with a number of holes that bring the river and man-made lakes into play. The 1st hole starts a round with a par 3 that requires an accurate drive across the river, to land the ball on a sculptured green beside a reed fringed lake. To end the round at the 18th hole, you need to make a straight drive past the ruined belfry to allow a second shot back over the river to land the ball on a recessed green.

18 Holes, 5881yds, Par 71, SSS 69, Course record 63.
Club membership 400.
Visitors contact course for details. **Societies** booking required. **Green Fees** not confirmed **Prof** Gary Stangoe/Ian Ellis **Facilities** 🍴 🛒
🍴 ⚐ 🍴 ⚑ ✎ 🚗 ✎ **Conf** facs Corporate Hospitality Days
Location 4.5m NW of Norwich. A1074 onto Longwater Ln, left onto West End, club on left
Hotel ★★ 85% HL Stower Grange, School Road, Drayton, NORWICH
☎ 01603 860210 📄 01603 860464 11 en suite

De Vere Dunston Hall Hotel Ipswich Rd NR14 8PQ
☎ 01508 470444   📄 01508 471499
web: www.devereonline.co.uk
18 Holes, 6300yds, Par 71, SSS 70, Course record 68.
Course Designer M Shaw **Location** on A140
Telephone for further details
Hotel ★★★★ 79% HL De Vere Dunston Hall, Ipswich Road, NORWICH ☎ 01508 470444 📄 01508 471499 169 en suite

Save on Hotels. Book at **theAA.com/hotel**

NORFOLK

Eaton Golf Club Newmarket Rd NR4 6SF
☎ 01603 451686 📠 01603 457539
web: www.eatongc.co.uk

18 Holes, 6118yds, Par 70, SSS 70, Course record 64.
Location 1.5m SW of city centre off A11
Telephone for further details
Hotel ★★★★ 76% HL Park Farm Hotel, HETHERSETT
☎ 01603 810264 📠 01603 812104 53 en suite

Marriott Sprowston Manor Hotel & Country Club
Wroxham Rd NR7 8RP
☎ 01603 410871 📠 01603 423911
web: www.marriottsprowstonmanor.co.uk

18 Holes, 6464yds, Par 71, SSS 71, Course record 64.
Course Designer Ross McMurray **Location** 4m NE from city centre on A1151, signed
Telephone for further details
Hotel ★★ SHL The Old Rectory, 103 Yarmouth Road, Thorpe St Andrew, NORWICH ☎ 01603 700772 📠 01603 300772 8 en suite

Royal Norwich Golf Club Drayton High Rd, Hellesdon NR6 5AH
☎ 01603 429928 📠 01603 417945
e-mail: mail@royalnorwichgolf.co.uk
web: www.royalnorwichgolf.co.uk

Undulating mature parkland course complimented with gorse. Largely unchanged since the alterations carried out by James Braid in 1924. A challenging test of golf.

18 Holes, 6506yds, Par 72, SSS 72, Course record 65.
Club membership 575.

Visitors Mon-Sun & BHs. Booking required. Dress code.
Societies booking required. **Green Fees** £48 per day, £30 per round (£48/£40 weekends) **Course Designer** James Braid **Prof** Simon Youd
Facilities 🛈 🍴 by prior arrangement 🖥 ☂ 🏌 ⚲ 🎒 ⛳
🛏 ⚑ **Conf** facs Corporate Hospitality Days **Location** 2.5m NW of city centre on A1067
Hotel ★★★★ 71% HL Holiday Inn Norwich-North, Cromer Road, NORWICH ☎ 01603 410544 📠 01603 487701 121 en suite

Wensum Valley Hotel, Golf & Country Club Beech Av, Taverham NR8 6HP
☎ 01603 261012 📠 01603 261664
e-mail: enqs@wensumvalleyhotel.co.uk
web: www.wensumvalleyhotel.co.uk

Two picturesque and contrasting courses set in 350 acres of the attractive Wensum Valley and designed and built to compliment the natural landscape. The shorter Valley course has narrow fairways with strategic bunkers to catch any loose drive. The greens, although generous in size, have some interesting undulations, putting a premium on iron play. The Wensum course has smaller well protected greens making approach play tricky. The 7th hole is a short par 3 that plays onto an island green over the river, which also comes into play throughout the 8th and 16th holes.

Valley Course: 18 Holes, 6223yds, Par 72, SSS 70,
Course record 62.
Wensum Course: 18 Holes, 6922yds, Par 72, SSS 73,
Course record 64. Club membership 500.

Visitors Mon-Sun & BHs. Dress code. **Societies** booking required.
Green Fees £40 per day/ £25 per round inc bar meal. Twilight £15
Course Designer B Todd **Prof** Brad Jordan **Facilities** 🛈 🍴 🖥 ☂ 🏌 ⚲ 🎒 ⛳ ◇ 🛏 ⚑ ⚑ **Leisure** heated indoor swimming pool, fishing, sauna, gymnasium **Conf** facs Corporate Hospitality Days
Location 5m N of Norwich off A1067
Hotel ★★ 85% HL Stower Grange, School Road, Drayton, NORWICH
☎ 01603 860210 📠 01603 860464 11 en suite

SHERINGHAM
Map 9 TG14

Sheringham Golf Club Weybourne Rd NR26 8HG
☎ 01263 823488 📄 01263 826129
e-mail: info@sheringhamgolfclub.co.uk
web: www.sheringhamgolfclub.co.uk
The course is laid out along a rolling, gorse-clad cliff top from where the sea is visible on every hole. The par 4 holes are outstanding with a fine view along the cliffs from the 5th tee.

18 Holes, 6456yds, Par 70, SSS 71, Course record 64.
Club membership 760.

Visitors Mon-Sun & BHs. Booking required. Dress code.
Societies booking required. **Green Fees** not confirmed 🅟 **Course Designer** Tom Dunn **Prof** M W Jubb **Facilities** ⑪ ⑩ 🛒 ⬜
🍴 ⌂ 🖻 ⛳ ✔ 🚃 ✔ **Conf** Corporate Hospitality Days
Location W of town centre on A149
Hotel ★★★ 79% SHL Roman Camp Inn, Holt Road, Aylmerton, SHERINGHAM ☎ 01263 838291 📄 01263 837071 15 en suite

SWAFFHAM
Map 5 TF80

Swaffham Golf Club Cley Rd PE37 8AE
☎ 01760 721621 📄 01760 721621
web: www.club-noticeboard.co.uk
18 Holes, 6525yds, Par 71, SSS 71.

Course Designer Jonathan Gaunt **Location** 1.5m SW of town centre
Telephone for further details
Hotel ★★★ 77% HL Best Western George Hotel, Station Road, SWAFFHAM ☎ 01760 721238 📄 01760 725333 29 en suite

THETFORD
Map 5 TL88

Feltwell Golf Club Thor Ave (off Wilton Rd), Feltwell IP26 4AY
☎ 01842 827644 📄 01842 829065
e-mail: sec.feltwellgc@virgin.net
web: www.club-noticeboard.co.uk/feltwell
Inland links course with quality fairways and greens. Well drained for winter play.

9 Holes, 6488yds, Par 72, SSS 72, Course record 67.
Club membership 320.

Visitors Mon-Sun & BHs. Dress code. **Societies** booking required.
Green Fees £22 per 18 holes (£30 weekends & BHs) **Prof** Jonathan Moore **Facilities** ⑪ ⑩ 🛒 ⬜ 🍴 ⌂ 🖻 ⛳ ✔ ✔ **Conf**
Corporate Hospitality Days **Location** on B1112 next to RAF Feltwell
Hotel ★★★ 73% HL Castle Hotel, High Street, DOWNHAM MARKET
☎ 01366 384311 📄 01366 384311 12 en suite

Thetford Golf Club Brandon Rd IP24 3NE
☎ 01842 752169 📄 01842 766212
e-mail: thetfordgolfclub@btconnect.com
web: www.thetfordgolfclub.co.uk
The course has a good pedigree. It was laid out by the fine golfer CH Mayo, later altered by James Braid and then again altered by another famous course designer, Mackenzie Ross. It is a testing heathland course with a particularly stiff finish.

18 Holes, 6849yds, Par 72, SSS 73.
Club membership 750.

Visitors After 10am Mon & Wed-Fr. After 2pm Tue, weekends & BHs. Booking required Mon & Wed-Fri. Handicap certificate, Dress code. **Societies** booking required. **Green Fees** £50 per day, £40 per round **Course Designer** James Braid **Prof** Gary Kitley **Facilities** ⑪
⑩ 🛒 ⬜ 🍴 ⌂ 🖻 ⛳ 🚃 ✔ **Leisure** short game area
Location 2m W of Thetford on B1107
Hotel ★★★ 83% HL The Olde Bull Inn, The Street, Barton Mills, MILDENHALL ☎ 01638 711001 📄 01638 712003 14 en suite

WATTON
Map 5 TF90

Richmond Park Golf Club Saham Rd IP25 6EA
☎ 01953 881803 📄 01953 881817
e-mail: info@richmondpark.co.uk
web: www.richmondpark.co.uk
Compact parkland course with mature and young trees set around the Little Wissey river and spread over 100 acres of Norfolk countryside. The river and other water hazards create an interesting but not daunting challenge.

18 Holes, 6258yds, Par 71, SSS 71, Course record 65.
Club membership 600.

Visitors Mon-Sun & BHs. Booking required weekends & BHs.
Societies booking required. **Green Fees** £45 per day, £30 per round (£45 per day/round weekends & BHs) **Course Designer** D Jessup/D Scott **Facilities** ⑪ ⑩ 🛒 ⬜ 🍴 ⌂ 🖻 ⛳ ◇ 🚃 ✔ ✔
Conf facs Corporate Hospitality Days **Location** 500yds NW of town centre
Hotel ★★★ 77% HL Best Western George Hotel, Station Road, SWAFFHAM ☎ 01760 721238 📄 01760 725333 29 en suite

WEST RUNTON
Map 9 TG14

Links Country Park Hotel & Golf Club NR27 9QH
☎ 01263 838383 📄 01263 838264
e-mail: sales@links-hotel.co.uk
web: www.links-hotel.co.uk
Parkland course 500yds from the sea, with superb views overlooking West Runton and The Wash.

9 Holes, 4842yds, Par 66, SSS 64, Course record 64.
Club membership 110.

Visitors Mon-Sun & BHs. Dress code. **Societies** booking required.
Green Fees £30 per round/day. Twilight £20 after 4pm. **Course Designer** J.H Taylor **Facilities** ⑪ ⑩ 🛒 ⬜ 🍴 ⌂ 🖻 ⛳
✔ 🚃 ✔ **Leisure** hard tennis courts, heated indoor swimming pool, sauna, gymnasium **Conf** facs Corporate Hospitality Days **Location** S of village off A149
Hotel ★★ 79% HL Beaumaris Hotel, South Street, SHERINGHAM
☎ 01263 822370 📄 01263 821421 21 en suite

WESTON LONGVILLE
Map 9 TG11

Weston Park Golf Club NR9 5JW
☎ 01603 872363 📠 01603 873040
e-mail: golf@weston-park.co.uk
web: www.weston-park.co.uk

Superb, challenging course, set in 200 acres of magnificent, mature woodland and parkland.

18 Holes, 6648yds, Par 72, SSS 72, Course record 67.
Club membership 480.

Visitors Mon-Sun & BHs. Booking required. Handicap certificate. Dress code. **Societies** booking required. **Green Fees** £55 per day, £45 per 18 holes (£47 weekends) **Course Designer** Golf Technology **Prof** Michael Few **Facilities** ⊗ 🍴 ⚒ ☕ 🍺 👤 🏠 🏌 🚲 **Leisure** hard tennis courts, croquet lawn **Conf** facs Corporate Hospitality Days **Location** brown tourist signs off A1067 or A47
Hotel ★★★ 68% HL Old Brewery House, Market Place, REEPHAM ☎ 01603 870881 📠 01603 870969 23 en suite

NORTHAMPTONSHIRE

CHACOMBE
Map 4 SP44

Cherwell Edge Golf Club OX17 2EN
☎ 01295 711591 📠 01295 713674
e-mail: enquiries@cherwelledgegolfclub.co.uk
web: www.cherwelledgegolfclub.co.uk

Parkland course over chalk giving good drainage. The back nine is short and tight with mature trees. The front nine is longer and more open. The course is well bunkered with three holes where water can catch the wayward golfer.

18 Holes, 6085yds, Par 70, SSS 69, Course record 62.
Club membership 500.

Visitors Mon-Sun & BHs. Dress code. **Societies** booking required. **Green Fees** not confirmed **Course Designer** R Davies **Prof** Jason Newman **Facilities** ⊗ 🍴 ⚒ ☕ 🍺 👤 🏠 🏌 🚲 **Conf** facs Corporate Hospitality Days **Location** M40 junct 11, 0.5m S off B4525, 2m from Banbury
Hotel ★★★ 74% HL Mercure Whately Hall, Banbury Cross, BANBURY ☎ 01295 253261 69 en suite

COLD ASHBY
Map 4 SP67

Cold Ashby Golf Club Stanford Rd NN6 6EP
☎ 01604 740548
e-mail: info@coldashbygolfclub.com
web: www.coldashbygolfclub.com

Undulating parkland course, nicely matured, with superb views. The 27 holes consist of three loops of nine, which can be interlinked with each other. All three loops have their own challenge and any combination of two loops will give an excellent course. The start of the Elkington loop offers five holes of scenic beauty and testing golf and the 3rd on the Winwick loop is a 200yd par 3 from a magnificent plateau tee.

Ashby/Elkington: 18 Holes, 6308yds, Par 72, SSS 71, Course record 67.
Elkington/Winwick: 18 Holes, 6293yds, Par 70, SSS 71, Course record 67.
Winwick/Ashby: 18 Holes, 6047yds, Par 70, SSS 70, Course record 64. Club membership 500.

Visitors Mon-Sun & BHs. Booking required. **Societies** booking required
Green Fees not confirmed **Course Designer** David Croxton **Prof** Shane

Rose **Facilities** ⊗ 🍴 ⚒ ☕ 🍺 👤 🏠 🏌 🚲
Conf facs Corporate Hospitality Days **Location** M1 junct 18 or A14 junct 1
Hotel BUD Ibis Rugby, Parklands, CRICK ☎ 01788 824331 📠 01788 824332 111 en suite

COLLINGTREE
Map 4 SP75

Collingtree Park Golf Course Windingbrook Ln NN4 0XN
☎ 01604 700000 & 701202 📠 01604 702600
web: www.collingtreeparkgolf.com

18 Holes, 6776yds, Par 72, SSS 72, Course record 66.
Course Designer Johnny Miller **Location** M1 junct 15, on A508 to Northampton
Telephone for further details
Hotel ★★★★ 75% HL Northampton Marriott Hotel, Eagle Drive, NORTHAMPTON ☎ 01604 768700 📠 01604 769011 120 en suite

See advert on this page

CORBY
Map 4 SP88

Priors Hall Golf Club Stamford Rd, Weldon NN17 3JH
☎ 01536 260756 📠 01536 260756
web: www.priorshallgolfclub.com
Parkland course with generous fairways, mature trees and 58 bunkers.
18 Holes, 6631yds, Par 72, SSS 72, Course record 68.
Club membership 600.
Visitors Mon-Sun & BHs. Booking required. **Societies** booking
required. **Green Fees** £17 per 18 holes, £11.40 per 9 holes (£21/£13
weekends) **Course Designer** F Hawtree **Prof** Jeff Bradbrook
Facilities 🕙 🍴 🍺 ☕ 🍴 🏌 🎯 🛍 ☕ ⛳ **Conf**
Corporate Hospitality Days **Location** 4m NE on A43
Hotel ★★★ 71% HL Holiday Inn Corby-Kettering A43, Geddington
Road, CORBY ☎ 01536 401020 📠 01536 400767 105 en suite

DAVENTRY
Map 4 SP56

Daventry & District Golf Club Norton Rd NN11 2LS
☎ 01327 702829
e-mail: ddgc@hotmail.co.uk
An undulatory course providing panoramic views and whose tight
fairways and small fast greens with large borrows provide a good test
of golf. 6 holes on the back nine have different teeing areas giving
them a totally different aspect.
9 Holes, 5808yds, Par 69, SSS 68. Club membership 285.
Visitors Mon-Sun & BHs. Booking required Sun. Dress code.
Societies booking required. **Green Fees** £15 per day (£20 weekends)
🎯 **Prof** Shay Brennan / Aaron Sheppard **Facilities** ☕ 🍴 🏌
Conf facs **Location** 0.5m E of Daventry
Hotel ★★★★ 71% HL Barceló Daventry Hotel, Sedgemoor Way,
DAVENTRY ☎ 01327 307000 📠 01327 706313 155 en suite

FARTHINGSTONE
Map 4 SP65

Farthingstone Hotel & Golf Course Everdon Rd NN12 8HA
☎ 01327 361291 📠 01327 361645
web: www.farthingstone.co.uk
A mature and challenging course set in picturesque countryside.
Woodland, water, naturally sweeping fairways and carefully crafted
greens make for a memorable golfing experience. Popular golf breaks
venue.
Farthingstone: 18 Holes, 6299yds, Par 70, SSS 70,
Course record 63. Club membership 350.
Visitors Mon-Sun & BHs. Dress code. **Societies** booking required.
Green Fees Mon-Thu £32 per day, £20 per 18 holes, £12.50 per 9
holes, Fri £35/£22/£15. Weekends before 10am £50 per day, £35 per
18 holes, after 10am £40 per day, £28 per 18 holes, £17 per 9 holes
Course Designer Don Donaldson **Prof** Mike Gallagher **Facilities** 🕙
🍴 🍺 ☕ 🍴 🏌 🎯 🛍 ☕ 🚻 🍴 ⛳ 🎣 **Leisure** squash,
snooker room **Conf** facs Corporate Hospitality Days **Location** M40
junct 11, E near Farthingstone
Hotel ★★★★ HL Fawsley Hall, Fawsley, DAVENTRY
☎ 01327 892000 📠 01327 892001 58 en suite

HELLIDON
Map 4 SP55

Hellidon Lakes Golf & Spa Hotel NN11 6GG
☎ 01327 262551 📠 01327 262559
e-mail: hellidonlakesgolf@qhotels.co.uk
web: www.qhotels.co.uk
Nestling in its own peaceful valley, a course of 27 holes running
through 220 acres and designed to test golfers of all levels. From
the elevated position of the first tee, the eye can wander over the
shimmering lakes below, which are a highlight of the course.
Many of the holes feature water hazards offering the choice of
challenging carries for the bold and daring or safer routes for the less
adventurous.
Red & Blue: 18 Holes, 6082yds, Par 72, SSS 70,
Course record 71.
Green: 9 Holes, 2791yds, Par 35. Club membership 209.
Visitors Mon-Sun & BHs. Booking required. Dress code.
Societies booking required. **Green Fees** £35 per 18 holes (£40
weekends). Nov-Mar £17.50/£25 **Course Designer** D Snell **Prof** Gary
Wills **Facilities** 🕙 🍴 🍺 ☕ 🍴 🏌 🎯 🛍 ☕ 🍴 🚻 ⛳ 🎣
Leisure hard tennis courts, heated indoor swimming pool, fishing,
gymnasium, steam room **Conf** facs Corporate Hospitality Days
Location off A361 into Hellidon, 2nd right
Hotel ★★★★ 74% HL Hellidon Lakes Golf & Spa Hotel, HELLIDON
☎ 01327 262550 📠 01327 262559 110 en suite

KETTERING
Map 4 SP87

Kettering Golf Club Headlands NN15 6XA
☎ 01536 511104 📠 01536 523788
e-mail: secretary@kettering-golf.co.uk
web: www.kettering-golf.co.uk
A mature woodland course with gentle slopes, established in 1891.
Easy walking. Quality greens
18 Holes, 6057yds, Par 69, SSS 69, Course record 63.
Club membership 600.
Visitors Mon, Wed-Fri & BHs. Booking required. **Societies** booking
required. **Green Fees** £36 per round summer, £25 winter **Course
Designer** Tom Morris **Prof** Kevin Theobald **Facilities** 🕙 🍴 🍺
☕ 🍴 🏌 🎯 🛍 ⛳ 🚻 ⛳ **Conf** facs Corporate Hospitality Days
Location A14 junct 8, take A43 towards Kettering and follow golf club
signs
Hotel ★★★★ 79% HL Kettering Park Hotel & Spa, Kettering
Parkway, KETTERING ☎ 01536 416666 📠 01536 416171
119 en suite

Pytchley Golf Lodge Kettering Rd, Pytchley NN14 1EY
☎ 01536 511527 📠 01536 790266
e-mail: info@pytchleygolflodgekettering.co.uk
web: www.pytchleygolflodgekettering.co.uk
Academy nine-hole pay-and-play course, offering a challenge to both
experienced and novice players.
9 Holes, 2574yards, Par 34. Club membership 200.
Visitors Mon-Sun & BHs. **Societies** welcome. **Green Fees** not
confirmed **Course Designer** Roger Griffiths Associates **Prof** Peter
Machin **Facilities** 🕙 🍺 ☕ 🍴 🏌 🎯 🛍 ⛳ 🎣
Location A14 junct 9, A509 towards Kettering signed
Hotel ★★★★ 79% HL Kettering Park Hotel & Spa, Kettering
Parkway, KETTERING ☎ 01536 416666 📠 01536 416171
119 en suite

ENGLAND

NORTHAMPTON   Map 4 SP76

rampton Heath Golf Centre Sandy Ln, Church Brampton
N6 8AX
☎ 01604 843939 📄 01604 843885
-mail: info@bhgc.co.uk
eb: www.bhgc.co.uk

opealing to both the novice and experienced golfer, this beautiful,
ell drained heathland course affords panoramic views over
orthampton. It plays like an inland links in the summer - fast
nning fairways, true rolling greens with the wind always providing
challenge. Excellent play all year round. Hosts of the Lee Westwood
cademy.

8 Holes, 6662yds, Par 72, SSS 72, Course record 66.
:lub membership 600.

isitors Mon-Sun & BHs. **Societies** booking required. **Green Fees** £21
er 18 holes (£26 weekends) **Course Designer** D Snell **Prof** Carl
ainsbury **Facilities** ⓣ ⑩ ▣ ▱ ▰ ⟰ ⌂ ⊶ ✿ ⛳
✸ ✦ **Leisure** 9 hole short course (814 yds) **Conf facs** Corporate
ospitality Days **Location** signed off A5199 2m N of Kingsthorpe
otel ★★★ 72% HL Best Western Lime Trees, 8 Langham Place,
arrack Road, NORTHAMPTON ☎ 01604 632188 📄 01604 233012
B en suite

Delapre Golf Centre Eagle Dr, Nene Valley Way NN4 7DU
☎ 01604 764036 📄 01604 706378
e-mail: delapre@jbgolf.co.uk
web: www.jackbarker.com

The Oaks is set in 260 acres of mature parkland with ditches, streams
and bunkers. The Hardingstone Nine is a short but testing nine hole
course situated on a hillside with a pond and some challenging lies
that require good course management. There are also two 9 hole par 3
courses of similar length but very different character.

The Oaks: 18 Holes, 5947yds, Par 69, SSS 69.
The Hardingstone: 9 Holes, 2109yds, Par 32.
Club membership 500.

Visitors Mon-Sun & BHs. **Societies** booking required. **Green
Fees** phone **Course Designer** John Jacobs/John Corby **Prof** J
Cuddihy/M Chapman/P Machin **Facilities** ⓣ ⑩ ▣ ▱ ⊶ ⟰
⌂ ⊶ ⛳ ✿ ✦ **Leisure** two 9 hole par 3 courses **Conf** facs
Corporate Hospitality Days **Location** M1 junct 15, 3m on A508/A45
Hotel ★★★★ 75% HL Northampton Marriott Hotel, Eagle Drive,
NORTHAMPTON ☎ 01604 768700 📄 01604 769011   120 en suite

Kingsthorpe Golf Club Kingsley Rd NN2 7BU
☎ 01604 710610 📄 01604 710610
e-mail: secretary@kingsthorpe-golf.co.uk
web: www.kingsthorpe-golf.co.uk

A compact, undulating parkland course set within the town boundary.
Not a long course but the undulating terrain provides a suitable
challenge for golfers of all standards. The 18th hole is claimed to be
the longest 400yds in the county when played into the wind and is
among the finest finishing holes in the area.

18 Holes, 5903yds, Par 69, SSS 69, Course record 63.
Club membership 500.

Visitors Mon-Fri, Sun & BHs. Booking required Sun & BHs. Dress code.
Societies booking required. **Green Fees** £40 per day, £30 per round.
£20 per round winter **Course Designer** Mr Alison/ H Colt **Prof** Paul
Armstrong **Facilities** ⓣ ⑩ ▣ ▱ ⊶ ⟰ ⌂ ⛳ ✿ **Conf**
Corporate Hospitality Days **Location** N of town centre on A5095
between Kingsthorpe and racecourse
Hotel ★★★ 72% HL Best Western Lime Trees, 8 Langham Place,
Barrack Road, NORTHAMPTON ☎ 01604 632188 📄 01604 233012
28 en suite

Northampton Golf Club Harlestone NN7 4EF
☎ 01604 845155 📄 01604 820262
e-mail: golf@northamptongolfclub.co.uk
web: www.northamptongolfclub.co.uk

Parkland with water in play on four holes.

18 Holes, 6515yds, Par 72, SSS 72, Course record 65.
Club membership 750.

Visitors Mon-Fri except BHs. Booking advisable. Handicap certificate.
Dress code. **Societies** booking required. **Green Fees** £40 per 18 holes
Course Designer Sinclair Steel **Prof** Nick Soto **Facilities** ⓣ ⑩ by
prior arrangement ▣ ▱ ⊶ ⟰ ⌂ ✿ ⛳ ✿ **Conf** facs
Corporate Hospitality Days **Location** NW of town centre on A428
Hotel ★★★ 72% HL Best Western Lime Trees, 8 Langham Place,
Barrack Road, NORTHAMPTON ☎ 01604 632188 📄 01604 233012
28 en suite

Northamptonshire County Golf Club Golf Ln, Church Brampton NN6 8AZ

☎ 01604 843025 📄 01604 843463
e-mail: secretary@countygolfclub.org.uk
web: www.countygolfclub.org.uk

A fine, traditional championship course situated on undulating heathland with areas of gorse, heather and extensive coniferous and deciduous woodland. A river and a railway line pass through the course and there is a great variety of holes. There are three additional holes providing a 9 hole loop returning to the clubhouse, for those wishing to play 9 or 27 holes. Par 3 course with artificial greens and tees. The club celebrated its centenary in 2009.

18 Holes, 6721yds, Par 70, SSS 73, Course record 68.
Club membership 750.

Visitors Handicap certificate. Dress code. **Societies** welcome. **Green Fees** £80 per 27/36, £70 per 18 holes. Winter £40 per day/round **Course Designer** H S Colt **Prof** Tim Rouse **Facilities** ⑪ ⭢ ᴸ 🖫 ⟒ 🖭 ⚲ 🏚 ⁿ⁺ ✔ 🍴 **Leisure** 6 hole par 3 course with artificial tees/greens **Conf** Corporate Hospitality Days **Location** 5m NW of Northampton off A5199

Hotel ★★★ 72% HL Best Western Lime Trees, 8 Langham Place, Barrack Road, NORTHAMPTON ☎ 01604 632188 📄 01604 233012 28 en suite

Overstone Park Hotel, Golf & Leisure Resort Billing Ln NN6 0AS

☎ 01604 643555 📄 01604 642635
e-mail: enquiries@overstonepark.com
web: www.overstonepark.com

A testing parkland course, gently undulating within panoramic views of local stately home. Excellent drainage and fine greens make the course great all year round. Water comes into play on three holes.

18 Holes, 6472yds, Par 72, SSS 72, Course record 69.
Club membership 600.

Visitors contact for details **Societies** booking required. **Green Fees** from £23 per round **Course Designer** Donald Steel **Prof** Stuart Keir **Facilities** ⑪ ⭢ ᴸ 🖫 ⟒ 🖭 ⚲ 🏚 ⁿ⁺ ◇ ✔ 🚗 ✔ **Leisure** hard tennis courts, heated indoor swimming pool, fishing, sauna, gymnasium **Conf** facs Corporate Hospitality Days **Location** M1 junct 15, A45 to Billing Aquadrome turn off, course 2m off A5076 Gt Billing Way

Hotel ★★★ 72% HL Best Western Lime Trees, 8 Langham Place, Barrack Road, NORTHAMPTON ☎ 01604 632188 📄 01604 233012 28 en suite

OUNDLE
Map 4 TL08

Oundle Golf Club Benefield Rd PE8 4EZ

☎ 01832 273267 📄 01832 273267
web: www.oundlegolfclub.com

18 Holes, 6265yds, Par 72, SSS 70, Course record 63.
Location 1m W on A427
Telephone for further details
Hotel ★★★ 71% HL Holiday Inn Corby-Kettering A43, Geddington Road, CORBY ☎ 01536 401020 📄 01536 400767 105 en suite

STAVERTON
Map 4 SP56

Staverton Park Golf Club Staverton Park NN11 6JT

☎ 01327 705506 📄 01327 311428

18 Holes, 6593yds, Par 71, SSS 72, Course record 65.
Course Designer Cmdr John Harris **Location** 0.75m NE on A425
Telephone for further details
Hotel ★★★★ 71% HL Barceló Daventry Hotel, Sedgemoor Way, DAVENTRY ☎ 01327 307000 📄 01327 706313 155 en suite

WELLINGBOROUGH
Map 4 SP86

Rushden Golf Club Kimbolton Rd, Chelveston NN9 6AN

☎ 01933 418511 📄 01933 418511
e-mail: secretary@rushdengolfclub.org
web: www.rushdengolfclub.org

Undulating parkland with a brook bisecting the course.

10 Holes, 6001yds, Par 71, SSS 69, Course record 65.
Club membership 400.

Visitors Mon, Tue, Thu, Fri & Sun except BHs. Wed am only. Booking required. Dress code. **Societies** booking required. **Green Fees** £25 per 18 holes, £13 per 9 holes 🚬 **Prof** Adrian Clifford **Facilities** ⑪ ⭢ ᴸ 🖫 ⟒ ⚲ **Conf** Corporate Hospitality Days **Location** 6m E of Wellingborough off B645

Hotel ★★★★ 79% HL Kettering Park Hotel & Spa, Kettering Parkway, KETTERING ☎ 01536 416666 📄 01536 416171 119 en suite

Wellingborough Golf Club Great Harrowden Hall NN9 5AD

☎ 01933 677234 📄 01933 679379
e-mail: info@wellingboroughgolfclub.com
web: www.wellingboroughgolfclub.com

Undulating parkland with many trees set in the grounds of Harrowden Hall with an 18th century clubhouse.

18 Holes, 6721yds, Par 72, SSS 72, Course record 68.
Club membership 820.

Visitors contact club for details. **Societies** booking required. **Green Fees** £48 per day **Course Designer** Hawtree **Prof** David Clifford **Facilities** ⑪ ⭢ ᴸ 🖫 ⟒ ⚲ 🏚 ✔ 🚗 ✔ **Leisure** outdoor swimming pool **Conf** facs Corporate Hospitality Days **Location** 2m N of Wellingborough on A509

Hotel ★★★★ 79% HL Kettering Park Hotel & Spa, Kettering Parkway, KETTERING ☎ 01536 416666 📄 01536 416171 119 en suite

Save on Hotels. Book at **theAA.com/hotel**

NORTHAMPTONSHIRE – NORTHUMBERLAND

ENGLAND

WHITTLEBURY   Map 4 SP64

Whittlebury Park Golf & Country Club NN12 8WP
☎ 01327 850000 📄 01327 850001
e-mail: enquiries@whittlebury.com
web: www.whittlebury.com
The 36 holes incorporate three loops of tournament-standard nines plus a short course. The 1905 course is a reconstruction of the original parkland course built at the turn of the century, the Royal Whittlewood is a lakeland course playing around copses and the Grand Prix, next to Silverstone Circuit, has a strong links feel playing over gently undulating grassland with many challenging features.

Grand Prix: 9 Holes, 3339yds, Par 36, SSS 36.
Royal Whittlewood: 9 Holes, 3323yds, Par 36, SSS 36.
1905: 9 Holes, 3256yds, Par 36, SSS 36.
Club membership 500.

Visitors Mon-Sun & BHs. Dress code. **Societies** booking required.
Green Fees phone for details **Course Designer** Cameron Sinclair
Prof Jim Hetherington/Richard Cartwright **Facilities** Ⓟ ⏀ ﹗
⌴ ﹗ ⚲ 🏠 ⑨ ◇ ✦ 🚗 ✦ ✦ **Leisure** heated indoor swimming pool, sauna, gymnasium, halfway house for refreshments
Conf facs Corporate Hospitality Days **Location** M1 junct 15a, on A413 Buckingham Road
Hotel ★★★★ 79% HL Whittlebury Hall, WHITTLEBURY
☎ 01327 857857 📄 01327 857987 211 en suite

NORTHUMBERLAND

ALLENDALE   Map 12 NY85

Allendale Golf Club High Studdon, Allenheads Rd
NE47 9DH
☎ 07005 808246
e-mail: secretary@allendale-golf.co.uk
web: www.allendale-golf.co.uk

Challenging and hilly parkland course set 1000ft above sea level with superb views of East Allen Valley.

9 Holes, 4541yds, Par 66, SSS 64. Club membership 130.

Visitors Contact club for details. **Societies** welcome. **Green Fees** £15 per day (£18 weekends) 🌐 **Facilities** ⌴ ﹗ ⚲ **Conf** Corporate Hospitality Days **Location** 1m S of Allendale on B6295
Hotel ★★★ 80% HL Best Western Beaumont Hotel, Beaumont Street, HEXHAM ☎ 01434 602331 📄 01434 606184 34 en suite

ALNMOUTH   Map 12 NU21

Alnmouth Golf Club Foxton Hall NE66 3BE
☎ 01665 830231 📄 01665 830922
e-mail: secretary@alnmouthgolfclub.com
web: www.alnmouthgolfclub.com
Situated on the magnificent Northumberland coast, the course was established in 1869, being the fourth oldest in England. It is widely regarded as one of the finest golf courses in the North-East of England.

18 Holes, 6500yds, Par 71, SSS 71, Course record 63.
Club membership 800.

Visitors Mon-Thu, Sun & BHs. Booking required. Dress code.
Societies booking required. **Green Fees** £40 per day, £35 per round
Course Designer H S Colt **Prof** Linzi Hardy **Facilities** Ⓟ ⏀ ﹗
⌴ ﹗ ⚲ 🏠 ◇ ✦ **Leisure** snooker room **Conf** Corporate Hospitality Days **Location** 5m E of Alnwick and A1
Hotel ★★★ 79% HL White Swan Hotel, Bondgate Within, ALNWICK
☎ 01665 602109 📄 01665 510400 56 en suite

Alnmouth Village Golf Club Marine Rd NE66 2RZ
☎ 01665 830370
web: www.alnmouthvillagegolfclub.co.uk

9 Holes, 6090yds, Par 70, SSS 70, Course record 63.

Course Designer Mungo Park **Location** E of village
Telephone for further details
Hotel ★★★ 79% HL White Swan Hotel, Bondgate Within, ALNWICK
☎ 01665 602109 📄 01665 510400 56 en suite

ALNWICK   Map 12 NU11

Alnwick Castle Golf Club Swansfield Park NE66 2AB
☎ 01665 602632
e-mail: secretary@alnwickgolfclub.co.uk
web: www.alnwickcastlegolfclub.co.uk
A mixture of mature parkland, open grassland and gorse bushes with panoramic views out to sea 5 miles away. Offers a fair test of golf.

18 Holes, 6250yds, Par 70, SSS 70, Course record 65.
Club membership 220.

Visitors Contact club for details. **Societies** booking required.
Green Fees £25 per day (£27 weekends) **Course Designer** Alistair
Rae **Facilities** Ⓟ ⏀ ﹗ ⌴ ﹗ ⚲ 🏠 ✦ 🚗 ✦ **Conf**
Corporate Hospitality Days **Location** S of town centre off B6341. Take
S exit from A1 and follow signs
Hotel ★★★ 79% HL White Swan Hotel, Bondgate Within, ALNWICK
☎ 01665 602109 📄 01665 510400 56 en suite

BAMBURGH
Map 12 NU13

Bamburgh Castle Golf Club The Club House, 40 The Wynding NE69 7DE
☎ 01668 214378 (club) & 214321 (sec)
📄 01668 214607
e-mail: sec@bamburghcastlegolfclub.co.uk
web: www.bamburghcastlegolfclub.co.uk
Superb coastal course with excellent greens that are both fast and true; natural hazards of heather and whin bushes abound. Magnificent views of the Farne Islands, Holy Island, Lindisfarne Castle, Bamburgh Castle and the Cheviot Hills.
18 Holes, 5621yds, Par 68, SSS 67, Course record 62. Club membership 785.
Visitors Mon-Fri, Sun & BHs. Booking required Sun & BHs. Dress code. **Societies** booking required. **Green Fees** not confirmed **Course Designer** George Rochester **Facilities** ⓘ 🍴 🖴 ⌂ 🍺 ⚖ 🏌 ⛳ **Conf** Corporate Hospitality Days **Location** 6m E of A1 via B1341 or B1342
Hotel ★★ 81% HL The Lord Crewe, Front Street, BAMBURGH
☎ 01668 214243 & 214613 📄 01668 214273 17 en suite

BEDLINGTON
Map 12 NZ28

Bedlingtonshire Golf Club Acorn Bank, Hartford Rd NE22 6AA
☎ 01670 822457 📄 01670 823048
e-mail: secretary@bedlingtongolfclub.com
web: www.bedlingtongolfclub.com
Meadowland and parkland with easy walking. Under certain conditions the wind can be a distinct hazard.
18 Holes, 6813yards, Par 73, SSS 73, Course record 64. Club membership 800.
Visitors Mon-Sun & BHs. Dress code. **Societies** booking required. **Green Fees** not confirmed 🅿 **Course Designer** Frank Pennink **Prof** Marcus Webb **Facilities** ⓘ 🍴 by prior arrangement 🖴 ⌂ 🍺 ⚖ 🏠 🍴 🏌 ⛳ **Conf** Corporate Hospitality Days **Location** 1m SW on A1068
Hotel ★★★ 78% HL Holiday Inn Newcastle upon Tyne, Great North Road, Seaton Burn, NEWCASTLE UPON TYNE ☎ 0871 423 4818 & 0191 201 9988 📄 0191 236 8091 154 en suite

BELFORD
Map 12 NU13

The Belford Golf Club South Rd NE70 7DP
☎ 01668 213232 📄 01668 213282
web: www.thebelford.co.uk
9 Holes, 3227yds, Par 71, SSS 71.
Course Designer Nigel Williams **Location** off A1 between Alnwick and Berwick on Tweed
Telephone for further details
Hotel ★★ 76% HL Purdy Lodge, Adderstone Services, BELFORD
☎ 01668 213000 📄 01668 213111 20 en suite

BELLINGHAM
Map 12 NY88

Bellingham Golf Club Boggle Hole NE48 2DT
☎ 01434 220530 (Secretary)
web: www.bellinghamgolfclub.com

18 Holes, 6093yds, Par 70, SSS 70, Course record 64.
Course Designer E Johnson/I Wilson **Location** N of village on B6320
Telephone for further details
Hotel ★★★ 78% HL The Otterburn Tower Hotel, OTTERBURN
☎ 01830 520620 📄 01830 521504 18 en suite

BERWICK-UPON-TWEED
Map 12 NT95

Berwick-upon-Tweed (Goswick) Golf Club Goswick TD15 2RW
☎ 01289 387256 📄 01289 387392
e-mail: goswickgc@btconnect.com
web: www.goswicklinksgc.co.uk
Natural seaside championship links course, with undulating fairways, elevated tees and good greens. Qualifying course for the Open Championship from 2008. Hosted English Golf Union boys' county finals 2010.
18 Holes, 6803yds, Par 72, SSS 72, Course record 72. Club membership 700.
Visitors Mon-Sun & BHs. Booking required. Dress code. **Societies** booking required. **Green Fees** £45 per day, £35 per round (£50/£40 weekends) **Course Designer** James Braid **Prof** Paul Terras **Facilities** ⓘ 🍴 🖴 🍺 ⚖ 🏠 🍴 🏌 ⛳ **Conf** Corporate Hospitality Days **Location** 6m S of Berwick off A1
Hotel ★★★ 74% CHH Marshall Meadows Country House, BERWICK-UPON-TWEED ☎ 01289 331133 📄 01289 331438 19 en suite

Magdalene Fields Golf Club Magdalene Fields TD15 1NE
☎ 01289 306130 📄 01289 306384
e-mail: mail@magdalene-fields.co.uk
web: www.magdalene-fields.co.uk
Seaside course on a clifftop with natural hazards formed by bays. All holes open to winds. Testing 8th hole over bay (par 3). Scenic views to Holy Island and north to Scotland.
18 Holes, 6575yds, Par 72, SSS 72, Course record 64. Club membership 350.
Visitors Mon-Sun & BHs. Booking required. Dress code. **Societies** booking required. **Green Fees** £27 per round (£32 weekends) **Course Designer** Willie Park **Facilities** ⓘ 🍴 🖴 ⌂ 🍺 🏠 🍴 🏌 🏌 ⛳ **Conf** Corporate Hospitality Days **Location** 0.5m E of town centre
Hotel ★★★ 86% CHH Tillmouth Park Country House, CORNHILL-ON-TWEED ☎ 01890 882255 📄 01890 882540 14 en suite

Save on Hotels. Book at **theAA.com/hotel**

NORTHUMBERLAND

ENGLAND

BLYTH
Map 12 NZ38

Blyth Golf Club New Delaval NE24 4DB
☎ 01670 540110 (sec) & 356514 (pro)
🖹 01670 540134
web: www.blythgolf.co.uk

18 Holes, 6424yds, Par 72, SSS 71, Course record 63.

Course Designer Hamilton Stutt **Location** 1m S of town centre
Telephone for further details
Hotel ★★★ 78% HL Holiday Inn Newcastle upon Tyne, Great North
Road, Seaton Burn, NEWCASTLE UPON TYNE ☎ 0871 423 4818 &
0191 201 9988 🖹 0191 236 8091 154 en suite

CRAMLINGTON
Map 12 NZ27

Arcot Hall Golf Club NE23 7QP
☎ 0191 236 2794 🖹 0191 217 0370
e-mail: arcothall@tiscali.co.uk
web: www.arcothallgolfclub.com

Wooded parkland, reasonably flat.

18 Holes, 6329yds, Par 70, SSS 70, Course record 60.
Club membership 695.

Visitors dress code. **Societies** booking required. **Green Fees** not
confirmed **Course Designer** James Braid **Prof** Carl Nichols
Facilities ⓣ ⓞ 🝙 ⌷ 🏐 ⚲ 🏠 🏴 🚗 ✐ **Conf** facs
Location 2m SW off A1
Hotel ★★★ 78% HL Holiday Inn Newcastle upon Tyne, Great North
Road, Seaton Burn, NEWCASTLE UPON TYNE ☎ 0871 423 4818 &
0191 201 9988 🖹 0191 236 8091 154 en suite

EMBLETON
Map 12 NU22

Dunstanburgh Castle Golf Club NE66 3XQ
☎ 01665 576562 🖹 01665 576562
e-mail: enquiries@dunstanburgh.com
web: www.dunstanburgh.com

Rolling links designed by James Braid, adjacent to the beautiful
Embleton Bay. Historic Dunstansburgh Castle is at one end of the
course and a National Trust lake and bird sanctuary at the other.
Superb views.

18 Holes, 6353yds, Par 70, SSS 70, Course record 67.
Club membership 323.

Visitors Mon-Sun & BHs. **Societies** welcome. **Green Fees** £32 per day,
£25 per round (£38/£30 weekends & BHs) **Course Designer** James
Braid **Facilities** ⓣ ⓞ 🝙 ⌷ 🏐 ⚲ 🏠 🏴 🚗 ✐
Conf facs Corporate Hospitality Days **Location** 7m NE of Alnwick off A1
Hotel ★★ 82% HL Dunstanburgh Castle Hotel, EMBLETON
☎ 01665 576111 🖹 0870 706 0394 32 en suite

FELTON
Map 12 NU10

Burgham Park Golf & Leisure Club NE65 9QP
☎ 01670 787898 (office) & 787978 (pro shop)
🖹 01670 787164
e-mail: info@burghampark.co.uk
web: www.burghampark.co.uk

PGA associates designed course, making the most of the gentle rolling
landscape with views to the sea and the Northumbrian hills.

Aidan Course: 18 Holes, 7065yards, Par 71, SSS 74,
Course record 72. Club membership 560.

Visitors Mon-Sun & BHs. Booking required. Handicap certificate.
Dress code. **Societies** booking required. **Green Fees** not confirmed
Course Designer Andrew Mair **Prof** David Mather **Facilities** ⓣ ⓞ
🝙 ⌷ 🏐 ⚲ 🏠 🏴 ✐ 🚗 ✐ ⚑ **Leisure** par 3 course **Conf**
Corporate Hospitality Days **Location** 5m N of Morpeth, 0.5m off A1
Hotel ★★★★ 82% HL Macdonald Linden Hall, Golf & Country
Club, LONGHORSLEY ☎ 01670 500000 & 0844 879 9084
🖹 01670 500001 50 en suite

HEDDON-ON-THE-WALL
Map 12 NZ16

Close House Hotel & Golf NE15 0HT
☎ 01661 852255 🖹 01661 853322
e-mail: ellie.barnett@closehouse.co.uk
web: www.closehouse.co.uk

Situated in the grounds of the Close House Estate with stunning views
of the River Tyne and surrounding area. The original course dates back
to 1964 but a substantial recent development has produced one of the
finest courses in the county. The new course offers a great challenge
to golfers of all abilities with its USGA specification sloping greens
and longer length.

Filly:, 5956yds, Par 70, SSS 70, Course record 65.
Club membership 400.

Visitors Mon-Sun & BHs. Booking required. Dress code.
Societies booking required. **Green Fees** not confirmed **Course**
Designer Hawtrees **Prof** Jonathan Lupton **Facilities** ⓣ ⓞ 🝙 ⌷
🏐 ⚲ 🏠 🏴 ✐ 🚗 ✐ ⚑ **Conf** facs Corporate Hospitality
Days **Location** From A1/A69 rdbt, follow A69 W for 4m to junct signed
Close House (B6528). Left at junct. Close House Hotel signed on left
Hotel ★★★★ 74% HL Close House, HEDDON-ON-THE-WALL
☎ 01661 852255 🖹 01661 853322 31 en suite

HEXHAM
Map 12 NY96

De Vere Slaley Hall, Golf Resort & Spa Slaley NE47 0BY
☎ 01434 673154 📄 01434 673152
web: www.deveregolf.co.uk
*Hunting Course: 18 Holes, 7088yds, Par 72, SSS 74,
Course record 63.
Priestman Course: 18 Holes, 6951yds, Par 72, SSS 72,
Course record 63.*
Course Designer Dave Thomas/Neil Coles **Location** 8m S of Hexham
off A68
Telephone for further details
Hotel ★★★★ 80% HL De Vere Slaley Hall, Slaley, HEXHAM
☎ 01434 673350 📄 01434 673962 142 en suite

Hexham Golf Club Spital Park NE46 3RZ
☎ 01434 603072 📄 01434 601865
e-mail: info@hexhamgolf.co.uk
web: www.hexhamgolf.co.uk
A very pretty, well-drained course with interesting natural contours.
Exquisite views from parts of the course of the Tyne Valley below. As
good a parkland course as any in the north of England.
*18 Holes, 6294yds, Par 70, SSS 70, Course record 61.
Club membership 700.*
Visitors Mon-Fri, Sun & BHs. Booking required. Dress code.
Societies booking required. **Green Fees** £35 per round (£45
Sun & BHs) **Course Designer** Vardon/Caird **Prof** Andrew
Paisley **Facilities** ⊕ ⑪ ⓘ 🏌 ☐ 🏐 🏖 🏠 🏴 ◇ 🏌 🚜 🏌
Leisure squash, squash courts **Conf** facs Corporate Hospitality Days
Location 1m NW on B6531
Hotel ★★★ 80% HL Best Western Beaumont Hotel, Beaumont
Street, HEXHAM ☎ 01434 602331 📄 01434 606184 34 en suite

LONGHORSLEY
Map 12 NZ19

Macdonald Linden Hall, Golf & Country Club NE65 8XF
☎ 01670 500011 📄 01670 500001
e-mail: golf.lindenhall@macdonald-hotels.co.uk
web: www.macdonaldhotels.co.uk/lindenhall
Set within the picturesque Linden Hall Estate on a mixture of mature
woodland and parkland, established lakes and burns provide
interesting water features to match the peaceful surroundings. This
award-winning course is a pleasure to play for all standards of golfer.
18 Holes, 6846yds, Par 72, SSS 73. Club membership 250.
Visitors Mon-Sun & BHs. Booking required. Dress code.
Societies booking required. **Green Fees** £36 (from £25 weekends)
Course Designer Jonathan Gaunt **Prof** Sam Oliver & Gordon Morrison
Facilities ⊕ ⑪ ⓘ 🏌 ☐ 🏐 🏖 🏠 🏴 ◇ 🏌 🚜 🏌
Leisure hard tennis courts, sauna, gymnasium, chipping green
Conf facs Corporate Hospitality Days **Location** from A1 take A697,
0.5m from village of Longhorsley
Hotel ★★★★ 82% HL Macdonald Linden Hall, Golf & Country
Club, LONGHORSLEY ☎ 01670 500000 & 0844 879 9084
📄 01670 500001 50 en suite

MATFEN
Map 12 NZ07

Matfen Hall Country House Hotel & Golf Club NE20 0RH
☎ 01661 886400 📄 01661 886055
e-mail: golf@matfenhall.com
web: www.matfenhall.com
A 27-hole parkland course set in beautiful countryside with many
natural and man-made hazards. The course is an enjoyable test
for players of all abilities but it does incorporate challenging water
features in the shape of a large lake and a fast flowing river. The dry
stone wall presents a unique obstacle on several holes. The 4th, 9th,
12th and 14th holes are particularly testing for 4s, the dog-leg 16th
is the pick of the par 5s but Matfen's signature hole is the long par 3
17th with its narrow green teasingly sited just over the river.
*Douglas: 9 Holes, 3339yds, Par 36, SSS 36.
Standing Stone: 9 Holes, 3361yds, Par 36, SSS 36.
Dewlaw: 9 Holes, 3357yds, Par 36, SSS 36.*
Visitors Mon-Sun & BHs. Booking required. Dress code.
Societies booking required. **Green Fees** not confirmed **Course
Designer** Mair/James/Gaunt/Harrison/Parkinson **Prof** John Harrison
Facilities ⑪ ⓘ 🏌 ☐ 🏐 🏖 🏠 🏴 ◇ 🏌 🚜 🏌 🏌
Leisure heated indoor swimming pool, sauna, gymnasium, 9 hole par
3 course. 10 bay covered driving range. Leisure complex & health spa
Conf facs Corporate Hospitality Days **Location** off B6318
Hotel ★★★★ 81% HL Matfen Hall, MATFEN ☎ 01661 886500 &
855708 📄 01661 886055 53 en suite

MORPETH
Map 12 NZ28

Morpeth Golf Club The Clubhouse NE61 2BT
☎ 01670 504942 📄 01670 504918
e-mail: admin@morpethgolf.co.uk
web: www.morpethgolf.co.uk
Parkland course with views of the Cheviots.
*18 Holes, 6206yds, Par 71, SSS 69, Course record 65.
Club membership 700.*
Visitors contact club for details. **Societies** welcome. **Green Fees** not
confirmed **Course Designer** Harry Vardon **Prof** Martin Jackson
Facilities ⑪ ⓘ 🏌 ☐ 🏐 🏖 🏠 🏌 🏌 **Location** S of town
centre on A197
Hotel ★★★★ 82% HL Macdonald Linden Hall, Golf & Country
Club, LONGHORSLEY ☎ 01670 500000 & 0844 879 9084
📄 01670 500001 50 en suite

NEWBIGGIN-BY-THE-SEA
Map 12 NZ38

Newbiggin Golf Club Prospect Place NE64 6DW
☎ 01670 817344
e-mail: info@newbiggingolfclub.co.uk
web: www.newbiggingolfclub.co.uk
Seaside-links course.
*18 Holes, 6516yds, Par 72, SSS 72, Course record 65.
Club membership 694.*
Visitors Mon-Sun except BHs. Dress code. **Societies** booking required.
Green Fees £27 per day, £20 per round (£27/£25 weekends) **Course
Designer** Willie Park **Prof** James Kerr **Facilities** ⑪ ⓘ 🏌 ☐ 🏐
🏖 🏠 🏌 🚜 🏌 **Leisure** snooker **Conf** facs Corporate Hospitality
Days **Location** N of town centre
Hotel ★★★★ 82% HL Macdonald Linden Hall, Golf & Country
Club, LONGHORSLEY ☎ 01670 500000 & 0844 879 9084
📄 01670 500001 50 en suite

Save on Hotels. Book at **theAA.com/hotel**

NORTHUMBERLAND

ENGLAND

PONTELAND
Map 12 NZ17

Ponteland Golf Club 53 Bell Villas NE20 9BD
☎ 01661 822689 📄 01661 860077
e-mail: secretary@thepontelandgolfclub.co.uk
web: www.thepontelandgolfclub.co.uk
Open parkland course offering testing golf and good views.
18 Holes, 6611yds, Par 72, SSS 72, Course record 65.
Club membership 1500.
Visitors Tue, Thu, Sun & BHs. Booking preferable. Handicap certificate preferred. Dress code. **Societies** booking required. **Green Fees** not confirmed **Course Designer** Harry Fernie **Prof** Alan Robson-Crosby
Facilities 🕪 🍴 🛒 ➔ 🖥 🏠 ⚙ 🛄 ⚙ 🏌 **Conf** facs
Corporate Hospitality Days **Location** 0.5m E on A696
Hotel ★★★ 77% HL Novotel Newcastle Airport, Ponteland Road, Kenton, NEWCASTLE UPON TYNE ☎ 0191 214 0303 📄 0191 214 0633 126 en suite

ROTHBURY
Map 12 NU00

Rothbury Golf Club Whitton Rd NE65 7RX
☎ 01669 621271
e-mail: secretary@rothburygolfclub.com
web: www.rothburygolfclub.com
Scenic, flat parkland course set alongside the River Coquet, surrounded by Simonside hills and Cragside Hall.
18 Holes, 6168yds, Par 71, SSS 70, Course record 71.
Club membership 306.
Visitors Mon-Sun & BHs. Booking required Sat & Sun. Dress code. **Societies** booking required. **Green Fees** not confirmed **Course Designer** J Radcliffe **Facilities** 🕪 🍴 🛒 ➔ 🖥 🏠 🛄 ⚙
🏌 **Conf** Corporate Hospitality Days **Location** SW of town off B6342
Hotel ★★★★ 82% HL Macdonald Linden Hall, Golf & Country Club, LONGHORSLEY ☎ 01670 500000 & 0844 879 9084
📄 01670 500001 50 en suite

SEAHOUSES
Map 12 NU23

Seahouses Golf Club Beadnell Rd NE68 7XT
☎ 01665 720794
e-mail: secretary@seahousesgolf.co.uk
web: www.seahousesgolf.co.uk
Traditional links course with many hazards. Signature holes are the famous par 3 10th hole, Logans Loch, water hole and the par 3 15th, nominated as one of the most difficult holes in the world. Spectacular views of the coastline to the Farne Islands and Lindisfarne.
18 Holes, 5542yds, Par 67, SSS 66, Course record 63.
Club membership 550.
Visitors Mon-Sun & BHs. Booking required. Dress code.
Societies booking required **Green Fees** not confirmed **Facilities** 🕪
🍴 🛒 ➔ 🖥 🏠 🛄 ⚙ **Location** S of village on B1340, 5m E of A1
Hotel ★★ 78% HL Beach House, Sea Front, SEAHOUSES
☎ 01665 720337 📄 01665 720921 27 en suite

STOCKSFIELD
Map 12 NZ06

Stocksfield Golf Club New Ridley Rd NE43 7RE
☎ 01661 843041 📄 01661 843046
e-mail: info@sgcgolf.co.uk
web: www.sgcgolf.co.uk
Challenging course: parkland (nine holes), woodland (nine holes). Some elevated greens, giving fine views, and water hazards.
18 Holes, 5967yds, Par 70, SSS 69, Course record 61.
Club membership 550.
Visitors Booking advisable. Dress code. **Societies** welcome. **Green Fees** £30 per day, £20 per round (£30 weekends & BHs) **Course Designer** Pennick **Prof** Steven Harrison **Facilities** 🕪 🍴 🛒 🖥
🍴 🏠 📷 🛄 ⚙ **Leisure** snooker **Conf** Corporate Hospitality Days **Location** 1.5m S off A695
Hotel ★★★ 80% HL Best Western Beaumont Hotel, Beaumont Street, HEXHAM ☎ 01434 602331 📄 01434 606184 34 en suite

SWARLAND
Map 12 NU10

Percy Wood Golf & Country Retreat Coast View NE65 9JG
☎ 01670 787010
web: www.percywood.co.uk
18 Holes, 6335yds, Par 72, SSS 72.
Location 1m W of A1
Telephone for further details
Hotel ★★★★ 82% HL Macdonald Linden Hall, Golf & Country Club, LONGHORSLEY ☎ 01670 500000 & 0844 879 9084
📄 01670 500001 50 en suite

WOOLER
Map 12 NT92

Wooler Golf Club Dod Law, Doddington NE71 6AN
☎ 01668 282135
web: www.woolergolf.co.uk
Hilltop, moorland course with spectacular views over the Glendale Valley. Nine greens played from 18 tees. A very challenging course when windy with one par 5 of 580yds. The course is much under used during the week so is always available.
9 Holes, 6411yds, Par 72, SSS 72, Course record 68.
Club membership 300.
Visitors Dress code. **Societies** booking required. **Green Fees** £20 per 18 holes, £15 per 9 holes 🏠 **Facilities** 🕪 by prior arrangement 🍴 by prior arrangement 🛒 🖥 🍴 🏠 ⚙ 🛄 ⚙ **Location** at Doddington on B6525
Hotel ★★ 76% HL Purdy Lodge, Adderstone Services, BELFORD
☎ 01668 213000 📄 01668 213111 20 en suite

NOTTINGHAMSHIRE

CALVERTON
Map 8 SK64

Ramsdale Park Golf Centre Oxton Rd NG14 6NU
☎ 0115 965 5600 📄 0115 965 4105
e-mail: info@ramsdaleparkgc.co.uk
web: www.ramsdaleparkgc.co.uk

The Seely Course is a challenging and comprehensive test for any standard of golf. A relatively flat front nine is followed by an undulating back nine that is renowned as one of the best in the county. The Lee Course is an 18-hole par 3 course with holes of varying lengths, suitable for beginners and those wishing to improve their short game.

Seely Course: 18 Holes, 6674yds, Par 71, SSS 72.
Club membership 400.

Visitors Mon-Sun & BHs. Booking required. Dress code.
Societies booking required. **Green Fees** not confirmed **Course Designer** Hawtree **Prof** Robert Macey **Facilities** ⓣ ⑩ ⯑ ⬜ ⯑ ⯑ ⯑ ⯑ ⯑ **Leisure** fishing, 18 hole par 3 Lee Course **Conf** facs Corporate Hospitality Days **Location** 8m NE of Nottingham off B6386
Hotel ★★★ 71% HL Best Western Bestwood Lodge, Bestwood Country Park, Arnold, NOTTINGHAM ☎ 0115 920 3011 📄 0115 964 9678 39 en suite

Springwater Golf Club Moor Ln NG14 6FZ
☎ 0115 965 2129 (pro shop) & 965 4946
📄 0115 965 2344
e-mail: dave.pullan@springwatergolfclub.com
web: www.springwatergolfclub.com

This attractive course set in rolling countryside overlooking the Trent Valley, offers an interesting and challenging game of golf to players of all handicaps. The 18th hole is particularly noteworthy, a 183yd par 3 over two ponds

18 Holes, 6262yds, Par 71, SSS 71, Course record 66.
Club membership 440.

Visitors Mon-Sun & BHs. Dress code. **Societies** booking required.
Green Fees £22 per round (£27 weekends & BHs) **Course Designer** Neil Footitt/Paul Wharmsby **Prof** Paul Drew **Facilities** ⓣ ⑩ ⯑ ⬜ ⯑ ⯑ ⯑ ⯑ ⯑ ⯑ ⯑ **Leisure** short game academy **Conf** facs Corporate Hospitality Days **Location** off A6097 to Calverton, 600yds on left
Hotel ★★★★ RR Cockliffe Country House, Burntstump Country Park, Burntstump Hill, Arnold, NOTTINGHAM ☎ 0115 968 0179 📄 0115 968 0623 11 rooms

EAST LEAKE
Map 8 SK52

The Rushcliffe Golf Club Stocking Ln LE12 5RL
☎ 01509 852959 📄 01509 852688
e-mail: secretary@rushcliffegolfclub.com
Hilly, tree-lined and picturesque parkland.

18 Holes, 6013yds, Par 70, SSS 71, Course record 63.
Club membership 750.

Visitors contact club for details **Societies** booking required. **Green Fees** not confirmed **Course Designer** Tom Williamson **Prof** Chris Hall **Facilities** ⓣ ⑩ ⯑ ⬜ ⯑ ⯑ ⯑ ⯑ ⯑ **Location** M1 junct 24
Hotel ★★★★ 79% HL Best Western Premier Yew Lodge Hotel & Spa, Packington Hill, KEGWORTH ☎ 01509 672518 📄 01509 674730 103 en suite

HUCKNALL
Map 8 SK54

Hucknall Golf Centre Wigwam Ln NG15 7TA
☎ 0115 964 2037 📄 0115 964 2724
web: www.jackbarker.com
18 Holes, 6026yds, Par 70, SSS 70.

Course Designer Tom Hodgetts **Location** 0.5m from town centre, signs for railway station, right onto Wigwam Ln
Telephone for further details
Hotel ★★★ 71% HL Best Western Bestwood Lodge, Bestwood Country Park, Arnold, NOTTINGHAM ☎ 0115 920 3011 📄 0115 964 9678 39 en suite

KEYWORTH
Map 8 SK63

Stanton on the Wolds Golf Club Golf Course Rd NG12 5BH
☎ 0115 937 4885 📄 0115 937 1652
18 Holes, 6369yds, Par 73, SSS 71, Course record 67.
Course Designer Tom Williamson **Location** E side of village off A606
Telephone for further details
Hotel ★★★ 81% HL Langar Hall, LANGAR ☎ 01949 860559 📄 01949 861045 12 en suite

KIRKBY IN ASHFIELD
Map 8 SK55

Notts Golf Club (Hollinwell) Derby Rd NG17 7QR
☎ 01623 753225 📄 01623 753655
e-mail: office@nottsgolfclub.co.uk
web: www.nottsgolfclub.co.uk
Undulating heathland championship course. Host to 2012 British Boys Championships.

18 Holes, 7250yds, Par 72, SSS 76, Course record 67.
Club membership 340.

Visitors Mon-Fri & Sun except BHs. Booking required. Handicap certificate. Dress code. **Societies** booking required. **Green Fees** £105 per day, £75 per round **Course Designer** Willie Park **Prof** Mike Bradley **Facilities** ⓣ ⑩ ⯑ ⬜ ⯑ ⯑ ⯑ ⯑ ⯑ **Conf** Corporate Hospitality Days **Location** 2m SE of Mansfield off A611
Hotel ★★ 70% SHL Pine Lodge, 281-283 Nottingham Road, MANSFIELD ☎ 01623 622308 📄 01623 656819 20 en suite

Save on Hotels. Book at **theAA.com/hotel**

NOTTINGHAMSHIRE

ENGLAND

MANSFIELD

Map 8 SK56

Sherwood Forest Golf Club Eakring Rd NG18 3EW

☎ 01623 627403 📄 01623 420412

e-mail: info@sherwoodforestgolfclub.co.uk

web: www.sherwoodforestgolfclub.co.uk

As the name suggests, the forest is the main feature of this natural heathland course with its heather, silver birch and pine trees. The homeward nine holes are particularly testing. The 11th to the 14th are notable par 4 holes on this well-bunkered course.

18 Holes, 6861yds, Par 73, SSS 73, Course record 64. Club membership 750.

Visitors Mon-Fri except BHs. Booking required. Handicap certificate. Dress code. **Societies** booking required. **Green Fees** £80 per day, £60 per round **Course Designer** H S Colt/James Braid **Prof** Ken Hall **Facilities** 🕙 🍴 🖺 🖵 🍴 🎿 🛋 ✔ 🛺 ✔ **Leisure** snooker **Conf** facs Corporate Hospitality Days **Location** E of Mansfield

Hotel ★★ 70% SHL Pine Lodge, 281-283 Nottingham Road, MANSFIELD ☎ 01623 622308 📄 01623 656819 20 en suite

NEWARK-ON-TRENT

Map 8 SK75

Newark Golf Club Coddington NG24 2QX

☎ 01636 626282 📄 01636 626497

e-mail: manager@newarkgolfclub.co.uk

web: www.newarkgolfclub.co.uk

Wooded parkland in a secluded position with easy walking, and of high quality.

18 Holes, 6488yds, Par 71, SSS 72. Club membership 650.

Visitors Mon, Wed-Sun except BHs. Booking required **Societies** booking required. **Green Fees** £42 per day, £35 per round (£50/£42 weekends) **Course Designer** T Williamson **Prof** Robert Ellis **Facilities** 🕙 🍴 🖺 🖵 🍴 🎿 🛋 ✔ 🛺 ✔ **Leisure** snooker **Conf** facs Corporate Hospitality Days **Location** 4m E of Newark on Sleaford road

Hotel ★★★ 82% HL The Grange Hotel, 73 London Road, NEWARK ☎ 01636 703399 📄 01636 702328 19 en suite

NOTTINGHAM

Map 8 SK53

Beeston Fields Golf Club Old Dr, Wollaton Rd, Beeston NG9 3DD

☎ 0115 925 7062 📄 0115 925 4280

e-mail: info@beestonfields.co.uk

web: www.beestonfields.co.uk

Parkland course with sandy subsoil and wide, tree-lined fairways. The par 3 14th has an elevated tee and a small bunker-guarded green.

18 Holes, 6404yds, Par 71, SSS 72, Course record 63. Club membership 600.

Visitors Mon,Wed & Fri except BHs.. Booking required. Dress code. **Societies** booking required. **Green Fees** £35 per day, £27.50 per round **Course Designer** Tom Williamson **Prof** Alun Wardle **Facilities** 🕙 🍴 by prior arrangement 🖺 🖵 🍴 🎿 🛋 🛺 ✔ **Conf** facs Corporate Hospitality Days **Location** 400yds SW off A52 Nottingham-Derby road

Hotel ★★★ 74% HL Risley Hall Hotel & Spa, Derby Road, RISLEY ☎ 0115 939 9000 & 921 8523 📄 0115 939 7766 35 en suite

Bulwell Forest Golf Club Hucknall Rd, Bulwell NG6 9LQ

☎ 0115 976 3172 (pro shop) 📄 0115 977 0576

e-mail: secretary@bulwellforestgolfclub.co.uk

web: www.bulwellforestgolfclub.com

Municipal heathland course with many natural hazards. Very tight fairways and subject to wind. Five challenging par 3s. Excellent drainage with no winter greens or tees.

18 Holes, 5726yds, Par 68, SSS 68. Club membership 180.

Visitors Mon-Sun & BHs. Booking required. **Societies** booking required. **Green Fees** phone **Course Designer** John Doleman **Prof** Ian Brown **Facilities** 🕙 🖺 🖵 🍴 🎿 🛋 🛺 ✔ **Leisure** hard tennis courts, children's playground **Conf** Corporate Hospitality Days **Location** 4m NW of city on A611

Hotel ★★★ 71% HL Best Western Bestwood Lodge, Bestwood Country Park, Arnold, NOTTINGHAM ☎ 0115 920 3011 📄 0115 964 9678 39 en suite

Chilwell Manor Golf Club Meadow Ln, Chilwell NG9 5AE

☎ 0115 925 8958 📄 0115 922 0575

e-mail: info@chilwellmanorgolfclub.co.uk

web: www.chilwellmanorgolfclub.co.uk

Flat parkland. Some water, plenty of trees and narrow fairways.

18 Holes, 6248yds, Par 70, SSS 71, Course record 64. Club membership 750.

Visitors Mon, Wed-Fri except BHs, Tue pm only. Dress code. **Societies** booking required **Green Fees** £30 per day, £25 per round (weekends £30 per round) 🖼 **Course Designer** Tom Williamson **Prof** Paul Wilson **Facilities** 🕙 🍴 🖺 🖵 🍴 🎿 🛋 ✔ **Conf** facs Corporate Hospitality Days **Location** 4m SW on A6005

Hotel ★★★ 74% HL Risley Hall Hotel & Spa, Derby Road, RISLEY ☎ 0115 939 9000 & 921 8523 📄 0115 939 7766 35 en suite

Edwalton Municipal Golf Course Wellin Ln, Edwalton NG12 4AS

☎ 0115 923 4775 📄 0115 923 1647

e-mail: edwalton@glendale-services.co.uk

web: www.glendale-golf.com

Gently sloping, challenging nine-hole parkland course. Also a nine-hole par 3.

9 Holes, 3336yds, Par 72, SSS 72, Course record 71. Club membership 650.

Visitors dress code. **Societies** booking required. **Green Fees** not confirmed **Prof** Mike Pashley/Daniel Parkes **Facilities** 🕙 🍴 by prior arrangement 🖺 🖵 🍴 🎿 🛋 🛺 ✔ 🛺 ✔ **Leisure** par 3 course **Conf** facs Corporate Hospitality Days **Location** S of Nottingham off A606

Hotel ★★★ 67% HL Swans Hotel & Restaurant, 84-90 Radcliffe Road, West Bridgford, NOTTINGHAM ☎ 0115 981 4042 📄 0115 945 5745 30 en suite

Mapperley Golf Club Central Av, Plains Rd, Mapperley NG3 6RH

☎ 0115 955 6673 (pro) & 955 6672 (sec)
🖨 0115 955 6670
e-mail: secretary@mapperleygolfclub.org
web: www.mapperleygolfclub.org

Hilly meadowland course but with easy walking.

18 Holes, 6307yds, Par 71, SSS 70, Course record 65.
Club membership 700.

Visitors contact club for details **Societies** booking required. **Green Fees** not confirmed **Course Designer** John Mason **Prof** John Newham **Facilities** ⑪ ⑩ ⬛ ⬜ ⬜ ⬜ ⬜ ⬜ ⬜ �🏌 **Leisure** pool room **Conf** facs Corporate Hospitality Days **Location** 3m NE of city centre off B684
Hotel ★★★ 71% HL Best Western Bestwood Lodge, Bestwood Country Park, Arnold, NOTTINGHAM ☎ 0115 920 3011 🖨 0115 964 9678 39 en suite

Nottingham City Golf Club Sandhurst Rd, Bulwell Hall Park NG6 8LF

☎ 0115 927 2767 & 07740 688694
e-mail: garyandkate1@talktalk.net
web: www.nottinghamcitygolfclub.co.uk

A pleasant parkland course on the city outskirts.

18 Holes, 6200yds, Par 69, SSS 70, Course record 64.
Club membership 390.

Visitors Sat am booking required. **Societies** booking required. **Green Fees** phone **Course Designer** Tom Williamson **Facilities** ⑪ ⑩ ⬛ ⬜ ⬜ ⬜ ⬜ **Conf** facs Corporate Hospitality Days **Location** 4m NW of city centre off A6002
Hotel ★★★ 71% HL Best Western Bestwood Lodge, Bestwood Country Park, Arnold, NOTTINGHAM ☎ 0115 920 3011 🖨 0115 964 9678 39 en suite

Wollaton Park Golf Club Limetree Av, Wollaton Park NG8 1BT

☎ 0115 978 7574 🖨 0115 970 0736
e-mail: secretary@wollatonparkgolfclub.com
web: www.wollatonparkgolfclub.com

A traditional parkland course on gently undulating land, winding through historic woodland and set in a historic deer park. Fine views of 16th-century Wollaton Hall.

18 Holes, 6445yds, Par 71, SSS 71.
Club membership 700.

Visitors Mon-Sun & BHs. Dress code. **Societies** booking required. **Green Fees** £52 per day, £38 per round (£58/£42 weekends & BHs) **Course Designer** T Williamson **Prof** John Lower **Facilities** ⑪ ⑩ ⬛ ⬜ ⬜ ⬜ ⬜ ✔ **Conf** Corporate Hospitality Days **Location** 2.5m W of city centre off ring road at junct A52
Hotel ★★★ 67% HL Swans Hotel & Restaurant, 84-90 Radcliffe Road, West Bridgford, NOTTINGHAM ☎ 0115 981 4042 🖨 0115 945 5745 30 en suite

OLLERTON
Map 8 SK66

Rufford Park Golf & Country Club Rufford Ln, Rufford NG22 9DG

☎ 01623 825253 🖨 01623 825254
e-mail: enquiries@ruffordpark.co.uk
web: www.ruffordpark.co.uk

Set in the heart of Sherwood Forest, Rufford Park is noted for its picturesque 18 holes with its especially challenging par 3s. From the unique 175yd par 3 17th over water to the riverside 641yd 13th, the course offers everything the golfer needs from beginner to professional.

18 Holes, 6368yds, Par 70, SSS 71, Course record 66.
Club membership 600.

Visitors Contact club for details. **Societies** booking required. **Green Fees** £35 per day, £22 per 18 holes (£28 weekends) **Course Designer** David Hemstock/Ken Brown **Prof** John Vaughan/James Thompson **Facilities** ⑪ ⑩ ⬛ ⬜ ⬜ ⬜ ⬜ ⬜ ✔ **Conf** facs Corporate Hospitality Days **Location** S of Ollerton, off A614 for Rufford Mill
Hotel ★★★ 78% HL Clumber Park, Clumber Park, WORKSOP ☎ 01623 835333 🖨 01623 835525 73 en suite

OXTON
Map 8 SK65

Oakmere Park Golf Club Oaks Ln NG25 0RH

☎ 0115 965 3545 🖨 0115 965 5628
e-mail: enquiries@oakmerepark.co.uk
web: www.oakmerepark.co.uk

Twenty-seven holes set in rolling heathland in the heart of picturesque Robin Hood country. Renowned for its all weather playing qualities.

Admirals: 18 Holes, 6739yds, Par 73, SSS 73, Course record 65.
Commanders: 9 Holes, 6407yds, Par 72, SSS 71, Course record 69. Club membership 900.

Visitors Mon-Sun & BHs. Booking required. **Societies** booking required. **Green Fees** Admirals £24 per 18 holes (£34 weekends). Commanders £14/£18 **Course Designer** Frank Pennick **Prof** Daryl St-John Jones **Facilities** ⑪ ⑩ ⬛ ⬜ ⬜ ⬜ ⬜ ✔ ✔ **Conf** facs Corporate Hospitality Days **Location** 1m NW of Oxton off A6097 or A614
Hotel ★★★★ RR Cockliffe Country House, Burntstump Country Park, Burntstump Hill, Arnold, NOTTINGHAM ☎ 0115 968 0179 🖨 0115 968 0623 11 rooms

Save on Hotels. Book at **theAA.com/hotel**

NOTTINGHAMSHIRE

ENGLAND

RADCLIFFE ON TRENT — Map 8 SK63

Cotgrave Place Golf Club, Stragglethorpe, Nr Cotgrave Village NG12 3HB
☎ 0115 933 3344 📠 0115 933 4567
e-mail: general@thenottinghamshire.com
web: www.thenottinghamshire.com

The course offers 36 holes of championship golf. The front nine of the Open course is placed around a beautiful lake, man-made ponds and the Grantham Canal. The back nine is set in magnificent parkland with mature trees and wide fairways. Masters has an opening nine set among hedgerows and coppices. The huge greens with their interesting shapes are a particularly challenging test of nerve. The par 5 17th hole is one of the toughest in the country.

Masters: 18 Holes, 5946yds, Par 70, SSS 69.
Open: 18 Holes, 6302yds, Par 71, SSS 71.
Club membership 850.

Visitors Mon-Sun & BHs. Booking required. Dress code. **Societies** booking required. **Green Fees** phone **Course Designer** Peter Aliss/John Small **Prof** Robert Smith **Facilities** ⊕ ⊮ ⊾ ⊡ ⊮ ⊿ ⊕ ✦ ⊕ ✦ ⊱ **Conf** facs Corporate Hospitality Days **Location** 2m SW of Radcliffe off A52
Hotel ★★★ 81% HL Langar Hall, LANGAR ☎ 01949 860559 📠 01949 861045 12 en suite

Radcliffe-on-Trent Golf Club Dewberry Ln, Cropwell Rd NG12 2JH
☎ 0115 933 3000 📠 0115 911 6991
e-mail: manager@radcliffeontrentgc.co.uk
web: www.radcliffeontrentgc.co.uk

Fairly flat, parkland course with three good finishing holes: 16th (423 yds) par 4; 17th (174 yds) through spinney, par 3; 18th (336 yds) dog-leg par 4. Excellent views.

18 Holes, 6374yds, Par 70, SSS 71, Course record 64.
Club membership 700.

Visitors Mon-Sun & BHs. Booking required Tue, weekends & BHs. Handicap certificate. Dress code **Societies** booking required. **Green Fees** £40 per day, £30 per 18 holes **Course Designer** Tom Williamson **Prof** Craig George **Facilities** ⊕ ⊮ ⊾ ⊡ ⊮ ⊿ ⊕ ⊮ ✦ ⊕ ✦ **Conf** Corporate Hospitality Days **Location** 0.5m SE of town centre off A52
Hotel ★★★ 67% HL Swans Hotel & Restaurant, 84-90 Radcliffe Road, West Bridgford, NOTTINGHAM ☎ 0115 981 4042 📠 0115 945 5745 30 en suite

RETFORD — Map 8 SK78

Retford Golf Club Brecks Rd, Ordsall DN22 7UA
☎ 01777 711188 (Secretary) 📠 01777 710412
e-mail: retfordgolfclub@lineone.net
web: www.retfordgolfclub.co.uk

Wooded parkland.

18 Holes, 6507yds, Par 72, SSS 72, Course record 65.
Club membership 700.

Visitors booking required. **Societies** welcome. **Green Fees** £37 per day, £32 per round **Course Designer** Tom Williamson **Prof** Craig Morris **Facilities** ⊕ ⊮ ⊾ ⊡ ⊮ ⊿ ⊕ ⊮ ✦ ⊕ ✦ **Conf** Corporate Hospitality Days **Location** 1.5m S A620, between Worksop & Gainsborough
Hotel ★★★ 77% HL Best Western West Retford, 24 North Road, RETFORD ☎ 01777 706333 📠 01777 709951 63 en suite

RUDDINGTON — Map 8 SK53

Ruddington Grange Golf Club Wilford Rd NG11 6NB
☎ 0115 921 1951 (pro shop) & 984 6141 (society) bkgs
📠 0115 940 5165
e-mail: info@ruddingtongrange.com
web: www.ruddingtongrange.com

Undulating parkland with many mature trees and water hazards on eight holes. Challenging but fair layout.

18 Holes, 6515yds, Par 72, SSS 72, Course record 69.
Club membership 650.

Visitors Mon-Fri except BHs. Booking required. Dress code. **Societies** booking required. **Green Fees** £40 per day, £28 per 18 holes **Course Designer** E MacAusland/J Small **Prof** Robert Simpson **Facilities** ⊕ ⊮ ⊾ ⊡ ⊮ ⊿ ⊕ ✦ ⊕ ✦ **Conf** facs Corporate Hospitality Days **Location** 4m S of city centre
Hotel ★★★ 67% HL Swans Hotel & Restaurant, 84-90 Radcliffe Road, West Bridgford, NOTTINGHAM ☎ 0115 981 4042 📠 0115 945 5745 30 en suite

SERLBY — Map 8 SK68

Serlby Park Golf Club DN10 6BA
☎ 01777 818268
e-mail: serlbysec@talktalkbusiness.net

Peaceful, picturesque setting on well-drained areas of woodland, parkland and farmland on the Serlby Hall Estate. Easy walking.

Serlby Park: 9 Holes, 5396yds, Par 66, SSS 66, Course record 62. Club membership 260.

Visitors Mon-Sun & BHs. Booking required. Handicap certificate. Dress code. **Societies** booking required. **Green Fees** £15 per round (£20 weekends & BHs) 🍴 **Course Designer** Tom Williamson **Facilities** ⊕ ⊮ ⊾ ⊡ ⊮ ⊿ **Conf** Corporate Hospitality Days **Location** from A1(M) Blyth take A614 E towards Bawtry for 1m. Right signed Serlby, clubhouse 0.75 on right
Hotel ★★★ 82% HL Best Western Charnwood Hotel, Sheffield Road, BLYTH ☎ 01909 591610 📠 01909 591429 45 en suite

SOUTHWELL — Map 8 SK65

Norwood Park Golf Course Norwood Park NG25 0PF
☎ 01636 816626
web: www.norwoodpark.co.uk

18 Holes, 6805yds, Par 72, SSS 72, Course record 68.

Course Designer Clyde B Johnston **Location** off A617 Newark to Mansfield road. Take turning to Southwell in Kirklington, golf course 5m on right
Telephone for further details
Hotel ★★★ 73% HL Saracens Head, Market Place, SOUTHWELL ☎ 01636 812701 📠 01636 815408 27 en suite

SUTTON IN ASHFIELD　　　　Map 8 SK45

Coxmoor Golf Club Coxmoor Rd NG17 5LF
☎ 01623 557359 📠 01623 557435
web: www.coxmoorgolfclub.co.uk

18 Holes, 6577yds, Par 73, SSS 72, Course record 65.
Location M1 junct 27/28, exit for Mansfield, entrance to club on B6139
Telephone for further details
Hotel ★★ 70% SHL Pine Lodge, 281-283 Nottingham Road, MANSFIELD ☎ 01623 622308 📠 01623 656819　20 en suite

WORKSOP　　　　Map 8 SK57

Bondhay Golf Club Bondhay Ln, Whitwell S80 3EH
☎ 01909 723608 📠 01909 720226
e-mail: enquiries@bondhay.com
web: www.bondhay.com

The wind usually plays quite an active role in making this flat championship course testing. Signature holes are the 10th which requires a second shot over water into a basin of trees; the 11th comes back over the same expanse of water and requires a mid to short iron to a long, narrow green; the 18th is a par 5 with a lake - the dilemma is whether to lay up short or go for the carry. The par 3s are generally island-like in design, requiring accuracy to avoid the many protective bunker features.

Devonshire Course: 18 Holes, 6820yds, Par 72, SSS 74, Course record 69. Club membership 600.
Visitors Mon-Sun & BHs. Dress code. **Societies** booking required.
Green Fees 18 holes Mon-Tues £17, Wed-Fri £20, weekends £27.
Par 3 course £6 **Course Designer** Donald Steel **Prof** Michael Ramsden **Facilities** ⊕ ⦾ ⓛ ⌂ ⛳ ⚐ 🏌 ♢ ✦ 🏁 ⛱ 🥢
Leisure fishing, 9 hole par 3 academy course **Conf** facs Corporate Hospitality Days **Location** M1 junct 30, 5m W of Worksop off A619
Hotel ★★★ 70% HL Sitwell Arms Hotel, Station Road, RENISHAW ☎ 01246 641263 & 435226 📠 01246 433915　31 en suite

College Pines Golf Course Worksop College Dr S80 3AL
☎ 01909 501431 📠 01909 481227
e-mail: snelljunior@btinternet.com
web: www.collegepinesgolfclub.co.uk

A fine heathland course set in majestic surroundings. Its free draining characteristics make it suitable for all year round play and full tees and greens remain open throughout.

18 Holes, 6801yards, Par 73, SSS 73.
Club membership 500.
Visitors Mon-Sun & BHs. Booking required **Societies** booking required.
♲ **Course Designer** David Snell **Prof** Charles Snell **Facilities** ⊕ ⦾ ⓛ ⌂ ⛳ 🏌 ⛱ ⚐ 🥢 🏌 🏁 **Leisure** short game practise area **Conf** Corporate Hospitality Days **Location** M1 junct 30/31, S of Worksop on B6034 Edwinstowe road
Hotel ★★★ 78% HL Clumber Park, Clumber Park, WORKSOP ☎ 01623 835333 📠 01623 835525　73 en suite

Lindrick Golf Club Lindrick Common S81 8BH
☎ 01909 475820
e-mail: johnking@lindrickgolfclub.co.uk
web: www.lindrickgolfclub.co.uk

Heathland course, with some trees and masses of gorse, which has hosted many major golf tournaments including the Ryder Cup.

18 Holes, 6271yds, Par 71, SSS 71.
Club membership 510.
Visitors Mon, Wed-Fri except BHs. Booking required. Dress code.
Societies booking required. **Green Fees** not confirmed **Prof** John R King **Facilities** ⊕ ⦾ ⓛ ⌂ ⛳ ⚐ 🏌 🏁 **Leisure** buggies for disabled only **Conf** Corporate Hospitality Days **Location** M1 junct 31, 4m NW of Worksop on A57
Hotel ★★★ 80% HL Best Western Lion, 112 Bridge Street, WORKSOP ☎ 01909 477925 📠 01909 479038　46 en suite

Worksop Golf Club Windmill Ln S80 2SQ
☎ 01909 477731 📠 01909 530917
e-mail: thesecretary@worksopgolfclub.co.uk
web: www.worksopgolfclub.com

Adjacent to Clumber Park, this course has heathland terrain, with gorse, broom, oak and birch trees. Fast, true greens, dry all year round.

18 Holes, 6660yds, Par 72, SSS 72. Club membership 600.
Visitors Mon, Wed, Fri-Sun except BHs. Booking required. Dress code.
Societies welcome. **Green Fees** not confirmed **Course Designer** Tom Williamson **Prof** K Crossland **Facilities** ⊕ ⦾ ⓛ ⌂ ⛳ 🏌 ⛱ 🏁 **Leisure** snooker **Conf** facs Corporate Hospitality Days **Location** A57 ring road onto B6034 to Edwinstowe
Hotel ★★★ 78% HL Clumber Park, Clumber Park, WORKSOP ☎ 01623 835333 📠 01623 835525　73 en suite

OXFORDSHIRE

ABINGDON　　　　Map 4 SU49

Drayton Park Golf Course Steventon Rd, Drayton OX14 4LA
☎ 01235 550607 (Pro Shop) 📠 01235 525731
e-mail: draytonpark@btclick.com
web: www.draytonparkgolfclubabingdon.co.uk

Set in the heart of Oxfordshire, an 18-hole parkland course designed by Hawtree. Five lakes and sand-based greens.

18 Holes, 5704yds, Par 69, SSS 69, Course record 67.
Club membership 400.
Visitors Mon-Sun & BHs. Booking required. Dress code.
Societies booking required. **Green Fees** not confirmed **Course Designer** Hawtree **Prof** Jonathan Draycott **Facilities** ⊕ ⦾ ⓛ ⌂ ⛳ 🏌 ⛱ 🏁 ⚐ 🏌 **Leisure** 9 hole par 3 course **Conf** facs Corporate Hospitality Days **Location** off A34 at Didcot
Hotel ★★★ 75% HL Abingdon Four Pillars Hotel, Marcham Road, ABINGDON ☎ 0800 374 692 & 01235 553456 📠 01235 554117　66 en suite

Save on Hotels. Book at **theAA.com/hotel**   **OXFORDSHIRE**

ENGLAND

BANBURY — Map 4 SP44

See also **Chacombe (Northamptonshire)**

Banbury Golf Club Aynho Rd, Adderbury OX17 3NT
☎ 01295 810419 & 812880   📠 01295 810056
e-mail: banburygolfclub@googlemail.com
web: www.banburygolfclub.co.uk
Undulating wooded course with water features and USGA specification greens.

Red & Yellow: 18 Holes, 6597yds, Par 71, SSS 71.
Yellow & Blue: 18 Holes, 6603yds, Par 71, SSS 71.
Red & Blue: 18 Holes, 6746yds, Par 72, SSS 72.
Club membership 300.

Visitors Mon-Sun & BHs. Booking required. Dress code casual. **Societies** booking required. **Green Fees** £18 per 18 holes **Course Designer** Reed/Payn **Prof** Mark McGeehan **Facilities** ⊕ ⑩↑ ⓘ ⓓ ⑪ ⚲ ⑪ ⚲ ⚲ **Conf** Corporate Hospitality Days **Location** M40 junct 10, off B4100 between Adderbury & Aynho **Hotel** ★★★ 79% HL Cartwright Hotel, 1-5 Croughton Road, AYNHO ☎ 01869 811885 📠 01869 812809 21 en suite

Rye Hill Golf Club Milcombe OX15 4RU
☎ 01295 721818   📠 01295 720089
e-mail: info@ryehill.co.uk
web: www.ryehill.co.uk
Well-drained course, set in 200 acres of rolling countryside, with both parkland and heathland features, including wide fairways, large undulating greens, dramatic lakes, and fine views of the surrounding countryside.

18 Holes, 6960yds, Par 72, SSS 73, Course record 63.
Club membership 400.

Visitors Mon-Sun & BHs. Booking advisable. **Societies** booking required. **Green Fees** £25 per 18 holes, £15 per 10 holes, £10 per 5 holes (£30/£20/£15 weekends) **Course Designer** Donald Steel **Prof** Mark Wheeler/Tony Pennock **Facilities** ⊕ ⑩↑ by prior arrangement ⓘ ⓓ ⑪ ⚲ ⑪ ⚲ ⚲ **Leisure** fishing, tri-golf 9 hole family course, 3 hole academy course **Conf** facs Corporate Hospitality Days **Location** M40 junct 11, A361 towards Chipping Norton, signed 1m out of Bloxham, head into Milcome village **Hotel** ★★★ 81% HL Best Western Wroxton House, Wroxton St Mary, BANBURY ☎ 01295 730777 📠 01295 730800 32 en suite

BURFORD — Map 4 SP21

Burford Golf Club Swindon Rd OX18 4JG
☎ 01993 822583   📠 01993 822801
e-mail: secretary@burfordgolfclub.co.uk
web: www.burfordgolfclub.co.uk
Parkland with mature, tree-lined fairways and high quality greens.

18 Holes, 6401yds, Par 71, SSS 71, Course record 64.
Club membership 770.

Visitors Mon, Wed & Fri. Other days & BHs limited play. Dress code. **Societies** booking required. **Green Fees** £40 per day **Course Designer** John H Turner **Prof** Michael Ridge **Facilities** ⊕ ⑩↑ ⓘ ⓓ ⑪ ⚲ ⑪ **Location** 0.5m S off A361 **Hotel** ★★★ 83% SHL The Lamb Inn, Sheep Street, BURFORD ☎ 01993 823155 📠 01993 822228 17 en suite

CHESTERTON — Map 4 SP52

Bicester Golf & Country Club OX26 1TE
☎ 01869 241204
e-mail: jamie.herbert@bicesterhotelgolfandspa.com
web: www.bicesterhotelgolfandspa.com
Testing course set in 135 acres of beautiful Oxfordshire countryside, complemented by 11 lakes strategically placed around the course and providing a challenge to every kind of golfer. Several new look holes will impress newcomers and all those who are re-visiting. All the greens are now built to USGA specifications.

18 Holes, 6255yds, Par 71, SSS 71, Course record 63.
Club membership 700.

Visitors Mon-Sun & BHs. Booking required. Dress code **Societies** booking required. **Green Fees** not confirmed **Course Designer** R Stagg **Prof** Peter Thompson **Facilities** ⊕ ⑩↑ ⓘ ⓓ ⑪ ⚲ ⑪ ⚲ ◇ ⚲ **Leisure** hard tennis courts, heated indoor swimming pool, sauna, gymnasium, spa **Conf** facs Corporate Hospitality Days **Location** 0.5m W off A4095 **Hotel** ★★ 76% HL Best Western Jersey Arms, BICESTER ☎ 01869 343234 & 343270 📠 01869 343565 20 en suite

CHIPPING NORTON — Map 4 SP32

Chipping Norton Golf Club Southcombe OX7 5QH
☎ 01608 642383   📠 01608 645422
e-mail: golfadmin@chippingnortongolfclub.com
web: www.chippingnortongolfclub.com
Downland course situated at 800ft above sea level, its undulations providing a good walk. On a limestone base, the course dries quickly in wet conditions. The opening few holes provide a good test of golf made more difficult when the prevailing wind makes the player use the extremes of the course.

18 Holes, 6241yds, Par 71, SSS 70, Course record 62.
Club membership 900.

Visitors Mon-Fri except BHs. Dress code. **Societies** welcome. **Green Fees** not confirmed **Prof** Neil Rowlands **Facilities** ⊕ ⑩↑ ⓘ ⓓ ⑪ ⚲ ◇ ⚲ ⚲ **Location** 1.5m E on A44 **Hotel** ★★★ 77% HL Mill House Hotel & Restaurant, KINGHAM ☎ 01608 658188 📠 01608 658492 23 en suite

Heythrop Park Golf Resort Enstone OX7 5UF
☎ 01608 673488
e-mail: golf@heythroppark.co.uk
web: www.heythropparkresort.co.uk

This new course meanders through ancient woodland, lakes and streams and the design echoes the original landscape plan drawn up in 1706 with its historical bridges and monuments. The course has an overtly English design with several holes that really stand out. The first is the 314yd par 4 6th, where the green is perched on the edge of an 18th century fishing lake, and the 528yd par 5 14th, which sweeps left around an ancient woodland to a green that sits close to an 18th century stone bridge. The fine set of challenging par 3s are also memorable as is the unique 596yd par 5 closing hole, which is as straight as a die and has the 18th century Main House as its impressive backdrop.

Bainbridge: 18 Holes, 7088yds, Par 72, SSS 72, Course record 71.

Visitors Contact resort for details. **Societies** booking required. **Green Fees** £25 (£35 weekends) **Course Designer** Tom Mackenzie **Prof** Gareth Ward **Facilities** ⑪ ⑩ ⓵ ⌴ 🍴 ⏟ 🏠 ⛶ ◇ 🛒 🏌 **Leisure** heated indoor swimming pool, fishing, sauna, gymnasium, on site tuition, spa treatment rooms **Conf** facs Corporate Hospitality Days **Location** A44 (signed Woodstock) for approx 12m to Enstone. Pass petrol station on left and continue through village. Turn right at bottom of hill by Harrow pub, entrance at x-rds **Hotel** U Crowne Plaza Heythrop Park - Oxford, Heythrop Park Resort, Enstone, CHIPPING NORTON ☎ 01608 673333 🖹 01608 673799 197 en suite

Wychwood Golf Club Lyneham OX7 6QQ
☎ 01993 831841 🖹 01993 831775
e-mail: info@thewychwood.com
web: www.thewychwood.com

Wychwood was designed to use the natural features of its location. It is set in 170 acres on the fringe of the Cotswolds and blends superbly with its surroundings. Lakes and streams enhance the challenge of the course with water coming into play on eight of the 18 holes. All greens are sand based, built to USGA specification.

18 Holes, 6885yds, Par 72, SSS 72. Club membership 650.
Visitors Mon-Sun & BHs. Booking required. Dress code. **Societies** booking required. **Green Fees** not confirmed **Prof** Adam Souter **Facilities** ⑪ ⑩ ⓵ ⌴ 🍴 ⏟ 🏠 ⛶ ◇ 🛒 🏌 **Leisure** fishing **Conf** facs Corporate Hospitality Days **Location** off A361 between Burford & Chipping Norton **Hotel** ★★★ 77% HL Mill House Hotel & Restaurant, KINGHAM ☎ 01608 658188 🖹 01608 658492 23 en suite

DIDCOT
Map 4 SU59

Hadden Hill Golf Club Wallingford Rd OX11 9BJ
☎ 01235 510410 🖹 01235 511260
e-mail: info@haddenhillgolf.co.uk
web: www.haddenhillgolf.co.uk

A challenging course on undulating terrain with excellent drainage. Superb greens and fairways.

18 Holes, 6563yds, Par 71, SSS 71, Course record 65. Club membership 400.

Visitors Mon-Sun & BHs. Booking required. **Societies** booking required. **Green Fees** £20 per 18 holes, £12 per 9 holes (£25/£15 weekends) **Course Designer** Michael V Morley **Prof** Ian Mitchell/Steve Laidler **Facilities** ⑪ ⑩ by prior arrangement ⓵ ⌴ 🍴 ⏟ 🏠 ⛶ 🛒 🏌 **Leisure** 6 hole par 3 academy course, teaching academy **Conf** Corporate Hospitality Days **Location** A34 Milton interchange, follow A4130, course 1m E of Didcot on Wallingford Road **Hotel** ★★★ 75% HL Abingdon Four Pillars Hotel, Marcham Road, ABINGDON ☎ 0800 374 692 & 01235 553456 🖹 01235 554117 66 en suite

FARINGDON
Map 4 SU29

Carswell Golf & Country Club Carswell SN7 8PU
☎ 01367 870422
e-mail: info@carswellgolfandcountryclub.co.uk
web: www.carswellgolfandcountryclub.co.uk

An attractive course set in undulating wooded countryside close to Faringdon. Mature trees, five lakes and well-placed bunkers add interest to the course. Floodlit driving range.

18 Holes, 6528yds, Par 72, SSS 71, Course record 69. Club membership 520.

Visitors Mon-Sun & BHs. Booking required except Mon. Dress code. **Societies** welcome. **Green Fees** not confirmed **Course Designer** J & E Ely **Prof** John Strode **Facilities** ⑪ ⑩ ⓵ ⌴ 🍴 ⏟ 🏠 ◇ 🏌 🛒 🏌 **Leisure** sauna, gymnasium **Conf** facs Corporate Hospitality Days **Location** off A420 **Hotel** ★★★ 74% HL Best Western Sudbury House Hotel & Conference Centre, London Street, FARINGDON ☎ 01367 241272 🖹 01367 242346 49 en suite

FRILFORD Map 4 SU49

Frilford Heath Golf Club OX13 5NW
☎ 01865 390864 Fax 01865 390823
e-mail: events@frilfordheath.co.uk
web: www.frilfordheath.co.uk

Fifty-four holes in three layouts of differing character. The Green course is a fully mature heathland course. The Red Course is of championship length with a parkland flavour and a marked degree of challenge. The Blue Course is of modern design and incorporates water hazards and large shallow sand traps.

Red Course: 18 Holes, 6961yds, Par 73, SSS 73, Course record 64.
Green Course: 18 Holes, 6006yds, Par 69, SSS 69, Course record 65.
Blue Course: 18 Holes, 6761yds, Par 72, SSS 72, Course record 65. Club membership 1300.

Visitors Mon-Sun & BHs. Booking required weekends & BHs. Dress code **Societies** booking required. **Green Fees** £80 per day (£95 weekends) **Course Designer** J Taylor/D Cotton/S Gidman/J Turner **Prof** Derek Craik Jnr **Facilities** **Conf** facs Corporate Hospitality Days **Location** 2m W of A34
Hotel ★★★ 78% HL Westwood Country Hotel, Hinksey Hill, Boars Hill, OXFORD ☎ 01865 735408 Fax 01865 736536 20 en suite

HENLEY-ON-THAMES Map 4 SU78

Badgemore Park Golf Club Badgemore RG9 4NR
☎ 01491 637300 Fax 01491 576899
e-mail: info@badgemorepark.com
web: www.badgemorepark.com

Formerly a country estate, Badgemore Park was transformed in 1971 into a beautiful parkland golf course, cleverly designed to challenge golfers of all standards.

18 Holes, 6129yds, Par 69, SSS 69, Course record 64. Club membership 600.

Visitors Mon-Fri anytime, Sat-Sun & BHs after 11am. Booking required. Dress code. **Societies** booking required. **Green Fees** £30 per day/round (£40 weekends) **Course Designer** Robert Sandow **Prof** Jonathan Dunn **Facilities** **Conf** facs Corporate Hospitality Days **Location** N from Henley towards Rotherfield Greys, 1.5m on right
Hotel ★★★★ 76% TH Hotel du Vin Henley-on-Thames, New Street, HENLEY-ON-THAMES ☎ 01491 848400 Fax 01491 848401 43 en suite

Henley Golf Club Harpsden RG9 4HG
☎ 01491 575742 Fax 01491 412179
e-mail: admin@henleygc.com
web: www.henleygc.com

Designed by James Braid in 1907, the course retains many of his classic features, while being a challenge for all golfers even with modern technology. The first four holes are considered the hardest opening holes of any course in Oxfordshire and possibly the UK. The club celebrated its centenary in 2007.

18 Holes, 6264yds, Par 70, SSS 70, Course record 62. Club membership 700.

Visitors Mon-Fri except BHs. Weekends pm. Booking required weekends. Handicap certificate. Dress code. **Societies** booking required. **Green Fees** £55 per day, £45 per round, £35 after 4pm **Course Designer** James Braid **Prof** Mark Howell **Facilities** **Conf** Corporate Hospitality Days **Location** 1.25m S off A4155
Hotel ★★★★ 76% TH Hotel du Vin Henley-on-Thames, New Street, HENLEY-ON-THAMES ☎ 01491 848400 Fax 01491 848401 43 en suite

HORTON-CUM-STUDLEY Map 4 SP51

Studley Wood Golf Club The Straight Mile OX33 1BF
☎ 01865 351122 & 351144 Fax 01865 351166
web: www.studleywoodgolf.co.uk.

18 Holes, 6811yds, Par 72, SSS 72, Course record 65.

Course Designer Simon Gidman **Location** M40 junct 8/9, from N take A34 then B4027, from S take A40 then B4027
Telephone for further details
Hotel ★★★★ 77% HL Barceló Oxford Hotel, Godstow Road, Wolvercote Roundabout, OXFORD ☎ 01865 489988 Fax 01865 489952 168 en suite

KIRTLINGTON

Map 4 SP41

Kirtlington Golf Club OX5 3JY
☎ 01869 351133 📠 01869 351143
e-mail: info@kirtlingtongolfclub.com
web: www.kirtlingtongolfclub.com

An inland links-type course with challenging greens. The course incorporates many natural features and has 102 bunkers and a 110yd par 3 19th when an extra hole is required to determine a winner. The 9 hole course has three par 4s and six par 3s with all year round buggy track.

18 Holes, 6107yds, Par 70, SSS 69.
Academy Course: 9 Holes, 1535yds, Par 30.
Club membership 400.

Visitors Mon-Sun & BHs. Booking required. Dress code.
Societies booking required. **Green Fees** £26 per 18 holes (£32 weekends & BHs). Academy £10 per 9 holes (£12 weekends & BHs)
Course Designer Graham Webster **Prof** Andy Taylor **Facilities** ⓣ
🍴 ☕ 🍳 ⚲ 🏠 ⛳ ✎ 🚗 ✦ ⚑ **Conf** facs Corporate Hospitality Days **Location** M40 junct 9, on A4095 outside Kirtlington
Hotel ★★★ 64% HL The Oxfordshire Inn, Heathfield Village,
BLETCHINGDON ☎ 01869 351444 📠 01869 351555 28 en suite

MILTON COMMON

Map 4 SP60

The Oxfordshire Golf Club Rycote Ln OX9 2PU
☎ 01844 278300 📠 01844 278003
e-mail: info@theoxfordshire.com
web: www.theoxfordshire.com

Designed by Rees Jones, The Oxfordshire is considered to be one of the most exciting courses in the country. The strategically contoured holes blend naturally into the surrounding countryside to provide a challenging game of golf. With four lakes and 135 bunkers, the course makes full use of the terrain and the natural elements to provide characteristics similar to those of a links course.

18 Holes, 7313yds, Par 72, SSS 73, Course record 63.
Club membership 420.

Visitors Mon, Wed & Fri. Tue & Thu pm. Weekends & BHs after 10.30 am. Booking required. Handicap certificate. Dress code.
Societies booking required. **Green Fees** not confirmed **Course Designer** Rees Jones **Prof** Justin Barns **Facilities** ⓣ 🍴 🍽 by prior arrangement 🍴 ☕ 🍳 ⚲ 🏠 ⛳ ◔ ✎ 🚗 ✦ ⚑
Leisure heated indoor swimming pool, sauna, gymnasium, Japanese ofuro baths, halfway house **Conf** facs Corporate Hospitality Days
Location M40 junct 7, 1.5m on A329
Hotel ★★★★ 82% HL The Oxfordshire, Rycote Lane, MILTON COMMON ☎ 01844 278300 📠 01844 278003 50 en suite

NUFFIELD

Map 4 SU68

Huntercombe Golf Club RG9 5SL
☎ 01491 641207 📠 01491 642060
web: www.huntercombegolfclub.co.uk

18 Holes, 6271yds, Par 70, SSS 70, Course record 63.
Course Designer Willie Park jnr **Location** off A4130 at Nuffield
Telephone for further details
Hotel ★★★ 73% HL Shillingford Bridge, Shillingford,
WALLINGFORD ☎ 01865 858567 📠 01865 858636 40 en suite

OXFORD

Map 4 SP50

Hinksey Heights Golf Course South Hinksey OX1 5AB
☎ 01865 327775
e-mail: sec@oxford-golf.co.uk
web: www.oxford-golf.co.uk

Undulating heathland and links-type course with a number of interesting and distinctive holes that reward the thoughtful golfer tempting boldness with the option of playing safe. Fairways and greens encourage golfers to employ their course management skills. Unsurpassed views of Oxford's Dreaming Spires and the beautiful Thames Valley.

Championship: 18 Holes, 6388yds, Par 72, SSS 71,
Course record 66.
Spires Course: 9 Holes, 2617yds, Par 35, SSS 33.
Club membership 600.

Visitors Mon-Sun & BHs. Booking required. Dress code.
Societies booking required. **Green Fees** £20 Mon-Fri (£25 weekends & BHs). Twilight 3 hours before sunset £12 (£16 weekends) **Course Designer** David Heads **Prof** Dean Davis **Facilities** ⓣ 🍽 🍴 ☕
🍳 ⚲ 🏠 ⛳ 🚗 ✎ ⚑ **Leisure** The Spires course 9 holes par 35, par 3 pitch & putt course par 27 **Conf** facs Corporate Hospitality Days **Location** on A34 Oxford bypass between Hinksey Hill and Botley. Take South Hinksey turning also signed for Garden Centre
Hotel ★★★ 77% HL Hawkwell House, Church Way, Iffley Village,
OXFORD ☎ 01865 749988 📠 01865 748525 66 en suite

North Oxford Golf Club Banbury Rd OX2 8EZ
☎ 01865 554924 📄 01865 515921
e-mail: manager@nogc.co.uk
web: www.nogc.co.uk
Gently undulating parkland.
18 Holes, 5702yds, Par 67, SSS 67, Course record 61.
Club membership 600.
Visitors Mon-Wed, Fri & BHs. Thu & weekends pm. Booking required
Tue, Thu, weekends & BHs. Handicap certificate. Dress code.
Societies booking required. **Green Fees** £35 per day, £30 per 18
holes, £19 after 2pm (weekends £38/£35/£22) **Prof** Lee Jackson
Facilities ⊕ ⑩ 🏌 ☐ 🏌 ⚐ 🏌 ✔ **Conf** Corporate
Hospitality Days **Location** 3m N of city centre on A4165
Hotel ★★★★ 77% HL Barceló Oxford Hotel, Godstow Road,
Wolvercote Roundabout, OXFORD ☎ 01865 489988 📄 01865 489952
168 en suite

Southfield Golf Club Hill Top Rd OX4 1PF
☎ 01865 242158 📄 01865 250023
e-mail: sgcltd@btopenworld.com
web: www.southfieldgolf.com

Home of the City, University and Ladies Clubs, and well-known
to graduates throughout the world. A classic Harry Colt designed
course, in a varied parkland setting, providing a real test for
players.
18 Holes, 6325yds, Par 70, SSS 70, Course record 63.
Club membership 550.
Visitors Mon-Fri except BHs. Weekends after 4pm. Dress code
Societies booking required. **Green Fees** £35 per day/round **Course**
Designer H S Colt **Prof** Tony Rees **Facilities** ⊕ ⑩ 🏌 ☐ 🏌
🟊 ⚐ 🏌 ✔ 🏌 **Conf facs** Corporate Hospitality Days
Location 1.5m SE of city centre off B480
Hotel ★★★ 78% HL Westwood Country Hotel, Hinksey Hill, Boars
Hill, OXFORD ☎ 01865 735408 📄 01865 736536　20 en suite

SHRIVENHAM　　　　　　　　　Map 4 SU28

Shrivenham Park Golf Club Penny Hooks Ln SN6 8EX
☎ 01793 783853
e-mail: info@shrivenhampark.com
web: www.shrivenhampark.com
A flat, mature parkland course with excellent drainage. A good
challenge for all standards of golfer.
18 Holes, 5769yds, Par 69, SSS 69, Course record 64.
Club membership 250.
Visitors Mon-Sun & BHs. Booking required Fri-Sun & BHs. Dress
code. Societies booking required. **Green Fees** £15 per 18 holes £12

per 9 holes (£25/£16 weekends & BHs) **Course Designer** Gordon Cox
Prof Richard Jefferies **Facilities** ⊕ ⑩ 🏌 ☐ 🏌 🟊 ⚐ 🏌
🟊 ✔ **Conf** Corporate Hospitality Days **Location** 0.5m NE of town
centre on A420 towards Oxford
Hotel ★★★ 74% HL Best Western Sudbury House Hotel &
Conference Centre, London Street, FARINGDON ☎ 01367 241272
📄 01367 242346　49 en suite

TADMARTON　　　　　　　　　Map 4 SP33

Tadmarton Heath Golf Club OX15 5HL
☎ 01608 737278 📄 01608 730548
e-mail: secretary@tadmartongolf.com
web: www.tadmartongolf.com
A mixture of heath and sandy land on a plateau in the Cotswolds.
The course opens gently before reaching the scenic 7th hole across
a trout stream close to the clubhouse. The course then progressively
tightens through the gorse before a challenging 430yd dog-leg
completes the round.
18 Holes, 5926yds, Par 69, SSS 69, Course record 62.
Club membership 630.
Visitors Mon-Wed, Fri-Sun except BHs. Thu pm. Booking required.
Handicap certificate. Dress code. Societies booking required.
Green Fees £50 per day, £40 after 10am (£60 weekends, £40 after
12pm). Reduced winter rates **Course Designer** Col C K Hutchison
Prof John Stubbs **Facilities** ⊕ ⑩ by prior arrangement 🏌 ☐
🏌 🟊 ⚐ 🏌 🟊 ✔ 🏌 Leisure fishing **Conf facs** Corporate
Hospitality Days **Location** 1m SW of Lower Tadmarton off B4035,
6m from Banbury
Hotel ★★★ 81% HL Best Western Wroxton House, Wroxton St
Mary, BANBURY ☎ 01295 730777 📄 01295 730800　32 en suite

WALLINGFORD　　　　　　　　Map 4 SU68

The Springs Hotel & Golf Club Wallingford Rd,
North Stoke OX10 6BE
☎ 01491 827310 📄 01491 827312
e-mail: proshop@thespringshotel.com
web: www.thespringshotel.com
The 133 acres of parkland are bordered by the River Thames, within
which lie three lakes and challenging wetland areas. The course has
traditional features like a double green and sleepered bunker with
sleepered lake edges of typical American design.
The Springs: 18 Holes, 6470yds, Par 72, SSS 71,
Course record 65. Club membership 610.
Visitors Mon-Sun & BHs. Booking required. Dress code.
Societies booking required. **Green Fees** £25 per day (£30 weekends
& BHs) **Course Designer** Brian Hugget **Prof** Jamie Clutterbuck
Facilities ⊕ ⑩ 🏌 ☐ 🏌 🟊 ⚐ 🏌 ◇ 🟊 ✔
Leisure heated outdoor swimming pool, fishing, sauna, croquet lawn
Conf facs Corporate Hospitality Days **Location** 2m SE of town centre
over River Thames
Hotel ★★★ 80% HL The Springs Hotel & Golf Club, Wallingford
Road, North Stoke, WALLINGFORD ☎ 01491 836687 📄 01491 836877
32 en suite

WATERSTOCK
Map 4 SP60

Waterstock Golf Course Thame Rd OX33 1HT
☎ 01844 338093 📠 01844 338036
e-mail: wgc_oxfordgolf@btinternet.com
web: www.waterstockgolf.co.uk

Course designed by Donald Steel with USGA greens and tees fully computer irrigated. Four par 3s facing north, south, east and west. A brook and hidden lake affect six holes, with dog-legs being 4th and 10th holes. Five par 4s on the course, making it a challenge for players of all standards.

18 Holes, 6535yds, Par 72, SSS 71, Course record 64.
Club membership 500.

Visitors Mon-Sun & BHs. Booking required. **Societies** welcome. **Green Fees** £30 per day, £23 per round, £17.50 twilight, £13 for 9 holes (£35/£28/£17.50 weekends & BHs) **Course Designer** Donald Steel **Prof** Paul Bryant **Facilities** 🍸 🍴 🏌 🖥 🍴 🛅 🏌 🚗 🚲 ⚙ 🏌 **Leisure** fishing **Conf** facs Corporate Hospitality Days **Location** M40 junct 8/8A, E of Oxford near Wheatley **Hotel** BUD Days Inn Oxford - M40, M40 junction 8A, Waterstock, OXFORD ☎ 01865 877000 📠 01865 877016 59 en suite

WITNEY
Map 4 SP31

Witney Lakes Golf Course Downs Rd OX29 0SY
☎ 01993 893011 📠 01993 778866
web: www.witney-lakes.co.uk

18 Holes, 6700yds, Par 71, Course record 67.

Course Designer Simon Gidman **Location** 2m W of Witney town centre, off B4047 Witney/Burford road
Telephone for further details
Hotel ★★★★ 72% HL Oxford Witney Four Pillars Hotel, Ducklington Lane, WITNEY ☎ 0800 374692 & 01993 779777 📠 01993 703467 87 en suite

RUTLAND

GREAT CASTERTON
Map 4 TF00

Rutland County Golf Club Pickworth PE9 4AQ
☎ 01780 460330 📠 01780 460437
e-mail: info@rutlandcountygolf.co.uk
web: www.rutlandcountygolf.co.uk

Inland links-style course with gently rolling fairways, large tees and greens. Playable all year round due to good drainage.

Main Course: 18 Holes, 6202yds, Par 71, SSS 69,
Course record 64. Club membership 500.

Visitors Mon-Sun & BHs. Booking required. Relaxed dress code on par 3, driving range, practice facilities & clubhouse. **Societies** booking required. **Green Fees** £30 per day, £20 per round (£25 weekends). £10 per 9 holes (£14 weekends) **Course Designer** Cameron Sinclair **Prof** Clive Fromant **Facilities** 🍸 🍴 🏌 🖥 🍴 🛅 🏌 🚗 ⚙ 🏌 **Leisure** par 3 course **Conf** facs Corporate Hospitality Days **Location** A1 exit for Pickworth Woolfox Depot. Mobile telephone masts at entrance
Hotel ★★★ 71% HL Greetham Valley, Wood Lane, GREETHAM ☎ 01780 460444 📠 01780 460623 35 en suite

GREETHAM
Map 8 SK91

Greetham Valley Hotel, Golf & Conference Centre
Wood Ln LE15 7NP
☎ 01780 460444 📠 01780 460623
e-mail: info@greethamvalley.co.uk
web: www.greethamvalley.co.uk

Set in 276 acres of attractive undulating countryside. Both courses feature numerous water hazards including ponds, lakes and the meandering North Brook. Renowned for hand cut greens which are fast and true.

Lakes: 18 Holes, 6769yds, Par 72, SSS 72.
Valley: 18 Holes, 5595yds, Par 68, SSS 67.
Academy: 18 Holes, 1218yds, Par 27.
Club membership 900.

Visitors Mon-Sun & BHs. Booking required. Dress code. **Societies** Booking required. **Green Fees** not confirmed **Course Designer** F E Hinch/B Stephens **Prof** Neil Evans **Facilities** 🍸 🍴 🏌 🖥 🍴 🛅 🏌 🚗 ◇ ⚙ 🚲 ⚙ 🏌 **Leisure** fishing, gymnasium, bowls green, 9 hole par 3, quad biking, 4x4 off-roading, fishing **Conf** facs Corporate Hospitality Days **Location** A1 onto B668 Oakham road, course signed
Hotel ★★★★ CHH Hambleton Hall, Hambleton, OAKHAM ☎ 01572 756991 📠 01572 724721 17 en suite

KETTON
Map 4 SK90

Luffenham Heath Golf Club PE9 3UU
☎ 01780 720205 📠 01780 722146
e-mail: jringleby@theluffenhamheathgc.co.uk
web: www.luffenhamheath.co.uk

A James Braid course with firm driving fairways framed by swaying fescue, cross bunkers, grassy wastes and subtly undulating greens, hemmed in by sculpted traps. Many outstanding and challenging holes, placing a premium on accuracy. The 17th par 3 signature hole is downhill over a tangle of mounds and studded with tricky bunkers.

18 Holes, 6563yds, Par 70, SSS 72.
Club membership 550.

Visitors Mon, Wed-Fri. Weekends & BHs restricted play. Booking required weekends & BHs. Handicap certificate. Dress code. **Societies** booking required. **Green Fees** not confirmed **Course Designer** James Braid **Prof** Ian Burnett **Facilities** 🍸 🍴 🏌 🖥 🍴 🛅 🏌 🚗 ⚙ **Conf** Corporate Hospitality Days **Location** 1.5m SW of Ketton on A6121 by Foster's Bridge
Hotel ★★★ 86% HL The George of Stamford, 71 St Martins, STAMFORD ☎ 01780 750750 & 750700 (res) 📠 01780 750701 47 en suite

Save on Hotels. Book at **theAA.com/hotel**

SHROPSHIRE

ENGLAND

SHROPSHIRE

BRIDGNORTH
Map 7 SO79

Bridgnorth Golf Club Stanley Ln WV16 4SF
☎ 01746 763315 ▤ 01746 763315
e-mail: secretary.bgc@tiscali.co.uk
web: www.bridgnorthgolfclub.co.uk
Pleasant parkland by the River Severn.

18 Holes, 6582yds, Par 73, SSS 72, Course record 68.
Club membership 725.

Visitors Mon, Tue, Thu, Fri & Sun except BHs. **Societies** welcome.
Green Fees not confirmed **Prof** Steve Russell **Facilities** ⑪ ⑩
⊞ ⌨ ⑭ ⊿ 🖻 ✔ ✔ **Leisure** fishing **Conf** Corporate
Hospitality Days **Location** 1m N off B4373
Hotel ★★★★ GH The Laurels, Broadoak, Six Ashes, BRIDGNORTH
☎ 01384 221546 & 07813 925319 7 rooms

CHURCH STRETTON
Map 7 SO49

Church Stretton Golf Club Trevor Hill SY6 6JH
☎ 01694 722281
web: www.churchstrettongolfclub.co.uk

18 Holes, 5020yds, Par 66, SSS 65, Course record 57.

Course Designer James Braid **Location** W of town. From Cardington
Valley up steep Trevor Hill
Telephone for further details
Hotel ★★★ 73% HL Longmynd Hotel, Cunnery Road, CHURCH
STRETTON ☎ 01694 722244 ▤ 01694 722718 50 en suite

CLEOBURY MORTIMER
Map 7 SO67

Cleobury Mortimer Golf Club Wyre Common DY14 8HQ
☎ 01299 271112 ▤ 01299 271468
e-mail: secretary@cleoburygolfclub.com
web: www.cleoburygolfclub.com
Well-designed 27-hole parkland course set in undulating countryside
with fine views from all holes. An interesting challenge to golfers of
all abilities.

Foxes Run: 9 Holes, 2980yds, Par 34, SSS 34.
Badgers Sett: 9 Holes, 3271yds, Par 36, SSS 36.
Deer Park: 9 Holes, 3167yds, Par 35, SSS 35.
Club membership 650.

Visitors Mon-Sun & BHs. Booking required. Dress code.
Societies Booking required. **Green Fees** not confirmed **Course
Designer** E.G.U **Prof** Tim Hall **Facilities** ⑪ ⑩ ⊞ ⌨ ⑭ ⊿
🖻 ◇ ✔ ⛟ ✔ **Leisure** fishing **Conf** facs Corporate Hospitality
Days **Location** on A4117 1m N of Cleobury Mortimer
Hotel ★★★ 78% HL Gainsborough House Hotel, Bewdley Hill,
KIDDERMINSTER ☎ 01562 820041 ▤ 01562 66179 42 en suite

LILLESHALL
Map 7 SJ71

Lilleshall Hall Golf Club TF10 9AS
☎ 01952 604776 ▤ 01952 604272
e-mail: honsec@lhgc.entadsl.com
web: www.lilleshallhallgolfclub.co.uk
Wooded parkland course. Easy walking.

18 Holes, 5813yds, Par 68, SSS 68, Course record 64.
Club membership 650.

Visitors Mon-Fri except BHs. Dress code. **Societies** booking required.
Green Fees contact club for details **Course Designer** H S Colt
Prof Robert Bluck **Facilities** ⑪ ⑩ ⊞ ⌨ ⑭ ⊿ 🖻 🖻 ✔
Conf Corporate Hospitality Days **Location** 3m SE of Lilleshall off
Lilleyhurst Rd
Hotel ★★★ 81% HL Hadley Park House, Hadley Park, TELFORD
☎ 01952 677269 ▤ 01952 676938 22 en suite

LUDLOW
Map 7 SO57

Ludlow Golf Club Bromfield SY8 2BT
☎ 01584 856366 ▤ 01584 856366
e-mail: secretary@ludlowgolfclub.com
web: www.ludlowgolfclub.com
A long-established heathland course in the middle of the racecourse.
Very flat, quick drying, with broom and gorse-lined fairways, excellent
playing surfaces all year round.

18 Holes, 6277yds, Par 70, SSS 70, Course record 65.
Club membership 600.

Visitors Mon-Sun & BHs. Dress code. **Societies** booking required.
Green Fees £35 per day, £28 per round (£35 per round weekends &
BHs) ⊗ **Prof** Russell Price **Facilities** ⑪ ⑩ ⊞ ⌨ ⑭ ⊿ 🖻
✔ ⛟ ✔ **Conf** facs Corporate Hospitality Days **Location** 1m N of
Ludlow off A49
Hotel ★★★ 80% HL Feathers, The Bull Ring, LUDLOW
☎ 01584 875261 ▤ 01584 876030 40 en suite

MARKET DRAYTON
Map 7 SJ63

Market Drayton Golf Club Sutton Ln TF9 2HX
☎ 01630 652266
e-mail: market.draytongc@btconnect.com
web: www.marketdraytongolfclub.co.uk
Undulating parkland course with two steep banks in quiet,
picturesque surroundings, providing a good test of golf.

18 Holes, 6295yds, Par 71, SSS 71. Club membership 600.

Visitors contact club for details. **Societies** booking required.
Green Fees summer £30 per round, winter £25 ⊗ **Prof** Russell
Clewes **Facilities** ⑪ ⑩ ⊞ ⌨ ⑭ ⊿ 🖻 ◇ ✔ **Conf**
Corporate Hospitality Days **Location** 1m S off A41/A529
Hotel ★★★ 83% HL Goldstone Hall, Goldstone, MARKET DRAYTON
☎ 01630 661202 ▤ 01630 661585 12 en suite

NEWPORT
Map 7 SJ72

Aqualate Golf Centre Stafford Rd TF10 9DB
☎ 01952 811699

9 Holes, 5659yds, Par 69, SSS 67, Course record 67.

Location 2m E of town centre on A518, 400yds from junct A41
Telephone for further details
Hotel ★★★ 81% HL Hadley Park House, Hadley Park, TELFORD
☎ 01952 677269 ▤ 01952 676938 22 en suite

OSWESTRY   Map 7 SJ22

Mile End Golf Course Mile End, Old Shrewsbury Rd SY11 4JF
☎ 01691 671246 📄 01691 670580
e-mail: info@mileendgolfclub.co.uk
web: www.mileendgolfclub.co.uk

A gently undulating parkland-type course covering over 135 acres and including a number of water features, notably the 3rd, 8th and 17th holes, which have greens protected by large pools. The longest hole is the par 5, 542yd 14th, complete with its two tiered green. New 16 bay, two tier driving range opened 2010.

18 Holes, 6233yds, Par 71, SSS 70. Club membership 560.
Visitors Mon-Sun & BHs. Booking advisable. Dress code.
Societies booking required. **Green Fees** £21 per round, £23 Fri, £29 weekends & BHs **Course Designer** Price/Gough **Prof** Scott Carpenter **Facilities** ⑪ by prior arrangement 🖫 ⌨ 🍴 ⚤ 🖻 🅿 ✐ **Conf** facs Corporate Hospitality Days **Location** 1m SE of Oswestry, signed off A5/A483
Hotel ★★★★ 74% HL Wynnstay Hotel, Church Street, OSWESTRY
☎ 01691 655261 📄 01691 670606   34 en suite

Oswestry Golf Club Aston Park, Queens Head SY11 4JJ
☎ 01691 610535 📄 01691 610535
e-mail: secretary@oswestrygolfclub.co.uk
web: www.oswestrygolfclub.co.uk

Gently undulating mature parkland course set in splendid Shropshire countryside. Free draining soils make Oswestry an ideal year round test of golf.

18 Holes, 6051yds, Par 70, SSS 69, Course record 62.
Club membership 910.
Visitors Mon-Sun & BHs. Booking required. Handicap certificate. Dress code. **Societies** booking required. **Green Fees** £46 per day, £35 per round (£51/£41 Sat) **Course Designer** James Braid **Prof** Jason Davies **Facilities** ⑪ 🍴 🖫 ⌨ 🍴 ⚤ 🖻 ✐ ⚐ ✐ **Conf** facs Corporate Hospitality Days **Location** 2m SE on A5
Hotel ★★★★ 74% HL Wynnstay Hotel, Church Street, OSWESTRY
☎ 01691 655261 📄 01691 670606   34 en suite

SHIFNAL   Map 7 SJ70

Shifnal Golf Club Decker Hill TF11 8QL
☎ 01952 460330 📄 01952 460330
web: www.shifnalgolf.com

Well-wooded parkland. Walking is easy and an attractive country mansion serves as the clubhouse.

18 Holes, 6465yds, Par 71, SSS 71. Club membership 750.
Visitors Mon-Fri, Sun & BHs. Booking required. Dress code.
Societies booking required. **Green Fees** £50 per day, £40 per 18 holes **Course Designer** Pennick **Prof** Neil Allsebrook **Facilities** ⑪ 🍴 🖫 ⌨ 🍴 ⚤ 🖻 ✐ ⚐ ✐ **Conf** Corporate Hospitality Days **Location** 1m N off B4379
Hotel ★★★★ 77% HL Park House, Park Street, SHIFNAL
☎ 01952 460128 📄 01952 461658   54 en suite

SHREWSBURY   Map 7 SJ41

Arscott Golf Club Arscott, Pontesbury SY5 0XP
☎ 01743 860114 📄 01743 860881
e-mail: golf@arscott.dydirect.net
web: www.arscottgolfclub.co.uk

At 365ft above sea level, the views from the course of the hills of south Shropshire and Wales are superb. Arscott is set in mature parkland with water features and holes demanding all sorts of club choice. A challenge to all golfers both high and low handicap.

18 Holes, 6201yds, Par 70, SSS 69. Club membership 500.
Visitors Mon-Sun & BHs. Booking required Tue, Thu & weekends.
Dress code. **Societies** booking required. **Green Fees** £24 per round (£29 weekends & BHs) ⊛ **Course Designer** M Hamer **Prof** Glyn Sadd **Facilities** ⑪ 🍴 🖫 ⌨ 🍴 ⚤ 🖻 🅿 🖩 ✐ **Leisure** fishing **Conf** facs Corporate Hospitality Days **Location** off A488 S of town
Hotel ★★★ 78% HL The Lion, Wyle Cop, SHREWSBURY
☎ 01743 353107 📄 01743 352744   59 en suite

Shrewsbury Golf Club Condover SY5 7BL
☎ 01743 872977 📄 01743 872977
web: www.shrewsburygolfclub.co.uk

18 Holes, 6207yds, Par 70, SSS 70.

Location 4m S off A49
Telephone for further details
Hotel ★★★ 83% HL Prince Rupert, Butcher Row, SHREWSBURY
☎ 01743 499955 📄 01743 357306   70 en suite

TELFORD   Map 7 SJ60

Shropshire Golf Centre Granville Park TF2 8PQ
☎ 01952 677800 📄 01952 677622
web: www.theshropshire.co.uk

Blue: 9 Holes, 3286yds, Par 35, SSS 35.
Silver: 9 Holes, 3303yds, Par 36, SSS 36.
Gold: 9 Holes, 3334yds, Par 36, SSS 36.

Course Designer Martin Hawtree **Location** M54/A5 onto B5060 towards Donnington, 3rd exit at Granville rdbt
Telephone for further details
Hotel ★★★ 81% HL Hadley Park House, Hadley Park, TELFORD
☎ 01952 677269 📄 01952 676938   22 en suite

Telford Hotel & Golf Resort Great Hay Dr TF7 4DT
☎ 01952 429977 📄 01952 586602
web: www.qhotels.co.uk

18 Holes, 6809yds, Par 72, SSS 72, Course record 66.

Course Designer Bryan Griffiths/John Harris **Location** M54 junct 4, follow signs for A442 towards Bridgnorth, exit at sign for Madeley/ Ironbridge Gorge. Turn right at first rdbt, left at next rdbt, take 3rd road on left (Great Hay Drive)
Telephone for further details
Hotel ★★★★ 75% HL Telford Hotel & Golf Resort, Great Hay Drive, Sutton Heights, TELFORD ☎ 01952 429977 📄 01952 586602 114 en suite

Save on Hotels. Book at **theAA.com/hotel**

SHROPSHIRE

ENGLAND

WELLINGTON
Map 7 SJ61

Wrekin Golf Club Ercall Woods, Golf Links Ln TF6 5BX
☎ 01952 244032 ☐ 01952 252906
e-mail: wrekingolfclub@btconnect.com
web: www.wrekingolfclub.co.uk

Downland course with some hard walking but superb views.

18 Holes, 5570yds, Par 66, SSS 68, Course record 62.
Club membership 650.

Visitors Mon, Wed-Sun & BHs. Booking required. Dress code.
Societies booking required. **Green Fees** £35 per day, £27 per round
(£35 per round weekends & BHs) **Prof** M Lea **Facilities** ⓣ ⓞ ⓛ
▯ ⓠ ⓐ ⓑ ✦ ⓔ ✦ **Location** M54 junct 7, 1.25m S off
B5061

Hotel ★★★ 81% HL Hadley Park House, Hadley Park, TELFORD
☎ 01952 677269 ☐ 01952 676938 22 en suite

WESTON-UNDER-REDCASTLE
Map 7 SJ52

Hawkstone Park Hotel & Golf Centre SY4 5UY
☎ 01948 841700 ☐ 01939 200335
e-mail: info.hawkstonepark@principal-hayley.com
web: www.hawkstone.co.uk

The Hawkstone Course plays through the English Heritage
designated Grade I landscape of the historic park and follies,
providing a beautiful, tranquil yet dramatic back drop to a round
of golf. The Championship Course utilises many American style
features and extensive water hazards and is a challenging
alternative.

Hawkstone Course: 18 Holes, 6497yds, Par 72, SSS 71,
Course record 62.
Championship Course: 18 Holes, 6763yds, Par 72,
SSS 73. Club membership 550.

Visitors Mon-Sun & BHs. Booking required. Dress code.
Societies booking required. **Green Fees** Hawkstone £45 per round.
Championship £35 (£45 weekends) **Course Designer** J Braid/B
Huggatt **Prof** Frank Kiddie **Facilities** ⓣ ⓞ ⓛ ▯ ⓠ ⓐ
ⓐ ⓟ ◈ ⓔ ✦ **Leisure** 6 hole par 3 course, snooker.
Conf facs Corporate Hospitality Days **Location** off A49/A442
Hotel ★★★ 75% HL Hawkstone Park Hotel, WESTON
☎ 01948 841700 ☐ 01939 200335 67 en suite

WHITCHURCH
Map 7 SJ54

Hill Valley Golf & Country Club Terrick Rd SY13 4JZ
☎ 01948 663584 & 667788 ☐ 01948 665927
web: www.hill-valley.co.uk
Emerald: 18 Holes, 6628yds, Par 73, SSS 72,
Course record 64.
Sapphire: 18 Holes, 4800yds, Par 66, SSS 64.
Course Designer Peter Alliss/Dave Thomas **Location** 1m N. Follow
signs from bypass
Telephone for further details
Hotel ★★★★ 76% HL Macdonald Hill Valley Spa, Hotel & Golf,
Tarporley Road, WHITCHURCH ☎ 0844 879 9049 ☐ 01948 667373
80 en suite

WORFIELD
Map 7 SO79

Chesterton Valley Golf Club Chesterton WV15 5NX
☎ 01746 783682
Dry course built on sandy soil giving excellent drainage. No temporary
greens and no trolley ban.

18 Holes, 6048yds, Par 71, SSS 69, Course record 63.
Club membership 450.

Visitors Mon-Sun & BHs. Booking required day before.
Societies booking required. **Green Fees** phone **Course Designer** Mike
Davis **Prof** Philip HInton **Facilities** ▯ ⓠ ⓐ ⓐ ◈ ⓔ ✦
Location on B4176
Hotel ★★★ 83% SHL Old Vicarage Hotel, Worfield, BRIDGNORTH
☎ 01746 716497 ☐ 01746 716552 14 en suite

Worfield Golf Course Roughton WV15 5HE
☎ 01746 716372 ☐ 01746 716302
e-mail: enquiries@worfieldgolf.co.uk
web: www.worfieldgolf.co.uk

A parkland links mix with three large lakes, many bunkers and large
trees giving a challenge to golfers. Superb views and drainage which
allows play on full greens and tees all year. Water comes into play
on four holes, including the short par 4 18th where it lies in front of
the green.

18 Holes, 6460yds, Par 73, SSS 72, Course record 68.
Club membership 520.

Visitors Mon-Sun & BHs. Booking required. Dress code.
Societies booking required. **Green Fees** not confirmed **Course
Designer** T Williams **Prof** Nick Doody **Facilities** ⓣ ⓞ ⓛ ▯
ⓠ ⓐ ⓐ ◈ ⓔ ✦ **Conf** facs Corporate Hospitality Days
Location 3m W of Bridgnorth, off A454
Hotel ★★★ 83% SHL Old Vicarage Hotel, Worfield, BRIDGNORTH
☎ 01746 716497 ☐ 01746 716552 14 en suite

SOMERSET

BACKWELL   Map 3 ST46

Tall Pines Golf Club Cooks Bridle Path, Downside BS48 3DJ
☎ 01275 472076 ▤ 01275 474869
e-mail: proshop@tallpinesgolf.co.uk
web: www.tallpinesgolf.co.uk

Free draining parkland with views over the Bristol Channel.

18 Holes, 6059yds, Par 70, SSS 70, Course record 65.
Club membership 500.

Visitors Mon-Sun & BHs. Booking required weekends. Dress code.
Societies welcome. **Green Fees** £20 per 18 holes (£25 weekends)
Course Designer T Murray **Prof** Alex Murray **Facilities** ⑪ †◎¶ ▯
▯ ¶ ⏄ ▥ ◇ ✂ ▦ ✦ **Conf** Corporate Hospitality Days
Location next to Bristol Airport, 1m off A38/A370
Hotel ★★★ 70% HL Beachlands Hotel, 17 Uphill Road North,
WESTON-SUPER-MARE ☎ 01934 621401 ▤ 01934 621966
21 en suite

BATH   Map 3 ST76

Bath Golf Club Sham Castle, North Rd BA2 6JG
☎ 01225 463834 ▤ 01225 331027
e-mail: enquiries@bathgolfclub.org.uk
web: www.bathgolfclub.org.uk

Considered to be one of the finest courses in the west, this is the site of Bath's oldest golf club. Situated on high ground overlooking the city and with splendid views over the surrounding countryside. The rocky ground supports good quality turf and there are many good holes. A stern but fair test of golf, rewarding the straight hitter, while any green achieved in par will feel like a real achievement. The 17th is a dog-leg right past, or over the corner of an out of bounds wall, and then on to an undulating green.

18 Holes, 6505yds, Par 71, SSS 71.
Club membership 770.

Visitors Mon-Sun & BHs. Booking required Sat & BHs. Handicap certificate. Dress code. **Societies** Booking required. **Green Fees** not confirmed **Course Designer** Colt & others **Prof** Russell Covey **Facilities** ⑪ †◎¶ ▯ ▯ ¶ ⏄ ▥ ¶ ▦ ✂ ✦
Conf facs Corporate Hospitality Days **Location** 1.5m SE city centre off A36
Hotel ★★★★★ 86% HL Macdonald Bath Spa, Sydney Road, BATH ☎ 0844 879 9106 & 01225 444424 ▤ 01225 444006
129 en suite

Entry Hill Golf Course BA2 5NA
☎ 01225 834248

9 Holes, 2065yds, Par 33, SSS 30.

Location off A367
Telephone for further details
Hotel ★★★ 78% MET Haringtons, 8-10 Queen Street, BATH
☎ 01225 461728 & 445883 ▤ 01225 444804 13 en suite

Lansdown Golf Club Lansdown BA1 9BT
☎ 01225 422138 ▤ 01225 339252
e-mail: admin@lansdowngolfclub.co.uk
web: www.lansdowngolfclub.co.uk

A level parkland course situated 800ft above sea level, providing a challenge to both low and high handicap golfers. Stunning views from the 5th and 14th holes.

18 Holes, 6428yds, Par 71, SSS 70, Course record 64.
Club membership 600.

Visitors Mon-Sun & BHs. Booking required weekends. Dress code.
Societies welcome. **Green Fees** not confirmed **Course Designer** C A Whitcombe **Prof** Scott Readman **Facilities** ⑪ †◎¶ ▯ ▯ ¶ ⏄
▥ ✂ ▦ ✦ **Leisure** 6 hole academy course **Conf** facs Corporate Hospitality Days **Location** M4 junct 18, 6m SW by Bath racecourse
Hotel ★★★ 72% HL Pratt's Hotel, South Parade, BATH
☎ 01225 460441 ▤ 01225 448807 46 en suite

BRIDGWATER   Map 3 ST23

Cannington Golf Course Cannington Centre for Land Based Studies, Cannington TA5 2LS
☎ 01278 655050 ▤ 01278 655055
e-mail: macrowr@bridgwater.ac.uk

Nine-hole links-style course with 18 tees. The 4th hole is a challenging 464 yd par 4, slightly uphill and into the prevailing wind.

9 Holes, 6072yds, Par 68, SSS 70, Course record 64.
Club membership 300.

Visitors Tue-Sun & BHs. Booking required weekends & BHs.
Societies Booking required. **Green Fees** not confirmed **Course Designer** Martin Hawtree **Prof** Ron Macrow **Facilities** ▥ ▯ ⏄
▦ ¶ ✂ ✦ **Location** 4m NW off A39
Hotel ★★★ 75% HL Combe House, HOLFORD ☎ 01278 741382 &
741213 ▤ 01278 741322 18 en suite

BURNHAM-ON-SEA   Map 3 ST34

Brean Golf Club at Brean Leisure Park Coast Rd, Brean Sands TA8 2QY
☎ 01278 752111 (pro shop) ▤ 01278 752111
e-mail: proshop@brean.com
web: www.breangolfclub.co.uk

Level moorland course with water hazards. Facilities of Brean Leisure Park adjoining.

18 Holes, 5893yds, Par 71, SSS 71, Course record 61.
Club membership 350.

Visitors booking preferred weekends & BHs. Dress code.
Societies booking required. **Green Fees** not confirmed **Course Designer** In house **Prof** David Haines **Facilities** ⑪ †◎¶ ▯ ▯ ¶ ▯
⏄ ▦ ¶ ◇ ✂ ▦ ✦ **Leisure** heated swimming pool and outdoor swimming pool, fishing **Conf** facs Corporate Hospitality Days
Location M5 junct 22, 4m on coast road
Hotel ★★★ 70% HL Beachlands Hotel, 17 Uphill Road North,
WESTON-SUPER-MARE ☎ 01934 621401 ▤ 01934 621966
21 en suite

Burnham & Berrow Golf Club St Christopher's Way TA8 2PE
☎ 01278 785760 📠 01278 795440
e-mail: secretary.bbgc@btconnect.com
web: www.burnhamandberrowgolfclub.co.uk
Natural championship links course with panoramic views of the Somerset hills and the Bristol Channel. A true test of golf suitable only for players with a handicap of 22 or better.
Championship Course: 18 Holes, 6658yds, Par 71, SSS 73, Course record 67.
Channel Course: 9 Holes, 5819yds, Par 70, SSS 69.
Club membership 900.
Visitors Mon-Sun & BHs. Booking required. **Societies** booking required. **Green Fees** Championship Course £90 per day, £70 per round (£80 per round Sat) **Course Designer** H S Colt **Prof** Mark Crowther-Smith **Facilities** ⓣ ⫟ ⓕ ⛳ ▨ ⬚ ▦ ⚑ 🗑 ⬦ ⬧ ⯐ **Location** 1m N of town on B3140
Hotel ★★★ 74% SHL Woodlands Country House Hotel, Hill Lane, BRENT KNOLL ☎ 01278 760232 📠 01278 769090 9 en suite

---

CHARD Map 3 ST30

Windwhistle Golf Club Cricket St Thomas TA20 4DG
☎ 01460 30231 📠 01460 30055
e-mail: info@windwhistlegolfclub.co.uk
web: www.windwhistlegolfclub.co.uk
Parkland course at 735ft above sea level with outstanding views over the Somerset Levels to the Bristol Channel and south Wales.
East/West Course: 18 Holes, 5969yds, Par 70, SSS 69, Course record 66. Club membership 500.
Visitors Mon-Sun & BHs. Booking required. Dress code.
Societies booking required. **Green Fees** £25 per 18 holes (£30 weekends) **Course Designer** Braid & Taylor/Fisher **Prof** Paul Deeprose **Facilities** ⓣ ▨ ⬚ ▦ ⚑ ⬚ ▦ ⯐ **Leisure** squash **Conf** facs Corporate Hospitality Days **Location** 3m E of Chard on A30
Hotel ★★★★ 73% CHH Cricket St Thomas Hotel, CHARD ☎ 01460 30111 📠 01460 30817 239 en suite

---

CLEVEDON Map 3 ST47

Clevedon Golf Club Castle Rd, Walton St Mary BS21 7AA
☎ 01275 874057 📠 01275 341228
e-mail: secretary@clevedongolfclub.co.uk
web: www.clevedongolfclub.co.uk
Situated on the cliff overlooking the Severn estuary with distant views of the Welsh coast. Excellent parkland course in first-class condition. Magnificent scenery and some tremendous drop holes.
18 Holes, 6557yds, Par 72, SSS 72, Course record 65. Club membership 750.
Visitors Mon-Sun & BHs. Booking required Sat. Dress code.
Societies booking required. **Green Fees** £35 per day (£45 weekends) 🅿 **Course Designer** J H Taylor **Prof** Robert Scanlan **Facilities** ⓣ ⫟ ▨ ⬚ ▦ ⚑ ⬚ ▦ ⯐ 🗑 ⯐
Leisure snooker table **Conf** Corporate Hospitality Days **Location** M5 junct 20, 1m NE of town centre
Hotel ★★★★ 80% HL Doubletree by Hilton Cadbury House, Frost Hill, Congresbury, BRISTOL ☎ 01934 834343 📠 01934 834390 72 en suite

---

CONGRESBURY Map 3 ST46

Mendip Spring Golf Club Honeyhall Ln BS49 5JT
☎ 01934 852322 📠 01934 853021
e-mail: info@mendipspringgolfclub.com
web: www.mendipspringgolfclub.com
Set in peaceful countryside with the Mendip Hills as a backdrop, the course includes lakes and numerous water hazards covering some 12 acres of the course. The 11th hole has a stroke index of 1 and there are long drives on the 7th and 13th. The nine-hole Lakeside course is easy walking, mainly par 4. Floodlit driving range.
Brinsea Course: 18 Holes, 6412yds, Par 71, SSS 71.
Lakeside: 9 Holes, 2329yds, Par 34, SSS 66.
Club membership 500.
Visitors Mon-Sun & BHs. Booking required. Dress code.
Societies booking required. **Green Fees** Brinsea £30 (£40 weekends). Lakeside £9.50/£10 **Prof** John Blackburn/Robert Moss/P Baker **Facilities** ⓣ ⫟ ▨ ⬚ ▦ ⚑ ⬚ ▦ ⯐ ⬦ ⯐ 🗑 ⯐
Conf facs Corporate Hospitality Days **Location** between A370 & A38 on B3133
Hotel ★★★★ 80% HL Doubletree by Hilton Cadbury House, Frost Hill, Congresbury, BRISTOL ☎ 01934 834343 📠 01934 834390 72 en suite

---

ENMORE Map 3 ST23

Enmore Park Golf Club TA5 2AN
☎ 01278 672100 📠 01278 672101
e-mail: manager@enmorepark.co.uk
web: www.enmorepark.co.uk
A parkland course on the foothills of the Quantocks, with water features. Wooded countryside and views of the Mendips; 1st and 10th are testing holes.
18 Holes, 6411yds, Par 71, SSS 71, Course record 64.
Club membership 700.
Visitors Mon-Sun & BHs. Booking required. Dress code.
Societies booking required. **Green Fees** £50 per day £37 per round **Course Designer** Hawtree **Prof** Nigel Wixon **Facilities** ⓣ ⫟ ▨ ⬚ ▦ ⚑ ⬚ ▦ ⯐ 🗑 ⯐ **Conf** facs Corporate Hospitality Days **Location** M5 junct 24, A38 into Bridgwater, left at lights onto A39 for Minehead. Left at next lights signed Spaxton. After 1m turn left signed Enmore. Course 2m on right
Hotel ★★★ 75% HL Combe House, HOLFORD ☎ 01278 741382 & 741213 📠 01278 741322 18 en suite

FARRINGTON GURNEY
Map 3 ST65

Farrington Golf & Country Club Marsh Ln BS39 6TS
☎ 01761 451596 📄 01761 451021
e-mail: info@farringtongolfclub.net
web: www.farringtongolfclub.net

USGA greens on both challenging nine and 18-hole courses. The 18-hole course has computerised irrigation, six lakes, four tees per hole and excellent views. Testing holes include the 12th (282yds) with the green set behind a lake at the base of a 100ft drop, and the 17th which is played between two lakes.

Duchy: 18 Holes, 6328yds, Par 72, SSS 71, Course record 63. Club membership 750.

Societies welcome except Sat. **Green Fees** not confirmed **Course Designer** Peter Thompson **Prof** Jon Lawrence **Facilities** 🏌 🍴 ⛳ 🖥 🍴 👥 🏠 ⛳ ✂ 🛺 ✂ 🏌 **Leisure** sauna, gymnasium, video teaching studio, 9 hole par 3 Manor course **Conf** facs Corporate Hospitality Days **Location** SE of village off A37
Hotel ★★★★ CHH Ston Easton Park, STON EASTON
☎ 01761 241631 📄 01761 241377 22 en suite

FROME
Map 3 ST74

Frome Golf Club Critchill Manor BA11 4LJ
☎ 01373 453410
e-mail: fromegolfclub@yahoo.co.uk
web: www.fromegolfclub.fsnet.co.uk

Attractive parkland course, founded in 1992, situated in a picturesque valley just outside the town, complete with practice areas and a driving range.

18 Holes, 5527yds, Par 69, SSS 67, Course record 64. Club membership 500.

Visitors Mon-Sun & BHs. Booking required weekends & BHs. Dress code. **Societies** booking required. **Green Fees** phone 📧 **Prof** Lawrence Wilkin **Facilities** 🏌 ⛳ 🖥 🍴 👥 🏠 ✂ **Location** 1m SW of town centre
Hotel ★★★★★ BB Lullington House, Lullington, FROME
☎ 01373 831406 & 07979 290146 📄 01373 831406 3 rooms

Orchardleigh Golf Club BA11 2PH
☎ 01373 454200 📄 01373 454202
e-mail: info@orchardleighgolf.co.uk
web: www.orchardleighgolf.co.uk

An 18-hole parkland course set amid Somerset countryside routed through mature trees with water coming into play on seven holes.

18 Holes, 6824yds, Par 72, SSS 73, Course record 68. Club membership 475.

Visitors Mon-Sun & BHs. Booking required. Dress code. **Societies** booking required. **Green Fees** not confirmed **Course Designer** Brian Huggett **Prof** Stuart Clark **Facilities** 🏌 🍴 ⛳ 🖥 🍴 👥 🏠 ⛳ ◇ ✂ 🛺 ✂ 🏌 **Conf** facs Corporate Hospitality Days **Location** on A362 Frome to Radstock road near village of Buckland Dinham
Hotel ★★★ CHH Homewood Park, HINTON CHARTERHOUSE
☎ 01225 723731 📄 01225 723820 21 en suite

GURNEY SLADE
Map 3 ST64

Mendip Golf Club BA3 4UT
☎ 01749 840570 📄 01749 841439
e-mail: secretary@mendipgolfclub.com
web: www.mendipgolfclub.com

Undulating downland course offering an interesting test of golf on superb fairways and extensive views over the surrounding countryside.

18 Holes, 6383yds, Par 71, SSS 71, Course record 65. Club membership 900.

Visitors Contact club for details. **Societies** booking required. **Green Fees** £25 per round (£36 weekends) **Course Designer** C K Cotton **Prof** Adrian Marsh **Facilities** 🏌 🍴 ⛳ 🖥 🍴 👥 🏠 ✂ 🏌 **Conf** facs Corporate Hospitality Days **Location** 1.5m S off A37
Hotel ★★★★ CHH Ston Easton Park, STON EASTON
☎ 01761 241631 📄 01761 241377 22 en suite

KEYNSHAM
Map 3 ST66

Stockwood Vale Golf Club Stockwood Ln BS31 2ER
☎ 0117 986 6505 📄 0117 986 8974
web: www.stockwoodvale.com

18 Holes, 6031yds, Par 71, SSS 69.

Location A4 W from Bath to the Bristol Ring Road (A4174) at the Hicks Gate rdbt. Left at rdbt for Keynsham. After 1m turn right at mini rdbt, club signed
Telephone for further details
Hotel ★★★★ GH Grasmere Court, 22-24 Bath Road, KEYNSHAM
☎ 0117 986 2662 📄 0117 986 2762 16 rooms

LONG ASHTON
Map 3 ST57

Long Ashton Golf Club The Clubhouse, Clarken Coombe BS41 9DW
☎ 01275 392229 📄 01275 394395
e-mail: secretary@longashtongolfclub.co.uk
web: www.longashtongolfclub.co.uk

Wooded parkland course with fine turf, wonderful views of Bristol and surrounding areas, and a spacious practice area. Good testing holes, especially the back nine, in prevailing south-west wind. Good drainage ensures pleasant winter golf.

Long Ashton: 18 Holes, 6368yds, Par 71, SSS 71. Club membership 700.

Visitors Contact club for details. **Societies** booking required. **Green Fees** phone **Course Designer** J H Taylor **Prof** Mike Hart **Facilities** 🏌 🍴 by prior arrangement ⛳ 🖥 🍴 👥 🏠 ✂ 🏌 **Conf** Corporate Hospitality Days **Location** 0.5m N on B3128
Hotel ★★★ 74% HL The Avon Gorge, Sion Hill, Clifton, BRISTOL
☎ 0117 973 8955 📄 0117 923 8125 75 en suite

Save on Hotels. Book at **theAA.com/hotel**

SOMERSET

ENGLAND

Woodspring Golf & Country Club Yanley Ln BS41 9LR
☎ 01275 394378 📄 01275 394473
e-mail: info@woodspring-golf.com
web: www.woodspring-golf.com

Set in 245 acres of undulating Somerset countryside, featuring superb natural water hazards, protected greens and a rising landscape. The course has three individual nine-hole courses, the Avon, Severn and Brunel. The 9th hole on the Brunel Course is a feature hole, with an elevated tee shot over a natural gorge. Long carries to tight fairways, elevated island tees and challenging approaches to greens make the most of the 27 holes.

Avon Course: 9 Holes, 2942yds, Par 35.
Brunel Course: 9 Holes, 3395yds, Par 37.
Severn Course: 9 Holes, 3267yds, Par 36.
Club membership 300.

Visitors Contact club for details. **Societies** booking required. **Green Fees** £16 weekdays (£18 weekends & BHs) **Course Designer** Clarke/Alliss/Steel **Prof** David Morgan **Facilities** ⑪ ⑭ ⓛ ⌷ ⑲
⚒ ☎ ⑲ ✦ 🏌 ⚒ ✦ 🏌 **Conf** facs Corporate Hospitality Days
Location off A38 Bridgwater Road
Hotel ★★★ 74% HL The Avon Gorge, Sion Hill, Clifton, BRISTOL
☎ 0117 973 8955 📄 0117 923 8125 75 en suite

MIDSOMER NORTON   Map 3 ST65

Fosseway Golf Course Charlton Ln BA3 4BD
☎ 01761 412214 📄 01761 418357
e-mail: club@centurionhotel.co.uk
web: www.centurionhotel.co.uk

Very attractive tree-lined parkland course, not demanding but with lovely views towards the Mendip Hills.

9 Holes, 4568yds, Par 67, SSS 63, Course record 57.
Club membership 180.

Visitors Mon-Sat & BHs. Sun pm. Dress code. **Societies** booking required. **Green Fees** £14 per 18 holes, £9 per 9 holes, Twilight from 4pm (except Wed) £8 (weekends £15/£10/£9) **Course Designer** C K Cotton/F Pennink **Facilities** ⑪ ⑭ ⓛ ⌷ ⑲ ⚒ ◇
Leisure outdoor and indoor heated swimming pool, sauna, gymnasium
Conf facs Corporate Hospitality Days **Location** SE of town centre off A367
Hotel ★★★★ CHH Ston Easton Park, STON EASTON
☎ 01761 241631 📄 01761 241377 22 en suite

MINEHEAD   Map 3 SS94

Minehead & West Somerset Golf Club The Warren TA24 5SJ
☎ 01643 702057 📄 01643 705095
web: www.minehead-golf-club.co.uk
18 Holes, 6153yds, Par 71, SSS 69, Course record 65.
Location E end of esplanade
Telephone for further details
Hotel ★★★ 74% SHL Channel House, Church Path, MINEHEAD
☎ 01643 703229 8 en suite

SALTFORD   Map 3 ST66

Saltford Golf Club Golf Club Ln BS31 3AA
☎ 01225 873513 📄 01225 873525
e-mail: mike@saltfordgolfclub.co.uk
web: www.saltfordgolfclub.co.uk

Set in 150 acres of attractive countryside, the course nestles in a natural wooded setting with extensive views over Bath and the Avon Valley. Notable holes are the long par 4 6th hole and the two delightful finishing holes.

18 Holes, 6398yds, Par 71, SSS 71, Course record 65.
Club membership 600.

Visitors Mon-Sun & BHs. Booking required weekends. Dress code. **Societies** booking required. **Green Fees** £30 per round (£35 weekends). Winter £22/£28 **Course Designer** Harry Vardon
Prof Darren Read **Facilities** ⑪ ⓛ ⌷ ⑲ ⚒ ☎ ⑲ ✦
⚒ ✦ 🏌 **Leisure** snooker **Conf** facs Corporate Hospitality Days
Location S of village, off A4
Hotel ★★★★★ 85% HL The Royal Crescent, 16 Royal Crescent,
BATH ☎ 01225 823333 📄 01225 339401 45 en suite

SOMERTON   Map 3 ST42

Long Sutton Golf Club Long Sutton TA10 9JU
☎ 01458 241017 📄 01458 241022
web: www.longsuttongolf.com
18 Holes, 6369yds, Par 71, SSS 70, Course record 64.
Course Designer Patrick Dawson **Location** 3.5m E of Langport, 0.5m S of Long Sutton on B3165
Telephone for further details
Hotel ★★★★ INN The Devonshire Arms, Long Sutton, LANGPORT
☎ 01458 241271 📄 01458 241037 9 rooms (8 en suite)

Wheathill Golf Club Wheathill TA11 7HG
☎ 01963 240667 📄 01963 240230
e-mail: wheathill@wheathill.fsnet.co.uk
web: www.wheathillgc.co.uk

A parkland course set in quiet countryside. Gently sloping land with the River Cary flowing next to the 13th and 14th holes. There is an 8 hole academy course and an expansive driving range.

18 Holes, 5381yds, Par 68, SSS 65, Course record 63.
Club membership 550.

Visitors Mon-Sun & BHs. Booking required Fri-Sun & BHs. Dress code. **Societies** welcome. **Green Fees** not confirmed **Course Designer** J Pain
Prof A England **Facilities** ⑪ ⑭ ⓛ ⌷ ⑲ ⚒ ☎ ✦ ⚒ ✦
🏌 **Leisure** 8 hole academy course. **Conf** facs Corporate Hospitality
Days **Location** 2m off A37, on B3153 between Somerton and Castle Cary
Hotel ★★ 81% HL Walnut Tree, Fore Street, WEST CAMEL
☎ 01935 851292 📄 01935 852119 13 en suite

TAUNTON
Map 3 ST22

Oake Manor Golf Club Oake TA4 1BA
☎ 01823 461993 🖹 01823 461995
e-mail: russell@oakemanor.com
web: www.oakemanor.com

An attractive and popular parkland and lakeland course situated in breathtaking Somerset countryside with views of the Quantock, Blackdown and Brendon hills. Ten holes feature water hazards such as lakes, cascades and a trout stream. The 15th hole (par 5, 476yds) is bounded by water all down the left with a carry over another lake on to an island green. The course is challenging yet great fun for all standards of golfer. Host of the PGA Total Triumph Classic and other amateur championships.

18 Holes, 6142yds, Par 70, SSS 70, Course record 63. Club membership 600.

Visitors Mon-Sun & BHs. Booking required. Dress code. **Societies** booking required **Green Fees** £29 per 18 holes, £31 Fri, £35 weekends **Course Designer** Adrian Stiff **Prof** R Gardner/J Smallacombe **Facilities** 🏌 🏌 🍴 🍴 ⚑ 🏌 ⚑ 🥓 🏌 🥓 **Leisure** 6 hole academy course, short game area, putting green, 11 bay covered driving range **Conf** facs Corporate Hospitality Days **Location** M5 junct 26, A38 N towards Taunton. Signed at World's End pub

Hotel ★★★ INN The Globe, Fore Street, MILVERTON ☎ 01823 400534 3 rooms

Taunton & Pickeridge Golf Club Corfe TA3 7BY
☎ 01823 421537 🖹 01823 421742
e-mail: mail@tauntongolf.co.uk
web: www.tauntongolf.co.uk

Downland course established in 1892 with extensive views of the Quantock and Mendip hills. Renowned for its excellent greens.

18 Holes, 6109yds, Par 69, SSS 70, Course record 62. Club membership 950.

Visitors Mon-Sun except Sat. Advance booking required. Dress code. **Societies** booking required. **Green Fees** not confirmed **Course Designer** Henry Fowler **Prof** Simon Stevenson **Facilities** 🏌 🍴 🍴 ⚑ 🏌 ⚑ 🥓 **Conf** facs Corporate Hospitality Days **Location** 4m S off B3170

Hotel ★★★ 83% HL The Mount Somerset, Lower Henlade, TAUNTON ☎ 01823 442500 🖹 01823 442900 11 en suite

Taunton Vale Golf Club Creech Heathfield TA3 5EY
☎ 01823 412220 🖹 01823 413583
e-mail: admin@tauntonvalegolf.co.uk
web: www.tauntonvalegolf.co.uk

An 18-hole and a nine-hole course in a parkland complex occupying 156 acres in the Vale of Taunton. Views of the Blackdown and Quantock Hills. Floodlit driving range.

Charlton Course: 18 Holes, 6237yds, Par 70, SSS 70.
Durston Course: 9 Holes, 2004yds, Par 32.
Club membership 700.

Visitors Mon-Sun & BHs. Booking required. Dress code. **Societies** booking required. **Green Fees** 18 hole course £26 per round (£32 weekends & BHs). 9 hole course £12 per round (£14 weekends) **Course Designer** John Payne **Prof** Martin Keitch **Facilities** 🏌 🍴 by prior arrangement 🍴 ⚑ 🏌 ⚑ 🥓 🏌 🥓 🏌 **Conf** facs Corporate Hospitality Days **Location** M5 junct 24 or 25, off A38/A361

Hotel ★★★ 83% HL The Mount Somerset, Lower Henlade, TAUNTON ☎ 01823 442500 🖹 01823 442900 11 en suite

Vivary Park Golf Course Fons George TA1 3JU
☎ 01823 333875
e-mail: r.coffin@toneleisure.com
web: www.toneleisure.co.uk

Tree-lined, flat parkland course with water features.

18 Holes, 4742yds, Par 66, SSS 63, Course record 58. Club membership 800.

Visitors Moderate dress code. **Societies** booking required. **Green Fees** £16 per round (£18 weekends) **Course Designer** W H Fowler **Prof** Richard Coffin **Facilities** 🏌 🍴 🍴 ⚑ 🏌 ⚑ 🥓 🏌 **Leisure** hard tennis courts, golf lessons **Conf** facs Corporate Hospitality Days **Location** S of town centre off A38

Hotel ★★★ 71% HL Corner House Hotel, Park Street, TAUNTON ☎ 01823 284683 🖹 01823 323464 44 en suite

WEDMORE
Map 3 ST44

Isle of Wedmore Golf Club Lineage BS28 4QT
☎ 01934 712222 (office) & 712452 (pro shop)
e-mail: info@wedmoregolfclub.com
web: www.wedmoregolfclub.com

Gently undulating course designed to maintain natural environment. Existing woodland and hedgerow enhanced by new planting. Magnificent panoramic views of Cheddar Valley and Glastonbury Tor from the back nine. The course design provides two loops of nine holes both starting and finishing at the clubhouse.

18 Holes, 6057yds, Par 70, SSS 69, Course record 67. Club membership 728.

Visitors Mon-Sun & BHs. Booking required Mon, Thu, weekends & BHs. Dress code. **Societies** booking required. **Green Fees** £32 per day, £24 per round. Reduced winter rates **Course Designer** Terry Murray **Prof** Nick Pope **Facilities** 🏌 🍴 🍴 ⚑ 🏌 ⚑ 🥓 🏌 🥓 **Leisure** indoor teaching studio & custom fitting centre **Conf** facs Corporate Hospitality Days **Location** 0.5m N of Wedmore

Hotel ★★★ 86% HL Best Western Swan, Sadler Street, WELLS ☎ 01749 836300 🖹 01749 836301 49 en suite

WELLS
Map 3 ST54

Wells (Somerset) Golf Club Blackheath Ln, East Horrington BA5 3DS
☎ 01749 675005 🖹 01749 683170
e-mail: secretary@wellsgolfclub.co.uk
web: www.wellsgolfclub.co.uk

Beautiful wooded course with wonderful views. The prevailing SW wind complicates the 448yd 3rd. Good drainage and paths for trolleys constructed all round the course.

18 Holes, 6004yds, Par 70, SSS 69, Course record 63. Club membership 670.

Visitors Mon-Sun & BHs. Booking required. Dress code. **Societies** booking required. **Green Fees** £30 per 18 holes (£35 weekends & BHs) 🏌 **Prof** Adrian Bishop **Facilities** 🏌 🍴 🍴 ⚑ 🏌 ⚑ 🥓 🏌 **Conf** facs Corporate Hospitality Days **Location** 1.5m E off B3139

Hotel ★★ 69% HL Ancient Gate House Hotel, 20 Sadler Street, WELLS ☎ 01749 672029 🖹 01749 670319 9 en suite

WESTON-SUPER-MARE   Map 3 ST36

Weston-Super-Mare Golf Club Uphill Road North BS23 4NQ
☎ 01934 626968 & 633360 (pro)   📠 01934 621360
e-mail: wsmgolfclub@eurotelbroadband.com
web: www.westonsupermaregolfclub.com
A compact and interesting layout with the opening hole adjacent to the beach. The sandy, links-type course is slightly undulating and has beautifully maintained turf and greens. The 15th is a testing 155yd par 4. Superb views across the Bristol Channel to Cardiff.
18 Holes, 6245yds, Par 70, SSS 70, Course record 69. Club membership 750.
Visitors Mon-Sun & BHs. Dress code. Societies welcome **Green Fees** £49 per day, £37 per round **Course Designer** T Dunne/Dr MacKenzie **Prof** Mike Laband **Facilities** ⏱ ⛳ 🍴 🏆 🎯 🏠 🍺 ⛳ **Location** S of town centre off A370
Hotel ★★★ 70% HL Beachlands Hotel, 17 Uphill Road North, WESTON-SUPER-MARE ☎ 01934 621401 📠 01934 621966
21 en suite

Worlebury Golf Club Monks Hill BS22 9SX
☎ 01934 625789   📠 01934 621935
e-mail: secretary@worleburygc.co.uk
web: www.worleburygc.co.uk
Parkland course on the ridge of Worlebury Hill, with fairly easy walking and extensive views of the Severn estuary and Wales.
18 Holes, 5843yds, Par 70, SSS 69, Course record 66. Club membership 650.
Visitors Mon-Sun & BHs. Booking required weekends & BHs. Dress code **Societies** welcome. **Green Fees** not confirmed **Course Designer** H Vardon **Prof** Gary Marks **Facilities** ⏱ 🍴 ⛳ ⛳ 🍺 ⛳ ⛳ **Conf** facs Corporate Hospitality Days **Location** 2m E off A370
Hotel ★★★ 70% HL Beachlands Hotel, 17 Uphill Road North, WESTON-SUPER-MARE ☎ 01934 621401 📠 01934 621966
21 en suite

YEOVIL   Map 3 ST51

Yeovil Golf Club Sherborne Rd BA21 5BW
☎ 01935 422965   📠 01935 411283
e-mail: office@yeovilgolfclub.com
web: www.yeovilgolfclub.com
On the Old Course the opener lies by the River Yeo before the gentle climb to high downs with good views. The outstanding 14th and 15th holes present a challenge, being below the player with a deep railway cutting on the left of the green. The 1st on the Newton Course is played over the river which then leads to a challenging but scenic course.
Old Course: 18 Holes, 6087yds, Par 71, SSS 70, Course record 64.
Newton Course: 9 Holes, 4856yds, Par 68, SSS 64, Course record 63. Club membership 1000.
Visitors Mon-Fri, Sun & BHs. Booking required. Handicap certificate. Dress code. **Societies** booking required. **Green Fees** not confirmed

Course Designer Hugh Allison **Prof** Geoff Kite **Facilities** ⏱ 🍴 ⛳ ⛳ 🍴 🏠 🍺 ⛳ 🍺 ⛳ 🚩 **Conf** Corporate Hospitality Days **Location** 1m E on A30
Hotel ★★★ 79% HL The Yeovil Court Hotel & Restaurant, West Coker Road, YEOVIL ☎ 01935 863746 📠 01935 863990
30 en suite

STAFFORDSHIRE

BROCTON   Map 7 SJ91

Brocton Hall Golf Club ST17 0TH
☎ 01785 661901   📠 01785 661591
e-mail: secretary@broctonhall.com
web: www.broctonhall.com
Parkland with gentle slopes in places, easy walking.
18 Holes, 6064yds, Par 69, SSS 69, Course record 66. Club membership 665.
Visitors Mon-Sun & BHs. Booking required Tue, Thu-Fri. Handicap certificate. Dress code. **Societies** booking required. **Green Fees** not confirmed **Course Designer** Harry Vardon **Prof** Nevil Bland **Facilities** ⏱ 🍴 ⛳ ⛳ 🍴 🏠 🍺 ⛳ ⛳ **Leisure** snooker **Conf** Corporate Hospitality Days **Location** NW of village off A34
Hotel ★★★★ 84% HL The Moat House, Lower Penkridge Road, Acton Trussell, STAFFORD ☎ 01785 712217 📠 01785 715344
41 en suite

BURTON UPON TRENT   Map 8 SK22

Belmont Driving Range & Golf Course Belmont Rd, Needwood DE13 9PH
☎ 01283 814381   📠 01283 814381
e-mail: belmontpro@belmontgolf.co.uk
web: www.belmontgolf.co.uk
A nine-hole course with five par 4s, the longest being 430 yards. Also a par 5 of 510 yards. The course comprises trees, bunkers, some water and great views.
9 Holes, 2415yds, Par 68, SSS 66, Course record 62. Club membership 55.
Visitors Mon-Sun & BHs. Dress code. **Societies** booking required. **Green Fees** £12.50 per 18 holes, £8 per 9 holes (£14.50/£9.50 weekends) 🅿 **Course Designer** R Coy **Prof** R Coy/C Roberts **Facilities** ⛳ 🏠 🍺 ⛳ 🚩 **Leisure** fishing **Conf** Corporate Hospitality Days **Location** 3m NW of Tutbury, off B5017 towards Tutbury
Hotel ★★★ 75% HL The Boars Head, Lichfield Road, SUDBURY ☎ 01283 820344 📠 01283 820075   23 en suite

217

Branston Golf & Country Club Burton Rd, Branston DE14 3DP

☎ 01283 512211 📠 01283 566984
e-mail: info@branstonclub.co.uk
web: www.branstonclub.co.uk

Semi-parkland course on undulating ground next to the River Trent. Natural water hazards on 13 holes. A nine-hole course has been opened.

Branston: 18 Holes, 6393yds, Par 72, SSS 70.
Academy Course: 9 Holes, 1684yds, Par 30, SSS 30.
Club membership 800.

Visitors Mon-Sun & BHs. Booking required. **Societies** Booking required. **Green Fees** £40 Mon-Thu, £50 Fri-Sun per 18 holes. £7/£11 per 9 holes **Course Designer** G Ramshall **Prof** Iain Ross **Facilities** ⊕ ⍩ ⛳ ⌨ ⛴ ⚑ ⌂ ⛴ ⚐ ⚲ ⚘ ⛴ **Leisure** heated indoor swimming pool, sauna, gymnasium, 9 hole course **Conf** facs Corporate Hospitality Days **Location** 1.5m SW on A5121
Hotel ★★★ 78% HL Three Queens, One Bridge Street, BURTON UPON TRENT ☎ 01283 523800 & 0845 230 1332 📠 01283 523823 38 en suite

Burton-upon-Trent Golf Club 43 Ashby Road East DE15 0PS

☎ 01283 544551 (secretary) & 562240 (pro)
e-mail: the secretary@burtonontrentgolfclub.co.uk
web: www.burtonontrentgolfclub.co.uk

Undulating parkland course with notable trees and water features on two holes. Testing par 3s at 10th and 12th. The signature hole is the 18th, played over a lake to a green just below the clubhouse.

18 Holes, 6579yds, Par 71, SSS 72, Course record 67.
Club membership 660.

Visitors Mon, Tue & Fri-Sun except BHs. Booking required weekends & BHs. Handicap certificate. Dress code. **Societies** booking required. **Green Fees** £52 per day, £40 per round (£59/£46 weekends & BHs) **Course Designer** H S Colt **Prof** Gary Stafford **Facilities** ⊕ ⍩ ⛳ ⌨ ⛴ ⚑ ⌂ ⛴ ⚐ ⚲ ⚘ **Conf** Corporate Hospitality Days **Location** 3m E of Burton on A511
Hotel ★★★ 78% HL Three Queens, One Bridge Street, BURTON UPON TRENT ☎ 01283 523800 & 0845 230 1332 📠 01283 523823 38 en suite

The Craythorne Craythorne Rd, Rolleston on Dove DE13 0AZ

☎ 01283 564329
e-mail: admin@craythorne.co.uk
web: www.craythorne.co.uk

A relatively short and challenging parkland course with tight fairways and views of the Trent Valley. Excellent greens giving all year play.

Suits all standards but particularly good for society players. The course has matured following development over many years and recent improvements to tees, paths and greens make the course a good test of golf.

18 Holes, 5641yds, Par 68, SSS 68, Course record 64.
Club membership 350.

Visitors Mon-Sun & BHs. Booking required. Dress code. **Societies** booking required. **Green Fees** not confirmed ⍩ **Course Designer** A A Wright **Prof** Steve Hadfield **Facilities** ⊕ ⍩ ⛳ ⌨ ⛴ ⚑ ⌂ ⛴ ⚐ ⚲ ⚘ ⛴ **Conf** facs Corporate Hospitality Days **Location** off A38 through Stretton, tourist signs
Hotel ★★★ 78% HL Three Queens, One Bridge Street, BURTON UPON TRENT ☎ 01283 523800 & 0845 230 1332 📠 01283 523823 38 en suite

CANNOCK   Map 7 SJ91

Beau Desert Golf Club Rugeley Rd WS12 0PJ

☎ 01543 422626 📠 01543 451137
web: www.bdgc.co.uk

18 Holes, 6310yds, Par 70, SSS 71, Course record 64.
Course Designer Herbert Fowler **Location** off A460 NE of Hednesford
Telephone for further details
Hotel ★★★★ GH Colton House, Colton, RUGELEY ☎ 01889 578580 📠 01889 578580 9 rooms

Cannock Park Golf Course Stafford Rd WS11 2AL

☎ 01543 578850

18 Holes, 5200yds, Par 67, SSS 65, Course record 62.
Course Designer John Mainland **Location** 0.5m N of town centre on A34
Telephone for further details
Hotel ★★★★ 84% HL The Moat House, Lower Penkridge Road, Acton Trussell, STAFFORD ☎ 01785 712217 📠 01785 715344 41 en suite

ENVILLE   Map 7 SO88

Enville Golf Club Highgate Common DY7 5BN

☎ 01384 872074 (office) & 873396 (pro shop)
📠 01384 873396
e-mail: secretary@envillegolfclub.com
web: www.envillegolfclub.com

Easy walking on two fairly flat woodland and heathland courses. Qualifying course for the Open Championship. Two quality courses, with the Highgate being in the top 200 UK courses. Enville also has a substantial practice facility comprising three chipping greens and an extensive driving range.

Highgate Course: 18 Holes, 6695yds, Par 72, SSS 73.
Lodge Course: 18 Holes, 6417yds, Par 71, SSS 71.
Club membership 900.

Visitors Mon-Fri except BHs. Dress code. **Societies** booking required. **Green Fees** £60 per 36 holes, £50 per 18 holes **Prof** Sean Power **Facilities** ⊕ ⍩ ⛳ ⌨ ⛴ ⚑ ⌂ ⚐ ⚲ ⚘ ⛴ **Conf** Corporate Hospitality Days **Location** 2m NE of Enville off A458
Hotel ★★★★ 78% HL Mill Hotel & Restaurant, ALVELEY ☎ 01746 780437 📠 01746 780850 41 en suite

ave on Hotels. Book at **theAA.com/hotel**

STAFFORDSHIRE

ENGLAND

GOLDENHILL

Map 7 SJ85

Goldenhill Golf Course Mobberley Rd ST6 5SS
☎ 01782 787678 📄 01782 787678
web: www.jackbarker.com
18 Holes, 5957yds, Par 71, SSS 69.
Location on A50 4m N of Stoke
Telephone for further details
Hotel ★★★★ 73% HL Best Western Stoke-on-Trent Moat
House, Etruria Hall, Festival Way, Etruria, STOKE-ON-TRENT
☎ 0870 225 4601 & 01782 206101 📄 01782 206101 147 en suite

HIMLEY

Map 7 SO89

Himley Hall Golf Centre Log Cabin, Himley Hall Park
DY3 4DF
☎ 01902 895207 & 0715284196
e-mail: bernie@bsparrow.wanadoo.co.uk
web: www.himleygolf.com
Parkland course set in the grounds of Himley Hall Park, with lovely
views. Large practice area including a pitch and putt.
9 Holes, 6216yds, Par 72, SSS 70, Course record 68.
Club membership 120.
Visitors Mon-Sun & BHs. Booking required weekends & BHs. Dress
code. Societies welcome. Green Fees not confirmed 🏌 Course
Designer A Baker Prof Mark Sparrow Facilities 🏌 🖥 📷 ✨
Location 0.5m E on B4176
Hotel ★★★★ 73% HL Copthorne Hotel Merry Hill - Dudley, The
Waterfront, Level Street, Brierley Hill, DUDLEY ☎ 01384 482882
📄 01384 482773 138 en suite

LEEK

Map 7 SJ95

Leek Golf Club Birchall ST13 5RE
☎ 01538 384779 & 384767 (pro) 📄 01538 384779
web: www.leekgolfclub.co.uk
18 Holes, 6218yds, Par 70, SSS 70, Course record 63.
Location 0.75m S on A520
Telephone for further details
Hotel ★★★ 77% HL Three Horseshoes Inn & Country Hotel, Buxton
Road, Blackshaw Moor, LEEK ☎ 01538 300296 📄 01538 300320
16 en suite

Westwood (Leek) Golf Course Newcastle Rd ST13 7AA
☎ 01538 398385 (office) & 398897 (pro)
📄 01538 382485
e-mail: westwoodgolfclubleek@btconnect.com
web: www.westwoodgolfclubleek.co.uk
A challenging moorland and parkland course set in beautiful open
countryside with an undulating front nine. The back nine is more open
and longer with the River Churnet coming into play on several holes.
18 Holes, 6105yds, Par 70, SSS 70, Course record 63.
Club membership 530.
Visitors Mon-Sat & BHs. Booking required Sat. Dress code.
Societies booking required. Green Fees £22 per 18 holes, £15 per 9
holes. (Sat £28 per 18 holes) Prof Greg Rogula Facilities 🏌 🍽 🅿
🖥 🍴 🧗 📷 🔧 🚜 ✨ Conf facs Corporate Hospitality Days
Location on A53 S of Leek
Hotel ★★★ 77% HL Three Horseshoes Inn & Country Hotel, Buxton
Road, Blackshaw Moor, LEEK ☎ 01538 300296 📄 01538 300320
16 en suite

LICHFIELD

Map 7 SK10

Lichfield Golf & Country Club Elmhurst WS13 8HE
☎ 01543 417333 📄 01543 418098
web: www.theclubcompany.com
Mill Course: 18 Holes, 6042yds, Par 72, SSS 70,
Course record 67.
Course Designer Hawtree & Son Location 3m N of Lichfield off B5014
Telephone for further details
Hotel ★★★ 77% HL Best Western The George, 12-14 Bird Street,
LICHFIELD ☎ 01543 414822 📄 01543 415817 45 en suite

Whittington Heath Golf Club Tamworth Rd WS14 9PW
☎ 01543 432317 📄 01543 433962
e-mail: info@whittingtonheathgc.co.uk
web: www.whittingtonheathgc.co.uk
The 18 magnificent holes wind through heathland and trees,
presenting a good test for the serious golfer. Leaving the fairway
can be severely punished. The dog-legs are most tempting,
inviting the golfer to chance his arm. Local knowledge is a definite
advantage. Clear views of the famous three spires of Lichfield
Cathedral.
18 Holes, 6490yds, Par 70, SSS 71, Course record 64.
Club membership 660.
Visitors Mon-Fri except BHs. Booking required. Handicap certificate.
Dress code. Societies booking required. Green Fees £55 per 36
holes, £48 per 27 holes, £40 per 18 holes. Course Designer Colt
Prof Mike Raj Facilities 🏌 🍽 🖥 🖥 🍴 🧗 📷 📷 ✨
Conf Corporate Hospitality Days Location 2.5m SE on A51
Hotel ★★★ 77% HL Best Western The George, 12-14 Bird Street,
LICHFIELD ☎ 01543 414822 📄 01543 415817 45 en suite

NEWCASTLE-UNDER-LYME

Map 7 SJ84

Jack Barkers Keele Golf Centre Newcastle Rd, Keele
ST5 5AB
☎ 01782 627596 📄 01782 714555
e-mail: keele@jackbarker.com
web: www.jackbarker.com
Parkland with mature trees and great views of Stoke-on-Trent and the
surrounding area.
18 Holes, 6346yds, Par 72, SSS 71, Course record 67.
Club membership 200.
Visitors Mon-Sun & BHs. Societies welcome. Green Fees £11 per
round, £14 Fri, £16 weekends Course Designer Hawtree Facilities 🏌
🍽 🖥 🖥 🍴 🧗 📷 🔧 ✨ 🚜 ✨ Leisure 9 hole par 3
academy course Conf Corporate Hospitality Days Location 2m W on
A525 opp Keele University
Hotel ★★★★ BB The Lodge, Red Hall Lane, HALMER END
☎ 01782 729047 & 07973 776797 📄 01782 729047 2 rooms

ENGLAND

Newcastle-Under-Lyme Golf Club Whitmore Rd ST5 2QB
☎ 01782 617006 📠 01782 617531
e-mail: info@newcastlegolfclub.co.uk
web: www.newcastlegolfclub.co.uk
Parkland course.

18 Holes, 6395yds, Par 72, SSS 71, Course record 66.
Club membership 600.

Visitors Mon-Fri except BHs. Handicap certificate. Dress code.
Societies booking required. **Green Fees** £35 per 18 holes, £40 per 36
holes 🅿 **Prof** David Cooper **Facilities** 🕦 🍴 🍺 ⬜ 🍷 🔺 🏠
🚚 🖋 **Conf** Corporate Hospitality Days **Location** 1m SW on A53
Hotel ★★★ 75% HL Holiday Inn Stoke-on-Trent, Clayton Road,
Clayton, NEWCASTLE-UNDER-LYME ☎ 01782 557000 & 557018
📠 01782 717138 118 en suite

Wolstanton Golf Club Dimsdale Old Hall, Hassam Pde,
Wolstanton ST5 9DR
☎ 01782 622413 (Sec) 📠 01782 622413
e-mail: wolstanton.golf.club.ltd@unicombox.co.uk
web: www.wolstantongolfclub.com
A challenging undulating suburban course incorporating six difficult
par 3 holes. The 6th hole (par 3) is 233yds from the Medal Tee.

18 Holes, 5533yds, Par 68, SSS 68, Course record 63.
Club membership 700.

Visitors Mon-Fri except BHs. Booking required. Handicap certificate.
Dress code. **Societies** booking required. **Green Fees** £35 per 18 holes
Prof Simon Arnold **Facilities** 🕦 🍴 🍺 ⬜ 🍷 🔺 🏠 🖋
Conf facs Corporate Hospitality Days **Location** 1.5m from town centre.
Turn off A34 at MacDonalds
Hotel ★★★★ 73% HL Best Western Stoke-on-Trent Moat
House, Etruria Hall, Festival Way, Etruria, STOKE-ON-TRENT
☎ 0870 225 4601 & 01782 206101 📠 01782 206101 147 en suite

ONNELEY
Map 7 SJ74

Onneley Golf Club CW3 5QF
☎ 01782 750577 & 846759
e-mail: admin@onneleygolfclub.co.uk
web: www.onneleygolf.co.uk
Parkland having panoramic views to the Welsh hills.

18 Holes, 5740yds, Par 70, SSS 67, Course record 62.
Club membership 410.

Visitors contact club for details. **Societies** booking required. **Green
Fees** Winter per 18 holes £15 (weekends £17.50). Summer £24.50
(£27) 🅿 **Course Designer** A Benson/G Marks **Facilities** 🕦 🍺 ⬜
🍷 🔺 **Conf** Corporate Hospitality Days **Location** 2m from Woore
on A525
Hotel ★★★★ 77% HL Crewe Hall, Weston Road, CREWE
☎ 01270 253333 📠 01270 253322 117 en suite

PATTINGHAM
Map 7 SO89

Patshull Park Hotel Golf & Country Club Patshull Rd
WV6 7HR
☎ 01902 700100 📠 01902 700874
e-mail: sales@patshull-park.co.uk
web: www.patshull-park.co.uk
Picturesque course set in 280 acres of glorious 'Capability' Brown
landscaped parkland. Designed by John Jacobs, the course meanders
alongside trout fishing lakes. Water comes into play alongside the 3rd
and 5th holes and there are challenging drives over water on the 13th
and 14th. Wellingtonia and Cedar trees prove an obstacle to wayward
drives. The 12th is the toughest hole on the course and the tee shot is
vital, anything wayward and the trees block out the second to the green

18 Holes, 6400yds, Par 72, SSS 72, Course record 63.
Club membership 300.

Visitors Mon-Sun & BHs. Booking required. Handicap certificate. Dress
code. **Societies** booking required. **Green Fees** not confirmed **Course
Designer** John Jacobs **Prof** Richard Bissell **Facilities** 🕦 🍴 🍺 ⬜
🍷 🔺 🏠 🤵 ♦ 🚚 🖋 🏌 **Leisure** heated indoor swimming
pool, fishing, sauna, gymnasium **Conf** facs Corporate Hospitality
Days **Location** 1.5m W of Pattingham, at Pattingham Church take the
Patshull Rd, hotel on right
Hotel ★★★ 79% HL Patshull Park Hotel Golf & Country Club,
Patshull Park, PATTINGHAM ☎ 01902 700100 📠 01902 700874
49 en suite

PENKRIDGE
Map 7 SJ91

The Chase Golf Club Pottal Pool Rd ST19 5RN
☎ 01785 712888 📠 01785 712692
e-mail: manager@thechasegolf.co.uk
web: www.thechasegolf.co.uk
Parkland course with links characteristics.

18 Holes, 6641yds, Par 73, SSS 72, Course record 65.
Club membership 850.

Visitors Mon-Sun & BHs. Booking required. Dress code.
Societies booking required. **Green Fees** not confirmed **Prof** Craig
Thomas **Facilities** 🕦 🍴 🍺 ⬜ 🍷 🔺 🏠 🖋 🚚 🖋 🏌
Leisure gymnasium, indoor teaching academy **Conf** facs Corporate
Hospitality Days **Location** 2m E off B5012
Hotel ★★★★ 84% HL The Moat House, Lower Penkridge Road,
Acton Trussell, STAFFORD ☎ 01785 712217 📠 01785 715344
41 en suite

PERTON
Map 7 SO89

Perton Park Golf Club Wrottesley Park Rd WV6 7HL
☎ 01902 380073 📠 01902 326219
e-mail: admin@pertongolfclub.co.uk
web: www.pertongolfclub.co.uk
Challenging inland links style course set in picturesque Staffordshire
countryside.

18 Holes, 6500yds, Par 71. Club membership 600.

Visitors Mon-Sun & BHs. **Societies** booking required. **Green Fees** £20
per round (£25 weekends & BHs). **Prof** Jeremy Harrold **Facilities** 🕦
🍴 🍺 ⬜ 🍷 🔺 🏠 🤵 ♦ 🚚 🖋 🏌 **Leisure** hard tennis
courts **Conf** facs Corporate Hospitality Days **Location** SE of Perton
off A454
Hotel ★★★ 88% HL The Elms Hotel, Stockton Road, ABBERLEY
☎ 01299 896666 📠 01299 896804 23 en suite

ave on Hotels. Book at **theAA.com/hotel**

STAFFORDSHIRE

ENGLAND

RUGELEY
Map 7 SK01

St Thomas's Priory Golf Club Hawkesyard Estate, Armitage Park WS15 1ED
☎ 01543 491911 📄 0870 300 7166
e-mail: info@hawkesyardestate.com
web: www.hawkesyardestate.com

A parkland course set in the historic Hawkesyard Estate with ancient woodland and lakes built by Dominican monks in the 19th century. Undulating fairways and excellent drainage facilitating golf all year round.

18 Holes, 5907yds, Par 70, SSS 70, Course record 65. Club membership 400.
Visitors Mon-Sun & BHs. Booking required Fri-Sun & BHs. Dress code. **Societies** booking required. **Green Fees** £30 (weekends £35) **Course Designer** P I Mulholland **Prof** Jon Watts **Facilities** ⊕ ⑨⑪ ⓵ ⊐ ⓵ ⌂ 🗑 ◇ 🏌 🛒 ∮ 🎿 **Leisure** fishing **Conf** facs Corporate Hospitality Days **Location** A51 onto A513
Hotel ★★★ 67% HL Cathedral Lodge Hotel, 62 Beacon Street, LICHFIELD ☎ 01543 414500 📄 01543 415734 36 en suite

STAFFORD
Map 7 SJ92

Stafford Castle Golf Club Newport Rd ST16 1BP
☎ 01785 223821 📄 01785 223821
web: www.staffordcastlegolf.com

Undulating parkland-type course built around Stafford Castle.

9 Holes, 6082yds, Par 71, SSS 69. Club membership 400.
Visitors Mon-Sat & BHs. Sun pm. Booking required. Dress code. **Societies** booking required. **Green Fees** £18 per day (£22 Sat) **Facilities** ⊕ ⓵ ⊐ ⑨⑪ 🎿 **Conf** Corporate Hospitality Days **Location** SW of town centre off A518
Hotel ★★★ 80% HL The Swan, 46 Greengate Street, STAFFORD ☎ 01785 258142 📄 01785 223372 31 en suite

STOKE-ON-TRENT
Map 7 SJ84

Burslem Golf Club Wood Farm, High Ln, Tunstall ST6 7JT
☎ 01782 837006
e-mail: alanporterburslemgc@yahoo.co.uk

On the outskirts of Tunstall, a moorland course with hard walking.

9 Holes, 5354yds, Par 66, SSS 66, Course record 66. Club membership 250.
Visitors Mon-Fri except BHs. Booking required. Dress code. **Societies** booking required. **Green Fees** not confirmed 🅿 **Facilities** ⊕ by prior arrangement ⑨⑪ by prior arrangement ⓵ ⊐ 🎿 **Location** 4m N of city centre on B5049
Hotel ★★★ 71% HL Quality Hotel Stoke, 66 Trinity Street, Hanley, STOKE-ON-TRENT ☎ 01782 202361 📄 01782 286464 136 en suite

Greenway Hall Golf Club Stanley Rd ST9 9LJ
☎ 01782 503158 📄 01782 504691
web: www.jackbarker.com

18 Holes, 5678yds, Par 68, SSS 67, Course record 65.
Location 5m NE off A53
Telephone for further details
Hotel ★★★ 71% HL Quality Hotel Stoke, 66 Trinity Street, Hanley, STOKE-ON-TRENT ☎ 01782 202361 📄 01782 286464 136 en suite

Trentham Golf Club 14 Barlaston Old Rd, Trentham ST4 8HB
☎ 01782 658109 📄 01782 644024
e-mail: generalmanager@trenthamgolf.org
web: www.trenthamgolf.org

Traditional parkland course with mature trees lining most fairways. A well placed approach shot is required to help navigate the many undulating greens. An Open Championship regional qualifying course for five years.

18 Holes, 6622yds, Par 72, SSS 72. Club membership 600.
Visitors contact club for details **Societies** booking required. **Green Fees** phone **Course Designer** Colt & Alison **Prof** Shane Owen **Facilities** ⊕ ⑨⑪ ⓵ ⊐ ⑨⑪ 🎿 🗑 ◇ ∮ 🛒 ⌂ 🏌 **Leisure** squash **Conf** Corporate Hospitality Days **Location** off A5035 in Trentham

Trentham Park Golf Club Trentham Park ST4 8AE
☎ 01782 658800 📄 01782 658800
web: www.trenthamparkgolfclub.com
18 Holes, 6425yds, Par 71, SSS 71, Course record 67.
Location M6 junct 15, 1m E. 3m SW of Stoke off A34
Telephone for further details

STONE
Map 7 SJ93

Barlaston Golf Club Meaford Rd ST15 8UX
☎ 01782 372795 & 372867 📄 01782 373648
e-mail: barlaston.gc@virgin.net
web: www.barlastongolfclub.co.uk

Picturesque parkland course designed by Peter Alliss. A number of water features come into play on several holes.

18 Holes, 5801yds, Par 69, SSS 68, Course record 64.
Club membership 600.

Visitors Mon-Sun & BHs. Dress code. **Societies** booking required.
Green Fees not confirmed **Course Designer** Peter Alliss **Prof** Ian Rogers **Facilities** ⓣ †◎⌐ 🍴 ⌐ 🛒 ⚒ 🚶 🗄 🛒 ✎ 🏌 **Conf** Corporate Hospitality Days **Location** M6 junct 15, 5m S
Hotel ★★★ 68% HL Stone House, Stafford Road, STONE
☎ 01785 815531 & 0844 414 6580 📄 01785 814764 50 en suite

Izaak Walton Golf Club Eccleshall Rd, Cold Norton ST15 0NS
☎ 01785 760900
e-mail: secretary@izaakwaltongolfclub.co.uk
web: www.izaakwaltongolfclub.co.uk

A gently undulating meadowland course set out in two loops of nine both returning to the clubhouse. The front nine lulls you into a false sense of security with its well defined and open fairways. The back nine tests you with tighter landing areas, water in abundance and holes which reward brave play.

18 Holes, 6370yds, Par 72, SSS 72, Course record 63.
Club membership 500.

Visitors Booking required. Dress code. **Societies** booking required.
Green Fees £30 per day (Wed £12.50 all day), £20 per round (£35/£25weekends & BHs) **Prof** Rob Grier **Facilities** ⓣ †◎⌐ 🛒 ⌐ 🍴 🚶 🗄 🛒 ✎ 🏌 **Conf** Corporate Hospitality Days **Location** on B5026 between Stone & Eccleshall
Hotel ★★★ 68% HL Stone House, Stafford Road, STONE
☎ 01785 815531 & 0844 414 6580 📄 01785 814764 50 en suite

Stone Golf Club Filleybrooks ST15 0NB
☎ 01785 813103
e-mail: enquiries@stonegolfclub.co.uk
web: www.stonegolfclub.co.uk

Nine-hole parkland course with easy walking and 18 different tees.

9 Holes, 6307yds, Par 71, SSS 70, Course record 65.
Club membership 310.

Visitors Mon-Sun except BHs. Booking required weekends. Dress code.
Societies welcome. **Green Fees** £20 per day ⊕ **Facilities** ⓣ †◎⌐ 🛒 ⌐ 🍴 🚶 ✎ **Conf** Corporate Hospitality Days **Location** 0.5m W on A34
Hotel ★★★ 68% HL Stone House, Stafford Road, STONE
☎ 01785 815531 & 0844 414 6580 📄 01785 814764 50 en suite

TAMWORTH
Map 7 SK20

Drayton Park Golf Club Drayton Park, Fazeley B78 3TN
☎ 01827 251139 📄 01827 284035
e-mail: draytonparkgc.co.uk
web: www.draytonparkgc.co.uk

Parkland course designed by James Braid. Club established since 1897.

18 Holes, 6439yds, Par 71, SSS 71, Course record 62.
Club membership 550.

Visitors dress code. **Societies** welcome. **Green Fees** £40 per day **Course Designer** James Braid **Prof** M W Passmore **Facilities** ⓣ †◎⌐ 🛒 ⌐ 🍴 🚶 🗄 🛒 ✎ **Conf** Corporate Hospitality Days **Location** 2m S on A4091, next to Drayton Manor Leisure Park
Hotel ★★ 82% HL Drayton Court Hotel, 65 Coleshill Street, Fazeley, TAMWORTH ☎ 01827 285805 📄 01827 284842 19 en suite

Tamworth Golf Centre Eagle Dr, Amington B77 4EG
☎ 01827 709303 📄 01827 709305
web: www.tamworth.gov.uk

This parkland course boasts five par 5s and a 17th hole par 3 of 231 yards that provides a challenge to any level of golfer. This course has played host to the NAPGC Junior Championships for over 25 years.

18 Holes, 6488yds, Par 73, SSS 72, Course record 65.
Club membership 250.

Visitors Mon-Sun & BHs. Booking required. **Societies** booking required. **Green Fees** £18.50 per 18 holes (£20.50 weekends & BHs)
Course Designer Hawtree & Son **Prof** Wayne Alcock **Facilities** ⓣ 🛒 ⌐ 🚶 🗄 🍴 ✎ 🛒 ✎ **Conf** facs Corporate Hospitality Days **Location** 2.5m E off B5000 (Glascote Road) onto Mercian Way. Straight across at rdbt then 1st right onto Eagle Drive
Hotel ★★ 82% HL Drayton Court Hotel, 65 Coleshill Street, Fazeley, TAMWORTH ☎ 01827 285805 📄 01827 284842 19 en suite

UTTOXETER
Map 7 SK03

Manor Golf Club Leese Hill ST14 8QT
☎ 01889 563234 📄 01889 563234
web: www.manorgolfclub.org.uk

18 Holes, 6206yds, Par 71, SSS 70, Course record 63.

Course Designer Various **Location** 2m from Uttoxeter on A518 towards Stafford
Telephone for further details
Hotel ★★★ 75% HL The Boars Head, Lichfield Road, SUDBURY ☎ 01283 820344 📄 01283 820075 23 en suite

ttoxeter Golf Club Wood Ln ST14 8JR
☎ 01889 564884 (Pro) & 566552 (Office)
📠 01889 566552
-mail: admin@uttoxetergolfclub.com
eb: www.uttoxetergolfclub.com
ndulating, challenging course with excellent putting surfaces,
anicured fairways, uniform rough and extensive views across the
ove Valley to the rolling hills of Staffordshire and Derbyshire.
8 Holes, 5801yds, Par 69, SSS 69. Club membership 500.
isitors Mon-Sun & BHs. Booking required weekends & BHs. Handicap
ertificate. Dress code. **Societies** booking required. **Green Fees** £28
er day (£30 weekends) **Course Designer** G Rothera **Prof** Adam
cCandless **Facilities** 🍴 🌐 🍺 🛒 ⚑ ♿ 🏠 🚌 🐾 **Conf**
orporate Hospitality Days **Location** near A50, 0.5m beyond main
ntrance to racecourse
otel ★★★ 75% HL The Boars Head, Lichfield Road, SUDBURY
☎ 01283 820344 📠 01283 820075 23 en suite

ESTON   Map 7 SJ92

ngestre Park Golf Club ST18 0RE
☎ 01889 270845 📠 01889 271434
-mail: office@ingestregolf.co.uk
eb: www.ingestregolf.co.uk
arkland course set in the grounds of Ingestre Hall, former home of
he Earl of Shrewsbury, with mature trees and pleasant views.
8 Holes, 6352yds, Par 70, SSS 70, Course record 67.
Club membership 750.
isitors Mon-Fri except BHs. Handicap certificate. Dress code.
ocieties welcome. **Green Fees** £50 per day, £40 per round 🍴
ourse Designer Hawtree **Prof** Danny Scullion **Facilities** 🍴 🌐 🍺
🛒 ♿ 🏠 🚌 🐾 **Conf** facs Corporate Hospitality Days
ocation 2m SE off A51
otel ★★★ 80% HL The Swan, 46 Greengate Street, STAFFORD
☎ 01785 258142 📠 01785 223372 31 en suite

HISTON   Map 7 SK04

Whiston Hall Golf Club Mansion Court Hotel ST10 2HZ
☎ 01538 266260 📠 01538 266820
eb: www.whistonhall.com
8 Holes, 5742yds, Par 71, SSS 69, Course record 70.
ourse Designer T Cooper **Location** E of village centre off A52
elephone for further details
otel ★★★ 80% HL Izaak Walton, Dovedale, ASHBOURNE
☎ 01335 350555 📠 01335 350539 35 en suite

SUFFOLK

LDEBURGH   Map 5 TM45

Aldeburgh Golf Club Saxmundham Rd IP15 5PE
☎ 01728 452890 📠 01728 452937
e-mail: info@aldeburghgolfclub.co.uk
web: www.aldeburghgolfclub.co.uk
Good natural drainage provides year round golf in links-type
conditions. Accuracy is the first challenge on well-bunkered,
heathland course. Fine views over an Area of Outstanding Natural
Beauty.

WENTWORTH
HOTEL ★★★
Aldeburgh, Suffolk
Tel: (01728) 452312 Fax: (01728) 454343
E-mail: stay@wentworth-aldeburgh.co.uk
Website: www.wentworth-aldeburgh.com

Enjoy the comfort and style of a country house. Two
lounges, with open fires and antique furniture, provide
ample space to relax. The individually decorated
bedrooms, many with sea views, are equipped with a
colour TV, radio, hairdryer and tea-making facilities.
The Restaurant serves a variety of fresh produce whilst
the Bar menu offers a light lunch, and can be eaten
outside on the sunken terrace garden. The timeless
and unhurried Aldeburgh provides quality shopping,
two excellent golf courses within a short distance, long
walks and birdwatching at nearby Minsmere Bird
Reserve. The internationally famous Snape Malting
Concert Hall offers music and the arts and there are
miles of beach to sit upon and watch the sea.

*Main Course: 18 Holes, 6603yds, Par 68, SSS 73,
Course record 65.*
River Course: 9 Holes, 2015yds, Par 32, SSS 30.
Club membership 900.
Visitors Mon-Sun & BHs. Booking required. Dress code.
Societies booking required. **Green Fees** £70 per day, £50 after
12 noon (weekends £75/£55) **Course Designer** Thompson, Fernie,
Taylor, Park. **Prof** Keith Preston **Facilities** 🍴 🍺 🛒 🏠 ♿
🏠 🚌 🐾 **Conf** Corporate Hospitality Days **Location** 1m W
on A1094
Hotel ★★★ 88% HL Wentworth, Wentworth Road, ALDEBURGH
☎ 01728 452312 📠 01728 454343 35 en suite

See advert on this page

BECCLES
Map 5 TM48

Beccles Golf Club The Common NR34 9BX
☎ 01502 712244
web: www.clubnoticeboard.com/becclesgc
Commons course with gorse bushes, no water hazards or bunkers.

9 Holes, 2500yds, Par 68, SSS 66, Course record 64.
Club membership 76.

Visitors Mon-Fri except BHs. Weekends pm. Dress code.
Societies welcome **Green Fees** not confirmed **Facilities** 🅱 🖥 🍴
⛳ **Location** NE of town centre
Hotel ★★★ 83% HL Waveney House, Puddingmoor, BECCLES
☎ 01502 712270 📄 01502 470370 12 en suite

BUNGAY
Map 5 TM38

Bungay & Waveney Valley Golf Club Outney Common NR35 1DS
☎ 01986 892337 📄 01986 892222
e-mail: bungaygolfclub@uwclub.net
web: www.club-noticeboard.co.uk
Heathland course, lined with fir trees and gorse. Excellent greens all-year-round, easy walking.

18 Holes, 6044yds, Par 69, SSS 69, Course record 64.
Club membership 730.

Visitors contact club for details **Societies** booking required. **Green Fees** not confirmed 🆓 **Course Designer** James Braid **Prof** Andrew Collison **Facilities** 🕎 🍴 🅱 🖥 🍴 ⛳ 🏨 ✦ 🛺 ✦ **Conf** Corporate Hospitality Days **Location** 0.5m NW on A143 at junct with A144
Hotel ★★★★ BB Heath Farmhouse, Homersfield, HARLESTON
☎ 01986 788417 2 rooms (2 pri facs)

BURY ST EDMUNDS
Map 5 TL86

Bury St Edmunds Golf Club Tut Hill IP28 6LG
☎ 01284 755979 📄 01284 763288
e-mail: info@burygolf.co.uk
web: www.burystedmundsgolfclub.co.uk
A mature, undulating course, full of character with some challenging holes. The nine-hole pay-and-play course consists of five par 3s and four par 4s with modern construction greens.

18 Holes, 6675yds, Par 72, SSS 72, Course record 65.
9 Holes, 2184yds, Par 62, SSS 62. Club membership 850.

Visitors Mon-Fri except BHs. 9 hole course Mon-Sun & BHs. Dress code. **Societies** booking required. **Green Fees** 18 hole course £45 per day, £37 per round, 9 hole course £16 per round (£18 weekends) **Course Designer** Ted Ray **Prof** Mark Jillings **Facilities** 🕎 🍴 by prior arrangement 🅱 🖥 🍴 ⛳ 🏨 🛺 ✦ 🛺 ✦ **Leisure** snooker table **Conf** Corporate Hospitality Days **Location** A14 junct 42, 0.5m NW on B1106
Hotel ★★★★ 83% TH Angel Hotel, Angel Hill, BURY ST EDMUNDS
☎ 01284 714000 📄 01284 714001 75 en suite

Suffolk Hotel Golf & Leisure Club Fornham St Genevieve IP28 6JQ
☎ 01284 706801 📄 01284 706721
e-mail: proshop.suffolkgolf@ohiml.com
web: www.oxfordhotelsandinns.com
A classic parkland course with the River Lark running through it. Criss-crossed by ponds and streams with rich fairways. Considerable upgrading of the course in recent years and the three finishing holes are particularly challenging.

The Genevieve: 18 Holes, 6392yds, Par 72, SSS 71.
Club membership 600.

Visitors Mon-Sun & BHs. Booking required. Dress code.
Societies booking required. **Green Fees** £32 per day (£37 weekends & BHs). £15 Dec-Mar **Prof** Steve Hall **Facilities** 🕎 🍴 🅱 🖥 🍴 ⛳ 🏨 🛺 ✦ 🛺 🛺 ✦ **Leisure** heated indoor swimming pool, sauna, gymnasium **Conf** facs Corporate Hospitality Days **Location** off A14 at Bury St Edmunds, W onto B1106 towards Brandon, club 2.5m on right
Hotel ★★★ 74% HL Suffolk Hotel Golf & Leisure Club, Fornham St Genevieve, BURY ST EDMUNDS ☎ 01284 706777 📄 01284 754767 40 en suite

CRETINGHAM
Map 5 TM26

Cretingham Golf Club IP13 7BA
☎ 01728 685275 📄 01728 685488
e-mail: cretinghamgolf@tiscali.co.uk
web: www.cretinghamgolfclub.co.uk
Parkland course, tree-lined with numerous water features, including the River Deben which runs through part of the course.

18 Holes, 6052yds, Par 71, SSS 70, Course record 67.
Club membership 350.

Visitors Mon-Sun & BHs. **Societies** welcome. **Green Fees** £20 per 18 holes, £11 per 9 holes (£22/£12 weekends) **Course Designer** J Austin **Prof** Neil Jackson/Rob Pritchard **Facilities** 🕎 🍴 🅱 🖥 🍴 ⛳ 🏨 🛺 ✦ 🛺 ✦ ✦ **Leisure** hard tennis courts, fishing **Conf** facs Corporate Hospitality Days **Location** NE of village off A1120
Hotel ★★★ 74% HL Cedars, Needham Road, STOWMARKET
☎ 01449 612668 📄 01449 674704 25 en suite

FELIXSTOWE
Map 5 TM33

Felixstowe Ferry Golf Club, Ferry Rd IP11 9RY
☎ 01394 286834 📄 01394 273679
e-mail: secretary@felixstowegolf.co.uk
web: www.felixstowegolf.co.uk
A seaside links with pleasant views, easy walking. Nine-hole pay-and-play course. Both courses a good test of golf.

Martello Course: 18 Holes, 6387yds, Par 72, SSS 71.
Kingsfleet: 9 Holes, 2986yds, Par 70, SSS 69.
Club membership 900.

Visitors Mon-Fri. Limited play weekends & BHs. Dress code. **Societies** booking required. **Green Fees** Martello £48 per day, £36 per 18 holes (£50 weekends & BHs). Kingsfleet £14 **Course Designer** Henry Cotton **Prof** Ian MacPherson **Facilities** 🕎 🍴 🅱 🖥 🍴 ⛳ 🏨 🛺 ✦ ✦ **Conf** facs Corporate Hospitality Days **Location** NE of town centre, signed from A14
Hotel ★★★ 77% HL The Brook Hotel, Orwell Road, FELIXSTOWE
☎ 01394 278441 📄 01394 670422 25 en suite

ave on Hotels. Book at **theAA.com/hotel**

SUFFOLK

ENGLAND

LEMPTON

Map 5 TL86

lempton Golf Club IP28 6EQ
☎ 01284 728291
e-mail: secretary@flempton.com
web: flemptongolfclub.co.uk

Breckland course with gorse and wooded areas. Very little water but surrounded by woodland and Suffolk Wildlife Trust lakes.

9 Holes, 6184yds, Par 70, SSS 70, Course record 64. Club membership 260.

Visitors Mon-Sun except BHs. Booking required. Handicap certificate. Dress code **Green Fees** £45 per day, £35 per 18 holes ⊛ **Course Designer** J H Taylor **Prof** Matthew Alderton **Facilities** ⑪ ⑩ 🍺 ☕ 🍴 ⚓ 🏠 ✏ **Location** 0.5m W on A1101

Hotel ★★★ 83% HL Best Western Priory, Mildenhall Road, BURY ST EDMUNDS ☎ 01284 766181 🖹 01284 767604 36 en suite

HALESWORTH

Map 5 TM37

Halesworth Golf Club Bramfield Rd IP19 9XA
☎ 01986 875567 🖹 01986 874565
e-mail: info@halesworthgc.co.uk
web: www.halesworthgc.co.uk

Situated in the heart of the Suffolk countryside with fine views over the Blyth Valley. Both courses offers golfers of all levels a challenge but the 9 hole Valley course is particularly suitable for the less experienced golfer.

Blyth: 18 Holes, 6512yds, Par 72, SSS 71, Course record 67. Valley: 9 Holes, 2280yds, Par 33. Club membership 400.

Visitors Mon-Sun & BHs. Dress code. **Societies** booking advised. **Green Fees** not confirmed **Course Designer** J W Johnson **Prof** Richard Davies **Facilities** ⑪ ⑩ 🍺 ☕ 🍴 ⚓ 🏠 ✏ 🏕 **Conf** facs Corporate Hospitality Days **Location** 0.75m S of town, signed A144 to Bramfield

Hotel ★★★★ 78% HL Swan Hotel, Market Place, SOUTHWOLD ☎ 01502 722186 🖹 01502 724800 42 en suite

HAVERHILL

Map 5 TL64

Haverhill Golf Club Coupals Rd CB9 7UW
☎ 01440 761951 🖹 01440 761951
e-mail: haverhillgolf@coupalsroad.eclipse.co.uk
web: www.club-noticeboard.co.uk

An 18-hole course lying across two valleys in pleasant parkland. The front nine with undulating fairways is complemented by a saucer-shape back nine, bisected by the River Stour, presenting a challenge to golfers of all standards.

18 Holes, 5986yds, Par 70, SSS 69, Course record 64. Club membership 750.

Visitors Mon-Sun & BHs. Dress code. **Societies** booking required. **Green Fees** phone **Course Designer** P Pilgrem/C Lawrie **Prof** Paul Wilby **Facilities** ⑪ ⑩ 🍺 ☕ 🍴 ⚓ 🏠 ✏ 🏕 **Leisure** chipping green. **Conf** facs **Location** 1m SE off A1017

Hotel BUD Days Inn Haverhill, Phoenix Road & Bumpstead Road, Haverhill Business Park, HAVERHILL ☎ 01440 716950 🖹 01440 716951 80 en suite

HINTLESHAM

Map 5 TM04

Hintlesham Golf Club IP8 3JG
☎ 01473 652761 🖹 01473 652750
e-mail: sales@hintleshamgolfclub.com
web: www.hintleshamgolfclub.com

Magnificent championship length course blending harmoniously with the ancient parkland surroundings. Opened in 1991 but seeded two years beforehand, this parkland course has reached a level maturity that allows it to be rivalled in the area only by a few ancient courses. The signature holes are the 4th and 17th, both featuring water at very inconvenient interludes.

18 Holes, 6580yds, Par 72, SSS 72, Course record 64. Club membership 470.

Visitors Mon-Sun & BHs. Booking required. Handicap certificate. Dress code. **Societies** booking required. **Green Fees** not confirmed **Course Designer** Hawtree & Sons **Prof** Henry Roblin **Facilities** ⑪ ⑩ 🍺 ☕ 🍴 ⚓ 🏠 ✏ 🏕 ✏ **Leisure** sauna **Conf** facs Corporate Hospitality Days **Location** in village on A1071

Hotel ★★★★ HL Hintlesham Hall Hotel, George Street, HINTLESHAM ☎ 01473 652334 🖹 01473 652463 33 en suite

IPSWICH

Map 5 TM14

Alnesbourne Priory Golf Course Priory Park IP10 0JT
☎ 01473 727393 🖹 01473 278372
e-mail: jwl@priory-park.com
web: www.priory-park.com

A fabulous outlook facing due south across the River Orwell is one of the many good features of this course set in woodland. All holes run among trees with some fairways requiring straight shots. The 8th green is on saltings by the river.

9 Holes, 1800yds, Par 30, SSS 30. Club membership 30.

Visitors Mon-Sun & BHs. Dress code. **Societies** booking required. **Green Fees** not confirmed ⊛ **Facilities** ⑪ ⑩ 🍺 ☕ 🍴 ⚓ 🏕 **Leisure** practice net **Conf** facs Corporate Hospitality Days **Location** 3m SE off A14

Hotel ★★★★ TH Salthouse Harbour, No 1 Neptune Quay, IPSWICH ☎ 01473 226789 🖹 01473 226927 70 en suite

Fynn Valley Golf Club IP6 9JA
☎ 01473 785267 📄 01473 785632
e-mail: enquiries@fynn-valley.co.uk
web: www.fynn-valley.co.uk

Undulating parkland alongside a protected river valley. The course has matured into an excellent test of golf enhanced by more than 100 bunkers, 3 water features and protected greens that have tricky slopes and contours.
18 Holes, 6391yds, Par 70, SSS 72, Course record 64.
Par Three Course: 9 Holes, 957yds, Par 27, SSS 27,
Course record 20. Club membership 680.
Visitors Mon-Sun & BHs. **Societies** booking required. **Green Fees** £36 per day, £26 per 18 holes (£40/£32 weekends & BHs) **Course Designer** Antonio Primavera **Prof** A Spink/C Smith **Facilities** ⊕ ⓘⓞ 🔥 ⌷ 🗜 🏌 🏠 🏌 🏌 🚩 **Leisure** 9 hole par 3 course, practice bunker **Conf** facs Corporate Hospitality Days **Location** 2m N of Ipswich on B1077
Hotel ★★★ 82% HL Best Western Claydon Country House Hotel, 16-18 Ipswich Road, Claydon, IPSWICH ☎ 01473 830382 📄 01473 832476 36 en suite

Ipswich Golf Club Bucklesham Rd, Purdis Heath IP3 8UQ
☎ 01473 728941 📄 01473 715236
e-mail: neill@ipswichgolfclub.com
web: www.ipswichgolfclub.com
Many golfers are surprised when they hear that Ipswich has, at Purdis Heath, a first-class course. In some ways it resembles some of Surrey's better courses; a beautiful heathland course with two lakes and easy walking.
Purdis Heath: 18 Holes, 6439yds, Par 71, SSS 72,
Course record 66.
9 Hole Course: 9 Holes, 1930yds, Par 31, SSS 59.
Club membership 926.
Visitors Mon-Sun except BHs. Booking required & Handicap certificate for main course. Dress code. 9 hole course available on 'pay & play' basis. **Societies** booking required. **Green Fees** 18 hole course £70 per day, £50 per round (£75/£55 weekends). 9 hole course £10 per day (£15 weekends & BHs) **Course Designer** James Braid **Prof** Kevin Lovelock **Facilities** ⊕ ⓘⓞ 🔥 ⌷ 🗜 🏌 🏠 🚩 🏌 **Location** 3m E of town centre off A1156
Hotel ★★★★ TH Salthouse Harbour, No 1 Neptune Quay, IPSWICH ☎ 01473 226789 📄 01473 226927 70 en suite

Rushmere Golf Club Rushmere Heath IP4 5QQ
☎ 01473 725648 📄 01473 273852
e-mail: rushmeregolfclub@btconnect.com
web: www.club-noticeboard.co.uk/rushmere
Heathland course with gorse and prevailing winds. A good test of golf.
18 Holes, 6265yds, Par 70, SSS 70, Course record 64.
Club membership 700.
Visitors Mon-Fri & Sun except BHs. Booking required Wed & Sun. Dress code **Societies** booking required. **Green Fees** £42 per day, £25 per round **Course Designer** James Braid **Prof** K. Vince **Facilities** ⊕ ⓘⓞ 🔥 ⌷ 🗜 🏌 🏠 🏌 **Conf** facs Corporate Hospitality Days **Location** on A1214 Woodbridge road near hospital, signed
Hotel ★★★★ TH Salthouse Harbour, No 1 Neptune Quay, IPSWICH ☎ 01473 226789 📄 01473 226927 70 en suite

LOWESTOFT   Map 5 TM59

Rookery Park Golf Club Beccles Rd NR33 8HJ
☎ 01502 509190 📄 01502 509191
web: www.club-noticeboard.co.uk
18 Holes, 6714yds, Par 72, SSS 72.
Course Designer C D Lawrie **Location** 3.5m SW of Lowestoft on A146
Telephone for further details
Hotel ★★★ 83% HL Ivy House Country Hotel, Ivy Lane, Beccles Road, Oulton Broad, LOWESTOFT ☎ 01502 501353 & 588144 📄 01502 501539 20 en suite

MILDENHALL   Map 5 TL77

West Suffolk Golf Centre New Drove, Beck Row IP28 8RN
☎ 01638 718972 📄 01353 675447
e-mail: golfinsuffolk1@btconnect.com
web: www.golfinsuffolk.com
This course has been gradually improved to provide a unique opportunity to play an inland course in all weather conditions. Situated on the edge of the Breckland, the dry nature of the course makes for easy walking with rare flora and fauna.
18 Holes, 5487yds, Par 69, SSS 66.
Visitors Contact centre for details. **Societies** booking required. **Green Fees** £15 per day (£19 weekends & BHs). £12 per 9 holes **Prof** Duncan Abbott **Facilities** ⊕ 🔥 ⌷ 🗜 🏌 🏠 🚩 🏌 🚩 **Leisure** fishing, pitch and putt practice area **Conf** facs Corporate Hospitality Days **Location** A1101 from Mildenhall to Beck Row, 1st left after Beck Row signed to West Row/Golf Centre, 0.5m on right
Hotel ★★★ 83% HL The Olde Bull Inn, The Street, Barton Mills, MILDENHALL ☎ 01638 711001 📄 01638 712003 14 en suite

Save on Hotels. Book at **theAA.com/hotel**

SUFFOLK

ENGLAND

NEWMARKET
Map 5 TL66

Links Golf Club Cambridge Rd CB8 0TG
☎ 01638 663000 🖹 01638 661476
e-mail: office@linksgolfclub.co.uk
web: www.linksgolfclub.co.uk

Gently undulating parkland.

18 Holes, 6643yds, Par 72, SSS 73, Course record 64.
Club membership 780.

Visitors Mon-Sun & BHs. Booking required. Handicap certificate. Dress code. **Societies** welcome. **Green Fees** £42 per day, £36 per round (£46/£42 weekends) **Course Designer** Col. Hotchkin **Prof** John Sharkey **Facilities** ⓣ ⁱⓄⅼ ⓛ ⲗ ⲡ ⲯⅼ ⳬ Ⳙ ⳥ Ⳟ ⳯ **Location** 1m SW on A1034

Hotel ★★★ 78% HL Rutland Arms, High Street, NEWMARKET
☎ 01638 664251 🖹 01638 666298 46 en suite

NEWTON
Map 5 TL94

Newton Green Golf Club Newton Green CO10 0QN
☎ 01787 377217 & 377501   🖹 01787 377549
e-mail: info@newtongreengolfclub.co.uk
web: www.newtongreengolfclub.co.uk

Flat course with pond. First nine holes are open with bunkers and trees. Second nine holes are tight with ditches and gorse.

18 Holes, 5961yds, Par 69, SSS 68. Club membership 500.

Visitors Mon, Wed-Sun & BHs. Tue pm. Booking advisable. Dress code. **Societies** booking required. **Green Fees** not confirmed **Prof** Tim Cooper **Facilities** ⓣ ⁱⓄⅼ ⓛ ⲗ ⲡ ⲯⅼ ⳬ Ⳙ ⳥ **Location** W of village on A134

Hotel ★★★ 82% HL Stoke by Nayland Hotel, Golf & Spa, Keepers Lane, Leavenheath, COLCHESTER ☎ 01206 262836 🖹 01206 265840 80 en suite

RAYDON
Map 5 TM03

Brett Vale Golf Club Noakes Rd IP7 5LR
☎ 01473 310718
web: www.brettvalegolf.co.uk

18 Holes, 5864yds, Par 70, SSS 69, Course record 65.

Course Designer Howard Swan **Location** A12 onto B1070 towards Hadleigh, left at Raydon, by water tower
Telephone for further details
Hotel ★★★ CHH Maison Talbooth, Stratford Road, DEDHAM
☎ 01206 322367 🖹 01206 322752 12 en suite

SOUTHWOLD
Map 5 TM57

Southwold Golf Club The Common IP18 6TB
☎ 01502 723234
e-mail: mail@southwoldgolfclub.co.uk
web: www.southwoldgolfclub.co.uk

Trustland course with fine greens and panoramic views of the sea. Over 125 years old.

18 Holes, 6052yds, Par 70, SSS 69, Course record 66.
Club membership 350.

Visitors Mon-Sun & BHs. Dress code. **Societies** booking required. **Green Fees** £30 per 18 holes, £16 per 9 holes (£33/£17 weekends). Reduced rate pm ⳯ **Course Designer** J Braid **Prof** Robin Mann **Facilities** ⓣ ⁱⓄⅼ by prior arrangement ⳬ Ⳙ ⳥ ⲗ Ⳟ ⳯ ⳯ **Conf** Corporate Hospitality Days **Location** S of town off A1095. Past water towers on right

Hotel ★★★★ 78% HL Swan Hotel, Market Place, SOUTHWOLD
☎ 01502 722186 🖹 01502 724800 42 en suite

STOWMARKET
Map 5 TM05

Stowmarket Golf Club Lower Rd, Onehouse IP14 3DA
☎ 01449 736473   🖹 01449 736826
e-mail: mail@stowmarketgolfclub.co.uk
web: www.club-noticeboard.co.uk

Parkland course in rolling countryside with river in play on three holes. Many majestic trees and fine views of the Suffolk countryside.

18 Holes, 6107yds, Par 69, SSS 70, Course record 64.
Club membership 630.

Visitors Mon-Sun & BHs. Handicap certificate. Dress code **Societies** welcome. **Green Fees** £45 per day, £35 per round (£55/£45 weekends) **Prof** Duncan Burl **Facilities** ⓣ ⁱⓄⅼ ⓛ ⲗ ⲡ ⲯⅼ ⳬ Ⳙ ⳥ Ⳟ ⳯ **Location** 2.5m SW off B1115

Hotel ★★★ 74% HL Cedars, Needham Road, STOWMARKET
☎ 01449 612668 🖹 01449 674704 25 en suite

STUSTON
Map 5 TM17

Diss Stuston IP21 4AA
☎ 01379 641025   🖹 01379 644586
e-mail: sec.dissgolf@virgin.net
web: www.club-noticeboard.co.uk

Picturesque heath and parkland course located on the Norfolk/Suffolk border, alongside the River Waveney and providing challenging golf for all standards of player. Excellent standards of greens with holes ranging from the scenic but difficult 468 yard par 4 13th hole, to the pretty 15th at 146 yards.

18 Holes, 6206yds, Par 70, SSS 70, Course record 65.
Club membership 750.

Visitors Mon-Sun & BHs. Booking required weekends & BHs. Dress code. **Societies** welcome. **Green Fees** not confirmed **Prof** N J Taylor **Facilities** ⓣ ⁱⓄⅼ ⓛ ⲗ ⲡ ⲯⅼ ⳬ Ⳙ ⳥ Ⳟ ⳯ **Leisure** driving nets **Conf** facs Corporate Hospitality Days **Location** 1.5m SE on B1118

Hotel ★★★★ INN The White Horse Inn, Stoke Ash, EYE
☎ 01379 678222 🖹 01379 678800 11 rooms (11 en suite)

THORPENESS
Map 5 TM45

Thorpeness Golf Club & Hotel Lakeside Av IP16 4NH
☎ 01728 452176 📠 01728 453868
e-mail: lyn@thorpeness.co.uk
web: www.thorpeness.co.uk

A coastal heathland course, designed in 1923 by James Braid. The course is easy to walk with free draining soils and offers a wide variety of different holes lined with heather, gorse and silver birch.

18 Holes, 6444yds, Par 69, SSS 72, Course record 66.
Club membership 700.

Visitors Mon-Sun & BHs. Handicap certificate. Dress code. Societies booking required. Green Fees £40 (£45 weekends). After 3pm £25. Course Designer James Braid Prof Frank Hill Facilities ⑪ ⍟ ⓛ ☐ 🍴 ⚁ ◇ 🐄 ♂ Leisure hard and grass tennis courts, fishing, snooker room Conf facs Corporate Hospitality Days Location off A1094 to Aldeburgh, signed
Hotel ★★★ 80% HL Thorpeness Hotel, Lakeside Avenue, THORPENESS ☎ 01728 452176 📠 01728 453868 36 en suite

WALDRINGFIELD
Map 5 TM24

Waldringfield Golf Club Newbourne Rd IP12 4PT
☎ 01473 736768
e-mail: enquiries@waldringfieldgc.co.uk
web: www.waldringfieldgc.co.uk

Easy walking heathland course with long drives on 1st and 13th (590yds) and some ponds.

18 Holes, 6085yds, Par 71, SSS 69, Course record 67.
Club membership 550.

Visitors Mon-Sun & BHs. Booking required. Societies booking required. Green Fees 18 holes £23 (£28 weekends & BHs). Fees include food voucher. Course Designer Phillip Pilgrem Prof Alex Lucas Facilities ⑪ ⍟ ⓛ ☐ 🍴 ⚁ 🐄 ♂ Conf facs Location 1m W of village off A12
Hotel ★★★★ 76% HL Seckford Hall, WOODBRIDGE ☎ 01394 385678 📠 01394 380610 32 en suite

WOODBRIDGE
Map 5 TM24

Best Western Ufford Park Hotel Golf & Spa Yarmouth Rd, Melton IP12 1QW
☎ 0844 4776495 📠 0844 4773727
e-mail: golf@uffordpark.co.uk
web: www.uffordpark.co.uk

Course is set in 120 acres of ancient parkland with 12 water features and voted one of the best British winter courses. The course enjoys

excellent natural drainage and a large reservoir supplements a spring feed pond to ensure ample water for irrigation. Two storey floodlit driving range, golf academy and American golf superstore on site.

18 Holes, 6312yds, Par 71, SSS 71, Course record 61.
Club membership 400.

Visitors Mon-Sun & BHs. Booking preferred weekends & BHs. Handicap certificate. Dress code. Societies booking required. Green Fees £20 per 18 holes (£30 weekends & BHs) Course Designer Phil Pilgrim Prof Stuart Robertson Facilities ⑪ ⍟ ⓛ ☐ 🍴 ⚁ ⚈ ◇ ♂ 🐄 ♂ Leisure heated indoor swimming pool, sauna, gymnasium, golf academy, health club & spa Conf facs Corporate Hospitality Days Location A12 onto B1438
Hotel ★★★ 82% HL Best Western Ufford Park Hotel Golf & Spa, Yarmouth Road, Ufford, WOODBRIDGE ☎ 01394 383555 📠 0844 4773727 87 en suite

Seckford Golf Club Seckford Hall Rd, Great Bealings IP13 6NT
☎ 01394 388000 📠 01394 382818
e-mail: secretary@seckfordgolf.co.uk
web: www.seckfordgolf.co.uk

An enjoyable course interspersed with maturing tree plantations, numerous bunkers, water hazards and undulating fairways, providing a challenge for all levels of golfer.

18 Holes, 4981yds, Par 66, SSS 65, Course record 63.
Club membership 600.

Visitors Mon-Sun & BHs. Booking required Tue, Fri-Sun & BHs. Handicap certificate. Dress code. Societies booking required. Green Fees phone Course Designer J Johnson Prof Simon Jay Facilities ⑪ ⍟ by prior arrangement ⓛ ☐ 🍴 ⚁ ⚈ ⚈ ◇ 🐄 ♂ Conf Corporate Hospitality Days Location 1m W of Woodbridge off A12, next to Seckford Hall Hotel
Hotel ★★★★ 76% HL Seckford Hall, WOODBRIDGE ☎ 01394 385678 📠 01394 380610 32 en suite

Woodbridge Golf Club Bromeswell Heath IP12 2PF
☎ 01394 382038 📠 01394 382392
e-mail: Info@woodbridgegolfclub.co.uk
web: www.woodbridgegolfclub.co.uk

Courses in a classic heathland setting with fine views. The 18 hole Heath course requires strategic golfing skill to manoeuvre around and the Forest is a full length 9 hole course of note.

Heath Course: 18 Holes, 6299yds, Par 70, SSS 71, Course record 64.
Forest Course: 9 Holes, 3191yds, Par 70, SSS 68.
Club membership 700.

Visitors Heath course Mon-Fri except BHs. Handicap certificate. Dress code. Societies booking required. Green Fees Heath course £45 per round, Forest Course £15 per round Course Designer James Braid/Davie Grant Prof Tim Johnson Facilities ⑪ ⍟ by prior arrangement ⓛ ☐ 🍴 ⚁ ⚈ ⚈ ◇ ♂ Conf Corporate Hospitality Days Location 2.5m NE off A1152
Hotel ★★★★ 76% HL Seckford Hall, WOODBRIDGE ☎ 01394 385678 📠 01394 380610 32 en suite

WORLINGTON   Map 5 TL67

Royal Worlington & Newmarket Golf Club Golf Links Rd
IP28 8SD
☎ 01638 712216 & 717787
web: www.royalworlington.co.uk
Inland links course, renowned as one of the best nine-hole
courses in the world. Well drained, giving excellent winter playing
conditions.
*9 Holes, 3123yds, Par 35, SSS 35, Course record 28.
Club membership 350.*
Visitors Mon, Thu-Sun except BHs. Booking required. Dress code.
Societies booking required. **Green Fees** £60 per day, £45 for
18 holes ⊛ **Course Designer** Tom Dunn **Prof** Richard Beadles
Facilities ⓘ by prior arrangement 🍴 ⌨ 🍽 ⚖ 🖼 ⛴ 🏌
⚐ **Location** 0.5m SE of Worlington near Mildenhall
Hotel ★★★ 83% HL The Olde Bull Inn, The Street, Barton Mills,
MILDENHALL ☎ 01638 711001 📠 01638 712003 14 en suite

SURREY

ADDLESTONE   Map 4 TQ06

New Zealand Golf Club Woodham Ln KT15 3QD
☎ 01932 345049 📠 01932 342891
e-mail: roger.marrett@nzgc.org
Heathland course set in trees and heather.
*18 Holes, 6073yds, Par 68, SSS 69, Course record 66.
Club membership 320.*
Visitors Mon-Fri except BHs. Booking required. Handicap certificate.
Dress code. **Societies** booking required. **Green Fees** £95 per day
⊛ **Course Designer** Mure Fergusson/Simpson **Prof** Vic Elvidge
Facilities ⓘ 🍴 ⌨ 🍽 ⚖ 🖼 ⛴ ⚐ 🏌 **Conf**
Corporate Hospitality Days **Location** 1.5m E of Woking
Hotel ★★★ 77% HL Best Western Ship Hotel, Monument Green,
WEYBRIDGE ☎ 01932 848364 📠 01932 857153 76 en suite

ASHFORD   Map 4 TQ07

Ashford Manor Golf Club Fordbridge Rd TW15 3RT
☎ 01784 424644 📠 01784 424649
e-mail: secretary@amgc.co.uk
web: www.amgc.co.uk
Tree-lined parkland course is built on gravel and drains well, never
needing temporary tees or greens. A heavy investment in fairway
irrigation and an extensive woodland management programme
over the past few years have formed a strong future for this course,
originally built over a 100 years ago.
18 Holes, 6073yds, Par 70, SSS 70. Club membership 700.
Visitors Mon-Fri except BHs. Booking required. Handicap certificate.
Dress code. **Societies** booking required. **Green Fees** £45 per round
Mon-Fri ex BHs **Course Designer** Tom Hogg **Prof** Robert Walton
Facilities ⓘ 🍴 ⌨ 🍽 ⚖ 🖼 🏌 **Leisure** swing studio
with video coaching and club fitting **Conf** facs Corporate Hospitality
Days **Location** 2m E of Staines via A308 Staines bypass
Hotel ★★★ 73% HL Mercure Thames Lodge, Thames Street,
STAINES ☎ 01784 464433 📠 01784 454858 79 en suite

BAGSHOT   Map 4 SU96

Windlesham Golf Course Grove End GU19 5HY
☎ 01276 452220 📠 01276 452290
web: www.windleshamgolf.com
18 Holes, 6650yds, Par 72, SSS 72, Course record 69.
Course Designer Tommy Horton **Location** M3 junct 3, on A30 between
Sunningdale and Camberley
Telephone for further details
Hotel ★★★★★ CHH Pennyhill Park Hotel & The Spa, London
Road, BAGSHOT ☎ 01276 471774 📠 01276 473217 123 en suite

BANSTEAD   Map 4 TQ25

Banstead Downs Golf Club Burdon Ln, Belmont, Sutton
SM2 7DD
☎ 020 8642 2284 📠 020 8642 5252
e-mail: secretary@bansteaddowns.com
web: www.bansteaddowns.com
A natural downland course set on a site of botanic interest. A
challenging 18 holes with narrow fairways and tight lies.
18 Holes, 6192yds, Par 69. Club membership 850.
Visitors Mon-Thu except BHs. Dress code. **Societies** booking required.
Green Fees £50 per 18 holes Mon-Thu **Course Designer** J H Taylor/
James Braid **Prof** Ian Golding **Facilities** ⓘ 🍽 by prior arrangement
🍴 ⌨ ⚖ 🖼 🏌 **Conf** facs Corporate Hospitality Days
Location M25 junct 8, A217 N for 6m
Hotel ★★★ 79% HL Holiday Inn London-Sutton, Gibson Road,
SUTTON ☎ 020 8234 1100 & 8234 1104 📠 020 8770 1539
119 en suite

Cuddington Golf Club Banstead Rd SM7 1RD
☎ 020 8393 0952 📠 020 8786 7025
e-mail: secretary@cuddingtongc.co.uk
Downland with easy walking and good views. Reputed to have the
longest start, over the first three holes, in Surrey. Well drained and
plays all year round with no temporary greens.
18 Holes, 6614yds, Par 71, SSS 71. Club membership 700.
Visitors Mon-Sun & BHs. Booking required weekends & BHs.
Societies booking required. **Green Fees** not confirmed **Course
Designer** H S Colt **Prof** Mark Warner **Facilities** ⓘ 🍽 🍴 ⌨ 🍽
⚖ 🖼 ⛴ 🏌 **Conf** facs Corporate Hospitality Days **Location** N
of Banstead station on A2022
Hotel ★★★ 79% HL Holiday Inn London-Sutton, Gibson Road,
SUTTON ☎ 020 8234 1100 & 8234 1104 📠 020 8770 1539
119 en suite

BLETCHINGLEY   Map 5 TQ35

Bletchingley Golf Club Church Ln RH1 4LP
☎ 01883 744666 📠 01883 744284
web: www.bletchingleygolf.co.uk
18 Holes, 6600yds, Par 72, SSS 72, Course record 69.
Location A25 onto Church Ln in Bletchingley
Telephone for further details
Hotel ★★★★ 82% HL Nutfield Priory, Nutfield, REDHILL
☎ 01737 824400 & 0845 072 7485 📠 01737 824410 60 en suite

BRAMLEY

Map 4 TQ04

Bramley Golf Club GU5 0AL
☎ 01483 892696 📠 01483 894673
e-mail: secretary@bramleygolfclub.co.uk
web: www.bramleygolfclub.co.uk

Parkland course. From the high ground picturesque views of the Wey Valley on one side, and the Hog's Back. Full on course irrigation system with three reservoirs on the course.

18 Holes, 5990yds, Par 69, SSS 69, Course record 61. Club membership 850.

Visitors Mon-Fri except BHs. Dress code. **Societies** booking required. **Green Fees** £50 per 36 holes, £40 per round **Course Designer** Charles Mayo/James Braid **Prof** Simon Iliffe **Facilities** ⑪ ⑥ 🏌 ☕ 🍽 🏌 🏡 ☂ 🏌 🛎 🏌 🏌 **Conf** Corporate Hospitality Days **Location** 3m S of Guildford on A281
Hotel ★★★ 80% HL Holiday Inn Guildford, Egerton Road, GUILDFORD ☎ 0871 942 9036 📠 01483 457256 168 en suite

BROOKWOOD

Map 4 SU95

West Hill Golf Club Bagshot Rd GU24 0BH
☎ 01483 474365 📠 01483 474252
e-mail: secretary@westhill-golfclub.co.uk
web: www.westhill-golfclub.co.uk

A challenging course with fairways lined with heather and tall pines, one of Surrey's finest courses. Demands every club in the bag to be played.

18 Holes, 6378yds, Par 69, SSS 71. Club membership 500.

Visitors Mon-Fri except BHs. Booking required. Dress code. **Societies** booking required. **Green Fees** £90 per day, £70 per round. £50 per round winter **Course Designer** C Butchart/W Parke **Prof** Guy Shoesmith **Facilities** ⑪ ⑥ by prior arrangement 🏌 ☕ 🍽 🏌 🏡 🏌 **Leisure** halfway hut **Conf** facs Corporate Hospitality Days **Location** E of village on A322
Hotel ★★★★★ CHH Pennyhill Park Hotel & The Spa, London Road, BAGSHOT ☎ 01276 471774 📠 01276 473217 123 en suite

CAMBERLEY

Map 4 SU86

Camberley Heath Golf Club Golf Dr GU15 1JG
☎ 01276 23258 📠 01276 692505
e-mail: info@camberleyheathgolfclub.co.uk
web: www.camberleyheathgolfclub.co.uk

Set in attractive Surrey countryside, a challenging golf course that features an abundance of pine and heather. A true classic heathland course with many assets, including the mature fairways.

18 Holes, 6147yds, Par 71, SSS 70, Course record 65. Club membership 600.

Visitors Mon-Thu except BHs. Booking required. Dress code. **Societies** booking required. **Green Fees** £55 per round **Course Designer** Harry S Colt **Prof** Steve Speller **Facilities** ⑪ ⑥ 🏌 ☕ 🍽 🏌 🏡 🏌 **Conf** facs Corporate Hospitality Days **Location** 1.25m SE of town centre off A325
Hotel ★★★★ 76% HL Macdonald Frimley Hall Hotel & Spa, Lime Avenue, CAMBERLEY ☎ 0844 879 9110 📠 01276 670362 98 en suite

Pine Ridge Golf Club Old Bisley Rd, Frimley GU16 9NX
☎ 01276 675444 📠 01276 678837
e-mail: pineridge@crown-golf.co.uk
web: www.pineridgegolf.co.uk

Pay-and-play heathland course cut through a pine forest with challenging par 3s, deceptively demanding par 4s and several birdiable par 5s. Easy walking, but gently undulating.

18 Holes, 6458yds, Par 72, SSS 71. Club membership 200.

Visitors Mon-Sun & BHs. Booking required. Dress code. **Societies** booking required. **Green Fees** not confirmed **Course Designer** Clive D Smith **Prof** Peter Sefton **Facilities** ⑪ ⑥ 🏌 ☕ 🍽 🏌 🏡 🏌 🏌 **Leisure** 6 lane ten pin bowling alley **Conf** facs Corporate Hospitality Days **Location** off B3015, near A30
Hotel ★★★★ 76% HL Macdonald Frimley Hall Hotel & Spa, Lime Avenue, CAMBERLEY ☎ 0844 879 9110 📠 01276 670362 98 en suite

ave on Hotels. Book at **theAA.com/hotel**

SURREY

CATERHAM Map 5 TQ35

Surrey National Golf Club Rook Ln, Chaldon CR3 5AA
☎ 01883 344555 📄 01883 344422
e-mail: caroline@surreynational.co.uk
web: www.surreynational.co.uk
Opened in April 1999, this American-style course is set in beautiful
countryside and features fully irrigated greens and fairways. The
setting is dramatic with rolling countryside, thousands of mature trees
and water features. The chalk based sub-soil, computerised irrigation
and buggy paths combine to make the course enjoyable to play at any
time of year.

18 Holes, 6612yds, Par 72, SSS 72.

Visitors Mon-Sun & BHs. Dress code. **Societies** booking
required **Green Fees** £22-£24 per round (£35 weekends) **Course
Designer** David Williams **Prof** Matthew Stock **Facilities** ⓣ ℐ○ℐ
by prior arrangement 🏌 🖵 ℐ 🏌 🖾 ℐ 🏌 ℐ
Conf facs Corporate Hospitality Days **Location** M25 junct 7, A23/M25
junct 6, A22

Hotel ★★★★ 70% HL Coulsdon Manor, Coulsdon Court
Road, Coulsdon, CROYDON ☎ 020 8668 0414 📄 020 8668 3118
37 en suite

CHERTSEY Map 4 TQ06

Laleham Golf Club Laleham Reach KT16 8RP
☎ 01932 564211
e-mail: info@laleham-golf.co.uk
web: www.laleham-golf.co.uk
Well-bunkered parkland and meadowland course. The prevailing
wind and strategic placement of hazards makes it a fair but testing
challenge. Natural drainage due to the underlying gravel. No
temporary tees or greens in winter months.

*18 Holes, 6291yds, Par 70, SSS 70, Course record 65.
Club membership 600.*

Visitors Mon-Fri & BHs. Weekends pm (11am low season). Dress
code. **Societies** booking required **Green Fees** not confirmed **Course
Designer** Jack White **Prof** Paul Smith **Facilities** ⓣ 🏌 🖵 ℐ
🏌 🖾 ℐ 🏌 ℐ **Conf** facs Corporate Hospitality Days
Location M25 junct 11, A320 to Thorpe Park rdbt, exit Penton Marina,
club signed
Hotel ★★★ 73% HL Mercure Thames Lodge, Thames Street,
STAINES ☎ 01784 464433 📄 01784 454858 79 en suite

CHIDDINGFOLD Map 4 SU93

Chiddingfold Golf Course Petworth Rd GU8 4SL
☎ 01428 685888 📄 01428 685939
web: www.chiddingfoldgc.co.uk
18 Holes, 5568yds, Par 70, SSS 67.
Course Designer Johnathan Gaunt **Location** off A283
Telephone for further details
Hotel ★★★★ 74% HL Lythe Hill Hotel and Spa, Petworth Road,
HASLEMERE ☎ 01428 651251 📄 01428 644131 41 en suite

CHIPSTEAD Map 4 TQ25

Chipstead Golf Club How Ln CR5 3LN
☎ 01737 555781 📄 01737 555404
e-mail: office@chipsteadgolf.co.uk
web: www.chipsteadgolf.co.uk
Testing downland course with good views.

*18 Holes, 5504yds, Par 68, SSS 68, Course record 61.
Club membership 475.*

Visitors Mon-Sun except BHs. Booking required. **Societies** welcome.
Green Fees £40 per day, £30 per round **Prof** Gary Torbett **Facilities** ⓣ
ℐ○ℐ 🏌 🖵 ℐ 🏌 🖾 ℐ 🏌 **Conf** facs Corporate
Hospitality Days **Location** 0.5m N of village
Hotel ★★★★ 70% HL Coulsdon Manor, Coulsdon Court
Road, Coulsdon, CROYDON ☎ 020 8668 0414 📄 020 8668 3118
37 en suite

CHOBHAM Map 4 SU96

Chobham Golf Club Chobham Rd, Knaphill GU21 2TZ
☎ 01276 855584 📄 01276 855663
e-mail: info@chobhamgolfclub.co.uk
web: www.chobhamgolfclub.co.uk
Designed by Peter Alliss and Clive Clark, Chobham course sits among
mature oaks and tree nurseries offering tree-lined fairways, together
with six man-made lakes.

*18 Holes, 5863yds, Par 69, SSS 68, Course record 64.
Club membership 630.*

Visitors Mon-Fri except BHs. Booking required. Handicap certificate.
Dress code. **Societies** booking required. **Green Fees** phone **Course
Designer** Peter Alliss/Clive Clark **Prof** Michael Harrison **Facilities** ⓣ
ℐ○ℐ by prior arrangement 🏌 🖵 ℐ 🏌 🖾 ℐ **Conf** facs
Corporate Hospitality Days **Location** on Chobham road between
Chobham and Knaphill
Hotel ★★★ 79% HL Holiday Inn Woking, Victoria Street, WOKING
☎ 01483 221000 📄 01483 221021 161 en suite

COBHAM Map 4 TQ16

Silvermere Golf Club Redhill Rd KT11 1EF
☎ 01932 584300 📄 01932 584301
web: www.silvermere-golf.co.uk
18 Holes, 6430yds, Par 71.
Course Designer Neil Coles **Location** 0.5m from M25 junct 10, off
A245
Telephone for further details
Hotel ★★★★ 80% HL Woodlands Park Hotel, Woodlands
Lane, STOKE D'ABERNON ☎ 01372 843933 & 0845 072 7581
📄 01372 842704 57 en suite

CRANLEIGH
Map 4 TQ03

Cranleigh Golf and Leisure Club Barhatch Ln GU6 7NG
☎ 01483 268855 📄 01483 267251
web: www.cranleighgolfandleisure.co.uk
18 Holes, 5263yds, Par 68, SSS 65, Course record 62.
Location 0.5m N of town centre
Telephone for further details
Hotel ★★★ **80%** HL Gatton Manor Hotel & Golf Club, Standon
Lane, OCKLEY ☎ 01306 627555 📄 01306 627713 18 en suite

Wildwood Golf & Country Club Horsham Rd, Alfold
GU6 8JE
☎ 01403 753255 📄 01403 752005
e-mail: info@wildwoodgolf.co.uk
web: www.wildwoodgolf.co.uk
Parkland with stands of old oaks dominating several holes, a stream
fed by a natural spring winds through a series of lakes and ponds.
The greens are smooth, undulating and large. Course consists of three
loops of nine holes with a signature hole on each.
Parkland/Lakes: 18 Holes, 6663yds, Par 72, SSS 73.
Parkland/Woodland: 18 Holes, 6485yds, Par 72, SSS 71.
Woodland/Lakes: 18 Holes, 6346yds, Par 72, SSS 71.
Club membership 600.
Visitors Mon-Sun & BHs. Booking required. Dress code.
Societies welcome. **Green Fees** not confirmed **Course
Designer** Hawtree & Sons **Prof** Phil Harrison **Facilities** 🎌 🍴 🏌
🍺 🎏 ⚐ 🏚 ⛳ 🏌 🏌 ⚑ **Leisure** gymnasium, par 3
course **Conf** facs Corporate Hospitality Days **Location** on A281 3m SW
of Cranleigh
Hotel ★★★ **80%** HL Gatton Manor Hotel & Golf Club, Standon
Lane, OCKLEY ☎ 01306 627555 📄 01306 627713 18 en suite

DORKING
Map 4 TQ14

Betchworth Park Golf Club Reigate Rd RH4 1NZ
☎ 01306 882052 📄 01306 877462
e-mail: manager@betchworthparkgc.co.uk
web: www.betchworthparkgc.co.uk
Established, well presented, parkland course with beautiful views, on
the southern side of the North Downs near Boxhill. True test of golf
for all levels of golfer. Hosted the PGA Senior Open Championship
Qualifier in 2011.
18 Holes, 6329yds, Par 69, SSS 71, Course record 64.
Club membership 800.
Visitors Mon-Sun & BHs. Booking required. Handicap certificate. Dress
code. **Societies** welcome. **Green Fees** £50 per round, £30 after 4pm
(£75/£45 Fri-Sun & BHs) **Course Designer** Harry Colt **Prof** Andy Tocher
Facilities 🎌 🏌 🍺 🎏 🏌 🏚 ⚐ ⛳ 🏌 ⚑ **Conf** facs
Corporate Hospitality Days **Location** 1m E of Dorking on A25 towards
Reigate, juncts 8/9
Hotel ★★★ **68%** HL Mercure White Horse, High Street, DORKING
☎ 01306 881138 📄 01306 887241 78 en suite

Dorking Golf Club Chart Park RH5 4BX
☎ 01306 886917
web: www.dorkinggolfclub.co.uk
9 Holes, 5120yds, Par 66, SSS 65, Course record 62.
Course Designer J Braid/Others **Location** 1m S on A24
Telephone for further details
Hotel ★★★★ **76%** HL Mercure Burford Bridge, Burford Bridge,
Box Hill, DORKING ☎ 01306 884561 📄 01306 880386 57 en suite

EFFINGHAM
Map 4 TQ15

Effingham Golf Club Guildford Rd KT24 5PZ
☎ 01372 452203 📄 01372 459959
e-mail: secretary@effinghamgolfclub.com
web: www.effinghamgolfclub.com
Easy-walking downland course laid out on 270 acres with tree-
lined fairways. It is one of the longest of the Surrey courses with
wide subtle greens that provide a provocative but by no means
exhausting challenge. Fine views of the London skyline.
18 Holes, 6554yds, Par 71, SSS 71, Course record 63.
Club membership 800.
Visitors Mon-Fri except BHs. Handicap certificate. Dress code.
Societies booking required. **Green Fees** £62.50 per day, £47.50
per round after 1pm, £25 after 3.30pm **Course Designer** H S Colt
Prof Steve Hoatson **Facilities** 🎌 🍴 by prior arrangement 🏌
🍺 🎏 🏌 🏚 ⚐ ⛳ 🏌 ⚑ **Leisure** hard tennis courts,
snooker table **Conf** Corporate Hospitality Days **Location** W of village
on A246
Hotel ★★ **67%** HL Bookham Grange Hotel, Little Bookham
Common, Bookham, LEATHERHEAD ☎ 01372 452742 & 459899
📄 01372 450080 27 en suite

ENTON GREEN
Map 4 SU94

West Surrey Golf Club GU8 5AF
☎ 01483 421275 📄 01483 415419
e-mail: office@wsgc.co.uk
web: www.wsgc.co.uk
An attractive course with tree-lined fairways and contrasting views
of the Surrey landscape. The course winds slowly upwards towards
its highest point 440ft above sea level.
18 Holes, 6477yds, Par 71, SSS 72, Course record 64.
Club membership 600.
Visitors Mon,Tue, Thu, weekends except BHs. Booking required.
Dress code. **Societies** booking required. **Green Fees** not confirmed
Course Designer Herbert Fowler **Prof** Alister Tawse **Facilities** 🎌
🍴 🏌 🍺 🎏 🏌 🏚 ⛳ 🏌 ⚑ **Leisure** hard tennis
courts **Conf** Corporate Hospitality Days **Location** S of village
Hotel ★★★ **77%** HL Mercure Bush Hotel, The Borough, FARNHAM
☎ 01252 715237 📄 01252 719297 94 en suite

Save on Hotels. Book at **theAA.com/hotel**

SURREY

EPSOM
Map 4 TQ26

Epsom Golf Club Longdown Lane South KT17 4JR
☎ 01372 721666 📠 01372 817183
e-mail: stuartwalker@epsomgolfclub.co.uk
web: www.epsomgolfclub.co.uk
Traditional downland course with many mature trees and fast undulating greens. Thought must be given to every shot to play to one's handicap.

18 Holes, 5656yds, Par 69, SSS 67, Course record 63.
Club membership 770.
Visitors Mon, Wed-Fri & BHs. Sat/Sun pm only. Booking required. Dress code. **Societies** booking required. **Green Fees** not confirmed **Course Designer** Willie Dunne **Prof** Stuart Walker **Facilities** ⑪ ⑩ ⑬ 🍴 人 🖼 ㆆ ♂ **Conf** facs Corporate Hospitality Days **Location** SE of town centre on B288
Hotel ★★★★ **80%** HL Woodlands Park Hotel, Woodlands Lane, STOKE D'ABERNON ☎ 01372 843933 & 0845 072 7581 📠 01372 842704 57 en suite

Horton Park Golf Club Hook Rd KT19 8QG
☎ 020 8393 8400 & 8394 2626 📠 020 8394 1369
e-mail: info@hortonparkgolf.com
web: www.hortonparkgolf.com
Parkland course in picturesque Country Park. Natural lake, dog-legs and many mature trees make an excellent challenge for all abilities. The signature hole is the 10th, with an island green. Separate par 3 nine hole course with holes up to 200 yards.

Millennium: 18 Holes, 5950yds, Par 70, SSS 69,
Course record 66.
Academy: 9 Holes, 1354yds, Par 27. Club membership 350.
Visitors Contact club for details. **Societies** booking required. **Green Fees** £20 (£26 weekends). Twilight from 1pm £15 (£18 weekends). Super Twilight after 5pm £10. **Course Designer** Dr Peter Nicholson **Prof** John Terrell **Facilities** ⑪ ⑬ ⑬ 🍴 人 🖼 ㆆ 🛒 ♂ ♂ **Conf** facs Corporate Hospitality Days **Location** junct Hook Road & Chessington Road.
Hotel ★★★★ **80%** HL Woodlands Park Hotel, Woodlands Lane, STOKE D'ABERNON ☎ 01372 843933 & 0845 072 7581 📠 01372 842704 57 en suite

ESHER
Map 4 TQ16

Moore Place Golf Club Portsmouth Rd KT10 9LN
☎ 01372 463533
web: www.mooreplacegolf.co.uk
9 Holes, 2103yds, Par 66, SSS 62, Course record 58.
Course Designer H Vardon/D Allen/N Gadd **Location** 0.5m from town centre on A307
Telephone for further details
Hotel ★★★ **77%** HL Best Western Ship Hotel, Monument Green, WEYBRIDGE ☎ 01932 848364 📠 01932 857153 76 en suite

Thames Ditton & Esher Golf Club Portsmouth Rd KT10 9AL
☎ 020 8398 1551
18 Holes, 5149yds, Par 66, SSS 65, Course record 61.
Location 1m NE on A307, next to Marquis of Granby pub
Telephone for further details
Hotel ★★★★ **71%** HL The Carlton Mitre, Hampton Court Road, HAMPTON COURT ☎ 020 8979 9988 & 8783 3505 📠 020 8979 9777 36 en suite

FARLEIGH
Map 5 TQ36

Farleigh Court Golf Club Farleigh Common CR6 9PE
☎ 01883 627711 📠 01883 627722
web: www.farleighcourtgolf.com
18 Holes, 6409yds, Par 72, SSS 70, Course record 67.
9 Holes, 3281yds, Par 36.
Course Designer John Jacobs **Location** 1.5m from Selsdon
Telephone for further details
Hotel ★★★ **73%** HL South Park Hotel, 3-5 South Park Hill Road, South Croydon, CROYDON ☎ 020 8688 5644 📠 020 8760 0861 30 en suite

FARNHAM
Map 4 SU84

Blacknest Golf Club Binsted GU34 4QL
☎ 01420 22888 📠 01420 22001
18 Holes, 5938yds, Par 69, SSS 69, Course record 64.
Course Designer Mr Nicholson **Location** 5m SW of Farnham, leave A325 at A31 Bentley
Telephone for further details
Hotel ★★★ **79%** HL Best Western Frensham Pond Hotel, Bacon Lane, CHURT ☎ 01252 795161 📠 01252 792631 51 en suite

Farnham Golf Club The Sands GU10 1PX
☎ 01252 782109 📠 01252 781185
e-mail: farnhamgolfclub@tiscali.co.uk
web: www.farnhamgolfclub.co.uk
Course is a mixture of parkland, pine and heather with gentle rolling undulations.

18 Holes, 6613yds, Par 72, SSS 72.
Club membership 700.
Visitors Mon-Sun & BHs. Booking required weekends & BHs. Dress code **Societies** booking required. **Green Fees** £65 per day, £45 per round **Course Designer** Donald Steel **Prof** Rob Colborne **Facilities** ⑪ 🍴 by prior arrangement 🖼 ⑬ 🍴 人 🖼 ♂ ♂ **Conf** Corporate Hospitality Days **Location** 3m E off A31
Hotel ★★★ **77%** HL Mercure Bush Hotel, The Borough, FARNHAM ☎ 01252 715237 📠 01252 719297 94 en suite

Farnham Park Golf Course Folly Hill GU9 0AU
☎ 01252 715216
9 Holes, 1163yds, Par 27, SSS 48, Course record 48.
Course Designer Henry Cotton **Location** N of town centre on A287, next to Farnham Castle
Telephone for further details
Hotel ★★★ **77%** HL Mercure Bush Hotel, The Borough, FARNHAM ☎ 01252 715237 📠 01252 719297 94 en suite

GODALMING
Map 4 SU94

Broadwater Park Golf Club & Driving Range
Guildford Rd, Farncombe GU7 3BU
☎ 01483 429955 📄 01483 429955
web: www.broadwaterparkgolf.co.uk
A par 3 public course with floodlit driving range and putting green.

9 Holes, 1271yds, Par 27, SSS 25, Course record 22.
Club membership 160.

Visitors Mon-Sun & BHs **Societies** welcome. **Green Fees** £6.75 (£8 weekends & BHs). 18 holes £11.50/£13.50 **Course Designer** Kevin Milton **Prof** Kevin D Milton/Nick English **Facilities** ⓣ by prior arrangement 🖪 🖵 🖭 🖨 🖵 🖋 🖝 **Conf** Corporate Hospitality Days **Location** NE of Godalming on A3100
Hotel ★★★ 80% HL Holiday Inn Guildford, Egerton Road, GUILDFORD ☎ 0871 942 9036 📄 01483 457256 168 en suite

Hurtmore Golf Club Hurtmore Rd, Hurtmore GU7 2RN
☎ 01483 426492 📄 01483 426121
e-mail: general@hurtmore-golf.co.uk
web: www.hurtmore-golf.co.uk

A Peter Alliss and Clive Clark pay-and-play course with several lakes that come into play more than once. Many well placed bunkers catch any errant shots. The par 5, 15th hole is the longest on the course. A narrow drive, long sweeping fairway, cross bunker and out of bounds to the left provide a daunting challenge to those who are too ambitious.

18 Holes, 5254yds, Par 70, SSS 67, Course record 65.
Club membership 200.

Visitors Mon-Sun & BHs. Booking required. Dress code. **Societies** booking required. **Green Fees** £25 per 18 holes, £13 per 9 holes (£30/£16 weekends). Twilight £15 per day **Course Designer** Peter Alliss/Clive Clark **Prof** Maxine Burton **Facilities** ⓣ 🖭 🖪 🖵 🖭 🛆 🖨 🖵 🖋 **Leisure** practice nets **Conf** Corporate Hospitality Days **Location** 2m NW of Godalming off A3
Hotel ★★★ 80% HL Holiday Inn Guildford, Egerton Road, GUILDFORD ☎ 0871 942 9036 📄 01483 457256 168 en suite

GODSTONE
Map 5 TQ35

Godstone Golf Club Rooks Nest Park RH9 8BZ
☎ 01883 742333 📄 01883 740227
e-mail: admin@godstone-golfclub.co.uk
web: www.godstone-golfclub.co.uk

Godstone offers three tees per hole, making it possible to play the 9 holes twice, with varying tee positions. The three new lakes, linked by a freshwater stream, add interest and a degree of difficulty to the course.

9 Holes, 3040yds, Par 72, SSS 69.

Visitors Mon-Sun & BHs. Booking required. Dress code. **Societies** booking required. **Green Fees** not confirmed **Course Designer** David Williams **Facilities** 🖪 🖵 🖵 🖨 🖋 **Location** M25 junct 6, situated on A22 towards Oxted
Hotel ★★★★ 82% HL Nutfield Priory, Nutfield, REDHILL ☎ 01737 824400 & 0845 072 7485 📄 01737 824410 60 en suite

GUILDFORD
Map 4 SU94

Guildford Golf Club High Path Rd, Merrow GU1 2HL
☎ 01483 563941 📄 01483 453228
e-mail: secretary@guildfordgolfclub.co.uk
web: www.guildfordgolfclub.co.uk

The course is on Surrey downland bordered by attractive woodlands. Situated on chalk, it is acknowledged to be one of the best all-weather courses in the area, and the oldest course in Surrey. Although not a long course, the prevailing winds across the open downs make low scoring difficult. It is possible to see four counties on a clear day.

18 Holes, 6160yds, Par 69, SSS 70, Course record 65.
Club membership 700.

Visitors Mon-Fri except BHs. Handicap certificate. Dress code. **Societies** booking required. **Green Fees** £35 per round **Course Designer** J H Taylor/Hawtree **Prof** A Kirk **Facilities** ⓣ 🖭 🖪 🖵 🖭 🛆 🖨 🖋 🖝 **Conf** facs Corporate Hospitality Days **Location** E of town centre off A246
Hotel ★★★ 80% HL Holiday Inn Guildford, Egerton Road, GUILDFORD ☎ 0871 942 9036 📄 01483 457256 168 en suite

Merrist Wood Golf Club Holly Ln GU3 3PE
☎ 01483 238890 📄 01483 238896
web: www.merristwood-golfclub.co.uk

18 Holes, 6600yds, Par 72, SSS 71, Course record 69.
Course Designer David Williams **Location** 3m from Guildford on A323 to Aldershot
Telephone for further details
Hotel ★★★ 80% HL Holiday Inn Guildford, Egerton Road, GUILDFORD ☎ 0871 942 9036 📄 01483 457256 168 en suite

Milford Golf Club Station Ln GU8 5HS
☎ 01483 419200 📄 01483 419199
web: www.crowngolf.com/milford

18 Holes, 5960yds, Par 69, SSS 68, Course record 64.
Course Designer Peter Alliss **Location** 6m SW Guildford. Off A3 into Milford, E towards station
Telephone for further details
Hotel ★★★ 80% HL Holiday Inn Guildford, Egerton Road, GUILDFORD ☎ 0871 942 9036 📄 01483 457256 168 en suite

Rokers Golf Course Rokers Farm, Aldershot Rd GU3 3PB
☎ 01483 236677 📄 01483 232324
e-mail: info@rokersgolf.co.uk
web: www.rokersgolf.co.uk

A pay-and-play nine-hole parkland course. A challenging course with two par 5 holes.

9 Holes, 3037yds, Par 72, SSS 69, Course record 67.
Club membership 200.

Visitors Contact course for details. Dress code. **Societies** booking required. **Green Fees** £9.50 per 9 holes (£11 weekends) **Course Designer** W V Roker **Prof** Adrian Carter **Facilities** ⓣ 🖭 🖪 🖵 🖭 🛆 🖨 🖵 🖋 🖝 **Location** 3m NW of Guildford on A323
Hotel ★★★ 80% HL Holiday Inn Guildford, Egerton Road, GUILDFORD ☎ 0871 942 9036 📄 01483 457256 168 en suite

Save on Hotels. Book at theAA.com/hotel

SURREY

ENGLAND

HINDHEAD　　　　Map 4 SU83

The Hindhead Golf Club Churt Rd GU26 6HX
☎ 01428 604614　🖷 01428 608508
e-mail: secretary@the-hindhead-golf-club.co.uk
web: www.the-hindhead-golf-club.co.uk

A picturesque Surrey heathland course. The front nine holes follow heather lined valleys which give the players a very remote and secluded feel. For the back nine play moves on to a plateau which offers a more traditional game before the tough challenge of the final two finishing holes.

18 Holes, 6356yds, Par 71, SSS 71.
Club membership 610.

Visitors Mon-Sun & BHs. Booking required. Dress code.
Societies booking required. **Green Fees** £70 per day, £60 per round (£80/£70 weekends & BHs) **Course Designer** J H Taylor **Prof** Ian Benson **Facilities** ⊕ ⊙ 🖿 ⊑ 🏌 ⏛ 🖼 ⏛ ⏛
Leisure snooker **Conf** Corporate Hospitality Days **Location** 1.5m NW of Hindhead on A287
Hotel ★★★★ 74% HL Lythe Hill Hotel and Spa, Petworth Road, HASLEMERE ☎ 01428 651251 🖷 01428 644131　41 en suite

KINGSWOOD　　　　Map 4 TQ25

Kingswood Golf and Country House Sandy Ln KT20 6NE
☎ 01737 832188　🖷 01737 833920
e-mail: sales@kingswood-golf.co.uk
web: www.kingswood-golf.co.uk

Mature parkland course sited on a plateau with delightful views of the Chipstead Valley. The course features lush, shaped fairways, testing bunkers positions and true greens. Recently re-designed by Howard Swan.

18 Holes, 6916yds, Par 72, SSS 73, Course record 66.
Club membership 650.

Visitors Mon-Sun & BHs. Booking required. Dress code.
Societies booking required. **Green Fees** not confirmed **Course Designer** James Braid **Prof** Terry Sims **Facilities** 🖿 ⊑ 🏌 ⏛ ⏛ 🖼 ⏛ ⏛ ⏛ **Leisure** squash, 3 snooker tables. **Conf** facs Corporate Hospitality Days **Location** 0.5m S of village off A217
Hotel ★★★ 73% HL Best Western Reigate Manor, Reigate Hill, REIGATE ☎ 01737 240125 🖷 01737 223883　50 en suite

Surrey Downs Golf Club Outwood Ln KT20 6JS
☎ 01737 839090　🖷 01737 839080
e-mail: booking@surreydownsgc.co.uk
web: www.surreydownsgc.co.uk

A challenging downland course with fine views over the Surrey countryside and first class facilities.

18 Holes, 6303yards, Par 71, SSS 70, Course record 64.
Club membership 652.

Visitors Mon-Sun & BHs. Booking required. Dress code.
Societies booking required. **Green Fees** £25 per round (£35 weekends & BHs) **Course Designer** Aliss/Clarke **Prof** Stephen Blacklee **Facilities** ⊕ ⊙ 🖿 ⊑ 🏌 ⏛ ⏛ ⏛ 🖼 ⏛ ⏛ **Leisure** sauna **Conf** facs Corporate Hospitality Days **Location** off A217 E onto B2032 at Kingswood for 1m, club on right after Eyhurst Park
Hotel ★★★ 73% HL Best Western Reigate Manor, Reigate Hill, REIGATE ☎ 01737 240125 🖷 01737 223883　50 en suite

LEATHERHEAD　　　　Map 4 TQ15

Leatherhead Golf Club Kingston Rd KT22 0EE
☎ 01372 843966 & 843956　🖷 01372 842241
e-mail: sales@lgc-golf.co.uk
web: www.lgc-golf.co.uk

Undulating, 100-year-old parkland course with tree-lined fairways and strategically placed bunkers. Easy walking.

18 Holes, 6203yds, Par 70, SSS 68, Course record 63.
Club membership 450.

Visitors Mon, Tue, Thu & Fri. Wed, weekends & BHs pm. Dress code. **Societies** booking required. **Green Fees** £38 per round (£40 weekends) **Prof** Timothy Lowe **Facilities** ⊕ ⊙ 🖿 ⊑ 🏌 ⏛ ⏛ 🖼 ⏛ ⏛ ⏛ **Conf** facs Corporate Hospitality Days **Location** 0.25m from junct 9 of M25, on A243
Hotel ★★ 67% HL Bookham Grange Hotel, Little Bookham Common, Bookham, LEATHERHEAD ☎ 01372 452742 & 459899 🖷 01372 450080　27 en suite

Pachesham Park Golf Complex Oaklawn Rd KT22 0BP
☎ 01372 843453
e-mail: enquiries@pacheshamgolf.co.uk
web: www.pacheshamgolf.co.uk

An undulating parkland course starting with five shorter but tight holes on one side of the road, followed by four longer more open but testing holes to finish.

Pachesham: 9 Holes, 2801yds, Par 35, SSS 67.
Club membership 140.

Visitors Mon-Sun & BHs. Booking required. Dress code.
Societies welcome. **Green Fees** £18 per 18 holes, £10 per 9 holes (£20/£14 weekends & BHs) **Course Designer** Phil Taylor **Prof** Philip Taylor **Facilities** ⊕ ⊙ by prior arrangement 🖿 ⊑ 🏌 ⏛ ⏛ 🖼 ⏛ ⏛ **Leisure** fitting centre **Conf** facs Corporate Hospitality Days **Location** M25 junct 9, 0.5m off A244 or A245
Hotel ★★★★ 80% HL Woodlands Park Hotel, Woodlands Lane, STOKE D'ABERNON ☎ 01372 843933 & 0845 072 7581 🖷 01372 842704　57 en suite

Tyrrells Wood Golf Club The Drive KT22 8QP
☎ 01372 376025　🖷 01372 360836
e-mail: general.manager@tyrrellswoodgolfclub.com
web: www.tyrrellswoodgolfclub.com

Easy walking course set in 276 acres of parkland with fine views and a Grade II listed clubhouse.

18 Holes, 6282yds, Par 71, SSS 70, Course record 65.
Club membership 780.

Visitors Mon-Fri except BHs. Booking required. Handicap certificate. Dress code. **Societies** booking required. **Green Fees** not confirmed **Course Designer** James Braid **Prof** Rob Humphrey **Facilities** ⊕ ⊙ 🖿 ⊑ 🏌 ⏛ ⏛ 🖼 ⏛ **Conf** facs Corporate Hospitality Days **Location** M25 junct 9, 2m SE of town off A24
Hotel ★★★★ 76% HL Mercure Burford Bridge, Burford Bridge, Box Hill, DORKING ☎ 01306 884561 🖷 01306 880386　57 en suite

LIMPSFIELD

Map 5 TQ45

Limpsfield Chart Golf Club Westerham Rd RH8 0SL
☎ 01883 723405 & 722106
e-mail: secretary@limpsfieldchartgolf.co.uk
web: www.limpsfieldchartgolf.co.uk

Attractive heathland course on National Trust land, easy walking with tree-lined fairways.

9 Holes, 5718yds, Par 70, SSS 68. Club membership 300.

Visitors Mon-Wed & Fri. Thu after 2.30pm. Booking required weekends & BHs. Dress code. **Societies** booking required. **Green Fees** £20 per day, £13 after 3pm 🅿 **Prof** Mike McLean **Facilities** 🆓 🖵 🍴 ⛳ **Conf** Corporate Hospitality Days **Location** M25 junct 6, 1m E on A25

LINGFIELD

Map 5 TQ34

Lingfield Park Golf Club Lingfield Rd, Racecourse Rd RH7 6PQ
☎ 01342 831761 📠 01342 831762
e-mail: cmorley@lingfieldpark.co.uk
web: www.lingfieldpark.co.uk

Difficult and challenging tree-lined parkland course, set in 210 acres of beautiful Surrey countryside with water features and 60 bunkers.

18 Holes, 6487yds, Par 72, SSS 71, Course record 64. Club membership 700.

Visitors Mon-Sun & BHs. Booking required. **Societies** booking required. **Green Fees** not confirmed **Course Designer** Chris Morley **Prof** Christopher Morley **Facilities** 🆓 🍽 🖵 🍴 ⛳ 🖾 🏇 ⛳ **Leisure** heated indoor swimming pool, sauna, gymnasium, horse racing **Conf** facs Corporate Hospitality Days **Location** M25 junct 6, signs to racecourse
Hotel ★★★★ 86% HL Felbridge Hotel & Spa, London Road, EAST GRINSTEAD ☎ 01342 337700 📠 01342 337715 120 en suite

NEWDIGATE

Map 4 TQ14

Rusper Golf Course Rusper Rd RH5 5BX
☎ 01293 871871 (shop) 📠 01293 871456
e-mail: nikki@ruspergolfclub.co.uk
web: www.ruspergolfclub.co.uk

The 18-hole course is set in countryside and offers golfers of all abilities a fair and challenging test. After a gentle start the holes wind through picturesque scenery, tree-lined fairways and natural water hazards.

18 Holes, 6724yds, Par 72, SSS 72. Club membership 300.
Visitors Mon-Sun & BHs. Booking required weekends & BHs.

Societies booking required. **Green Fees** not confirmed **Course Designer** A Blunden **Prof** Janice Arnold **Facilities** 🆓 🍽 🖵 🖾 🍴 ⛳ 🖾 🏇 ⛳ **Conf** Corporate Hospitality Days
Location off A24 between Newdigate & Rusper
Hotel ★★★★ 76% HL Mercure Burford Bridge, Burford Bridge, Box Hill, DORKING ☎ 01306 884561 📠 01306 880386 57 en suite

OCKLEY

Map 4 TQ14

Gatton Manor Hotel & Golf Club Standon Ln RH5 5PQ
☎ 01306 627555 📠 01306 627713
e-mail: info@gattonmanor.co.uk
web: www.gattonmanor.co.uk

A mature woodland course, formerly part of the Abinger estate. The challenging course makes imaginative use of the various streams, lakes and woodlands. A good scorecard can be suddenly ruined if the individual challenges each hole presents are not carefully considered.

18 Holes, 6563yds, Par 72, SSS 72, Course record 67. Club membership 350.

Visitors Contact club for details **Societies** booking required **Green Fees** not confirmed **Course Designer** John D Harris **Prof** Max Newman **Facilities** 🆓 🍽 🖵 🖾 🍴 ⛳ 🖾 🏇 ⛳ 🖾 ⛳ **Leisure** gymnasium **Conf** facs Corporate Hospitality Days **Location** 1.5m SW off A29
Hotel ★★★ 80% HL Gatton Manor Hotel & Golf Club, Standon Lane, OCKLEY ☎ 01306 627555 📠 01306 627713 18 en suite

OTTERSHAW

Map 4 TQ06

Foxhills Club and Resort Stonehill Rd KT16 0EL
☎ 01932 704465 📠 01932 875200
e-mail: golf@foxhills.co.uk
web: www.foxhills.co.uk

The Longcross course threads its way through pine trees and is a typical Surrey heathland course. The longer Bernard Hunt course is parkland with several lakes and ponds. The two courses complement each other and offer different challenges.

Bernard Hunt Course: 18 Holes, 6892yds, Par 73, SSS 73. Longcross Course: 18 Holes, 6750yds, Par 72, SSS 72.

Visitors Mon-Sun & BHs. Booking required. Dress code **Societies** booking required. **Green Fees** phone **Course Designer** F W Hawtree **Prof** R Summerscales **Facilities** 🆓 🍽 🖵 🍴 ⛳ 🖾 🏇 🖾 ⛳ ⛳ **Leisure** hard tennis courts, outdoor and indoor heated swimming pool, squash, sauna, gymnasium, par 3 course **Conf** facs Corporate Hospitality Days **Location** 1m NW of Ottershaw. M25 junct 11, signed
Hotel ★★★★ 80% HL Foxhills Club and Resort, Stonehill Road, OTTERSHAW ☎ 01932 872050 & 704500 📠 01932 874762 70 en suite

PIRBRIGHT

Map 4 SU95

Goal Farm Golf Club Gole Rd GU24 0PZ
☎ 01483 473183 📠 01483 473205
web: www.gfgc.co.uk

9 Holes, 1273yds, Par 54, SSS 48, Course record 50.

Course Designer Bill Cox **Location** 1.5m NW on B3012
Telephone for further details
Hotel ★★★ 75% HL Lakeside International, Wharf Road, Frimley Green, CAMBERLEY ☎ 01252 838000 📠 01252 837857 98 en suite

relax-on-thames

come and mess around beside the river...
come and stay at our newly revived hotel, the
runnymede-on-thames, just minutes from
The Wentworth Club. We've got gorgeous new
contemporary interiors, new bars and restaurants
with al fresco dining... all with dramatic riverside
views. But at heart we're still the same; our
friendly team are just as welcoming as ever. Our
handy location makes it easy to reach us by road,
rail and air. Whether you come with your partner
or family, there's so much to do here... and it's
also perfect for relaxing and doing nothing at all!

make more of your time here...
pamper yourself silly in our award-winning spa,
take a dip in our outdoor pool, relax by the river,
hire a boat and float away or go for a stroll along
the towpath. Unleash the kids in the children's
play area or tuck into a picnic on the riverbank.

and just around the corner...
why not have a whale of a time at one of the local
attractions, wind back the clock at Windsor Castle,
or take a turn around local gardens and lakes.

**To book or for more information
please call the reservations
team on: 01784 220980**

the runnymede-on-thames

Windsor Road Egham Surrey TW20 0AG
telephone: 01784 220600 email: info@therunnymede.co.uk www.therunnymede.co.uk

PUTTENHAM
Map 4 SU94

Puttenham Golf Club Heath Rd GU3 1AL
☎ 01483 810498 🖹 01483 810988
e-mail: enquiries@puttenhamgolfclub.co.uk
web: www.puttenhamgolfclub.co.uk

Mixture of heathland and woodland - undulating layout with stunning views across the Hog's Back and towards the South Downs. Sandy subsoil provides free drainage for year round play.

18 Holes, 6214yds, Par 71, SSS 70, Course record 65.
Club membership 650.

Visitors Mon-Fri except BHs. Booking required. Dress code.
Societies booking required. **Green Fees** £60 per day, £40 per round.
Prof Dean Lintott **Facilities** Ⓣ ⑪ by prior arrangement 🝙 🖵
🍴 🎍 🏠 🛠 🛒 🛠 🏳 **Conf** Corporate Hospitality Days
Location 1m SE on B3000
Hotel ★★★ 77% HL Mercure Bush Hotel, The Borough, FARNHAM
☎ 01252 715237 🖹 01252 719297 94 en suite

REDHILL
Map 4 TQ25

Redhill & Reigate Golf Club Clarence Lodge,
Pendelton Rd RH1 6LB
☎ 01737 240777 🖹 01737 242117
e-mail: mail@rrgc.net
web: www.rrgc.net

Flat picturesque tree-lined course, well over 100 years old.

18 Holes, 5272yds, Par 68, SSS 66, Course record 59.
Club membership 300.

Visitors Mon-Sun & BHs. Booking required weekends & BHs.
Societies booking required. **Green Fees** Oct-Mar £15 (weekends £20),
Apr-Sep £20 (£25) **Course Designer** James Braid **Prof** Joel Dowland
Facilities ⑪ by prior arrangement 🝙 🖵 🍴 🎍 🏠 🛒
🛠 **Conf** facs Corporate Hospitality Days **Location** 1m S on A23
Hotel ★★★ 73% HL Best Western Reigate Manor, Reigate Hill,
REIGATE ☎ 01737 240125 🖹 01737 223883 50 en suite

REIGATE
Map 4 TQ25

Reigate Heath Golf Club Flanchford Rd RH2 8QR
☎ 01737 242610 & 226793
web: www.reigateheathgolfclub.co.uk

9 Holes, 5658yds, Par 67, SSS 68, Course record 65.
Location 1.5m W off A25
Telephone for further details
Hotel ★★★ 73% HL Best Western Reigate Manor, Reigate Hill,
REIGATE ☎ 01737 240125 🖹 01737 223883 50 en suite

Reigate Hill Golf Club Gatton Bottom RH2 0TU
☎ 01737 646070 🖹 01737 642650
e-mail: proshop@reigatehillgolfclub.co.uk
web: www.reigatehillgolfclub.co.uk

A challenging course that can be enjoyed by all handicap levels. Tees and greens have been built with USGA specification and can be played all year round. Feature holes include two par fives; the 7th has two parallel fairways and the 14th has a large lake that has to be carried with the approach shot to the green.

18 Holes, 6246yds, Par 72, SSS 71. Club membership 450.
Visitors Mon-Sun & BHs. Booking required. Dress code.
Societies booking required. **Green Fees** £27 per 18 holes (£32

weekends & BHs) **Course Designer** David Williams **Prof** Mike
Lovegrove **Facilities** Ⓣ ⑪ 🝙 🖵 🍴 🎍 🏠 🛒 🛠 🛒 🛠
Conf facs Corporate Hospitality Days **Location** M25 junct 8 Reigate.
Stay in left lane heading along Gatton Bottom, entrance on right
Hotel ★★★ 73% HL Best Western Reigate Manor, Reigate Hill,
REIGATE ☎ 01737 240125 🖹 01737 223883 50 en suite

SHEPPERTON
Map 4 TQ06

Sunbury Golf Centre Charlton Ln TW17 8QA
☎ 01932 771414 🖹 01932 789300
web: www.crown-golf.co.uk

18 Holes, 5103yds, Par 68, SSS 65, Course record 60.
Academy: 9 Holes, 2444yds, Par 33, SSS 32.

Course Designer Peter Alliss **Location** M3, junct 1, 1m N off A244
Telephone for further details
Hotel ★★★ 73% HL Mercure Thames Lodge, Thames Street,
STAINES ☎ 01784 464433 🖹 01784 454858 79 en suite

SOUTH GODSTONE
Map 5 TQ34

Horne Park Golf Club Croydon Barn Ln, Horne RH9 8JP
☎ 01342 844443 🖹 01342 841828
e-mail: info@hornepark.co.uk
web: www.hornepark.co.uk

Set in attractive Surrey countryside with water coming into play in 5 holes. Relatively flat for easy walking. A different set of tees pose an intriguing second 9 holes.

9 Holes, 5436yds, Par 68, SSS 66, Course record 62.
Club membership 350.

Visitors Mon-Sun & BHs. Booking required. **Societies** welcome. **Green Fees** £16 per 18 holes, £11.50 per 9 holes (£17/£12.50 weekends)
Course Designer Howard Swan **Prof** Neil Burke **Facilities** ⑪ ⓉⓁ
by prior arrangement 🝙 🖵 🍴 🎍 🏠 🛒 🛠 🛒 🛠 🏳
Leisure swing analysis system, teaching academy **Conf** Corporate Hospitality Days **Location** A22, signed 3m N of East Grinstead
Hotel ★★★★ 71% HL Copthorne Hotel Effingham Gatwick,
West Park Road, COPTHORNE ☎ 01342 714994 🖹 01342 716039
122 en suite

SUTTON GREEN
Map 4 TQ05

Sutton Green Golf Club New Ln GU4 7QF
☎ 01483 747898 🖹 01483 750289
e-mail: admin@suttongreengc.co.uk
web: www.suttongreengc.co.uk

Set in the Surrey countryside, a challenging course with many water features. Excellent year round conditions with fairway watering. Many testing holes with water surrounding greens and fairways, making accuracy a premium.

18 Holes, 6400yds, Par 71, SSS 70, Course record 64.
Club membership 600.

Visitors contact club for details **Societies** booking required. **Green Fees** phone **Course Designer** David Walker/Laura Davies **Prof** Peter
Fuller **Facilities** ⓉⓁ ⑪ 🝙 🖵 🍴 🎍 🏠 🛒 🛠 🛒
Conf facs Corporate Hospitality Days **Location** off A320 between
Woking & Guildford
Hotel ★★★★★ CHH Pennyhill Park Hotel & The Spa, London
Road, BAGSHOT ☎ 01276 471774 🖹 01276 473217 123 en suite

WENTWORTH

SURREY - VIRGINIA WATER - MAP 4 TQ06

Wentworth Club, the home of the PGA and World Match Play championships, is a very special venue for any sporting, business or social occasion. The West Course is familiar to millions of television viewers who have followed the championships here. In recent years it was felt that in certain key areas the West course no longer played quite as Colt had intended and so a process of modernisation and restoration was undertaken by Ernie Els, involving extensive re-bunkering and lengthening of certain holes, where appropriate. There are two other excellent courses, the East Course and the Edinburgh Course, and a nine-hole par 3 executive course. The courses cross Surrey heathland with woods of pine, oak and birch.

Wentworth Dr GU25 4LS ☎ 01344 842201 🖨 01344 842804
e-mail: reception@wentworthclub.com **web:** www.wentworthclub.com
West Course: 18 Holes, 7308yds, Par 72, Course record 63.
East Course: 18 Holes, 6201yds, Par 68, SSS 70, Course record 62.
Edinburgh Course: 18 Holes, 7004yds, Par 72, Course record 67. Club membership 4300.
Visitors Mon-Fri. Booking required. Handicap certificate. Dress code. **Societies** booking required.
Green Fees West Course, 1 Jun-Oct £360, Nov £240, Dec-March £195 (fees include compulsory Wentworth caddy), Edinburgh & East Course, Apr £125, Jun-Oct £160, Nov £110, Dec-Mar £95 **Course Designer** Colt/Jacobs/Gallacher/Player **Prof** Stephen Gibson **Facilities** ⓘ ⍾ ⌾ ⌿ ⍀ ⍁ ⍂ ⍃ ⍄ ⍅ ⍆ ⍇ ⍈
Leisure hard and grass tennis courts, outdoor and indoor heated swimming pool, fishing, sauna, gymnasium, spa with 6 treatment rooms **Conf** facs Corporate Hospitality Days **Location** Main gate directly opposite turning for A329 on main A30
Hotel ★★★★ 80% HL the runnymede-on-thames, Windsor Road, EGHAM ☎ 01784 220600 🖨 01784 436340 181 en suite

TANDRIDGE   Map 5 TQ35

Tandridge Golf Club RH8 9NQ
☎ 01883 712274   📄 01883 730537
e-mail: secretary@tandridgegolfclub.com
web: www.tandridgegolfclub.com

A parkland course with two loops of nine holes from the clubhouse. The first nine are relatively flat. The second nine undulate with outstanding views of the North Downs.

18 Holes, 6277yds, Par 70, SSS 71, Course record 65. Club membership 750.

Visitors Mon-Fri except BHs. Booking required. Handicap certificate. Dress code. **Societies** booking required. **Green Fees** £68 per day, £48 after noon. Winter £38 per round **Course Designer** H S Colt **Prof** Chris Evans **Facilities** ⊕ ⊾ ☐ ☜ � 🖻 ☝ ✐ **Conf** Corporate Hospitality Days **Location** M25 junct 6, 2m SE on A25
Hotel ★★★★ 82% HL Nutfield Priory, Nutfield, REDHILL
☎ 01737 824400 & 0845 072 7485 📄 01737 824410   60 en suite

TILFORD   Map 4 SU84

Hankley Common Golf Club The Club House GU10 2DD
☎ 01252 792493   📄 01252 795699
e-mail: jhay@hankley-commongc.co.uk
web: www.hankley.co.uk

A natural heathland course subject to wind. Greens are first rate. The 18th, a long par 4, is most challenging, the green being beyond a deep chasm which traps any but the perfect second shot. The 7th is a spectacular one-shotter.

18 Holes, 6782yds, Par 71, SSS 73, Course record 65. Club membership 700.

Visitors Mon-Fri except BHs. Booking required Tue & Wed. Dress code. **Societies** booking required. **Green Fees** not confirmed **Course Designer** James Braid **Prof** Peter Stow **Facilities** ⊕ ☜ ゑ 🖻 ☝ ✐ 🖻 ✐ ☝ **Location** 0.75m SE of Tilford
Hotel ★★★ 77% HL Mercure Bush Hotel, The Borough, FARNHAM
☎ 01252 715237 📄 01252 719297   94 en suite

VIRGINIA WATER   Map 4 TQ06

Wentworth Club see page 239
Wentworth Dr GU25 4LS
☎ 01344 842201   📄 01344 842804
e-mail: reception@wentworthclub.com
web: www.wentworthclub.com
Hotel ★★★★ 80% HL the runnymede-on-thames, Windsor Road, EGHAM ☎ 01784 220600 📄 01784 436340   181 en suite

See advert on page 237

WALTON-ON-THAMES   Map 4 TQ16

Burhill Golf Club Burwood Rd KT12 4BL
☎ 01932 227345   📄 01932 267159
e-mail: info@burhillgolf-club.co.uk
web: www.burhillgolf-club.co.uk

The Old Course is a mature tree-lined parkland course with some of the finest greens in Surrey. The New Course, opened in 2001, is a modern course built to USGA specifications has many bunkers and water hazards, including the River Mole.

Old Course: 18 Holes, 6500yds, Par 70, SSS 71, Course record 60.
New Course: 18 Holes, 6600yds, Par 72, SSS 72, Course record 64. Club membership 1300.

Visitors Mon-Fri. Weekends & BHs pm. Booking required. Dress code. **Societies** booking required. **Green Fees** Old Course £110 per day, £90 per 18 holes. New Course £75 per 18 holes **Course Designer** Willie Park/Simon Gidman **Prof** Pip Elson **Facilities** ⊕ ☜ ⊾ ☐ ☜ ゑ 🖻 ☝ ✐ 🖻 ✐ ☝ **Conf** facs Corporate Hospitality Days **Location** M25 junct 10, take A3 towards London, 1st exit (Painshill junct) towards Byfleet. Follow signs to club.
Hotel ★★★ 77% HL Best Western Ship Hotel, Monument Green, WEYBRIDGE ☎ 01932 848364 📄 01932 857153   76 en suite

WALTON-ON-THE-HILL   Map 4 TQ25

Walton Heath Golf Club see page 241
Deans Ln, Walton-on-the-Hill KT20 7TP
☎ 01737 812380   📄 01737 814225
e-mail: secretary@waltonheath.com
web: www.waltonheath.com

WEST BYFLEET   Map 4 TQ06

West Byfleet Golf Club Sheerwater Rd KT14 6AA
☎ 01932 343433
e-mail: admin@wbgc.co.uk
web: www.wbgc.co.uk

An attractive course set against a background of woodland and gorse. The 13th is the famous pond shot with a water hazard and two bunkers fronting the green. No less than six holes of 420yds or more.

18 Holes, 6197yds, Par 70, SSS 70, Course record 62. Club membership 600.

Visitors Mon-Fri except BHs. Booking required. Dress code. **Societies** booking required. **Green Fees** £75 per day, £50 per round (£97.50/£65 weekends) **Course Designer** C S Butchart **Prof** David Regan **Facilities** ⊕ ☜ ⊾ ☐ ☜ ゑ 🖻 ☝ ✐ 🖻 ✐ ☝ **Conf** facs Corporate Hospitality Days **Location** W of village on A245
Hotel ★★★ 79% HL Holiday Inn Woking, Victoria Street, WOKING
☎ 01483 221000 📄 01483 221021   161 en suite

WALTON HEATH

SURREY - WALTON-ON-THE-HILL - MAP 4 TQ25

Walton Heath, a traditional member club, has two extremely challenging courses. Enjoying an enviable international reputation, the club was founded in 1903. It has played host to over 60 major amateur and professional championships, including the 1981 Ryder Cup and five European Open Tournaments (1991, 1989, 1987, 1980 and 1977); among the many prestigious amateur events, Walton Heath hosted the English Amateur in 2002. In recent years the club has hosted the European qualification for the U.S. Open Championship. The Old Course is popular with visitors, while the New Course is very challenging, requiring subtle shots to get the ball near the hole. Straying from the fairway brings gorse, bracken and heather to test the golfer.

Deans Ln, Walton-on-the-Hill KT20 7TP ☎ 01737 812380 📄 01737 814225
e-mail: secretary@waltonheath.com **web:** www.waltonheath.com
Old Course: 18 Holes, 7406yds, Par 72, SSS 76.
New Course: 18 Holes, 7175yds, Par 72, SSS 75. Club membership 1000.
Visitors Mon-Fri. Weekends & BHs after 11.30am. Booking required. **Societies** booking required.
Green Fees £115 each course (£145) winter, £125 (£155) weekends **Course Designer** Herbert Fowler
Prof Simon Peaford **Facilities** 🏆 🍴 🍺 🍴 🚶 🏠 📷 ⚡ **Conf** Corporate Hospitality Days **Location** M25 junct 8, SE of village off B2032
Hotel ★★★ 80% HL Chalk Lane Hotel, Chalk Lane, Woodcote End, EPSOM ☎ 01372 721179
📄 01372 727878 22 en suite

WEST CLANDON

Map 4 TQ05

Clandon Regis Golf Club Epsom Rd GU4 7TT
☎ 01483 224888 📄 01483 211781
e-mail: office@clandonregis-golfclub.co.uk
web: www.clandonregis-golfclub.co.uk
High quality parkland course with challenging lake holes on the back nine. European Tour specification tees and greens.
18 Holes, 5917yds, Par 72, SSS 69. Club membership 692.
Visitors Mon-Sun & BHs. Booking required. Dress code.
Societies Booking required **Green Fees** £50 per day, £40 per 18 holes (weekends & BHs £50 per 18 holes) **Course Designer** David Williams
Prof Steve Lloyd **Facilities** ⓔ ⓘ ⓛ ⓒ ⓟ ⓐ ⓔ ⓟ ⓕ
ⓕ **Leisure** sauna **Conf** facs Corporate Hospitality Days **Location** SE of village off A246
Hotel ★★★ INN The Drummond at Albury, High Street, ALBURY
☎ 01483 202039 📄 01483 205361   9 rooms

WEST END

Map 4 SU96

Windlemere Golf Club Windlesham Rd GU24 9QL
☎ 01276 858727 📄 01276 858271
A parkland course, undulating in parts with natural water hazards. There is also a floodlit driving range.
9 Holes, 2673yds, Par 34, SSS 33, Course record 30.
Visitors contact club for details. **Green Fees** £12.25 per 9 holes (£13.75 weekends) **Course Designer** Clive Smith **Prof** David Thomas **Facilities** ⓛ ⓒ ⓟ ⓐ ⓔ ⓟ ⓕ
ⓕ **Leisure** pool/snooker tables **Location** N of village at junct A319
Hotel ★★★★★ CHH Pennyhill Park Hotel & The Spa, London Road, BAGSHOT ☎ 01276 471774 📄 01276 473217   123 en suite

WEYBRIDGE

Map 4 TQ06

St George's Hill Golf Club Golf Club Rd, St George's Hill KT13 0NL
☎ 01932 847758 📄 01932 821564
e-mail: admin@stgeorgeshillgolfclub.co.uk
web: www.stgeorgeshillgolfclub.co.uk
Comparable and similar to Wentworth, a feature of this course is the number of long and difficult par 4s. To score well it is necessary to place the drive - and long driving pays handsomely. Walking is hard on this undulating, heavily wooded course with plentiful heather and rhododendrons.
Red & Blue: 18 Holes, 6526yds, Par 70, SSS 71.
Green: 9 Holes, 2897yds, Par 70, SSS 70.
Club membership 700.
Visitors Wed-Fri except BHs. Booking required. Dress code.
Societies booking required. **Green Fees** not confirmed **Course Designer** H S Colt **Prof** A C Rattue **Facilities** ⓔ ⓛ ⓒ ⓟ ⓐ
ⓔ ⓟ ⓕ **Conf**   Corporate Hospitality Days **Location** 2m S off B374
Hotel ★★★ 77% HL Best Western Ship Hotel, Monument Green, WEYBRIDGE ☎ 01932 848364 📄 01932 857153   76 en suite

WOKING

Map 4 TQ05

Hoebridge Golf Centre Old Woking Rd GU22 8JH
☎ 01483 722611 📄 01483 740369
e-mail: info@hoebridgegc.co.uk
web: www.hoebridgegc.co.uk
The setting encompasses 200 acres of mature parkland and includes 3 golf courses containing 45 holes. The Hoebridge course has tree-lined fairways, challenging bunkers and fine views. The testing 9 hole Shey Copse is a par 4/par 3 course which winds around the woodland. The Maybury is an 18 holes par 3 course for beginners or golfers wishing to improve their short game.
Hoebridge: 18 Holes, 6549yds, SSS 71.
Shey Copse: 9 Holes, 2294yds, SSS 31.
Maybury Course: 18 Holes, 2181yds, SSS 54.
Club membership 750.
Visitors Mon-Sun & BHs. Booking required. Dress code.
Societies booking required. **Green Fees** Hoebridge £26 (£35 weekends), Shey £13.50 (£16.50 weekends), Maybury £12 (£15 weekends) **Course Designer** John Jacobs **Prof** Ian Hayward
Facilities ⓔ ⓘ ⓛ ⓒ ⓟ ⓐ ⓔ ⓟ ⓕ ⓔ ⓕ ⓕ
Leisure sauna, gymnasium, health & fitness club **Conf** facs Corporate Hospitality Days **Location** M25 junct 11, follow signs for Woking, then Old Woking, then Hoebridge
Hotel ★★★★★ CHH Pennyhill Park Hotel & The Spa, London Road, BAGSHOT ☎ 01276 471774 📄 01276 473217   123 en suite

Pyrford Golf Club Warren Ln GU22 8XR
☎ 01483 723555 📄 01483 729777
web: www.pyrfordgolf.co.uk
18 Holes, 6256yds, Par 72, SSS 70, Course record 64.
Course Designer Peter Alliss & Clive Clark **Location** off A3 Ripley to Pyrford
Telephone for further details
Hotel ★★★★★ CHH Pennyhill Park Hotel & The Spa, London Road, BAGSHOT ☎ 01276 471774 📄 01276 473217   123 en suite

Traditions Golf Course Pyrford Rd, Pyrford GU22 8UE
☎ 01932 350355 📄 01932 350234
e-mail: traditions@crown-golf.co.uk
web: www.traditionsgolf.co.uk
Situated in the heart of the Surrey countryside with a mature setting which includes various woodland and water features. A course with many challenges which can be enjoyed by golfers of all levels and experience.
18 Holes, 6304yds, Par 71, SSS 70. Club membership 400.
Visitors Mon-Sun & BHs. Booking required. **Societies** booking required. **Green Fees** not confirmed **Course Designer** Peter Alliss
Facilities ⓔ ⓘ ⓛ ⓒ ⓟ ⓐ ⓔ ⓟ ⓕ ⓔ ⓕ **Conf** facs Corporate Hospitality Days **Location** M25 junct 10, A3, signs to RHS Garden Wisley, through Wisley to Pyford, course 0.5m
Hotel ★★★★★ CHH Pennyhill Park Hotel & The Spa, London Road, BAGSHOT ☎ 01276 471774 📄 01276 473217   123 en suite

Save on Hotels. Book at **theAA.com/hotel**

SURREY – SUSSEX, EAST

ENGLAND

Woking Golf Club Pond Rd GU22 0JZ
☎ 01483 760053 📄 01483 772441
web: www.wokinggolfclub.co.uk
18 Holes, 6340yds, Par 70, SSS 70, Course record 65.
Course Designer Tom Dunn **Location** W of town centre in area of
St Johns Heath
Telephone for further details
Hotel ★★★★★ CHH Pennyhill Park Hotel & The Spa, London
Road, BAGSHOT ☎ 01276 471774 📄 01276 473217 123 en suite

Worplesdon Golf Club Heath House Rd GU22 0RA
☎ 01483 472277
web: www.worplesdon.co.uk
18 Holes, 6431yds, Par 71, SSS 71, Course record 66.
Course Designer J F Abercromby **Location** 1.5m N of village off
A322
Telephone for further details
Hotel ★★★★★ CHH Pennyhill Park Hotel & The Spa, London
Road, BAGSHOT ☎ 01276 471774 📄 01276 473217 123 en suite

WOLDINGHAM   Map 5 TQ35

North Downs Golf Club Northdown Rd CR3 7AA
☎ 01883 652057 📄 01883 652832
e-mail: manager@northdownsgolfclub.co.uk
web: www.northdownsgolfclub.co.uk
Parkland course, 850ft above sea level, with several testing holes
and magnificent views. Probably the highest golf course in the south
of England.
18 Holes, 5815yds, Par 69, SSS 69, Course record 64.
Club membership 460.
Visitors Mon-Wed, Fri & BHs. Thu & Sun pm. Booking required
Sun. Handicap certificate. Dress code. County cards accepted.
Societies booking required. **Green Fees** £40 per day, £33 per round
(£25 per round Sun) **Course Designer** Pennink **Prof** M Homewood
Facilities ⊕ ⏽⏺ ⛾ ◻ ⋈ ⟁ 🖾 ⛳ ✆ **Conf** facs
Corporate Hospitality Days **Location** 0.75m S of Woldingham

Woldingham Golf Club Halliloo Valley Rd CR3 7HA
☎ 01883 653501 📄 01883 653502
e-mail: info@woldingham-golfclub.co.uk
web: www.woldingham-golfclub.co.uk
Located in Halliloo Valley and designed by the American architect
Bradford Benz, this pleasant course utilises all the contours and
features of the valley. The chalk base gives excellent drainage for all
year play.
18 Holes, 6393yds, Par 71, SSS 70, Course record 64.
Club membership 500.
Visitors Mon-Sun & BHs. Booking required. Dress code.
Societies booking required. **Green Fees** £44 per day, £32 per
round (£35 per round weekends) **Course Designer** Bradford Benz
Facilities ⊕ ⏽⏺ ⛾ ◻ ⋈ ⟁ 🖾 ⛙ 🖦 ✆ ✆ **Conf** facs
Corporate Hospitality Days **Location** M25 junct 6, A22 N, 1st rdbt onto
Woldingham Rd, Halliloo Valley Rd, on left
Hotel ★★★★ 70% HL Coulsdon Manor, Coulsdon Court
Road, Coulsdon, CROYDON ☎ 020 8668 0414 📄 020 8668 3118
37 en suite

SUSSEX, EAST

BEXHILL   Map 5 TQ70

Cooden Beach Golf Club Cooden Sea Rd TN39 4TR
☎ 01424 842040 & 843938 (Pro Shop)
📄 01424 842040
e-mail: enquiries@coodenbeachgc.com
web: www.coodenbeachgc.com
Downland links course running alongside the sea but separated by
the main rail line. A dry course that plays well throughout the year
with some excellent testing holes, particularly the par 4 1st. The 4th
and 11th are both played to built up greens and the final three holes
required careful club selection.
18 Holes, 6504yds, Par 72, SSS 72, Course record 65.
Club membership 850.
Visitors Mon-Fri & BHs. Booking required. Handicap certificate.
Dress code. **Societies** booking required. **Green Fees** £48 per day,
£42 per round **Course Designer** W Herbert Fowler **Prof** Jeffrey Sim
Facilities ⊕ ⏽⏺ ⛾ ◻ ⋈ ⟁ 🖾 🖦 ✆ ✆
Leisure indoor practice facility **Conf** facs Corporate Hospitality Days
Location 2m W on A259
Hotel ★★★ 80% HL Cooden Beach Hotel, Cooden Beach,
BEXHILL ☎ 01424 842281 📄 01424 846142 41 en suite

Highwoods Golf Club Ellerslie Ln TN39 4LJ
☎ 01424 212625 📄 01424 216866
e-mail: highwoods@btconnect.com
web: www.highwoodsgolfclub.co.uk
Undulating parkland with water on eight holes.
18 Holes, 6218yds, Par 70, SSS 70. Club membership 750.
Visitors Mon-Sat & BHs. Sun pm. Booking advisable Handicap
certificate. Dress code. **Societies** welcome. **Green Fees** £35 per 18
holes (£40 weekends & BHs) **Course Designer** J H Taylor **Prof** Mike
Andrews **Facilities** ⊕ ⏽⏺ ⛾ ◻ ⋈ ⟁ 🖾 🖦 ✆ **Conf** facs
Corporate Hospitality Days **Location** 1.5m NW
Hotel ★★★ 73% HL Best Western Royal Victoria, Marina, St
Leonards-on-Sea, HASTINGS ☎ 01424 445544 📄 01424 721995
50 en suite

BRIGHTON & HOVE   Map 4 TQ30

Brighton & Hove Golf Club Devils Dyke Rd BN1 8YJ
☎ 01273 556482 📄 01273 554247
e-mail: phil@brightongolf.co.uk
web: www.brightonandhovegolfclub.co.uk
Testing nine-hole course with glorious views over the Downs and
the sea. Famous par 3 6th hole considered to be one of the most
extraordinary holes in golf.
9 Holes, 5704yds, Par 68, SSS 67, Course record 64.
Club membership 400.
Visitors Mon-Sun & BHs. Booking required Wed, Fri-Sun & BHs. Dress
code. **Societies** booking required **Green Fees** not confirmed **Course**
Designer James Braid **Prof** Phil Bonsall **Facilities** ⊕ ⏽⏺ ⛾ ◻
⋈ ⟁ 🖾 ⛙ 🖦 ✆ **Conf** facs Corporate Hospitality Days
Location 4m NW of Brighton, 1m from A27 & A23
Hotel ★★★ 78% HL Best Western Old Tollgate Restaurant & Hotel,
The Street, Bramber, STEYNING ☎ 01903 879494 📄 01903 813399
38 en suite

Dyke Golf Club Devils Dyke BN1 8YJ
☎ 01273 857296 (office) & 857260 (pro shop)
🖹 01273 857078
web: www.dykegolf.com

18 Holes, 6627yds, Par 72, SSS 72, Course record 66.

Course Designer Fred Hawtree **Location** 4m N of Brighton, between A23 & A27

Telephone for further details
Hotel ★★★ 78% HL Best Western Old Tollgate Restaurant & Hotel, The Street, Bramber, STEYNING ☎ 01903 879494
🖹 01903 813399 38 en suite

Hollingbury Park Golf Club Ditchling Rd BN1 7HS
☎ 01273 552010 (sec) & 500086 (pro)
🖹 01273 552010
web: www.hollingburyparkgolf.org.uk

18 Holes, 6500yds, Par 72, SSS 71, Course record 65.

Location 2m N of town centre
Telephone for further details
Hotel ★★ 67% HL Preston Park Hotel, 216 Preston Road, BRIGHTON ☎ 01273 507853 🖹 01273 540039 33 en suite

Waterhall Golf Club Saddlescombe Rd BN1 8YN
☎ 01273 508658
e-mail: golf@brighton-hove.gov.uk
web: www.waterhall.org.uk

Hilly downland course with hard walking and open to the wind. Private club playing over municipal course.

18 Holes, 5773yds, Par 69, SSS 68, Course record 66.
Club membership 150.

Visitors Mon-Sun & BHs. Dress code **Societies** booking required.
Green Fees not confirmed **Facilities** ⏱ ⑩ 🍴 ⓛ ♿ 🛈 🍸
🍴 ♿ **Conf** Corporate Hospitality Days **Location** 2m NE from A27
Hotel ★★★ 78% HL Best Western Old Tollgate Restaurant & Hotel, The Street, Bramber, STEYNING ☎ 01903 879494 🖹 01903 813399 38 en suite

West Hove Golf Club Badgers Way, Hangleton BN3 8EX
☎ 01273 419738 & 413494 (pro) 🖹 01273 439988
e-mail: info@westhovegolfclub.co.uk
web: www.westhovegolfclub.co.uk

Founded in 1910 the course stands in the South Downs, an Area of Outstanding Natural Beauty. Laid out over rolling chalk downland, it is a challenging par 70 and the terrain makes it playable all year.

18 Holes, 6260yds, Par 71, SSS 70. Club membership 600.

Visitors Mon-Sun & BHs but restrictions apply. Booking required. Dress code. **Societies** booking required. **Green Fees** not confirmed
Course Designer Hawtree & Sons **Prof** Darren Cook **Facilities** ⏱
⑩ ⓛ 🍴 ⓛ ♿ 🛈 🍸 ♿ 🍴 **Conf** facs Corporate
Hospitality Days **Location** off A27 N of Brighton
Hotel ★★★ 64% HL The Courtlands Hotel & Conference Centre, 15-27 The Drive, HOVE ☎ 01273 731055 🖹 01273 328295
67 en suite

CROWBOROUGH
Map 5 TQ53

Crowborough Beacon Golf Club Beacon Rd TN6 1UJ
☎ 01892 661511
e-mail: secretary@cbgc.co.uk
web: www.cbgc.co.uk

Standing some 800ft above sea level, this is a testing heathland course where accuracy off the tee rather than distance is paramount. Panoramic views of the South Downs, Eastbourne and even the sea on a clear day.

18 Holes, 6319yds, Par 71, SSS 71.
Club membership 600.

Visitors Contact club for details. **Societies** booking required. **Green Fees** £60 per day, £40 per round (£45 per round weekends & BHs)
Prof Mr D C Newnham **Facilities** ⏱ ⑩ by prior arrangement
ⓛ ⓛ 🍴 ♿ 🛈 🍴 ♿ 🍴 **Conf** facs Corporate
Hospitality Days **Location** 9m S of Tunbridge Wells on A26
Hotel ★★★★ HL Ashdown Park Hotel & Country Club, Wych Cross, FOREST ROW ☎ 01342 824988 🖹 01342 826206 106 en suite

Dewlands Manor Golf Course Cottage Hill, Rotherfield TN6 3JN
☎ 01892 852266 🖹 01892 853015

A meadowland course built on land surrounding a 15th-century manor. The short par 4 4th can be played by the brave by launching a driver over the trees; the 7th requires accurate driving on a tight fairway; and the final two holes are sweeping par 5s travelling parallel to each other, a small stream guarding the front of the 9th green.

9 Holes, 3186yds, Par 36, SSS 35. Club membership 400.

Visitors Mon-Sun & BHs. Booking required. **Societies** booking required
Green Fees phone **Course Designer** R M & N M Godin **Prof** Nick Godin
Facilities ⏱ ⓛ ⓛ 🍴 ♿ 🛈 🍴 🍸 ♿ **Leisure** indoor
teaching facilities with computer analysis. **Conf** facs Corporate
Hospitality Days **Location** 0.5m S of Rotherfield
Hotel ★★★ INN Plough & Horses, Walshes Road, CROWBOROUGH
☎ 01892 652614 🖹 01892 652614 15 rooms

DITCHLING
Map 5 TQ31

Mid Sussex Golf Club Spatham Ln BN6 8XJ
☎ 01273 846567 🖹 01273 847815
web: www.midsussexgolfclub.co.uk

18 Holes, 6462yds, Par 71, SSS 71, Course record 65.

Course Designer David Williams **Location** 1m E of Ditchling
Telephone for further details
Hotel ★★★★ 76% HL Shelleys Hotel, 136 High Street, LEWES
☎ 01273 472361 & 483403 🖹 01273 483152 19 en suite

EASTBOURNE   Map 5 TV69

Eastbourne Downs Golf Club East Dean Rd BN20 8ES
☎ 01323 720827 📄 01323 412506
e-mail: secretary@ebdownsgolf.co.uk
web: www.ebdownsgolf.co.uk

This downland course has spectacular views over the South Downs
and Channel. Situated in an Area of Outstanding Natural Beauty 1m
behind Beachy Head. The club celebrated its centenary in 2008.

18 Holes, 6158yds, Par 72, SSS 69. Club membership 600.

Visitors Mon-Fri. Weekends & BHs after 11am. **Societies** booking
required. **Green Fees** not confirmed **Course Designer** J H Taylor
Prof T Marshall **Facilities** ⊕ ⦿ ⅃ ▱ ⅋ 🖻 ✈ 🏌 **Conf**
Corporate Hospitality Days **Location** 0.5m W of town centre on A259
Hotel ★★★ 78% HL Best Western Lansdowne, King Edward's
Parade, EASTBOURNE ☎ 01323 725174 & 745483 📄 01323 739721
102 en suite

Royal Eastbourne Golf Club Paradise Dr BN20 8BP
☎ 01323 744045 📄 01323 744048
web: www.regc.co.uk

*Devonshire Course: 18 Holes, 6077yds, Par 70, SSS 69,
Course record 62.*

Hartington Course: 9 Holes, 2147yds, Par 64, SSS 61.

Course Designer Arthur Mayhewe **Location** 0.5m W of town centre
Telephone for further details
Hotel ★★★ 73% HL New Wilmington, 25-27 Compton Street,
EASTBOURNE ☎ 01323 721219 📄 01323 746255 40 en suite

Willingdon Golf Club Southdown Rd, Willingdon BN20 9AA
☎ 01323 410981 📄 01323 411510
e-mail: secretary@willingdongolfclub.co.uk
web: www.willingdongolfclub.co.uk

Unique downland course set in an oyster-shaped amphitheatre.

*18 Holes, 6158yds, Par 69, SSS 69, Course record 61.
Club membership 600.*

Visitors Mon-Sun & BHs. Booking required weekends & BHs. Dress
code. **Societies** booking required. **Green Fees** £24 per round (£35
weekends) **Course Designer** J Taylor/Dr MacKenzie **Prof** Ally Mellor
Facilities ⊕ ⦿ ⅃ ▱ ⅋ 🖻 ✈ 🏌 **Conf**
Corporate Hospitality Days **Location** 0.5m N of town centre off A22
Hotel ★★★ 80% HL Hydro, Mount Road, EASTBOURNE
☎ 01323 720643 📄 01323 641167 84 en suite

FOREST ROW   Map 5 TQ43

Ashdown Park Hotel & Country Club Wych Cross
RH18 5JR
☎ 01342 824988 📄 01342 826206
e-mail: reservations@ashdownpark.com
web: www.ashdownpark.com

Set in 186 acres of landscaped Sussex countryside at the heart of
Ashdown Forest.

18 Holes, 2310yds, Par 54.

Societies booking required. **Green Fees** £16 per 18 holes for
hotel guests (£9 per 9 holes). £35 day membership including golf
Facilities ⊕ ⦿ ⅃ ▱ ⅋ 🖻 🖳 ⬦ ✦ 🏌 **Leisure** hard
tennis courts, heated indoor swimming pool, sauna, gymnasium
Conf facs Corporate Hospitality Days **Location** A264 to East Grinstead,

then A22 to Eastbourne, 2m S of Forest Row at Wych Cross lights, left
to Hartfied, 0.75m on right
Hotel ★★★★ HL Ashdown Park Hotel & Country Club, Wych Cross,
FOREST ROW ☎ 01342 824988 📄 01342 826206 106 en suite

Royal Ashdown Forest Golf Club Chapel Ln RH18 5LR
☎ 01342 822018 📄 01342 825211
e-mail: office@royalashdown.co.uk
web: www.royalashdown.co.uk

Old Course is on undulating heathland with no bunkers. Long
carries off the tees and magnificent views over the Forest. Not a
course for the high handicapper. West Course on natural heathland
with no bunkers. Less demanding than Old Course although
accuracy is at a premium.

*Old Course: 18 Holes, 6530yds, Par 72, SSS 72,
Course record 69.*

*West Course: 18 Holes, 5606yds, Par 68, SSS 67,
Course record 64. Club membership 450.*

Visitors Mon-Sun & BHs. Booking required. Dress code.
Societies booking required. **Green Fees** Old Course £65 per round
(£80 weekends). West Course £30 per round (£35 weekends).
Reduced winter rates **Course Designer** Archdeacon Scott
Prof Martyn Landsborough **Facilities** ⊕ ⦿ by prior arrangement
⅃ ▱ ⅋ 🖻 ✈ 🖻 🏌 ✦ 🏌 ✦ **Leisure** computerised video
swing analysis **Conf** Corporate Hospitality Days **Location** on B2110
in Forest Row

Hotel ★★★★ HL Ashdown Park Hotel & Country Club,
Wych Cross, FOREST ROW ☎ 01342 824988 📄 01342 826206
106 en suite

HAILSHAM   Map 5 TQ50

Wellshurst Golf & Country Club North St, Hellingly
BN27 4EE
☎ 01435 813456 (pro shop) 📄 01435 812444
e-mail: info@wellshurst.com
web: www.wellshurst.com

There are outstanding views of the South Downs and the Weald from
this well-manicured, undulating 18-hole course. There are varied
features and some water hazards.

18 Holes, 6084yds, Par 70, SSS 69. Club membership 400.

Visitors Mon-Sun & BHs. Dress code **Societies** welcome. **Green
Fees** £24 per 18 holes (£28 weekends) **Course Designer** The Golf
Corporation **Prof** Richard Holland **Facilities** ⊕ ⦿ ⅃ ▱ ⅋ 🖻
⅃ 🖻 🖳 ⬦ ✦ 🖻 🏌 **Conf** facs Corporate Hospitality
Days **Location** 2.5m N off A22 junct at Hailsham, on A267
Hotel ★★ 79% HL The Olde Forge Hotel & Restaurant, Magham
Down, HAILSHAM ☎ 01323 842893 📄 01323 842893 7 en suite

HASTINGS & ST LEONARDS — Map 5 TQ80

Beauport Golf Club Battle Rd TN37 7BP
☎ 01424 854245 🖹 01424 854245
e-mail: info@beauportparkgolf.co.uk
web: www.beauportparkgolf.co.uk
Course on Beauport Park Estate. Undulating parkland with stream and fine views.

18 Holes, 6180yds, Par 71, SSS 70, Course record 69. Club membership 250.

Visitors Contact club for details. **Societies** booking required.
Green Fees £18 per 18 holes, £14 per 9 holes (weekends £23/£16)
Prof Charles Giddins **Facilities** ⓘ ⦵ 🍴 🏌 ♨ 🍴 ⚲ 👤 🏠
🍴 ♢ 🏌 🛏 🏌 ⚑ **Leisure** hard tennis courts, heated indoor swimming pool, sauna, gymnasium, 9 hole pitch & putt course
Conf facs Corporate Hospitality Days **Location** 3m N of Hastings on A2100

Hotel ★★★ 80% HL Powder Mills, Powdermill Lane, BATTLE
☎ 01424 775511 🖹 01424 774540 40 en suite

HEATHFIELD — Map 5 TQ52

Horam Park Golf Course Chiddingly Rd, Horam TN21 0JJ
☎ 01435 813477 🖹 01435 813677
e-mail: horamgolfclub@hotmail.co.uk
web: www.horamparkgolfclub.co.uk
A pretty, woodland course with lakes and quality fast-running greens.

9 Holes, 6128yds, Par 70, SSS 69, Course record 65. Club membership 350.

Visitors Mon-Sun & BHs. Dress code. **Societies** booking required.
Green Fees £18 per 18 holes, £12 per 9 holes (£20/£13 weekends).
Twilight £11 **Course Designer** Glen Johnson **Prof** Giles Velvick
Facilities ⓘ ⦵ 🏌 ♨ 🍴 👤 🏠 🍴
Leisure pitch & putt, digital coaching room, custom fit clubs service
Conf Corporate Hospitality Days **Location** off A267 Hailsham to Heathfield
Hotel ★★★ 72% HL Boship Farm Hotel, Lower Dicker, HAILSHAM
☎ 01323 844826 & 442600 🖹 01323 843945 47 en suite

HOLTYE — Map 5 TQ43

Holtye Golf Club TN8 7ED
☎ 01342 850635 🖹 01342 851139
e-mail: secretary@holtye.com
web: www.holtye.com
Undulating forest and heathland course with tree-lined fairways providing testing golf. Different tees on the back nine.

9 Holes, 5260yds, Par 66, SSS 66, Course record 62. Club membership 300.

Visitors Contact club for details. Dress code **Societies** booking required. **Green Fees** £16 per 18 holes, £10 per 9 holes (£18/£14 weekends) **Prof** Kevin Hinton **Facilities** ⓘ 🏌 ♨ 🍴 👤 🏠 🍴
🏌 🛏 🏌 ⚑ **Location** 4m E of East Grinstead on A264
Hotel ★★★★ HL Ashdown Park Hotel & Country Club, Wych Cross, FOREST ROW ☎ 01342 824988 🖹 01342 826206 106 en suite

LEWES — Map 5 TQ41

Lewes Golf Club Chapel Hill BN7 2BB
☎ 01273 483474 🖹 01273 483474
e-mail: secretary@lewesgolfclub.co.uk
web: www.lewesgolfclub.co.uk
Downland course with undulating fairways. Fine views. Main greens and tees all-year-round.

18 Holes, 6248yds, Par 71, SSS 70, Course record 61. Club membership 440.

Visitors dress code. **Societies** booking required. **Green Fees** £42 per day, £30 per round, £17 Mon, £16 Twilight **Course Designer** Jack Rowe **Prof** Tony Hilton **Facilities** ⓘ by prior arrangement 🏠 🍴
🍴 👤 🏠 🍴 🏌 🛏 🏌 ⚑ **Conf** Corporate Hospitality Days
Location E of town centre
Hotel ★★★ 86% HL Deans Place, Seaford Road, ALFRISTON
☎ 01323 870248 🖹 01323 870918 36 en suite

NEWHAVEN — Map 5 TQ40

Peacehaven Golf Club Brighton Rd BN9 9UH
☎ 01273 514049 🖹 01273 512571
web: www.golfatpeacehaven.co.uk

9 Holes, 5488yds, Par 70, SSS 66, Course record 65.

Course Designer James Braid **Location** 0.75m W on A259
Telephone for further details
Hotel ★★★ 86% HL Deans Place, Seaford Road, ALFRISTON
☎ 01323 870248 🖹 01323 870918 36 en suite

RYE — Map 5 TQ92

Rye Golf Club New Lydd Rd, Camber TN31 7QS
☎ 01797 225241 🖹 01797 225460
e-mail: links@ryegolfclub.co.uk
web: www.ryegolfclub.co.uk
Unique links course with superb undulating greens set among ridges of sand dunes alongside Rye Harbour. Fine views over Romney Marsh and towards Fairlight and Dungeness.

Old Course: 18 Holes, 6497yds, Par 68, SSS 71.
Jubilee Course: 11 Holes, 5864yds, Par 69, SSS 68.
Club membership 1200.

Visitors Mon-Sun & BHs. Booking required. Dress code.
Green Fees advised on application **Course Designer** H S Colt
Prof Michael Lee **Facilities** ⓘ 🏌 🍴 🍴 👤 🏠 🍴 ♢ 🏌
Location 2.75m SE off A259
Hotel ★★★★ 76% HL George in Rye, 98 High Street, RYE
☎ 01797 222114 🖹 01797 224065 34 en suite

EAST SUSSEX NATIONAL GOLF RESORT & SPA

EAST SUSSEX - UCKFIELD - MAP 5 TQ42

East Sussex National offers two huge courses ideal for big-hitting professionals. The European Open has been staged here and it is home to the European Headquarters of the David Leadbetter Golf Academy, with indoor and outdoor video analysis. Bob Cupp designed the courses using 'bent' grass from tee to green, resulting in an American-style course to test everyone. The greens on both the East and West courses are immaculately maintained. The West Course, with stadium design and chosen for major events, is reserved for members and their guests; visitors are welcome on the East Course, also with stadium design, and which was the venue for the 1993 and 1994 European Open.

Little Horsted TN22 5ES ☎ 01825 880088 📄 01825 880066
e-mail: golf@eastsussexnational.co.uk web: www.eastsussexnational.co.uk
East Course: 18 Holes, 7138yds, Par 72, SSS 74.
West Course: 18 Holes, 7154yds, Par 72, SSS 72, Course record 65. Club membership 650.
Visitors Mon-Sun & BHs. Booking required. Handicap certificate. Dress code. Societies booking required.
Green Fees Sun-Thu £50, Fri-Sat £60. Twilight £30-£35. Reduced winter rates Course Designer Bob Cupp
Prof Sarah Maclennan/Jack Budgen Facilities ⊕ ⫶⊙⫶ 🍺 ⌨ 🍴 🏌 🏠 ⛳ ◇ 🛒 🚲 🏌 ℱ Leisure hard tennis courts, heated indoor swimming pool, fishing, sauna, gymnasium, golf academy, health club and spa Conf facs Corporate Hospitality Days Location 2m S of Uckfield on A22
Hotel ★★★ HL Horsted Place, Little Horsted, UCKFIELD ☎ 01825 750581 📄 01825 750459 20 en suite

SEAFORD
Map 5 TV49

Seaford Golf Club Firle Rd BN25 2JD
☎ 01323 892442 📠 01323 894113
e-mail: secretary@seafordgolfclub.co.uk
web: www.seafordgolfclub.co.uk

The great J H Taylor did not perhaps design as many courses as his friend and rival, James Braid, but Seaford's original design was Taylor's. It is a splendid downland course with magnificent views and some fine holes.

18 Holes, 6546yds, Par 69, SSS 71.
Club membership 600.

Visitors contact club for details. **Societies** booking required. **Green Fees** £40 per 18 holes (£30 winter) **Course Designer** J H Taylor **Prof** Chris Lovis **Facilities** ⊕ ⊖ by prior arrangement 🏌 ⌑ 🥤 ⚲ 🏠 ◇ ⚘ 🛒 ⚘ ⚲ **Conf** Corporate Hospitality Days **Location** turn inland off A259 at war memorial
Hotel ★★★ 86% HL Deans Place, Seaford Road, ALFRISTON
☎ 01323 870248 📠 01323 870918 36 en suite

Seaford Head Golf Course Southdown Rd BN25 4JS
☎ 01323 890139 📠 01323 894491
web: www.seafordheadgolfcourse.co.uk

18 Holes, 5848yds, Par 71, SSS 68, Course record 62.
Location E of Seaford on A259
Telephone for further details
Hotel ★★★ 86% HL Deans Place, Seaford Road, ALFRISTON
☎ 01323 870248 📠 01323 870918 36 en suite

TICEHURST
Map 5 TQ63

Dale Hill Hotel & Golf Club TN5 7DQ
☎ 01580 200112 📠 01580 201249
e-mail: info@dalehill.co.uk
web: www.dalehill.co.uk

Dale Hill is set in over 350 acres, high on the Weald in an Area of Outstanding Natural Beauty. Offering two 18-hole courses, one of which has been designed by Ian Woosnam to USGA specifications.

Dale Hill: 18 Holes, 5856yds, Par 69, SSS 69,
Course record 65.
Ian Woosnam: 18 Holes, 6512yds, Par 71, SSS 71,
Course record 64. Club membership 850.

Visitors Mon-Sun & BHs. Dress code. **Societies** booking required. **Green Fees** not confirmed **Course Designer** Ian Woosnam **Prof** Mark Wood **Facilities** ⊕ ⊖ 🏌 ⌑ 🥤 ⌑ 🏠 ⚲ ◇ 🛒 ⚘ ⚲ **Leisure** heated indoor swimming pool, sauna, gymnasium **Conf** facs Corporate Hospitality Days **Location** M25 junct 5, A21, B2087 left after 1m
Hotel ★★★★ 81% HL Dale Hill Hotel & Golf Club, TICEHURST
☎ 01580 200112 📠 01580 201249 35 en suite

UCKFIELD
Map 5 TQ42

East Sussex National Golf Resort & Spa see page 247
Little Horsted TN22 5ES
☎ 01825 880088 📠 01825 880066
e-mail: golf@eastsussexnational.co.uk
web: www.eastsussexnational.co.uk

Piltdown Golf Club Piltdown TN22 3XB
☎ 01825 722033 📠 01825 724192
e-mail: info@piltdowngolfclub.co.uk
web: www.piltdowngolfclub.co.uk

A course built on rolling Sussex countryside. The terrain is fairly level but the narrow fairways, small greens and an abundance of heather and gorse make for challenging golf. Easy walking and fine views.

18 Holes, 6076yds, Par 68, SSS 69, Course record 64.
Club membership 400.

Visitors Mon-Sun & BHs. Booking required. Dress code.
Societies booking required. **Green Fees** £55 per day, £40 per round, £35 after 1.30pm, £20 after 4pm **Prof** Jason Partridge **Facilities** ⊕ ⊖ 🏌 ⌑ 🥤 ⌑ 🏠 ⚘ 🛒 ⚘ ⚲ **Conf** facs Corporate Hospitality Days **Location** 2m W of Uckfield off A272, club signed
Hotel ★★★ HL Horsted Place, Little Horsted, UCKFIELD
☎ 01825 750581 📠 01825 750459 20 en suite

ANGMERING
Map 4 TQ00

Ham Manor Golf Club West Dr BN16 4JE
☎ 01903 783288 📠 01903 850886
e-mail: secretary@hammanor.co.uk
web: www.hammanor.co.uk

Two miles from the sea, this parkland course has fine springy turf and provides an interesting test in two loops of nine holes each.

18 Holes, 6230yds, Par 70, SSS 70.
Club membership 780.

Visitors Mon-Sun & BHs. Handicap certificate. Dress code.
Societies booking required. **Green Fees** £35 (£50 weekends) **Course Designer** Harry Colt **Prof** Simon Buckley **Facilities** ⊕ ⊖ 🏌 ⌑ 🥤 ⌑ 🏠 ⚘ 🛒 ⚘ **Conf** facs Corporate Hospitality Days **Location** off A259
Hotel ★★★★★ GA Angmering Manor, High Street, ANGMERING
☎ 01903 859849 📠 01903 783268 17 rooms

ARUNDEL
Map 4 TQ00

Avisford Park Golf Course Yapton Ln BN18 0LS
☎ 01243 554611 📠 01243 555580
18 Holes, 5703yds, Par 68, SSS 66.
Location off A27 towards Yapton
Telephone for further details
Hotel ★★★ 74% HL Norfolk Arms, High Street, ARUNDEL
☎ 01903 882101 📠 01903 884275 33 en suite

Save on Hotels. Book at **theAA.com/hotel**

SUSSEX, WEST

BOGNOR REGIS

Map 4 SZ99

Bognor Regis Golf Club Downview Rd, Felpham
PO22 8JD
☎ 01243 821929 (Secretary) 📄 01243 860719
e-mail: sec@bognorgolfclub.co.uk
web: www.bognorgolfclub.co.uk

This flattish, well tree-lined, parkland course has more variety than is to be found on some other south coast courses. The course is open to the prevailing wind and the River Rife and many water ditches need negotiation.

18 Holes, 6121yds, Par 70, SSS 69, Course record 62.
Club membership 500.

Visitors Mon, Tue pm, Wed-Sun & BHs. Booking required. Dress code. **Societies** booking required. **Green Fees** £30. Twilight after 4pm £15 **Course Designer** James Braid **Prof** Matthew Kirby **Facilities** ⓣ ⓣⓄ ⓛ ▽ ⓟ ⌲ 🏠 🍴 🍺 🏌 **Conf** facs Corporate Hospitality Days **Location** 0.5m N at Felpham lights on A259

Hotel ★★★ 71% HL Best Western Beachcroft Hotel, Clyde Road, Felpham Village, BOGNOR REGIS ☎ 01243 827142 📄 01243 863500 35 en suite

BURGESS HILL

Map 4 TQ31

Burgess Hill Golf Course, Cuckfield Rd RH15 8RE
☎ 01444 258585 📄 01444 247318
e-mail: enquiries@burgesshillgolfcentre.co.uk
web: www.burgesshillgolfcentre.co.uk

Very challenging nine-hole course. Gently undulating layout with trees and water. Used for PGA short course championships

9 Holes, 1280yds, Par 27, Course record 22.

Visitors Mon-Sun & BHs. **Societies** welcome. **Green Fees** £10 per 9 holes **Course Designer** Donald Steel **Prof** Mark Collins **Facilities** ⓣ ⓣⓄ ⓛ ▽ ⓟ ⌲ 🏠 🍴 🍺 🏌 **Leisure** pitching & chipping green **Conf** facs Corporate Hospitality Days **Location** N of town on B2036

Hotel ★★★ 78% CHH Hickstead, Jobs Lane, Bolney, HICKSTEAD ☎ 01444 248023 📄 01444 245280 52 en suite

CHICHESTER

Map 4 SU80

Chichester Golf Club Hunston Village PO20 1AX
☎ 01243 533833 📄 01243 539922
web: www.chichestergolf.co.uk

Tower Course: 18 Holes, 6175yds, Par 72, SSS 69,
Course record 67.
Cathedral Course: 18 Holes, 6461yds, Par 72, SSS 71,
Course record 65.

Course Designer Philip Saunders **Location** 3m S of Chichester on B2145

Telephone for further details
Hotel ★★★ 81% HL Crouchers Country Hotel & Restaurant, Birdham Road, CHICHESTER ☎ 01243 784995 📄 01243 539797 26 en suite

COPTHORNE

Map 5 TQ33

Copthorne Golf Club Borers Arms Rd RH10 3LL
☎ 01342 712033 & 712508 📄 01342 717682
e-mail: info@copthornegolfclub.co.uk
web: www.copthornegolfclub.co.uk

Despite it having been in existence since 1892, this club remains one of the lesser known Sussex courses. It is hard to know why because it is most attractive with plenty of trees and much variety.

18 Holes, 6435yds, Par 71, SSS 71, Course record 64.
Club membership 550.

Visitors Mon-Sun & BHs. Booking required. Dress code.
Societies welcome. **Green Fees** £40 **Course Designer** James Braid **Prof** Joe Burrell **Facilities** ⓣ ⓣⓄ ⓛ ▽ ⓟ ⌲ 🏠 🍴 🏌 **Conf** Corporate Hospitality Days **Location** M23 junct 10, E of village off A264

Hotel ★★★★ 72% HL Copthorne Hotel London Gatwick, Copthorne Way, COPTHORNE ☎ 01342 348800 & 348888 📄 01342 348833 227 en suite

Effingham Park Golf Club The Copthorne Hotel Effingham Gatwick, West Park Rd RH10 3EU
☎ 01342 716528 📄 0870 8900 215
web: www.effinghamparkgc.co.uk

Parkland course with good green conditions. Water comes into play on five holes.

9 Holes, 1851yds, Par 30, SSS 57. Club membership 230.

Visitors Mon-Sun & BHs. **Societies** welcome. **Green Fees** not confirmed **Course Designer** Francisco Escario **Prof** Mark Root **Facilities** ⓣ ⓣⓄ ⓛ ▽ ⓟ ⌲ 🏠 🍴 ◇ 🏌 **Leisure** hard tennis courts, heated indoor swimming pool, sauna, gymnasium **Conf** facs Corporate Hospitality Days **Location** 2m E on B2028

Hotel ★★★★ 71% HL Copthorne Hotel Effingham Gatwick, West Park Road, COPTHORNE ☎ 01342 714994 📄 01342 716039 122 en suite

CRAWLEY
Map 4 TQ23

Cottesmore Hotel Golf & Country Club Buchan Hill, Pease Pottage RH11 9AT
☎ 01293 528256 📠 01293 522819
e-mail: cottesmore@crown-golf.co.uk
web: www.cottesmoregolf.co.uk

Challenging tree-lined golf course where position off the tee is key. Set in 247 acres of Sussex countryside offering great views of the Sussex Downland.

Griffin: 18 Holes, 6070yds, Par 71, SSS 70, Course record 67.
Phoenix: 18 Holes, 5053yds, Par 68, SSS 65. Club membership 1250.

Visitors Visitors after midday at weekends **Societies** Booking required. **Green Fees** Griffin Course £34 (£40 weekends), Phoenix Course £16 (£20 weekends) per 18 holes **Course Designer** Michael J Rogerson **Prof** Calum J Callan **Facilities** ⊕ ⊙ 🍴 🍺 ☕ 🦐 🏌 🏡 ⛳ ◇ 🛒 ✦ **Leisure** hard tennis courts, heated indoor swimming pool, sauna, gymnasium, Chipping green & bunker **Conf** facs Corporate Hospitality Days **Location** M23 junct 11, through village of Pease Pottage, 2m on right
Hotel ★★★★ HL Alexander House Hotel & Utopia Spa, East Street, TURNERS HILL ☎ 01342 714914 📠 01342 717328 38 en suite

Ifield Golf Club Rusper Rd, Ifield RH11 0LN
☎ 01293 520222 📠 01293 612973
Parkland course.

Ifield: 18 Holes, 6319yds, Par 70, SSS 70, Course record 63. Club membership 750.

Visitors Mon-Fri except BHs. Sun pm. Booking required. Dress code. **Societies** booking required. **Green Fees** £27 per 18 holes **Course Designer** Hawtree & Taylor **Prof** Jonathan Earl **Facilities** ⊕ ⊙ 🍺 ☕ 🦐 🏌 🏡 ✦ 🛒 ✦ **Conf** Corporate Hospitality Days **Location** 1m W side of town centre off A23
Hotel ★★★★ HL Alexander House Hotel & Utopia Spa, East Street, TURNERS HILL ☎ 01342 714914 📠 01342 717328 38 en suite

Tilgate Forest Golf Centre Titmus Dr RH10 5EU
☎ 01293 530103 📠 01293 523478
e-mail: tilgate@glendale-services.co.uk
web: www.glendale-golf.com
Designed by former Ryder Cup players Neil Coles and Brian Huggett, the course has been carefully cut through a silver birch and pine forest. It is possibly one of the most beautiful public courses in the country. The 17th is a treacherous par 5 demanding an uphill third shot to a green surrounded by rhododendrons.

Tilgate Forest: 18 Holes, 6317yds, Par 71, SSS 70, Course record 68. Club membership 200.

Visitors Mon-Sun & BHs. Booking required. Dress code. **Societies** welcome. **Green Fees** £20 per 18 holes (£25 weekends) **Course Designer** Neil Coles/Brian Huggett **Prof** William Easdale **Facilities** ⊕ ⊙ 🍺 ☕ 🦐 🏌 🏡 ⛳ 🛒 ✦ 🏌 **Leisure** par 3 9 hole course **Conf** Corporate Hospitality Days **Location** 2m E of town centre
Hotel ★★★★ HL Alexander House Hotel & Utopia Spa, East Street, TURNERS HILL ☎ 01342 714914 📠 01342 717328 38 en suite

EAST GRINSTEAD
Map 5 TQ33

Chartham Park Golf & Country Club Felcourt Rd, Felcourt RH19 2JT
☎ 01342 870340 & 870008 (pro shop) 📠 01342 870719
e-mail: charthampk.retail@theclubcompany.com
web: www.theclubcompany.com
Mature parkland course surrounded by ancient woodland with fine views across the North Downs. The course features an abundance of mature trees, carp filled lakes and several heathland holes on the back nine. The course has buggy paths and the latest draining features.

18 Holes, 6680yards, Par 72, SSS 72, Course record 64. Club membership 740.

Visitors Mon-Sun & BHs. Booking required **Societies** welcome. **Green Fees** not confirmed **Course Designer** Neil Coles **Prof** David Hobbs **Facilities** ⊕ ⊙ 🍺 ☕ 🦐 🏌 🏡 ⛳ ✦ 🛒 ✦ 🏌 **Leisure** sauna, gymnasium **Conf** Corporate Hospitality Days **Location** 2m N from town centre towards Felcourt, on right
Hotel ★★★★ 86% HL Felbridge Hotel & Spa, London Road, EAST GRINSTEAD ☎ 01342 337700 📠 01342 337715 120 en suite

HASSOCKS
Map 4 TQ31

Hassocks Golf Club London Rd BN6 9NA
☎ 01273 846630 & 846990 📠 01273 846070
e-mail: hassocksgolfclub@btconnect.com
web: www.hassocksgolfclub.co.uk
Set against the backdrop of the South Downs, Hassocks is a course designed and contoured to blend naturally with the surrounding countryside and appealing to golfers of all ages and abilities.

18 Holes, 5703yds, Par 70, SSS 68, Course record 65. Club membership 400.

Visitors Mon-Sun & BHs. Booking required. Dress code. **Societies** booking required. **Green Fees** £17.50 per 18 holes (£22.50 weekends & BHs) **Course Designer** Paul Wright **Prof** Mike Ovett **Facilities** ⊕ ⊙ 🍺 ☕ 🦐 🏌 🏡 ⛳ ✦ 🛒 ✦ 🏌 **Conf** facs Corporate Hospitality Days **Location** on A273 between Burgess Hill and Hassocks
Hotel ★★★ 78% CHH Hickstead, Jobs Lane, Bolney, HICKSTEAD ☎ 01444 248023 📠 01444 245280 52 en suite

HAYWARDS HEATH   Map 5 TQ32

Haywards Heath Golf Club High Beech Ln RH16 1SL
☎ 01444 414457 ᐧ 01444 458319
e-mail: info@haywardsheathgolfclub.co.uk
web: www.haywardsheathgolfclub.co.uk
Pleasant undulating parkland course with easy walking. Several
challenging par 4s and 3s - a test for high and low handicap golfers.
*18 Holes, 6216yds, Par 71, SSS 70, Course record 65.
Club membership 770.*
Visitors Mon-Fri except BHs. Dress code. **Societies** booking required.
Green Fees £32 per 18 holes **Course Designer** James Braid
Prof Michael Henning **Facilities** ⑪ ⍾ ᐧ ☐ ⍾ ⏁ ☖ ⌕ ⌀
ᐟ **Conf** Corporate Hospitality Days **Location** 1.25m N of Haywards
Heath off B2028
Hotel ★★★ 74% HL Best Western The Birch Hotel, Lewes Road,
HAYWARDS HEATH ☎ 01444 451565 ᐧ 01444 440109 51 en suite

Lindfield Golf Club East Mascalls Ln, Lindfield RH16 2QN
☎ 01444 484467 ᐧ 01444 482709
e-mail: info@thegolfcollege.com
web: www.thegolfcollege.com
A downland course in two loops of nine in an Area of Outstanding
Natural Beauty. Home to the Golf College which provides 'A' level
education to talented young golfers.
*18 Holes, 5957yds, Par 70, SSS 68, Course record 63.
Club membership 240.*
Visitors Mon-Sun & BHs. Booking required. Dress code
Societies welcome. **Green Fees** £15 **Course Designer** P Tallack
Prof Paul Lyons **Facilities** ⑪ ⍾ ᐧ ☐ ⍾ ⏁ ☖ ⌕ ⊟
⌀ ᐟ **Conf** facs Corporate Hospitality Days **Location** 2m NE of
Haywards Heath, E of Lindfield off B2011
Hotel ★★★ 74% HL Best Western The Birch Hotel, Lewes Road,
HAYWARDS HEATH ☎ 01444 451565 ᐧ 01444 440109 51 en suite

HORSHAM   Map 4 TQ13

See Slinfold

Horsham Golf & Fitness Worthing Rd RH13 7AX
☎ 01403 271525 ᐧ 01403 274528
web: www.horshamgolfandfitness.co.uk
9 Holes, 4122yds, Par 33, SSS 30, Course record 55.
Location A24 rdbt onto B2237, by garage
Telephone for further details
Hotel ★★★★★ 87% CHH South Lodge Hotel, Brighton Road,
LOWER BEEDING ☎ 01403 891711 ᐧ 01403 891766 89 en suite

HURSTPIERPOINT   Map 4 TQ21

Singing Hills Golf Course Muddleswood Rd, Albourne
BN6 9EB
☎ 01273 835353 ᐧ 01273 835444
e-mail: info@singinghills.co.uk
web: www.singinghills.co.uk
Three distinct nines (Lake, River and Valley) can be combined to make
a truly varied game. Gently undulating fairways and spectacular
waterholes make Singing Hills a test of accurate shot making. The
opening two holes of the River nine have long drives, while the
second hole on the Lake course is an island green where the tee
is also protected by two bunkers. The Valley course demands long,
accurate tee shots. The water hazards are picturesque and harbour an
abundance of wildlife and golf balls.
*Lake: 9 Holes, 3200yds, Par 35.
River: 9 Holes, 2861yds, Par 35.
Valley: 9 Holes, 3362yds, Par 36. Club membership 496.*
Visitors Mon-Sun & BHs. Booking required. **Societies** booking
required. **Green Fees** not confirmed **Course Designer** M R M Sandow
Prof Wallace Street **Facilities** ⑪ ⍾ ᐧ ☐ ⍾ ⏁ ☖ ⌕ ⌀
ᐟ **Conf** facs Corporate Hospitality Days **Location** A23 onto B2117
Hotel ★★★ 78% CHH Hickstead, Jobs Lane, Bolney, HICKSTEAD
☎ 01444 248023 ᐧ 01444 245280 52 en suite

LITTLEHAMPTON   Map 4 TQ00

Littlehampton Golf Club 170 Rope Walk, Riverside West
BN17 5DL
☎ 01903 717170 ᐧ 01903 726629
e-mail: lgc@talk21.com
web: www.littlehamptongolf.co.uk

A delightful seaside links in an equally delightful setting - and the
only links course in the area.
*18 Holes, 6226yds, Par 70, SSS 68, Course record 61.
Club membership 600.*
Visitors Mon-Fri. Weekends pm. BHs on application. Handicap
certificate. Dress code. **Societies** booking required. **Green Fees** not
confirmed **Course Designer** Hawtree & J H Taylor Ltd **Prof** Stuart
Fallow **Facilities** ⑪ ⍾ ᐧ ☐ ⍾ ⏁ ☖ ⌕ ⊟ ⌀ **Conf** facs
Corporate Hospitality Days **Location** 1m W off A259
Hotel ★★★ HL Bailiffscourt Hotel & Spa, Climping Street,
CLIMPING ☎ 01903 723511 ᐧ 01903 723107 39 en suite

LOWER BEEDING   Map 4 TQ22

Mannings Heath Hotel, Winterpit Ln RH13 6LY
☎ 01403 891191 ᐧ 01403 891499
e-mail: info@manningsheathhotel.com
web: www.manningsheathhotel.com
A nine-hole, 18-tee course with three par 4s set in glorious
countryside.
9 Holes, 3335yds, Par 60. Club membership 150.
Visitors Mon-Sun & BHs. **Societies** welcome. **Green Fees** not
confirmed **Prof** Terry Betts **Facilities** ⑪ ⍾ ᐧ ☐ ⍾ ⌕ ◇
Leisure fishing **Conf** facs Corporate Hospitality Days **Location** off
A281 S of Horsham
Hotel ★★★★★ 87% CHH South Lodge Hotel, Brighton Road,
LOWER BEEDING ☎ 01403 891711 ᐧ 01403 891766 89 en suite

MANNINGS HEATH
Map 4 TQ22

Mannings Heath Golf Club Fullers, Hammerpond Rd RH13 6PG
☎ 01403 210228 🖷 01403 270974
e-mail: enquiries@manningsheath.com
web: www.exclusivehotels.co.uk

The Waterfall course is set amid acres of mature deciduous woodland and streams with patchwork fairways. Due to its location on the rolling Sussex Downs, the course is a hybrid mix of heathland, downland and parkland and provides golfers with an exciting and entertaining course holding the interest of the golfer all the way round. May only be played by members and their guests but is available for corporate golf days. The Kingfisher course, with breathtaking views, may be played by visitors and is suitable for all levels of golfer.

Waterfall: 18 Holes, 6683yds, Par 72, SSS 72.
Kingfisher: 18 Holes, 6217yds, Par 70, SSS 70.
Club membership 600.

Visitors Mon-Sun & BHs - Kingfisher course only. Booking required. Dress code. **Societies** booking required. **Green Fees** Kingfisher from £18 **Course Designer** David Williams/Harry Colt **Prof** Neil Darnell **Facilities** ⊕ ⊩○⊩ ⅃⊩ ⊑ ⊮⅃ ⌿⊥ ⌒ ⊓ ⌷ ◇ ⏚ ⌖ ⌀ ⌶ **Leisure** hard tennis courts, fishing, sauna, chipping practice area, driving range open to public **Conf** facs Corporate Hospitality Days **Location** off A281 on N side of village
Hotel ★★★★★ 87% CHH South Lodge Hotel, Brighton Road, LOWER BEEDING ☎ 01403 891711 🖷 01403 891766   89 en suite

MIDHURST
Map 4 SU82

Cowdray Park Golf Club Petworth Rd GU29 0BB
☎ 01730 813599 🖷 01730 815900
web: www.cowdraygolf.co.uk

18 Holes, 6265yds, Par 70, SSS 70, Course record 65.
Course Designer Jack White **Location** 1m E of Midhurst on A272 **Telephone for further details**
Hotel ★★★ 81% HL Spread Eagle Hotel and Spa, South Street, MIDHURST ☎ 01730 816911 🖷 01730 815668   38 en suite

PULBOROUGH
Map 4 TQ01

West Sussex Golf Club Golf Club Ln, Wiggonholt RH20 2EN
☎ 01798 872563 🖷 01798 872033
e-mail: secretary@westsussexgolf.co.uk
web: www.westsussexgolf.co.uk

An outstanding beautiful heathland course occupying an oasis of sand, heather and pine in the middle of attractive countryside.

18 Holes, 6264yds, Par 68, SSS 70, Course record 61.
Club membership 850.

Visitors Mon-Thu, weekends & BHs. Booking required. Handicap certificate. Dress code. **Societies** booking required. **Green Fees** not confirmed 😊 **Course Designer** Campbell/Hutcheson/Hotchkin **Prof** Tim Packham **Facilities** ⊕ ⅃⊩ ⊑ ⊮⅃ ⌿⊥ ⌒ ⊓ ⌷ ⌀ ⌶ **Location** 1.5m E of Pulborough off A283
Hotel ★★★★ BB Woody Banks Cottage, Crossgates, AMBERLEY ☎ 01798 831295 & 07719 916703   2 rooms (2 pri facs)

PYECOMBE
Map 4 TQ21

Pyecombe Golf Club Clayton Hill BN45 7FF
☎ 01273 845372 🖷 01273 843338
e-mail: office@pyecombegolf.co.uk
web: www.pyecombegolfclub.com

Typical downland course on the inland side of the South Downs with panoramic views of the Weald.

18 Holes, 6266yds, Par 71, SSS 70, Course record 65.
Club membership 525.

Visitors Mon-Fri. Restricted weekends & BHs. Dress code. **Societies** booking required. **Green Fees** £25 per round, £30 per day (weekends £33/£38) **Course Designer** James Braid **Prof** J Bowen **Facilities** ⊕ by prior arrangement ⊩○⊩ by prior arrangement ⅃⊩ ⊑ ⊮⅃ ⌿⊥ ⌒ ⊓ ⌷ ⌀ **Location** E of village on A273
Hotel ★★★ 64% HL The Courtlands Hotel & Conference Centre, 15-27 The Drive, HOVE ☎ 01273 731055 🖷 01273 328295   67 en suite

SELSEY
Map 4 SZ89

Selsey Golf Club Golf Links Ln PO20 9DR
☎ 01243 608935 🖷 01243 607101
e-mail: secretary@selseygolfclub.co.uk
web: www.selseygolfclub.co.uk

Fairly difficult links type seaside course, exposed to wind and has natural ditches.

18 Holes, 5833yds, Par 68, SSS 68, Course record 62.
Club membership 300.

Visitors Mon-Sun & BHs. Booking required. **Societies** booking required. **Green Fees** not confirmed **Course Designer** J H Taylor **Prof** Peter Grindley **Facilities** ⊕ ⊩○⊩ ⅃⊩ ⊑ ⊮⅃ ⌿⊥ ⌒ ⌀ **Leisure** hard tennis courts **Location** 1m N off B2145
Hotel ★★★ 81% HL Crouchers Country Hotel & Restaurant, Birdham Road, CHICHESTER ☎ 01243 784995 🖷 01243 539797   26 en suite

SLINFOLD
Map 4 TQ13

Slinfold Golf & Country Club Stane St RH13 0RE
☎ 01403 791154 🖷 01403 791465
e-mail: web.slinfold@ccgclubs.com
web: www.ccgslinfold.com

Slinfold course enjoys splendid views among mature trees. The 10th tee is spectacularly located on the centre of one of the two large landscaped lakes. The 166-yard 16th has water running in front of the tee and everything sloping towards it!

Main Course: 18 Holes, 6424yds, Par 72, SSS 71, Course record 65.
Academy Course: 9 Holes, 1315yds, Par 28.
Club membership 750.

Visitors Mon-Sun & BHs. Booking required. Dress code. **Societies** booking required. **Green Fees** not confirmed **Course Designer** John Fortune **Prof** Ryan Fenwick **Facilities** ⊕ ⊩○⊩ ⅃⊩ ⊑ ⊮⅃ ⌿⊥ ⌒ ⊓ ⌷ ⌀ ⌶ **Leisure** heated indoor swimming pool, gymnasium **Conf** facs Corporate Hospitality Days **Location** 4m W of Horsham on A29
Hotel ★★★ 80% HL Gatton Manor Hotel & Golf Club, Standon Lane, OCKLEY ☎ 01306 627555 🖷 01306 627713   18 en suite

VEST CHILTINGTON Map 4 TQ01

Vest Chiltington Golf Club Broadford Bridge Rd
H20 2YA
☎ 01798 812115 (bookings) & 813574
📠 01798 812631
veb: www.westchiltgolf.co.uk
Vindmill: 18 Holes, 5967yds, Par 70, SSS 69,
ourse record 66.
ourse Designer Brian Barnes **Location** N of village
elephone for further details
otel ★★★★ BB Woody Banks Cottage, Crossgates, AMBERLEY
☎ 01798 831295 & 07719 916703 2 rooms (0 en suite)

VORTHING Map 4 TQ10

Hill Barn Golf Club Hill Barn Ln BN14 9QF
☎ 01903 237301 📠 01903 217613
-mail: info@hillbarngolf.com
veb: www.hillbarngolf.com
ownland course with views of both Isle of Wight and Brighton.
8 Holes, 6229yds, Par 70, SSS 70, Course record 63.
lub membership 500.
isitors Mon-Sun & BHs. Booking required. Dress code. **ocieties** booking required. **Green Fees** not confirmed **Course esigner** Fred Hawtree **Facilities** 🍴 🍽 by prior arrangement 🫖 ☕ 🍷 🧥 🏪 ⛳ 🚗 🛒 **Leisure** croquet **Conf** facs Corporate ospitality Days **Location** signposted from Grove Lodge roundabout by orwich Union on A27
otel ★★★ 70% HL Findon Manor Hotel, High Street, Findon, VORTHING ☎ 01903 872733 📠 01903 877473 11 en suite

Worthing Golf Club Links Rd BN14 9QZ
☎ 01903 260801 📠 01903 694664
e-mail: enquiries@worthinggolf.com
web: www.worthinggolf.co.uk
The Lower Course is considered to be one of the best Downland courses with its undulating greens. The Upper Course is shorter but compensates with tricky approaches to the greens and fine views of the English Channel.
Lower Course: 18 Holes, 6505yds, Par 71, SSS 72.
Upper Course: 18 Holes, 5211yds, Par 66, SSS 65.
Club membership 1200.
Visitors Mon-Sun except BHs. Dress code. **Societies** booking required. **Green Fees** Lower Course £35 per round, Upper Course £30 per round, both courses £50 (weekends £50/£40/£55) **Course Designer** H S Colt **Prof** Stephen Rolley **Facilities** 🍴 🫖 ☕ 🍷 🧥 🏪 ⛳ 🚗 🛒 🏌 **Conf** facs Corporate Hospitality Days **Location** N of town centre off A27 & close to end of A24
Hotel ★★★ 80% HL Ardington Hotel, Steyne Gardens, WORTHING ☎ 01903 230451 📠 01903 526526 45 en suite

TYNE & WEAR

BIRTLEY Map 12 NZ25

Birtley Golf Club Birtley Ln DH3 2LR
☎ 0191 410 2207
e-mail: birtleygolfclub@aol.com
web: www.birtleyportobellogolfclub.co.uk
A nine-hole parkland course. Good test of golf with challenging par 3 and par 4 holes.
9 Holes, 5729yds, Par 67, SSS 67, Course record 63.
Club membership 350.
Visitors contact club for details. **Societies** booking required. **Green Fees** £15 per 18 holes 🚫 **Facilities** ☕ 🍷 🧥 **Location**
Hotel ★★★ 75% HL Holiday Inn Washington, Emerson District 5, WASHINGTON ☎ 0871 942 9084 📠 0191 415 3371 136 en suite

BOLDON Map 12 NZ36

Boldon Golf Club Dipe Ln, East Boldon NE36 0PQ
☎ 0191 536 5360 📠 0191 537 2270
e-mail: info@boldongolfclub.co.uk
web: www.boldongolfclub.co.uk
Parkland links course, easy walking, distant sea views.
18 Holes, 6414yds, Par 72, SSS 71, Course record 65.
Club membership 700.
Visitors Mon-Sun & BHs. Booking required weekends & BHs. Dress code. **Societies** welcome. **Green Fees** £24 per day (£27 weekends & BHs) 🚫 **Course Designer** Harry Vardon **Facilities** 🍴 🍽 🫖 ☕ 🍷 🧥 🏪 ⛳ 🛒 🚗 🛒 🏌 **Leisure** snooker **Conf** facs Corporate Hospitality Days **Location** 1m from A19, 3m S of Tyne Tunnel
Hotel ★★★★ 73% HL Sunderland Marriott, Queen's Parade, Seaburn, SUNDERLAND ☎ 0191 529 2041 📠 0191 529 4227 82 en suite

CHOPWELL Map 12 NZ15

Garesfield Golf Club NE17 7AP
☎ 01207 561309 📠 01207 561309
e-mail: garesfieldgc@btconnect.com
web: www.garesfieldgolfclub.co.uk
The course winds its way through the mature trees which form a natural, tranquil and beautiful setting. All the holes have their own individual challenge and there are fine views of the surrounding countryside.
18 Holes, 6458yds, Par 72, SSS 71. Club membership 400.
Visitors Booking required weekends & BHs. **Societies** booking required. **Green Fees** £20 per 18 holes (£25 weekends) 🚫 **Course Designer** Harry Fernie **Facilities** 🍴 🍽 🫖 ☕ 🍷 🧥 🏪 🚗 **Conf** Corporate Hospitality Days **Location** off B6315 in High Spen at Bute Arms for Chopwell
Hotel ★★★★ 74% HL Close House, HEDDON-ON-THE-WALL ☎ 01661 852255 📠 01661 853322 31 en suite

FELLING
Map 12 NZ26

Heworth Golf Club Gingling Gate, Heworth NE10 8XY
☎ 0191 469 9832 🖹 0191 469 9898
e-mail: secretary@theheworthgolfclub.co.uk
web: www.theheworthgolfclub.co.uk
Fairly flat parkland.

18 Holes, 6180yds, Par 71, SSS 69, Course record 64.
Club membership 800.

Visitors Mon-Fri & BHs. Booking required Tue, Thu & Fri. Dress code
Societies booking required. **Green Fees** £25 per day **Prof** Adrian
Marshall **Facilities** ⓣ ⦿ ⓛ ⛛ ⓣ ⓛ ⓗ ⓛ ⓗ ⓛ
Conf facs Corporate Hospitality Days **Location** on A195, 0.5m NW of
junc with A1(M)
Hotel ★★★ 81% HL Mercure Newcastle George Washington Hotel,
Stone Cellar Road, High Usworth, WASHINGTON ☎ 0191 402 9988
🖹 0191 415 1166 103 en suite

GATESHEAD
Map 12 NZ26

Ravensworth Golf Club Angel View, Longbank, Wrekenton
NE9 7NE
☎ 0191 487 6014 🖹 0191 487 6014
e-mail: secretary@ravensworthgolfclub.co.uk
web: www.ravensworthgolfclub.co.uk
Moorland and parkland 600ft above sea level with fine views,
overlooking the Angel of the North. Testing 5th and 7th holes (par 3s).

18 Holes, 5874yds, Par 70, SSS 70, Course record 63.
Club membership 700.

Visitors Mon-Sun & BHs. Booking required Tue & Thu-Sun.
Societies booking required. **Green Fees** £25 per 36 holes, £15 per
18 holes (£25 per 18 holes weekends & BHs) **Course Designer** J W
Fraser **Facilities** ⓣ ⦿ ⓛ ⛛ ⓛ ⓗ **Conf** Corporate
Hospitality Days **Location** leave A1(M) at junct for A167 (Angel of the
North) take A1295 for 300 yds
Hotel ★★★ 79% HL Eslington Villa Hotel, 8 Station Road, Low
Fell, GATESHEAD ☎ 0191 487 6017 & 420 0666 🖹 0191 420 0667
17 en suite

GOSFORTH
Map 12 NZ26

Gosforth Golf Club Broadway East NE3 5ER
☎ 0191 285 3495 🖹 0191 284 6274
e-mail: gosforth.golf@virgin.net
web: www.gosforthgolfclub.com
Easy walking parkland with natural water hazards.

18 Holes, 6031yds, Par 69, SSS 69, Course record 62.
Club membership 500.

Visitors Mon-Sun & BHs. Booking required. Handicap certificate. Dress
code. **Societies** booking required. **Green Fees** £30 per day, £25 per
round (£32/£28 weekends) **Prof** G Garland **Facilities** ⓣ ⦿ ⓛ ⛛
ⓣ ⓛ ⓗ ⓛ **Conf** Corporate Hospitality Days **Location** N of town
centre off A6125
Hotel ★★★★ 78% HL Newcastle Marriott Hotel Gosforth
Park, High Gosforth Park, Gosforth, NEWCASTLE UPON TYNE
☎ 0191 236 4111 🖹 0191 236 8192 178 en suite

HOUGHTON-LE-SPRING
Map 12 NZ34

Elemore Golf Course Elemore Ln DH5 0QB
☎ 0191 517 3061 🖹 0191 517 3054
18 Holes, 6003yds, Par 69, Course record 68.
Course Designer J Gaunt **Location** 4m S of Houghton-le-Spring on
A182
Telephone for further details
Hotel ★★ 76% HL Chilton Country Pub & Hotel, Black Boy Road,
Chilton Moor, Fencehouses, HOUGHTON-LE-SPRING ☎ 0191 385 269◄
🖹 0191 385 6762 25 en suite

Houghton-le-Spring Golf Club Copt Hill DH5 8LU
☎ 0191 584 7421
e-mail: houghton.golf@virgin.net
web: www.houghtongolfclub.co.uk
Hilly, downland course with natural slope hazards and excellent
greens.

18 Holes, 6101yds, Par 72, SSS 71. Club membership 680.
Visitors Mon-Sat & BHs. Booking required. Dress code.
Societies booking required **Green Fees** not confirmed **Prof** Graeme
Robinson **Facilities** ⓣ ⦿ ⓛ ⛛ ⓣ ⓛ ⓗ ⓛ ⓗ
Conf facs Corporate Hospitality Days **Location** 0.5m E on B1404
Hotel ★★ 76% HL Chilton Country Pub & Hotel, Black Boy Road,
Chilton Moor, Fencehouses, HOUGHTON-LE-SPRING ☎ 0191 385 269◄
🖹 0191 385 6762 25 en suite

NEWCASTLE UPON TYNE
Map 12 NZ26

City of Newcastle Golf Club Three Mile Bridge NE3 2DR
☎ 0191 285 1775
e-mail: info@cityofnewcastlegolfclub.com
web: www.cityofnewcastlegolfclub.com
A well-manicured woodland course in the Newcastle suburbs.

18 Holes, 6523yds, Par 72, SSS 71, Course record 63.
Club membership 600.

Visitors Contact club for details. **Societies** welcome. **Green Fees** £40
per day, £25 per round **Course Designer** Harry Vardon **Prof** Steve
McKenna **Facilities** ⓣ ⦿ ⓛ ⛛ ⓣ ⓛ ⓗ ⓛ
Conf facs Corporate Hospitality Days **Location** 3m N on B1318
Hotel ★★★ 71% HL The Caledonian Hotel, Newcastle, 64
Osborne Road, Jesmond, NEWCASTLE UPON TYNE ☎ 0191 281 7881
🖹 0191 281 6241 90 en suite

Northumberland Golf Club High Gosforth Park NE3 5HT
☎ 0191 236 2498 🖹 0191 236 2036
e-mail: sec@thengc.co.uk
web: www.thengc.co.uk
Predominantly a level heathland style course, the firm, fast greens
are a particular feature.

Summer Course: 18 Holes, 6680yds, Par 72, SSS 72,
Course record 65. Club membership 580.
Visitors Mon-Sun & BHs. Booking required. Dress code.
Societies booking required. **Green Fees** £60 per day, £50 per
round (£60 per round weekends) ⓦ **Course Designer** Colt/
Braid **Facilities** ⓣ ⦿ ⓛ ⛛ ⓣ ⓛ ⓗ **Conf** Corporate
Hospitality Days **Location** 4m N of city centre off A1
Hotel ★★★★ 78% HL Newcastle Marriott Hotel Gosforth
Park, High Gosforth Park, Gosforth, NEWCASTLE UPON TYNE
☎ 0191 236 4111 🖹 0191 236 8192 178 en suite

Save on Hotels. Book at **theAA.com/hotel**

TYNE & WEAR

Westerhope Golf Club Whorlton Grange, Westerhope NE5 1PP

☎ 0191 286 7636 📠 0191 2146287

e-mail: wgc@btconnect.com

web: www.westerhopegolfclub.com

Attractive, easy walking parkland with tree-lined fairways. Good open views towards the airport.

18 Holes, 6392yds, Par 72, SSS 71, Course record 64. Club membership 750.

Visitors Mon-Sun & BHs. Booking required. Dress code. **Societies** booking required. **Green Fees** £26 per round (£30 per round BHs) **Prof** Michael Nesbit **Facilities** ⊕ †⊘↑ ⓑ ⬜ ⬛↑ ⳺ 📦 ⛳ ⬢ ⬟ **Conf** Corporate Hospitality Days **Location** 4.5m NW of city centre off B6324

Hotel ★★★★ 78% HL Newcastle Marriott Hotel Gosforth Park, High Gosforth Park, Gosforth, NEWCASTLE UPON TYNE ☎ 0191 236 4111 📠 0191 236 8192 178 en suite

RYTON
Map 12 NZ16

Ryton Golf Club Clara Vale NE40 3TD

☎ 0191 413 3253 📠 0191 413 1642

e-mail: secretary@rytongolfclub.co.uk

web: www.rytongolfclub.co.uk

Parkland course set in the heart of the Tyne Valley and bordered by the river. Tight fairways on some holes add to the challenge.

18 Holes, 6031yds, Par 70, SSS 69, Course record 64. Club membership 400.

Visitors Mon-Fri & BHs. Dress code. **Societies** booking required. **Green Fees** £28 per day, £22 per round **Prof** Gary Shipley **Facilities** ⊕ †⊘↑ ⓑ ⬜ ⬛↑ ⳺ **Conf** Corporate Hospitality Days **Location** NW of town centre off A695

Hotel ★★★ 74% HL Gibside, Front Street, WHICKHAM ☎ 0191 488 9292 📠 0191 488 8000 44 en suite

Tyneside Golf Club Westfield Ln NE40 3QE

☎ 0191 413 2742 📠 0191 413 0199

e-mail: secretary.tynesidegolfclub@odysseydsl.co.uk

web: www.tynesidegolfclub.co.uk

Open, part hilly parkland course with a water hazard.

18 Holes, 6103yds, Par 70, SSS 69, Course record 65. Club membership 641.

Visitors Mon-Fri, Sun & BHs. Booking required. Dress code. **Societies** booking required. **Green Fees** £30 per 18 holes (Sun £36) **Course Designer** H S Colt **Prof** Gary Vickers **Facilities** ⊕ †⊘↑ ⓑ ⬜ ⬛↑ ⳺ 📦 ⬛ ⛳ **Conf** Corporate Hospitality Days **Location** NW of town centre off A695

Hotel ★★★ 74% HL Gibside, Front Street, WHICKHAM ☎ 0191 488 9292 📠 0191 488 8000 44 en suite

SOUTH SHIELDS
Map 12 NZ36

South Shields Golf Club Cleadon Hills NE34 8EG

☎ 0191 456 8942 📠 0191 456 8942

e-mail: ssgcsecy@gmail.com

web: www.ssgc.co.uk

A slightly undulating downland course on a limestone base ensuring good conditions underfoot. Open to strong winds, the course is testing but fair. There are fine views of the coastline.

18 Holes, 6174yds, Par 71, SSS 70, Course record 64. Club membership 700.

Visitors Mon-Fri & BHs. Handicap certificate. **Societies** welcome. **Green Fees** not confirmed **Course Designer** McKenzie-Braid **Prof** Glyn Jones **Facilities** ⊕ †⊘↑ ⓑ ⬜ ⬛↑ ⳺ 📦 ⛳ **Conf** facs Corporate Hospitality Days **Location** SE of town centre off A1300

Hotel ★★★ 75% HL Best Western Sea Hotel, Sea Road, SOUTH SHIELDS ☎ 0191 427 0999 📠 0191 454 0500 37 en suite

Whitburn Golf Club Lizard Ln NE34 7AF

☎ 0191 529 4944 (Sec) 📠 0191 529 4944

e-mail: wgcsec@hotmail.com

web: www.golf-whitburn.co.uk

Parkland with sea views. Situated on limestone making it rarely unplayable.

18 Holes, 5899yds, Par 70, SSS 69, Course record 64. Club membership 590.

Visitors Mon-Sat & BHs. Sun in winter. Booking required. Dress code. **Societies** booking required. **Green Fees** £18.50 (£25.50 Sat & BHs, Sat after 2pm £13). Winter £15.50 (weekends & BHs £20.50, Sat after 1pm £10.50). Twilight after 4pm summer £10.50. **Course Designer** Colt, Alison & Morrison **Prof** Neil Whinham **Facilities** ⊕ †⊘↑ ⓑ ⬜ ⳺ 📦 ⛳ ⬛ ⛳ **Leisure** practice net **Conf** Corporate Hospitality Days **Location** 2.5m SE off A183

Hotel ★★★★ 73% HL Sunderland Marriott, Queen's Parade, Seaburn, SUNDERLAND ☎ 0191 529 2041 📠 0191 529 4227 82 en suite

SUNDERLAND
Map 12 NZ35

Wearside Golf Club Coxgreen SR4 9JT

☎ 0191 534 2518 📠 0191 534 6186

e-mail: wearside_golf@yahoo.co.uk

web: www.wearsidegolfclub.co.uk

Open, undulating parkland rolling down to the River Wear beneath the shadow of the famous Penshaw Monument. Built on the lines of a Greek temple it is a well-known landmark. Two ravines cross the course presenting a variety of challenging holes.

18 Holes, 6427yds, Par 72, SSS 71, Course record 64. Club membership 648.

Visitors Mon-Sun & BHs. Handicap certificate. Dress code. **Societies** booking required. **Green Fees** phone ⓔ **Prof** Doug Brolls **Facilities** †⊘↑ ⓑ ⬜ ⬛↑ ⳺ 📦 ⬛ ⛳ **Location** 3.5m W off A183

Hotel ★★★★ 73% HL Sunderland Marriott, Queen's Parade, Seaburn, SUNDERLAND ☎ 0191 529 2041 📠 0191 529 4227 82 en suite

ENGLAND

TYNEMOUTH
Map 12 NZ36

Tynemouth Golf Club Spital Dene NE30 2ER
☎ 0191 257 4578 📄 0191 259 5193
e-mail: secretary@tynemouthgolfclub.com
web: www.tynemouthgolfclub.com
Well-drained parkland course, not physically demanding but providing a strong challenge to both low and high handicap players.
18 Holes, 6343yds, Par 70, SSS 70, Course record 65.
Club membership 850.
Visitors Mon, Wed-Fri except BHs. Tue & Sun pm. Booking required.
Dress code. **Societies** welcome. **Green Fees** £30.50 per day,
£25.50 per 18 holes **Course Designer** Willie Park **Prof** J P McKenna
Facilities ⑪ ⑩ ⑤ ⑤ ⑤ ⑤ ⑤ ⑤ ⑤ ⑤ ✱ **Conf**
Corporate Hospitality Days **Location** 0.5m W
Hotel ★★★ 79% HL Grand, Grand Parade, TYNEMOUTH
☎ 0191 293 6666 📄 0191 293 6665 45 en suite

WALLSEND
Map 12 NZ26

Centurion Park Golf Club Rheydt Av, Bigges Main
NE28 8SU
☎ 0191 262 1973
web: www.centurionparkwallsend.co.uk
Parkland course.
18 Holes, 6031yds, Par 70, SSS 69. Club membership 655.
Visitors Mon-Sun & BHs. Booking required. Dress code.
Societies welcome. **Green Fees** not confirmed ⑭ **Course Designer** A
Snowball **Prof** Craig Fetherston **Facilities** ⑪ ⑩ ⑤ ⑤ ⑤
⑤ ⑤ ✱ 🏌 **Leisure** squash **Conf** Corporate Hospitality Days
Location NW of town centre off A193
Hotel ★★★ 71% HL The Caledonian Hotel, Newcastle, 64
Osborne Road, Jesmond, NEWCASTLE UPON TYNE ☎ 0191 281 7881
📄 0191 281 6241 90 en suite

WASHINGTON
Map 12 NZ25

George Washington Golf & Country Club Stone Cellar Rd,
High Usworth NE37 1PH
☎ 0191 417 8346 📄 0191 415 1166
e-mail: reservations@georgewashington.co.uk
web: www.georgewashington.co.uk
The course is set in 150 acres of rolling parkland. Wide generous fairways and large greens. Trees feature on most holes, penalising the wayward shot.
18 Holes, 6604yds, Par 73, SSS 71. Club membership 550.
Visitors Mon-Sun & BHs. Booking required Fri-Sun & BHs.
Societies booking required. **Green Fees** not confirmed **Course
Designer** Eric Watson **Facilities** ⑪ ⑩ ⑤ ⑤ ⑤ ⑤ ⑤ ⑤
◇ ✱ 🏌 ✱ 🏌 **Leisure** heated indoor swimming pool, sauna,
gymnasium, 9 hole par 3 course, hair & beauty salon **Conf** facs
Corporate Hospitality Days **Location** from A195 signed Washington
North take last exit on rdbt, then right at mini-rdbt
Hotel ★★★ 81% HL Mercure Newcastle George Washington Hotel,
Stone Cellar Road, High Usworth, WASHINGTON ☎ 0191 402 9988
📄 0191 415 1166 103 en suite

WHICKHAM
Map 12 NZ26

Whickham Golf Club Hollinside Park, Fellside Rd
NE16 5BA
☎ 0191 488 1576 📄 0191 488 1577
e-mail: enquiries@whickhamgolfclub.co.uk
web: www.whickhamgolfclub.co.uk
Undulating parkland set on the east bank of the beautiful Derwent Valley with fine views of surrounding countryside. Its undulating fairways and subtly contoured greens create an interesting challenge for players of all abilities.
Nordmann Course: 18 Holes, 6666yds, Par 72, SSS 72.
Club membership 543.
Visitors Mon-Fri, Sun & BHs. Booking required. Dress code.
Societies booking required. **Green Fees** £22 per 18 holes ⑭
Prof Simon Williamson **Facilities** ⑪ ⑩ ⑤ ⑤ ⑤ ⑤ ⑤ ✱
🏌 ✱ **Location** exit A1 for Whickham. Club is 1m from junct off Front
St signed Burnopfield
Hotel ★★★ 74% HL Gibside, Front Street, WHICKHAM
☎ 0191 488 9292 📄 0191 488 8000 44 en suite

WHITLEY BAY
Map 12 NZ37

Whitley Bay Golf Club Claremont Rd NE26 3UF
☎ 0191 252 0180 📄 0191 297 0030
e-mail: whtglfclb@aol.com
web: www.whitleybaygolfclub.co.uk
An 18-hole links type course, close to the sea, with a stream running through the undulating terrain.
18 Holes, 6579yds, Par 71, SSS 71, Course record 66.
Club membership 800.
Visitors contact club for details. **Societies** booking required. **Green
Fees** £30 per round (£35 Sun pm) ⑭ **Prof** Peter Crosby **Facilities** ⑪
⑩ ⑤ ⑤ ⑤ ⑤ ⑤ ⑤ ✱ **Location** NW of town centre off
A1148
Hotel ★★★ 79% HL Grand, Grand Parade, TYNEMOUTH
☎ 0191 293 6666 📄 0191 293 6665 45 en suite

WARWICKSHIRE

ATHERSTONE
Map 4 SP39

Atherstone Golf Club The Outwoods, Coleshill Rd CV9 2RL
☎ 01827 713110 📄 01827 715686
e-mail: agc.golf@btconnect.com
web: www.atherstonegolfclub.com
Scenic parkland course, established in 1894 and laid out on hilly ground. Interesting challenge on every hole.
18 Holes, 6012yds, Par 72, SSS 70. Club membership 450.
Visitors Mon-Fri & BHs. Booking required BHs. **Societies** welcome.
Green Fees not confirmed **Course Designer** Hawtree & Gaunt Mornoch
Facilities ⑪ ⑩ ⑤ ⑤ ⑤ ⑤ ⑤ **Conf** Corporate Hospitality
Days **Location** 0.5m S, A5 onto B4116
Hotel ★★★★ 76% HL Lea Marston Hotel, Haunch Lane, LEA
MARSTON ☎ 01675 470468 📄 01675 470871 88 en suite

COLESHILL   Map 4 SP28

Maxstoke Park Golf Club Castle Ln B46 2RD
☎ 01675 466743   📄 01675 466185
web: www.maxstokeparkgolfclub.com
18 Holes, 6442yds, Par 71, SSS 71, Course record 64.
Location 3m E of Coleshill, off B4114 for Maxstoke
Telephone for further details
Hotel ★★★ 71% CHH Grimstock Country House, Gilson Road,
Gilson, COLESHILL ☎ 01675 462121 📄 01675 467646 44 en suite

HENLEY-IN-ARDEN   Map 4 SP16

Henley Golf & Country Club Birmingham Rd B95 5QA
☎ 01564 793715   📄 01564 795754
e-mail: enquiries@henleygcc.co.uk
web: www.henleygcc.co.uk
Attractive course in peaceful rural location which can be played off 4
different tee positions allowing golfers to play the course at varying
length to suit different playing and physical abilities.
18 Holes, 6893yds, Par 73, SSS 73, Course record 65.
Club membership 500.
Visitors Mon-Sun & BHs. Booking required. Dress code.
Societies booking required. **Green Fees** £30 (£40 weekends). 2-4-1
vouchers accepted **Course Designer** N Selwyn Smith **Prof** Neale
Hyde **Facilities** ⊕ �🍴 📙 ♿ 🏌 👤 🍴 🏌
Leisure hard tennis courts, 9 hole par 3 course, beauty salon
Conf facs Corporate Hospitality Days **Location** on A3400 just N of
Henley-in-Arden
Hotel ★★★★ 77% HL Ardencote Manor Hotel, Country
Club & Spa, The Cumsey, Lye Green Road, Claverdon, WARWICK
☎ 01926 843111 📄 01926 842646 110 en suite

KENILWORTH   Map 4 SP27

Kenilworth Golf Club Crewe Ln CV8 2EA
☎ 01926 858517   📄 01926 864453
e-mail: secretary@kenilworthgolfclub.co.uk
web: www.kenilworthgolfclub.co.uk
A mature parkland course with tree-lined fairways that provide a
tough but fair test of golf for all standards of golfer. The course is
centrally located close to the M6, M40, A45 and M1 and is an ideal
venue for a corporate golf day or a conference. Club founded in 1889.
18 Holes, 6308yds, Par 71, SSS 71, Course record 64.
Club membership 755.
Visitors Mon-Sun & BHs. Booking required weekends & BHs.
Societies booking required. **Green Fees** £40 per day **Course
Designer** Hawtree **Prof** Steve Yates **Facilities** ⊕ �🍴 📙 ♿ 🏌
👤 🍴 🏌 🏌 🏌 **Leisure** par 3 chipping green **Conf** facs
Corporate Hospitality Days **Location** 0.5m NE
Hotel ★★★ 78% HL Best Western Peacock Hotel, 149 Warwick
Road, KENILWORTH ☎ 01926 851156 & 864500 📄 01926 864644
29 en suite

LEA MARSTON   Map 4 SP29

Lea Marston Hotel Haunch Ln B76 0BY
☎ 01675 470468   📄 01675 470871
e-mail: info@leamarstonhotel.co.uk
web: www.leamarstonhotel.co.uk
The Marston Lakes course was opened in April 2001. The layout
includes many water and sand hazards through undulating parkland.
While short by modern standards, it is a good test for even low
handicap players, requiring virtually everything in the bag. Tees and
greens have been built to championship course specifications.
Marston Lakes: 9 Holes, 2059yds, Par 31, SSS 30,
Course record 57. Club membership 330.
Visitors Mon-Sun & BHs. Booking required. Dress code.
Societies booking required. **Green Fees** £14 per 18 holes, £9 per 9
holes (£18/£12 weekends) **Course Designer** Contour Golf **Prof** Darren
Lewis **Facilities** ⊕ �🍴 📙 ♿ 🏌 👤 🍴 🏌 ◇ 🏌 🏌
🏌 **Leisure** hard tennis courts, heated indoor swimming pool, sauna,
gymnasium, 9 hole par 3 academy course, golf simulator, golf lessons,
spa **Conf** facs Corporate Hospitality Days **Location** M42 junct 9, A4097
towards Kingsbury, 1m right
Hotel ★★★★ 76% HL Lea Marston Hotel, Haunch Lane, LEA
MARSTON ☎ 01675 470468 📄 01675 470871 88 en suite

LEAMINGTON SPA   Map 4 SP36

Leamington & County Golf Club Golf Ln, Whitnash
CV31 2QA
☎ 01926 425961
e-mail: office@leamingtongolf.co.uk
web: www.leamingtongolf.co.uk
Undulating parkland with extensive views.
18 Holes, 6418yds, Par 72, SSS 71, Course record 63.
Club membership 854.
Visitors Mon-Sun except BHs. Dress code. **Societies** booking required.
Green Fees not confirmed **Course Designer** H S Colt **Prof** Julian
Mellor **Facilities** ⊕ �🍴 📙 ♿ 🏌 👤 🍴 🏌 🏌
Leisure snooker. **Conf** facs Corporate Hospitality Days **Location** S of
town centre
Hotel ★★★ HL Mallory Court, Harbury Lane, Bishop's Tachbrook,
LEAMINGTON SPA ☎ 01926 330214 📄 01926 451714 30 en suite

Newbold Comyn Golf Club Newbold Terrace East
CV32 4EW
☎ 01926 421157
e-mail: ian@viscount5.freeserve.co.uk
Parkland course with a hilly front nine and little room for error. A
downhill par 3 of 107 yards is the signature hole here and the par 4
9th which is a 467yd testing hole. The back nine is rather flat and
slightly more forgiving but includes two par 5s.
18 Holes, 6315yds, Par 70, SSS 70, Course record 67.
Club membership 150.
Visitors Mon-Sun & BHs. Booking required. **Societies** welcome. **Green
Fees** not confirmed **Facilities** ⊕ �🍴 📙 ♿ 🏌 👤 🍴 🏌
🏌 **Leisure** heated indoor swimming pool, gymnasium **Location** 0.75m
E of town centre off B4099
Hotel ★★★ 77% HL Angel Hotel, 143 Regent Street, ROYAL
LEAMINGTON SPA ☎ 01926 881296 📄 01926 313853 48 en suite

LEEK WOOTTON
Map 4 SP26

The Warwickshire Golf & Country Club CV35 7QT
☎ 01926 409409 📄 01926 408409
e-mail: p.taylor@theclubcompany.com
web: www.theclubcompany.com

Two courses, the Kings which is an American style course with lots of water and the Earls, which is mainly a woodland course.

Kings: 18 Holes, 6821yds, Par 72, SSS 73.
Earls: 18 Holes, 7108yds, Par 72, SSS 74.
Club membership 1500.

Visitors Mon-Sun & BHs. Booking required. Dress code.
Societies booking required. Green Fees not confirmed Course Designer Karl Litten Prof Mark Dulson Facilities ⑪ ⑩ ⓛ ☐ 🍴 ⚲ 🏠 ⛳ ✦ 🚌 ✦ ✦ Leisure heated indoor swimming pool, sauna, gymnasium, health club Conf facs Corporate Hospitality Days Location S of village off A46
Hotel ★★★★ 79% HL Chesford Grange, Chesford Bridge, KENILWORTH ☎ 01926 859331 📄 01926 859272 205 en suite

LOWER BRAILES
Map 4 SP33

Brailes Golf Club Feldon Valley, Sutton Ln, Lower Brailes OX15 5BB
☎ 01608 685633
e-mail: steve.hutchinson@feldonvalley.co.uk

Undulating meadowland on 105 acres of Cotswold countryside. Sutton Brook passes through the course and must be crossed five times. The par 5 17th offers the most spectacular view of three counties from the tee. Challenging par 3 short holes. Suitable for golfers of all standards.

18 Holes, 6304yds, Par 70, SSS 70, Course record 65.
Club membership 600.

Visitors Mon-Sun & BHs. Booking required. Dress code.
Societies welcome. Green Fees not confirmed Course Designer R Baldwin/Steve Ritson Prof Steve Hutchinson Facilities ⑪ ⑩ ⓛ ☐ 🍴 ⚲ 🏠 ⛳ ✦ 🚌 ✦ ✦ Conf facs Corporate Hospitality Days Location S of Lower Brailes off B4035
Hotel ★★★★ INN The Red Lion, Main Street, SHIPSTON ON STOUR ☎ 01608 684221 📄 01608 684968 5 rooms

NUNEATON
Map 4 SP39

Oakridge Golf Course Arley Ln, Ansley Village CV10 9PH
☎ 01676 541389 & 540542 📄 01676 542709
e-mail: shane.lovric@golfatoakridge.com
web: www.oakridgegolf.fsnet.co.uk

The water hazards on the back nine add to the natural beauty of the countryside. The undulating course is affected by winter cross winds on several holes. Overall it will certainly test golfing skills.

18 Holes, 6208yds, Par 71, SSS 71. Club membership 500.

Visitors Mon-Sun & BHs. Booking required Fri-Sun & BHs. Dress code Societies welcome. Green Fees not confirmed Course Designer Algy Jayes Facilities ⑪ ⑩ ⓛ ☐ 🍴 ⚲ 🏠 ⛳ ✦ 🚌 ✦ Conf Corporate Hospitality Days Location 4m W
Hotel ★★★ 73% HL Best Western Weston Hall, Weston Lane, Bulkington, NUNEATON ☎ 024 7631 2989 📄 024 7664 0846 40 en suite

RUGBY
Map 4 SP57

Rugby Golf Club Clifton Rd CV21 3RD
☎ 01788 542306 & 575134 (Pro) 📄 01788 542306
e-mail: info@rugbygolfclub.co.uk
web: www.rugbygolfclub.co.uk

A short parkland course across the undulating Clifton Valley. Clifton brook runs through the lower level of the course and comes into play on seven holes. Accuracy is the prime requirement for a good score.

18 Holes, 5457yds, Par 68, SSS 67, Course record 60.
Club membership 600.

Visitors Mon-Sun & BHs. Booking required. Dress code.
Societies booking required. Green Fees not confirmed Prof David Quinn Facilities ⑪ ⑩ ⓛ ☐ 🍴 ⚲ 🏠 ⛳ ✦ ✦ Conf facs Corporate Hospitality Days Location 1m NE on B5414. M6 junct 1, take 3rd turning at rdbt. Over next 2 rdbts 1st left at 3rd rdbt. Follow road to end and turn right, golf club 50 mtrs on left
Hotel ★★★ 78% HL Brownsover Hall Hotel, Brownsover Lane, Old Brownsover, RUGBY ☎ 0844 855 9123 📄 01788 535367 47 en suite

Whitefields Golf Course London Rd, Thurlaston CV23 9LF
☎ 01788 521800 📄 01788 521695
e-mail: mail@draycotehotel.co.uk
web: www.whitefieldsgolfclub.co.uk

Whitefields has superb natural drainage. There are many water features and the 13th has a stunning dog-leg 442yd par 4 with a superb view across Draycote Water. The 16th is completely surrounded by water and is particularly difficult.

18 Holes, 6289yds, Par 71, SSS 71, Course record 64.
Club membership 400.

Visitors Mon-Sun & BHs. Booking required weekends & BHs.
Societies booking required. Green Fees not confirmed Course Designer Reg Mason Prof David Mills Facilities ⑪ ⑩ ⓛ ☐ 🍴 ⚲ 🏠 ⛳ ◇ ✦ 🚌 ✦ ✦ Leisure gymnasium Conf facs Corporate Hospitality Days Location M45 junct 1, 0.5m on A45, on left. W of Dunchurch
Hotel ★★★ 64% HL Draycote, London Road, THURLASTON ☎ 01788 521800 📄 01788 521695 49 en suite

THE BELFRY
WARWICKSHIRE - WISHAW - MAP 7 SP19

he Belfry is unique as the only venue to have staged the biggest golf event in the world, the Ryder Cup matches, an unprecedented four times, most recently in 2002. The Brabazon is regarded throughout the world as great championship course with some of the most demanding holes in golf; the 10th (Ballesteros's Hole) and he 18th, with its dangerous lakes and its amphitheatre around the final green, are world famous. Alternatively, ou can pit your wits against a new legend in the making, the PGA National Course, which has won plaudits rom near and far. The Dave Thomas-designed course has been used for professional competition and is already stablished as one of Britain's leading courses. For those who like their golf a little easier or like to get back into he swing gently, The Derby is ideal and can be played by golfers of any standard.

Wishaw B76 9PR ☎ 01675 470301 🖹 01675 470178
-mail: enquiries@thebelfry.com web: www.thebelfry.com
he Brabazon: 18 Holes, 7235yds, Par 72.
PGA National: 18 Holes, 7053yds, Par 72.
he Derby: 18 Holes, 6057yds, Par 70, SSS 70. Club membership 230.
Visitors Advance booking essential. Dress code. Societies booking required. Green Fees Brabazon from £75, PGA from £45, Derby from £25 Course Designer Dave Thomas/Peter Alliss Facilities 🍴 🍽 🛒 🖥 🍴 🏖 🎒 🖥 ⛳
🏌 🏌 🛶 🏌 🎣 Leisure heated indoor swimming pool, squash, sauna, gymnasium, PGA National Golf Academy
Conf facs Corporate Hospitality Days Location M42 junct 9, 4m E on A446
Hotel ★★★★ 76% HL Lea Marston Hotel, Haunch Lane, LEA MARSTON ☎ 01675 470468 🖹 01675
-70871 88 en suite

STONELEIGH
Map 4 SP37

Stoneleigh Deer Park Golf Club The Clubhouse, The Old Deer Park, Coventry Rd CV8 3DR

☎ 024 7663 9991 & 7663 9912 📠 024 7651 1533

e-mail: info@stoneleighdeerparkgolfclub.com

web: www.stoneleighdeerparkgolfclub.com

Parkland course in old deer park with many mature trees. The River Avon meanders through the course and comes into play on four holes. Also a nine-hole par 3 course.

Tantara Course: 18 Holes, 6056yds, Par 71, SSS 69.
Avon: 9 Holes, 1251yds, Par 27. Club membership 750.

Visitors Mon-Thu. Fri-Sun & BHs restrictions from 1pm. Booking required. Dress code. **Societies** booking required. **Green Fees** £20 (£22 Fri, £30 weekends & BHs) **Prof** Matt McGuire **Facilities** ⊕ ⏀ ▐ ⊑ ⏧ ⋏ ▭ ⬟ **Leisure** 9 hole par 3 Avon Course **Conf** facs Corporate Hospitality Days **Location** 3m NE of Kenilworth **Hotel** ★★★★ 79% HL Chesford Grange, Chesford Bridge, KENILWORTH ☎ 01926 859331 📠 01926 859272 205 en suite

STRATFORD-UPON-AVON
Map 4 SP25

Ingon Manor Golf & Country Club Ingon Ln, Snitterfield CV37 0QE

☎ 01789 731857 📠 01789 731657

e-mail: info@ingonmanor.co.uk

web: www.ingonmanor.co.uk

Nestling in the Welcombe Hills, a short distance from the town. The Manor, dating back to the 14th century, lies within 171 acres of land. The championship course is open all year round and has been designed to test all standards of golfers with a variety of challenging holes.

18 Holes, 6623yds, Par 72. Club membership 400.

Visitors Mon-Sun & BHs. Booking required. Dress code. **Societies** welcome. **Green Fees** £30 per 18 holes (£40 weekends) **Prof** Richard Hampton **Facilities** ⊕ ⏀ ▐ ⊑ ⏧ ⋏ ▭ ⬟ ⬟ ⬟ **Conf** facs Corporate Hospitality Days **Location** off A46 **Hotel** ★★★★ 83% HL Menzies Welcombe Hotel Spa & Golf Club, Warwick Road, STRATFORD-UPON-AVON ☎ 01789 295252 📠 01789 414666 78 en suite

Menzies Welcombe Hotel Spa and Golf Club Warwick Rd CV37 0NR

☎ 01789 413800 📠 01789 262028

web: www.menzieshotels.co.uk

18 Holes, 6288yds, Par 70, SSS 69, Course record 64.

Course Designer Thomas Macauley **Location** 1.5m NE off A46 **Telephone for further details** **Hotel** ★★★★ 83% HL Menzies Welcombe Hotel Spa & Golf Club, Warwick Road, STRATFORD-UPON-AVON ☎ 01789 295252 📠 01789 414666 78 en suite

Stratford Oaks Golf Club Bearley Rd, Snitterfield CV37 0EZ

☎ 01789 731980 📠 01789 731981

e-mail: admin@stratfordoaks.co.uk

web: www.stratfordoaks.co.uk

American-style, level parkland course with some water features designed by Howard Swan.

18 Holes, 6232yds, Par 70, SSS 70. Club membership 700.

Visitors Mon-Sun & BHs. Booking required. Dress code. **Societies** booking required. **Green Fees** not confirmed **Course Designer** H Swan **Prof** Andrew Dunbar **Facilities** ⊕ ⏀ ▐ ⊑ ⏧ ⋏ ▭ ⬟ **Leisure** gymnasium, massage and physiotherapy facility **Conf** Corporate Hospitality Days **Location** 4m NE of Stratford-upon-Avon **Hotel** ★★★★ 77% HL Stratford Manor, Warwick Road, STRATFORD-UPON-AVON ☎ 01789 731173 📠 01789 731131 104 en suite

Stratford-on-Avon Golf Club Tiddington Rd CV37 7BA

☎ 01789 205749 📠 01789 414909

web: www.stratfordgolf.co.uk

18 Holes, 6274yds, Par 72, SSS 70, Course record 63.

Course Designer Taylor **Location** 0.75m E on B4086 **Telephone for further details** **Hotel** ★★★★ 79% HL Macdonald Alveston Manor, Clopton Bridge, STRATFORD-UPON-AVON ☎ 0844 879 9138 📠 01789 41409⬚ 113 en suite

TANWORTH IN ARDEN
Map 7 SP17

Ladbrook Park Golf Club Poolhead Ln B94 5ED

☎ 01564 742264 📠 01564 742909

e-mail: secretary@ladbrookparkgolf.co.uk

web: www.ladbrookparkgolf.co.uk

Parkland course lined with mature trees up to 100 years old. Harry Colt designed.

18 Holes, 6502yds, Par 71, SSS 72, Course record 63.
Club membership 700.

Visitors Mon-Fri & BHs. Booking required. Handicap certificate. Dress code. **Societies** booking required. **Green Fees** £45 per 36 holes, £45 per 27 holes, £40 per 18 holes **Course Designer** H S Colt **Prof** Gary Allis **Facilities** ⊕ ⏀ ▐ ⊑ ⏧ ⋏ ▭ ⬟ ⬟ ⬟ ⬟ **Conf** Corporate Hospitality Days **Location** M42 junct 3, 2.5m SE **Hotel** ★★★ 86% HL Nuthurst Grange Country House & Restaurant, Nuthurst Grange Lane, HOCKLEY HEATH ☎ 01564 783972 📠 01564 783919 19 en suite

WARWICK
Map 4 SP26

Warwick Golf Club The Racecourse CV34 6HW

☎ 01926 494316

Easy walking parkland. Driving range with floodlit bays.

9 Holes, 2682yds, Par 34, SSS 66. Club membership 150.

Visitors Mon-Sat & BHs, Sun after 12.30pm. Booking required Sat. **Societies** welcome. **Green Fees** £8 per 9 holes (£8.50 weekends) ⬚ **Course Designer** D G Dunkley **Prof** Mario Luca **Facilities** ⏧ ⋏ ▭ ⬟ ⬟ **Location** W of town centre **Hotel** ★★★★ 77% HL Ardencote Manor Hotel, Country Club & Spa, The Cumsey, Lye Green Road, Claverdon, WARWICK ☎ 01926 843111 📠 01926 842646 110 en suite

WISHAW
Map 7 SP19

The Belfry see page 259
Wishaw B76 9PR

☎ 01675 470301 📠 01675 470178

e-mail: enquiries@thebelfry.com

web: www.thebelfry.com

ENGLAND

WEST MIDLANDS

ALDRIDGE   Map 7 SK00

Druids Heath Golf Club Stonnall Rd WS9 8JZ
☎ 01922 455595 (Office) 📠 01922 452887
e-mail: admin@druidsheathgc.co.uk
web: www.druidsheathgc.co.uk

Testing, undulating heathland course. Large greens with subtle slopes. Excellent natural drainage gives good winter play.

18 Holes, 6665yds, Par 72, SSS 73, Course record 67. Club membership 660.

Visitors Mon-Fri except BHs Weekends pm. Booking required Fri-Sun. **Dress code. Societies** booking required. **Green Fees** £37 per day (£40 weekends pm only) **Prof** Glenn Williams **Facilities** ⑪ ⅋ ⅃ ⌾ ⅃ ⌾ ✎ **Leisure** snooker room with 2 tables **Conf** Corporate Hospitality Days **Location** NE of town centre off A454 & A452
Hotel ★★★ 85% HL Fairlawns Hotel & Spa, 178 Little Aston Road, WALSALL ☎ 01922 455122 📠 01922 743148 58 en suite

BIRMINGHAM   Map 7 SP08

Cocks Moors Woods Golf Club Alcester Road South, Kings Heath B14 4ER
☎ 0121 464 3584 📠 0121 441 1305
e-mail: steve.ellis@birmingham.co.uk
web: www.golfbirmingham.co.uk

Opened in 1927, this is a modest course which requires accurate play in order to avoid the "chinn" brook, which meanders across 11 fairways. The course adjoins a modern leisure centre. Despite its modest length the course provides an excellent challenge for golfers of all abilities.

18 Holes, 5784yds, Par 69, SSS 68. Club membership 300.

Visitors Mon-Sun excluding BHs. **Societies** booking required. **Green Fees** £16 per 18 holes, £10 per 9 holes (winter reductions available) **Course Designer** Hawtree & J H Taylor **Prof** Steve Ellis **Facilities** ⑪ ⅃ ⌾ ⅃ ✎ ⅃ ⌾ ✎ **Leisure** heated indoor swimming pool, gymnasium **Location** M42 junct 3, 4m N on A435
Hotel ★★★ 82% HL Best Western Westley, 80-90 Westley Road, Acocks Green, BIRMINGHAM ☎ 0121 706 4312 📠 0121 706 2824 37 en suite

---

Edgbaston Golf Club Church Rd, Edgbaston B15 3TB
☎ 0121 454 1736 📠 0121 454 2395
e-mail: secretary@edgbastongc.co.uk
web: www.edgbastongc.co.uk

Set in 144 acres of woodland, lake and parkland, 2m from the centre of Birmingham, this delightful course utilises the wealth of natural features to provide a series of testing and adventurous holes set in the traditional double loop that starts directly in front of the clubhouse, an imposing Georgian mansion.

18 Holes, 6132yds, Par 69, SSS 70, Course record 64. Club membership 920.

Visitors Mon-Sun & BHs. **Dress code. Societies** booking required. **Green Fees** £47 per 18 holes (£57 weekends & BHs) **Course Designer** H S Colt **Prof** Jamie Cundy **Facilities** ⑪ ⅃ ⌾ ⅃ ⌾ ✎ ⅃ ⌾ ✎ **Conf** facs Corporate Hospitality Days **Location** 2m S of city centre on B4217, off A38
Hotel ★★★ 75% HL Menzies Strathallan, 225 Hagley Road, Edgbaston, BIRMINGHAM ☎ 0121 455 9777 📠 0121 454 9432 135 en suite

---

Great Barr Golf Club Chapel Ln B43 7BA
☎ 0121 358 4376 📠 0121 358 4376
web: www.greatbarrgolfclub.co.uk

18 Holes, 6523yds, Par 72, SSS 72, Course record 67.
Location 6m N of city centre off A 34
Telephone for further details
Hotel ★★★ 72% HL Holiday Inn Birmingham M6 Jct 7, Chapel Lane, Great Barr, BIRMINGHAM ☎ 0871 942 9009 & 0121 357 7303 📠 0121 357 7503 190 en suite

Handsworth Golf Club 11 Sunningdale Close, Handsworth Wood B20 1NP
☎ 0121 554 3387 📠 0121 554 6144
e-mail: info@handsworthgolfclub.net
web: www.handsworthgolfclub.co.uk

Undulating parkland with some tight fairways and strategic bunkering with a number of well-placed water features.

18 Holes, 6325yds, Par 70, SSS 71, Course record 64. Club membership 730.

Visitors Mon-Sun & BHs. Booking required. Handicap certificate. Dress code. **Societies** booking required. **Green Fees** £40 per day ⊕ **Course Designer** H S Colt **Prof** Lee Bashford **Facilities** ⑪ ⅃ ⌾ ⅃ ⌾ ✎ ⅃ ⌾ ✎ **Leisure** squash, fishing **Conf** Corporate Hospitality Days **Location** 3.5m NW of city centre off A4040
Hotel ★★★ 67% HL Great Barr Hotel & Conference Centre, Pear Tree Drive, Newton Road, Great Barr, BIRMINGHAM ☎ 0121 357 1141 📠 0121 357 7557 92 en suite

Harborne Church Farm Golf Club Vicarage Rd, Harborne B17 0SN
☎ 0121 427 1204

Parkland with two brooks running through. Course is small but tight.

9 Holes, 2441yds, Par 66, SSS 64, Course record 63. Club membership 100.

Visitors Mon-Sun & BHs. Booking preferred. **Societies** booking required. Fees not confirmed **Prof** Mark Hampton **Facilities** ⑪ ⅃ ⌾ ⅃ ⌾ ✎ **Leisure** practice net **Location** 3.5m SW of city centre off A4040
Hotel ★★★ 75% HL Menzies Strathallan, 225 Hagley Road, Edgbaston, BIRMINGHAM ☎ 0121 455 9777 📠 0121 454 9432 135 en suite

Harborne Golf Club 40 Tennal Rd, Harborne B32 2JE
☎ 0121 427 3058 📠 0121 427 4039
e-mail: adrian@harbornegolfclub.org
web: www.harbornegolfclub.org.uk

Parkland course in a hilly location, with a brook running through.

18 Holes, 6180yds, Par 70, SSS 70, Course record 64. Club membership 600.

Visitors Mon-Fri except BHs. **Dress code. Societies** welcome. **Green Fees** not confirmed **Course Designer** Harry Colt **Prof** Stewart Mathews **Facilities** ⑪ ⅃ ⌾ ⅃ ⌾ ✎ ⅃ ⌾ ✎ **Conf** facs Corporate Hospitality Days **Location** 3.5 m SW of city centre off A4040
Hotel ★★★ 75% HL Menzies Strathallan, 225 Hagley Road, Edgbaston, BIRMINGHAM ☎ 0121 455 9777 📠 0121 454 9432 135 en suite

Hatchford Brook Golf Course Coventry Rd, Sheldon B26 3PY
☎ 0121 743 9821 📄 0121 743 3420
e-mail: hatchfordbrook_golf@birmingham.gov.uk
Fairly flat, municipal parkland course.
Hatchford Brook: 18 Holes, 6137yds, Par 70, SSS 69, Course record 65. Club membership 250.
Visitors Mon-Sun & BHs. Dress code. **Societies** booking required. **Green Fees** phone **Prof** Mark Hampton **Facilities** ⑪ ⓑ ⏍ ⑨ ⚐ ⌂ ⌁ *Location* 6m E of city centre on A45
Hotel ★★★★ 71% HL Novotel Birmingham Airport, BIRMINGHAM AIRPORT ☎ 0121 782 7000 & 782 4111 📄 0121 782 0445
195 en suite

Hilltop Public Golf Course Park Ln, Handsworth B21 8LJ
☎ 0121 554 4463
A good test of golf with interesting layout, undulating fairways and large greens, located in the Sandwell Valley conservation area.
18 Holes, 6209yds, Par 71, SSS 70. Club membership 200.
Visitors Mon-Sun & BHs. Booking required. **Societies** booking required. **Green Fees** not confirmed **Course Designer** Hawtree **Prof** Kevin Highfield **Facilities** ⑪ ⓣⓞⓛ ⓑ ⏍ ⑨ ⌂ ⌁ ⌁ **Conf** facs Corporate Hospitality Days **Location** M5 junct 1, 1m on A41
Hotel ★★★ 67% HL Great Barr Hotel & Conference Centre, Pear Tree Drive, Newton Road, Great Barr, BIRMINGHAM ☎ 0121 357 1141 📄 0121 357 7557 92 en suite

Lickey Hills Golf Course Rosehill B45 8RR
☎ 0121 453 3159 📄 0121 457 8779
18 Holes, 5835yds, Par 69, SSS 68.
Location 10m SW of city centre on B4096
Telephone for further details
Hotel ★★★★ 71% HL Holiday Inn Birmingham - Bromsgrove, Kidderminster Road, BROMSGROVE ☎ 01527 576600 & 0871 942 9142 📄 01527 878981 110 en suite

Moseley Golf Club Springfield Rd, Kings Heath B14 7DX
☎ 0121 444 4957 📄 0121 441 4662
e-mail: secretary@moseleygolfclub.co.uk
web: www.moseleygolfclub.co.uk
Parkland with a lake, pond and a stream providing natural hazards. The par 3 4th goes through a cutting in woodland to a tree and garden-lined amphitheatre, and the par 4 5th entails a drive over a lake to a dog-leg fairway.
18 Holes, 6300yds, Par 70, SSS 71, Course record 63. Club membership 600.
Visitors Handicap certificate. Dress code. **Societies** booking required. **Green Fees** £45 per round **Course Designer** H S Colt with others **Prof** Martin Griffin **Facilities** ⑪ ⓣⓞⓛ ⓑ ⏍ ⑨ ⌂ ⌁ ⌁ **Conf** facs Corporate Hospitality Days **Location** 4m S of city centre on B4146
Hotel ★★★ 82% HL Best Western Westley, 80-90 Westley Road, Acocks Green, BIRMINGHAM ☎ 0121 706 4312 📄 0121 706 2824
37 en suite

North Worcestershire Golf Course Frankley Beeches Rd, Northfield B31 5LP
☎ 0121 475 1047 📄 0121 476 8681
e-mail: secretary@nwgolfclub.com
web: www.nwgolfclub.com
Designed by James Braid and established in 1907, this is a mature parkland course. Tree plantations rather than heavy rough are the main hazards.
18 Holes, 5959yds, Par 69, SSS 68, Course record 64. Club membership 600.
Visitors contact course for details. **Societies** welcome. **Green Fees** £37 per day, £25 per round 🅴 **Course Designer** James Braid **Prof** Richard Davies **Facilities** ⑪ ⓣⓞⓛ ⓑ ⏍ ⑨ ⌂ ⌁ ⌁ **Conf** facs Corporate Hospitality Days **Location** 7m SW of Birmingham city centre, off A38
Hotel ★★★ 72% HL Edgbaston Palace, 198-200 Hagley Road, Edgbaston, BIRMINGHAM ☎ 0121 452 1577 📄 0121 455 7933
48 en suite

Queslett Park Golf Centre Host Centre, Queslett Park, Great Barr B42 2RG
☎ 0121 360 7600 📄 0121 360 7603
web: www.queslettpark.co.uk
This golf academy consists of a nine-hole short game improvement course, a covered floodlit driving range and teaching and training facilities.
9 Holes, 905yds, Par 27, SSS 27, Course record 21.
Visitors contact centre for details. **Societies** booking required. **Green Fees** 18 holes Adult £10 (9 holes £7), Junior £10 (£6), Senior £10 (£6) **Prof** Andy Gorman/Daniel Grant **Facilities** ⓑ ⏍ ⑨ ⌂ ⌁ ⌁ **Conf** facs Corporate Hospitality Days **Location** M6 junct 7
Hotel ★★★ 72% HL Holiday Inn Birmingham M6 Jct 7, Chapel Lane, Great Barr, BIRMINGHAM ☎ 0871 942 9009 & 0121 357 7303 📄 0121 357 7503 190 en suite

Warley Woods Golf Course The Pavilion, 101 Lightwoods Hill, Smethwick B67 5ED
☎ 0121 429 2440
e-mail: golfshop@warleywoods.org.uk
web: www.warleywoods.org.uk/golf
Municipal parkland course in Warley Woods. New out of bounds areas and bunkers have tightened the course considerably with further improvement following tree planting. Part of a community trust in liaison with English Heritage.
9 Holes, 2646yds, Par 34, SSS 68, Course record 62. Club membership 200.
Visitors Mon-Sun & BHs. Booking required weekends & BHs. Dress code. **Societies** welcome. **Green Fees** phone **Prof** G Lynch **Facilities** ⑪ ⓑ ⏍ ⌂ ⌁ ⌁ ⌁ **Leisure** practice nets **Conf** facs Corporate Hospitality Days **Location** 4m W of city centre off A456
Hotel ★★★★★ GA Westbourne Lodge, 25-31 Fountain Road, Edgbaston, BIRMINGHAM ☎ 0121 429 1003 📄 0121 429 7436
18 rooms

ave on Hotels. Book at **theAA.com/hotel**   **WEST MIDLANDS**

ENGLAND

OVENTRY   Map 4 SP37

nsty Golf Centre Brinklow Rd, Ansty CV7 9JL
☎ 024 7662 1341 📄 024 7660 2568
-mail: info@anstygolfcentre.co.uk
pay-and-play parkland course of two nine-hole loops. Open all year
ound.
8 Holes, 6079yds, Par 71, SSS 69, Course record 66.
isitors Mon-Sun & BHs. Dress code. **Societies** booking required.
reen Fees £15 per 18 holes (£20 weekends & BHs). Academy £5
£6 weekends and BHs) **Course Designer** David Morgan **Prof** M
oodwin/S Webster **Facilities** ⊕ ⊗ ⊑ ⊑ ⊒ ⊿ ⊑ ⊕ ⊘
⊕ ⊘ ⚑ **Leisure** par 3 course **Conf** facs Corporate Hospitality Days
ocation M6/M69 junct 2, 1m signed
otel ★★★ 75% HL Novotel Coventry, Wilsons Lane, COVENTRY
☎ 024 7636 5000 📄 024 7636 2422 98 en suite

Coventry Golf Club St Martins Rd, Finham CV3 6RJ
☎ 024 7641 4152 📄 024 7669 0131
e-mail: secretary@coventrygolfclub.net
web: www.coventrygolfclub.net
The scene of several major professional events, this undulating
parkland course has a great deal of quality. More than that, it
usually plays its length, and thus scoring is never easy, as many
professionals have found to their cost.
18 Holes, 6590yds, Par 73, SSS 72.
Club membership 750.
Visitors Mon-Fri except BHs. Dress code. **Societies** booking
required. **Green Fees** £50 per day **Course Designer** Vardon Bros/
Hawtree **Prof** Philip Weaver **Facilities** ⊕ ⊗ ⊑ ⊑ ⊒ ⊿ ⊑
⊑ ⊕ ⊘ **Conf** Corporate Hospitality Days **Location** 3m S of city
centre on B4113
Hotel ★★★ 78% HL Best Western Peacock Hotel, 149 Warwick
Road, KENILWORTH ☎ 01926 851156 & 864500 📄 01926 864644
29 en suite

Coventry Hearsall Golf Club Beechwood Av CV5 6DF
☎ 024 7671 3470 📄 024 7669 1534
e-mail: secretary@hearsallgolfclub.co.uk
web: www.hearsallgolfclub.co.uk
Parkland with fairly easy walking. A brook provides an interesting
hazard.
18 Holes, 6005yds, Par 70, SSS 69. Club membership 650.
Visitors Mon-Sun & BHs. Booking required. Handicap certificate. Dress
code. **Societies** welcome. **Green Fees** not confirmed **Prof** Mike Tarn
Facilities ⊕ ⊗ ⊑ ⊑ ⊒ ⊿ ⊑ ⊕ ⊘ **Conf** facs Corporate
Hospitality Days **Location** 1.5m SW of city centre off A429
Hotel ★★★ 64% HL Quality Hotel, Birmingham Road, Allesley,
COVENTRY ☎ 024 7640 3835 📄 024 7640 3081 80 en suite

Windmill Village Hotel Golf & Leisure Club
Birmingham Rd, Allesley CV5 9AL
☎ 024 7640 4041 📄 024 7640 4042
e-mail: leisure@windmillvillagehotel.co.uk
web: www.windmillvillagehotel.co.uk
An attractive 18-hole course over rolling parkland with plenty of trees
and two lakes that demand shots over open water. Four challenging
par 5 holes.
18 Holes, 5184yds, Par 70, SSS 66, Course record 63.
Club membership 500.

Visitors Mon-Sun & BHs. Booking advisable. Dress code.
Societies booking required. **Green Fees** not confirmed **Course
Designer** Robert Hunter **Prof** Robert Hunter **Facilities** ⊕ ⊗
⊑ ⊑ ⊒ ⊿ ⊑ ⊕ ⊘ ⊘ ⊘ ⊘ **Leisure** heated indoor
swimming pool, sauna, gymnasium, practice nets. **Conf** facs
Corporate Hospitality Days **Location** 3m from the NEC on A45
Hotel Ⓤ Windmill Village Hotel, Golf & Leisure Club, Birmingham
Road, Allesley, COVENTRY ☎ 02476 404040 📄 02476 404042
105 en suite

DUDLEY   Map 7 SO99

Dudley Golf Club Turner's Hill B65 9DP
☎ 01384 233877 📄 01384 233877
web: www.dudleygolfclub.com
18 Holes, 5714yds, Par 69, SSS 68, Course record 63.
Location 2m S of town centre off B4171
Telephone for further details
Hotel ★★★★ 73% HL Copthorne Hotel Merry Hill - Dudley, The
Waterfront, Level Street, Brierley Hill, DUDLEY ☎ 01384 482882
📄 01384 482773 138 en suite

Swindon Golf Club Bridgnorth Rd, Swindon DY3 4PU
☎ 01902 897031 📄 01902 326219
e-mail: admin@swindongolfclub.co.uk
web: www.swindongolfclub.co.uk
Attractive, undulating woodland and parkland with spectacular views.
Old Course: 18 Holes, 6121yds, Par 71.
Club membership 600.
Visitors Mon-Sun & BHs. Booking required. Dress code.
Societies booking required. **Green Fees** £25 per round (£30 weekends
& BHs) **Prof** James Wright **Facilities** ⊕ ⊗ ⊑ ⊑ ⊒ ⊿ ⊑
⊑ ⊘ **Leisure** fishing **Conf** facs Corporate Hospitality Days
Location 4m W of Dudley on B4176
Hotel ★★★ 79% HL Patshull Park Hotel Golf & Country Club,
Patshull Park, PATTINGHAM ☎ 01902 700100 📄 01902 700874
49 en suite

HALESOWEN   Map 7 SO98

Halesowen Golf Club The Leasowes, Leasowes Ln
B62 8QF
☎ 0121 501 3606
e-mail: office@halesowengc.co.uk
web: www.halesowengc.co.uk
Parkland course within the only Grade I listed park in the Midlands.
18 Holes, 5754yds, Par 69, SSS 69, Course record 64.
Club membership 468.
Visitors contact club for details. **Societies** booking required. **Green
Fees** £34 per day, £28 per round ⓦ **Prof** Jon Nicholas **Facilities** ⊕
⊗ ⊑ ⊑ ⊒ ⊿ ⊑ ⊘ ⊑ ⊘ **Conf** facs Corporate
Hospitality Days **Location** M5 junct 3, 1m E, off Manor Ln
Hotel ★★★ 72% HL Edgbaston Palace, 198-200 Hagley Road,
Edgbaston, BIRMINGHAM ☎ 0121 452 1577 📄 0121 455 7933
48 en suite

KNOWLE
Map 7 SP17

Copt Heath Golf Club 1220 Warwick Rd B93 9LN
☎ 01564 731620 📠 01564 731621
e-mail: golf@copt-heath.co.uk
web: www.coptheathgolf.co.uk
Flat heathland and parkland course designed by H Vardon.

Copt Heath Golf Club: 18 Holes, 6528yds, Par 71, SSS 71, Course record 65. Club membership 700.

Visitors Mon, Wed-Fri. Tue pm. Limited play weekends & BHs. Booking required. Dress code. **Societies** booking required. **Green Fees** £55 per day, £45 per round ☺ **Course Designer** H Vardon **Prof** Brian J Barton **Facilities** ⊕ ⊗ ⤓ ⌂ ☐ ☕ ⚑ ⚒ ⚐ **Conf** Corporate Hospitality Days **Location** M42 junct 5, 0.5m S on A4141
Hotel ★★★★ 71% HL Holiday Inn Solihull, 61 Homer Road, SOLIHULL ☎ 0871 942 9201 & 0121 623 9988 📠 0121 711 2696 120 en suite

MERIDEN
Map 4 SP28

Forest of Arden, A Marriott Hotel & Country Club see page 265
Maxstoke Ln CV7 7HR
☎ 01676 522335 📠 0870 400 7372
web: www.marriotthotels.com

North Warwickshire Golf Club Hampton Ln CV7 7LL
☎ 01676 522259 (shop) & 522915 (sec)
📠 01676 523004

9 Holes, 6402yds, Par 72, SSS 71, Course record 65.
Location 1m SW on B4102
Telephone for further details
Hotel ★★★★ 73% HL Manor Hotel, Main Road, MERIDEN ☎ 01676 522735 📠 01676 522186 110 en suite

Stonebridge Golf Club Somers Rd CV7 7PL
☎ 01676 522442 📠 01676 522447
e-mail: info@stonebridgegolf.co.uk
web: www.stonebridgegolf.co.uk
A parkland course set in 170 acres with towering oak trees, lakes, and the River Blythe on its borders. An additional 9 holes were added in 2007 to make this a 27 hole course, the new holes are very distinctive and blend with the original18 holes. New lakes have been constructed with water coming in to play on three of the new holes.

Hampton: 9 Holes, 2786yds, Par 33.
Blythe: 9 Holes, 2757yds, Par 33.
Somers: 9 Holes, 3316yds, Par 37. Club membership 500.
Visitors Mon-Sun & BHs. Booking required. Dress code.
Societies booking required. **Green Fees** £20 per 18 holes (£25 Fri-Sun) **Course Designer** Mark Jones **Prof** Darren Murphy **Facilities** ⊕ ⊗ ⤓ ⌂ ☐ ☕ ⚑ ☖ ⚒ ⚐ **Leisure** fishing, golf academy **Conf** facs Corporate Hospitality Days **Location** M42 junct 6, 3m
Hotel ★★★ 74% HL Best Western Stade Court, Stade Street, West Parade, HYTHE ☎ 01303 268263 📠 01303 261803 42 en suite

SEDGLEY
Map 7 SO99

Sedgley Golf Centre Sandyfields Rd DY3 3DL
☎ 01902 880503
9 Holes, 3147yds, Par 72, SSS 70.
Course Designer W G Cox **Location** 0.5m from town centre off A463
Telephone for further details
Hotel ★★★★ 73% HL Copthorne Hotel Merry Hill - Dudley, The Waterfront, Level Street, Brierley Hill, DUDLEY ☎ 01384 482882 📠 01384 482773 138 en suite

SOLIHULL
Map 7 SP17

Olton Golf Club Mirfield Rd B91 1JH
☎ 0121 704 1936 📠 0121 711 2010
e-mail: secretary@oltongolfclub.co.uk
web: www.oltongolfclub.co.uk
Testing parkland course, over 100 years old, close to the town centre but in a secluded position.

18 Holes, 6254yds, Par 69, SSS 70, Course record 63. Club membership 700.

Visitors Mon-Fri except BHs. Booking required. Handicap certficate. Dress code. **Societies** booking required. **Green Fees** £50 per 36 holes, £45 per 27 holes, £40 per 18 holes ☺ **Course Designer** J H Taylor **Prof** Charles Haynes **Facilities** ⊕ ⊗ ⤓ ⌂ ☐ ☕ ⚑ ☖ ⚒ ⚐ **Leisure** snooker **Conf** Corporate Hospitality Days **Location** M42 junct 5, A41 for 1.5m
Hotel ★★★★ 76% HL St Johns Hotel, 651 Warwick Road, SOLIHULL ☎ 0121 711 3000 📠 0121 705 6629 180 en suite

Robin Hood Golf Club St Bernards Rd B92 7DJ
☎ 0121 706 0061 📠 0121 700 7502
e-mail: manager@robinhoodgolfclub.co.uk
web: www.robinhoodgolfclub.co.uk
Pleasant parkland with easy walking and good views. Tree-lined fairways and varied holes, culminating in three excellent finishing holes.

18 Holes, 6506yds, Par 72, SSS 72. Club membership 650.

Visitors Mon-Fri & Sun except BHs. Booking required Sun. Dress code. **Societies** booking required. **Green Fees** £40 per 18 holes **Course Designer** H S Colt **Prof** Alan Harvey **Facilities** ⊕ ⊗ ⤓ ☐ ☕ ⚑ ☖ ⚒ ⚐ **Conf** facs Corporate Hospitality Days **Location** 2m W off B4025
Hotel ★★★ 82% HL Best Western Westley, 80-90 Westley Road, Acocks Green, BIRMINGHAM ☎ 0121 706 4312 📠 0121 706 2824 37 en suite

FOREST OF ARDEN, A MARRIOTT HOTEL & COUNTRY CLUB
WEST MIDLANDS - MERIDEN - MAP 4 SP28

This is one of the finest golf destinations in the UK, with a range of facilities to impress every golfer. The jewel in the crown is the Arden championship parkland course, set in 10,000 acres of the Packington Estate. Designed by Donald Steel, it presents one of the country's most spectacular challenges and has hosted a succession of international tournaments, including the British Masters and English Open. Beware the 18th hole, which is enough to stretch the nerves of any golfer. The shorter Aylesford Course offers a varied and enjoyable challenge, which golfers of all abilities will find rewarding. Golf events are a speciality, and there is a golf academy and extensive leisure facilities.

Maxstoke Ln CV7 7HR ☎ 01676 522335 📄 0870 400 7372
web: www.marriotthotels.com
Aylesford Course: 18 Holes, 5801yds, Par 69, SSS 68.
Arden Course: 18 Holes, 7213yds, Par 72, SSS 73. Club membership 800.
Visitors Mon-Sun & BHs. Booking required. Handicap certificate. Dress code. **Societies** booking required.
Green Fees phone **Course Designer** Donald Steele **Prof** K Thomas **Facilities** ⚲ 🏠 🏌 ♦ 🏌 🛄 🏌 ⚐
Leisure hard tennis courts, heated indoor swimming pool, fishing, sauna, gymnasium, croquet lawn, health and beauty salon **Conf** facs Corporate Hospitality Days **Location** M42 junct 6, follow A45 to Coventry. Straight over Stonebridge flyover, then turn left into Shepherds Lane before Little Chef. Hotel 2m on left
Hotel ★★★★ 82% CHH Forest of Arden, A Marriott Hotel & Country Club, Maxstoke Lane, MERIDEN ☎ 01676 522335 📄 01676 523711 214 en suite

Shirley Golf Club Stratford Rd, Monkspath, Shirley B90 4EW

☎ 0121 744 6001 ▤ 0121 746 5645

e-mail: enquiries@shirleygolfclub.co.uk

web: www.shirleygolfclub.co.uk

Undulating parkland course in the Blythe Valley, with water features and surrounded by woodland.

18 Holes, 5600yds, Par 72, SSS 72, Course record 66. Club membership 600.

Visitors Mon-Fri & BHs. Weekends pm. Booking required weekends. Handicap certificate. Dress code. **Societies** booking required. **Green Fees** £38 per day (£40 weekends) **Prof** S Bottrill **Facilities** ⑪ ⑨ ⊚ ▯ ▯ ⚑ ⚐ ⚑ ⚑ ⚑ ⚑ **Leisure** halfway house **Conf** facs Corporate Hospitality Days **Location** M42 junct 4, 0.5m N on A34

Hotel ★★★★ 71% HL Holiday Inn Solihull, 61 Homer Road, SOLIHULL ☎ 0871 942 9201 & 0121 623 9988 ▤ 0121 711 2696 120 en suite

West Midlands Golf Club Marsh House Farm Ln B92 0LB

☎ 01675 444890 ▤ 01675 444891

web: www.wmgc.co.uk

18 Holes, 6624yds, Par 72, SSS 72, Course record 65.

Course Designer Nigel & Mark Harrhy/David Griffith **Location** from NEC A45 towards Coventry for 0.5m, onto A452 towards Leamington, club on right behind Mercedes dealership

Telephone for further details

Hotel ★★★ 73% HL Arden Hotel & Leisure Club, Coventry Road, Bickenhill, SOLIHULL ☎ 01675 443221 ▤ 01675 445604 216 en suite

See advert on opposite page

Widney Manor Golf Club Saintbury Dr B91 3SZ

☎ 0121 704 0704 ▤ 0121 704 7999

web: www.wmgc.co.uk

18 Holes, 5654yards, Par 71, SSS 66.

Course Designer Nigel & Mark Harrhy **Location** M42 junct 4, signs to Monkspath

Telephone for further details

Hotel ★★★★ 71% HL Holiday Inn Solihull, 61 Homer Road, SOLIHULL ☎ 0871 942 9201 & 0121 623 9988 ▤ 0121 711 2696 120 en suite

STOURBRIDGE
Map 7 SO88

Hagley Golf & Country Club Wassell Grove Ln, Hagley DY9 9JW

☎ 01562 883701 ▤ 01562 887518

e-mail: manager@hagleygcc.freeserve.co.uk

web: www.hagleygolfandcountryclub.co.uk

Undulating parkland course beneath the Clent Hills with superb views. Challenging, especially the testing 15th, par 5, 559yds, named Monster or Card Destroyer.

18 Holes, 6376yds, Par 72, SSS 72. Club membership 700.

Visitors dress code. **Societies** booking required **Green Fees** not confirmed **Course Designer** Garratt & Co **Prof** Paul Johnson **Facilities** ⑪ ⑨ ⊚ ▯ ▯ ⚑ ⚐ ⚑ ⚑ **Leisure** squash **Conf** facs Corporate Hospitality Days **Location** 1m E of Hagley off A456. 2m from junct 3 on M5

Hotel ★★★★ 73% HL Copthorne Hotel Merry Hill - Dudley, The Waterfront, Level Street, Brierley Hill, DUDLEY ☎ 01384 482882 ▤ 01384 482773 138 en suite

Stourbridge Golf Club Worcester Ln, Pedmore DY8 2RB

☎ 01384 395566 ▤ 01384 444660

e-mail: secretary@stourbridge-golf-club.co.uk

web: www.stourbridge-golf-club.co.uk

Parkland course playable all year. Not long by today's standards but accuracy is the key to returning a good score.

18 Holes, 6231yds, Par 70, SSS 69, Course record 67. Club membership 729.

Visitors Mon-Fri except BHs. Handicap certificate. Dress code **Societies** booking required. **Green Fees** £32 per 18 holes, £37.50 per day ⊚ **Prof** M Male **Facilities** ⑪ ⑨ ⊚ ▯ ▯ ⚑ ⚐ ⚑ ⚑ **Conf** Corporate Hospitality Days **Location** 2m S from town centre

Hotel ★★★★ 73% HL Copthorne Hotel Merry Hill - Dudley, The Waterfront, Level Street, Brierley Hill, DUDLEY ☎ 01384 482882 ▤ 01384 482773 138 en suite

SUTTON COLDFIELD
Map 7 SP19

Boldmere Golf Course Monmouth Dr B73 6JL

☎ 0121 354 3379 ▤ 0121 355 4534

e-mail: boldmere_golf@birmingham.gov.uk

web: www.golfbirmingham.co.uk

Established municipal course with 10 par 3s and a lake coming into play on the 16th and 18th holes.

18 Holes, 4202yds, Par 62, SSS 60, Course record 56. Club membership 300.

Visitors phone to book tee time. **Societies** booking required. **Green Fees** £16 per 18 holes (£12 after 2pm) **Prof** Trevor Short **Facilities** ⑪ ⊚ ▯ ▯ ⚑ ⚐ ⚑ ⚑ **Location** next to Sutton Park. Turn off A452 onto Monmouth Drive

Hotel ★★★★ 75% HL Best Western Premier Moor Hall Hotel & Spa, Moor Hall Drive, Four Oaks, SUTTON COLDFIELD ☎ 0121 308 3751 ▤ 0121 308 8974 82 en suite

Little Aston Golf Club Roman Rd, Streetly B74 3AN

☎ 0121 353 2942 ▤ 0121 580 8387

e-mail: manager@littleastongolf.co.uk

web: www.littleastongolf.co.uk

This parkland course is set in the rolling countryside of the former Little Aston Hall and there is a wide variety of mature trees. There are

continued

three par 3 holes and three par 5 holes and although the fairways are not unduly narrow there are rewards for accuracy - especially from the tee. The course features two lakes. At the par 5 12th the lake cuts into the green and at the par 4 17th the green is partially in the lake.

18 Holes, 6813yds, Par 72, SSS 74, Course record 65. Club membership 350.

Visitors Mon-Fri, Sun & BHs. Booking required. Handicap certificate. Dress code. **Societies** booking required. **Green Fees** £110 per day, £80 per round **Course Designer** H Vardon/H Colt **Prof** Brian Rimmer **Facilities** ⏀ ⏀ ⏀ ⏀ ⏀ ⏀ ⏀ ⏀ ⏀ ⏀ **Conf** Corporate Hospitality Days **Location** 3.5m NW of Sutton Coldfield off A454

Hotel ★★★★ 75% HL Best Western Premier Moor Hall Hotel & Spa, Moor Hall Drive, Four Oaks, SUTTON COLDFIELD ☎ 0121 308 3751 📄 0121 308 8974　82 en suite

Moor Hall Golf Club Moor Hall Dr B75 6LN
☎ 0121 308 6130 📄 0121 308 9560
e-mail: secretary@moorhallgolfclub.co.uk
Outstanding parkland course with mature trees lining the fairways. The 14th hole is notable and is part of a challenging finish to the round.

18 Holes, 6293yds, Par 70, SSS 70, Course record 64. Club membership 600.

Visitors Mon-Wed & Fri except BHs. Booking required. **Societies** booking required. **Green Fees** £60 per day, £45 per round **Course Designer** Hawtree & Taylor **Prof** Cameron Clark **Facilities** ⏀ ⏀ ⏀ ⏀ ⏀ ⏀ ⏀ ⏀ **Conf** Corporate Hospitality Days **Location** 2.5m N of town centre off A453

Hotel ★★★★ 75% HL Best Western Premier Moor Hall Hotel & Spa, Moor Hall Drive, Four Oaks, SUTTON COLDFIELD ☎ 0121 308 3751 📄 0121 308 8974　82 en suite

Pype Hayes Golf Club Eachel Hurst Rd B76 1EP
☎ 0121 351 1014 📄 0121 313 0206

18 Holes, 5927yds, Par 71, SSS 69, Course record 65.
Course Designer Bobby Jones **Location** 2.5m S off B4148
Telephone for further details
Hotel ★★★★ 75% HL Best Western Premier Moor Hall Hotel & Spa, Moor Hall Drive, Four Oaks, SUTTON COLDFIELD ☎ 0121 308 3751 📄 0121 308 8974　82 en suite

Sutton Coldfield Golf Club 110 Thornhill Rd, Streetly B74 3ER
☎ 0121 353 9633 📄 0121 353 5503
e-mail: admin@suttoncoldfieldgc.com
web: www.suttoncoldfieldgc.com
A fine natural, all-weather, heathland course, with tight fairways, gorse, heather and trees. A good challenge for all standards of golfer.

18 Holes, 6548yds, Par 72, SSS 72, Course record 64. Club membership 600.

Visitors Mon-Sun & BHs. Booking required. Dress code. **Societies** booking required. **Green Fees** Nov-Feb £45 per day, £35 per round (£45 weekends). Mar-Oct £50 per day, £40 per round (£50 weekends) **Course Designer** Dr A McKenzie **Prof** Jerry Hayes **Facilities** ⏀ ⏀ ⏀ ⏀ ⏀ ⏀ ⏀ ⏀ **Conf** facs Corporate Hospitality Days **Location** M6 junct 7, A34 towards Birmingham, 1st lights left onto A4041 Queslett Rd, Thornhill Rd, entrance after 4th left
Hotel ★★★★ 75% HL Best Western Premier Moor Hall Hotel & Spa, Moor Hall Drive, Four Oaks, SUTTON COLDFIELD ☎ 0121 308 3751 📄 0121 308 8974　82 en suite

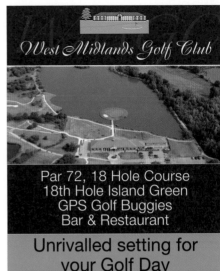

Walmley Golf Club Brooks Rd, Wylde Green B72 1HR
☎ 0121 373 0029 📄 0121 377 7272
e-mail: walmleygolfclub@aol.com
web: www.walmleygolfclub.co.uk
Rolling parkland course with mature woodlands. Two medium lakes cross three holes and two small lakes cross another hole.

18 Holes, 6603yds, Par 72, SSS 72, Course record 67. Club membership 700.

Visitors Mon-Fri except BHs. Booking required. Dress code. **Societies** booking required. **Green Fees** £36 per 18 holes **Course Designer** Neil Coles/Brian Huggett **Prof** M Morris **Facilities** ⏀ ⏀ ⏀ ⏀ ⏀ ⏀ ⏀ **Leisure** 2 snooker tables **Conf** Corporate Hospitality Days **Location** 2m S off A5127
Hotel ★★★★ 75% HL Best Western Premier Moor Hall Hotel & Spa, Moor Hall Drive, Four Oaks, SUTTON COLDFIELD ☎ 0121 308 3751 📄 0121 308 8974　82 en suite

Wishaw Golf Club Bulls Ln, Wishaw B76 9QW
☎ 0121 313 2110 📄 0121 313 2110
e-mail: golf@wishawgolfclub.co.uk
web: www.wishawgc.co.uk
Parkland with excellent water features and tight driving holes.

18 Holes, 6069yards, Par 70, SSS 69, Course record 68. Club membership 420.

Visitors Booking required weekends. Dress code. **Societies** booking required. **Green Fees** £18 per round (£25 weekends). Winter Nov-Mar £15 (£20) **Course Designer** R. Wallis **Prof** Alan Partridge **Facilities** ⏀ ⏀ ⏀ ⏀ ⏀ ⏀ ⏀ ⏀ ⏀ **Conf** facs Corporate Hospitality Days **Location** W of village off A4097
Hotel ★★★★ 80% HL New Hall, Walmley Road, SUTTON COLDFIELD ☎ 08450 727577 📄 08450 727578　60 en suite

WALSALL   Map 7 SP09

Bloxwich Golf Club 136 Stafford Rd, Bloxwich WS3 3PQ
☎ 01922 476593 📠 01922 493449
e-mail: secretary@bloxwichgolfclub.com
web: www.bloxwichgolfclub.com
Undulating parkland with natural hazards and subject to prevailing westerly winds, which in 2011 underwent a major course layout change.

18 Holes, 6269yds, Par 71, SSS 71, Course record 65.
Club membership 680.

Visitors Mon-Fri & BHs. Booking required. Dress code.
Societies booking required. **Green Fees** Mon £30 per 18 holes, Tue-Thu £33, Fri £35. **Prof** Richard J Dance **Facilities** ⊕ ⚑ 🍴 🏪 ☐ 🍴 🛄 🏧 🛒 **Conf** facs Corporate Hospitality Days **Location** M 6 junct 11/M6 (toll) T7, 3m N of town centre on A34
Hotel ★★★ 85% HL Fairlawns Hotel & Spa, 178 Little Aston Road, WALSALL ☎ 01922 455122 📠 01922 743148 58 en suite

Calderfields Golf Academy Aldridge Rd WS4 2JS
☎ 01922 632243 📠 01922 640540
web: www.calderfieldsgolf.com
18 Holes, 6509yds, Par 73, SSS 71.
Course Designer Roy Winter **Location** on A454
Telephone for further details
Hotel ★★★ 85% HL Fairlawns Hotel & Spa, 178 Little Aston Road, WALSALL ☎ 01922 455122 📠 01922 743148 58 en suite

Walsall Golf Club The Broadway WS1 3EY
☎ 01922 613512 📠 01922 616460
e-mail: secretary@walsallgolfclub.co.uk
web: www.walsallgolfclub.co.uk
Well-wooded parkland course with easy walking.

18 Holes, 6219yds, Par 70, SSS 70, Course record 63.
Club membership 600.

Visitors Mon-Fri except BHs. Handicap certificate preferred. Dress code. **Societies** booking required. **Green Fees** £46 per 18 holes **Course Designer** McKenzie **Prof** Richard Lambert **Facilities** ⊕ 🍴 🏪 ☐ 🍴 🛄 🏧 🛒 **Conf** Corporate Hospitality Days **Location** 1m S of town centre off A34
Hotel ★★★ 72% HL Holiday Inn Birmingham M6 Jct 7, Chapel Lane, Great Barr, BIRMINGHAM ☎ 0871 942 9009 & 0121 357 7303 📠 0121 357 7503 190 en suite

WEST BROMWICH   Map 7 SP09

Dartmouth Golf Club Vale St B71 4DW
☎ 0121 588 5746 & 588 2131
web: www.dartmouthgolfclub.co.uk
Very tight meadowland course with undulating but easy walking. The 675 yd par 5 1st hole is something of a challenge.

9 Holes, 5766yds, Par 71, SSS 69. Club membership 250.
Visitors Mon-Sun & BHs. Booking required. Dress code.
Societies booking required **Green Fees** not confirmed 🏧 **Course Designer** H Walker **Facilities** ⊕ 🏪 ☐ 🍴 🛄 🏧 **Conf** facs Corporate Hospitality Days **Location** E of town centre off A4041
Hotel ★★★ 67% HL Great Barr Hotel & Conference Centre, Pear Tree Drive, Newton Road, Great Barr, BIRMINGHAM ☎ 0121 357 1141 📠 0121 357 7557 92 en suite

Sandwell Park Golf Club Birmingham Rd B71 4JJ
☎ 0121 553 4637 📠 0121 525 1651
e-mail: secretary@sandwellparkgolfclub.co.uk
web: www.sandwellparkgolfclub.co.uk
A picturesque course wandering over wooded heathland and utilising natural features. Each hole is entirely separate, shielded from the others by either natural banks or lines of trees. A course that demands careful placing of shots that have been given a great deal of thought. Natural undulating fairways create difficult and testing approach shots to the greens.

18 Holes, 6468yds, Par 71, SSS 73.
Club membership 550.

Visitors Mon-Fri except BHs. Handicap certificate. Dress code.
Societies booking required. **Green Fees** £35 per 18 holes Mon-Fri. Winter specials & group rates available 🏧 **Course Designer** H S Colt **Prof** Daniel Lowe **Facilities** ⊕ 🍴 🏪 ☐ 🍴 🛄 🏧 🛒 **Leisure** practice chipping area **Conf** facs Corporate Hospitality Days **Location** M5 junct 1, 200yds on A41
Hotel ★★★ 67% HL Great Barr Hotel & Conference Centre, Pear Tree Drive, Newton Road, Great Barr, BIRMINGHAM ☎ 0121 357 1141 📠 0121 357 7557 92 en suite

WOLVERHAMPTON   Map 7 SO99

3 Hammers Golf Complex Old Stafford Rd, Coven WV10 7PP
☎ 01902 790428 📠 01902 791777
e-mail: info@3hammers.co.uk
web: www.3hammers.co.uk
Well maintained short course designed by Henry Cotton and providing a unique challenge to golfers of all standards.

18 Holes, 1410yds, Par 54, SSS 54, Course record 42.
Visitors Mon-Sun & BHs. Dress code **Societies** booking required.
Green Fees not confirmed **Course Designer** Henry Cotton **Prof** Piers Ward/Andy Proudman **Facilities** ⊕ 🍴 🏪 ☐ 🍴 🛄 🏧 🛒 **Conf** Corporate Hospitality Days **Location** M54 junct 2, on A449 N
Hotel ★★★ 71% HL Holiday Inn Wolverhampton, Dunstall Park, WOLVERHAMPTON ☎ 01902 390004 📠 01902 714364 54 en suite

Oxley Park Golf Club Stafford Rd WV10 6DE
☎ 01902 773989 📠 01902 773981
web: www.oxleyparkgolfclub.co.uk
18 Holes, 6226yds, Par 71, SSS 71, Course record 66.
Course Designer H S Colt **Location** M54 junct 2, 2m S
Telephone for further details
Hotel ★★★ 71% HL Holiday Inn Wolverhampton, Dunstall Park, WOLVERHAMPTON ☎ 01902 390004 📠 01902 714364 54 en suite

Penn Golf Club Penn Common, Penn WV4 5JN
☎ 01902 341142 📠 01902 620504
e-mail: secretary@penngolfclub.co.uk
web: www.penngolfclub.co.uk
Heathland course just outside the town.

18 Holes, 6453yds, Par 70, SSS 72, Course record 65.
Club membership 650.

Visitors Mon-Fri except BHs, Sun after 2pm. **Societies** booking required. **Green Fees** £28 per round, £35 per day **Prof** Guy Dean **Facilities** ⊕ 🍴 🏪 ☐ 🍴 🛄 🏧 🛒 **Location** SW of town centre off A449
Hotel ★★★ 70% HL The Connaught Hotel, Tettenhall Road, WOLVERHAMPTON ☎ 01902 424433 📠 01902 710353 87 en suite

South Staffordshire Golf Club Danescourt Rd, Tettenhall WV6 9BQ
☎ 01902 751065 📄 01902 751159
e-mail: suelebeau@southstaffsgc.co.uk
web: www.southstaffordshiregolfclub.co.uk

A wooded parkland course.
18 Holes, 6512yds, Par 71, SSS 72, Course record 64.
Club membership 500.
Visitors Mon-Sun & BHs. Booking required. Dress code.
Societies booking required. **Green Fees** £40 per round **Course Designer** Harry Vardon **Prof** Peter Baker **Facilities** ⑨ ⑩ ⬛
⬜ 🏴 ⅄ 🏠 🚅 ♂ ✦ **Conf** Corporate Hospitality Days
Location 3m NW of town centre, off A41
Hotel ★★★ 71% HL Holiday Inn Wolverhampton, Dunstall Park, WOLVERHAMPTON ☎ 01902 390004 📄 01902 714364 54 en suite

Wergs Golf Club Keepers Ln, Tettenhall WV6 8UA
☎ 01902 742225 📄 01902 844553
e-mail: wergs.golfclub@btinternet.com
web: www.wergs.com

Gently undulating parkland with streams and ditches, a mix of evergreen and deciduous trees, large greens and wide fairways.
18 Holes, 6949yds, Par 72, SSS 73. Club membership 100.
Visitors Mon-Sun & BHs. Booking required weekends. Dress code.
Societies booking required. **Green Fees** not confirmed **Course Designer** C W Moseley **Prof** Steve Weir **Facilities** ⑨ ⬛ ⬜ 🏴
⅄ 🏠 ♂ 🚅 ✦ **Conf** Corporate Hospitality Days **Location** 3m W of Wolverhampton off A41
Hotel ★★★ 71% HL Holiday Inn Wolverhampton, Dunstall Park, WOLVERHAMPTON ☎ 01902 390004 📄 01902 714364 54 en suite

WIGHT, ISLE OF

COWES   Map 4 SZ49

Cowes Golf Club Crossfield Av PO31 8HN
☎ 01983 292303 (secretary) 📄 01983 292303
e-mail: secretary@cowesgolfclub.co.uk
web: www.cowesgolfclub.co.uk

Fairly level, tight parkland course with difficult par 3s and Solent views.
9 Holes, 5672yds, Par 70, SSS 67, Course record 62.
Club membership 350.
Visitors Mon-Wed, Fri, Sat & BHs. Sun pm. Booking required. Dress code. **Societies** booking required. **Green Fees** not confirmed **Course Designer** Hamilton-Stutt **Facilities** ⑨ ⑩ ⬛ ⬜ 🏴 ⅄ ⅊
✦ **Conf** Corporate Hospitality Days **Location** NW of town centre next to Cowes High School
Hotel ★★★ 72% HL Best Western New Holmwood, Queens Road, Egypt Point, COWES ☎ 01983 292508 📄 01983 295020 26 en suite

EAST COWES   Map 4 SZ59

Osborne Golf Club Osborne House Estate PO32 6JX
☎ 01983 295421 📄 01983 292781
e-mail: manager@osbornegolfclub.co.uk
web: www.osbornegolfclub.co.uk

Undulating parkland course in the grounds of Osborne House. Quiet and peaceful situation with outstanding views.
9 Holes, 6381yds, Par 70, SSS 70, Course record 67.
Club membership 450.
Visitors Mon-Sun & BHs. Booking required. Dress code.
Societies booking required. **Green Fees** £27.50 per day (£32 weekends & BHs) **Prof** Derry Goodburn **Facilities** ⑨ ⬛ ⬜ 🏴
⅄ 🏠 ✦ **Location** E of town centre off A3021, in Osborne House Estate
Hotel ★★★ 72% HL Best Western New Holmwood, Queens Road, Egypt Point, COWES ☎ 01983 292508 📄 01983 295020 26 en suite

FRESHWATER   Map 4 SZ38

Freshwater Bay Golf Club Afton Down PO40 9TZ
☎ 01983 752955 📄 01983 752955
e-mail: secretary@freshwaterbaygolfclub.co.uk
web: www.freshwaterbaygolfclub.co.uk

A downland/seaside links with wide fairways and spectacular coastal views of the Solent and Channel.
18 Holes, 5725yds, Par 69, SSS 68, Course record 65.
Club membership 350.
Visitors Mon-Sun & BHs. Dress code **Societies** booking required.
Green Fees £34 per day (£38 weekends & BHs) **Course Designer** J H Taylor **Prof** James Veal **Facilities** ⑨ ⑩ ⬛ ⬜ 🏴 ⅄ ⅊
♂ 🚅 ✦ **Conf** Corporate Hospitality Days **Location** 0.5m E of village off A3055
Hotel ★★★ HL George Hotel, Quay Street, YARMOUTH
☎ 01983 760331 📄 01983 760425 19 en suite

ENGLAND

NEWPORT   Map 4 SZ58

Newport Golf Club St George's Down, Shide PO30 3BA
☎ 01983 525076
e-mail: mail@newportgolfclub.co.uk
web: www.newportgolfclub.co.uk
Challenging nine-hole course with water hazards, dog-legs and fine views.

9 Holes, 5350yds, Par 68, SSS 66. Club membership 350.
Visitors Mon-Wed, Fri except BHs. Thu & Sun pm only. Booking required. **Societies** booking required. **Green Fees** not confirmed 📷
Course Designer Guy Hunt **Prof** Graham Darke **Facilities** ⓨ ⓑ ⌑
🍴 ⌲ 🏠 ⛳ ✂ 🏌 **Location** 1.5m S off A3020, 200yds past Newport Football Club on left
Hotel ★★★ 72% HL Best Western New Holmwood, Queens Road, Egypt Point, COWES ☎ 01983 292508 📄 01983 295020 26 en suite

RYDE   Map 4 SZ59

Ryde Golf Club Binstead Rd PO33 3NF
☎ 01983 614809 📄 01983 567418
web: www.rydegolf.co.uk
9 Holes, 5587yds, Par 70, SSS 69, Course record 65.
Course Designer Hamilton-Stutt **Location** 1m W from town centre on A3054
Telephone for further details
Hotel ★★★ 73% HL Yelf's Hotel, Union Street, RYDE
☎ 01983 564062 📄 01983 563937 40 en suite

SANDOWN   Map 4 SZ58

Shanklin & Sandown Golf Club The Fairway, Lake PO36 9PR
☎ 01983 403217 (office) & 404424 (pro)
📄 01983 403007 (office)/404424 (pro)
e-mail: club@ssgolfclub.com
web: www.ssgolfclub.com
A county championship course, recognised for its natural heathland beauty, spectacular views and challenging qualities. The course demands respect, with accurate driving and careful club selection the order of the day.

18 Holes, 6044yds, Par 70, SSS 70. Club membership 700.
Visitors Mon, Wed-Fri, Sun & BHs. Tue pm. Sat after 1pm. Dress code. **Societies** booking required. **Green Fees** £36 (£40 weekends & BHs) **Course Designer** Braid **Prof** Peter Hammond **Facilities** ⓨ
🍽 ⓑ ⌑ 🍴 ⌲ 🏠 ⛳ ✂ **Conf** Corporate Hospitality Days
Location from Sandown towards Shanklin past Heights Leisure Centre, 200yds right into Fairway for 1m
Hotel ★★★ 80% HL Melville Hall Hotel & Utopia Spa, Melville Street, SANDOWN ☎ 01983 400500 & 406526 📄 01983 407093 30 en suite

VENTNOR   Map 4 SZ57

Ventnor Golf Club Steephill Down Rd PO38 1BP
☎ 01983 853326 & 853388 📄 01983 853326
web: www.ventnorgolfclub.co.uk
12 Holes, 5767yds, Par 70, SSS 68, Course record 64.
Location 1m NW off B3327, turn at chip shop
Telephone for further details
Hotel ★★★★ 79% HL The Royal Hotel, Belgrave Road, VENTNOR
☎ 01983 852186 📄 01983 855395 53 en suite

WILTSHIRE

BISHOPS CANNINGS   Map 4 SU06

North Wilts Golf Club SN10 2LP
☎ 01380 860627 📄 01380 860877
e-mail: secretary@northwiltsgolf.com
web: www.northwiltsgolf.com
Established in 1890 and one of the oldest courses in Wiltshire, North Wilts is situated high on the downlands of Wiltshire, with spectacular views over the surrounding countryside. The chalk base allows free draining and the course provides a challenge to golfers of all abilities.

18 Holes, 6414yds, Par 71, SSS 71, Course record 65. Club membership 700.
Visitors dress code. **Societies** welcome. **Green Fees** £40 per day (£40 per round weekends) **Course Designer** H S Colt **Prof** Graham Laing **Facilities** ⓨ 🍽 ⓑ ⌑ 🍴 ⌲ 🏠 ⛳ ✂ 🏌
Conf Corporate Hospitality Days **Location** 2m NW of Devizes between A4 & A361
Hotel ★★★ 80% HL Bear Hotel, Market Place, DEVIZES
☎ 01380 722444 📄 01380 722450 25 en suite

BRADFORD-ON-AVON   Map 3 ST86

Cumberwell Park Golf Club BA15 2PQ
☎ 01225 863322 📄 01225 868160
web: www.cumberwellpark.com

Red: 9 Holes, 3296yds, Par 35.
Yellow: 9 Holes, 3139yds, Par 36.
Blue: 9 Holes, 3291yds, Par 36.
Orange: 9 Holes, 3061yds, Par 35.
Course Designer Adrian Stiff **Location** 1.5m N on A363
Telephone for further details
Hotel ★★★ 82% HL Woolley Grange, Woolley Green, BRADFORD-ON-AVON ☎ 01225 864705 📄 01225 864059 26 en suite

Save on Hotels. Book at **theAA.com/hotel**

WILTSHIRE

ENGLAND

CALNE
Map 3 ST97

Bowood Hotel, Spa & Golf Resort Derry Hill SN11 9PQ
☎ 01249 822228 ▤ 01249 822218
e-mail: golfclub@bowood.org
web: www.bowood.org

This Dave Thomas designed course weaves through 200 acres of 'Capability' Brown's mature woodland with cavernous moulded bunkers, skilfully planned hillocks defining the fairways and vast rolling greens. Numerous doglegs, bunkers, tees and lakes will prove a test for any golfer.

Bowood Championship Course: 18 Holes, 7317yds, Par 72, SSS 73, Course record 63. Club membership 500.

Visitors Mon-Fri & BHs. Weekends pm. Booking required. Dress code. **Societies** booking required. **Green Fees** £60 per round **Course Designer** Dave Thomas **Prof** Paul McLean **Facilities** ⓣ ⑩ ᴸ ⊑ ▥ ⅄ 🖻 ⅌ ◇ ♂ 🛒 ♂ ✔ **Leisure** heated indoor swimming pool, sauna, gymnasium, halfway house **Conf** facs Corporate Hospitality Days **Location** signed from M4 junct 17, 2.5m W of Calne off A4

Hotel ★★★★ 82% CHH Bowood Hotel, Spa and Golf Resort, Derry Hill, CALNE ☎ 01249 822228 ▤ 01249 822218 43 en suite

CASTLE COMBE
Map 3 ST87

Manor House Hotel and Golf Club SN14 7JW
☎ 01249 782982 ▤ 01249 782992
e-mail: enquiries@manorhousegolfclub.co.uk
web: www.exclusivehotels.co.uk

Set in a wonderful location within the wooded estate of the 14th-century Manor House, this course includes five par 5s and some spectacular par 3s. Manicured fairways and hand-cut greens, together with the River Bybrook meandering through the middle make for a picturesque and dramatic course.

18 Holes, 6500yds, Par 72, SSS 72.
Club membership 450.

Visitors Mon, Tue, Thu, Fri & BHs. Other days pm only. Booking required. Handicap certificate. Dress code. **Societies** booking required. **Green Fees** not confirmed **Course Designer** Peter Alliss/Clive Clark **Prof** P Green/A Ryan **Facilities** ⓣ ⑩ ᴸ ⊑ ▥ ⅄ 🖻 ⅌ ◇ ♂ 🛒 ♂ ✔ **Leisure** hard tennis courts, fishing, sauna, croquet **Conf** facs Corporate Hospitality Days **Location** M4 junct 17/18, 5m NW of Chippenham on B4039

Hotel ★★★★ CHH Manor House Hotel and Golf Club, CASTLE COMBE ☎ 01249 782206 ▤ 01249 782159 48 en suite

CHIPPENHAM
Map 3 ST97

Chippenham Golf Club Malmesbury Rd SN15 5LT
☎ 01249 652040 ▤ 01249 446681
e-mail: chippenhamgolf@btconnect.com
web: www.chippenhamgolfclub.com

Easy walking on mixed parkland/heathland course. Nine of the holes will test the best golfer and the remaining holes will give everyone a chance for pars and birdies.

18 Holes, 5783yds, Par 69, SSS 67, Course record 62.
Club membership 650.

Visitors Mon-Sun & BHs. Booking required weekends. **Societies** booking required. **Green Fees** £32 per day, £30 per round (£38 weekends & BHs) **Prof** Bill Creamer **Facilities** ⓣ ⑩ ᴸ ⊑ ▥ ⅄ 🖻 ♂ ✔ **Conf** facs Corporate Hospitality Days **Location** 2m S of M4 junct 17, 1m N of Chippenham on A350

Hotel ★★★★ CHH Manor House Hotel and Golf Club, CASTLE COMBE ☎ 01249 782206 ▤ 01249 782159 48 en suite

CRICKLADE
Map 4 SU09

Cricklade House Common Hill SN6 6HA
☎ 01793 750751 ▤ 01793 751767
e-mail: reception@crickladehotel.co.uk
web: www.crickladehotel.co.uk

A challenging nine-hole course with undulating greens and beautiful views. Par 3 6th (128yds) signature hole from an elevated tee to a green protected by a deep pot bunker and a water hazard.

9 Holes, 1830yds, Par 62, SSS 58. Club membership 60.

Visitors Dress code. **Societies** booking required. **Green Fees** £9 pay and play **Course Designer** Ian Bolt/Colin Smith **Facilities** ⓣ ⑩ ᴸ ⊑ ▥ ⅄ 🖻 ♂ ✔ **Leisure** hard tennis courts, heated indoor swimming pool, gymnasium, snooker, pool, jacuzzi, tennis, steam room **Conf** facs Corporate Hospitality Days **Location** on B4040 from Cricklade towards Malmesbury

Hotel ★★★ 78% HL Cricklade House, Common Hill, CRICKLADE ☎ 01793 750751 ▤ 01793 751767 46 en suite

ERLESTOKE
Map 3 ST95

Erlestoke Golf Club SN10 5UB
☎ 01380 831069 ▤ 01380 831284
e-mail: info@erlestokegolfclub.co.uk
web: www.erlestokegolfclub.co.uk

The course is set on the lower slopes of Salisbury Plain with distant views to the Cotswolds and the Marlborough Downs. The 7th plunges from an elevated three-tiered tee, high in the woods, to a large green with a spectacular backdrop of a meandering river and hills. The course was built to suit every standard of golfer from the novice to the very low handicapper and its two tiers offer lakes and rolling downland.

18 Holes, 6759yds, Par 72, SSS 72. Club membership 720.

Visitors Mon-Sun & BHs. Booking required. Dress code. **Societies** booking required. **Green Fees** £26 per 18 holes (£31 weekends and BHs) **Course Designer** Adrian Stiff **Prof** Steve Blazey **Facilities** ⓣ ⑩ ᴸ ⊑ ▥ ⅄ 🖻 ⅌ 🛒 ♂ ✔ **Conf** facs Corporate Hospitality Days **Location** on B3098 Devizes-Westbury road

Hotel ★★★ 80% HL Bear Hotel, Market Place, DEVIZES ☎ 01380 722444 ▤ 01380 722450 25 en suite

GREAT DURNFORD
Map 4 SU13

High Post Golf Club SP4 6AT
☎ 01722 782356 📠 01722 782674
e-mail: admin@highpostgolfclub.co.uk
web: www.highpostgolfclub.co.uk
Established in 1922, a championship downland course which offers summer tees and greens all year. Free draining and easy walking. The opening three holes, usually played with the wind, get you to off to a flying start, but the closing three provide a tough finish. Peter Alliss has rated the 9th among his dream holes. The club welcomes golfers of all abilities.
18 Holes, 6305yds, Par 70, SSS 70, Course record 64. Club membership 625.
Visitors Mon-Sun & BHs. Booking required weekends & BHs. **Societies** welcome. **Green Fees** not confirmed **Course Designer** Hawtree & Ptrs **Prof** Tony Isaacs **Facilities** ⓣ ⓘⓞⓘ ⓛ ⓒ ⓟⓘ ⓛ ⓐ ⓒ ⓕ **Conf** facs Corporate Hospitality Days
Location on A345 between Sailsbury and Amesbury
Hotel ★★★ 62% HL Quality Hotel Andover, Micheldever Road, ANDOVER ☎ 01264 369111 📠 01264 369000 49 en suite

HIGHWORTH
Map 4 SU29

Wrag Barn Golf & Country Club Shrivenham Rd SN6 7QQ
☎ 01793 861327 📠 01793 861325
e-mail: info@wragbarn.com
web: www.wragbarn.com
A fast maturing parkland course in an Area of Outstanding Natural Beauty with views to the Lambourne Hills and Vale of the White Horse.
18 Holes, 6633yds, Par 72, SSS 72, Course record 65. Club membership 700.
Visitors Mon-Sun & BHs. Booking required weekends & BHs. Dress code. **Societies** booking required **Green Fees** not confirmed **Course Designer** Hawtree **Prof** Ian Ridsdale **Facilities** ⓣ ⓘⓞⓘ ⓛ ⓒ ⓟⓘ ⓛ ⓐ ⓒ ⓕ **Conf** facs Corporate Hospitality Days
Location on B4000 from Highworth, signed
Hotel ★★★ 77% HL Stanton House, The Avenue, Stanton Fitzwarren, SWINDON ☎ 0870 084 1388 📠 01793 861857 82 en suite

KINGSDOWN
Map 3 ST86

Kingsdown Golf Club SN13 8BS
☎ 01225 743472 📠 01225 743472
e-mail: kingsdowngc@btconnect.com
web: www.kingsdowngolfclub.co.uk
Fairly flat, open downland course with very sparse tree cover but surrounding wood. Many interesting holes with testing features.
18 Holes, 6445yds, Par 72, SSS 71. Club membership 800.
Visitors Mon-Fri except BHs. Dress code. **Societies** booking required. **Green Fees** £36 per day **Prof** Andrew Butler **Facilities** ⓣ ⓛ ⓒ ⓟⓘ ⓐ ⓒ ⓕ **Location** W of village between Corsham and Bathford
Hotel ★★★★★ CHH Lucknam Park, COLERNE ☎ 01225 742777 📠 01225 743536 42 en suite

LANDFORD
Map 4 SU21

Hamptworth Golf & Country Club Hamptworth Rd, Hamptworth SP5 2DU
☎ 01794 390155
e-mail: info@hamptworthgolf.co.uk
web: www.hamptworthgolf.co.uk
Hamptworth enjoys ancient woodland and an abundance of wildlife in a beautiful setting on the northern edge of the New Forest. Many holes play alongside or over the Blackwater river with mature forest oaks guarding almost every fairway.
18 Holes, 6004yds, Par 70, SSS 69. Club membership 750.
Visitors Mon-Sun & BHs. Booking required. Dress code.
Societies booking required **Green Fees** Mon-Wed £20 per 18 holes, Thu & Fri £29, weekends £40. Twilight after 3pm, Mon-Wed £15 per 18 holes, £8 per 9 holes, Sun £25/£10 **Course Designer** Philip Sanders/Brian Pierson **Prof** Nick Stoner **Facilities** ⓣ ⓘⓞⓘ ⓛ ⓒ ⓟⓘ ⓐ ⓒ ⓕ ⓕ **Leisure** hard tennis courts, gymnasium, croquet lawns, physiotherapy **Conf** facs Corporate Hospitality Days
Location 1.5m W of Landford off B3079
Hotel ★★★ 80% HL Bartley Lodge Hotel, Lyndhurst Road, CADNAM ☎ 023 8081 2248 📠 023 8081 2075 40 en suite

MARLBOROUGH
Map 4 SU16

Marlborough Golf Club The Common SN8 1DU
☎ 01672 512147 📠 01672 513164
e-mail: contactus@marlboroughgolfclub.co.uk
web: www.marlboroughgolfclub.co.uk
Undulating downland course with extensive views over the Og Valley and the Marlborough Downs.
18 Holes, 6433yds, Par 72, SSS 71, Course record 68. Club membership 800.
Visitors Mon-Sun & BHs. Dress code. **Societies** booking required. **Green Fees** not confirmed **Prof** S Amor **Facilities** ⓣ ⓘⓞⓘ ⓛ ⓒ ⓟⓘ ⓐ ⓒ ⓕ ⓒ ⓕ **Conf** facs Corporate Hospitality Days
Location N of town centre on A346
Hotel ★★★ 70% HL The Castle & Ball, High Street, MARLBOROUGH ☎ 01672 515201 📠 01672 515895 35 en suite

OGBOURNE ST GEORGE
Map 4 SU27

Ogbourne Downs Golf Club SN8 1TB
☎ 01672 841327
e-mail: office@ogbournedowns.co.uk
web: www.ogbournedowns.co.uk
Downland turf and magnificent greens. Wind and slopes make this one of the most challenging courses in Wiltshire. Extensive views. No temporary greens or tees.
18 Holes, 6422yds, Par 71, SSS 71. Club membership 650.
Visitors Mon-Sun & BHs. Booking required. Dress code.
Societies booking required. **Green Fees** £25 per 18 holes (£35 weekends) **Course Designer** J H Taylor **Prof** Craig Bell/Ben Newman **Facilities** ⓣ ⓘⓞⓘ ⓛ ⓒ ⓟⓘ ⓐ ⓒ ⓕ ⓒ ⓕ **Conf** facs Corporate Hospitality Days **Location** N of village on A346
Hotel ★★★ 75% HL Chiseldon House, New Road, Chiseldon, SWINDON ☎ 01793 741010 & 07770 853883 📠 01793 741059 21 en suite

ALISBURY　　　　　　　　　Map 4 SU12

alisbury & South Wilts Golf Club Netherhampton
P2 8PR
☎ 01722 742645 📄 01722 742676
-mail: mail@salisburygolf.co.uk
eb: www.salisburygolf.co.uk

ently undulating and well-drained parkland courses in country
etting with panoramic views of the cathedral and surrounding
ountryside. Never easy with six excellent opening holes and four
qually testing closing holes. Both these mature courses are
aintained to a very high standard and are in excellent condition all
ear round.

*athedral Course: 18 Holes, 6485yds, Par 71, SSS 71,
ourse record 62.
ibury Course: 9 Holes, 2837yds, Par 34, SSS 67.
lub membership 900.*

isitors Mon-Sun & BHs. Booking required weekends & BHs.
andicap certificate. Dress code. **Societies** booking required.
reen Fees Cathedral course £40 per day, £35 per round (£60/£50
eekends). Bibury £15/£12 (£16/£13 weekends) **Course Designer** J
H Taylor/S Gidman **Prof** Jon Waring **Facilities** ⓘ 🍴 🍺 🖥 🍴
🏌 🍴 ⛳ 🍴 **Leisure** snooker table **Conf** facs Corporate
ospitality Days **Location** 2m SW of Salisbury on A3094
otel ★★★ 68% HL Grasmere House Hotel, Harnham Road,
ALISBURY ☎ 01722 338388 📄 01722 333710　38 en suite

SWINDON　　　　　　　　　Map 4 SU18

Broome Manor Golf Complex Pipers Way SN3 1RG
☎ 01793 532403 (bookings) & 495761 (enquiries)
📄 01793 433255
e-mail: broomegolfshop@swindon.gov.uk
web: www.swindon.gov.uk/broome

Two courses and a 34-bay floodlit driving range. Parkland with water
hazards, open fairways and short cut rough. Walking is easy on gentle
slopes.

*Broome Manor 1: 18 Holes, 6366yds, Par 71, SSS 70,
Course record 61.
Broome Manor 2: 9 Holes, 2690yds, Par 66, SSS 66.
Club membership 800.*

Visitors Mon-Sun & BHs. Booking required. **Societies** booking
required. **Green Fees** contact club for details **Course
Designer** Hawtree **Prof** Barry Sandry **Facilities** ⓘ 🍴 🍺 🖥 🍴
🏌 🍴 ⛳ 🍴 **Leisure** gymnasium **Conf** facs Corporate
ospitality Days **Location** 1.75m SE of town centre off B4006
otel ★★★★ 76% HL Swindon Marriott Hotel, Pipers Way,
SWINDON ☎ 01793 512121 📄 01723 513114　156 en suite

TIDWORTH　　　　　　　　　Map 4 SU24

Tidworth Garrison Golf Club Bulford Rd SP9 7AF
☎ 01980 842301 📄 01980 842301
e-mail: secretary@tidworthgolfclub.co.uk
web: www.tidworthgolfclub.co.uk

A breezy, dry downland course with lovely turf, fine trees and
views over Salisbury Plain and the surrounding area. The 4th and
12th holes are notable. The 565yd 14th, going down towards the
clubhouse, gives the big hitter a chance to let fly.

*18 Holes, 6320yds, Par 70, SSS 70, Course record 65.
Club membership 700.*

Visitors Mon-Sun & BHs. Booking required. Handicap certificate.
Dress code. **Societies** booking required. **Green Fees** £35 before
noon, £25 after noon **Course Designer** Donald Steel **Prof** Terry
Gosden **Facilities** ⓘ 🍴 🍺 🖥 🍴 🏌 🍴 ⛳ 🍴
Location W of village off A338
Hotel ★★★ 62% HL Quality Hotel Andover, Micheldever Road,
ANDOVER ☎ 01264 369111 📄 01264 369000　49 en suite

TOLLARD ROYAL　　　　　　　Map 3 ST91

Rushmore Golf Club SP5 5QB
☎ 01725 516326 📄 01725 516437
e-mail: golf@rushmoreuk.com
web: www.rushmoregolfclub.co.uk

Peaceful and testing parkland course situated on Cranborne Chase
with far-reaching views. An undulating course with avenues of trees
and well-drained greens. With water on seven out of 18 holes, it will
test the most confident of golfers.

18 Holes, 6131yds, Par 71, SSS 70. Club membership 650.

Visitors Mon-Sun & BHs. Booking required. Dress code.
Societies booking required. **Green Fees** £30 per round (£40
weekends). £80 4 ball (£100 weekends) **Course Designer** David
Pottage/John Jacobs Developments **Prof** Jason Sherman **Facilities** ⓘ
🍴 by prior arrangement 🍺 🖥 🍴 🏌 🍴 ⛳ 🍴 ⛳
Conf facs Corporate Hospitality Days **Location** N off B3081 between
Sixpenny Handley & Tollard Royal
Hotel ★★★ 72% HL Best Western Royal Chase, Royal Chase
Roundabout, SHAFTESBURY ☎ 01747 853355 📄 01747 851969
33 en suite

UPAVON　　　　　　　　　Map 4 SU15

Upavon Golf Club Douglas Av SN9 6BQ
☎ 01980 630787 & 630281 📄 01980 635103
e-mail: play@upavongolfclub.co.uk
web: www.upavongolfclub.co.uk

Free-draining course on chalk downland with panoramic views over
the Vale of Pewsey and the Alton Barnes White Horse. A fair test of golf
with a good mixture of holes including a 602yd par 5 and an excellent
finishing hole, a par 3 of 169yds across a valley.

*18 Holes, 6402yds, Par 71, SSS 71, Course record 66.
Club membership 520.*

Visitors Mon-Sun & BHs. Booking required weekends & BHs. Dress
code. **Societies** booking required. **Green Fees** £36 per day (£46
weekends) 🌐 **Course Designer** Richard Blake **Prof** Richard Blake
Facilities ⓘ 🍴 by prior arrangement 🍺 🖥 🍴 🏌 🍴 ⛳
🍴 ⛳ **Location** 1.5m SE of Upavon on A342
Hotel ★★★ 80% HL Bear Hotel, Market Place, DEVIZES
☎ 01380 722444 📄 01380 722450　25 en suite

ENGLAND

WARMINSTER — Map 3 ST84

West Wilts Golf Club Elm Hill BA12 0AU
☎ 01985 213133
e-mail: sec@westwiltsgolfclub.co.uk
web: www.westwiltsgolfclub.co.uk

A hilltop chalk downland course among the Wiltshire downs. Free draining, short, but a very good test of accurate iron play. Excellent fairways and greens all year round.

18 Holes, 5754yds, Par 70, SSS 68, Course record 61.
Club membership 700.

Visitors Mon-Fri, Sun & BHs. Booking required Sun. County cards accepted. **Societies** booking required. **Green Fees** £25 per 18 holes, £40 per 36 holes. County card £20, Juniors £17.50 **Course Designer** J H Taylor **Facilities** ⑪ ⑩ by prior arrangement ⓘ ⓛ ⑨ ⓙ ⓐ ⓔ ⑨ ⓕ **Leisure** indoor practice facility **Conf** Corporate Hospitality Days **Location** N of town centre, 1m off A350 **Hotel** ★★★★ 78% HL Bishopstrow House Hotel, WARMINSTER ☎ 01985 212312 ⓙ 01985 216769 32 en suite

WOOTTON BASSETT — Map 4 SU08

The Wiltshire Golf Club Vastern SN4 7PB
☎ 01793 849999 ⓙ 01793 849988
e-mail: reception@the-wiltshire.co.uk
web: www.the-wiltshire.co.uk

A Peter Alliss and William Swan design set in rolling Wiltshire downland. A number of lakes add a challenge for both low and high handicappers.

The Garden Course: 9 Holes, 3027yds, Par 71, SSS 69.
The Lakes Course: 18 Holes, 6628yds, Par 72, SSS 72.
Club membership 450.

Visitors Mon-Sun & BHs. Booking required. Dress code.
Societies booking required. **Green Fees** Lakes £24 per 18 holes (£33 weekends & BHs). Garden £15 per 9 holes (£20 weekends & BHs) **Course Designer** Peter Alliss & William Swan **Prof** Richard Lawless **Facilities** ⑪ ⑩ ⓘ ⓛ ⑨ ⓙ ⓐ ⓔ ⑨ ⓞ ⓕ ⓖ ⑨ **Leisure** heated indoor swimming pool, sauna, gymnasium, halfway house **Conf** facs Corporate Hospitality Days **Location** M4 exit junct 16, off A3102 SW of Wootton Bassett **Hotel** ★★★ 78% HL The Wiltshire, WOOTTON BASSETT ☎ 01793 849999 ⓙ 01793 849988 58 en suite

Woodbridge Park Golf Club Longmans Farm SN15 5DG
☎ 01666 510277
web: www.woodbridgepark.co.uk
18 Holes, 5884yds, Par 70, SSS 70.
Course Designer Chris Kane **Location** off B4042 between Malmesbury and Wootton Bassett
Telephone for further details
Hotel ★★★ 72% HL Marsh Farm, Coped Hall, WOOTTON BASSETT ☎ 01793 842800 & 848044 ⓙ 01793 851528 50 en suite

WORCESTERSHIRE

ALVECHURCH — Map 7 SP07

Kings Norton Golf Club Brockhill Ln, Weatheroak B48 7ED
☎ 01564 826706 & 826789 ⓙ 01564 826955
e-mail: info@kingsnortongolfclub.co.uk
web: www.kingsnortongolfclub.co.uk

Parkland with water hazards. A 27-hole championship venue playing as three combinations of nine holes.

Weatheroak: 18 Holes, 6700yds, Par 72, SSS 72,
Course record 65.
Brockhill: 18 Holes, 6603yds, Par 72, SSS 72,
Course record 66.
Wythall: 18 Holes, 6551yds, Par 72, SSS 72.
Club membership 1000.

Visitors Mon-Fri except BHs. Dress code. **Societies** booking required. **Green Fees** £35 per day. Winter £22 **Course Designer** F Hawtree **Prof** Kevin Hayward **Facilities** ⑪ ⑩ ⓘ ⓛ ⑨ ⓙ ⓐ ⓔ ⑨ ⓕ ⓖ ⑨ **Leisure** 12 hole par 3 course **Conf** facs Corporate Hospitality Days **Location** M42 junct 3, off A435 **Hotel** ★★★★ 71% HL Holiday Inn Birmingham - Bromsgrove, Kidderminster Road, BROMSGROVE ☎ 01527 576600 & 0871 942 9142 ⓙ 01527 878981 110 en suite

BEWDLEY — Map 7 SO77

Bewdley Pines Golf Club Habberley Rd DY12 1LY
☎ 01299 404744 (Pro shop) & 409098 (club house)
ⓙ 01299 861578
e-mail: contact@bewdleypines.com
web: www.bewdleypines.com

Taking full advantage of the rolling terrain, the course is laid out over sandy, well draining land alongside the scenic Habberley Valley Country Park. The cunningly enhanced natural hazards ensure that no hole resembles another, each presenting its own test of skill and nerve. Two holes that deserve special mention are the 3rd par 4 367yds, a 'thread needle' hole onto a sloping fairway which bounces wayward shots out of bounds. The 14th par 3 151yds has a 30 foot drop from tee to green on to a pocket handkerchief green. Overhanging trees and steep banks ensure a reward only for a well struck tee shot.

18 Holes, 5398yds, Par 69, SSS 67. Club membership 550.

Visitors Mon-Fri, Sun & BHs. Sat pm. Booking required. Dress code. **Societies** booking required. **Green Fees** £20 per 18 holes, £13 per 9 holes (£25/£15 weekends) **Prof** Mark Slater **Facilities** ⑪ ⑩ ⓘ ⑨ ⓙ ⓐ ⓔ ⑨ ⓕ ⓖ ⑨ **Conf** Corporate Hospitality Days **Location** A456 past West Midland Safari Park, then take B4190 **Hotel** ★★★ 78% HL Gainsborough House Hotel, Bewdley Hill, KIDDERMINSTER ☎ 01562 820041 ⓙ 01562 66179 42 en suite

Little Lakes Golf and Country Club Lye Head DY12 2UZ
☎ 01299 266385 ⓙ 01299 266398
web: www.little-lakes.co.uk
18 Holes, 6298yds, Par 71, SSS 70, Course record 68.
Course Designer M Laing **Location** 2.25m W of Bewdley off A456
Telephone for further details
Hotel ★★★★ INN Royal Forester Country Inn, Callow Hill, BEWDLEY ☎ 01299 266286 7 rooms

Wharton Park Golf & Country Club Longbank DY12 2QW
☎ 01299 405163 📄 01299 405121
e-mail: enquiries@whartonpark.co.uk
web: www.whartonpark.co.uk

An 18-hole championship-standard course set in beautiful Worcestershire countryside, with stunning views. Some long par 5s such as the 9th (594yds) as well as superb par 3 holes at 3rd, 10th and 15th make this a challenging course.

18 Holes, 6468yds, Par 71, SSS 71. Club membership 500.

Visitors Mon-Sun & BHs. Booking required. Dress code.
Societies booking required. **Green Fees** £17.50-£22.50 per round
Course Designer Howard Swan **Prof** Angus Hoare **Facilities** ⊕ ⫶⊙⫶
⊪ ⊡ ⫽ ⊿ 🖾 ⫽ ◇ ⊘ ⊨ ⊘ ⌇ **Conf facs** Corporate
Hospitality Days **Location** off A456 Bewdley bypass
Hotel ★★★★ GH Welchgate Guest House, 1 Welch Gate, BEWDLEY
☎ 01299 402655   4 rooms

BISHAMPTON   Map 3 SO95

Vale Golf Club Hill Furze Rd WR10 2LZ
☎ 01386 462781 📄 01386 462597
e-mail: membership.manager@thevalegolf.co.uk
web: www.thevalegolf.co.uk

This course offers an American-style layout, with large greens, trees and bunkers and several water hazards. Its rolling fairways provide a testing round, as well as superb views of the Malvern Hills. Picturesque and peaceful.

International Course: 18 Holes, 7154yds, Par 74, SSS 74, Course record 68.
Lenches Course: 9 Holes, 5518yds, Par 70, SSS 66.
Club membership 1050.

Visitors Mon-Sun & BHs. Booking required. Dress code.
Societies booking required. **Green Fees** International £28 per round, Lenches 9 holes £12 (£36/£13 weekends) **Course Designer** Bob Sandow **Prof** Richard Jenkins **Facilities** ⊕ ⫶⊙⫶ ⊪ ⊡ ⫽
⊿ 🖾 ⫽ ⊘ ⊨ ⊘ ⌇ **Leisure** fishing **Conf facs** Corporate
Hospitality Days **Location** signed off A44
Hotel ★★★ 77% HL The Evesham, Coopers Lane, Off Waterside, EVESHAM ☎ 01386 765566 & 0800 716969 (Res) 📄 01386 765443
40 en suite

BROADWAY   Map 4 SP03

Broadway Golf Club Willersey Hill WR12 7LG
☎ 01386 853683 📄 01386 858643
e-mail: secretary@broadwaygolfclub.co.uk
web: www.broadwaygolfclub.co.uk

Uniquely located at the edge of the Cotswolds this course lies at an altitude of 850ft above sea level, with extensive views over the Vale of Evesham. The inland links style provides a challenge for golfers of all abilities. It offers holes that with their natural and artificial hazards require drives that are skilfully placed, approaches carefully judged and undulating greens expertly read. The rolling fairways are intersected by Cotswold dry stone walls.

18 Holes, 6228yds, Par 72, SSS 71, Course record 63.
Club membership 700.

Visitors Mon-Fri except BHs. Weekends pm. Booking required weekends. Handicap certificate. Dress code. **Societies** booking required. **Green Fees** £42 per day, £35 per round (£42 weekends)
Course Designer James Braid **Prof** Martyn Freeman **Facilities** ⊕

⫶⊙⫶ ⊪ ⊡ ⫽ ⊿ 🖾 ⫽ ◇ ⊘ ⊨ ⊘ ⌇ **Conf facs** Corporate
Hospitality Days **Location** 1.5m E on A44, at top of Fish Hill take left turning opposite Broadway Tower signed Saintbury. After 0.5m turn left as road bends sharply right. Club just past Dormy House Hotel on left
Hotel ★★★★ 77% HL Dormy House, Willersey Hill, BROADWAY
☎ 01386 852711 📄 01386 858636   45 en suite

BROMSGROVE   Map 7 SO97

The Blackwell Golf Club Agmore Rd, Blackwell B60 1PY
☎ 0121 445 1994 📄 0121 445 4911
e-mail: info@blackwellgolfclub.com
web: www.blackwellgolfclub.co.uk

Mature undulating parkland course over 117 years old, with a variety of trees. Laid out in two nine-hole loops.

18 Holes, 6260yds, Par 70, SSS 71, Course record 64.
Club membership 338.

Visitors Mon, Wed-Fri except BHs. Booking required. Dress code.
Societies booking required. **Green Fees** not confirmed ⊛ **Course Designer** Herbert Fowler/Tom Simpson **Prof** Finlay Clark **Facilities** ⊕
by prior arrangement ⫶⊙⫶ by prior arrangement ⊪ ⊡ ⫽ ⊿
🖾 ⫽ ◇ ⊘ ⌇ **Conf** Corporate Hospitality Days **Location** 2.5m
NE of Bromsgrove off B4096
Hotel ★★★★ 71% HL Holiday Inn Birmingham - Bromsgrove, Kidderminster Road, BROMSGROVE ☎ 01527 576600 & 0871 942
9142 📄 01527 878981   110 en suite

Bromsgrove Golf Centre Stratford Rd B60 1LD
☎ 01527 575886 & 570505   📄 01527 570964
e-mail: enquiries@bromsgrovegolfcentre.com
web: www.bromsgrovegolfcentre.com

This gently undulating course with superb views over Worcestershire is not to be underestimated. Creative landscaping and a selection of well-defined bunkers ensure that the course delivers a uniquely satisfying experience through a variety of challenging, yet enjoyable, holes.

18 Holes, 5969yds, Par 68, SSS 69. Club membership 900.

Visitors Mon-Sun & BHs. Dress code. **Societies** booking required.
Green Fees £21.70 per 18 holes (£28.90 weekends) **Course Designer** Hawtree & Son **Prof** Graeme Long/Danny Wall **Facilities** ⊕
⫶⊙⫶ ⊪ ⊡ ⫽ ⊿ 🖾 ⫽ ⊨ ◇ ⌇ **Conf facs** Corporate
Hospitality Days **Location** 1m from town centre at junct A38/A448, signed
Hotel ★★★★ 71% HL Holiday Inn Birmingham - Bromsgrove, Kidderminster Road, BROMSGROVE ☎ 01527 576600 & 0871 942
9142 📄 01527 878981   110 en suite

DROITWICH
Map 3 SO86

Droitwich Golf & Country Club Ford Ln WR9 0BQ
☎ 01905 774344 ▤ 01905 796503
e-mail: secretary@droitwichgolfclub.co.uk
Mature parkland with scenic views from the highest points.
18 Holes, 5990yds, Par 70, SSS 70. Club membership 732.
Visitors Mon-Fri except BHs. Handicap certificate. Dress code.
Societies Booking required. **Green Fees** £35 per day, £30 per round
Course Designer J Braid/G Franks **Prof** Phil Cundy **Facilities** ⓣ
⊗ 🖐 ⚑ ☺ ⚐ ✆ **Leisure** snooker **Conf** Corporate
Hospitality Days **Location** M5 junct 5, off A38 at Droitwich opposite
Chateau Impney Hotel
Hotel ★★★ 79% HL Pear Tree Inn & Country Hotel, Smite,
WORCESTER ☎ 01905 756565 ▤ 01905 756777 24 en suite

Gaudet Luce Golf Club Middle Ln WR9 7DP
☎ 01905 796375 ▤ 01905 797245
web: www.gaudet-luce.co.uk
18 Holes, 6040yds, Par 70, SSS 68.
Course Designer M A Laing **Location** M5 junct 5, left at Tagwell Rd
onto Middle Ln, 1st driveway on left
Telephone for further details
Hotel ★★★ 79% HL Pear Tree Inn & Country Hotel, Smite,
WORCESTER ☎ 01905 756565 ▤ 01905 756777 24 en suite

Ombersley Golf Club Bishops Wood Rd WR9 0LE
☎ 01905 620747 ▤ 01905 620047
web: www.ombersleygolfclub.co.uk
18 Holes, 6139yds, Par 72, SSS 69, Course record 67.
Course Designer David Morgan **Location** 3m W of Droitwich off A449.
At Mitre Oak pub A4025 to Stourport, signed 400yds on left
Telephone for further details
Hotel ★★★★ 77% HL Menzies Stourport Manor, 35 Hartlebury
Road, STOURPORT-ON-SEVERN ☎ 01299 289955 ▤ 01299 878520
68 en suite

HOLLYWOOD
Map 7 SP07

Gay Hill Golf Club Hollywood Ln B47 5PP
☎ 0121 430 8544 & 474 6001 (pro) ▤ 0121 436 7796
e-mail: secretary@ghgc.org.uk
web: www.ghgc.org.uk
Parkland course with some 10,000 trees and a brook running through.
Gently undulating so a good test of golf rather than stamina.
18 Holes, 6406yds, Par 72, SSS 72, Course record 64.
Club membership 700.
Visitors Mon-Sun except BHs. Booking required weekends. Handicap
certificate. **Societies** booking required. **Green Fees** £35.50 per round
(£40.50 weekends) **Prof** Chris Harrison **Facilities** ⓣ ⊗ 🖐 ☐
☐ ☺ ⚐ ☐ ✆ **Location** Just off M42 junct 3
Hotel ★★★ 82% HL Best Western Westley, 80-90 Westley Road,
Acocks Green, BIRMINGHAM ☎ 0121 706 4312 ▤ 0121 706 2824
37 en suite

KIDDERMINSTER
Map 7 SO87

Churchill and Blakedown Golf Club Churchill Ln, Blakedown DY10 3NB
☎ 01562 700018
e-mail: admin@churchillblakedowngolfclub.co.uk
web: www.churchillblakedowngolfclub.co.uk
Mature hilly course, playable all year round, with good views.
9 Holes, 6491yds, Par 72, SSS 71, Course record 65.
Club membership 410.
Visitors Mon-Fri & BHs. Booking required. Handicap certificate. Dress
code. **Societies** Booking required. **Green Fees** £20 per 18 holes ✆
Prof Debbie Garbett **Facilities** ⓣ ⊗ 🖐 ☐ ☐ ☺ ⚐ ✆
Conf Corporate Hospitality Days **Location** W of village off A456
Hotel ★★★★ 78% HL Stone Manor, Stone, KIDDERMINSTER
☎ 01562 777555 ▤ 01562 777834 57 en suite

Habberley Golf Club Low Habberley, Trimpley Rd DY11 5RF
☎ 01562 745756 ▤ 01562 745756
e-mail: dave.mcdermott1@blueyonder.co.uk
web: www.habberleygolfclub.co.uk
Wooded, undulating parkland.
9 Holes, 5401yds, Par 69, SSS 67, Course record 62.
Club membership 108.
Visitors Mon, Wed-Sun & BHS. Booking required weekends.
Societies booking required. **Green Fees** £15 per day (£10 winter)
☺ **Facilities** ⓣ ⊗ 🖐 ☐ ☐ ☺ ⚐ **Location** 2m NW of
Kidderminster
Hotel ★★★★ 78% HL Stone Manor, Stone, KIDDERMINSTER
☎ 01562 777555 ▤ 01562 777834 57 en suite

Kidderminster Golf Club Russell Rd DY10 3HT
☎ 01562 822303 ▤ 01562 827866
web: www.kidderminstergolfclub.com
18 Holes, 6422yds, Par 72, SSS 71, Course record 65.
Location 0.5m SE of town centre, signed off A449
Telephone for further details
Hotel ★★★★ 78% HL Stone Manor, Stone, KIDDERMINSTER
☎ 01562 777555 ▤ 01562 777834 57 en suite

Wyre Forest Golf Club Zortech Av DY11 7EX
☎ 01299 822682 ▤ 01299 879433
e-mail: wyreforestgc@hotmail.co.uk
web: www.wyreforestgolf.co.uk
Making full use of the existing contours, this interesting and
challenging course is bounded by woodland and gives extensive views
over the surrounding area. Well drained fairways and greens give an
inland links style.
18 Holes, 6018yds, Par 71, SSS 70, Course record 69.
Club membership 397.
Visitors Mon-Sun & BHs. Booking required weekends & BHs. Dress
code. **Societies** booking required. **Green Fees** £15 per 18 holes (£20
weekends) **Prof** Chris Botterill **Facilities** ⓣ 🖐 ☐ ☐ ☺ ⚐ ☐
⚐ ✆ ☺ ✆ ✆ **Conf** Corporate Hospitality Days **Location** on
A451 between Kidderminster and Stourport
Hotel ★★★ 78% HL Gainsborough House Hotel, Bewdley Hill,
KIDDERMINSTER ☎ 01562 820041 ▤ 01562 66179 42 en suite

Save on Hotels. Book at **theAA.com/hotel**

WORCESTERSHIRE

ENGLAND

MALVERN
Map 3 SO74

The Worcestershire Golf Club Wood Farm, Wood Farm Rd WR14 4PP
☎ 01684 575992 📄 01684 893334
e-mail: secretary@worcsgolfclub.co.uk
web: www.worcsgolfclub.co.uk

Fairly easy walking on windy downland course with trees, ditches and other natural hazards. Outstanding views of the Malvern Hills and the Severn Valley. The 17th hole (par 5) is approached over a small lake.

The Worcestershire: 18 Holes, 6455yds, Par 71, SSS 72, Course record 64. Club membership 750.

Visitors Mon-Fri except BHs. Booking required. Handicap certificate. Dress code. **Societies** booking required. **Green Fees** £42 per day, £36 per round 🏌 **Course Designer** Hawtree **Prof** Richard Lewis **Facilities** ⓦ ⓧ ⓑ ⓓ 🍴 ⓐ 🎒 ⚬ ⚬ **Leisure** indoor teaching facility **Conf** facs Corporate Hospitality Days **Location** 2m S of Gt Malvern on B4209

Hotel ★★★ 85% HL The Cottage in the Wood Hotel, Holywell Road, Malvern Wells, MALVERN ☎ 01684 588860 📄 01684 560662 30 en suite

REDDITCH
Map 7 SP06

Abbey Hotel Golf & Country Club Dagnell End Rd, Hither Green Ln B98 9BE
☎ 01527 406600 & 406500 📄 01527 406514
e-mail: info@theabbeyhotel.co.uk
web: www.theabbeyhotel.co.uk

Championship standard parkland course extensively upgraded and lengthened in recent years. The layout includes mature trees, lakes and on the whole the fairways are wide with the rough not too punishing. The picturesque 7th is a 192 yard drive from the medal tee with the green surrounded on three sides by the River Arrow. The 13th is a challenging uphill par 4 drive between two mature oak trees at 250 yards, with the green concealed out of sight at the top of the hill.

The Abbey Course: 18 Holes, 6500yds, Par 72. Club membership 397.

Visitors Mon-Sun & BHs. Booking required. Dress code.
Societies booking required. **Green Fees** not confirmed **Course Designer** Donald Steele **Prof** R Davies **Facilities** ⓦ ⓧ ⓑ ⓓ 🍴 ⓐ 🎒 ⚬ ⚬ ⚬ **Leisure** heated indoor swimming pool, fishing, sauna, gymnasium **Conf** facs Corporate Hospitality Days **Location** A441 N from town, onto B4101 signed Beoley, right onto Hither Green Ln

Hotel ★★★★ 78% HL Abbey Hotel Golf & Country Club, Hither Green Lane, Dagnell End Road, Bordesley, REDDITCH ☎ 01527 406600 📄 01527 406514 100 en suite

Pitcheroak Golf Club Plymouth Rd B97 4PB
☎ 01527 541054 📄 01527 65216

Woodland course, hilly in places. There is also a putting green and a practice ground.

9 Holes, 4561yds, Par 65, SSS 62. Club membership 210.

Visitors Mon-Sun & BHs. **Societies** booking required. **Green Fees** not confirmed **Prof** Chris Stanley **Facilities** ⓦ ⓧ ⓑ ⓓ 🍴 ⓐ 🎒 ⚬ ⚬ **Conf** Corporate Hospitality Days **Location** SW of town centre off A448

Hotel BUD Holiday Inn Express Birmingham - Redditch, 2 Hewell Road, Enfield, REDDITCH ☎ 01527 584658 📄 01527 597905 100 en suite

Redditch Golf Club Lower Grinsty, Green Ln, Callow Hill B97 5PJ
☎ 01527 543079 (sec) 📄 01527 547413
e-mail: lee@redditchgolfclub.com
web: www.redditchgolfclub.com

Parkland with many tree-lined fairways, excellent greens, and a particularly tough finish. The par 3s are all long and demanding.

18 Holes, 6494yds, Par 72, SSS 72, Course record 68. Club membership 650.

Visitors Mon-Fri except BHs. Booking required. Dress code.
Societies booking required. **Green Fees** £45 per day, £35 per round **Course Designer** F Pennick **Prof** David Down **Facilities** ⓦ ⓧ ⓑ ⓓ 🍴 ⓐ 🎒 ⚬ ⚬ ⚬ **Conf** Corporate Hospitality Days **Location** 2m SW

Hotel BUD Holiday Inn Express Birmingham - Redditch, 2 Hewell Road, Enfield, REDDITCH ☎ 01527 584658 📄 01527 597905 100 en suite

TENBURY WELLS
Map 7 SO56

Cadmore Lodge Hotel & Country Club St Michaels WR15 8TQ
☎ 01584 810044 📄 01584 810044
web: www.cadmorelodge.com

9 Holes, 5132yds, Par 68, SSS 65.

Course Designer G Farr, J Weston **Location** A4112 from Tenbury to Leominster, 2m right for Berrington, 0.75m on left
Telephone for further details
Hotel ★★ 74% HL Cadmore Lodge Hotel & Country Club, Berrington Green, St Michaels, TENBURY WELLS ☎ 01584 810044 📄 01584 810044 15 en suite

WORCESTER
Map 3 SO85

Best Western Bank House Hotel Golf & Country Club Bransford WR6 5JD
☎ 01886 833545 📄 01886 832461
e-mail: bransfordgolfclub@brook-hotels.co.uk
web: www.brook-hotels.co.uk

The Bransford Course is designed as a Florida-style course with fairways weaving between water courses, 14 lakes and sculpted mounds. The course has dog-legs, island greens and tight fairways to challenge all standards of player and comprises 6 par 3s, 6 par 4s and 6 par 5s. The 10th, 16th and 18th (The Devil's Elbow) are particularly tricky.

Bransford Course: 18 Holes, 6172yds, Par 72, SSS 70, Course record 64. Club membership 414.

Visitors Mon-Sun & BHs. Booking required. Dress code.
Societies welcome. **Green Fees** not confirmed **Course Designer** Bob Sandow **Prof** Matt Nixon **Facilities** ⓦ ⓧ ⓑ ⓓ 🍴 ⓐ 🎒 ⚬ ⚬ ⚬ **Leisure** outdoor swimming pool, sauna, gymnasium **Conf** facs Corporate Hospitality Days **Location** M5 junct 7, A4103 3m S of Worcester

Hotel ★★★★ INN The Dewdrop Inn, Bell Lane, Lower Broadheath, WORCESTER ☎ 01905 640012 📄 01905 640265 7 rooms

Perdiswell Park Golf Course Bilford Rd WR3 8DX
☎ 01905 754668 & 457189

18 Holes, 5297yds, Par 68, SSS 66.
Location N of city centre off A30
Telephone for further details
Hotel ★★★ 79% HL Pear Tree Inn & Country Hotel, Smite,
WORCESTER ☎ 01905 756565 📄 01905 756777 24 en suite

Worcester Golf & Country Club Boughton Park WR2 4EZ
☎ 01905 422555 📄 01905 749090
e-mail: worcestergcc@btconnect.com
web: www.worcestergcc.co.uk

Fine parkland course with many varieties of trees, lakes and fine views
of the Malvern Hills. Narrow approaches to the greens provide a good
test of golf accuracy.

18 Holes, 6251yds, Par 70, SSS 70, Course record 64.
Club membership 900.

Visitors Mon-Fri & BHs. Booking required. Handicap certificate.
Dress code. **Societies** booking required. **Green Fees** £50 per day,
£40 per round ♨ **Course Designer** Dr A MacKenzie **Prof** Graham
Farr **Facilities** ⑪ ⑩ ⓑ ⏛ 🕪 ⌸ 🖼 ⌕ **Leisure** hard and
grass tennis courts, squash **Conf** facs Corporate Hospitality Days
Location 1.5m from city centre on A4103
Hotel ★★★ 79% HL Pear Tree Inn & Country Hotel, Smite,
WORCESTER ☎ 01905 756565 📄 01905 756777 24 en suite

WYTHALL   **Map 7 SP07**

Fulford Heath Golf Club Tanners Green Ln B47 6BH
☎ 01564 824758 📄 01564 822629
e-mail: secretary@fulfordheathgolfclub.co.uk
web: www.fulfordheathgolfclub.co.uk

A mature parkland course encompassing two classic par 3s. The 11th,
a mere 149yds, shoots from an elevated tee through a channel of trees
to a well-protected green. The 16th, a 167yd par 3, elevated green,
demands a 140yd carry over an imposing lake.

18 Holes, 6174yds, Par 70, SSS 70, Course record 64.
Club membership 850.

Visitors Mon-Sun except BHs. Booking required weekends. Dress
code. **Societies** booking required. **Green Fees** £30-£36 per day ♨
Course Designer Braid/Hawtree **Prof** Sam Johnson **Facilities** ⑪
⑩ ⓑ ⏛ 🕪 ⌸ 🖼 ⌕ **Conf** Corporate Hospitality Days
Location 1m SE off A435
Hotel ★★★★ 78% HL Abbey Hotel Golf & Country Club,
Hither Green Lane, Dagnell End Road, Bordesley, REDDITCH
☎ 01527 406600 📄 01527 406514 100 en suite

ALLERTHORPE   **Map 8 SE85**

Allerthorpe Park Golf Club Allerthorpe Park YO42 4RL
☎ 01759 306686 📄 01759 305106
e-mail: enquiries@allerthorpeparkgolfclub.com
web: www.allerthorpeparkgolfclub.com

A picturesque parkland course, maintained to a high standard, with
many interesting features, including a meandering beck and the 18th
hole over the lake. Relatively new but with a maturity which offers a
challenging game of golf.

18 Holes, 6430yds, Par 70, SSS 70, Course record 67.
Club membership 500.

Visitors Mon-Sun & BHs. Dress code. **Societies** booking required
Green Fees £25 per 18 holes (£30 weekends). Winter £18/£20 **Course
Designer** J G Hatcliffe & Partners **Prof** James Drinkall **Facilities** ⑪
⑩ ⓑ ⏛ 🕪 ⌸ 🖼 ⌕ 🖼 ⌕ **Conf** facs Corporate
Hospitality Days **Location** 2m SW of Pocklington off A1079
Hotel ★★ 68% HL Feathers, 56 Market Place, POCKLINGTON
☎ 01759 303155 📄 01759 304382 16 en suite

AUGHTON   **Map 8 SE73**

The Oaks Golf Club & Spa Aughton Common, Long Ln
YO42 4PW
☎ 01757 288577 📄 01757 288232
e-mail: sheila@theoaksgolfclub.co.uk
web: www.theoaksgolfclub.co.uk

The course is built in harmony with its natural wooded parkland
setting, near to the Derwent Ings. The wide green fairways blend and
bend with the gentle countryside. Seven lakes come into play.

The Oaks: 18 Holes, 6849yds, Par 72, SSS 72,
Course record 63. Club membership 650.

Visitors Mon-Fri excluding BHs. Booking required. Handicap
certificate. Dress code.. **Societies** booking required. **Green Fees** £32
Course Designer Fox Plant **Prof** Graham Walker/Lysa Jones/John
Mellor **Facilities** ⑪ ⑩ ⓑ ⏛ 🕪 ⌸ 🖼 🖼 ⌕ ⌕
Leisure heated indoor swimming pool, sauna, gymnasium **Conf** facs
Corporate Hospitality Days **Location** 1m N of Bubwith on B1228
Hotel ★★★ 78% CHH Parsonage Country House Hotel, York Road,
ESCRICK ☎ 01904 728111 📄 01904 728151 50 en suite

BEVERLEY   **Map 8 TA03**

Beverley & East Riding Golf Club The Westwood
HU17 8RG
☎ 01482 868757 📄 01482 868757
e-mail: golf@beverleygolfclub.karoo.co.uk
web: www.beverleygolfclub.co.uk

Picturesque parkland with some hard walking and natural hazards
- trees and gorse bushes. Only two fairways adjoin. Cattle (spring to
autumn) and horseriders are occasional early morning hazards.

Westwood: 18 Holes, 5696yds, Par 69, SSS 67,
Course record 63. Club membership 530.

Visitors Mon-Sun & BHs. Booking required weekends. Dress code.
Societies welcome. **Green Fees** £26 per day, £17 per round (£26/£17
weekends) **Prof** Alex Ashby **Facilities** ⑪ ⑩ ⓑ ⏛ 🕪 ⌸ 🖼
🖼 ⌕ **Conf** Corporate Hospitality Days **Location** 1m SW on B1230
Hotel ★★★ 82% HL Tickton Grange, Tickton, BEVERLEY
☎ 01964 543666 📄 01964 542556 20 en suite

Save on Hotels. Book at **theAA.com/hotel**

YORKSHIRE, EAST RIDING OF

ENGLAND

BRANDESBURTON
Map 8 TA14

Hainsworth Park Golf Club Burton Holme YO25 8RT
☎ 01964 542362
e-mail: info@hainsworthparkgolfclub.co.uk
web: www.hainsworthparkgolfclub.co.uk
A parkland course based on sand and gravel giving excellent drainage. Demands straight driving due to mature trees.
18 Holes, 6362yds, Par 71, SSS 71. Club membership 500.
Visitors Mon-Sun & BHs. Booking required. Dress code.
Societies booking required. **Green Fees** £24 per day, £20 per round (£29/£24 weekends) **Prof** Peter Myers **Facilities** ⑪ ⑩ ⓛ ☐ ⒄ ⏚ ⓘ ☖ ◈ ⌀ ⇶ ⌀ **Location** SW of village on A165
Hotel ★★ 71% HL Burton Lodge, BRANDESBURTON
☎ 01964 542847 📄 01964 544771 9 en suite

BRIDLINGTON
Map 8 TA16

Bridlington Golf Club Belvedere Rd YO15 3NA
☎ 01262 606367
web: www.bridlingtongolfclub.co.uk
18 Holes, 6638yds, Par 72, SSS 72, Course record 64.
Course Designer James Braid **Location** 1m S off A165
Telephone for further details
Hotel ★★★ 75% HL Expanse, North Marine Drive, BRIDLINGTON
☎ 01262 675347 📄 01262 604928 47 en suite

Bridlington Links Flamborough Rd, Marton YO15 1DW
☎ 01262 401584 📄 01262 401702
e-mail: info@bridlington-links.co.uk
web: www.bridlington-links.co.uk
Coastal links type course with large greens, numerous water hazards and splendid views towards Flamborough Head. When the wind blows off the sea, the course becomes a challenging test of golf for even the experienced golfer.
Main: 18 Holes, 6719yds, Par 72, SSS 72, Course record 66. Club membership 401.
Visitors Mon-Sun & BHs. Booking required. Dress code.
Societies booking required. **Green Fees** not confirmed **Course Designer** Swan **Prof** Wayne Stephens **Facilities** ⑪ ⑩ ⓛ ☐ ⒄ ⏚ ⓘ ☖ ⌀ ⇶ ⌀ **Leisure** gymnasium, 9 hole par 26 short course **Conf** facs Corporate Hospitality Days **Location** on B1255 between Bridlington & Flamborough Head
Hotel ★★★ 75% HL Expanse, North Marine Drive, BRIDLINGTON
☎ 01262 675347 📄 01262 604928 47 en suite

BROUGH
Map 8 SE92

Brough Golf Club Cave Rd HU15 1HB
☎ 01482 667291 📄 01482 669873
e-mail: gt@brough-golfclub.co.uk
web: www.brough-golfclub.co.uk
Parkland course, where accurate positioning of the tee ball is required for good scoring. Testing for the scratch player without being too difficult for the higher handicap.
18 Holes, 6064yds, Par 68, SSS 69, Course record 61. Club membership 680.
Visitors Mon-Sun & BHs. Booking required. Handicap certificate. Dress code. **Societies** booking required. **Green Fees** £60 per day, £35 per round (£70/£50 weekends) ⊛ **Prof** Gordon Townhill **Facilities** ⑪ ⑩

⏚ ☐ ⒄ ⓘ ☖ ⓘ ☖ ◈ ⌀ ⇶ ⌀ **Conf** Corporate Hospitality Days **Location** 8m W of Hull off A63
Hotel ★★★ 72% HL Cave Castle Hotel & Country Club, Church Hill, SOUTH CAVE ☎ 01430 422245 📄 01430 421118 70 en suite

BURSTWICK
Map 8 TA22

Burstwick Country Golf Ellifoot Ln HU12 9EF
☎ 01964 670112 📄 01964 670116
e-mail: info@burstwickcountrygolf.com
web: www.burstwickcountrygolf.co.uk
A course with 72 bunkers, 5 lakes and 4,500 trees set in attractive countryside. Challenging with well-guarded greens, exposed tee shots and sharp dog-legs. A modern yet natural design with each bunker and water feature strategically placed around the landing areas and undulating greens. All greens to full USGA specification.
18 Holes, 6000yds, Par 70, SSS 69, Course record 65. Club membership 400.
Visitors Mon-Sun & BHs. Booking required. Dress code.
Societies booking required. **Green Fees** £18 per 18 holes (£22 weekends). Winter £13/£18 **Course Designer** Gaunt Golf Design Ltd **Prof** Stewart Fraser **Facilities** ⑪ ⓛ ⏚ ☐ ⒄ ⏚ ⓘ ☖ ⌀ ⇶ ⌀ **Conf** facs Corporate Hospitality Days **Location** 10 miles E of Hull, A63 towards Hull, then A1033 to Hedon. Follow minor roads signed for Burstwick
Hotel ★★★★ 73% HL Portland, Paragon Street, HULL
☎ 01482 326462 📄 01482 213460 126 en suite

COTTINGHAM
Map 8 TA03

Cottingham Parks Golf & Leisure Club Woodhill Way HU16 5SW
☎ 01482 846030 📄 01482 845932
e-mail: enquiries@cottinghamparks.co.uk
web: www.cottinghamparks.co.uk
Gently undulating parkland course incorporating many natural features, including lateral water hazards, several ponds on the approach to greens, and rolling fairways.
Cottingham: 18 Holes, 6453yds, Par 72, SSS 71, Course record 65.
Skidby Lakes: 18 Holes, 6158yds, Par 70, SSS 70, Course record 66. Club membership 600.
Visitors Mon-Sun & BHs. Booking required. Dress code.
Societies booking required. **Green Fees** £22 per round (£32 weekends & BHs) **Course Designer** Terry Litten **Prof** Chris Gray **Facilities** ⑪ ⑩ ⏚ ☐ ⒄ ⏚ ⓘ ☖ ◈ ⌀ ⇶ ⌀ **Leisure** heated indoor swimming pool, sauna, gymnasium, jacuzzi, remedial masseur **Conf** facs Corporate Hospitality Days **Location** A164 onto B1233 towards Cottingham, 100yds left onto Woodhill Way
Hotel ★★★ 83% HL Best Western Willerby Manor Hotel, Well Lane, WILLERBY ☎ 01482 652616 📄 01482 653901 63 en suite

DRIFFIELD (GREAT)　Map 8 TA05

Driffield Golf Club Sunderlandwick YO25 9AD
☎ 01377 253116 📠 01377 240599
e-mail: info@driffieldgolfclub.co.uk
web: www.driffieldgolfclub.co.uk
An easy walking, mature parkland course set within the beautiful
Sunderlandwick Estate, including numerous water features, one of
which is a renowned trout stream.
18 Holes, 6215yds, Par 70, SSS 70, Course record 62.
Club membership 670.
Visitors Mon-Sun & BHs (times vary). Booking required. Dress code.
Societies booking required. **Green Fees** Summer £30 per day, £25
per round (£40/£30 weekends & BH). Winter £15 per round (£20
weekends & BHs) 🅿 **Course Designer** Keith Gray **Prof** Kenton
Wright **Facilities** ⑪ ⑩ ⮂ ⛁ 🍴 ⮂ 🏠 ⛳ 🏌 ⚒
Leisure fishing, golf practice nets **Conf** facs Corporate Hospitality
Days **Location** 0.5m S of Driffield, off A164, Beverley Rd, follow brown
sign
Hotel ★★★ 78% HL Best Western Bell Hotel, 46 Market Place,
DRIFFIELD ☎ 01377 256661 📠 01377 253228　16 en suite

FLAMBOROUGH　Map 8 TA27

Flamborough Head Golf Club Lighthouse Rd YO15 1AR
☎ 01262 850333
e-mail: enquiries@flamboroughheadgolfclub.co.uk
web: www.flamboroughheadgolfclub.co.uk

This east coast links course moulds itself around the contours of
the cliffs which form part of the famous Flamborough Head and has
panoramic sea views. The course provides a demanding but enjoyable
test of golfing skills and the unwary can be forgiven for standing on
the 1st tee and being deceived by the apparent gentleness of the view
across the course.
18 Holes, 6185yds, Par 71, SSS 70, Course record 64.
Club membership 345.
Visitors Booking recommended. Dress code. **Societies** welcome. **Green
Fees** £36 per day, £22 per round (£42/£31 weekends & BHs). Twilight
£10 **Prof** Chris Feast **Facilities** ⑪ ⑩ ⮂ ⛁ 🍴 ⮂ 🏠 ⛳
⚒ 🏌 ⚒ **Leisure** golf coaching & lessons **Conf** facs Corporate
Hospitality Days **Location** B1255 E of Bridlington to Flamborough
village church. Right into Lighthouse Rd, golf club approx 1m on left
before historic lighthouse
Hotel ★★ 76% SHL North Star, North Marine Drive, FLAMBOROUGH
☎ 01262 850379 📠 01262 850379　7 en suite

See advert on opposite page

HORNSEA　Map 8 TA14

Hornsea Golf Club Rolston Rd HU18 1XG
☎ 01964 532020 📠 01964 532080
e-mail: hornseagolfclub@aol.com
web: www.hornseagolfclub.co.uk
Easy walking parkland course with good drainage and renowned for
the quality of its hand cut greens.
18 Holes, 6647yds, Par 72, SSS 72, Course record 66.
Club membership 600.
Visitors Mon, Wed-Fri-Sun & BHs. Tue after 12.30pm. Sat after 3pm,
Sun after 11am. Booking required. Dress code. **Societies** booking
required. **Green Fees** not confirmed **Course Designer** Herd/MacKenzie/
Braid **Prof** Stretton Wright **Facilities** ⑪ ⑩ by prior arrangement
⮂ ⛁ 🍴 ⮂ 🏠 ⛳ 🏌 ⚒ **Conf** Corporate Hospitality Days
Location 1m S on B1242, signs for Hornsea Freeport
Hotel ★★ 71% HL Burton Lodge, BRANDESBURTON
☎ 01964 542847 📠 01964 544771　9 en suite

HOWDEN　Map 8 SE72

Boothferry Golf Club Spaldington Ln DN14 7NG
☎ 01430 430364
e-mail: info@boothferrygolfclub.co.uk
web: www.boothferrygolfclub.co.uk
Pleasant, meadowland course in the Vale of York with interesting
natural dykes, creating challenges on some holes. The par 5 9th is
a test for any golfer with its dyke coming into play on the tee shot,
second shot and approach. Easy walking.
18 Holes, 6684yds, Par 73, SSS 72, Course record 66.
Eagles: 9 Holes, 1741yds, Par 29. Club membership 370.
Visitors Mon-Sun & BHs. Dress code for main course.
Societies booking required. **Green Fees** £20 per 18 holes, £14 per
9 holes (£25/£18 weekends). Eagles £8 per 18 holes, £5 per 9 holes
Course Designer Donald Steel **Prof** Ben McAllister **Facilities** ⑪ ⑩
⮂ ⛁ 🍴 ⮂ 🏠 ⛳ 🏌 ⚒ 🏌 **Conf** facs Corporate
Hospitality Days **Location** M62 junct 37, 2.5m N of Howden off B1228
Hotel ★★★ 78% CHH Parsonage Country House Hotel, York Road,
ESCRICK ☎ 01904 728111 📠 01904 728151　50 en suite

KINGSTON UPON HULL　Map 8 TA02

Ganstead Park Golf Club Longdales Ln, Coniston
HU11 4LB
☎ 01482 817754 📠 01482 817754
e-mail: secretary@gansteadpark.co.uk
web: www.gansteadpark.co.uk
Easy walking parkland with many water features.
18 Holes, 6801yds, Par 72, SSS 72. Club membership 650.
Visitors Mon, Tue, Thu & Fri. Wed, weekends & BHs pm. Booking
required. **Societies** booking required. **Green Fees** £30 per day, £24
per round **Course Designer** P Green **Prof** Michael J Smee **Facilities** ⑪
⑩ ⮂ ⛁ 🍴 ⮂ 🏠 ⛳ 🏌 ⚒ 🏌 **Conf** Corporate
Hospitality Days **Location** A165 Hull exit, pass Ganstead, right onto
B1238 to Bilton, course on right
Hotel ★★★★ 73% HL Portland, Paragon Street, HULL
☎ 01482 326462 📠 01482 213460　126 en suite

Hull Golf Club (1921) The Hall, 27 Packman Ln HU10 7TJ
☎ 01482 660970 📄 01482 660978
e-mail: secretary@hullgolfclub1921.karoo.co.uk
web: www.hullgolfclub.com

Attractive mature parkland course.

18 Holes, 6278yds, Par 70, SSS 70, Course record 64.
Club membership 693.

Visitors Mon, Tue, Thu, Fri, Sun & BHs. Booking required. Handicap certificate. Dress code. **Societies** booking required. **Green Fees** Nov-Feb £20 per round. Mar-Oct £40 per day, £30 per round (£35 per day/round weekends) **Course Designer** James Braid **Prof** David Jagger **Facilities** ⑪ ⛶ 🏌 ☐ ⛴ ⚐ 📧 ☞ ⚙ 🛺 ☞ **Leisure** snooker **Conf** Corporate Hospitality Days **Location** 5m W of city off A164

Hotel ★★★ 83% HL Best Western Willerby Manor Hotel, Well Lane, WILLERBY ☎ 01482 652616 📄 01482 653901 63 en suite

Springhead Park Golf Club Willerby Rd HU5 5JE
☎ 01482 656309 📄 01482 656309
e-mail: secretary@springheadparkgolfclub.co.uk
Municipal parkland course with tight, undulating tree-lined fairways.

18 Holes, 6401yds, Par 71, SSS 71, Course record 65.
Club membership 200.

Visitors Mon-Sun & BHs. Booking required. Dress code.
Societies welcome. **Green Fees** £12.50 per round (£14.50 weekends) **Facilities** 🏌 ☐ ⛴ ⚐ 📧 ☞ **Conf** facs Corporate Hospitality Days **Location** 5m W off A164

Hotel ★★★ 83% HL Best Western Willerby Manor Hotel, Well Lane, WILLERBY ☎ 01482 652616 📄 01482 653901 63 en suite

POCKLINGTON Map 8 SE84

KP Golf Club Kilnwick Percy YO42 1UF
☎ 01759 303090 📄 01759 303090
e-mail: info@kpclub.co.uk
web: www.kpclub.co.uk
Attractive parkland course on the edge of the Wolds above Pocklington which has undergone a major redevelopment in recent years and offers a great golf experience.

18 Holes, 6140yds, Par 70, SSS 70, Course record 65.
Club membership 600.

Visitors Mon-Sun & BHs. Booking required. Dress code.
Societies welcome. **Green Fees** not confirmed **Course Designer** John Day **Prof** Aaron Pheasant **Facilities** ⑪ ⛶ 🏌 ☐ ⛴ ⚐ 📧 ☞ ♦ ☞ 🛺 ☞ **Conf** facs Corporate Hospitality Days **Location** 1m E of Pocklington off B1246

Hotel ★★ 68% HL Feathers, 56 Market Place, POCKLINGTON ☎ 01759 303155 📄 01759 304382 16 en suite

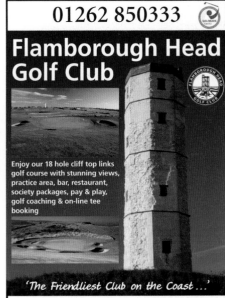

01262 850333
Flamborough Head Golf Club

Enjoy our 18 hole cliff top links golf course with stunning views, practice area, bar, restaurant, society packages, pay & play, golf coaching & on-line tee booking

'The Friendliest Club on the Coast...'

Lighthouse Road Flamborough YO15 1AR
enquiries@flamboroughheadgolfclub.co.uk
www.flamboroughheadgolfclub.co.uk

RAYWELL Map 8 TA02

Hessle Golf Club Westfield Rd HU16 5YL
☎ 01482 306840 & 306842 (Prof) 📄 01482 652679
e-mail: secretary@hessle-golf-club.co.uk
web: www.hessle-golf-club.co.uk
Well-wooded downland course with easy walking. The greens, conforming to USGA specification, are large and undulating with excellent drainage, enabling play throughout the year. Two lakes were added in 2007.

18 Holes, 6621yds, Par 72, SSS 72, Course record 65.
Club membership 720.

Visitors Mon-Sun & BHs. Handicap certificate. Dress code.
Societies booking required. **Green Fees** £45 per day; £35 per round (£45 per round weekends) **Course Designer** D Thomas/P Alliss **Prof** Grahame Fieldsend **Facilities** ⑪ ⛶ 🏌 ☐ ⛴ ⚐ 📧 🛺 ☞ ☞ **Conf** facs Corporate Hospitality Days **Location** 3m SW of Cottingham

Hotel ★★★ 83% HL Best Western Willerby Manor Hotel, Well Lane, WILLERBY ☎ 01482 652616 📄 01482 653901 63 en suite

SKIDBY
Map 8 TA03

Skidby Lakes Golf Club Woodhill Way HU16 5SW
☎ 01482 844270 & 844003   🖹 01482 844269
e-mail: info@skidbylakes.co.uk
web: www.skidbylakes.co.uk

An interesting parkland course with narrow fairways and three large lakes that come into play on several holes whilst playing the well guarded undulating greens.

18 Holes, 6188yds, Par 70, SSS 70, Course record 66.
Club membership 400.

Visitors Mon-Sun & BHs. Dress code. **Societies** booking required.
Green Fees £16 per round (£21 weekends & BHs) **Course Designer** Wilf Adamson **Prof** Karl Worby **Facilities** ⓧ 🍴 ⌸ ⌷ 🔲 ♨ 🪑 🏠 ⛴ ♦ ✦ **Leisure** heated indoor swimming pool, sauna, gymnasium **Conf** facs Corporate Hospitality Days **Location** from Humber Bridge proceed N on A164 towards Beverley. At Skidby rdbt take B1233 towards Cottingham for 100yds then left into Woodhill Way, entrance 3rd on right
Hotel ★★★ 83% HL Best Western Willerby Manor Hotel, Well Lane, WILLERBY ☎ 01482 652616 🖹 01482 653901 63 en suite

SOUTH CAVE
Map 8 SE93

Cave Castle Hotel & Country Club Church Hill, South Cave HU15 2EU
☎ 01430 421286   🖹 01430 421118
e-mail: admin@cavecastlegolf.co.uk
web: www.cavecastlegolf.co.uk

Undulating meadow and parkland at the foot of the Wolds, with superb views.

18 Holes, 6524yds, Par 72, SSS 71, Course record 67.
Club membership 340.

Visitors Mon-Sun & BHs. Booking required. Dress code.
Societies booking required. **Green Fees** phone **Course Designer** Mrs N Freling **Prof** Stephen MacKinder **Facilities** ⓧ 🍴 ⌸ ⌷ 🔲 🪑 🏠 ⛴ ♦ 🛒 ✦ **Leisure** heated indoor swimming pool, sauna, gymnasium **Conf** facs Corporate Hospitality Days **Location** 1m from A63
Hotel ★★★ 72% HL Cave Castle Hotel & Country Club, Church Hill, SOUTH CAVE ☎ 01430 422245 🖹 01430 421118 70 en suite

WITHERNSEA
Map 8 TA32

Withernsea Golf Club Chestnut Av HU19 2PG
☎ 01964 612078 & 612258   🖹 01964 612078
e-mail: info@withernseagolfclub.co.uk
web: www.withernseagolfclub.co.uk

Exposed seaside links with narrow, undulating fairways, bunkers and small greens.

9 Holes, 6207yds, Par 72, SSS 69. Club membership 200.
Visitors Mon-Fri except BHs. Dress code. **Societies** booking required.
Green Fees £15 per 18 holes **Facilities** ⓧ 🍴 ⌸ ⌷ 🔲 🪑 ✦ 🛺 **Conf** facs Corporate Hospitality Days **Location** S of town centre off A1033, signed from Victoria Av
Hotel ★★★★ 73% HL Portland, Paragon Street, HULL
☎ 01482 326462 🖹 01482 213460 126 en suite

YORKSHIRE, NORTH

ALDWARK
Map 8 SE46

Aldwark Manor Golf & Spa Hotel YO61 1UF
☎ 01347 838353   🖹 01347 833991
web: www.qhotels.co.uk

18 Holes, 6187yds, Par 72, SSS 70, Course record 67.
Location 5m SE of Boroughbridge off A1
Telephone for further details
Hotel ★★★★ 74% HL Aldwark Manor Golf & Spa Hotel, ALDWARK
☎ 01347 838146 🖹 01347 833950 54 en suite

BEDALE
Map 8 SE28

Bedale Golf Club Leyburn Rd DL8 1EZ
☎ 01677 422451 (sec)   🖹 01677 427143
e-mail: office@bedalegolfclub.com
web: www.bedalegolfclub.com

One of North Yorkshire's most picturesque and interesting courses. The course is in parkland with tree-lined fairways and receptive greens protected by bunkers providing a good golfing test.

Bedale: 18 Holes, 6580yds, Par 72, SSS 70.
Club membership 600.

Visitors Mon-Sun & BHs. Booking required. Handicap certificate. Dress code. **Societies** booking required. **Green Fees** £37 per day, £32 per round (£39/£34 weekends) 🌐 **Course Designer** Hawtree **Prof** Tony Johnson **Facilities** ⓧ 🍴 ⌸ ⌷ 🔲 🪑 🏠 ♦ 🛺 ✦ **Conf** facs Corporate Hospitality Days **Location** A1 onto A684 at Leeming Bar to Bedale
Hotel ★★ 71% HL Lodge at Leeming Bar, The Great North Road, LEEMING BAR ☎ 01677 422122 🖹 01677 424507 39 en suite

BENTHAM
Map 7 SD66

Bentham Golf Club Robin Ln LA2 7AG
☎ 015242 62455
e-mail: secretary@benthamgolfclub.co.uk
web: www.benthamgolfclub.co.uk

Moorland course with glorious views and excellent greens.

18 Holes, 6033yds, Par 71, SSS 69. Club membership 335.
Visitors Mon-Sun & BHs. Booking required. Dress code.
Societies booking required. **Green Fees** £35 per day, £30 per round (£35 weekends) **Prof** Chris Cousins **Facilities** ⓧ 🍴 ⌸ ⌷ 🔲 🪑 🏠 ⛴ ♦ ✦ 🛒 ✦ **Conf** facs Corporate Hospitality Days **Location** N side of High Bentham, 12m E of Lancaster
Hotel ★★ 76% HL The Whoop Hall, Burrow with Burrow, KIRKBY LONSDALE ☎ 015242 71284 🖹 015242 72154 24 en suite

CATTERICK GARRISON — Map 8 SE29

Catterick Golf Club Leyburn Rd DL9 3QE
☎ 01748 833268
e-mail: secretary@catterickgolfclub.co.uk
web: www.catterickgolfclub.co.uk

Scenic parkland and moorland course of championship standard, with good views of the Pennines and the Cleveland hills. A cunning and subtle design, with strategically placed bunkers and cleverly guarded enlarged greens which combine with the undulating terrain to create a tough but rewarding test of skill for all standards of golfer.

18 Holes, 6378yds, Par 71, SSS 70. Club membership 400.

Visitors Mon-Sun & BHs. Dress code. **Societies** booking required. **Green Fees** £30 per day, £25 per 18 holes **Course Designer** Arthur Day **Prof** Andy Marshall **Facilities** 🍴 🍽 🛋 ☕ 🍷 👔 🏪 ⛳ 🛒 🚗 🔋 **Conf** facs Corporate Hospitality Days **Location** 0.5m W of Catterick Garrison
Hotel ★★ 71% HL Lodge at Leeming Bar, The Great North Road, LEEMING BAR ☎ 01677 422122 📠 01677 424507 39 en suite

COPMANTHORPE — Map 8 SE54

Pike Hills Golf Club Tadcaster Rd YO23 3UW
☎ 01904 700797 📠 01904 700797
e-mail: secretary@pikehillsgolfclub.co.uk
web: www.pikehillsgolfclub.co.uk

Parkland course surrounding a nature reserve. Level terrain.

18 Holes, 6146yds, Par 71, SSS 70. Club membership 750.

Visitors Mon-Fri except BHs. Booking required. Dress code. **Societies** booking required. **Green Fees** £36 per day, £30 per round **Prof** Ian Tailby **Facilities** 🍴 🍽 🛋 ☕ 🍷 👔 🏪 ⛳ 🛒 🚗 🔋 🏌 **Conf** facs Corporate Hospitality Days **Location** 3m SW of York on A64 westbound carriageway
Hotel ★★★★ 77% HL York Marriott Hotel, Tadcaster Road, YORK ☎ 01904 701000 📠 01904 702308 151 en suite

EASINGWOLD — Map 8 SE56

Easingwold Golf Club Stillington Rd YO61 3ET
☎ 01347 821964 (Pro) & 822474 (Sec)
e-mail: enquiries@easingwoldgolfclub.co.uk
web: www.easingwoldgolfclub.co.uk

Parkland with easy walking. Trees are a major feature and on six holes water hazards come into play.

18 Holes, 6699yds, Par 73, SSS 72. Club membership 600.

Visitors Mon-Sun except BHs. Dress code. **Societies** booking required. **Green Fees** £35 per day, £28 per round (£40 weekends) 💳 **Course Designer** Hawtree **Prof** John Hughes **Facilities** 🍴 🍽 🛋 ☕ 🍷 👔 🏪 ⛳ 🛒 🚗 🔋 🏌 **Conf** Corporate Hospitality Days **Location** 1m S of Easingwold
Hotel ★★ 76% SHL George Hotel, Market Place, EASINGWOLD ☎ 01347 821698 📠 01347 823448 15 en suite

FILEY — Map 8 TA18

Filey Golf Club West Av YO14 9BQ
☎ 01723 513293
e-mail: secretary@fileygolfclub.com
web: www.fileygolfclub.com

Links and parkland course with good views. Stream runs through course. Testing 9th and 13th holes.

18 Holes, 6129yds, Par 70, SSS 69, Course record 65.
Academy Course: 9 Holes, 1570yds, Par 30.
Club membership 600.

Visitors Mon-Sun & BHs. Booking weekends & BHs. Dress code. **Societies** booking required. **Green Fees** £32 per round (£38 weekends), Academy £7.50 per round **Course Designer** Braid **Prof** Darren Squire **Facilities** 🍴 🍽 🛋 ☕ 🍷 👔 🏪 ⛳ 🛒 🚗 🔋 **Conf** Corporate Hospitality Days **Location** 0.5m S of Filey
Hotel ★★★ 75% HL Ambassador Hotel, Esplanade, SCARBOROUGH ☎ 01723 362841 📠 01723 366166 59 en suite

GANTON — Map 8 SE97

Ganton Golf Club YO12 4PA
☎ 01944 710329 📠 01944 710922
e-mail: secretary@gantongolfclub.com
web: www.gantongolfclub.com

Championship course, heathland, gorse-lined fairways and heavily bunkered; variable winds. The opening holes make full use of the contours of the land and the approach to the second demands the finest touch. The 4th is considered one of the best holes on the outward half with its shot across a valley to a plateau green, the surrounding gorse punishing anything less than a perfect shot. The finest hole is possibly the 18th, requiring an accurately placed drive to give a clear shot to the sloping, well-bunkered green.

18 Holes, 6724yds, Par 73, SSS 73, Course record 66.
Club membership 500.

Visitors Mon-Sun & BHs. Booking required. Dress code. **Societies** booking required. **Green Fees** £85 per day (£90 weekends) **Course Designer** Dunn/Vardon/Braid/Colt **Prof** Gary Brown **Facilities** 🍴 🍽 🛋 ☕ 🍷 👔 🏪 ⛳ 🛒 🚗 🔋 **Conf** Corporate Hospitality Days **Location** N of village off A64
Hotel ★★★★ GA Orchard Lodge, North Street, FLIXTON ☎ 01723 890202 📠 01723 890202 6 rooms

ENGLAND

HARROGATE
Map 8 SE35

Harrogate Golf Club Forest Lane Head, Starbeck HG2 7TF
☎ 01423 862999 📠 01423 860073
e-mail: secretary@harrogate-gc.co.uk
web: www.harrogate-gc.co.uk

Course on fairly flat terrain with MacKenzie-style greens and tree-lined fairways. While not a long course, the layout penalises the golfer who strays off the fairway. Subtly placed bunkers and copses of trees require the golfer to adopt careful thought and accuracy if par is be bettered. The last six holes include five par 4s, of which four exceed 400yds.

18 Holes, 6241yds, Par 69, SSS 70.
Club membership 700.

Visitors Mon, Wed-Fri, Sun & BHs. Tue pm only. Handicap certificate. Dress code. **Societies** booking required. **Green Fees** £45 per day, £40 per round (£50 Sun) **Course Designer** Sandy Herd **Prof** Gary Stothard, Sam Evison **Facilities** 🕦 🍴 🛍 🗆 🖥 ⚒ 🏠 🍴 🐜 ✍ **Leisure** snooker **Conf** Corporate Hospitality Days **Location** 2.25m N on A59
Hotel ★★★★ 70% HL Best Western Cedar Court Hotel, Queens Buildings, Park Parade, HARROGATE ☎ 01423 858585 & 858595 (Res) 📠 01423 504950 100 en suite

Oakdale Golf Club Oakdale Glen HG1 2LN
☎ 01423 567162 📠 01423 536030
e-mail: manager@oakdalegolfclub.co.uk
web: www.oakdalegolfclub.co.uk

A pleasant, undulating parkland course which provides a good test of golf for the low handicap player without intimidating the less proficient. A special feature is an attractive stream which comes in to play on four holes. Excellent views from the clubhouse.

18 Holes, 6456yds, Par 71, SSS 71.
Club membership 900.

Visitors Mon-Sun & BHs. Booking required weekends & BHs. Handicap certificate. Dress code. **Societies** booking required. **Green Fees** £60 for 27 holes, £50 per 18 holes (£65 weekends & BHs) **Course Designer** Dr McKenzie **Prof** Clive Dell **Facilities** 🕦 🍴 🛍 🗆 🖥 ⚒ 🏠 🍴 🐜 ✍ **Conf** Corporate Hospitality Days **Location** N of town centre off A61
Hotel ★★★★ 75% HL Studley Hotel, Swan Road, HARROGATE ☎ 01423 560425 📠 01423 530967 30 en suite

Rudding Park Hotel, Spa & Golf Follifoot HG3 1JH
☎ 01423 872100 📠 01423 872286
e-mail: golf@ruddingpark.com
web: www.ruddingpark.co.uk

The Hawtree course runs through 18th century parkland and provides a challenge for the most seasoned golfer with mature trees, attractive lakes and water features. The Repton 6 hole short course includes a signature island hole based on the notorious 17th at Sawgrass, Florida.

Hawtree Course: 18 Holes, 6883yds, Par 72.
Club membership 650.

Visitors Mon-Sun & BHs. Booking required. Dress code. **Societies** booking required. **Green Fees** from £12 per 18 holes depending on day/time **Course Designer** Martin Hawtree **Prof** D Fountain **Facilities** 🕦 🍴 🛍 🗆 🖥 ⚒ 🏠 🍴 ◇ ✍ 🐜 ✍ 🏌 **Leisure** 6 hole par 3 short course **Conf** facs Corporate Hospitality Days **Location** 2m SE of Harrogate town centre, off A658, brown tourist signs
Hotel ★★★★ HL Rudding Park Hotel, Spa & Golf, Rudding Park, Follifoot, HARROGATE ☎ 01423 871350 📠 01423 872286 90 en suite

KIRKBYMOORSIDE
Map 8 SE68

Kirkbymoorside Golf Club Manor Vale YO62 6EG
☎ 01751 430402 📠 01751 433190
e-mail: enqs@kirkbymoorsidegolf.co.uk
web: www.kirkbymoorsidegolf.co.uk

Challenging hilly parkland course with narrow fairways, gorse and hawthorn bushes. Beautiful views and several interesting holes.

Kirkbymoorside: 18 Holes, 6207yds, Par 69, SSS 70,
Course record 65. Club membership 600.

Visitors Mon-Sun & BHs. Booking required BHs. Dress code. **Societies** booking required. **Green Fees** £30 per day, £24 per round (£35 weekends & BHs). **Prof** John Hinchliffe **Facilities** 🕦 🍴 🛍 🗆 🖥 ⚒ 🏠 🍴 🐜 ✍ **Leisure** snooker room **Conf** facs Corporate Hospitality Days **Location** N of village
Hotel ★★ 82% HL Fox & Hounds Country Inn, Main Street, Sinnington, YORK ☎ 01751 431577 📠 01751 432791 10 en suite

KNARESBOROUGH   Map 8 SE35

Knaresborough Golf Club Boroughbridge Rd HG5 0QQ
☎ 01423 862690 📄 01423 869345
e-mail: secretary@kgc.uk.com
web: www.knaresboroughgolfclub.co.uk

Pleasant and well-presented parkland course in a rural setting. The first 11 holes are tree-lined and are constantly changing direction around the clubhouse. The closing holes head out overlooking the old quarry with fine views.

18 Holes, 6800yds, Par 72, SSS 73, Course record 68. Club membership 625.

Visitors Mon-Sun & BHs. Booking required. Handicap certificate. Dress code. **Societies** booking required. **Green Fees** £50 per day, £37 per round (£50 weekends) **Course Designer** Hawtree **Prof** Andrew Turner **Facilities** ⊕ ⑩ 🍴 ⌂ ⛳ ☂ 🏪 🛒 ⛳ **Conf** Corporate Hospitality Days **Location** 1.25m N on A6055
Hotel ★★★★ 75% CHH Nidd Hall Hotel, Nidd, HARROGATE
☎ 01423 771598 📄 01423 770931 183 en suite

MALTON   Map 8 SE77

Malton & Norton Golf Club Welham Park, Norton YO17 9QE
☎ 01653 697912 📄 01653 697844
e-mail: maltonandnorton@btconnect.com
web: www.maltonandnortongolfclub.co.uk

Parkland course, consisting of three nine-hole loops, with panoramic views of the moors. Very testing 1st hole (564yd dog-leg, left) on the Welham Course.

Welham Course: 18 Holes, 6456yds, Par 72, SSS 71, Course record 66.
Park Course: 18 Holes, 6251yds, Par 72, SSS 70, Course record 67.
Derwent Course: 18 Holes, 6295yds, Par 72, SSS 70, Course record 66. Club membership 880.

Visitors Mon-Fri & Sun. Sat & BHs after 1.30pm. Booking required. Dress code. **Societies** booking required. **Green Fees** £37 per day, £32 per round (£42/£37 weekends & BHs) **Prof** M Brooks **Facilities** ⊕ ⑩ 🍴 ⌂ ⛳ ☂ 🏪 🛒 ⛳ ⛳ **Conf** Corporate Hospitality Days **Location** 0.75m from Malton
Hotel ★★★★ FH Woodhouse Farm, WESTOW ☎ 01653 618378 & 07904 293422 📄 01653 618378 2 rooms

MASHAM   Map 8 SE28

Masham Golf Club Burnholme, Swinton Rd HG4 4NS
☎ 01765 688054
e-mail: info@mashamgolfclub.co.uk
web: www.mashamgolfclub.co.uk

Flat parkland crossed by River Burn, which comes into play on six holes.

9 Holes, 3102yds, Par 70, SSS 70. Club membership 270.

Visitors Mon-Fri except BHs. Dress code. **Societies** booking required. **Green Fees** £25 per day, £20 per 18 holes 🏷 **Facilities** ⊕ by prior arrangement ⑩ by prior arrangement 🍴 ☂ 🏪 ⛳ **Conf** Corporate Hospitality Days **Location** SW of Masham centre off A6108
Hotel ★★★★ HL Swinton Park, MASHAM ☎ 01765 680900 📄 01765 680901 30 en suite

MIDDLESBROUGH   Map 8 NZ41

Middlesbrough Golf Club Brass Castle Ln, Marton TS8 9EE
☎ 01642 311515 📄 01642 319607
e-mail: enquiries@middlesbroughgolfclub.co.uk
web: www.middlesbroughgolfclub.co.uk

Undulating wooded parkland affected by the wind. Testing 6th, 8th and 12th holes. (USGA greens).

18 Holes, 6328yds, Par 70, SSS 70, Course record 63. Club membership 950.

Visitors Mon, Wed-Fri, Sun & BHs. Booking required. Handicap certificate. Dress code. **Societies** booking required. **Green Fees** £39 per round (£44 Sun) **Course Designer** James Baird **Prof** Gordon Cattrell **Facilities** ⊕ ⑩ 🍴 ⌂ ⛳ ☂ 🏪 ⛳ **Leisure** snooker table **Conf** facs Corporate Hospitality Days **Location** 6m S of Middlesbrough
Hotel ★★★ 79% HL Best Western Parkmore Hotel & Leisure Club, 636 Yarm Road, Eaglescliffe, STOCKTON-ON-TEES ☎ 01642 786815 📄 01642 790485 55 en suite

Middlesbrough Municipal Golf Centre Ladgate Ln TS5 7YZ
☎ 01642 315533 📄 01642 300726
web: www.middlesbrough.gov.uk

18 Holes, 6333yds, Par 71, SSS 70, Course record 67.

Course Designer Shuttleworth **Location** 2m S of Middlesbrough on the A174
Telephone for further details
Hotel ★★★ 79% HL Best Western Parkmore Hotel & Leisure Club, 636 Yarm Road, Eaglescliffe, STOCKTON-ON-TEES ☎ 01642 786815 📄 01642 790485 55 en suite

NORTHALLERTON   Map 8 SE39

Romanby Golf & Country Club Yafforth Rd DL7 0PE
☎ 01609 778855 📄 01609 779084
web: www.romanby.com

18 Holes, 6663yds, Par 72, SSS 72, Course record 72.

Course Designer Will Adamson **Location** 1m W of Northallerton on B6271
Telephone for further details
Hotel ★★ 71% HL Lodge at Leeming Bar, The Great North Road, LEEMING BAR ☎ 01677 422122 📄 01677 424507 39 en suite

PANNAL
Map 8 SE35

Pannal Golf Club Follifoot Rd HG3 1ES
☎ 01423 872628 📠 01423 870043
e-mail: secretary@pannalgolfclub.co.uk
web: www.pannalgolfclub.co.uk

Fine championship course chosen as a regional qualifying venue for the Open Championship. Moorland turf but well-wooded with trees closely involved with play. Excellent views enhance the course.

18 Holes, 6614yds, Par 72, SSS 72, Course record 63.
Club membership 800.

Visitors Mon-Fri except BHs. Booking required. Dress code.
Societies booking required. **Green Fees** £45 per round May & Oct, £25 Nov-Apr **Course Designer** Sandy Herd **Prof** David Padgett
Facilities ⓣ ⍟ ⓛ ⌷ ⍝ ⍨ 🏠 ⍦ 🚂 ⍦ 🌳 **Conf**
Corporate Hospitality Days **Location** 2m S of Harrogate, E of village off A61

Hotel ★★★ 75% HL The Yorkshire Hotel, Prospect Place, HARROGATE ☎ 0845 906 9966 📠 01423 500082 80 en suite

RAVENSCAR
Map 8 NZ90

Raven Hall Hotel Golf Course YO13 0ET
☎ 01723 870353 📠 01723 870072
e-mail: enquiries@ravenhall.co.uk
web: www.ravenhall.co.uk

Opened by the Earl of Cranbrook in 1898, this nine-hole clifftop course is sloping and with good quality small greens. Because of its clifftop position it is subject to strong winds which make it great fun to play, especially the 6th hole.

9 Holes, 1894yds, Par 32, SSS 32.

Visitors Mon-Sun & BHs. **Societies** welcome. **Green Fees** £8 per round
Facilities ⓣ ⍟ ⓛ ⌷ ⍝ ⍨ ⍦ **Leisure** hard tennis courts, heated indoor swimming pool, sauna, croquet, bowls, games room
Conf facs Corporate Hospitality Days **Location** A171 from Scarborough towards Whitby, through Cloughton, right to Ravenscar, hotel on clifftop

Hotel ★★★ 75% HL Raven Hall Country House, RAVENSCAR
☎ 01723 870353 📠 01723 870072 60 en suite

REDCAR
Map 8 NZ62

Cleveland Golf Club Majuba Rd TS10 5BJ
☎ 01642 471798 📠 01642 471798
e-mail: secretary@clevelandgolfclub.co.uk
web: www.clevelandgolfclub.co.uk

The oldest golf club in Yorkshire playing over the only links championship course in the county. A true test of traditional golf, especially when windy. Flat seaside links with easy walking.

18 Holes, 6696yds, Par 72, SSS 73, Course record 67.
Club membership 480.

Visitors contact club for details. **Societies** booking required. **Green Fees** £20 (£25 Sun) **Course Designer** Donald Steel (new holes)
Prof Tim Jenkins **Facilities** ⓣ ⍟ ⓛ ⌷ ⍝ ⍨ 🏠 🚂 ⍦
🌳 **Conf** Corporate Hospitality Days **Location** 8m E of Middlesborough, at N end of Redcar

Hotel ★★★★ 80% HL Macdonald Gisborough Hall, Whitby Lane, GUISBOROUGH ☎ 0844 879 9149 📠 01287 610844 71 en suite

Wilton Golf Club Wilton TS10 4QY
☎ 01642 465265 (Secretary) 📠 01642 465463
e-mail: secretary@wiltongolfclub.co.uk
web: www.wiltongolfclub.co.uk

Parkland with some fine views and an abundance of trees and shrubs.

18 Holes, 6540yds, Par 70, SSS 69, Course record 64.
Club membership 650.

Visitors Mon-Fri, Sun & BHs. Dress code. **Societies** booking required
Green Fees £26 per day ⍟ **Prof** P D Smillie **Facilities** ⓣ ⍟ ⍟
by prior arrangement ⓛ ⌷ ⍝ ⍨ 🏠 ⍦ ⍦ 🚂 ⍦
Leisure snooker **Conf** Corporate Hospitality Days **Location** 3m W of Redcar on A174

Hotel ★★★★ 80% HL Macdonald Gisborough Hall, Whitby Lane, GUISBOROUGH ☎ 0844 879 9149 📠 01287 610844 71 en suite

RICHMOND
Map 7 NZ10

Richmond Golf Club Bend Hagg DL10 5EX
☎ 01748 823231 (Secretary) 📠 01748 821709
e-mail: secretary@richmondyorksgolfclub.co.uk
web: www.richmondyorksgolfclub.co.uk

Undulating parkland. Ideal to play 27 holes, not too testing but very interesting.

18 Holes, 6073yds, Par 71, SSS 69, Course record 63.
Club membership 600.

Visitors Mon-Sat & BHs. Sun after 3.30pm. Booking required. Dress code. **Societies** booking required. **Green Fees** not confirmed **Course Designer** F Pennink **Prof** James Cousins **Facilities** ⓣ ⍟ ⓛ ⌷
⍝ ⍨ 🏠 ⍦ 🚂 ⍦ **Conf** facs **Location** 0.75m N
Hotel ★★★★ 77% HL The Morritt, Greta Bridge, BARNARD CASTLE
☎ 01833 627232 📠 01833 627392 27 en suite

RIPON
Map 8 SE37

Ripon City Golf Club Palace Rd HG4 3HH
☎ 01765 603640 📠 01765 692880
e-mail: secretary@riponcitygolfclub.com
web: www.riponcitygolfclub.com

Moderate walking on undulating parkland course; four testing par 3s at 1st, 5th, 7th and 14th.

18 Holes, 6084yds, Par 70, SSS 69. Club membership 600.

Visitors Mon-Fri, Sun & BHs. Booking required. Dress code.
Societies booking required **Green Fees** £32 per 18 holes ⍟ **Course Designer** H Varden **Prof** S T Davis **Facilities** ⓣ ⍟ ⓛ ⌷ ⍝
⍨ 🏠 ⍦ ⍦ 🚂 ⍦ 🌳 **Conf** facs Corporate Hospitality Days
Location 1m NW on A6108

Hotel ★★★ 81% HL The Ripon Spa Hotel, Park Street, RIPON
☎ 01765 602172 📠 01765 690770 40 en suite

Save on Hotels. Book at **theAA.com/hotel**

YORKSHIRE, NORTH

SALTBURN-BY-THE-SEA
Map 8 NZ62

Hunley Hotel & Golf Club Ings Ln, Brotton TS12 2FT
☎ 01287 676216 📠 01287 678250
e-mail: enquiries@hhgc.co.uk
web: www.hhgc.co.uk

A picturesque coastal course with panoramic views of the countryside and coastline. It offers golfers flexibility with several courses available from the 29 interchangeable holes, providing a good test of golf and a rewarding game for all.

Morgans: 18 Holes, 6872yds, Par 73, SSS 73, Course record 63.
Millennium: 18 Holes, 5945yds, Par 68, SSS 68.
Jubilee: 18 Holes, 6289yds, Par 71, SSS 70.
Imperial: 18 Holes, 6543yds, Par 72. Club membership 550.
Visitors Mon-Sun & BHs. Dress code. **Societies** booking required.
Green Fees £25 per day (£35 weekends & BHs) **Course Designer** John Morgan **Prof** Andrew Brook **Facilities** ⊕ ⊘ ⊾ ⊑ ⊓ ⊿ ⊟ ⊹ ◇ ⬚ ✗ ꝼ **Conf** facs Corporate Hospitality Days
Location from N A1(M) junct 60, A689 to A19. From S A1(M) junct 49, A168 to A19. Take Saltburn junct to A174, travel through Saltburn and Brotton, 2nd left for St Margarets Way, signed.
Hotel ★★★ 75% HL Hunley Hotel & Golf Club, Ings Lane, Brotton, SALTBURN ☎ 01287 676216 📠 01287 678250 27 en suite

Saltburn by the Sea Golf Club Hob Hill, Guisborough Rd TS12 1NJ
☎ 01287 622812 📠 01287 625988
e-mail: secretary@saltburngolf.co.uk
web: www.saltburngolf.co.uk

Parkland course surrounded by woodland. Particularly attractive in autumn. There are fine views of the Cleveland Hills and of Tees Bay.

18 Holes, 5974yds, Par 70, SSS 70, Course record 63.
Club membership 900.
Visitors Mon-Fri, Sun & BHs. Booking required. Dress code.
Societies booking required. **Green Fees** from £21 per day **Course Designer** J Braid **Prof** Mike Howes **Facilities** ⊕ ⊾ ⊑ ⊓ ⊿ ⊟ ✗ ⬚ ꝼ **Leisure** 2 snooker tables **Conf** facs Corporate Hospitality Days **Location** 0.5m S from Saltburn
Hotel ★★★ 75% HL Hunley Hall Golf Club & Hotel, Ings Lane, Brotton, SALTBURN ☎ 01287 676216 📠 01287 678250 27 en suite

SCARBOROUGH
Map 8 TA08

Scarborough North Cliff Golf Club North Cliff Av YO12 6PP
☎ 01723 355397 📠 01723 362134
e-mail: info@northcliffgolfclub.co.uk
web: www.northcliffgolfclub.co.uk

Seaside course beginning on clifftop overlooking North Bay and castle winding inland through parkland with stunning views of the North Yorkshire moors and coast.

18 Holes, 6493yds, Par 72, SSS 71, Course record 63.
Club membership 850.
Visitors Mon-Sun & BHs. Dress code. **Societies** booking required.
Green Fees £40 per day, £35 per round (£45/£40 Fri-Sun & BHs).
Course Designer James Braid **Prof** Simon N Deller **Facilities** ⊕ ⊙ ⊾ ⊑ ⊓ ⊿ ⊟ ⊹ ✗ ⬚ ꝼ **Conf** Corporate Hospitality Days **Location** 2m N of town centre off A165
Hotel ★★★★ INN Blacksmiths Arms, High Street, CLOUGHTON ☎ 01723 870244 10 rooms

Scarborough South Cliff Golf Club Deepdale Av YO11 2UE
☎ 01723 360522 📠 01723 360523
e-mail: clubsecretary@southcliffgolf.com
web: www.southcliffgolfclub.com

Parkland and seaside course which falls into two parts, divided from one another by the main road from Scarborough to Filey. On the seaward side of the road lie holes 4 to 10. On the landward side the first three holes and the last eight are laid out along the bottom of a rolling valley, stretching southwards into the hills.

18 Holes, 6432yds, Par 72, SSS 71, Course record 63.
Club membership 450.
Visitors Mon-Sun & BHs. Booking required. **Societies** booking required. **Green Fees** £44 per day, £36 per round (£50/£40 Fri-Sun & BHs) **Course Designer** McKenzie **Prof** Tony Skingle **Facilities** ⊕ ⊙ ⊾ ⊑ ⊓ ⊿ ⊟ ✗ ⬚ ꝼ **Leisure** 6 hole pitch & putt course **Conf** Corporate Hospitality Days **Location** 1m S on A165
Hotel ★★★ 79% HL Palm Court, St Nicholas Cliff, SCARBOROUGH ☎ 01723 368161 📠 01723 371547 40 en suite

ENGLAND

SELBY
Map 8 SE63

Selby Golf Club Mill Ln, Brayton YO8 9LD
☎ 01757 228622 📄 01757 228622
e-mail: secretary@selbygolfclub.co.uk
web: www.selbygolfclub.co.uk
Mainly flat, links-type course; prevailing south-west wind. Testing holes including the 3rd, 7th and 16th.
18 Holes, 6374yds, Par 71, SSS 71. Club membership 840.
Visitors Mon, Wed-Fri except BHs. Booking required. Handicap certificate. Dress code. **Societies** booking required. **Green Fees** £37 per day, £33 per round **Course Designer** J Taylor & Hawtree
Prof Nick Ludwell **Facilities** ⓨ 🍴 🍺 ⌨ 🍴 🏊 🏠 ✎ ✦
Location off A63 Selby bypass
Hotel ★★★ 81% CHH Monk Fryston Hall, MONK FRYSTON
☎ 01977 682369 📄 01977 683544   29 en suite

SETTLE
Map 7 SD86

Settle Golf Club Buckhaw Brow, Giggleswick BD24 0DH
☎ 01729 825288 & 822858 (sec)   📄 01729 825288
web: www.settlegolfclub.com
Picturesque parkland with several water courses affecting play on four holes in an Area of Outstanding Natural Beauty.
9 Holes, 6262yds, Par 72. Club membership 160.
Visitors Mon-Sun & BHs. Booking required Sun. Dress code.
Societies booking required. **Green Fees** £20 per round **Course Designer** Tom Vardon **Facilities** 🏊 **Location** 1m W of Settle on Kendal Rd
Hotel ★★★★ 77% HL The Coniston, Coniston Cold, SKIPTON
☎ 01756 748080 📄 01756 749487   50 en suite

SKIPTON
Map 7 SD95

Skipton Golf Club Short Lee Ln BD23 3LF
☎ 01756 795657 📄 01756 796665
e-mail: enquiries@skiptongolfclub.co.uk
web: www.skiptongolfclub.co.uk
Undulating parkland with some water hazards and panoramic views.
18 Holes, 6090yds, Par 70, SSS 69. Club membership 800.
Visitors Mon-Sun & BHs. Booking required. Dress code.
Societies booking required. **Green Fees** not confirmed **Prof** Peter Robinson **Facilities** ⓨ 🍴 🍺 ⌨ 🍴 🏊 🏠 🍴 ✎
Leisure snooker **Conf** Corporate Hospitality Days **Location** 1m N of Skipton on A59
Hotel ★★★★ HL The Devonshire Arms Country House Hotel & Spa, BOLTON ABBEY ☎ 01756 710441 & 718111 📄 01756 710564 40 en suite

TADCASTER
Map 8 SE44

Scarthingwell Golf Course Scarthingwell LS24 9PF
☎ 01937 557864 (pro) & 557878 (club)
📄 01937 557909
e-mail: ben.burlingham@scarthingwellgolfcourse.co.uk
web: www.scarthingwellgolfcourse.co.uk
Testing water hazards and well-placed bunkers and trees provide a challenging test of golf for all handicaps at this scenic parkland course. Easy walking.
18 Holes, 6771yds, Par 72, SSS 72. Club membership 500.
Visitors contact course for details. **Societies** Booking required. **Green Fees** not confirmed **Prof** Simon Danby **Facilities** ⓨ 🍺 ⌨ 🍴 🏊 🏠 ✎ **Leisure** snooker **Conf** facs Corporate Hospitality Days
Location 4m S of Tadcaster on A162 Tadcaster-Ferrybridge road
Hotel ★★★ 81% HL Best Western Milford Hotel, A1 Great North Road, Peckfield, LEEDS ☎ 01977 681800 📄 01977 681245 46 en suite

THIRSK
Map 8 SE48

Thirsk & Northallerton Golf Club Thornton-le-Street YO7 4AB
☎ 01845 525115 📄 01845 525119
e-mail: secretary@tngc.co.uk
web: www.tngc.co.uk
The course has good views of the nearby Hambleton Hills to the east and Wensleydale to the west. Testing course, mainly flat.
18 Holes, 6533yds, Par 72, SSS 72. Club membership 600.
Visitors Mon-Sun & BHs. Dress code. **Societies** welcome. **Green Fees** £38 per day, £32 per round (£48/£38 weekends) **Course Designer** ADAS **Prof** Robert Garner **Facilities** ⓨ 🍴 🍺 ⌨ 🍴 🏊 🏠 🍴 ✎ ✦ **Conf** Corporate Hospitality Days
Location 2m N on A168
Hotel ★★★★★ GA Spital Hill, York Road, THIRSK
☎ 01845 522273 📄 01845 524970   5 rooms (4 en suite)

WHITBY
Map 8 NZ81

Whitby Golf Club Low Straggleton, Sandsend Rd YO21 3SR
☎ 01947 600660 📄 01947 600660
e-mail: office@whitbygolfclub.co.uk
web: www.whitbygolfclub.co.uk
Seaside course with four holes along clifftops and over ravines. Good views and a fresh sea breeze.
18 Holes, 6259yds, Par 71, SSS 70, Course record 67. Club membership 400.
Visitors Mon-Sun & BHs. Dress code. **Societies** booking required.
Green Fees £27 per day (£30 weekends) 🍴 **Course Designer** Simon Gidman **Prof** Tony Mason **Facilities** ⓨ 🍴 🍺 ⌨ 🍴 🏊 🏠 🍴 ✎ **Leisure** full size snooker table **Conf** Corporate Hospitality Days **Location** 1.5m NW on A174
Hotel ★★★ 82% CHH Dunsley Hall, Dunsley, WHITBY
☎ 01947 893437 📄 01947 893505   26 en suite

ave on Hotels. Book at **theAA.com/hotel**

YORKSHIRE, NORTH

ENGLAND

ORK
Map 8 SE65

orest of Galtres Golf Club Moorlands Rd, Skelton
032 2RF
☎ 01904 766198 🖨 01904 769400
-mail: secretary@forestofgaltres.co.uk
web: www.forestofgaltres.co.uk

evel parkland in the heart of the ancient Forest of Galtres, with
ature oak trees and interesting water features coming into play on
he 6th, 14th and 17th holes. Views of York Minster.

8 Holes, 6534yds, Par 72, SSS 71, Course record 65.
Club membership 450.

Visitors Mon-Sun & BHs. Booking required. Dress code.
ocieties booking required. **Green Fees** £32 per day, £25 per
ound (£42/£32 weekends & BHs) **Course Designer** Simon Gidman
rof Alastair Grindlay **Facilities** ⓉⒾ ⑩ by prior arrangement 🝙
⛳ 🕯 🛋 🏠 ♈ ☙ **Conf** Corporate Hospitality Days
ocation 0.5m from the York ring road B1237, just off A19 Thirsk road
hrough the village of Skelton
otel ★★★★ 72% CHH Fairfield Manor, Shipton Road, Skelton,
ORK ☎ 01904 670222 🖨 01904 670311 89 en suite

orest Park Golf Club Stockton-on-the-Forest YO32 9UW
☎ 01904 400425
-mail: admin@forestparkgolfclub.co.uk
web: www.forestparkgolfclub.co.uk

lat parkland 27-hole course with large greens and narrow tree-lined
airways. The Old Foss beck meanders through the course, creating a
atural hazard on many holes.

Old Foss Course: 18 Holes, 6673yds, Par 71, SSS 72.
The West Course: 9 Holes, 6372yds, Par 70, SSS 70.
Club membership 600.

Visitors Mon-Sun & BHs. Dress code. **Societies** welcome. **Green
ees** £25 per 18 holes (£30 weekends), 9 holes £10/£12 **Prof** Mark
Winterburn **Facilities** ⓉⒾ ⑩ 🝙 🕯 🛋 🏠 ♈ ☙ 🛋 ☙
` **Conf** facs Corporate Hospitality Days **Location** 4m NE of York off
.64 York bypass
otel ★★★ 80% HL Best Western Monkbar, Monkbar, YORK
☎ 01904 638086 🖨 01904 629195 99 en suite

Fulford Golf Club Heslington Ln YO10 5DY
☎ 01904 413579 🖨 01904 416918
e-mail: gary@fulfordgolfclub.co.uk
web: www.fulfordgolfclub.co.uk

A flat, parkland and heathland course well-known for the superb
quality of its turf, particularly the greens, and famous as the venue

for some of the best professional golf tournaments in the British
Isles in recent years.

*Championship Course: 18 Holes, 6900yds, Par 72,
SSS 74, Course record 62. Club membership 700.*

Visitors Mon-Fri & Sun except BHs. Booking required. Handicap
certificate. Dress code. **Societies** booking required **Green
Fees** Summer from £55, Winter from £30 **Course Designer** C.
MacKenzie **Prof** Guy Wills **Facilities** ⓉⒾ ⑩ 🝙 🛋 🕯 🛋 🏠
⛳ 🛋 ☙ **Conf** facs Corporate Hospitality Days **Location** 2m S of
York off A19
Hotel ★★★★ 77% HL York Marriott Hotel, Tadcaster Road,
YORK ☎ 01904 701000 🖨 01904 702308 151 en suite

Heworth Golf Club Muncaster House YO31 9JY
☎ 01904 422389 🖨 01904 426156
web: www.theheworthgolfclub.co.uk

12 Holes, 6105yds, Par 69, SSS 69, Course record 68.

Course Designer B Cheal **Location** 1.5m NE of city centre on A1036
Telephone for further details
Hotel ★★★ 80% HL Best Western Monkbar, Monkbar, YORK
☎ 01904 638086 🖨 01904 629195 99 en suite

Swallow Hall Golf Course Crockey Hill YO19 4SG
☎ 01904 448889 🖨 01904 448219
e-mail: jtscores@hotmail.com
web: www.swallowhall.co.uk

A small 18-hole, par 3 course with three par 4s. Attached to a caravan
park and holiday cottages.

18 Holes, 3600yds, Par 57, SSS 56, Course record 58.
Club membership 100.

Visitors Mon-Sun & BHs. **Societies** Booking required. **Green Fees** not
confirmed **Course Designer** Brian Henry **Prof** Dan Moodie **Facilities** ⓉⒾ
⑩ 🝙 🛋 🕯 🏠 ♈ ◇ 🛋 ⛳ ☙ **Leisure** fishing, par 3
academy course **Conf** facs Corporate Hospitality Days **Location** off
A19 signed Wheldrake
Hotel ★★★ 74% HL Best Western York Pavilion, 45 Main Street,
Fulford, YORK ☎ 01904 622099 & 239900 🖨 01904 626939
57 en suite

York Golf Club Lords Moor Ln, Strensall YO32 5XF
☎ 01904 491840 (Sec) & 490304 (Pro)
🖨 01904 491852
e-mail: secretary@yorkgolfclub.co.uk
web: www.yorkgolfclub.co.uk

A pleasant, well-designed, heathland course with easy walking. The
course is of good length but is flat so not too tiring. The course is well
bunkered with excellent greens and there are two testing pond holes.

18 Holes, 6118yds, Par 70, SSS 69, Course record 65.
Club membership 750.

Visitors Mon-Fri & Sun except BHs. Dress code. **Societies** welcome.
Green Fees £58 for 36 holes, £52 for 27 holes, £44 for 18 holes
Course Designer J H Taylor **Prof** Mark Rogers **Facilities** ⓉⒾ ⑩
🝙 🛋 🕯 🏠 🏠 ♈ ☙ 🛋 ☙ ⛳ **Conf** facs Corporate
Hospitality Days **Location** 6m NE of York, E of Strensall
Hotel ★★★★ 76% HL Best Western Dean Court, Duncombe Place,
YORK ☎ 01904 625082 🖨 01904 620305 37 en suite

YORKSHIRE, SOUTH

BARNSLEY
Map 8 SE30

Barnsley Golf Club Wakefield Rd, Staincross S75 6JZ
☎ 01226 382856 🗎 01226 382856
e-mail: barnsleygolfclub@hotmail.com
Undulating municipal parkland course with easy walking apart from last 4 holes. Testing 8th and 18th holes.

18 Holes, 5951yds, Par 69, SSS 69, Course record 61.
Club membership 350.

Visitors Mon-Sun & BHs. Booking required. Dress code.
Societies booking required. **Green Fees** £17 per 18 holes (£19 weekends) **Prof** Shaun Wyke **Facilities** ⓣ by prior arrangement ⦿ by prior arrangement 🏠 ⬚ 🍴 🔺 🏠 🏌 ⚡ 🛒 ⚡ **Conf** Corporate Hospitality Days **Location** 3m N on A61
Hotel ★★★ 79% HL Best Western Ardsley House Hotel, Doncaster Road, Ardsley, BARNSLEY ☎ 01226 309955 🗎 01226 205374 75 en suite

Sandhill Golf Club Middlecliffe Ln, Little Houghton S72 0HW
☎ 01226 753444 🗎 01226 753444
web: www.sandhillgolfclub.co.uk
Attractive, easy walking parkland with views of the surrounding countryside. Designed with strategically placed bunkers, the 4th hole having a deep bunker directly in front of the green. Very fine views from the 17th tee.

18 Holes, 6309yds, Par 71, SSS 70, Course record 62.
Club membership 450.

Visitors Mon-Sun & BHs. Booking required. Dress code.
Societies booking required. **Green Fees** £17.50 per round (£22.50 weekends & BHs) **Course Designer** John Royston **Facilities** ⓣ ⦿ 🏠 ⬚ 🍴 🔺 🏠 ⚡ 🏌 **Conf** Corporate Hospitality Days **Location** 5m E of Barnsley off A635
Hotel ★★★ 79% HL Best Western Ardsley House Hotel, Doncaster Road, Ardsley, BARNSLEY ☎ 01226 309955 🗎 01226 205374 75 en suite

BAWTRY
Map 8 SK69

Bawtry Golf Club Cross Ln, Austerfield DN10 6RF
☎ 01302 711409 & 711445
web: www.bawtrygolfclub.co.uk
Championship moorland course featuring the 618yd 7th and the Postage Stamp 8th. Well drained and easy walking with attached driving range.

18 Holes, 7000yds, Par 73, SSS 73, Course record 66.
Club membership 600.

Visitors Mon-Fri & BHs. Weekends after 12.30pm. Booking required weekends. Dress code. **Societies** booking required. **Green Fees** not confirmed **Prof** Daniel Gregory/Mick Beck **Facilities** ⓣ ⦿ 🏠 ⬚ 🍴 🔺 🏠 ⚡ 🛒 ⚡ **Conf** Corporate Hospitality Days **Location** 2m from Bawtry on A614
Hotel ★★★★ 76% HL Best Western Premier Mount Pleasant Hotel, Great North Road, DONCASTER ☎ 01302 868696 & 868219 🗎 01302 865130 56 en suite

CONISBROUGH
Map 8 SK59

Crookhill Park Municipal Golf Course Carr Ln DN12 2AH
☎ 01709 862979 🗎 01709 866455
18 Holes, 5849yds, Par 70, SSS 68, Course record 64.
Location 1.5m SE on B6094
Telephone for further details
Hotel ★★★ 80% HL Best Western Pastures, Pastures Road, MEXBOROUGH ☎ 01709 577707 🗎 01709 577795 60 en suite

DONCASTER
Map 8 SE50

Doncaster Golf Club 278 Bawtry Rd, Bessacarr DN4 7PD
☎ 01302 865632 🗎 01302 865994
e-mail: info@doncastergolfclub.co.uk
web: www.doncastergolfclub.co.uk
Pleasant undulating heathland course with wooded surroundings. Quick drying, ideal all year round course.

18 Holes, 6244yds, Par 69, SSS 70. Club membership 500.

Visitors Tue-Sun except BHs. Dress code. **Societies** booking required. **Green Fees** £40 per day, £36 per round (£40 per round weekends) **Course Designer** MacKenzie/Hawtree **Prof** Graham Bailey **Facilities** ⓣ ⦿ 🏠 ⬚ 🍴 🔺 🏠 ⚡ 🛒 ⚡ **Conf** facs Corporate Hospitality Days **Location** 4m SE on A638
Hotel ★★★★ 76% HL Best Western Premier Mount Pleasant Hotel, Great North Road, DONCASTER ☎ 01302 868696 & 868219 🗎 01302 865130 56 en suite

Doncaster Town Moor Golf Club Bawtry Rd, Belle Vue DN4 5HU
☎ 01302 533167 🗎 01302 533448
e-mail: dtmgc@btconnect.com
web: www.doncastertownmoorgolfclub.co.uk
Easy walking, but testing, heathland course with good true greens. Notable hole is 11th (par 4), 464yds. Situated in centre of racecourse. Open all winter.

18 Holes, 6072yds, Par 69, SSS 69, Course record 63.
Club membership 520.

Visitors Mon-Sat & BHs. Booking required. Dress code.
Societies booking required. **Green Fees** not confirmed **Prof** Steven Shaw **Facilities** ⓣ ⦿ 🏠 ⬚ 🍴 🔺 🏠 🛒 ⚡ **Conf** facs Corporate Hospitality Days **Location** 1.5m E at racecourse on A638
Hotel BUD Campanile Doncaster, Doncaster Leisure Park, Bawtry Road, DONCASTER ☎ 01302 370770 🗎 01302 370813 50 en suite

Owston Park Golf Course Owston Ln, Owston DN6 8EF
☎ 01302 330821
e-mail: michael.parker@foremostgolf.com
web: www.owstonparkgolfcourse.co.uk
A flat easy walking course surrounded by woodland. A lot of mature trees and a few ditches in play.

9 Holes, 2866yds, Par 35, SSS 70.

Visitors Mon-Sun & BHs. **Societies** welcome. **Green Fees** phone **Course Designer** M Parker **Prof** Mike Parker **Facilities** ⬚ 🔺 🏠 🍴 ⚡ 🛒 ⚡ **Location** 5m N of Doncaster off A19
Hotel ★★★ 68% HL Danum, High Street, DONCASTER ☎ 01302 342261 🗎 01302 329034 64 en suite

Thornhurst Park Golf Club Holme Ln, Owston DN5 0LR
☎ 01302 337799
e-mail: info.thornhurst@virgin.net
Surrounded by Owston Wood, this scenic parkland course has numerous strategically placed bunkers, and a lake comes into play at the 7th and 8th holes.

18 Holes, 6456yds, Par 72, SSS 71, Course record 67. Club membership 160.
Visitors Mon-Sun & BHs. Booking required weekends & BHs. Dress code. **Societies** booking required. **Green Fees** £12 per 18 holes, £7 per 9 holes (£15/£8 weekends & BHs) **Prof** Kevin Pearce **Facilities** ⓧ 🍴 ▙ 🖳 🖭 ⚐ 🏌 ⛳ 🏨 ⚒ **Conf** facs Corporate Hospitality Days **Location** on A19 between Bentley and Askern
Hotel ★★★ 68% HL Danum, High Street, DONCASTER ☎ 01302 342261 📠 01302 329034 64 en suite

Wheatley Golf Club Armthorpe Rd DN2 5QB
☎ 01302 831655 📠 01302 812736
web: www.wheatleygolfclub.co.uk
18 Holes, 6405yds, Par 71, SSS 71, Course record 64.
Course Designer George Duncan **Location** NE of town centre off A18
Telephone for further details
Hotel ★★★ 68% HL Danum, High Street, DONCASTER ☎ 01302 342261 📠 01302 329034 64 en suite

HATFIELD Map 8 SE60

Kings Wood Golf Course Thorne Rd DN7 6EP
☎ 01405 741343 📠 01405 741343
e-mail: chris.mann@foremostgolf.com
web: www.kingswoodgolfcentre.co.uk
An undulating course with ditches that come into play on several holes, especially on the testing back nine. Notable holes are the 12th par 4, 16th and par 5 18th. Water is a prominent feature with several large lakes strategically placed.

18 Holes, 6001yds, Par 71, SSS 71, Course record 67. Club membership 150.
Visitors Mon-Sun & BHs. **Societies** booking required. **Green Fees** £9 per 18 holes, £5.50 per 9 holes (£10/£6 weekends & BHs) **Designer** John Hunt **Prof** Chris Mann **Facilities** ⓧ 🍴 ▙ 🖳 🖭 ▟ 🏌 ⚒ **Conf** facs Corporate Hospitality Days **Location** M180 junct 1, A614 towards Thorne, onto A1146 towards Hatfield for 0.8m

HICKLETON Map 8 SE40

Hickleton Golf Club Lidgett Ln DN5 7BE
☎ 01709 896081 📠 01709 896083
web: www.hickletongolfclub.co.uk
18 Holes, 6434yds, Par 71, SSS 71, Course record 64.
Course Designer Huggett/Coles **Location** 3m W from A1(M) junct 37, off A635
Telephone for further details
Hotel ★★★ 68% HL Danum, High Street, DONCASTER ☎ 01302 342261 📠 01302 329034 64 en suite

HIGH GREEN Map 8 SK39

Tankersley Park Golf Club S35 4LG
☎ 0114 246 8247 📠 0114 245 7818
e-mail: secretary@tpgc.freeserve.co.uk
web: www.tankersleyparkgolfclub.org.uk
Rolling parkland course that demands accuracy rather than length. Lush fairways. The 18th hole considered to be one of the best last hole tests in Yorkshire.

Tankersley Park: 18 Holes, 6244yds, Par 70, SSS 70, Course record 634. Club membership 634.
Visitors Mon-Fri except BHs. Booking required. Dress code. **Societies** booking required. **Green Fees** £36 per day; £27 per round (£36 weekends) **Course Designer** Hawtree **Prof** Ian Kirk **Facilities** ⓧ 🍴 ▙ 🖳 🖭 ⚐ ▟ 🏨 🏌 ⛳ ⚒ **Conf** Corporate Hospitality Days **Location** A61/M1 onto A616 Stocksbridge bypass
Hotel ★★★★ 77% HL Tankersley Manor, Church Lane, TANKERSLEY ☎ 01226 744700 📠 01226 745405 99 en suite

RAWMARSH Map 8 SK49

Wath Golf Club Abdy Ln S62 7SJ
☎ 01709 878609 📠 01709 877097
e-mail: golf@wathgolfclub.co.uk
web: www.wathgolfclub.co.uk
Parkland course, not easy in spite of its length. Testing course with narrow fairways and small greens. Many dikes crisscross fairways, making playing for position paramount. Strategically placed copses reward the golfer who is straight off the tee. Playing over a pond into a prevailing wind on the 12th hole to a postage stamp size green, will test the most accomplished player.

18 Holes, 6096yds, Par 70, SSS 69, Course record 65. Club membership 625.
Visitors Mon-Fri & BHs. Sun pm. Booking required Sun & BHs. Dress code. **Societies** booking required. **Green Fees** £36 per 18 holes **Prof** Chris Bassett **Facilities** ⓧ 🍴 ▙ 🖳 🖭 ▟ 🏨 🏌 ⛳ 🚜 ⚒ **Conf** facs Corporate Hospitality Days **Location** 2m N of Rotherham on B6089
Hotel ★★★ 79% HL Carlton Park, 102/104 Moorgate Road, ROTHERHAM ☎ 01709 849955 📠 01709 368960 80 en suite

ROTHERHAM Map 8 SK49

Grange Park Golf Club Upper Wortley Rd S61 2SJ
☎ 01709 559497
18 Holes, 6421yds, Par 71, SSS 71, Course record 65.
Course Designer Fred Hawtree **Location** 3m NW off A629
Telephone for further details
Hotel ★★★★ 77% HL Tankersley Manor, Church Lane, TANKERSLEY ☎ 01226 744700 📠 01226 745405 99 en suite

Phoenix Golf Club Pavilion Ln S60 5PA
☎ 01709 382624
web: www.phoenixgolfclub.co.uk
18 Holes, 6182yds, Par 71, SSS 70, Course record 65.
Course Designer C K Cotton **Location** SW of Rotherham off A630
Telephone for further details
Hotel ★★★ 79% HL Carlton Park, 102/104 Moorgate Road, ROTHERHAM ☎ 01709 849955 📠 01709 368960 80 en suite

Rotherham Golf Club Thrybergh Park S65 4NU
☎ 01709 859500 📄 01709 859517
web: www.rotherhamgolfclub.com
18 Holes, 6324yds, Par 70, SSS 70, Course record 65.
Course Designer Sandy Herd **Location** 3.5m E on A630
Telephone for further details
Hotel ★★★ **80%** HL Best Western Elton House Hotel, Main
Street, Bramley, ROTHERHAM ☎ 01709 545681 📄 01709 549100
29 en suite

Sitwell Park Golf Club Shrogswood Rd S60 4BY
☎ 01709 541046 📄 01709 703637
e-mail: secretary@sitwellgolf.co.uk
web: www.sitwellgolf.co.uk
Undulating parkland course designed in 1913 by Dr Alister MacKenzie
and retaining many of his greens and complete with its own 'Amen
Corner' aptly named 'The Jungle'. Good test of golf for all levels of
player.
18 Holes, 5960yds, Par 71, SSS 69. Club membership 500.
Visitors Mon-Fri, Sun & BHs. Booking required. Dress code.
Societies booking required. **Green Fees** £34 per day, £26 per round
(£40/£32 Sun). **Course Designer** A MacKenzie **Prof** Nic Taylor
Facilities ⊕ ⦿I ᴌ ⊑ ⦿I ⌲ 🖻 ꝗ ⧉ 🛒 ⧉ **Conf** facs
Corporate Hospitality Days **Location** 2m SE of Rotherham centre off
A631
Hotel ★★★★ **71%** HL Hellaby Hall, Old Hellaby Lane, Hellaby,
ROTHERHAM ☎ 01709 702701 📄 01709 700979 90 en suite

SHEFFIELD   Map 8 SK38

Abbeydale Golf Club Twentywell Ln, Dore S17 4QA
☎ 0114 236 0763 📄 0114 236 0762
e-mail: abbeygolf@btconnect.com
web: www.abbeydalegolfclub.co.uk
Well presented undulating parkland course set in the Beauchief Estate
with fine views over Sheffield and the Derbyshire countryside.
18 Holes, 6261yds, Par 71, SSS 70, Course record 66.
Club membership 700.
Visitors Mon, Tue, Fri, Sun & BHs. Booking required Fri, Sun &
BHs. Handicap certificate. Dress code. **Societies** booking required.
Green Fees £45 per day, £36 per round (£45 Sun, £35 after
2.30pm). Twilight by arrangement after 4.30pm £20 ⊛ **Course
Designer** Herbert Fowler **Prof** Nigel Perry **Facilities** ⊕ ⦿I ᴌ
⊑ ⦿I ⌲ 🖻 ⧉ 🛒 ⧉ **Leisure** snooker **Conf** facs Corporate
Hospitality Days **Location** 4m SW of city off A621
Hotel ★★★★ **77%** HL Doubletree by Hilton, Chesterfield Road
South, SHEFFIELD ☎ 0114 282 9988 📄 0114 237 8140 95 en suite

Beauchief Golf Course Abbey Ln S8 0DB
☎ 0114 236 7274
web: www.beauchiefgolfclub.co.uk
Pay-and-play course with natural water hazards. The rolling land looks
west to the Pennines and a 12th-century abbey adorns the course.
18 Holes, 5586yds, Par 67, SSS 66, Course record 63.
Club membership 450.
Visitors Mon-Sun & BHs. Booking required. **Societies** booking
required. **Green Fees** not confirmed **Prof** M C Trippett **Facilities** ⊕
⦿I ᴌ ⊑ ⦿I ⌲ 🖻 ⧉ **Conf** facs Corporate
Hospitality Days **Location** 4m SW of city off A621
Hotel ★★★★ **77%** HL Doubletree by Hilton, Chesterfield Road
South, SHEFFIELD ☎ 0114 282 9988 📄 0114 237 8140 95 en suite

Birley Wood Golf Club Birley Ln S12 3BP
☎ 0114 264 7262
web: www.birleywood.com
Fairway course: 18 Holes, 5734yds, Par 69, SSS 67,
Course record 64.
Birley Course: 18 Holes, 5037, Par 66, SSS 65.
Location 4.5m SE of city off A616
Telephone for further details
Hotel ★★★ **80%** HL Best Western Mosborough Hall, High Street,
Mosborough, SHEFFIELD ☎ 0114 248 4353 📄 0114 247 9759
43 en suite

Concord Park Golf Club Shiregreen Ln S5 6AE
☎ 0114 257 7378
Hilly municipal parkland course with some fairways wood-flanked,
good views, often windy. Seven par 3 holes.
18 Holes, 4886yds, Par 67, SSS 64, Course record 58.
Club membership 220.
Visitors Mon-Sun & BHs. Booking required. **Societies** welcome.
Green Fees not confirmed **Prof** W Allcroft **Facilities** ⊕ ⦿I ᴌ
⊑ ⦿I ⌲ 🖻 ꝗ ⧉ 🛒 ⧉ **Leisure** hard tennis courts,
heated indoor swimming pool, squash, sauna, gymnasium **Conf** facs
Corporate Hospitality Days **Location** 3.5m N of city on B6086, off
A6135
Hotel ★★★★ **79%** HL Copthorne Hotel Sheffield, Sheffield
United Football Club, Bramhall Lane, SHEFFIELD ☎ 0114 252 5480
📄 0114 252 5490 158 en suite

Dore & Totley Golf Club Bradway Rd, Bradway S17 4QR
☎ 0114 2366 844 📄 0114 2353 436
e-mail: dore.totley@btconnect.com
web: www.doreandtotleygolfclub.co.uk
Flat parkland course upgraded with the addition of 5 holes making the
course 500 yards longer.
18 Holes, 6763yds, Par 72, SSS 73, Course record 66.
Club membership 580.
Visitors Mon-Fri. Sun & BHs pm. Booking required. **Societies** booking
required. **Green Fees** not confirmed **Prof** Gregg Roberts **Facilities** ⊕
⦿I ᴌ ⊑ ⦿I ⌲ 🖻 ⧉ 🛒 ⧉ **Leisure** snooker **Conf** facs
Corporate Hospitality Days **Location** 7m S of city on B6054, off A61
Hotel ★★★★ **77%** HL Doubletree by Hilton, Chesterfield Road
South, SHEFFIELD ☎ 0114 282 9988 📄 0114 237 8140 95 en suite

Hallamshire Golf Club Sandygate S10 4LA
☎ 0114 230 2153 📄 0114 230 5413
e-mail: secretary@hallamshiregolfclub.co.uk
web: www.hallamshiregolfclub.co.uk
Situated on a shelf of land at a height of 850ft. Magnificent views
to the west. Moorland turf, long carries over ravine and small and
quick greens. Not suitable for high handicap golfers.
18 Holes, 6346yds, Par 71, SSS 71, Course record 65.
Club membership 600.
Visitors Mon-Sun except BHs. Booking required. Dress code.
Societies booking required. **Green Fees** not confirmed ⊛ **Course
Designer** Harry Colt **Prof** G R Tickell **Facilities** ⊕ ⦿I ᴌ ⊑
⦿I ⌲ 🖻 ⧉ **Conf** Corporate Hospitality Days **Location** off
A57 at Crosspool onto Sandygate Rd, clubhouse 0.75m on right
Hotel ★★★★ **79%** HL Copthorne Hotel Sheffield, Sheffield
United Football Club, Bramhall Lane, SHEFFIELD ☎ 0114 252 5480
📄 0114 252 5490 158 en suite

Save on Hotels. Book at **theAA.com/hotel**

YORKSHIRE, SOUTH

ENGLAND

Hillsborough Golf Club Worrall Rd S6 4BE
☎ 0114 234 9151 (Sec) 📠 0114 229 4105
web: www.hillsboroughgolfclub.co.uk
18 Holes, 6345yards, Par 71, SSS 70, Course record 63.
Location 3m NW of city off A616
Telephone for further details
Hotel ★★★★ 77% HL Tankersley Manor, Church Lane,
TANKERSLEY ☎ 01226 744700 📠 01226 745405 99 en suite

Lees Hall Golf Club Hemsworth Rd, Norton S8 8LL
☎ 0114 255 4402
e-mail: secretary@leeshallgolfclub.co.uk
web: www.leeshallgolfclub.co.uk
Parkland/meadowland course with panoramic view of city.
18 Holes, 6171yds, Par 71, SSS 70, Course record 63.
Club membership 538.
Visitors Mon-Fri, Sun & BHs. Booking required. Dress code.
Societies booking required. **Green Fees** £25 per 18 holes (£35 weekends) **Prof** A Rossington **Facilities** ⓣ ⦿ 🍴 ☕ 🍽 ⛱
🖼 🖋 🛒 🖋 **Conf** Corporate Hospitality Days **Location** 3.5m S of city off A6102
Hotel ★★★★ 77% HL Doubletree by Hilton, Chesterfield Road South, SHEFFIELD ☎ 0114 282 9988 📠 0114 237 8140 95 en suite

Rother Valley Golf Centre Mansfield Rd, Wales Bar S26 5PQ
☎ 0114 247 3000 📠 0114 247 6000
e-mail: rother@jbgolf.co.uk
web: www.jackbarker.com
The challenging Blue Monster parkland course features a variety of water hazards. Notable holes include the 7th, with its island green fronted by water and dominated by bunkers to the rear. Look out for the water on the par 5 18th.
18 Holes, 6397yds, Par 72, SSS 72, Course record 68.
Club membership 300.
Visitors Dress code. **Societies** booking required. **Green Fees** £17.50 per 18 holes (£20 Fri, £22.50 weekends and BHs) **Course Designer** Michael Shattock & Mark Roe **Prof** Jason Ripley **Facilities** ⓣ ⦿ 🍴 ☕ 🍽 ⛱ 🖼 🖋 **Conf** facs Corporate Hospitality Days **Location** M1 junct 31, signs to Rother Valley Country Park
Hotel ★★★ 80% HL Best Western Mosborough Hall, High Street, Mosborough, SHEFFIELD ☎ 0114 248 4353 📠 0114 247 9759 43 en suite

Tinsley Park Municipal Golf Club High Hazels Park S9 4PE
☎ 0114 244 8974
18 Holes, 6064yds, Par 70, SSS 68, Course record 66.
Location 4m E of city off A630
Telephone for further details
Hotel ★★★ 80% HL Best Western Mosborough Hall, High Street, Mosborough, SHEFFIELD ☎ 0114 248 4353 📠 0114 247 9759 43 en suite

SILKSTONE Map 8 SE20

Silkstone Golf Club Field Head, Elmhirst Ln S75 4LD
☎ 01226 790328 📠 01226 794902
e-mail: silkstonegolf@hotmail.co.uk
web: www.silkstone-golf-club.co.uk
Parkland and downland course, fine views over the Pennines. Testing golf. Seven holes built to USGA specifications recently opened.
18 Holes, 6648yds, Par 73, SSS 73, Course record 67.
Club membership 530.
Visitors Mon-Fri. Limited availability weekends. Booking preferred. Dress code. **Societies** booking required. **Green Fees** £36 per day, £29 per round 🏌 **Course Designer** Jonathan Gaunt **Prof** Kevin Guy **Facilities** ⓣ ⦿ 🍴 ☕ 🍽 ⛱ 🖼 🖋 🛒 🖋 **Conf** Corporate Hospitality Days **Location** M1 junct 37, 1m W off A628
Hotel ★★★ 79% HL Best Western Ardsley House Hotel, Doncaster Road, Ardsley, BARNSLEY ☎ 01226 309955 📠 01226 205374 75 en suite

STOCKSBRIDGE Map 8 SK29

Stocksbridge & District Golf Club Royd Ln S36 2RZ
☎ 0114 288 2003 (office) 📠 0114 283 1460
web: www.stocksbridgegolfclub.co.uk
18 Holes, 5200yds, Par 65, SSS 65, Course record 60.
Course Designer Dave Thomas **Location** S of town centre
Telephone for further details
Hotel ★★★★ 78% HL Whitley Hall Hotel, Elliott Lane, Grenoside, SHEFFIELD ☎ 0114 245 4444 & 246 0456 📠 0114 245 5414 32 en suite

THORNE Map 8 SE61

Thorne Golf Club Kirton Ln DN8 5RJ
☎ 01405 812084 📠 01405 741899
e-mail: edward@highfield247.fsworld.co.uk
web: www.thornegolf.co.uk
Picturesque parkland with 6000 trees. Water hazards on 11th, 14th and 18th holes.
18 Holes, 5294yds, Par 68, SSS 68, Course record 62.
Club membership 300.
Visitors Contact club for details. **Societies** booking required. **Green Fees** £12 per round (£14 weekends) **Course Designer** R D Highfield **Prof** Edward Highfield **Facilities** ⓣ ⦿ 🍴 ☕ 🍽 ⛱ 🖼 🖇 🖋 🛒 🖋 **Conf** facs Corporate Hospitality Days **Location** M18 junct 1, A614 into Thorne, left onto Kirton Ln
Hotel ★★★ 73% HL Ramada Encore Doncaster Airport, Robin Hood Airport, DONCASTER ☎ 01302 718520 📠 01302 772045 102 en suite

WORTLEY
Map 8 SK39

Wortley Golf Club Hermit Hill Ln S35 7DF
☎ 0114 288 8469 📄 0114 288 8488
e-mail: wortley.golfclub@btconnect.com
web: www.wortleygolfclub.co.uk
Well-wooded, undulating parkland, sheltered from the prevailing wind. Excellent greens in a totally pastoral setting.

18 Holes, 6035yds, Par 68, SSS 68, Course record 64.
Club membership 600.

Visitors Mon-Fri & BHs. Weekends pm. Booking required except Mon & Fri. **Societies** booking required. **Green Fees** £30 per day (£35 per round weekends) 🏌 **Prof** Ian Kirk **Facilities** ⓣ ⓞ ⓛ ⓓ ⓟ 🚗 📷 ✦ 📷 ✦ **Conf** Corporate Hospitality Days **Location** 0.5m NE of village off A629

Hotel ★★★★ 78% HL Whitley Hall Hotel, Elliott Lane, Grenoside, SHEFFIELD ☎ 0114 245 4444 & 246 0456 📄 0114 245 5414 32 en suite

YORKSHIRE, WEST

ADDINGHAM
Map 7 SE04

Bracken Ghyll Golf Club Skipton Rd LS29 0SL
☎ 01943 831207 📄 01943 839453
e-mail: office@brackenghyll.co.uk
web: www.brackenghyll.co.uk
On the edge of the Yorkshire Dales, the course commands superb views over Ilkley Moor and the Wharfe Valley. The demanding 18-hole layout is a test of both golfing ability and sensible course management.

18 Holes, 5624yds, Par 68, SSS 68, Course record 64.
Club membership 460.

Visitors Mon-Fri & BHs. Weekends pm. Booking required. Dress code. **Societies** booking required. **Green Fees** £36 per day, £25 per 18 holes. £72 per 4-ball **Prof** Chris Hughes **Facilities** ⓣ ⓞ ⓛ ⓓ ⓟ 🚗 📷 📷 ✦ **Conf** facs Corporate Hospitality Days **Location** off A65 between Ilkley and Skipton

Hotel ★★★ 83% HL Best Western Rombalds Hotel & Restaurant, 11 West View, Wells Road, ILKLEY ☎ 01943 603201 📄 01943 816586 15 en suite

ALWOODLEY
Map 8 SE24

Alwoodley Golf Club Wigton Ln LS17 8SA
☎ 0113 268 1680
e-mail: alwoodley@btconnect.com
web: www.alwoodley.co.uk
Natural heathland course with heather, whins and shrubs. Plentifully and cunningly bunkered with undulating and interesting greens.

18 Holes, 6338yds, Par 70, SSS 71.
Club membership 483.

Visitors Mon-Sun except BHs. Booking required. Dress code. **Societies** booking required. **Green Fees** £80 per day/round (£95 weekends). £45 after 4.10pm. Winter £57 (£75 weekends) **Course Designer** Dr Alister MacKenzie **Prof** John R Green **Facilities** ⓣ ⓞ ⓛ ⓓ ⓟ 🚗 📷 📷 ✦ **Conf** facs Corporate Hospitality Days **Location** 5m N off A61

Hotel ★★★★ 71% HL Park Plaza Leeds, Boar Lane, LEEDS ☎ 0113 380 4000 📄 0113 380 4100 185 en suite

BAILDON
Map 7 SE13

Baildon Golf Club Moorgate BD17 5PP
☎ 01274 584266
e-mail: secretary@baildongolfclub.com
web: www.baildongolfclub.com

Moorland course set out in links style with the outward front nine looping back to clubhouse. Panoramic views with testing short holes in prevailing winds. The 2nd hole has been described as one of Britain's scariest.

18 Holes, 6322yds, Par 70, SSS 70, Course record 63.
Club membership 629.

Visitors Mon-Sun & BHs. Booking required Tue, Wed, weekends & BHs. Dress code. **Societies** booking required. **Green Fees** Apr-Sep £18 per round, Oct-Mar £15 **Course Designer** James Braid/Tom Morris **Prof** Richard Masters **Facilities** ⓣ ⓞ ⓛ ⓓ ⓟ 🚗 📷 🚜 ✦ **Leisure** snooker table **Conf** facs Corporate Hospitality Days **Location** 3m N of Bradford off A6038 at Shipley

Hotel ★★★★ 76% HL Hollins Hall, A Marriott Hotel & Country Club, Hollins Hill, Baildon, SHIPLEY ☎ 01274 530053 📄 01274 534251 122 en suite

BINGLEY
Map 7 SE13

Bingley St Ives Golf Club Golf Club House BD16 1AT
☎ 01274 562436 📄 01274 511788
web: www.bingleystivesgc.co.uk

18 Holes, 6485yds, Par 71, SSS 71, Course record 69.
Course Designer Alister MacKenzie **Location** 0.75m W off B6429
Telephone for further details
Hotel ★★ 70% HL Dalesgate, 406 Skipton Road, Utley, KEIGHLEY ☎ 01535 664930 📄 01535 611253 20 en suite

Save on Hotels. Book at **theAA.com/hotel**   **YORKSHIRE, WEST**

ENGLAND

Shipley Golf Club Beckfoot Ln BD16 1LX
☎ 01274 568652 (Secretary) & 563674 (pro)
e-mail: office@shipleygc.co.uk
web: www.shipleygolfclub.com
Laid out by the renowned golf course architect Alister MacKenzie, this parkland course is set in a beautiful wooded valley on the outskirts of Bingley.
18 Holes, 6220yds, Par 71, SSS 70, Course record 65.
Club membership 600.
Visitors Mon, Wed-Fri, Sun & BHs. Tue pm. Booking required. Dress code. **Societies** booking required. **Green Fees** £45 per day, £39 per round, Mon £35/£29 **Course Designer** Colt/Allison/MacKenzie/Braid **Prof** Nathan Stead **Facilities** ⓉⒾ Ⓨ ⓁⒷ ⬜ Ⓨ Ⓛ Ⓑ Ⓨ Ⓒ Ⓕ **Conf** facs Corporate Hospitality Days **Location** 6m N of Bradford on A650
Hotel ★★★ 75% SHL Five Rise Locks Hotel & Restaurant, Beck Lane, BINGLEY ☎ 01274 565296 🖹 01274 568828   9 en suite

---

BRADFORD   Map 7 SE13

Bradford Moor Golf Club Scarr Hall, Pollard Ln BD2 4RW
☎ 01274 771716 & 771693 (office)
e-mail: bfdmoorgc@hotmail.co.uk
web: www.bradfordmoorgolfclub.co.uk
Moorland course with tricky undulating greens.
9 Holes, 5900yds, Par 70, SSS 68, Course record 65.
Club membership 300.
Visitors Mon-Fri except BHs. Dress code. **Societies** booking required.
Green Fees £12 ⓈFacilities ⬜ Ⓨ Ⓛ **Conf** Corporate Hospitality Days **Location** 2m NE of city centre off A658
Hotel ★★★ 80% HL Midland Hotel, Forster Square, BRADFORD
☎ 01274 735735 🖹 01274 720003   90 en suite

Clayton Golf Club Thornton View Rd BD14 6JX
☎ 01274 880047
9 Holes, 6300yds, Par 72, SSS 72.
Location 2.5m SW of city centre on A647
Telephone for further details
Hotel ★★★ 73% HL Campanile Bradford, 6 Roydsdale Way, Euroway Estate, BRADFORD ☎ 01274 683683 🖹 0844 800 5769 130 en suite

East Bierley Golf Club South View Rd BD4 6PP
☎ 01274 681023 🖹 01274 683666
9 Holes, 4700yds, Par 64, SSS 63, Course record 59.
Location 4m SE of city centre off A650
Telephone for further details
Hotel ★★★ 73% HL Campanile Bradford, 6 Roydsdale Way, Euroway Estate, BRADFORD ☎ 01274 683683 🖹 0844 800 5769 130 en suite

Headley Golf Club Headley Ln, Thornton BD13 3LX
☎ 01274 833481 🖹 01274 833481
e-mail: admin@headleygolfclub.co.uk
web: www.headleygolfclub.co.uk
Hilly moorland course, short but very testing, windy, fine views.
9 Holes, 4864yds, Par 65, SSS 65, Course record 57.
Club membership 256.
Visitors Booking required Sat & Sun. Dress code. **Societies** booking required. **Green Fees** £10 per 18 holes (£15 weekends) Ⓢ
Facilities ⓉⒾ Ⓨ ⓁⒷ ⬜ Ⓨ Ⓛ **Conf** Corporate Hospitality Days **Location** 4m W of city centre off B6145 at Thornton
Hotel ★★★ 80% HL Midland Hotel, Forster Square, BRADFORD
☎ 01274 735735 🖹 01274 720003   90 en suite

Queensbury Golf Club Brighouse Rd, Queensbury BD13 1QF
☎ 01274 882155 & 816864   🖹 01274 882155
web: www.queensburygc.co.uk
Undulating woodland and parkland.
9 Holes, 5008yds, Par 66, SSS 65, Course record 62.
Club membership 350.
Visitors Mon-Sun & BHs. Booking required Thu & weekends.
Societies booking required. **Green Fees** not confirmed Ⓢ **Course Designer** Jonathan Gaunt **Prof** Gareth Murray **Facilities** ⓉⒾ ⓁⒷ ⬜ Ⓨ Ⓛ Ⓑ Ⓒ Ⓕ Ⓑ Ⓒ **Conf** Corporate Hospitality Days **Location** 4m from Bradford on A647
Hotel ★★★ 80% HL Midland Hotel, Forster Square, BRADFORD
☎ 01274 735735 🖹 01274 720003   90 en suite

South Bradford Golf Club Pearson Rd, Odsal BD6 1BH
☎ 01274 679195
Hilly course with good greens, trees and ditches. Interesting short 2nd hole (par 3) 200yds, well-bunkered and played from an elevated tee.
9 Holes, 6076yds, SSS 69. Club membership 300.
Visitors Mon-Fri. Restricted play weekends & BHs. Dress code.
Societies welcome. **Green Fees** phone Ⓢ **Prof** Paul Cooke **Facilities** ⓉⒾ by prior arrangement ⓁⒷ ⬜ Ⓨ Ⓛ Ⓑ Ⓒ **Location** 2m S of city centre off A638
Hotel ★★★ 73% HL Campanile Bradford, 6 Roydsdale Way, Euroway Estate, BRADFORD ☎ 01274 683683 🖹 0844 800 5769 130 en suite

West Bradford Golf Club Chellow Grange Rd BD9 6NP
☎ 01274 542767 🖹 01274 482079
web: www.westbradfordgolfclub.co.uk
18 Holes, 5738yds, Par 69, SSS 68, Course record 63.
Location 3.5 m W of city centre off B6144
Telephone for further details
Hotel ★★★★ 76% HL Hollins Hall, A Marriott Hotel & Country Club, Hollins Hill, Baildon, SHIPLEY ☎ 01274 530053 🖹 01274 534251 122 en suite

BRIGHOUSE
Map 7 SE12

Willow Valley Golf Highmoor Ln, Clifton HD6 4JB
☎ 01274 878624
e-mail: sales@wvgc.co.uk
web: www.wvgc.co.uk

A championship length course offering a unique golfing experience, featuring island greens, shaped fairways, water in play on eleven of its holes, bunkers, and multiple teeing areas. Pine Valley is an intermediate 18 hole course, suitable for golfers of all abilities. The nine-hole course offers an exciting challenge to less experienced golfers or for a short game. Yorkshire's largest golfing venue with a choice of three courses, and home of the YPGA Championship.

Willow Valley: 18 Holes, 6496yds, Par 72, SSS 72, Course record 69.
Pine Valley: 18 Holes, 5032yds, Par 67, SSS 64, Course record 60.
Fountain Ridge: 9 Holes, 1592yds, Par 30, SSS 30.
Club membership 350.

Visitors Mon-Sun & BHs. Dress code for Willow Valley & Pine Valley. **Societies** booking required. **Green Fees** Willow Valley £26 per round, Pine Valley £16 per round, Fountain Ridge £7.50 per round (£38/£18/£9 weekends & BHs) **Course Designer** Jonathan Gaunt **Prof** Julian Haworth **Facilities** ⑪ ⑭ by prior arrangement ⬛ ⬜ 🍴 🧑 🏠 ♂ 🎣 **Leisure** 3 hole floodlit academy course **Conf** Corporate Hospitality Days **Location** M62 junct 25, A644 towards Brighouse, right at rdbt onto A643, course 1m on right
Hotel ★★★ 77% HL Healds Hall Hotel & Restaurant, Leeds Road, LIVERSEDGE ☎ 01924 409112 🖨 01924 401895 24 en suite

CLECKHEATON
Map 8 SE12

Cleckheaton & District Golf Club Bradford Rd BD19 6BU
☎ 01274 851266 🖨 01274 871382
web: www.cleckheatongolfclub.co.uk

18 Holes, 5706yds, Par 70, SSS 68, Course record 61.
Course Designer Dr A MacKenzie **Location** M62 junct 26, towards Oakenshaw, 100yds on left, signed Low Moor
Telephone for further details
Hotel ★★★ 79% HL Gomersal Park, Moor Lane, GOMERSAL ☎ 01274 869386 🖨 01274 861042 100 en suite

DEWSBURY
Map 8 SE22

Hanging Heaton Golf Club White Cross Rd WF12 7DT
☎ 01924 461606 🖨 01924 430100
e-mail: derek.atkinson@hhgc.org
web: www.hhgc.org

Arable land, easy walking, fine views. Testing 4th hole (par 3).

9 Holes, 5836yds, Par 69, SSS 68. Club membership 500.
Visitors Mon-Sun except BHs. Booking required Wed & weekends. Dress code. **Societies** welcome. **Green Fees** not confirmed 📧 **Prof** Gareth Moore **Facilities** ⑪ by prior arrangement 🍴 by prior arrangement ⬛ ⬜ 🍴 🧑 🏠 ♂ **Conf** facs Corporate Hospitality Days **Location** 0.75m NE off A653
Hotel ★★★ 77% HL Healds Hall Hotel & Restaurant, LIVERSEDGE ☎ 01924 409112 🖨 01924 401895 24 en suite

ELLAND
Map 7 SE12

Elland Golf Club Hammerstone, Leach Ln HX5 0TA
☎ 01422 372505 & 374886 (pro)
e-mail: ellandgolfclub@ellandgolfclub.plus.com
web: www.ellandgolfclub.plus.com
Nine-hole parkland course played off 18 tees.

9 Holes, 5498yds, Par 66, SSS 67, Course record 65. Club membership 450.
Visitors Mon-Wed, Fri & Sun except BHs. Booking required. Handicap certificate. Dress code. **Societies** booking required. **Green Fees** £20 per round/day (£30 weekends & BHs) 📧 **Prof** N Krzywicki **Facilities** ⑪ 🍴 ⬛ ⬜ 🍴 🧑 🏠 ♂ **Conf** facs Corporate Hospitality Days **Location** M62 junct 24, signs to Blackley
Hotel ★★★ 77% HL Pennine Manor Hotel, Nettleton Hill Road, Scapegoat Hill, HUDDERSFIELD ☎ 01484 642368 🖨 01484 642866 30 en suite

FENAY BRIDGE
Map 8 SE11

Woodsome Hall Golf Club HD8 0LQ
☎ 01484 602739 🖨 01484 608260
web: www.woodsome.co.uk

18 Holes, 6096yds, Par 70, SSS 69, Course record 67.
Location 1.5m SW off A629
Telephone for further details
Hotel ★★★ 74% HL Bagden Hall, Wakefield Road, Scissett, HUDDERSFIELD ☎ 01484 865330 🖨 01484 861001 36 en suite

GARFORTH
Map 8 SE43

Garforth Golf Club Long Ln LS25 2DS
☎ 0113 286 3308 🖨 0113 286 3308
e-mail: garforthgcltd@lineone.net
web: www.garforthgolfclub.co.uk
Gently undulating parkland with fine views and easy walking.

18 Holes, 6304yds, Par 70, SSS 71, Course record 64. Club membership 600.
Visitors Mon-Sun except BHs. Booking required. Dress code. **Societies** welcome. **Green Fees** £38 per round. Winter £20 per round **Course Designer** Dr Alister MacKenzie **Prof** Ken Findlater **Facilities** ⑪ 🍴 ⬛ ⬜ 🍴 🧑 🏠 ♂ **Conf** Corporate Hospitality Days **Location** 6m E of Leeds, next to A1/M1 link road between Garforth and Barwick in Elmet
Hotel ★★★ 81% HL Best Western Milford Hotel, A1 Great North Road, Peckfield, LEEDS ☎ 01977 681800 🖨 01977 681245 46 en suite

UISELEY Map 8 SE14

radford (Hawksworth) Golf Club Hawksworth Ln
S20 8NP
☎ 01943 875570 📠 01943 875570
-mail: secretary@bradfordgolfclub.co.uk
web: www.bradfordgolfclub.co.uk
et in undulating countryside, the course is a moorland links laid out
n the southern slope of a wooded ridge about 650ft above sea level.
he spacious greens with their subtle borrows, together with some
ough and uncompromising par 4s make this a challenging course.
he testing par 4 10th and the par 3 14th require accurate shots to
well-protected greens.

Hawksworth: 18 Holes, 6303yds, Par 71, SSS 71,
Course record 65. Club membership 685.

Visitors Mon-Sun & BHs. Booking required. Handicap certificate. Dress
ode. **Societies** booking required. **Green Fees** £45 per day (£50 Sun
BHs). Twilight £20 **Course Designer** W H Fowler **Prof** Andrew Hall
acilities ⓘ ⓘ 🅿 ⌺ 🍴 🏌 🏠 ✦ 🏊 ✦ **Conf** facs
orporate Hospitality Days **Location** SW of town centre off A6038
otel ★★★★ 76% HL Hollins Hall, A Marriott Hotel &
ountry Club, Hollins Hill, Baildon, SHIPLEY ☎ 01274 530053
📠 01274 534251 122 en suite

HALIFAX Map 7 SE02

Halifax Golf Club Union Ln HX2 8XR
☎ 01422 244171
web: www.halifaxgolfclub.co.uk
8 Holes, 6037yds, Par 70, SSS 69, Course record 65.
Course Designer A Herd/J Braid **Location** 4m from Halifax on A629
Halifax-Keighley road
Telephone for further details
otel ★★★ 86% HL Holdsworth House, Holdsworth, HALIFAX
☎ 01422 240024 📠 01422 245174 40 en suite

Halifax West End Golf Club Paddock Ln, Highroad Well
HX2 0NT
☎ 01422 341878 📠 01422 341878
e-mail: westendgc@btinternet.com
web: www.westendgc.co.uk
Semi-moorland course. Tree-lined. Two ponds.
8 Holes, 5893yds, Par 69, SSS 68. Club membership 650.
Visitors Mon-Fri, Sun & BHs. Booking required. Dress code.
Societies booking required. **Green Fees** £30 per round **Prof** David
Rishworth/Darren Arber **Facilities** ⓘ ⓘ 🅿 ⌺ 🍴 🏌 🏠
✦ 🍽 ✦ **Conf** facs Corporate Hospitality Days **Location** W of town
centre off A646
Hotel ★★★ 86% HL Holdsworth House, Holdsworth, HALIFAX
☎ 01422 240024 📠 01422 245174 40 en suite

Lightcliffe Golf Club Knowle Top Rd HX3 8SW
☎ 01422 202459 & 204081
9 Holes, 5388mtrs, Par 68, SSS 68.
Location 3.5m E of Halifax on A58
Telephone for further details
Hotel ★★★ 86% HL Holdsworth House, Holdsworth, HALIFAX
☎ 01422 240024 📠 01422 245174 40 en suite

HEBDEN BRIDGE Map 7 SD92

Hebden Bridge Golf Club Great Mount HX7 8PH
☎ 01422 842896 & 842732
web: www.hebdenbridgegolfclub.co.uk
9 Holes, 5242yds, Par 68, SSS 67, Course record 61.
Location 1.5m E off A6033
Telephone for further details
Hotel ★★★ 86% HL Holdsworth House, Holdsworth, HALIFAX
☎ 01422 240024 📠 01422 245174 40 en suite

HOLYWELL GREEN Map 7 SE01

Halifax Bradley Hall Golf Club HX4 9AN
☎ 01422 374108
e-mail: bhgc@gotadsl.co.uk
web: www.bradleyhallgolf.co.uk
Moorland and parkland course, tightened by tree planting. Easy
walking.
18 Holes, 6138yds, Par 70, SSS 70, Course record 64.
Club membership 600.
Visitors Mon-Fri, Sun & BHs. Booking required Sun & BHs. Dress
code. **Societies** booking required **Green Fees** not confirmed **Course
Designer** Alexander Herd **Prof** Peter Wood **Facilities** ⓘ ⓘ 🅿 ⌺
🍴 🏌 🏠 ✦ **Conf** facs Corporate Hospitality Days **Location** M62
junct 24 (Huddersfield) follow exit to rdbt. Take 2nd exit off rdbt
signed Halifax, onto A629 for 2.5m to lights and turn left. Left again
off mini rdbt onto the B6117 towards West Vale & Stainland. Pass
through 2 sets of lights, club 1m on right
Hotel ★★★ 77% HL Pennine Manor Hotel, Nettleton Hill Road,
Scapegoat Hill, HUDDERSFIELD ☎ 01484 642368 📠 01484 642866
30 en suite

HUDDERSFIELD Map 7 SE11

Bagden Hall Hotel & Golf Course Wakefield Rd HD8 9LE
☎ 01484 865330 📠 01484 861001
web: www.bagdenhallhotel.co.uk
9 Holes, 3002yds, Par 56, SSS 55, Course record 60.
Course Designer F O'Donnell/R Braithwaite **Location** A636 Wakefield-
Denby Dale
Telephone for further details
Hotel ★★★ 74% HL Bagden Hall, Wakefield Road, Scissett,
HUDDERSFIELD ☎ 01484 865330 📠 01484 861001 36 en suite

Bradley Park Golf Course Off Bradley Rd HD2 1PZ
☎ 01484 223772 📠 01484 451613
web: www.bradleyparkgolf.co.uk
Parkland course, challenging with good mix of long and short holes.
Superb views.
18 Holes, 6284yds, Par 70, SSS 70, Course record 65.
Club membership 300.
Visitors Mon-Sun & BHs. Booking required weekends & BHs
Societies booking required. **Green Fees** £17.50 (£19 weekends & BHs)
Course Designer Cotton/Pennick/Lowire & Ptnrs **Prof** Parnell E Reilly
Facilities ⓘ ⓘ 🅿 ⌺ 🍴 🏌 🏠 🍽 🚆 ✦ 🏊 **Leisure** 9
hole par 3 course **Conf** facs Corporate Hospitality Days **Location** M62
junct 25, 2.5m
Hotel ★★★ 81% HL Holiday Inn Leeds-Brighouse, Clifton Village,
BRIGHOUSE ☎ 0871 942 9013 📠 01484 400068 94 en suite

Crosland Heath Golf Club Felk Stile Rd, Crosland Heath HD4 7AF

☎ 01484 653216

e-mail: golf@croslandheath.co.uk

web: www.croslandheath.co.uk

Heathland course with fine views over valley.

18 Holes, 6082yds, Par 71, SSS 70. Club membership 650.

Visitors Mon-Fri & Sun except BHs. Booking required. Dress code. **Societies** booking required. **Green Fees** £37 per day (£42 Sun) 🅱 **Course Designer** Dr. McKenzie **Prof** Richard Lambert **Facilities** ⊕ 🏮 🍴 ▆ ▭ 🐿 ⚙ 🚇 ✆ **Conf** facs Corporate Hospitality Days **Location** SW off A62

Hotel ★★★ 77% HL Pennine Manor Hotel, Nettleton Hill Road, Scapegoat Hill, HUDDERSFIELD ☎ 01484 642368 📄 01484 642866 30 en suite

Huddersfield Golf Club Fixby Hall, Lightridge Rd, Fixby HD2 2EP

☎ 01484 426203 📄 01484 424623

e-mail: secretary@huddersfield-golf.co.uk

web: www.huddersfield-golf.co.uk

A testing heathland course of championship standard, laid out in 1891.

18 Holes, 6466yds, Par 71, SSS 71, Course record 63. Club membership 760.

Visitors Mon-Sun & BHs. Dress code. **Societies** booking required. **Green Fees** £55 per day, £45 per round (£65/£55 weekends & BHs) **Prof** Paul Carman **Facilities** ⊕ 🍴 🏮 ▭ 🐿 ⚙ 🚇 🚌 ✆ **Conf** facs Corporate Hospitality Days **Location** 2m N off A641

Hotel ★★★ 81% HL Holiday Inn Leeds-Brighouse, Clifton Village, BRIGHOUSE ☎ 0871 942 9013 📄 01484 400068 94 en suite

Longley Park Golf Club Maple St, Aspley HD5 9AX

☎ 01484 422304 📄 01484 515280

e-mail: longleyparkgolfclub@12freeukisp.co.uk

Lowland course, surrounded by mature woodland.

9 Holes, 5212yds, Par 66, SSS 66, Course record 61. Club membership 440.

Visitors Mon-Wed, Fri Sun & BHs. Booking required. Dress code. **Societies** booking required. **Green Fees** phone 🅱 **Prof** John Ambler **Facilities** ⊕ 🍴 🏮 ▭ 🐿 ⚙ 🚇 ✆ **Conf** facs Corporate Hospitality Days **Location** 0.5m SE of town centre off A629

Hotel ★★★★ 71% HL Cedar Court, Ainley Top, HUDDERSFIELD ☎ 01422 375431 📄 01422 314050 113 en suite

ILKLEY

Map 7 SE14

Ben Rhydding Golf Club High Wood, Ben Rhydding LS29 8SB

☎ 01943 608759

e-mail: secretary@benrhyddinggc.freeserve.co.uk

Moorland and parkland with splendid views over the Wharfe Valley. A compact but testing course.

9 Holes, 4611yds, Par 65, SSS 63, Course record 64. Club membership 250.

Visitors Mon-Sun & BHs. Booking required Tue-Thu, Sun & BHs. Handicap certificate. Dress code. **Societies** booking required. **Green Fees** £18 per day (£22 weekends & BHs) 🅱 **Course Designer** William Dell **Facilities** ▭ 🐿 **Conf** Corporate Hospitality Days **Location** E of town centre. Off Wheatley Ln onto Wheatley Grove, left onto High Wood, clubhouse on left

Hotel ★★★ 83% HL Best Western Rombalds Hotel & Restaurant, 11 West View, Wells Road, ILKLEY ☎ 01943 603201 📄 01943 81658 15 en suite

Ilkley Golf Club Nesfield Rd, Myddleton LS29 0BE

☎ 01943 600214 📄 01943 816130

e-mail: honsec@ilkleygolfclub.co.uk

web: www.ikleygolfclub.co.uk

A beautiful parkland course in Wharfedale. The Wharfe is a hazard on the first seven holes - in fact, the 3rd is laid out entirely on an island in the river. Originally designed by Dr Alister Mackenzie.

18 Holes, 6235yds, Par 69, SSS 70, Course record 65. Club membership 450.

Visitors Mon-Sun & BHs. Booking required. **Societies** booking required. **Green Fees** £50 (£55 weekends) **Course Designer** MacKenzie **Prof** John L Hammond **Facilities** ⊕ 🍴 🏮 ▭ 🐿 ⚙ 🚇 ✆ **Leisure** fishing **Conf** facs Corporate Hospitality Days **Location** W side of town centre off A65

Hotel ★★★ 83% HL Best Western Rombalds Hotel & Restaurant, 11 West View, Wells Road, ILKLEY ☎ 01943 603201 📄 01943 816586 15 en suite

KEIGHLEY

Map 7 SE04

Keighley Golf Club Howden Park, Utley BD20 6DH

☎ 01535 604778 📄 01535 604778

e-mail: manager@keighleygolfclub.com

web: www.keighleygolfclub.com

A riverside, valley-bottom parkland course with quality summer greens. Mature trees and lengthy par 4s on this 100 year old course provides an enjoyable and varied golfing experience. The 17th, 'one of the most difficult finishing holes in Yorkshire' ensures an exciting round of golf will be had by all.

Howden Park: 18 Holes, 6141yds, Par 69, SSS 70. Club membership 650.

Visitors Sun-Fri & BHs. Sat limited. Booking required Sat. Dress code. **Societies** booking required. **Green Fees** £22-£35 depending on day/time **Course Designer** Henry Smith **Prof** Andrew Rhodes **Facilities** ⊕ 🍴 🏮 ▭ 🐿 ⚙ 🚇 🚌 ✆ **Leisure** snooker table, Sky Sports tv **Conf** facs Corporate Hospitality Days **Location** 1m NW of town centre off B6265, turn N at Roebuck pub

Hotel ★★ 70% HL Dalesgate, 406 Skipton Road, Utley, KEIGHLEY ☎ 01535 664930 📄 01535 611253 20 en suite

LEEDS   Map 8 SE33

Brandon Golf Course Hollywell Ln LS17 8EZ
☎ 0113 273 7471
18 Holes, 6700yds, Par 72.
Village/Wike: 12 Holes, 3000yds, Par 34.
Course Designer William Binner **Location** off A58 into Shadwell, onto Main St, right at Red Lion pub
Telephone for further details
Hotel ★★★★ HL Wood Hall Hotel, Trip Lane, Linton, WETHERBY
☎ 01937 587271 📠 01937 584353 44 en suite

Cookridge Hall Golf Club Cookridge Ln LS16 7NL
☎ 0113 230 0641 📠 0113 203 0198
e-mail: info@cookridgehall.co.uk
web: www.cookridgehall.co.uk
American-style course with intimidating water hazards strewn across the course and strategic bunkering, providing a true test for golfers of all abilities. Spectacular views of the Yorkshire Dales.
18 Holes, 6498yds, Par 72, SSS 72, Course record 65.
Club membership 550.
Visitors Mon-Sun & BHs. Booking required weekends & BHs. Dress code. **Societies** booking required. **Green Fees** £25 per round (£30 weekends & BHs) **Course Designer** Karl Litten **Prof** Mark Ankett **Facilities** ⊕ ⦿ ⓛ ⛟ ⛊ ⊿ 🏌 ✆ ✆ 🏌 ✆
Leisure chipping and practice bunker **Conf** Corporate Hospitality Days
Location 6m NW of Leeds, off A660
Hotel ★★★ 74% HL Chevin Country Park Hotel & Spa, Yorkgate, OTLEY ☎ 01943 467818 📠 01943 850335 49 en suite

De Vere Oulton Hall Golf Course Rothwell Ln, Oulton LS26 8HN
☎ 0113 282 3152 📠 0113 282 6290
web: www.devere-hotels.com
27 holes of championship standard golf with a state of the art 16 bay golf academy.
*Park Course: 18 Holes, 6500yds, Par 71, SSS 71,
Course record 69.*
Hall Course: 9 Holes, 3300yds, Par 36.
Club membership 550.
Visitors Mon-Sun & BHs. Booking required. Handicap certificate. Dress code. **Societies** booking required. **Green Fees** Park £60 per 18 holes (£65 weekends). Hall £20 per 9 holes (£25 weekends) **Course Designer** Dave Thomas **Prof** Keith Pickard **Facilities** ⊕ ⦿ ⓛ ⛟ ⛊ ⊿ 🏌 ✆ 🏌 ✆ 🏌 **Leisure** heated indoor swimming pool, sauna, gymnasium **Conf** facs Corporate Hospitality Days **Location** M62 junct 30
Hotel ★★★★ 83% HL De Vere Oulton Hall, Rothwell Lane, Oulton, LEEDS ☎ 0113 282 1000 📠 0113 282 8066 152 en suite

Gotts Park Golf Club Armley Ridge Rd LS12 2QX
☎ 0113 231 1896 & 0798 3008044
Municipal parkland course; hilly and windy with narrow fairways. Some very steep hills to some greens. A challenging course requiring accuracy rather than length from the tees.
18 Holes, 4960yds, Par 65, SSS 64, Course record 63.
Club membership 120.
Visitors contact club for details. **Societies** welcome. **Green Fees** phone **Facilities** ⊕ ⛟ 🏌 ⛊ 🏌 ✆ **Location** 3m W of city centre off A647
Hotel ★★★★ 80% HL The Queens, City Square, LEEDS
☎ 0113 243 1323 📠 0113 243 5315 215 en suite

Headingley Golf Club Back Church Ln, Adel LS16 8DW
☎ 0113 267 9573 📠 0113 281 7334
e-mail: manager@headingleygolfclub.co.uk
web: www.headingleygolfclub.co.uk
Dramatic course with a wealth of natural features offering fine views from higher ground. Its most striking hazard is the famous ravine at the 18th. Leeds's oldest course, founded in 1892.
18 Holes, 6566yds, Par 71, SSS 72, Course record 65.
Club membership 655.
Visitors Mon-Fri, Sun & BHs. Booking required. **Societies** booking required. **Green Fees** not confirmed **Course Designer** Dr MacKenzie **Prof** Neil M Harvey **Facilities** ⊕ ⦿ ⓛ ⛟ ⛊ ⊿ 🏌 ✆
✆ **Location** 5.5m N of city centre. A660 to Skipton, right at lights junct Farrar Ln and Church Ln, follow Eccup signs
Hotel BUD Holiday Inn Express Leeds City Centre, Cavendish Street, LEEDS ☎ 0113 242 6200 📠 0113 242 6300 112 en suite

Horsforth Golf Club Layton Rise, Layton Rd, Horsforth LS18 5EX
☎ 0113 258 6819 📠 0113 258 9336
e-mail: secretary@horsforthgolfclub.co.uk
web: www.horsforthgolfclub.co.uk
Moorland and parkland course combining devilish short holes with some more substantial challenges. Extensive views across Leeds and on a clear day York Minster can be seen from the 14th tee.
18 Holes, 6258yds, Par 71, SSS 70, Course record 65.
Club membership 750.
Visitors Mon-Fri, Sun & BHs. Booking required. Dress code. **Societies** booking required. **Green Fees** £42 per day **Course Designer** Alister MacKenzie **Prof** Dean Stokes/Simon Booth **Facilities** ⊕ ⦿ ⓛ ⛟ ⛊ ⊿ 🏌 🏌 ✆ **Conf** facs Corporate Hospitality Days **Location** 6.5m NW of city centre off A65
Hotel ★★★ 74% HL Chevin Country Park Hotel & Spa, Yorkgate, OTLEY ☎ 01943 467818 📠 01943 850335 49 en suite

Leeds Golf Centre, Wike Ridge Wike Ridge Ln LS17 9JW
☎ 0113 288 6000 📠 0113 288 6185
web: www.leedsgolfcentre.com
*Wike Ridge Course: 18 Holes, 6332yds, Par 72, SSS 71,
Course record 64.*
Oaks: 12 Holes, 1610yds, Par 36, SSS 35, Course record 29.
Course Designer Donald Steel **Location** 5m N, A58, course on N side of Shadwell
Telephone for further details
Hotel ★★★★ HL Wood Hall Hotel, Trip Lane, Linton, WETHERBY
☎ 01937 587271 📠 01937 584353 44 en suite

Leeds Golf Club Elmete Ln LS8 2LJ
☎ 0113 265 8786 & 265 9203 📄 0113 232 3369
e-mail: secretary@leedsgolfclub.co.uk
web: www.leedsgolfclub.co.uk
Parkland with pleasant views.
18 Holes, 6115yds, Par 69, SSS 69, Course record 63.
Club membership 600.
Visitors Mon-Fri & Sun except BHs. Booking required. Handicap
certificate. Dress code. **Societies** booking required. **Green Fees** £40
per round (£45 weekends) 🍴 **Course Designer** Alister McKenzie
Prof Simon Longster **Facilities** ⓣ ⎰ 🍴 🖢 🍴 🏌 🏠 🚡
🏌 **Location** 5m NE of city centre on A6120, off A58
Hotel ★★★★ 84% HL Thorpe Park Hotel & Spa, Century
Way, Thorpe Park, LEEDS ☎ 0113 264 1000 📄 0113 264 1010
111 en suite

Moor Allerton Golf Club Coal Rd, Wike LS17 9NH
☎ 0113 266 1154 📄 0113 268 0589
e-mail: info@magc.co.uk
web: www.magc.co.uk
The Moor Allerton Club, established in 1923, has 27 holes set in
220 acres of undulating parkland, with testing water hazards
and magnificent views extending across the Vale of York. The
championship course was designed by Robert Trent Jones, the
famous American course architect, and provides a challenge to both
high and low handicapped golfers.
Lakes Course: 18 Holes, 6470yds, Par 71, SSS 72.
Blackmoor Course: 18 Holes, 6673yds, Par 71, SSS 73.
High Course: 18 Holes, 6841yds, Par 72, SSS 74.
Club membership 500.
Visitors Mon-Sun & BHs. Dress code. **Societies** welcome. **Green
Fees** not confirmed **Course Designer** Robert Trent Jones **Prof** James
Whitaker **Facilities** ⓣ ⎰ 🍴 🖢 🍴 🏌 🚡
🏌 🚢 ⚘ **Leisure** sauna **Conf** facs Corporate Hospitality Days
Location 5.5m N of city centre on A61
Hotel ★★★★ HL Wood Hall Hotel, Trip Lane, Linton, WETHERBY
☎ 01937 587271 📄 01937 584353 44 en suite

Moortown Golf Club Harrogate Rd, Alwoodley LS17 7DB
☎ 0113 268 6521 📄 0113 268 0986
e-mail: secretary@moortown-gc.co.uk
web: www.moortown-gc.co.uk
Championship course, tough but fair. Springy moorland turf, natural
hazards of heather, gorse and streams, cunningly placed bunkers
and immaculate greens. No winter tees or greens. Home of Ryder
Cup in 1929.
18 Holes, 6767yds, Par 71, SSS 74, Course record 65.
Club membership 585.
Visitors Mon-Sun & BHs (after 2.30pm Sat). Booking required.
Strict dress code. **Societies** booking required. **Green Fees** May-
Sep £80 per day/round. (Apr & Oct £60, Nov-Mar £45) **Course
Designer** Alistair MacKenzie **Prof** Martin Heggie **Facilities** ⓣ ⎰
🖢 🍴 🏌 🏠 🚡 ⚘ 🚢 ⚘ **Conf** facs Corporate
Hospitality Days **Location** 6m N of Leeds city centre on A61
Harrogate Road
Hotel ★★★★ 71% HL Park Plaza Leeds, Boar Lane, LEEDS
☎ 0113 380 4000 📄 0113 380 4100 185 en suite

Roundhay Golf Club Park Ln LS8 2EJ
☎ 0113 266 2695 & 266 4225
Attractive municipal parkland course, natural hazards, easy walking
9 Holes, 5223yds, Par 70, SSS 65, Course record 61.
Club membership 240.
Visitors contact club for details. **Societies** welcome. **Green
Fees** phone **Prof** Adrian Newboult **Facilities** 🖢 🖢 🍴 🏠 🏠
🚡 🏌 **Location** 4m NE of city centre off A58
Hotel ★★★★ 74% HL Leeds Marriott Hotel, 4 Trevelyan Square,
Boar Lane, LEEDS ☎ 0113 236 6366 📄 0113 236 6367 244 en suite

Sand Moor Golf Club Alwoodley Ln LS17 7DJ
☎ 0113 268 5180 📄 0113 266 1105
e-mail: jackie@sandmoorgolf.co.uk
web: www.sandmoorgolf.co.uk
A beautiful, inland course situated next to Eccup reservoir on the
north side of Leeds. It has been described as the finest example
of golfing paradise being created out of a barren moor. With
magnificent views of the surrounding countryside, the course has
sandy soil and drains exceptionally well.
18 Holes, 6446yds, Par 71, SSS 71, Course record 63.
Club membership 600.
Visitors Mon-Fri, Sun & BHs. Booking required. Dress code.
Societies booking required. **Green Fees** £60 per day, £50 per
round (£60 per round Sun & BHs) **Course Designer** Dr A MacKenzie
Prof Frank Houlgate **Facilities** ⓣ ⎰ 🖢 🍴 🏌 🏠 🚡
🏌 🚢 🏌 **Conf** Corporate Hospitality Days **Location** 5m N of city
centre off A61
Hotel ★★★★ 73% HL Cedar Court Hotel Wakefield, Denby Dale
Road, WAKEFIELD ☎ 01924 276310 📄 01924 280221 149 en suite

South Leeds Golf Club Gipsy Ln LS11 5TU
☎ 0113 272 3757
web: www.southleedsgolfclub.co.uk
18 Holes, 5865yds, Par 69, SSS 68, Course record 63.
Course Designer Dr Alister MacKenzie **Location** 3m S of city centre
off A653
Telephone for further details
Hotel ★★★★ 80% HL The Queens, City Square, LEEDS
☎ 0113 243 1323 📄 0113 243 5315 215 en suite

Temple-Newsam Golf Club Temple-Newsam Rd LS15 0LN
☎ 0113 264 7362
e-mail: ady@templenewsamgolfcourse.co.uk
web: www.templenewsamgolfcourse.co.uk
Two parkland courses. Testing long 13th (563yds) on second course.
Lord Irwin: 18 Holes, 5806yds, Par 70, SSS 68.
Lady Dorothy: 18 Holes, 5571yds, Par 70, SSS 67.
Club membership 520.
Visitors Mon-Sun & BHs. Booking required weekends & BHs.
Societies booking required. **Green Fees** not confirmed **Course
Designer** MacKenzie **Prof** Adrian Newboult **Facilities** 🍴 🏠 🏠
🚡 🚢 🏌 **Location** 3.5m E of city centre off A63
Hotel ★★★★ 84% HL Thorpe Park Hotel & Spa, Century
Way, Thorpe Park, LEEDS ☎ 0113 264 1000 📄 0113 264 1010
111 en suite

MARSDEN   Map 7 SE01

Marsden Golf Club Hemplow Mount Rd HD7 6NN
☎ 01484 844253
web: www.marsdengolf.co.uk

Holes, 5702yds, Par 68, SSS 68, Course record 64.

Course Designer Dr McKenzie **Location** S side off A62
Telephone for further details
Hotel ★★★★ RR The Olive Branch Restaurant with Rooms,
Manchester Road, MARSDEN ☎ 01484 844487 3 rooms

MELTHAM   Map 7 SE01

Meltham Golf Club Thick Hollins Hall HD9 4DQ
☎ 01484 850227 (office) & 851521 (pro)
▤ 01484 850227
e-mail: admin@meltham-golf.co.uk
web: www.meltham-golf.co.uk

Challenging blend of heath/parkland with babbling brooks and lake
feature. Tree-lined fairways with natural slopes, fast and true greens.

*Thick Hollins: 18 Holes, 6407yds, Par 71, SSS 70,
Course record 65. Club membership 595.*

Visitors Mon, Tue, Thu, Fri, Sun & BHs. Booking required Sun.
Handicap certificate. Dress code. **Societies** booking required. **Green
Fees** £33 per day, £28 per round (£38/£33 Sun & BHs). **Course
Designer** Alex Herd **Prof** Paul Davies **Facilities** ⑪ ⑨ ▤ ▱ ▤
⚑ ⚐ **Conf** facs Corporate Hospitality Days **Location** 0.5m E of
Meltham on B6107
Hotel ★★★★ RR The Olive Branch Restaurant with Rooms,
Manchester Road, MARSDEN ☎ 01484 844487 3 rooms

MIRFIELD   Map 8 SE21

Dewsbury District Golf Club Sands Ln WF14 8HJ
☎ 01924 492399 & 496030   ▤ 01924 491928
e-mail: info@dewsburygolf.co.uk
web: www.dewsburygolf.co.uk

Moorland or parkland terrain with panoramic views. Ponds in middle
of 3rd fairway, left of 5th green and 17th green. A challenging test
of golf.

*18 Holes, 6360yds, Par 71, SSS 71, Course record 63.
Club membership 700.*

Visitors Mon-Sun & BHs. Booking required weekends & BHs. Dress
code. **Societies** booking required. **Green Fees** £30 per day, £25 per
round (£17.50 weekends) **Course Designer** Old Tom Morris/Alister
MacKenzie/Ted Ray **Prof** Nigel P Hirst **Facilities** ⑪ ⑨ ▤ ▱ ▤ by prior
arrangement ▤ ⑨ ▱ ▤ ⚐ **Leisure** snooker
tables **Conf** facs Corporate Hospitality Days **Location** off A644, 4 m
from M62 junct 25 and 6m from M1 junct 40
Hotel ★★★ 77% HL Healds Hall Hotel & Restaurant, Leeds Road,
LIVERSEDGE ☎ 01924 409112 ▤ 01924 401895 24 en suite

MORLEY   Map 8 SE22

Howley Hall Golf Club Scotchman Ln LS27 0NX
☎ 01924 350100 ▤ 01924 350104
e-mail: office@howleyhall.co.uk
web: www.howleyhall.co.uk

Easy walking parkland with superb views of the Pennines and the
Calder Valley.

*18 Holes, 6383yds, Par 71, SSS 71, Course record 64.
Club membership 700.*

Visitors Mon-Fri, Sun & BHs. Booking required. Dress code.
Societies booking required. **Green Fees** £40 (£50 Sun & BHs) ⚑
Course Designer MacKenzie **Prof** Gary Watkinson **Facilities** ⑪ ⑨
by prior arrangement ▤ ▱ ⑨ ▱ ▤ ⚑ ⚐ ⚐ **Conf** facs
Corporate Hospitality Days **Location** 1.5m S on B6123
Hotel ★★★ 77% HL Healds Hall Hotel & Restaurant, Leeds Road,
LIVERSEDGE ☎ 01924 409112 ▤ 01924 401895 24 en suite

OSSETT   Map 8 SE22

Low Laithes Golf Club Parkmill Ln, Flushdyke WF5 9AP
☎ 01924 274667 & 266067   ▤ 01924 266266
e-mail: info@lowlaithesgolfclub.co.uk
web: www.lowlaithesgolfclub.co.uk

Testing parkland course.

*18 Holes, 6445yds, Par 72, SSS 71, Course record 66.
Club membership 600.*

Visitors Mon-Sun & BHs. Booking required weekends & BHs. Dress
code. **Societies** booking required. **Green Fees** not confirmed ⚑
Course Designer Dr MacKenzie **Prof** Paul Browning **Facilities** ⑪ ⑨
▤ ▱ ⑨ ▱ ▤ ⚑ ⚑ ⚐ **Conf** Corporate Hospitality Days
Location M1 junct 40, 0.5m on Dewsbury road, signed
Hotel ★★★ 72% HL Heath Cottage Hotel & Restaurant, Wakefield
Road, DEWSBURY ☎ 01924 465399 ▤ 01924 459405 28 en suite

OTLEY   Map 8 SE24

Otley Golf Club Off West Busk Ln LS21 3NG
☎ 01943 465329 ▤ 01943 850387
e-mail: office@otleygolfclub.co.uk
web: www.otleygolfclub.co.uk

An expansive course with magnificent views across Wharfedale. It
is well wooded with streams crossing the fairway. The 4th is a fine
hole which generally needs two woods to reach the plateau green.
The 17th is a good short hole. A test of golf as opposed to stamina.

*18 Holes, 6211yds, Par 70, SSS 70, Course record 64.
Club membership 700.*

Visitors Mon, Wed-Fri except BHs. Booking required. Dress code.
Societies booking required. **Green Fees** £46 per day, £39 per 18/27
holes **Prof** Steven Tomkinson **Facilities** ⑪ ⑨ ▤ ▱ ⑨ ▱
▤ ▱ ⚑ ⚑ ⚐ **Leisure** practice bunker **Conf** facs Corporate
Hospitality Days **Location** 1m W of Otley off A6038
Hotel ★★★ 74% HL Chevin Country Park Hotel & Spa, Yorkgate,
OTLEY ☎ 01943 467818 ▤ 01943 850335 49 en suite

OUTLANE — Map 7 SE01

Outlane Golf Club Slack Ln, Off New Hey Rd HD3 3FQ
☎ 01422 374762 📠 01422 311789
e-mail: secretary@outlanegolfclub.ltd.uk
web: www.outlanegolfclub.ltd.uk

A moorland course with undulating fairways. Four par 3 holes with an 8th hole of 249yds regarded as the hardest par 3 in Yorkshire. The three par 5s may be reachable on a good day in two strokes but in adverse conditions will take more than three. Smaller than average greens on some holes, which makes for accurate second shots.

18 Holes, 6015yds, Par 71, SSS 69, Course record 66. Club membership 680.

Visitors Mon-Sun & BHs. Booking required. Dress code.
Societies booking required. **Green Fees** not confirmed **Prof** David Chapman **Facilities** ⓣ �🍽 ⓑ ⌨ 🍴 ⚴ 🏠 ⛴ 🛥 ⚲ **Location** M62 junct 23, A640 New Hey Rd through Outlane
Hotel ★★★ 77% HL Pennine Manor Hotel, Nettleton Hill Road, Scapegoat Hill, HUDDERSFIELD ☎ 01484 642368 📠 01484 642866 30 en suite

PONTEFRACT — Map 8 SE42

Mid Yorkshire Golf Club Havercroft Ln, Darrington WF8 3BP
☎ 01977 704522 📠 01977 600823
e-mail: admin@midyorkshiregolfclub.com
web: www.midyorkshiregolfclub.com

A championship-standard course opened in 1993, and widely considered to be one of the finest newer courses in Yorkshire.

18 Holes, 6308yds, Par 70, SSS 70, Course record 68. Club membership 500.

Visitors Mon-Sun & BHs. Booking required. Dress code.
Societies welcome. **Green Fees** £25 per 18 holes (£30 weekends)
Course Designer Steve Marnoch **Prof** Michael Hessay **Facilities** ⓣ 🍽 ⓑ ⌨ 🍴 ⚴ 🏠 ⛴ ⚴ 🛥 ⚲ 🏌 **Conf** facs Corporate Hospitality Days **Location** on A1 0.5m S junct A1/M62
Hotel ★★★★ 77% HL Wentbridge House, Wentbridge, PONTEFRACT ☎ 01977 620444 📠 01977 620148 41 en suite

Pontefract & District Golf Club Park Ln WF8 4QS
☎ 01977 792241 📠 01977 792241
e-mail: manager@pdgc.co.uk
web: www.pdgc.co.uk

Undulating parkland course with some elevated tees. The tight fairways present a challenge.

18 Holes, 6519yds, Par 72, SSS 72, Course record 67. Club membership 800.

Visitors Mon-Fri except BHs. Dress code. **Societies** welcome.
Green Fees not confirmed **Course Designer** A McKenzie **Prof** Ian Marshall **Facilities** ⓣ 🍽 ⓑ ⌨ 🍴 ⚴ 🏠 ⚴ 🛥 ⚴
Conf Corporate Hospitality Days **Location** W of Pontefract. A639 onto B6134, club 1m on right
Hotel ★★★★ 77% HL Wentbridge House, Wentbridge, PONTEFRACT ☎ 01977 620444 📠 01977 620148 41 en suite

PUDSEY — Map 8 SE2:

Calverley Golf Club Woodhall Ln LS28 5QY
☎ 0113 256 9244 📠 0113 256 4362
e-mail: danny@calverleygolf.co.uk
web: www.calverleygolf.co.uk

Gently undulating parkland. The small greens require accurate approach shots.

18 Holes, 5626yds, Par 68, SSS 67, Course record 64.
9 Holes, 3000yds, Par 36. Club membership 350.

Visitors Mon-Sun & BHs. Booking required weekends. Dress code.
Societies booking required. **Green Fees** £16 per round (£20 weekends) **Course Designer** Peter McAvoy **Prof** Neil Wendel-Jones
Facilities ⓣ 🍽 ⓑ ⌨ 🍴 ⚴ 🏠 ⚴ 🛥 ⚴ **Conf** facs
Corporate Hospitality Days **Location** signed Calverley from A647
Hotel ★★★ 80% HL Midland Hotel, Forster Square, BRADFORD
☎ 01274 735735 📠 01274 720003 90 en suite

Fulneck Golf Club LS28 8NT
☎ 0113 256 5191
e-mail: fulneck golf@aol.com
web: www.fulneckgolfclub.co.uk

Picturesque parkland course, established 1892.

9 Holes, 5456yds, Par 66, SSS 67, Course record 65. Club membership 250.

Visitors Mon-Sun & BHs. Booking required weekends & BHs.
Societies booking required. **Green Fees** £12 (£18 weekends)
ⓖ **Prof** Jeff Whittam **Facilities** ⓣ 🍽 ⓑ ⌨ 🍴 ⚴
Location Pudsey, between Leeds and Bradford
Hotel ★★★ 73% HL Campanile Bradford, 6 Roydsdale Way, Euroway Estate, BRADFORD ☎ 01274 683683 📠 0844 800 5769 130 en suite

Woodhall Hills Golf Club Calverley LS28 5UN
☎ 0113 255 4594 📠 0113 255 4594
e-mail: woodhallgolf@btconnect.com
web: www.woodhallhillsgc.co.uk

Meadowland course, recently redeveloped with an improved layout an open ditches around the course. A challenging opening hole, a good variety of par 3s and testing holes at the 6th and 11th.

18 Holes, 6397yds, Par 71, SSS 71, Course record 67. Club membership 550.

Visitors Mon-Fri. Sun & BHs. Booking required. Dress code.
Societies booking required. **Green Fees** £26 per round (£30 Sun). £1 Twilight **Prof** Richard Hedley **Facilities** ⓣ 🍽 ⓑ ⌨ 🍴 ⚴
🏠 ⚴ 🛥 ⚴ **Leisure** snooker room **Conf** facs Corporate Hospitalit Days **Location** 1m NW off A647
Hotel ★★★ 80% HL Midland Hotel, Forster Square, BRADFORD
☎ 01274 735735 📠 01274 720003 90 en suite

Save on Hotels. Book at **theAA.com/hotel**   **YORKSHIRE, WEST**

ENGLAND

RIDDLESDEN   Map 7 SE04

Riddlesden Golf Club Howden Rough BD20 5QN
☎ 01535 602148
18 Holes, 4295yds, Par 63, SSS 61, Course record 59.
Location 1m NW
Telephone for further details
Hotel ★★ 70% HL Dalesgate, 406 Skipton Road, Utley, KEIGHLEY
☎ 01535 664930 📄 01535 611253 20 en suite

SCARCROFT   Map 8 SE34

Scarcroft Golf Club Syke Ln LS14 3BQ
☎ 0113 289 2311 📄 0113 289 3835
e-mail: secretary@scarcroftgolfclub.com
web: www.scarcroftgolfclub.com
Undulating parkland course with prevailing west wind and easy
walking.
18 Holes, 6456yds, Par 71, SSS 71, Course record 65.
Club membership 650.
Visitors Mon-Sun & BHs. Booking required. Dress code.
Societies booking required. **Green Fees** not confirmed 🏌 **Course**
Designer Charles Mackenzie **Prof** David Hughes **Facilities** ⑪ ⑩!
🏌 ☂ 🍴 🛎 🏌 🥤 **Location** 0.5m N of village off A58
Hotel ★★★★ HL Wood Hall Hotel, Trip Lane, Linton, WETHERBY
☎ 01937 587271 📄 01937 584353 44 en suite

SHIPLEY   Map 7 SE13

Hollins Hall, A Marriott Hotel & Country Club Hollins Hill
BD17 7QW
☎ 01274 534212 📄 01274 534220
web: www.hollinshallgolf.com
18 Holes, 6671yds, Par 71, SSS 71, Course record 65.
Course Designer Ross McMurray **Location** 3m N on the A6038
Telephone for further details
Hotel ★★★★ 76% HL Hollins Hall, A Marriott Hotel &
Country Club, Hollins Hill, Baildon, SHIPLEY ☎ 01274 530053
📄 01274 534251 122 en suite

Northcliffe Golf Club High Bank Ln BD18 4LJ
☎ 01274 596731 📄 01274 584148
e-mail: northcliffegc@hotmail.com
web: www.northcliffegc.org.uk
Parkland with magnificent views of moors. Testing 1st hole, dog-leg
left over a ravine. The 18th hole is one of the most picturesque and
difficult par 3s in the country, with a green 100 feet below the tee and
protected by bunkers, water and trees.
18 Holes, 6113yds, Par 71, SSS 70. Club membership 700.
Visitors Mon-Fri, Sun & BHs. Dress code. **Societies** booking required.
Green Fees £30 per day, £25 per round (£30 per round Sun & BHs).
🏌 **Course Designer** James Braid **Prof** M Hillas **Facilities** ⑪ ⑩!
🏌 ☂ 🍴 🛎 🏌 🥤 ⌚ 🥤 **Conf** Corporate Hospitality Days
Location 1.25m SW of Shipley, off A650
Hotel ★★★★ 76% HL Hollins Hall, A Marriott Hotel &
Country Club, Hollins Hill, Baildon, SHIPLEY ☎ 01274 530053
📄 01274 534251 122 en suite

SILSDEN   Map 7 SE04

Silsden Golf Club Brunthwaite Ln, Brunthwaite BD20 0ND
☎ 01535 652998
e-mail: info@silsdengolfclub.co.uk
web: www.silsdengolfclub.co.uk
Short parkland course that provides a good tesy for golfers of all
standards. Good views of the Aire Valley.
18 Holes, 5136yds, Par 67, SSS 66, Course record 64.
Club membership 350.
Visitors Mon-Sun & BHs. Booking required weekends. Dress code.
Societies booking required. **Green Fees** £15 per round (£20 weekend
& BHs) 🏌 **Facilities** ⑪ ⑩! 🏌 ☂ 🍴 🏌 🥤 **Conf** facs
Corporate Hospitality Days **Location** E of town off Howden Rd onto
Hawber Ln
Hotel ★★ 70% HL Dalesgate, 406 Skipton Road, Utley, KEIGHLEY
☎ 01535 664930 📄 01535 611253 20 en suite

SOWERBY   Map 7 SE02

Ryburn Golf Club The Shaw, Norland HX6 3QP
☎ 01422 831355
Moorland course, easy walking. Panoramic views of the Ryburn and
Calder valleys.
9 Holes, 5127yds, Par 66, SSS 65, Course record 56.
Club membership 300.
Visitors Mon-Fri except BHs. Booking required. Dress code.
Societies booking required. **Green Fees** £20 per round 🏌 **Course**
Designer Dr Alister MacKenzie **Facilities** ⑪ ⑩! 🏌 ☂ 🍴 🥤
Conf Corporate Hospitality Days **Location** 1m S of Sowerby Bridge
off A58
Hotel ★★★ 74% HL The White Swan Hotel, Princess Street,
HALIFAX ☎ 01422 355541 📄 01422 357311 40 en suite

TODMORDEN   Map 7 SD92

Todmorden Golf Club Rive Rocks, Cross Stone Rd
OL14 8RD
☎ 01706 812986 📄 01706 812986
e-mail: secretary@todmordengolfclub.co.uk
web: www.todmordengolfclub.co.uk
A challenging but fair moorland course with spectacular scenery.
Exceptionally well maintained course with narrow fairways testing
rough and excellent sculptured greens.
18 Holes, 5874yds, Par 68, SSS 68, Course record 62.
Club membership 240.
Visitors Mon-Sun & BHs. Booking required weekends & BHs. Dress
code. **Societies** booking required. **Green Fees** £15 per day (£20
weekends) 🏌 **Facilities** ⑪ 🏌 ☂ 🍴 🥤 **Conf** Corporate
Hospitality Days **Location** NE off A646, E of town centre
Hotel ★★★ 86% HL Holdsworth House, Holdsworth, HALIFAX
☎ 01422 240024 📄 01422 245174 40 en suite

ENGLAND

WAKEFIELD
Map 8 SE32

City of Wakefield Golf Club Horbury Rd WF2 8QS
☎ 01924 360282
Mature, level parkland course.
18 Holes, 6319yds, Par 72, SSS 70, Course record 64.
Club membership 600.
Visitors contact club for details. **Societies** booking required. **Green**
Fees £16 weekends **Course Designer** J S F Morrison **Prof** David Bagg
Facilities ⑪ ⑩ 🍴 ⬛ ⬜ ⬛ 🏌 ➡ ⚑ 🚜 ⚙ **Location** 1.5m
W of city centre on A642
Hotel ★★★★ 75% HL Waterton Park, Walton Hall, The Balk,
Walton, WAKEFIELD ☎ 01924 257911 & 249800 📄 01924 259686
65 en suite

Lofthouse Hill Golf Club Leeds Rd WF3 3LR
☎ 01924 823703 📄 01924 823703
e-mail: lofthousehillgolfclub@fsmail.net
web: www.lofthousehillgolfclub.co.uk
New parkland course.
18 Holes, 5957yds, Par 70, SSS 69.
Visitors Mon-Sun & BHs. Booking required. Dress code.
Societies booking required. **Green Fees** £15 per 18 holes, £9 per
9 holes **Prof** Peter Rishworth/Derek Johnson **Facilities** ⑪ ⑩ 🍴
⬜ 🏌 ➡ ⚑ 🚜 **Conf** facs Corporate Hospitality Days
Location 2m from Wakefield off A61 to Leeds
Hotel ★★★★ 75% HL Waterton Park, Walton Hall, The Balk,
Walton, WAKEFIELD ☎ 01924 257911 & 249800 📄 01924 259686
65 en suite

Normanton Golf Club Hatfield Hall, Aberford Rd WF3 4JP
☎ 01924 377943 📄 01924 200777
e-mail: office@normantongolf.co.uk
web: www.normantongolf.co.uk
A championship course occupying 145 acres of the Hatfield Hall
Estate. A blend of parkland and elevations, the course incorporates
impressive lakes and benefits from the sympathetic preservation of
long established trees and wildlife. The large undulating greens are
built to USGA standards and are playable all year.
18 Holes, 6200yds, Par 72, SSS 71. Club membership 800.
Visitors dress code. **Societies** booking required. **Green Fees** £35 per
day. Reduced winter rates. **Course Designer** Patrick Dawson **Prof** Gary
Pritchard **Facilities** ⑪ ⑩ 🍴 ⬛ ⬜ 🏌 ➡ ⚑ 🚜 ⚙
Conf facs **Location** M62 junct 30, A642 towards Wakefield, 2m on
right
Hotel ★★★★ 83% HL De Vere Oulton Hall, Rothwell Lane, Oulton,
LEEDS ☎ 0113 282 1000 📄 0113 282 8066 152 en suite

Painthorpe House Golf & Country Club Painthorpe Ln
WF4 3HE
☎ 01924 254737 & 255083 📄 01924 252022
9 Holes, 4544yds, Par 62, SSS 62, Course record 63.
Location 2m S off A636
Telephone for further details
Hotel ★★★★ 73% HL Cedar Court Hotel Wakefield, Denby Dale
Road, WAKEFIELD ☎ 01924 276310 📄 01924 280221 149 en suite

Wakefield Golf Club Woodthorpe Ln, Sandal WF2 6JH
☎ 01924 258778 (sec) 📄 01924 242752
e-mail: office@wakefieldgolfclub.co.uk
web: www.wakefieldgolfclub.co.uk
Well-sheltered meadowland and parkland with easy walking and good
views.
18 Holes, 6663yds, Par 72, SSS 72, Course record 65.
Club membership 540.
Visitors Mon-Sun & BHs. Booking required. Handicap certificate.
Dress code. **Societies** booking required. **Green Fees** not confirmed ⚙
Course Designer A McKenzie/S Herd **Prof** Ian M Wright **Facilities** ⑪
⑩ 🍴 ⬛ ⬜ 🏌 ➡ ⚑ ⚙ **Conf** Corporate Hospitality Days
Location 3m S of Wakefield, off A61
Hotel ★★★★ 75% HL Waterton Park, Walton Hall, The Balk,
Walton, WAKEFIELD ☎ 01924 257911 & 249800 📄 01924 259686
65 en suite

WETHERBY
Map 8 SE44

Wetherby Golf Club Linton Ln LS22 4JF
☎ 01937 580089 📄 01937 581915
e-mail: manager@wetherbygolfclub.co.uk
web: www.wetherbygolfclub.co.uk
A medium length parkland course renowned for its lush fairways.
Particularly memorable holes are the 6th, a par 4 which follows the
sweeping bend of the River Wharfe.
18 Holes, 6288yds, Par 72, SSS 71. Club membership 950.
Visitors Mon-Fri, Sun except BHs. Booking required. Dress code.
Societies booking required. **Green Fees** £44 per day, £34 per round
(£47/£38 Sun) **Prof** Mark Daubney **Facilities** ⑪ ⑩ 🍴 ⬛ ⬜ 🏌
➡ ⚑ ⚙ 🚜 ⚙ **Conf** facs Corporate Hospitality Days
Location 1m W off A661, 2m W off A1
Hotel ★★★★ HL Wood Hall Hotel, Trip Lane, Linton, WETHERBY
☎ 01937 587271 📄 01937 584353 44 en suite

WIKE
Map 8 SE34

The Village Golf Course Backstone Gill Ln LS17 9JU
☎ 0113 273 7471 & 07759012364
A 12 hole pay-and-play course in an elevated position enjoying long
panoramic views. The holes are par 3, 4 and 5s and include water
hazards and shaped large greens.
12 Holes, 5780yds, Par 75, SSS 68, Course record 66.
Visitors Mon-Sun & BHs. Dress code. **Societies** welcome.
Green Fees not confirmed ⚙ **Course Designer** William Binner
Prof Deborah Snowden **Facilities** ⑪ ⬜ ⚑ 🚜 ⚙ **Leisure** fishing
Location signed, 1m off A61, 2m off A58
Hotel ★★★★ HL Wood Hall Hotel, Trip Lane, Linton, WETHERBY
☎ 01937 587271 📄 01937 584353 44 en suite

Save on Hotels. Book at **theAA.com/hotel**

YORKSHIRE, WEST – CHANNEL ISLANDS

ENGLAND

WOOLLEY

Map 8 SE31

Woolley Park Golf Course New Rd WF4 2JS
☎ 01226 380144 01226 390295
e-mail: woolleyparkgolf@yahoo.co.uk
web: www.woolleyparkgolfclub.co.uk

A demanding course set in a mature wooded parkland. With many water features in play and undulating greens, the course offers a challenge to all golfers.

18 Holes, 6636yds, Par 71, SSS 72, Course record 70.

Visitors Mon-Sun & BHs. Booking required. Dress code.
Societies booking required. **Green Fees** £21 per 18 holes (£29 weekends & BHs). Academy course £7.50 per 9 holes **Course Designer** M Shattock **Prof** Jon Baldwin **Facilities** ⑪ ⓗ ♿ ⛳ ⓣ
⛏ ⌂ ⛳ ⛳ ⛳ ⛳ ⛳ **Leisure** 9 hole par 3 academy course
Conf Corporate Hospitality Days **Location** M1 junct 38, off A61 between Wakefield and Barnsley
Hotel ★★★★ 73% HL Cedar Court Hotel Wakefield, Denby Dale Road, WAKEFIELD ☎ 01924 276310 01924 280221 149 en suite

CHANNEL ISLANDS
GUERNSEY

L'ANCRESSE VALE

Map 16

Royal Guernsey Golf Club GY3 5BY
☎ 01481 246523 01481 243960
e-mail: roy.rggc@cwgsy.net
web: www.royalguernseygolfclub.com

Not quite as old as its neighbour Royal Jersey, Royal Guernsey is a sporting course which was redesigned after World War II by Mackenzie Ross, who has many fine courses to his credit. It is a pleasant and well-maintained links. The 8th hole, a good par 4, requires an accurate second shot to the green set among the gorse and thick rough. The 18th, with lively views, needs a strong shot to reach the green well down below. The course is windy, with hard walking.

18 Holes, 6215yds, Par 70, SSS 70, Course record 63.
Club membership 934.

Visitors Mon-Wed, Fri & BHs. Handicap certificate. Dress code.
Green Fees not confirmed **Course Designer** Mackenzie Ross
Prof Christopher Douglas **Facilities** ⑪ ⓣⓞⓘ ⓗ ♿ ⓣ ⛏ ⌂
⛳ ⛳ ⛳ **Location** 3m N of St Peter Port
Hotel ★★★★ 73% HL St Pierre Park Hotel, Rohais, ST PETER PORT ☎ 01481 728282 01481 712041 131 en suite

CASTEL

Map 16

La Grande Mare Hotel Golf & Country Club Vazon Bay GY5 7LL
☎ 01481 253544 01481 255197
e-mail: golf@lagrandemare.com
web: www.lagrandemare.com

This hotel and golf complex is set in over 120 acres of grounds. The Hawtree designed parkland course opened in 1994 and was originally designed around 14 holes with four double greens. Water hazards on 15 holes.

18 Holes, 4761yds, Par 64, SSS 64, Course record 63.
Club membership 800.

Visitors Mon-Sun & BHs. Dress code. **Societies** booking required
Green Fees not confirmed **Course Designer** Hawtree **Prof** Matt Groves **Facilities** ⑪ ⓣⓞⓘ ⓗ ♿ ⓣ ⛏ ⌂ ⛳ ⛳ ⛳ ⛳ ⛳
Leisure outdoor and indoor heated swimming pool, fishing, sauna, gymnasium, sports massage **Conf** facs Corporate Hospitality Days
Location
Hotel ★★★★ 71% HL La Grande Mare Hotel Golf & Country Club, The Coast Road, Vazon Bay, CASTEL ☎ 01481 256576
 01481 256532 24 en suite

ST PETER PORT

Map 16

St Pierre Park Golf Club Rohais GY1 1FD
☎ 01481 728282 01481 712041
e-mail: gary.roberts@stpierrepark.co.uk
web: www.stpierrepark.co.uk

Challenging par 3 parkland course in a delightful setting, with lakes, streams and superb greens.

9 Holes, 2758yds, Par 54, SSS 50, Course record 53.
Club membership 200.

Visitors Mon-Sun & BHs. Booking required. **Societies** welcome.
Green Fees from £20 per 18 holes, from £15 per 9 holes. **Course Designer** Jacklin **Facilities** ⑪ ⓣⓞⓘ ⓗ ♿ ⓣ ⛏ ⌂ ⛳ ⛳
⛳ ⛳ **Leisure** hard tennis courts, heated indoor swimming pool, sauna, gymnasium, spa pool **Conf** facs Corporate Hospitality Days
Location 1m W off Rohais Rd
Hotel ★★★★ 73% HL St Pierre Park Hotel, Rohais, ST PETER PORT ☎ 01481 728282 01481 712041 131 en suite

JERSEY

GROUVILLE
Map 16

Royal Jersey Golf Club Le Chemin au Greves JE3 9BD
☎ 01534 854416
e-mail: thesecretary@royaljersey.com
web: www.royaljersey.com
A seaside links - its centenary was celebrated in 1978. It is also
famous for the fact that Britain's greatest golfer, Harry Vardon,
was born in a little cottage on the edge of the course and learned
his golf here.
18 Holes, 6120yds, Par 70, SSS 71, Course record 64.
Club membership 1300.
Visitors Mon-Sun & BHs. Booking advised. Handicap certificate.
Dress code. **Societies** booking required. **Green Fees** £60 per round
Prof David Morgan **Facilities** ⚐ ⛳ ⛳ ⛳ ⛳ ⛳ ⛳ ⛳ ⛳
⛳ ⛳ **Conf** Corporate Hospitality Days **Location** 4m E of St Helier
off coast road
Hotel ★★★ 71% HL Old Court House, GOREY ☎ 01534 854444
📄 01534 853587 58 en suite

LA MOYE
Map 16

La Moye Golf Club La Route Orange JE3 8GQ
☎ 01534 743401 📄 01534 747289
web: www.lamoyegolfclub.co.uk
18 Holes, 6664yds, Par 72, SSS 73, Course record 65.
Course Designer James Braid **Location** W of village off A13
Telephone for further details
Hotel ★★★★ HL The Atlantic, Le Mont de la Pulente, ST
BRELADE ☎ 01534 744101 📄 01534 744102 50 en suite

ST CLEMENT
Map 16

St Clements Golf & Sports Centre Plat Douet Rd JE2 6PN
☎ 01534 721938 📄 01534 721012
web: www.stclementsgolfandsportscentre.co.uk
The most southerly course in the British Isles. Testing 9 hole parkland
course and three hole academy course suitable for all types of players
and ages.
9 Holes, 2568yds, Par 35, SSS 35. Club membership 500.
Visitors Booking required. Course closed Sun am & Tue am.
Societies booking required. **Green Fees** £25 per day, £15 per 9 holes
(Junior £18/£10) **Prof** Lee Elstone & Steve Whiteside **Facilities** ⚐
⛳ ⛳ ⛳ ⛳ ⛳ ⛳ ⛳ ⛳ **Leisure** hard tennis
courts, squash, 3 hole academy course. **Conf** facs **Location** E of St
Helier on A5
Hotel ★★★★★ HL Longueville Manor, ST SAVIOUR
☎ 01534 725501 📄 01534 731613 30 en suite

ST OUEN
Map 16

Les Mielles Golf & Country Club JE3 7FQ
☎ 01534 482787 📄 01534 485414
e-mail: enquiry@lesmielles.co.je
web: www.lesmielles.com
Challenging championship course with bent grass greens, dwarf
rye fairways and picturesque ponds situated in the Island's largest
conservation area within St Ouen's Bay.
18 Holes, 5770yds, Par 70, SSS 68, Course record 62.
Club membership 1500.
Visitors Mon-Sun & BHs. Booking required weekends.
Societies booking required. **Green Fees** not confirmed **Course
Designer** J Le Brun/R Whitehead **Prof** W Osmand/L Cummins
Facilities ⚐ ⛳ ⛳ ⛳ ⛳ ⛳ ⛳ ⛳ ⛳ ⛳
Leisure Laser clay pigeon shooting, 18 hole miniature golf course
Conf facs Corporate Hospitality Days **Location** centre of St Ouen's Bay
Hotel ★★★★ 85% HL L'Horizon Hotel and Spa, St Brelade's Bay,
ST BRELADE ☎ 01534 743101 📄 01534 746269 106 en suite

ISLE OF MAN

CASTLETOWN
Map 6 SC26

Castletown Golf Links Fort Island, Derbyhaven IM9 1UA
☎ 01624 822211
e-mail: 1sttee@manx.net
web: www.golfiom.com
Set on the Langness peninsula, this superb championship course is
surrounded on three sides by the sea, and holds many surprises from
its Championship tees. A bunker redevelopment programme has seen
22 additional bunkers added to this historic links course.
18 Holes, 6707yds, Par 72, SSS 72, Course record 64.
Club membership 300.
Visitors Mon-Sun & BHs. Booking required. Handicap certificate.
Dress code. **Societies** booking required. **Green Fees** £39 per round
(£49 weekends) **Course Designer** McKenzie Ross/Old Tom Morris
Prof Andy Patterson **Facilities** ⛳ ⛳ ⛳ ⛳ ⛳ ⛳ ⛳ ⛳
Leisure snooker **Conf** Corporate Hospitality Days **Location** Close to
airport
Hotel ★★ 71% HL Falcon's Nest, The Promenade, PORT ERIN
☎ 01624 834077 📄 01624 835370 39 en suite

DOUGLAS
Map 6 SC37

Douglas Golf Club Pulrose Park IM2 1AE
☎ 01624 675952 📄 01624 616865
web: www.isleofmangolf.com
Parkland and moorland course under the control of Douglas
Corporation.
18 Holes, 5947yds, Par 69, SSS 69, Course record 64.
Club membership 250.
Visitors Mon-Sun & BHs. Booking required Tue & weekends.
Societies booking required. **Green Fees** not confirmed **Course
Designer** Dr A MacKenzie **Prof** Mike Vipond **Facilities** ⚐ ⛳ ⛳
⛳ ⛳ ⛳ ⛳ ⛳ **Conf** facs Corporate Hospitality Days
Location 1m from Douglas on Castletown road on Pulrose Estate
Hotel ★★★★ 81% HL Sefton, Harris Promenade, DOUGLAS
☎ 01624 645500 📄 01624 676004 96 en suite

Save on Hotels. Book at **theAA.com/hotel**

ISLE OF MAN

Mount Murray Hotel & Country Club Mount Murray, Santon IM4 2HT

☎ 01624 661111 📄 01624 611116

e-mail: hotel@mountmurray.com

web: www.mountmurray.com

A challenging course with many natural features, lakes, streams etc. Five par 5s, six par 3s and the rest par 4. Fine views over the whole island.

18 Holes, 6356yds, Par 71, SSS 71, Course record 66. Club membership 300.

Visitors Mon-Sun & BHs. Booking required. Dress code. **Societies** booking required. **Green Fees** from £30 per round (from £35 weekends) **Course Designer** Bingley Sports Research **Prof** Allyn Laing **Facilities** ⊕ ⓑ ☐ ☜ 🍴 ♨ ☂ ⚑ ♣ 🍺 🏌 ➴ **Leisure** heated indoor swimming pool, squash, sauna, gymnasium **Conf** facs Corporate Hospitality Days **Location** 5m from Douglas towards airport

Hotel ★★★★ 73% HL Mount Murray Hotel and Country Club, Santon, DOUGLAS ☎ 01624 661111 📄 01624 611116   100 en suite

PEEL

Map 6 SC28

Peel Golf Club Rheast Ln IM5 1BG

☎ 01624 842227 & 843456   📄 01624 843456

e-mail: peelgc@manx.net

web: www.peelgolfclub.com

Moorland course, with natural hazards and easy walking. Good views. The drop down to the 12th and climb back up to the 13th interrupt an otherwise fairly level course. The long, dog-legged 11th hole is an outstanding par 4, where the gorse must be carried to get a good second shot to the green. Most notable of the short holes are the 10th and 17th where an errant tee shot finds bunker, gorse or thick rough.

18 Holes, 5874yds, Par 69, SSS 69, Course record 62. Club membership 856.

Visitors Mon-Sun & BHs. Booking required. Dress code. **Societies** booking required. **Green Fees** £22 per round (£30 weekends) **Course Designer** James Braid **Prof** Paul O'Reilly **Facilities** ⊕ ⓑ ☐ ☜ 🍴 ☂ ⚑ 🏌 **Leisure** snooker **Conf** Corporate Hospitality Days **Location** SE of town centre on A1

Hotel ★★ 71% HL Falcon's Nest, The Promenade, PORT ERIN ☎ 01624 834077 📄 01624 835370   39 en suite

PORT ERIN

Map 6 SC16

Rowany Golf Club Rowany Dr IM9 6LN

☎ 01624 834108 & 834072   📄 01624 834072

e-mail: rowany@iommail.net

web: www.rowanygolfclub.com

Undulating seaside course with testing later holes, which cut through gorse and rough. However, those familiar with this course maintain that the 7th and 12th holes are the most challenging.

18 Holes, 5840yds, Par 70, SSS 69, Course record 62. Club membership 500.

Visitors contact club for details. **Societies** welcome. **Green Fees** phone **Course Designer** G Lowe **Facilities** ⊕ 🍴 by prior arrangement ⓑ ☐ ☜ 🍴 ☂ ⚑ ♣ 🍺 🏌 **Conf** Corporate Hospitality Days **Location** N of village off A32

Hotel ★★ 71% HL Falcon's Nest, The Promenade, PORT ERIN ☎ 01624 834077 📄 01624 835370   39 en suite

PORT ST MARY

Map 6 SC26

Port St Mary Golf Club Kallow Point Rd IM9 5EJ

☎ 01624 834932

Slightly hilly course with beautiful scenic views over Port St Mary and the Irish Sea.

9 Holes, 5570yds, Par 68, SSS 68, Course record 63. Club membership 324.

Visitors Mon-Sun & BHs. **Societies** welcome. **Green Fees** not confirmed **Course Designer** George Duncan **Facilities** ⊕ 🍴 ⓑ ☐ ☜ 🍴 ☂ ⚑ 🏌 **Leisure** hard tennis courts, croquet lawn **Conf** Corporate Hospitality Days **Location** signed entering Port St Mary, one-way system, 2nd left to end, 1st right

Hotel ★★★★★ GH Aaron House, The Promenade, PORT ST MARY ☎ 01624 835702 📄 01624 837731   4 rooms (3 en suite)

RAMSEY

Map 6 SC49

Ramsey Golf Club Brookfield Av IM8 2AH

☎ 01624 812244   📄 01624 815833

e-mail: ramseygolfclub@manx.net

web: www.ramseygolfclub.im

Parkland with easy walking and good views. Testing holes: 1st, par 5; 18th, par 3.

18 Holes, 5982yds, Par 70. Club membership 700.

Visitors Mon-Sun & BHs. Dress code. **Societies** booking required. **Green Fees** £25 per day (£34 per 18 holes weekends & BHs). Winter £22/£30 **Course Designer** James Braid **Prof** Andrew Dyson **Facilities** ⊕ 🍴 by prior arrangement ⓑ ☐ ☜ 🍴 ☂ ⚑ 🏌 🍺 🏌 **Conf** Corporate Hospitality Days **Location** SW of town centre

Hotel ★★★★ 73% HL Mount Murray Hotel and Country Club, Santon, DOUGLAS ☎ 01624 661111 📄 01624 611116   100 en suite

Scotland

Buachaille Etive Beag, Glen Coe, Highlands

CITY OF ABERDEEN

ABERDEEN
Map 15 NJ90

Auchmill Golf Course Bonnyview Rd, West Heatheryfold AB16 7FQ
☎ 01224 714577 & 01224 715214 (clubhouse)
📠 01224 648693
e-mail: auchmill.golf@btconnect.com
web: www.auchmill.co.uk

A young parkland course providing an enjoyable challenge for all golfers, with fine views of Aberdeen and the surrounding area. Over recent years the course has improved significantly, making it more adventurous, with tree-lined fairways, open drainage ditches and tightly cut greens and fairways.

18 Holes, 5939yds, Par 71, SSS 69, Course record 63.
Club membership 428.

Visitors Mon-Sun & BHs. Booking advisable weekends. Dress code. **Societies** booking required **Green Fees** £25 per day, £15 per 18 holes **Course Designer** Neil Coles/Brian Hugget **Facilities** ⑪ ⑧ ⓑ ⬜ 🍴 🍺 ⬟ ⛳ **Conf** Corporate Hospitality Days **Location** from A90 North Anderson Drive turn W at Rosehill rdbt along Provost Rust Drive for approx 1m, turn right into Bonnyview Rd and keep left
Hotel ★★★ 78% HL The Craighaar, Waterton Road, Bucksburn, ABERDEEN ☎ 01224 712275 📠 01224 716362 53 en suite

Balnagask Golf Course St Fitticks Rd AB11 3QT
☎ 01224 876407 📠 01224 648693

Links course with fine views over the harbour and beach. Very hilly with lots of hidden holes.

18 Holes, 5606yds, Par 70, SSS 68, Course record 63.

Visitors Mon-Fri, Sun & BHs. **Societies** welcome. **Green Fees** phone ⊛ **Facilities** ⑪ ⑧ ⓑ ⬜ ⬟ ⛳ **Leisure** 9 hole pitch & putt course **Location** 2m E of city centre
Hotel ★★★★ 71% HL Maryculter House Hotel, South Deeside Road, Maryculter, ABERDEEN ☎ 01224 732124 📠 01224 733510 40 en suite

Craibstone Golf Centre Craibstone Estate AB21 9YA
☎ 01224 716777 📠 01224 711298
web: www.craibstone.com

18 Holes, 5757yards, Par 69, SSS 69, Course record 66.

Location NW of city off A96 Aberdeen-Inverness road. A96 through Bucksburn. Before next rdbt left signed Forrit Brae. At top of road club signed
Telephone for further details
Hotel ★★★★ 75% HL Aberdeen Marriott Hotel, Overton Circle, Dyce, ABERDEEN ☎ 01224 770011 📠 01224 722347 155 en suite

Deeside Golf Club Golf Rd AB15 9DL
☎ 01224 869457 📠 01224 861800
web: www.deesidegolfclub.com

Haughton: 18 Holes, 6286yds, Par 70, SSS 71,
Course record 65.

Blairs: 9 Holes, 5042yds, Par 68, SSS 64.

Course Designer Archie Simpson **Location** 3m W of city centre off A93
Telephone for further details
Hotel ★★★★ 74% HL Mercure Ardoe House Hotel & Spa, South Deeside Road, Blairs, ABERDEEN ☎ 01224 860600 📠 01224 861283 109 en suite

Hazlehead Golf Course Hazlehead Av AB15 8BD
☎ 01224 321830 📠 01224 810452
e-mail: golf@aberdeencity.gov.uk
web: www.aberdeencity.gov.uk

Three picturesque courses and a pitch and putt course which provide a true test of golfing skills,s with gorse and woodlands being a hazard for any wayward shots.

No 1 Course: 18 Holes, 6224yds, Par 70, SSS 70,
Course record 61.

No 2 Course: 18 Holes, 5764yds, Par 67, SSS 68,
Course record 62.

Visitors Mon-Sun & BHs. **Societies** booking required. **Green Fees** not confirmed **Prof** C Nelson **Facilities** ⓑ ⬜ 🍴 ⬟ ⛳ **Leisure** 9 hole pitch & putt course **Conf** Corporate Hospitality Days **Location** 4m W of city centre off A944
Hotel ★★★★ 74% HL Mercure Ardoe House Hotel & Spa, South Deeside Road, Blairs, ABERDEEN ☎ 01224 860600 📠 01224 861283 109 en suite

Murcar Links Golf Club Bridge of Don AB23 8BD
☎ 01224 704354 📠 01224 704354
e-mail: golf@murcarlinks.com
web: www.murcarlinks.com

Seaside links course with a prevailing south-west wind. Its main attraction is the challenge of playing round and between gorse, heather and sand dunes. The additional hazards of burns and out of bounds give any golfer a testing round of golf.

Murcar: 18 Holes, 6516yds, Par 71, SSS 73.
Strabathie: 9 Holes, 5364yds, Par 70, SSS 71.
Club membership 650.

Visitors Mon-Sun & BHs. Booking required. Handicap certificate. Dress code. **Societies** booking required. **Green Fees** £95 per day, £75 per round (£90 per round weekends). Strabathie £38 per day, £15 per round (£45/£22.50 weekends) **Course Designer** A Simpson/J Braid/G Webster **Prof** Gary Forbes **Facilities** ⑪ ⑧ ⓑ ⬜ 🍴 ⬟ 🏠 ⛳ ✎ ✦ **Location** 5m NE of city centre off A90
Hotel ★★★ 78% HL The Craighaar, Waterton Road, Bucksburn, ABERDEEN ☎ 01224 712275 📠 01224 716362 53 en suite

Royal Aberdeen Golf Club Links Rd, Balgownie, Bridge of Don AB23 8AT
☎ 01224 702571 📠 01224 826591
e-mail: admin@royalaberdeengolf.com
web: www.royalaberdeengolf.com

Championship genuine links course with undulating dunes. Windy, easy walking.

Balgownie Course: 18 Holes, 6861yds, Par 71, SSS 74,
Course record 63.

Silverburn Course: 18 Holes, 4021yds, Par 64, SSS 61.
Club membership 500.

Visitors After 3pm weekends. Handicap certificate. **Societies** booking required. **Green Fees** £150 per day, £100 per round (£120 per round weekends) **Course Designer** Braid & Simpson **Prof** David Ross **Facilities** ⑪ ⓑ ⬜ 🍴 ⬟ 🏠 ⛳ ✦ **Location** 2.5m N of city centre off A92
Hotel ★★★ 79% HL The Mariner Hotel, 349 Great Western Road, ABERDEEN ☎ 01224 588901 📠 01224 571621 25 en suite

Save on Hotels. Book at **theAA.com/hotel**

CITY OF ABERDEEN – ABERDEENSHIRE

SCOTLAND

Westhill Golf Club Westhill Heights, Westhill AB32 6RY
☎ 01224 740159 🖻 01224 749124
e-mail: westhillgolf@btconnect.com
web: www.westhillgolfclub.co.uk
A challenging parkland course.

18 Holes, 5849yds, Par 69, SSS 69, Course record 64.
Club membership 808.

Visitors Mon-Sun & BHs. Dress code. **Societies** welcome. **Green Fees** £25 per day, £20 per round (£30/£25 weekends) **Course Designer** Charles Lawrie **Prof** George Bruce **Facilities** ⊕ ⊙ ⅃ ⊑ 🏌 ⅄ 🛍 ⅂ ⅄ 🛒 ⅄ **Leisure** snooker table **Conf** facs Corporate Hospitality Days **Location** 7m NW of city centre off A944
Hotel ★★★ 78% HL The Craighaar, Waterton Road, Bucksburn, ABERDEEN ☎ 01224 712275 🖻 01224 716362 53 en suite

PETERCULTER — Map 15 NJ80

Peterculter Golf Course Oldtown, Burnside Rd AB14 0LN
☎ 01224 734994 (shop) & 735245 (office)
🖻 01224 735580
e-mail: info@petercultergolfclub.co.uk
web: www.petercultergolfclub.co.uk
Surrounded by wonderful scenery and bordered by the River Dee, a variety of birds, deer and foxes may be seen on the course, which also has superb views up the Dee Valley.

18 Holes, 6226yds, Par 71, SSS 70, Course record 64.
Club membership 1035.

Visitors Mon-Sun & BHs. Booking required. Dress code **Societies** booking required. **Green Fees** £46 per day, £36 per round **Course Designer** Greens of Scotland **Prof** Dean Vannet **Facilities** ⊕ ⊙ ⅃ ⊑ 🏌 ⅄ 🛍 ⅄ 🛒 ⅄ **Location** on A93
Hotel ★★★★ 71% HL Maryculter House Hotel, South Deeside Road, Maryculter, ABERDEEN ☎ 01224 732124 🖻 01224 733510 40 en suite

ABERDEENSHIRE

ABOYNE — Map 15 NO59

Aboyne Golf Club Formaston Park AB34 5HP
☎ 013398 86328 🖻 013398 87592
e-mail: aboynegolfclub@btconnect.com
web: www.aboynegolfclub.co.uk
Beautiful parkland with outstanding views. Two lochs on course.

18 Holes, 6009yds, Par 68, SSS 69, Course record 62.
Club membership 920.

Visitors dress code **Societies** booking required. **Green Fees** £40 per day, £30 per round (£50/£35 weekends) **Prof** Stephen Moir **Facilities** ⊕ ⊙ ⅃ ⊑ 🏌 ⅄ 🛍 ⅄ 🛒 **Conf** Corporate Hospitality Days **Location** E side of village, N of A93
Hotel ★★★ 80% HL Loch Kinord, Ballater Road, Dinnet, BALLATER ☎ 013398 85229 🖻 013398 87007 20 en suite

ALFORD — Map 15 NJ51

Alford Golf Club Montgarrie Rd AB33 8AE
☎ 019755 62178 🖻 019755 64910
web: www.alford-golf-club.co.uk
18 Holes, 5483yds, Par 69, SSS 65, Course record 64.
Location in village centre on A944
Telephone for further details
Hotel ★★ 64% SHL Gordon Arms Hotel, The Square, HUNTLY ☎ 01466 792288 🖻 01466 794556 13 en suite

AUCHENBLAE — Map 15 NO77

Auchenblae Golf Course AB30 1TX
☎ 01561 320002
web: www.auchenblaegolfcourse.co.uk
Short but demanding course set in spectacular scenery and renowned for its excellent greens. A mixture of short and long holes, small and large greens add to the challenge and enjoyment of the course.

Auchenblae: 9 Holes, 3933yds, Par 64, SSS 61,
Course record 60. Club membership 500.

Visitors Contact course for details. **Societies** booking required. **Green Fees** £15 per day (£18 weekends) 🎯 **Course Designer** Robin Hiseman **Facilities** ⅃ ⊑ ⅄ 🛍 ⅄ **Leisure** hard tennis courts **Location** 10m S of Stonehaven off A90

BALLATER — Map 15 NO39

Ballater Golf Club Victoria Rd AB35 5LX
☎ 013397 55567
e-mail: sec@ballatergolfclub.co.uk
web: www.ballatergolfclub.co.uk
Heathland course with testing long and short holes and glorious views of the nearby hills.

18 Holes, 5582yds, Par 67, SSS 67, Course record 61.
Club membership 750.

Visitors Mon-Sun & BHs. Booking required. Dress code.
Societies booking required. **Green Fees** £28 per round (£32 weekends) **Course Designer** Alister McKenzie **Prof** Bill Yule **Facilities** ⊕ ⊙ ⅃ ⊑ 🏌 ⅄ 🛍 ⅄ 🛒 ⅄ **Leisure** hard tennis courts, snooker, bowls **Conf** facs Corporate Hospitality Days **Location** W side of town
Hotel ★★★ 80% HL Loch Kinord, Ballater Road, Dinnet, BALLATER ☎ 013398 85229 🖻 013398 87007 20 en suite

SCOTLAND

BANCHORY Map 15 NO69

Banchory Golf Club Kinneskie Rd AB31 5TA
☎ 01330 822365 🖹 01330 822491
e-mail: info@banchorygolfclub.co.uk
web: www.banchorygolfclub.co.uk

Sheltered parkland beside the River Dee, with easy walking and woodland scenery. Strategically placed bunkers and the river itself are among the challenges.

18 Holes, 5801yds, Par 69, SSS 68, Course record 63.
Club membership 975.

Visitors Mon-Sun & BHs. Booking required weekends. Handicap certificate. Dress code. **Societies** welcome. **Green Fees** £40 per day, £30 per round (£50/£40 weekends) **Prof** David Naylor **Facilities** ⑪
🏦 🍴 🍺 ☱ 🍷 ⚖ 🏠 ♈ ⚐ ♂ **Conf** facs **Location** A93, 300yds from W end of High St

Hotel ★★★ **70%** SHL Best Western Burnett Arms Hotel, 25 High Street, BANCHORY ☎ 01330 824944 🖹 01330 825553 18 en suite

Inchmarlo Resort & Golf Club Inchmarlo AB31 4BQ
☎ 01330 826424 & 826422/826427 🖹 01330 826425
e-mail: secretary@inchmarlo.com
web: www.inchmarlogolf.com

The Laird's course is laid out on the gentle parkland slopes of the Inchmarlo Estate in the Dee Valley and the designer has taken advantage of the natural contours of the land and its many mature trees. The nine-hole Queen's course is a tricky and testing course with ponds, meadering burns and dry stone dykes combining with the more traditional bunkers to test the skill of even the most accomplished player.

Laird's Course: 18 Holes, 6063yards, Par 70, SSS 70,
Course record 66.
Queen's Course: 9 Holes, 2150yds, Par 32, SSS 31.
Club membership 800.

Visitors Mon-Sun & BHs. Dress code. **Societies** booking required. **Green Fees** not confirmed **Course Designer** Graeme Webster **Prof** Andrew Locke **Facilities** ⑪ 🏦 🍴 🍺 ☱ 🍷 ⚖ 🏠 ♈ ◇ ♂ 🛒 ♂ **Conf** facs Corporate Hospitality Days **Location** 0.5m from A93 Aberdeen-Braemar road

Hotel ★★★ **70%** SHL Best Western Burnett Arms Hotel, 25 High Street, BANCHORY ☎ 01330 824944 🖹 01330 825553 18 en suite

BANFF Map 15 NJ66

Duff House Royal Golf Club The Barnyards AB45 3SX
☎ 01261 812062 🖹 01261 812224
e-mail: info@duffhouseroyal.com
web: www.duffhouseroyal.com

Well-manicured flat parkland course, bounded by woodlands and the River Deveron. Well bunkered and renowned for its large, two-tier greens. The river is a hazard for those who wander off the tee at the 7th, 16th and 17th holes. True to design of legendary course architect, Dr Alister MacKenzie.

18 Holes, 6161yds, Par 68, SSS 69, Course record 60.
Club membership 1200.

Visitors Contact club for details. **Societies** welcome. **Green Fees** £40 per day, £30 per round (£50/£36 weekends) **Course Designer** Dr Alister MacKenzie **Prof** Gary Holland **Facilities** ⑪ 🏦 🍺 ☱ 🍷 ⚖ 🏠 ♂ 🛒 ♂ 🗝 **Conf** facs Corporate Hospitality Days **Location** 0.5m S on A98

BRAEMAR Map 15 NO19

Braemar Golf Club Cluniebank Rd AB35 5XX
☎ 013397 41618 🖹 013397 41400
e-mail: info@braemargolfclub.co.uk
web: www.braemargolfclub.co.uk

Flat course, set amid beautiful countryside on Royal Deeside, with River Clunie running through several holes. The 2nd hole is one of the most testing in the area.

18 Holes, 5000yds, Par 65, SSS 64, Course record 59.
Club membership 450.

Visitors contact club for details. **Societies** booking required. **Green Fees** not confirmed **Course Designer** Joe Anderson **Facilities** ⑪ 🏦 🍺 ☱ 🍷 ⚖ 🏠 ♈ ♂ **Location** 0.5m S

Hotel ★★★★ GH Callater Lodge Guest House, 9 Glenshee Road, BRAEMAR ☎ 013397 41275 6 rooms

CRUDEN BAY Map 15 NK03

Cruden Bay Golf Club Aulton Rd AB42 0NN
☎ 01779 812285 🖹 01779 812945
e-mail: secretary@crudenbaygolfclub.co.uk
web: www.crudenbaygolfclub.co.uk

A typical links course which epitomises the old fashioned style of rugged links golf. The drives require accuracy with bunkers and protecting greens, blind holes and undulating greens. The 10th provides a panoramic view of half the back nine down at beach level, and to the east can be seen the outline of the spectacular ruin of Slains Castle featured in Bram Stoker's *Dracula*.

Main Course: 18 Holes, 6287yds, Par 70, SSS 71,
Course record 64.
St Olaf Course: 9 Holes, 2463yds, Par 32, SSS 32.
Club membership 1100.

Visitors Mon-Sun & BHs. Booking required. Handicap certificate. Dress code. **Societies** booking required. **Green Fees** £70 per day (£75 per round weekends) **Course Designer** Thomas Simpson **Prof** Neil Murray **Facilities** ⑪ 🏦 🍺 ☱ 🍷 ⚖ 🏠 ♈ ⚐ ♂ 🗝 **Conf** Corporate Hospitality Days **Location** SW side of village on A975

Hotel 70% Ⓤ The Udny Arms Hotel, Main Street, NEWBURGH ☎ 01358 789444 🖹 01358 789012 30 en suite

ELLON Map 15 NJ93

McDonald Golf Club Hospital Rd AB41 9AW
☎ 01358 720576 🖹 01358 720001
e-mail: mcdonald.golf@virgin.net
web: www.ellongolfclub.co.uk

Tight, parkland course with streams.

18 Holes, 5942yds, Par 70, SSS 70. Club membership 710.

Visitors Mon-Sun & BHs. Booking required. **Societies** booking required. **Green Fees** £30 per day (£40 weekends) **Prof** Sandy Aird **Facilities** ⑪ 🏦 🍺 ☱ 🍷 ⚖ 🏠 ♈ ♂ **Conf** Corporate Hospitality Days **Location** 0.25m N on A948

Hotel 70% Ⓤ The Udny Arms Hotel, Main Street, NEWBURGH ☎ 01358 789444 🖹 01358 789012 30 en suite

SCOTLAND

FRASERBURGH
Map 15 NJ96

Fraserburgh Golf Club Philorth Links AB43 8TL
☎ 01346 516616
e-mail: secretary@fraserburghgolfclub.org
web: www.fraserburghgolfclub.org

Testing seaside course, natural links. An extremely scenic course, surrounded and protected by substantial sand dunes. Fraserburgh is the seventh oldest golf club in the world, founded in 1777.

Corbiehill: 18 Holes, 6308yds, Par 70, SSS 71, Course record 62.
Rosehill: 9 Holes, 4832yds, Par 66, SSS 63, Course record 58. Club membership 650.

Visitors Mon-Sun & BHs. Booking required. Dress code. **Societies** welcome. **Green Fees** not confirmed **Course Designer** James Braid **Facilities** ⊕ ⑩ ⓘ ▯ ⧖ ♨ ⛳ ✦ **Conf** Corporate Hospitality Days **Location** 1m SE on B9033

HUNTLY
Map 15 NJ53

Huntly Golf Club Cooper Park AB54 4SH
☎ 01466 792643   📄 01466 793852
e-mail: huntlygc@btconnect.com
web: www.huntlygc.com

Parkland between the rivers Deveron and Bogie.

18 Holes, 5359yds, Par 67, SSS 66, Course record 61.
Club membership 500.

Visitors Mon-Sun & BHs. Booking preferred **Societies** Booking required. **Green Fees** not confirmed **Facilities** ⊕ ⑩ ⓘ ▯ ⧖ ♨ ✦ **Location** N side of Huntly, turn off A96 at bypass rdbt

Hotel ★★ 64% SHL Gordon Arms Hotel, The Square, HUNTLY ☎ 01466 792288 📄 01466 794556   13 en suite

INSCH
Map 15 NJ62

Insch Golf Club Golf Ter AB52 6JY
☎ 01464 820363
e-mail: administrator@inschgolfclub.co.uk
web: www.inschgolfclub.co.uk

A challenging course, a mixture of flat, undulating parkland, with trees, stream and pond. The most challenging hole of the course is the 9th, a testing par 5 of 534yds requiring long and accurate play. This follows the par 3 8th, a hole which demands a well-positioned tee shot played over a large water hazard to a long narrow green. Although a relatively short course, the natural woodland, water hazards and large contoured greens require accurate play.

18 Holes, 5350yds, Par 69, SSS 67, Course record 64.
Club membership 400.

Visitors Mon-Sun & BHs. Booking required. Dress code. **Societies** booking required. **Green Fees** not confirmed **Course Designer** Greens of Scotland **Facilities** ⊕ by prior arrangement ⑩ by prior arrangement ⓘ ▯ ⧖ ♨ ✦ **Conf** Corporate Hospitality Days **Location** from A96 turn left onto B992 at Kellockbank for 1.9m. Turn right at x-rds into Market St, then 1st left into Golf Terrace. Course on right.

Hotel ★★★★ 74% HL Macdonald Pittodrie House, Chapel of Garioch, Pitcaple, INVERURIE ☎ 0870 1942111 & 01467 681744 📄 01467 681648   27 en suite

INVERALLOCHY
Map 15 NK06

Inverallochy Golf Club Whitelink AB43 8XY
☎ 01346 582000
e-mail: inverallochygolf@btconnect.com
web: www.inverallochygolfclub.co.uk

Seaside links course with natural hazards, tricky par 3s and easy walking.

18 Holes, 5370yds, Par 67, SSS 66, Course record 57.
Club membership 600.

Visitors Mon-Sun & BHs. Booking required Mon, Tue & Sat. **Societies** booking required. **Green Fees** £25 per day, £20 per round (£30/£25 weekends). £10 after 2pm Sat & Sun ⊛ **Facilities** ⊕ ⑩ ⓘ ▯ ⧖ ♨ **Leisure** bowling green **Location** E side of village off B9107

INVERURIE
Map 15 NJ72

Inverurie Golf Club Davah Wood AB51 5JB
☎ 01467 624080   📄 01467 672869
e-mail: administrator@inveruriegc.co.uk
web: www.inveruriegc.co.uk

Parkland course, part of which is through a wood.

18 Holes, 5664yds, Par 69, SSS 68, Course record 63.
Club membership 750.

Visitors Mon-Sun & BHs. Booking required weekends & BHs. **Societies** booking required. **Green Fees** £25 per day/round (£40 per day, £30 per round weekends) **Prof** Steven McLean **Facilities** ⊕ ⑩ ⓘ ▯ ⧖ ♨ ⛳ ✦ **Location** off Blackhall rdbt off A96 bypass

Hotel ★★★★ 74% HL Macdonald Pittodrie House, Chapel of Garioch, Pitcaple, INVERURIE ☎ 0870 1942111 & 01467 681744 📄 01467 681648   27 en suite

KEMNAY
Map 15 NJ71

Kemnay Golf Club Monymusk Rd AB51 5RA
☎ 01467 642225 (shop)   📄 01467 643746
e-mail: administrator@kemnaygolfclub.co.uk
web: www.kemnaygolfclub.co.uk

Parkland with stunning views, incorporating tree-lined and open fairways, and a stream crossing four holes. The course is not physically demanding but a challenge is presented to every level of golfer due to the diverse characteristics of each hole.

18 Holes, 6362yds, Par 71, SSS 71, Course record 65.
Club membership 800.

Visitors Mon-Sun & BHs. Booking required. Dress code. **Societies** booking required. **Green Fees** £33 per day, £27 per round (£39/£33 weekends) **Course Designer** Greens of Scotland **Prof** David J Brown **Facilities** ⊕ ⑩ ⓘ ▯ ⧖ ♨ ✦ ⛳ ✦ **Conf** Corporate Hospitality Days **Location** W side of village on B993 **Hotel** ★★★★ 74% HL Macdonald Pittodrie House, Chapel of Garioch, Pitcaple, INVERURIE ☎ 0870 1942111 & 01467 681744 📄 01467 681648   27 en suite

KINTORE
Map 15 NJ71

Kintore Golf Course Balbithan AB51 0UR
☎ 01467 632631 📠 01467 632995
e-mail: kintoregolfclub@lineone.net
web: www.kintoregolfclub.net

The course covers a large area of ground, from the Don Basin near the clubhouse, to mature woodland at the far perimeter. The 1st is one of the toughest opening holes in the North East, and the 7th requires an accurate drive followed by a second shot over a burn which runs diagonally across the front of the green. The 11th is the longest hole on the course, made longer by the fact that it slopes upwards all the way to the green. The final holes are short, relatively hilly and quite tricky but offer spectacular views to the Bennachie and Grampian hills.

18 Holes, 6019yds, Par 70, SSS 69, Course record 62. Club membership 700.

Visitors Mon-Fri, Sun & BHs. Dress code **Societies** booking required. **Green Fees** £30 per day, £25 per round. **Facilities** ⑪ ⑩l ㏇ ▱ ▯ ⚲ ㋡ 🍴 🛏 ⚶ **Conf** Corporate Hospitality Days **Location** 1m from village centre on B977
Hotel ★★★★ 78% HL Thistle Aberdeen Airport, Aberdeen Airport, Argyll Road, ABERDEEN ☎ 0871 376 9001 📠 0871 376 9101 147 en suite

MACDUFF
Map 15 NJ76

Royal Tarlair Golf Club Buchan St AB44 1TA
☎ 01261 832897 📠 01261 833455
e-mail: info@royaltarlair.co.uk
web: www.royaltarlair.co.uk

Parkland clifftop course. Testing 13th, Clivet (par 3).

18 Holes, 5866yds, Par 71, SSS 68, Course record 68. Club membership 400.

Visitors Mon-Sun & BHs. Booking required weekends. **Societies** booking required. **Green Fees** not confirmed 🚗
Facilities ⑪ ⑩l ㏇ ▱ ⚲ ㋡ 🍴 🛏 ⚶ **Conf** Corporate Hospitality Days **Location** 0.75m E off A98

MINTLAW
Map 15 NJ94

Longside Golf Club West End, Longside AB42 4XJ
☎ 01779 821558
e-mail: info@longsidegolf.wanadoo.co.uk

Flat parkland course with a river winding through, providing a challenging course which requires accurate play.

18 Holes, 5225yds, Par 66, SSS 66, Course record 64. Club membership 700.

Visitors Mon-Sun & BHs. **Societies** booking required. **Green Fees** £20 per day, £15 per round (£30/£20 weekends) 🚗 **Facilities** ⑪ ⑩l ㏇ ▱ ⚲ ㋡ ⚶ **Location** 4m W of Peterhead on New Pitsligo road
Hotel ★★★ 80% HL Palace, Prince Street, PETERHEAD ☎ 01779 474821 📠 01779 476119 64 en suite

NEWBURGH
Map 15 NJ92

Newburgh on Ythan Golf Club Beach Rd AB41 6BY
☎ 01358 789058 & 789084
e-mail: secretary@newburghgolfclub.co.uk
web: www.newburghgolfclub.co.uk

This seaside course was founded in 1888 and is adjacent to a bird sanctuary. The course was extended in 1996 and the nine newer holes, the outward half, are characterised by undulations and hills, with elevated tees and greens requiring a range of shot making. The original inward nine demands accurate golf from tee to green. The 18th is a testing 550yd dog-leg (par 5), at one time the longest hole in Scotland.

18 Holes, 6423yds, Par 72, SSS 72. Club membership 630.

Visitors Mon-Sun & BHs. Booking required. Dress code..
Societies booking required. **Green Fees** £45 per day, £35 per round (£55/£45 weekends) **Course Designer** J H Taylor **Prof** Ian Bratton
Facilities ⑪ ⑩l ㏇ ▱ ⚲ ㋡ 🍴 🛏 ⚶
Leisure hard tennis courts, fishing, indoor swing studio, 6 hole practice course **Conf** facs Corporate Hospitality Days **Location** 10m N of Aberdeen on A975
Hotel 70% 🅄 The Udny Arms Hotel, Main Street, NEWBURGH ☎ 01358 789444 📠 01358 789012 30 en suite

NEWMACHAR
Map 15 NJ81

Newmachar Golf Club Swailend AB21 7UU
☎ 01651 863002 📠 01651 863055
e-mail: info@newmachargolfclub.co.uk
web: www.newmachargolfclub.co.uk

Hawkshill is a championship-standard parkland course designed by Dave Thomas. Several lakes affect five of the holes and there are well-developed birch and Scots pine trees. Swailend is a parkland course, also designed by Dave Thomas. It provides a test all of its own with some well-positioned bunkering and testing greens.

Hawkshill: 18 Holes, 6730yds, Par 72, SSS 74, Course record 64.

Swailend: 18 Holes, 6388yds, Par 72, SSS 71, Course record 64. Club membership 1200.

Visitors Mon-Sun & BHs. Booking required. Handicap certificate. Dress code. **Societies** booking required. **Green Fees** Hawkshill £70 per day, £50 per round. (£70 per round weekends). Swailend £40 per day, £30 per round. (£50 per day, £40 per round weekends). **Course Designer** Dave Thomas/Peter Alliss **Prof** Andrew Cooper **Facilities** ⑪ ⑩l ㏇ ▱ ⚲ ㋡ 🍴 🛏 ⚶ ⚓ **Conf** Corporate Hospitality Days **Location** 2m N of Dyce, off A947
Hotel ★★★★ 75% HL Aberdeen Marriott Hotel, Overton Circle, Dyce, ABERDEEN ☎ 01224 770011 📠 01224 722347 155 en suite

OLDMELDRUM
Map 15 NJ82

Old Meldrum Golf Club Kirk Brae AB51 0DJ
☎ 01651 872648 📠 01651 872896
e-mail: admin@oldmeldrumgolf.co.uk
web: www.oldmeldrumgolf.co.uk

Parkland with tree-lined fairways and superb views. Challenging 196yd, par 3 11th over two ponds to a green surrounded by bunkers.

18 Holes, 6100yds, Par 70, SSS 70, Course record 63. Club membership 750.

continued

SCOTLAND

Save on Hotels. Book at **theAA.com/hotel**

ABERDEENSHIRE

Visitors Mon-Sun & BHs. Booking required. **Societies** booking required. **Green Fees** £24 per round (£30 weekends) **Prof** Hamish Love **Facilities** ⒯ ⑴ ⓲ ⌨ ⑪ ⌂ ⍾ 🛏 ♂ 🏌 **Location** E side of village off A947
Hotel ★★★★ 78% CHH Meldrum House Hotel Golf & Country Estate, OLD MELDRUM ☎ 01651 872294 🖺 01651 872464 22 en suite

---

PETERHEAD
Map 15 NK14

Peterhead Golf Club Craigewan Links, Riverside Dr AB42 1LT
☎ 01779 472149 & 480725 🖺 01779 480725
e-mail: enquiries@peterheadgolfclub.co.uk
web: www.peterheadgolfclub.co.uk
The Old Course is a natural links course bounded by the sea and the River Ugie. Varying conditions of play depending on wind and weather. The New Course is more of a parkland course.
Old Course: 18 Holes, 6173yds, Par 70, SSS 71,
Course record 63.
New Course: 9 Holes, 2228yds, Par 31.
Club membership 650.
Visitors Mon-Sun & BHs. Booking required weekends.
Societies welcome. **Green Fees** not confirmed **Course Designer** W Park/ L Auchterconie/J Braid **Prof** Harry Dougal **Facilities** ⒯ ⑴ ⓲ ⌨ ⑪ ⌂ ⍾ ♂ **Location** N side of town centre off A90
Hotel ★★★ 80% HL Palace, Prince Street, PETERHEAD
☎ 01779 474821 🖺 01779 476119 64 en suite

PORTLETHEN
Map 15 NO99

Portlethen Golf Club Badentoy Rd AB12 4YA
☎ 01224 782575 & 781090 🖺 01224 783383
web: www.portlethenclub.com
18 Holes, 6707yds, Par 72, SSS 72, Course record 63.
Course Designer Cameron Sinclair **Location** off A90 S of Aberdeen
Telephone for further details
Hotel ★★★★ 77% HL Norwood Hall, Garthdee Road, Cults, ABERDEEN ☎ 01224 868951 🖺 01224 869868 73 en suite

---

STONEHAVEN
Map 15 NO88

Stonehaven Golf Club Cowie AB39 3RH
☎ 01569 762124 🖺 01569 765973
e-mail: info@stonehavengolfclub.com
web: www.stonehavengolfclub.com
Challenging meadowland course overlooking sea with three gullies and splendid views.
18 Holes, 5103yds, Par 66, SSS 65, Course record 61.
Club membership 500.
Visitors Dress code. **Societies** booking required. **Green Fees** £35 per day, £30 per round (£40/£35 weekends) **Course Designer** C Simpson **Facilities** ⒯ ⑴ ⓲ ⌨ ⑪ ⌂ ⍾ **Leisure** snooker **Conf** Corporate Hospitality Days **Location** 1m N off A92
Hotel ★★★★ 71% HL Maryculter House Hotel, South Deeside Road, Maryculter, ABERDEEN ☎ 01224 732124 🖺 01224 733510 40 en suite

---

TARLAND
Map 15 NJ40

Tarland Golf Club Aberdeen Rd AB34 4TB
☎ 013398 81000 🖺 013398 81000
web: www.tarlandgolfclub.co.uk
9 Holes, 5888yds, Par 67, SSS 68, Course record 65.
Course Designer Tom Morris **Location** E side of village off B9119
Telephone for further details
Hotel ★★★ 80% HL Loch Kinord, Ballater Road, Dinnet, BALLATER ☎ 013398 85229 🖺 013398 87007 20 en suite

---

TORPHINS
Map 15 NJ60

Torphins Golf Club Bog Rd AB31 4JU
☎ 013398 82115
e-mail: stuartmacgregor5@btinternet.com
Heathland and parkland course built on a hill with views of the Cairngorms.
9 Holes, 4738yds, Par 64, SSS 64, Course record 62.
Club membership 310.
Visitors Mon-Sun & BHs. **Societies** welcome. **Green Fees** £15 per day (£16 weekends). £9 per 9 holes ⓼ **Facilities** ⓲ ⌨ ⌂ ♂ **Location** 0.25m W of village off A980
Hotel ★★★ 70% SHL Best Western Burnett Arms Hotel, 25 High Street, BANCHORY ☎ 01330 824944 🖺 01330 825553 18 en suite

---

TURRIFF
Map 15 NJ75

Turriff Golf Club Rosehall AB53 4HD
☎ 01888 562982 🖺 01888 568050
e-mail: grace@turriffgolf.sol.co.uk
web: www.turriffgolfclub.com

An inland course with tight fairways, well-paced greens and well-sighted bunkers to test all golfers. The par 5 12th hole sets a challenge for the longest driver while the short par 3 4th, with its green protected by bunkers is a challenge in its own right.
18 Holes, 6118yds, Par 70, SSS 70, Course record 64.
Club membership 650.
Visitors Mon-Sun & BHs. Booking required. Handicap certificate. Dress code. **Societies** booking required. **Green Fees** not confirmed **Prof** Gordon Dunn **Facilities** ⒯ ⑴ ⓲ ⌨ ⑪ ⌂ ♂ 🛏 ♂ **Conf** Corporate Hospitality Days **Location** 1m W off B9024

ANGUS

ARBROATH
Map 12 NO64

Arbroath Golf Course Elliot DD11 2PE
☎ 01241 875837 📄 01241 875837
e-mail: lindsay.ewart@btconnect.com
web: www.arbroathgolfcourse.co.uk

A typical links layout, predominately flat, with the prevailing south westerly wind facing for the first seven holes, making a big difference to how certain holes play. When the wind is in a northerly direction the back nine holes are very tough. The greens are well protected by deep riveted pot bunkers. Fast tricky greens make for difficult putting.

18 Holes, 6200yds, Par 70, SSS 70, Course record 63. Club membership 550.

Visitors Mon-Sun & BHs. Booking required. Dress code.
Societies booking required. **Green Fees** £35 per day, £30 per round (£45/£35 weekends). £15 per round winter **Course Designer** Braid **Prof** Lindsay Ewart **Facilities** ⓣ ⓨ ⓛ ⓓ ⓟ ⓧ ⓐ ⓨ ⓯
🛒 ⓧ 🏌 **Location** 1m SW on A92
Hotel ★★★★ 73% HL Carnoustie Golf Hotel & Spa, The Links, CARNOUSTIE ☎ 0844 414 6520 📄 0844 414 6519 85 en suite

Letham Grange Golf Colliston DD11 4RL
☎ 01241 890373 📄 01241 890725

Old Course: 18 Holes, 6632yds, Par 73, SSS 73, Course record 66.
Glens Course: 18 Holes, 5528yds, Par 68, SSS 68, Course record 60.

Course Designer G K Smith/Donald Steel **Location** 4m N on A933
Telephone for further details
Hotel ★★★★ 73% HL Carnoustie Golf Hotel & Spa, The Links, CARNOUSTIE ☎ 0844 414 6520 📄 0844 414 6519 85 en suite

BARRY
Map 12 NO53

Panmure Golf Club Burnside Rd DD7 7RT
☎ 01241 855120 📄 01241 859737
e-mail: secretary@panmuregolfclub.co.uk
web: www.panmuregolfclub.co.uk

A nerve-testing, adventurous course which opens quietly and builds its challenge amongst the sandhills further out. The course is used for Open Championship final qualifying rounds.

18 Holes, 6550yds, Par 70, SSS 70, Course record 67. Club membership 700.

Visitors Mon, Wed-Fri, Sun & BHs. Booking required. Dress code.
Societies booking required. **Green Fees** £95 per day, £75 per round **Course Designer** James Braid **Prof** Andrew Crerar **Facilities** ⓣ ⓨ ⓛ ⓓ ⓟ ⓧ ⓐ ⓨ 🛒 ⓧ 🏌 **Conf** Corporate Hospitality Days **Location** S side of village off A930
Hotel ★★★★ 73% HL Carnoustie Golf Hotel & Spa, The Links, CARNOUSTIE ☎ 0844 414 6520 📄 0844 414 6519 85 en suite

BRECHIN
Map 15 NO56

Brechin Golf & Squash Club Trinity DD9 7PD
☎ 01356 622383 & 625270 (pro shop) 📄 01356 625270
e-mail: brechingolfclub@tiscali.co.uk
web: www.brechingolfclub.co.uk

Rolling parkland with easy walking and good views of the Grampian mountains. Set among many lush green tree-lined fairways with excellent greens. A wide variation of holes with dog-legs, long par 3s, tricky par 4s and reachable in two par 5s, where the longer hitters can take a more challenging tee shot.

18 Holes, 6092yds, Par 72, SSS 70, Course record 66. Club membership 850.

Visitors Mon-Sun & BHs. Booking required. Dress code.
Societies booking required. **Green Fees** £40 per day, £33 per round (£45/£35 weekends) **Course Designer** James Braid (partly) **Prof** Stephen Rennie **Facilities** ⓣ ⓨ ⓛ ⓓ ⓟ ⓧ ⓐ ⓯ ⓧ 🛒 ⓧ **Leisure** squash **Conf** Corporate Hospitality Days **Location** 1m N on B966
Hotel ★★★★ RR Gordon's, Main Street, INVERKEILOR ☎ 01241 830364 📄 01241 830364 5 rooms

CARNOUSTIE
Map 12 NO53

Carnoustie Golf Links see page 317
20 Links Pde DD7 7JF
☎ 01241 802270 (bookings) 📄 01241 802271
e-mail: golf@carnoustiegolflinks.co.uk
web: www.carnoustiegolflinks.co.uk

EDZELL
Map 15 NO66

Edzell Golf Club High St DD9 7TF
☎ 01356 647283 (Secretary) 📄 01356 648094
e-mail: secretary@edzellgolfclub.com
web: www.edzellgolfclub.com

This delightful, gentle, flat course is situated in the foothills of the Highlands and provides good golf as well as conveying a feeling of peace and quiet to everyone who plays here. The village of Edzell is one of the most picturesque in Scotland.

18 Holes, 6455yds, Par 71, SSS 71, Course record 62.
West Water: 9 Holes, 2057yds, Par 32, SSS 60.
Club membership 855.

Visitors Mon-Sun & BHs. Handicap certificate. Dress code.
Societies booking required. **Green Fees** £52 per day, £40 per round (£60/£44 weekends). West Water £20 per 18 holes, £15 per 9 holes **Course Designer** Bob Simpson **Prof** A J Webster **Facilities** ⓣ ⓨ ⓛ ⓓ ⓟ ⓧ ⓐ ⓯ ⓧ 🛒 ⓧ 🏌 **Location** B966 north of Brechin Bypass on A90, 4 miles, club entrance is on left after arch
Hotel ★★★ GH Oaklands, 10 Rossie Island Road, MONTROSE ☎ 01674 672018 📄 01674 672018 7 rooms

CARNOUSTIE GOLF LINKS

ANGUS - CARNOUSTIE - MAP 12 NO53

This Championship Course has been voted the top course in Britain by many golfing greats and described as Scotland's ultimate golfing challenge. The course developed from origins in the 1560s; James Braid added new bunkers, greens and tees in the 1920s. The Open Championship first came to the course in 1931, and Carnoustie hosted the Scottish Open in 1995 and 1996, was the venue for the 1999 Open Championship, and again in 2007. The Burnside Course (6028yds) is enclosed on three sides by the Championship Course and has been used for Open Championship qualifying rounds. The Buddon Course (5420yds) has been extensively remodelled, making it ideal for mid to high handicappers.

20 Links Pde DD7 7JF ☎ 01241 802270 (bookings) 🖷 01241 802271
e-mail: golf@carnoustiegolflinks.co.uk web: www.carnoustiegolflinks.co.uk
Championship: 18 Holes, 6955yds, Par 72, SSS 75, Course record 64.
Burnside: 18 Holes, 6028yds, Par 68, SSS 70.
Buddon Links: 18 Holes, 5420yds, Par 66, SSS 67.
Visitors Mon-Sun & BHs. Booking required. Dress code. **Societies** booking required. **Green Fees** Championship course £135, Burnside £37, Buddon £32. Play all 3 courses £160 **Course Designer** James Braid
Prof Colin Sinclair **Facilities** ⑪ ⑩ 🍴 ➗ 🍽 ⚑ ⛳ ◇ ✎ ⚑ **Leisure** heated indoor swimming pool, sauna, gymnasium **Conf** facs Corporate Hospitality Days **Location** SW of town centre off A930
Hotel ★★★★ 73% HL Carnoustie Golf Hotel & Spa, The Links, CARNOUSTIE ☎ 0844 414 6520
🖷 0844 414 6519 85 en suite

KIRRIEMUIR
Map 15 NO35

Kirriemuir Golf Club Shielhill Rd DD8 4LN
☎ 01575 573317 📄 01575 574608
web: www.kirriemuirgolfclub.co.uk
18 Holes, 5553yds, Par 68, SSS 67, Course record 62.
Course Designer James Braid **Location** 1m N off B955
Telephone for further details
Hotel ★★★★★ GA Tigh Na Leigh Guesthouse, 22-24 Airlie Street,
ALYTH ☎ 01828 632372 📄 01828 632279 5 rooms

MONIFIETH
Map 12 NO43

Monifieth Golf Links Princes St DD5 4AW
☎ 01382 532767 📄 01382 535816
e-mail: monifiethgolf@freeuk.com
web: www.monifiethgolf.co.uk

The chief of the two courses at Monifieth is the Medal Course. It
has been one of the qualifying venues for the Open Championship
on more than one occasion. A seaside links, but divided from the
sand dunes by a railway which provides the principal hazard for the
first few holes. The 10th hole is outstanding, the 17th is excellent
and there is a delightful finishing hole. The other course here is the
Ashludie.
Medal Course: 18 Holes, 6655yds, Par 71, SSS 72.
Ashludie Course: 18 Holes, 5123yds, Par 68, SSS 65.
Club membership 1500.
Visitors Mon-Sun & BHs. Booking required. Handicap certificate.
Dress code. **Societies** booking required. **Green Fees** not confirmed
Course Designer James Braid **Prof** Ian McLeod **Facilities** ⓘ �𝄃○
⯊ ⬜ 🍴 ⬘ 🖼 ⯑ 🏌 Location NE side of town on
A930
Hotel ★★★★ 73% HL Carnoustie Golf Hotel & Spa, The Links,
CARNOUSTIE ☎ 0844 414 6520 📄 0844 414 6519 85 en suite

MONTROSE
Map 15 NO75

Montrose Golf Links Traill Dr DD10 8SW
☎ 01674 672932 📄 01674 671800
e-mail: secretary@montroselinks.co.uk
web: www.montroselinks.co.uk
The links at Montrose like many others in Scotland are on
commonland. The Medal Course at Montrose - the fifth oldest in the
world - is typical of Scottish links, with narrow, undulating fairways
and problems from the first hole to the last. The Broomfield course
is flatter and easier.
Medal Course: 18 Holes, 6544yds, Par 71, SSS 72,
Course record 63.
Broomfield Course: 18 Holes, 4825yds, Par 66, SSS 63.
Club membership 1300.
Visitors Mon-Sun & BHs. Booking recommended. Dress code. Medal
- Sat (1444-1540 only) **Societies** welcome. **Green Fees** Medal £65
Sun-Fri, £50 per round (£75/£55 Sat). Broomfield £35/£30 (£22 Sat)
Course Designer W Park/Tom Morris **Prof** Jason J Boyd **Facilities** ⓘ
�𝄃○ ⯊ ⬜ 🍴 ⬘ 🖼 ⯑ 🏌 🏌 Location NE side of
town off A92
Hotel ★★★★ RR Gordon's, Main Street, INVERKEILOR
☎ 01241 830364 📄 01241 830364 5 rooms

ARGYLL & BUTE

CARDROSS
Map 10 NS37

Cardross Golf Club Main Rd G82 5LB
☎ 01389 841754 📄 01389 842162
e-mail: golf@cardross.com
web: www.cardross.com
Undulating, testing parkland course with good views.
18 Holes, 6447yds, Par 71, SSS 72, Course record 64.
Club membership 800.
Visitors Mon-Fri except BHs. Booking required. Dress code.
Societies booking required. **Green Fees** not confirmed **Course
Designer** James Braid **Prof** Robert Farrell **Facilities** ⓘ �𝄃○ by prior
arrangement ⯊ ⬜ 🍴 ⬘ 🖼 ⯑ 🏌 **Conf** Corporate
Hospitality Days **Location** in village centre on A814
Hotel ★★★★★ 85% HL Cameron House on Loch Lomond,
BALLOCH ☎ 01389 755565 📄 01389 759522 96 en suite

CARRADALE
Map 10 NR83

Carradale Golf Club PA28 6RY
☎ 01583 431788
Pleasant seaside course built on a promontory overlooking the Isle of
Arran. Natural terrain and small greens are the most difficult natural
hazards. Described as the most sporting nine-hole course in Scotland.
Testing 7th hole (240yds), par 3.
9 Holes, 4550yds, Par 65, SSS 62, Course record 61.
Club membership 280.
Visitors Mon-Sun & BHs. **Societies** booking required. **Green Fees** £20
per day, £16 per 9 holes ⚐ **Facilities** ⯊ ⯑ 🏌 **Location** S side
of village, on B842
Hotel ★★★ 80% HL Best Western Kinloch, BLACKWATERFOOT
☎ 01770 860444 📄 01770 860447 37 en suite

DALMALLY Map 10 NN12

Dalmally Golf Course Old Saw Mill PA33 1AE
☎ 01838 200619
e-mail: dalmallygolfclub@btinternet.com
web: www.dalmallygolfclub.co.uk
A nine-hole flat parkland course bounded by the River Orchy and surrounded by mountains. Many water hazards and bunkers.
9 Holes, 4528yds, Par 64, SSS 63. Club membership 130.
Visitors Mon-Fri & BHs. Booking required weekends. Dress code.
Societies booking required. **Green Fees** £15 per round/day ⊗
Course Designer MacFarlane Barrow Co **Facilities** 🍴 ♨ ♈ ✈ ✓
Location on A85, 1.5m W of Dalmally
Hotel ★★★ CHH The Ardanaiseig, by Loch Awe, KILCHRENAN
☎ 01866 833333 🖹 01866 833222 18 en suite

DUNOON Map 10 NS17

Cowal Golf Club Ardenslate Rd PA23 8LT
☎ 01369 705673 🖹 01369 705673
e-mail: secretary@cowalgolfclub.com
web: www.cowalgolfclub.com
Moorland course. Panoramic views of the Clyde estuary and surrounding hills.
18 Holes, 6063yds, Par 70, SSS 70, Course record 63.
Club membership 348.
Visitors contact club for details. **Societies** welcome. **Green Fees** not confirmed **Course Designer** James Braid **Prof** Russell Weir
Facilities 🍴 ♨ ♈ ✈ ✓ **Conf** Corporate Hospitality Days **Location** 1m N of pier
Hotel ★★ 74% HL Selborne, Clyde Street, West Bay, DUNOON
☎ 01369 702761 🖹 01369 704032 98 en suite

ERISKA Map 10 NM94

Isle of Eriska Hotel, Spa & Island PA37 1SD
☎ 01631 720371 & 720802 🖹 01631 720531
e-mail: office@eriska-hotel.co.uk
web: www.eriska-hotel.co.uk
This remote and most beautiful course is set around the owners' hotel, with stunning views. The signature 5th hole provides a 140yd carry to a green on a hill surrounded by rocks and bunkers.
9 Holes, 2588yds, Par 35. Club membership 60.
Visitors Mon-Sun & BHs. **Societies** welcome. **Green Fees** £15 per day
Course Designer H Swan **Facilities** 🍴 ♨ ♈ ✈ ✓
✈ **Leisure** hard tennis courts, heated indoor swimming pool, sauna, gymnasium, multipurpose sports hall **Conf** facs Corporate Hospitality Days **Location** A828 Connel-Fort William, signed 4m N of Benderloch
Hotel ★★★★★ CHH Isle of Eriska, Eriska, BY OBAN
☎ 01631 720371 🖹 01631 720531 23 en suite

GIGHA ISLAND Map 10 NR64

Isle of Gigha Golf Club PA41 7AA
☎ 01583 505242 🖹 01583 505244
e-mail: golf@gigha.net
web: www.gigha.org
A nine-hole course with scenic views of the Sound of Gigha and Kintyre. Ideal for the keen or occasional golfer.
9 Holes, 5042yds, Par 66, SSS 65, Course record 71.
Club membership 40.
Visitors Mon-Sun & BHs. **Societies** booking required. **Green Fees** £15 per day ⊗ **Course Designer** Members **Facilities** ♨ ♈
Location near ferry landing

HELENSBURGH Map 10 NS28

Helensburgh Golf Club 25 East Abercromby St G84 9HZ
☎ 01436 674173 🖹 01436 671170
e-mail: thesecretary@helensburghgolfclub.co.uk
web: www.helensburghgolfclub.co.uk
Testing moorland course with superb views of Loch Lomond and River Clyde.
18 Holes, 5942yds, Par 69, SSS 69, Course record 62.
Club membership 875.
Visitors dress code. **Societies** booking required. **Green Fees** not confirmed **Course Designer** Old Tom Morris **Prof** Fraser Hall
Facilities 🍴 ♨ ♈ ✈ ✓ **Conf**
Corporate Hospitality Days **Location** NE side of town off B832, turn off Sinclair St into East Abercromby St
Hotel ★★★★★ 85% HL Cameron House on Loch Lomond,
BALLOCH ☎ 01389 755565 🖹 01389 759522 96 en suite

INNELLAN Map 10 NS17

Innellan Golf Course Knockamillie Rd PA23 7SG
☎ 01369 830242 & 830415
e-mail: innellangolfclub@btconnect.com
Situated above the village of Innellan, this undulating hilltop, parkland course has extensive views of the Firth of Clyde.
9 Holes, 2343yds, Par 64, SSS 64, Course record 61.
Club membership 199.
Visitors Mon-Sun & BHs. Booking required weekends & BHs. Dress code. **Societies** welcome. **Green Fees** not confirmed ⊗ **Facilities** ♨ ✈ ✓ **Location** 4m S of Dunoon
Hotel ★★ 74% HL Selborne, Clyde Street, West Bay, DUNOON
☎ 01369 702761 🖹 01369 704032 98 en suite

INVERARAY Map 10 NN00

Inveraray Golf Course North Cromalt PA32 8XT
☎ 01499 600286
Testing parkland course with beautiful views overlooking Loch Fyne.
9 Holes, 5628yds, Par 70, SSS 69, Course record 69.
Club membership 120.
Visitors contact course for details. **Societies** welcome. **Green Fees** not confirmed ⊗ **Facilities** ♨ ✈ **Location** 1m S of Inveraray
Hotel ★★★ 82% HL Creggans Inn, STRACHUR ☎ 01369 860279
🖹 01369 860637 14 en suite

SCOTLAND

SCOTLAND

LOCHGILPHEAD
Map 10 NR88

Lochgilphead Golf Course PA31 8LE
☎ 01546 602340 & 600104
9 Holes, 2242yds, Par 64, SSS 63, Course record 58.
Course Designer Dr I McCamond **Location** next to hospital, signed from village
Telephone for further details
Hotel ★★★ 78% HL Cairnbaan, Crinan Canal, Cairnbaan, LOCHGILPHEAD ☎ 01546 603668 📄 01546 606045 12 en suite

MACHRIHANISH
Map 10 NR62

The Machrihanish Golf Club PA28 6PT
☎ 01586 810213 📄 01586 810221
e-mail: secretary@machgolf.com
web: www.machgolf.com
Magnificent natural links of championship status. The 1st hole is the famous drive across the Atlantic. Sandy soil allows for play all year round. Large greens, easy walking, windy.
18 Holes, 6225yds, Par 70, SSS 71, Course record 63.
The Pans Course: 9 Holes, 2376yds, Par 34, SSS 69.
Club membership 1300.
Visitors contact club for details. **Societies** booking required. **Green Fees** Mon-Fri & Sun £80 per day, £50 per round. (Sat £90/£70). The Pans course £12 per day. **Course Designer** Tom Morris **Prof** Ken Campbell **Facilities** ⑪ ⭐ 🏐 ➗ 🍴 🏌 🏛 ⛳ 🚂 ⚒
Location 5m W of Campbeltown on B843

OBAN
Map 10 NM83

Glencruitten Golf Club Glencruitten Rd PA34 4PU
☎ 01631 564604
web: www.obangolf.com
18 Holes, 4452yds, Par 61, SSS 63, Course record 55.
Course Designer James Braid **Location** NE side of town centre off A816
Telephone for further details
Hotel ★★★ 83% HL Manor House, Gallanach Road, OBAN
☎ 01631 562087 📄 01631 563053 11 en suite

SOUTHEND
Map 10 NR60

Dunaverty Golf Club PA28 6RW
☎ 01586 830677 📄 01586 830677
e-mail: dunavertygc@aol.com
web: www.dunavertygolfclub.com
Undulating, seaside course with spectacular views of Ireland and the Ayrshire coast.
18 Holes, 4577yds, Par 66, SSS 66, Course record 57.
Club membership 400.
Visitors Mon-Sun & BHs. **Societies** booking required. **Green Fees** not confirmed 🅿 **Facilities** ⑪ ⭐ 🏐 ➗ 🏌 🏛 ⛳ ⚒
Leisure fishing **Location** 10m S of Campbeltown on B842

TARBERT
Map 10 NR86

Tarbert Golf Club PA29 6XX
☎ 01546 606896
Hilly parkland with views over West Loch Tarbert.
9 Holes, 4460yds, Par 66, SSS 63, Course record 62.
Club membership 90.
Visitors Mon-Sun & BHs. **Societies** welcome. **Green Fees** £20 per day, £10 per round 🅿 **Location** N 1m W on B8024
Hotel ★★★★ 73% HL Stonefield Castle, TARBERT
☎ 01880 820836 📄 01880 820929 32 en suite

TIGHNABRUAICH
Map 10 NR97

Kyles of Bute Golf Club PA21 2AB
☎ 01700 811603 (secretary)
web: www.kylesofbutegolfclub.com
Moorland course which is hilly and exposed. Fine mountain and sea views. Heather, whin and burns provide heavy penalties for inaccuracy. Wild life abounds.
9 Holes, 4748yds, Par 66, SSS 64, Course record 62.
Club membership 150.
Visitors No play Sun 9.30am-1.30pm & Wed 5pm. **Societies** booking required. **Green Fees** £15 per 18 holes, £10 per 9 holes 🅿 **Facilities** 🏌 ⛳ ⚒ **Location** 1.25m S off B8000
Hotel ★★★★ 73% HL Stonefield Castle, TARBERT
☎ 01880 820836 📄 01880 820929 32 en suite

CLACKMANNANSHIRE

ALLOA
Map 11 NS89

Alloa Golf Club Schawpark FK10 3AX
☎ 01259 724476 📄 01259 724476
web: www.alloagolfpage.co.uk
18 Holes, 6229yds, Par 69, SSS 71, Course record 63.
Course Designer James Braid **Location** 1.5m NE on A908
Telephone for further details
Hotel BUD Holiday Inn Express - Stirling, Springkerse Business Park, STIRLING ☎ 01786 449922 📄 01786 449932 80 en suite

Braehead Golf Club Cambus FK10 2NT
☎ 01259 725766 📄 01259 214070
e-mail: enquiries@braeheadgolfclub.co.uk
web: www.braeheadgolfclub.co.uk
Attractive parkland at the foot of the Ochil Hills, having spectacular views.
18 Holes, 6053yds, Par 70, SSS 69, Course record 60.
Club membership 800.
Visitors Mon-Sun & BHs. Dress code. **Societies** booking required. **Green Fees** £32 per day, £24 per round (£40/£32 weekends) **Course Designer** Robert Tait **Prof** Jamie Stevenson **Facilities** ⑪ ⭐ 🏐 ➗ 🍴 🏌 🏛 ⛳ ⚒ 🚂 ⚒ **Conf** Corporate Hospitality Days **Location** 1m W on A907
Hotel BUD Holiday Inn Express - Stirling, Springkerse Business Park, STIRLING ☎ 01786 449922 📄 01786 449932 80 en suite

ALVA
Map 11 NS89

Alva Golf Club Beauclerc St FK12 5LD
☎ 01259 760431
e-mail: alva@alvagolfclub.wanadoo.com
web: www.alvagolfclub.com
A nine-hole course at the foot of the Ochil Hills, which gives it its characteristic sloping fairways and fast greens.
9 Holes, 2423yds, Par 66, SSS 64, Course record 61.
Club membership 318.
Visitors contact club for details. **Societies** welcome. **Green Fees** phone **Facilities** 🏌 ☕ 🍴 ⚲ **Location** 7m from Stirling, A91 Stirling-St Andrews
Hotel BUD Holiday Inn Express - Stirling, Springkerse Business Park, STIRLING ☎ 01786 449922 📠 01786 449932 80 en suite

DOLLAR
Map 11 NS99

Dollar Golf Club Brewlands House FK14 7EA
☎ 01259 742400
e-mail: info@dollargolfclub.com
web: www.dollargolfclub.com
Compact hillside course with magnificent views along the Ochil Hills.
18 Holes, 5242yds, Par 69, SSS 66, Course record 57.
Club membership 450.
Visitors Contact club for details. **Societies** booking required. **Green Fees** phone 🅿 **Course Designer** Ben Sayers **Facilities** ⓣ 🍴 🏌 ☕ ⚲ ♦ ⚄ **Leisure** snooker table **Conf** Corporate Hospitality Days **Location** 0.5m N off A91
Hotel ★★★★★ HL The Gleneagles Hotel, AUCHTERARDER ☎ 01764 662231 📠 01764 662134 232 en suite

MUCKHART
Map 11 NO00

Muckhart Golf Club Drumburn Rd FK14 7JH
☎ 01259 781423 & 781493
e-mail: enquiries@muckhartgolf.com
web: www.muckhartgolf.com
Scenic heathland and parkland course comprising 27 holes in three combinations of 18, all of which start and finish close to the clubhouse. Each requires a different approach, demanding tactical awareness and a skilful touch with all the clubs in the bag. There are superb views from the course's many vantage points, including the aptly named Arndean 5th 'Top of the World'.
Arndean/Cowden Course: 18 Holes, 6086yds, Par 71, SSS 70.
Naemoor/Cowden Course: 18 Holes, 6456yds, Par 71, SSS 72.
Arndean/Naemoor Course: 18 Holes, 6040yds, Par 70, SSS 70. Club membership 910.
Visitors Mon-Sun & BHs. Booking required. Dress code.
Societies booking required. **Green Fees** £40 per 36 holes, £30 per 18 holes (£45/£35 weekends) **Prof** Keith Salmoni **Facilities** ⓣ 🍴 🏌 ☕ 🍴 ⚲ 🛒 ⚄ **Conf** Corporate Hospitality Days **Location** S of village between A91 & A911
Hotel ★★★★ 73% HL The Green Hotel, 2 The Muirs, KINROSS ☎ 01577 863467 📠 01577 863180 46 en suite

TILLICOULTRY
Map 11 NS99

Tillicoultry Golf Club Alva Rd FK13 6BL
☎ 01259 750124 📠 01259 750124
e-mail: golf@tillygc.freeserve.co.uk
web: www.tillygc.co.uk
Parkland at foot of the Ochil Hills. Some hard walking but fine views.
9 Holes, 5475yards, Par 68, SSS 67, Course record 61.
Club membership 400.
Visitors Mon-Sun & BHs. Booking required weekends. Dress code. **Societies** booking required. **Green Fees** £12 per 18 holes (£18 weekends & BHs) ⚄ **Facilities** ☕ ⚲ **Location** A91, 9m E of Stirling
Hotel BUD Holiday Inn Express - Stirling, Springkerse Business Park, STIRLING ☎ 01786 449922 📠 01786 449932 80 en suite

DUMFRIES & GALLOWAY

CASTLE DOUGLAS
Map 11 NX76

Castle Douglas Golf Club Abercromby Rd DG7 1BA
☎ 01556 502801 & 503527
e-mail: cdgolfclub@aol.com
web: www.cdgolfclub.co.uk
The original course was laid out in 1905 and many changes have taken place over the years. The small but fast greens reward accuracy and a good short game is needed. The 359 yard par 4 3rd hole has a green protected by a raised plateau and even the biggest hitters have a tricky second shot. The subtle challenge of the 316 yard 5th, with its up-turned saucer green can leave even the best drive leaving the golfer with a hard job to get par.
9 Holes, 5390yds, Par 68, SSS 66, Course record 61.
Club membership 300.
Visitors Mon-Sun & BHs. Booking required Tue & Thu.
Societies booking required. **Green Fees** £20 per day, £12 per 9 holes ⚄ **Facilities** ⓣ 🍴 🏌 ☕ 🍴 ⚲ 🛒 ⚄ **Leisure** pool table **Conf** Corporate Hospitality Days **Location** 0.5m from town centre on A713 Abercrombie road
Hotel ★★ 75% HL Arden House Hotel, Tongland Road, KIRKCUDBRIGHT ☎ 01557 330544 📠 01557 330742 9 en suite

COLVEND
Map 11 NX85

Colvend Golf Club Sandyhills DG5 4PY
☎ 01556 630398 📠 01556 630495
e-mail: secretary@colvendgolfclub.co.uk
web: www.colvendgolfclub.co.uk
Picturesque and challenging course on the Solway coast. Superb views.
18 Holes, 5341yds, Par 69, SSS 67. Club membership 300.
Visitors Mon-Sun & BHs. Dress code. **Societies** welcome. **Green Fees** £30 per day, £30 per round **Course Designer** Alliss & Thomas **Facilities** ⓣ 🍴 🏌 ☕ ⚲ ♦ 🛒 ⚄ **Location** 6m SE from Dalbeattie on A710
Hotel ★★★ 86% HL Balcary Bay Hotel, AUCHENCAIRN ☎ 01556 640217 & 640311 📠 01556 640272 20 en suite

SCOTLAND

CUMMERTREES
Map 11 NY16

Powfoot Golf Club DG12 5QE
☎ 01461 204100 ▤ 01461 204111
e-mail: info@powfootgolfclub.com
web: www.powfootgolfclub.com

This championship course is on the Solway Firth and playing at this delightfully compact semi-links seaside course is a scenic treat. Lovely holes include the 2nd, the 8th and the 11th. The 9th includes a Second World War bomb crater.

18 Holes, 5980yds, Par 69, SSS 70.
Club membership 630.

Visitors Mon-Sun & BHs. Booking required. Handicap certificate. Dress code. Societies booking required. Green Fees £50 per day, £39 per round (£60/£45 weekends) Course Designer J Braid Facilities ⓣ ⑩ ⓑ ☐ ⑪ ⌿ 🍴 🛏 ⌒ ⌿ ⚑ Location 0.5m off B724
Hotel ★★★ 78% HL Powfoot Golf Hotel, Links Avenue, POWFOOT ☎ 01461 700254 & 207580 ▤ 01461 700288 24 en suite

DALBEATTIE
Map 11 NX86

Dalbeattie Golf Club 19 Maxwell Park DG5 4LR
☎ 01556 610666 ▤ 01556 612247
web: www.dalbeattiegc.co.uk

This nine-hole course provides an excellent challenge for golfers of all abilities. There are a few gentle slopes to negotiate but compensated by fine views along the Urr Valley. The 363yd 4th hole is a memorable par 4, with views across to the Lake District.

9 Holes, 5710yds, Par 68, SSS 68. Club membership 250.

Visitors Mon-Sun & BHs. Booking required Wed & Thu. Dress code. Societies booking required. Green Fees not confirmed ⊛ Course Designer Bryan C Moor Facilities ⑪ ⌒ ⌿ ⌒ Location signed off B794. Access by Maxwell Park
Hotel ★★★ 86% HL Balcary Bay Hotel, AUCHENCAIRN ☎ 01556 640217 & 640311 ▤ 01556 640272 20 en suite

DUMFRIES
Map 11 NX97

The Dumfries & County Golf Club Nunfield, Edinburgh Rd DG1 1JX
☎ 01387 253585 ▤ 01387 253585
e-mail: admin@thecounty.co.uk
web: www.thecounty.org.uk

Parkland alongside the River Nith, with views of the Queensberry Hills. Greens built to USPGA specifications. Nature trails link the fairways and the Burns Walk is incorporated within the course.

Nunfield: 18 Holes, 5918yds, Par 69, SSS 69.
Club membership 800.

Visitors Mon-Fri, Sun & BHs. Booking required. Dress code. Societies booking required. Green Fees £49 per day, £38 per round (£60/£45 Sun) Course Designer William Fernie Prof Stuart Syme Facilities ⓣ ⑩ ⓑ ☐ ⑪ ⌒ 🛏 ⌿ Conf Corporate Hospitality Days Location 1m NE of Dumfries on A701
Hotel ★★★ 80% HL Cairndale Hotel & Leisure Club, English Street, DUMFRIES ☎ 01387 254111 ▤ 01387 240288 91 en suite

Dumfries & Galloway Golf Club 2 Laurieston Av DG2 7NY
☎ 01387 263848 ▤ 01387 263848
e-mail: info@dandggolfclub.co.uk
web: www.dandggolfclub.co.uk

Attractive parkland course, a good test of golf but not physically demanding.

18 Holes, 6222yds, Par 70, SSS 71. Club membership 800.
Visitors Mon-Fri & BHs. Restricted play weekends. Booking required. Handicap certificate. Dress code. Societies booking required. Green Fees £38 per day, £30 per round (£45/£35 weekends) ⊛ Course Designer W Fernie Prof Joe Fergusson Facilities ⓣ ⑩ ⓑ ☐ ⑪ ⌒ 🛏 ⌿ 🛏 ⌿ Location W of town centre on A780
Hotel ★★★ 80% HL Cairndale Hotel & Leisure Club, English Street, DUMFRIES ☎ 01387 254111 ▤ 01387 240288 91 en suite

Dumfriesshire Golf Centre Lockerbie Rd DG1 3PF
☎ 01387 247444 ▤ 01387 254892
e-mail: admin@pinesgolf.com
web: www.dumfriesshiregolfcentre.com

A mixture of parkland and woodland with numerous water features. Excellent greens with many subtle undulations. This course cannot be overpowered, so must be played strategically.

Burns Heritage: 18 Holes, 5730yds, Par 69, SSS 69.
Course record 65. Club membership 280.

Visitors Mon-Sun & BHs. Booking required. Dress code Societies booking required. Green Fees not confirmed Course Designer Duncan Gray Prof Gareth Dick Facilities ⓣ ⑩ ⓑ ☐ ⑪ ⌒ 🛏 ⌒ ◇ ⌿ 🛏 ⌿ ⚑ Conf Corporate Hospitality Days Location off A701 Lockerbie Road, beside A75 Dumfries bypass
Hotel ★★★ 79% HL Best Western Station Hotel, 49 Lovers Walk, DUMFRIES ☎ 01387 254316 ▤ 01387 250388 32 en suite

GATEHOUSE OF FLEET
Map 11 NX55

Cally Palace Hotel & Golf Course DG7 2DL
☎ 01557 814341 ▤ 01557 814522
e-mail: info@callypalace.co.uk
web: www.mcmillanhotels.co.uk

18 hole parkland course for the exclusive use of guests of McMillan Hotels. Sculptured into the parkland surrounding the hotel, the course uses the natural contours of the land, the magnificent trees, the hidden burns and the Cally lake.

Societies booking required. Green Fees not confirmed Course Designer Tom Macaulay Facilities ⓣ ⑩ ⓑ ☐ ⑪ ⌒ 🛏 ◇ 🛏 ⌿ Leisure hard tennis courts, heated indoor swimming pool, sauna Conf facs Corporate Hospitality Days Location From M6 & A74, signed A75 Dumfries then Stranraer. At Gatehouse-of-Fleet right onto B727, left at Cally
Hotel ★★★★ 76% CHH Cally Palace, GATEHOUSE OF FLEET ☎ 01557 814341 ▤ 01557 814522 55 en suite

Gatehouse Golf Club Laurieston Rd DG7 2BE
☎ 01557 814766
web: www.gatehousegolfclub.com

9 Holes, 2521yds, Par 66, SSS 66, Course record 62.
Course Designer Tom Fernie Location 0.25m N of town
Telephone for further details
Hotel ★★★★ 76% CHH Cally Palace, GATEHOUSE OF FLEET ☎ 01557 814341 ▤ 01557 814522 55 en suite

Save on Hotels. Book at **theAA.com/hotel**

DUMFRIES & GALLOWAY

GLENLUCE
Map 10 NX15

Wigtownshire County Golf Club Mains of Park DG8 0NN
☎ 01581 300420 📄 01581 300420
e-mail: enquiries@wigtownshirecountygolfclub.com
web: www.wigtownshirecountygolfclub.com
Seaside links course on the shores of Luce Bay, easy walking but
affected by winds. The 12th hole, a dog-leg with out of bounds to the
right, is named after the course's designer, Gordon Cunningham.
18 Holes, 6104yds, Par 70, SSS 70, Course record 63.
Club membership 450.
Visitors Mon-Sun & BHs. Booking required weekends & BHs.
Societies welcome. Green Fees not confirmed Course Designer W
Gordon Cunningham Facilities ⚐ ⏰ ☕ 🏌 🛒 ⛳ 🎯 🍴
🏌 ⛳ Conf Corporate Hospitality Days Location 1.5m W off A75,
200yds off A75 on shores of Luce Bay

KIRKCUDBRIGHT
Map 11 NX65

Brighouse Bay Golf Course & Driving Range
Brighouse Bay DG6 4TS
☎ 01557 870409 📄 01557 870409
web: www.brighousebay-golfclub.co.uk.
18 Holes, 6501yds, Par 73, SSS 72.
Course Designer D Gray Location 3m S of Borgue off B727
Telephone for further details
Hotel ★★ 75% HL Arden House Hotel, Tongland Road,
KIRKCUDBRIGHT ☎ 01557 330544 📄 01557 330742 9 en suite

Kirkcudbright Golf Club Stirling Crescent DG6 4EZ
☎ 01557 330314 📄 01557 330314
e-mail: kbtgolfclub@lineone.net
web: www.kirkcudbrightgolf.com
Parkland with exceptional views over the harbour town of
Kirkcudbright, the Dee Estuary and the Galloway Hills. A challenging
course with subtle greens, offering a great day out for golfers of all
abilities.
18 Holes, 5717yds, Par 69, SSS 69. Club membership 400.
Visitors Mon-Sun & BHs. Booking required at weekends. Dress code.
Societies booking required. Green Fees £35 per day, £28 per round
⚐ Course Designer E. Shamash Facilities ⚐ ⏰ 🏌 ☕
🛒 🎯 🏌 ⛳ 🏌 Conf Corporate Hospitality Days Location NE
side of town off A711. Club off Stirling Crescent
Hotel ★★ 75% HL Arden House Hotel, Tongland Road,
KIRKCUDBRIGHT ☎ 01557 330544 📄 01557 330742 9 en suite

LANGHOLM
Map 11 NY38

Langholm Golf Club Whitaside DG13 0JR
☎ 07724 875151
e-mail: golf@langholmgolfclub.co.uk
web: www.langholmgolfclub.co.uk
Hillside course with fine views, easy to medium walking.
9 Holes, 6180yds, Par 70, SSS 69, Course record 65.
Club membership 200.
Visitors Mon-Sun & BHs. Booking required Sat. Societies booking
required. Green Fees phone ⚐ Facilities 🏌 Location E side of
village off A7
Hotel ★★★★ INN Liddesdale, Douglas Sq, NEWCASTLETON
☎ 01387 375255 📄 01387 752577 6 rooms

LOCHMABEN
Map 11 NY08

Lochmaben Golf Club Castlehillgate DG11 1NT
☎ 01387 810552
e-mail: enquiries@lochmabengolf.co.uk
web: www.lochmabengolf.co.uk
Attractive parkland surrounding Kirk Loch. Excellent views from this
well-maintained course.
18 Holes, 5933yds, Par 70, SSS 70, Course record 62.
Club membership 660.
Visitors Mon-Sun & BHs. Booking required. Societies booking
required. Green Fees £38 per day, £30 per round (£43/£33 weekends)
Course Designer James Braid Facilities ⚐ ⏰ 🏌 ☕ 🎯
🛒 🏌 Leisure fishing Conf Corporate Hospitality Days Location 4m
from Lockerbie on A74. S side of village off A709
Hotel ★★★★ 73% HL Dryfesdale Country House, Dryfebridge,
LOCKERBIE ☎ 01576 202427 📄 01576 204187 29 en suite

LOCKERBIE
Map 11 NY18

Lockerbie Golf Club DG11 2ND
☎ 01576 203363 📄 01576 203363
e-mail: enquiries@lockerbiegolf.com
web: www.lockerbiegolf.co.uk
Parkland course with excellent views from the course and featuring a
pond hole which comes into play at 3 holes.
18 Holes, 5463yds, Par 67, SSS 67, Course record 63.
Club membership 350.
Visitors Mon-Sat & BHs. Sun after 11.30am. Booking required. Dress
code. Societies booking required. Green Fees £28 per 18 holes
(£32 weekends) Course Designer James Braid Facilities ⚐ by
prior arrangement ⏰ 🏌 ☕ 🎯 🏌 Conf Corporate
Hospitality Days Location E side of town centre off B7068
Hotel ★★★★ 73% HL Dryfesdale Country House, Dryfebridge,
LOCKERBIE ☎ 01576 202427 📄 01576 204187 29 en suite

MOFFAT
Map 11 NT00

The Moffat Golf Club DG10 9SB
☎ 01683 220020
e-mail: bookings@moffatgolfclub.co.uk
web: www.moffatgolfclub.co.uk
Scenic moorland course overlooking the town, with panoramic views of
southern uplands.
Moffat: 18 Holes, 5276yds, Par 69, SSS 67.
Club membership 350.
Visitors Mon-Sun & BHs. Booking required. Societies booking
required. Green Fees £30 per day, £25 per round (£36/£30 weekends
and BHs) Course Designer Ben Sayers Facilities ⚐ ⏰ 🏌 ☕
🎯 🏌 🏌 ⛳ 🏌 Leisure snooker Conf Corporate Hospitality
Days Location from A74(M) junct 15, take A701 to Moffat, course
signed on left after 30mph limit sign
Hotel ★★★ 78% HL Annandale Arms Hotel, High Street, MOFFAT
☎ 01683 220013 📄 01683 221395 16 en suite

MONREITH
Map 10 NX34

St Medan Golf Club DG8 8NJ
☎ 01988 700358
e-mail: mail@stmedangolfclub.com
web: www.stmedangolfclub.com

Scotland's most southerly course. This links nestles in Monreith Bay with panoramic views across to the Isle of Man. The testing nine-hole course, with 18 tees, is a challenge to both high and low handicaps.

9 Holes, 4520yds, Par 64, SSS 64, Course record 60.
Club membership 200.

Visitors Mon, Thu, Fri-Sun & BHs. Dress code. **Societies** booking required. **Green Fees** £30 per day, £20 per 18 holes, £12 per 9 holes 🏌 **Course Designer** James Braid **Facilities** Ⓟ ⑩ 🍴 ⬜ 🍺 ⚲ ⚑ 🏐 **Leisure** practice net **Location** 3m S of Port William off A747

NEW GALLOWAY
Map 11 NX67

New Galloway Golf Club High St DG7 3RN
☎ 01644 420737 & 450685   📄 01644 450685
web: www.nggc.com

9 Holes, 5006yds, Par 68, SSS 67, Course record 64.

Course Designer James Braid **Location** S side of town on A762
Telephone for further details

NEWTON STEWART
Map 10 NX46

Newton Stewart Golf Club Kirroughtree Av DG8 6PF
☎ 01671 402172   📄 01671 402172
web: www.newtonstewartgolfclub.com

18 Holes, 5903yds, Par 69, SSS 70, Course record 66.

Location 0.5m N of town centre off A75
Telephone for further details
Hotel ★★★ CHH Kirroughtree House, Minnigaff, NEWTON STEWART ☎ 01671 402141 📄 01671 402425   17 en suite

PORTPATRICK
Map 10 NX05

Lagganmore Hotel DG9 9AB
☎ 01776 810499
web: www.lagganmoregolf.co.uk

18 Holes, 5698yds, Par 69, SSS 68, Course record 66.

Course Designer Stephen Hornby **Location** on A77
Telephone for further details
Hotel ★★★ HL Knockinaam Lodge, PORTPATRICK ☎ 01776 810471 📄 01776 810435   10 en suite

Portpatrick Golf Club Golf Course Rd DG9 8TB
☎ 01776 810273   📄 01776 810811
e-mail: enquiries@portpatrickgolfclub.com
web: www.portpatrickgolfclub.com

Situated on the south-west coast, overlooking the North Channel, Portpatrick benefits from the temperate climate, which allows golf to be played all year round. The two courses are a mix of rolling moorland and seaside heath, and afford some magnificent views of the Irish coastline.

Dunskey Course: 18 Holes, 5913yds, Par 70, SSS 69, Course record 64.
Dinvin Course: 9 Holes, 1346yds, Par 27, SSS 27.
Club membership 550.

Visitors Mon-Sun & BHs. Booking advisable. **Societies** Booking required. **Green Fees** £42.50 per day, £32 per round (£48.50/£37.50 weekends) **Course Designer** Charles Hunter **Prof** James Erskine **Facilities** Ⓟ ⑩ 🍴 ⬜ 🍺 ⚲ 🏠 ⚑ 🚂 🏐 **Leisure** 9 hole par 3 Dinvin Course **Conf** Corporate Hospitality Days **Location** entering village fork right at war memorial - 600yds **Hotel** ★★★ HL Knockinaam Lodge, PORTPATRICK ☎ 01776 810471 📄 01776 810435   10 en suite

SANQUHAR
Map 11 NS70

Sanquhar Golf Club Euchan Golf Course, Blackaddie Rd DG4 6JZ
☎ 01659 50577
e-mail: tich@rossirence.fsnet.co.uk

Easy walking parkland, fine views. A good test for all standards of golfer.

9 Holes, 5646yds, Par 70, SSS 68, Course record 66.
Club membership 200.

Visitors Mon-Sun & BHs. Dress code. **Societies** booking required. **Green Fees** £15 per day 🏌 **Course Designer** Willie Fernie **Facilities** Ⓟ by prior arrangement ⑩ by prior arrangement 🍺 ⬜ ⚲ **Leisure** snooker, pool. **Conf** Corporate Hospitality Days **Location** 0.5m SW off A76 **Hotel** ★★★★★ GA Gillbank House, 8 East Morton Street, THORNHILL ☎ 01848 330597 📄 01848 331713   6 rooms

SOUTHERNESS
Map 11 NX95

Solway Links Golf Course Kirkbean DG2 8BE
☎ 01387 880323 & 880623   📄 01387 880555
e-mail: info@solwaygolf.co.uk
web: www.solwaygolf.co.uk

Solway Links is a pay-and-play links golf course in a stunning coastal location near Southerness holiday village and beaches. The golf course overlooks the Solway Firth with spectacular views of the surrounding countryside and across the sea to the Lake District. Built on an ancient raised beach with excellent, well drained, undulating fairways.

18 Holes, 5037yds, Par 67.

Visitors Mon-Sun & BHs. **Societies** booking required. **Green Fees** not confirmed **Course Designer** Gordon Gray **Facilities** ⬜ ⚑ 🏐 🚂 🏐 **Leisure** clay pigeon shooting **Location** On A710 Dumfries to Dalbeattie road. **Hotel** ★★★ CHH Cavens, KIRKBEAN ☎ 01387 880234 📄 01387 880467   6 en suite

Southerness Golf Club DG2 8AZ
☎ 01387 880677 📄 01387 880644
e-mail: admin@southernessgc.sol.co.uk
web: www.southernessgolfclub.com
Natural links, championship course with panoramic views. Heather
and bracken abound.

18 Holes, 6566yds, Par 69, SSS 73, Course record 64.
Club membership 830.

Visitors Mon-Sun & BHs. Booking required. Handicap certificate.
Dress code. **Societies** booking required. **Green Fees** £65 per day;
£50 per round (£75/£60 weekends) **Course Designer** McKenzie Ross
Facilities ⑪ ⑩ 🍴 ⛳ 🏌 ⚐ ⚑ **Location** 3.5m S of Kirkbean
off A710
Hotel ★★★ CHH Cavens, KIRKBEAN ☎ 01387 880234
📄 01387 880467 6 en suite

STRANRAER   Map 10 NX06

Stranraer Golf Club Creachmore DG9 0LF
☎ 01776 870245 📄 01776 870445
e-mail: stranraergolf@btclick.com
web: www.stranraergolfclub.net
Parkland with beautiful views over Loch Ryan to Ailsa Craig, Arran and
beyond. Several notable holes including the 3rd, where a winding burn
is crossed three times to a green set between a large bunker and a
steep bank sloping down to the burn; the scenic 5th with spectacular
views; the 11th requiring a demanding tee shot with trees and out of
bounds to the left, then a steep rise to a very fast green. The 15th is a
difficult par 3 where accuracy is paramount with ground sloping away
either side of the green.

Creachmore: 18 Holes, 6308yds, Par 70, SSS 72,
Course record 64. Club membership 600.

Visitors Mon-Sun & BHs. Booking required. Dress code
Societies booking required. **Green Fees** £45 per day, £35 per
round (£50/£40 weekends). Seasonal variations may apply **Course
Designer** James Braid **Facilities** ⑪ ⑩ 🍴 ⛳ 🏌 ⚐ 🏠 ⚑
⚑ 🚗 ⚑ **Location** 2.5m NW on A718 from Stranraer
Hotel ★★★ 80% HL Corsewall Lighthouse Hotel, Corsewall
Point, Kirkcolm, STRANRAER ☎ 01776 853220 📄 01776 854231
11 en suite

THORNHILL   Map 11 NX89

Thornhill Golf Club Blacknest DG3 5DW
☎ 01848 331779 & 330546
e-mail: info@thornhillgolfclub.co.uk
web: www.thornhillgolfclub.co.uk
Moorland and parkland with fine views of the southern uplands.

Blacknest: 18 Holes, 6102yds, Par 71, SSS 70,
Course record 63. Club membership 570.

Visitors Mon-Sun & BHs. Booking required. Dress code.
Societies booking required. **Green Fees** not confirmed **Course
Designer** Willie Fernie **Facilities** ⑪ ⑩ 🍴 ⛳ 🏌 ⚐ ⚑ ⚑
🚗 ⚑ **Conf** Corporate Hospitality Days **Location** 1m E of town off
A76
Hotel ★★★★ GA Gillbank House, 8 East Morton Street,
THORNHILL ☎ 01848 330597 📄 01848 331713 6 rooms (6 en suite)

WIGTOWN   Map 10 NX45

Wigtown & Bladnoch Golf Club Lightlands Ter DG8 9DY
☎ 01988 403354
Slightly hilly parkland with fine views over Wigtown Bay to the
Galloway Hills.

9 Holes, 5200yds, Par 68, SSS 67, Course record 63.
Club membership 150.

Visitors Mon-Sun & BHs. **Societies** booking required. **Green Fees** £22
for 18 holes, £13 for 9 holes 🍴 **Course Designer** W Muir **Facilities**
⛳ 🏌 🏠 ⚑ **Location** SW on A714
Hotel ★★★ CHH Kirroughtree House, Minnigaff, NEWTON STEWART
☎ 01671 402141 📄 01671 402425 17 en suite

CITY OF DUNDEE

DUNDEE   Map 11 NO43

Ballumbie Castle Golf Course 3 Old Quarry Rd DD4 0SY
☎ 01382 730026 (club) & 770028 (pro)
📄 01382 730008
e-mail: ballumbie2000@yahoo.com
web: www.ballumbiecastlegolfclub.com
Parkland/heathland course built in 2000. No two holes go in the same
direction and every golf club is required. Water comes into play on 4
holes.

18 Holes, 6157yds, Par 69, SSS 70, Course record 65.
Club membership 550.

Visitors Mon-Sun & BHs. Booking required weekends. Dress code.
Societies welcome. **Green Fees** not confirmed **Prof** Lee Sutherland
Facilities ⑪ ⑩ 🍴 ⛳ 🏌 ⚐ 🏠 ⚑ ⚑ 🚗 ⚑ **Conf**
Corporate Hospitality Days **Location** NE outskirts of town, signed off
A90
Hotel ★★★★ 77% HL Apex City Quay Hotel & Spa, 1 West
Victoria Dock Road, DUNDEE ☎ 0845 365 0000 & 01382 202404
📄 01382 201401 151 en suite

Caird Park Golf Course Mains Loan DD4 9BX
☎ 01382 438871 📄 01382 433211
web: www.dundeecity.gov.uk/golf
18 Holes, 6280yds, Par 72, SSS 69, Course record 65.
Location off A90 Kingsway onto Forfar Rd, left onto Claverhouse Rd,
1st left into Caird Park
Telephone for further details
Hotel ★★★★ 77% HL Apex City Quay Hotel & Spa, 1 West
Victoria Dock Road, DUNDEE ☎ 0845 365 0000 & 01382 202404
📄 01382 201401 151 en suite

Downfield Golf Club Turnberry Av DD2 3QP
☎ 01382 825595 📠 01382 813111
e-mail: downfieldgc@aol.com
web: www.downfieldgolf.co.uk

Past Open Qualifying venue. A course with championship credentials providing an enjoyable test for all golfers.

18 Holes, 6820yds, Par 73, SSS 73, Course record 65. Club membership 750.

Visitors Mon-Fri, Sun & BHs. Booking required. Societies booking required. Green Fees £50-£66 per day, £45-£55 per round Course Designer James Braid Prof Kenny Hutton Facilities ⓣ ⑩ ⓛ ⓓ ⓟ ⓛ ⓐ ⓔ 🍴 ✪ 🚌 ✪ Leisure snooker room Conf Corporate Hospitality Days Location N of city centre, signed at junct A90

Hotel ★★★★ 77% HL Apex City Quay Hotel & Spa, 1 West Victoria Dock Road, DUNDEE ☎ 0845 365 0000 & 01382 202404 📠 01382 201401 151 en suite

EAST AYRSHIRE

GALSTON — Map 11 NS53

Loudoun Golf Club Edinburgh Rd KA4 8PA
☎ 01563 821993 📠 01563 820011
e-mail: secy@loudoungowfclub.co.uk
web: www.loudoungowfclub.co.uk

Pleasant, fairly flat parkland with many mature trees, in the Irvine Valley. Excellent test of golf skills without being too strenuous.

Loudoun: 18 Holes, 6005yds, Par 68, SSS 69, Course record 60. Club membership 850.

Visitors Mon-Fri except BHs. Booking required. Dress code. Societies booking required. Green Fees £40 per day, £30 per 18 holes Facilities ⓣ ⑩ ⓛ ⓓ ⓟ ⓛ ⓐ ⓔ 🚌 ✪ Location NE side of town on A71

Hotel ★★★ 78% HL The Fenwick Hotel, Fenwick, KILMARNOCK ☎ 01560 600478 📠 01560 600334 30 en suite

KILMARNOCK — Map 10 NS43

Annanhill Golf Club Irvine Rd KA1 2RT
☎ 01563 521644 & 521512 (starter)
e-mail: annanhillgolfclub@btconnect.com

Municipal, tree-lined parkland course.

18 Holes, 6224yds, Par 71, SSS 70, Course record 65. Club membership 135.

Visitors Mon-Sun & BHs. Booking required. Societies booking required. Green Fees phone Course Designer Jack McLean Facilities ⓐ 🚌 Location 1m N on B7081

Hotel ★★★ 78% HL The Fenwick Hotel, Fenwick, KILMARNOCK ☎ 01560 600478 📠 01560 600334 30 en suite

Caprington Golf Club Ayr Rd KA1 4UW
☎ 01563 523702 & 521915 (enquiries)
e-mail: caprington.golf@btconnect.com

Municipal parkland course.

18 Holes, 5062yds, Par 68, SSS 68, Course record 63. Club membership 400.

Visitors Mon-Sun & BHs. Dress code. Societies booking required. Green Fees not confirmed 😊 Facilities ⓣ by prior arrangement ⑩ ⓛ ⓓ ⓟ ⓛ ⓐ ⓔ 🚌 ✪ Location 1.5m S on B7038 (Ayr road) at the Caprington Gates

Hotel ★★★ 78% HL The Fenwick Hotel, Fenwick, KILMARNOCK ☎ 01560 600478 📠 01560 600334 30 en suite

MAUCHLINE — Map 11 NS42

Ballochmyle Golf Club Catrine Rd KA5 6LE
☎ 01290 550469
e-mail: ballochmylegolf@btconnect.com
web: www.ballochmylegolfclub.co.uk

Tree-lined parkland course with undulating terrain and small tricky greens.

18 Holes, 5951yds, Par 70, SSS 69, Course record 63. Club membership 730.

Visitors Sun-Fri & BHs. Booking required. Handicap certificate. Dress code. Societies booking required. Green Fees £32.50 per 36 holes, £22.50 per 18 holes (£37.50/£27.50) Facilities ⓣ ⑩ ⓛ ⓓ ⓟ ⓛ ⓐ ⓔ 🚌 ✪ Leisure games room, 2 full size snooker tables Conf Corporate Hospitality Days Location 1m SE on B705

Hotel ★★★★ 76% CHH Enterkine Country House, Annbank, AYR ☎ 01292 520580 📠 01292 521582 14 en suite

PATNA — Map 10 NS41

Doon Valley Golf Course Hillside Park KA6 7JT
☎ 01292 531607

Established parkland course located on an undulating hillside.

9 Holes, 5886yds, Par 70, SSS 70, Course record 56. Club membership 100.

Visitors contact club for details. Societies booking required. Green Fees not confirmed Facilities 🍴 ⓐ Leisure fishing, fitness and games hall nearby Location 10m S of Ayr on the A713

Hotel ★★★★ TH Hotel du Vin at One Devonshire Gardens, 1 Devonshire Gardens, GLASGOW ☎ 0141 339 2001 📠 0141 337 1663 49 en suite

EAST DUNBARTONSHIRE

BALMORE — Map 11 NS57

Balmore Golf Club Golf Course Rd G64 4AW
☎ 01360 620284 📠 01360 622742
web: www.balmoregolfclub.co.uk

18 Holes, 5530yds, Par 66, SSS 67, Course record 61.

Course Designer Harry Vardon Location N off A807
Telephone for further details
Hotel ★★★ 78% CHH Strathblane Country House, Milngavie Road, STRATHBLANE ☎ 01360 770491 📠 01360 770345 10 en suite

Save on Hotels. Book at **theAA.com/hotel**

EAST DUNBARTONSHIRE

BEARSDEN
Map 11 NS57

Bearsden Golf Club Thorn Rd G61 4BP
☎ 0141 586 5300
e-mail: secretary@bearsdengolfclub.com
web: www.bearsdengolfclub.com
Parkland course with 16 greens and 11 teeing areas. Easy walking and views of city and the Campsie Hills.

9 Holes, 6012yds, SSS 69, Course record 64. Club membership 560.
Visitors Mon & Wed. Booking required. Handicap certificate. Dress code. **Societies** booking required. **Green Fees** phone 🏌 **Facilities** 🏌 🍴 🛒 🐾 Location 1m W off A809
Hotel ★★★★ TH Hotel du Vin at One Devonshire Gardens, 1 Devonshire Gardens, GLASGOW ☎ 0141 339 2001 📠 0141 337 1663 49 en suite

Douglas Park Golf Club Hillfoot G61 2TJ
☎ 0141 942 2220 (Clubhouse) 📠 0141 942 0985
e-mail: secretary@douglasparkgolfclub.co.uk
web: www.douglasparkgolfclub.co.uk
Undulating parkland course with a variety of holes.

18 Holes, 5962yds, Par 69, SSS 69, Course record 64. Club membership 900.
Visitors Mon-Sun & BHs. Dress code. **Societies** booking required. **Green Fees** not confirmed **Course Designer** Willie Fernie **Prof** Robert Irvine **Facilities** 🏌 🍴 🛒 🐾 🏠 📷 ⛳ **Location** E side of town on A81
Hotel ★★★★ TH Hotel du Vin at One Devonshire Gardens, 1 Devonshire Gardens, GLASGOW ☎ 0141 339 2001 📠 0141 337 1663 49 en suite

Glasgow Golf Club Killermont G61 2TW
☎ 0141 942 2011 📠 0141 942 0770
e-mail: secretary@glasgowgolfclub.com
web: www.glasgowgolfclub.com
One of the finest parkland courses in Scotland.

Killermont: 18 Holes, 5973yds, Par 70, SSS 69, Course record 63. Club membership 800.
Visitors Mon-Fri except BHs. Booking required. Handicap certificate. Dress code. **Societies** booking required **Green Fees** £85 per day, £70 per round **Course Designer** Tom Morris Snr **Prof** J Greaves **Facilities** 🏌 🍴 🛒 🐾 🏠 📷 ⛳ 🏌 Conf Corporate Hospitality Days **Location** SE side off A81
Hotel ★★★★ 76% HL Menzies Irvine, 46 Annick Road, IRVINE ☎ 01294 274272 📠 01294 277287 128 en suite

Windyhill Golf Club Baljaffray Rd G61 4QQ
☎ 0141 942 2349 📠 0141 942 5874
e-mail: secretary@windyhill.co.uk
web: www.windyhillgolfclub.co.uk
Interesting parkland and moorland course with panoramic views of Glasgow and beyond; testing 12th hole.

18 Holes, 6254yds, Par 71, SSS 70, Course record 64. Club membership 800.
Visitors Mon-Fri except BHs. Handicap certificate. Dress code. **Societies** booking required. **Green Fees** £25 per round, £35 per day **Course Designer** James Braid **Prof** Chris Duffy **Facilities** 🏌 🍴 🛒 🐾 🏠 ⛳ **Conf** Corporate Hospitality Days **Location** 2m NW off B8050, 1.5m from Bearsden cross, just off Drymen road
Hotel ★★★★ 77% HL Beardmore Hotel, Beardmore Street, CLYDEBANK ☎ 0141 951 6000 📠 0141 951 6018 166 en suite

BISHOPBRIGGS
Map 11 NS67

Bishopbriggs Golf Club Brackenbrae Rd G64 2DX
☎ 0141 772 1810 & 772 8938 📠 0141 762 2532
web: www.bishopbriggsgolfclub.com
18 Holes, 6262yds, Par 71, SSS 70, Course record 63.
Course Designer James Braid **Location** 0.5m NW off A803
Telephone for further details
Hotel ★★★★ 78% HL Glasgow Marriott Hotel, 500 Argyle Street, Anderston, GLASGOW ☎ 0141 226 5577 📠 0141 221 9202 300 en suite

Cawder Golf Club Cadder Rd G64 3QD
☎ 0141 761 1281 📠 0141 761 1285
e-mail: secretary@cawdergolfclub.com
web: www.cawdergolfclub.com
Two parkland courses: The Cawder Course is an excellent test of golfing skill, the 14th and 15th being particularly challenging. The Keir Course shorter and flatter, but the smaller greens make for a challenging short game.

Cawder Course: 18 Holes, 6295yds, Par 70, SSS 70, Course record 63.
Keir Course: 18 Holes, 5877yds, Par 68, SSS 68. Club membership 1150.
Visitors Mon-Fri & BHs. Dress code. **Societies** booking required. **Green Fees** £35 per round/£45 per day **Course Designer** James Braid **Prof** Gordon Stewart **Facilities** 🏌 🍴 🛒 🐾 🏠 ⛳ 🏌 **Conf** facs Corporate Hospitality Days **Location** 5 m NE off A803
Hotel ★★★★ 78% HL Glasgow Marriott Hotel, 500 Argyle Street, Anderston, GLASGOW ☎ 0141 226 5577 📠 0141 221 9202 300 en suite

Littlehill Golf Course Auchinairn Rd G64 1UT
☎ 0141 772 1916
18 Holes, 6240yds, Par 70, SSS 70.
Location 3m NE of Glasgow city centre on A803
Telephone for further details
Hotel ★★★★ 78% HL Glasgow Marriott Hotel, 500 Argyle Street, Anderston, GLASGOW ☎ 0141 226 5577 📠 0141 221 9202 300 en suite

KIRKINTILLOCH　　　　　　Map 11 NS67

Hayston Golf Club Campsie Rd G66 1RN
☎ 0141 776 1244 📠 0141 776 9030
web: www.haystongolf.com

18 Holes, 6042yds, Par 70, SSS 70, Course record 60.

Course Designer James Braid **Location** 1m NW off A803
Telephone for further details
Hotel ★★★★ 81% HL The Westerwood Hotel & Golf Resort, 1
St Andrews Drive, Westerwood, CUMBERNAULD ☎ 01236 457171
📠 01236 738478 148 en suite

Kirkintilloch Golf Club Todhill, Campsie Rd G66 1RN
☎ 0141 776 1256 & 775 2387 📠 0141 775 2424
e-mail: secretary@kirkintillochgolfclub.co.uk
web: www.kirkintillochgolfclub.co.uk

Rolling parkland in the foothills of the Campsie Fells. The course was extended some years ago giving testing but enjoyable holes over the whole 18.

18 Holes, 5860yds, Par 70, SSS 69, Course record 64.
Club membership 650.

Visitors Mon-Fri & BHs. Booking required. Handicap certificate. Dress code. **Societies** Booking required. **Green Fees** not confirmed **Course Designer** James Braid **Facilities** ⓦ 🍴 ▤ ☂ 🍷 🏌 📷 ✦
Conf Corporate Hospitality Days **Location** 1m NW off A803
Hotel ★★★★ 81% HL The Westerwood Hotel & Golf Resort, 1
St Andrews Drive, Westerwood, CUMBERNAULD ☎ 01236 457171
📠 01236 738478 148 en suite

LENNOXTOWN　　　　　　Map 11 NS67

Campsie Golf Club Crow Rd G66 7HX
☎ 01360 310244 📠 01360 310244
e-mail: campsiegolfclub@aol.com
web: www.campsiegolfclub.org.uk

Scenic hillside course.

18 Holes, 5507yds, Par 70, SSS 68, Course record 69.
Club membership 300.

Visitors Mon-Sun & BHs. Booking required weekends & BHs.
Societies booking required **Green Fees** £15 per round (£20 weekends)
🍷 **Course Designer** W Auchterlonie **Facilities** ⓦ 🍴 ▤ ☂ 🍷
🏌 📷 **Conf** Corporate Hospitality Days **Location** 0.5m N on B822
Hotel ★★★★ 81% HL The Westerwood Hotel & Golf Resort, 1
St Andrews Drive, Westerwood, CUMBERNAULD ☎ 01236 457171
📠 01236 738478 148 en suite

LENZIE　　　　　　Map 11 NS67

Lenzie Golf Club 19 Crosshill Rd G66 5DA
☎ 0141 776 1535 📠 0141 777 7748
e-mail: club.secretary@ntlbusiness.com
web: www.lenziegolfclub.co.uk

The course is parkland and prominent features include the old beech trees, which line some of the fairways together with thorn hedges and shallow ditches. Extensive larch and fir plantations have also been created. The course is relatively flat apart from a steep hill to the green at the 5th hole.

18 Holes, 5813yds, Par 69, SSS 68, Course record 61.
Club membership 890.

Visitors Mon-Fri, Sun & BHs. Booking required. Handicap certificate. Dress code. **Societies** booking required. **Green Fees** not confirmed **Prof** Jim McCallum **Facilities** ⓦ 🍴 ▤ ☂ 🍷 🏌 📷 ✦
Conf facs Corporate Hospitality Days **Location** N of Glasgow, M80 exit Kirkintilloch
Hotel ★★★★ 81% HL The Westerwood Hotel & Golf Resort, 1
St Andrews Drive, Westerwood, CUMBERNAULD ☎ 01236 457171
📠 01236 738478 148 en suite

MILNGAVIE　　　　　　Map 11 NS57

Clober Golf Club Craigton Rd G62 7HP
☎ 0141 956 1685 📠 0141 955 1416
e-mail: clobergolfclub@btopenworld.com
web: www.clobergc.co.uk

Short parkland course that requires skill in chipping with eight par 3s. Testing 5th hole, par 3 with out of bounds left and right and a burn in front of the tee.

18 Holes, 4963yds, Par 66, SSS 65, Course record 59.
Club membership 600.

Visitors Mon-Fri except BHs. Booking required. Dress code.
Societies booking required. **Green Fees** not confirmed 🍷 **Course Designer** George Lyle **Prof** Gary McFarlane **Facilities** ⓦ 🍴 ▤ ☂
🍷 🏌 📷 🎌 ✦ **Location** NW side of town
Hotel ★★★★ 77% HL Beardmore Hotel, Beardmore Street,
CLYDEBANK ☎ 0141 951 6000 📠 0141 951 6018 166 en suite

Esporta, Dougalston Golf Club Strathblane Rd G62 8HJ
☎ 0141 956 6161
e-mail: golfinghouse@btconnect.com
web: www.esporta.com

A course of tremendous character set in 300 acres of beautiful woodland dotted with drumlins, lakes and criss-crossed by streams and ditches. The course makes excellent use of the natural features to create mature, tree-lined fairways and provides a tough but fair test for the enthusiastic golfer.

Esporta: 18 Holes, 6120yds, Par 70, SSS 71.
Club membership 400.

Visitors Mon-Sun & BHs. Booking required weekends & BHs. Dress code. **Societies** booking required. **Green Fees** £32 per 18 holes (£40 weekends) **Course Designer** Commander Harris **Prof** Daryn Cochrane **Facilities** ⓦ 🍴 ▤ ☂ 🍷 🏌 📷 🎌 ⛳ 🚗 ✦
Leisure hard tennis courts, heated indoor swimming pool, sauna, gymnasium **Conf** facs Corporate Hospitality Days **Location** NE side of town on A81
Hotel ★★★ 78% CHH Strathblane Country House, Milngavie Road, STRATHBLANE ☎ 01360 770491 📠 01360 770345 10 en suite

Hilton Park Golf Club Auldmarroch Estate G62 7HB
☎ 0141 956 4657 📠 0141 956 1215
web: www.hiltonpark.co.uk
Hilton Course: 18 Holes, 6054yds, Par 70, SSS 70,
Course record 65.
Allander Course: 18 Holes, 5487yards, Par 69, SSS 67,
Course record 65.
Course Designer James Braid **Location** 3m NW of Milngavie, on A809
Telephone for further details
Hotel ★★★★ 77% HL Beardmore Hotel, Beardmore Street,
CLYDEBANK ☎ 0141 951 6000 📠 0141 951 6018 166 en suite

EAST LOTHIAN

ABERLADY   Map 12 NT47

Kilspindie Golf Club EH32 0QD
☎ 01875 870358
e-mail: kilspindie@btconnect.com
web: www.kilspindiegolfclub.co.uk
Traditional Scottish seaside links, short but good challenge of golf
and well-bunkered. Situated on the shores of the River Forth with
panoramic views.
18 Holes, 5502yds, Par 69, SSS 66, Course record 59.
Club membership 900.
Visitors contact club for details **Societies** booking required. **Green**
Fees £65 per day, £40 per round (£75/£50 weekends) **Course**
Designer Park & Ross with additions by Braid **Prof** Graham J
Sked **Facilities** ⊕ ⭑◎ 🍴 ⌨ 🍺 ⎍ 🏌 📷 ⛳ ⛳
Leisure driving nets **Conf** Corporate Hospitality Days **Location** N side
of village off A198. Private access at E end of Aberlady
Hotel ★★★★ 82% HL Macdonald Marine Hotel & Spa, Cromwell
Road, NORTH BERWICK ☎ 0844 879 9130 📠 01620 894480
83 en suite

Luffness New Golf Club EH32 0QA
☎ 01620 843336 📠 01620 842933
e-mail: secretary@luffnessnew.com
web: www.luffnessgolf.com
Links course, national final qualifying course for the Open
Championship.
18 Holes, 6328yds, Par 70, SSS 71, Course record 63.
Club membership 750.
Visitors Sun-Fri & BHs. Booking required. Dress code.
Societies booking required. **Green Fees** £95 per day, £80 per round
Course Designer Tom Morris **Facilities** ⊕ ⭑◎ ⌨ 🍺 🍴 ⎍
🍺 ⛳ **Conf** Corporate Hospitality Days **Location** 1m E Aberlady
on A198
Hotel ★★★★ 82% HL Macdonald Marine Hotel & Spa, Cromwell
Road, NORTH BERWICK ☎ 0844 879 9130 📠 01620 894480
83 en suite

DUNBAR   Map 12 NT67

Dunbar Golf Club East Links EH42 1LL
☎ 01368 862317 📠 01368 865202
e-mail: manager@dunbargolfclub.com
web: www.dunbargolfclub.com
Another of Scotland's old links. It is said that it was some Dunbar
members who first took the game of golf to the north of England.
A natural links course on a narrow strip of land, following the
contours of the sea shore. There is a wall bordering one side and the
shore on the other side making this quite a challenging course for
all levels of player. The wind, if blowing from the sea, is a problem.
Qualifying course for the Open Championship.
18 Holes, 6597yds, Par 71, SSS 72, Course record 62.
Club membership 1080.
Visitors Mon-Wed, Fri-Sun & BHs. Booking required.
Societies booking required. **Green Fees** £80 per day, £60 per round
(£105/£85 weekends). Discounts after 3pm **Course Designer** Tom
Morris **Prof** Jacky Montgomery **Facilities** ⊕ ⭑◎ 🍺 ⌨ 🍴
⎍ 📷 🍺 ⛳ 🏌 🍺 🌿 **Conf** Corporate Hospitality Days
Location 0.5m E off A1087
Hotel ★★★★ 82% HL Macdonald Marine Hotel & Spa, Cromwell
Road, NORTH BERWICK ☎ 0844 879 9130 📠 01620 894480
83 en suite

Winterfield Golf Club North Rd EH42 1AU
☎ 01368 863562
e-mail: kevinphillips@tiscali.co.uk
web: www.winterfieldgolfclub.info
Seaside course with superb views.
18 Holes, 5155yds, Par 65, SSS 65, Course record 60.
Club membership 240.
Visitors dress code. **Societies** booking required. **Green Fees** not
confirmed **Course Designer** James Braid **Prof** Kevin Phillips
Facilities ⊕ ⭑◎ 🍺 ⌨ 🍴 ⎍ 📷 🍺 🌿 **Location** W
side of town off A1087
Hotel ★★★★ 82% HL Macdonald Marine Hotel & Spa, Cromwell
Road, NORTH BERWICK ☎ 0844 879 9130 📠 01620 894480
83 en suite

GIFFORD   Map 12 NT56

Castle Park Golf Club Castlemains EH41 4PL
☎ 01620 810733
e-mail: castleparkgolf@hotmail.com
web: www.castleparkgolfclub.co.uk
Naturally undulating parkland course in beautiful setting with much
wild life. Wide rolling fairways on the first nine with tantalising water
and dyke hazards. The mature back nine is shorter but full of hidden
surprises requiring good golfing strategy when passing Yester Castle.
18 Holes, 6443yds, Par 72, SSS 71, Course record 65.
Club membership 430.
Visitors Mon-Sun & BHs. Booking required weekends & BHs.
Societies booking required. **Green Fees** £35 per day, £24 per round
(weekends £45/£32) **Course Designer** Archie Baird **Prof** Derek
Small **Facilities** ⊕ ⭑◎ 🍺 ⌨ 🍴 ⎍ 📷 🌿 **Conf**
Corporate Hospitality Days **Location** off B6355, 2m S of Gifford
Hotel ★★★★ FH The Old Farmhouse, Redshill Farm, GIFFORD
☎ 01620 810406 & 07971 115848 3 rooms

Gifford Golf Club Edinburgh Rd EH41 4JE
☎ 01620 810591
e-mail: secretary@giffordgolfclub.com
web: www.giffordgolfclub.com
One of the oldest clubs in East Lothian. A gently undulating 9 hole course in the picturesque setting of the Lammermuir Hills, providing a challenging round of golf in relaxed and peaceful surroundings.
9 Holes, 6057yds, Par 71, SSS 69. Club membership 600.
Visitors contact club for details **Societies** booking required **Green Fees** not confirmed **Facilities** 🍴 ⛳ 🚻 👤 ⛳ ♂ ♂ **Location** 1m SW of village, off B6355
Hotel ★★★★ FH The Old Farmhouse, Redshill Farm, GIFFORD ☎ 01620 810406 & 07971 115848   3 rooms

GULLANE
Map 12 NT48

Gullane Golf Club West Links Rd EH31 2BB
☎ 01620 842255 📄 01620 842327
e-mail: bookings@gullanegolfclub.com
web: www.gullanegolfclub.com
Gullane is a delightful village and one of Scotland's great golf centres. The game has been played on the three links courses for over 300 years and the club was formed in 1882. The No. 1 course (a Final Qualifier when The Open is played at Muirfield) is literally in the village and the three courses stretch out along the coast line. All have magnificent views over the Firth of Forth, standing on the highest point at the 7th tee is reported as one of the "finest views in golf".
Course No 1: 18 Holes, 6466yds, Par 71, SSS 72, Course record 65.
Course No 2: 18 Holes, 6385yds, Par 71, SSS 71.
Course No 3: 18 Holes, 5259yds, Par 68.
Club membership 1200.
Visitors Mon-Sun & BHs. Booking preferred. Dress code. **Societies** welcome. **Green Fees** Course 1 £90 per round (£105 weekends). Course 2 £45 per round (£50 weekends). Course 3 £29 per round (£35 weekends) Prof Alasdair Good **Facilities** 🍴 🍽 🍴 ⛳ 🚻 👤 ⛳ ♂ ♂ 🏌 Leisure golf museum
Conf Corporate Hospitality Days **Location** W end of village on A198
Hotel ★★★★ 82% HL Macdonald Marine Hotel & Spa, Cromwell Road, NORTH BERWICK ☎ 0844 879 9130 📄 01620 894480   83 en suite

Muirfield (Honourable Company of Edinburgh Golfers) see page 331
Duncur Rd, Muirfield EH31 2EG
☎ 01620 842123 📄 01620 842977
e-mail: hceg@muirfield.org.uk
web: www.muirfield.org.uk

HADDINGTON
Map 12 NT57

Haddington Golf Club Amisfield Park EH41 4PT
☎ 01620 822727 & 823627 📄 01620 826580
web: www.haddingtongolf.co.uk
18 Holes, 6335yds, Par 71, SSS 71, Course record 63.
Location E side of town centre
Telephone for further details
Hotel ★★★★ 82% HL Macdonald Marine Hotel & Spa, Cromwell Road, NORTH BERWICK ☎ 0844 879 9130 📄 01620 894480   83 en suite

LONGNIDDRY
Map 12 NT47

Longniddry Golf Club Links Rd EH32 0NL
☎ 01875 852141 📄 01875 853371
e-mail: secretary@longniddrygolfclub.co.uk
web: www.longniddrygolfclub.co.uk
Undulating seaside links and partial woodland course with no par 5s. One of the numerous courses which stretch east from Edinburgh to Dunbar. The inward half is more open than the wooded outward half, but can be difficult in prevailing west wind.
Longniddry: 18 Holes, 6044yds, Par 68, SSS 70, Course record 62. Club membership 1100.
Visitors Mon-Fri & BHs. Limited play weekends.. Booking required. Handicap certificate. Dress code. **Societies** booking required. **Green Fees** not confirmed **Course Designer** H S Colt Prof John Gray **Facilities** 🍴 🍽 🍴 ⛳ 🚻 👤 🏠 ⛳ ♂ ♂ Conf Corporate Hospitality Days **Location** N side of village off A198
Hotel ★★★ 79% HL Best Western Kings Manor, 100 Milton Road East, EDINBURGH ☎ 0131 669 0444 & 468 8003 📄 0131 669 6650   95 en suite

MUSSELBURGH
Map 11 NT37

Musselburgh Golf Club Monktonhall EH21 6SA
☎ 0131 665 2005 📄 0131 665 4435
e-mail: secretary@themusselburghgolfclub.com
web: www.themusselburghgolfclub.com
Testing parkland course with natural hazards including trees and a burn; easy walking.
18 Holes, 6725yds, Par 71, SSS 72, Course record 64. Club membership 1000.
Visitors Mon-Fri, Sun & BHs. Dress code **Societies** booking required. **Green Fees** not confirmed **Course Designer** James Braid Prof Norman Huguet **Facilities** 🍴 🍽 🍴 ⛳ 🚻 👤 🏠 ⛳ ♂ 🚜 ♂ Conf Corporate Hospitality Days **Location** 1m S on B6415
Hotel ★★★ 79% HL Best Western Kings Manor, 100 Milton Road East, EDINBURGH ☎ 0131 669 0444 & 468 8003 📄 0131 669 6650   95 en suite

MUIRFIELD
(HONOURABLE COMPANY OF EDINBURGH GOLFERS)
EAST LOTHIAN - GULLANE - MAP 12 NT48

The original course at Muirfield was designed by Old Tom Morris in 1891 but the current course was designed by Harry Colt. It is generally considered to be one of the top ten courses in the world. The club itself has an excellent pedigree: it was founded in 1744, making it just 10 years older than the Royal and Ancient. Muirfield is the only course to have hosted the Open (15 times, the most recent in 2002), the Amateur, the Mid Amateur, the Senior British Open, the Ryder Cup, the Walker Cup, the Home Internationals and the Curtis Cup. It is consistently ranked as one of the world's most exclusive golf courses and is hosting the Open Championship in 2013. The course has recently been re-designed by Martin Hawtree.

Duncur Rd, Muirfield EH31 2EG ☎ 01620 842123 📄 01620 842977
e-mail: hceg@muirfield.org.uk web: www.muirfield.org.uk
Muirfield Course: 18 Holes, 6673yds, Par 70, SSS 73, Course record 68. Club membership 700.
Visitors Tue & Thu. Booking required. Handicap certificate. Dress code. **Green Fees** £240 per 36 holes, £190 per 18 holes **Course Designer** Harry Colt/Martin Hawtree **Facilities** ℗ by prior arrangement 🖥 🍴 ⚑ ⛳ ✦
Location NE of village, off A198 next to Greywalls Hotel
Hotel ★★★★ 82% HL Macdonald Marine Hotel & Spa, Cromwell Road, NORTH BERWICK ☎ 0844 879 9130 📄 01620 894480 83 en suite

Musselburgh Old Course & Golf Club 10 Balcarres Rd EH21 7SD
☎ 0131 665 5438 (starter) & 665 6981(club)
🖷 0131 653 1770
web: www.mocgc.com

9 Holes, 2874yds, Par 34, SSS 34, Course record 29.

Location 1m E of town off A1
Telephone for further details
Hotel ★★★ 79% HL Best Western Kings Manor, 100 Milton Road East, EDINBURGH ☎ 0131 669 0444 & 468 8003 🖷 0131 669 6650 95 en suite

NORTH BERWICK   Map 12 NT58

Glen Golf Club East Links, Tantallon Ter EH39 4LE
☎ 01620 892726 🖷 01620 895447
e-mail: secretary@glengolfclub.co.uk
web: www.glengolfclub.co.uk

A popular course with a good variety of holes including the famous 13th, par 3 Sea Hole. The views of the town, the Firth of Forth and the Bass Rock are breathtaking.

18 Holes, 6275yds, Par 70, SSS 70. Club membership 650.

Visitors Mon-Sun & BHs. Booking required. Dress code.
Societies welcome. **Green Fees** £56 per day, £42 per round (£70/£55 Sat & Sun) **Course Designer** Ben Sayers/James Braid **Facilities** ⊕ ⏿⚞ 🍴 🏌 🛒 🚻 ☂ 🚗 ✆ **Conf** facs Corporate Hospitality Days **Location** A1 onto A198 to North Berwick. Right at seabird centre, sea-wall road
Hotel ★★★★ 82% HL Macdonald Marine Hotel & Spa, Cromwell Road, NORTH BERWICK ☎ 0844 879 9130 🖷 01620 894480 83 en suite

North Berwick Golf Club Beach Rd EH39 4BB
☎ 01620 892135 🖷 01620 893274
e-mail: secretary@northberwickgolfclub.com
web: www.northberwickgolfclub.com

Another of East Lothian's famous courses, the links at North Berwick is still popular. A classic championship links, it has many hazards including the beach, streams, bunkers, light rough and low walls. The great hole on the course is the 15th, the famous Redan. Hosted the Amateur Championship in 2010 and will host Final Qualifying for the Open Championship in 2013.

West Links: 18 Holes, 6458yds, Par 71, SSS 71, Course record 63. Club membership 730.

Visitors Mon-Sun & BHs. Booking required. Handicap certificate. Dress code. **Societies** welcome. **Green Fees** £110 per day, £85 per round (£95 weekends) **Course Designer** David Strath & others **Prof** M Huish **Facilities** ⊕ ⏿⚞ 🏌 🛒 🚻 ☂ 🚗 ✆ **Location** W side of town on A198
Hotel ★★★★ 82% HL Macdonald Marine Hotel & Spa, Cromwell Road, NORTH BERWICK ☎ 0844 879 9130 🖷 01620 894480 83 en suite

Whitekirk Golf & Country Club EH39 5PR
☎ 01620 870300 🖷 01620 870330
e-mail: countryclub@whitekirk.com
web: www.whitekirk.com

Scenic coastal course with lush green fairways, gorse covered rocky banks and stunning views. Natural water hazards and strong sea breezes make this well-designed course a good test of golf.

18 Holes, 6526yds, Par 72, SSS 72, Course record 64. Club membership 400.

Visitors Mon-Sun & BHs. Booking required weekends. Dress code. **Societies** booking required. **Green Fees** £52.50 per day, £35 per round (£58.50/£39 weekends) **Course Designer** Cameron Sinclair **Prof** Paul Wardell **Facilities** ⊕ ⏿⚞ 🏌 🛒 🚻 ☂ 🚗 ✆ **Leisure** sauna, gymnasium, health spa **Conf** facs Corporate Hospitality Days **Location** on A198 E of North Berwick and 3m off A199. Leave A1 Expressway, Edinburgh to Berwick Upon Tweed road to Dunbar or Haddington onto A199
Hotel ★★★★ 82% HL Macdonald Marine Hotel & Spa, Cromwell Road, NORTH BERWICK ☎ 0844 879 9130 🖷 01620 894480 83 en suite

PRESTONPANS   Map 11 NT37

Royal Musselburgh Golf Club Prestongrange House EH32 9RP
☎ 01875 810276 🖷 01875 810276
e-mail: royalmusselburgh@btinternet.com
web: www.royalmusselburgh.co.uk

Tree-lined parkland course, home to the fifth oldest club in the world, and overlooking the Firth of Forth. Well maintained and providing an excellent challenge. The final third of the course can make or break a score. The tough six hole finish stretches from the long par 4 13th including The Gully, a par 3 14th where to be short is to court disaster, followed by the par 4 15th huddled tight beside trees to the left. A precision drive is required to find the rollercoaster fairway and from there a long iron or fairway wood is played over an uphill approach to a tilting green.

18 Holes, 6237yds, Par 70, SSS 70, Course record 64. Club membership 1000.

Visitors Mon-Thu, weekends & BHs. Fri am. Booking require weekends. Dress code. **Societies** booking required. **Green Fees** £48 per day, £38 per round (£45 per round weekends) 🚭 **Course Designer** James Braid **Prof** John Henderson **Facilities** ⊕ ⏿⚞ 🏌 🛒 🚻 ☂ 🚗 ✆ ✆ **Conf** facs Corporate Hospitality Days **Location** W of town centre on B1361 to North Berwick
Hotel ★★★ 79% HL Best Western Kings Manor, 100 Milton Road East, EDINBURGH ☎ 0131 669 0444 & 468 8003 🖷 0131 669 6650 95 en suite

EAST RENFREWSHIRE

BARRHEAD   Map 11 NS45

Fereneze Golf Club Fereneze Av G78 1HJ
☎ 0141 880 7058 🖷 0141 881 7149
web: www.ferenezegolfclub.co.uk

18 Holes, 5962yds, Par 71, SSS 69, Course record 65.

Location NW side of town off B774
Telephone for further details
Hotel ★★★ 80% HL Uplawmoor Hotel, Neilston Road, UPLAWMOOR ☎ 01505 850565 🖷 01505 850689 14 en suite

CLARKSTON   Map 11 NS55

Cathcart Castle Golf Club Mearns Rd G76 7YL
☎ 0141 638 9449 ▤ 0141 638 1201
e-mail: secretary@cathcartcastle.com
web: www.cathcartcastle.com
Tree-lined parkland course, with undulating terrain.
18 Holes, 5861yds, Par 69, SSS 69. Club membership 995.
Visitors Mon-Fri except BHs. Booking required. Dress code.
Societies booking required. **Green Fees** £45 per day, £30 per round
Course Designer James Braid **Prof** Stephen Duncan **Facilities** ⒯
†◎ ⅃ ☐ ⌱ ⅄ 🖿 ✔ ✔ **Location** 0.75m SW off A726
Hotel ★★★★ 76% HL Menzies Glasgow, 27 Washington Street,
GLASGOW ☎ 0141 222 2929 & 270 2323 ▤ 0141 270 2301
141 en suite

EAGLESHAM   Map 11 NS55

Bonnyton Golf Club Kirktonmoor Rd G76 0QA
☎ 01355 303030 ▤ 01355 303151
e-mail: secretarybgc@btconnect.com
web: www.bonnytongolfclub.com
Dramatic moorland course offering spectacular views of beautiful
countryside as far as snow-capped Ben Lomond. Tree-lined fairways,
plateau greens, natural burns and well-situated bunkers and a unique
variety of holes offer golfers both challenge and reward.
18 Holes, 6231yds, Par 72, SSS 71, Course record 63.
Club membership 960.
Visitors Mon, Wed-Fri except BHs. Booking required. Handicap
certificate. Dress code. **Societies** booking required. **Green Fees** £47
per round **Course Designer** Alister MacKenzie **Prof** David Andrews
Facilities ⒯ †◎ ⅃ ☐ ⌱ ⅄ 🖿 ✔ **Conf** Corporate
Hospitality Days **Location** 0.25m SW off B764
Hotel ★★★★ 76% HL Menzies Glasgow, 27 Washington Street,
GLASGOW ☎ 0141 222 2929 & 270 2323 ▤ 0141 270 2301
141 en suite

NEWTON MEARNS   Map 11 NS55

East Renfrewshire Golf Club Pilmuir G77 6RT
☎ 01355 500256 ▤ 01355 500323
e-mail: secretary@eastrengolfclub.co.uk
web: www.eastrengolfclub.co.uk
Undulating moorland with loch; prevailing south-west wind. Extensive
views of Glasgow and the southern Highlands. Each hole has its own
unique challenge. Course well maintained and presented.
18 Holes, 6107yds, Par 70, SSS 70, Course record 63.
Club membership 900.
Visitors Mon-Fri & BHs. Booking required. Handicap certificate.
Dress code. **Societies** booking required. **Green Fees** £60 per day,
£45 per round **Course Designer** James Braid **Prof** Stewart Russell
Facilities ⒯ †◎ ⅃ ☐ ⌱ ⅄ 🖿 ✔ **Conf** Corporate
Hospitality Days **Location** 3m SW of Newton Mearns on A77, junct 5
Hotel ★★★ 80% HL Uplawmoor Hotel, Neilston Road, UPLAWMOOR
☎ 01505 850565 ▤ 01505 850689 14 en suite

Eastwood Golf Club Muirshield, Loganswell G77 6RX
☎ 01355 500280 ▤ 01355 500333
e-mail: eastwoodgolfclub@btconnect.com
web: www.eastwoodgolfclub.co.uk
An undulating moorland course situated in a scenic setting. Originally
built in 1937, the course was redesigned in 2003. The greens are now
of modern design, built to USGA specification.
18 Holes, 6071yds, Par 70, SSS 70. Club membership 900.
Visitors Mon-Sun & BHs. Booking required. Dress code.
Societies Booking required. **Green Fees** £40 per day, £30 per 18 holes
Course Designer Graeme J. Webster/Theodore Moone **Prof** Stuart
Wilson **Facilities** ⒯ †◎ ⅃ ☐ ⌱ ⅄ 🖿 ✔ **Location** 2.5m S
of Newton Mearns, on A77
Hotel ★★★ 80% HL Uplawmoor Hotel, Neilston Road, UPLAWMOOR
☎ 01505 850565 ▤ 01505 850689 14 en suite

UPLAWMOOR   Map 10 NS45

Caldwell Golf Club G78 4AU
☎ 01505 850366 (Secretary) & 850616 (Pro)
▤ 01505 850604
web: www.caldwellgolfclub.com
18 Holes, 6294yds, Par 71, SSS 71, Course record 62.
Course Designer W. Fernie **Location** 5m SW of Barrhead on A736
Irvine road
Telephone for further details
Hotel ★★★ 80% HL Uplawmoor Hotel, Neilston Road, UPLAWMOOR
☎ 01505 850565 ▤ 01505 850689 14 en suite

CITY OF EDINBURGH

EDINBURGH   Map 11 NT27

Baberton Golf Club 50 Baberton Av, Juniper Green
EH14 5DU
☎ 0131 453 4911 ▤ 0131 453 4678
e-mail: manager@baberton.co.uk
web: www.baberton.co.uk
Heathland course offering the golfer a variety of interesting and
challenging holes. The outward half follows the boundary of the course
and presents some demanding par 3 and 4 holes over the undulating
terrain. The inward half has some longer, equally challenging holes
contained within the course and presents some majestic views of the
Pentland Hills and the Edinburgh skyline.
18 Holes, 6129yds, Par 69, SSS 70, Course record 64.
Club membership 900.
Visitors Mon-Fri, Sun & BHs. Dress code. **Societies** welcome. **Green
Fees** £60 per day, £40 per round **Course Designer** Willie Park Jnr
Prof Ken Kelly **Facilities** ⒯ †◎ ⅃ ☐ ⌱ ⅄ 🖿 ⏣ 🖨 ✔
Leisure snooker **Conf** Corporate Hospitality Days **Location** 5m W of
city centre off A70
Hotel ★★★★ 80% HL Edinburgh Marriott Hotel, 111 Glasgow
Road, EDINBURGH ☎ 0131 334 9191 ▤ 0131 316 4507 245 en suite

SCOTLAND

SCOTLAND

Braid Hills Golf Course 27 Braid Hills Approach EH10 6JY
☎ 0131 447 6666 📄 0131 651 2299
web: www.edinburghleisure.co.uk
18 Holes, 5345yds, Par 70, SSS 66.
Course Designer Peter McEwan & Bob Ferguson **Location** 2.5m S of city centre off A702
Telephone for further details
Hotel ★★★ 82% HL Best Western Braid Hills Hotel, 134 Braid Road, EDINBURGH ☎ 0131 447 8888 📄 0131 452 8477 67 en suite

Bruntsfield Links Golfing Society 32 Barnton Av EH4 6JH
☎ 0131 336 1479 📄 0131 336 5538
e-mail: secretary@bruntsfield.sol.co.uk
web: www.bruntsfieldlinks.co.uk
Mature parkland course with magnificent views over the Firth of Forth and to the west. Greens and fairways are generally immaculate. Challenging for all categories of handicap. Open Championship regional qualifying course from 2011
Bruntsfield: 18 Holes, 6446yds, Par 71, SSS 71, Course record 63. Club membership 1200.
Visitors Mon-Sun & BHs. Booking required. Handicap certificate. Dress code. Societies booking required. **Green Fees** £85 per day, £60 per round (£90/£65 weekends) **Course Designer** Willie Park Jr/A Mackenzie/Hawtree **Prof** Richard Brian **Facilities** ⊕ ⦿| ⓘ ⌣ ☀| ⛳ 🖼 ⊶ ❍ 🛒 ⛳ **Conf** Corporate Hospitality Days
Location 4m NW of city centre off A90
Hotel ★★★ 75% HL Holiday Inn Edinburgh West, 107 Queensferry Road, EDINBURGH ☎ 0871 942 9025 📄 0131 332 3408 101 en suite

Carrick Knowe Golf Course Carrick Knowe EH12 5UZ
☎ 0131 337 1096 📄 0131 651 2299
18 Holes, 5697yds, Par 70, SSS 69.
Location 3m W of city centre, S of A8
Telephone for further details
Hotel ★★★★ 75% HL Holiday Inn Edinburgh, Corstorphine Road, EDINBURGH ☎ 0871 942 9026 📄 0131 334 9237 303 en suite

Craigentinny Golf Course Fillyside Rd EH7 6RG
☎ 0131 554 7501 📄 0131 651 2299
web: www.edinburghleisure.co.uk
18 Holes, 5205yds, Par 67, SSS 65, Course record 62.
Location NE side of city, between Leith & Portobello
Telephone for further details
Hotel ★★★ 79% HL Best Western Kings Manor, 100 Milton Road East, EDINBURGH ☎ 0131 669 0444 & 468 8003 📄 0131 669 6650 95 en suite

Craigmillar Park Golf Club 1 Observatory Rd EH9 3HG
☎ 0131 667 0047 📄 0131 662 8091
e-mail: secretary@craigmillarpark.co.uk
web: www.craigmillarpark.co.uk
Parkland with good views.
18 Holes, 5825yds, Par 70, SSS 68. Club membership 850.
Visitors contact club for details. Societies booking required. **Green Fees** £40 per day, £30 per round (£40 per round Sun after 3pm) **Course Designer** James Braid **Prof** Scott Gourlay **Facilities** ⊕ ⦿| ⓘ ⌣ ☀| ⛳ 🖼 ⊶ ❍ 🛒 ⛳ **Location** 2m S of city centre off A7
Hotel ★★★ 82% HL Best Western Braid Hills Hotel, 134 Braid Road, EDINBURGH ☎ 0131 447 8888 📄 0131 452 8477 67 en suite

Duddingston Golf Club Duddingston Road West EH15 3QD
☎ 0131 661 4301 📄 0131 661 4301
e-mail: duddingstonproshop@hotmail.com
web: www.duddingstongolfclub.com
Easy walking parkland with a burn as a natural hazard. Testing 11th hole.
18 Holes, 6525yds, Par 72, SSS 72. Club membership 700.
Visitors Mon-Sun & BHs. Booking required. Dress code
Societies welcome. **Green Fees** not confirmed **Course Designer** Willie Park Jnr **Prof** Alastair McLean **Facilities** ⊕ ⦿| ⓘ ⌣ ☀| ⛳ 🖼 ⊶ ❍ 🛒 ⛳ **Conf** facs Corporate Hospitality Days
Location 2.5m SE of city centre off A1
Hotel ★★★ 79% HL Best Western Kings Manor, 100 Milton Road East, EDINBURGH ☎ 0131 669 0444 & 468 8003 📄 0131 669 6650 95 en suite

Kingsknowe Golf Club 326 Lanark Rd EH14 2JD
☎ 0131 441 1145 (Sec) 📄 0131 441 2079
e-mail: louis@kingsknowe.com
web: www.kingsknowe.com

Picturesque parkland course set amid gently rolling hills. This course provides a varied and interesting challenge for all levels of golfers.
18 Holes, 5938yds, Par 69, SSS 69, Course record 63. Club membership 930.
Visitors Mon-Fri & BHs. Dress code. Societies booking required. **Green Fees** not confirmed **Course Designer** A Herd/James Braid **Prof** Chris Morris **Facilities** ⊕ ⦿| ⓘ ⌣ ☀| ⛳ 🖼 ⊶ ❍ 🛒 ⛳ **Leisure** indoor teaching/practice facility **Conf** Corporate Hospitality Days **Location** 4m SW of city centre on A70
Hotel ★★★★ 80% HL Edinburgh Marriott Hotel, 111 Glasgow Road, EDINBURGH ☎ 0131 334 9191 📄 0131 316 4507 245 en suite

Liberton Golf Club 297 Gilmerton Rd EH16 5UJ
☎ 0131 664 3009 (sec)
e-mail: info@libertongc.co.uk
web: www.libertongc.co.uk
Gentle, undulating, wooded parkland with tight fairways and well guarded greens suitable for all standards of golfer.
18 Holes, 5344yds, Par 67, SSS 66. Club membership 846.
Visitors Mon-Sun & BHs. Booking required weekends & BHs. Handicap certificate. Dress code. Societies welcome. **Green Fees** not confirmed **Prof** Iain Seath **Facilities** ⊕ ⦿| ⓘ ⌣ ☀| ⛳ 🖼 ⊶ ❍ **Conf** facs Corporate Hospitality Days **Location** 3m SE of city centre on A7
Hotel ★★★ 82% HL Dalhousie Castle and Aqueous Spa, Bonnyrigg, EDINBURGH ☎ 01875 820153 📄 01875 821936 36 en suite

MARRIOTT DALMAHOY HOTEL GOLF & COUNTRY CLUB
CITY OF EDINBURGH - MAP 11 NT27

The Championship East Course has hosted many major events including the Solheim Cup and the Charles Church Seniors PGA Championship of Scotland. The course has long sweeping fairways and generous greens protected by strategic bunkers. Many of the long par 4 holes offer a serious challenge to any golfer. The signature 18th hole has the green set in front of Dalmahoy's historic hotel with a testing approach over a wide ravine. The shorter West Course offers a different test with tighter fairways requiring more accuracy from the tee. The finishing holes incorporate the Gogar burn meandering through the fairway to create a tough finish.

Kirknewton EH27 8EB ☎ 0131 335 8010 📄 0131 335 3577
e-mail: mbrs.edigs.golf@marriotthotels.com web: www.dalmahoygolf.com
East Course: 18 Holes, 7055yds, Par 73, SSS 74, Course record 69.
West Course: 18 Holes, 5168yds, Par 68, SSS 65, Course record 60. Club membership 748.
Visitors Mon-Sun & BHs. Booking required. Dress code. Societies booking required. Green Fees East Course £70 per 18 holes (£85 weekends). West £40 (£45 weekends). Reduced winter rates Course Designer James Braid Prof Scott Dixon Facilities ⑪ 🍴 ⅃ ☕ 🛋 🏌 🏡 ⚑ ◇ ✦ 🛒 ✦ 🏌 Leisure hard tennis courts, heated indoor swimming pool, sauna, gymnasium, fitness studio, golf academy, health salon Conf facs Corporate Hospitality Days Location 7m W of city on A71
Hotel ★★★★ 80% HL Marriott Dalmahoy Hotel & Country Club, Kirknewton, EDINBURGH ☎ 0131 333 1845 📄 0131 333 1433 215 en suite

Lothianburn Golf Club 106A Biggar Rd, Fairmilehead EH10 7DU

☎ 0131 445 2288 📠 0131 445 5067

e-mail: info@lothianburngc.co.uk

web: www.lothianburngc.co.uk

Situated to the south-west of Edinburgh, on the slopes of the Pentland Hills, the course rises from the clubhouse some 300ft to its highest point at the 13th green. There is only one real climb of note, after playing the 2nd shot to the 9th green. The course is noted for its excellent greens, and challenging holes include the 5th, where one drives for position in order to pitch at almost right angles to a plateau green; and the 14th, longest hole on the course, three-quarters of which is downhill with out of bounds on both sides of the fairway.

18 Holes, 5662yds, Par 71, SSS 69, Course record 64. Club membership 500.

Visitors dress code. **Societies** booking required. **Green Fees** £25 per round (£30 weekends) **Course Designer** J Braid (re-designed 1928) **Prof** Kurt Mungall **Facilities** ⚑ 🍴 🍽 🗪 🛒 👤 🏠 📷 🥤 🍺 🥤 **Conf** Corporate Hospitality Days **Location** 4.5m S of city centre on A702

Hotel ★★★ 82% HL Best Western Braid Hills Hotel, 134 Braid Road, EDINBURGH ☎ 0131 447 8888 📠 0131 452 8477 67 en suite

Marriott Dalmahoy Hotel Golf & Country Club see page 335

Kirknewton EH27 8EB

☎ 0131 335 8010 📠 0131 335 3577

e-mail: mbrs.edigs.golf@marriotthotels.com

web: www.dalmahoygolf.com

Merchants of Edinburgh Golf Club 10 Craighill Gardens EH10 5PY

☎ 0131 447 1219 📠 0131 446 9833

e-mail: admin@merchantsgolf.com

web: www.merchantsgolf.com

Fairly short but testing hill course with superb views over the city and surrounding countryside.

18 Holes, 4889yds, Par 65, SSS 64, Course record 59. Club membership 980.

Visitors contact club for details **Societies** booking required. **Green Fees** not confirmed **Course Designer** Ben Sayers **Prof** Neil Colquhoun **Facilities** ⚑ 🍴 🍽 🗪 🛒 👤 🏠 📷 🥤 **Leisure** snooker room **Conf** facs Corporate Hospitality Days **Location** 2m SW of city centre off A702

Hotel ★★★ 82% HL Best Western Braid Hills Hotel, 134 Braid Road, EDINBURGH ☎ 0131 447 8888 📠 0131 452 8477 67 en suite

Mortonhall Golf Club 231 Braid Rd EH10 6PB

☎ 0131 447 6974 📠 0131 447 8712

e-mail: clubhouse@mortonhallgc.co.uk

web: www.mortonhallgc.co.uk

Moorland and parkland with views over Edinburgh.

18 Holes, 6273yds, Par 72, SSS 71, Course record 62. Club membership 1089.

Visitors Mon, Tue, Thu, Fri & Sun except BHs. Booking required. Handicap certificate. Dress code. **Societies** booking required. **Green Fees** £65 per day, £45 per round (£55 per round weekends) **Course Designer** James Braid/F Hawtree **Prof** Malcolm Leighton **Facilities** ⚑ 🍴 🗪 🛒 👤 🏠 📷 🥤 🚗 🥤 **Location** 3m S of city centre off A702

Hotel ★★★ 82% HL Best Western Braid Hills Hotel, 134 Braid Road, EDINBURGH ☎ 0131 447 8888 📠 0131 452 8477 67 en suite

Murrayfield Golf Club 43 Murrayfield Rd EH12 6EU

☎ 0131 337 3478 📠 0131 313 0721

e-mail: john@murrayfieldgolfclub.co.uk

web: www.murrayfieldgolfclub.co.uk

Parkland on the side of Corstorphine Hill, with fine views.

18 Holes, 5725yds, Par 70, SSS 69. Club membership 815.

Visitors Mon-Sun & BHs. Booking required. Handicap certificate. Dress code. **Societies** booking required. **Green Fees** £50 per day, £40 per round **Prof** Jonnie Cliff **Facilities** ⚑ 🍴 🗪 🛒 👤 🏠 📷 🥤 **Conf** Corporate Hospitality Days **Location** 2m W of city centre off A8

Hotel ★★★ 75% HL Holiday Inn Edinburgh West, 107 Queensferry Road, EDINBURGH ☎ 0871 942 9025 📠 0131 332 3408 101 en suite

Prestonfield Golf Club 6 Priestfield Road North EH16 5HS

☎ 0131 667 9665 📠 0131 667 9665

e-mail: gavincook@prestonfieldgolfclub.co.uk

web: www.prestonfieldgolfclub.co.uk

Parkland with beautiful views, set under the extinct volcano of Arthur's Seat. The course is a gentle walk, but a challenge for golfers of all levels.

18 Holes, 6212yds, Par 70, SSS 70, Course record 66. Club membership 850.

Visitors contact club for details. **Societies** welcome. **Green Fees** £32 per round (£42 per day) **Course Designer** James Braid **Prof** Gavin Cook **Facilities** ⚑ 🍴 🗪 🛒 👤 🏠 📷 🥤 🍺 🥤 **Conf** facs Corporate Hospitality Days **Location** 1.5m S of city centre off A68

Hotel ★★★★★ TH Prestonfield, Priestfield Road, EDINBURGH ☎ 0131 225 7800 📠 0131 220 4392 23 en suite

Ravelston Golf Club 24 Ravelston Dykes Rd EH4 3NZ

☎ 0131 315 2486 📠 0131 315 2486

e-mail: ravelstongc@hotmail.com

Parkland on the north-east side of Corstorphine Hill, overlooking the Firth of Forth.

9 Holes, 5230yds, Par 66, SSS 66, Course record 63. Club membership 610.

Visitors Mon-Fri except BHs. Handicap certificate. Dress code. **Green Fees** £30 per day 🅿 **Course Designer** James Braid **Facilities** 🗪 🛒 👤 **Location** 3m W of city centre off A90

Hotel ★★★★ 80% HL Edinburgh Marriott Hotel, 111 Glasgow Road, EDINBURGH ☎ 0131 334 9191 📠 0131 316 4507 245 en suite

Royal Burgess Golfing Society of Edinburgh 181 Whitehouse Rd, Barnton EH4 6BU
☎ 0131 339 2075 📄 0131 339 3712
e-mail: generalmanager@royalburgess.co.uk
web: www.royalburgess.co.uk

No mention of golf clubs would be complete without the Royal Burgess, which was instituted in 1735 and is the oldest golfing society in Scotland. Its course is a pleasant parkland, and one with a great deal of variety. A club which anyone interested in the history of the game should visit.

18 Holes, 6486yds, Par 71, SSS 71.
Club membership 635.

Visitors Mon-Fri & BHs.Booking required. Dress code.
Societies booking required. **Green Fees** £60 per day **Course Designer** Tom Morris **Prof** Steven Brian **Facilities** ⑪ ⑪ ⓛ ⊡ 🎏 ⚖ 🏠 ⛳ 🚌 ⛳ **Conf** facs Corporate Hospitality Days **Location** 5m W of city centre off A90
Hotel ★★★★ 80% HL Edinburgh Marriott Hotel, 111 Glasgow Road, EDINBURGH ☎ 0131 334 9191 📄 0131 316 4507 245 en suite

---

Silverknowes Golf Course Silverknowes EH4 5ET
☎ 0131 336 3843
web: www.edinburghleisure.co.uk

18 Holes, 6070yds, Par 71, SSS 70.

Location 4m NW of city centre, easy access from city bypass
Telephone for further details
Hotel ★★★ 75% HL Holiday Inn Edinburgh West, 107 Queensferry Road, EDINBURGH ☎ 0871 942 9025 📄 0131 332 3408 101 en suite

Swanston New Golf Club 111 Swanston Rd, Fairmilehead EH10 7DS
☎ 0131 445 2239 📄 0131 445 2239
e-mail: stewart.snedden@swanston.co.uk
web: www.swanstongolf.co.uk

The Swanston is a short yet challenging course situated on the lower slopes of the Pentland Hills with fine views over the city of Edinburgh and the Firth of Forth. The course has recently been re-modelled with 6 new holes on the lower level. The Templar is a par 3 short course with features streams, ponds, full sand based USGA specification greens, bunkers and wide fairways.

Swanston: 18 Holes, 5544yds, Par 68, SSS 67,
Course record 58.
Templar: 9 Holes, 1059yds, Par 27, SSS 30,
Course record 22. Club membership 800.

Visitors Booking required. **Societies** booking required. **Green Fees** From £15 per round (£20 weekends) **Course Designer** Herbert More **Prof** Stuart J Campbell/Oliver Morton **Facilities** ⑪ ⑪ ⓛ ⊡ 🎏 ⚖ 🏠 ⛳ ◇ ⛳ 🚌 ⛳ **Leisure** gymnasium, 9 hole par 3 Templar Course **Conf** facs Corporate Hospitality Days **Location** 4m S of city centre off B701
Hotel ★★★ 82% HL Best Western Braid Hills Hotel, 134 Braid Road, EDINBURGH ☎ 0131 447 8888 📄 0131 452 8477 67 en suite

Torphin Hill Golf Club Torphin Rd, Colinton EH13 0PG
☎ 0131 441 1100 📄 0131 441 7166
e-mail: torphinhillgc@btconnect.com
web: www.torphin.com

Beautiful hillside, heathland course, with fine views of Edinburgh and the Forth Estuary. From 600 to 700ft above sea level with 14 holes set on a relatively flat plateau.

18 Holes, 5285yds, Par 68, SSS 67, Course record 64.
Club membership 450.

Visitors Mon-Sun & BHs. Booking required weekends. Dress code.
Societies welcome. **Green Fees** £25 per day, £18 per round (£25 per round weekends) **Facilities** ⑪ ⑪ ⓛ ⊡ 🎏 ⚖ 🏠 ⛳ ⛳ **Conf** Corporate Hospitality Days **Location** 5m SW of city centre S of A720
Hotel ★★★ 82% HL Best Western Braid Hills Hotel, 134 Braid Road, EDINBURGH ☎ 0131 447 8888 📄 0131 452 8477 67 en suite

Turnhouse Golf Club 154 Turnhouse Rd EH12 0AD
☎ 0131 339 1014 📄 0131 339 5141
e-mail: secretary@turnhousegc.com
web: www.turnhousegc.com

Challenging tree-lined course with numerous par 4s in excess of 400yds. Large sloping greens give a real challenge and the golfer is virtually guaranteed to use all the clubs in the bag.

18 Holes, 6060yds, Par 69, SSS 70, Course record 63.
Club membership 800.

Visitors Mon-Fri & Sun except BHs. Dress code. **Societies** booking required. **Green Fees** £40 per day, £30 per round (£40 per round Sun) **Course Designer** J Braid **Prof** Scott Greive **Facilities** ⑪ ⑪ ⓛ ⊡ 🎏 ⚖ 🏠 ⛳ ⛳ 🚌 ⛳ **Conf** facs Corporate Hospitality Days **Location** 6m W of city centre N of A8
Hotel ★★★★ 80% HL Edinburgh Marriott Hotel, 111 Glasgow Road, EDINBURGH ☎ 0131 334 9191 📄 0131 316 4507 245 en suite

RATHO   Map 11 NT17

Ratho Park Golf Club EH28 8NX
☎ 0131 335 0068 & 335 0069 📄 0131 333 1752
e-mail: secretary@rathoparkgolfclub.co.uk
web: www.rathoparkgolfclub.co.uk

Easy walking parkland, with a converted mansion as the clubhouse.

18 Holes, 5960yds, Par 69, SSS 68, Course record 62.
Club membership 850.

Visitors Mon-Sun & BHs. Booking required. Dress code.
Societies booking required. **Green Fees** £46 per day, £33 per round (£46 per round weekends) **Course Designer** James Braid **Prof** Alan Pate **Facilities** ⑪ ⑪ ⓛ ⊡ 🎏 ⚖ 🏠 ⛳ ⛳ **Conf** Corporate Hospitality Days **Location** 0.75m E, N of A71
Hotel ★★★★ HL Norton House, Ingliston, EDINBURGH ☎ 0131 333 1275 📄 0131 333 5305 83 en suite

SCOTLAND

SOUTH QUEENSFERRY
Map 11 NT17

Dundas Parks Golf Club Dundas Estate EH30 9SS
☎ 0131 331 4252
e-mail: cmkwood@btinternet.com
Parkland course situated on the estate of Dundas Castle, with excellent views.

9 Holes, 6100yds, Par 70, SSS 69, Course record 62.
Club membership 500.

Visitors Mon-Fri & BHs. Booking required. Dress code.
Societies booking required. **Green Fees** £15 per round 🏌
Facilities ⑪ by prior arrangement 🍽 by prior arrangement 🖳
⛏ **Location** 0.5m S on A8000
Hotel ★★★★ HL Norton House, Ingliston, EDINBURGH
☎ 0131 333 1275 🗎 0131 333 5305 83 en suite

FALKIRK

FALKIRK
Map 11 NS88

Falkirk Golf Club Carmuirs, 136 Stirling Rd, Camelon FK2 7YP
☎ 01324 611061 (club) 🗎 01324 639573 (sec)
e-mail: secretary@falkirkgolfclub.co.uk
web: www.falkirkgolfclub.co.uk
Parkland with gorse and streams.

18 Holes, 6230yds, Par 71, SSS 70, Course record 63.
Club membership 800.

Visitors Mon-Fri, Sun & BHs. Booking required Sun. Dress code.
Societies booking required. **Green Fees** £40 per day, £30 per round (£55/£45 Sun) **Course Designer** James Braid **Prof** Stewart Craig
Facilities ⑪ 🍽 🏪 🖳 🍴 ⛏ 🏡 ✂ ⚙ **Conf** Corporate Hospitality Days **Location** 1.5m W on A9
Hotel ★★★★ 72% HL Macdonald Inchyra Grange, Grange Road, POLMONT ☎ 01324 711911 🗎 01324 716134 98 en suite

LARBERT
Map 11 NS88

Falkirk Tryst Golf Club 86 Burnhead Rd FK5 4BD
☎ 01324 562054 🗎 01324 562054
18 Holes, 6053yds, Par 70, SSS 69, Course record 62.
Location on A88
Telephone for further details
Hotel ★★★★ 72% HL Macdonald Inchyra Grange, Grange Road, POLMONT ☎ 01324 711911 🗎 01324 716134 98 en suite

Glenbervie Golf Club Stirling Rd FK5 4SJ
☎ 01324 562605 🗎 01324 551054
web: www.glenberviegolfclub.com
18 Holes, 6438yds, Par 71, SSS 70, Course record 62.
Course Designer James Braid **Location** 2m NW on A9
Telephone for further details
Hotel ★★★★ 72% HL Macdonald Inchyra Grange, Grange Road, POLMONT ☎ 01324 711911 🗎 01324 716134 98 en suite

POLMONT
Map 11 NS97

Grangemouth Golf Club Polmont Hill FK2 0YE
☎ 01324 503840 🗎 01324 503841
18 Holes, 6314yds, Par 71, SSS 71, Course record 65.
Location M9 junct 4, 0.5m N
Telephone for further details
Hotel ★★★★ 72% HL Macdonald Inchyra Grange, Grange Road, POLMONT ☎ 01324 711911 🗎 01324 716134 98 en suite

Polmont Golf Club Manuelrigg, Maddiston FK2 0LS
☎ 01324 711277 🗎 01324 712504
e-mail: polmontgolfclub@btconnect.com
Hilly parkland with small greens protected by bunkers. Views of the River Forth and the Ochil Hills.

9 Holes, 6092yds, Par 72, SSS 70. Club membership 300.
Visitors Mon-Fri & BHs. Sun by arrangement. Dress code.
Societies welcome. **Green Fees** not confirmed 🏌 **Facilities** 🏪
🍴 ⛏ **Location** A805 from Falkirk, 1st right after fire brigade headquarters
Hotel ★★★★ 72% HL Macdonald Inchyra Grange, Grange Road, POLMONT ☎ 01324 711911 🗎 01324 716134 98 en suite

FIFE

ABERDOUR
Map 11 NT18

Aberdour Golf Club Seaside Place KY3 0TX
☎ 01383 860080 🗎 01383 860050
e-mail: manager@aberdourgolfclub.co.uk
web: www.aberdourgolfclub.co.uk
Parkland with lovely views over Firth of Forth.

18 Holes, 5447yds, Par 67, SSS 67, Course record 59.
Club membership 800.

Visitors Mon-Sun & BHs. Booking required. Dress code.
Societies booking required. **Green Fees** Mon-Thu £42 per day, £32 per round, Fri £45/£35, weekends £50/£40 **Prof** David Gemmell
Facilities ⑪ 🍽 🏪 🖳 🍴 ⛏ 🏡 🎯 ✂ 🚜 ⚙ **Location** S side of village
Hotel ★★★ 75% HL Kingswood, Kinghorn Road, BURNTISLAND
☎ 01592 872329 🗎 01592 873123 13 en suite

ANSTRUTHER
Map 12 NO50

Anstruther Golf Club Marsfield, Shore Rd KY10 3DZ
☎ 01333 310956
e-mail: captain@anstruthergolf.co.uk
web: www.anstruthergolf.co.uk
A tricky links course with some outstanding views of the River Forth. The nine holes consist of four par 4s and five par 3s. The 5th hole is rated one of the hardest par 3s anywhere, measuring 245yds from the medal tees.

9 Holes, 4690yds, Par 62, Course record 59.
Club membership 550.

Visitors Mon-Fri, Sat (after 4.30pm), Sun & BHs. Dress code
Societies booking required. **Green Fees** £28 per round (free soft drink), £18 per 9 holes **Course Designer** Tom Morris **Facilities** ⑪
🍽 🏪 🖳 🍴 ⛏ 🎯 ⚙ **Location** turn right at Craw's Hotel, SW off A917
Hotel ★★ 74% SHL Balcomie Links Hotel, Balcomie Road, CRAIL
☎ 01333 450237 🗎 01333 450540 14 en suite

Save on Hotels. Book at **theAA.com/hotel**

FIFE

BURNTISLAND

Map 11 NT28

Burntisland Golf House Club Dodhead, Kirkcaldy Rd
KY3 9LQ
☎ 01592 874093 (Office) & 872116 (Golf)
e-mail: info@burntislandgolfhouseclub.co.uk
web: www.burntislandgolfhouseclub.co.uk
A lush, testing course offering magnificent views over the Forth
estuary.
18 Holes, 5993yds, Par 70, SSS 70, Course record 61.
Club membership 600.
Visitors Mon-Sun & BHs. Booking required. Handicap certificate. Dress
code. **Societies** booking required. **Green Fees** £39 per day, £29 per
round (£48/£36 Fri-Sun) **Course Designer** Willie Park Jnr **Prof** Paul
Wytrazek **Facilities** ⓣ †○† ⓑ ⬚ ¶ ⌿ ⚑ ⚑ ⚑
Conf facs Corporate Hospitality Days **Location** 1m E on B923
Hotel ★★★ 75% HL Kingswood, Kinghorn Road, BURNTISLAND
☎ 01592 872329 ◻ 01592 873123 13 en suite

COLINSBURGH

Map 12 NO40

Charleton Golf Club Charleton KY9 1HG
☎ 01333 340505 ◻ 01333 340583
e-mail: clubhouse@charleton.co.uk
web: www.charleton.co.uk
Parkland course with undulating links style greens and wonderful
views over the Firth of Forth.
18 Holes, 6446yds, Par 72, SSS 72, Course record 65.
Club membership 400.
Visitors Mon-Sun & BHs. Dress code. **Societies** booking required.
Green Fees £44 per day, £27 per round (£54/£32 weekends) **Course
Designer** J Salvesen **Prof** George Finlayson **Facilities** ⓣ †○† ⓑ
⬚ ¶ ⚑ ⚑ ⌿ **Leisure** 9 hole pitch & putt
course. **Conf** Corporate Hospitality Days **Location** off B942, NW of
Colinsburgh
Hotel ★★★★ HL Rufflets Country House, Strathkinness Low Road,
ST ANDREWS ☎ 01334 472594 ◻ 01334 478703 24 en suite

COWDENBEATH

Map 11 NT19

Cowdenbeath Golf Club Seco Place KY4 8PD
☎ 01383 511918
web: www.cowdenbeath-golfclub.com
Dora Course: 18 Holes, 6300yds, Par 71, SSS 70,
Course record 64.
Location off A92 into Cowdenbeath, 2nd right signed
Telephone for further details
Hotel BUD Holiday Inn Express Dunfermline, Lauder College, Halbeath,
DUNFERMLINE ☎ 01383 748220 ◻ 01383 748221 82 en suite

CRAIL

Map 12 NO60

Crail Golfing Society Balcomie Clubhouse, Fifeness
KY10 3XN
☎ 01333 450686 & 450960 ◻ 01333 450416
e-mail: info@crailgolfingsociety.co.uk
web: www.crailgolfingsociety.co.uk
Perched on the edge of the North Sea, the Crail Golfing Society's
courses at Balcomie are picturesque and sporting. Crail Golfing
Society began its life in 1786 and the course is highly thought of by
students of the game both for its testing holes and the standard of
its greens. Craighead Links has panoramic seascape and country
views. With wide sweeping fairways and USGA specification greens
it is a testing but fair challenge.
Balcomie Links: 18 Holes, 5861yds, Par 69, SSS 70,
Course record 64.
Craighead Links: 18 Holes, 6722yds, Par 72, SSS 74,
Course record 68. Club membership 1600.
Visitors Mon-Sun & BHs. Booking required. **Societies** welcome.
Green Fees not confirmed **Course Designer** Tom Morris
Prof Graeme Lennie **Facilities** ⓣ †○† ⓑ ⬚ ¶ ⚑ ⚑ ¶
⌿ ⚑ ⌿ ⚑ **Location** 2m NE off A917
Hotel ★★ 74% SHL Balcomie Links Hotel, Balcomie Road, CRAIL
☎ 01333 450237 ◻ 01333 450540 14 en suite

CUPAR

Map 11 NO31

Cupar Golf Club Hilltarvit KY15 5JT
☎ 01334 653549 ◻ 01334 653549
e-mail: cupargc@fsmail.net
web: www.cupargolfclub.co.uk
Hilly parkland with fine views over north-east Fife. The 5th/14th hole
is most difficult - uphill into the prevailing wind. Said to be the oldest
nine-hole club in the UK.
9 Holes, 5153yds, Par 68, SSS 66, Course record 62.
Club membership 400.
Visitors Sun-Fri & BHs. Booking required. **Societies** booking required.
Green Fees £20 per day ⚑ **Course Designer** Allan Robertson
Facilities ⓣ ⓑ ⬚ ¶ ⚑ ¶ ⌿ **Location** 0.75m S off A92
Hotel ★★★★ HL Rufflets Country House, Strathkinness Low Road,
ST ANDREWS ☎ 01334 472594 ◻ 01334 478703 24 en suite

Elmwood Golf Course Stratheden KY15 5RS
☎ 01334 658780 ◻ 01334 658781
web: www.elmwoodgc.co.uk
18 Holes, 6002yds, Par 70, SSS 68.
Course Designer John Salveson/Howard Swan **Location** M90 junct 8,
A91 to St Andrews, 0.5m before Cupar. At Wisemans Dairy right, right
at next junct, course 400yds on left
Telephone for further details
Hotel ★★★★ CHH Balbirnie House, Balbirnie Park, MARKINCH
☎ 01592 610066 ◻ 01592 610529 30 en suite

SCOTLAND

DUNFERMLINE
Map 11 NT08

Canmore Golf Club Venturefair Av KY12 0PE
☎ 01383 724969 ▤ 01383 731649
e-mail: canmoregolfclub@btconnect.com
web: www.canmoregolfclub.co.uk

Parkland course with excellent turf, moderate in length but a good test of accuracy demanding a good short game. Ideal for 36-hole play, and suitable for all ages.

18 Holes, 5400yds, Par 67, SSS 66, Course record 61. Club membership 650.

Visitors dress code. **Societies** welcome. **Green Fees** £20 per round midweek (£25 weekends). £60 midweek four ball offer (£80 weekends) **Course Designer** Ben Sayers & others **Prof** Daryn Cochrane **Facilities** ⑪ ⑩ ⓫ ☕ ⑭ ⑮ ᔕ ⑯ ⑰ ᕦ **Conf** Corporate Hospitality Days **Location** 1m N on A823
Hotel ★★★ 73% HL King Malcolm, Queensferry Road, DUNFERMLINE ☎ 01383 722611 ▤ 01383 730865 48 en suite

Dunfermline Golf Club Pitfirrane KY12 8QW
☎ 01383 723534 & 729061 ▤ 01383 723547
web: www.dunfermlinegolfclub.com

18 Holes, 6121yds, Par 72, SSS 70, Course record 65.

Course Designer J R Stutt **Location** 2m W of Dunfermline on A994
Telephone for further details
Hotel ★★★ 73% HL King Malcolm, Queensferry Road, DUNFERMLINE ☎ 01383 722611 ▤ 01383 730865 48 en suite

Forrester Park Golf Course Pitdinnie Rd, Cairneyhill KY12 8RF
☎ 01383 880505 ▤ 01383 882430
e-mail: info@forresterparkresort.co.uk
web: www.forresterparkresort.com

Set in the heart of 350 acres of parkland on what was originally the Keavil Estate. Ponds and streams come into play on 9 holes and all greens have been constructed to USGA specifications giving full play all year.

18 Holes, 6296yds, Par 72, SSS 72, Course record 69. Club membership 700.

Visitors Mon-Sun & BHs. Booking required. **Societies** booking required. **Green Fees** not confirmed **Prof** Paul Edgcombe **Facilities** ⑪ ⑩ ⓫ ☕ ⑭ ᔕ ⑯ ⑰ ᕦ ᕤ ᕦ **Conf** facs Corporate Hospitality Days **Location** 2.5m W of Dunfermline in village of Cairneyhill
Hotel ★★★ 73% HL King Malcolm, Queensferry Road, DUNFERMLINE ☎ 01383 722611 ▤ 01383 730865 48 en suite

Pitreavie Golf Club Queensferry Rd KY11 8PR
☎ 01383 722591 ▤ 01383 722592
web: www.pitreaviegolfclub.co.uk

Picturesque woodland course with panoramic view of the Forth Valley. Testing golf.

18 Holes, 6032yds, Par 71, SSS 69. Club membership 700.

Visitors contact club for details. Dress code. **Societies** booking required. **Green Fees** not confirmed **Course Designer** Dr Alister MacKenzie **Prof** Paul Brookes **Facilities** ⑪ ⑩ ⓫ ☕ ⑭ ᔕ ⑯ ᕤ **Conf** Corporate Hospitality Days **Location** M90 junct 2. SE side of town on A823
Hotel ★★★ 73% HL King Malcolm, Queensferry Road, DUNFERMLINE ☎ 01383 722611 ▤ 01383 730865 48 en suite

ELIE
Map 12 NO40

Golf House Club KY9 1AS
☎ 01333 330301 ▤ 01333 330895
web: www.golfhouseclub.org
18 Holes, 6273yds, Par 70, SSS 70, Course record 62.
Location W side of village off A917
Telephone for further details
Hotel ★★★★ INN The Inn at Lathones, Largoward, ST ANDREWS ☎ 01334 840494 ▤ 01334 840694 21 rooms

FALKLAND
Map 11 NO20

Falkland Golf Club The Myre KY15 7AA
☎ 01337 857404
e-mail: falklandgolfclub@gmail.com

A flat, well-kept course with excellent greens and views of East Lomond Hill and Falkland Palace.

9 Holes, 4988yds, Par 67, SSS 65, Course record 62. Club membership 150.

Visitors Mon-Sun & BHs. Booking required Sat. **Societies** welcome. **Green Fees** £15 per 18 holes ⊛ **Facilities** ⑪ by prior arrangement ⓫ ☕ ⑯ ᔕ **Location** N side of town on A912
Hotel ★★★★ CHH Balbirnie House, Balbirnie Park, MARKINCH ☎ 01592 610066 ▤ 01592 610529 30 en suite

GLENROTHES
Map 11 NO20

Glenrothes Golf Club Golf Course Rd KY6 2LA
☎ 01592 754561 ▤ 01592 754561
web: www.glenrothesgolf.org.uk
18 Holes, 6444yds, Par 71, SSS 71, Course record 67.
Course Designer J R Stutt **Location** W side of town off B921
Telephone for further details
Hotel ★★★★ CHH Balbirnie House, Balbirnie Park, MARKINCH ☎ 01592 610066 ▤ 01592 610529 30 en suite

KINCARDINE
Map 11 NS98

Tulliallan Golf Club Alloa Rd FK10 4BB
☎ 01259 730798 ▤ 01259 733950
web: www.tulliallangolf.co.uk
18 Holes, 5965yds, Par 69, SSS 69, Course record 63.
Location 1m NW on A977
Telephone for further details
Hotel ★★★★ 76% HL The Grange Manor, Glensburgh, GRANGEMOUTH ☎ 01324 474836 ▤ 01324 665861 36 en suite

Save on Hotels. Book at **theAA.com/hotel**

FIFE

KINGHORN

Map 11 NT28

Kinghorn Golf Club Burntisland Rd KY3 9RS
☎ 01592 890345 & 890978
e-mail: kgclub@tiscali.co.uk
Municipal course, semi links and parkland, 300ft above sea level with views over the Firth of Forth and the North Sea. Undulating and quite testing.
18 Holes, 5141yds, Par 66, SSS 66, Course record 62.
Club membership 190.
Visitors Mon-Sun & BHs. Dress code. **Societies** booking required.
Green Fees £15 per round, Juniors £5 (£20/£8 weekends) **Course Designer** Tom Morris **Facilities** 🏳 🍴 👤 **Location** N side of town on A921
Hotel ★★★ 78% HL Dean Park, Chapel Level, KIRKCALDY
☎ 01592 261635 🖨 01592 261371 34 en suite

KINGSBARNS

Map 12 NO51

Kingsbarns Golf Links KY16 8QD
☎ 01334 460860 🖨 01334 460877
web: www.kingsbarns.com
18 Holes, 7152yds, Par 72, Course record 62.
Course Designer Kyle Phillips **Location** from St Andrews take A917 toward Crail, pass through village of Kingsbarns, entrance to links signed on left
Telephone for further details
Hotel ★★★★ HL Rufflets Country House, Strathkinness Low Road, ST ANDREWS ☎ 01334 472594 🖨 01334 478703 24 en suite

KIRKCALDY

Map 11 NT29

Dunnikier Park Golf Club Dunnikier Way KY1 3LP
☎ 01592 261599 🖨 01592 642541
e-mail: dunnikierparkgolfclub@btinternet.com
web: www.dunnikierparkgolfclub.com
Parkland, rolling fairways, not heavily bunkered, views of the Firth of Forth.
18 Holes, 6500yds, Par 72, SSS 72, Course record 65.
Club membership 700.
Visitors Mon-Sun & BHs. Booking required. Dress code.
Societies welcome. **Green Fees** phone **Course Designer** R Stutt **Prof** Ian Mair **Facilities** ⓗ 🍴 👤 🏳 🍴 👤 📷 ✦ **Conf** facs
Location 2m N on B981, next to Kirkcaldy High School
Hotel ★★★ 78% HL Dean Park, Chapel Level, KIRKCALDY
☎ 01592 261635 🖨 01592 261371 34 en suite

Kirkcaldy Golf Club Balwearie Rd KY2 5LT
☎ 01592 205240 & 203258 (Pro Shop)
e-mail: enquiries@kirkcaldygolfclub.co.uk
web: www.kirkcaldygolfclub.co.uk
A challenging parkland course in countryside, with beautiful views. A burn meanders by five holes. The club celebrated its centenary in 2004.
18 Holes, 6086yds, Par 71, SSS 70, Course record 64.
Club membership 713.
Visitors Mon-Sun & BHs. Booking required. Dress code.
Societies booking required. **Green Fees** £44 per day, £34 per round (weekends £54/£44) **Course Designer** Tom Morris **Prof** Anthony Caira
Facilities ⓗ 🍴 👤 🏳 🍴 👤 📷 ♟ ✦ ✦ **Conf** facs
Corporate Hospitality Days **Location** SW side of town off A910
Hotel ★★★ 78% HL Dean Park, Chapel Level, KIRKCALDY
☎ 01592 261635 🖨 01592 261371 34 en suite

LADYBANK

Map 11 NO30

Ladybank Golf Club Annsmuir KY15 7RA
☎ 01337 830814 🖨 01337 831505
e-mail: info@ladybankgolf.co.uk
web: www.ladybankgolf.co.uk

Picturesque classic heathland course of championship status set among heather, Scots pines and silver birch and comprising two loops of nine holes. The drive at the dog-leg 3rd and 9th holes requires extreme care as do the 15th and 16th on the back nine. The greens are compact and approach shots require precision to find the putting surface. Open qualifying course since 1978 and again in 2010.
18 Holes, 6602yds, Par 71, SSS 72, Course record 63.
Club membership 1000.
Visitors Sun-Fri & BHs. Booking required. Handicap certificate.
Dress code. **Societies** booking required. **Green Fees** £53 per round weekdays, £43 Apr & Oct (£63 weekends, £53 Apr & Oct). £79 per 36 holes weekdays (£69 Apr & Oct) **Course Designer** Tom Morris **Prof** Sandy Smith **Facilities** ⓗ 🍴 👤 🏳 🍴 👤 📷 ♟ ✦ ✦ **Conf** facs Corporate Hospitality Days **Location** N of town off A92
Hotel ★★★★ CHH Balbirnie House, Balbirnie Park, MARKINCH
☎ 01592 610066 🖨 01592 610529 30 en suite

LESLIE
Map 11 NO20

Leslie Golf Club Balsillie Laws KY6 3EZ
☎ 01592 620040

Challenging parkland course.

9 Holes, 4572yds, Par 68, SSS 65, Course record 59. Club membership 230.

Visitors Mon-Sun & BHs. **Societies** welcome. **Green Fees** not confirmed ⊛ **Course Designer** Tom Morris **Facilities** ⑪ by prior arrangement ᵀ⊙ᵀ by prior arrangement 🏠 ⬜ 🍴 ⚒ **Conf** Corporate Hospitality Days **Location** N side of town off A911 **Hotel** ★★★★ CHH Balbirnie House, Balbirnie Park, MARKINCH ☎ 01592 610066 📄 01592 610529 30 en suite

LEUCHARS
Map 12 NO42

Drumoig Hotel & Golf Course Drumoig KY16 0BE
☎ 01382 541800 (Starter) & 541898 📄 01382 541898
e-mail: drumoig@btconnect.com
web: www.drumoigleisure.com

Set in a parkland environment but plays like a links course in places. Features include Whinstone Quarries and views over to St Andrews and Carnoustie. Water features are demanding, especially on the 9th where the fairway runs between two tiny lochs, also on the 10th and 11th holes.

18 Holes, 6835yds, Par 72, SSS 73, Course record 67. Club membership 350.

Visitors Mon-Sun & BHs. Booking required weekends & BHs. Dress code **Societies** booking required **Green Fees** not confirmed **Facilities** ⑪ ᵀ⊙ᵀ 🏠 ⬜ 🍴 ⚒ 🏠 ⛳ ◆ 🚲 ⚐ ☂ **Conf** facs Corporate Hospitality Days **Location** on A914 between St Andrews & Dundee

Hotel ★★★★ HL Rufflets Country House, Strathkinness Low Road, ST ANDREWS ☎ 01334 472594 📄 01334 478703 24 en suite

St Michaels Golf Club KY16 0DX
☎ 01334 838666 (office) 📄 01334 838789
e-mail: stmichaelsgc@btclick.com
web: www.stmichaelsgolf.co.uk

Parkland with open views over Fife and Tayside. The undulating course weaves its way through tree plantations. The par 3 15th hole is the signature hole and the short par 4 17th, parallel to the railway and over a pond to a stepped green, poses an interesting challenge.

18 Holes, 5806yds, Par 70, SSS 68. Club membership 290.

Visitors Mon-Sun & BHs. Booking required weekends & BHs. **Societies** booking required. **Green Fees** £28 per 18 holes (£32 weekends) **Course Designer** Old Tom Morris **Facilities** ⑪ ᵀ⊙ᵀ by prior arrangement 🏠 ⬜ 🍴 ⚒ ⚐ 🚲 ◆ **Conf** Corporate Hospitality Days **Location** NW side of village on A919 **Hotel** ★★★★ HL Rufflets Country House, Strathkinness Low Road, ST ANDREWS ☎ 01334 472594 📄 01334 478703 24 en suite

LEVEN
Map 11 NO30

Leven Links Golf Course The Promenade KY8 4HS
☎ 01333 428859 & 421390 📄 01333 428859
web: www.leven-links.com

18 Holes, 6506yds, Par 71, SSS 72, Course record 63.

Course Designer Tom Morris **Location** off the A915 Kikcaldy to St Andrews road
Telephone for further details
Hotel ★★★★ CHH Balbirnie House, Balbirnie Park, MARKINCH ☎ 01592 610066 📄 01592 610529 30 en suite

Scoonie Golf Course KY8 4SP
☎ 01333 307007 & 423437 (Starter) 📄 01333 307008
web: www.scooniegolfclub.com

18 Holes, 5494mtrs, Par 67, SSS 66, Course record 62.

Location on coastal road to St. Andrews
Telephone for further details
Hotel ★★★★ CHH Balbirnie House, Balbirnie Park, MARKINCH ☎ 01592 610066 📄 01592 610529 30 en suite

LOCHGELLY
Map 11 NT19

Lochgelly Golf Club Cartmore Rd KY5 9PB
☎ 01592 780174 & 782589 (Pro)

Easy walking parkland, often windy, with spectacular views.

18 Holes, 5491yds, Par 68, SSS 67. Club membership 150.

Visitors Mon-Sun & BHs. Booking required. Handicap certificate. Dress code. **Societies** welcome. **Green Fees** £12 per 18 holes (£20 weekends) **Course Designer** Ian Marchbanks **Prof** Stuart Nellies **Facilities** ⑪ ᵀ⊙ᵀ 🏠 ⬜ 🍴 ⚒ 🏠 ◆ 🚲 ◆ **Location** W side of town off A910, signed
Hotel ★★★ 78% HL Dean Park, Chapel Level, KIRKCALDY ☎ 01592 261635 📄 01592 261371 34 en suite

Lochore Meadows Country Park Golf Course Lochore Meadows Country Park, Crosshill KY5 8BA
☎ 01592 583343 📄 01592 583647
e-mail: info@lochore-meadows.co.uk
web: www.lochore-meadows.co.uk

Lochside course with a stream running through it and woodland nearby. Country park offers many leisure facilities.

9 Holes, 3207yds, Par 72, SSS 71. Club membership 240.

Visitors contact course for details. **Societies** booking required. **Green Fees** £12 per round (weekends £15) **Facilities** ⑪ ⬜ 🏠 **Leisure** fishing, outdoor education centre, childrens play park **Conf** facs **Location** 0.5m W off B920 **Hotel** ★★★★ 73% HL The Green Hotel, 2 The Muirs, KINROSS ☎ 01577 863467 📄 01577 863180 46 en suite

ave on Hotels. Book at **theAA.com/hotel**

FIFE

LUNDIN LINKS
Map 12 NO40

Lundin Golf Club, Golf Rd KY8 6BA
☎ 01333 320202 🖨 01333 329743
e-mail: secretary@lundingolfclub.co.uk
web: www.lundingolfclub.co.uk
A complex links course with open burns, an internal out of bounds
(the old railway line), and strategic bunkering. Lundin presents a
challenge for the thinking golfer where position from the tee rather
than distance will yield just rewards on the scorecard. Renowned
for its beautiful greens and some of the most demanding short par
4s in the game.
18 Holes, 6371yds, Par 71, SSS 71, Course record 62.
Club membership 950.
Visitors Mon-Sun & BHs. Booking required. Dress code.
Societies booking required. **Green Fees** not confirmed **Course
Designer** James Braid **Prof** Ron Walker **Facilities** ⓣ 🏌 ⬛ ☕
🏌 ⬛ 🏠 ⛳ **Location** W side of village off A915
Hotel ★★★★ CHH Balbirnie House, Balbirnie Park, MARKINCH
☎ 01592 610066 🖨 01592 610529 30 en suite

Lundin Ladies Golf Club Woodielea Rd KY8 6AR
☎ 01333 320832 & 320022
e-mail: llgolfclub@tiscali.co.uk
Short, lowland course with Bronze Age standing stones on the second
fairway and coastal views.
9 Holes, 2365yds, Par 68, SSS 68, Course record 64.
Club membership 260.
Visitors Mon, Tue, Thu-Sun & BHs. **Societies** welcome. **Green
Fees** £16 per 18 holes, £9 per 9 holes (£18/£10 weekends) 🅿 **Course
Designer** James Braid **Facilities** ⬛ ⬛ 🏠 ⛳ **Location** W side
of village off A915
Hotel ★★★★ CHH Balbirnie House, Balbirnie Park, MARKINCH
☎ 01592 610066 🖨 01592 610529 30 en suite

MARKINCH
Map 11 NO20

Balbirnie Park Golf Club Balbirnie Park KY7 6NR
☎ 01592 612095 & 752006 (tee times)
🖨 01592 612383/752006
e-mail: golfpro@balbirniegolf.com
web: www.balbirniegolf.com
Set in the magnificent Balbirnie Park, a fine example of the best in
traditional parkland design, with natural contours the inspiration
behind the layout. A course that will suit all standards of golfers.
18 Holes, 6313yds, Par 71, SSS 71. Club membership 900.
Visitors Mon-Sun & BHs. **Societies** welcome. **Green Fees** £40 per
round, £50 per day (£45/£60 weekends) **Course Designer** Fraser
Middleton **Prof** Craig Donnelly **Facilities** ⓣ 🏌 ⬛ ⬛ 🏌
⬛ 🏠 ⛳ ◇ ⛳ 🚿 ⛳ **Conf** facs Corporate Hospitality Days
Location 2m E of Glenrothes, off A92
Hotel ★★★★ CHH Balbirnie House, Balbirnie Park, MARKINCH
☎ 01592 610066 🖨 01592 610529 30 en suite

ST ANDREWS
Map 12 NO51

British Golf Museum (situated opposite Royal & Ancient
Golf Club)
☎ 01334 460046
web: www.britishgolfmuseum.co.uk
The British Golf Museum sits at the heart of the home of golf, just
67 yards from the famous Old Course. 2010 marked the 150th
Anniversary of The Open Championship and the 20th Anniversary of
the British Golf Museum. Imaginative exhibitions, hands on activities
and stunning multimedia displays bring to life over 500 years of
golfing history.
Open all year: Apr-Oct, Mon-Sat 9.30am-5.30pm, Sun 10am-5pm.
Nov-Mar 10am-4pm. There is a charge.

The Duke's Craigtoun KY16 8NS
☎ 01334 470214 🖨 01334 479456
e-mail: reservations@oldcoursehotel.co.uk
web: www.playthedukes.com

Now owned and managed by The Old Course Hotel, with a
spectacular setting above St Andrews, this is one of the finest
heathland courses in the UK, and the only one in St Andrews. Five
sets of tees are on offer, with something for every ability. Rated as
one of the UK's top 100 courses.
The Duke's Course: 18 Holes, 7512yds, Par 71, SSS 73,
Course record 71. Club membership 300.
Visitors contact course for details. **Societies** welcome. **Green
Fees** £115 per round Jun-Oct, Winter rates available **Course
Designer** Tim Liddy **Prof** Ayden Roberts-Jones **Facilities** ⓣ 🏌
⬛ ⬛ 🏌 ⬛ 🏠 🏠 ◇ ⛳ 🚿 ⛳ ⛳ **Leisure** sauna,
gymnasium **Conf** facs Corporate Hospitality Days **Location** A91 to
St Andrews, turn off for Strathkiness, follow signs to The Duke's,
Craigtoun
Hotel ★★★★★ HL The Old Course Hotel, Golf Resort & Spa, ST
ANDREWS ☎ 01334 474371 🖨 01334 477668 144 en suite

SCOTLAND

Fairmont St Andrews KY16 8PN
☎ 01334 837000 📠 01334 471115
e-mail: standrews.scotland@fairmont.com
web: www.fairmontgolf.com

Two championship seaside courses overlooking the town and the North Sea coastline. The Torrance has recently been redeveloped to give one of the finest new courses in Scotland and is a Open Championship qualifying course. The Kittocks course, a stunning clifftop course with unique characteristics, has a new layout, providing a challenge to all levels of golfer.

Torrance: 18 Holes, 7230yds, Par 72, SSS 75, Course record 66.
Kittocks: 18 Holes, 7192yds, Par 71, SSS 75.

Visitors Contact club for details. **Societies** booking required. **Green Fees** £45-£120 **Course Designer** S Torrance/G Sarazen/B Devlin **Prof** John Kerr **Facilities** ⑪ †◎¶ 🏌 ⬜ 🍴 ⚐ 🏠 ⛳ ♦ 🚶 🛌 ⚘ 🐾 **Leisure** heated indoor swimming pool, sauna, gymnasium, steam room **Conf** facs Corporate Hospitality Days **Location** On A917 from St Andrews to Kingsbarns. On outskirts of town on Crail road
Hotel ★★★★★ 85% HL Fairmont St Andrews, Scotland, ST ANDREWS ☎ 01334 837000 📠 01334 471115 209 en suite

See advert on this page

St Andrews Links see page 345
Pilmour House KY16 9SF
☎ 01334 466666 📠 01334 479555
e-mail: enquiries@standrews.org.uk
web: www.standrews.org.uk

SALINE
Map 11 NT09

Saline Golf Club Kinneddar Hill KY12 9LT
☎ 01383 852591 📠 01383 852591
e-mail: salinegolfclub@btconnect.com
web: www.saline-golf-club.co.uk

Hillside parkland course with excellent turf and panoramic view of the Forth Valley.

9 Holes, 5384yds, Par 68, SSS 66. Club membership 300.

Visitors Mon-Fri & Sun except BHs. Booking required Sun. Dress code **Societies** booking required. **Green Fees** £12.50 per day, £9.50 per 9 holes (£14.50 Sun) 🅿 **Facilities** ⑪ by prior arrangement †◎¶ by prior arrangement 🏌 ⬜ 🍴 ⚐ **Location** M90 junct 4, 7m W following signs for Dollar
Hotel ★★★ 73% HL King Malcolm, Queensferry Road, DUNFERMLINE ☎ 01383 722611 📠 01383 730865 48 en suite

TAYPORT
Map 12 NO42

Scotscraig Golf Club Golf Rd DD6 9DZ
☎ 01382 552515 📠 01382 553130
e-mail: scotscraig@scotscraiggolfclub.com
web: www.scotscraiggolfclub.com

Combined with heather and rolling fairways, the course is part heathland, part links, with the greens being renowned for being fast and true. Qualifying course for the Open Championship.

18 Holes, 6330yds, Par 71, SSS 72, Course record 65. Club membership 835.

Visitors Mon-Sun & BHs. Booking required. Dress code. **Societies** booking required. **Green Fees** £75 per day, £56 per round (£100/£72 am/£62 pm weekends) **Course Designer** James Braid **Prof** Craig Mackie **Facilities** ⑪ †◎¶ 🏌 ⬜ 🍴 ⚐ 🏠 ⛳ ♦ 🚶 ⚘ **Conf** Corporate Hospitality Days **Location** S side of village off B945
Hotel ★★★★ 77% HL Apex City Quay Hotel & Spa, 1 West Victoria Dock Road, DUNDEE ☎ 0845 365 0000 & 01382 202404 📠 01382 201401 151 en suite

ST ANDREWS LINKS

FIFE - ST ANDREWS - MAP 12 NO51

Golf was first played here around 1400 and the Old Course is acknowledged worldwide as the Home of Golf. The Old Course has played host to the greatest golfers in the world and many of golf's most dramatic moments. The New Course (6625yds) was opened in 1895, having been laid out by Old Tom Morris. The Jubilee was opened in 1897 and is 6742yds long from the medal tees. A shorter version of the Jubilee Course is also available, known as the Bronze Course, measuring 5573yds. There is no handicap limit for the shorter course and it is best for lower and middle handicap golfers. The Strathtyrum has a shorter, less testing layout, best for high handicap golfers. The nine-hole Balgrove Course, upgraded and re-opened in 1993, is best for beginners and children. The cliff top Castle Course opened in 2008. The facilities and courses at St Andrews make this the largest golf complex in Europe.

Pilmour House KY16 9SF ☎ 01334 466666 🖷 01334 479555
e-mail: enquiries@standrews.org.uk **web:** www.standrews.org.uk
Old Course: 18 Holes, 6721yds, Par 72, SSS 73, Course record 64.
New Course: 18 Holes, 6625yds, Par 71, SSS 73, Course record 64.
Jubilee Course: 18 Holes, 6742yds, Par 72, SSS 73, Course record 63.
Eden Course: 18 Holes, 6112yds, Par 70, SSS 70.
Strathtyrum Course: 18 Holes, 5094yds, Par 69, SSS 69.
Balgove Course: 9 Holes, 1530yds, Par 30, SSS 30.
Castle Course: 18 Holes, 7200yds, Par 72.
Visitors Old Course Mon-Sat & BHs. Other courses Mon-Sun & BHs. Handicap certificate required for Old Course. Dress code. **Societies** welcome. **Green Fees** contact course for details **Prof** Steve North **Facilities** ⑪ ⑩ ⓛ ☐ ▦ ⚲ ⚑ 🛢 ⚘ ⚹ **Conf** Corporate Hospitality Days **Location** off A91
Hotel ★★★★★ HL The Old Course Hotel, Golf Resort & Spa, ST ANDREWS ☎ 01334 474371 🖷 01334 477668 144 en suite

SCOTLAND

THORNTON

Map 11 NT29

Thornton Golf Club Station Rd KY1 4DW
☎ 01592 771111 🖹 01592 774955
e-mail: thorntongolf@btconnect.com
web: www.thorntongolfclub.co.uk

A relatively flat, lightly tree-lined parkland course, bounded on three sides by a river that comes into play at holes 14 to 16.

18 Holes, 6210yds, Par 70, SSS 70, Course record 61.
Club membership 700.

Visitors Mon-Sun & BHs. Booking required. Dress code.
Societies booking required. **Green Fees** £35 per day, £25 per round (£50/£35 weekends) 🅿 **Facilities** ⓘ ⑩ ⓛ ⬛ ⑪ ⬠ 🛶 ⚐
Conf Corporate Hospitality Days **Location** 1m E of town off A92
Hotel ★★★★ CHH Balbirnie House, Balbirnie Park, MARKINCH
☎ 01592 610066 🖹 01592 610529 30 en suite

CITY OF GLASGOW

GLASGOW

Map 11 NS56

Alexandra Golf Club Alexandra Park G31 8SE
☎ 0141 276 0600

9 Holes, 2800yds, Par 31, Course record 25.

Course Designer G McArthur **Location** 2m E of city centre off M8/A8
Telephone for further details
Hotel ★★★ 83% HL Holiday Inn Glasgow City Centre-Theatreland, 161 West Nile Street, GLASGOW ☎ 0141 352 8300 🖹 0141 332 7447 113 en suite

Cowglen Golf Club Barrhead Rd G43 1AU
☎ 0141 632 7463 🖹 0141 632 7463
e-mail: secretary@cowglengolfclub.co.uk
web: www.cowglengolfclub.co.uk

Undulating and challenging parkland course with good views over the Clyde Valley to the Campsie Hills. Club and line selection is most important on many holes due to the strategic placing of copses on the course.

18 Holes, 6105yds, Par 70, SSS 70, Course record 64.
Club membership 650.

Visitors Booking required. Dress code **Societies** booking required.
Green Fees £45 per day, £35 per round **Course Designer** David Adams/James Braid **Prof** Simon Payne **Facilities** ⓘ ⑩ ⓛ ⬛
⑪ ⬠ 🖼 ⚒ ⚐ ⚐ 🏌 **Conf** facs Corporate Hospitality Days
Location M77 S from Glasgow, Pollok/Barrhead slip road, left at lights, club 0.5m right
Hotel ★★★★ 77% HL Mint Hotel Glasgow, Finnieston Quay, GLASGOW ☎ 0141 240 1002 & 227 1026 🖹 0141 248 2754 164 en suite

Haggs Castle Golf Club 70 Dumbreck Rd, Dumbreck G41 4SN
☎ 0141 427 1157 🖹 0141 427 1157
e-mail: secretary@haggscastlegolfclub.com
web: www.haggscastlegolfclub.com

Wooded, parkland course where Scottish National Championships and the Glasgow and Scottish Open have been held.

18 Holes, 6426yds, Par 72, SSS 72.
Club membership 900.

Visitors Weekends & BHs. Booking required. Dress code.
Societies booking required. **Green Fees** £40 per round, £60 per day **Course Designer** Dave Thomas (1998) **Prof** Campbell Elliott **Facilities** ⓘ ⑩ ⓛ ⬛ ⑪ ⬠ 🖼 ⚒ ⚐ **Conf**
Corporate Hospitality Days **Location** M77 junct 1, 2.5m SW of city centre
Hotel ★★★★ 76% HL Menzies Glasgow, 27 Washington Street, GLASGOW ☎ 0141 222 2929 & 270 2323 🖹 0141 270 2301 141 en suite

Kirkhill Golf Club Greenless Rd, Cambuslang G72 8YN
☎ 0141 641 8499 🖹 0141 641 8499
e-mail: carol.downes@btconnect.com
web: www.kirkhillgolfclub.org.uk

Meadowland course designed by James Braid.

18 Holes, 6030yds, Par 70, SSS 70, Course record 63.
Club membership 650.

Visitors Mon-Fri. Booking required. Handicap certificate. Dress code. **Societies** booking required. **Green Fees** not confirmed **Course Designer** J Braid **Prof** Duncan Williamson **Facilities** ⓘ ⑩ ⓛ ⬛
⑪ ⬠ 🖼 🛶 ⚐ **Location** 5m SE of city centre off A749
Hotel ★★★ 80% HL Bothwell Bridge Hotel, 89 Main Street, BOTHWELL ☎ 01698 852246 🖹 01698 854686 90 en suite

Lethamhill Golf Club 1240 Cumbernauld Rd, Millerston G33 1AH
☎ 0141 276 0810 🖹 0141 770 0520

Municipal parkland course.

18 Holes, 5836yds, Par 70.

Visitors Mon-Sun & BHs. Booking required BHs. **Societies** must contact in advance. **Green Fees** not confirmed 🅿 **Prof** Gary Taggart **Facilities** ⬠ **Location** 3m NE of city centre on A80
Hotel ★★★★ 74% HL Millennium Hotel Glasgow, George Square, GLASGOW ☎ 0141 332 6711 🖹 0141 332 4264 116 en suite

Linn Park Golf Club Simshill Rd G44 5EP
☎ 0141 276 0702
web: www.glasgowlife.org.uk

Municipal parkland/woodland course with six par 3s in outward half.

18 Holes, 5132yds, Par 68, SSS 64. Club membership 83.

Visitors Mon-Sun & BHs. Booking required. **Societies** booking required. **Green Fees** £10.40 per round summer, £9.40 winter 🅿
Facilities ⬠ **Location** 4m S of city centre off B766, between Castle Milk and Cathcart
Hotel ★★★★ 75% HL Holiday Inn Glasgow-East Kilbride, Stewartfield Way, EAST KILBRIDE ☎ 01355 236300 🖹 01355 233552 101 en suite

Save on Hotels. Book at **theAA.com/hotel**

CITY OF GLASGOW – HIGHLAND

Pollok Golf Club 90 Barrhead Rd G43 1BG

☎ 0141 632 4351 📄 0141 649 1398

e-mail: secretary@pollokgolf.com

web: www.pollokgolf.com

Parkland with woods and river. Gentle walking until the 18th hole.

18 Holes, 6358yds, Par 71, SSS 71, Course record 62.
Club membership 620.

Visitors contact club for details. Dress code. **Societies** welcome. **Green Fees** not confirmed **Course Designer** J Douglas & Alistair McKenzie **Facilities** ⓣ ⅃ 🍷 🏌 ⚑ 🍴 ⚫ ⚫ **Conf** facs Corporate Hospitality Days **Location** M77 junct 2, S to A762 Barrhead Rd, 1m E

Hotel ★★★★ 76% HL Menzies Glasgow, 27 Washington Street, GLASGOW ☎ 0141 222 2929 & 270 2323 📄 0141 270 2301 141 en suite

Williamwood Golf Club Clarkston Rd G44 3YR

☎ 0141 637 1783 📄 0141 571 0166

e-mail: secretary@williamwoodgc.co.uk

web: www.williamwoodgc.co.uk

Undulating parkland with mature woods.

18 Holes, 6050yds, Par 69, SSS 69, Course record 61.
Club membership 800.

Visitors Mon-Fri except BHs. Booking required. Dress code. **Societies** booking required. **Green Fees** not confirmed **Course Designer** James Braid **Prof** Stewart Marshall **Facilities** ⓣ 🍴 ⅃ 🍷 🏌 🏠 ⚫ **Location** 5m S of city centre on B767

Hotel ★★★★ 76% HL Menzies Glasgow, 27 Washington Street, GLASGOW ☎ 0141 222 2929 & 270 2323 📄 0141 270 2301 141 en suite

HIGHLAND

ALNESS

Map 14 NH66

Alness Golf Club Ardross Rd IV17 0QA

☎ 01349 883877

e-mail: info@alness-golfclub.co.uk

web: www.alness-golfclub.co.uk

A testing, parkland course with beautiful views over the Cromarty Firth and the Black Isle. It is located on the north west edge of the village of Alness and four holes run parallel to the gorge of the River Averon. Golfers of all abilities will find the course interesting and challenging. A particular test of skill is required at the 14th hole where the tee is located far above the green which lies beside the gorge at a distance of 406yds.

18 Holes, 4976yds, Par 67, SSS 64, Course record 64.
Club membership 350.

Visitors Mon-Sun & BHs. Booking required weekends & BHs. **Societies** welcome. **Green Fees** not confirmed **Prof** Gary Lister **Facilities** ⓣ 🍴 ⅃ 🍷 🏌 🏠 ⚑ ⚫ 🛺 ⚫ 🏐 **Leisure** fishing **Conf** facs Corporate Hospitality Days **Location** 0.5m N off A9

Hotel ★★★★ 78% CHH Kincraig Castle Hotel, INVERGORDON ☎ 01349 852587 📄 01349 852193 15 en suite

ARISAIG

Map 13 NM68

Traigh Golf Course Traigh PH39 4NT

☎ 01687 450337

web: www.traighgolf.co.uk

Traigh lies alongside sandy beaches with views to Skye and the Inner Hebrides. The feature of the course is a line of grassy hills, originally sand dunes, that rise to some 60ft, and provide a challenge to the keenest golfer.

9 Holes, 2456yds, Par 34, SSS 65. Club membership 150.

Visitors Mon-Sun & BHs. **Societies** booking required. **Green Fees** not confirmed ⚫ **Course Designer** John Salvesen 1994 **Facilities** 🍷 🏠 ⚑ ⚫ **Location** A830 to Arisaig, signed onto B8008, 2m N of Arisaig

Hotel ★★★★ INN Cnoc-na-Faire, Back of Keppoch, ARISAIG ☎ 01687 450249 📄 01687 450249 6 rooms

AVIEMORE

Map 14 NH81

Spey Valley Golf Course Aviemore Highland Resort PH22 1PJ

☎ 01479 815100 📄 01479 812128

web: www.macdonaldhotels.co.uk

Opened in Spring 2006 with a total length of 7200 yards and featuring one of the longest par 5 holes in the country, Creag Eabraich, which measures 641 yards from the championship tee. Situated beneath the Cairngorm Mountains with breathtaking views.

18 Holes, 7200yds, Par 72, SSS 74, Course record 64.
Club membership 300.

Visitors Mon-Sun & BHs. Handicap certificate preferred. Dress code. **Societies** booking required. **Green Fees** not confirmed **Course Designer** Dave Thomas **Prof** Murray Urquhart **Facilities** ⓣ 🍴 ⅃ 🍷 🏌 🏠 ⚑ ◇ ⚫ ⚫ 🏐 **Leisure** squash, sauna, gymnasium **Conf** facs Corporate Hospitality Days **Location** leave A9 signed Aviemore on B970. Follow road to village then turn off for Dalfaber and follow signs for golf course

Hotel ★★★★ 75% HL Macdonald Highlands, Aviemore Highland Resort, AVIEMORE ☎ 01479 815100 📄 01479 815101 151 en suite

BOAT OF GARTEN

Map 14 NH91

Boat of Garten Golf Club PH24 3BQ

☎ 01479 831282 📄 01479 831523

e-mail: office@boatgolf.com

web: www.boatgolf.com

In the heart of the Cairngorm National Park, this prime example of James Braid's design genius is cut through moorland and birch forest, maximising the natural landscape. A beautiful and challenging course set amid stunning scenery.

18 Holes, 5876yds, Par 70, SSS 69, Course record 67.
Club membership 650.

Visitors Mon-Sun & BHs. Booking required. Dress code. **Societies** booking required. **Green Fees** £49 per day, £37 per round (£54/£42 weekends) **Course Designer** James Braid **Prof** Ross Harrower **Facilities** ⓣ 🍴 ⅃ 🍷 🏌 🏠 ⚑ ⚫ **Leisure** hard tennis courts **Conf** Corporate Hospitality Days **Location** E side of village

Hotel ★★★ 80% HL Boat Hotel, BOAT OF GARTEN ☎ 01479 831258 & 831696 📄 01479 831414 34 en suite

BONAR BRIDGE · Map 14 NH69

Bonar Bridge-Ardgay Golf Club Migdale Rd IV24 3EJ
☎ 01863 766199
e-mail: bonar-ardgay-golf@tiscali.co.uk
Wooded moorland course with picturesque views of hills and loch.
9 Holes, 5162yds, Par 68, SSS 63, Course record 63.
Club membership 210.
Visitors Contact club for details. **Societies** booking required.
Green Fees £20 per day ⊗ **Facilities** ⑪ ⓛ ⊡ ⚲ ⚲ ⚲
Location 0.5m E. From bridge in village up hill past church. Course on right opposite school.
Hotel ★★★ GA Kyle House, Dornoch Road, BONAR BRIDGE
☎ 01863 766360 5 rooms (3 en suite)

BRORA · Map 14 NC90

Brora Golf Club Golf Rd KW9 6QS
☎ 01408 621417 ▤ 01408 622157
web: www.broragolf.co.uk

18 Holes, 6110yds, Par 69, SSS 70, Course record 61.
Course Designer James Braid **Location** E side of village, signs to Beach Car Park
Telephone for further details
Hotel ★★★★ 75% HL Royal Marine Hotel, Restaurant & Spa, Golf Road, BRORA ☎ 01408 621252 ▤ 01408 621181 21 en suite

CARRBRIDGE · Map 14 NH92

Carrbridge Golf Club Inverness Rd PH23 3AU
☎ 01479 841623
e-mail: secretary@carrbridgegolf.co.uk
web: www.carrbridgegolf.co.uk
Challenging part-parkland, part-moorland course with magnificent views of the Cairngorms, this is a fine 9-hole course that is a challenge for more experienced golfers, and loads of fun for the less experienced.
9 Holes, 5300yds, Par 71, SSS 68, Course record 61.
Club membership 450.
Visitors Mon-Sun & BHs. Booking required. Dress code.
Societies booking required. **Green Fees** £23 per day, £15 per 9 holes
Facilities ⑪ ⓧ by prior arrangement ⓛ ⊡ ⚲ ▤ ⚲ ⚲
Conf Corporate Hospitality Days **Location** N side of village
Hotel ★★★ 80% HL Boat Hotel, BOAT OF GARTEN
☎ 01479 831258 & 831696 ▤ 01479 831414 34 en suite

DORNOCH · Map 14 NH78

Royal Dornoch Golf Club see page 349
Golf Rd IV25 3LW
☎ 01862 810219 ext.1 ▤ 01862 810792
e-mail: bookings@royaldornoch.com
web: www.royaldornoch.com

DURNESS · Map 14 NC46

Durness Golf Club Balnakeil IV27 4PG
☎ 01971 511364 ▤ 01971 511321
e-mail: lucy@durnessgolfclub.org
web: www.durnessgolfclub.org
Set in tremendous scenery overlooking Balnakeil Bay. Part links and part inland with water hazards. Off alternative tees for second nine holes giving surprising variety. Tremendous last hole played over a deep gully to the green over 100yds away.
9 Holes, 5555yds, Par 70, SSS 67, Course record 69.
Club membership 150.
Visitors Mon-Sat & Sun pm. Booking appreciated. **Societies** booking required. **Green Fees** £20 per day, £18 per 18 holes, £15 per 9 holes
⊗ **Course Designer** F Keith/L Ross/I Morrison **Facilities** ⑪ ⊡ ⚲
⚲ ⚲ **Leisure** fishing **Conf** Corporate Hospitality Days **Location** 1m W of village overlooking Balnakeil Bay

FORT AUGUSTUS · Map 14 NH30

Fort Augustus Golf Club Markethill PH32 4DS
☎ 01320 366660
e-mail: fortaugustusgc@aol.com
web: www.fortaugustusgc.webeden.co.uk
Fort Augustus is a traditional heathland course, which many consider the most challenging 9 hole in Scotland. The dense gorse and heather that line the long narrow fairways demand accurate driving. The course is also bordered by the tree-lined Caledonian canal.
9 Holes, 5423yds, Par 68, SSS 67. Club membership 119.
Visitors Check weekend availability **Societies** booking required.
Green Fees £25 per day, £18 per 18 holes, £15 per 9 holes ⊗ **Course Designer** Colt **Facilities** ⓛ ⊡ ⚲ ⚲ ⚲ ⚲ **Location** 1m SW on A82
Hotel ★★★ 82% CHH Glengarry Castle, INVERGARRY
☎ 01809 501254 ▤ 01809 501207 26 en suite

FORTROSE · Map 14 NH75

Fortrose & Rosemarkie Golf Club Ness Road East IV10 8SE
☎ 01381 620529 ▤ 01381 621328
web: www.fortrosegolfclub.co.uk
18 Holes, 5890yds, Par 71, SSS 69, Course record 63.
Course Designer James Braid **Location** A9 N over Kessock Bridge, signs to Munlochy
Telephone for further details

ROYAL DORNOCH

HIGHLAND - DORNOCH - MAP 14 NH78

The championship course is rated among the world's top courses and is a links of rare subtlety. It appears amicable but proves very challenging in play with stiff breezes and tight lies. It is wild and isolated with a pure white sandy beach dividing it from the Dornoch Firth and has hosted golfers since 1616. It was granted a Royal Charter by King Edward VII in 1906. The unique features of the links land have been used to create a magical golfing experience. The 18-hole Struie links course provides, in a gentler style, an enjoyable test of a golfer's accuracy for players of all abilities. Every golfer should make at least one pilgrimage to this superb setting.

Golf Rd IV25 3LW ☎ 01862 810219 ext.1 📄 01862 810792
e-mail: bookings@royaldornoch.com **web:** www.royaldornoch.com
Championship Course: 18 Holes, 6595yds, Par 70, SSS 73.
Struie Course: 18 Holes, 6192yds, Par 71, SSS 70. Club membership 1700.
Visitors Mon-Fri, Sun & BHs.Sat pm. Booking recommended. Dress code. **Societies** booking required. **Green Fees** Championship course £90 per round (£100 weekends), Struie course £35 all week. **Course Designer** Tom Morris **Prof** Andrew Skinner **Facilities** ⑪ 🍴 🍔 ☕ 🍺 🏌 🏠 🎯 ⛳ 🛒 🏌 **Leisure** hard tennis courts
Conf facs Corporate Hospitality Days **Location** E side of town
Hotel ★★★ 75% HL Dornoch Castle Hotel, Castle Street, DORNOCH ☎ 01862 810216 📄 01862 810981 22 en suite

FORT WILLIAM
Map 14 NN17

Fort William Golf Club Torlundy PH33 6SN
☎ 01397 704464
web: www.fortwilliamgolf.co.uk

18 Holes, 6217yds, Par 72, SSS 71, Course record 67.

Course Designer Hamilton Stutt **Location** 3m NE on A82
Telephone for further details
Hotel ★★★ 82% HL Moorings, Banavie, FORT WILLIAM
☎ 01397 772797 🖹 01397 772441 27 en suite

GAIRLOCH
Map 14 NG87

Gairloch Golf Club IV21 2BE
☎ 01445 712407
e-mail: gairlochgolfclub@hotmail.co.uk
web: www.gairlochgolfclub.co.uk

Fine seaside links course running along Gairloch Sands with good views over the sea to Skye. In windy conditions each hole is affected. Founded in 1898, the course, although short, is challenging for all golfers.

9 Holes, 4534yds, Par 63, SSS 63, Course record 62.
Club membership 250.

Visitors Mon-Sun & BHs. Booking required. **Societies** booking required. **Green Fees** £25 per day, £18 per 18 holes **Course Designer** Capt Burgess **Facilities** ⑪ ⓫ ⌷ 🗋 ⚒ 🏠 ⛏ ✦ **Conf** Corporate Hospitality Days **Location** 1m S on A832
Hotel ★★★★★ GA Pool House, POOLEWE ☎ 01445 781272 🖹 01445 781403 6 rooms

GOLSPIE
Map 14 NH89

Golspie Golf Club Ferry Rd KW10 6ST
☎ 01408 633266
e-mail: info@golspie-golf-club.co.uk
web: www.golspie-golf-club.co.uk

Founded in 1889, laid out by Archibald Simpson in 1908 and redesigned in 1926 by James Braid, Golspie's seaside links course offers easy walking and natural hazards including beach, heather, and woodland. Spectacular scenery.

18 Holes, 6021yds, Par 70, SSS 70. Club membership 363.

Visitors Mon-Sun & BHs. Booking advisable. **Societies** booking required. **Green Fees** £50 per day, £40 per round **Course Designer** Archibald Simpson/James Braid **Facilities** ⑪ ⓉⓄⓁ ⓫ ⌷ 🗋 ⚒ 🏠 ⛏ ◇ ✦ 🚡 ✦ **Conf** Corporate Hospitality Days **Location** 0.5m off A9 at S entry to Golspie
Hotel ★★★★ 75% HL Royal Marine Hotel, Restaurant & Spa, Golf Road, BRORA ☎ 01408 621252 🖹 01408 621181 21 en suite

GRANTOWN-ON-SPEY
Map 14 NJ02

Craggan Golf Course Craggan PH26 3NT
☎ 01479 873283 🖹 01479 872325
e-mail: fhglaing@btopenworld.com
web: www.cragganforleisure.co.uk

A golf course in miniature set in stunning scenery on the edge of the Cairngorms National Park.

18 Holes, 2500yds, Par 54, Course record 52.
Club membership 400.

Visitors Contact course for details. **Societies** booking required. **Green Fees** £25 per day, £17.50 per round 🌐 **Course Designer** Bill Mitchel **Facilities** ⑪ ⓫ ⌷ 🗋 🏠 ⛏ ✦ **Leisure** fishing **Conf** facs Corporate Hospitality Days **Location** off A95, 1m S of Grantown-on-Spey
Hotel ★★★★ GA Holmhill House, Woodside Avenue, GRANTOWN-ON-SPEY ☎ 01479 873977 3 rooms (3 en suite)

Grantown-on-Spey Golf Club Golf Course Rd PH26 3HY
☎ 01479 872079 🖹 01479 873725
e-mail: secretary@grantownonspeygolfclub.co.uk
web: www.grantownonspeygolfclub.co.uk

Parkland and woodland course. Part easy walking, remainder hilly. The 7th to 13th holes really sort out the golfers.

18 Holes, 5710yds, Par 70, SSS 68, Course record 60.
Club membership 750.

Visitors Mon-Sun & BHs. Booking advisable. Dress code. **Societies** booking required. **Green Fees** £37 per day, £30 per round (£42/£35 weekends) **Course Designer** A Brown/W Park/J Braid **Facilities** ⑪ ⓉⓄⓁ by prior arrangement ⓫ ⌷ 🗋 🏠 🏠 ⛏ ✦ 🚡 ✦ **Conf** Corporate Hospitality Days **Location** NE side of town centre
Hotel ★★★ 79% HL Grant Arms Hotel, 25-27 The Square, GRANTOWN-ON-SPEY ☎ 01479 872526 🖹 01479 873589 50 en suite

HELMSDALE
Map 14 ND01

Helmsdale Golf Club Golf Rd KW8 6JL
☎ 01431 821063
web: www.helmsdale.org

Sheltered, undulating course following the line of the Helmsdale River.

9 Holes, 1860yds, Par 60, SSS 60. Club membership 58.

Visitors Mon-Sun & BHs. **Societies** booking required. **Green Fees** £15 per 18 holes 🌐 **Facilities** 🏠 **Location** NW side of town on A896
Hotel ★★★★ 75% HL Royal Marine Hotel, Restaurant & Spa, Golf Road, BRORA ☎ 01408 621252 🖹 01408 621181 21 en suite

Save on Hotels. Book at **theAA.com/hotel**

HIGHLAND

INVERGORDON

Map 14 NH76

Invergordon Golf Club King George St IV18 0BD
☎ 01349 852715
e-mail: invergordongolf@tiscali.co.uk
web: www.invergordongolf.co.uk

A windy 18-hole parkland course, with woodland and good views over Cromarty Firth to the distant mountains. Very good greens and a fair challenge for all golfers, especially if the wind is from the south west. Four par 3s and one par 5.

18 Holes, 6900yds, Par 69, SSS 69, Course record 63.
Club membership 266.

Visitors Mon-Sun & BHs. Booking required Sat. **Societies** booking required. **Green Fees** £25 per day, £20 per 18 holes **Course Designer** A Rae **Facilities** ⑪ ⓛ ⌷ ⓣ ⓛ ⓐ ⓣ ⚡ **Conf** Corporate Hospitality Days **Location** from A9 take B817 for 2m entering town via High St, after approx 300 yds turn left into Albany Rd then left again over railway bridge. Continue for 0.6m into club car park

Hotel ★★★★ 78% CHH Kincraig Castle Hotel, INVERGORDON
☎ 01349 852587 ▤ 01349 852193 15 en suite

INVERNESS

Map 14 NH64

Inverness Golf Club Culcabock IV2 3XQ
☎ 01463 239882 ▤ 01463 240616
e-mail: manager@invernessgolfclub.co.uk
web: www.invernessgolfclub.co.uk

A parkland course with tree-lined fairways. The Mill burn meanders through the course, posing a challenge at several holes. The 313yd 6th hole requires caution from the tee as a long drive may reach the burn that guards the green. The 14th (Midmills) is a hole of exceptional quality with a dog-leg to the right which obscures a view of the green with a wayward shot. At 461yds the long par 4 18th is a demanding finish, especially into a north east breeze.

18 Holes, 6256yds, Par 69, SSS 70, Course record 61.
Club membership 1250.

Visitors Mon-Sun & BHs. Booking required Thu & weekends. Handicap certificate. Dress code. **Societies** booking required. **Green Fees** £55 per day, £42 per round **Course Designer** J Fraser/G Smith **Prof** Alistair P Thomson **Facilities** ⑪ ⓧ ⓛ ⌷ ⓣ ⓛ ⓐ ⚡ **Leisure** chipping green **Conf** Corporate Hospitality Days **Location** A96 towards Inverness. Pass retail park on left and straight on at rdbt. At next rdbt take 2nd exit (B865), then at next rdbt take 1st exit (B9006). At next rdbt take 2nd exit into Culcabock Rd, golf club 200 yds on left
Hotel ★★★ 77% HL Royal Highland, Station Square, Academy Street, INVERNESS ☎ 01463 231926 & 251451 ▤ 01463 710705 85 en suite

Loch Ness Golf Course Fairways, Castle Heather IV2 6AA
☎ 01463 713335 ▤ 01463 712695
e-mail: info@golflochness.com
web: www.golflochness.com

An 18 hole course and a 9 hole family course with seven par 3s and two par 4s and small undulating greens and deep bunkers to test short game skills. The New course offers great variety from the 550 yard 2nd hole to the 76 yard hole called Chance which is played over a deep gully.

New Course: 18 Holes, 5943yds, Par 70, SSS 69,
Course record 67.
Family Course: 9 Holes, 1440yds, Par 29.
Club membership 600.

Visitors Mon-Sun & BHs. Booking required weekends & BHs. Dress code. **Societies** welcome. **Green Fees** £45-£55 per day, £30-£35 per round. Family Course £10 **Course Designer** Caddies Golf Course Design **Prof** Martin Piggot **Facilities** ⑪ ⓧ ⓛ ⌷ ⓣ ⓛ ⓐ ⓣ ◇ ⚡ ⌂ ⚡ ⓕ **Leisure** sports injury clinic, indoor bowls. **Conf** facs Corporate Hospitality Days **Location** SW outskirts of Inverness, along bypass
Hotel ★★★ 77% HL Royal Highland, Station Square, Academy Street, INVERNESS ☎ 01463 231926 & 251451 ▤ 01463 710705 85 en suite

Torvean Golf Club Glenurquhart Rd IV3 8JN
☎ 01463 225651 (Office) ▤ 01463 711417
web: www.torveangolfclub.co.uk

18 Holes, 5799yds, Par 69, SSS 68, Course record 63.

Course Designer Hamilton **Location** 1.5m SW on A82
Telephone for further details
Hotel ★★★ 77% HL Royal Highland, Station Square, Academy Street, INVERNESS ☎ 01463 231926 & 251451 ▤ 01463 710705 85 en suite

KINGUSSIE

Map 14 NH70

Kingussie Golf Club Gynack Rd PH21 1LR
☎ 01540 661600 ▤ 01540 662066
e-mail: sec@kingussie-golf.co.uk
web: www.kingussie-golf.co.uk

Upland course with natural hazards and magnificent views. Stands about 1000ft above sea level at its highest point, and the River Gynack, which runs through the course, comes into play on five holes. Golf has been played here for over 100 years and some tight fairways and deceptive par threes make the course a challenge for all golfers.

18 Holes, 5501yds, Par 67, SSS 68, Course record 64.
Club membership 650.

Visitors Mon-Sun & BHs. Booking required. **Societies** welcome. **Green Fees** not confirmed **Course Designer** Vardon **Facilities** ⑪ ⓧ ⓛ ⌷ ⓣ ⓛ ⓐ ⓣ ⌂ ⚡ **Location** 0.25m N off A86
Hotel ★★★★★ RR The Cross at Kingussie, Tweed Mill Brae, Ardbroilach Road, KINGUSSIE ☎ 01540 661166 ▤ 01540 661080 8 rooms

SCOTLAND

LOCHCARRON
Map 14 NG83

Lochcarron Golf Club IV54 8YS
☎ 01599 577219
e-mail: bill1@btinternet.com
web: www.lochcarrongolf.co.uk

Seaside links course with some parkland with an interesting 1st hole. A short course but great accuracy is required.

9 Holes, 3575yds, Par 60, SSS 60, Course record 57. Club membership 130.

Visitors Contact club for details. Societies booking required. Green Fees £15 per day, £10 per 9 holes (half price for under 16s) Facilities ⑪ †◎¹ ₪ ☐ ⚲ 盒 ⑨ 🏌 Location 1m E of Lochcarron by A896
Hotel ★★★ 75% SHL The Plockton, 41 Harbour Street, PLOCkTON ☎ 01599 544274 🗎 01599 544475 15 en suite

LYBSTER
Map 15 ND23

Lybster Golf Club Main St KW3 6AE
☎ 01593 721486 & 721316
web: www.lybstergolfclub.co.uk

Picturesque, short heathland course, easy walking.

9 Holes, 2002yds, Par 62, SSS 61, Course record 57. Club membership 140.

Visitors contact club for details. Societies welcome. Green Fees not confirmed Facilities ⚲ Location E side of village
Hotel ★★★ 75% HL Mackay's, Union Street, WICK ☎ 01955 602323 🗎 01955 605930 30 en suite

MUIR OF ORD
Map 14 NH55

Muir of Ord Golf Club Great North Rd IV6 7SX
☎ 01463 870825
e-mail: muir.golf@btconnect.com
web: www.muirofordgolfclub.com

Long-established (1875) heathland course with tight fairways and easy walking. Playable all year.

18 Holes, 5542yds, Par 68, SSS 68, Course record 62. Club membership 750.

Visitors Mon-Sun except BHs. Booking required. Dress code. Societies booking required Green Fees £32 per day, £28 per round (weekends £44/£40) Course Designer James Braid Facilities ⑪ by prior arrangement †◎¹ by prior arrangement ₪ ☐ ⚲ 盒 🏌 ⚲ Location S side of village on A862
Hotel ★★★ 74% HL Priory, The Square, BEAULY ☎ 01463 782 309 🗎 01463 782531 37 en suite

NAIRN
Map 14 NH85

Nairn Dunbar Golf Club Lochloy Rd IV12 5AE
☎ 01667 452741 🗎 01667 456897
e-mail: secretary@nairndunbar.com
web: www.nairndunbar.com

Traditional Scottish links course with testing gorse and whin-lined fairways. Fairly flat with big greens. Championship course.

18 Holes, 6765yds, Par 72, SSS 74, Course record 64. Club membership 1200.

Visitors Mon-Sun & BHs. Booking required. Societies booking required. Green Fees £62 per day, £47 per round (£72/£52 weekends) Prof David Torrance Facilities ⑪ †◎¹ ₪ ☐ ⚲ 盒 ⑨ ⚲ 🚗 ⚲ Conf facs Corporate Hospitality Days Location E side of town off A96
Hotel ★★★★ 74% HL Newton, Inverness Road, NAIRN ☎ 01667 453144 🗎 01667 454026 56 en suite

The Nairn Golf Club Seabank Rd IV12 4HB
☎ 01667 453208 🗎 01667 456328
e-mail: bookings@nairngolfclub.co.uk
web: www.nairngolfclub.co.uk

Championship, seaside links founded in 1887 and created from a wilderness of heather and whin. Designed by Archie Simpson, Old Tom Morris and James Braid. Opening holes stretch out along the shoreline with the turn for home at the 10th.

18 Holes, 6430yds, Par 71, SSS 73, Course record 64. Newton: 9 Holes, 3542yds, Par 58, SSS 57. Club membership 1150.

Visitors Mon-Sun & BHs. Booking required. Dress code. Societies welcome. Green Fees phone Course Designer A Simpson/ Old Tom Morris/James Braid Prof Robin P Fyfe Facilities ⑪ †◎¹ ₪ ☐ ⚲ ⚲ 盒 ⑨ ⚲ 🏌 Location 16m E of Inverness on A96
Hotel ★★★★ 72% HL Golf View Hotel & Leisure Club, The Seafront, NAIRN ☎ 01667 452301 🗎 01667 455267 42 en suite

NETHY BRIDGE
Map 14 NJ02

Abernethy Golf Club PH25 3EB
☎ 01479 821305 🗎 01479 821305
e-mail: info@abernethygolfclub.com
web: www.abernethygolfclub.com

Traditional Highland course built on moorland surrounded by pine trees and offering a great variety of shot making for the low handicapped or casual visitor. The 2nd hole, although very short is played across bogland and a B road to a two-tiered green. The small and fast greens are the most undulating and tricky in the valley. The Abernethy forest lies on the boundary and from many parts of the course there are splendid views of Strathspey.

9 Holes, 2526yds, Par 66, SSS 66. Club membership 400.

Visitors Mon-Sun & BHs. Societies welcome. Green Fees £22 per day (£25 weekends). Twilight £11 (£12 weekends) ⊛ Facilities ⑪ †◎¹ ₪ ☐ ⚲ 盒 ⑨ ⚲ Conf Corporate Hospitality Days Location N side of village on B970
Hotel ★★ 78% HL The Mountview Hotel, Grantown Road, NETHY BRIDGE ☎ 01479 821248 🗎 01479 821515 12 en suite

NEWTONMORE   Map 14 NN79

Newtonmore Golf Club Golf Course Rd PH20 1AT
☎ 01540 673878
e-mail: secretary@newtonmoregolf.com
web: www.newtonmoregolf.com
Inland course beside the River Spey. Beautiful views and easy walking.
Testing 17th hole (par 3).
18 Holes, 5515mtrs, Par 70, SSS 69, Course record 62.
Club membership 420.

Visitors Mon-Sun & BHs. **Societies** Booking required **Green Fees** £36
per day, £30 per 18 holes (£40/£33 weekends) **Prof** Robert Henderson
Facilities ⓑ ⓞ ⓛ ☐ ⓟ ⓛ ⓔ ⓟ ⓔ ⓔ ⓔ **Location** E
side of town off A9
Hotel ★★★★★ RR The Cross at Kingussie, Tweed Mill Brae,
Ardbroilach Road, KINGUSSIE ☎ 01540 661166 ▤ 01540 661080
8 rooms

REAY   Map 14 NC96

Reay Golf Club KW14 7RE
☎ 01847 811288 ▤ 01847 894189
web: www.reaygolfclub.co.uk
18 Holes, 5831yds, Par 69, SSS 69, Course record 64.
Course Designer Braid **Location** 11m W of Thurso on A836
Telephone for further details
Hotel ★★★★ 76% SHL Forss House, Forss, THURSO
☎ 01847 861201 ▤ 01847 861301 14 en suite

STRATHPEFFER   Map 14 NH45

Strathpeffer Spa Golf Club IV14 9AS
☎ 01997 421219 & 421011 ▤ 01997 421011
e-mail: mail@strathpeffergolf.co.uk
web: www.strathpeffergolf.co.uk
Beautiful, testing upland course in this historic village. Many natural
hazards alongside eight sand bunkers on the course and the course's
claim to fame is the 1st hole which features the longest drop from tee
to green in Scotland. Stunning views.
18 Holes, 5001yds, Par 67, SSS 65, Course record 61.
Club membership 400.

Visitors Mon-Sun & BHs. Booking required Sat. Dress code.
Societies booking required. **Green Fees** £38 per day, £28 per
round (£40/£30 weekends) **Course Designer** Willie Park/Tom Morris
Facilities ⓑ ⓛ ☐ ⓟ ⓛ ⓔ ⓟ ⓔ ⓔ **Conf** Corporate
Hospitality Days **Location** 0.25m N of village off A834, signed
Hotel ★★★ GH Inver Lodge, STRATHPEFFER ☎ 01997 421392
2 rooms (2 pri facs)

TAIN   Map 14 NH78

Tain Golf Club Chapel Rd IV19 1JE
☎ 01862 892314 ▤ 01862 892099
e-mail: info@tain-golfclub.co.uk
web: www.tain-golfclub.co.uk
Links course with river affecting three holes; easy walking, fine views.
Many of the original Old Tom Morris-designed holes are still in play.
18 Holes, 6404yds, Par 70, SSS 72, Course record 64.
Club membership 600.

Visitors Contact club for details. **Societies** booking required. **Green
Fees** £65 per day, £48 per round (£65/£48 weekends) **Course
Designer** Old Tom Morris **Prof** Stuart Morrison **Facilities** ⓑ ⓞ
ⓛ ☐ ⓟ ⓛ ⓔ ⓟ ⓔ ⓔ **Leisure** 3 practice nets, 3
bay driving unit, short game area **Conf** Corporate Hospitality Days
Location E side of town centre off B9174
Hotel ★★★ 75% HL Dornoch Castle Hotel, Castle Street, DORNOCH
☎ 01862 810216 ▤ 01862 810981 22 en suite

THURSO   Map 15 ND16

Thurso Golf Club Newlands of Geise KW14 7XD
☎ 01847 893807
web: www.ebigh.com/thursogolf
Parkland course, windy, but with fine views of Dunnet Head and the
Orkney Islands. Tree-lined fairways but 4th and 16th holes are testing
into the prevailing wind. The 13th is a short par 4 but has a testing
drive over a burn with heather on left and punishing rough on right.
18 Holes, 5820yds, Par 69, SSS 69, Course record 63.
Club membership 320.

Visitors Mon-Sun & BHs. **Societies** welcome. **Green Fees** not
confirmed ⓔ **Course Designer** W S Stewart **Facilities** ☐ ⓟ ⓛ
ⓟ ⓔ **Conf** Corporate Hospitality Days **Location** 2m SW of Thurso
on B874
Hotel ★★★★ 76% SHL Forss House, Forss, THURSO
☎ 01847 861201 ▤ 01847 861301 14 en suite

ULLAPOOL   Map 14 NH19

Ullapool Golf Course The Clubhouse, North Rd, Morefield
IV26 2TH
☎ 01854 613323
e-mail: mail@ullapoolgolfclub.co.uk
web: www.ullapoolgolfclub.co.uk
Seaside/parkland course with fine views.
9 Holes, 5299yds, Par 70, SSS 67, Course record 71.
Club membership 120.

Visitors Contact club for details. **Societies** booking required. **Green
Fees** £22.50 per day, £15 per 9 holes ⓔ **Course Designer** Souters
Facilities ⓛ ☐ ⓟ ⓛ ⓔ ⓟ ⓔ **Conf** Corporate Hospitality
Days **Location** on A835 at N end of village

SCOTLAND

SCOTLAND

WICK
Map 15 ND35

Wick Golf Club Reiss KW1 4RW
☎ 01955 602726
web: www.wickgolfclub.com
18 Holes, 6123yds, Par 69, SSS 71, Course record 63.
Location 3.5m N off A9
Telephone for further details
Hotel ★★★ 75% HL Mackay's, Union Street, WICK
☎ 01955 602323 📄 01955 605930 30 en suite

INVERCLYDE

GOUROCK
Map 10 NS27

Gourock Golf Club Cowal View PA19 1HD
☎ 01475 631001 & 636834 (pro) 📄 01475 638307
web: www.gourockgolfclub.com
18 Holes, 6408yds, Par 73, SSS 72, Course record 64.
Course Designer J Braid/H Cotton Location SW side of town off A770
Telephone for further details
Hotel ★★ 74% HL Selborne, Clyde Street, West Bay, DUNOON
☎ 01369 702761 📄 01369 704032 98 en suite

GREENOCK
Map 10 NS27

Greenock Golf Club Forsyth St PA16 8RE
☎ 01475 787236
e-mail: secretary@greenockgolfclub.co.uk
web: www.greenockgolfclub.co.uk
Testing moorland courses with panoramic views of Clyde Estuary.
18 Holes, 5838yds, Par 68, SSS 69, Course record 62.
Wee Course: 9 Holes, 2160yds, Par 32, SSS 32,
Course record 29. Club membership 700.
Visitors Mon, Tue, Thu, Fri, Sun & BHs. Dress code. Societies booking required. Green Fees not confirmed 🅿 Course Designer James Braid Prof Kevin Campbell Facilities ⓣ ⅋ ⓘ 🏌 🖵 🍴 🏖 🏠 🍴
🏌 🏌 🍴 Conf Corporate Hospitality Days Location SW side of town off A770
Hotel ★★ 74% HL Selborne, Clyde Street, West Bay, DUNOON
☎ 01369 702761 📄 01369 704032 98 en suite

Greenock Whinhill Golf Club Beith Rd PA16 9LN
☎ 01475 719260
18 Holes, 5504yds, Par 68, SSS 67, Course record 64.
Course Designer William Fernie Location 1.5m SW off B7054
Telephone for further details
Hotel BUD Holiday Inn Express Greenock, Cartsburn, GREENOCK
☎ 01475 786666 📄 01475 786777 71 en suite

PORT GLASGOW
Map 10 NS37

Port Glasgow Golf Club Devol Rd PA14 5XE
☎ 01475 704181
web: www.portglasgowgolfclub.com
18 Holes, 5712yds, Par 68, SSS 68.
Location 1m S
Telephone for further details
Hotel ★★★★ 73% HL Best Western Gleddoch House, LANGBANK
☎ 01475 540711 📄 01475 540201 70 en suite

MIDLOTHIAN

BONNYRIGG
Map 11 NT36

Broomieknowe Golf Club 36 Golf Course Rd EH19 2HZ
☎ 0131 663 9317 📄 0131 663 2152
e-mail: administrator@broomieknowe.com
web: www.broomieknowe.com
Easy walking mature parkland course laid out by Ben Sayers and extended by James Braid. Elevated site with excellent views.
18 Holes, 6150yds, Par 70, SSS 70, Course record 63.
Club membership 900.
Visitors Mon-Sun & BHs. Booking required weekends & BHs. Dress code. Societies booking required. Green Fees phone Course Designer Ben Sayers/Hawtree Prof Mark Patchett Facilities ⓣ ⓘ
🏌 🖵 🍴 🏖 🏠 🍴 🏌 🏌 🍴 Conf Corporate Hospitality Days Location 0.5m NE off B704
Hotel ★★★ 82% HL Dalhousie Castle and Aqueous Spa, Bonnyrigg, EDINBURGH ☎ 01875 820153 📄 01875 821936 36 en suite

DALKEITH
Map 11 NT36

Newbattle Golf Club Abbey Rd EH22 3AD
☎ 0131 663 2123 & 663 1819 📄 0131 654 1810
e-mail: mail@newbattlegolfclub.com
web: www.newbattlegolfclub.com
Gently undulating parkland course, dissected by the South Esk river and surrounded by woods.
18 Holes, 5912yds, Par 69, SSS 69, Course record 61.
Club membership 700.
Visitors Mon-Fri & BHs. Sun pm. Dress code. Societies booking required. Green Fees £40 per day, £30 per round Course Designer H S Colt Prof Scott McDonald Facilities ⓣ ⓘ 🏌 🖵 🍴 🏖 🏠
🏖 🍴 Location SW side of town off A68
Hotel ★★★ 82% HL Dalhousie Castle and Aqueous Spa, Bonnyrigg, EDINBURGH ☎ 01875 820153 📄 01875 821936 36 en suite

GOREBRIDGE
Map 11 NT36

Vogrie Golf Course Vogrie Estate Country Park EH23 4NU
☎ 01875 821716 📄 01875 823958
web: www.midlothian.gov.uk
9 Holes, 2530yds, Par 33.
Location off B6372
Telephone for further details
Hotel ★★★ 82% HL Dalhousie Castle and Aqueous Spa, Bonnyrigg, EDINBURGH ☎ 01875 820153 📄 01875 821936 36 en suite

Save on Hotels. Book at **theAA.com/hotel**

MIDLOTHIAN – MORAY

LASSWADE
Map 11 NT36

Kings Acre Golf Course & Academy EH18 1AU
☎ 0131 663 3456 📄 0131 663 7076
e-mail: info@kings-acregolf.com
web: www.kings-acregolf.com

Parkland course set in countryside location and making excellent use of the natural contours of the land with strategically placed water hazards and over 50 bunkers leading to large undulating greens. The naturally sandy based soil ensures excellent play all year.

18 Holes, 6031yds, Par 70, SSS 69. Club membership 300.

Visitors Mon-Sun & BHs. **Societies** welcome. **Green Fees** £38 per day, £28 per round **Course Designer** Graeme Webster **Prof** Alan Murdoch **Facilities** ⚑ 🍴 🛒 ⬛ 🍽 ⛱ 🏠 ⛿ ♦ 🏌 🏌 ⚑ **Conf** facs Corporate Hospitality Days **Location** off A720, City of Edinburgh bypass road
Hotel ★★★ 82% HL Dalhousie Castle and Aqueous Spa, Bonnyrigg, EDINBURGH ☎ 01875 820153 📄 01875 821936 36 en suite

PENICUIK
Map 11 NT25

Glencorse Golf Club Milton Bridge EH26 0RD
☎ 01968 677189 & 676481 📄 01968 674399
e-mail: secretary@glencorsegolfclub.com
web: www.glencorsegolfclub.com

Picturesque parkland with a burn affecting 10 holes. Testing 5th hole (237yds) par 3.

18 Holes, 5217yds, Par 64, SSS 66, Course record 60. Club membership 700.

Visitors Mon-Fri & BHs. Sun pm. Booking required. **Societies** welcome. **Green Fees** £32 per day, £25 per round (BHs £32 per round) **Course Designer** Willie Park **Prof** Cliffe Jones **Facilities** ⚑ 🍴 🛒 ⬛ 🍽 ⛱ 🏠 ⛿ ♦ 🏌 **Location** 9m S of Edinburgh on A701 Peebles Road
Hotel ★★★★ INN The Original Rosslyn Inn, 4 Main Street, ROSLIN ☎ 0131 440 2384 📄 0131 440 2514 6 rooms (6 en suite)

MORAY

BALLINDALLOCH
Map 15 NJ13

Ballindalloch Castle Golf Course Lagmore AB37 9AA
☎ 01807 500305 📄 01807 500210
e-mail: golf@ballindallochcastle.co.uk
web: www.ballindallochcastle.co.uk

Course nestling among mature trees on the banks of the river Avon with fine views of the surrounding hills and woods.

18 Holes, 6495yds, Par 72.

Visitors contact course for details. **Societies** booking required. **Green Fees** £20 per 18 holes, £15 per 9 holes **Course Designer** Donald Steel **Facilities** ⚑ ⬛ 🍽 ⛱ 🏠 ⛿ ♦ **Conf** Corporate Hospitality Days **Location** off A95 13m NE of Grantown-on-Spey
Hotel ★★★ 77% SHL Archiestown Hotel, ARCHIESTOWN ☎ 01340 810218 📄 01340 810239 11 en suite

BUCKIE
Map 15 NJ46

Buckpool Golf Club Barhill Rd, Buckpool AB56 1DU
☎ 01542 832236 📄 01542 832236
e-mail: golf@buckpoolgolf.com
web: www.buckpoolgolf.com

Links course with superlative view over Moray Firth, easy walking.

18 Holes, 6097yds, Par 70, SSS 69, Course record 63. Club membership 430.

Visitors Mon-Sun & BHs. **Societies** booking required. **Green Fees** £28 per day, £22 per round **Course Designer** J H Taylor **Facilities** ⚑ ⬛ 🍽 ⛱ 🏠 ⛿ **Leisure** squash, snooker **Location** off A98, after Arradoul signed Hospital, Golf Club. Continue straight to end of road
Hotel ★★★ 75% SHL Cullen Bay Hotel, A98, CULLEN ☎ 01542 840432 📄 01542 840900 14 en suite

Strathlene Buckie Golf Club Portessie AB56 2DJ
☎ 01542 831798 📄 01542 831798
web: www.strathlenegolfclub.co.uk

Raised seaside links course with magnificent view. A special feature of the course is approach shots to raised greens (holes 4, 5, 6 and 13).

18 Holes, 5977yds, Par 69, SSS 69, Course record 64.

Visitors Mon-Sun & BHs. Dress code **Societies** booking required. **Green Fees** £24 per day, £20 per round (£32/£23 weekends) 🚫 **Course Designer** George Smith **Facilities** ⚑ ⬛ 🍽 ⛱ 🏠 ⛿ 🏌 **Conf** Corporate Hospitality Days **Location** 2m E of Buckie on A942
Hotel ★★★ 75% SHL Cullen Bay Hotel, A98, CULLEN ☎ 01542 840432 📄 01542 840900 14 en suite

CULLEN
Map 15 NJ56

Cullen Golf Club The Links AB56 4WB
☎ 01542 840685
web: www.cullengolfclub.co.uk

18 Holes, 4610yds, Par 63, SSS 62, Course record 55.

Course Designer Tom Morris/Charlie Neaves **Location** 0.5m W off A98 **Telephone for further details**
Hotel ★★★ 75% SHL Cullen Bay Hotel, A98, CULLEN ☎ 01542 840432 📄 01542 840900 14 en suite

DUFFTOWN
Map 15 NJ34

Dufftown Golf Club Tomintoul Rd AB55 4BS
☎ 01340 820325 📄 01340 820325
e-mail: admin@dufftowngolfclub.com
web: www.dufftowngolfclub.com

A short and undulating inland course with spectacular views. The tee of the highest hole, the 9th, is over 1200ft above sea level.

18 Holes, 5308yds, Par 67, SSS 67, Course record 64. Club membership 350.

Visitors Mon-Sun & BHs. Booking required. **Societies** booking required. **Green Fees** £20 per day/round **Course Designer** Members **Facilities** ⚑ by prior arrangement 🍴 by prior arrangement ⬛ 🍽 ⛱ 🏠 ⛿ ♦ **Conf** facs Corporate Hospitality Days **Location** 0.75m SW off B9009
Hotel ★★★★ 72% HL Craigellachie, CRAIGELLACHIE ☎ 01340 881204 📄 01340 881253 26 en suite

SCOTLAND

ELGIN
Map 15 NJ26

Elgin Golf Club Hardhillock, Birnie Rd, New Elgin IV30 8SX
☎ 01343 542884 ▤ 01343 542341
e-mail: secretary@elgingolfclub.com
web: www.elgingolfclub.com

Possibly the finest inland course in the north of Scotland, with undulating greens and compact holes that demand the highest accuracy. There are 13 par 4s and one par 5 hole on its parkland layout, eight of the par 4s being over 400yds long.

Hardhillock: 18 Holes, 6416yds, Par 68, SSS 69, Course record 63. Club membership 1000.

Visitors handicap certificate. Dress code. **Societies** booking required. **Green Fees** £47 per day, £37 per round (weekends £49/£39) **Course Designer** John Macpherson **Prof** Kevin Stables **Facilities** ⓣ ⓄⓄ ⓛ ⯑ ⯑ ⯑ ⯑ ⯑ **Conf** facs Corporate Hospitality Days **Location** 1m S on A941
Hotel ★★★ 79% HL Mansion House, The Haugh, ELGIN
☎ 01343 548811 ▤ 01343 547916 23 en suite

FORRES
Map 14 NJ05

Forres Golf Course Muiryshade IV36 2RD
☎ 01309 672250 ▤ 01309 672250
e-mail: sandy@forresgolf.demon.co.uk
web: www.forresgolfclub.co.uk

An all-year parkland course laid on light, well-drained soil in wooded countryside. Walking is easy despite some hilly holes. A test for all golfers.

18 Holes, 6236yds, Par 70, SSS 70, Course record 60. Club membership 800.

Visitors Mon-Sun & BHs. Booking required. **Societies** welcome. **Green Fees** £50 per day, £35 per round **Course Designer** James Braid/Willie Park **Prof** Sandy Aird **Facilities** ⓣ ⓄⓄ ⓛ ⯑ ⯑ ⯑ ⯑ ⯑ ⯑ ⯑ **Conf** Corporate Hospitality Days
Location SE side of town centre off B9010
Hotel ★★★ HL Boath House, Auldearn, NAIRN ☎ 01667 454896 ▤ 01667 455469 8 en suite

GARMOUTH
Map 15 NJ36

Garmouth & Kingston Golf Club Spey St IV32 7NJ
☎ 01343 870388 ▤ 01343 870388
e-mail: garmouthgolfclub@aol.com
web: www.garmouthkingstongolfclub.com

Flat seaside course with several parkland holes and tidal waters. The 8th hole measures only 328yds from the medal tee but the fairway is bounded by a ditch on either side, the left hand one being out of bounds for the entire length of the hole. The par 5 17th Whinny Side has gorse bordering on both sides of the fairway which can be intimidating to any level of golfer.

18 Holes, 5554yds, Par 69, SSS 67. Club membership 500.

Visitors Mon-Sun & BHs. Booking required. **Societies** booking required. **Green Fees** £25 per day, £20 per round (£28/£25 weekends) **Course Designer** George Smith **Facilities** ⓣ by prior arrangement ⓄⓄ by prior arrangement ⓛ ⯑ ⯑ ⯑ ⯑ **Conf** Corporate Hospitality Days **Location** in village on B9015
Hotel ★★★ 79% HL Mansion House, The Haugh, ELGIN
☎ 01343 548811 ▤ 01343 547916 23 en suite

HOPEMAN
Map 15 NJ16

Hopeman Golf Club Clubhouse IV30 5YA
☎ 01343 830578 ▤ 01343 830152
e-mail: hopemangc@aol.com
web: www.hopemangc.co.uk

Links-type course with beautiful views over the Moray Firth. The 12th hole, called the Priescach, is a short hole with a drop of 100ft from te to green. It can require anything from a wedge to a wood depending on the wind.

18 Holes, 5624yds, Par 68, SSS 68, Course record 64. Club membership 700.

Visitors Mon-Sun & BHs. **Societies** booking required. **Green Fees** £23 per round (£30 Sat, £22 Sun) **Course Designer** Charles Neaves **Facilities** ⓣ ⓄⓄ ⓛ ⯑ ⯑ ⯑ ⯑ ⯑ **Location** E side of village off B9040
Hotel ★★★ 79% HL Mansion House, The Haugh, ELGIN
☎ 01343 548811 ▤ 01343 547916 23 en suite

KEITH
Map 15 NJ45

Keith Golf Club Fife Park AB55 5DF
☎ 01542 882469
e-mail: secretary@keithgolfclub.org.uk
web: www.keithgolfclub.org.uk

Parkland course, with natural hazards over first 9 holes. Testing 7th hole, 232 yds, par 3.

18 Holes, 5802yds, Par 69, SSS 68, Course record 65. Club membership 500.

Visitors Mon-Sun & BHs. Booking required weekends.
Societies welcome. **Green Fees** not confirmed **Course Designer** Roy Phimister **Facilities** ⓣ ⓄⓄ ⯑ ⯑ ⯑ ⯑ **Location** NW of town centre, A96 onto B9014 right
Hotel ★★★★ 72% HL Craigellachie, CRAIGELLACHIE
☎ 01340 881204 ▤ 01340 881253 26 en suite

LOSSIEMOUTH
Map 15 NJ27

Moray Golf Club Stotfield Rd IV31 6QS
☎ 01343 812018 ▤ 01343 815102
e-mail: secretary@moraygolf.co.uk
web: www.moraygolf.co.uk

Two fine Scottish Championship links courses, known as Old and New (Moray), and situated on the Moray Firth where the weather is unusually mild. The Old course was designed by Old Tom Morris, and includes seven par fours over 400 yards. The New course is the work of Henry Cotton, who has designed a tighter and smaller course.

Old Course: 18 Holes, 6687yds, Par 71, SSS 73, Course record 67.
New Course: 18 Holes, 6068yds, Par 70, SSS 69, Course record 62. Club membership 1550.

Visitors Mon-Sun & BHs. Booking required weekends. Dress code. **Societies** booking required. **Green Fees** Old course Mon-Fri £55 (weekends & BHs £65). New course Mon-Fri £25, (weekends & BHs £30) **Course Designer** Tom Morris & Henry Cotton **Prof** John Murray **Facilities** ⓣ ⓄⓄ ⓛ ⯑ ⯑ ⯑ ⯑ ⯑ ⯑ ⯑ **Conf** Corporate Hospitality Days **Location** N side of town
Hotel ★★★ 79% HL Mansion House, The Haugh, ELGIN
☎ 01343 548811 ▤ 01343 547916 23 en suite

Save on Hotels. Book at theAA.com/hotel

MORAY – NORTH AYRSHIRE

ROTHES
Map 15 NJ24

Rothes Golf Club Blackhall AB38 7AN
☎ 01340 831443 (evenings) 📠 01340 831443
e-mail: enquiries@rothesgolfclub.co.uk
web: www.rothesgolfclub.co.uk
A parkland course on an elevated site with fine views over the Spey Valley Lush tree-lined fairways and well maintained greens.
9 Holes, 5230yds, Par 70, SSS 65, Course record 68.
Club membership 260.
Visitors Mon-Sun & BHs. Booking required weekends. Societies booking required. Green Fees not confirmed Course Designer John Souter Facilities ⑪ ⑨ 🏌 ☕ 🍴 ⚘ Conf Corporate Hospitality Days Location on A941 10m S of Elgin
Hotel ★★★★ 72% HL Craigellachie, CRAIGELLACHIE
☎ 01340 881204 📠 01340 881253 26 en suite

NORTH AYRSHIRE

BEITH
Map 10 NS35

Beith Golf Club Threepwood Rd KA15 2JR
☎ 01505 503166 & 506814 📠 01505 506814
e-mail: beith_secretary@btconnect.com
web: www.beithgc.webs.com
Hilly course, with panoramic views over seven counties.
18 Holes, 5684yds, Par 69. Club membership 487.
Visitors Mon-Sun & BHs. Booking required weekends & BHs. Societies booking required. Green Fees £20 per round, £28 per day (weekend £25 per round) Course Designer Members Facilities ⑪ ⑨ 🏌 ☕ 🍴 ⚘ Conf Corporate Hospitality Days Location 1st left on Beith bypass, S on A737
Hotel ★★★ 80% HL Bowfield Hotel & Country Club, HOWWOOD
☎ 01505 705225 📠 01505 705230 23 en suite

GREAT CUMBRAE ISLAND (MILLPORT)
Map 10 NS15

Millport Golf Club Golf Rd KA28 0HB
☎ 01475 530306 📠 01475 530306
e-mail: secretary@millportgolfclub.co.uk
web: www.millportgolfclub.co.uk
Pleasantly situated on the west side of Cumbrae looking over Bute to Arran and the Mull of Kintyre. Exposed, so conditions can vary according to wind strength and direction. A typical seaside resort course welcoming visitors.
18 Holes, 5828yds, Par 68, SSS 69, Course record 62.
Club membership 460.
Visitors Mon-Sun & BHs. Societies welcome. Green Fees £24 per round (£32 weekends) Course Designer James Braid Facilities ⑪ ⑨ 🏌 ☕ 🍴 ⚘ 🏠 🏌 ⚘ Conf Corporate Hospitality Days Location 4m from ferry slip
Hotel ★★★ 75% HL Willowbank Hotel, 96 Greenock Road, LARGS
☎ 01475 672311 & 675435 📠 01475 689027 30 en suite

IRVINE
Map 10 NS34

Glasgow Golf Club Gailes KA11 5AE
☎ 0141 942 2011 📠 0141 942 0770
web: www.glasgowgailes-golf.com
18 Holes, 6535yds, Par 71, SSS 72, Course record 63.
Course Designer W Park Jnr Location off A78 at Newhouse junct, S of Irvine
Telephone for further details
Hotel ★★★★ 76% HL Menzies Irvine, 46 Annick Road, IRVINE
☎ 01294 274272 📠 01294 277287 128 en suite

Irvine Golf Club Bogside KA12 8SN
☎ 01294 275979 📠 01294 278209
e-mail: secretary@theirvinegolfclub.co.uk
web: www.theirvinegolfclub.co.uk
Testing links course; only two short holes.
18 Holes, 6400yds, Par 71, SSS 73, Course record 65.
Club membership 450.
Visitors contact club for details. Societies welcome. Green Fees not confirmed Course Designer James Braid Prof Jim McKinnon Facilities ⑪ ⑨ 🏌 ☕ 🍴 ⚘ 🏠 ⚘ Location N side of town off A737
Hotel ★★★★ 76% HL Menzies Irvine, 46 Annick Road, IRVINE
☎ 01294 274272 📠 01294 277287 128 en suite

Irvine Ravenspark Golf Club 13 Kidsneuk KA12 8SR
☎ 01294 271293
e-mail: secretary@irgc.co.uk
web: www.irgc.co.uk
Parkland course except final 5 holes (links).
18 Holes, 6457yds, Par 71, SSS 71, Course record 64.
Club membership 500.
Visitors Mon-Sun & BHs. Dress code. Societies booking required. Green Fees not confirmed 🏌 Prof Peter Bond Facilities ⑪ ⑨ 🏌 ☕ 🍴 ⚘ 🏠 ⚘ Conf Corporate Hospitality Days Location N side of town on A737
Hotel ★★★★ 76% HL Menzies Irvine, 46 Annick Road, IRVINE
☎ 01294 274272 📠 01294 277287 128 en suite

Western Gailes Golf Club Gailes by Irvine KA11 5AE
☎ 01294 311649 📠 01294 312312
e-mail: enquiries@westerngailes.com
web: www.westerngailes.com
A magnificent seaside links with glorious turf and wonderful greens. The view is open across the Firth of Clyde to the neighbouring islands. It is a well-balanced course crossed by three burns. There are two par 5s, the 6th and 14th, and the 11th is a testing 445yd par 4 dog-leg.
18 Holes, 6640yds, Par 71, SSS 74, Course record 65.
Club membership 475.
Visitors Mon, Wed, Fri-Sun except BHs. Sun pm. Sat twilight in summer. Booking required. Dress code. Societies booking required. Green Fees £120 per 18 holes, £170 per 36 holes (both including lunch). £125 Sun (no lunch), Sat twilight £125 (no food) Facilities ⑪ ⑨ by prior arrangement 🏌 ☕ 🍴 ⚘ 🏠 🏌 ⚘ ⚘ Location 2m S off A737
Hotel ★★★★ 76% HL Menzies Irvine, 46 Annick Road, IRVINE
☎ 01294 274272 📠 01294 277287 128 en suite

SCOTLAND

KILBIRNIE
Map 10 NS35

Kilbirnie Place Golf Club Largs Rd KA25 7AT
☎ 01505 684444 & 683398
e-mail: kilbirnie.golfclub@tiscali.co.uk
web: www.kilbirnieplacegolfclub.webs.com

Easy walking parkland. The fairways are generally narrow and burns come into play on five holes and the greens are generally small with fairly tricky borrows. Two par 5 holes, both 500 yds.

18 Holes, 5524yds, Par 69, SSS 67, Course record 62.
Club membership 340.

Visitors Sun-Fri & BHs. Booking required Sun & BHs. Dress code. **Societies** booking required. **Green Fees** not confirmed **Facilities** ⊕ ⦿ ⬛ ▭ ⬚ ⚲ **Location** 1m W from Kilbirnie Cross on A760
Hotel ★★★ 75% HL Willowbank Hotel, 96 Greenock Road, LARGS
☎ 01475 672311 & 675435 ▤ 01475 689027 30 en suite

LARGS
Map 10 NS25

Largs Golf Club Irvine Rd KA30 8EU
☎ 01475 673594 ▤ 01475 673594
e-mail: secretary@largsgolfclub.co.uk
web: www.largsgolfclub.co.uk

A parkland, tree-lined course with views to the Clyde coast and the Isle of Arran.

Largs Kelburn: 18 Holes, 6150yds, Par 70, SSS 71,
Course record 65. Club membership 850.

Visitors Mon, Tue, Thu, Fri & Sun. Booking required. Dress code **Societies** Booking required. **Green Fees** £48 per day, £36 per round (£48 per round Sun) **Course Designer** H Stutt **Prof** Andrew Fullen **Facilities** ⊕ ⦿ ⬛ ▭ ⬚ ⚲ 🏠 ⛳ ✦ **Location** 1m S of town centre on A78
Hotel ★★★ 75% HL Willowbank Hotel, 96 Greenock Road, LARGS
☎ 01475 672311 & 675435 ▤ 01475 689027 30 en suite

Routenburn Golf Club Routenburn Rd KA30 8QA
☎ 01475 686475 ▤ 01475 687240

Heathland course with panoramic views over the Firth of Clyde and the Argyll peninsula to the Isle of Arran.

18 Holesyds, Par 67, SSS 68, Course record 63.
Club membership 300.

Visitors Mon-Sun & BHs. Booking required Wed, weekends & BHs. **Societies** booking required. **Green Fees** not confirmed **Course Designer** J Braid **Prof** J Grieg McQueen **Facilities** ⊕ by prior arrangement ⬛ ▭ ⬚ ⚲ 🏠 ⛳ ✦ **Conf** Corporate Hospitality Days **Location** 1m N off A78
Hotel ★★★ 75% HL Willowbank Hotel, 96 Greenock Road, LARGS
☎ 01475 672311 & 675435 ▤ 01475 689027 30 en suite

SKELMORLIE
Map 10 NS16

Skelmorlie Golf Club Beithglass PA17 5ES
☎ 01475 520152
e-mail: sgcsec@yahoo.co.uk
web: www.skelmorliegolf.co.uk

Parkland and moorland course with magnificent views over the Firth of Clyde.

18 Holes, 5030yds, Par 65, SSS 65, Course record 63.
Club membership 450.

Visitors Mon-Fri except BHs. Dress code. **Societies** booking required. **Green Fees** £27 per day, £22 per round (£32/£27 weekends) ⚲ **Course Designer** James Braid **Facilities** ⊕ by prior arrangement ⦿ by prior arrangement ⬛ ▭ ⬚ ⚲ ✦ **Conf** Corporate Hospitality Days **Location** E side of village off A78
Hotel ★★★ 75% HL Willowbank Hotel, 96 Greenock Road, LARGS
☎ 01475 672311 & 675435 ▤ 01475 689027 30 en suite

STEVENSTON
Map 10 NS24

Ardeer Golf Club Greenhead KA20 4LB
☎ 01294 464542 ▤ 01294 464542
e-mail: info@ardeergolf.co.uk
web: www.ardeergolfclub.co.uk

Parkland with natural hazards, including several water features. Trees are a feature of the course.

18 Holes, 6401yds, Par 72, SSS 71, Course record 66.
Club membership 550.

Visitors Mon-Sun & BHs. Sat after 3pm. Booking required weekends & BHs. Dress code. **Societies** booking required **Green Fees** £40 per day, £25 per round (£50/£35 Sun). £50 per 4 ball Tue & Thu, £15 per round **Course Designer** Stutt **Facilities** ⊕ ⬛ ▭ ⬚ ⚲ 🏠 ⛳ ✦ **Leisure** snooker **Conf** Corporate Hospitality Days **Location** 0.5m N off A78
Hotel ★★★★ 76% HL Menzies Irvine, 46 Annick Road, IRVINE
☎ 01294 274272 ▤ 01294 277287 128 en suite

WEST KILBRIDE
Map 10 NS24

West Kilbride Golf Club 33-35 Fullerton Dr, Seamill KA23 9HT
☎ 01294 823911 ▤ 01294 829573
e-mail: golf@westkilbridegolfclub.com
web: www.westkilbridegolfclub.com

Seaside links course on the Firth of Clyde, with fine views of Isle of Arran from every hole.

18 Holes, 6548yds, Par 71, SSS 71, Course record 63.
Club membership 840.

Visitors Mon-Fri except BHs. Booking required. Handicap certificate. Dress code. **Societies** welcome. **Green Fees** not confirmed **Course Designer** James Braid **Prof** Iain Darroch **Facilities** ⊕ ⦿ ⬛ ▭ ⬚ ⚲ 🏠 ⛳ 🚃 ✦ **Location** W side of town off A78
Hotel ★★★ 75% HL Willowbank Hotel, 96 Greenock Road, LARGS
☎ 01475 672311 & 675435 ▤ 01475 689027 30 en suite

SCOTLAND

NORTH LANARKSHIRE

AIRDRIE   Map 11 NS76

Airdrie Golf Club Rochsoles ML6 0PQ
☎ 01236 762195 📄 01236 760584
18 Holes, 6004yds, Par 69, SSS 68, Course record 61.
Course Designer J Braid **Location** 1m N on B802
Telephone for further details
Hotel ★★★★ 81% HL The Westerwood Hotel & Golf Resort, 1
St Andrews Drive, Westerwood, CUMBERNAULD ☎ 01236 457171
📄 01236 738478 148 en suite

Easter Moffat Golf Club Mansion House, Station Rd,
Plains ML6 8NP
☎ 01236 842878 📄 01236 842904
e-mail: secretary@emgc.org.uk
A challenging moorland and parkland course which enjoys good views
of the Campsie and Ochil hills. Although fairways are generous,
accurate placement from the tee is essential on most holes. The
signature hole on the course, the 18th is a truly memorable par
3, played from an elevated tee, to a receptive green in front of the
clubhouse.
18 Holes, 6221yds, Par 72, SSS 70, Course record 66.
Club membership 500.
Visitors Mon-Fri except BHs. Dress code. **Societies** welcome. **Green
Fees** £35 per day, £23 per round 🅿 **Prof** Graham King **Facilities** ⓣ
🍽 🍺 ☕ 🍴 ⚒ 🏠 ⚡ **Location** 2m E of Airdrie on A89
Hotel ★★★★ 81% HL The Westerwood Hotel & Golf Resort, 1
St Andrews Drive, Westerwood, CUMBERNAULD ☎ 01236 457171
📄 01236 738478 148 en suite

BELLSHILL   Map 11 NS76

Bellshill Golf Club Community Rd, Orbiston ML4 2RZ
☎ 01698 745124 📄 01698 292576
e-mail: info@bellshillgolfclub.com
web: www.bellshillgolfclub.com
Tree-lined course situated in the heart of Lanarkshire near Strathclyde
Park. First opened for play in 1905 and extended in 1970. The 2nd hole
has been redesigned by Mark James and Andrew Mair. The first five
holes are extremely demanding but are followed by the gentler birdie
alley where shots can be recovered. The signature hole is the 17th, a
par 3 which involves a tricky tee shot from an elevated tee to a small
well-bunkered green with out of bounds on the right.
18 Holes, 5818yds, Par 69, SSS 68, Course record 63.
Club membership 700.
Visitors Mon-Fri, Sun & BHs. Sat after 3pm. **Societies** booking
required. **Green Fees** Summer £25 per day, £20 per round (£30/£25
weekends & BHs) **Facilities** ⓣ 🍽 🍺 ☕ 🍴 ⚒ **Location** 1m
SE off A721
Hotel ★★★★ 78% HL Alona Hotel, Strathclyde Country Park,
MOTHERWELL ☎ 01698 333888 📄 01698 338720 51 en suite

COATBRIDGE   Map 11 NS76

Drumpellier Golf Club Drumpellier Av ML5 1RX
☎ 01236 424139 📄 01236 428723
e-mail: administrator@drumpelliergolfclub.com
Parkland with rolling fairways and fast greens.
18 Holes, 6227yds, Par 71, SSS 70, Course record 62.
Club membership 827.
Visitors Mon-Fri & BHs. Booking required. Handicap certificate. Dress
code. **Societies** booking required. **Green Fees** £50 per day, £35
per round **Course Designer** W Fernie **Prof** Ian Taylor **Facilities** ⓣ
🍽 🍺 ☕ 🍴 ⚒ 🏠 ⚡ ⚡ **Conf** facs Corporate
Hospitality Days **Location** 0.75m W off A89
Hotel ★★★ 80% HL Bothwell Bridge Hotel, 89 Main Street,
BOTHWELL ☎ 01698 852246 📄 01698 854686 90 en suite

CUMBERNAULD   Map 11 NS77

Dullatur Golf Club 1A Glen Douglas Dr G68 0DW
☎ 01236 723230 📄 01236 727271
web: www.dullaturgolf.com
Dullatur Carrickstone is a parkland course, with natural hazards
and wind. Dullatur Antonine, designed by Dave Thomas, is a modern
course.
Carrickstone: 18 Holes, 6204yds, Par 70, SSS 70,
Course record 68.
Antonine: 18 Holes, 5875yds, Par 69, SSS 68.
Club membership 700.
Visitors Booking required. **Societies** booking required. **Green Fees** not
confirmed **Course Designer** James Braid **Prof** Duncan Sinclair
Facilities ⓣ 🍽 🍺 ☕ 🍴 ⚒ 🏠 ⚡ ⚡ **Leisure** hard
tennis courts, sauna, gymnasium, bowling green **Conf** facs Corporate
Hospitality Days **Location** 1.5m N of A80 at Cumbernauld
Hotel ★★★★ 81% HL The Westerwood Hotel & Golf Resort, 1
St Andrews Drive, Westerwood, CUMBERNAULD ☎ 01236 457171
📄 01236 738478 148 en suite

Palacerigg Golf Club Palacerigg Country Park G67 3HU
☎ 01236 734969 & 721461 📄 01236 721461
e-mail: palacerigg-golfclub@lineone.net
web: www.palacerigg.co.uk
Well-wooded parkland course set in Palacerigg Country Park, with
good views to the Campsie Hills.
18 Holes, 6444yds, Par 72, SSS 72, Course record 66.
Club membership 300.
Visitors Mon-Sun & BHs. Booking required. **Societies** booking
required. **Green Fees** £15 per day, £10 per round (weekend £12 per
round) **Course Designer** Henry Cotton **Facilities** ⓣ 🍽 🍺 ☕ 🍴
⚒ 🏠 ⚡ ⚡ **Conf** Corporate Hospitality Days **Location** 2m S of
Cumbernauld on Palacerigg road off Lenziemill road B8054, within
Palacerigg Country Park
Hotel ★★★★ 81% HL The Westerwood Hotel & Golf Resort, 1
St Andrews Drive, Westerwood, CUMBERNAULD ☎ 01236 457171
📄 01236 738478 148 en suite

SCOTLAND

Westerwood Hotel & Golf Resort 1 St Andrews Dr, Westerwood G68 0EW
☎ 01236 725281 📄 01236 738478
e-mail: westerwoodgolf@qhotels.co.uk
web: www.qhotels.co.uk

Undulating parkland and woodland course designed by Dave Thomas and Seve Ballasteros. Holes meander through silver birch, firs, heaths and heather, and the spectacular 15th, The Waterfall, has its green set against a 40ft rockface. Buggie track.

18 Holes, 6144yds, Par 71, SSS 71. Club membership 400.
Visitors contact hotel for details. **Societies** welcome. **Green Fees** Apr-Oct £35 per round (£40 weekends). Nov-Mar £20 **Course Designer** Seve Ballasteros/Dave Thomas **Prof** Vincent Brown **Facilities** ⊕ †◎¶ 🅱 ⌁ 🗗 👤 🖼 🍴 ◇ 🍷 🍺 🏌 **Leisure** hard tennis courts, heated indoor swimming pool, sauna, gymnasium **Conf** facs Corporate Hospitality Days **Location** by A80, 14m from Glasgow
Hotel ★★★★ 81% HL The Westerwood Hotel & Golf Resort, 1 St Andrews Drive, Westerwood, CUMBERNAULD ☎ 01236 457171 📄 01236 738478 148 en suite

GARTCOSH
Map 11 NS66

Mount Ellen Golf Club Johnston Rd G69 8BD
☎ 01236 872277 📄 01236 872277
e-mail: secretary@mountellengolfclub.co.uk
web: www.mountellengolfclub.co.uk

Downland course with 73 bunkers. Testing 10th (Bedlay), 156yds, par 3.

18 Holes, 5426yds, Par 68, SSS 67, Course record 61. Club membership 500.
Visitors Mon-Fri, Sun & BHs. Booking required Sun & BHs. Dress code. **Societies** booking required. **Green Fees** not confirmed **Prof** Iain Bilsborough **Facilities** ⊕ †◎¶ 🅱 ⌁ 🗗 👤 🖼 🍷 🍺 🏌 **Conf** Corporate Hospitality Days **Location** M73 junct 2A
Hotel ★★★★ 74% HL Millennium Hotel Glasgow, George Square, GLASGOW ☎ 0141 332 6711 📄 0141 332 4264 116 en suite

KILSYTH
Map 11 NS77

Kilsyth Lennox Golf Club Tak Ma Doon Rd G65 0RS
☎ 01236 824115 📄 01236 823089
web: www.kilsythlennox.com

18 Holes, 6612yds, Par 71, SSS 71, Course record 66.
Course Designer Rocky Roquemore **Location** N side of town off A803
Telephone for further details
Hotel ★★★★ 81% HL The Westerwood Hotel & Golf Resort, 1 St Andrews Drive, Westerwood, CUMBERNAULD ☎ 01236 457171 📄 01236 738478 148 en suite

MOTHERWELL
Map 11 NS75

Colville Park Golf Club New Jerviston House, Jerviston Estate, Merry St ML1 4UG
☎ 01698 265779 (pro) 📄 01698 230418
web: www.colvillepark.co.uk

Parkland course. First nine, tree-lined, second nine, more exposed. Testing 10th hole par 3, 16th hole par 4.

18 Holes, 6352yds, Par 71, SSS 71, Course record 63. Club membership 900.
Visitors Mon-Fri & BHs, Booking required Fri & BHs. Dress Code **Societies** apply in writing. **Green Fees** not confirmed **Course Designer** James Braid **Prof** Sam Cairns **Facilities** ⊕ †◎¶ 🅱 ⌁ 🗗 👤 🖼 🏌 **Location** 1.25m NE of Motherwell town centre on A723
Hotel ★★★ 80% HL Bothwell Bridge Hotel, 89 Main Street, BOTHWELL ☎ 01698 852246 📄 01698 854686 90 en suite

MUIRHEAD
Map 11 NS66

Crow Wood Golf Club Garnkirk House, Cumbernauld Rd G69 9JF
☎ 0141 779 2011 📄 0141 779 4873
e-mail: secretary@crowwood-golfclub.co.uk
web: www.crowwood-golfclub.co.uk

Parkland course.

18 Holes, 6168yds, Par 71, SSS 70, Course record 63. Club membership 800.
Visitors booking required weekends & BHs. Dress code. **Societies** booking required. **Green Fees** not confirmed **Course Designer** James Braid **Prof** Ian Graham **Facilities** ⊕ †◎¶ 🅱 ⌁ 🗗 👤 🖼 🏌 **Leisure** snooker,pool **Conf** facs Corporate Hospitality Days **Location** First left off the A80 immediately after end of M80 Stepps bypass towards Stirling.
Hotel ★★★ 82% HL Malmaison Glasgow, 278 West George Street, GLASGOW ☎ 0141 572 1000 📄 0141 572 1002 72 en suite

SHOTTS
Map 11 NS86

Shotts Golf Club Blairhead ML7 5BJ
☎ 01501 822658 📄 01501 822650
web: www.shottsgolfclub.co.uk

18 Holes, 6205yds, Par 70, SSS 70, Course record 63.
Course Designer James Braid **Location** 2m from M8 off Benhar Road
Telephone for further details
Hotel ★★★★ FH East Badallan Farm, FAULDHOUSE ☎ 01501 770251 3 rooms

WISHAW
Map 11 NS75

Wishaw Golf Club 55 Cleland Rd ML2 7PH
☎ 01698 372869 (club house) & 357480 (admin)
▤ 01698 356930
e-mail: jwdouglas@btconnect.com
web: www.wishawgolfclub.com
Parkland with many tree-lined fairways. Bunkers protect 17 of the 18 greens.

18 Holes, 5999yds, Par 69, SSS 69, Course record 62.
Club membership 984.

Visitors Mon-Fri, Sun & BHs. Dress code. **Societies** booking required.
Green Fees not confirmed 🏌 **Course Designer** James Braid
Prof Stuart Adair **Facilities** ⊕ ⍾ ▤ ⏣ ⍾ ⊿ 🏠 ⚐ 🏌
⚐ **Location** NW side of town off A721
Hotel ★★★★ 78% HL Alona Hotel, Strathclyde Country Park,
MOTHERWELL ☎ 01698 333888 ▤ 01698 338720 51 en suite

PERTH & KINROSS

ABERFELDY
Map 14 NN84

Aberfeldy Golf Club Taybridge Rd PH15 2BH
☎ 01887 820535 ▤ 01887 820535
e-mail: abergc@tiscali.com.uk
web: www.aberfeldygolf.co.uk
Founded in 1895, this flat, parkland course is situated by the River Tay near the famous Wade Bridge and Black Watch Monument, and enjoys some splendid scenery. The layout will test the keen golfer.

18 Holes, 5283yds, Par 68, SSS 66, Course record 64.
Club membership 140.

Visitors Mon-Sun & BHs. Booking required Sat. Dress code.
Societies booking required. **Green Fees** £27.50 per round (£30 weekends & BHs) **Course Designer** Soutars **Facilities** ⊕ ⍾
▤ ⏣ ⍾ ⊿ 🏠 🍴 **Conf** Corporate Hospitality Days
Location N side of town centre
Hotel ★★★ 78% HL Kenmore Hotel, The Square, KENMORE
☎ 01887 830205 ▤ 01887 830262 40 en suite

ALYTH
Map 15 NO24

The Alyth Golf Club 1894 Pitcrocknie PH11 8HF
☎ 01828 632268 ▤ 01828 633491
e-mail: enquiries@alythgolfclub.co.uk
web: www.alythgolfclub.co.uk
Windy, heathland course with easy walking.

18 Holes, 6205yds, Par 71, SSS 71, Course record 64.
Club membership 1000.

Visitors contact club for details. **Societies** welcome. **Green
Fees** phone **Course Designer** James Braid **Prof** Tom Melville
Facilities ⊕ ⍾ ▤ ⏣ ⍾ ⊿ 🏠 🍴 ⚐ 🏌 🏌
Location 1m E on B954
Hotel ★★★★★ GA Tigh Na Leigh Guesthouse, 22-24 Airlie Street,
ALYTH ☎ 01828 632372 ▤ 01828 632279 5 rooms

Strathmore Golf Centre Leroch PH11 8NZ
☎ 01828 633322 ▤ 01828 633533
e-mail: enquiries@strathmoregolf.com
web: www.strathmoregolf.com

The Rannaleroch Course is set on rolling parkland and heath with splendid views over Strathmore. It is generous off the tee but beware of the undulating, links-style greens. Among the challenging holes is the 480yd 5th with a 180yd carry over water from a high tee position. The nine-hole Leitfie Links has been specially designed with beginners, juniors and older golfers in mind.

Rannaleroch Course: 18 Holes, 6454yds, Par 72, SSS 72,
Course record 64.
Leitfie Links: 9 Holes, 1666yds, Par 29.
Club membership 520.

Visitors Contact centre for details. **Societies** booking required. **Green
Fees** £32 per round. Leitfie £12 per round (£38/£14 weekends) **Course
Designer** John Salvesen **Prof** Andy Lamb/Gareth Couzens **Facilities** ⊕
⍾ ▤ ⏣ ⍾ ⊿ 🏠 🏌 ⚐ 🏌 **Conf** facs Corporate
Hospitality Days **Location** 2m SE of Alyth, B954 at Meigle onto A926,
signed from Blairgowrie
Hotel ★★★★★ GA Tigh Na Leigh Guesthouse, 22-24 Airlie Street,
ALYTH ☎ 01828 632372 ▤ 01828 632279 5 rooms

AUCHTERARDER
Map 11 NN91

Auchterarder Golf Club Orchil Rd PH3 1LS
☎ 01764 662804 (Sec) ▤ 01764 664423 (Sec)
e-mail: secretary@auchterardergolf.co.uk
web: www.auchterardergolf.co.uk
Flat parkland course, part woodland with pine, larch and silver birch.
It may be short but tricky with cunning dog-legs and guarded greens that require accuracy rather than sheer power. The 14th Punchbowl hole is perhaps the trickiest. A blind tee shot needs to be hit accurately over the left edge of the cross bunker to a long and narrow green - miss and you face a difficult downhill chip shot.

18 Holes, 5750yds, Par 69, SSS 69, Course record 61.
Club membership 820.

Visitors Mon-Sun & BHs. Dress code. **Societies** booking required.
Green Fees Mon-Thu £45 per day, £35 per round, Fri-Sun £55/£40
Course Designer Ben Sayers **Prof** Gavin Baxter **Facilities** ⊕ ⍾
▤ ⏣ ⍾ ⊿ 🏠 🏌 ⚐ **Conf** Corporate Hospitality Days
Location 0.75m SW on A824
Hotel ★★★★★ HL The Gleneagles Hotel, AUCHTERARDER
☎ 01764 662231 ▤ 01764 662134 232 en suite

SCOTLAND

The Gleneagles Hotel see page 363
PH3 1NF
☎ 01764 662231 📄 01764 662134
e-mail: resort.sales@gleneagles.com
web: www.gleneagles.com

BLAIR ATHOLL   Map 14 NN86

Blair Atholl Golf Club Invertilt Rd PH18 5TG
☎ 01796 481407 📄 01796 481292
Easy walking parkland with a river alongside three holes.

9 Holes, 5816yds, Par 70, SSS 68. Club membership 309.
Visitors Mon-Sun & BHs. Booking required weekends.
Societies welcome. **Green Fees** not confirmed **Course Designer** Tom
Morriss **Facilities** ⑪ 🍴 🍺 ⬜ 🏧 ⚲ ㄱ ℱ **Location** 0.5m
S off B8079
Hotel ★★★ 72% HL Atholl Arms Hotel, Old North Road, BLAIR
ATHOLL ☎ 01796 481205 📄 01796 481550 30 en suite

BLAIRGOWRIE   Map 15 NO14

Blairgowrie Golf Club Golf Course Rd, Rosemount
PH10 6LG
☎ 01250 872622 📄 01250 875451
e-mail: office@theblairgowriegolfclub.co.uk
web: www.theblairgowriegolfclub.co.uk
Two 18-hole championship heathland/woodland courses, also a
nine-hole course.

Rosemount Course: 18 Holes, 6630yds, Par 72, SSS 72.
Lansdowne Course: 18 Holes, 6866yds, Par 72, SSS 73.
Wee Course: 9 Holes, 2352yds, Par 64, SSS 63.
Club membership 1800.
Visitors Mon-Sun & BHs. Booking required. Dress code.
Societies booking required. **Green Fees** phone **Course Designer** J
Braid/P Alliss/D Thomas/Old Tom Morris **Prof** Charles Dernie
Facilities ⑪ 🍴 🍺 ⬜ 🏧 ⚲ 🏠 ㄱ ℱ 🚜 ℱ ⚓
Conf Corporate Hospitality Days **Location** off A93 Rosemount
Hotel ★★★★ 78% CHH Ballathie House Hotel, KINCLAVEN
☎ 01250 883268 📄 01250 883396 41 en suite

COMRIE   Map 11 NN72

Comrie Golf Club Laggan Braes PH6 2LR
☎ 01764 670055
e-mail: comriegolf@tiscali.co.uk
web: www.comriegolf.co.uk
Challenging 9-hole course with two tricky par 3s. Fine views of
highland scenery from most holes.

9 Holes, 6016yds, Par 70, SSS 70, Course record 63.
Club membership 350.
Visitors Mon-Sun & BHs. Booking required Mon-Tue. **Societies** booking
required. **Green Fees** £22 per day, £20 per 18 holes, £15 per 9 holes
(£26/£22/£18 weekends and BHs) **Course Designer** Col. Williamson
Facilities ⑪ 🍴 🍺 ⬜ ⚲ ㄱ 🚜 ℱ **Conf** Corporate
Hospitality Days **Location** E side of village off A85
Hotel ★★★ 83% HL The Four Seasons Hotel, Loch Earn, ST FILLANS
☎ 01764 685333 📄 01764 685444 18 en suite

CRIEFF   Map 11 NN82

Crieff Golf Club Ferntower, Perth Rd PH7 3LR
☎ 01764 652909 📄 01764 653803
e-mail: bookings@crieffgolf.co.uk
web: www.crieffgolf.co.uk

Set in dramatic countryside, Crieff Golf Club was established in
1891. The Ferntower championship course has magnificent views
over the Strathearn Valley and offers all golfers an enjoyable round.
The short nine-hole Dornock course, which incorporates some of the
James Braid designed holes from the original 18 holes, provides an
interesting challenge for juniors, beginners and others short of time.
Ferntower Course: 18 Holes, 6493yds, Par 71, SSS 72.
Dornoch Course: 9 Holes, 4540yds, Par 64, SSS 63.
Club membership 720.
Visitors Mon-Sun & BHs. Booking required. Handicap certificate.
Dress code. **Societies** booking required. **Green Fees** Ferntower £34
May & Oct, £37 Jun-Sep (£40/£43 weekends). Dornock £12 for 9
holes, £16 for 18 holes **Course Designer** James Braid **Prof** David
Murchie **Facilities** ⑪ 🍴 🍺 ⬜ 🏧 ⚲ 🏠 ㄱ ℱ 🚜 ℱ
Conf Corporate Hospitality Days **Location** 0.5m NE on A85
Hotel ★★★ 83% HL Royal, Melville Square, COMRIE
☎ 01764 679200 📄 01764 679219 13 en suite

GLENEAGLES HOTEL

PERTH & KINROSS - AUCHTERARDER - MAP 11 NN91

The PGA Centenary Course, created by Jack Nicklaus, and launched in style in May 1993, has an American-Scottish layout with many water hazards, elevated tees and raised contoured greens. It is the selected venue for the Ryder Cup 2014. It has a five-tier tee structure making it both the longest and shortest playable course, as well as the most accommodating to all standards of golfer. The King's Course, with its abundance of heather, gorse, raised greens and plateau tees, is set within the valley of Strathearn with the Grampian mountains spectacularly in view to the north. The shorter Queen's Course, with fairways lined with Scots pines and water hazards, is set within a softer landscape and is considered an easier test of golf. You can improve your game at the golf academy at Gleneagles where the philosophy is that golf should be fun and fun in golf comes from playing better. A complete corporate golf package is available.

PH3 1NF ☎ 01764 662231 🖷 01764 662134
e-mail: resort.sales@gleneagles.com **web:** www.gleneagles.com
King's Course: 18 Holes, 6471yds, Par 70, SSS 73, Course record 60.
Queen's Course: 18 Holes, 5965yds, Par 68, SSS 70, Course record 61.
PGA Centenary Course: 18 Holes, 6815yds, Par 73, SSS 74, Course record 65. Club membership 600.
Visitors Mon-Sun & BHs. Booking required. Dress code. **Societies** booking required. **Green Fees** Apr-mid May & mid-end Oct £98, mid May-mid Oct £155. Wee Course £30 all year **Course Designer** James Braid/Jack Nicklaus **Prof** Russell Smith **Facilities** **Leisure** hard tennis courts, heated indoor swimming pool, fishing, sauna, gymnasium, halfway house, golf academy, horse riding, shooting, falconry, off road driving **Conf** facs Corporate Hospitality Days **Location** 2m SW of A823
Hotel ★★★★★ HL The Gleneagles Hotel, AUCHTERARDER ☎ 01764 662231 🖷 01764 662134 232 en suite

DUNKELD — Map 11 NO04

Dunkeld & Birnam Golf Club Fungarth PH8 0ES
☎ 01350 727524 📄 01350 728660
e-mail: secretary-dunkeld@tiscali.co.uk
web: www.dunkeldandbirnamgolfclub.co.uk

Interesting and challenging course. Each hole has its own character and the course affords spectacular views over the dramatic countryside and overlooks the historic Dunkeld Cathedral and Loch of the Lowes Nature Reserve, where the osprey come to nest and can often be seen flying overhead.

18 Holes, 5511yds, Par 69, SSS 67, Course record 61.
Visitors contact club for details. **Societies** welcome. **Green Fees** phone **Course Designer** D A Tod **Facilities** ⓣ 🍴 🛒 ⬚ 🔧 👤 🏠 ⛳ 🏌 🚌 ⛳ **Conf** Corporate Hospitality Days **Location** 1m N of village on A923
Hotel ★★★★ 78% CHH Ballathie House Hotel, KINCLAVEN
☎ 01250 883268 📄 01250 883396 41 en suite

DUNNING — Map 11 NO01

Dunning Golf Club Rollo Park, Station Rd PH2 0QX
☎ 01764 684747
e-mail: secretary@dunninggolfclub.co.uk
web: www.dunninggolfclub.co.uk
A pleasant parkland course with some testing holes, complicated by the burn which is a feature of four of the nine holes.

9 Holes, 4894yds, Par 66, SSS 64. Club membership 460.
Visitors Mon-Sun & BHs (after 3pm on Sat). Booking required. Dress code. **Societies** booking required. **Green Fees** £18 per 18 holes (£20 weekends). £10 per 9 holes 😊 **Prof** Stuart Barker **Facilities** 🛒 ⬚ 👤 🏠 ⛳ **Location** 4m N of Auchterarder, 1.5m off A9 on B9146
Hotel ★★★★★ HL The Gleneagles Hotel, AUCHTERARDER
☎ 01764 662231 📄 01764 662134 232 en suite

Whitemoss Golf Course Whitemoss Rd PH2 0QX
☎ 01738 730300 📄 01738 730490
web: www.whitemossgolf.com
18 Holes, 5595yds, Par 68, SSS 68, Course record 63.
Course Designer Whitemoss Leisure **Location** off A9 at Whitemoss Rd junct, 3m N of Gleneagles
Telephone for further details
Hotel ★★★★★ HL The Gleneagles Hotel, AUCHTERARDER
☎ 01764 662231 📄 01764 662134 232 en suite

GLENSHEE (SPITTAL OF) — Map 15 NO17

Dalmunzie Golf Club Dalmunzie Estate PH10 7QE
☎ 01250 885226
e-mail: enquiries@dalmunziecottages.com
web: www.dalmunziecottages.com
Well-maintained highland course. Testing short course with small but good greens. One of the highest courses in Britain at 1200ft.

9 Holes, 2099yds, Par 30, SSS 30, Course record 29.
Club membership 90.
Visitors Contact club for details. **Societies** welcome. **Green Fees** £15 per day **Course Designer** Alistair Campbell **Facilities** ⓣ 🍴 🛒 ⬚ 🔧 🏠 ⛳ ◇ **Leisure** hard tennis courts, fishing, clay target shooting **Conf** facs Corporate Hospitality Days **Location** 2m NW of Spittal of Glenshee
Hotel ★★★ 80% CHH Dalmunzie Castle, SPITTAL OF GLENSHEE
☎ 01250 885224 📄 01250 885225 17 en suite

KENMORE — Map 14 NN74

Kenmore Golf Course PH15 2HN
☎ 01887 830226 📄 01887 830775
e-mail: info@taymouth.co.uk
web: www.taymouth.co.uk
Testing course in mildly undulating natural terrain. Beautiful views in tranquil setting by Loch Tay. The par 5 4th is 560yds and only one of the par 4s, the 2nd, is under 400yds - hitting from the tee out of a mound of trees down a snaking banking fairway which encourages the ball to stay on the fairway. The slightly elevated green is surrounded by banks to help hold the ball on the green. The fairways are generous and the rough short, which tends to encourage an unhindered round.

9 Holes, 6052yds, Par 70, SSS 69, Course record 67.
Club membership 200.
Visitors Mon-Sun & BHs. Booking advised weekends & BHs. **Societies** booking required. **Green Fees** £30 per day, £20 per 18 holes, £15 per 9 holes (£35/£25/£17 weekends) **Course Designer** Robin Menzies **Facilities** ⓣ 🍴 🛒 ⬚ 🔧 👤 🏠 ⛳ ◇ 🚌 ⛳ **Leisure** fishing, horse riding **Conf** Corporate Hospitality Days **Location** on A827, beside Kenmore Bridge at Mains of Taymouth
Hotel ★★★ 78% HL Kenmore Hotel, The Square, KENMORE
☎ 01887 830205 📄 01887 830262 40 en suite

Save on Hotels. Book at **theAA.com/hotel**

PERTH & KINROSS

KINROSS
Map 11 NO10

The Green Hotel Golf & Leisure Resort 2 The Muirs KY13 8AS
☎ 01577 863407 🖹 01577 863180
e-mail: bookings@golfkinross.com
web: www.golfkinross.com

Two interesting and picturesque parkland courses, with easy walking. Many of the fairways are bounded by trees and plantations. A number of holes have views over Loch Leven to the hills beyond. The more challenging of the two is the Montgomery which has been enhanced by the addition of a pond in front of the 11th green and 19 extra bunkers. The Bruce is slightly shorter but still provides a stern test of golf with notable features being the 6th Pond Hole and the run of four par 5s in six holes on the front nine.

Bruce: 18 Holes, 6231yds, Par 73, SSS 72.
Montgomery: 18 Holes, 6508yds, Par 72, SSS 72.
Club membership 600.

Visitors Mon-Sun & BHs. Booking required. Dress code.
Societies booking required. **Green Fees** Individual rounds £35 per day, (£45 weekends). Day tickets £48, (£58 weekends) **Course Designer** Sir David Montgomery **Prof** Greig McSporran **Facilities** 🍴 🍸 🖥 🛄 🛅 🏌 🍴 💠 **Leisure** heated indoor swimming pool, fishing, sauna, gymnasium, 4 sheet curling rink, croquet **Conf** facs Corporate Hospitality Days **Location** M90 junct 6, NE side of town on B996
Hotel ★★★★ 73% HL The Green Hotel, 2 The Muirs, KINROSS
☎ 01577 863467 🖹 01577 863180 46 en suite

MILNATHORT
Map 11 NO10

Milnathort Golf Club South St KY13 9XA
☎ 01577 864069
e-mail: milnathort.gc@btconnect.com
Undulating inland course with lush fairways and excellent greens. Strategically placed copses require accurate tee shots. Different tees and greens for some holes will make for more interesting play.

9 Holes, 5985yds, Par 71, SSS 69, Course record 61.
Club membership 575.

Visitors Sun-Fri & BHs. Booking required. Dress code.
Societies booking required. **Green Fees** Weekdays £22 per day, £15 per round (weekends £25/£17) **Facilities** 🍴 🍴 🖥 🍸 🛄 🛅 🏌 💠 🍴 **Conf** Corporate Hospitality Days **Location** S side of town on A922
Hotel ★★★★ 73% HL The Green Hotel, 2 The Muirs, KINROSS
☎ 01577 863467 🖹 01577 863180 46 en suite

MUTHILL
Map 11 NN81

Muthill Golf Club Peat Rd PH5 2DA
☎ 01764 681523 🖹 01764 681557
e-mail: muthillgolfclub@btconnect.com
web: www.muthillgolfclub.co.uk
A nine-hole course that, although short, requires accurate shot making to match the SSS. The three par 3s are all challenging holes with the 9th, a 205yd shot to a small well-bunkered green making a fitting end to nine holes characterised by great views and springy well-maintained fairways.

9 Holes, 4673yds, Par 66, SSS 63. Club membership 285.

Visitors Mon-Sun & BHs. Booking required. **Societies** booking required. **Green Fees** not confirmed 🅿 **Course Designer** Members **Facilities** 🍴 🍸 🛄 🏌 🍴 **Location** W side of village off A822
Hotel ★★★★ 73% HL The Green Hotel, 2 The Muirs, KINROSS
☎ 01577 863467 🖹 01577 863180 46 en suite

PERTH
Map 11 NO12

Craigie Hill Golf Club Cherrybank PH2 0NE
☎ 01738 622644 (pro) 🖹 01738 620829
e-mail: admin@craigiehill.co.uk
web: www.craigiehill.com
Slightly hilly, heathland course. Panoramic views of Perth and the surrounding hills.

18 Holes, 5386yds, Par 66, SSS 67, Course record 60.
Club membership 600.

Visitors Mon-Sun & BHs. Booking required Wed & weekends. Dress code. **Societies** booking required. **Green Fees** £32 per day, £24 per round (£37/£29 weekends) **Course Designer** Fernie/Anderson **Prof** Niall McGill **Facilities** 🍴 🍴 🖥 🍸 🛄 🛅 🏌 🍴 **Conf** facs Corporate Hospitality Days **Location** 1m SW of city centre off A952
Hotel ★★★ 75% HL Best Western Queens Hotel, Leonard Street, PERTH ☎ 01738 442222 🖹 01738 638496 50 en suite

King James VI Golf Club Moncreiffe Island PH2 8NR
☎ 01738 632460
e-mail: mansec@kingjamesvi.com
web: www.kingjamesvi.com
Parkland course on island in the River Tay. Easy walking.

18 Holes, 6038yds, Par 70, SSS 69, Course record 62.
Club membership 650.

Visitors Mon-Sun & BHs. Booking required. Dress code. **Societies** welcome. **Green Fees** £34 per day, £25 per round (£36/£28 weekends) **Course Designer** Tom Morris **Prof** Allan Knox **Facilities** 🍴 🍴 🛄 🍸 🛅 🏌 💠 🍴 **Conf** Corporate Hospitality Days **Location** SE side of city centre
Hotel ★★★ 75% HL Best Western Queens Hotel, Leonard Street, PERTH ☎ 01738 442222 🖹 01738 638496 50 en suite

Murrayshall House Hotel & Golf Course Murrayshall, Scone PH2 7PH

☎ 01738 552784 & 551171   📠 01738 552595

e-mail: info@murrayshall.com

web: www.murrayshall.com

Set within 350 acres of undulating parkland, Murrayshall offers 36 holes of outstanding golf. The original championship course is set out within the parkland estate and the Lynedoch is a woodland-style course, full of natural features. Many of the fairways are lined by majestic trees while white sand bunkers and water hazards with natural stone bridges protecting the generous greens.

Murrayshall Course: 18 Holes, 6489yds, Par 73, SSS 73, Course record 64.

Lynedoch Course: 18 Holes, 5800yds, Par 69.

Club membership 350.

Visitors Mon-Sun & BHs. Booking required. Dress code. **Societies** booking required. **Green Fees** not confirmed **Course Designer** Hamilton Stutt **Prof** Alan Reid **Facilities** ⊕ ⑩ ☕ 🍴 ⚐ 🏪 ᵠ ◇ 🛒 ⚒ **Leisure** hard tennis courts **Conf facs** Corporate Hospitality Days **Location** E side of village off A94 **Hotel** ★★★★ 76% HL Murrayshall House Hotel & Golf Course, New Scone, PERTH ☎ 01738 551171 📠 01738 552595 41 en suite

PITLOCHRY   Map 14 NN95

Pitlochry Golf Golf Course Rd PH16 5QY

☎ 01796 472792   📠 01796 473947

e-mail: pro@pitlochrygolf.co.uk

web: www.pitlochrygolf.co.uk

A varied and interesting heathland course with fine views and posing many problems. Its SSS permits few errors in its achievement.

18 Holes, 5681yds, Par 69, SSS 69, Course record 60.

Club membership 400.

Societies booking required. **Green Fees** £40 per day, £30 per round (£48/£38 weekends). Low season £34/£25 (£40/£33 weekends) **Course Designer** Willie Fernie **Prof** Mark Pirie **Facilities** ⊕ ⑩ ᵯ ⚐ 🍴 ᵠ 🏪 ◇ ⚒ 🛒 ⚒ **Conf** Corporate Hospitality Days **Location** off A924 onto Larchwood Rd then on to Golf Course Rd **Hotel** ★★★ 75% HL Moulin Hotel, 11-13 Kirkmichael Road, Moulin, PITLOCHRY ☎ 01796 472196 📠 01796 474098 15 en suite

ST FILLANS   Map 11 NN62

St Fillans Golf Club South Loch Earn Rd PH6 2NJ

☎ 01764 685312   📠 01764 685312

web: www.stfillans-golf.com

9 Holes, 6054yds, Par 69, SSS 69, Course record 73.

Course Designer W Auchterlonie **Location** E side of village off A85 **Telephone for further details** **Hotel** ★★★ 83% HL The Four Seasons Hotel, Loch Earn, ST FILLANS ☎ 01764 685333 📠 01764 685444 18 en suite

STRATHTAY   Map 14 NN95

Strathtay Golf Club Upper Derculich PH9 0LR

☎ 01887 840493

e-mail: strathtay@aol.com

web: www.strathtaygolfclub.com

Very attractive highland course in a charming location. Steep in places but with fine views of surrounding hills and the Tay Valley.

9 Holes, 3826yds, Par 63, SSS 61. Club membership 150.

Visitors Contact club for details. **Societies** welcome. **Green Fees** £15 per day (£20 weekends) 🍴 **Facilities** ⚐ ⚒ **Location** E of village centre off A827 **Hotel** ★★★ 87% CHH Green Park, Clunie Bridge Road, PITLOCHRY ☎ 01796 473248 📠 01796 473520 51 en suite

RENFREWSHIRE

BISHOPTON   Map 10 NS47

Erskine Golf Club PA7 5PH

☎ 01505 862108   📠 01505 862302

e-mail: peter@erskinegc.wanadoo.co.uk

web: www.erskinegolfclublimited.co.uk

Parkland on the south bank of the River Clyde, with views of the hills beyond.

18 Holes, 6372yds, Par 71, SSS 71. Club membership 800.

Visitors Mon-Fri & BHs. Dress code. **Societies** welcome **Green Fees** not confirmed **Prof** Peter Thomson **Facilities** ⊕ ⑩ ᵯ ⚐ 🍴 🏪 ᵠ ◇ ⚒ **Conf** Corporate Hospitality Days **Location** 0.75 NE off B815 **Hotel** ★★★★ 77% HL Beardmore Hotel, Beardmore Street, CLYDEBANK ☎ 0141 951 6000 📠 0141 951 6018 166 en suite

BRIDGE OF WEIR   Map 10 NS36

Old Course Ranfurly Golf Club Ranfurly Place PA11 3DE

☎ 01505 613612   📠 01505 613214

web: www.oldranfurly.com

18 Holes, 6061yds, Par 70, SSS 70, Course record 63.

Course Designer W Park **Location** 6m S of Glasgow Airport **Telephone for further details** **Hotel** ★★★ 80% HL Bowfield Hotel & Country Club, HOWWOOD ☎ 01505 705225 📠 01505 705230 23 en suite

Ranfurly Castle Golf Club The Clubhouse, Golf Rd PA11 3HN

☎ 01505 612609   📠 01505 610406

e-mail: secretary@ranfurlycastlegolfclub.co.uk

web: www.ranfurlycastlegolfclub.co.uk

A picturesque, highly challenging 240-acre moorland course.

18 Holes, 6261yds, Par 70, SSS 71, Course record 64. Club membership 824.

Visitors Mon-Fri & BHs. Booking required Wed & BHs. Dress code. **Societies** booking required. **Green Fees** £45 per day, £35 per round **Course Designer** A Kirkcaldy/W Auchterlomie **Prof** Tom Eckford **Facilities** ⊕ ⑩ ᵯ ⚐ 🍴 ⚒ 🏪 ᵠ ◇ 🛒 ⚒ **Location** 5m NW of Johnstone **Hotel** ★★★ 80% HL Bowfield Hotel & Country Club, HOWWOOD ☎ 01505 705225 📠 01505 705230 23 en suite

JOHNSTONE　　　　　　　　　Map 10 NS46

Cochrane Castle Golf Club Scott Av, Craigston PA5 0HF
☎ 01505 328465 🖹 01505 325338
web: www.cochranecastle.co.uk
Fairly hilly parkland, wooded with two small streams running through.
18 Holes, 6194yds, Par 71, SSS 71, Course record 63.
Club membership 721.
Visitors Mon-Fri & BHs. Booking required. Dress code.
Societies booking required. **Green Fees** £35 per day, £25 per round
🌐 **Course Designer** J Hunter **Prof** Alan J Logan **Facilities** ⑪ ℍ ⬚
☐ ⅌ ⬭ 🏡 ✦ **Location** 1m from town centre, off Beith Rd
Hotel ★★★ 80% HL Bowfield Hotel & Country Club, HOWWOOD
☎ 01505 705225 🖹 01505 705230　23 en suite

Elderslie Golf Club 63 Main Rd, Elderslie PA5 9AZ
☎ 01505 320032 🖹 01505 340346
e-mail: eldersliegolfclub@btconnect.com
web: www.eldersliegolfclub.net
Undulating parkland with good views.
18 Holes, 6175yds, Par 70, SSS 71, Course record 62.
Club membership 940.
Visitors Mon-Fri except BHs. Booking required. Dress code.
Societies booking required. **Green Fees** not confirmed **Course
Designer** J Braid **Prof** Richard Bowman **Facilities** ⑪ ℍ ⬭ ☐
⅌ ⬭ 🏡 ✦ **Leisure** snooker table **Conf** Corporate Hospitality
Days **Location** E side of town on A737
Hotel ★★★ 79% HL Holiday Inn Glasgow Airport, Abbotsinch,
PAISLEY ☎ 0871 942 9031 & 0141 887 1266 🖹 0141 887 3738
300 en suite

LOCHWINNOCH　　　　　　　　Map 10 NS35

Lochwinnoch Golf Club Burnfoot Rd PA12 4AN
☎ 01505 842153 & 01505 843029　🖹 01505 843668
e-mail: admin@lochwinnochgolf.co.uk
web: www.lochwinnochgolf.co.uk
Well-maintained parkland course incorporating natural burns.
Throughout the course the majority of fairways are wide with tricky
greens, but always in good condition. Very scenic with lots of bunkers.
18 Holes, 6002yds, Par 71, SSS 70, Course record 63.
Club membership 650.
Visitors dress code. **Societies** booking required. **Green Fees** £25
per round, £35 per day **Prof** Gerry Reilly **Facilities** ⑪ ℍ ⬭ ☐
⅌ ⬭ 🏡 ⚲ ✦ 🚌 ✦ **Conf** facs Corporate Hospitality Days
Location W side of town off A760
Hotel ★★★ 80% HL Bowfield Hotel & Country Club, HOWWOOD
☎ 01505 705225 🖹 01505 705230　23 en suite

PAISLEY　　　　　　　　　　　Map 11 NS46

Barshaw Golf Club Barshaw Park PA1 3TJ
☎ 0141 889 2908
Municipal parkland course.
18 Holes, 5703yds, Par 68, SSS 68, Course record 56.
Club membership 100.
Visitors contact club for details. **Societies** booking required. **Green
Fees** not confirmed 🌐 **Course Designer** J R Stutt **Facilities** ⬭
Location 1m E off A737
Hotel ★★★ 79% HL Holiday Inn Glasgow Airport, Abbotsinch,
PAISLEY ☎ 0871 942 9031 & 0141 887 1266 🖹 0141 887 3738
300 en suite

Paisley Golf Club Braehead Rd PA2 8TZ
☎ 0141 884 3903 & 884 2292　🖹 0141 884 3903
e-mail: paisleygolfclub@btconnect.com
web: www.paisleygolfclub.co.uk
Moorland course with good views which suits all handicaps. The
course has been designed in two loops of nine holes. Holes feature
trees and gorse.
18 Holes, 6479yds, Par 71, SSS 72, Course record 63.
Club membership 810.
Visitors Mon-Fri & Sun except BHs. Booking required. Handicap
certificate. Dress code. **Societies** booking required. **Green Fees** not
confirmed **Course Designer** John Stutt **Facilities** ⑪ ℍ ⬭ ☐
⅌ ⬭ 🏡 ⅌ ⬭ ✦ **Conf** facs **Location** Exit M8 junct 27,
Renfrew Rd and continue through lights. Left at Causeyside St, right
before Gleniffer Hotel, left at rdbt, at top of hill
Hotel ★★★ 79% HL Holiday Inn Glasgow Airport, Abbotsinch,
PAISLEY ☎ 0871 942 9031 & 0141 887 1266 🖹 0141 887 3738
300 en suite

Ralston Golf Club Strathmore Av, Ralston PA1 3DT
☎ 0141 882 1349 🖹 0141 883 9837
e-mail: thesecretary@ralstongolf.co.uk
web: www.ralstongolfclub.com
Parkland course.
18 Holes, 6119yds, Par 70, SSS 69, Course record 62.
Club membership 750.
Visitors Mon-Sun & BHs. Booking required Mon-Fri. Handicap
certificate. Dress code. **Societies** booking required. **Green Fees** £42
per day, £27 per round **Course Designer** J Braid **Prof** Colin Munro
Facilities ⑪ ℍ ⬭ ☐ ⅌ ⬭ 🏡 ⚲ ✦ **Conf** facs
Corporate Hospitality Days **Location** 2m E of Paisley town centre on
A761
Hotel ★★★ 79% HL Holiday Inn Glasgow Airport, Abbotsinch,
PAISLEY ☎ 0871 942 9031 & 0141 887 1266 🖹 0141 887 3738
300 en suite

RENFREW　　　　　　　　　　Map 11 NS46

Renfrew Golf Club Blythswood Estate, Inchinnan Rd
PA4 9EG
☎ 0141 886 6692 🖹 0141 886 1808
e-mail: andy.mclaughlin@renfrewgolfclub.net
web: www.renfrewgolfclub.net
A tree-lined parkland course.
18 Holes, 6818yds, Par 72, SSS 73, Course record 65.
Club membership 800.
Visitors Mon-Sun & BHs. Booking required. Dress code.
Societies booking required. **Green Fees** £45 per day, £35 per round
🌐 **Course Designer** Commander Harris **Prof** Ricky Gray **Facilities** ⑪
ℍ ⬭ ☐ ⅌ ⬭ 🏡 ✦ **Conf** facs Corporate Hospitality Days
Location 0.75m W off A8
Hotel ★★★★ 77% HL Beardmore Hotel, Beardmore Street,
CLYDEBANK ☎ 0141 951 6000 🖹 0141 951 6018　166 en suite

SCOTLAND

SCOTTISH BORDERS

ASHKIRK
Map 12 NT42

Woll Golf Course New Woll Estate TD7 4PE
☎ 01750 32711
e-mail: wollclubhouse@tiscali.co.uk
web: www.wollgolf.co.uk
Flat parkland course with mature trees and a natural burn and ponds. The course is gentle but testing for all standards of golfer. Set in the private grounds of New Woll Estate in outstanding countryside in the Ale Valley.

18 Holes, 6051yds, Par 70, SSS 70. Club membership 500.
Visitors Mon-Sun & BHs. Booking required Fri-Sun & BHs. Dress code. **Societies** booking required. **Green Fees** £40 per day, £28 per 18 holes (weekend £32 per 18 holes) **Course Designer** Alec Cleghorn **Prof** Murray Cleghorn **Facilities** ⑪ ⑩ ⓑ ⓓ ⑨ ⌂ 🖻 ⑨ ◇ ✔ 🚍 ✔ **Leisure** sauna **Conf** facs Corporate Hospitality Days **Location** off A7 at village of Ashkirk, between the towns of Selkirk and Hawick
Hotel ★★★ 77% HL Kingsknowes, Selkirk Road, GALASHIELS ☎ 01896 758375 🖺 01896 750377 12 en suite

COLDSTREAM
Map 12 NT83

Hirsel Golf Club Kelso Rd TD12 4NJ
☎ 01890 882678 🖺 01890 882233
e-mail: bookings@hirselgc.co.uk
web: www.hirselgc.co.uk
A beautifully situated parkland course set in the Hirsel Estate, with panoramic views of the Cheviot Hills. Each hole offers a different challenge especially the 7th, a 170yd par 3 demanding accuracy of flight and length from the tee to ensure achieving a par.

18 Holes, 6024yds, Par 70, SSS 70, Course record 64. Club membership 500.
Visitors Mon-Sun & BHs. Booking required. Dress code.
Societies booking required. **Green Fees** £38 per day, £30 per round (£44/£34 weekends) **Facilities** ⑪ ⑩ ⓑ ⓓ ⑨ ⌂ 🖻 ✔ 🚍 ✔ **Conf** facs Corporate Hospitality Days **Location** on A697 at W end of Coldstream
Hotel ★★★ 86% CHH Tillmouth Park Country House, CORNHILL-ON-TWEED ☎ 01890 882255 🖺 01890 882540 14 en suite

DUNS
Map 12 NT75

Duns Golf Club Hardens Rd TD11 3NR
☎ 01361 882194 & 883599
e-mail: secretary@dunsgolfclub.com
web: www.dunsgolfclub.com
Interesting upland course, with natural hazards of water and hilly slopes. Views south to the Cheviot Hills. A burn comes into play at seven of the holes. The signature hole is the short 116 yard 15th, named 'Double Trouble', due to a two tier green and burn at the front and rear of the green.

18 Holes, 6298yds, Par 71, SSS 70, Course record 65. Club membership 400.
Visitors Mon-Sun & BHs. Booking required. **Societies** booking required. **Green Fees** £40 per day, £30 per round (£45/£35 weekends & BHs) **Course Designer** A H Scott **Facilities** ⑪ ⑩ ⓑ ⓓ ⑨ ⌂ ⑨ 🚍 ✔ **Conf** Corporate Hospitality Days **Location** 1m W off A6105

Hotel ★★★ 74% CHH Marshall Meadows Country House, BERWICK-UPON-TWEED ☎ 01289 331133 🖺 01289 331438 19 en suite

EYEMOUTH
Map 12 NT96

Eyemouth Golf Club Gunsgreen Hill TD14 5SF
☎ 01890 750551 (clubhouse) & 750004 (Pro)
web: www.eyemouthgolfclub.co.uk
18 Holes, 6520yds, Par 72, SSS 72, Course record 66.
Course Designer J R Bain **Location** E side of town, 8m N of Berwick and 2m off A1
Telephone for further details
Hotel ★★★ 74% CHH Marshall Meadows Country House, BERWICK-UPON-TWEED ☎ 01289 331133 🖺 01289 331438 19 en suite

GALASHIELS
Map 12 NT43

Galashiels Golf Club Ladhope Recreation Ground TD1 2NJ
☎ 01896 753724
e-mail: secretary@galashiels-golfclub.co.uk
web: www.galashiels-golfclub.co.uk
Hillside course with superb views from the top, recently redeveloped.

9 Holes, 3000yds, Par 68, SSS 68. Club membership 186.
Visitors Mon-Sun & BHs. Booking required Sat. **Societies** booking required. **Green Fees** not confirmed **Course Designer** James Braid **Facilities** ⑪ by prior arrangement ⑩ by prior arrangement ⓑ ⓓ ⑨ ⌂ ✔ **Location** N side of town centre off A7, opposite Ladhope Inn
Hotel ★★★ 77% HL Kingsknowes, Selkirk Road, GALASHIELS ☎ 01896 758375 🖺 01896 750377 12 en suite

Torwoodlee Golf Club Edinburgh Rd TD1 2NE
☎ 01896 752260 🖺 01896 752306
e-mail: torwoodleegolfclub@btconnect.com
web: www.torwoodleegolfclub.co.uk
A picturesque course flanked by the River Gala and set among a mix of mature woodland and rolling parkland.

18 Holes, 6021yds, Par 69, SSS 70, Course record 64. Club membership 550.
Visitors Mon-Sun & BHs. Booking required. Dress code. **Societies** booking required. **Green Fees** £42 per day, £32 per round **Course Designer** Willie Park **Facilities** ⑪ ⑩ ⓑ ⓓ ⑨ ⌂ 🚍 ✔ **Conf** Corporate Hospitality Days **Location** 1.75m NW of Galashiels off A7
Hotel ★★★ 77% HL Kingsknowes, Selkirk Road, GALASHIELS ☎ 01896 758375 🖺 01896 750377 12 en suite

HAWICK
Map 12 NT51

Hawick Golf Club Vertish Hill TD9 0NY
☎ 01450 372293
e-mail: thesecretary@hawickgolfclub.com
web: www.hawickgolfclub.com
Hill course with good views.

Vertish Hill: 18 Holes, 5933yds, Par 68, SSS 68, Course record 66. Club membership 600.
Visitors Mon-Sun & BHs. Booking required. Handicap certificate. Dress code. **Societies** booking required. **Green Fees** £36 per day, £30 per round **Facilities** ⑪ ⑩ ⓑ ⓓ ⑨ ⌂ 🖻 ⑨ ✔ 🚍 ✔ **Conf** Corporate Hospitality Days **Location** SW side of town

SCOTLAND

Save on Hotels. Book at **theAA.com/hotel**

SCOTTISH BORDERS

INNERLEITHEN
Map 11 NT33

Innerleithen Golf Club Leithen Water EH44 6NL
☎ 01896 830951

9 Holes, 6066yds, Par 70, SSS 69, Course record 64.
Course Designer Willie Park **Location** 1.5m N on B709
Telephone for further details
Hotel ★★★★ 77% HL Macdonald Cardrona Hotel & Golf Course,
Cardrona, PEEBLES ☎ 01896 833600 ▤ 01896 831166 99 en suite

JEDBURGH
Map 12 NT62

Jedburgh Golf Club Dunion Rd TD8 6TA
☎ 01835 863587
e-mail: info@jedburghgolfclub.co.uk
web: www.jedburghgolfclub.co.uk
Undulating parkland/moorland course with superb views over
surrounding countryside. The course offers an excellent variety of holes
with water hazards coming into play on many of the holes.
Dunion Course: 18 Holes, 5819yds, Par 69, SSS 69,
Course record 70. Club membership 220.
Visitors Mon-Sun & BHs. Booking required. Dress code.
Societies booking required. **Green Fees** not confirmed 🌐 **Course**
Designer William Park **Facilities** ⑪ ⑩ ⅃ ⌴ ⊓ ⌳ 👜 ✂
Conf Corporate Hospitality Days **Location** 1m W on B6358
Hotel ★★★★ 77% CHH The Roxburghe Hotel & Golf Course,
Heiton, KELSO ☎ 01573 450331 ▤ 01573 450611 22 en suite

KELSO
Map 12 NT73

The Roxburghe Hotel & Golf Course Heiton TD5 8JZ
☎ 01573 450333 ▤ 01573 450611
e-mail: golf@roxburghe.net
web: www.roxburghegolfclub.co.uk

An exceptional parkland layout designed by Dave Thomas and
opened in 1997. Surrounded by natural woodland on the banks
of the River Teviot. Owned by the Duke of Roxburghe, this course
has numerous bunkers, wide rolling and sloping fairways and
strategically placed water features. The signature hole is the 14th.
18 Holes, 6925yds, Par 72, SSS 74, Course record 66.
Club membership 325.
Visitors Mon-Sun & BHs. Booking required. Handicap certificate.
Dress code. **Societies** booking required. **Green Fees** £90 per day, £70
per round **Course Designer** Dave Thomas **Prof** Craig Montgomerie
Facilities ⑪ ⑩ ⅃ ⌴ ⊓ ⌳ 👜 ⋔ ◇ ✂ 👜 ✂ 🏇
Leisure fishing, clay pigeon shooting, falconry, archery, mountain bikes
Conf facs Corporate Hospitality Days **Location** 2m W of Kelso on A698
Hotel ★★★★ 77% CHH The Roxburghe Hotel & Golf Course,
Heiton, KELSO ☎ 01573 450331 ▤ 01573 450611 22 en suite

LAUDER
Map 12 NT54

Lauder Golf Course Galashiels Rd TD2 6RS
☎ 01578 722426 ▤ 01578 722526
e-mail: secretary@laudergolfclub.org.uk
web: www.laudergolfclub.org.uk
Inland course and practice area on gently sloping hill with stunning
views of the Lauderdale district. The signature holes are The Wood, a
dog-leg par 4 played round the corner of a wood which is itself out of
bounds, and The Quarry, a 150yd par 3 played over several old quarry
holes into a bowl shaped green.
9 Holes, 6030yds, Par 70, SSS 69. Club membership 220.
Visitors Mon-Sun & BHs. Booking required Sun. **Societies** booking
required. **Green Fees** not confirmed 🌐 **Course Designer** Willie Park
Jnr **Facilities** ⅃ ⌴ ⌳ **Location** off A68, 0.5m from Lauder, on
Galashiels Road
Hotel ★★★ 70% HL Lauderdale, 1 Edinburgh Road, LAUDER
☎ 01578 722231 ▤ 01578 718642 10 en suite

MELROSE
Map 12 NT53

Melrose Golf Club Dingleton TD6 9HS
☎ 01896 822855 ▤ 01896 822855
e-mail: melrosegolfclub@tiscali.co.uk
Undulating tree-lined fairways with splendid views. Many bunkers.
Ponds and streams cross and border four of the holes.
9 Holes, 5545yds, Par 70, SSS 68, Course record 64.
Club membership 300.
Visitors Mon-Sun & BHs. Booking required Wed & Sat.
Societies booking required. **Green Fees** £25 per day. Reductions for 9
holes. 🌐 **Course Designer** James Braid **Facilities** ⌴ ⊓ ⌳ ✂
Location S side of town centre on B6359
Hotel ★★★ 78% HL Burt's, Market Square, MELROSE
☎ 01896 822285 ▤ 01896 822870 20 en suite

MINTO
Map 12 NT52

Minto Golf Club TD9 8SH
☎ 01450 870220 ▤ 01450 870126
e-mail: pat@mintogolfclub.freeserve.co.uk
web: www.mintogolf.co.uk
Pleasant, undulating parkland, featuring mature trees and panoramic
views of the border country. Short but quite testing course.
18 Holes, 5658yds, Par 69, SSS 68. Club membership 500.
Visitors Mon-Sun & BHs. Booking required weekends & BHs. Dress
code. **Societies** booking required. **Green Fees** not confirmed **Course**
Designer Thomas Telford **Facilities** ⑪ ⑩ ⅃ ⌴ ⊓ ⌳ 👜
✂ **Conf** Corporate Hospitality Days **Location** 5m NE from Hawick off
B6405
Hotel ★★★★ 73% CHH Dryburgh Abbey Hotel, ST BOSWELLS
☎ 01835 822261 ▤ 01835 823945 38 en suite

SCOTLAND

NEWCASTLETON
Map 12 NY48

Newcastleton Golf Club Holm Hill TD9 0QD
☎ 01387 375608

Hilly course with scenic views over the Liddesdale Valley and Newcastleton.

9 Holes, 5491yds, Par 69, SSS 70, Course record 67. Club membership 100.

Visitors contact club for details. **Societies** booking required. **Green Fees** £12 all week per 18 holes, £8 per 9 holes 🅿 **Course Designer** J Shade **Facilities** ⛳ 🍴 **Leisure** fishing **Location** W side of village **Hotel** ★★★ 75% HL Garden House, Sarkfoot Road, GRETNA ☎ 01461 337621 📄 01461 337692 38 en suite

PEEBLES
Map 11 NT24

Macdonald Cardrona Hotel & Golf Course Cardrona EH45 8NE
☎ 01896 833701 (Pro shop) 📄 01896 831166
e-mail: golf.cardrona@macdonald-hotels.co.uk
web: www.macdonaldhotels.co.uk

Opened for play in 2001 and already a settled and inspiring test. The terrain is a mixture of parkland, heathland and woodland with an additional 20,000 trees planted. The USPGA specification greens are mostly raised and mildly contoured with no two being the same shape.

18 Holes, 6643yds, Par 72, SSS 73, Course record 67. Club membership 200.

Visitors Mon-Sun & BHs. Booking required. Dress code. **Societies** welcome. **Green Fees** £45 per round (£55 weekends) **Course Designer** Dave Thomas **Facilities** 🏌 🍴 🍺 🖥 🍴 ⛳ 🏊 ◇ 🏌 🚌 🏌 🎯 **Leisure** heated indoor swimming pool, fishing, sauna, gymnasium **Conf** facs Corporate Hospitality Days **Location** off A72, 3m S of Peebles **Hotel** ★★★★ 77% HL Macdonald Cardrona Hotel & Golf Course, Cardrona, PEEBLES ☎ 01896 833600 📄 01896 831166 99 en suite

Peebles Golf Club Kirkland St EH45 8EU
☎ 01721 720197
e-mail: secretary@peeblesgolfclub.co.uk
web: www.peeblesgolfclub.co.uk

This parkland course is one of the most picturesque courses in Scotland, shadowed by the rolling border hills and Tweed Valley and set high above the town. The tough opening holes are balanced by a more generous stretch through to the 14th hole but from here the closing five prove a challenging test.

18 Holes, 6160yds, Par 70, SSS 70, Course record 63. Club membership 750.

Visitors Mon-Fri, Sun & BHs. Handicap certificate. Dress code. **Societies** booking required. **Green Fees** £55 per day, £40 per round **Course Designer** H S Colt **Prof** Craig Imlah **Facilities** 🏌 🍴 🍺 🖥 🍴 ⛳ 🏊 🏠 ⛳ 🏌 🏌 🏌 **Conf** Corporate Hospitality Days **Location** W side of town centre off A72 **Hotel** ★★★ 82% HL Tontine, High Street, PEEBLES ☎ 01721 720892 📄 01721 729732 36 en suite

ST BOSWELLS
Map 12 NT53

St Boswells Golf Club Braeheads TD6 0DE
☎ 01835 823527 📄 01835 823527
e-mail: secretary@stboswellsgolfclub.co.uk
web: www.stboswellsgolfclub.co.uk

Attractive, easy walking parkland by the River Tweed.

9 Holes, 5274yds, Par 68, SSS 66. Club membership 350.

Visitors Mon-Sun & BHs. **Societies** booking required. **Green Fees** £35 per day, £25 per 18 holes, £15 per 9 holes 🅿 **Course Designer** W Park **Facilities** 🏌 by prior arrangement 🍺 🖥 🍴 ⛳ **Location** 500yds off A68 east end of village **Hotel** ★★★★ 73% CHH Dryburgh Abbey Hotel, ST BOSWELLS ☎ 01835 822261 📄 01835 823945 38 en suite

SELKIRK
Map 12 NT42

Selkirk Golf Club Selkirk Hill TD7 4NW
☎ 01750 20621
e-mail: secretary@selkirkgolfclub.co.uk
web: www.selkirkgolfclub.co.uk

Pleasant moorland course with gorse and heather, set around Selkirk Hill. A testing course for all golfers. Unrivalled views.

9 Holes, 5575yds, Par 68, SSS 68, Course record 61. Club membership 300.

Visitors Mon-Wed, Fri, Sun & BHs. Thu am. Booking required. **Societies** booking required. **Green Fees** £22 per 18 holes, £12 per 9 holes 🅿 **Facilities** 🍴 ⛳ **Location** 1m S on A7 **Hotel** ★★★ 78% HL Burt's, Market Square, MELROSE ☎ 01896 822285 📄 01896 822870 20 en suite

WEST LINTON
Map 11 NT15

Rutherford Castle Golf Club EH46 7AS
☎ 01968 661233 📄 01968 661233
e-mail: clubhouse@rutherfordcastlegc.org.uk
web: www.rutherfordcastlegc.org.uk

Undulating parkland set beneath the Pentland Hills. The many challenging holes are a good test for the better player while offering great enjoyment to the average player.

18 Holes, 6525yds, Par 72, SSS 71. Club membership 120.

Visitors Mon-Sun & BHs. Booking required. Dress code. **Green Fees** not confirmed 🅿 **Course Designer** Bryan Moore **Facilities** 🖥 🏌 🚌 ⛳ **Location** on A702 towards Carlisle **Hotel** ★★★★ CHH Cringletie House, Edinburgh Road, PEEBLES ☎ 01721 725750 📄 01721 725751 13 en suite

West Linton Golf Club EH46 7HN
☎ 01968 660970 📄 01968 660622
e-mail: secretarywlgc@btinternet.com
web: www.wlgc.co.uk

Moorland course with beautiful views of Pentland Hills. This well-maintained course offers a fine challenge to all golfers with ample fairways and interesting layouts. The wildlife and natural scenery give added enjoyment.

18 Holes, 6161yds, Par 69, SSS 70, Course record 63. Club membership 850.

Visitors Mon-Sun & BHs. **Societies** booking required. **Green Fees** £40 per day, £30 per round (£40 per round weekends) **Course Designer** Millar/Braid/Fraser **Prof** Ian Wright **Facilities** 🏌 🍴 🍺 🖥 🍴 ⛳ 🏠 🏌 🏌 🏌 **Conf** Corporate Hospitality Days **Location** NW side of village off A702 **Hotel** ★★★★ CHH Cringletie House, Edinburgh Road, PEEBLES ☎ 01721 725750 📄 01721 725751 13 en suite

SCOTLAND

ROYAL TROON

SOUTH AYRSHIRE - TROON - MAP 10 NS33

Troon was founded in 1878 with just five holes on linksland. In its first decade it grew from five holes to six, then 12, and finally 18 holes. It became Royal Troon in 1978 on its 100th anniversary. Royal Troon's reputation is based on its combination of rough and sandy hills, bunkers, and a severity of finish that has diminished the championship hopes of many. The most successful players have relied on an equal blend of finesse and power. The British Open Championship has been played at Troon eight times - in 1923, 1950, 1962, 1973, 1982, 1989, 1997, and lastly in 2004 when it hosted the 133rd tournament. It has the shortest hole of courses hosting the Open. It is recommended that you apply to the course in advance for full visitor information.

Craigend Rd KA10 6EP ☎ 01292 311555 ▤ 01292 318204
e-mail: bookings@royaltroon.com web: www.royaltroon.com
Old Course: 18 Holes, 6641yds, Par 71, SSS 73, Course record 64.
Portland: 18 Holes, 6289yds, Par 71, SSS 71.
Craigend: 9 Holes, 1539yds, Par 29. Club membership 800.
Visitors Mon-Tue & Thu. Booking required. Handicap certificate. Dress code. **Societies** booking required.
Green Fees £175 per day, 1 round over Old & 1 round over Portland **Course Designer** C Hunter/G Strath/W Fernie **Prof** Kieron Stevenson **Facilities** ⑨ ⑩ ⓛ ⬚ ⬚ ⬚ ⬚ ⬚ ⬚ ✦ ⛳ **Location** S of town on B749. 3m from Prestwick airport
Hotel ★★★★ 78% HL Barceló Troon Marine Hotel, Crosbie Road, TROON ☎ 01292 314444
▤ 01292 316922 89 en suite

SOUTH AYRSHIRE

AYR
Map 10 NS32

Belleisle Golf Course Belleisle Park KA7 4DU
☎ 01292 441258 📄 01292 442632
web: www.golfsouthayrshire.com
Belleisle Course: 18 Holes, 6431yds, Par 71, SSS 72,
Course record 63.
Seafield Course: 18 Holes, 5498yds, Par 68, SSS 67.
Course Designer James Braid **Location** 2m S of Ayr on A719
Telephone for further details
Hotel ★★★★ 79% HL Fairfield House, 12 Fairfield Road, AYR
☎ 01292 267461 📄 01292 261456 44 en suite

Dalmilling Golf Club Westwood Av KA8 0QY
☎ 01292 263893 📄 01292 610543
web: www.golfsouthayrshire.com/dalmilling.html
18 Holes, 5724yds, Par 69, SSS 68, Course record 61.
Location 1.5m E of town centre off A77
Telephone for further details
Hotel ★★★★ 79% HL Fairfield House, 12 Fairfield Road, AYR
☎ 01292 267461 📄 01292 261456 44 en suite

BARASSIE
Map 10 NS33

Kilmarnock (Barassie) Golf Club 29 Hillhouse Rd
KA10 6SY
☎ 01292 313920 📄 01292 318300
e-mail: secretary@kbgc.co.uk
web: www.kbgc.co.uk
The club has a 27-hole layout. Magnificent seaside links, relatively
flat with much heather and small, undulating greens.
Barassie Links: 18 Holes, 6484yds, Par 72, SSS 74,
Course record 64.
Hillhouse Course: 9 Holes, 2756yds, Par 34, SSS 34.
Club membership 600.
Visitors Mon-Sun & BHs. Booking required. Dress code.
Societies booking required. **Green Fees** £82 per 36 holes, £57 per
round (£67 per round weekends) **Course Designer** Prof Gregor Howie **Facilities** ⊕ ⦿ ▥ ⊑ ▯ ⅄ 🖼 🛢
✍ Conf Corporate Hospitality Days **Location** E side of village on
B746, 2m N of Troon
Hotel ★★★★ 78% HL Barceló Troon Marine Hotel, Crosbie
Road, TROON ☎ 01292 314444 📄 01292 316922 89 en suite

GIRVAN
Map 10 NX19

Brunston Castle Golf Course Golf Course Rd KA26 9GD
☎ 01465 811471 & 811825 📄 01465 811545
web: www.brunstoncastle.co.uk
Burns: 18 Holes, 6662yds, Par 72, SSS 72,
Course record 63.
Course Designer Donald Steel **Location** 5m E of Girvan
Telephone for further details
Hotel ★★★ 83% HL Malin Court, TURNBERRY ☎ 01655 331457
📄 01655 331072 18 en suite

MAYBOLE
Map 10 NS20

Maybole Municipal Golf Club Memorial Park KA19 7DX
☎ 01655 889770
web: www.south-ayrshiregolf.co.uk
Hilly parkland course with wonderful views over the Carrick Hills.
9 Holes, 5226yds, Par 66, SSS 66, Course record 65.
Club membership 100.
Visitors Mon-Sun & BHs. **Societies** booking required. **Green
Fees** £6.50 per 18 holes, £4.50 per 9 holes (£8/£6 weekends) ⊕
Leisure heated indoor swimming pool, bowling green **Location** off
A77 S of town
Hotel ★★★ 83% HL Malin Court, TURNBERRY ☎ 01655 331457
📄 01655 331072 18 en suite

PRESTWICK
Map 10 NS32

Prestwick Golf Club 2 Links Rd KA9 1QG
☎ 01292 477404 📄 01292 477255
e-mail: bookings@prestwickgc.co.uk
web: www.prestwickgc.co.uk
Seaside links with natural hazards, tight fairways and difficult fast
undulating greens.
18 Holes, 6544yds, Par 71, SSS 73, Course record 67.
Club membership 575.
Visitors Mon-Sun & BHs. Dress code. **Societies** booking required.
Green Fees £175 per day, £120 per round (weekends £145 per
round) **Course Designer** Tom Morris **Prof** D A Fleming **Facilities** ⊕
▥ ⊑ ▯ ⅄ 🖼 ⅋ ✍ 🛢 ✍ Conf Corporate Hospitality
Days **Location** in town centre off A79
Hotel ★★★ 77% HL Parkstone, Esplanade, PRESTWICK
☎ 01292 477286 📄 01292 477671 30 en suite

Prestwick St Cuthbert Golf Club East Rd KA9 2SX
☎ 01292 477101 📄 01292 671730
e-mail: secretary@stcuthbert.co.uk
web: www.stcuthbert.co.uk
Parkland with easy walking and natural hazards. Tree-lined fairways,
nine dog-legs and well bunkered.
18 Holes, 6159yds, Par 70, SSS 70, Course record 64.
Club membership 884.
Visitors Mon-Fri, Sun & BHs. Booking required. Dress code.
Societies booking required. **Green Fees** £48 per day, £35 per
round (Mon-Fri). £45 per round (Sun) **Course Designer** Stutt & Co
Facilities ⊕ ⦿ ▥ ⊑ ▯ ⅄ ✍ 🛢 ✍ Conf Corporate
Hospitality Days **Location** 0.5m E of town centre off A77
Hotel ★★★ 77% HL Parkstone, Esplanade, PRESTWICK
☎ 01292 477286 📄 01292 477671 30 en suite

TURNBERRY RESORT

SOUTH AYRSHIRE - TURNBERRY - MAP 10 NS20

For thousands of players of all nationalities, Turnberry is one of the finest of all golf destinations, where some of the most remarkable moments in Open history have taken place. The legendary Ailsa Course is complemented by the highly acclaimed Kintyre Course, while the nine-hole Arran Course, created by Donald Steel and Colin Montgomerie, has similar challenges such as undulating greens, tight tee shots, pot bunkers and thick Scottish rough. With the famous hotel on the left and the magnificent Ailsa Craig away to the right, there are few vistas in world golf to match the 1st tee here. To help you prepare for your game the Colin Montgomerie Links Golf Academy, alongside the luxurious and extensive clubhouse, was opened in April 2000; it features 12 driving bays, four short-game bays, two dedicated teaching rooms and a group teaching room. The Open returned to the Ailsa in 2009.

Maidens Rd KA26 9LT ☎ 01655 331000 📄 01655 331069
web: www.turnberryresort.co.uk
Ailsa Course: 18 Holes, 7211yds, Par 70.
Kintyre Course: 18 Holes, 6921yds, Par 72.
Arran Course: 9 Holes, 1996yds, Par 31, SSS 31.
Visitors Mon-Sun & BHs. Booking required. Dress code. **Societies** booking required. **Green Fees** contact course for details. **Course Designer** Mackenzie Ross/Donald Steel **Prof** Richard Hall **Facilities** 🍴 🍽 🍦 🖥 🍴 🏌 📁 🏑 ◇ 🏌 🏌 🏌 🏌 **Leisure** hard tennis courts, heated indoor swimming pool, fishing, sauna, gymnasium, Colin Montgomerie Links Golf Academy, Tailor made performance lab **Conf** facs Corporate Hospitality Days
Location 15m SW of Ayr on A77
Hotel ★★★★★ HL Turnberry Resort, Scotland, TURNBERRY ☎ 01655 331000 📄 01655 331706 207 en suite

SCOTLAND

Prestwick St Nicholas Golf Club Grangemuir Rd KA9 1SN
☎ 01292 477608 📄 01292 473900
e-mail: secretary@prestwickstnicholas.com
web: www.prestwickstnicholas.com

Classic seaside links course with views across the Firth of Clyde to the Isle of Arran to the west and Ailsa Craig to the south.

18 Holes, 6044yds, Par 69, SSS 69, Course record 63.
Club membership 750.

Visitors Mon-Sun & BHs. Booking required. Dress code.
Societies booking required. **Green Fees** £75 per day, £55 per round (£60 per round weekends) **Course Designer** Charles Hunter **Facilities** ⑨ ⑩ 🍴 🖥 🥤 🏌 🏠 ⛳ ✆ **Location** S side of town off A79
Hotel ★★★ 77% HL Parkstone, Esplanade, PRESTWICK
☎ 01292 477286 📄 01292 477671 30 en suite

TROON Map 10 NS33

Royal Troon Golf Club see page 371
Craigend Rd KA10 6EP
☎ 01292 311555 📄 01292 318204
e-mail: bookings@royaltroon.com
web: www.royaltroon.com

Troon Municipal Golf Club Harling Dr KA10 6NE
☎ 01292 312464 📄 01292 312578
web: www.golfsouthayrshire.com

Lochgreen Course: 18 Holes, 6820yds, Par 74, SSS 73.
Darley Course: 18 Holes, 6360yds, Par 71, SSS 63.
Fullarton Course: 18 Holes, 4870yds, Par 66, SSS 64.
Location 100yds from railway station
Telephone for further details
Hotel ★★★★ 78% HL Barceló Troon Marine Hotel, Crosbie Road, TROON ☎ 01292 314444 📄 01292 316922 89 en suite

---

TURNBERRY Map 10 NS20

Turnberry Resort see page 373
Maidens Rd KA26 9LT
☎ 01655 331000 📄 01655 331069
web: www.turnberryresort.co.uk

SOUTH LANARKSHIRE

BOTHWELL Map 11 NS75

Bothwell Castle Golf Club Uddingston Rd G71 8TD
☎ 01698 801971 & 801972 📄 01698 801971
e-mail: matchsecretary@bcgolf.co.uk
web: www.bcgolf.co.uk

Flat tree-lined parkland course in a residential area.

18 Holes, 6224yds, Par 70, SSS 71. Club membership 1000.
Visitors Mon-Fri except BHs. Booking required. Dress code.
Societies booking required. **Green Fees** £48 per day, £35 per round
Prof Alan McCloskey **Facilities** ⑨ ⑩ 🍴 🖥 🥤 🏌 🏠 ✆
Conf facs Corporate Hospitality Days **Location** NW of village off B7071
Hotel ★★★ 80% HL Bothwell Bridge Hotel, 89 Main Street, BOTHWELL ☎ 01698 852246 📄 01698 854686 90 en suite

---

BURNSIDE Map 11 NS65

Blairbeth Golf Club Fernbrae Av G73 4SF
☎ 0141 634 3355 & 634 3325
web: www.blairbethgolfclub.co.uk

18 Holes, 5537yds, Par 70, SSS 68, Course record 63.
Location 2m S of Rutherglen off Burnside Rd
Telephone for further details
Hotel ★★★★ 75% HL Holiday Inn Glasgow-East Kilbride, Stewartfield Way, EAST KILBRIDE ☎ 01355 236300 📄 01355 233552 101 en suite

Cathkin Braes Golf Club Cathkin Rd G73 4SE
☎ 0141 634 6605
e-mail: secretary@cathkinbraesgolfclub.co.uk
web: www.cathkinbraesgolfclub.co.uk

Moorland course, 600ft above sea level but relatively flat with a prevailing westerly wind and views over Glasgow. A small loch hazard at 5th hole. Very strong finishing holes.

18 Holes, 6200yds, Par 71, SSS 71, Course record 63.
Club membership 1020.

Visitors Mon-Fri & BHs. Dress code **Societies** booking required. **Green Fees** £45 per day, £35 per round 🅿 **Course Designer** James Braid **Prof** Stephen Bree **Facilities** ⑨ ⑩ 🍴 🖥 🥤 🏌 🏠 ✆ 🚜 ✆ **Conf** Corporate Hospitality Days **Location** 1m S on B759
Hotel ★★★★ 75% HL Holiday Inn Glasgow-East Kilbride, Stewartfield Way, EAST KILBRIDE ☎ 01355 236300 📄 01355 233552 101 en suite

---

CARLUKE Map 11 NS85

Carluke Golf Club, Mauldslie Rd, Hallcraig ML8 5HG
☎ 01555 770574 & 771070
e-mail: carlukegolfsecy@tiscali.co.uk
web: www.carlukegolfclub.com/

Parkland course with views over the Clyde Valley. Testing 11th hole, par 3.

18 Holes, 5936yds, Par 70, SSS 69, Course record 64.
Club membership 750.

Visitors Mon-Fri & BHs. booking required. Dress code.
Societies booking required **Green Fees** £35 per day, £25 per round
Prof Craig Ronald **Facilities** ⑨ ⑩ 🍴 🖥 🥤 🏌 🏠 ✆ 🚜 ✆ **Location** 1m W off A73
Hotel ★★★ 75% CHH Best Western Cartland Bridge Hotel, Glasgow Road, LANARK ☎ 01555 664426 📄 01555 663773 20 en suite

Save on Hotels. Book at **theAA.com/hotel**

SOUTH LANARKSHIRE

CARNWATH
Map 11 NS94

Carnwath Golf Club 1 Main St ML11 8JX
☎ 01555 840251 📄 01555 841070
e-mail: carnwathgc@hotmail.com
web: www.carnwathgc.co.uk
Picturesque parkland, slightly hilly, panoramic views. The small
greens call for accuracy.

18 Holes, 5222yds, Par 66, SSS 66, Course record 63.
Club membership 586.

Visitors Mon-Fri, Sun & BHs. Booking required. Dress code.
Societies booking required. **Green Fees** £35 per day, £25 per
round (£40/£30 Sun) 🏌 **Facilities** ⓣ 🍽 ⓛ ⓓ ⓨ ⓛ ⓢ
Location W side of village on A70
Hotel ★★★ 75% CHH Best Western Cartland Bridge Hotel,
Glasgow Road, LANARK ☎ 01555 664426 📄 01555 663773
20 en suite

EAST KILBRIDE
Map 11 NS65

East Kilbride Golf Club Chapelside Rd, Nerston G74 4PF
☎ 01355 247728 📄 01355 247728
e-mail: secretary@ekgolfclub.co.uk
web: www.ekgolfclub.com
Parkland course of variable topography. Generous fairways and greens
but a challenging test of golf.

18 Holes, 6419yds, Par 71, SSS 71, Course record 63.
Club membership 850.

Visitors Mon-Fri & BHs. Booking required. Dress code.
Societies booking required. **Green Fees** £40 per day, £30 per round
Course Designer Charles Hawtree **Prof** Paul McKay **Facilities** ⓣ 🍽
ⓛ ⓓ ⓨ ⓛ ⓢ 🏠 🎯 ⓢ **Conf** Corporate Hospitality Days
Location 0.5m N off A749, adjacent to Nerston village
Hotel ★★★★ 75% HL Holiday Inn Glasgow-East Kilbride,
Stewartfield Way, EAST KILBRIDE ☎ 01355 236300 📄 01355 233552
101 en suite

Torrance House Golf Course Calderglen Country Park
G75 0QZ
☎ 01355 248638 📄 01355 570916
18 Holes, 6476yds, Par 72, SSS 69, Course record 71.
Course Designer Hawtree & Son **Location** 1.5m SE of East Kilbride
on A726
Telephone for further details
Hotel ★★★★ 74% HL Macdonald Crutherland House, Strathaven
Road, EAST KILBRIDE ☎ 0844 879 9039 📄 01355 577047
75 en suite

HAMILTON
Map 11 NS75

Hamilton Golf Club Carlisle Rd, Ferniegair ML3 7UE
☎ 01698 282872 📄 01698 204650
e-mail: secretary@hamiltongolfclub.co.uk
web: www.hamiltongolfclub.co.uk
Beautiful parkland.

18 Holes, 6498yds, Par 70, SSS 70, Course record 62.
Visitors Mon-Sun & BHs. Booking required. Dress code.
Societies booking required. **Green Fees** £45 per day. £35 per round
(£60/£45 weekends) **Course Designer** James Braid **Prof** Derek Wright
Facilities ⓣ 🍽 ⓛ ⓓ ⓨ ⓛ ⓢ 🏠 🎯 ⓢ 🎯 **Conf** facs
Corporate Hospitality Days **Location** 1.5m SE on A72
Hotel BUD Express by Holiday Inn Hamilton, Keith Street, HAMILTON
☎ 0141 419 3500 📄 0141 419 3500 104 en suite

Strathclyde Park Golf Club Mote Hill ML3 6BY
☎ 01698 429350
Municipal wooded parkland course with views of the Strathclyde Park
sailing loch. With its undulating fairways, every shot in the book is
required. Surrounded by a nature reserve and Hamilton racecourse.

9 Holes, 3051yds, Par 36, SSS 70, Course record 68.
Club membership 120.

Visitors Mon-Sun & BHs. Booking required. Dress code.
Societies booking required. **Green Fees** not confirmed 🏌
Prof William Walker **Facilities** ⓓ ⓢ 🏠 ⓢ 🎯 **Location** N side
of town off B7071
Hotel ★★★★ 78% HL Alona Hotel, Strathclyde Country Park,
MOTHERWELL ☎ 01698 333888 📄 01698 338720 51 en suite

LANARK
Map 11 NS84

Lanark Golf Club The Moor, Whitelees Rd ML11 7RX
☎ 01555 663219 & 661456 📄 01555 663219
e-mail: lanarkgolfclub@supanet.com
web: www.lanarkgolfclub.co.uk
Lanark is renowned for its smooth fast greens, natural moorland
fairways and beautiful scenery. The course is built on a substrata of
glacial sands, providing a unique feeling of tackling a links course
at 600ft above sea level. The par of 70 can be a real test when the
prevailing wind blows.

Old Course: 18 Holes, 6306yds, Par 70, SSS 71,
Course record 62.
Wee Course: 9 Holes, 1337yds, Par 28.
Club membership 880.

Visitors Mon-Fri & BHs. Booking required. Dress code.
Societies booking required. **Green Fees** £50 per day, £40 per round.
Wee Course £8 per day **Course Designer** Tom Morris **Prof** Alan
White **Facilities** ⓣ 🍽 ⓛ ⓓ ⓨ ⓛ ⓢ 🏠 ⓢ 🚜 ⓢ **Conf**
Corporate Hospitality Days **Location** E side of town centre off A73
Hotel ★★★ 75% CHH Best Western Cartland Bridge Hotel,
Glasgow Road, LANARK ☎ 01555 664426 📄 01555 663773
20 en suite

SCOTLAND

LARKHALL
Map 11 NS75

Larkhall Golf Club Burnhead Rd ML9 3AA
☎ 01698 889597 & 881113 (bookings)
9 Holes, 6234yds, Par 70, SSS 70, Course record 69.
Location E side of town on B7019
Telephone for further details
Hotel BUD Express by Holiday Inn Hamilton, Keith Street, HAMILTON
☎ 0141 419 3500 📠 0141 419 3500 104 en suite

LEADHILLS
Map 11 NS81

Leadhills Golf Club 51 Main St ML12 6XP
☎ 07939 435784
e-mail: leadhillsgolfclub@hotmail.co.uk
At 1500ft above sea level it is the highest golf course in Scotland. A natural, old fashioned style course which makes use of the contours of the land producing a unique experience and enjoyable gold.
9 Holes, 2304yds, Par 68, SSS 64. Club membership 50.
Visitors Mon-Sat & BHs. Sun pm **Societies** booking required. **Green Fees** £10 per day, £3 per day juniors 😊 **Location** E side of village off B797. Turn left after Hopeton Arms Hotel, clubhouse is 300yds up hill
Hotel ★★★ 79% CHH Blackaddie House Hotel, Blackaddie Road, SANQUHAR ☎ 01659 502700 9 en suite

LESMAHAGOW
Map 11 NS83

Hollandbush Golf Club Acretophead ML11 0JS
☎ 01555 893484 & 893646
e-mail: mail@hollandbushgolfclub.co.uk
web: www.hollandbushgolfclub.co.uk
Fairly difficult, tree-lined municipal parkland and moorland course. First half is relatively flat, while second half is hilly.
18 Holes, 6183yds, Par 72, SSS 70. Club membership 400.
Visitors Mon-Sun & BHs. Booking required. Dress code.
Societies booking required. **Green Fees** phone 😊 **Course Designer** J Lawson/K Pate **Facilities** ⑪ ⑩ 🍴 🖥 🍽 🏃 🍴 🏌
Location 3m S of Lesmahagow on Coalburn Rd
Hotel ★★★ 83% HL New Lanark Mill Hotel, Mill One, New Lanark Mills, LANARK ☎ 01555 667200 📠 01555 667222 38 en suite

RIGSIDE
Map 11 NS83

Douglas Water Golf Club, Ayr Rd ML11 9NP
☎ 01555 880361 📠 01555 880361
A 9-hole course with good variety and some hills and spectacular views. An interesting course with a challenging longest hole of 564 yards but, overall, not too testing for average golfers.
9 Holes, 5890yds, Par 72, SSS 69, Course record 63. Club membership 150.
Visitors Mon-Fri, Sun & BHs. **Societies** welcome. **Green Fees** not confirmed **Facilities** 🖥 🏃 **Location** on A70
Hotel ★★★ 75% CHH Best Western Cartland Bridge Hotel, Glasgow Road, LANARK ☎ 01555 664426 📠 01555 663773 20 en suite

STRATHAVEN
Map 11 NS74

Strathaven Golf Club Glasgow Rd ML10 6NL
☎ 01357 520421 📠 01357 520539
e-mail: info@strathavengc.com
web: www.strathavengc.com
Gently undulating, tree-lined, championship parkland course with views over the town and the Avon Valley.
18 Holes, 6265yds, Par 71, SSS 71. Club membership 1050.
Visitors Mon-Fri except BHs. Dress code. **Societies** welcome. **Green Fees** not confirmed **Course Designer** Willie Fernie/J Stutt **Prof** Stuart Kerr **Facilities** ⑪ ⑩ 🍴 🖥 🍽 🏃 🍴 🏌 🍴
Location NE side of town on A726
Hotel ★★★★ 74% HL Macdonald Crutherland House, Strathaven Road, EAST KILBRIDE ☎ 0844 879 9039 📠 01355 577047 75 en suite

UDDINGSTON
Map 11 NS66

Calderbraes Golf Club 57 Roundknowe Rd G71 7TS
☎ 01698 813425
Parkland with good views of Clyde Valley. Testing 4th hole (par 4), hard uphill.
9 Holes, 5186yds, Par 66, SSS 67, Course record 65. Club membership 230.
Visitors Mon-Sun & BHs. Booking required weekends.
Societies booking required. **Green Fees** £15 per day 😊 **Facilities** 🖥 🍽 🏃 **Location** 1.5m NW off A74
Hotel ★★★ 80% HL Bothwell Bridge Hotel, 89 Main Street, BOTHWELL ☎ 01698 852246 📠 01698 854686 90 en suite

STIRLING

ABERFOYLE
Map 11 NN50

Aberfoyle Golf Club Braeval FK8 3UY
☎ 01877 382493
e-mail: secretary@aberfoylegolf.co.uk
web: www.aberfoylegolf.co.uk
Scenic heathland course with mountain views, sitting at the foot of the Monteith Hills, on the southern border of Loch Lomond and the Trossachs.
18 Holes, 5158yds, Par 66, SSS 66, Course record 64. Club membership 450.
Visitors Contact club for details. **Societies** booking required. **Green Fees** £25 per day, £20 per round (£30/25 weekends) **Facilities** ⑪ ⑩ 🖥 🍽 🏃 🍴 🍴 **Conf** Corporate Hospitality Days **Location** 1m E on A81
Hotel ★★★★ 76% HL Macdonald Forest Hills Hotel & Resort, Kinlochard, ABERFOYLE ☎ 0844 879 9057 & 01877 389500 📠 01877 387307 49 en suite

BANNOCKBURN　　　　　　　　Map 11 NS89

Brucefields Family Golf Centre Pirnhall Rd FK7 8EH
☎ 01786 818184 📄 01786 817770
e-mail: info@brucefields.co.uk
web: www.brucefields.co.uk
Gently rolling parkland with fine views. Most holes can be played without too much difficulty with the exception of the 2nd which is a long and tricky par 4 and the 6th, a par 3, which requires exact club selection and a straight shot.

Main Course: 9 Holes, 5025yds, Par 68, SSS 66.
Club membership 300.
Visitors Mon-Sun & BHs. Booking required. Dress code.
Societies Booking required. **Green Fees** not confirmed **Course Designer** Souters Sportsturf **Prof** Gregor Monks/Graham Gormley
Facilities ⓣ ⏀ 🍴 🗒 🖳 🏐 🛒 ⬇ 🏠 ♿ ⚲ ⚡
Leisure golf academy, par 3 9 hole course **Conf** facs Corporate Hospitality Days **Location** M80/M9 junct 9, A91, 1st left signed
Hotel ★★★★ 75% HL Barceló Stirling Highland Hotel, Spittal Street, STIRLING ☎ 01786 272727 📄 01786 272829 96 en suite

BRIDGE OF ALLAN　　　　　　　Map 11 NS79

Bridge of Allan Golf Club Sunnylaw FK9 4LY
☎ 01786 832332
e-mail: secretary@bofagc.com
web: www.bofagc.co.uk
Very hilly parkland with good views of Stirling Castle and beyond to the Trossachs. Testing par 3 1st hole, 221yds uphill, with a 6ft wall 25yds before green.

9 Holes, 4932yds, Par 66, SSS 66, Course record 59.
Club membership 400.
Visitors contact club for details. **Societies** welcome. **Green Fees** not confirmed ♿ **Course Designer** Tom Morris **Facilities** 🖳 🖵 🛒 ⬇
⚲ **Location** 0.5m N off A9
Hotel ★★★★ 75% HL Barceló Stirling Highland Hotel, Spittal Street, STIRLING ☎ 01786 272727 📄 01786 272829 96 en suite

CALLANDER　　　　　　　　　　Map 11 NN60

Callander Golf Club Aveland Rd FK17 8EN
☎ 01877 330090 & 330975 📄 01877 330062
e-mail: callandergolf@btconnect.com
web: www.callandergolfclub.co.uk
Challenging parkland course with tight fairways and a number of interesting holes. Designed by Tom Morris Snr and overlooked by the Trossachs.

18 Holes, 5151yds, Par 66, SSS 65, Course record 59.
Club membership 600.
Visitors Contact club for details. **Societies** booking required. **Green Fees** £30 per day, £25 per round (weekends £35/£40) **Course Designer** Morris/Fernie **Prof** Allan Martin **Facilities** ⓣ ⏀ 🍴 🖳 🖵
🏐 ⬇ 🏠 🛒 ⚲ 🚠 ⚲ ⚡ **Location** E side of town off A84
Hotel ★★★ CHH Roman Camp Country House, CALLANDER
☎ 01877 330003 📄 01877 331533 15 en suite

DRYMEN　　　　　　　　　　　　Map 11 NS48

Buchanan Castle Golf Club G63 0HY
☎ 01360 660307 📄 01360 660993
web: www.buchanancastlegolfclub.com
18 Holes, 6059yds, Par 70, SSS 69.
Course Designer James Braid **Location** 1m W
Telephone for further details
Hotel ★★★ 75% HL Winnock Hotel, The Square, DRYMEN
☎ 01360 660245 📄 01360 660267 73 en suite

Strathendrick Golf Club G63 0AA
☎ 01360 660695
web: www.strathendrickgolfclub.co.uk
Hillside course with breathtaking views of the Campsie and Luss Hills and Ben Lomond. Mainly natural hazards with few bunkers. Greens are comparatively small but in immaculate condition.

9 Holes, 2491yards, Par 66, SSS 64. Club membership 470.
Visitors Mon-Fri except BHs. Dress code. **Societies** booking required. **Green Fees** £15 per 18 holes, £10 per 9 holes ♿ **Course Designer** Willie Fernie **Facilities** ⬇ 🛒 ⚲ **Leisure** hard tennis courts, driving net **Location** 0.5m S of Drymen via access lane E of A811
Hotel ★★★★★ 85% HL Cameron House on Loch Lomond, BALLOCH ☎ 01389 755565 📄 01389 759522 96 en suite

DUNBLANE　　　　　　　　　　Map 11 NN70

Dunblane New Golf Club Perth Rd FK15 0LJ
☎ 01786 821521 📄 01786 825066
e-mail: secretary@dngc.co.uk
web: www.dngc.co.uk
Well-maintained parkland course. Testing par 3 holes. On-line tee booking available.

18 Holes, 5600yds, Par 69, SSS 68, Course record 63.
Club membership 1000.
Visitors Mon-Fri, Sun & BHs. Booking required. Dress code.
Societies booking required. **Green Fees** £32-£45 per day **Course Designer** James Braid **Prof** Bob Jamieson **Facilities** ⓣ ⏀ 🍴 🖳
🖵 🏐 ⬇ 🏠 🛒 🚠 ⚲ **Conf** facs Corporate Hospitality Days
Location off fourways rdbt in town centre
Hotel ★★★★ 75% HL Barceló Stirling Highland Hotel, Spittal Street, STIRLING ☎ 01786 272727 📄 01786 272829 96 en suite

KILLIN　　　　　　　　　　　　Map 11 NN53

Killin Golf Club FK21 8TX
☎ 01567 820312 📄 01567 820312
e-mail: info@killingolfclub.co.uk
web: www.killingolfclub.co.uk
Parkland course at the west end of Loch Tay with outstanding views. Challenging nine-hole course with 15 different tees. Final hole considered one of the best finishing holes in Scotland.

9 Holes, 5136yds, Par 66, SSS 65, Course record 57.
Club membership 200.
Visitors Mon-Sun & BHs. Dress code. **Societies** booking required.
Green Fees £27 per day, £20 per 18 holes, £12 per 9 holes
(£30/£24/£14 weekends) **Course Designer** John Duncan/J Braid
Facilities ⓣ ⏀ 🍴 🖳 🖵 🏐 ⬇ 🏠 🛒 ⚲ 🚠 ⚲ **Conf**
Corporate Hospitality Days **Location** 0.5m N of village centre on A827
Hotel ★★★ 83% HL The Four Seasons Hotel, Loch Earn, ST FILLANS
☎ 01764 685333 📄 01764 685444 18 en suite

SCOTLAND

STIRLING
Map 11 NS79

Stirling Golf Club Queens Rd FK8 3AA
☎ 01786 464098 📄 01786 460090
e-mail: enquiries@stirlinggolfclub.tv
web: www.stirlinggolfclub.com

Undulating parkland with magnificent views of Stirling Castle and the Grampian Mountains. Testing 15th, Cotton's Fancy, 384yds (par 4).

18 Holes, 6187yds, Par 72, SSS 69, Course record 64.
Club membership 1100.

Visitors Mon-Fri & Sun except BHs. Booking required. Dress code. **Societies** booking required. **Green Fees** £52 per day, £35 per round **Course Designer** Henry Cotton **Prof** Ian Collins **Facilities** ⑪ ⑩⎮ ⒧ ⬜ ⑪ ⬠ ⌂ ⑪ ✆ ⍨ ✆ **Conf** Corporate Hospitality Days **Location** W side of town on B8051

Hotel ★★★★ 75% HL Barceló Stirling Highland Hotel, Spittal Street, STIRLING ☎ 01786 272727 📄 01786 272829 96 en suite

WEST DUNBARTONSHIRE

BALLOCH
Map 10 NS48

The Carrick on Loch Lomond G83 8RE
☎ 01389 713655
web: www.devere.co.uk

The Carrick on Loch Lomond: 18 Holes, 7082yds, Par 71, SSS 74.

Wee Demon: 9 Holes, 3200yds, Par 29.

Course Designer Doug Carrick **Location** M8 (W) junct 30 for Erskine Bridge, then A82 for Crainlarich. Course 1m past Balloch rdbt
Telephone for further details

Hotel ★★★★★ 85% HL Cameron House on Loch Lomond, BALLOCH ☎ 01389 755565 📄 01389 759522 96 en suite

BONHILL
Map 10 NS37

Vale of Leven Golf Club North Field Rd G83 9ET
☎ 01389 752351 📄 01389 758866
e-mail: rbarclay@volgc.org
web: www.volgc.org

Moorland course, tricky with many natural hazards - gorse, burns, trees. Overlooks Loch Lomond.

Northfield Course: 18 Holes, 5330yds, Par 67, SSS 67, Course record 62. Club membership 750.

Visitors Mon-Fri, Sun & BHs. Booking required Fri, Sun & BHs. Dress code. **Societies** booking required. **Green Fees** £32 per day, £22 per round (£40/£27 Sun) **Prof** Barry Campbell **Facilities** ⑪ ⑩⎮ ⒧ ⬜ ⑪ ⬠ ⌂ ⑪ ✆ **Conf** facs Corporate Hospitality Days **Location** E side of town off A813

Hotel ★★★★★ 85% HL Cameron House on Loch Lomond, BALLOCH ☎ 01389 755565 📄 01389 759522 96 en suite

CLYDEBANK
Map 11 NS56

Clydebank & District Golf Club Glasgow Rd G81 5QY
☎ 01389 383831 & 383833 📄 01389 383831

18 Holes, 5825yds, Par 68, SSS 69, Course record 63.

Course Designer Members **Location** 2m E of Erskine Bridge
Telephone for further details
Hotel ★★★★ 77% HL Beardmore Hotel, Beardmore Street, CLYDEBANK ☎ 0141 951 6000 📄 0141 951 6018 166 en suite

Clydebank Municipal Golf Course Overtoun Rd G81 3RE
☎ 0141 952 6372 📄 0141 9526372

18 Holes, 5349yds, Par 67, SSS 66, Course record 61.

Location 2m NW of town centre
Telephone for further details
Hotel ★★★★ 77% HL Beardmore Hotel, Beardmore Street, CLYDEBANK ☎ 0141 951 6000 📄 0141 951 6018 166 en suite

DUMBARTON
Map 10 NS37

Dumbarton Golf Club Broadmeadow G82 2BQ
☎ 01389 732830 & 765995
e-mail: secretary@dumbartongolfclub.co.uk
web: www.dumbartongolfclub.co.uk

Flat parkland with many trees.

18 Holes, 5934yds, Par 70, SSS 69, Course record 62. Club membership 700.

Visitors Mon-Fri except BHs. Dress code. **Societies** booking required. **Green Fees** £30 per day, £20 per round **Prof** David Muir **Facilities** ⑪ ⑩⎮ ⒧ ⬜ ⑪ ⬠ ⌂ ✆ **Conf** Corporate Hospitality Days **Location** 0.25m N off A814 & A82

Hotel ★★★★ 73% HL Best Western Gleddoch House, LANGBANK ☎ 01475 540711 📄 01475 540201 70 en suite

WEST LOTHIAN

BATHGATE
Map 11 NS96

Bathgate Golf Club Edinburgh Rd EH48 1BA
☎ 01506 630505 📄 01506 636775
e-mail: bathgate.golfclub@lineone.net
web: www.bathgategolfclub.co.uk

Moorland course. Easy walking. Testing 11th hole, par 3.

18 Holes, 6328yds, Par 71, SSS 71, Course record 58. Club membership 900.

Visitors Mon-Sat & BHs. Dress code. **Societies** booking required. **Green Fees** £35 per day, £30 per round (£45/£35 Sat) **Course Designer** W Park **Prof** Stuart Callan **Facilities** ⑪ ⑩⎮ ⒧ ⬜ ⑪ ⬠ ⌂ ⑪ ✆ ⍨ ✆ **Conf** Corporate Hospitality Days **Location** E side of town off A89

Hotel ★★★★ 78% HL Macdonald Houstoun House, UPHALL ☎ 0844 879 9043 📄 01506 854220 73 en suite

BROXBURN
Map 11 NT07

Niddry Castle Golf Club Castle Rd, Winchburgh EH52 6RQ
☎ 01506 891097 📄 01506 891097
e-mail: info@niddrycastlegc.co.uk
web: www.niddrycastlegc.co.uk
An 18-hole parkland course, requiring accurate golf to score well.
18 Holes, 5914yds, Par 70, SSS 69, Course record 65.
Club membership 300.
Visitors Mon-Sun. **Societies** booking required. **Green Fees** £22 per 18 holes (£29 weekends) 🏌 **Course Designer** A Scott **Facilities** ⊕ ⥮ ⤏ ⤶ ⤷ ⤸ ⟡ **Location** 9m W of Edinburgh on B9080
Hotel ★★★★ 78% HL Macdonald Houstoun House, UPHALL
☎ 0844 879 9043 📄 01506 854220 73 en suite

FAULDHOUSE
Map 11 NS96

Greenburn Golf Club 6 Greenburn Rd EH47 9HJ
☎ 01501 770292 📄 01501 772615
e-mail: administrator@greenburngolfclub.co.uk
web: www.greenburngolfclub.co.uk
A testing course, with a mixture of parkland and moorland. Water features on 14 of the 18 holes, with a burn crossing most of the holes on the back 9.
18 Holes, 6067yds, Par 71, SSS 70, Course record 63.
Club membership 750.
Visitors Mon-Sun & BHs. Booking required weekends & BHs. Handicap certificate. Dress code. **Societies** booking required. **Green Fees** £32 per day, £24 per round (weekends £40/£32) **Prof** Scott Catlin **Facilities** ⊕ ⥮ ⤏ ⤶ ⤷ ⤸ ⟡ **Location** 3m SW of Whitburn
Hotel ★★★★ 78% HL Macdonald Houstoun House, UPHALL
☎ 0844 879 9043 📄 01506 854220 73 en suite

LINLITHGOW
Map 11 NS97

Linlithgow Golf Club Braehead EH49 6QF
☎ 01506 844356 (pro) & 842585 (sec)
📄 01506 842764
e-mail: info@linlithgowgolf.co.uk
web: www.linlithgowgolf.co.uk
A short but testing undulating parkland course with panoramic views of the Forth Valley.
18 Holes, 5851yds, Par 70, SSS 68, Course record 64.
Club membership 450.
Visitors Mon, Tue, Thu, Fri, Sun & BHs. Booking required. Dress code. **Societies** booking required. **Green Fees** £35 per day, £25 per round (£40/£30 Sun) 🏌 **Course Designer** R Simpson of Carnoustie **Prof** Graeme Bell **Facilities** ⊕ ⥮ ⤏ ⤶ ⤷ ⤸ ⟡ **Conf** Corporate Hospitality Days **Location** 1m S off A706
Hotel ★★★★ 72% HL Macdonald Inchyra Grange, Grange Road, POLMONT ☎ 01324 711911 📄 01324 716134 98 en suite

West Lothian Golf Club Airngath Hill EH49 7RH
☎ 01506 826030 📄 01506 826030
web: www.westlothiangc.com
Challenging 18 holes with fantastic views over the river Forth from Wallace Monument to the Bass Rock.
18 Holes, 6249yds, Par 71, SSS 71. Club membership 800.
Visitors Mon-Sun & BHs. Booking required. Handicap certificate. Dress code. **Societies** booking required. **Green Fees** phone **Course Designer** Fraser Middleton **Prof** Alan Reid **Facilities** ⊕ ⥮ ⤏ ⤶ ⤷ ⤸ ⟡ **Conf** facs Corporate Hospitality Days **Location** 1m N off A706
Hotel ★★★★ 72% HL Macdonald Inchyra Grange, Grange Road, POLMONT ☎ 01324 711911 📄 01324 716134 98 en suite

LIVINGSTON
Map 11 NT06

Deer Park Golf & Country Club Golf Course Rd EH54 8AB
☎ 01506 446699 📄 01506 435608
e-mail: deerpark@muir-group.co.uk
web: www.deer-park.co.uk
Championship golf course with panoramic views over the Pentlands. No individual hole stands out, they are all wonderful. But if one had to be chosen, it would be the 4th, a challenging par 4 that brings water into play twice and really rewards the well-played shot.
18 Holes, 6727yds, Par 72, SSS 72, Course record 63.
Club membership 1500.
Visitors Mon-Sun & BHs. Booking required Thu-Sun & BHs. Dress code. **Societies** booking required. **Green Fees** £30 per 18 holes (£40 weekends) **Course Designer** Alliss/Thomas **Prof** Sandy Strachan **Facilities** ⊕ ⥮ ⤏ ⤶ ⤷ ⤸ ⟡ **Leisure** heated indoor swimming pool, squash, sauna, gymnasium, snooker table, ten pin bowling **Conf** facs Corporate Hospitality Days **Location** M8 junct 3, off A899
Hotel ★★★★ 78% HL Macdonald Houstoun House, UPHALL
☎ 0844 879 9043 📄 01506 854220 73 en suite

Pumpherston Golf Club Drumshoreland Rd, Pumpherston EH53 0LH
☎ 01506 433336 (office) & 433337 (pro)
📄 01506 438250
e-mail: sheena.corner@tiscali.co.uk
web: www.pumpherstongolfclub.co.uk
Undulating, well-bunkered parkland course with very testing 2nd and 15th holes. The course has water features at five holes and has won several environmental awards. Panoramic views of Edinburgh and the Pentland Hills.
18 Holes, 6006yds, Par 70, SSS 72. Club membership 800.
Visitors Mon-Sun & BHs. Booking required. Handicap certificate. Dress code. **Societies** booking required. **Green Fees** phone **Course Designer** G Webster **Prof** Richard Fyvie **Facilities** ⊕ ⥮ by prior arrangement ⤏ ⤶ ⤷ ⤸ ⟡ **Conf** Corporate Hospitality Days **Location** 1m E of Livingston off B8046
Hotel ★★★★ 78% HL Macdonald Houstoun House, UPHALL
☎ 0844 879 9043 📄 01506 854220 73 en suite

SCOTLAND

UPHALL
Map 11 NT07

Uphall Golf Club EH52 6JT
☎ 01506 856404 📄 01506 855358
web: www.uphallgolfclub.com
18 Holes, 5588yds, Par 69, SSS 67, Course record 61.
Location W side of village on A899
Telephone for further details
Hotel ★★★★ 78% HL Macdonald Houstoun House, UPHALL
☎ 0844 879 9043 📄 01506 854220 73 en suite

WEST CALDER
Map 11 NT06

Harburn Golf Club EH55 8RS
☎ 01506 871131 & 871256 📄 01506 870286
e-mail: info@harburngolfclub.co.uk
web: www.harburngolfclub.co.uk
Parkland with a variety of beech, oak and pine trees. Fine views of the Pentlands and the Ochil Hills.
18 Holes, 5309yds, Par 71, SSS 70. Club membership 700.
Visitors Mon,Tue, Thu-Sun & BHs. Booking required. Dress code.
Societies booking required. **Green Fees** £35 per day, £30 per round (Fri £40/£35, Sat-Sun £45/£40) **Prof** Stephen Mills **Facilities** ⊕ 🍴 🛅 ⌷ ▥ 🏌 🏮 ⚑ 🛒 ✪ 🚙 ✪ **Conf** facs Corporate Hospitality Days **Location** 2m S of West Calder on B7008
Hotel ★★★★ 78% HL Macdonald Houstoun House, UPHALL
☎ 0844 879 9043 📄 01506 854220 73 en suite

WHITBURN
Map 11 NS96

Polkemmet Country Park EH47 0AD
☎ 01501 743905 📄 01506 846256
e-mail: mail@beecraigs.com
web: www.beecraigs.com
Public parkland course surrounded by mature woodland and rhododendron bushes and bisected by a river. Interesting and demanding last hole.
9 Holes, 3247mtrs, Par 37. Club membership 100.
Visitors Mon-Sun & BHs. **Societies** welcome. **Green Fees** not confirmed **Prof** David Burns **Facilities** ⊕ 🛅 ⌷ 🏮 ▥ ✪ ⚑ **Leisure** bowling green **Conf** Corporate Hospitality Days **Location** 2m W of Whitburn on B7066
Hotel ★★★★ 78% HL Macdonald Houstoun House, UPHALL
☎ 0844 879 9043 📄 01506 854220 73 en suite

SCOTTISH ISLANDS

ARRAN, ISLE OF

BLACKWATERFOOT
Map 10 NR92

Shiskine Golf Club Shore Rd KA27 8HA
☎ 01770 860226 📄 01770 860205
web: www.shiskinegolf.com
12 Holes, 2990yds, Par 42, SSS 42, Course record 38.
Course Designer W Fernie **Location** W side of village off A841
Telephone for further details
Hotel ★★★ CHH Kilmichael Country House, Glen Cloy, BRODICK
☎ 01770 302219 📄 01770 302068 8 en suite

LAMLASH
Map 10 NS03

Lamlash Golf Club KA27 8JU
☎ 01770 600296
e-mail: lamlashgolfclub@btconnect.com
web: www.lamlashgolfclub.co.uk
Undulating heathland course with magnificent views of the mountains and sea.
18 Holes, 4510yds, Par 61, SSS 61, Course record 58.
Club membership 450.
Visitors Mon-Sun & BHs. Booking required Fri-Sun & BHs.
Societies welcome. **Green Fees** not confirmed **Course Designer** Auchterlonie/Fernie **Facilities** ⊕ 🍴 🛅 ⌷ ▥ ⌂ 🏮 ✪ 🚙 ✪ **Location** 0.75m N of Lamlash on A841
Hotel ★★★ CHH Kilmichael Country House, Glen Cloy, BRODICK
☎ 01770 302219 📄 01770 302068 8 en suite

LOCHRANZA
Map 10 NR95

Lochranza Golf Course KA27 8HL
☎ 01770 830273
e-mail: office@lochgolf.demon.co.uk
web: www.lochranzagolf.com
Lochranza is a 9 hole pay-and-play course, stretching along the flat floor of the glen to the head of the loch with views of the medieval castle. Wild red deer graze the fairways and golden eagles soar overhead. The course has water hazards including the Lochranza burn which is lined by mature trees.
9 Holes, 2332yds, Par 31.
Visitors contact course for details. **Societies** welcome. **Green Fees** £15 per day, £10 per 9 holes **Course Designer** relaid 1991 by I Robertson **Facilities** ⊕ 🛅 ⌷ 🏮 ✪ **Location** in Lochranza village, opposite Isle of Arran Distillery
Hotel ★★★ CHH Kilmichael Country House, Glen Cloy, BRODICK
☎ 01770 302219 📄 01770 302068 8 en suite

Save on Hotels. Book at **theAA.com/hotel**

SCOTTISH ISLANDS

MACHRIE
Map 10 NR83

Machrie Bay Golf Course KA27 8DZ
☎ 01770 840259 📄 01770 840266
web: www.dougarie.com

9 Holes, 4556yds, Par 66, SSS 63, Course record 63.
Course Designer W Fernie **Location** 9m W of Brodick via String Rd
Telephone for further details
Hotel ★★★ CHH Kilmichael Country House, Glen Cloy, BRODICK
☎ 01770 302219 📄 01770 302068 8 en suite

SANNOX
Map 10 NS04

Corrie Golf Club KA27 8JD
☎ 01770 810223 & 810652
e-mail: guy.murray1@virgin.net
web: www.corriegolf.com

A heathland course on the coast with beautiful mountain scenery. An upward climb to 6th hole then a descent from the 7th. All these holes are subject to strong winds in bad weather.

9 Holes, 3830yds, Par 63, SSS 62, Course record 51.
Club membership 300.
Visitors Mon-Sun & BHs. Booking required weekends.
Societies booking required. **Green Fees** £20 per day, £10 per 9 holes
🍽 **Facilities** ⑪ ⑩ ⌑ ⚐ ☂ ✆ **Location** 6m N of A841
Hotel ★★★ CHH Kilmichael Country House, Glen Cloy, BRODICK
☎ 01770 302219 📄 01770 302068 8 en suite

WHITING BAY
Map 10 NS02

Whiting Bay Golf Club KA27 8QT
☎ 01770 700487
e-mail: info@whitingbaygolfclub.org.uk
web: www.whitingbaygolfclub.org.uk

Founded in 1895, the course is set high on the south east coast of Arran, with spectacular views over the Firth of Clyde. Although modest in length, the heathland course features some challenging par 3s.

18 Holes, 4063yds, Par 63, SSS 63, Course record 58.
Club membership 350.
Visitors Mon-Sun & BHs. Booking required weekends & BHs.
Societies booking required. **Green Fees** £21 per day per 18 holes (£24 weekends) **Facilities** ⓑ ⌑ ⑩ ☂ 🍴 ✆ 🍺 ✆
Leisure snooker room **Location** NW side of village off A841
Hotel ★★★ CHH Kilmichael Country House, Glen Cloy, BRODICK
☎ 01770 302219 📄 01770 302068 8 en suite

BARRA, ISLE OF

CASTLEBAY
Map 13 NL69

Barra Golf Club Cleat HS9 5XX
☎ 01871 810944
e-mail: duncanmackinnon@live.co.uk
web: www.isleofbarra.com

A 9 hole course with spectacular views of the Atlantic. The greens are fenced to stop the cattle entering the greens. Visitors are always pleased to have played the most westerly course on the British Isles.

9 Holes, 5200yds, Par 64, SSS 64, Course record 68.
Club membership 22.
Visitors Contact club for details. **Societies** welcome. **Green Fees** £10 per day **Facilities** ⚐ ✆ ✆ **Conf** Corporate Hospitality Days
Location 4m from Castlebay going west

BUTE, ISLE OF

KINGARTH
Map 10 NS05

Bute Golf Club St Ninians, 32 Marine Place, Ardbeg, Rothesay PA20 0LF
☎ 01700 503091
e-mail: administrator@butegolfclub.com
web: www.butegolfclub.com

Flat seaside course with good greens and fine views over the Sound of Bute to Isle of Arran. Challenging par 3 along sea.

9 Holes, 4722yds, Par 68, SSS 64, Course record 61.
Club membership 200.
Visitors Mon-Fri, Sun & BHs. Sat after 11am. **Societies** booking required. **Green Fees** not confirmed **Facilities** ▲ **Location** 6m from Rothesay pier on A845
Hotel ★★ 74% HL Selborne, Clyde Street, West Bay, DUNOON
☎ 01369 702761 📄 01369 704032 98 en suite

PORT BANNATYNE
Map 10 NS06

Port Bannatyne Golf Club Bannatyne Mains Rd PA20 0PH
☎ 01700 505142
web: www.portbannatynegolf.co.uk

Seaside hill course with panoramic views. Almost unique in having 13 holes, with the first five being played again before a separate 18th. Difficult 4th (par 3).

13 Holes, 5085yds, Par 68, SSS 65, Course record 62.
Club membership 170.
Visitors Mon-Sun & BHs. Booking required. **Societies** booking required **Green Fees** £17 per day, £12 per round. (£22/£18 weekends) 🐕
Course Designer Peter Morrison **Facilities** ⑪ ⓑ ⌑ ⑩ ▲
Location W side of village off A886
Hotel ★★ 74% HL Selborne, Clyde Street, West Bay, DUNOON
☎ 01369 702761 📄 01369 704032 98 en suite

SCOTLAND

ROTHESAY
Map 10 NS06

Rothesay Golf Club Canada Hill PA20 9HN
☎ 01700 503554 📠 01700 503554
web: www.rothesaygolfclub.com
18 Holes, 5419yds, Par 69, SSS 66, Course record 62.
Course Designer James Braid & Ben Sayers **Location** 500yds SE from main ferry terminal
Telephone for further details
Hotel ★★★ 75% HL Willowbank Hotel, 96 Greenock Road, LARGS
☎ 01475 672311 & 675435 📠 01475 689027 30 en suite

COLONSAY, ISLE OF

SCALASAIG
Map 10 NR39

Colonsay Golf Club Machrins Farm PA61 7YR
☎ 01951 200290 📠 01951 200290
18 Holes, 4775yds, Par 72, SSS 72.
📶 **Location** 2m W on A870
Telephone for further details

ISLAY, ISLE OF

PORT ELLEN
Map 10 NR34

Machrie Hotel & Golf Links Machrie PA42 7AN
☎ 01496 302310 📠 01496 302404
web: www.machrie.com
18 Holes, 6324yds, Par 71, SSS 71, Course record 66.
Course Designer W Campbell **Location** 4m N off A846
Telephone for further details

LEWIS, ISLE OF

STORNOWAY
Map 13 NB43

Stornoway Golf Club Lady Lever Park HS2 0XP
☎ 01851 702240
e-mail: admin@stornowaygolfclub.co.uk
web: www.stornowaygolfclub.co.uk
A short but tricky undulating parkland course set in the grounds of Lewis Castle with fine views over the Minch to the mainland. The terrain is peat based and there has been substantial investment in drainage works.
18 Holes, 5252yds, Par 68, SSS 67, Course record 62.
Club membership 500.
Visitors Mon-Sat & BHs. Booking required Sat. **Societies** welcome.
Green Fees £30 per day, £25 per round **Course Designer** J & R Stutt
Facilities 🕙 by prior arrangement 🖴 ⚑ 🍴 ⚐ 🖻 🏴 ⚅
Conf facs **Location** 0.5m from town centre off A857

MULL, ISLE OF

CRAIGNURE
Map 10 NM73

Craignure Golf Club Scallastle PA65 6BA
☎ 01680 812370
9 Holes, 5357yds, Par 69, SSS 66, Course record 72.
Location 1.5m N of Craignure A849
Telephone for further details

TOBERMORY
Map 13 NM55

Tobermory Golf Club PA75 6PS
☎ 01688 302741 📠 01688 302741
e-mail: enquiries@tobermorygolfclub.com
web: www.tobermorygolfclub.com
A beautifully maintained hilltop course with superb views over the Sound of Mull. Testing 7th hole (par 3).
9 Holes, 4912yds, Par 64, SSS 64, Course record 65.
Club membership 150.
Visitors Limited play on competition days. **Societies** booking required.
Green Fees £20 per day 📶 **Course Designer** David Adams **Facilities**
🖴 ⚑ 🍴 ⚐ 🏴 ♦ ⚅ **Location** 0.5m N off A848
Hotel ★★★ SHL Highland Cottage, Breadalbane Street,
TOBERMORY ☎ 01688 302030 6 en suite

ORKNEY

KIRKWALL
Map 16 HY41

Orkney Golf Club Grainbank KW15 1RB
☎ 01856 872457
web: www.orkneygolfclub.co.uk
18 Holes, 5411yds, Par 70, SSS 67, Course record 63.
Location 0.5m W off A965
Telephone for further details

STROMNESS
Map 16 HY20

Stromness Golf Club, Ness KW16 3DW
☎ 01856 850772
e-mail: enquiries@stromnessgc.co.uk
web: www.stromnessgc.co.uk
Testing parkland and seaside course with easy walking. Magnificent views of Scapa Flow.
18 Holes, 4762yds, Par 65, SSS 64, Course record 61.
Club membership 350.
Visitors Mon-Sun & BHs. **Societies** booking required. **Green Fees** £25 per day 📶 **Facilities** ⚑ 🍴 ⚐ 🏴 ⚅ **Leisure** hard tennis courts, Bowling **Location** S end of town at Ness

SHETLAND

LERWICK   Map 16 HU44

Shetland Golf Club Dale Golf Course ZE2 9SB
☎ 01595 840369 📠 01595 840369
web: www.shetlandgolfclub.co.uk

Dale Course: 18 Holes, 5562yds, Par 68, SSS 68,
Course record 68.

Course Designer Fraser Middleton **Location** 4m N on A970
Telephone for further details
Hotel ★★★ 73% HL Shetland, Holmsgarth Road, LERWICK
☎ 01595 695515 📠 01595 695828 64 en suite

WHALSAY, ISLAND OF   Map 16 HU56

Whalsay Golf Club Skaw Taing ZE2 9AA
☎ 01806 566450 & 566481

18 Holes, 6140yds, Par 71, SSS 69, Course record 69.
Location 5m N from Symbister ferry terminal
Telephone for further details

SKYE, ISLE OF

SCONSER   Map 13 NG53

Isle of Skye Golf Club IV48 8TD
☎ 01478 650414
e-mail: info@isleofskyegolfclub.co.uk
web: www.isleofskyegolfclub.co.uk

Seaside course with spectacular views; nine holes with 18 tees,
different settings on the back nine. Suitable for golfers of all abilities.

18 Holes, 4775yds, Par 67, SSS 65, Course record 63.
Club membership 150.

Visitors Mon-Sun & BHs. **Societies** booking required. **Green Fees** not
confirmed **Facilities** 🏌 🖤 🛝 🏠 ⛳ 🏌 **Conf** Corporate
Hospitality Days **Location** on A87 between Broadford
Hotel ★★★ 73% HL Rosedale, Beaumont Crescent, PORTREE
☎ 01478 613131 📠 01478 612531 18 en suite

SOUTH UIST

DALIBURGH   Map 13 NF72

Askernish Golf Club HS8 5SY
☎ 07900 387167
e-mail: info@askernishgolfclub.com
web: www.askernishgolfclub.com

Originally laid out in 1891 by 'old' Tom Morris and re-opened in
2008, Askernish Golf Course has been received to wide acclaim
internationally. Described as 'the most natural links course in the
world' by environmental experts and 'closer to a perfect ten than any
other course' by golf writer John Garrity.

Askernish Old: 18 Holes, 6315yds, Par 72, SSS 71,
Course record 69.

Visitors contact club for details. **Societies** welcome. **Green Fees** Day
ticket £50, Scottish resident day ticket £35 🎫 **Course Designer** Old
Tom Morris/Martin Robert **Facilities** 🅿 🏌 🖤 🛝 🏠 ⛳ 🏌
🏌 **Leisure** coastal & beach walking routes **Conf** facs Corporate
Hospitality Days **Location** 1.5m north of Daliburgh

Wales

St Non's, Pembrokeshire National Park

ANGLESEY, ISLE OF

AMLWCH
Map 6 SH49

Bull Bay Golf Club LL68 9RY
☎ 01407 830960 📠 01407 832612
e-mail: info@bullbaygc.co.uk
web: www.bullbaygc.co.uk
Wales's northernmost course, Bull Bay is a pleasant coastal, heathland course with natural rock, gorse and wind hazards. Views from several tees across the Irish Sea to the Isle of Man, and across Anglesey to Snowdonia.

18 Holes, 6276yds, Par 70, SSS 72, Course record 60. Club membership 700.

Visitors Mon-Sun & BHs. Handicap certificate. Dress code. **Societies** welcome. **Green Fees** £45 per day, £35 per round (£50/£40 weekends & BHs) **Course Designer** W H Fowler **Prof** John Burns **Facilities** ⊕ ⊚ ⊨ ⊑ ⊒ ⅄ 🖻 ⁊ ⚑ 🛒 ⚐ **Conf** Corporate Hospitality Days **Location** 1m W of Amlwch on A5025
Hotel ★★★★ BB Hafod Country House, CEMAES BAY
☎ 01407 711645 3 rooms (3 en suite)

BEAUMARIS
Map 6 SH67

Baron Hill Golf Club LL58 8YW
☎ 01248 810231 📠 01248 810231
e-mail: golf@baronhill.co.uk
web: www.baronhill.co.uk
Undulating course with natural hazards of rock and gorse. Testing 3rd and 4th holes (par 4s). Hole 5/14 plays into the prevailing wind with an elevated tee across two streams. The hole is between two gorse covered mounds and considered one of the best par 3 holes in North Wales.

9 Holes, 5572yds, Par 68, SSS 68, Course record 65. Club membership 350.

Visitors Mon-Sun & BHs. Booking required. Dress code. **Societies** welcome. **Green Fees** £20 per day, £12.50 per 9 holes ⊛ **Course Designer** R Dawson **Facilities** ⊕ ⊚ ⊨ ⊑ ⊒ ⅄ ⁊ ⚐ **Conf** Corporate Hospitality Days **Location** A545 from Menai Bridge to Beaumaris, course signed on approach to town
Hotel ★★ 85% SHL Bishopsgate House Hotel, 54 Castle Street, BEAUMARIS ☎ 01248 810302 📠 01248 810166 9 en suite

Henllys Golf Club Henllys Hall LL58 8HU
☎ 01248 811717 📠 01248 811511
e-mail: hg@hpb.co.uk
web: www.henllysgolfclub.co.uk
The Menai Straits and the Snowdonia mountains form a magnificent backdrop to the course. Full use has been made of the mature parkland trees and natural water hazards to provide a really testing and enjoyable game of golf.

18 Holes, 5821yds, Par 71, SSS 69, Course record 65. Club membership 300.

Visitors Mon-Sun & BHs. Booking required. Dress code. **Societies** booking required. **Green Fees** not confirmed **Course Designer** Roger Jones **Prof** Peter Maton & David Gadsby **Facilities** ⊕ ⊚ ⊨ ⊑ ⊒ ⅄ 🖻 ⚑ 🛒 ⚐ **Location** A545 through Beaumaris, 0.25m Henllys Hall signed on left
Hotel ★★★ 77% HL Best Western Bulkeley Hotel, Castle Street, BEAUMARIS ☎ 01248 810415 📠 01248 810146 43 en suite

BRYNTEG
Map 6 SH48

Storws Wen Golf Club LL78 8JY
☎ 01248 852673
e-mail: storws.wen@hotmail.co.uk
web: www.storwswen.org
Parkland course with mountain views. Water hazards on some holes.

9 Holes, 2801yds, Par 70, SSS 68. Club membership 200.

Visitors Mon-Sun & BHs. Booking required. **Societies** booking required. **Green Fees** From £7 per 9 holes **Course Designer** K Jones **Facilities** ⊕ ⊚ ⊨ ⊑ ⊒ ⅄ ⁊ ⚐ **Conf** facs Corporate Hospitality Days **Location** 1.75m along the B5108 from Benllech to Brynteg
Hotel ★★★★ FH Tre-Wyn, Maenaddwyn, LLANERCHYMEDD
☎ 01248 470875 3 rooms

HOLYHEAD
Map 6 SH28

Holyhead Golf Club Lon Garreg Fawr, Trearddur Bay LL65 2YL
☎ 01407 763279 📠 01407 763279
e-mail: holyheadgolfclub@tiscali.co.uk
web: www.holyheadgolfclub.co.uk
Treeless, undulating seaside course which provides a varied and testing game, particularly in a south wind. The fairways are bordered by gorse, heather and rugged outcrops of rock. Accuracy from most tees is paramount as there are 43 fairway and greenside bunkers and lakes. Designed by James Braid.

18 Holes, 6058yds, Par 70, SSS 70, Course record 64. Club membership 962.

Visitors Mon-Sun & BHs. Booking required. Handicap certificate. Dress code. **Societies** booking required. **Green Fees** £35 per day (£40 weekends) **Course Designer** James Braid **Prof** Stephen Elliott **Facilities** ⊕ ⊚ ⊨ ⊑ ⊒ ⅄ 🖻 ⁊ ⚑ 🛒 ⚐ **Conf** facs Corporate Hospitality Days **Location** A55 to rdbt at Holyhead, left onto B4545 to Trearddur Bay 1m
Hotel ★★★★ BB Hafod Country House, CEMAES BAY
☎ 01407 711645 3 rooms

RHOSNEIGR
Map 6 SH37

Anglesey Golf Club Station Rd LL64 5QX
☎ 01407 811127 📠 01407 811127
e-mail: info@theangleseygolfclub.com
web: www.theangleseygolfclub.co.uk

An interesting 18-hole links course set among sand dunes and heather, renowned for its excellent greens and numerous streams.

continued

The whole course has an abundance of wildlife and is an important conservation area.

18 Holes, 6330yds, Par 70, SSS 71, Course record 64. Club membership 500.

Visitors contact club for details. **Societies** booking required. **Green Fees** phone **Course Designer** H Hilton **Facilities** ⓣ ℃ ⓛ ⓣ ⓣ ⓣ ⓛ ⓣ ⓛ **Location** NE side of village on A4080
Hotel ★★★★ FH Tre-Wyn, Maenaddwyn, LLANERCHYMEDD ☎ 01248 470875 3 rooms

BLAENAU GWENT

NANTYGLO   Map 3 SO11

West Monmouthshire Golf Club Golf Rd NP23 4QT
☎ 01495 310233
web: www.westmongolfclub.co.uk
18 Holes, 6300yds, Par 71, SSS 69, Course record 65.
Course Designer Ben Sayers **Location** 0.25m W off A467
Telephone for further details
Hotel ★★★ 75% HL The Old Rectory Country Hotel & Golf Club, LLANGATTOCK ☎ 01873 810373 23 en suite

TREDEGAR   Map 3 SO10

Tredegar and Rhymney Golf Club Cwmtysswg, Rhymney NP22 5HA
☎ 01685 840743 (club)
e-mail: tandrgc@googlemail.com
web: www.tandrgc.co.uk
Mountain course with lovely views. The course has now been developed into an 18-hole course with easy walking.
18 Holes, 5500yds, Par 67, SSS 67, Course record 64. Club membership 150.
Visitors Mon-Sun & BHs. Booking required weekends. Dress code. **Societies** booking required. **Green Fees** £15 per day winter, £20 per day summer ⓛ **Facilities** ⓣ ℃ ⓛ ⓣ ⓣ ⓛ ⓛ **Conf** facs Corporate Hospitality Days **Location** 1.75m SW on B4256
Hotel ★★★★ 78% HL Best Western Parkway, Cwmbran Drive, CWMBRAN ☎ 01633 871199 ⓛ 01633 869160 70 en suite

BRIDGEND

BRIDGEND   Map 3 SS97

Coed-Y-Mwstwr Golf Club The Clubhouse, Bryn Rd, Coychurch CF35 6AF
☎ 01656 864934 ⓛ 01656 864934
e-mail: secretary@coed-y-mwstwr.co.uk
web: www.coed-y-mwstwr.co.uk
Course extended to 18 holes during 2005 and the new holes are now fully bedded in. The 2nd hole, a 212 yard par 3 to a well guarded green is a real tester. The fairways are lush and generous fairways allow the golfer to open their shoulders but the surrounding woodland is a trap for the wayward drive. A conservatory gives fine views over the course and surrounding hills.
18 Holes, 5703yds, Par 69, SSS 68, Course record 69. Club membership 300.
Visitors Mon-Sun & BHs. Booking required weekends & BHs. Handicap certificate. Dress code. **Societies** booking required. **Green Fees** £22 per 18 holes (£26.50 weekends & BHs) **Course Designer** Chapman/Warren **Prof** Paul Thomas **Facilities** ⓣ ⓛ ⓣ ⓣ ⓛ ⓛ ⓛ **Conf** facs Corporate Hospitality Days **Location** M4 junct 35, A473 into Coychurch, course 1m N
Hotel ★★★★ 79% CHH Coed-Y-Mwstwr, Coychurch, BRIDGEND ☎ 01656 860621 ⓛ 01656 863122 35 en suite

Southerndown Golf Club Ogmore By Sea CF32 0QP
☎ 01656 880476 ⓛ 01656 880317
e-mail: admin@southerndowngolfclub.com
web: www.southerndowngolfclub.com
Downland-links championship course with rolling fairways and fast greens. Golfers who successfully negotiate the four par 3s still face a testing finish with three of the last four holes played into the prevailing wind. The par 3 5th is played across a valley and the 18th, with its split-level fairway, is a demanding finishing hole. Superb views.
18 Holes, 6449yds, Par 70, SSS 72. Club membership 710.
Visitors Mon-Sun & BHs. Booking required. Handicap certificate. Dress code. **Societies** booking required. **Green Fees** £55 per 18 holes, £50 pm & £20 extra holes (£75/£70 & £25 extra holes weekends) **Course Designer** W Park/W Fernie & others **Prof** D G McMonagle **Facilities** ⓣ ℃ ⓛ ⓣ ⓣ ⓛ ⓛ ⓛ ⓛ ⓛ **Conf** Corporate Hospitality Days **Location** 3m SW of Bridgend on B4524
Hotel ★★★ 75% HL Best Western Heronston, Ewenny Road, BRIDGEND ☎ 01656 668811 & 666085 ⓛ 01656 767391 75 en suite

WALES

387

MAESTEG
Map 3 SS89

Maesteg Golf Club Mount Pleasant, Neath Rd CF34 9PR
☎ 01656 734106 📠 01656 731822
e-mail: ijm@fsmail.net
web: www.maesteg-golf.co.uk
Reasonably flat hill-top course with scenic views. Caters to all levels of golf.

18 Holes, 5889yds, Par 70, SSS 69, Course record 63.
Club membership 500.

Visitors Mon-Sun & BHs. Booking required weekends & BHs. Handicap certificate. Dress code. **Societies** booking required. **Green Fees** not confirmed **Course Designer** James Braid **Prof** Tom Davies **Facilities** ⊕ ⊚ by prior arrangement 🍴 🖥 🏌 🏖 🛒 **Conf** facs Corporate Hospitality Days **Location** 0.5m W off B4282
Hotel ★★★ 79% HL Best Western Aberavon Beach Hotel, Neath, PORT TALBOT ☎ 01639 884949 📠 01639 897885 52 en suite

PENCOED
Map 3 SS98

St Mary's Hotel & Country Club St Mary Hill CF35 5EA
☎ 01656 868900 📠 01656 863400
e-mail: stmarys.reception@btopenworld.com
web: www.stmaryshotel.com
A parkland course with many American-style features. The par 3 10th, called Alcatraz, has a well-deserved reputation.

St Mary's Course: 18 Holes, 5142yds, Par 68, SSS 66, Course record 65.
Kingfisher: 12 Holes, 2838yds, Par 44.
Club membership 300.

Visitors Mon-Sun & BHs. Booking required. Dress code. **Societies** booking required. **Green Fees** not confirmed **Course Designer** Peter Johnson **Prof** Leighton Janes **Facilities** ⊕ ⊚ 🍴 🖥 🏌 🏖 🛒 🚐 **Conf** facs Corporate Hospitality Days **Location** M4 junct 35, 5m
Hotel ★★★ 72% HL St Mary's Hotel & Country Club, St Marys Golf Club, PENCOED ☎ 01656 861100 📠 01656 863400 24 en suite

PORTHCAWL
Map 3 SS87

Royal Porthcawl Golf Club Rest Bay CF36 3UW
☎ 01656 782251 📠 01656 771687
e-mail: office@royalporthcawl.com
web: www.royalporthcawl.com
One of the great links courses, Royal Porthcawl is unique in that the sea is in full view from every single hole. The course enjoys a substantial reputation with heather, broom, gorse and a challenging wind demanding a player's full skill and attention.

18 Holes, 6578yds, Par 72, SSS 73, Course record 65.
Club membership 800.

Visitors Tue, Thur & Fri. Wed am. Mon, weekends & BHs pm. Booking required. Dress code. Booking required. Dress code. **Societies** booking required. **Green Fees** £150 per day, £105 per round (£185/£125 weekends). Weekday rates include 2 course lunch **Course Designer** Ramsey Hunter **Prof** Peter Evans **Facilities** ⊕ ⊚ by prior arrangement 🍴 🖥 🏌 🏖 🛒 🚐 **Conf** Corporate Hospitality Days **Location** M4 junct 37, proceed to Rest Bay
Hotel ★★ 64% HL Seabank Hotel, Esplanade, PORTHCAWL ☎ 01656 782261 📠 01656 785363 87 en suite

PYLE
Map 3 SS88

Pyle & Kenfig Golf Club Waun-Y-Mer CF33 4PU
☎ 01656 783093 📠 01656 772822
e-mail: secretary@pandkgolfclub.co.uk
web: www.pandkgolfclub.co.uk
Links and downland course, with dunes. Easy walking.

18 Holes, 6824yds, Par 71, SSS 71, Course record 69.
Club membership 933.

Visitors Mon-Sun & BHs. Booking required. Handicap certificate. Dress code. **Societies** welcome. **Green Fees** £55 weekdays (£70 Sun) max 27 holes **Course Designer** Colt **Prof** Dylan Williams **Facilities** ⊕ ⊚ 🍴 🖥 🏌 🏖 🛒 🚐 **Conf** facs Corporate Hospitality Days **Location** M4 junct 37, off A4229
Hotel ★★ 64% HL Seabank Hotel, Esplanade, PORTHCAWL ☎ 01656 782261 📠 01656 785363 87 en suite

CAERPHILLY

BARGOED
Map 3 ST19

Bargoed Golf Club Heolddu CF81 9GF
☎ 01443 836179
Mountain parkland course, a challenging par 70 with panoramic views.

18 Holes, 6086yds, Par 70, SSS 70. Club membership 600.

Visitors Mon-Fri & BHs. Sat pm. **Societies** booking required. **Green Fees** not confirmed **Prof** Craig Easton **Facilities** ⊕ ⊚ 🍴 🖥 🏌 🏖 🛒 🚐 **Conf** facs Corporate Hospitality Days **Location** NW side of town
Hotel ★★★ 74% CHH Llechwen Hall, Llanfabon, PONTYPRIDD ☎ 01443 742050 & 743020 📠 01443 742189 20 en suite

BLACKWOOD
Map 3 ST19

Blackwood Golf Club Cwmgelli NP12 1BR
☎ 01495 222121 (Office) & 223152 (Club)
Heathland course with sand bunkers. Undulating, with hard walking. Testing 2nd hole par 4. Good views.

9 Holes, 5332yds, Par 66. Club membership 310.

Visitors Mon-Fri except BHs. Booking required. Dress code. **Societies** booking required. **Green Fees** £25 per round 🚐 **Facilities** ⊕ 🍴 🖥 🏌 🏖 **Conf** Corporate Hospitality Days **Location** 0.25m N of Blackwood, off A4048
Hotel ★★★ 74% CHH Llechwen Hall, Llanfabon, PONTYPRIDD ☎ 01443 742050 & 743020 📠 01443 742189 20 en suite

WALES

Save on Hotels. Book at **theAA.com/hotel**

CAERPHILLY – CARDIFF

CAERPHILLY
Map 3 ST18

Caerphilly Golf Club Pencapel, Mountain Rd CF83 1HJ
☎ 029 2088 3481 & 2086 3441 🖨 029 2086 3441
web: www.caerphillygolfclub.com

Undulating mountain course with woodland affording good views especially from 9th hole, 700 ft above sea level.

18 Holes, 5728yds, Par 69, SSS 71, Course record 64.
Club membership 650.

Visitors Mon-Sun & BHs. Booking required weekends & BHs. Handicap certificate. Dress code. **Societies** booking required. **Green Fees** not confirmed 🅿 **Prof** Joel Hill **Facilities** ⓣ by prior arrangement 🍴 by prior arrangement 🍺 ☕ 🏌 🏃 🛏 ✂ 🚗 ✂ **Conf** facs Corporate Hospitality Days **Location** 0.5m S on A469
Hotel ★★★ 70% HL The Legacy Cardiff International Hotel, Merthyr Road, Tongwynlais, CARDIFF ☎ 0844 411 9074 & 0330 333 2874 🖨 0844 411 9075 95 en suite

Mountain Lakes & Castell Heights Blaengwynlais CF83 1NG
☎ 029 2086 1128 & 2088 6666 🖨 029 2086 3243
web: www.golfclub.co.uk

Mountain Lakes Course: 18 Holes, 6046mtrs, Par 74, SSS 73, Course record 69.
Castell Heights Course: 9 Holes, 2751mtrs, Par 35, SSS 32, Course record 32.

Course Designer Bob Sandow **Location** M4 junct 32, near Black Cock Inn, Caerphilly Mountain
Telephone for further details
Hotel ★★★ 70% HL The Legacy Cardiff International Hotel, Merthyr Road, Tongwynlais, CARDIFF ☎ 0844 411 9074 & 0330 333 2874 🖨 0844 411 9075 95 en suite

MAESYCWMMER
Map 3 ST19

Bryn Meadows Golf Hotel & Spa CF82 7FN
☎ 01495 225590 🖨 01495 228272
web: www.brynmeadows.com

18 Holes, 6021yds, Par 71, SSS 70, Course record 68.
Course Designer Mayo/Jeffries **Location** on A4048 Blackwood-Ystrad Mynach road
Telephone for further details
Hotel ★★★★ 80% HL Bryn Meadows Golf, Hotel & Spa, Maesycwmmer, Ystrad Mynach, HENGOED ☎ 01495 225590 🖨 01495 228272 43 en suite

NELSON
Map 3 ST19

Whitehall Golf Club The Pavilion CF46 6ST
☎ 01443 740245
e-mail: mwilde001@tiscali.co.uk
web: www.whitehallgolfclub1922.co.uk

Hilltop course. Testing 4th hole (225yds) par 3, and 6th hole (402yds) par 4. Pleasant views.

9 Holes, 5666yds, Par 69, SSS 68, Course record 63.
Club membership 200.

Visitors Mon-Sat & BHs. Booking required Fri, Sat & BHs. Handicap certificate. Dress code. **Societies** booking required. **Green Fees** £10 per round (9 or 18 holes) 🅿 **Facilities** ⓣ 🍴 🍺 ☕ 🏌 🏃 **Leisure** snooker **Conf** facs Corporate Hospitality Days **Location** 1m SW of Nelson off A4054
Hotel ★★★ 74% CHH Llechwen Hall, Llanfabon, PONTYPRIDD ☎ 01443 742050 & 743020 🖨 01443 742189 20 en suite

OAKDALE
Map 3 ST19

Oakdale Golf Course Llwynon Ln NP12 0NF
☎ 01495 220044 & 220440

A challenging parkland course for players of all abilities. Well-maintained mature greens. Floodlit 18 bay driving range.

9 Holes, 1760yds.

Visitors Mon-Sun & BHs. **Societies** welcome. **Green Fees** £7.50 per 9 holes 🅿 **Course Designer** Ian Goodenough **Prof** Mathew Griffiths **Facilities** 🍺 ☕ 🏌 🏃 🛏 ✂ 🚗 ✂ 🏃 **Leisure** fishing, snooker **Location** off B4251 at Oakdale
Hotel ★★★ 74% CHH Llechwen Hall, Llanfabon, PONTYPRIDD ☎ 01443 742050 & 743020 🖨 01443 742189 20 en suite

CARDIFF

CARDIFF
Map 3 ST17

Cardiff Golf Club Sherborne Av, Cyncoed CF23 6SJ
☎ 029 2075 3320 🖨 029 2068 0011
e-mail: cardiff.golfclub@virgin.net
web: www.cardiffgolfclub.co.uk

Parkland where trees form natural hazards. Interesting variety of holes, mostly bunkered. A stream flows through the course and comes into play on nine separate holes.

18 Holes, 6146yds, Par 70, SSS 70, Course record 62.
Club membership 600.

Visitors Mon, Wed-Fri, Sun & BHs. Booking required. Handicap certificate. Dress code. **Societies** booking required. **Green Fees** £40 per round **Prof** Terry Hanson **Facilities** ⓣ 🍴 🍺 ☕ 🏌 🏃 🛏 ✂ **Conf** facs Corporate Hospitality Days **Location** 3m N of city centre
Hotel BUD Ibis Cardiff Gate, Malthouse Avenue, Cardiff Gate Business Park, Pontprennau, CARDIFF ☎ 029 2073 3222 🖨 029 2073 4222 78 en suite

WALES

Llanishen Golf Club Cwm Lisvane CF14 9UD
☎ 029 2075 5078
e-mail: secretary.llanishengc@virgin.net
web: www.llanishengc.co.uk
Picturesque sloping course overlooking England and the Bristol Channel.
18 Holes, 5301yds, Par 68, SSS 67. Club membership 900.
Visitors Tue, Thu, Fri & Sun. Booking required. Handicap certificate. Dress code. **Societies** Booking required. **Green Fees** £25 per round (£30 Sun) **Prof** Adrian Jones **Facilities** ⑪ ⑩ ⒧ ⌺ ⑪ ⌲ ⌸ ⑲ ⌷ ⒧ **Conf** facs Corporate Hospitality Days **Location** 5m N of city off A469
Hotel BUD Ibis Cardiff Gate, Malthouse Avenue, Cardiff Gate Business Park, Pontprennau, CARDIFF ☎ 029 2073 3222 🖷 029 2073 4222 78 en suite

Peterstone Lakes Golf Club Peterstone CF3 2TN
☎ 01633 680009 & 680075 (pro) 🖷 01633 680563
web: www.peterstonelakes.com
18 Holes, 6569yds, Par 72.
Course Designer Bob Sandow **Location** 3m from Castleton off A48
Telephone for further details
Hotel ★★★ 70% HL Best Western St Mellons Hotel & Country Club, Castleton, CARDIFF ☎ 01633 680355 🖷 01633 680399 41 en suite

Radyr Golf Club The Clubhouse, Drysgol Rd, Radyr CF15 8BS
☎ 029 2084 2408 🖷 029 2084 3914
e-mail: manager@radyrgolf.co.uk
web: www.radyrgolf.co.uk
Parkland course that celebrated its centenary in 2002. Good views. Venue for many county and national championships.
18 Holes, 6100yds, Par 69, SSS 70, Course record 62. Club membership 935.
Visitors Mon-Fri & BHs. Booking required Fri. Dress code. **Societies** welcome. **Green Fees** not confirmed **Course Designer** Colt **Prof** Simon Swales **Facilities** ⑪ ⑩ ⒧ ⌺ ⑪ ⌲ ⌸ ⑲ **Leisure** Table tennis **Conf** facs Corporate Hospitality Days **Location** M4 junct 32, 4.5m NW of city off A4119
Hotel ★★★★ 68% HL Barceló Cardiff Angel Hotel, Castle Street, CARDIFF ☎ 029 2064 9200 🖷 029 2039 6212 102 en suite

St Mellons Golf Club St Mellons CF3 2XS
☎ 01633 680408 🖷 01633 681219
web: www.stmellonsgolfclub.co.uk
18 Holes, 6275yds, Par 70, SSS 70, Course record 63.
Course Designer Colt & Morrison **Location** M4 junct 30, 2m E off A48
Telephone for further details
Hotel ★★★ 70% HL Best Western St Mellons Hotel & Country Club, Castleton, CARDIFF ☎ 01633 680355 🖷 01633 680399 41 en suite

Whitchurch Cardiff Golf Club Pantmawr Rd, Whitchurch CF14 7TD
☎ 029 2062 0985 📄 029 2052 9860
e-mail: secretary@whitchurchcardiffgolfclub.com
web: www.whitchurchcardiffgolfclub.com

This undulating parkland course is an urban oasis and offers panoramic views of the city. It is an easy walk and always in good condition with excellent drainage and smooth, quick greens.

18 Holes, 6278yds, Par 71, SSS 71, Course record 63.
Club membership 750.

Visitors Mon-Fri except BHs. Sun pm Booking required. Handicap certificate. Dress code. **Societies** booking required. **Green Fees** £50 per day **Course Designer** F Johns **Prof** Rhys Davies **Facilities** ⑪ ⑩ ⓛ ☐ 🍴 ⚲ 🖼 ⚙ **Conf** Corporate Hospitality Days **Location** M4 junct 32, 0.5m S on A470
Hotel ★★★★ 68% HL Barceló Cardiff Angel Hotel, Castle Street, CARDIFF ☎ 029 2064 9200 📄 029 2039 6212 102 en suite

CREIGIAU (CREIYIAU)   Map 3 ST08

Creigiau Golf Club Llantwit Rd CF15 9NN
☎ 029 2089 0263 📄 029 2089 0706
e-mail: creigiaugolfclub@btconnect.com
web: www.creigiaugolf.co.uk

Downland course, with small greens and many interesting water hazards.

18 Holes, 6063yds, Par 71, SSS 70. Club membership 800.

Visitors Mon-Sun except BHs. Handicap certificate. Dress code. **Societies** welcome **Green Fees** £40 per day **Prof** Iain Luntz **Facilities** ⑪ ⑩ ⓛ ☐ 🍴 ⚲ 🖼 ⚙ ⚙ **Location** 6m NW of Cardiff on A4119
Hotel ★★★★ 75% CHH Miskin Manor Country Hotel, Pendoylan Road, MISKIN ☎ 01443 224204 📄 01443 237606 43 en suite

---

CARMARTHENSHIRE

AMMANFORD   Map 3 SN61

Glynhir Golf Club Glynhir Rd, Llandybie SA18 2TF
☎ 01269 851365 📄 01269 851365
e-mail: glynhir.golfclub@tiscali.co.uk
web: www.glynhirgolfclub.co.uk

Parkland with good views. Last holes close to Upper Loughor River and the 14th is a 394yd dog-leg.

18 Holes, 5917yds, Par 69, SSS 70, Course record 66.
Club membership 450.

Visitors Mon-Sun & BHs. Booking required Wed, Fri-Sun & BHs. Handicap certificate. Dress code. **Societies** booking required. **Green Fees** Winter £13, Summer £20 (£16/£25 weekends) **Course Designer** F Hawtree **Prof** Richard Herbert **Facilities** ⑪ ⑩ ⓛ ☐ 🍴 ⚲ 🖼 ◇ 🍴 ⚙ 🐾 **Conf** facs Corporate Hospitality Days **Location** 2m N of Ammanford
Hotel ★★★★ 77% HL The Plough Inn, Rhosmaen, LLANDEILO ☎ 01558 823431 📄 01558 823969 14 en suite

BURRY PORT   Map 2 SN40

Ashburnham Golf Club Cliffe Ter SA16 0HN
☎ 01554 832269 & 833846 📄 01554 836974
web: www.ashburnhamgolfclub.co.uk
18 Holes, 6950yds, Par 72, SSS 74, Course record 66.
Course Designer J H Taylor **Location** W of town centre on A484
Telephone for further details
Hotel ★★ 75% HL Ashburnham Hotel, Ashburnham Road, Pembrey, LLANELLI ☎ 01554 834343 & 834455 📄 01554 834483 13 en suite

CARMARTHEN   Map 2 SN42

Carmarthen Golf Club Blaenycoed Rd SA33 6EH
☎ 01267 281588 📄 01267 281493
e-mail: info@carmarthengolfclub.co.uk
web: www.carmarthengolfclub.com

A well maintained heathland course with tricky greens. Magnificent clubhouse and scenery.

18 Holes, 6242yds, Par 71, SSS 71. Club membership 450.

Visitors Mon-Sun & BHs. Booking required weekends.
Societies welcome. **Green Fees** £29.50 (£34.50 weekends) **Course Designer** J H Taylor **Prof** Darren Griffiths **Facilities** ⑪ ⑩ ⓛ ☐ 🍴 ⚲ 🖼 🐾 ⚙ ⚙ 🐾 **Leisure** 5 hole beginners course **Conf** facs Corporate Hospitality Days **Location** 4m N of town
Hotel ★★ 80% HL Falcon, Lammas Street, CARMARTHEN ☎ 01267 234959 & 237152 📄 01267 221277 16 en suite

Derllys Court Golf Club Llysonnen Rd, Bancyfelin SA33 5DT
☎ 01267 211575 📄 01267 211575
e-mail: derllys@hotmail.com
web: www.derllyscourtgolfclub.com

The back and front halves provide an interesting contrast. The greens on the front 9 are undulating as opposed to the relatively flat greens of the back 9. Water hazards and bunkers come into play providing an interesting challenge. Fine views.

18 Holes, 5847yds, Par 70, SSS 68, Course record 69.
Club membership 300.

Visitors Mon-Sun & BHs. Booking required weekends. Dress code. **Societies** welcome. **Green Fees** phone **Course Designer** Peter Johnson/Stuart Finney **Prof** Robert Ryder **Facilities** ⑪ ⓛ ☐ 🍴 ⚲ 🖼 🐾 ⚙ **Conf** Corporate Hospitality Days **Location** off A40 between Carmarthen and St Clears
Hotel ★★ 80% HL Falcon, Lammas Street, CARMARTHEN ☎ 01267 234959 & 237152 📄 01267 221277 16 en suite

GARNANT   Map 3 SN61

Garnant Park Golf Club Dinefwr Rd SA18 1NP
☎ 01269 823365
web: www.parcgarnantgolf.co.uk
18 Holes, 6670yds, Par 72, SSS 72, Course record 69.
Course Designer Roger Jones **Location** M4 junct 48, off A474 in village of Garnant, signed
Telephone for further details
Hotel ★★ 71% HL White Hart Inn, 36 Carmarthen Road, LLANDEILO ☎ 01558 823419 📄 01558 823089 11 en suite

WALES

KIDWELLY

Map 2 SN40

Glyn Abbey Golf Club Trimsaran SA17 4LB
☎ 01554 810278 📄 01554 810889
e-mail: course-enquiries@glynabbey.co.uk
web: www.glynabbey.co.uk

Beautiful parkland course with spectacular views of the Gwendraeth Valley, set in 200 acres with mature wooded backdrops. USGA greens and tees. Welsh Golf Club of the Year 2009.

The Abbey: 18 Holes, 6202yds, Par 70, SSS 70, Course record 64.
The Mission: 9 Holes, 657yds. Club membership 300.

Visitors Mon-Sun & BHs. Dress code. **Societies** booking required.
Green Fees £25 per round (£30 weekends & BHs). Par 3 course £5 per round **Course Designer** Hawtree **Prof** Mike Davies **Facilities** ⑪ ⑩Ⓘ 🍴 🖢 📺 🛠 🏠 ⛳ ♦ 🛒 ✏ 🏌 **Leisure** gymnasium, 9 hole par 3 course **Conf** facs Corporate Hospitality Days **Location** E of Kidwelly on B4317 between Trimsaran & Carway, opposite Ffos Las Racecourse
Hotel ★★ 75% HL Ashburnham Hotel, Ashburnham Road, Pembrey, LLANELLI ☎ 01554 834343 & 834455 📄 01554 834483 13 en suite

LLANELLI

Map 2 SS59

Machynys Peninsula Golf & Country Club Nicklaus Av SA15 2DG
☎ 01554 744888 📄 01554 744680
web: www.machynys.com

18 Holes, 7051yds, Par 72, SSS 75.

Course Designer Gary Nicklaus **Location** M4 junct 47/48, follow directions for Llanelli. Take B4034 to Machynys, golf club on left
Telephone for further details
Hotel ★★★ 78% HL Best Western Diplomat Hotel, Felinfoel, LLANELLI ☎ 01554 756156 📄 01554 751649 50 en suite

RHOS

Map 2 SN44

Saron Golf Club Saron, Penwern SA44 5EL
☎ 01559 370705 📄 01559 370705
web: www.saron-golf.com

Set in 50 acres of mature parkland with large trees and magnificent Teifi Valley views. Numerous water hazards and bunkers.

9 Holes, 2091yds, Par 32.

Visitors Mon-Sun & BHs. **Societies** welcome. **Green Fees** £12 per 18 holes, £9 per 9 holes ⓔ **Course Designer** Adas **Facilities** 🛠 ♦ ⛳ **Location** off A484 at Saron, between Carmarthen and Newcastle Emlyn
Hotel ★★★ 78% HL Gwesty'r Emlyn Hotel, Bridge Street, NEWCASTLE EMLYN ☎ 01239 710317 📄 01239 710792 21 en suite

CEREDIGION

ABERYSTWYTH

Map 6 SN58

Aberystwyth Golf Club Brynmor Rd SY23 2HY
☎ 01970 615104 📄 01970 626622
e-mail: aberystwythgolf@talk21.com
web: www.aberystwythgolfclub.com

Undulating meadowland course. Testing holes: 16th (The Loop), par 3; 17th, par 4; 18th, par 3. Good views over Cardigan Bay.

18 Holes, 6119yds, Par 70, SSS 71, Course record 64.
Club membership 300.

Visitors Mon-Sun & BHs. Booking required. Dress code.
Societies booking required. **Green Fees** £30 per round (£35 weekends & BHs). £15 per round Mon & Fri before 11 am ⓔ **Course Designer** Harry Vardon **Prof** Jim McLeod **Facilities** ⑪ ⑩Ⓘ 🍴 🖢 📺 🛠 🏠 ⛳ 🛒 ✏ 🏌 **Leisure** 6 hole par 3 course **Conf** facs Corporate Hospitality Days **Location** N side of town near Constitution Hill and Cliff Railway
Hotel ★★★ 77% SHL Richmond, 44-45 Marine Terrace, ABERYSTWYTH ☎ 01970 612201 📄 01970 626706 15 en suite

BORTH

Map 6 SN69

Borth & Ynyslas Golf Club SY24 5JS
☎ 01970 871202 📄 01970 871202
e-mail: secretary@borthgolf.co.uk
web: www.borthgolf.co.uk

Traditional championship links course with superb scenery. Provides a true test of golf for all standards of player.

18 Holes, 6116yds, Par 70, SSS 70, Course record 63.
Club membership 500.

Visitors handicap certificate. Dress code. **Societies** booking required. **Green Fees** Winter £30 per round, Summer £40 **Course Designer** Harry Colt **Prof** J G Lewis **Facilities** ⑪ ⑩Ⓘ by prior arrangement 🍴 🖢 📺 🛠 🏠 ⛳ ♦ 🛒 **Conf** facs Corporate Hospitality Days **Location** 0.5m N on B4353
Hotel ★★★ CHH Ynyshir Hall, EGLWYS FACH ☎ 01654 781209 & 781268 📄 01654 781366 9 en suite

CARDIGAN

Map 2 SN14

Cardigan Golf Club Gwbert-on-Sea SA43 1PR
☎ 01239 621775 & 612035 📄 01239 621775
web: www.cardigangolf.co.uk

18 Holes, 6455yds, Par 72, SSS 73, Course record 67.

Course Designer Grant/Hawtree **Location** 3m N off A487
Telephone for further details
Hotel ★★★ 75% HL The Cliff Hotel, GWBERT-ON-SEA
☎ 01239 613241 📄 01239 615391 70 en suite

GWBERT ON SEA   Map 2 SN15

Cliff Hotel Golf Course SA43 1PP
☎ 01239 613241 ▤ 01239 615391
e-mail: reservations@cliffhotel.com
web: www.cliffhotel.com

This is a short course with two par 4s and the remainder are
challenging par 3s. Particularly interesting holes are played across the
sea on to a small island.

9 Holes, 1545yds, Par 29.

Visitors contact hotel for details. **Societies** booking required. **Green
Fees** from £7 ⊛ **Facilities** ⑪ ⫯◎⫯ ▯ ⬚ ⫯▯ ⫯⫯ ◇ ⬚ ⫯
Leisure outdoor and indoor heated swimming pool, fishing, sauna,
gymnasium, spa facility **Conf** facs Corporate Hospitality Days
Location 3m N of Cardigan off B4548
Hotel ★★★ 75% HL The Cliff Hotel, GWBERT-ON-SEA
☎ 01239 613241 ▤ 01239 615391 70 en suite

LLANRHYSTUD   Map 6 SN56

Penrhos Golf & Country Club SY23 5AY
☎ 01974 202999 ▤ 01974 202100
e-mail: info@penrhosgolf.co.uk
web: www.penrhosgolf.co.uk

Beautifully scenic course incorporating lakes and spectacular coastal
and inland views.

Penrhos: 18 Holes, 6660yds, Par 72, SSS 73,
Course record 68.
Academy: 9 Holes, 1784yds, Par 31. Club membership 300.

Visitors Mon-Sun & BHs. Booking required weekends & BHs. Dress
code. **Societies** booking required. **Green Fees** Championship £35
per day (£45 weekends). Academy £6 per round **Course Designer** Jim
Walters **Prof** Paul Diamond **Facilities** ⑪ ⫯◎⫯ ▯ ⬚ ⫯▯ ⤳
⬚ ⫯⫯ ◇ ⬚ ⫯ ⫯ **Leisure** hard tennis courts, heated indoor
swimming pool, sauna, gymnasium, bowling green **Conf** facs
Corporate Hospitality Days **Location** A487 onto B4337 in Llanrhystud,
course 0.25m on left
Hotel ★★★ BB Aromatherapy Reflexology Centre, The Barn House,
Pennant Road, ABERAERON ☎ 01974 202581 3 rooms (2 en suite)

CONWY

ABERGELE   Map 6 SH97

Abergele Golf Club Tan-y-Gopa Rd LL22 8DS
☎ 01745 824034 ▤ 01745 824772
e-mail: secretary@abergelegolfclub.co.uk
web: www.abergelegolfclub.co.uk

A beautiful parkland course with views of the Irish Sea and Gwyrch
Castle. There are splendid finishing holes: a testing par 5 16th; a
185yd 17th to an elevated green; and a superb par 5 18th with out of
bounds just behind the green.

18 Holes, 6396yds, Par 71, SSS 72, Course record 64.
0 Holes, 0. Club membership 1250.

Visitors Mon-Fri, Sun & BHs. Sat late pm. Booking required. Handicap
certificate. Dress code. **Societies** booking required. **Green Fees** £30
(£35 weekends) **Course Designer** Hawtree/D Williams **Prof** Iain R
Runcie **Facilities** ⑪ ⫯◎⫯ ▯ ⬚ ⫯▯ ⤳ ⬚ ⫯ ⫯
Conf facs Corporate Hospitality Days **Location** 0.5m W off A547
Hotel ★★★ 73% HL Kinmel Manor, St George's Road, ABERGELE
☎ 01745 832014 ▤ 01745 832014 51 en suite

BETWS-Y-COED   Map 6 SH75

Betws-y-Coed Golf Club LL24 0AL
☎ 01690 710556
e-mail: info@betws-y-coed.co.uk
web: www.betws-y-coedgolfclub.co.uk

Attractive flat meadowland course set between two rivers in
Snowdonia National Park, known as the Jewel of the Nines.

9 Holes, 4998yds, Par 64, SSS 64, Course record 63.
Club membership 300.

Visitors contact club for details. **Societies** welcome. **Green Fees** £20
per 18 holes, £10 per 9 holes ⊛ **Facilities** ⑪ ⫯◎⫯ ▯ ⬚ ⫯▯ ⤳
⬚ ⫯ **Leisure** Practice nets **Location** NE side of village off A5
Hotel ★★★ 86% HL Royal Oak, Holyhead Road, BETWS-Y-COED
☎ 01690 710219 ▤ 01690 710603 27 en suite

COLWYN BAY   Map 6 SH87

Old Colwyn Golf Club Woodland Av, Old Colwyn LL29 9NL
☎ 01492 515581 & 07799 575 369
e-mail: colwyngolfclub@tiscali.co.uk
web: www.oldcolwyngolfclub.co.uk

Hilly, meadowland course.

9 Holes, 5268yds, Par 68, SSS 66. Club membership 276.

Visitors Sun-Fri & BHs. **Societies** booking required. **Green Fees** £15
per day (£18 per round weekends & BHs) ⊛ **Course Designer** James
Braid **Facilities** ⑪ ⫯◎⫯ ▯ ⬚ ⫯▯ ⤳ **Location** E of town centre
on B5383
Hotel ★★★★★ GA Plas Rhos, Cayley Promenade, RHOS-ON-SEA
☎ 01492 543698 ▤ 01492 540088 7 rooms (7 en suite)

WALES

CONWY Map 6 SH77

Conwy (Caernarvonshire) Golf Club Beacons Way, Morfa LL32 8ER
☎ 01492 592423 📠 01492 593363
e-mail: secretary@conwygolfclub.com
web: www.conwygolfclub.com

Founded in 1890, Conwy has hosted national and international championships since 1898. Set among sand hills, possessing true links greens and a profusion of gorse on the latter holes. This course provides the visitor with real golfing enjoyment in stunning scenery. In 2006 the course became the first in Wales to stage the final qualifying rounds for the Open Championship and has since staged several major events.

18 Holes, 6647yds, Par 72, SSS 74, Course record 64. Club membership 1050.

Visitors Mon-Sun & BHs. Booking required. Dress code. Societies booking required. Green Fees £50 per day, £45 per round (£50 weekends & BHs) Prof Peter Lees Facilities ⑪ ⑩ ᕯ ☐ 🍷 ⚂ 🏠 ♈ 🛺 ✦ 🏌 Leisure snooker tables Conf facs Corporate Hospitality Days Location 1m W of town centre on A55, junct 17

Hotel ★★★★ 75% HL Empire Hotel & Spa, Church Walks, LLANDUDNO ☎ 01492 860555 📠 01492 860791 60 en suite

LLANDUDNO Map 6 SH78

Llandudno (Maesdu) Golf Club Hospital Rd LL30 1HU
☎ 01492 876450 📠 01492 876450
e-mail: secretary@maesdugolfclub.co.uk
web: www.maesdugolfclub.co.uk

Part links, part parkland, this championship course starts and finishes on one side of the main road, the remaining holes, more seaside in nature, being played on the other side. The holes are pleasantly undulating and present a pretty picture when the gorse is in bloom. Often windy, this varied and testing course is not for beginners.

18 Holes, 6545yds, Par 72, SSS 72, Course record 62. Club membership 1120.

Visitors Mon-Sun & BHs. Societies welcome. Green Fees not confirmed Prof Simon Boulden Facilities ⑪ ⑩ ᕯ ☐ 🍷 ⚂ 🏠 ♈ ✦ 🛺 ✦ Leisure snooker Location S of town centre on A546

Hotel ★★★★ 79% HL Imperial, The Promenade, LLANDUDNO ☎ 01492 877466 📠 01492 878043 98 en suite

North Wales Golf Club 72 Bryniau Rd, West Shore LL30 2DZ
☎ 01492 875325 📠 01492 873355
e-mail: enquiries@northwalesgolfclub.co.uk
web: www.northwalesgolfclub.co.uk

Situated on the west coast of Llandudno with excellent views over the Conwy estuary to Anglesey and Snowdonia. It is a true links course of championship standard and provides an invigorating and challenging experience for all levels of player.

18 Holes, 5883yds, Par 71, SSS 69, Course record 65. Club membership 650.

Visitors Mon-Sun & BHs. Booking required. Dress code. Societies booking required. Green Fees £30 per round (£35-£42 weekends and BHs), £12 after 3pm Course Designer Tancred Cummins Prof Richard Bradbury Facilities ⑪ ⑩ ᕯ ☐ 🍷 ⚂ 🏠 ♈ 🛺 ✦ 🏌 Leisure snooker, custom fit and indoor teaching studio Conf facs Corporate Hospitality Days Location W side of town on A546

Hotel ★★★ HL St Tudno Hotel and Restaurant, The Promenade, LLANDUDNO ☎ 01492 874411 📠 01492 860407 18 en suite

Rhos-on-Sea Golf Club Penryhn Bay LL30 3PU
☎ 01492 548115 (pro) & 549641 (clubhouse) 📠 01492 549100
web: www.rhosgolf.co.uk

18 Holes, 6064yds, Par 69, SSS 69, Course record 68.

Course Designer J J Simpson Location 0.5m W of Llandudno off A55
Telephone for further details
Hotel ★★★★ 79% HL Imperial, The Promenade, LLANDUDNO ☎ 01492 877466 📠 01492 878043 98 en suite

LLANFAIRFECHAN Map 6 SH67

Llanfairfechan Golf Club Llannerch Rd LL33 0ES
☎ 01248 680144 & 680524

9 Holes, 3119yds, Par 54, SSS 57, Course record 53.

Location W side of town on A55
Telephone for further details
Hotel ★★★ 77% HL Best Western Bulkeley Hotel, Castle Street, BEAUMARIS ☎ 01248 810415 📠 01248 810146 43 en suite

PENMAENMAWR Map 6 SH77

Penmaenmawr Golf Club Conway Old Rd LL34 6RD
☎ 01492 623330 📠 01492 622105
e-mail: clubhouse@pengolf.co.uk
web: www.pengolf.co.uk

Hilly course with magnificent views across the bay to Llandudno and Anglesey. Drystone wall hazards.

9 Holes, 5372yds, Par 67, SSS 66, Course record 62. Club membership 600.

Visitors Mon-Sun & BHs. Booking required weekends & BHs. Handicap certificate. Dress code. Societies booking required. Green Fees not confirmed Facilities ⑪ ⑩ by prior arrangement ᕯ ☐ 🍷 ⚂ 🛺 ✦ Conf Corporate Hospitality Days Location 1.5m NE off A55

Hotel ★★★★ 79% TH Castle Hotel Conwy, High Street, CONWY ☎ 01492 582800 📠 01492 582300 28 en suite

WALES

DENBIGHSHIRE

BODELWYDDAN
Map 6 SJ07

Kinmel Park Golf Course & Driving Range LL18 5SR
☎ 01745 833548
e-mail: info@kinmelgolf.co.uk
web: www.kinmelgolf.co.uk

Flat nine hole pay-and-play course, ideal for all levels of golfing ability.

9 Holes, 1080yds, Par 27.

Visitors contact course for details. **Societies** welcome. **Green Fees** £5 per 18 holes (£6 weekends & BHs) ⊛ **Prof** Rhodri Lloyd Jones **Facilities** ▢ ⚲ ⛳ ♂ ⚑ **Leisure** golf academy **Location** A55 junct 25
Hotel ★★★★ 74% HL The Oriel, Upper Denbigh Road, ST ASAPH
☎ 01745 582716 📄 01745 585208 33 en suite

DENBIGH
Map 6 SJ06

Bryn Morfydd Hotel & Golf Club LL16 4NP
☎ 01745 589090 📄 01745 589093
web: www.byrnmorfyddhotelgolf.co.uk

Dukes Course: 18 Holes, 5650yds, Par 70, SSS 67,
Course record 74.
Duchess Course: 9 Holes, 2098yds, Par 27.

Course Designer Peter Alliss **Location** on A525 between Denbigh and Ruthin
Telephone for further details
Hotel ★★★★ INN The Wynnstay Arms, Well Street, RUTHIN
☎ 01824 703147 📄 01824 705428 7 rooms

Denbigh Golf Club Henllan Rd LL16 5AA
☎ 01745 814159 & 816669 📄 01745 814888
e-mail: denbighgolfclub@aol.com
web: www.denbighgolfclub.co.uk

Parkland course with stunning views across the Vale of Clwyd down to the coast, giving a testing and varied game.

18 Holes, 5712yds, Par 69, SSS 68, Course record 64.
Club membership 500.

Visitors Mon-Sun & BHs. Handicap certificate. Society certificate. Dress code. **Societies** booking required. **Green Fees** £32 per 27 holes, £26 per round (£37/£32 weekends) **Course Designer** John Stockton **Prof** Mike Jones **Facilities** ⊕ ⦿ ⚲ ▢ ⛳ ⚲ 🏡 ⛳ 🍴
♂ **Leisure** function room for hire **Conf** facs Corporate Hospitality Days **Location** 1.5m NW on B5382
Hotel ★★★★ 74% HL The Oriel, Upper Denbigh Road, ST ASAPH
☎ 01745 582716 📄 01745 585208 33 en suite

LLANGOLLEN
Map 7 SJ24

Vale of Llangollen Golf Club Holyhead Rd LL20 7PR
☎ 01978 860906
e-mail: info@vlgc.co.uk
web: www.vlgc.co.uk

Parkland in superb scenery by the River Dee. Favoured venue for national and county competitions.

18 Holes, 6672yds, Par 72, SSS 73, Course record 64.
Club membership 800.

Visitors Mon-Sun & BHs. Booking required. Handicap certificate. Dress code. **Societies** booking required. **Green Fees** £38 per round (£43 weekends) **Prof** David Vaughan **Facilities** ⊕ ⦿ ⚲ ▢ ⛳ 🍴 ⚲
🏡 ♂ 🚬 ♂ **Conf** Corporate Hospitality Days **Location** 1.5m E on A5 from Llangollen
Hotel ★★★★ BB Tyn Celyn Farmhouse, Tyndwr, LLANGOLLEN
☎ 01978 861117 3 rooms

PRESTATYN
Map 6 SJ08

Prestatyn Golf Club Marine Road East LL19 7HS
☎ 01745 854320 📄 01745 854320
web: www.prestatyngolfclub.co.uk

18 Holes, 6568yds, Par 72, SSS 72, Course record 65.

Course Designer S Collins **Location** 0.5m N off A548
Telephone for further details
Hotel ★★★★ RR Barratt's of Ty'n Rhyl, Ty'n Rhyl, 167 Vale Road, RHYL ☎ 01745 344138 & 0773 095 4994 📄 01745 344138 3 rooms

St Melyd Golf Club The Paddock, Meliden Rd LL19 8NB
☎ 01745 854405 📄 01745 856908
e-mail: enquiries@stmelydgolfltd.co.uk
web: www.stmelydgolf.co.uk

Parkland with good views of mountains and the Irish Sea. Testing 1st hole (423yds) par 4.

9 Holes, 5829yds, Par 68, SSS 68, Course record 65.
Club membership 400.

Visitors Mon-Fri, Sun & BHs. Dress code. **Societies** booking required. **Green Fees** not confirmed ⊛ **Facilities** ⊕ ⦿ ⚲ ▢ 🍴
⚲ 🚬 ♂ **Leisure** snooker **Conf** facs Corporate Hospitality Days **Location** 0.5m S on A547
Hotel ★★★★ 74% HL The Oriel, Upper Denbigh Road, ST ASAPH
☎ 01745 582716 📄 01745 585208 33 en suite

RHUDDLAN
Map 6 SJ07

Rhuddlan Golf Club Meliden Rd LL18 6LB
☎ 01745 590217 (Sec) & 590898(Pro) 📄 01745 590472
e-mail: secretary@rhuddlangolfclub.co.uk
web: www.rhuddlangolfclub.co.uk

Attractive, gently undulating parkland with good views. Well bunkered with trees and water hazards. The 476yd 8th and 431yd 11th require both length and accuracy.

18 Holes, 6471yds, Par 71, SSS 71, Course record 66.
Club membership 1133.

Visitors Mon-Sat & BHs. Booking required. **Societies** welcome. **Green Fees** not confirmed **Course Designer** Hawtree & Son **Prof** Andrew Carr **Facilities** ⊕ ⦿ ⚲ ▢ ⛳ 🍴 ⚲ 🏡 ♂ 🚬 ♂ **Conf** Corporate Hospitality Days **Location** from A55 take Rhyl junct and follow dual carriageway to rdbt, take 3rd exit into Rhuddlan. Follow A547, club on right
Hotel ★★★ 73% HL Kinmel Manor, St George's Road, ABERGELE
☎ 01745 832014 📄 01745 832014 51 en suite

WALES

RHYL
Map 6 SJ08

Rhyl Golf Club Coast Rd LL18 3RE
☎ 01745 353171
e-mail: rhylgolfclub@btconnect.com
web: www.rhylgolfclub.co.uk
Flat links course with challenging holes.

9 Holes, 6220yds, Par 71, SSS 70, Course record 64.
Club membership 500.

Visitors Mon-Sun & BHs. Booking required Thu, Sat & BHs. Handicap certificate. Dress code. **Societies** Booking required. **Green Fees** not confirmed **Course Designer** James Braid **Prof** Robert Dunbar **Facilities** ⑨ ⑩ by prior arrangement ⓑ ⛾ ⑩ 丄 ☎ ⚑ ⛟ ⚌ **Conf** facs Corporate Hospitality Days **Location** 1m E on A548
Hotel ★★★★ RR Barratt's of Ty'n Rhyl, Ty'n Rhyl, 167 Vale Road, RHYL ☎ 01745 344138 & 0773 095 4994 🖹 01745 344138 3 rooms

RUTHIN
Map 6 SJ15

Ruthin-Pwllglas Golf Club Pwllglas LL15 2PE
☎ 01824 702296
e-mail: neillroberts@aol.com
web: www.ruthinpwllglasgc.co.uk
Parkland course established in 1905 with panoramic views of the Vale of Clwyd. Three testing par 3 holes.

10 Holes, 5362yds, Par 70, SSS 66, Course record 62.
Club membership 380.

Visitors Mon-Sun & BHs. Booking required. Dress code.
Societies booking required. **Green Fees** not confirmed ⊗ **Course Designer** Dai Rees **Prof** Richard Heginbotham **Facilities** ⑨ ⑩ ⓑ ⛾ ⑩ 丄 ⚑ ⚌ ⛟ **Conf** Corporate Hospitality Days **Location** 2.5m S off A494
Hotel ★★★★ FH Tyddyn Chambers, Pwllglas, RUTHIN ☎ 01824 750683 & 07745 589946 3 rooms

ST ASAPH
Map 6 SJ07

Llannerch Park Golf Course North Wales Golf Range LL17 0BD
☎ 01745 730805
web: www.parkgolf.co.uk
9 Holes, 1587yds, Par 30, Course record 27.

Course Designer B Williams **Location** 200yds S off A525
Telephone for further details
Hotel ★★★★ 74% HL The Oriel, Upper Denbigh Road, ST ASAPH ☎ 01745 582716 🖹 01745 585208 33 en suite

FLINTSHIRE

BRYNFORD
Map 7 SJ17

Holywell Golf Club Brynford CH8 8LQ
☎ 01352 710040
web: www.hoywellgc.co.uk
18 Holes, 6100yds, Par 70, SSS 70, Course record 67.

Location 1.25m SW off B5121
Telephone for further details
Hotel ★★★ 74% HL Beaufort Park Hotel, Alltami Road, New Brighton, MOLD ☎ 01352 758646 🖹 01352 757132 106 en suite

FLINT
Map 7 SJ27

Flint Golf Club Cornist Park CH6 5HJ
☎ 01352 732327
e-mail: secretary@flintgolfclub.co.uk
web: www.flintgolfclub.co.uk
Parkland incorporating woods and streams. Excellent views of Dee estuary and the Welsh hills.

9 Holes, 5980yds, Par 70, SSS 70, Course record 62.
Club membership 200.

Visitors Mon-Sat & BHs. Sun pm only. Booking required. Handicap certificate. Dress code. **Societies** booking required. **Green Fees** £12 per day, £10 per 18 holes, £5 per 9 holes ⊗ **Course Designer** H G Griffith **Prof** Anthony Middleton **Facilities** ⑨ ⑩ ⓑ ⛾ ⑩ 丄 ☎ **Conf** facs Corporate Hospitality Days **Location** 1m W of Flint, signs for Cornist Hall Golf Club
Hotel ★★★ 74% HL Beaufort Park Hotel, Alltami Road, New Brighton, MOLD ☎ 01352 758646 🖹 01352 757132 106 en suite

HAWARDEN
Map 7 SJ36

Hawarden Golf Club Groomsdale Ln CH5 3EH
☎ 01244 531447 & 520809   🖹 01244 536901
e-mail: secretary@hawardengolfclub.co.uk
web: www.hawardengolfclub.co.uk
Parkland course with comfortable walking and good views.

18 Holes, 5842yds, Par 69, SSS 69. Club membership 500.

Visitors Sun-Fri & BHs. Booking required. Dress code.
Societies booking required. **Green Fees** £50 per 4 ball ex BHs. Mon-Tue £14, Wed-Fri £20, Sat-Sun £25 **Prof** Alex Rowland **Facilities** ⑨ ⑩ ⓑ ⛾ ⑩ 丄 ☎ ⚑ ⚌ ⛟ **Location** W side of town off B5125
Hotel ★★★ 74% HL Beaufort Park Hotel, Alltami Road, New Brighton, MOLD ☎ 01352 758646 🖹 01352 757132 106 en suite

MOLD
Map 7 SJ26

Mold Golf Club Cilcain Rd, Pantymwyn CH7 5EH
☎ 01352 741513 🖹 01352 741517
e-mail: info@moldgolfclub.co.uk
web: www.moldgolfclub.co.uk
Parkland course with magnificent views of 5 counties.

18 Holes, 5524yds, Par 69, SSS 69. Club membership 700.

Visitors Mon-Sun & BHs. Booking required Fri-Sun & BHs.
Societies welcome. **Green Fees** £30 per day, £25 per round (£36/£30 weekends). Winter £20 per round (£22 weekends) **Course Designer** Hawtree **Facilities** ⑨ ⑩ ⓑ ⛾ ⑩ 丄 ☎ ⛟ ⚑ ⚌ **Conf** facs Corporate Hospitality Days **Location** E side of village
Hotel ★★★ 74% HL Beaufort Park Hotel, Alltami Road, New Brighton, MOLD ☎ 01352 758646 🖹 01352 757132 106 en suite

Save on Hotels. Book at **theAA.com/hotel**

FLINTSHIRE – GWYNEDD

Old Padeswood Golf Club Station Ln, Padeswood CH7 4JL
☎ 01244 547401 & 547701 📠 01244 545082
web: www.oldpadeswoodgolfclub.co.uk
Situated in the beautiful Alyn Valley, part bounded by the River Alyn, this challenging course suits all categories of golfers. Nine holes are flat and nine are gently undulating. The signature hole is the 18th, a par 3 that needs a carry to the green as a valley waits below.

18 Holes, 6200yds, Par 72, SSS 72, Course record 65.
Club membership 600.

Visitors Mon-Sun & BHs. Booking advisable. **Societies** booking required. **Green Fees** not confirmed **Course Designer** Jeffries
Prof Tony Davies **Facilities** ⓘ 🏵 ▮ 🖵 🍴 ⚱ 🏠 🍸 ⚘
🛒 ⚘ **Conf** facs Corporate Hospitality Days **Location** 3m SE off A5118
Hotel ★★★ 74% HL Beaufort Park Hotel, Alltami Road, New Brighton, MOLD ☎ 01352 758646 📠 01352 757132 106 en suite

Padeswood & Buckley Golf Club The Caia, Station Ln, Padeswood CH7 4JD
☎ 01244 550537 📠 01244 541600
e-mail: admin@padeswoodgolf.plus.com
web: www.padeswoodgolfclub.com
Bounded by the banks of the River Alyn, gently undulating parkland with natural hazards and good views of the Welsh hills.

18 Holes, 6052yds, Par 70, SSS 70, Course record 67.
Club membership 800.

Visitors Mon-Fri & BHs. Dress code. **Societies** booking required. **Green Fees** £30 per round (£36 Sat) **Course Designer** Williams Partnership
Prof David Ashton **Facilities** ⓘ 🏵 ▮ 🖵 🍴 ⚱ 🏠 ⚘ 🚜
⚘ **Leisure** snooker tables, pool table **Conf** Corporate Hospitality Days
Location 3m SE off A5118
Hotel ★★★ 74% HL Beaufort Park Hotel, Alltami Road, New Brighton, MOLD ☎ 01352 758646 📠 01352 757132 106 en suite

NORTHOP   Map 7 SJ26

Northop Golf & Country Club CH7 6WA
☎ 01352 840440 📠 01352 840445
web: www.northoppark.co.uk
18 Holes, 6750yds, Par 72, SSS 73, Course record 64.
Course Designer John Jacobs **Location** 150yds from Connahs Quay turning on A55
Telephone for further details
Hotel ★★★ 74% HL Beaufort Park Hotel, Alltami Road, New Brighton, MOLD ☎ 01352 758646 📠 01352 757132 106 en suite

WHITFORD   Map 6 SJ17

Pennant Park Golf Club CH8 9AE
☎ 01745 563000
web: www.pennant-park.co.uk
18 Holes, 6059yds, Par 70, SSS 70, Course record 66.
Course Designer Roger Jones **Location** from Chester take A55 towards Holyhead. Exit at junct 32 to Holywell, follow signs for Pennant Park
Telephone for further details
Hotel ★★★★ GA The Old Mill Guest Accommodation, Melin-Y-Wern, Denbigh Road, NANNERCH ☎ 01352 741542 6 rooms

GWYNEDD

ABERDYFI   Map 6 SN69

Aberdovey Golf Club see page 399
LL35 0RT
☎ 01654 767493 📠 01654 767027
e-mail: sec@aberdoveygolf.co.uk
web: www.aberdoveygolf.co.uk

ABERSOCH   Map 6 SH32

Abersoch Golf Club LL53 7EY
☎ 01758 712636 (office) & 712622 (shop)
📠 01758 712777
web: www.abersochgolf.co.uk

18 Holes, 5819yds, Par 69, SSS 68, Course record 66.
Course Designer Harry Vardon **Location** S side of village
Telephone for further details
Hotel ★★ 81% HL Neigwl, Lon Sarn Bach, ABERSOCH
☎ 01758 712363 📠 01758 712544 9 en suite

See advert on page 398

BALA   Map 6 SH93

Bala Golf Club Penlan LL23 7YD
☎ 01678 520359 & 521361 📠 01678 521361
e-mail: balagolf@btconnect.com
web: www.balagolf.co.uk
Upland course with natural hazards. All holes except first and last affected by wind. First hole is a most challenging par 3. Irrigated greens and spectacular views of surrounding countryside.

10 Holes, 4962yds, Par 66, SSS 64, Course record 64.
Club membership 235.

Visitors Mon-Sun & BHs. Booking required weekends & BHs.
Societies booking required. **Green Fees** £15 (£20 weekends & BHs)
🍽 **Course Designer** Syd Collins **Facilities** ⓘ by prior arrangement
🏵 by prior arrangement ▮ 🖵 🍴 ⚱ 🏠 🍸 ⚘ **Conf**
Corporate Hospitality Days **Location** 0.5m SW off A494
Hotel ★★★★★ GA Penmachno Hall, Penmachno, BETWS-Y-COED
☎ 01690 760410 📠 01690 760410 3 rooms

WALES

BANGOR — Map 6 SH57

St Deiniol Golf Club Penybryn LL57 1PX
☎ 01248 353098 ▤ 01248 370792
e-mail: secretary@st-deiniol.co.uk
web: www.st-deiniol.co.uk

Parkland course with panoramic views of Snowdonia, the Menai Strait and Anglesey. Designed by James Braid in 1906 this course is a test test of accuracy and course management. The 3rd has a narrow driving area and a shot to an elevated green. The 4th, one of six par 3s, provides a choice of pitching the green or utilising the contours, making it one of the most difficult holes on the course. The 13th, a dog-leg par 4, is the last hole of the course's own Amen Corner with its out of bounds to the right and left.

18 Holes, 5652yds, Par 68, SSS 68, Course record 60.
Club membership 300.

Visitors Mon-Sun & BHs. Booking required. **Societies** booking required. **Green Fees** not confirmed **Course Designer** James Braid **Facilities** ⑪ ⑩ ⓑ ⎁ ⑩ ⚐ ⎈ ⓟ ⎈ ✐ **Location** A55 junct 11, E of town centre off A5122
Hotel ★★ 85% SHL Bishopsgate House Hotel, 54 Castle Street, BEAUMARIS ☎ 01248 810302 ▤ 01248 810166 9 en suite

CAERNARFON — Map 6 SH46

Royal Town of Caernarfon Golf Club, Llanfaglan LL54 5RP
☎ 01286 673783 ▤ 01286 673783
e-mail: secretary@caernarfongolfclub.co.uk
web: www.caernarfongolfclub.co.uk

Parkland with gentle gradients. Immaculately kept course with excellent greens and tree-lined fairways.

18 Holes, 5969yds, Par 69, SSS 69, Course record 64.
Club membership 600.

Visitors Mon-Sun & BHs. Booking required Tue-Sun & BHs. Handicap certificate. Dress code. **Societies** welcome. **Green Fees** £28 per day, £32 per round (£32 per round weekends) **Prof** Aled Owen **Facilities** ⑪ ⑩ ⓑ ⎁ ⑩ ⚐ ✐ ⎈ ✐ **Conf** facs Corporate Hospitality Days **Location** 1.75m SW of Caernarfon
Hotel ★★★ 80% HL Celtic Royal Hotel, Bangor Street, CAERNARFON ☎ 01286 674477 ▤ 01286 674139 110 en suite

CRICCIETH — Map 6 SH43

Criccieth Golf Club Ednyfed Hill LL52 0PH
☎ 01766 522154
e-mail: aaguide@cricciethgolfclub.co.uk
web: www.cricciethgolfclub.co.uk

Hilly course on high ground, with generous fairways and natural hazards. The 16th tee has panoramic views in all directions.

18 Holes, 5787yds, Par 69, SSS 68.

Visitors Mon-Sun & BHs. **Societies** booking required. **Green Fees** not confirmed ⊛ **Facilities** ⑪ ⑩ ⓑ ⎁ ⚐ ✐ **Location** 1m NE
Hotel ★★★ 87% CHH Bron Eifion Country House, CRICCIETH ☎ 01766 522385 ▤ 01766 523796 18 en suite

---

— Clwb Golf Abersoch —

Located at Abersoch on the Llyn Peninsula in Gwynedd, Wales, UK – Clwb Golff Abersoch / Abersoch Golf Club offers-18 holes of links and parkland golf.

Designed by Harry Varden in 1907, the original 9 hole links course opened in 1908. Today we offer a full 18 holes of links and parkland golf. The sandy soil and the unique microclimate ensures golf for 365-days a year.

We pride ourselves in the condition of the course and the warm welcome extended to members and visitors alike.

Please browse the website for all the latest information, green fees and facilities offered, then visit the local www.abersoch.co.uk website for further details about the resort's surrounding area.

Clwb Golf Abersoch	Tel: Admin 01758 712636
Abersoch	Email: admin@abersochgolf.co.uk
Pwllheli	Web: www.abersochgolf.co.uk
Gwynedd	Pro: Tel: 01758 712622
LL53 7NN	Email: pro@abersochgolf.co.uk

DOLGELLAU — Map 6 SH71

Dolgellau Golf Club Pencefn Rd LL40 2ES
☎ 01341 422603 ▤ 01341 422603
e-mail: richard@dolgellaugolfclub.com
web: www.dolgellaugolfclub.com

Set amidst spectacular mountain scenery, the club is considered to be one of the most beautiful courses in Wales. Do not be fooled by its lack of length, this 9 hole course with alternating tees for the second nine provides a true test of golf for all standards of golfer.

9 Holes, 4696yds, Par 66, SSS 64, Course record 61.
Club membership 300.

Visitors Mon-Sun & BHs. Booking advised weekends & BHs. **Societies** booking required. **Green Fees** £18 per day (£22.50 weekends & BHs). £12 per 9 holes **Course Designer** Jack Jones **Prof** Mark White **Facilities** ⑪ ⑩ ⓑ ⎁ ⑩ ⚐ ✐ ⎈ ✐ **Conf** facs Corporate Hospitality Days **Location** 0.5m N, near Town Bridge
Hotel ★★★ CHH Penmaenuchaf Hall, Penmaenpool, DOLGELLAU ☎ 01341 422129 ▤ 01341 422787 14 en suite

WALES

ABERDOVEY

GWYNEDD - ABERDYFI - MAP 6 SN69

Golf was first played at Aberdovey in 1886, with the club founded six years later. The links has since developed into one of the finest championship courses in Wales. The club has hosted many prestigious events over the years, and is popular with golfing societies and clubs who regularly return here. Golfers can enjoy spectacular views and easy walking alongside the dunes of this characteristic seaside links. Fine holes include the 3rd, 11th and a good short hole at the 12th.

LL35 0RT ☎ 01654 767493 🖹 01654 767027
e-mail: sec@aberdoveygolf.co.uk   web: www.aberdoveygolf.co.uk
18 Holes, 6615yds, Par 71, SSS 72, Course record 66. Club membership 1000.
Visitors Mon-Sun & BHs. Booking required. Dress code. Societies booking required. Green Fees £65 per day,
£50 per round Course Designer J Braid Prof John Davies Facilities ⑪ ⑩ 🛏 ⬜ 🍴 ♨ 🏠 ◇ ✦ 🛒 ✦
Conf facs Corporate Hospitality Days Location 0.5m W on A493
Hotel ★★★ CHH Ynyshir Hall, EGLWYS FACH ☎ 01654 781209 & 781268 🖹 01654 781366 9 en suite

WALES

FFESTINIOG
Map 6 SH93

Ffestiniog Golf Club Y Cefn LL41 4LS
☎ 01766 762637
e-mail: info@ffestinioggolf.org
web: www.ffestiniog.org
Moorland course set in Snowdonia National Park.

9 Holes, 4570yds, Par 68, SSS 66. Club membership 150.
Visitors contact club for details. **Societies** welcome. **Green Fees** £10 per day **Facilities** ⚲ **Location** 1m E of Ffestiniog on B4391
Hotel ★★★★ 77% HL Castell Deudraeth, PORTMEIRION
☎ 01766 770000 🖹 01766 771771   11 en suite

HARLECH
Map 6 SH53

Royal St Davids Golf Club LL46 2UB
☎ 01766 780361   🖹 01766 781110
web: www.royalstdavids.co.uk
18 Holes, 6225yds, Par 69, SSS 71, Course record 61.
Course Designer Harold Finch-Hatton **Location** W side of town on A496
Telephone for further details
Hotel ★★ 74% SHL Ty Mawr, LLANBEDR ☎ 01341 241440
🖹 01341 241440   10 en suite

MORFA NEFYN
Map 6 SH24

Nefyn & District Golf Club LL53 6DA
☎ 01758 720966   🖹 01758 720476
web: www.nefyn-golf-club.co.uk
Old Course: 18 Holes, 6201yds, Par 71, SSS 71, Course record 67.
New Course: 18 Holes, 6317yds, Par 71, SSS 71, Course record 66.
Course Designer James Braid **Location** 0.75m NW
Telephone for further details
Hotel ★★★ 87% CHH Bron Eifion Country House, CRICCIETH
☎ 01766 522385 🖹 01766 523796   18 en suite

PORTHMADOG
Map 6 SH53

Porthmadog Golf Club Morfa Bychan LL49 9UU
☎ 01766 514124   🖹 01766 514124
e-mail: secretary@porthmadog-golf-club.co.uk
web: www.porthmadog-golf-club-co.uk
A mixture of heathland and links with beautiful scenery.

18 Holes, 6322yds, Par 71, SSS 72, Course record 65.
Club membership 700.
Visitors Mon-Sun & BHs. Booking required. Dress code.
Societies booking required. **Green Fees** £47 per day, £37 per round (£52/£42 weekends & BHs) **Course Designer** James Braid **Prof** Peter L Bright **Facilities** ⑪ ⑩ 🍴 ⬤ 🛒 ⚲ 🏠 🛺 ✍ ⚙
Leisure snooker **Conf** Corporate Hospitality Days **Location** 1.5m SW of Porthmadog
Hotel ★★★ 87% CHH Bron Eifion Country House, CRICCIETH
☎ 01766 522385 🖹 01766 523796   18 en suite

PWLLHELI
Map 6 SH33

Pwllheli Golf Club Golf Rd LL53 5PS
☎ 01758 701644   🖹 01758 701644
e-mail: admin@pwllheligolfclub.co.uk
web: www.pwllheligolfclub.co.uk
Easy walking on flat seaside course, 9 holes links, 9 holes parkland. Outstanding views of Snowdon, Cader Idris and Cardigan Bay.

18 Holes, 6100yds, Par 69, SSS 69, Course record 65.
Club membership 780.
Visitors Mon-Sun & BHs. Dress code. **Societies** booking required.
Green Fees £34 per day (£37 weekends & BHs), £20 twilight rate per round **Course Designer** Tom Morris & James Braid **Prof** Stuart Pilkington **Facilities** ⑪ ⑩ 🍴 ⬤ 🛒 🍴 ⚲ 🏠 🛺 🛺 ✍
Location 0.5m SW off A497
Hotel ★★★ 80% CHH Porth Tocyn, Bwlch Tocyn, ABERSOCH
☎ 01758 713303 & 07789 994942 🖹 01758 713538   17 en suite

MERTHYR TYDFIL

MERTHYR TYDFIL
Map 3 S000

Merthyr Tydfil Golf Club Cilsanws Mountain, Cefn Coed CF48 2NU
☎ 01685 723308
Mountain-top course in the Brecon Beacons National Park with beautiful views of the surrounding area. The course plays longer than its card length and requires accuracy off the tee. A real test of golf.

18 Holes, 5652yds, Par 69, Course record 64.
Club membership 100.
Visitors Mon-Sun & BHs. Booking required weekends & BHs. Dress code. **Societies** welcome. **Green Fees** £10 per day (£15 weekends & BHs) **Course Designer** V Price/R Mathias **Facilities** ⑪ by prior arrangement ⑩ by prior arrangement ⬤ 🛒 🍴 ⚲
Location off A470 at Cefn Coed to Cloth Hall Lane and top of hill.
Hotel ★★★ 74% CHH Llechwen Hall, Llanfabon, PONTYPRIDD
☎ 01443 742050 & 743020 🖹 01443 742189   20 en suite

Morlais Castle Golf Club Pant CF48 2UY
☎ 01685 722822
web: www.morlaiscastlegolf.co.uk
18 Holes, 6550yds, Par 71, SSS 72, Course record 65.
Course Designer Donald Steel **Location** 2.5m N off A465. Follow signs for Mountain Railway. Course entrance opposite railway car park
Telephone for further details
Hotel ★★★★ GH Penrhadw Farm, Pontsticill, MERTHYR TYDFIL
☎ 01685 723481 & 722461 🖹 01685 722461   10 rooms

ST PIERRE, A MARRIOTT HOTEL & COUNTRY CLUB
MONMOUTHSHIRE - CHEPSTOW - MAP 3 ST59

Set in 400 acres of beautiful parkland, Marriott St Pierre offers two 18-hole courses. The Old Course is one of the finest in the country and has played host to over 14 European Tour events. The par 3 18th hole is famous for its tee shot over the lake to an elevated green. The Mathern has its own challenges and is highly enjoyable for golfers of all abilities.

St Pierre Park NP16 6YA ☎ 01291 625261 📄 01291 627977
e-mail: mhrs.cwlas.golf@marriotthotels.com web: www.stpierregolf.com
Old Course: 18 Holes, 7090yds, Par 72, SSS 73, Course record 64.
Mathern Course: 18 Holes, 5730yds, Par 68, SSS 68, Course record 63. Club membership 800.
Visitors Mon-Sun & BHs. Booking required. Dress code. Societies booking required. Green Fees Old £50, Mathern from £35. Winter Old from £25, Mathern from £15 Course Designer H Cotton Prof Craig Dun
Facilities ⊕ ⏐◎⏐ ⛴ ⏢ ⑨⎞ ⤳ 🗄 ☌ ◇ 🛒 ✐ ⸙ Leisure hard tennis courts, heated indoor swimming pool, fishing, sauna, gymnasium, halfway house on Old Course, health & beauty suite, chipping green. Conf facs Corporate Hospitality Days Location M48 junct 2, A466 towards Chepstow, at 2nd rdbt take exit for Caerwent. Hotel after 2m
Hotel ★★★★ 79% CHH St Pierre, A Marriott Hotel & Country Club, St Pierre Park, CHEPSTOW
☎ 01291 625261 📄 01291 629975 148 en suite

MONMOUTHSHIRE

ABERGAVENNY   Map 3 SO21

Monmouthshire Golf Club Gypsy Ln, LLanfoist NP7 9HE
☎ 01873 852606 📄 01873 850470
e-mail: monmouthshiregc@btconnect.com
web: www.monmouthshiregolfclub.co.uk
This parkland course is very picturesque, with the beautifully
wooded River Usk running alongside. There are a number of par 3
holes and a testing par 4 at the 15th.
18 Holes, 5776yds, Par 70, SSS 69, Course record 65.
Club membership 600.
Visitors handicap certificate. Dress code. **Societies** booking
required. **Green Fees** £30 per 18 holes (£35 weekends) **Course
Designer** James Braid **Prof** B Edwards **Facilities** ⊕ ⓣⓞⓛ by prior
arrangement ⬚ ☐ ⛳️ ⤳ ⬚ 🛢 ♪ **Conf** Corporate
Hospitality Days **Location** 2m S off B4269
Hotel ★★★ 78% HL Angel Hotel, 15 Cross Street, ABERGAVENNY
☎ 01873 857121 📄 01873 858059 35 en suite

Wernddu Golf Centre Old Ross Rd NP7 8NG
☎ 01873 856223 📄 01873 852177
e-mail: info@wernddu-golf-club.co.uk
web: www.wernddu-golf-club.co.uk
A parkland course with magnificent views, wind hazards on several
holes in certain conditions, and water hazards on four holes. This
gently undulating course has a long front nine and a shorter back
nine, while the final hole, a par 3, is an outstanding finish.
Wernddu: 18 Holes, 5613yds, Par 69, SSS 68,
Course record 64. Club membership 500.
Visitors Mon-Sun & BHs. Booking required. Dress code.
Societies booking required. **Green Fees** £18 per round **Course
Designer** G Watkins **Prof** Tina Tetley **Facilities** ⊕ ⬚ ☐ ⛳️ ⤳
⬚ ♪ 🛒 ♪ 🏌 **Leisure** 9 hole pitch & putt course **Location** 1.5m
NE on B4521
Hotel ★★★★ 78% CHH Llansantffraed Court, Llanvihangel
Gobion, Clytha, ABERGAVENNY ☎ 01873 840678 📄 01873 840674
21 en suite

BETTWS NEWYDD   Map 3 SO30

Alice Springs Golf Club Kemeys Commander NP15 1PP
☎ 01873 880914
e-mail: golf@alicespringsgolfclub.co.uk
web: www.alicespringsgolfclub.co.uk
Two 18-hole undulating parkland courses set back to back with
magnificent views of the Usk Valley. The Monnow course has testing
7th and 15th holes, the Usk 3rd, 12th and 13th.
Monnow Course: 18 Holes, 5321yds, Par 69, SSS 67.
Usk Course: 18 Holes, 5967yds, Par 70, SSS 69.
Club membership 380.
Visitors Mon-Sun & BHs. Booking required weekends & BHs. Dress
code. **Societies** booking required. **Green Fees** £20 weekdays (£30
weekends) **Course Designer** Keith Morgan **Prof** James Morgan
Facilities ⊕ ⓣⓞⓛ ⬚ ☐ ⛳️ ⤳ ⬚ ♪ ◇ ♪ 🛢 ♪ 🏌
Conf facs Corporate Hospitality Days **Location** N of Usk on B4598
Hotel ★★★ 79% HL Glen-yr-Afon House, Pontypool Road, USK
☎ 01291 672302 & 673202 📄 01291 672597 28 en suite

CAERWENT   Map 3 ST49

Dewstow Golf Club NP26 5AH
☎ 01291 430444 📄 01291 425816
web: www.dewstow.co.uk
Valley Course: 18 Holes, 6110yds, Par 72, SSS 70,
Course record 64.
Park Course: 18 Holes, 6226yds, Par 69, SSS 69,
Course record 67.
Location 0.5m S of Caerwent
Telephone for further details
Hotel ★★★★ 79% CHH St Pierre, A Marriott Hotel & Country
Club, St Pierre Park, CHEPSTOW ☎ 01291 625261 📄 01291 629975
148 en suite

CHEPSTOW   Map 3 ST59

St Pierre, A Marriott Hotel & Country Club
see page 401
St Pierre Park NP16 6YA
☎ 01291 625261 📄 01291 627977
e-mail: mhrs.cwlas.golf@marriotthotels.com
web: www.stpierregolf.com

MONMOUTH   Map 3 SO51

Monmouth Golf Club Leasbrook Ln NP25 3SN
☎ 01600 712212 (clubhouse) 📄 01600 772399
e-mail: sec@monmouthgolfclub.co.uk
web: www.monmouthgolfclub.co.uk

Parkland on high undulating land with beautiful views. The 8th hole,
Cresta Run, is renowned as one of Britain's most extraordinary golf
holes.
18 Holes, 5582yds, Par 69, SSS 68, Course record 62.
Club membership 484.
Visitors Mon-Sun & BHs. **Societies** booking required. **Green
Fees** £34 per day, £24 per round (£38/£28 weekends & BHs) **Course
Designer** George Walden **Prof** Richard Ballard **Facilities** ⊕ ⓣⓞⓛ
⬚ ☐ ⛳️ ⤳ ⬚ ♪ ◇ ♪ 🛢 ♪ **Conf** Corporate Hospitality
Days **Location** turn into Leasbrook Lane, 150 yds past Dixon rdbt on
Monmouth to Ross on Wye dual carriageway. Club 0.5m up lane on
right
Hotel ★★★★ RR The Stonemill & Steppes Farm Cottages,
ROCKFIELD ☎ 01600 775424 6 rooms

The Rolls of Monmouth Golf Club The Hendre NP25 5HG
☎ 01600 715353 📄 01600 713115
web: www.therollsgolfclub.co.uk
18 Holes, 6733yds, Par 72, SSS 73, Course record 69.
Location 4m W on B4233
Telephone for further details
Hotel ★★★ 75% HL The Beaufort Arms Coaching Inn &
Brasserie, High Street, RAGLAN ☎ 01291 690412 📄 01291 690935
15 en suite

NEATH PORT TALBOT

GLYNNEATH   Map 3 SN80

Glynneath Golf Club Pen-y-graig SA11 5UH
☎ 01639 720452 & 720872   📄 01639 720452
web: www.glynneathgolfclub.co.uk
18 Holes, 6211yds, Par 71, SSS 70, Course record 69.
Course Designer Cotton/Pennick/Lawrie/Williams **Location** 2m NE of
Glynneath on B4242 then take Pontneath Vaughan Rd
Telephone for further details
Hotel ★★★ 71% HL Castle Hotel, The Parade, NEATH
☎ 01639 641119 📄 01639 641624   29 en suite

MARGAM   Map 3 SS78

Lakeside Golf Course Water St SA13 2PA
☎ 01639 899959
web: www.lakesidegolf.co.uk
18 Holes, 4550yds, Par 63, SSS 63, Course record 65.
Course Designer Matthew Wootton **Location** M4 junct 38, off B4283
Telephone for further details
Hotel ★★★ 79% HL Best Western Aberavon Beach Hotel, Neath,
PORT TALBOT ☎ 01639 884949 📄 01639 897885   52 en suite

NEATH   Map 3 SS79

Earlswood Golf Course Jersey Marine SA10 6JP
☎ 01792 321578
Earlswood is a hillside course offering spectacular scenic views
over Swansea Bay. The terrain is gently undulating downs with
natural hazards and is designed to appeal to both the new and the
experienced golfer.
18 Holes, 5084yds, Par 68, SSS 68.
Visitors contact course for details. **Societies** welcome. **Green Fees** not
confirmed **Course Designer** Gorvett Estates **Prof** Mike Day **Facilities**
🏌 ⛳ 🏠 ⛽ 🎯 **Location** 4m E of Swansea, off A483
Hotel ★★★ 71% HL Castle Hotel, The Parade, NEATH
☎ 01639 641119 📄 01639 641624   29 en suite

Neath Golf Club Cadoxton SA10 8AH
☎ 01639 632759 (sec) & 643615 (clubhouse)
📄 01639 639955
e-mail: info@neathgolfclub.co.uk
web: www.neathgolfclub.co.uk

Historic heathland course, with spectacular views of the Brecon
Beacons to the north and the Bristol Channel to the south. Magnificent
test of golf offering a different challenge on every hole. Classic par 72
layout, suitable for golfers of all levels.
18 Holes, 6490yds, Par 72, SSS 72, Course record 66.
Club membership 700.
Visitors Mon-Sun & BHs. Booking required. Handicap certificate
required. Dress code. **Societies** booking required. **Green Fees** Apr-Sep
£35 per 18 holes (£40 weekends), Oct-Mar £25. Additional £10 for 36
holes 🅿 **Course Designer** James Braid **Prof** R Bennett **Facilities** 🛈
🍴 🏌 ⛳ 🎯 🏠 🎯 **Leisure** snooker **Conf** Corporate
Hospitality Days **Location** In Cadoxton opposite St Catwg Church.
Cwmbach Rd between Crown & Septre Inn & Green Dragon Hotel
Hotel ★★★ 71% HL Castle Hotel, The Parade, NEATH
☎ 01639 641119 📄 01639 641624   29 en suite

Swansea Bay Golf Club Jersey Marine SA10 6JP
☎ 01792 812198 & 814153
e-mail: swanseabaygolfclub@hotmail.co.uk
Fairly level seaside links with part dunes.
18 Holes, 6459yds, Par 72, SSS 72, Course record 66.
Club membership 500.
Visitors Mon-Sun & BHs. Dress code. **Societies** booking required.
Green Fees £18 per round (£27 weekends & BHs) **Prof** Mike
Day **Facilities** 🛈 🍴 🏌 ⛳ 🎯 🏠 🎯 🚜 🎯
Leisure indoor bowls **Conf** facs Corporate Hospitality Days
Location M4 junct 42, onto A483, 1st right onto B4290 towards Jersey
Marine, 1st right to clubhouse
Hotel ★★★ 79% HL Best Western Aberavon Beach Hotel, Neath,
PORT TALBOT ☎ 01639 884949 📄 01639 897885   52 en suite

WALES

PONTARDAWE
Map 3 SN70

Pontardawe Golf Club Cefn Llan SA8 4SH
☎ 01792 863118 📄 01792 830041
web: www.pontardawegolfclub.co.uk
18 Holes, 6101yds, Par 70, SSS 70, Course record 64.
Location M4 junct 45, off A4067 N of town centre
Telephone for further details
Hotel ★★★ 71% HL Castle Hotel, The Parade, NEATH
☎ 01639 641119 📄 01639 641624 29 en suite

PORT TALBOT
Map 3 SS78

British Steel Port Talbot Golf Course SA13 2NF
☎ 01639 793194
9 Holes, 4726yds, Par 62, SSS 63, Course record 60.
Location M4 junct 40
Telephone for further details
Hotel ★★★ 79% HL Best Western Aberavon Beach Hotel, Neath,
PORT TALBOT ☎ 01639 884949 📄 01639 897885 52 en suite

YSTRADGYNLAIS
Map 3 SN71

Palleg and Swansea Valley Golf Course Lower Cwmtwrch
SA9 2QQ
☎ 01639 842193 📄 01639 845661
e-mail: gc.gcgs@btinternet.com
web: www.palleg-golf.com
Meadowland course set in 120 acres with spectacular views of the
Black Mountains and Swansea Valley situated at the foot of the
Brecon Beacons. An attractive ravine runs through the back nine
holes. A great experience for both beginners and advanced golfers.
18 Holes, 5902yds, Par 72, SSS 69, Course record 69.
Club membership 320.
Visitors Mon-Sun & BHs. Booking required weekends.
Societies booking required. **Green Fees** £24 per day, £18 per round,
£10 per 9 holes. £8 twilight ticket after 3pm **Course Designer** C H
Cotton **Prof** Graham Coombe **Facilities** ⊕ ⓘⓄ ⓛ ⨅ ⑨ 丄
🏠 ⑨ 🏌 🛒 🏌 **Leisure** practice nets **Conf** facs Corporate
Hospitality Days **Location** M4 junct 45, N on A4067 towards Brecon. At
6th rdbt (Powys sign) turn left to Cwmtwrch for 500 yds. Turn right at
mini rdbt, up hill into Palleg Rd. Course 1m on left
Hotel ★★★ 71% HL Castle Hotel, The Parade, NEATH
☎ 01639 641119 📄 01639 641624 29 en suite

NEWPORT

CAERLEON
Map 3 ST39

Caerleon Golf Course The Broadway NP618 1AY
☎ 01633 420342
e-mail: stephen.dennis70@ntlworld.com
web: www.caerleongolfclub.co.uk
Parkland course.
9 Holes, 2874yds, Par 34. Club membership 148.
Visitors Mon-Sun & BHs. **Societies** welcome. **Green Fees** £7 per
9 holes (£9 weekends) 🕲 **Course Designer** Steel **Prof** J. Pritchard
Facilities ⊕ ⓘⓄ ⓛ ⨅ ⑨ 🏌 **Location** M4 junct 24,
B4236 to Caerleon, 1st left after Priory Hotel, follow road to bottom
Hotel ★★★★★ 85% HL The Celtic Manor Resort, Coldra Woods,
NEWPORT ☎ 01633 413000 📄 01633 412910 400 en suite

LLANWERN
Map 3 ST38

Llanwern Golf Club Tennyson Av NP18 2DW
☎ 01633 412029 (sec) 📄 01633 412260
e-mail: llanwerngolfclub@btconnect.com
web: www.llanwerngolfclub.co.uk
Established in 1928, a mature, parkland course in a picturesque
village setting.
18 Holes, 6200yds, Par 70, SSS 69, Course record 65.
Club membership 500.
Visitors Mon-Fri & BHs. Sat pm. Dress code. **Societies** welcome.
Green Fees £20 per round (£25 weekends) **Prof** Stephen Truman
Facilities ⊕ ⓘⓄ ⓛ ⨅ ⑨ 丄 🏠 🏌 **Conf** Corporate
Hospitality Days **Location** 0.5m S off A455, signed
Hotel ★★★★★ 85% HL The Celtic Manor Resort, Coldra Woods,
NEWPORT ☎ 01633 413000 📄 01633 412910 400 en suite

NEWPORT
Map 3 ST38

The Celtic Manor see page 405
Coldra Woods NP18 1HQ
☎ 01633 413000 📄 01633 410269
e-mail: postbox@celtic-manor.com
web: www.celtic-manor.com

Newport Golf Club Great Oak NP10 9FX
☎ 01633 892643 📄 01633 896676
web: www.newportgolfclub.org.uk
18 Holes, 6500yds, Par 72, SSS 71, Course record 63.
Course Designer W Fernie **Location** M4 junct 27, 1m NW on B4591
Telephone for further details
Hotel ★★★★★ 85% HL The Celtic Manor Resort, Coldra
Woods, NEWPORT ☎ 01633 413000 📄 01633 412910 400 en suite

Parc Golf Course Church Ln, Coedkernew NP10 8TU
☎ 01633 680933 📄 01633 681011
web: www.parcgolf.co.uk
A challenging but enjoyable 18-hole course with water hazards and
accompanying wildlife which is in the process of being extended. The
38-bay driving range is floodlit until 10pm.
18 Holes, 5785yds, Par 70, SSS 68, Course record 64.
Club membership 400.
Visitors Mon-Sun & BHs. Booking required. Dress code.
Societies welcome. **Green Fees** not confirmed **Course Designer** B
Thomas/T F Hicks **Prof** R Dinsdale/J Wills/N Humphries **Facilities** ⊕
ⓘⓄ ⓛ ⨅ ⑨ 丄 🏠 🏌 🏌 🛒 🏌 **Leisure** 9 hole astra
turf short course **Conf** facs Corporate Hospitality Days **Location** 3m
SW of Newport, off A48
Hotel ★★★ 70% HL Best Western St Mellons Hotel & Country Club,
Castleton, CARDIFF ☎ 01633 680355 📄 01633 680399 41 en suite

Tredegar Park Golf Club Parc-y-Brain Rd NP10 9TG
☎ 01633 894433 📄 01633 897152
web: www.tredegarparkgolfclub.co.uk
18 Holes, 6545yds, Par 72, SSS 72.
Course Designer R Sandow **Location** M4 junct 27, B4591 N, club
signed
Telephone for further details
Hotel ★★★★ 78% HL Best Western Parkway, Cwmbran Drive,
CWMBRAN ☎ 01633 871199 📄 01633 869160 70 en suite

WALES

CELTIC MANOR RESORT

NEWPORT - MAP 3 ST38

This relatively new resort has quickly become a world-renowned venue for golf, set in 1400 acres of beautiful, unspoiled parkland at the southern gateway to Wales. Boasting three championship courses, Celtic Manor offers a challenge for all levels of play, complemented by a golf school and one of the largest clubhouses in Europe, as well as extensive leisure facilities. In 2010, The Celtic Manor Resort hosted the 38th Ryder Cup on the world's first ever course to be specifically designed for this prestigious tournament. The new course opened in spring 2007, featuring nine holes from the original Wentwood Hills course and nine spectacular new holes in the valley of the River Usk.

Coldra Woods NP18 1HQ ☎ 01633 413000 📄 01633 410269
e-mail: postbox@celtic-manor.com **web:** www.celtic-manor.com
Roman Road: 18 Holes, 6039yds, Par 70, SSS 70.
Montgomerie: 18 Holes, 5863yds, Par 69, SSS 69.
Twenty Ten Course: 18 Holes, 6570yds, Par 71, SSS 73. Club membership 720.
Visitors Contact resort for details. **Societies** booking required. **Green Fees** Twenty Ten from £56 per 18 holes, Roman Road/Montgomerie from £18 **Course Designer** Robert Trent Jones **Prof** Lee Jay Barnes **Facilities** ⑪ 🍽️ 🍺 🖥️ 🧖 🏌️ 🍳 🏖️ 🏌️ **Leisure** hard tennis courts, heated indoor swimming pool, fishing, sauna, gymnasium, health spa, golf academy, adventure golf course, high ropes course, shooting school **Conf** facs Corporate Hospitality Days **Location** M4 junct 24, B4237 towards Newport, 300yds right
Hotel ★★★★★ 85% HL The Celtic Manor Resort, Coldra Woods, NEWPORT ☎ 01633 413000
📄 01633 412910 400 en suite

PEMBROKESHIRE

HAVERFORDWEST
Map 2 SM91

Haverfordwest Golf Club Arnolds Down SA61 2XQ
☎ 01437 764523 & 768409 📄 01437 764143
e-mail: haverfordwestgc@btconnect.com
web: www.haverfordwestgolfclub.co.uk
Fairly flat parkland course, a good challenge for golfers of all
handicaps. Set in attractive surroundings with fine views over the
Preseli Hills.
18 Holes, 6002yds, Par 70, SSS 69, Course record 63.
Club membership 770.
Visitors Mon-Sun & BHs. Booking required. Dress code.
Societies booking required. **Green Fees** Mon £16, Tue-Fri £23,
weekends £26 **Prof** Alex Pile **Facilities** ⓣ ⚏ ⮨ ⯑ ⯑ ⯑ ⯑
⯑ ✔ ⯑ ✔ **Conf** facs Corporate Hospitality Days **Location** 1m E
on A40 of Haverfordwest
Hotel ★★★★ GH College Guest House, 93 Hill Street, St Thomas
Green, HAVERFORDWEST ☎ 01437 763710 📄 01437 763710
8 rooms

LETTERSTON
Map 2 SM92

Priskilly Forest Golf Club & Country House Castlemorris
SA62 5EH
☎ 01348 840276 📄 01348 840276
e-mail: jevans@priskilly-forest.co.uk
web: www.priskilly-forest.co.uk
Challenging parkland course with panoramic views and a stunning
18th hole. Immaculate greens and fairways surrounded by
rhododendrons, established shrubs and trees. Testing lies.
9 Holes, 5900yds, Par 70, SSS 69, Course record 70.
Club membership 180.
Visitors Mon-Wed, Fri-Sun & BHs. Booking required Thu, weekends &
BHs. **Societies** welcome. **Green Fees** £24 per day, £20 per 18 holes,
£14 per 9 holes **Course Designer** J Walters **Facilities** ⓣ ⮨ ⮨ ⯑
⯑ ⮨ ⯑ ⯑ ✔ ⯑ ✔ **Leisure** fishing **Conf** facs Corporate
Hospitality Days **Location** 2m off A40 at Letterston off B4331
Hotel ★★★ 78% CHH Wolfscastle Country Hotel, WOLF'S CASTLE
☎ 01437 741688 & 741225 📄 01437 741383 20 en suite

MILFORD HAVEN
Map 2 SM90

Milford Haven Golf Club Woodbine House SA73 3RX
☎ 01646 697762 📄 01646 697870
web: www.mhgc.co.uk
18 Holes, 6112yds, Par 71, SSS 70, Course record 64.
Course Designer David Williams **Location** 1.5m W of Milford Haven
Telephone for further details
Hotel ★★★ 79% HL Beggars Reach, BURTON ☎ 01646 600700
📄 01646 600560 30 en suite

NEWPORT (PEMBROKESHIRE)
Map 2 SN03

Newport Links Golf Club Newport Links Golf Club
SA42 0NR
☎ 01239 820244 📄 01239 821338
e-mail: info@newportlinks.co.uk
web: www.newportlinks.co.uk
Seaside links course situated in a National Park, with easy walking
and good view of the Preseli Hills and Newport Bay.
18 Holes, 6013yds, Par 71, SSS 70, Course record 65.
Club membership 246.
Visitors Mon-Sun & BHs. Booking required. Dress code.
Societies booking required. **Green Fees** £26 per round (£31 weekends
& BHs) **Course Designer** James Braid **Prof** Alun Evans **Facilities** ⓣ
⮨ ⮨ ⯑ ⯑ ⮨ ⯑ ⯑ ✔ ⯑ ✔ ⯑ **Conf** facs
Corporate Hospitality Days **Location** 1.25m N of Newport off A487
Hotel ★★★ 75% HL The Cliff Hotel, GWBERT-ON-SEA
☎ 01239 613241 📄 01239 615391 70 en suite

PEMBROKE DOCK
Map 2 SM90

South Pembrokeshire Golf Club Military Rd SA72 6SE
☎ 01646 621453 📄 01646 621453
web: www.southpembsgolf.co.uk
18 Holes, 6279yds, Par 70, SSS 69, Course record 65.
Course Designer Committee **Location** SW of town centre off B4322
Telephone for further details
Hotel ★★★ 79% HL Beggars Reach, BURTON ☎ 01646 600700
📄 01646 600560 30 en suite

TENBY
Map 2 SN10

Tenby Golf Club The Burrows SA70 7NP
☎ 01834 844447 & 842978 📄 01834 842978
e-mail: tenbygolfclub@uku.co.uk
web: www.tenbygolf.co.uk
The oldest club in Wales, this fine seaside links, with sea views and
natural hazards, provides good golf all the year round.
18 Holes, 6528yds, Par 72, SSS 72, Course record 69.
Club membership 700.
Visitors Mon-Sun & BHs. Booking required weekends & BHs.
Dress code. **Societies** welcome. **Green Fees** not confirmed **Course
Designer** James Braid **Prof** Rhys Harry **Facilities** ⓣ ⮨ ⮨ ⯑
⯑ ⮨ ⯑ ⯑ ✔ ⯑ ✔ ⯑ **Conf** Corporate Hospitality
Days **Location** near railway station
Hotel ★★★ 80% HL Atlantic Hotel, The Esplanade, TENBY
☎ 01834 842881 📄 01834 840911 42 en suite

Save on Hotels. Book at **theAA.com/hotel**

PEMBROKESHIRE – POWYS

Trefloyne Golf, Bar & Restaurant Trefloyne Park, Penally SA70 7RG
☎ 01834 842165 📄 01834 844288
e-mail: enquiries@trefloyne.com
web: www.trefloyne.com

Idyllic parkland course with backdrop of mature mixed woodlands and distant views of Tenby, Carmarthen Bay and Caldey Island. Natural features and hazards such as the Old Quarry make for exciting and challenging golf.

18 Holes, 6398yds, Par 72, SSS 72, Course record 68. Club membership 400.

Visitors Mon-Sun & BHs. Booking required Tue, Thu, weekends & BHs. Dress code. **Societies** booking required. **Green Fees** not confirmed **Course Designer** F H Gillman **Prof** Oliver Duckett **Facilities** ⓣ ⑪ ⬛ ☕ 🍴 🏌 ⚐ 🏠 ⛳ ✦ 🛒 ✦ **Location** in Trefloyne Park, just W of Tenby
Hotel ★★★ 80% HL Atlantic Hotel, The Esplanade, TENBY
☎ 01834 842881 📄 01834 840911 42 en suite

POWYS

BRECON
Map 3 SO02

Brecon Golf Club Newton Park LD3 8PA
☎ 01874 622004 & 611545
e-mail: info@brecongolfclub.co.uk
web: www.brecongolfclub.co.uk

Easy walking parkland. Natural hazards include two rivers on the boundary. Good river and mountain scenery.

9 Holes, 6068yds, Par 70, SSS 70. Club membership 210.

Visitors Mon-Sun & BHs. Booking required Tue, Thu, Sun & BHs. Dress code. **Societies** booking required. **Green Fees** £15 per day (£18 weekends & BHs) 🅿 **Course Designer** James Braid **Facilities** ⓣ ⑪ ⬛ ☕ 🍴 🏌 ⚐ 🏠 **Leisure** Junior par 3 course **Conf** Corporate Hospitality Days **Location** 0.75m W of town centre on A40
Hotel ★★★★★ GA The Coach House, Orchard Street, BRECON
☎ 01874 620043 & 07974 328437 6 rooms

Cradoc Golf Club Penoyre Park, Cradoc LD3 9LP
☎ 01874 623658 📄 01874 611711
e-mail: secretary@cradoc.co.uk
web: www.cradoc.co.uk

Parkland with wooded areas, ponds and spectacular views over the Brecon Beacons.

18 Holes, 6188yds, Par 71, SSS 71, Course record 65. Club membership 700.

Visitors Mon-Sun & BHs. Booking required Tue, Fri, weekends & BHs. Dress code. **Societies** booking required. **Green Fees** £28 per day (£34 weekends & BHs) **Course Designer** C K Cotton **Prof** Richard Davies **Facilities** ⓣ ⑪ ⬛ ☕ 🍴 🏌 ⚐ 🏠 ⛳ ✦ 🛒 ✦ 🏌
Location 2m N of Brecon off B4520
Hotel ★★★★★ GA The Coach House, Orchard Street, BRECON
☎ 01874 620043 & 07974 328437 6 rooms

BUILTH WELLS
Map 3 SO05

Builth Wells Golf Club Golf Links Rd LD2 3NF
☎ 01982 553296
e-mail: info@builthwellsgolf.co.uk
web: www.builthwellsgolf.co.uk

Well-guarded greens and a stream running through the centre of the course add interest to this 18-hole undulating parkland course. The clubhouse is a converted 15th-century Welsh longhouse.

18 Holes, 5424yds, Par 66, SSS 66, Course record 62. Club membership 380.

Visitors Mon-Sun & BHs. Booking required Wed-Sun & BHs. Dress code. **Societies** booking required. **Green Fees** £32 per day, £24 per round (£34/£27 weekends & BHs) **Prof** Simon Edwards **Facilities** ⑪ 🍴 ⬛ ☕ 🍴 🏌 ⚐ 🏠 ⛳ ✦ 🛒 ✦ **Conf** Corporate Hospitality Days **Location** N of A483
Hotel ★★★★ RR Lasswade Country House, Station Road, LLANWRTYD WELLS ☎ 01591 610515 📄 01591 610611 8 rooms

KNIGHTON
Map 7 SO27

Knighton Golf Club Ffrydd Wood LD7 1DL
☎ 01547 528046 (Sec)
web: www.knightongolfclub.co.uk

Upland course with some hard walking. Fine views over the England border.

9 Holes, 5362yds, Par 68, SSS 66, Course record 64. Club membership 150.

Visitors Mon-Sat & BHs. Booking required Sat & BHs. **Societies** booking required. **Green Fees** not confirmed **Course Designer** Harry Vardon **Facilities** ⑪ by prior arrangement ⬛ ☕ 🍴 🏌 **Location** 0.5m S off B4355
Hotel ★★★ 79% CHH Milebrook House, Milebrook, KNIGHTON
☎ 01547 528632 📄 01547 520509 10 en suite

LLANDRINDOD WELLS
Map 3 SO06

Llandrindod Wells Golf Club The Clubhouse LD1 5NY
☎ 01597 823873 (sec) 📄 01597 823873
web: www.lwgc.co.uk

18 Holes, 5759yds, Par 69, SSS 69, Course record 65.

Course Designer H Vardon **Location** 1m SE off A483
Telephone for further details
Hotel ★★★★ 77% HL The Metropole, Temple Street, LLANDRINDOD WELLS ☎ 01597 823700 📄 01597 824828 120 en suite

LLANGATTOCK
Map 3 SO21

Old Rectory Golf Club NP8 1PH
☎ 01873 810373 📄 018373 810373
web: www.rectoryhotel.co.uk

9 Holes, 2200yds, Par 54, SSS 59, Course record 53.

Location SW of village
Telephone for further details
Hotel ★★★ 75% HL The Old Rectory Country Hotel & Golf Club, LLANGATTOCK ☎ 01873 810373 23 en suite

WALES

LLANIDLOES
Map 6 SN98

St Idloes Golf Club Penrallt SY18 6LG
☎ 01686 412559
web: www.stidloesgolfclub.co.uk
9 Holes, 5540yds, Par 66, SSS 66, Course record 61.
Location 1m N off B4569
Telephone for further details
Hotel ★★★ INN Mount Inn, China Street, LLANIDLOES
☎ 01686 412247 ▤ 01686 412247 9 rooms (9 en suite)

LLANYMYNECH
Map 7 SJ22

Llanymynech Golf Club SY10 8LB
☎ 01691 830983 & 830542 ▤ 01691 839184
e-mail: secretary@llanymynechgolfclub.co.uk
web: www.llanymynechgolfclub.co.uk
Upland course on the site of a prehistoric hill fort with far-reaching views. With 15 holes in Wales and three in England, drive off in Wales and putt out in England on 4th hole. A quality mature course with a tremendous variety of holes.
18 Holes, 6036yds, Par 70, SSS 69, Course record 64.
Club membership 750.
Visitors Mon-Sun except BHs. Booking required. Dress code.
Societies booking required. Green Fees £42 per day, £32 per round (£42 Sun) Prof Andrew P Griffiths Facilities ⊕ ↻ ↳ ☐ ¶↿
⅄ ☖ ⌁ ⇒ ⌁ Conf Corporate Hospitality Days Location 6m S of Oswestry, off A483 in Pant at Cross Guns Inn
Hotel ★★★★ 74% HL Wynnstay Hotel, Church Street, OSWESTRY
☎ 01691 655261 ▤ 01691 670606 34 en suite

MACHYNLLETH
Map 6 SH70

Machynlleth Golf Club SY20 8UH
☎ 01654 702000
e-mail: machgolf2@tiscali.co.uk
web: www.machynllethgolf.co.uk
A heathland course surrounded by hills. The course is at its best in spring and summer with colour from the gorse and rhododendrons. Elevated tees on the 5th and 8th holes give wonderful views of the surrounding countryside.
9 Holes, 5726yds, Par 68, SSS 68, Course record 65.
Club membership 150.
Visitors Mon-Sun & BHs. Booking required Thu & Sun. Dress code.
Societies booking required. Green Fees £18 per day ⊚ Course Designer James Braid Facilities ⊕ ↻ ↳ ☐ ¶↿ ⅄ ⊓↿ ⌁
Leisure 3 hole par 3 course Location 0.5m E off A489
Hotel ★★★ CHH Ynyshir Hall, EGLWYS FACH ☎ 01654 781209 & 781268 ▤ 01654 781366 9 en suite

NEWTOWN
Map 6 SO19

St Giles Golf Club Pool Rd SY16 3AJ
☎ 01686 625844 ▤ 01686 625844
web: www.stgilesgolf.co.uk
9 Holes, 6012yds, Par 70, SSS 70, Course record 67.
Location 0.5m NE on A483
Telephone for further details
Hotel ★★ 79% HL Dragon Hotel, MONTGOMERY ☎ 01686 668359
▤ 0870 011 8227 20 en suite

WELSHPOOL
Map 7 SJ20

Welshpool Golf Club Golfa Hill SY21 9AQ
☎ 01938 850249 ▤ 01938 850249
e-mail: welshpool.golfclub@btconnect.com
web: www.welshpoolgolfclub.co.uk
Undulating, hilly, heathland course with spectacular views. Testing holes are 2nd (par 5), 14th (par 3), 17th (par 3) and a memorable 18th.
18 Holes, 5700yds, Par 70, SSS 69. Club membership 400.
Visitors Mon-Sun & BHs. Societies welcome. Green Fees £30 per round. (Winter £25 per round) Course Designer James Braid Facilities ⊕ ↻ ↳ ☐ ¶↿ ⅄ ☖ ⌁ ⇒ ⌁ Conf Corporate Hospitality Days Location 3m W off A458
Hotel ★★★ 77% HL Royal Oak, The Cross, WELSHPOOL
☎ 01938 552217 ▤ 01938 556652 25 en suite

RHONDDA CYNON TAFF

ABERDARE
Map 3 SO00

Aberdare Golf Club Abernant CF44 0RY
☎ 01685 872797 ▤ 01685 872797
e-mail: sec-age@btconnect.com
web: www.aberdaregolfclub.co.uk
Mountain course with parkland features overlooking the Brecon Beacons. Tree-lined with many mature oaks.
18 Holes, 5875yds, Par 69, SSS 69, Course record 63.
Club membership 450.
Visitors Mon-Fri, Sun & BHs. Booking required Sat & BHs.
Societies booking required. Green Fees £17 per day (£21 Sun & BHs) ⊛ Facilities ⊕ ↻ ↳ ☐ ¶↿ ⅄ ☖ ⌁ Leisure 3 practice nets Conf facs Corporate Hospitality Days Location 1m NE of town centre. Past hospital, 400yds on right
Hotel ★★★★ GH Llwyn Onn, Cwmtaf, MERTHYR TYDFIL
☎ 01685 384384 ▤ 01685 359310 11 rooms

WALES

MOUNTAIN ASH   Map 3 ST09

Mountain Ash Golf Club Cefnpennar CF45 4DT
☎ 01443 479459 📄 01443 479628
e-mail: sec@mountainashgc.co.uk
web: www.mountainashgc.co.uk

Mountain moorland course with panoramic views of the Brecon Beacons. Not long but testing and demands accuracy from the opening hole, a 390yd par 4 that rises up halfway down its length with woodland on the left and out of bounds on the right. The 10th hole is the highest point, hitting from an elevated platform with woodland on the left below. The 18th is a dramatic finale in the form of a 510yd, par 5, with a carry over gorse, a ditch crossing the fairway and bunkers and sand traps protecting the green.

18 Holes, 5553yds, Par 69, SSS 67, Course record 60.
Club membership 560.

Visitors contact club for details. **Societies** booking required. **Green Fees** not confirmed **Facilities** ⊕ ⌀ ▦ ▱ ⌷ ⤳ **Conf** facs Corporate Hospitality Days **Location** 1m NW off A4059
Hotel ★★★ 74% CHH Llechwen Hall, Llanfabon, PONTYPRIDD
☎ 01443 742050 & 743020 📄 01443 742189 20 en suite

PENRHYS   Map 3 ST09

Rhondda Golf Club Golf Club House CF43 3PW
☎ 01443 441384 📄 01443 441384

18 Holes, 6205yds, Par 70, SSS 71, Course record 67.
Location 0.5m W off B4512
Telephone for further details
Hotel ★★★ 74% CHH Llechwen Hall, Llanfabon, PONTYPRIDD
☎ 01443 742050 & 743020 📄 01443 742189 20 en suite

PONTYPRIDD   Map 3 ST08

Pontypridd Golf Club Ty Gwyn Rd CF37 4DJ
☎ 01443 409904 📄 01443 491622
web: www.pontypriddgolfclub.co.uk

18 Holes, 5721yds, Par 69, SSS 68, Course record 65.
Location E of town centre off A470
Telephone for further details
Hotel ★★★ 74% CHH Llechwen Hall, Llanfabon, PONTYPRIDD
☎ 01443 742050 & 743020 📄 01443 742189 20 en suite

TALBOT GREEN   Map 3 ST08

Llantrisant & Pontyclun Golf Club Off Ely Valley Rd CF72 8AL
☎ 01443 228169
web: www.llantrisantgolfclub.co.uk

18 Holes, 5328yds, Par 68, SSS 66, Course record 62.
Location M4 junct 34, A4119 to Llantrisant, over 1st rdbt, left at 2nd lights to Talbot Green, right at mini-rdbt, club 50yds on left
Telephone for further details
Hotel ★★★★ 75% CHH Miskin Manor Country Hotel, Pendoylan Road, MISKIN ☎ 01443 224204 📄 01443 237606 43 en suite

SWANSEA

CLYDACH   Map 3 SN60

Tawe Vale Golf Club SA6 5QR
☎ 01792 842929
e-mail: secretarytawevalegolfclub@btconnect.com
web: www.tawevalegolfclub.co.uk

Flat meadowland course bordered by meandering River Tawe and the Swansea Valley.

18 Holes, 6015yds, Par 70, SSS 69, Course record 68.
Club membership 450.

Visitors Mon-Sun & BHs. Dress code. **Societies** booking required. **Green Fees** £20 per round (£25 weekends) ⊕ **Facilities** ⊕ ⌀ ▦ ▱ ⌷ ⤳ ⌀ ⤳ ⤳ **Leisure** outdoor bowling green **Conf** Corporate Hospitality Days **Location** M4 junct 45, 1.5m NE on A4067
Hotel BUD Express by Holiday Inn Swansea - West, Neath Road, Llandarcy, SWANSEA ☎ 01792 818700 📄 01792 818718 91 en suite

SOUTHGATE   Map 2 SS58

Pennard Golf Club 2 Southgate Rd SA3 2BT
☎ 01792 233131 & 233451 📄 01792 235125
e-mail: sec@pennardgolfclub.com
web: www.pennardgolfclub.com

Undulating, cliff-top seaside links with good coastal views. At first sight it can be intimidating with steep hills that make club selection important - there are a few blind shots to contend with. The difficulties are not insurmountable unless the wind begins to blow in calm weather. Greens are slick and firm all year.

18 Holes, 6267yds, Par 71. Club membership 850.

Visitors Mon-Sun & BHs. Booking required. Handicap certificate. Dress code. **Societies** booking required. **Green Fees** £50 per 18 holes (£60 weekends) **Course Designer** James Braid **Prof** M V Bennett
Facilities ⊕ ⌀ ▦ ▱ ⌷ ⤳ ⌀ ⌷ ⤳ ⤳ **Conf** facs
Location 8m W of Swansea by A4067 and B4436
Hotel ★★★★★ RR Maes-Yr-Haf Restaurant with Rooms, PARKMILL ☎ 01792 371000 📄 01792 234922 5 rooms

SWANSEA   Map 3 SS69

Clyne Golf Club 120 Owls Lodge Ln, The Mayals, Blackpill SA3 5DP
☎ 01792 401989 📄 01792 401078
e-mail: clynegolfclub@supanet.com
web: www.clynegolfclub.com

Challenging moorland course with excellent greens and scenic views of Swansea Bay and the Gower. Many natural hazards with a large number of bunkers and gorse and bracken in profusion,

18 Holes, 6432yds, Par 72, SSS 72, Course record 64.
Club membership 700.

Visitors Mon-Sun & BHs. Booking required. Dress code.
Societies booking required. **Green Fees** £30 per round (£40 weekends & BHs), Winter £20 including bar meal ⊕ **Course Designer** H S Colt & Harries **Prof** Jonathan Clewett **Facilities** ⊕ ⌀ ▦ ▱ ⌷ ⤳ ⌀ ⌷ ⤳ ⤳ ⤳ **Leisure** chipping green, driving nets, indoor practice net **Conf** facs Corporate Hospitality Days **Location** 3.5m SW on B4436
Hotel ★★★★ 80% HL Swansea Marriott Hotel, The Maritime Quarter, SWANSEA ☎ 0870 400 7282 📄 0870 400 7382 119 en suite

WALES

Langland Bay Golf Club Langland Bay SA3 4QR
☎ 01792 361721 📄 01792 361082
e-mail: info@langlandbaygolfclub.com
web: www.langlandbaygolfclub.com

Situated on the cliff top on the Gower Peninsula, an Area of Outstanding Natural Beauty, this links course has 360 degree views across the Bristol Channel in on direction and the Brecon Beacons in the other. Created in 1904, it spreads over meadowland and the cliffs to challenge any golfer come rain or shine.

18 Holes, 5857yds, Par 70, SSS 70, Course record 63.
Club membership 850.

Visitors Mon-Sun & BHs. Booking required. Dress code.
Societies booking required. **Green Fees** £40 per day (£50 weekends & BHs). Society packages from £25 per person **Course Designer** James Braid **Prof** Mark Evans **Facilities** 🏤 🍽 🛒 ⛳ 🏌️ ⛱ 🏪 ⛳
⛳ **Conf** Corporate Hospitality Days **Location** M4 junct 42 to Swansea, then A4118 to Mumbles/Langland Bay
Hotel ★★★★★ GA Little Langland, 2 Rotherslade Road, Langland, MUMBLES ☎ 01792 369696 6 rooms (6 en suite)

Morriston Golf Club 160 Clasemont Rd, Morriston SA6 6AJ
☎ 01792 796528 📄 01792 796528
e-mail: morristongolf@btconnect.com
web: www.morristongolfclub.co.uk

Pleasant parkland course with a very difficult par 3 15th hole, one of the most challenging short holes in Wales. The 17th is aptly nicknamed Temple of Doom.

18 Holes, 5708yds, Par 68, SSS 68. Club membership 650.

Visitors Mon-Sun & BHs. Booking required. Dress code.
Societies booking required. **Green Fees** £25 per day (£35 weekends & BHs) **Prof** M. Govier **Facilities** 🏤 🍽 🛒 ⛳ 🏌️ ⛱ 🏪 ⛳
🚗 ⛳ **Conf** facs Corporate Hospitality Days **Location** M4 junct 46, 1m E on A48
Hotel ★★★★ 76% HL Dragon, The Kingsway Circle, SWANSEA
☎ 01792 657100 & 0870 4299 848 📄 01792 456044 106 en suite

THREE CROSSES
Map 2 SS59

Gower Golf Club Cefn Goleu SA4 3HS
☎ 01792 872480 📄 01792 875535
web: www.gowergolf.co.uk

18 Holes, 6441yds, Par 71, SSS 72, Course record 66.

Course Designer Donald Steel **Location** off A4118 Swansea to Gower, signed from Three Crosses
Telephone for further details
Hotel ★★★ 78% HL Best Western Diplomat Hotel, Felinfoel, LLANELLI ☎ 01554 756156 📄 01554 751649 50 en suite

UPPER KILLAY
Map 2 SS59

Fairwood Park Golf Club Blackhills Ln SA2 7JN
☎ 01792 297849 📄 01792 297849
e-mail: info@fairwoodpark.com
web: www.fairwoodpark.com

Parkland championship course on the beautiful Gower Peninsula, being both the flattest and the longest course in Swansea. Surrounded by vast areas of woodland on all sides, each fairway is well defined with strategically placed lakes to test the nerve of any golfer off the tee. The only PGA Championship course in the County of Swansea.

The Championship Course: 18 Holes, 6226yds, Par 71,
SSS 71, Course record 69. Club membership 500.

Visitors Mon-Sun & BHs. Booking required Fri-Sun & BHs. Dress code. **Societies** booking required. **Green Fees** £30 weekdays (£38 weekends) **Course Designer** Hawtree **Prof** Gary Hughes **Facilities** 🏤
🍽 🛒 ⛳ 🏌️ ⛱ 🏪 ⛳ ♦ ⛳ 🚗 ⛳ 🏌 **Conf** facs
Corporate Hospitality Days **Location** 1.5m S off A4118
Hotel ★★★★ 80% HL Swansea Marriott Hotel, The Maritime Quarter, SWANSEA ☎ 0870 400 7282 📄 0870 400 7382 119 en suite

TORFAEN

CWMBRAN
Map 3 ST29

Green Meadow Golf & Country Club, Treherbert Rd, Croesyceiliog NP44 2BZ
☎ 01633 869321 & 862626 📄 01633 868430
e-mail: info@greenmeadowgolf.com
web: www.greenmeadowgolf.com

Undulating parkland with panoramic views. Tree-lined fairways, water hazards and pot bunkers. The greens are excellent and are playable all year round.

18 Holes, 6078yds, Par 70, SSS 70, Course record 63.
Club membership 400.

Visitors Mon-Sun & BHs. Booking weekends. Dress code.
Societies booking required. **Green Fees** not confirmed **Course Designer** Peter Richardson **Prof** Dave Woodman **Facilities** 🏤 🍽
🛒 ⛳ 🏌️ ⛱ 🏪 ♦ 🚗 ⛳ 🏌 **Leisure** hard tennis courts, sauna, gymnasium **Conf** facs Corporate Hospitality Days **Location** NE of town off A4042
Hotel ★★★★ 78% HL Best Western Parkway, Cwmbran Drive, CWMBRAN ☎ 01633 871199 📄 01633 869160 70 en suite

Pontnewydd Golf Club Maesgwyn Farm, Upper Cwmbran NP44 1AB

☎ 01633 482170 🖨 01633 484447

e-mail: ct.phillips@virgin.net

web: www.pontnewyddgolf.co.uk.

Meadowland course with good views across the Severn estuary. Oldest golf course in Wales, established 1875. (11 separate holes with 7 played twice off different tees)

11 Holes, 5278yds, Par 68, SSS 67, Course record 61.
Club membership 420.

Visitors Mon-Sun & BHs. Booking required Wed, Sat & BHs. Handicap certificate. Dress code. **Societies** booking required. **Green Fees** £15 per round **Prof** Gavin Evans **Facilities** ⊕ ⁏⊙⊦ ⓑ ⬚ ⁏ ⬚ ⬚ ⬚ ⬚ ⬚ ✦ **Conf** facs Corporate Hospitality Days **Location** N of town centre

Hotel ★★★★ 78% HL Best Western Parkway, Cwmbran Drive, CWMBRAN ☎ 01633 871199 🖨 01633 869160　70 en suite

---

PONTYPOOL　　　　　Map 3 SO20

Pontypool Golf Club Lasgarn Ln, Trevethin NP4 8TR

☎ 01495 763655 🖨 01495 755564

e-mail: pontypoolgolf@btconnect.com

web: www.pontypoolgolf.co.uk

Undulating mountain course with magnificent views of the Bristol Channel.

18 Holes, 5963yds, Par 69, SSS 69, Course record 64.
Club membership 502.

Visitors Mon-Fri & Sun except BHs. Booking required. Dress code. **Societies** booking required. **Green Fees** not confirmed **Prof** Kyle Smith **Facilities** ⊕ ⁏⊙⊦ ⓑ ⬚ ⁏ ⬚ ⬚ ⬚ ✦ **Leisure** indoor teaching academy with video analysis **Conf** facs Corporate Hospitality Days **Location** 1.5m N off A4043

Hotel ★★★ 79% HL Glen-yr-Afon House, Pontypool Road, USK ☎ 01291 672302 & 673202 🖨 01291 672597　28 en suite

Woodlake Park Golf & Country Club Glascoed NP4 0TE

☎ 01291 673933 🖨 01291 673811

e-mail: golf@woodlake.co.uk

web: www.woodlake.co.uk

Undulating parkland with magnificent views over the Llandegfedd Reservoir. Superb greens constructed to USGA specification. Holes 4, 7 and 16 are par 3s, which are particularly challenging. Holes 6 and 17 are long par 4s, which can be wind affected.

Woodland Park: 18 Holes, 6400yds, Par 72, SSS 72, Course record 67. Club membership 500.

Visitors Mon-Sun & BHs. Booking required. Dress code. **Societies** booking required. **Green Fees** £35 per day, £25 per round (£42/£32 Fri-Sun & BHs) **Facilities** ⊕ ⁏⊙⊦ ⓑ ⬚ ⁏ ⬚ ⬚ ✦ ⬚ ✦ **Leisure** fishing **Conf** facs Corporate Hospitality Days **Location** overlooking Llandegfedd Reservoir, 3m from Usk

Hotel ★★★ 79% HL Glen-yr-Afon House, Pontypool Road, USK ☎ 01291 672302 & 673202 🖨 01291 672597　28 en suite

VALE OF GLAMORGAN

BARRY　　　　　Map 3 ST16

Brynhill Golf Club Port Rd CF62 8PN

☎ 01446 720277 🖨 01446 740422

web: www.brynhillgolfclub.co.uk

18 Holes, 6516yds, Par 72, SSS 71.

Course Designer David Thomas **Location** 1.25m N on B4050
Telephone for further details
Hotel ★★★ 73% HL Best Western Mount Sorrel, Porthkerry Road, BARRY ☎ 01446 740069 🖨 01446 746600　42 en suite

RAF St Athan Golf Club Clive Rd, St Athan CF62 4JD

☎ 01446 751043 🖨 01446 751862

e-mail: rafstathan@golfclub.fsbusiness.co.uk

Parkland affected by strong winds straight from the sea. Further interest is added by this being a very tight course with lots of trees. Beware of low-flying RAF jets.

9 Holes, 6480yds, Par 72, SSS 72. Club membership 450.

Visitors Mon-Sun & BHs. Booking required Sat. Handicap certificate. Dress code. **Societies** booking requested. **Green Fees** not confirmed **Course Designer** the members **Facilities** ⊕ ⁏⊙⊦ ⓑ ⬚ ⁏ ⬚ ⬚ **Location** between Barry & Llantwit Major

Hotel ★★★★ 85% HL Vale Resort, Hensol Park, HENSOL ☎ 01443 667800 🖨 01443 667801　143 en suite

St Andrews Major Golf Course Coldbrook Road East, Cadoxton CF63 1BL

☎ 01446 722227 🖨 01446 748953

e-mail: info@standrewsmajorgolfclub.com

web: www.standrewsmajorgolfclub.com

A scenic 18-hole parkland course, suitable for all standards of golfer. The greens are designed to US specifications. The course provides excellent challenges to all levels of golfers without being physically exerting.

St Andrews Major: 18 Holes, 5425yds, Par 69, SSS 66. Club membership 400.

Visitors Contact course for details. **Societies** welcome. **Green Fees** £18 per 18 holes (£20 weekends) **Course Designer** Richard Hurd **Prof** John Hastings **Facilities** ⊕ ⁏⊙⊦ ⓑ ⬚ ⁏ ⬚ ⬚ ✦ ⬚ ✦ **Conf** facs Corporate Hospitality Days **Location** M4 junct 33, follow signs for Cardiff Wales Airport, take A4231 and follow signs for golf club

Hotel ★★★★ 75% HL Copthorne Hotel Cardiff-Caerdydd, Copthorne Way, Culverhouse Cross, CARDIFF ☎ 029 2059 9100 🖨 029 2059 9080　135 en suite

WALES

DINAS POWYS
Map 3 ST17

Dinas Powis Golf Club High Walls Av CF64 4AJ
☎ 029 2051 2727 🖨 029 2051 2727
e-mail: dinaspowisgolfclub@yahoo.co.uk
web: www.dpgc.co.uk

Parkland/downland course with dramatic views over the Bristol Channel and the Vale of Glamorgan. Open all year with fine natural drainage.

18 Holes, 5595yds, Par 68, SSS 67. Club membership 550.

Visitors Mon-Sun & BHs. Booking required. Dress code.
Societies booking required **Green Fees** not confirmed **Course Designer** James Braid **Prof** Gareth Bennett **Facilities** ⓤ ⍁ ⍒ ⌂ ⍝ ⋏ ⌂ ✦ ⛟ ✦ **Conf** facs Corporate Hospitality Days **Location** NW side of village, turning opposite cenotaph
Hotel ★★★ 73% HL Best Western Mount Sorrel, Porthkerry Road, BARRY ☎ 01446 740069 🖨 01446 746600 42 en suite

HENSOL
Map 3 ST07

Vale Resort see page 413
Hensol Park CF72 8JY
☎ 01443 667733 & 665899 🖨 01443 665850
e-mail: smetson@vale-hotel.com
web: www.vale-hotel.com

See advert on page 390

PENARTH
Map 3 ST17

Glamorganshire Golf Club Lavernock Rd CF64 5UP
☎ 029 2070 1185 🖨 029 2071 3333
e-mail: glamgolf@btconnect.com
web: www.glamorganshiregolfclub.co.uk

Parkland overlooking the Bristol Channel.

18 Holes, 6184yds, Par 70, SSS 70, Course record 64.
Club membership 1000.

Visitors Mon, Wed-Sun except BHs. Booking required. Handicap certificate. Dress code **Societies** booking required. **Green Fees** not confirmed **Course Designer** James Braid **Prof** Andrew Kerr-Smith
Facilities ⓤ ⍁ ⍒ ⌂ ⍝ ⋏ ⌂ ⍝ ✦ ⛟ ✦ **Location** S of town centre on B4267
Hotel ★★★ 73% HL Best Western Mount Sorrel, Porthkerry Road, BARRY ☎ 01446 740069 🖨 01446 746600 42 en suite

ST NICHOLAS
Map 3 ST17

Cottrell Park Golf Resort Cottrell Park CF5 6SJ
☎ 01446 781781 🖨 01446 781187
e-mail: admin@cottrellpark.com
web: www.golfwithus.com

Two well-designed courses situated in historic parkland with spectacular views across the Brecon Beacons to the Mendips over the Bristol Channel. An enjoyable yet testing game of golf for players of all abilities.

Mackintosh: 18 Holes, 6529yds, Par 72, SSS 71.
Button Gwinnett: 18 Holes, 6183yds, Par 71, SSS 70.

Visitors Mon-Sun & BHs. Booking required. Dress code.
Societies booking required. **Green Fees** Per 18 holes: Mackintosh £29.95 (£39.95 weekends). Button Gwinnett £24.95 (£34.95 weekends) **Course Designer** MRM Sandow **Prof** Simon Cox/Wesley Vaughan **Facilities** ⓤ ⍁ ⍒ ⌂ ⍝ ⋏ ⌂ ⍝ ✦ ⛟ ✦ ✦ **Leisure** indoor surround golf simulators, segways for hire **Conf** facs Corporate Hospitality Days **Location** M4 junct 33, 6.5m W of Cardiff off A48, NW of St Nicholas
Hotel ★★★★ 75% HL Copthorne Hotel Cardiff-Caerdydd, Copthorne Way, Culverhouse Cross, CARDIFF ☎ 029 2059 9100 🖨 029 2059 9080 135 en suite

See advert on page 390

VALE RESORT

VALE OF GLAMORGAN - HENSOL - MAP 3 ST07

The Resort's two courses have both played host to PGA professional championships and are true tests for golfers of every level. The award-winning Wales National course at 7433 yards is destined to be one of the great UK inland courses; mature woodland, fearsome bunkers and water areas plus USGA standard greens combine to make a true test of golf. The Lake course, at 6436, whilst shorter is aptly named with water coming into play on 12 holes - the 12th green being an island; a well established par 72 course that guarantees a most memorable day's golf.

Hensol Park CF72 8JY ☎ 01443 667733 & 665899 🖷 01443 665850
e-mail: smetson@vale-hotel.com **web:** www.vale-hotel.com
Lake: 18 Holes, 6436yds, Par 72, SSS 72, Course record 64.
Wales National: 18 Holes, 7433yds, Par 73, SSS 75, Course record 65. Club membership 700.
Visitors Booking required. Handicap certificate. Dress code. **Societies** booking required **Green Fees** phone
Course Designer Terry Jones **Prof** Coombs, Simmonds, Williams **Facilities** ⑪ ⑩ 🖫 ⬚ 🖳 ⚲ 🖻 ⚐ ◇ ✦ 🖾
✦ ✦ **Leisure** hard tennis courts, heated indoor swimming pool, squash, fishing, sauna, gymnasium, spa, walks
Conf facs Corporate Hospitality Days **Location** M4 junct 34, signed
Hotel ★★★★ 85% HL Vale Resort, Hensol Park, HENSOL ☎ 01443 667800 🖷 01443 667801 143 en suite

WREXHAM

CHIRK
Map 7 SJ23

Chirk Golf Club LL14 5AD
☎ 01691 774407 📄 01691 773878
e-mail: enquiries@chirkgolfclub.co.uk
web: www.chirkgolfclub.co.uk

Overlooked by the National Trust's Chirk Castle, a championship-standard 18-hole course with a 664yd par 5 at the 9th - one of the longest in Europe. Also a nine-hole course, driving range and golf academy.

Captain Davids: 18 Holes, 7045yds, Par 72, SSS 74, Course record 68. Club membership 300.

Visitors Mon-Sun & BHs. Booking required. **Societies** booking required. **Green Fees** £25 per round (£30 weekends) **Prof** Chris Hodges **Facilities** ⊕ ⎢◎⎢ ⎢ 🖵 ⋔ ⚲ 🖾 ⋔ ❤ 🚗 ⚲ ➤ **Leisure** 9 hole par 3 course **Conf** facs Corporate Hospitality Days **Location** 1m NW of Chirk, near Chirk Castle
Hotel ★★★ 75% HL Moreton Park Lodge, Moreton Park, Gledrid, CHIRK ☎ 01691 776666 📄 01691 776655 45 en suite

EYTON
Map 7 SJ34

Plassey Oaks Golf Complex LL13 0SP
☎ 01978 780020 📄 01978 781397
e-mail: info@plassey-golf.co.uk
web: www.plassey-golf.co.uk

Picturesque nine-hole course in undulating parkland.

9 Holes, 5002yds, Par 68, SSS 66, Course record 62. Club membership 222.

Visitors Mon-Sun & BHs. Booking required. **Societies** booking required. **Green Fees** £20 per 18 holes, £10 per 9 holes **Course Designer** Welsh Golf Union **Prof** Richard Stockdale **Facilities** ⊕ ⎢◎⎢ ⎢ 🖵 ⋔ ⚲ 🖾 ⋔ ❤ 🚗 ⚲ ➤ **Leisure** fishing **Conf** facs Corporate Hospitality Days **Location** 4m S of Wrexham off B5426, signed
Hotel ★★★ 75% HL Best Western Cross Lanes Hotel & Restaurant, Cross Lanes, Bangor Road, Marchwiel, WREXHAM ☎ 01978 780555 📄 01978 780568 16 en suite

WREXHAM
Map 7 SJ35

Clays Golf Centre Bryn Estyn Rd, Llan-y-Pwll LL13 9UB
☎ 01978 661406 📄 01978 661406
e-mail: sales@claysgolf.co.uk
web: www.claysgolf.co.uk

Gently undulating parkland course in countryside with views of the Welsh mountains. Noted for its difficult par 3s.

18 Holes, 6000yds, Par 69, SSS 68, Course record 61. Club membership 500.

Visitors Mon-Sun & BHs. **Societies** booking required. **Green Fees** not confirmed **Course Designer** R D Jones **Prof** David Larvin **Facilities** ⊕ ⎢◎⎢ ⎢ 🖵 ⋔ ⚲ 🖾 ⋔ ❤ 🚗 ⚲ ➤ **Conf** facs Corporate Hospitality Days **Location** off A534
Hotel ★★★ 75% HL Best Western Cross Lanes Hotel & Restaurant, Cross Lanes, Bangor Road, Marchwiel, WREXHAM ☎ 01978 780555 📄 01978 780568 16 en suite

Wrexham Golf Club Holt Rd LL13 9SB
☎ 01978 364268 📄 01978 362168
e-mail: info@wrexhamgolfclub.co.uk
web: www.wrexhamgolfclub.co.uk

Inland, sandy course with easy walking. Testing dog-leg 7th hole (par 4), and short 14th hole (par 3) with full carry to green.

18 Holes, 6148yds, Par 70, SSS 70, Course record 64. Club membership 1000.

Visitors Mon-Fri except BHs. Handicap certificate. Dress code. **Societies** booking required. **Green Fees** £35 per day (£40 weekends) **Course Designer** James Braid **Prof** Paul Williams **Facilities** ⊕ ⎢◎⎢ ⎢ 🖵 ⋔ ⚲ 🖾 🚗 ⚲ **Conf** facs Corporate Hospitality Days **Location** 2m NE on A534
Hotel ★★★ 75% HL Best Western Cross Lanes Hotel & Restaurant, Cross Lanes, Bangor Road, Marchwiel, WREXHAM ☎ 01978 780555 📄 01978 780568 16 en suite

Northern Ireland

Slieve Donard, Co. Down

CO ANTRIM

ANTRIM
Map 1 D5

Massereene Golf Club 51 Lough Rd BT41 4DQ
☎ 028 9442 8096 🖷 028 9448 7661
e-mail: info@massereene.com
web: www.massereene.com

The first nine holes are parkland, while the second, adjacent to the shore of Lough Neagh, have more of a links character with sandy ground.

18 Holes, 6602yds, Par 72, SSS 72, Course record 63.
Club membership 1050.

Visitors Mon-Fri, Sun & BHs. Booking required. Dress code.
Societies booking required. **Green Fees** £25 per round (£35 weekends) **Course Designer** F Hawtree/H Swan **Prof** Jim Smyth **Facilities** ⓣ ⓨⓞ ⓛ ⓟ ⓢ ⓥ ⓕ ⓣ ⓤ ⓔ **Conf** facs Corporate Hospitality Days **Location** 1m SW of town
Hotel ★★★★ 82% HL Galgorm Resort & Spa, BALLYMENA
☎ 028 2588 1001 🖷 028 2588 0080 75 en suite

BALLYCASTLE
Map 1 D6

Ballycastle Golf Club Cushendall Rd BT54 6QP
☎ 028 2076 2536 🖷 028 2076 9909
e-mail: info@ballycastlegolfclub.com
web: www.ballycastlegolfclub.com

An unusual mixture of terrain beside the sea, lying at the foot of one of the nine glens of Antrim, with magnificent views from all parts. The first five holes are parkland with natural hazards; the middle holes are links type and the rest on adjacent upland. Accurate iron play is essential for good scoring while the undulating greens will test putting skills.

18 Holes, 5876yds, Par 71. Club membership 700.

Visitors Mon-Sun & BHs. Booking required. **Societies** booking required. **Green Fees** £28 per round (£38 weekends & BHs)
Prof Damien McEvoy **Facilities** ⓣ ⓨⓞ ⓛ ⓟ ⓢ ⓥ ⓕ ⓔ ⓕ **Conf** facs Corporate Hospitality Days **Location** between Portrush & Cushendall (A2)
Hotel ★★★★★ GA Whitepark House, 150 Whitepark Road, Ballintoy, BALLEYCASTLE ☎ 028 2073 1482 3 rooms

BALLYCLARE
Map 1 D5

Ballyclare Golf Club 25 Springvale Rd BT39 9JW
☎ 028 9332 2696 (office) & 028 9332 4541 (pro shop)
🖷 028 9332 2696
e-mail: info@ballyclaregolfclub.net
web: www.ballyclaregolfclub.net

Founded in 1923 and set in rolling green countryside, this mature parkland course makes good use of the natural features of its landscape, in particular the local river and stream with lakes in play on three holes, providing a fabulous setting and demanding challenge for all who play. The fairways are tree-lined and as expected, accurate driving is required for a good score.

18 Holes, 6339mtrs, Par 71, SSS 71, Course record 67.
Club membership 737.

Visitors Mon-Sun & BHs. Booking required weekends & BHs. Dress code. **Societies** booking required. **Green Fees** not confirmed **Course Designer** T McCauley **Prof** Colin Lyttle **Facilities** ⓣ ⓨⓞ ⓛ ⓟ ⓢ ⓥ ⓕ ⓔ ⓤ ⓕ **Conf** facs Corporate Hospitality Days **Location** 1.5m N of Ballyclare
Hotel ★★★★ 82% HL Galgorm Resort & Spa, BALLYMENA
☎ 028 2588 1001 🖷 028 2588 0080 75 en suite

Greenacres Golf Course 153 Ballyrobert Rd BT39 9RT
☎ 028 9335 4111 🖷 028 9334 4509
e-mail: info@greenacresgolfcentre.co.uk
web: www.greenacresgolfcentre.co.uk

Designed and built into the rolling countryside, and with the addition of lakes at five of the holes, provides a challenge for both the seasoned golfer and the higher-handicapped player.

Greenacres: 18 Holes, 6053yds, Par 70.
Lislea: 9 Holes, 2004yds, Par 54. Club membership 630.

Visitors Mon-Fri. Par 3 course Mon-Sun & BHs. Greenacres course Sun-Fri. Dress code **Societies** booking required. **Green Fees** not confirmed **Prof** John Foster **Facilities** ⓣ ⓨⓞ ⓛ ⓟ ⓢ ⓥ ⓕ ⓤ ⓕ ⓕ **Leisure** 18 hole mini golf & 9 hole par 3 course. **Conf** Corporate Hospitality Days **Location** 12m from Belfast city centre

BALLYGALLY
Map 1 D5

Cairndhu Golf Club 192 Coast Rd BT40 2QG
☎ 028 2858 3954 🖷 028 2858 3324
web: www.cairndhugolfclub.co.uk

18 Holes, 6120yds, Par 70, SSS 69, Course record 64.

Course Designer Mr Morrison **Location** 4m N of Larne on coast road
Telephone for further details
Hotel ★★★★ GH Manor Guest House, 23 Older Fleet Road, Harbour Highway, LARNE ☎ 028 2827 3305 🖷 028 2826 0505
8 rooms

BALLYMENA   Map 1 D5

Galgorm Castle Golf Club Galgorm Rd BT42 1HL
☎ 028 2564 6161 ▤ 028 2565 1151
e-mail: golf@galgormcastle.com
web: www.galgormcastle.com

An 18-hole USGA championship course set in 220 acres of mature parkland in the grounds of one of Ireland's most historic castles. The course is bordered by two rivers which come into play and includes five lakes. A course of outstanding beauty offering a challenge to both the novice and low handicapped golfer.

18 Holes, 6736yds, Par 72, SSS 73, Course record 63.
Club membership 750.

Visitors Mon-Fri & Sun (restrictions on Sat). Booking required.
Dress code. **Societies** booking required. **Green Fees** £45 weekdays (£55 weekends) **Course Designer** Simon Gidman **Prof** Phil Collins
Facilities ⑪ ⑩ ⒧ ⌨ ⑪ ⌁ ⚲ ⚲ ⚲ ⚲ ⚲ ⚲
Leisure fishing, PGA staffed Academy **Conf** facs Corporate Hospitality
Days **Location** 1m S of Ballymena on A42
Hotel ★★★★ 82% HL Galgorm Resort & Spa, BALLYMENA
☎ 028 2588 1001 ▤ 028 2588 0080 75 en suite

BALLYMONEY   Map 1 D6

Gracehill Golf Course 141 Ballinlea Rd, Stranocum
BT53 8PX
☎ 028 2075 1209 ▤ 028 2075 1074
e-mail: info@gracehillgolfclub.co.uk
web: www.gracehillgolfclub.co.uk

Challenging parkland course with some holes played over water and many mature trees coming into play.

18 Holes, 6553yds, Par 72, SSS 73, Course record 69.
Club membership 400.

Visitors Mon-Sun & BHs. Booking required weekends & BHs. Dress code. **Societies** booking required. **Green Fees** not confirmed **Course Designer** Frank Ainsworth **Prof** Ian Blair **Facilities** ⑪ ⑩ ⒧ ⌨
⑪ ⌁ ⚲ ⚲ **Conf** Corporate Hospitality Days **Location** M2 N from Belfast, onto A26 N to Ballymoney, signs for Coleraine. At Ballymoney bypass onto B147/A2 to Sranocum/Ballintoy
Hotel ★★★ 71% HL Brown Trout Golf & Country Inn, 209 Agivey Road, AGHADOWEY ☎ 028 7086 8209 ▤ 028 7086 8878 15 en suite

CARRICKFERGUS   Map 1 D5

Carrickfergus Golf Club 35 North Rd BT38 8LP
☎ 028 9336 3713 ▤ 028 9336 3023
e-mail: carrickfergusgc@btconnect.com
web: www.carrickfergusgolfclub.co.uk

Parkland course, fairly level but nevertheless demanding, with a notorious water hazard at the 1st. Well-maintained, with an interesting in-course riverway and fine views across Belfast Lough.

18 Holes, 5768yds, Par 68, SSS 68. Club membership 980.

Visitors Mon-Fri, Sun & BHs. Booking required Tue, Fri, Sun & BHs. **Societies** welcome. **Green Fees** £19 per day, £13 per round (£25/£16 Sun & BHs) **Prof** Colin Farr **Facilities** ⑪ ⑩ ⒧ ⌨ ⑪ ⌁ ⚲
⚲ **Conf** facs Corporate Hospitality Days **Location** 9m NE of Belfast on A2
Hotel ★★★★ 82% HL The Old Inn, 15 Main Street, CRAWFORDSBURN ☎ 028 9185 3255 ▤ 028 9185 2775 31 en suite

Greenisland Golf Club 156 Upper Rd, Greenisland
BT38 8RW
☎ 028 9086 2236
e-mail: greenislandgolf@btconnect.com
web: www.greenislandgolfclub.co.uk

A parkland course, with mature, tree-lined fairways, nestling at the foot of Knockagh Hill, with scenic views over Belfast Lough.

9 Holes, 6090yds, Par 71, SSS 69, Course record 66.
Club membership 600.

Visitors Mon-Fri, Sun & BHs. Sat after 4.30pm. Dress code.
Societies booking required. **Green Fees** not confirmed ⓖ
Facilities ⑪ ⑩ ⒧ ⌨ ⑪ ⌁ **Location** N of Belfast, close to Carrickfergus
Hotel ★★★★★ GH Rayanne House, 60 Desmesne Road, HOLYWOOD ☎ 028 9042 5859 ▤ 028 9042 5859 10 rooms

CUSHENDALL   Map 1 D6

Cushendall Golf Club 21 Shore Rd BT44 0NG
☎ 028 2177 1318 ▤ 028 2177 1318
e-mail: cushendallgc@btconnect.com

Scenic course with spectacular views over the Sea of Moyle and Red Bay to the Mull of Kintyre. The River Dall winds through the course, coming into play in seven of the nine holes. This demands a premium on accuracy rather than length. The signature hole is the par 3 2nd, requiring a tee shot across the river to a plateau green with a steep slope in front and out of bounds behind.

9 Holes, 4379mtrs, Par 66, SSS 63, Course record 59.
Club membership 680.

Visitors Mon-Sun & BHs. Booking required weekends. Dress code.
Societies booking required. **Green Fees** £15 per day (£20 BHs)
Course Designer D Delargy **Facilities** ⑪ ⑩ ⒧ ⌨ ⑪ ⌁ ⚲
Conf facs **Location** in Cushendall beside beach on Antrim coast road
Hotel ★★★ 74% HL Londonderry Arms, 20 Harbour Road, CARNLOUGH ☎ 028 2888 5255 ▤ 028 2888 5263 35 en suite

LARNE   Map 1 D5

Larne Golf Club 54 Ferris Bay Rd, Islandmagee BT40 3RT
☎ 028 9338 2228 ▤ 028 9338 2088
e-mail: info@larnegolfclub.co.uk
web: www.larnegolfclub.co.uk

An exposed part links, part heathland course, situated on the Island Magee Peninsula with magnificent views of the Antrim coast and across the Irish sea to Scotland. The course offers a fine challenge to all golfers with the 8th hole highlyregarded.

9 Holes, 6288yds, Par 70, SSS 68. Club membership 430.

Visitors Mon-Thu, Sun & BHs. **Societies** booking required. **Green Fees** £15 per day summer (£20 weekends & BHs). £10 per day winter (£15) ⓖ **Course Designer** G L Bailie **Facilities** ⑪ ⑩ ⒧ ⌨ ⑪
⌁ **Location** 6m N of Whitehead on Browns Bay road
Hotel ★★★★ GA Derrin House, 2 Princes Gardens, LARNE
☎ 028 2827 3269 ▤ 028 2827 3269 7 rooms (7 en suite)

IRELAND

LISBURN
Map 1 D5

Aberdelghy Golf Course Bell's Ln BT27 4QH
☎ 028 9266 2738 📄 028 9260 3432
web: www.customprogolf.co.uk

18 Holes, 4139mtrs, Par 66, SSS 62, Course record 64.
Course Designer Alec Blair **Location** 1.5m N of Lisburn off A1
Telephone for further details
Hotel ★★★★ 74% HL Malone Lodge, 60 Eglantine Avenue,
BELFAST ☎ 028 9038 8000 📄 028 9038 8088 46 en suite

Lisburn Golf Club 68 Eglantine Rd BT27 5RQ
☎ 028 9267 7216 📄 028 9260 3608
e-mail: lisburngolfclub@aol.com
web: www.lisburngolfclub.com

Meadowland course, fairly level, with plenty of trees and shrubs.
Challenging last three holes, the par 3 finishing hole is a spectacular
downhill hole and reaching par is a bonus.

18 Holes, 6647yds, Par 72, SSS 72, Course record 67.
Club membership 1200.

Visitors contact club for details **Societies** booking required.
Green Fees not confirmed **Course Designer** Hawtree **Prof** Stephen
Hamill **Facilities** 🕦 🍴 🛒 🖥 🏌 🛋 🏴 ✪ 🛺 ✪
Location 2m from town on A1
Hotel ★★★★ 74% HL Malone Lodge, 60 Eglantine Avenue,
BELFAST ☎ 028 9038 8000 📄 028 9038 8088 46 en suite

MAZE
Map 1 D5

Down Royal Park Golf Course 6 Dunygarton Rd BT27 5RT
☎ 028 9262 1339 📄 028 9262 1339

18 Holes, 6940yds, Par 72, SSS 72, Course record 69.
Valley Course: 9 Holes, 2019, Par 33.

Location inside Down Royal Race Course
Telephone for further details
Hotel ★★★★ 74% HL Malone Lodge, 60 Eglantine Avenue,
BELFAST ☎ 028 9038 8000 📄 028 9038 8088 46 en suite

PORTBALLINTRAE
Map 1 C6

Bushfoot Golf Club 50 Bushfoot Rd, Portballintrae BT57 8RR
☎ 028 2073 1317 📄 028 2073 1852
e-mail: bushfootgolfclub@btconnect.com

A seaside links course with superb views in an area of outstanding
beauty. A challenging par 3 7th is ringed by bunkers with out of
bounds beyond, while the 3rd has a blind approach. Also a putting
green and pitch and putt course.

9 Holes, 6075yds, Par 70, SSS 68, Course record 64.
Club membership 850.

Visitors Mon, Wed-Fri, Sun & BHs. **Societies** welcome. **Green
Fees** £16 per round (£20 Sun & BHs) **Facilities** 🕦 🍴 🛒 🖥 🏌
🛋 🏴 ✪ **Location** off Ballaghmore road
Hotel ★★★ GA Beulah Guest House, 16 Causeway Street,
PORTRUSH ☎ 028 7082 2413 9 rooms

PORTRUSH
Map 1 C6

Royal Portrush Golf Club see page 421
Dunluce Rd BT56 8JQ
☎ 028 7082 2311 📄 028 7082 3139
e-mail: info@royalportrushgolfclub.com
web: www.royalportrushgolfclub.com

WHITEHEAD
Map 1 D5

Bentra Golf Course Slaughterford Rd BT38 9TG
☎ 028 9337 8996 📄 028 9337 8996

9 Holes, 5952yds, Par 37, SSS 35.
Location 6m from Carrickfergus
Telephone for further details
Hotel ★★★★★ BB Hebron House, 68 Princetown Road, BANGOR
☎ 028 9146 3126 📄 028 9146 3126 3 rooms

Whitehead Golf Club McCrae's Brae BT38 9NZ
☎ 028 9337 0820 & 9337 0822 📄 028 9337 0825
e-mail: info@whiteheadgolfclub.com
web: www.whiteheadgolfclub.com

Undulating parkland course with magnificent sea views.

18 Holes, 5846yds, Par 70, SSS 69, Course record 63.
Club membership 962.

Visitors Mon-Fri, Sun & BHs. Booking required Sun. **Societies** Booking
required. **Green Fees** £20 per round (£24 Sun & BHs) ♨ **Course
Designer** A B Armstrong **Prof** Colin Farr **Facilities** 🕦 🍴 🛒
🖥 🏌 🛋 🏴 ✪ 🛺 ✪ **Conf** Corporate Hospitality Days
Location 1m from town
Hotel ★★★★ GH Manor Guest House, 23 Older Fleet Road,
Harbour Highway, LARNE ☎ 028 2827 3305 📄 028 2826 0505
8 rooms (8 en suite)

ROYAL PORTRUSH

CO ANTRIM - PORTRUSH - MAP 1 C6

This course, designed by Harry S Colt, is considered to be among the best six in the UK. Founded in 1888, it was the venue of the first professional golf event in Ireland, held in 1895, when Sandy Herd beat Harry Vardon in the final. Royal Portrush is spectacular and breathtaking, one of the tightest driving courses known to golfers. On a clear day there's a fine view of Islay and the Paps of Jura from the 3rd tee, and the Giant's Causeway from the 5th. While the greens have to be 'read' from the start, there are fairways up and down valleys, and holes called Calamity Corner and Purgatory (for good reason). The 2nd hole, Giant's Grave, is 509yds, but the 17th is even longer. The Dunluce course has recently been extended.

Dunluce Rd BT56 8JQ ☎ 028 7082 2311 ▤ 028 7082 3139
e-mail: info@royalportrushgolfclub.com web: www.royalportrushgolfclub.com
Dunluce: 18 Holes, 7143yds, Par 72.
Valley: 18 Holes, 6304yds, Par 70, SSS 69. Club membership 1300.
Visitors Mon-Sun & BHs. Booking required. Handicap certificate. Dress code. Societies welcome. Green
Fees Dunluce £125 per round (£140 weekends). Apr & Oct £75 per round. Valley £35 per round (£40 weekends).
Nov-Mar Dunluce £60 per round, Valley £25 per round Course Designer Harry Colt Prof Gary McNeill
Facilities ⑪ ⑩ ⓛ ⌹ ⑭ ⌱ ⑮ ⌤ ⚭ ❀ Conf Corporate Hospitality Days Location 0.8km from Portrush on
Bushmills road
Hotel ★★★ GA Beulah Guest House, 16 Causeway Street, PORTRUSH ☎ 028 7082 2413 ▤ 028 7082 2413
9 en suite

CO ARMAGH

ARMAGH
Map 1 C5

County Armagh Golf Club The Demesne, Newry Rd BT60 1EN
☎ 028 3752 5861 ▤ 028 3752 8768
e-mail: lynne@golfarmagh.co.uk
web: www.golfarmagh.co.uk

Mature parkland course with excellent views of Armagh city and its surroundings.

18 Holes, 6212yds, Par 70, SSS 69, Course record 63. Club membership 1300.

Visitors Mon-Wed, Fri, Sun & BHs. Booking required. Dress code. **Societies** welcome. **Green Fees** not confirmed **Prof** Alan Rankin **Facilities** ⑪ ⑩ 🏌 🛒 🍴 👥 🏠 🏌 🛒 🏌
Leisure snooker **Conf** Corporate Hospitality Days **Location** on Newry Rd
Hotel ★★ 72% HL Cohannon Inn & Auto Lodge, 212 Ballynakilly Road, DUNGANNON ☎ 028 8772 4488 ▤ 028 8775 2217 42 en suite

CULLYHANNA
Map 1 C5

Ashfield Golf Club 44 Cregganduff Rd BT35 0JJ
☎ 028 3086 8611

18 Holes, 5840yds, Par 69.

Course Designer Frank Ainsworth **Location**
Telephone for further details
Hotel ★★★★ 79% HL Ballymascanlon House Hotel, DUNDALK
☎ 042 9358200 ▤ 042 9371598 90 en suite

LURGAN
Map 1 D5

Craigavon Golf & Ski Centre Turmoyra Ln BT66 6NG
☎ 028 3832 6606 ▤ 028 3834 7272
web: www.craigavon.gov.uk
Silverwood: 18 Holes, 6496yds, Par 72, SSS 72, Course record 67.

Location 2m N at Silverwood off M1
Telephone for further details

Lurgan Golf Club The Demesne BT67 9BN
☎ 028 3832 2087 ▤ 028 3831 6166
e-mail: lurgangolfclub@btconnect.com
web: www.lurgangolfclub.com

Testing parkland course bordering Lurgan Park Lake with a need for accurate shots. Drains well in wet weather and suits a long straight hitter.

18 Holes, 6298yds, Par 70, SSS 70, Course record 64. Club membership 1019.

Visitors Mon-Sun & BHs. Booking required Tue & Wed. Dress code. **Societies** booking required. **Green Fees** £20 (£25 weekends & BHs) **Course Designer** A Pennink **Prof** Peter Hanna **Facilities** ⑪ ⑩ 🏌 🛒 🍴 👥 🏠 🏌 **Conf** facs **Location** 0.5m from town centre near Lurgan Park

PORTADOWN
Map 1 D5

Portadown Golf Club 192 Gilford Rd BT63 5LF
☎ 028 3835 5356 ▤ 028 3839 1394
e-mail: info@portadowngolfclub.co.uk
web: www.portadowngolfclub.co.uk

Nestled in the heart of Orchard County since 1900, a course of exceptional beauty and elegance, placed in a partial woodland setting, which will test abilities and skill at any standard.

18 Holes, 6118yds, Par 72, SSS 72, Course record 63. Club membership 711.

Visitors Mon, Wed-Fri, Sun & BHs. Booking required. Handicap certificate. Dress code. **Societies** booking required. **Green Fees** £18 (£22 weekends & BHs) 🏌 **Course Designer** Mr Wilson/Mr Jameson **Prof** Paul Stevenson **Facilities** ⑪ ⑩ 🏌 🛒 🍴 👥 🏠
🏌 🛒 🏌 **Leisure** squash **Conf** facs Corporate Hospitality Days **Location** A50 towards Banbridge from Portadown
Hotel ★★ 72% HL Cohannon Inn & Auto Lodge, 212 Ballynakilly Road, DUNGANNON ☎ 028 8772 4488 ▤ 028 8775 2217 42 en suite

TANDRAGEE
Map 1 D5

Tandragee Golf Club Markethill Rd BT62 2ER
☎ 028 3884 1272 ▤ 028 3884 0664
e-mail: office@tandragee.co.uk
web: www.tandragee.co.uk

This well-wooded parkland course is a good test of golf for any golfer. Tree-lined fairways will penalize the wayward shot and with an internal out of bounds straight shots are required. The four par 3s on the course provide differing approaches especially the 16th, one of the best par 3s in the country. Playing from an elevated tee to an elevated green, with the ground falling away on three sides, straight and true is the watchword playing this hole. The course provides excellent views of the rolling Armagh landscape.

18 Holes, 5736mtrs, Par 71, SSS 69, Course record 64. Club membership 848.

Visitors Mon-Fri & Sun. Dress code. **Societies** booking required. **Green Fees** £20 per day (£25 weekends & BHs) **Course Designer** John Stone **Prof** Dympna Keenan **Facilities** ⑪ ⑩ 🏌 🛒 🍴 👥 🏠 🏌
🛒 🏌 🏌 **Leisure** snooker **Conf** facs Corporate Hospitality Days **Location** on B3 from Tandragee towards Markethill

BELFAST

BELFAST
Map 1 D5

See also The Royal Belfast, Holywood, Co Down.

Dunmurry Golf Club 91 Dunmurry Ln, Dunmurry BT17 9JS
☎ 028 9061 0834 ▤ 028 9060 2540
e-mail: dunmurrygc@hotmail.com
web: www.dunmurrygolfclub.com

Maturing very nicely, this tricky parkland course has several memorable holes which call for skilful shots.

18 Holes, 6156yds, Par 70, SSS 70. Club membership 1100.

Visitors Mon-Fri, Sun & BHs. Booking required. **Societies** booking required **Green Fees** not confirmed 🏌 **Prof** John Dolan **Facilities** ⑪ ⑩ 🏌 🛒 🍴 👥 🏠 🏌 🛒 **Location**
Hotel ★★★★ 74% HL Malone Lodge, 60 Eglantine Avenue, BELFAST ☎ 028 9038 8000 ▤ 028 9038 8088 46 en suite

Fortwilliam Golf Club 8A Downview Ave BT15 4EZ
☎ 028 9037 0770 (Office) & 9077 0980 (Pro)
🖷 028 9078 1891
web: www.fortwilliam.co.uk
18 Holes, 5692yds, Par 70, SSS 68, Course record 63.
Location off Antrim road
Telephone for further details
Hotel ★★★ 83% HL Malmaison Belfast, 34 - 38 Victoria Street,
BELFAST ☎ 028 9022 0200 🖷 028 9022 0220 64 en suite

Malone Golf Club 240 Upper Malone Rd, Dunmurry
BT17 9LB
☎ 028 9061 2758 (Office) 🖷 028 9043 1394
e-mail: manager@malonegolfclub.co.uk
web: www.malonegolfclub.co.uk
Two parkland courses, extremely attractive with a large lake, mature
trees and flowering shrubs and bordered by the River Lagan. Very
well maintained and offering a challenging round.
Main Course: 18 Holes, 6448yds, Par 71, SSS 71,
Course record 65.
Edenderry: 9 Holes, 6422yds, Par 72, SSS 70.
Club membership 1450.
Visitors Mon, Thu, Fri, Sun & BHs. Wed am only. Sat pm
only. Booking required. Handicap certificate. Dress code.
Societies booking required. **Green Fees** Main Course £75 per day,
Edenderry £20 per day (£85/£25 weekends) **Course Designer** C
K Cotton **Prof** Michael McGee **Facilities** ⑪ †◯┃ ⌷ 🖫 ⤬ ⛳ 🏌 ⛳
⌷ 🏕 ⛳ ⛳ 🚲 ⛳ **Leisure** fishing, Outdoor bowling green.
Conf facs Corporate Hospitality Days **Location** 4.5m S opposite Lady
Dixon Park
Hotel ★★★★ 74% HL Malone Lodge, 60 Eglantine Avenue,
BELFAST ☎ 028 9038 8000 🖷 028 9038 8088 46 en suite

Mount Ober Golf & Country Club 24 Ballymaconaghy Rd
BT8 6SB
☎ 028 9040 1811 & 9079 5666 🖷 028 9070 5862
e-mail: mt.ober@ukonline.co.uk
web: www.mountober.com
Inland parkland course which is a great test of golf for all handicaps,
with fantastic panoramic views of Belfast.
18 Holes, 4949yds, Par 67, SSS 65, Course record 65.
Club membership 400.
Visitors Mon-Fri, Sun & BHs. Dress code. **Societies** booking required.
Green Fees £18 per round (£20 Sun & BHs) **Prof** Wesley Ramsay
Facilities ⑪ †◯┃ ⌷ 🖫 ⤬ ⛳ ⌷ ⛳ ⛳ **Leisure** American
billiards & snooker **Conf** facs Corporate Hospitality Days **Location** off
Saintfield road at Fourwinds rdbt
Hotel ★★★★★ 84% HL Merchant, 16 Skipper Street, BELFAST
☎ 028 9023 4888 🖷 028 9024 7775 63 en suite

Ormeau Golf Club 50 Park Rd BT7 2FX
☎ 028 9064 0700
e-mail: ormeau.golfclub@btconnect.com
web: www.ormeaugolfclub.co.uk
Parkland course which provides a challenge for low and high handicap
golfers, good shots being rewarded and those that stray offline
receiving due punishment. The long par 4 5th hole has an intimidating
out of bounds on the right and a narrow sloping green, well protected
by trees and bunkers. Two long par 3 holes each demand an accurate
drive and when playing the 3rd and 12th holes, visitors are advised
to look for the Fairy Tree which graces the middle of the fairway. Club
folklore states that if a golfer hits this tree he should apologise to the
fairies or his game will suffer!
9 Holes, 2688yds, Par 68, SSS 66. Club membership 520.
Visitors Sun-Fri & BHs. Dress code. **Societies** booking required.
Green Fees £12-£18 (£14-£20 weekends) **Prof** Mr Stephen Rourke
Facilities ⑪ †◯┃ ⌷ 🖫 ⤬ ⛳ **Leisure** snooker
room **Conf** facs Corporate Hospitality Days **Location** S of city centre
between Ravenhill & Ormeau roads
Hotel ★★★★★ 84% HL Merchant, 16 Skipper Street, BELFAST
☎ 028 9023 4888 🖷 028 9024 7775 63 en suite

Shandon Park Golf Club 73 Shandon Park BT5 6NY
☎ 028 9080 5030
e-mail: shandonpark@btconnect.com
web: www.shandonpark.net
Fairly level parkland with excellent greens, offering a pleasant
challenge.
18 Holes, 6119yds, Par 70, SSS 69, Course record 65.
Club membership 1100.
Visitors Mon-Sun & BHs. Booking required. Dress code.
Societies booking required. **Green Fees** £20 per round **Prof** Barry
Wilson **Facilities** ⑪ †◯┃ ⌷ 🖫 ⤬ ⛳ ⌷ ⛳ ⛳ 🚲 ⛳
Leisure indoor coaching facilities **Conf** facs Corporate Hospitality
Days **Location** off Knock road
Hotel ★★★★★ 84% HL Merchant, 16 Skipper Street, BELFAST
☎ 028 9023 4888 🖷 028 9024 7775 63 en suite

DUNDONALD   Map 1 D5

Knock Golf Club Summerfield BT16 2QX
☎ 028 9048 3251 🖷 028 9048 7277
e-mail: knockgolfclub@btconnect.com
web: www.knockgolfclub.co.uk
Parkland course with huge trees, deep bunkers and a river cutting
across several fairways. This is a hard but fair course and will test the
best of golfers.
18 Holes, 6435yds, Par 70, SSS 71, Course record 65.
Club membership 920.
Visitors Mon, Thu, Fri, Sun & BHs. Booking required. Handicap
certificate. Dress code. **Societies** booking required. **Green Fees** £26
per day (£55 weekends & BHs) **Course Designer** Colt, Allison &
McKenzie **Prof** Richard Whitford **Facilities** ⑪ †◯┃ ⌷ 🖫 ⤬ ⛳
🏕 ⛳ ⛳ 🚲 ⛳ **Conf** Corporate Hospitality Days **Location** 5m E
of Belfast
Hotel ★★★★ 82% HL The Old Inn, 15 Main Street,
CRAWFORDSBURN ☎ 028 9185 3255 🖷 028 9185 2775 31 en suite

IRELAND

NEWTOWNBREDA

Map 1 D5

Belvoir Park Golf Club 73 Church Rd BT8 7AN
☎ 028 9049 1693 ▤ 028 9064 6113
e-mail: info@belvoirparkgolfclub.com
web: www.belvoirparkgolfclub.com

This undulating parkland course is not strenuous to walk, but is certainly a test of your golf, with tree-lined fairways and a particularly challenging finish at the final four holes.

18 Holes, 6270yds, Par 70, SSS 71.
Club membership 1220.

Visitors Mon, Tue, Thu & BHs. Booking required. Handicap certificate. Dress code. **Societies** booking required. **Green Fees** not confirmed **Course Designer** H S Colt Prof Michael McGivern **Facilities** ⓣ ⓘⓞⓣ ☎ ⌨ 🍴 ♨ ☏ ✆ 🏌 🏌 **Conf** facs **Location** 2m from city centre off Saintfield-Newcastle road **Hotel** ★★★★ 80% HL Clandeboye Lodge, 10 Estate Road, Clandeboye, BANGOR ☎ 028 9185 2500 ▤ 028 9185 2772 43 en suite

CO DOWN

ARDGLASS

Map 1 D5

Ardglass Golf Club Castle Place BT30 7TP
☎ 028 4484 1219 ▤ 028 4484 1841
e-mail: info@ardglassgolfclub.com
web: www.ardglassgolfclub.com

A scenic clifftop seaside course with championship standard greens. The first five holes, with the Irish Sea and cliffs tight to the left, should be treated with respect as anything resembling a hook will meet with disaster. The 2nd hole is a daunting par 3. The tee shot must carry a cliff and canyon - meanwhile the superb views of the Mountains of Mourne should not be missed.

18 Holes, 6268yds, Par 70, SSS 69, Course record 69.
Club membership 900.

Visitors Mon-Fri & BHs. Weekends restricted. Booking required. Dress code. **Societies** booking required **Green Fees** £43 per round (£62 weekends) **Course Designer** David Jones **Prof** Philip Farrell **Facilities** ⓣ ⓘⓞⓣ ☎ ⌨ 🍴 ♨ ☏ 🏌 **Conf** facs **Location** 7m from Downpatrick on the B1 **Hotel** ★★★★ INN The Cuan Licensed Guest Inn, 6-12 The Square, STRANGFORD ☎ 028 4488 1222 9 rooms

BALLYNAHINCH

Map 1 D5

Spa Golf Club 20 Grove Rd BT24 8PN
☎ 028 9756 2365 ▤ 028 9756 4158
e-mail: spagolfclub@btconnect.com
web: www.spagolfclub.net

Parkland course with tree-lined fairways and scenic views of the Mourne Mountains. A long and demanding course and feature holes include the par 3 2nd and 405yd par 4 11th.

18 Holes, 6003mtrs, Par 72, SSS 72, Course record 65.
Club membership 700.

Visitors booking required. Dress code. **Societies** welcome. **Green Fees** £20 per round (£25 Sun & BHs) **Course Designer** F Ainsworth/T Magee/R Wallace **Facilities** ⓣ ⓘⓞⓣ ☎ ⌨ 🍴 ♨ ☏ 🏌 ✆ **Leisure** gymnasium, outdoor bowls **Conf** facs Corporate Hospitality Days **Location** 1m S

BANBRIDGE

Map 1 D5

Banbridge Golf Club 116 Huntly Rd BT32 3UR
☎ 028 4066 2211 ▤ 028 4066 9400
e-mail: info@banbridgegolfclub.net
web: www.banbridgegolfclub.net

A mature parkland course with excellent views of the Mourne Mountains. The holes are not long, but are tricky. Signature holes are the 6th with its menacing pond and the par 3 10th where playing for a safe 4 is usually the best option.

18 Holes, 5590yds, Par 69, SSS 67, Course record 62.
Club membership 800.

Visitors Mon-Fri, Sun & BHs. Booking required Tue, Sun & BHs. Dress code. **Societies** booking required. **Green Fees** not confirmed **Course Designer** F Ainsworth **Prof** Jason Greenaway **Facilities** ⓣ ⓘⓞⓣ ☎ ⌨ 🍴 ♨ ☏ 🏌 🏌 **Conf** facs **Location** 0.5m along Huntly Rd

BANGOR

Map 1 D5

Bangor Golf Club Broadway BT20 4RH
☎ 028 9127 0922 ▤ 028 9145 3394
e-mail: office@bangorgolfclubni.co.uk
web: www.bangorgolfclubni.co.uk

The course is continually maturing and the fairways and greens would do justice to many a more famous course. The signature hole is the par 4 5th (463 yards), the longest par 4 on the course where the player needs to keep left and lay up short of the path with the approach shot.

18 Holes, 6410yds, Par 71, SSS 71, Course record 62.
Club membership 1000.

Visitors Contact club for details. **Societies** booking required. **Green Fees** Mon-Fri £27 per round, Sun £35 **Course Designer** James Braid **Prof** Michael Bannon **Facilities** ⓣ ⓘⓞⓣ ☎ ⌨ 🍴 ♨ ☏ 🏌 **Leisure** Indoor/outdoor coaching **Conf** Corporate Hospitality Days **Location** 1m from town centre, 300yds off Donaghadee Rd **Hotel** ★★★★★ BB Hebron House, 68 Princetown Road, BANGOR ☎ 028 9146 3126 ▤ 028 9146 3126 3 rooms

Blackwood Golf Centre 150 Crawfordsburn Rd, Clandeboye BT19 1GB
☎ 028 9185 2706 ▤ 028 9185 3785
web: www.blackwoodgolfcentre.com

The golf centre is a pay-and-play development with a computerised booking system for the 18-hole championship-standard Hamilton Course. The course is built on mature woodland with man-made lakes that come into play on five holes. The Temple course is an 18-hole par 3 course with holes ranging from the 75yd 1st to the 185yd 10th, which has a lake on the right of the green. Banked by gorse with streams crossing throughout, this par 3 course is no pushover.

Hamilton Course: 18 Holes, 6392yds, Par 71.
Temple Course: 18 Holes, 2492yds, Par 54.

Visitors Mon-Sun & BHs. Booking required Fri-Sun & BHs. Dress code. **Societies** welcome. **Green Fees** not confirmed **Course Designer** Simon Gidman **Prof** Debbie Hanna **Facilities** ⓣ ⓘⓞⓣ ☎ ⌨ 🍴 ♨ ☏ 🏌 **Conf** Corporate Hospitality Days **Location** 2m from Bangor off A2 to Belfast **Hotel** ★★★★ 80% HL Clandeboye Lodge, 10 Estate Road, Clandeboye, BANGOR ☎ 028 9185 2500 ▤ 028 9185 2772 43 en suite

IRELAND

Save on Hotels. Book at **theAA.com/hotel**

CO DOWN

Carnalea Golf Club Station Rd BT19 1EZ

☎ 028 9127 0368 ▤ 028 9127 3989

e-mail: info@carnaleagolfclub.co.uk

web: www.carnaleagolfclub.co.uk

A scenic course on the shores of Belfast Lough.

18 Holes, 5716yds, Par 69. Club membership 1200.

Visitors Mon-Fri, Sun & BHs. Booking required. Dress code.
Societies welcome. **Green Fees** not confirmed ⊛ **Prof** Tom Loughran
Facilities ⑪ ⑩ ⓘ ▤ ⬜ ⬚ ▟ ⬚ ⬚ **Conf** facs
Corporate Hospitality Days **Location** 2m W next to railway station
Hotel ★★★★ 82% HL The Old Inn, 15 Main Street,
CRAWFORDSBURN ☎ 028 9185 3255 ▤ 028 9185 2775 31 en suite

Clandeboye Golf Club Tower Rd, Conlig, Newtownards BT23 3PN

☎ 028 9127 1767 ▤ 028 9147 3711

e-mail: office@cgc-ni.com

web: www.cgc-ni.com

Parkland and heathland courses. The Dufferin is the championship
course and offers a tough challenge demanding extreme accuracy,
with gorse, bracken and strategically placed trees that flank every
hole. Errors will be punished. The Ava compliments the Dufferin
perfectly. Accuracy is the key on this course with small targets and
demanding tee shots. Outstanding panoramic views.

Dufferin Course: 18 Holes, 6550yds, Par 71, SSS 72.
Ava Course: 18 Holes, 5755yds, Par 70, SSS 67.
Club membership 1238.

Visitors Mon-Fri, Sun & BHs. Booking required. Dress code.
Societies booking required. **Green Fees** Dufferin £40 (£45 weekends),
Ava £35 (£40 weekends) **Course Designer** Von Limburger/Alliss/
Thomas **Prof** Peter Gregory **Facilities** ⑪ ⑩ ⓘ ▤ ⬜ ⬚ ▟ ⬚
⬚ ⬚ ⬚ **Leisure** snooker, table tennis, indoor bowls **Conf** facs
Corporate Hospitality Days **Location** 2m S on A1 between Bangor &
Newtownards
Hotel ★★★★ 80% HL Clandeboye Lodge, 10 Estate Road,
Clandeboye, BANGOR ☎ 028 9185 2500 ▤ 028 9185 2772
43 en suite

Helen's Bay Golf Club Golf Rd, Helen's Bay BT19 1TL

☎ 028 9185 2815 & 9185 2601 ▤ 028 9185 2660

e-mail: mail@helensbaygc.com

web: www.helensbaygc.com

A parkland course on the shores of Belfast Lough with panoramic
views along the Antrim coast. The 4th hole par 3 is particularly
challenging as the green is screened by high trees.

9 Holes, 2795yds, Par 68, SSS 67, Course record 67.
Club membership 649.

Visitors Mon, Wed-Fri, Sun & BHs. Booking required. Dress code.
Societies Booking required. **Green Fees** £20 per 18 holes (£25 Fri-
Sun & BHs) ⊛ **Facilities** ⑪ ⑩ ⓘ ▤ ⬜ ⬚ ▟ ⬚ ⬚ ⬚
Conf facs **Location** A2 from Belfast
Hotel ★★★★ 82% HL The Old Inn, 15 Main Street,
CRAWFORDSBURN ☎ 028 9185 3255 ▤ 028 9185 2775 31 en suite

CARRYDUFF

Map 1 D5

Rockmount Golf Club 28 Drumalig Rd, Carryduff BT8 8EQ

☎ 028 9081 2279 ▤ 028 9081 5851

e-mail: rockmountgc@btconnect.com

web: www.rockmountgolfclub.com

A cleverly designed course incorporating natural features with water
coming into play as streams with a lake at the 11th and 14th.

18 Holes, 6373yds, Par 71, SSS 71, Course record 68.
Club membership 750.

Visitors Mon-Fri, Sun & BHs. **Societies** welcome. **Green Fees** £25
per round (£30 Sun) **Course Designer** Robert Patterson **Facilities** ⑪
⑩ ⓘ ▤ ⬜ ⬚ ▟ ⬚ ⬚ ⬚ **Conf** facs **Location** 10m S
of Belfast
Hotel ★★★ 83% HL Malmaison Belfast, 34 - 38 Victoria Street,
BELFAST ☎ 028 9022 0200 ▤ 028 9022 0220 64 en suite

CLOUGHEY

Map 1 D5

Kirkistown Castle Golf Club 142 Main Rd, Cloughey BT22 1JA

☎ 028 4277 1233 ▤ 028 4277 1699

e-mail: kirkistown@supanet.com

web: www.linksgolfkirkistown.com

A seaside part-links, designed by James Braid, popular with visiting
golfers because of its quiet location. The course is exceptionally dry
and remains open when others in the area have to close. The short but
treacherous par 4 15th hole was known as Braid's Hole. The 2nd and
10th holes are long par 4s with elevated greens, which are a feature
of the course. The 10th is particularly distinctive with a long drive and
a slight dog-leg to a raised green with a gorse covered motte waiting
for the wayward approach shot. It has the reputation of being one of
the hardest par 4s in Ireland.

18 Holes, 6167yds, Par 69, SSS 70, Course record 63.
Club membership 940.

Visitors Booking advisable. Dress code. **Societies** booking required.
Green Fees £25 per day (£30 weekends) **Course Designer** James
Braid **Prof** Neil Graham **Facilities** ⑪ ⑩ ⓘ ▤ ⬜ ⬚ ▟ ⬚
⬚ ⬚ ⬚ **Conf** Corporate Hospitality Days **Location** 16m from
Newtownards on A2
Hotel ★★★★ 82% HL The Old Inn, 15 Main Street,
CRAWFORDSBURN ☎ 028 9185 3255 ▤ 028 9185 2775 31 en suite

IRELAND

COMBER

Map 1 D5

Mahee Island Golf Club 14 Mahee Island, Comber BT23 6EP
☎ 028 9754 1234
e-mail: mahee_gents@hotmail.com
web: www.maheegolf.com

An undulating parkland course, almost surrounded by water, with magnificent views of Strangford Lough and its islands, with Scrabo Tower in the background. Undulating fairways and tricky greens make this a good test of golf.

9 Holes, 5882yds, Par 71, SSS 68, Course record 66.
Club membership 500.

Visitors Mon-Fri, Sun & BHs. Dress code **Societies** booking required. **Green Fees** £13 per round, £10 per 9 holes (£18/£13 Sun & BHs) **Course Designer** Mr Robinson **Facilities** ⊕ by prior arrangement ⊗ by prior arrangement ⬛ ⬚ 🏠 ⛳ ✦ **Location** off Comber-Killyleagh road, 0.5m from Comber
Hotel ★★★★ HL Clandeboye Lodge, 10 Estate Road, Clandeboye, BANGOR ☎ 028 9185 2500 ▤ 028 9185 2772 43 en suite

DONAGHADEE

Map 1 D5

Donaghadee Golf Club Warren Rd BT21 0PQ
☎ 028 9188 3624 ▤ 028 9188 8891
e-mail: office@donaghadeegolfclub.net
web: www.donaghadeegolfclub.com

Undulating seaside course, part links, part parkland, requiring a certain amount of concentration. Splendid views.

18 Holes, 5904yds, Par 71, SSS 70, Course record 63.
Club membership 1200.

Visitors dress code. **Societies** booking required. **Green Fees** £23 (£30 Sun) **Course Designer** Howard Swan **Prof** Gordon Drew **Facilities** ⊕ ⊗ ⬛ ⬚ 🏠 ⬚ ✦ ✦ **Conf** facs Corporate Hospitality Days **Location** 5m S of Bangor on Coast Rd
Hotel ★★★★ 82% HL The Old Inn, 15 Main Street, CRAWFORDSBURN ☎ 028 9185 3255 ▤ 028 9185 2775 31 en suite

DOWNPATRICK

Map 1 D5

Downpatrick Golf Club 43 Saul Rd BT30 6PA
☎ 028 44615947
e-mail: office@downpatrickgolfclub.org.uk
web: www.downpatrickgolfclub.org.uk

A classic parkland course with most holes boasting spectacular views of Co Down, Strangford Lough and even the Isle of Man, on a clear day. Undulating fairways, strategically placed sand traps and quick but true greens make the course a testing yet pleasurable challenge to golfers of all abilities.

18 Holes, 6020yds, Par 69, SSS 69, Course record 62.
Club membership 960.

Visitors Mon-Fri, Sun & BHs. Booking required Wed, Sun & BHs. Dress code. **Societies** booking required. **Green Fees** £23 per day (£28 Sun & BHs) **Course Designer** Hawtree & Son **Prof** Robert Hutton **Facilities** ⊕ ⊗ ⬛ ⬚ 🏠 ⬚ 🏠 ✦ ✦ **Location** 1.5m from town centre
Hotel ★★★★ INN The Cuan Licensed Guest Inn, 6-12 The Square, STRANGFORD ☎ 028 4488 1222 9 rooms

HOLYWOOD

Map 1 D5

Holywood Golf Club Nuns Walk, Demesne Rd BT18 9LE
☎ 028 9042 3135 ▤ 028 9042 5040
e-mail: mail@holywoodgolfclub.co.uk
web: www.holywoodgolfclub.co.uk

Hilly parkland course, providing some fine views and an interesting game. Several feature holes, including the short 6th 'Nuns Walk', fondly remembered by the many who have 'holed out in one'. In contrast, the treacherous 12th 'White House' is a most difficult par 4. The tee shot must be placed precisely on the fairway to allow the long approach to a green which is protected out of bounds to the right and a perilous drop to the left.

18 Holes, 6078mtrs, Par 69, SSS 68, Course record 62.
Club membership 950.

Visitors Contact club for details. **Societies** booking required. **Green Fees** phone **Prof** Stephen Crooks **Facilities** ⊕ ⊗ ⬛ ⬚ 🏠 ⬚ ✦ ✦ **Conf** Corporate Hospitality Days **Location** off Bangor dual carriageway
Hotel ★★★★ 82% HL The Old Inn, 15 Main Street, CRAWFORDSBURN ☎ 028 9185 3255 ▤ 028 9185 2775 31 en suite

The Royal Belfast Golf Club Station Rd BT18 0BP
☎ 028 9042 8165 ▤ 028 9042 1404
web: www.royalbelfast.com
18 Holes, 6185yds, Par 70, SSS 69.
Course Designer H C Colt **Location** 2m E on A2
Telephone for further details
Hotel ★★★★ 82% HL The Old Inn, 15 Main Street, CRAWFORDSBURN ☎ 028 9185 3255 ▤ 028 9185 2775 31 en suite

KILKEEL

Map 1 D5

Kilkeel Golf Club Mourne Park BT34 4LB
☎ 028 4176 5095 ▤ 028 4176 5579
e-mail: info@kilkeelgolfclub.org
web: www.kilkeelgolfclub

Picturesquely situated at the foot of the Mourne Mountains. Eleven holes have tree-lined fairways with the remainder in open parkland. A championship course which has hosted senior qualifying events.

18 Holes, 6579yds, Par 72, SSS 72, Course record 68.
Club membership 750.

Visitors Mon-Fri, Sun & BHs. Booking required. Dress code. **Societies** booking required. **Green Fees** not confirmed **Course Designer** Babington/Hackett **Facilities** ⊕ ⊗ ⬛ ⬚ 🏠 🏠 ✦ ✦ **Conf** facs Corporate Hospitality Days **Location** 3m from Kilkeel on Newry road

KILLYLEAGH

Map 1 D5

Ringdufferin Golf Course BT30 9PH
☎ 028 4482 8812 ▤ 028 4482 8972
web: www.ringdufferin.com
18 Holes, 5093mtrs, Par 68, SSS 66.
Course Designer Frank Ainsworth **Location** 2m N of Killyleagh
Telephone for further details
Hotel ★★★★ 85% CHH Ballynahinch Castle, Recess, Connemara, BALLYNAHINCH ☎ 095 31006 ▤ 095 31085 40 en suite

ROYAL COUNTY DOWN

CO DOWN - NEWCASTLE - MAP 1 D5

The Championship Course is consistently rated among the world's top ten courses. Laid out beneath the imperious Mourne Mountains, the course has a magnificent setting as it stretches out along the shores of Dundrum Bay. As well as being one of the most beautiful courses, it is also one of the most challenging, with great swathes of heather and gorse lining fairways that tumble beneath vast sand hills, and wild tussock-faced bunkers defending small, subtly contoured greens. The Annesley Links offers a less formidable yet extremely characterful game, played against the same incomparable backdrop. Substantially revised under the direction of Donald Steel, the course begins quite benignly before charging headlong into the dunes. Several charming and one or two teasing holes have been carved out amid the gorse, heather and bracken.

---

36 Golf Links Rd BT33 0AN ☎ 028 43723314 🖷 028 43726281
e-mail: golf@royalcountydown.org **web:** www.royalcountydown.org
Championship Course: 36 Holes, 6902yds, Par 71, SSS 74.
Annesley Links: 18 Holes, 4617yds, Par 66, SSS 65. Club membership 450.
Visitors Mon, Tue & Fri except BHs. Thu am. Sun pm. Booking required. Dress code. **Societies** booking required.
Green Fees Championship Course £165, £150 pm (£180 Sun). £250 per day per 36 holes **Course Designer** Tom Morris **Prof** Kevan Whitson **Facilities** ⑪ by prior arrangement ⓛ 🖵 🕾 ♨ 🏠 ♈ ✒ **Location** N of town centre off A24

MAGHERALIN
Map 1 D5

Edenmore Golf & Country Club Edenmore House, 70 Drumnabreeze Rd BT67 0RH
☎ 028 9261 9241 📄 028 9261 3310
e-mail: info@edenmore.com
web: www.edenmore.com

Set in mature parkland with gently rolling slopes. The front nine holes provide an interesting contrast to the back nine with more open play involved. Many paths and features have been added. The 13th hole, Edenmore, is the most memorable hole with a small lake protecting a contoured green.

18 Holes, 6278yds, Par 71, SSS 70. Club membership 650.

Visitors Mon-Sun & BHs. Booking required weekends & BHs. Dress code. **Societies** booking required. **Green Fees** £20 (£25 weekends & BHs) **Course Designer** F Ainsworth **Prof** Andrew Manson **Facilities** ⊕ ⏃ ⧠ ⊑ ⏦ ⎐ ⎔ ⧉ ☌ ⎔ ☌ **Leisure** sauna, gymnasium, 5 practice greens **Conf** facs Corporate Hospitality Days **Location** M1 Moira exit, through Moira towards Lurgan. Turn off in Magheralin, signed
Hotel ★★★★ 82% HL The Old Inn, 15 Main Street, CRAWFORDSBURN ☎ 028 9185 3255 📄 028 9185 2775 31 en suite

NEWCASTLE
Map 1 D5

Royal County Down Golf Club see page 427
36 Golf Links Rd BT33 0AN
☎ 028 43723314 📄 028 43726281
e-mail: golf@royalcountydown.org
web: www.royalcountydown.org

NEWTOWNARDS
Map 1 D5

Scrabo Golf Club 233 Scrabo Rd BT23 4SL
☎ 028 9181 2355 📄 028 9182 2919
e-mail: admin.scrabogc@btconnect.com
web: www.scrabo-golf-club.org

Hilly and picturesque, this heathland course stands on a 150-metre hill with rocky outcrops. The matured course has a totally natural layout with stunning views over the surrounding countryside.

18 Holes, 6270yds, Par 71, SSS 71, Course record 65. Club membership 700.

Visitors Mon-Sun & BHs. Booking required weekends & BHs. Dress code. Ladies day Wednesday. **Societies** booking required. **Green Fees** £19 per round (£24 Sun) **Prof** Scott Kirkpatrick **Facilities** ⊕ ⏦ ⊑ ⧠ ⏦ ⏃ ⎔ ⎔ ☌ **Conf** facs Corporate Hospitality Days **Location** outskirts of Newtownards on Ards peninsula, signs for Scrabo Country Park
Hotel ★★★★ 80% HL Clandeboye Lodge, 10 Estate Road, Clandeboye, BANGOR ☎ 028 9185 2500 📄 028 9185 2772 43 en suite

WARRENPOINT
Map 1 D5

Warrenpoint Golf Club Lower Dromore Rd BT34 3LN
☎ 028 4175 3695 📄 028 4175 2918
web: www.warrenpointgolf.com

18 Holes, 6108yds, Par 71, SSS 70, Course record 61.

Course Designer Tom Craddock/Pat Ruddy **Location** 1m W
Telephone for further details
Hotel ★★★★ 79% HL Ballymascanlon House Hotel, DUNDALK
☎ 042 9358200 📄 042 9371598 90 en suite

CO FERMANAGH

ENNISKILLEN
Map 1 C5

Ashwoods Golf Centre Sligo Rd BT74 7JY
☎ 028 6632 5321 & 6632 2908 📄 028 6632 9411

Only one mile from Enniskillen, this course is in open meadowland. It has been well planted with many young trees.

14 Holes, 1721yds, Par 42.

Visitors Mon-Sun & BHs. Booking required BHs. **Societies** booking required. **Green Fees** not confirmed ⊛ **Course Designer** P Loughran **Prof** L McCool **Facilities** ⊕ ⏦ by prior arrangement ⊑ ⧠ ⏃ ⎔ ⏦ ⎔ ☌ ⎔ **Conf** facs Corporate Hospitality Days **Location** 1.5m W of Enniskillen on Sligo road
Hotel ★★★★ 79% HL Killyhevlin Hotel & Health Club, ENNISKILLEN ☎ 028 6632 3481 📄 028 6632 4726 70 en suite

Castle Hume Golf Course Castle Hume, Belleek Rd BT93 7ED
☎ 028 6632 7077 📄 028 6632 7076
e-mail: info@castlehumegolf.com
web: www.castlehumegolf.com

Castle Hume is a particularly scenic and challenging course. Set in undulating parkland with large rolling greens, rivers, lakes and water hazards all in play on a championship standard course.

18 Holes, 5770mtrs, Par 72, SSS 70, Course record 69. Club membership 350.

Visitors handicap certificate. Dress code. **Societies** booking required. **Green Fees** £25/35 per 18 holes (£35/50 weekends and BHs) **Course Designer** B Browne **Prof** Shaun Donnelly **Facilities** ⊕ ⏦ ⊑ ⧠ ⏦ ⏃ ⎔ ⏦ ⎔ ☌ ⎔ ☌ **Leisure** heated indoor swimming pool, fishing, sauna, gymnasium **Conf** facs Corporate Hospitality Days **Location** 4m from Enniskillen on A46 Belleek-Donegal road
Hotel ★★★★ 79% HL Killyhevlin Hotel & Health Club, ENNISKILLEN ☎ 028 6632 3481 📄 028 6632 4726 70 en suite

Enniskillen Golf Club Castlecoole BT74 6HZ
☎ 028 6632 5250 📄 028 6632 5250
e-mail: enniskillengolfclub@mail.com
web: www.enniskillengolfclub.com
Tree-lined parkland course offering panoramic views of Enniskillen town and the surrounding lakeland area. Situated beside the National Trust's Castlecoole Estate.

18 Holes, 6145yds, Par 71, SSS 69. Club membership 550.

Visitors Mon-Sun & BHs. Booking required weekends & BHs. Dress code. **Societies** welcome. **Green Fees** £20 per day (£25 weekends & BHs) **Facilities** ⓘ by prior arrangement 🍴 by prior arrangement 🍺 🔽 🏌 ⚐ 🛒 🏌 **Conf** facs Corporate Hospitality Days **Location** 1m E of town centre
Hotel ★★★★ 79% HL Killyhevlin Hotel & Health Club, ENNISKILLEN ☎ 028 6632 3481 📄 028 6632 4726 70 en suite

Lough Erne Resort Belleek Rd BT93 7ED
☎ 028 6632 3230 📄 028 6634 5758
web: www.loughernegolfresort.com
Faldo Championship Course: 18 Holes, 7216yds, Par 72.
Course Designer Nick Faldo **Location** 4m N of Enniskillen on Enniskillen to Donegal road
Telephone for further details
Hotel ★★★★★ 86% HL Lough Erne Resort, Belleek Road, ENNISKILLEN ☎ 028 6632 3230 📄 028 6634 5758 120 en suite

---

CO LONDONDERRY

AGHADOWEY   Map 1 C6

Brown Trout Golf & Country Inn 209 Agivey Rd BT51 4AD
☎ 028 7086 8209 📄 028 7086 8878
web: www.browntroutinn.com
9 Holes, 5510yds, Par 70, SSS 68, Course record 64.
Course Designer Bill O'Hara Snr **Location** junct A54, 7m S of Coleraine
Telephone for further details
Hotel ★★★ 71% HL Brown Trout Golf & Country Inn, 209 Agivey Road, AGHADOWEY ☎ 028 7086 8209 📄 028 7086 8878 15 en suite

CASTLEDAWSON   Map 1 C5

Moyola Park Golf Club 15 Curran Rd BT45 8DG
☎ 028 7946 8468 & 7946 8830 (Prof) 📄 028 7946 8626
e-mail: moyolapark@btconnect.com
web: www.moyolapark.com
Parkland championship course with some difficult shots, calling for length and accuracy. The Moyola river provides a water hazard at the 8th. Newly designed par 3 17th demands good shot placement to a green on an island in the Moyola, when players' capabilities will be tested by the undulating green.

18 Holes, 6519yds, Par 71, SSS 71, Course record 67. Club membership 800.

Visitors Mon-Sun & BHs. Booking required. Dress code. **Societies** booking required. **Green Fees** Mon-Thu £24 per 18 holes (£30 Fri-Sun) **Course Designer** Don Patterson **Prof** Bob Cockcroft **Facilities** ⓘ 🍴 🏌 🔽 🍺 🏌 📷 ⚐ 🛒 🏌 **Conf** facs Corporate Hospitality Days **Location** club signed
Hotel ★★★★ 82% HL Galgorm Resort & Spa, BALLYMENA ☎ 028 2588 1001 📄 028 2588 0080 75 en suite

CASTLEROCK   Map 1 C6

Castlerock Golf Club 65 Circular Rd BT51 4TJ
☎ 028 7084 8314 📄 028 7084 9440
e-mail: info@castlerockgc.co.uk
web: www.castlerockgc.co.uk
A most exhilarating course with three superb par 4s, four testing short holes and five par 5s. After an uphill start, the hazards are many, including the river and a railway, and both judgement and accuracy are called for. The signature hole is the 4th, Leg of Mutton. A challenge in calm weather, any trouble from the elements will test your golf to the limits.

Mussenden Links: 18 Holes, 6747yds, Par 73, SSS 72, Course record 64.
Bann Course: 9 Holes, 4892yds, Par 68, SSS 66. Club membership 1251.

Visitors Mon-Sun & BHs. Booking required. Dress code. **Societies** booking required. **Green Fees** £80 per 36 holes, £65 per 18 holes (£80 day/round weekends & BHs) **Course Designer** Ben Sayers **Prof** Thomas Johnston **Facilities** ⓘ 🍴 🏌 🔽 🍺 🍵 📷 🛒 ⚐ 🛒 🏌 **Leisure** Short game practice area. **Conf** Corporate Hospitality Days **Location** 6m from Coleraine on A2
Hotel ★★★★★ FH Greenhill House, 24 Greenhill Road, Aghadowey, COLERAINE ☎ 028 7086 8241 📄 028 7086 8365 6 rooms

KILREA   Map 1 C5

Kilrea Golf Course 47a Lisnagrot Rd BT51 5TB
☎ 028 2954 0044
e-mail: kilreagc@hotmail.co.uk
web: www.kilreagolfclub.co.uk
Undulating inland course, winner of an environmental award and one of the driest to be found. Kilrea Golf Club was founded in 1919. Accuracy is required off the tee to give a fighting chance of par at most holes.

Kilrea: 9 Holes, 5696yds, Par 70, SSS 68. Club membership 300.

Visitors Mon-Sun & BHs. Booking required Tue, Wed & Sat. Dress code. **Societies** booking required. **Green Fees** £15 per day (£20 weekends) 🛒 **Course Designer** H McNeill **Facilities** ⓘ 🍴 🏌 🔽 🍺 🏌 **Location** From Kilrea town centre follow brown tourist signs for approx 0.5m
Hotel ★★★ 71% HL Brown Trout Golf & Country Inn, 209 Agivey Road, AGHADOWEY ☎ 028 7086 8209 📄 028 7086 8878 15 en suite

LIMAVADY   Map 1 C6

Benone Tourist Complex 53 Benone Ave BT49 0LQ
☎ 028 7775 0555 📄 028 7775 0919
9 Holes, 1459yds, Par 27.
Location between Coleraine & Limavady on A2
Telephone for further details
Hotel ★★★★ 75% HL Radisson Blu Roe Park Resort, LIMAVADY ☎ 028 7772 2222 📄 028 7772 2313 118 en suite

IRELAND

Radisson SAS Roe Park Resort BT49 9LB
☎ 028 7772 2222 📠 028 7772 2313
web: www.radissonroepark.com

18 Holes, 6283yds, Par 70, SSS 70, Course record 67.

Course Designer Frank Ainsworth **Location** just outside Limavady on A2 Ballykelly-Londonderry road
Telephone for further details
Hotel ★★★★ 75% HL Radisson Blu Roe Park Resort, LIMAVADY
☎ 028 7772 2222 📠 028 7772 2313 118 en suite

LONDONDERRY   Map 1 C5

City of Derry Golf Club 49 Victoria Rd BT47 2PU
☎ 028 7134 6369 📠 028 7131 0008
web: www.cityofderrygolfclub.com

Prehen Course: 18 Holes, 6406yds, Par 71, SSS 71, Course record 68.
Dunhugh Course: 9 Holes, 2354yds, Par 66, SSS 66.

Location 2m S
Telephone for further details
Hotel ★★★ 79% CHH Beech Hill Country House Hotel, 32 Ardmore Road, LONDONDERRY ☎ 028 7134 9279 📠 028 7134 5366 27 en suite

Foyle International Golf Centre 12 Alder Rd BT48 8DB
☎ 028 7135 2222 📠 028 7135 3967
e-mail: mail@foylegolf.club24.co.uk
web: www.foylegolfcentre.co.uk

Foyle International has a championship course, a nine-hole par 3 course and a driving range. It is a fine test of golf with water coming into play on the 3rd, 10th and 11th holes. The 6th green overlooks the Amelia Earhart centre.

Earhart: 18 Holes, 6639yds, Par 71, SSS 71, Course record 70.
Woodlands: 9 Holes, 1349yds, Par 27.
Club membership 320.

Visitors Mon-Sun & BHs. **Societies** booking required. **Green Fees** £17 (£20 weekends) **Course Designer** Frank Ainsworth **Prof** Derek Morrison & Sean Young **Facilities** ⊕ ⚑ ⓘ ⦾ 🏌 ♨ ⌂ 🍴 🏌 ♂
🏌 **Leisure** 9 hole par 3 course **Conf** facs Corporate Hospitality Days
Location 1.5m from Foyle Bridge towards Moville
Hotel ★★★★ 73% HL City Hotel, Queens Quay, LONDONDERRY
☎ 028 7136 5800 📠 028 7136 5801 146 en suite

PORTSTEWART   Map 1 C6

Portstewart Golf Club 117 Strand Rd BT55 7PG
☎ 028 7083 2015 & 7083 3839 📠 028 7083 4097
web: www.portstewartgc.co.uk

Strand Course: 18 Holes, 6784yds, Par 72, SSS 72, Course record 67.
Old Course: 18 Holes, 4733yds, Par 64, SSS 62.
Riverside: 9 Holes, 2622yds, Par 32.

Course Designer Des Giffin **Location**
Telephone for further details
Hotel ★★★ GA Beulah Guest House, 16 Causeway Street, PORTRUSH ☎ 028 7082 2413 9 rooms

CO TYRONE

COOKSTOWN   Map 1 C5

Killymoon Golf Club 200 Killymoon Rd BT80 8TW
☎ 028 8676 3762 & 8676 2254 📠 028 8676 3762
e-mail: killymoongolf@btconnect.com
web: www.killymoongolfclub.com

Parkland course on elevated, well-drained land. The signature hole is the aptly named 10th hole - the Giant's Grave. Accuracy is paramount here and a daunting tee shot into a narrow-necked fairway will challenge even the most seasoned golfer. The enclosing influence of the trees continues the whole way to the green.

18 Holes, 6202yds, Par 70, SSS 70, Course record 64.
Club membership 830.

Visitors Mon-Sun except BHs. Booking required. Dress code.
Societies booking required. **Green Fees** £16 per round Mon, £22 Tue-Fri, £28 weekends ⛳ **Course Designer** John Nash **Prof** Gary Chambers **Facilities** ⊕ ⓘ ⦾ 🏌 ♨ 🍴 ♨ ⌂ 🍴 ♂
Leisure snooker **Conf** facs Corporate Hospitality Days **Location** S of Cookstown
Hotel ★★ 72% HL Cohannon Inn & Auto Lodge, 212 Ballynakilly Road, DUNGANNON ☎ 028 8772 4488 📠 028 8775 2217 42 en suite

DUNGANNON   Map 1 C5

Dungannon Golf Club 34 Springfield Ln BT70 1QX
☎ 028 8772 2098 📠 028 8772 7338
e-mail: dungannongolfclub2009@hotmail.co.uk
web: www.dungannongolfclub.com

Parkland course with five par 3s and tree-lined fairways.

18 Holes, 6155yds, Par 72, SSS 70, Course record 62.
Club membership 1000.

Visitors Mon-Sun & BHs. Booking required. Dress code.
Societies booking required. **Green Fees** £20 per round (£25 weekends) ⛳ **Course Designer** Sam Bacon **Prof** Chris Jelly
Facilities ⊕ ⓘ ⦾ 🏌 ♨ 🍴 ♨ ⌂ 🍴 🚜 ♂ **Location** 0.5m outside town on Donaghmore road
Hotel ★★ 72% HL Cohannon Inn & Auto Lodge, 212 Ballynakilly Road, DUNGANNON ☎ 028 8772 4488 📠 028 8775 2217 42 en suite

NEWTOWNSTEWART   Map 1 C5

Newtownstewart Golf Club 38 Golf Course Rd BT78 4HU
☎ 028 8166 1466 📠 028 8166 2506
web: www.newtownstewartgolfclub.com

18 Holes, 5320mtrs, Par 70, SSS 69, Course record 65.

Course Designer Frank Pennick **Location** 2m SW on B84
Telephone for further details

OMAGH   Map 1 C5

Omagh Golf Club 83a Dublin Rd BT78 1HQ
☎ 028 8224 3160 📠 028 8224 3160
web: www.omaghgolfclub.co.uk

18 Holes, 5683mtrs, Par 71, SSS 70, Course record 65.

Course Designer Don Patterson **Location** S outskirts of town
Telephone for further details

IRELAND

Republic of

Ireland

Sally Gap, Co. Wicklow

CO CARLOW

BORRIS
Map 1 C3

Borris Golf Club Deerpark
☎ 059 9773310 📠 059 9773750
e-mail: borrisgolfclub@eircom.net

Testing parkland course with tree-lined fairways situated within the McMorrough Kavanagh Estate at the foot of Mount Leinster. Modern sand based greens.

9 Holes, 5680mtrs, Par 70, SSS 69. Club membership 550.

Visitors Mon-Sun & BHs. Booking required. Dress code.
Societies booking required. Green Fees not confirmed 😎
Facilities ⑪ 🍴 🖥 🔌 🏊 🛏 🚗 Location
Hotel ★★★★ CHH Mount Juliet Hotel, THOMASTOWN
☎ 056 7773000 📠 056 7773019 57 en suite

CARLOW
Map 1 C3

Carlow Golf Club Deerpark
☎ 059 9131695 📠 059 9140065
e-mail: carlowgolfclub@eircom.net
web: www.carlowgolfclub.com

Created in 1922 to a design by Cecil Barcroft, this testing and enjoyable course is set in a wild deer park, with beautiful dry terrain and a varied character. With sandy subsoil, the course is playable all year round. There are water hazards at the 2nd, 10th and 11th and only two par 5s, both offering genuine birdie opportunities.

18 Holes, 6025mtrs, Par 70, SSS 71. Course record 63. Oakpark: 9 Holes, 2564mtrs, Par 35, SSS 35, Course record 67. Club membership 1200.

Visitors Mon-Sat except BHs. Booking required. Handicap certificate. Dress code. Societies booking required. Green Fees 60 per round (70 Sat). Oakpark: 20 per 9/18 holes Course Designer Cecil Barcroft/Tom Simpson Prof Andrew Gilbert
Facilities ⑪ 🍴 🖥 🔌 🏊 🏇 🛏 🚗 🚙
Location 3km N of Carlow on N9
Hotel ★★★ 78% HL Seven Oaks, Athy Road, CARLOW
☎ 059 9131308 📠 059 9132155 89 en suite

TULLOW
Map 1 C3

Mount Wolseley Hotel, Spa, Golf & Country Club
☎ 059 9180100 📠 059 9152123
e-mail: sales@mountwolseley.ie
web: www.mountwolseley.ie

A magnificent setting, a few hundred yards from the banks of the River Slaney with its mature trees and lakes set against the backdrop of the East Carlow and Wicklow mountains. With wide landing areas the only concession for demanding approach shots to almost every green. There is water in play on 11 holes, with the 11th an all-water carry off the tee of 207yds. The 18th is a fine finishing hole - a fairway lined with mature oak trees, then a second shot uphill across a water hazard to a green.

18 Holes, 7198yds, Par 72, SSS 72, Course record 68. Club membership 300.

Visitors booking required weekends. Societies booking required.
Green Fees €40 per person Sun-Thu, €50 Fri & Sat Course Designer Christy O'Connor Jnr Facilities ⑪ 🍴 🖥 🔌 🏊 🛏
🚗 🚙 ♢ 🛏 🚗 Leisure heated indoor swimming pool, sauna, gymnasium, spa Conf facs Corporate Hospitality Days Location from Dublin take N7, then N9. At Castledermos take left
Hotel ★★★★ 80% HL Mount Wolseley Hotel, Spa & Country Club,
TULLOW ☎ 059 9180100 📠 059 9152123 143 en suite

CO CAVAN

BALLYCONNELL
Map 1 C4

Slieve Russell Hotel Golf & Country Club
☎ 049 9525090 📠 049 9526640
e-mail: slieve-golfclub@quinn-hotels.com
web: www.slieverussell.com

An 18-hole course opened in 1992 and rapidly establishing itself as one of the finest parkland courses in the country. Forming part of a 300 acre estate, including 50 acres of lakes, the course has been sensitively wrapped around the surrounding landscape. On the main course, the 2nd plays across water while the 16th has water surrounding the green. The course finishes with a 512 yard, par 5 18th.

18 Holes, 7001mtrs, Par 72, SSS 72, Course record 65. Club membership 700.

Visitors Contact club for details. Societies booking required. Green Fees 39 per round, 49 Sat (winter 35/ 45). Par 3 20 per 18 holes (winter 15) Course Designer Paddy Merrigan Prof Gordon Smyth
Facilities ⑪ 🍴 🖥 🔌 🏊 🏇 🛏 🚗 ♢ ♀ 🛏 🚗 ♀ 🏇
Leisure hard tennis courts, heated indoor swimming pool, sauna, gymnasium, par 3 nine hole course Conf facs Corporate Hospitality Days Location 4km E of Ballyconnell
Hotel ★★★★ BB Prospect Bay Lakeside Accommodation, Brackley Lake, BALLYCONNELL ☎ 049 9523930 4 rooms

BLACKLION
Map 1 C5

Blacklion Golf Club Toam
☎ 071 9853024 📠 071 9853024
e-mail: info@blacklion.ie
web: www.blackliongolf.com

Parkland course established in 1962, with coppices of woodland and mature trees. The lake comes into play on four holes and there are some magnificent views of the lake, islands and surrounding hills. It has been described as one of the best maintained scenic inland courses in Ireland.

9 Holes, 5858mtrs, Par 72, SSS 70. Club membership 350.

Visitors Mon-Sun & BHs. Societies booking required. Green Fees not confirmed Course Designer Eddie Hackett Facilities ⑪ 🍴 🖥 🔌
🔌 🏊 🛏 ♀ Leisure fishing, snooker Conf Corporate Hospitality Days Location from Blacklion village W towards Sligo on N16 for 0.5kms, course on right
Hotel ★★★★ 74% HL Sligo Park, Pearse Road, SLIGO
☎ 071 9190400 📠 071 9169556 137 en suite

CAVAN   Map 1 C4

County Cavan Golf Course Drumelis
☎ 049 4331541 ▤ 049 4331541
e-mail: cavangc@iol.ie
web: www.cavangolf.ie
Parkland course with number of mature trees, some over 100 years old. The closing six holes are an exacting challenge for both the handicap and professional golfer alike.

18 Holes, 5627mtrs, Par 70. Club membership 830.

Visitors Mon-Sun & BHs. Dress code. **Societies** welcome. **Green Fees** €20 per 18 holes before noon, €25 after noon **Course Designer** Eddie Hackett, Arthur Spring **Prof** Bill Noble **Facilities** ⓑ ▯ 🏐 🏌 🏠 ⛳ 🏌 🏌 **Location** on road towards Killeshandra

Hotel ★★★ 79% HL Kilmore, Dublin Road, CAVAN
☎ 049 4332288 ▤ 049 4332458 38 en suite

CO CLARE

ENNIS   Map 1 B3

Ennis Golf Club Drumbiggle
☎ 065 6824074 & 6865415   ▤ 065 6841848
e-mail: info@ennisgolfclub.com
web: www.ennisgolfclub.com
On rolling hills, this immaculately manicured course presents an excellent challenge to both casual visitors and aspiring scratch golfers, with tree-lined fairways and well-protected greens.

18 Holes, 5706mtrs, Par 70, SSS 70, Course record 66. Club membership 1313.

Visitors Mon-Sat & BHs. Booking required except Mon. Dress code. **Societies** welcome. **Green Fees** €30 per round (€35 Sat) **Prof** Martin Ward **Facilities** ⓑ �🍴 by prior arrangement 🏐 ▯ 🏌 🏌 🏠 🏌 🏌 ⛳ **Location** signed near town

Hotel ★★★ 80% HL Temple Gate, The Square, ENNIS
☎ 065 6823300 ▤ 065 6823322 70 en suite

Woodstock Golf and Country Club Shanaway Rd
☎ 065 6829463 & 6842406   ▤ 065 6820304
e-mail: proshopwoodstock@eircom.net
web: www.woodstockgolfclub.com
This parkland course is set in 63 hectares and includes four holes where water is a major hazard. The sand-based greens offer a consistent surface for putting. The layout takes in beautiful views of the surrounding countryside and the lake feature at the 7th hole is challenging.

18 Holes, 5864mtrs, Par 71, SSS 71. Club membership 350.

Visitors Mon-Sun & BHs. Booking required weekends & BHs. Dress code. **Societies** booking required. **Green Fees** €25 per 18 holes (€30 weekends & BHs), €15 per 9 holes **Course Designer** Arthur Spring **Facilities** ⓑ 🍴 🏐 ▯ 🏌 🏌 🏠 🏌 🏌 ⛳ 🏌 **Leisure** sauna, gymnasium **Conf** Corporate Hospitality Days **Location** off N85, follow signs for Caminch, left at garage off rdbt

Hotel ★★★ 80% HL Temple Gate, The Square, ENNIS
☎ 065 6823300 ▤ 065 6823322 70 en suite

KILKEE   Map 1 B3

Kilkee Golf Club East End
☎ 065 9056048 ▤ 065 9656977
web: www.kilkeegolfclub.ie
18 Holes, 5555mtrs, Par 70, SSS 69, Course record 68.
Course Designer Eddie Hackett **Location**
Telephone for further details

LAHINCH   Map 1 B3

Lahinch Golf Club
☎ 065 7081003 ▤ 065 7081592
e-mail: info@lahinchgolf.com
web: www.lahinchgolf.com
Originally designed by Tom Morris and later modified by Dr Alister MacKenzie, Lahinch has hosted every important Irish amateur fixture and the Home Internationals. The par five 4th - The Klondike - is played along a deep valley and over a huge dune; the par three 5th may be short, but calls for a blind shot over the ridge of a hill to a green hemmed in by hills on three sides.

Old Course: 18 Holes, 6349yds, Par 72, SSS 71.
Castle Course: 18 Holes, 5344yds, Par 69.
Club membership 1840.

Visitors Mon-Sun except BHs. Booking required. Handicap certificate. Dress code. **Societies** booking required. **Green Fees** Old Course 100, Castle Course 30 (125/ 30 weekends) **Course Designer** Alister MacKenzie/Old Tom Morris **Prof** R McCavery **Facilities** ⓑ 🍴 🏐 ▯ 🏌 🏌 🏠 🏌 🏌 ⛳ **Location** 3km W of Ennistymon on N67

Hotel ★★★ 78% HL Sheedys Country House, LISDOONVARNA
☎ 065 7074026 ▤ 065 7074555 11 en suite

MILLTOWN MALBAY   Map 1 B3

Spanish Point Golf Club
☎ 065 7084198 ▤ 065 7084263
web: www.spanish-point.com
9 Holes, 4950mtrs, Par 68, SSS 66, Course record 59.
Location 3km SW of Miltown Malbay on N67
Telephone for further details
Hotel ★★★★★ GH Moy House, LAHINCH ☎ 065 7082800
▤ 065 7082500 9 rooms

IRELAND

NEWMARKET-ON-FERGUS Map 1 B3

Dromoland Castle Golf & Country Club
☎ 061 368444 & 368144 ▤ 061 363355/368498
e-mail: golf@dromoland.ie
web: www.dromoland.ie

Set in 200 acres of parkland, the course is enhanced by numerous trees and a lake. Three holes are played around the lake which is in front of the castle.

18 Holes, 6240mtrs, Par 72, SSS 72, Course record 65. Club membership 500.

Visitors Mon-Sun & BHs. Booking required. Dress code. **Societies** booking required. **Green Fees** not confirmed **Course Designer** Ron Kirby & J. B. Carr **Prof** David Foley **Facilities** ⑪ ⑤l ⓗ ⬛ ⓗ ⬥ ⑭ ◇ ⑯ ⑰ ⑱ **Leisure** hard tennis courts, heated indoor swimming pool, fishing, sauna, gymnasium **Conf** facs Corporate Hospitality Days **Location** 3km N on Limerick-Galway road
Hotel ★★★★★ HL Dromoland Castle, NEWMARKET-ON-FERGUS ☎ 061 368144 ▤ 061 363355 99 en suite

CO CORK

BANDON Map 1 B2

Bandon Golf Club Castlebernard
☎ 023 884 1111 ▤ 023 884 4690
e-mail: enquiries@bandongolfclub.com
web: www.bandongolfclub.com

Lovely parkland in pleasant countryside. Hazards of water, sand and trees. The course has been extended around the picturesque ruin of Castle Barnard.

18 Holes, 5782mtrs, Par 71, SSS 71, Course record 66. Club membership 1100.

Visitors Mon, Tue, Fri & Sat except BHs. Dress code. **Societies** booking required. **Green Fees** €35 per 18 holes (€40 weekends) **Prof** Paddy O'Boyle **Facilities** ⑪ ⑤l ⓗ ⬛ ⓗ ⬥ ⑭ ◇ ⑯ ◇ **Leisure** hard tennis courts **Location** 2.5km W
Hotel ★★★★ BB Glebe Country House, Ballinadee, BANDON ☎ 021 4778294 ▤ 021 4778456 4 rooms

BANTRY Map 1 B2

Bantry Bay Golf Club Donemark
☎ 027 50579 ▤ 027 53790
e-mail: info@bantrygolf.com
web: www.bantrygolf.com

Designed by Christy O'Connor Jnr, this challenging and rewarding course is idyllically set at the head of Bantry Bay. Testing holes include the par 5 of 463 metres with the green on the shoreline and the par 3 ninth on top of a hill with stunning views of Bantry Bay.

18 Holes, 6144mtrs, Par 71, SSS 71, Course record 67. Club membership 600.

Visitors Booking required 24hrs in advance. **Societies** booking required. **Green Fees** €35 per 18 holes Oct-Apr (€40 May-Sep) **Course Designer** Christy O'Connor Jnr/Eddie Hackett **Facilities** ⑪ ⑤l ⓗ ⬛ ⓗ ⬥ ◇ **Conf** Corporate Hospitality Days **Location** 3km N of town on N71
Hotel ★★★ 74% HL Westlodge Hotel, BANTRY ☎ 027 50360 ▤ 027 50438 90 en suite

BLACKROCK Map 1 B2

Mahon Golf Course Clover Hill
☎ 021 4294280
e-mail: mahon@golfnet.ie
web: www.mahongolfclub.com

Parkland course along the Mahon estuary. Includes 6 holes where water makes a major contribution to the difficulty of play.

18 Holes, 5291metres, Par 70, SSS 68. Club membership 550.

Visitors Mon-Sun & BHs. Booking required. Dress code. **Societies** booking required. **Green Fees** not confirmed **Course Designer** Eddie Hackett **Facilities** ⑪ ⑤l ⓗ ⬛ ⓗ ⬥ ⑭ ◇ **Location**
Hotel ★★★★ 79% HL Ballymascanlon House Hotel, DUNDALK ☎ 042 9358200 ▤ 042 9371598 90 en suite

BLARNEY Map 1 B2

Blarney Golf Resort Tower
☎ 021 4384477 ▤ 021 4516453
e-mail: reservations@blarneygolfresort.com
web: www.blarneygolfresort.com

You will come across some of the best greens in Ireland as you wind your way along the course. Its location nestled in the stunning Shournagh Valley creates a great atmosphere with breathtaking views. The 601 yard par 5 has the signature of the designer, John Daly, written all over it.

18 Holes, 6712yds, Par 71, Course record 69.

Visitors Mon-Sun & BHs. Booking required. Handicap certificate. Dress code. **Societies** booking required. **Green Fees** not confirmed **Course Designer** John Daly **Prof** Alan O'Meara **Facilities** ⑪ ⑤l ⓗ ⬛ ⓗ ⬥ ⑭ ◇ ◇ ⑯ ◇ **Leisure** heated indoor swimming pool, sauna, gymnasium **Conf** facs Corporate Hospitality Days **Location**
Hotel ★★★★ 76% HL Blarney Golf Resort, Tower, BLARNEY ☎ 021 4384477 ▤ 021 4516453 117 en suite

FOTA ISLAND RESORT

CO CORK - CORK - MAP 1 B2

The landscape of this attractive course, set on a 780 acre island in Cork harbour, is magnificent. The Deerpark Course was designed in 1993 by Christy O'Connor and Peter McEvoy and upgraded in 1999 under the direction of the Canadian designer, Jeff Howes. In recent years it has been transformed by the addition of nine new holes. These have been incorporated into the original design, with the result that three courses have now been created, depending on how the new holes are combined with the existing ones. In addition to this innovative development, there is a hi-tech golf academy where computer systems can analyse your swing, either on the spot, or by e-mail! All this, coupled with the luxurious clubhouse and hotel complex, make this course akin to an American style country club.

Fota Island ☎ 021 4883700 🖹 021 4883713
e-mail: reservations@fotaisland.ie **web:** www.fotaisland.ie
Deerpark: 18 Holes, 6334mtrs, Par 71, SSS 73, Course record 63.
Belvelly: 18 Holes, 6511mtrs, Par 72.
Barryscourt: 18 Holes, 6732mtrs, Par 73. Club membership 600.
Visitors Mon-Sun & BHs. Booking required. Dress code. **Societies** welcome. **Green Fees** phone
Course Designer Jeff Howes **Prof** Kevin Morris **Facilities** ⊕ ⊗ ⊾ ⊡ ⊹ ⅄ 🖷 ⅊ ◇ ⅋ ⊜ ⟋ 🐾
Leisure heated indoor swimming pool, sauna, gymnasium, golf academy, spa treatments **Conf facs** Corporate Hospitality Days **Location** E of Cork. N25 exit for Cobh, 500mtrs on right
Hotel ★★★★ 78% HL Silver Springs Moran, Tivoli, CORK ☎ 021 4507533 🖹 021 4507641 109 en suite

CASTLETOWNBERE (CASTLETOWN BEARHAVEN)
Map 1 A2

Berehaven Golf Club Millcove
☎ 027 70700 🗐 027 71957
e-mail: info@berehavengolf.com
web: www.berehavengolf.com

Scenic seaside links founded in 1902. Moderately difficult with four holes over water. Testing nine-hole course with different tee positions for the back nine. Water is a dominant feature and comes into play at every hole.

9 Holes, 4793mtrs, Par 68, SSS 70. Club membership 200.

Visitors Mon-Sun & BHs. Dress code. **Societies** booking required. **Green Fees** not confirmed **Course Designer** Royal Navy **Facilities** ⑪ 🍽 🍺 ☕ 🍴 ⚐ ⚒ 🏌 **Leisure** hard tennis courts, sauna **Conf** facs Corporate Hospitality Days **Location** 3km E from Castletownbere on R572

Hotel ★★★ HL Sea View House Hotel, BALLYLICKEY ☎ 027 50073 & 50462 🗐 027 51555 25 en suite

CHARLEVILLE
Map 1 B2

Charleville Golf Club
☎ 063 81257 & 81515 🗐 063 81274
web: www.charlevillegolf.com

West Course: 18 Holes, 5680metres, Par 71, SSS 69, Course record 65.
East Course: 9 Holes, 6128metres, Par 72, SSS 72.

Course Designer Murphy/Barry (West)/Connaughton (East) **Location** 3km W of town centre
Telephone for further details
Hotel ★★★ 75% HL Springfort Hall Country House Hotel, MALLOW ☎ 022 21278 🗐 022 21557 49 en suite

CLONAKILTY
Map 1 B2

Dunmore Golf Course, Dunmore, Muckross
☎ 023 883 4644
e-mail: dunmoregolfclub@gmail.com
web: www.dunmoregolfclub.ie

A hilly, rocky 9-hole course overlooking the Atlantic.

9 Holes, 4082metres, Par 64, SSS 61, Course record 57. Club membership 380.

Visitors Mon-Fri except BHs. Dress code. **Societies** booking required. **Green Fees** not confirmed 🅿 **Course Designer** E Hackett **Facilities** ⑪ 🍽 🍺 ☕ 🍴 ⚐ ◇ 🏌 **Location** 5.5km S of Clonakilty

Hotel ★★★★ 83% HL Inchydoney Island Lodge & Spa, CLONAKILTY ☎ 023 8833143 🗐 023 8835229 67 en suite

CORK
Map 1 B2

Cork Golf Club Little Island
☎ 021 4353451 🗐 021 4353410
e-mail: info@corkgolfclub.ie
web: www.corkgolfclub.ie

This championship-standard course is kept in superb condition and is playable all year round. Memorable and distinctive features include holes at the water's edge and in a disused quarry. The 4th hole is considered to be among the most attractive and testing holes in Irish golf.

18 Holes, 5910mtrs, Par 72, SSS 72, Course record 67. Club membership 750.

Visitors booking required. Handicap certificate. Dress code. **Societies** booking required. **Green Fees** 85 (95 weekends) **Course Designer** Alister MacKenzie **Prof** Peter Hickey **Facilities** ⑪ 🍽 🍺 ☕ 🍴 ⚐ 🛆 🎣 🏌 **Conf** Corporate Hospitality Days **Location** 8km E of Cork on N25

Hotel ★★★★ 78% HL Silver Springs Moran, Tivoli, CORK ☎ 021 4507533 🗐 021 4507641 109 en suite

Fota Island see page 433
Fota Island
☎ 021 4883700 🗐 021 4883713
e-mail: reservations@fotaisland.ie
web: www.fotaisland.ie

Muskerry Golf Club Carrigrohane
☎ 021 4385297 🗐 021 4516860
e-mail: muskgc@eircom.net
web: www.muskerrygolfclub.ie

An adventurous game is guaranteed at this course, with its wooded hillsides and the meandering Shournagh River coming into play at a number of holes. The 15th is a notable hole - not long, but very deep - and after that all you need to do to get back to the clubhouse is stay out of the water.

18 Holes, 5520mtrs, Par 71, SSS 70. Club membership 851.

Visitors Mon & Tue. Wed & Thu am. Weekends pm. Booking required. Handicap certificate. Dress code. **Societies** booking required. **Green Fees** 30 per round (40 weekends) **Course Designer** Dr A McKenzie **Prof** W M Lehane **Facilities** ⑪ 🍺 ☕ 🍴 🛆 🏠 ⚐ 🏌 **Location** 4km W of Blarney

Hotel ★★★★ 76% HL Blarney Golf Resort, Tower, BLARNEY ☎ 021 4384477 🗐 021 4516453 117 en suite

The Ted McCarthy Municipal Golf Course Blackrock
☎ 021 4292543 🗐 021 4292604
web: www.mahongolfclub.com

18 Holes, 5033mtrs, Par 70, SSS 66, Course record 65.

Course Designer E Hackett **Location** 3km from city centre
Telephone for further details
Hotel ★★★★ 78% HL Silver Springs Moran, Tivoli, CORK ☎ 021 4507533 🗐 021 4507641 109 en suite

DOUGLAS — Map 1 B2

Douglas Golf Club
☎ 021 4895297 📠 021 4367200
e-mail: admin@douglasgolfclub.ie
web: www.douglasgolfclub.ie
Well-maintained, relatively flat parkland course with panoramic views from the clubhouse. All tees and greens constructed to full USGA specifications.

18 Holes, 6056mtrs, Par 72, SSS 71, Course record 64. Club membership 900.

Visitors Mon, Wed-Sun & BHs. Booking required. **Societies** booking required. **Green Fees** €40 per round (€45 weekends and BHs) **Course Designer** Peter McEvoy **Prof** Stephen Hayes **Facilities** ⊕ ℃ ⅃ ☐ ☐ ♨ ♨ ⚑ ✈ ✈ ✈ **Location** 6km S of Cork
Hotel ★★★★ 80% HL Maryborough Hotel & Spa, Maryborough Hill, DOUGLAS ☎ 021 4365555 📠 021 4365662 93 en suite

FERMOY — Map 1 B2

Fermoy Golf Club Corrin Cross
☎ 025 32694 (office) & 31472 (shop) 📠 025 33072
web: www.fermoygolfclub.ie
18 Holes, 5596mtrs, Par 70, SSS 69, Course record 66.
Course Designer John Harris **Location** S of town off N8, signed
Telephone for further details
Hotel ★★★★ BB Abbeyville House, Abercomby Place, FERMOY ☎ 025 32767 📠 025 32767 6 rooms

GLENGARRIFF — Map 1 B2

Glengarriff Golf Course
☎ 027 63150 📠 027 63575
9 Holes, 2042metres, Par 66, SSS 62.
Location on N71
Telephone for further details
Hotel ★★★ 74% HL Westlodge Hotel, BANTRY ☎ 027 50360 📠 027 50438 90 en suite

KANTURK — Map 1 B2

Kanturk Golf Club Fairyhill
☎ 029 50534 📠 029 20951
e-mail: kanturkgolfclub@eircom.net
web: www.kanturkgolf.com
Scenic parkland course set in the heart of the Duhallow region with superb mountain views. It provides a good test of skill for golfers of all standards, with tight fairways requiring accurate driving and precise approach shots to small and tricky greens.

18 Holes, 5433mtrs, Par 71, SSS 69, Course record 67. Club membership 600.

Visitors Mon-Sun & BHs. Booking required. **Societies** booking required **Green Fees** not confirmed 🔒 **Course Designer** Richard Barry **Facilities** ⊕ by prior arrangement ℃ by prior arrangement ⅃ ☐ ☐ ♨ ♨ ⚑ **Conf** Corporate Hospitality Days
Location 1.6km SW of Kanturk
Hotel ★★★ 75% HL Gougane Barra, Gougane Barra, BALLINGEARY ☎ 026 47069 📠 026 47226 26 en suite

KINSALE — Map 1 B2

Kinsale Golf Club Farrangalway
☎ 021 4774722 📠 021 4773114
web: www.kinsalegolf.com
Farrangalway: 18 Holes, 6043mtrs, Par 71, SSS 71, Course record 70.
Ringenane: 9 Holes, 4936mtrs, Par 70, SSS 66.
Course Designer Jack Kenneally **Location** Farrangalway course N off R607, Ringenane course N off R600
Telephone for further details

Old Head Golf Links
☎ 021 4778444 📠 021 4778022
e-mail: info@oldhead.com
web: www.oldhead.com
Spectacular location on a promontory jutting out into the Atlantic. As well as bringing the sea and cliffs into play, you have to contend with strong prevailing winds - a fine test for serious golfers.

18 Holes, 6583mtrs, Par 72, SSS 73. Club membership 420.

Visitors Mon-Sun & BHs. Booking required. Dress code.
Societies booking required. **Green Fees** €200 per 18 holes, €300 per 36 holes Twilight after 3pm €160 **Course Designer** R Kirby/J Carr/P Merrigan/E Hackett **Prof** Danny Brassil **Facilities** ⊕ ℃ ⅃ ☐ ♨ ⚑ ♦ ⚑ ✈ **Leisure** sauna, gymnasium, spa & beauty treatment rooms **Conf** facs Corporate Hospitality Days
Location On R600 towards Cork, signed
Hotel ★★★ 74% HL Blue Haven, 3 Pearse Street, KINSALE ☎ 021 4772209 📠 021 4774268 17 en suite

MACROOM — Map 1 B2

Macroom Golf Club, Lackaduve
☎ 026 41072 & 42615 📠 026 41391
e-mail: mcroomgc@iol.ie
web: www.macroomgolfclub.com
A particularly scenic parkland course located on undulating ground along the banks of the River Sullane. Bunkers and mature trees make a variable and testing course and the 12th has a 73-metre carry over the river to the green.

18 Holes, 5574mtrs, Par 71, SSS 69, Course record 65. Club membership 840.

Visitors booking required Wed, Fri-Sun & BHs. Dress code.
Societies booking required. **Green Fees** €30 per day (€35 weekends & BHs). Early Bird Mon-Thu until 10.30am €20 **Course Designer** Jack Kenneally/Eddie Hackett **Facilities** ⊕ ℃ ⅃ ☐ ☐ ♨ ♨ ⚑ **Location** through castle entrance in town square

IRELAND

MALLOW
Map 1 B2

Mallow Golf Club Ballyellis
☎ 022 21145 📠 022 42501
e-mail: mallowgolfclubmanager@eircom.net
web: www.mallowgolfclub.net

Mallow Golf Club was established in the late 19th century. A well-wooded parkland course overlooking the Blackwater Valley, Mallow is straightforward, but no less of a challenge for it. The front nine is by far the longer, but the back nine is demanding in its call for accuracy and the par 3 18th provides a tough finish.

18 Holes, 5960mtrs, Par 72, SSS 72, Course record 66. Club membership 800.

Visitors Mon-Sun & BHs. Booking required Tue, Fri-Sun & BHs. **Societies** booking required. **Green Fees** 35 per round (40 weekends & BHs). Special rates Mon-Fri before 11am. **Course Designer** D W Wishart **Prof** Sean Conway **Facilities** ⊕ ⊚ 🍴 🎮 🏌 ⛳ **Leisure** hard tennis courts, squash **Location** 1.6km E of Mallow
Hotel ★★★ 75% HL Gougane Barra, Gougane Barra, BALLINGEARY ☎ 026 47069 📠 026 47226 26 en suite

MIDLETON
Map 1 C2

East Cork Golf Club Gortacrue
☎ 021 4631687 & 4631273 📠 021 4613695
e-mail: eastcorkgolfclub@eircom.net
web: www.eastcorkgolfclub.com
A well-wooded course calling for accuracy of shots.

18 Holes, 5152mtrs, Par 69, SSS 66, Course record 64. Club membership 820.

Visitors Mon-Sun & BHs. Booking required Mon, weekends & BHs. **Societies** booking requested **Green Fees** not confirmed **Course Designer** E Hackett **Prof** Don MacFarlane **Facilities** ⊕ ⊚ 🍴 🎮 ⛳ **Location** 3km N of Midleton on A626
Hotel ★★★★ 75% HL Garryvoe, Ballycotton Bay, Castlemartyr, GARRYVOE ☎ 021 4646718 📠 021 4646824 82 en suite

Water Rock Golf Course Water Rock
☎ 021 4613499
web: www.waterrockgolfcourse.com
18 Holes, 5690mtrs, Par 70, SSS 70.
Course Designer Patrick Merrigan **Location** next to N25 on outskirts of Midleton
Telephone for further details
Hotel ★★★★★ GH Ballymaloe House, SHANAGARRY
☎ 021 4652531 📠 021 4652021 30 rooms

MITCHELSTOWN
Map 1 B2

Mitchelstown Golf Club Limerick Rd
☎ 025 24072 & 086 8263089 📠 025 86631
web: www.mitchelstown-golf.com
18 Holes, 5773mtrs, Par 71, SSS 71.
Course Designer David Jones **Location** 1km from Mitchelstown
Telephone for further details
Hotel ★★★★ BB Abbeyville House, Abercomby Place, FERMOY
☎ 025 32767 📠 025 32767 6 rooms

MONKSTOWN
Map 1 B2

Monkstown Golf Club Parkgariffe
☎ 021 4841376
web: www.monkstowngolfclub.com

18 Holes, 5441mtrs, Par 70, SSS 68, Course record 66.
Course Designer Peter O'Hare & Tom Carey **Location** 0.8km SE of Monkstown
Telephone for further details

SKIBBEREEN
Map 1 B2

Skibbereen & West Carbery Golf Club Licknavar
☎ 028 21227 📠 028 22994
web: www.skibbgolf.com
18 Holes, 5490mtrs, Par 71, SSS 69, Course record 66.
Course Designer Jack Kenneally **Location** 1.6km SW on R595
Telephone for further details
Hotel ★★★ BB Ilenroy House, 10 North Street, SKIBBEREEN
☎ 028 22751 & 22193 📠 028 23228 5 rooms

YOUGHAL
Map 1 C2

Youghal Golf Club Knockaverry
☎ 024 92787 & 92861 📠 024 92641
web: www.youghalgolfclub.ie
18 Holes, 5976mtrs, Par 71, SSS 71, Course record 66.
Course Designer Jeff Howes Golf Design **Location** off N25
Telephone for further details
Hotel ★★★★ 82% HL Cliff House, ARDMORE ☎ 024 87800 & 87801 📠 024 87820 39 en suite

IRELAND

CO DONEGAL

BALLYBOFEY   Map 1 C5

Ballybofey & Stranorlar Golf Club Stranorlar
☎ 074 9131093 ▯ 074 9130158
e-mail: info@ballybofeyandstranorlargolfclub.com
web: www.ballybofeyandstranorlargolfclub.com

A most scenic course incorporating pleasant valleys backed by mountains with three of its holes bordered by a lake. There are three par 3s on the first nine and two on the second. The most difficult hole is the long uphill par 4 16th. The only par 5 is the 7th.

18 Holes, 5366mtrs, Par 68, SSS 68, Course record 64. Club membership 648.

Visitors Mon-Sun & BHs. Booking required Tue, weekends & BHs. Timesheet in operation. **Societies** booking required. **Green Fees** €20 (€25 weekends) **Course Designer** P C Carr **Facilities** ⑪ ⑩ ⬛ 🖵 🗗 ⬜ 🛇 🗑 🎶 🦯 🦯 **Location** 0.4km E of Stranorlar

BALLYLIFFIN   Map 1 C6

Ballyliffin Golf Club
☎ 074 9376119 ▯ 074 9376672
e-mail: info@ballyliffingolfclub.com
web: www.ballyliffingolfclub.com

The Old links is a traditional course with rolling fairways, surrounded by sand dunes and bounded on one side by the ocean and has been upgraded by Nick Faldo. The 18-hole Glashedy course is a modern championship links with large greens and revetted bunkers. Both courses have hosted top Amateur and European Tour events.

Old Links: 18 Holes, 6318mtrs, Par 71, SSS 72, Course record 67.
Glashedy Links: 18 Holes, 6599mtrs, Par 72, SSS 74, Course record 67. Club membership 1400.

Visitors Mon-Sun & BHs. Booking required. Handicap certificate preferred. Dress code. **Societies** booking required. **Green Fees** Old Links €70. Glashedy €80 **Course Designer** Nick Faldo/Tom Craddock/ Pat Ruddy **Prof** John Farren **Facilities** ⑪ ⑩ ⬛ 🖵 🗗 ⬜ 🏠 🎶 🦯 🖻 🦯 🏌 **Conf** facs Corporate Hospitality Days **Location** off R238

BUNCRANA   Map 1 C6

Buncrana Golf Club Railway Rd, Ballymacarry
☎ 074 9362279 & 074 9320749
e-mail: buncranagc@eircom.net
web: www.buncranagolfclub.com

A nine-hole course with a very challenging par 3 3rd hole with all carry out of bounds on either side. Situated on the banks of The White Strand, overlooking the beautiful Lough Swilly. The 9 hole course offers a challenge to golfers of all ability.

9 Holes, 4492mtrs, Par 66, SSS 64, Course record 62. Club membership 200.

Visitors Mon-Sun & BHs. Booking required weekends & BHs. Handicap certificate. **Societies** booking required. **Green Fees** €8-€15 per round ⊛ **Prof** Jim Doherty **Facilities** 🖵 ⬜ 🏠 🦯 **Conf** facs **Location** 1st left on entering Buncrana beside Tourist Information Office
Hotel ★★★★ BB Mount Royd Country Home, CARRIGANS
☎ 074 914 0163 ▯ 074 914 0400 4 rooms

North West Golf Club Lisfannon
☎ 074 9361715 ▯ 074 9363284
web: www.northwestgolfclub.com

18 Holes, 5457mtrs, Par 70, SSS 70, Course record 64.

Course Designer Thompson Davy **Location** 1.6km S of Buncrana on R238
Telephone for further details
Hotel ★★★★ BB Mount Royd Country Home, CARRIGANS
☎ 074 914 0163 ▯ 074 914 0400 4 rooms (4 en suite)

BUNDORAN   Map 1 B5

Bundoran Golf Club
☎ 071 9841302 ▯ 071 9842014
e-mail: bundorangolfclub@eircom.net
web: www.bundorangolfclub.com

This popular course, acknowledged as one of the best in the country, runs along the high cliffs above Bundoran beach and has a difficult par of 70. Designed by Harry Vardon, it offers a challenging game of golf in beautiful surroundings and has been the venue for a number of Irish golf championships.

18 Holes, 5729metres, Par 70, SSS 71. Club membership 770.

Visitors Mon-Sun & BHs. Handicap certificate. Dress code. **Societies** welcome. **Green Fees** not confirmed **Course Designer** Harry Vardon **Prof** David T Robinson **Facilities** ⬛ 🖵 🗗 ⬜ 🏠 🎶 🖻 🦯 **Location** off Main St onto Sligo-Derry road
Hotel ★★★★ GH Dún Na Sí, Bundoran Road, BALLYSHANNON
☎ 071 985 2322 & 085 122 2813 7 rooms

DUNFANAGHY   Map 1 C6

Dunfanaghy Golf Club Kill
☎ 074 9136335 ▯ 074 9136684
web: www.dunfanaghygolfclub.com

18 Holes, 5247mtrs, Par 68, SSS 66, Course record 63.

Course Designer Harry Vardon **Location** 30m W of Letterkenny on N56
Telephone for further details
Hotel ★★★ 74% HL Arnold's Hotel, DUNFANAGHY ☎ 074 9136208 ▯ 074 9136352 30 en suite

GREENCASTLE   Map 1 C6

Greencastle Golf Club Greencastle
☎ 074 9381013 ▯ 074 9381015
e-mail: b_mc_caul@yahoo.com
web: www.greencastlegc.com

A links course along the shores of Lough Foyle, surrounded by rocky headlands and sandy beaches.

18 Holes, 5293mtrs, Par 69, SSS 68, Course record 66. Club membership 680.

Visitors Mon-Sun & BHs. Booking weekends. Dress code. **Societies** booking required. **Green Fees** €25 per day **Course Designer** E Hackett/D Jones **Facilities** ⑪ ⑩ ⬛ 🖵 🗗 ⬜ 🏠 🎶 🦯 🖻 🦯 **Location**
Hotel ★★★★ 75% HL Ballyliffin Lodge & Spa, Shore Road, BALLYLIFFIN ☎ 074 9378200 ▯ 074 9378985 40 en suite

IRELAND

GWEEDORE

Map 1 B6

Gweedore Golf Course Derrybeg
☎ 074 9531140
e-mail: eugenemccafferty@hotmail.com
web: www.gweedoregolfclub.com

With breathtaking scenery, this 9-hole links course provides plenty of challenge with two subtle par 3s and the par 5 5th/14th at 556yards into the prevailing west wind is a monster.

9 Holes, 5699mtrs, Par 71, SSS 68, Course record 65. Club membership 150.

Visitors Mon-Sun & BHs. Booking required. Dress code. **Societies** booking required. **Green Fees** €20 per day 🌐 **Course Designer** Danny Molloy **Facilities** 🅱 🖵 🍴 🏌 ⛳ 🏌 **Conf** Corporate Hospitality Days **Location** 37m NW of Letterkenny on N56

LETTERKENNY

Map 1 C5

Letterkenny Golf Club Barnhill
☎ 074 9121150 📠 074 9121175
e-mail: info@letterkennygolfclub.com
web: www.letterkennygolfclub.com

The fairways are wide and generous, but the rough, when you find it, is short, tough and mean. The flat and untiring terrain on the shores of Lough Swilly provides good holiday golf. The first 11 holes have been redesigned to incorporate seven lakes and five greens and bunkers on all holes. The next seven holes have also been redesigned with bunkers and fairway mounding and two new greens.

18 Holes, 5705mtrs, Par 72, SSS 71, Course record 65. Club membership 700.

Visitors booking required Tue-Thu pm & weekends am. Dress code. **Societies** booking required **Green Fees** €25 per 18 holes (€35 weekends & BHs) **Course Designer** Eddie Hacket/Declan Branigan **Facilities** 🍴 🖵 🅱 🖵 🍴 🏌 🛏 🏌 **Conf** facs Corporate Hospitality Days **Location** 3km NE of town on R245
Hotel ★★★ 74% HL Downings Bay, Downings, LETTERKENNY ☎ 074 9155586 & 9155770 📠 074 9154716 40 en suite

MOVILLE

Map 1 C6

Redcastle Golf Course
☎ 074 9385555 📠 074 9385444
web: www.carltonredcastlehotel.com

9 Holes, 2846mtrs, Par 35.

Location 6km SW on R238
Telephone for further details

NARIN (NARAN)

Map 1 B5

Narin & Portnoo Golf Club
☎ 074 9545107 📠 074 9545994
e-mail: narinportnoo@eircom.net
web: www.narinportnoogolfclub.ie

Seaside links with every hole presenting its own special feature, the signature hole being the chasm-crossing 8th. One of the few natural links layouts remaining, with undulating fairways and greens. Fine views of Gweebarra Bay are visible from the course with an adjacent award winning beach. The links will test a player's iron play, with raised greens a common feature.

18 Holes, 6269mtrs, Par 73, SSS 73, Course record 69. Club membership 700.

Visitors booking required weekends & BHs. **Societies** booking required. **Green Fees** not confirmed **Course Designer** Leo Wallace/Hugh McNeill **Prof** Connor Mallon **Facilities** 🍴 🅱 🖵 🍴 🏌 🛏 ⛳ 🏌 **Conf** Corporate Hospitality Days **Location** off R261
Hotel ★★★★ GH Dún Na Sí, Bundoran Road, BALLYSHANNON ☎ 071 985 2322 & 085 122 2813 7 rooms

PORTSALON

Map 1 C6

Portsalon Golf Club
☎ 074 9159459 📠 074 9159919
e-mail: portsalongolfclub@eircom.net
web: www.portsalongolfclub.com

Another course blessed by nature. The golden beaches of Ballymastocker Bay lie at one end, while the beauty of Lough Swilly and the Inishowen Peninsula beyond is a distracting but pleasant feature to the west. Situated on the Fanad Peninsula, this lovely links course provides untiring holiday golf at its best. North West Ireland European Golf Destination of the Year 2011.

18 Holes, 6200mtrs, Par 72, SSS 72, Course record 69. Club membership 450.

Visitors Mon-Sun & BHs. Booking required. Handicap certificate. Dress code. **Societies** booking required. **Green Fees** €40 per 18 holes (€50 weekends & BHs) **Course Designer** Pat Ruddy **Prof** Seamus Clinton **Facilities** 🍴 🅱 🖵 🍴 € 🛏 🏌 **Conf** Corporate Hospitality Days **Location** 22m N of Letterkenny on R246
Hotel ★★★ 80% HL Fort Royal Hotel, Fort Royal, RATHMULLAN ☎ 074 9158100 📠 074 9158103 15 en suite

RATHMULLAN

Map 1 C6

Otway Golf Course Whiteleas, Ramelton
☎ 074 9158319 & 9151665
e-mail: otway_golf_club@eircom.net

One of the oldest courses in Ireland, created in 1861 by British military personnel as a recreational facility.

9 Holes, 3872mtrs, Par 64, SSS 60, Course record 60. Club membership 112.

Visitors contact course for details **Societies** booking required. **Green Fees** not confirmed **Facilities** 🍴 🏌 **Conf** Corporate Hospitality Days **Location** In Rathmullan, turn left at Mace convenience store, head for Knockalla coast Rd. 2m signed
Hotel ★★★ 80% HL Fort Royal Hotel, Fort Royal, RATHMULLAN ☎ 074 9158100 📠 074 9158103 15 en suite

ROSEPENNA
Map 1 C6

Rosapenna Golf Club Downings
☎ 074 9155301 & 9155000 📠 074 9155128
e-mail: golf@rosapenna.ie
web: www.rosapenna.ie

Dramatic links courses offering a challenging round. Originally designed by Tom Morris and later modified by James Braid and Harry Vardon, it includes features such as bunkers in mid-fairway. The best part of the links runs in the low valley along the ocean. The Sandy Hills links course is newer, having opened in 2003. Both courses are considered among the best in Ireland.

Old Tom Morris: 18 Holes, 5734mtrs, Par 70, SSS 71. Sandy Hills Links: 18 Holes, 7177ydsmtrs, Par 71. Club membership 400.

Visitors contact club for details. **Societies** booking required **Green Fees** Old Tom Morris 45 per round (50 Sat, Sun & 60 BHs). Sandy Hills Links 60/ 80 **Course Designer** Old Tom Morris/Pat Ruddy **Prof** Noel Callan **Facilities** ⓣ 🍴 🛗 🖥 🖊 ⌁ 🏠 ⛳ ◇ 🏌 🛒 🏊 🏌 **Leisure** hard tennis courts, heated indoor swimming pool, 9 hole academy, 12 hole pitch & putt **Conf** facs Corporate Hospitality Days **Location** NE of village off R248
Hotel ★★★ 74% HL Downings Bay, Downings, LETTERKENNY ☎ 074 9155586 & 9155770 📠 074 9154716 40 en suite

CO DUBLIN

BALBRIGGAN
Map 1 D4

Balbriggan Golf Club Blackhall
☎ 01 8412229 📠 01 8413927
e-mail: balbriggangolfclub@eircom.net
web: www.balbriggangolfclub.com

A parkland course with great variations and good views of the Mourne and Cooley mountains.

18 Holes, 6069mtrs, Par 72, SSS 72. Club membership 750.

Visitors Mon-Fri except BHs. Booking required. Dress code. **Societies** booking required. **Green Fees** not confirmed **Course Designer** E. Connaughton **Prof** Nigel Howley **Facilities** ⓣ 🍴 🛗 🖥 🖊 ⌁ 🏠 🛒 ⛳ **Location** 1km S of Balbriggan on N1
Hotel ★★★ 71% HL Waterside House, DONABATE ☎ 01 8436153 📠 01 8436111 35 en suite

BALLYBOGHILL
Map 1 D4

Hollywood Lakes Golf Club
☎ 01 8433406 📠 01 8433002
e-mail: hollywoodlakesgc@eircom.net
web: www.hollywoodlakesgolfclub.com

A parkland course opened in 1992 with large USGA-type, sand-based greens and tees. There are water features on ten holes. The front nine requires accuracy while the second nine includes a 581 metre par 5.

18 Holes, 6100mtrs, Par 72, SSS 73. Club membership 780.

Visitors Mon-Fri. Weekends & BHs by arrangement. Dress code **Societies** telephone then write in advance. **Green Fees** not confirmed **Course Designer** Mel Flanagan **Prof** Sid Baldwin **Facilities** ⓣ 🍴 🛗 🖥 🖊 ⌁ 🏠 🛒 🏌 🛒 🏌 **Conf** Corporate Hospitality Days **Location** N of village on R108
Hotel ★★★ 71% HL Waterside House, DONABATE ☎ 01 8436153 📠 01 8436111 35 en suite

BRITTAS
Map 1 D4

Slade Valley Golf Club Lynch Park
☎ 01 4582183 & 4582739 📠 01 4582784
web: www.sladevalleygolfclub.ie

18 Holes, 5388mtrs, Par 69, SSS 68, Course record 65.

Course Designer W Sullivan & D O Brien **Location** off N81
Telephone for further details
Hotel ★★★ 72% HL Bewleys Hotel Newlands Cross, Newlands Cross, Naas Rd, DUBLIN 22 ☎ 01 4640140 & 4123301 📠 01 4640900 299 en suite

CASTLEKNOCK
Map 1 D4

Elm Green Golf Course
☎ 01 8200797 📠 01 8226668
e-mail: elmgreen@golfdublin.com
web: www.golfdublin.com

Located a short distance from Dublin, beside Phoenix Park, with a fine layout, tricky greens and year round playability.

18 Holes, 5850yds, Par 70, SSS 68, Course record 64. Club membership 800.

Visitors Mon-Sat & BHs. Sun pm. Booking required. **Societies** booking required. **Green Fees** not confirmed **Course Designer** Eddie Hackett **Prof** Paul McGahan & Karl Kelly **Facilities** ⓣ 🍴 🛗 🖥 🖊 ⌁ 🏠 🛒 🏌 🏌 🏌 **Leisure** pitch and putt course. **Conf** facs Corporate Hospitality Days **Location** off N3, Navan road
Hotel ★★★ 79% HL Finnstown Country House Hotel, Newcastle Road, LUCAN ☎ 01 6010700 & 6010708 📠 01 6281088 81 en suite

Luttrellstown Castle Golf & Country Club
☎ 01 8089988 📠 01 8089989
web: www.luttrellstown.ie

18 Holes, 6378metres, Par 72, SSS 73, Course record 66.

Course Designer Donald Steele **Location** W of town off R121
Telephone for further details
Hotel ★★★ 79% HL Finnstown Country House Hotel, Newcastle Road, LUCAN ☎ 01 6010700 & 6010708 📠 01 6281088 81 en suite

CLOGHRAN
Map 1 D4

Forrest Little Golf Club
☎ 01 8401183 & 8401763 📠 01 8908499
e-mail: margaret@forrestlittle.ie
web: www.forrestlittle.com

A well-manicured and mature parkland with many water features, large sand based greens and undulating fairways, playable all year.

18 Holes, 5902mtrs, Par 71, SSS 72, Course record 68. Club membership 900.

Visitors Mon-Fri excluding BHs. Booking required. Handicap certificate. Dress code. **Societies** booking required. **Green Fees** not confirmed **Course Designer** Mr Hawtree snr **Prof** Tony Judd **Facilities** ⓣ 🍴 🛗 🖥 🖊 ⌁ 🏠 🛒 🏌 🛒 🏌 **Location** N of Dublin Airport off R132
Hotel ★★★ 71% HL Waterside House, DONABATE ☎ 01 8436153 📠 01 8436111 35 en suite

IRELAND

DONABATE
Map 1 D4

Balcarrick Golf Club Corballis
☎ 01 8436957 🖹 01 8436228
e-mail: balcarr@iol.ie
web: www.balcarrickgolfclub.com
Fine 18-hole estuary course located close to the sea and exposed to the elements, featuring the best qualities of links and parkland play.
18 Holes, 6273mtrs, Par 73, SSS 71. Club membership 750.
Visitors Mon-Fri. Weekends & BHs restricted play. Booking required. Handicap certificate. Dress code. **Societies** booking required **Green Fees** not confirmed **Course Designer** Roger Jones **Prof** Stephen Rayfus **Facilities** ⓦ 🍴 🏌 ☕ 🍺 🏊 🏠 🏌 🚃 🏌 **Location** off R126
Hotel ★★★ 77% HL Deer Park Hotel, Golf & Spa, HOWTH
☎ 01 8322624 🖹 01 8392405 75 en suite

Donabate Golf Club, Balcarrick
☎ 01 8436346 🖹 01 8434488
e-mail: info@donabategolfclub.com
web: www.donabategolfclub.com
A challenging 27 hole golf course with mature tree-lined fairways which has been rebuilt to USGA specifications. All greens are sand based and the course is playable all year round.
27 Holes, 6094mtrs, Par 72, SSS 73, Course record 66. Club membership 1200.
Visitors dress code. **Societies** welcome. **Green Fees** not confirmed **Course Designer** Pat Suttle **Prof** Hugh Jackson **Facilities** ⓦ 🍴 🏌 ☕ 🍺 🏊 🏠 🏌 🏌 🚃 🏌 **Conf** Corporate Hospitality Days **Location** E of town off R126
Hotel ★★★ 77% HL Deer Park Hotel, Golf & Spa, HOWTH
☎ 01 8322624 🖹 01 8392405 75 en suite

The Island Golf Club Corballis
☎ 01 8436205 🖹 01 8436860
e-mail: info@theislandgolfclub.com
web: www.theislandgolfclub.com
One of Ireland's finest links courses, located across the estuary from Malahide and surrounded by the sea on three sides. The course enjoys a unique setting, nestled among the highest sand dunes of any links course in Ireland. The rugged nature and beauty of the course offers a true links golf experience.
18 Holes, 6206mtrs, Par 71, SSS 63. Club membership 1100.
Visitors Mon-Sun. Booking required. Dress code. **Societies** booking required. **Green Fees** 115 per 18 holes **Course Designer** Martin Hawtree **Prof** David Costigan **Facilities** ⓦ 🍴 🏌 ☕ 🍺 🏊 🏠 🏌 🏌 🚃 🏌 **Conf** facs Corporate Hospitality Days **Location**
Hotel ★★★ 77% HL Deer Park Hotel, Golf & Spa, HOWTH
☎ 01 8322624 🖹 01 8392405 75 en suite

Turvey Golf Club & Hotel Turvey Av
☎ 01 8435169 🖹 01 8435179
web: www.turveygolfclub.com
18 Holes, 6068mtrs, Par 71, SSS 72, Course record 64.
Course Designer P McGurk **Location** M1, 1st junct N after Dublin airport, 1m on N1 Turvey signed on right
Telephone for further details
Hotel ★★★ 77% HL Deer Park Hotel, Golf & Spa, HOWTH
☎ 01 8322624 🖹 01 8392405 75 en suite

DUBLIN
Map 1 D4

The Carrickmines Golf Club Carrickmines
☎ 01 2955972
Meadowland and partly hilly gorseland course.
9 Holes, 4644mtrs, Par 71, SSS 69. Club membership 600.
Visitors Mon, Tue, Thu, Fri & Sun except BHs. Dress code. **Green Fees** not confirmed 🍴 **Facilities** ☕ 🍺 🏊 🏌 **Location** 11km SE of city centre off N11
Hotel ★★★ 74% HL Bewleys Hotel Leopardstown, Central Park, Leopardstown, DUBLIN 18 ☎ 01 2935000 & 2935001 🖹 01 2935099 352 en suite

Castle Golf Club Woodside Dr, Rathfarnham
☎ 01 4904207 🖹 01 4920264
e-mail: office@castlegc.ie
web: www.castlegc.ie
A tight, tree-lined parkland course in an excellent location close to the city.
18 Holes, 5732mtrs, Par 70, SSS 71, Course record 66. Club membership 1350.
Visitors Mon-Sun & BHs. Booking required. Dress code. **Societies** Booking required. **Green Fees** not confirmed **Course Designer** Harry Colt **Prof** David Kinsella **Facilities** ⓦ 🍴 🏌 ☕ 🍺 🏊 🏠 **Conf** Corporate Hospitality Days **Location** off Dodder Park Rd
Hotel ★★★ 74% HL Mespil Hotel, Mespil Road, DUBLIN 4 ☎ 01 4884600 🖹 01 6671244 255 en suite

Clontarf Golf Club Donnycarney House
☎ 01 8331892 & 8331520 🖹 01 8331933
web: www.clontarfgolfclub.ie

18 Holes, 5317metres, Par 69, SSS 68, Course record 64.
Course Designer Harry Colt **Location** 4km NE of city centre via Fairway
Telephone for further details
Hotel ★★★★ 79% HL Clontarf Castle, Castle Avenue, Clontarf, DUBLIN 3 ☎ 01 8332321 & 8534336 🖹 01 8330418 111 en suite

IRELAND

Corrstown Golf Course Corrstown, Kilsallaghan
☎ 01 8640533 & 8640534 ⌨ 01 8640537
e-mail: info@corrstowngolfclub.com
web: www.corrstowngolfclub.com

The 18-hole course has a small river meandering through, coming into play at several holes culminating in a challenging island green finish. Orchard course has mature trees and rolling pastureland offering golfers a relaxing enjoyable game.

River Course: 18 Holes, 6077mtrs, Par 72, SSS 71,
Course record 69.
Orchard Course: 9 Holes, 2792metres, Par 35, SSS 69.
Club membership 1050.

Visitors Mon-Fri. Booking required. Dress code. **Societies** Booking required. **Green Fees** not confirmed **Course Designer** Eddie Connaughton **Prof** Pat Gittens **Facilities** ⑪ ⭥ ⬛ ⬜ ⬚ ⬚ ⬛ ✦ ⬛ ✦ **Location** 10km N of city centre via St Margarets
Hotel ★★★ 74% HL Mespil Hotel, Mespil Road, DUBLIN 4
☎ 01 4884600 ⌨ 01 6671244 255 en suite

Edmondstown Golf Club Edmondstown Rd, Edmondstown
☎ 01 4931082 & 4932461 ⌨ 01 4933152
e-mail: info@edmondstowngolfclub.ie
web: www.edmondstowngolfclub.ie

A popular and testing parkland course situated at the foot of the Dublin Mountains in the suburbs of the city. Now completely renovated and redesigned. All greens are now sand based to the highest standard. An attractive stream flows in front of the 4th and 6th greens calling for an accurate approach shot. The par 3 17th will test the best golfers and the 5th and 12th require thoughtful club selection to the green.

18 Holes, 6011mtrs, Par 71, SSS 73, Course record 66.
Club membership 750.

Visitors Mon, Thu, Fri & BHs. Sat am. Sun after 3.30pm. Booking required weekends & BHs. **Societies** booking required **Green Fees** €55 per round (€65 Sat & BHs) **Course Designer** McEvoy/Cooke **Prof** Gareth McShea **Facilities** ⑪ ⭥ ⬛ ⬜ ⬚ ⬚ ✦ ⬛ ✦ ⬚ **Conf** facs Corporate Hospitality Days **Location** M50 junct 12, follow signs to Edmondstown
Hotel ★★★★ 80% HL Nuremore, CARRICKMACROSS
☎ 042 9661438 ⌨ 042 9661853 72 en suite

Malahide Golf Club

Golfers visiting this 27-hole parkland course will find a scenically beautiful course, consistently maintained to the highest standards.

The motto of the club is "A light heart and a cheerful spirit", also reflected in the warmth of our welcome both to individuals and Societies, which sees many returning year after year.

For beginner or established players, our friendly Golf Professional John Murray is on hand to offer advice or lessons to improve your game.

From the Clubhouse there are breath-taking views of Howth Head and the Wicklow Mountains, matched by the hospitality cuisine found in out Restaurant and bar.

Beechwood, The Grange, Malahide, Co. Dublin
For bookings please contact Mark Gannon, General Manager
Email: manager@malahidegolfclub.ie
Tel: +353 (01) 846-1611 Fax: +353 (01) 846-1270
Website: www.malahidegoldclub.ie

Elm Park Golf & Sports Club Nutley House
☎ 01 2693438 ⌨ 01 2694505
web: www.elmparkgolfclub.ie

18 Holes, 5380mtrs, Par 69, SSS 69, Course record 64.

Course Designer Patrick Merrigan **Location** 5km SE of city centre off N11
Telephone for further details
Hotel ★★★ 74% HL Sandymount Hotel, Herbert Road, Sandymount, DUBLIN 4 ☎ 01 6142000 ⌨ 01 6607077 168 en suite

Howth Golf Club, Carrickbrack Rd, Sutton
☎ 01 8323055 ⌨ 01 8321793
e-mail: secretary@howthgolfclub.ie
web: www.howthgolfclub.ie

A hilly heathland course with scenic views of Dublin Bay. A good challenge to the novice or expert golfer.

18 Holes, 5618mtrs, Par 72, SSS 72, Course record 65.
Club membership 1400.

Visitors Mon-Tue, Thu-Sun, except BHs. Dress code. **Societies** booking required **Green Fees** €40 per day, €20 per 9 holes **Course Designer** James Braid **Prof** John McGuirk **Facilities** ⑪ by prior arrangement ⭥ by prior arrangement ⬛ ⬜ ⬚ ⬚ ⬛ ✦ ⬛ ✦ ✦ **Conf** facs Corporate Hospitality Days **Location** 14.5km NE of city centre
Hotel ★★★ 77% HL Deer Park Hotel, Golf & Spa, HOWTH
☎ 01 8322624 ⌨ 01 8392405 75 en suite

441

IRELAND

Milltown Golf Club Lower Churchtown Rd
☎ 01 4976090 🖷 01 4976008
web: www.milltowngolfclub.ie.

18 Holes, 5638mtrs, Par 71, SSS 70, Course record 64.

Course Designer Freddie Davis **Location**
Telephone for further details
Hotel ★★★ 74% HL Mespil Hotel, Mespil Road, DUBLIN 4
☎ 01 4884600 🖷 01 6671244 255 en suite

Newlands Golf Club Clondalkin
☎ 01 4593157 & 4593498 🖷 01 4593498
e-mail: info@newlandsgolfclub.com
web: www.newlandsgolfclub.com

Mature trees model and soften the landscape of this parkland course once the home of the Lord Chief Justice of Ireland. Recent improvements to the course include new fairway bunkers, USPGA specification greens and some new challenging holes.

18 Holes, 5982mtrs, Par 71, SSS 70.
Club membership 1000.

Visitors Mon, Thu & Fri. Booking required. Dress code.
Societies booking required **Green Fees** not confirmed **Course Designer** James Braid/Jeff Howe **Prof** Karl O'Donnell **Facilities** ⊕ ⧈ ⧈ ⧈ ⧈ ⧈ ⧈ ⧈ ⧈ ⧈ ⧈ **Conf** Corporate Hospitality Days **Location** 6m SW of Dublin at Newlands Cross N7
Hotel ★★★ 74% HL Mespil Hotel, Mespil Road, DUBLIN 4
☎ 01 4884600 🖷 01 6671244 255 en suite

Rathfarnham Golf Club Newtown
☎ 01 4931201 & 4931561 🖷 01 4931561
e-mail: rgc@oceanfree.net

Parkland course designed by John Jacobs in 1962. Set in the foothills of the Dublin mountains which provide a beautiful backdrop, the course offers a good and interesting test of golf.

18 Holes, 5579mtrs, Par 71, SSS 70, Course record 69.
Club membership 685.

Visitors Mon, Wed-Fri & Sun. Booking required. Dress code.
Societies booking required **Green Fees** not confirmed **Course Designer** John Jacobs/Jeff Howes **Prof** Brian O'Hara **Facilities** ⊕ ⧈ ⧈ ⧈ ⧈ ⧈ ⧈ **Location** 5km S of city centre off N81
Hotel ★★★ 74% HL Mespil Hotel, Mespil Road, DUBLIN 4
☎ 01 4884600 🖷 01 6671244 255 en suite

The Royal Dublin Golf Club North Bull Island Reserve, Dollymount
☎ 01 8336346 🖷 01 8336504
e-mail: info@theroyaldublingolfclub.com
web: www.theroyaldublingolfclub.com

A popular course with visitors, for its design subtleties, the condition of the links and the friendly atmosphere. Founded in 1885, the club moved to its present site in 1889 and received its Royal designation in 1891. A notable former club professional was Christy O'Connor, who was appointed in 1959 and immediately made his name. Along with its many notable holes, Royal Dublin has a fine and testing finish. The 18th is a sharp dog-leg par 4, with out of bounds along the right-hand side. The decision to try the long carry over the 'garden' is one many visitors have regretted.

18 Holes, 6647mtrs, Par 72. Club membership 1250.

Visitors Mon, Tue, Thu, Fri & Sun. Limited play Sat & BHs. Booking required. Handicap certificate. Dress code. **Societies** booking required. **Green Fees** not confirmed **Course Designer** H S Colt/ Martin Hawtree **Prof** Leonard Owens **Facilities** ⊕ ⧈ ⧈ ⧈

⧈ ⧈ ⧈ ⧈ ⧈ ⧈ ⧈ ⧈ **Conf** facs Corporate Hospitality Days **Location** 5.5km NE of city centre
Hotel ★★★★ 79% HL Clontarf Castle, Castle Avenue, Clontarf, DUBLIN 3 ☎ 01 8332321 & 8534336 🖷 01 8330418 111 en suite

St Margaret's Golf & Country Club St Margaret's
☎ 01 8640400 🖷 01 8640408
e-mail: reservations@stmargaretsgolf.com
web: www.stmargaretsgolf.com

A championship standard course which measures nearly 7,000 yards off the back tees, but flexible teeing offers a fairer challenge to the middle and high handicap golfer. The modern design makes wide use of water hazards and mounding. Dramatic 18th hole. Has hosted many international tournaments.

18 Holes, 6917yds, Par 73, SSS 73, Course record 65.
Club membership 260.

Visitors dress code. **Societies** welcome. **Green Fees** Low season 30- 50, high season 35- 65 **Course Designer** Craddock/Ruddy **Prof** Gary Kearney **Facilities** ⊕ ⧈ ⧈ ⧈ ⧈ ⧈ ⧈ ⧈ ⧈ ⧈ ⧈ ⧈ **Leisure** golf academy **Conf** facs Corporate Hospitality Days **Location** 9km N of city centre off R122. Adjacent to Dublin Airport
Hotel ★★★ 74% HL Mespil Hotel, Mespil Road, DUBLIN 4
☎ 01 4884600 🖷 01 6671244 255 en suite

Stackstown Golf Club Kellystown Rd
☎ 01 4942338 & 4941993 🖷 01 4933934
web: www.stackstowngolfclub.com

18 Holes, 5625mtrs, Par 72, SSS 72, Course record 63.

Course Designer Shaftrey **Location** 9km S of city centre. M50 junct 13, signs for Rathfarnham, 3rd lights left for Leopardstown, next lights follow road under M50, club 300mtrs
Telephone for further details
Hotel ★★★★ 77% HL Stillorgan Park, Stillorgan Road, Stillorgan, DUBLIN 4 ☎ 01 2001800 🖷 01 2831610 150 en suite

---

HOWTH
Map 1 D4

Deer Park Hotel, Golf & Spa
☎ 01 8322624 🖷 01 8392405
e-mail: sales@deerpark.iol.ie
web: www.deerpark-hotel.ie

Claiming to be Ireland's largest golf-hotel complex, Deer Park offers a challenge to all levels of golfer. Spectacular scenery within the parkland setting surrounding Howth Castle.

Deer Park: 18 Holes, 6293mtrs, Par 72.
Grace O'Malley: 18 Holes, 5927mtrs, Par 72.
Short Course: 12 Holes, 1598mtrs, Par 36.
Club membership 350.

Visitors Mon-Sun & BHs. **Societies** booking required. **Green Fees** not confirmed **Course Designer** Fred Hawtree **Facilities** ⊕ ⧈ ⧈ ⧈ ⧈ ⧈ ⧈ ⧈ ⧈ **Leisure** hard tennis courts, heated indoor swimming pool, sauna **Conf** facs Corporate Hospitality Days **Location** 14.5km NE of city centre, off coast road 0.8km before Howth Harbour
Hotel ★★★ 77% HL Deer Park Hotel, Golf & Spa, HOWTH
☎ 01 8322624 🖷 01 8392405 75 en suite

PORTMARNOCK

CO DUBLIN - PORTMARNOCK - MAP 1 D4

Universally acknowledged as one of the truly great links courses, Portmarnock has hosted many great events from the British Amateur Championships of 1949 and the Canada Cup in 1960, to 12 stagings of the revised Irish Open. Founded in 1894, the serpentine championship course offers a classic challenge: surrounded by water on three sides, no two successive holes play in the same direction. Unlike many courses that play nine out and nine home, Portmarnock demands a continual awareness of wind direction. Extraordinary holes include the 14th, which Henry Cotton regarded as the best hole in golf; the 15th, which Arnold Palmer regards as the best par 3 in the world; and the 5th, regarded as the best on the course by the late Harry Bradshaw. Bradshaw was for 40 years Portmarnock's golf professional and runner-up to AD Locke in the 1949 British Open, playing his ball from an empty bottle of stout.

☎ 01 8462968 📄 01 8462601
e-mail: info@portmarnockgolfclub.ie **web:** www.portmarnockgolfclub.ie
Red & Blue: 18 Holes, 6345metres, Par 72, SSS 74.
Red & Yellow: 18 Holes, 6292metres, Par 73, SSS 74.
Yellow & Blue: 18 Holes, 6188mtrs, Par 73, SSS 72. **Club membership** 1100.
Visitors Mon-Sun & BHs at set times. Booking required. Dress code. **Societies** booking required.
Green Fees €270 per 36 holes (weekdays), €180 per round (all including soup and sandwiches). Nov-Mar €120 per round weekdays **Course Designer** W Pickeman **Prof** Joey Purcell **Facilities** ⑪ 🍽 by prior arrangement 🛗 🖥 🍴 🧺 🏧 🏌 ⚓ 🛥 ✂ 🦮 **Conf** Corporate Hospitality Days **Location** S of town off R106

LUCAN
Map 1 D4

Hermitage Golf Club Ballydowd
☎ 01 6268491 📄 01 6238881
e-mail: hermitagegolf@eircom.net
web: www.hermitagegolf.ie

Part level, part undulating course bordered by the River Liffey and offering some surprises.

18 Holes, 6060mtrs, Par 71, SSS 72, Course record 64. Club membership 1100.

Visitors Mon, Thu & Fri. Booking required. Dress code.
Societies booking required. **Green Fees** €50 per round **Course Designer** J McKenna **Prof** Simon Byrne **Facilities** ⑪ 🍴 🍺 ☕ 🍷 ⌚ 🏠 ⛳ 🛒 ⛳ **Conf** facs Corporate Hospitality Days
Location On N4
Hotel ★★★ 79% HL Finnstown Country House Hotel, Newcastle Road, LUCAN ☎ 01 6010700 & 6010708 📄 01 6281088 81 en suite

Lucan Golf Club Celbridge Rd
☎ 01 6282106 📄 01 6282929
e-mail: lucangolf@eircom.net
web: www.lucangolfclub.ie

Founded in 1897 as a nine-hole course and extended to 18 holes in 1988, Lucan involves playing over a lane which bisects the 1st and 7th holes. The front nine is undulating while the back nine is flatter and features water hazards and a 531-metre par 5 18th hole.

18 Holes, 5958mtrs, Par 71, SSS 71, Course record 67. Club membership 920.

Visitors Mon-Fri. Booking required. **Societies** booking required. **Green Fees** not confirmed **Course Designer** Eddie Hackett **Facilities** ⑪ 🍴 🍺 ☕ 🍷 ⌚ 🏠 ⛳ 🛒 ⛳ **Location** W of town towards Celbridge
Hotel ★★★ 63% HL Lucan Spa, LUCAN ☎ 01 6280494 📄 01 6280841 71 en suite

MALAHIDE
Map 1 D4

Malahide Golf Club Beechwood
☎ 01 8461611 📄 01 8461270
web: www.malahidegolfclub.ie

Main Course: 18 Holes, 6066mtrs, Par 71.
Course Designer E Hackett **Location** 1.6km from R106 coast road at Portmarnock
Telephone for further details
See advert on page 441

PORTMARNOCK
Map 1 D4

Portmarnock Golf Club see page 443
☎ 01 8462968 📄 01 8462601
e-mail: info@portmarnockgolfclub.ie
web: www.portmarnockgolfclub.ie

Portmarnock Hotel & Golf Links Strand Rd
☎ 01 8460611 📄 01 8462442
web: www.portmarnock.com

18 Holes, 5992metres, Par 71, SSS 72, Course record 67.
Course Designer Bernhard Langer **Location** from Dublin Airport, N1, rdbt 1st exit, 2nd rdbt 2nd exit, next rdbt 3rd exit, left at T-junct, over x-rds. Hotel on left past Strand
Telephone for further details

RATHCOOLE
Map 1 D4

Beech Park Golf Club Johnstown
☎ 01 4580522 📄 01 4588365
web: www.beechpark.ie

18 Holes, 5753metres, Par 72, SSS 70, Course record 67.
Course Designer Eddie Hackett **Location** From N7, take exit signed Rathcoole North. Follow local signs.
Telephone for further details
Hotel ★★★ 79% HL Finnstown Country House Hotel, Newcastle Road, LUCAN ☎ 01 6010700 & 6010708 📄 01 6281088 81 en suite

RUSH
Map 1 D4

Rush Golf Club
☎ 01 8438177 (Office) & 8437548 📄 01 8438177
e-mail: info@rushgolfclub.com

Seaside borders three fairways on this links course. There are 28 bunkers and undulating fairways to add to the challenge of the variable and strong winds that blow at all times and change with the tides. There are no easy holes.

9 Holes, 5490mtrs, Par 70, SSS 71. Club membership 500.

Visitors contact club for details. **Societies** booking required. **Green Fees** €36 per 18 holes **Facilities** ⑪ 🍴 🍺 ☕ 🍷 🏠 ⛳ **Location** SW of town
Hotel ★★★ 71% HL Waterside House, DONABATE ☎ 01 8436153 📄 01 8436111 35 en suite

IRELAND

SAGGART   Map 1 D4

Citywest Hotel
☎ 01 4010500 & 4010878 (shop)   📠 01 4588565
e-mail: proshop@citywesthotel.com
web: www.citywesthotel.com

Course west of Dublin comprising 142 acres at the foothills of the Dublin mountains and built on fine parkland. Well wooded and enjoys natural drainage. The Lakes course is fairly short but a good test of golf with fine greens and fairways.

Championship: 18 Holes, 6019yds, Par 68, SSS 69.
Lakes: 18 Holes, 5154yds, Par 65, SSS 68.

Visitors Mon-Sun & BHs. Booking required weekends.
Societies booking required. **Green Fees** not confirmed **Course Designer** Christy O'Connor Jnr **Facilities** ⑪ ⑩ 🍴 📇 🖳 🗑 🛎 ♨ ♦ 🏌 🚗 ⚡ **Leisure** heated indoor swimming pool, fishing, sauna, gymnasium **Conf** facs Corporate Hospitality Days **Location** off N7, exit 3A, S to village
Hotel ★★★ 72% HL Bewleys Hotel Newlands Cross, Newlands Cross, Naas Rd, DUBLIN 22 ☎ 01 4640140 & 4123301 📠 01 4640900 299 en suite

SKERRIES   Map 1 D4

Skerries Golf Club Hacketstown
☎ 01 8491567 📠 01 8491591
web: www.skerriesgolfclub.ie

18 Holes, 6081mtrs, Par 73, SSS 72, Course record 67.

Location S of town off R127
Telephone for further details
Hotel ★★★ 71% HL Waterside House, DONABATE ☎ 01 8436153 📠 01 8436111 35 en suite

SWORDS   Map 1 D4

Swords Open Golf Course Balheary Av, Swords
☎ 01 8409819 & 8901030   📠 01 8901030
e-mail: info@swordsopengolfcourse.com
web: www.swordsopengolfcourse.com

Parkland beside the River Broadmeadow, in countryside, easily accessible from Dublin Airport and close to Swords Village.

18 Holes, 5613mtrs, Par 71, SSS 69, Course record 63.
Club membership 500.

Visitors Mon-Sun & BHs. Booking required. Dress code.
Societies booking required. **Green Fees** €20 per 18 holes (€25 weekends & BHs) **Course Designer** T Halpin **Facilities** 📇 🖳 🛎 ♨ ♦ 🚗 ⚡ **Leisure** sauna, gymnasium **Conf** Corporate Hospitality Days **Location** from M1 take Donabate/Skerries exit towards Swords Turn right at Estuary rdbt, right at lights, then second turning left, course 2km on left
Hotel ★★★ 75% HL Bewleys Hotel Dublin Airport, Baskin Lane, SWORDS ☎ 01 8711000 & 8711200 📠 01 8711001 466 en suite

TALLAGHT   Map 1 D4

Dublin City Golf Club Ballinascorney
☎ 01 4516430 📠 01 4598445
web: www.dublincitygolf.com

18 Holes, 5061mtrs, Par 69, SSS 67, Course record 63.

Course Designer Eddie Hackett **Location** 12km SW of city centre on R114
Telephone for further details
Hotel ★★★★ 76% HL Red Cow Moran, Red Cow Complex, Naas Road, DUBLIN 22 ☎ 01 4593650 📠 01 4591588 123 en suite

CO GALWAY

BALLYCONNEELY   Map 1 A4

Connemara Championship Links
☎ 095 23502 & 23602   📠 095 23662
e-mail: info@connemaragolflinks.net
web: www.connemaragolflinks.com

This championship links course has a spectacular setting by the Atlantic Ocean, with the Twelve Bens Mountains in the background. Established in 1973, it is a tough challenge, due in no small part to its exposed location, with the back nine the equal of any in the world. The last six holes are exceptionally long and offer a great challenge to golfers of all abilities. When the wind blows, club selection is crucial. Notable holes are the 13th (200yd par 3), the long par 5 14th, the 15th with a green nestling in the hills, the 16th guarded by water and the 17th and 18th, both par 5s over 500yds long.

AB: 18 Holes, 6095mtrs, Par 72, SSS 73,
Course record 67.
AC: 9 Holes, 5511mtrs, Par 70, SSS 73.
BC: 18 Holes, 5796mtrs, Par 72, SSS 73.
Club membership 970.

Visitors Mon-Sun & BHs. Booking required. Dress code.
Societies booking required. **Green Fees** not confirmed **Course Designer** Eddie Hackett **Prof** Hugh O'Neill **Facilities** ⑪ ⑩ 📇 🖳 🗑 🛎 🚗 ♨ ♦ 🏌 ⚡ 🏴 **Conf** Corporate Hospitality Days **Location** from Clifden take R341 to Bally Conneely, then fork right in village after Keogh's public house
Hotel ★★★★ BB Mallmore House, Ballyconneely Road, CLIFDEN ☎ 095 21460 6 rooms

IRELAND

445

BEARNA
Map 1 B3

Bearna Golf and Country Club Corboley
☎ 091 592677 ▤ 091 592674
web: www.bearnagolfclub.com

18 Holes, 5746metres, Par 72, SSS 72, Course record 68.
Course Designer Robert J Brown Location 3.5km N of Bearna, off R336
Telephone for further details

GALWAY
Map 1 B4

Galway Golf Club Blackrock, Salthill
☎ 091 522033 ▤ 091 529783
e-mail: info@galwaygolf.com
web: www.galwaygolf.com
Designed by Dr A MacKenzie, this course is inland by nature,
although some of the fairways run close to the ocean. The terrain
is of gently sloping hillocks with plenty of trees and furze bushes
to catch out the unwary. Although not a long course it continues to
delight visiting golfers.
18 Holes, 5974metres, Par 70, SSS 70.
Club membership 1238.
Visitors Mon, Wed-Sat & BHs. Booking required. Handicap
certificate. Dress code. Societies booking required. Green Fees 30
per 18 holes Course Designer McKenzie Prof Don Wallace
Facilities ⊕ ⊓⊙⊦ ⛳ ⬚ ⊓ ⊿ ⏢ ⊓ ✎ 🏌 ✎ Conf
Corporate Hospitality Days Location 3km W in Salthill
Hotel ★★★ 79% HL Claregalway, Claregalway Village, GALWAY
☎ 091 738300 & 738302▤ 091 738311 48 en suite

GORT
Map 1 B3

Gort Golf Club, Castlequarter
☎ 091 632244 ▤ 091 632387
e-mail: info@gortgolf.com
web: www.gortgolf.com
Set in 65 hectares of picturesque parkland. The 515-metre 9th and
the 472-metre 17th are played into a prevailing wind and the par 4
dog-leg 7th will test the best.
18 Holes, 5705mtrs, Par 71, SSS 69, Course record 67.
Club membership 978.
Visitors Mon-Sun & BHs. Booking required Mon, Tue, weekends & BHs.
Dress code. Societies booking required. Green Fees Oct-Mar €22 per
round (€25 weekends & BHs). Apr-Sep €25 (€30 weekends) Course
Designer Christy O'Connor Jnr Facilities ⊕ ⊓⊙⊦ ⛳ ⬚ ⊓ ⊿
⏢ ⊓ ✎ 🏌 ✎ Location located at Castlequarter, approx 2m
W of Gort

LOUGHREA
Map 1 B3

Loughrea Golf Club Bullaun Rd
☎ 091 841049 ▤ 091 847472
18 Holes, 5825mtrs, Par 71, SSS 70, Course record 68.
Course Designer Eddie Hackett Location Follow signs from bypass for
Mountbellew/New Inn. 1.5m N of town.
Telephone for further details

MOUNTBELLEW
Map 1 B4

Mountbellew Golf Course, Ballinasloe
☎ 090 9679259
e-mail: mountbellewgc@gmail.com
web: www.mountbellewgolfclub.com
A wooded parkland course with two quarries and water hazards in play
at six holes. Four par 5s. Sand based greens. Lots of wildlife. Lunch
and dinner only available on competition days and for groups.
Mountbellew: 18 Holes, 5567mtrs, Par 71, SSS 70.
Club membership 400.
Visitors Mon-Sun & BHs. Booking required. Societies booking
required. Green Fees €15 per day winter. €20 per day summer (€25
weekends) ⊛ Course Designer Ken Kearney Prof Ray Ryan Facilities
⛳ ⬚ ⊓⊙⊦ ⊿ ✎ 🏌 ✎ Conf Corporate Hospitality Days
Location off N63, 1m from Mountbellew

ORANMORE
Map 1 B3

Athenry Golf Club Palmerstown
☎ 091 794466 ▤ 091 794971
web: www.athenrygolfclub.net
18 Holes, 5687metres, Par 70, SSS 70, Course record 67.
Course Designer Eddie Hackett Location 6km E on R348
Telephone for further details

Galway Bay Golf Resort, Renville
☎ 091 790711 ▤ 091 792510
e-mail: info@galwaybaygolfresort.com
web: www.galwaybaygolfresort.com
A championship golf course surrounded on three sides by the
Atlantic Ocean and featuring water hazards on a number of holes.
Each hole has its own characteristics made more obvious by the
everchanging seaside winds. The design of the course highlights
and preserves the ancient historic features of the Renville
Peninsula. The spectacular setting and distractingly beautiful and
cleverly designed mix of holes presents a real golfing challenge,
demanding total concentration.
18 Holes, 6533metres, Par 72, SSS 73, Course record 68.
Club membership 280.
Visitors contact club for details. Societies booking required. Green
Fees €45 (€60 weeekends) Course Designer Christy O'Connor
Jnr Prof Eugene O'Connor Facilities ⊕ ⊓⊙⊦ ⛳ ⬚ ⊓ ⊿
⏢ ⊓ ◇ ✎ 🏌 ✎ 🚩 Conf Corporate Hospitality Days
Location 5km SW of village of Oranmore

PORTUMNA
Map 1 B3

Portumna Golf Club
☎ 090 9741059 📠 090 9741798
e-mail: info@portumnagolfclub.ie
web: www.portumnagolfclub.ie.
Parkland with mature trees and wildlife.
18 Holes, 6100mtrs, Par 72, SSS 72. Club membership 800.
Visitors Mon-Sat & BHs. Booking required Mon,Sat & BHs.
Societies booking required. **Green Fees** €30 **Course Designer** E
Connaughton **Facilities** ⊕ ⦿ ⛳ ☖ ▱ ⛴ ⚘ ⛟ ⚲
Location 4km W of town on R352

CO KERRY

BALLYBUNION
Map 1 A3

Ballybunion Golf Club see page 449
Sandhill Rd
☎ 068 27146 📠 068 27387
e-mail: info@ballybuniongolfclub.ie
web: www.ballybuniongolfclub.ie

BALLYFERRITER
Map 1 A2

Dingle Links Golf Club
☎ 066 9156255 📠 066 9156409
e-mail: dinglegc@iol.ie
web: www.dinglelinks.com
This most westerly course in Europe has a magnificent scenic location.
It is a traditional links course with beautiful turf, many bunkers, a
stream that comes into play on 14 holes and, usually, a prevailing wind.
18 Holes, 6737mtrs, Par 72, SSS 71, Course record 66.
Club membership 432.
Visitors Mon-Sun & BHs. Booking required weekends & BHs.
Dress code. Societies welcome. **Green Fees** not confirmed **Course**
Designer Hackett/O'Connor Jnr **Facilities** ⊕ ⦿ ⛳ ☖ ▱ ⛴ ⚘
⛟ ⛾ ⚲ ⚲ Leisure buggies for hire May-Oct **Location** 2.5km NW
of village off R559
Hotel ★★★★★ GH Gormans Clifftop House & Restaurant,
Glaise Bheag, Ballydavid, DINGLE ☎ 066 9155162 & 083 0033133
📠 066 9155003 8 rooms

CASTLEGREGORY
Map 1 A2

Castlegregory Golf Course Stradbally
☎ 066 7139444 📠 066 7139958
web: www.castlegregorygolflinks.com
9 Holes, 2569mtrs, Par 68, SSS 68, Course record 67.
Course Designer Dr Arthur Spring **Location** 3km W of town near
Stradbally
Telephone for further details
Hotel ★★★★ BB Sea-Mount House, Cappatigue, Conor Pass
Road, CASTLEGREGORY ☎ 066 7139229 📠 066 7139229 2 rooms

GLENBEIGH
Map 1 A2

Dooks Golf Links
☎ 066 9768205 📠 066 9768476
e-mail: office@dooks.com
web: www.dooks.com
Long-established course on the shore between the Kerry mountains
and Dingle Bay. Sand dunes are a feature (the name Dooks is a
derivation of the Gaelic word for sand bank) and the course offers a
fine challenge in a superb Ring of Kerry location.
18 Holes, 5944mtrs, Par 71, SSS 70, Course record 70.
Club membership 1000.
Visitors contact club for details. Societies booking required. **Green**
Fees not confirmed **Course Designer** Martin Hawtree **Facilities** ⊕
⦿ ⛳ ☖ ▱ ⛴ ⚘ ⛓ ⛾ ⛟ ⚲ **Conf** Corporate
Hospitality Days **Location** NE of village off on N70
Hotel ★★★★★ GH Carrig House Country House & Restaurant,
Caragh Lake, KILLORGLIN ☎ 066 9769100 📠 066 9769166 16 rooms

KENMARE
Map 1 B2

Ring of Kerry Golf & Country Club Templenoe
☎ 064 6642000 📠 064 6642533
web: www.ringofkerrygolf.com
18 Holes, 6353mtrs, Par 72, SSS 73, Course record 68.
Course Designer Eddie Hackett **Location** 6.5km W of Kenmare
Telephone for further details
Hotel ★★★★★ CHH Sheen Falls Lodge, KENMARE
☎ 06466 41600 📠 06466 41386 66 en suite

KILLARNEY
Map 1 B2

Beaufort Golf Resort Churchtown, Beaufort
☎ 064 6644440 📠 064 6644752
e-mail: info@beaufortgolfresort.com
web: www.beaufortgolfresort.com
A championship-standard parkland course designed by Dr Arthur
Spring. This course is in the centre of south-west Ireland's golfing
mecca. Ruins of a medieval castle dominate the back nine and the
whole course is overlooked by the mountains of MacGillycuddy's Reeks.
The par 3 10th and par 4 13th are two of the most memorable holes.
18 Holes, 6428mtrs, Par 71, SSS 73, Course record 69.
Club membership 350.
Visitors Mon-Sun & BHs. Booking required Fri & weekends. Dress
code. Societies booking required. **Green Fees** not confirmed **Course**
Designer Arthur Spring **Facilities** ⊕ ⦿ ⛳ ☖ ▱ ⛴ ⚘ ⛓ ⛾
⛟ ⚲ **Conf** Corporate Hospitality Days **Location** 11km W of Killarney
off N72
Hotel ★★★ 79% HL Castlerosse Hotel & Golf Resort, KILLARNEY
☎ 064 6631144 📠 064 6631031 120 en suite

IRELAND

447

Castlerosse Hotel & Golf Resort
☎ 064 6631144 📠 064 6631031
e-mail: res@castlerosse.ie
web: www.castlerosse.ie

Set in mature parkland, the course commands stunning views and has fully irrigated USGA standard greens plus a practice green.

9 Holes, 2761metres, Par 36. Club membership 80.
Visitors Mon-Sun & BHs. Booking required weekends & BHs. Handicap certificate. Dress code. **Societies** welcome. **Green Fees** €32 for 18 holes, €20 for 9 holes **Course Designer** H Wallace **Facilities** ⭑ ⓔ 🍴 👤 ⛳ 🛎 🏪 🚜 ⚒ **Leisure** hard tennis courts, heated indoor swimming pool, sauna, gymnasium **Conf** facs **Location** 2km from Killarney, off the Ring of Kerry road
Hotel ★★★ 79% HL Castlerosse Hotel & Golf Resort, KILLARNEY ☎ 064 6631144 📠 064 6631031 120 en suite

Killarney Golf & Fishing Club Mahony's Point
☎ 064 6631034 📠 064 6633065
e-mail: reservations@killarney-golf.com
web: www.killarney-golf.com

The three courses are lakeside with tree-lined fairways; many bunkers and small lakes provide no mean challenge. Mahoney's Point Course has a particularly testing par 5, 4, 3 finish and the courses call for great skill from the tee. Killarney has been the venue for many important events and is a favourite of many famous golfers.

Mahony's Point: 18 Holes, 6164mtrs, Par 72, SSS 72.
Killeen: 18 Holes, 6566mtrs, Par 73, SSS 73.
Lackabane: 18 Holes, 6410mtrs, Par 73, SSS 73.
Club membership 1600.
Visitors Mon-Sun & BHs. Booking required. Handicap certificate. Dress code. **Societies** welcome. **Green Fees** not confirmed **Course Designer** H Longhurst/Sir Guy Campbell **Prof** David Keating
Facilities ⓔ 🍴 🏪 🛎 👤 ⛳ ⚒ **Leisure** sauna, gymnasium **Conf** Corporate Hospitality Days
Location 3.5km W on N72
Hotel ★★★ 78% HL Killeen House, Lakes of Killarney, Aghadoe, KILLARNEY ☎ 064 6631711 & 6631773 📠 064 6631811 23 en suite

KILLORGLIN   Map 1 A2

Killorglin Golf Club Stealroe
☎ 066 9761979 📠 066 9761437
e-mail: kilgolf@iol.ie
web: www.killorglingolf.ie

A parkland course designed by Eddie Hackett as a challenging but fair test of golf, surrounded by magnificent views.

18 Holes, 6456yds, Par 72, Course record 63.
Club membership 510.
Visitors Mon-Sun & BHs. Booking required weekends. Dress code **Societies** Booking required. **Green Fees** not confirmed **Course Designer** Eddie Hackett **Prof** Hugh Duggan **Facilities** ⓔ 🍴 🏪 🛎 👤 ⚒ 🚜 ⚒ **Leisure** fishing **Location** 3km NE on N70
Hotel ★★★★ GH Grove Lodge, Killarney Road, KILLORGLIN ☎ 066 9761157 & 08720 73238 📠 066 9762726 10 rooms

TRALEE   Map 1 A2

Tralee Golf Club West Barrow
☎ 066 7136379 📠 066 7136008
e-mail: info@traleegolfclub.com
web: www.traleegolfclub.com

The first Arnold Palmer designed course in Europe, this magnificent 18-hole links is set in spectacular scenery on the Barrow peninsula, surrounded on three sides by the sea. Perhaps the most memorable hole is the par 4 17th which plays from a high tee, across a deep gorge to a green perched high against a backdrop of mountains. The back nine is very difficult and challenging. Not suitable for beginners.

18 Holes, 6378mtrs, Par 72, SSS 73.
Club membership 1306.
Visitors Mon-Fri & BHs. Dress code **Societies** booking required. **Green Fees** not confirmed **Course Designer** Arnold Palmer **Prof** David Power **Facilities** ⓔ 🍴 🏪 🛎 👤 ⚒ **Conf** facs Corporate Hospitality Days **Location** 13km NW of Tralee off R558
Hotel ★★★★ 78% HL Carlton Hotel Tralee, Fels Point, Dan Spring Road, TRALEE ☎ 066 7119986 & 7199100 📠 066 7119987 165 en suite

IRELAND

BALLYBUNION

CO KERRY - BALLYBUNION - MAP 1 A3

Two challenging and unique links courses, the Old Course and the Trent Jones Cashen Course, overlooking the Atlantic Ocean. The Old Course exudes a majestic feel that simply cannot be compared with any other. With beautifully contoured fairways that tumble down through a blanket of grassy dunes it's no surprise that these challenging holes have been consistently rated among the top courses in the world. The wild look of the Trent Jones Cashen Course, located along the sweeping undisturbed shoreline, offers breathtaking views throughout. Long grass covers the dunes that pitch and roll throughout the course. Golfers find themselves hitting uphill, downhill and sidehill shots, putting on relatively smalll but beautifully contoured greens. This is a course that rewards good play.

Sandhill Rd ☎ 068 27146 📄 068 27387
e-mail: info@ballybuniongolfclub.ie **web:** www.ballybuniongolfclub.ie
Old Course: 18 Holes, 6236mtrs, Par 71, SSS 72.
Cashen: 18 Holes, 5766mtrs, Par 72, SSS 73. Club membership 1500.
Visitors Mon-Sat except BHs. Booking required. Handicap certificate. Dress code. **Societies** booking required.
Green Fees Old Course €180 per round, Cashen Course €65 per round. Both courses: €180 **Course Designer** Simpson **Prof** Brian O'Callaghan **Facilities** ⑪ 🍴 🍺 ⬜ 🍽 ⛱ 🏪 ⛳ ✎ 🛒 ✎ 🏌 **Conf** Corporate Hospitality Days **Location** 2km S of Ballybunion town

WATERVILLE (AN COIREÁN)   Map 1 A2

Waterville House & Golf Links
☎ 066 9474102 📄 066 9474482
e-mail: wvgolf@iol.ie
web: www.watervillegolflinks.ie

On the western tip of the Ring of Kerry, this course is highly regarded by many top golfers. The feature holes are the par 5 11th, which runs along a rugged valley between towering dunes, and the par 3 17th, which features an exceptionally elevated tee. Needless to say, the surroundings are beautiful.

Waterville: 18 Holes, 6725mtrs, Par 72.
Club membership 600.

Visitors Contact club for details. **Societies** booking required. **Green Fees** 150 per 18 holes (170 weekends) **Course Designer** Eddie Hackett/Tom Fazio **Prof** Brian Higgins **Facilities** ⓣ ⦿ 🍴 ⛳ ▱ 🏌 ⚘ 🏠 ⛳ ♦ ⚙ 🏌 **Leisure** fishing, sauna, gymnasium, short game area **Location** 0.5km from Waterville on N70
Hotel ★★★ 75% HL Derrynane, CAHERDANIEL ☎ 066 9475136 📄 066 9475160 50 en suite

CO KILDARE

CARBURY   Map 1 C4

Highfield Golf & Country Club
☎ 046 9731021 📄 046 9731021
e-mail: highfieldgolf@eircom.ie
web: www.highfield-golf.ie

Environmentally friendly parkland course with interesting undulations, enhanced by the fast stream that runs through many holes. Many innovative water features and mature trees with naturally built greens. The 4th dog-legs over the lake, the 7th is a great par 5 with a challenging green, the 10th par 3 is over rushes onto a plateau green (out of bounds on left). The 1st tee is situated on top of the cedar log clubhouse, which provides a spectacular starting point.

18 Holes, 5493mtrs, Par 70, SSS 69. Club membership 500.

Visitors Mon-Sun & BHs. Booking required weekends. Dress code.. **Societies** welcome. **Green Fees** €30-€40 **Course Designer** Alan Duggan **Facilities** ⓣ ⦿ ⛳ ▱ 🍴 🏌 ⚘ ♦ 🏠 ⚙ **Leisure** hard tennis courts, gymnasium **Conf** facs Corporate Hospitality Days **Location** 4.5km NW of village off R402

DONADEA   Map 1 C4

Knockanally Golf & Country Club
☎ 045 869322 📄 045 869322
web: www.knockanally.com

18 Holes, 5930mtrs, Par 72, SSS 72, Course record 66.

Course Designer Noel Lyons **Location** 6km NW of village off M4
Telephone for further details
Hotel ★★★★ 80% HL Barberstown Castle, STRAFFAN
☎ 01 6288157 📄 01 6277027 58 en suite

KILDARE   Map 1 C3

Cill Dara Golf Course Cill Dara
☎ 045 521295 & 521433

9 Holes, 5852mtrs, Par 71, SSS 70, Course record 64.

Location 1.6km E of town
Telephone for further details

The Curragh Golf Club Curragh
☎ 045 441238 & 441714   📄 045 442476
e-mail: curraghgolf@eircom.net
web: www.curraghgolf.com

A particularly challenging course, well wooded and with lovely scenery all around.

18 Holes, 6021mtrs, Par 72, SSS 71, Course record 68.
Club membership 1040.

Visitors Mon & Wed-Fri & BHs. Booking required. Handicap certificate. Dress code. **Societies** booking required. **Green Fees** not confirmed **Prof** Gerry Burke **Facilities** ⓣ ⦿ ⛳ ▱ 🍴 🏌 ⚘ 🏠 ⛳ ⚙ 🏌 **Location** N7 junct 12, follow R413 E towards Kilcullen, turn right at x-roads
Hotel ★★★ 79% HL Maudlins House, Dublin Road, NAAS
☎ 045 896999 📄 045 906411 25 en suite

MAYNOOTH   Map 1 D4

Carton House Golf Club
☎ 01 5052000 📄 01 6286555
web: www.cartonhouse.com

O'Meara: 18 Holes, 6042mtrs, Par 72, SSS 72.
Montgomerie: 18 Holes, 6237mtrs, Par 72, SSS 73,
Course record 68.

Course Designer O'Meara/Lobb & Montgomerie/Edy **Location** N4 W from Dublin, exit Leixlip West, signed
Telephone for further details
Hotel ★★★★ 80% HL Barberstown Castle, STRAFFAN
☎ 01 6288157 📄 01 6277027 58 en suite

NAAS   Map 1 D4

Craddockstown Golf Club Blessington Rd
☎ 045 897610 📄 045 896968
web: www.craddockstown.com

18 Holes, 5748mtrs, Par 72, SSS 72, Course record 66.

Course Designer A Spring & R Jones **Location** SE of town off R410
Telephone for further details
Hotel ★★★ 79% HL Maudlins House, Dublin Road, NAAS
☎ 045 896999 📄 045 906411 25 en suite

THE K CLUB

CO KILDARE - STRAFFAN - MAP 1 D4

The K Club was the venue for the Ryder Cup in 2006, the first time that Ireland has hosted the event. The course reflects the personality of its architect, Arnold Palmer, covering 220 acres of Kildare woodland, with 14 man-made lakes and the River Liffey providing the water hazards. From the instant you arrive at the 1st tee, you are enveloped by a unique atmosphere: the courses are both cavalier and charismatic. The Palmer Course is one of Europe's most spectacular courses, charming, enticing, and invariably bringing out the very best in your game. The best way to describe the Smurfit Course is that of an inland links but its attributes do not stop there. The course has many dramatic landscapes with dunes moulding throughout, while some 14 acres of water have been worked in to the design, especially through the holes 13-18; a watery grave awaits many on the home stretch. The course is entirely different from the Palmer Course located just across the River Liffey.

☎ 01 6017200 📄 01 6017297
e-mail: resortsales@kclub.ie **web:** www.kclub.ie
Palmer Course: 18 Holes, 6709mtrs, Par 72, SSS 76, Course record 60.
Smurfit Course: 18 Holes, 6608mtrs, Par 72, SSS 75, Course record 63. Club membership 700.
Visitors Mon-Sun & BHs. Booking required. Dress code. **Societies** booking required. **Green Fees** Palmer Course from €140, Smurfit Course from €95 **Course Designer** Arnold Palmer **Prof** Michael Dixon **Facilities** ⊕ ⦿ ⓘ ⓛ ☐ ⓠ ⓛ ⓐ ⓔ ⓣ ◇ ◈ ⓕ ◈ ⓕ **Leisure** heated indoor swimming pool, fishing, sauna, gymnasium **Conf** facs Corporate Hospitality Days **Location** W of village off R403
Hotel ★★★★★ CHH The K Club, STRAFFAN ☎ 01 6017200 📄 01 6017298 79 en suite

Naas Golf Club Kerdiffstown
☎ 045 897509 & 874644 📠 045 896109
web: www.naasgolfclub.com

18 Holes, 5663mtrs, Par 71, SSS 69, Course record 65.

Course Designer E Hackett/A Spring/J Howes **Location** NE of town, off N7 onto Johnstown-Sallins road
Telephone for further details
Hotel ★★★ 79% HL Maudlins House, Dublin Road, NAAS
☎ 045 896999 📠 045 906411 25 en suite

STRAFFAN   Map 1 D4

Castlewarden Golf & Country Club
☎ 01 4589254 📠 01 4588972
e-mail: info@castlewardengolfclub.ie
web: www.castlewardengolfclub.ie

Founded in 1990, Castlewarden is maturing into a delightful parkland course with water features and excellent greens.

18 Holes, 5940mtrs, Par 72, SSS 70. Club membership 765.

Visitors Mon, Wed-Fri except BHs. Booking required. Dress code. **Societies** booking required. **Green Fees** €30-€35 **Course Designer** Tommy Halpin **Prof** Brian O'Brien **Facilities** ⑪ ⑩ ⓛ ⌷ ☏ ⚖ 🏠 ⑪ 🐴 ⚒ **Conf** Corporate Hospitality Days
Location 6km S of village off N7 exit 6
Hotel ★★★★ 80% HL Barberstown Castle, STRAFFAN
☎ 01 6288157 📠 01 6277027 58 en suite

The K Club see page 451
☎ 01 6017200 📠 01 6017297
e-mail: resortsales@kclub.ie
web: www.kclub.ie

CO KILKENNY

CALLAN   Map 1 C3

Callan Golf Course Geraldine
☎ 056 7725136 & 7725949 📠 056 7755155
web: www.callangolfclub.com

Meadowland course with well positioned spinneys and water hazards. Not difficult walking and a good test for golfers of all standards.

18 Holes, 5817mtrs, Par 71, SSS 69.
Club membership 1100.

Visitors Mon-Sun & BHs. Booking required. Handicap certificate. Dress code. **Societies** booking required. **Green Fees** not confirmed **Course Designer** B Moore/J Power **Prof** Michael O'Shea **Facilities** ⑪ ⑩ ⓛ ⌷ ☏ ⚖ 🏠 ⑪ ⚒ 🐴 ⚒ **Leisure** fishing **Location** 1.6km SE of village on R699
Hotel ★★★★ 72% HL Pembroke Hotel, Patrick Street, KILKENNY
☎ 056 7783500 📠 056 7783535 74 en suite

KILKENNY   Map 1 C3

Kilkenny Golf Club Glendine
☎ 056 7765400 📠 056 7723593
e-mail: enquiries@kilkennygolfclub.com
web: www.kilkennygolfclub.com

One of Ireland's most pleasant inland courses, noted for its tricky finishing holes and its par 3s. Features of the course are its long 11th and 13th holes and the challenge increases year by year as thousands of trees planted over the last 30 years or so are maturing. Sand based greens make the course playable all year round.

18 Holes, 5908mtrs, Par 71, SSS 70, Course record 67.
Club membership 1380.

Visitors Mon-Sun & BHs. Booking required Fri-Sun & BHs. Dress code. **Societies** booking required. **Green Fees** Apr-Oct 35 per 18 holes Mon-Thu, 35 Fri (45 weekends). Nov-Mar 30 (35 weekends)
Prof Jimmy Bolger **Facilities** ⑪ ⑩ ⓛ ⌷ ☏ ⚖ 🏠 🐴 ⚒ 🐴 ⚒ **Leisure** snooker & pool **Conf** facs Corporate Hospitality Days **Location** 1.6km N of town on N77
Hotel ★★★★ 78% HL Kilkenny River Court Hotel, The Bridge, John Street, KILKENNY ☎ 056 7723388 📠 056 7723389 90 en suite

THOMASTOWN   Map 1 C3

Mount Juliet Hotel & Golf Club see page 453
☎ 056 7773010
e-mail: golfreservations@mountjuliet.ie
web: www.mountjuliet.ie

CO LAOIS

ABBEYLEIX   Map 1 C3

Abbeyleix Golf Course Rathmoyle
☎ 057 8731450
e-mail: info@abbeyleixgolfclub.ie
web: www.abbeyleixgolfclub.ie

A pleasant, parkland course. Undulating with water features at five holes.

18 Holes, 5561mtrs, Par 72, SSS 70. Club membership 470.

Visitors Mon-Sun & BHs. Booking required Fri & Sun. Dress code. **Societies** booking required. **Green Fees** not confirmed **Course Designer** Mel Flanagan **Facilities** ⓛ ⌷ ☏ ⚖ ⚒ 🐴 ⚒ **Location** 0.6km from Abbeyleix on Ballyroan road
Hotel ★★★★ 73% HL Killeshin, Dublin Road, PORTLAOISE
☎ 057 8681870 📠 057 8681871 91 en suite

KILLENARD   Map 1 C3

The Heritage Golf & Spa Resort see page 455
☎ 057 864 5500 📠 057 864 2392
e-mail: golf@theheritage.com
web: www.theheritage.com

IRELAND

MOUNT JULIET HOTEL & GOLF CLUB
CO KILKENNY - THOMASTOWN - MAP 1 C3

Mount Juliet's superb 18-hole course was designed by Jack Nicklaus. It has also hosted many prestigious events including the Irish Open on three occasions. The course has a cleverly concealed drainage and irrigation system, perfect even when inclement weather would otherwise halt play. It takes advantage of the estate's mature landscape to provide a world-class 72-par challenge for professionals and high-handicap golfers alike. A unique three-hole golfing academy has been added to allow novice and experienced players ample opportunity to improve their game, while an 18-hole putting course provides an extra dimension of golfing pleasure and is the venue for the National Putting Championship.

☎ 056 7773010
e-mail: golfreservations@mountjuliet.ie   **web:** www.mountjuliet.ie
18 Holes, 6639metres, Par 72, SSS 75, Course record 62. Club membership 500.
Visitors Mon-Sun & BHs. Booking required weekends. Dress code. **Societies** booking required. **Green Fees** Apr & Oct Mon-Tue €70 per round, Wed-Thu & Sun €75, Fri-Sat €85. May-Sep Mon-Tue €75, Wed, Thu & Sun €80, Fri-Sat €90. Nov-Mar Sun-Thu €65, Fri-Sat €75 **Course Designer** Jack Nicklaus **Facilities** ⑨ ⑩ ⊫ ⊡ ⊠ ⊾ ⊜ ⊓ ◇ ✿ ⬤ ◈ ✦ **Leisure** hard tennis courts, heated indoor swimming pool, fishing, sauna, gymnasium, Archery/clay shooting/equestrian **Conf** facs Corporate Hospitality Days **Location** 4km S of town off N9
Hotel ★★★★ CHH Mount Juliet Hotel, THOMASTOWN ☎ 056 7773000 ▤ 056 7773019 57 en suite

MOUNTRATH
Map 1 C3

Mountrath Golf Club Knockanina
☎ 057 8732558 ▤ 057 8732643
web: www.mountrathgolfclub.ie

18 Holes, 5732mtrs, Par 71, SSS 70, Course record 68.

Location 2.5km SW of town off N7
Telephone for further details
Hotel ★★★★ 73% HL Killeshin, Dublin Road, PORTLAOISE
☎ 057 8681870 ▤ 057 8681871 91 en suite

PORTARLINGTON
Map 1 C3

Portarlington Golf Club Garryhinch
☎ 057 8623115 ▤ 057 8623044
e-mail: portalingtongc@eircom.net
web: www.portalingtongolf.com

Lovely parkland course designed around woodland with flat terrain. It is bounded on the 16th and 17th by the River Barrow which makes the back 9 very challenging. Club celebrated its centenary in 2008.

18 Holes, 5906mtrs, Par 71, SSS 71, Course record 66. Club membership 1080.

Visitors Mon-Sat & BHs. Booking required Wed, Sat & BHs. Handicap certificate. Dress code. **Societies** booking required. **Green Fees** €25 per round summer (€40 weekends). €20 winter **Course Designer** Eddie Hackett **Facilities** ⓣ ⓞ ▤ ⬜ ⓣ ⚒ ⬛ ⚔ 🛒 ⚔
Conf facs Corporate Hospitality Days **Location** 6.5km SW of town on R423
Hotel ★★★★ 73% HL Killeshin, Dublin Road, PORTLAOISE
☎ 057 8681870 ▤ 057 8681871 91 en suite

PORTLAOISE
Map 1 C3

The Heath Golf Club
☎ 057 8646533 ▤ 057 8646735
e-mail: info@theheathgc.ie
web: www.theheathgc.ie

Course noted for its rough heather and gorse and scenic views of the rolling hills of Co Laois. Remarkably dry conditions all year round.

18 Holes, 5866mtrs, Par 71, SSS 71, Course record 65. Club membership 850.

Visitors Mon-Sun & BHs. Booking required weekends & BHs. **Societies** booking required. **Green Fees** €25 per round (€35 weekends) **Course Designer** Jeff Howes Prof Mark O'Boyle
Facilities ⓣ ⓞ ▤ ⬜ ⓣ ⚒ ⬛ ⚔ 🛒 ⚔ ⚓
Leisure Billiard room **Location** M7 exit 16, 1.5m to club
Hotel ★★★★ 73% HL Killeshin, Dublin Road, PORTLAOISE
☎ 057 8681870 ▤ 057 8681871 91 en suite

RATHDOWNEY
Map 1 C3

Rathdowney Golf Club
☎ 0505 46170 ▤ 0505 46065
web: www.rathdowneygolfclub.com

18 Holes, 5894metres, Par 71, SSS 70, Course record 67.

Course Designer Eddie Hackett **Location** 0.8km SE, follow Johnstown signs from town square
Telephone for further details

CO LEITRIM

BALLINAMORE
Map 1 C4

Ballinamore Golf Club
☎ 071 9644346

9 Holes, 5194mtrs, Par 70, SSS 68, Course record 66.

Course Designer A Spring **Location** 3km W of town along Shannon-Erne canal
Telephone for further details
Hotel ★★★★ 78% HL Lough Rynn Castle, MOHILL
☎ 071 9632700 & 9632714 ▤ 071 9632710 43 en suite

CARRICK-ON-SHANNON
Map 1 C4

Carrick-on-Shannon Golf Club Woodbrook
☎ 071 9667015
e-mail: ckgc3@eircom.net
web: www.carrickgolfclub.ie

An 18 hole course with a delightful diversity of scenery. Extended from 9 holes on preserved marshland that sweeps down to a lake and the Boyle river. The original 9 holes are set in mature parkland and under the new layout constitute the first 5 and last 4 holes of the course. Two spectacular holes are the 8th where the tee is surrounded by water which requires a carry over the river and the 13th, a frightening par 3.

18 Holes, 5728mtrs, Par 70, SSS 68. Club membership 450.

Visitors contact club for details. **Societies** booking required. **Green Fees** €20 Mon-Thu Apr-Sep, (€35 Fri-Sun) **Course Designer** Eddie Hackett/ Marc Westenborg (new 9) **Facilities** ⓣ ⓞ ▤ ⬜ ⓣ €
⚒ 🛒 ⚔ ⚓ **Location** 6.5km W of town on N4
Hotel ★★★★ 74% HL The Landmark, CARRICK-ON-SHANNON
☎ 071 9622222 ▤ 071 9622233 60 en suite

CO LIMERICK

ADARE
Map 1 B3

Adare Manor Golf Club
☎ 061 396204 ▤ 061 396800
e-mail: info@adaremanorgolfclub.com
web: www.adaremanorgolfclub.com

A parkland course surrounding the ruins of a 13th-century castle and a 15th-century abbey.

18 Holes, 6058mtrs, Par 69, SSS 67, Course record 63. Club membership 750.

Visitors Mon-Wed, Fri & Sat except BHs. Booking required. **Societies** booking required **Green Fees** €40 per round **Course Designer** Ben Sayers/Eddie Hackett **Facilities** ⓣ ⓞ ▤ ⬜ ⓣ
⚒ ⬛ ⚓ ⚔ **Location** NE of town off N21
Hotel ★★★★ 82% HL Dunraven Arms, ADARE ☎ 061 605900
▤ 061 396541 86 en suite

IRELAND

THE HERITAGE GOLF & SPA RESORT

CO LAOIS - KILLENARD - MAP 1 C3

The Heritage Golf & Spa Resort, located in the village of Killenard, just an hour from Dublin, is home to the Heritage 72 par Championship course, co-designed by the late Seve Ballesteros and Jeff Howes. Set in beautiful rolling countryside, with the Slieve Bloom mountains as a backdrop, the course provides one of the most enjoyable experiences in Ireland for golfers of all standards. Five lakes and a stream bring water into play on 10 holes, while 98 bunkers and 7,000 trees adorn the gently undulating landscape. A variety of tees allow the course to be played from 5,747 to 7,319 yards. Also part of the resort, the Seve Ballesteros 'Natural' Golf School, the first of its kind in the UK and Ireland, makes use of cutting edge technology and personal tuition from PGA professionals to teach the principles of Ballesteros' own game. In addition you will find the Leix Course, a dedicated practice course.

☎ 057 864 5500   🖹 057 864 2392
e-mail: golf@theheritage.com   **web:** www.theheritage.com
18 Holes, 6889yds, Par 72, SSS 72. Club membership 220.
Visitors Contact club for details. **Societies** booking required. **Green Fees** Jan-Mar & Oct-Dec €50 per person, Apr-Sep €60 per person per 18 holes **Course Designer** Seve Ballesteros **Facilities** ⑪ 🍴 🔚 ⬜ 🍴 ⛱ 🗄 ⛳
◇ ✿ 🚗 ✿ 🏌 **Leisure** hard tennis courts, heated indoor swimming pool, fishing, sauna, gymnasium **Conf** facs Corporate Hospitality Days **Location** M7 exit 15, signed, approx 4m
Hotel ⛴ The Heritage Golf & Spa Resort, KILLENARD ☎ 057 8645500 🖹 057 8695037 98 en suite

LIMERICK
Map 1 B3

Castletroy Golf Club Castletroy
☎ 061 335753 ▤ 061 335373
e-mail: golf@castletroygolfclub.ie
web: www.castletroygolfclub.ie

Mature, parkland course extensively redeveloped in recent years. Out of bounds left of the first two holes and well maintained fairways demand accuracy off the tee. The long par 5 6th hole is set into water. The par 3 14th hole features a panoramic view from the tee with the green surrounded by water while the picturesque 18th is a stern test to finish with the green guarded by bunkers on both sides.

18 Holes, 6284mtrs, Par 72, SSS 73, Course record 69. Club membership 1000.

Visitors Mon, Wed, Fri, Sat & BHs. Booking required. Handicap certificate. Dress code. **Societies** booking required. **Green Fees** €40 per 18 holes (€50 Fri-Sat & BHs) **Course Designer** Eddie Connaughton **Prof** Denise O'Shea **Facilities** ⑪ ⑩ ⓛ ⓤ ⓛ ⚘ ⚘ ✦ **Conf** Corporate Hospitality Days **Location** 5km E of city centre **Hotel** ★★★★ 79% HL Carlton Castletroy Park Hotel, Dublin Road, LIMERICK ☎ 061 335566 & 508700 ▤ 061 331117 107 en suite

Limerick County Golf & Country Club Ballyneety
☎ 061 351881 ▤ 061 351384
e-mail: info@limerickcounty.com
web: www.limerickcounty.com

Limerick County was designed by Des Smyth and presents beautifully because of the strategic location of the main features. It stretches over undulating terrain with one elevated section providing views of the surrounding countryside. It features over 70 bunkers with six lakes and several unique design features.

18 Holes, 5417mtrs, Par 71, SSS 36. Club membership 800.

Visitors Mon-Sun & BHs. Booking required Fri-Sun & BHs. Dress code. **Societies** Booking required. **Green Fees** not confirmed **Course Designer** Des Smyth **Prof** Donal McSweeney **Facilities** ⑪ ⑩ ⓛ ⓤ ⓛ ⚘ ⚘ ✦ **Conf** facs Corporate Hospitality Days **Location** 8km SE of city on R512 **Hotel** ★★★★ 79% HL Carlton Castletroy Park Hotel, Dublin Road, LIMERICK ☎ 061 335566 & 508700 ▤ 061 331117 107 en suite

Limerick Golf Club Ballyclough
☎ 061 415146 ▤ 061 319219
e-mail: pat.murray@limerickgolfclub.ie
web: www.limerickgc.com

Tree-lined parkland course. The club is the only Irish winner of the European Cup Winners Team Championship.

18 Holes, 6601mtrs, Par 72, SSS 72, Course record 63. Club membership 1500.

Visitors Mon, Wed-Sun except BHs. Booking required. Dress code. **Societies** booking required. **Green Fees** not confirmed **Course Designer** A McKenzie **Prof** Lee Harrington **Facilities** ⑪ ⑩ ⓛ ⓤ ⓛ ⚘ ⚘ ✦ **Conf** facs Corporate Hospitality Days **Location** 5km S on R511 **Hotel** ★★★★ 79% HL Carlton Castletroy Park Hotel, Dublin Road, LIMERICK ☎ 061 335566 & 508700 ▤ 061 331117 107 en suite

NEWCASTLE WEST
Map 1 B3

Newcastle West Golf Club, Ardagh
☎ 069 76500 ▤ 069 76511
e-mail: info@newcastlewestgolf.com
web: www.newcastlewestgolf.com

Course set in 160 acres of countryside, built to the highest standards on sandy free draining soil. A practice ground and driving range are included. Hazards on the course include lakes, bunkers, streams and trees. A signature hole is the par 3 6th playing 185yds over a lake. New features on par 5, 8th hole including bunker and open drain.

18 Holes, 6000mtrs, Par 71, Course record 66. Club membership 1019.

Visitors Mon-Sun & BHs. Booking required Thu, weekends & BHs. **Societies** booking required. **Green Fees** €30 per 18 holes (€35 weekends) **Course Designer** Dr Arthur Spring **Prof** Conor McCormick **Facilities** ⑪ ⑩ ⓛ ⓤ ⓛ ⚘ ⚘ ⚘ ⚘ ✦ **Conf** facs Corporate Hospitality Days **Location** 3.5km off N21 **Hotel** ★★★★ 82% HL Dunraven Arms, ADARE ☎ 061 605900 ▤ 061 396541 86 en suite

LONGFORD
Map 1 C4

County Longford Golf Club, Glack, Dublin Rd
☎ 043 3346310 ▤ 043 3347082
e-mail: colonggolf@eircom.net
web: www.countylongfordgolfclub.com

A lovely parkland course with lots of trees founded in 1894. A stream comes into play at a number of holes including the last. Additional water features have also been introduced, especially at the signature 13th hole. Fine views of Longford and the surrounding countryside from almost every hole.

18 Holes, 5781mtrs, Par 72. Club membership 804.

Visitors Mon-Sun & BHs. Booking required. Dress code. **Societies** booking required. **Green Fees** €20 weekdays (€25 weekends & BHs) **Course Designer** Irish Golf Design **Prof** David Byrne **Facilities** ⑪ ⑩ ⓛ ⓤ ⓛ ⚘ ⚘ ⚘ ⚘ ✦ **Conf** facs Corporate Hospitality Days **Location** From Dublin take 1st exit at rdbt entering Longford. Continue for approx 0.5m along Dublin Rd, club entrance on left **Hotel** ★★★★ 76% HL Abbey Hotel, Galway Road, ROSCOMMON ☎ 090 6626240 ▤ 090 6626021 50 en suite

ARDEE
Map 1 D4

Ardee Golf Club Townparks
☎ 041 6853227 ▤ 041 6856137
web: www.ardeegolfclub.com

18 Holes, 5934mtrs, Par 71, SSS 72, Course record 64.

Course Designer Eddie Hackett & Declan Branigan **Location** N33 to Ardee, 400 metres from Fair Green
Telephone for further details
Hotel ★★★★ 79% HL Ballymascanlon House Hotel, DUNDALK ☎ 042 9358200 ▤ 042 9371598 90 en suite

BALTRAY   Map 1 D4

County Louth Golf Club
☎ 041 9881530 📠 041 9881531
e-mail: reservations@countylouthgolfclub.com
web: www.countylouthgolfclub.com

Generally held to have the best greens in Ireland, this links course was designed by Tom Simpson to have well-guarded and attractive greens without being overly dependant on bunkers. It provides a good test for modern championship play.

18 Holes, 6300mtrs, Par 72, SSS 72, Course record 64. Club membership 1342.

Visitors Mon, Wed-Sat excluding BHs. Booking required. Dress code. **Societies** welcome. **Green Fees** 100 (135 Sat) **Course Designer** Tom Simpson **Prof** Paddy McGuirk **Facilities** ⓣ ⓞ 🏋 ⛳ 🍴 ⚒ 🏠 ⚑ ◇ ⚙ 🚽 ⚙ 🏌 **Leisure** hard tennis courts **Conf** Corporate Hospitality Days **Location** 8km NE of Drogheda
Hotel ★★★★ BB Windsor Lodge, 1 The Court, DROGHEDA
☎ 041 9841966 📠 041 9841966 7 rooms

DUNDALK   Map 1 D4

Ballymascanlon House Hotel Golf Course Carlingford Rd (R173)
☎ 042 9358200 📠 042 9371598
e-mail: info@ballymascanlon.com
web: www.ballymascanlon.com

A testing parkland course with numerous water hazards and two difficult holes through woodland, this very scenic course is set at the edge of the Cooley Mountains.

Ballymascanlon: 18 Holes, 5073mtrs, Par 68, SSS 68.

Visitors Booking required Fri-Sun. **Societies** booking required. **Green Fees** From €25-€35 **Course Designer** Craddock/Ruddy **Facilities** ⓣ ⓞ 🏋 ⛳ 🍴 ⚒ 🏠 ⚑ ◇ ⚙ 🚽 ⚙ **Leisure** hard tennis courts, heated indoor swimming pool, sauna, gymnasium **Conf** facs Corporate Hospitality Days **Location** 5km NE of town on R173
Hotel ★★★★ 79% HL Ballymascanlon House Hotel, DUNDALK
☎ 042 9358200 📠 042 9371598 90 en suite

Killin Park Golf Club Killin Park
☎ 042 9339303 📠 042 9320848

18 Holes, 4840mtrs, Par 69, SSS 65, Course record 65.

Course Designer Eddie Hackett **Location** 4.5km NW of village off N53
Telephone for further details
Hotel ★★★★ 79% HL Ballymascanlon House Hotel, DUNDALK
☎ 042 9358200 📠 042 9371598 90 en suite

GREENORE   Map 1 D4

Greenore Golf Club
☎ 042 9373212 & 9373678 📠 042 9383898
web: www.greenoregolfclub.com

18 Holes, 6078mtrs, Par 71, SSS 73, Course record 69.

Course Designer Eddie Hackett **Location** near village off R175
Telephone for further details
Hotel ★★★★ 79% HL Ballymascanlon House Hotel, DUNDALK
☎ 042 9358200 📠 042 9371598 90 en suite

TERMONFECKIN   Map 1 D4

Seapoint Golf Club
☎ 041 9822333 📠 041 9822331
e-mail: golflinks@seapoint.ie
web: www.seapointgolfclub.com

A premier championship links course with a particularly interesting 17th hole. A testing course where all the clubs in the bag will be needed.

18 Holes, 6470mtrs, Par 72, SSS 74. Club membership 600.

Visitors Mon-Sat & BHs. Booking required. Dress code. **Societies** booking required. **Green Fees** €65 (€75 Sat) **Course Designer** Des Smyth **Prof** David Carroll **Facilities** ⓣ ⓞ 🏋 ⛳ 🍴 ⚒ 🏠 ⚑ ◇ ⚙ 🚽 ⚙ 🏌 **Conf** facs Corporate Hospitality Days **Location** 6.5km NE of Drogheda
Hotel ★★★★ BB Windsor Lodge, 1 The Court, DROGHEDA
☎ 041 9841966 📠 041 9841966 7 rooms

CO MAYO

BALLINA   Map 1 B4

Ballina Golf Club Mossgrove, Shanaghy
☎ 096 21050 📠 096 21718
e-mail: ballinagc@eircom.net
web: www.ballina-golf.com

Undulating parkland with fine views featuring mature and semi-mature tree-lined fairways. The par 3s are a special feature.

18 Holes, 5646mtrs, Par 71, SSS 69, Course record 64. Club membership 520.

Visitors Mon-Sun & BHs. Booking required weekends & BHs. Dress code. **Societies** booking required. **Green Fees** not confirmed **Course Designer** E Hackett **Facilities** ⓣ ⓞ 🏋 ⛳ 🍴 ⚒ 🏠 ⚑ ◇ ⚙ **Location** 1.5km W of town on R294
Hotel ★★★★ 83% HL Mount Falcon Estate, BALLINA
☎ 096 74472 📠 096 74473 32 en suite

BALLINROBE   Map 1 B4

Ballinrobe Golf Club Cloonacastle
☎ 094 9541118 📠 094 9541889
e-mail: info@ballinrobegolfclub.com
web: www.ballinrobegolfclub.com

A championship parkland course, set in the mature woodlands of a historic estate at Cloonacastle. The layout of the course incorporates seven man-made lakes with the River Robe flowing at the back of the 3rd and 5th greens. Ballinrobe is full of character, typified by the 19th-century residence now used as the clubhouse.

18 Holes, 6354mtrs, Par 73, SSS 73, Course record 67. Club membership 750.

Visitors Mon-Sat & BHs. Booking required Fri, Sat & BHs. Dress code. **Societies** booking required. **Green Fees** not confirmed **Course Designer** Eddie Hackett **Prof** Sean Whelan **Facilities** ⓣ ⓞ 🏋 ⛳ 🍴 ⚒ 🏠 ⚑ ◇ ⚙ **Conf** facs Corporate Hospitality Days **Location** NE of town on R331
Hotel ★★★ 70% HL Cill Aodain Court Hotel, Main Street, KILTIMAGH ☎ 094 9381761 📠 094 9381838 17 en suite

BELMULLET (BÉAL AN MHUIRTHEAD)　Map 1 A5

Carne Golf Links Carne
☎ 097 82292　📄 097 81477
web: www.carnegolflinks.com
18 Holes, 6119mtrs, Par 72, SSS 72, Course record 66.
Course Designer Eddie Hackett **Location** 3km W of town off R313
Telephone for further details
Hotel ★★★★ 83% HL Mount Falcon Estate, BALLINA
☎ 096 74472 📄 096 74473　32 en suite

CASTLEBAR　Map 1 B4

Castlebar Golf Club Hawthorn Av, Rocklands
☎ 094 9021649　📄 094 9026088
e-mail: info@castlebargolfclub.ie
web: www.castlebargolfclub.ie
Course opened September 2000. Fast greens with severe borrows. Accuracy is essential from the tee on most holes. Long difficult course from the championship tees.
18 Holes, 5870mtrs, Par 71, SSS 71. Club membership 650.
Visitors Mon-Sat & BHs. Booking required. **Societies** booking required.
Green Fees €25 per day (€35 Fri-Sat) **Course Designer** Peter McEvoy **Facilities** ⓣ 🍴 🍸 ⌸ 🍷 🏖 🏠 ⛳ 🚕 🏌️ 🏑
Location 1.6km SE of town off N84
Hotel ★★★ GH Kennys Guest House, Lucan Street, CASTLEBAR
☎ 094 9023091　8 rooms

CLAREMORRIS　Map 1 B4

Claremorris Golf Club Castlemacgarrett
☎ 094 9371527　📄 094 9372919
e-mail: info@claremorrisgolfclub.com
web: www.claremorrisgolfclub.com
A parkland course designed by Tom Craddock, designer of Druids Glen. It consists of many eye-catching water features, bunkers, trees and wooded backgrounds. The feature hole is the short par 4 14th with its island green.
18 Holes, 6131mtrs, Par 73, SSS 71. Club membership 675.
Visitors Mon-Sun & BHs. Booking required Thu-Sun & BHs.
Societies booking required. **Green Fees** Oct-Mar €20 per round, Apr-Sep €25 **Course Designer** Tom Craddock **Prof** Jimmy Heggarty **Facilities** ⓣ 🍴 🍸 ⌸ 🍷 🏖 🏠 ⛳ 🏌️ **Location** 2km S of town on N17
Hotel ★★★★ 77% HL McWilliam Park Hotel, CLAREMORRIS
☎ 094 9378000 📄 094 9378001　103 en suite

KEEL　Map 1 A4

Achill Golf Club Achill Island, Westport
☎ 098 43456　📄 098 43456
e-mail: achillislandgolfclub@gmail.com
web: www.achillgolfclub.com
Seaside links in a scenic location by the Atlantic Ocean overlooking Keel Strand with panoramic views of the Minaun Cliffs.
9 Holes, 5452mtrs, Par 70, SSS 67, Course record 70. Club membership 240.
Visitors Mon-Sun & BHs. **Societies** booking required. **Green Fees** not confirmed 🅿 **Course Designer** Paddy Skirrit **Facilities** ⌸ 🏖 ⛳ **Location** E of Keel on R319
Hotel ★★★★ 78% HL Hotel Westport Leisure, Spa & Conference, Newport Road, WESTPORT ☎ 098 25122 & 0870 876 5432 📄 098 25122　129 en suite

SWINFORD　Map 1 B4

Swinford Golf Club Brabazon Park
☎ 094 9251378　📄 094 9251378
web: www.swinfordgolf.com
9 Holes, 5542metres, Par 70, SSS 68.
Location S of town on R320
Telephone for further details
Hotel ★★★ 70% HL Cill Aodain Court Hotel, Main Street, KILTIMAGH ☎ 094 9381761 📄 094 9381838　17 en suite

WESTPORT　Map 1 B4

Westport Golf Club Carrowholly
☎ 098 28262 & 27070　📄 098 24648
e-mail: info@westportgolfclub.com
web: www.westportgolfclub.com
This is a beautiful course with wonderful views of Clew Bay, with its 365 islands, and the holy mountain Croagh Patrick, famous for the annual pilgrimage to its summit. Golfers indulge in a different kind of penance on this challenging course with many memorable holes. Perhaps the most exciting is the par 5 15th, 580yds long and featuring a long carry from the tee over an inlet of Clew Bay.
18 Holes, 6148mtrs, Par 73, SSS 71, Course record 61. Club membership 600.
Visitors Mon-Sun & BHs. Booking required. Dress code.
Societies booking required. **Green Fees** not confirmed **Course Designer** Fred Hawtree **Prof** Alex Mealia **Facilities** ⓣ 🍴 🍸 ⌸ 🍷 🏖 🏠 ⛳ 🏌️ 🏑 **Conf** Corporate Hospitality Days **Location** 4km from town off N59
Hotel ★★★★ 78% HL Hotel Westport Leisure, Spa & Conference, Newport Road, WESTPORT ☎ 098 25122 & 0870 876 5432 📄 098 25122　129 en suite

CO MEATH

BETTYSTOWN   Map 1 D4

Laytown & Bettystown Golf Club
☎ 041 9827170 📄 041 9828506
e-mail: links@landb.ie
web: www.landb.ie

A very competitive and trying links course.

18 Holes, 5875mtrs, Par 71, SSS 71. Club membership 950.

Visitors Mon-Sun & BHs. Booking required. Dress code.
Societies booking required. **Green Fees** €40 per 18 holes **Prof** Robert
J Browne **Facilities** ⑦ ⑩ 🍴 ▯ ⑪ ⚂ 🏠 🖇 ⚞ ⚒
Leisure hard tennis courts **Conf** facs Corporate Hospitality Days
Location N of village on R150
Hotel ★★★★ BB Windsor Lodge, 1 The Court, DROGHEDA
☎ 041 9841966 📄 041 9841966   7 rooms

DUNSHAUGHLIN   Map 1 D4

Black Bush Golf Club Thomastown
☎ 01 8250021 📄 01 8250400
web: www.blackbushgolfclub.ie

Black Bush: 18 Holes, 6337metres, Par 73, SSS 72.
Agore: 18 Holes, 6033metres, Par 71, SSS 69.
Thomastown: 18 Holes, 5882metres, Par 70, SSS 68.

Course Designer Bobby Browne **Location** 2.5km E of village on R125
Telephone for further details
Hotel ★★★ 79% HL Finnstown Country House Hotel, Newcastle
Road, LUCAN ☎ 01 6010700 & 6010708 📄 01 6281088   81 en suite

KELLS   Map 1 C4

Headfort Golf Club
☎ 046 9240146 📄 046 9249282
e-mail: info@headfortgolfclub.ie
web: www.headfortgolfclub.ie

Headfort Old Course is a delightful parkland course which is
regarded as one of the best of its kind in Ireland. There are ample
opportunities for birdies, but even if these are not achieved,
provides a challenging test. The New Course is a modern course
which criss-crosses the Blackwater river, making use of two
islands.

Old Course: 18 Holes, 5973mtrs, Par 72, SSS 71.
New Course: 18 Holes, 6515metres, Par 72, SSS 75.
Club membership 1700.

Visitors Mon-Sun & BHs. Booking required. **Societies** booking
required. **Green Fees** not confirmed **Course Designer** Christy
O'Connor jnr **Prof** Brendan McGovern **Facilities** ⑦ ⑩ 🍴 ▯
⑪ ⚂ 🏠 🖇 ⚞ ⚒ **Location** 0.8km E of village on N3
Hotel ★★★ 73% HL The Park Hotel, Virginia Park, VIRGINIA
☎ 049 8546100 📄 049 8547203   26 en suite

KILCOCK   Map 1 C4

Kilcock Golf Club, Gallow
☎ 01 6287592 📄 01 6287283
e-mail: kilcockgolfclub@eircom.net
web: www.kilcockgolfclub.ie

A parkland course with generous fairways, manicured greens and light
rough only. The course has undergone a major redevelopment with the
installation of USGA sand based tees and greens and a comprehensive
drainage programme.

18 Holes, 6046mtrs, Par 72, SSS 70, Course record 69.
Club membership 700.

Visitors Mon-Sun & BHs. Booking required. Dress code.
Societies booking required. **Green Fees** May-Oct €25 per day (€30
weekends & BHs). Nov-Mar €20 (€28) **Course Designer** Eddie Hackett
Facilities ⑦ ⑩ 🍴 ▯ ⑪ ⚂ ⚒ **Location** M4 exit Kilcock,
course 3km out on Summerhill/Trim Road
Hotel ★★★ 63% HL Lucan Spa, LUCAN ☎ 01 6280494
📄 01 6280841   71 en suite

NAVAN   Map 1 C4

Royal Tara Golf Club Bellinter
☎ 046 25508 & 25244   📄 046 25508
web: www.royaltaragolfclub.com

New Course: 18 Holes, 5757mtrs, Par 71, SSS 70.
Bellinter Nine: 9 Holes, 2911mtrs, Par 35, SSS 35.

Course Designer Des Smyth **Location** 20km from Navan on N3
Telephone for further details
Hotel ★★★★ GA Killyon, Dublin Road, NAVAN ☎ 046 9071224 &
08681 71061 📄 046 9072766   6 rooms

TRIM   Map 1 C4

County Meath Golf Club Newtownmoynagh
☎ 046 9431463 📄 046 9437554
web: www.trimgolf.net

18 Holes, 6088mtrs, Par 73, SSS 72, Course record 68.

Course Designer Eddie Hackett/Tom Craddock **Location** 5km SW of
town on R160
Telephone for further details
Hotel ★★★ GH Brogans, High Street, TRIM ☎ 046 9431237
📄 046 9437648   18 rooms

IRELAND

CO MONAGHAN

CARRICKMACROSS
Map 1 C4

Mannan Castle Golf Club Donaghmoyne
☎ 042 9663308 ▤ 042 9663308
e-mail: mannancastlegc@eircom.net
web: www.mannancastlegolfclub.ie

Parkland and picturesque, the course features the par 3 3rd to an island green. The short par 4 13th through the woods and the 14th to 18th, all crossing water at least once. A test of golf for both amateur and professional. A new Pro shop has been set up along with a new practice putting green and practice chipping area.

18 Holes, 5589mtrs, Par 70, SSS 69. Club membership 700.

Visitors Mon-Sun & BHs. Booking required. Dress code.
Societies booking required. **Green Fees** €25 per 18 holes (€35 weekends) **Course Designer** F Ainsworth **Prof** Kevin McGivern
Facilities ⑪ ⑩ ▐ ⬛ ☕ ⊿ ☖ ✐ 🚗 ✐ ☂ **Conf**
Corporate Hospitality Days **Location** 5km N of Carrickmacross, signed from N1
Hotel ★★★★ 79% HL Ballymascanlon House Hotel, DUNDALK
☎ 042 9358200 ▤ 042 9371598 90 en suite

Nuremore Hotel & Country Club
☎ 042 9671368 ▤ 042 9661853
e-mail: info@nuremore.com
web: www.nuremore.com

Picturesque parkland course of championship length incorporating the drumlins and lakes that are a natural feature of the Monaghan countryside. Precision is required on the 10th to drive over a large lake and between a narrow avenue of trees. Signature hole 18th.

18 Holes, 5870mtrs, Par 71, SSS 71. Club membership 250.

Visitors Mon-Sun & BHs. Booking required.
Societies welcome. **Green Fees** not confirmed **Course Designer** Eddie Hackett **Prof** Maurice Cassidy **Facilities** ⑪ ⑩ ▐ ⬛ ☕ ⊿ ☖ ☕ ♢ ✐ 🚗 ✐ **Leisure** hard tennis courts, heated indoor swimming pool, squash, fishing, sauna, gymnasium **Conf** facs Corporate Hospitality Days **Location** 1.6km SE of town on N2
Hotel ★★★★ 80% HL Nuremore, CARRICKMACROSS
☎ 042 9661438 ▤ 042 9661853 72 en suite

CLONES
Map 1 C5

Clones Golf Club Hilton Park
☎ 047 56017 & 56913 ▤ 047 56913
web: www.clonesgolfclub.com

18 Holes, 5980mtrs, Par 71, SSS 71, Course record 68.

Course Designer Dr Arthur Spring **Location** 5km S of town on R212
Telephone for further details
Hotel ★★★★ 77% HL Errigal Country House, Cavan Road, COOTEHILL ☎ 049 5556901 ▤ 049 5556902 29 en suite

MONAGHAN
Map 1 C5

Rossmore Golf Club Rossmore Park, Cootehill Rd
☎ 047 71222
e-mail: info@rossmoregc.com
web: www.rossmoregc.com

An undulating parkland course in beautiful countryside with views over Ulster and the surrounding area.

18 Holes, 5590mtrs, Par 70, SSS 69, Course record 68.
Club membership 650.

Visitors Mon-Sun & BHs. Booking required Thu, weekends & BHs.
Societies booking required. **Green Fees** €25 per round (€30 weekends & BHs) **Course Designer** Des Smyth **Prof** Ciaran Smyth **Facilities** ⑪ ⑩ ▐ ⬛ ☕ ⊿ ☖ ☕ ✐ 🚗 ✐ ☂ **Leisure** snooker
Location 3km S of town on R188
Hotel ★★★★★ GH The Castle at Castle Leslie Estate, GLASLOUGH ☎ 047 88100 ▤ 047 88256 20 rooms (19 en suite)

CO OFFALY

DAINGEAN
Map 1 C4

Castle Barna Golf Club Tullamore
☎ 057 9353384 ▤ 057 9353077
e-mail: info@castlebarna.ie
web: www.castlebarna.ie

Parkland beside the Grand Canal noted for its excellent greens and lush fairways. Many mature trees, natural streams and the naturally undulating landscape provide a great challenge for golfers of all abilities.

18 Holes, 5816mtrs, Par 72, SSS 71, Course record 66.
Club membership 600.

Visitors Mon-Sun & BHs. Booking required weekends & BHs.
Dress code. **Societies** booking required. **Green Fees** not confirmed
Course Designer Alan Duggan/Kieran Monahan **Facilities** ⑪ by prior arrangement ⑩ by prior arrangement ▐ ⬛ ☕ ⊿ ☕ ✐ 🚗 ✐ **Leisure** fishing **Conf** Corporate Hospitality Days
Location 11km off N6 Dublin-Galway road at Tyrells pass

EDENDERRY
Map 1 C4

Edenderry Golf Club
☎ 046 9731072 ▤ 046 9733911
web: www.edenderrygolfclub.com

18 Holes, 5815metres, Par 72, SSS 72, Course record 66.

Course Designer Havers/Hackett **Location** 1.2km outside Edenderry on Dublin route
Telephone for further details

IRELAND

TULLAMORE   Map 1 C4

Esker Hills Golf Club
☎ 057 9355999 ▤ 057 9355021
e-mail: info@eskerhillsgolf.com
web: www.eskerhillsgolf.com

Esker Hills is built on a landscape of plateaux, sweeping valleys and natural lakes created by the retreating glaciers of the ice age 10,000 years ago. In a unique setting with 18 challenging holes, no two of which are remotely alike. Plays as a parkland course with a links feel and sand based greens.

18 Holes, 6058yds, Par 71, SSS 72, Course record 67.
Club membership 280.

Visitors Mon-Sun & BHs. Booking required. **Societies** Booking required. **Green Fees** €35 per 18 holes (€45 weekends & BHs) **Course Designer** Christy O'Connor jnr **Facilities** ⑪ ⑩! ⓑ
▱ 🍴 ⚲ ⛳ ✦ **Location** 3m from Tullamore off N80 Tullamore to Clara road

Tullamore Golf Club Brookfield
☎ 057 9321439 ▤ 057 9341806
e-mail: tullamoregolfclub@eircom.net
web: www.tullamoregolfclub.ie

Course set in mature parkland of oak, beech and chestnut. The original design was by James Braid and this has been radically altered to meet the highest standards of the modern game, with sand-based undulating greens, lakes, bunkering, mounding and more trees.

18 Holes, 5918mtrs, Par 70, SSS 70, Course record 64.
Club membership 1200.

Visitors Mon-Sun & BHs. Booking required. Dress code **Societies** booking required. **Green Fees** €37 per 18 holes (€48 weekends & BHs) **Course Designer** James Braid/Paddy Merrigam **Prof** Donagh McArdle **Facilities** ⑪ ⑩! ⓑ ▱ 🍴 ⚲ 🏠 ⍾
✦ 🛎 ✦ **Location** N52 taking exit at Ballard rdbt onto R421 for Kinnitty. Club on right after approx 1.6km

CO ROSCOMMON

ATHLONE   Map 1 C4

Athlone Golf Club Hodson Bay
☎ 090 6492073 ▤ 090 6494080
e-mail: athlonegolfclub@eircom.net
web: www.athlonegolfclub.ie

A picturesque parkland course with a panoramic view of Lough Ree. Its tree-lined fairways and undulating terrain make it a true test of golf.

Championship Course: 18 Holes, 5983mtrs, Par 72, SSS 72.
Lough Ree Challenge: 18 Holes, 5698mtrs, Par 73, SSS 71.
Club membership 800.

Visitors Booking required. **Societies** booking required. **Green Fees** €25 (€35 weekends & BHs). Open day Wed €15 **Course Designer** J McAllister **Prof** Kevin Grealy **Facilities** ⑪ ⑩! ⓑ ▱
🍴 ⚲ 🏠 ⍾ ✦ 🛎 ✦ **Conf** Corporate Hospitality Days **Location** 6.5km from Athlone town beside Lough Ree off N61

BALLAGHADERREEN   Map 1 B4

Ballaghaderreen Golf Club
☎ 094 9860295
e-mail: info@ballaghaderreengolfclub.com
web: www.ballaghaderreengolfclub.com

Mature nine-hole course with an abundance of trees. Accuracy off the tee is vital for a good score. Small protected greens require a good short-iron plan. The par 3, 5th hole at 178yds has ruined many a good score.

9 Holes, 5339mtrs, Par 70, SSS 67, Course record 63.
Club membership 300.

Visitors Mon-Sun & BHs. Handicap certificate **Societies** booking required. **Green Fees** not confirmed 🍴 **Course Designer** Paddy Skerritt **Facilities** ⚲ ✦ **Location** 3.5km S of town

BOYLE   Map 1 B4

Boyle Golf Club Roscommon Rd
☎ 071 9662594
9 Holes, 5324mtrs, Par 68, SSS 66, Course record 65.
Course Designer E Hackett **Location** 3km S off N61
Telephone for further details
Hotel ★★★★ 74% HL The Landmark, CARRICK-ON-SHANNON
☎ 071 9622222 ▤ 071 9622233 60 en suite

CASTLEREA   Map 1 B4

Castlerea Golf Course Clonalis
☎ 094 9620068
e-mail: castlereagolf@oceanfree.net
web: www.castlereagolfclub.com

The clubhouse is virtually at the centre of Castlerea course with seven tees visible. A pleasant parkland course incorporating part of the River Francis.

9 Holes, 4974mtrs, Par 68, SSS 66, Course record 61.
Club membership 700.

Visitors Mon-Sat & BHs. **Societies** booking required. **Green Fees** €15 per day 🍴 **Facilities** ⓑ ▱ 🍴 ⚲ ✦ **Location** near town centre on N60
Hotel ★★★★ 76% HL Abbey Hotel, Galway Road, ROSCOMMON
☎ 090 6626240 ▤ 090 6626021 50 en suite

IRELAND

ROSCOMMON
Map 1 B4

Roscommon Golf Course Mote Park
☎ 090 6626382 📄 090 6626043
e-mail: rosegolfclub@eircom.net
web: www.golfclubireland.com/roscommon
Located on the rolling pastures of the Mote Park estate. Numerous water hazards, notably on the tricky 12th, multi-tiered greens and an excellent irrigation to give an all-weather surface. Nine newly designed greens which have added to the quality of the course.

18 Holes, 6290mtrs, Par 72, SSS 72, Course record 64. Club membership 700.

Visitors Mon–Sun & BHs. Booking required Thu, Fri & Sun. Open days usually Fri. Dress code. **Societies** booking required. **Green Fees** €30 per round (€35 weekends) 🏌 **Course Designer** E Connaughton **Facilities** 🍽 🅟 🍴 🛒 ⚑ 👜 🏌 **Location** 0.8km S of Roscommon
Hotel ★★★★ 76% HL Abbey Hotel, Galway Road, ROSCOMMON
☎ 090 6626240 📄 090 6626021 50 en suite

STROKESTOWN
Map 1 C4

Strokestown Golf Club Bumlin
☎ 071 9633528 & 9633660
web: www.strokesdowngolfclub.com
9 Holes, 2615mtrs, Par 70, SSS 67.

Course Designer Mel Flanagan **Location** 2.5km SW of village off R368
Telephone for further details
Hotel ★★★★ 76% HL Abbey Hotel, Galway Road, ROSCOMMON
☎ 090 6626240 📄 090 6626021 50 en suite

CO SLIGO

BALLYMOTE
Map 1 B4

Ballymote Golf Club Ballinascarrow
☎ 071 9183089
web: www.ballymotegolfclub.ie
9 Holes, 5302mtrs, Par 70, SSS 68, Course record 63.
Course Designer Eddie Hacket/Mel Flanagan **Location** 1.5km from Ballymote centre
Telephone for further details
Hotel ★★★★ 74% HL Sligo Park, Pearse Road, SLIGO
☎ 071 9190400 📄 071 9169556 137 en suite

INISHCRONE
Map 1 B5

Enniscrone Golf Club
☎ 096 36297 📄 096 36657
web: www.enniscronegolf.com
27 Holes, 6125metres, Par 73, SSS 72, Course record 70.
Course Designer E Hackett/Donald Steel **Location** 0.8km S of village
Telephone for further details
Hotel ★★★★ 83% HL Mount Falcon Estate, BALLINA
☎ 096 74472 📄 096 74473 32 en suite

SLIGO
Map 1 B5

County Sligo Golf Club Rosses Point
☎ 071 9177134 & 9177186 📄 071 9177460
e-mail: teresa@countysligogolfclub.ie
web: www.countysligogolfclub.ie
Now considered to be one of the top links courses in Ireland, County Sligo is host to a number of international competitions. Set in an elevated position on cliffs above three large beaches, the prevailing winds provide an additional challenge. Tom Watson described it as 'a magnificent links, particularly the stretch of holes from the 14th to the 17th'.

18 Holes, 6170mtrs, Par 71, SSS 72, Course record 66. Bomore: 9 Holes, 2785mtrs, Par 70, SSS 69, Course record 68. Club membership 1250.

Visitors Mon–Sun & BHs. Booking required. Dress code. **Societies** booking required. **Green Fees** Championship Course 70 per 18 holes. Bowmore 25 per 9 holes, 40 per 18 holes **Course Designer** Harry Colt **Prof** Jim Robinson **Facilities** 🍽 🅟 🍴 🅿 🛒 👜 ⚑ 🏌 👜 🏌 **Conf facs** Corporate Hospitality Days
Location N of town off N15
Hotel ★★★★ 79% HL Radisson Blu Hotel & Spa Sligo, Rosses Point Road, Ballincar, SLIGO ☎ 071 9140008 📄 071 9140005 132 en suite

Strandhill Golf Club Strandhill
☎ 071 9168188 📄 071 9168811
18 Holes, 5516mtrs, Par 69, SSS 68.
Location 8km W of town off R292
Telephone for further details
Hotel ★★★★ 74% HL Sligo Park, Pearse Road, SLIGO
☎ 071 9190400 📄 071 9169556 137 en suite

TOBERCURRY
Map 1 B4

Tubbercurry Golf Club
☎ 071 85849 📄 071 9185888
e-mail: contact@tubbercurrygolfclub.com
web: www.tubbercurrygolfclub.com
A parkland course designed by Edward Hackett. The 8th hole, a par 3, is regarded as being one of the most testing in the west of Ireland. An exceptionally dry course, playable all year round.

9 Holes, 5527mtrs, Par 70, SSS 69, Course record 63. Club membership 350.

Visitors Contact club for details. **Societies** booking required. **Green Fees** €15 per day 🏌 **Course Designer** Eddie Hackett **Facilities** 🍽 🅟 🅟 🛒 👜 🏌 **Conf** Corporate Hospitality Days
Location 0.4km from town centre

IRELAND

Save on Hotels. Book at **theAA.com/hotel**

CO TIPPERARY

CO TIPPERARY

CAHIR
Map 1 C3

Cahir Park Golf Club Kilcommon
☎ 052 41474 🖹 052 42717
web: www.cahirparkgolfclub.com

18 Holes, 5806mtrs, Par 71, SSS 71, Course record 66.

Course Designer Eddie Hackett **Location** 1.6km SW of town centre on R668

Telephone for further details
Hotel ★★★★ GH Hanoras Cottage, Nire Valley, BALLYMACARBRY ☎ 052 6136134 & 6136442 🖹 052 6136540 10 rooms

CLONMEL
Map 1 C2

Clonmel Golf Club Lyreanearla
☎ 052 24050 🖹 052 83349
web: www.clonmelgolfclub.com

18 Holes, 5804mtrs, Par 72, SSS 71.

Course Designer Eddie Hackett **Location** 5km from Clonmel off N24
Telephone for further details
Hotel ★★★★ 77% HL Hotel Minella, CLONMEL ☎ 052 22388 🖹 052 24381 70 en suite

MONARD
Map 1 B3

Ramada Hotel & Suites Ballykisteen
☎ 062 33333 🖹 062 31555
web: www.ramadaireland.com

18 Holes, 6186metres, Par 72, SSS 72.

Course Designer Des Smyth **Location** 1.6km SE of village on N24 towards Tipperary
Telephone for further details
Hotel ★★★ GH Ach-na-Sheen House, Clonmel Road, TIPPERARY ☎ 062 51298 🖹 062 80467 8 rooms

NENAGH
Map 1 B3

Nenagh Golf Club Beechwood
☎ 067 31476 🖹 067 34808
e-mail: nenaghgolfclub@eircom.net
web: www.nenaghgolfclub.com

The sand-based greens guarded by intimidating bunkers are a challenge for even the most fastidious putters. Excellent drainage and firm surfaces allow play all year round.

18 Holes, 6029mtrs, Par 72, SSS 72, Course record 68. Club membership 1100.

Visitors Mon-Sat. Booking required. Handicap certificate. Dress code. **Societies** booking required. **Green Fees** not confirmed **Course Designer** Patrick Merrigan **Prof** Ryan McCann **Facilities** ⓤ by prior arrangement 🍴 by prior arrangement 🏓 ⛳ 🎯 ⚑ 🏧 ⚐ **Location** 5km NE of town on R491
Hotel ★★★★ BB Ashley Park House, NENAGH ☎ 067 38223 & 38013 🖹 067 38013 5 rooms

ROSCREA
Map 1 C3

Roscrea Golf Club Derryvale
☎ 0505 21130 🖹 0505 23410
e-mail: info@roscreagolfclub.ie
web: www.roscreagolfclub.ie

Course situated on the eastern side of Roscrea in the shadows of the Slieve Bloom Mountains. A special feature of the course is the variety of the par 3 holes, most noteworthy of which is the 150-metre 4th, which is played almost entirely over a lake. It is widely recognised that the finishing six holes will prove a worthy challenge to even the best players. The most famous hole on the course is the 5th, referred to locally as the Burma Road, a par 5 of over 511 metres with the fairway lined with trees and out of bounds on the left side.

18 Holes, 5594mtrs, Par 71, SSS 70, Course record 67. Club membership 600.

Visitors booking required weekends & BHs. Dress code. **Societies** booking required. **Green Fees** not confirmed **Course Designer** A Spring **Facilities** ⓤ 🍴 🏓 ⛳ 🎯 ⚑ 🏧 ⚐ **Conf** facs Corporate Hospitality Days **Location** E of town on N7

TEMPLEMORE
Map 1 C3

Templemore Golf Club Manna South
☎ 0504 31400
e-mail: tmoregc1@eircom.net

Flat parkland course with many spinneys masking out the fairways. Drains cross the fairway on the 1st and 8th holes and require golfers to manage shot making to avoid ending up in the hazard. The 4th, a par 4 dog-leg and 5th, a par 3, while not very long, demand accuracy to avoid the influence of water hazards and the course boundary.

9 Holes, 5780mtrs, Par 71, SSS 71, Course record 68. Club membership 330.

Visitors contact club for details. **Societies** booking required. **Green Fees** €15 per day (€20 weekends) 🏐 **Facilities** ⚐ **Leisure** hard tennis courts **Location** 0.8km S of town on N62
Hotel ★★★★ 79% HL Horse & Jockey Hotel, Horse & Jockey, THURLES ☎ 0504 44192 🖹 0504 44747 67 en suite

TIPPERARY
Map 1 C3

County Tipperary Golf & Country Club
Dundrum House Hotel
☎ 062 71717 🖹 062 71718
web: www.dundrumhousehotel.com

18 Holes, 6447metres, Par 72, SSS 72.

Course Designer Philip Walton **Location** 12km NE of town on R505
Telephone for further details
Hotel ★★★ GH Ach-na-Sheen House, Clonmel Road, TIPPERARY ☎ 062 51298 🖹 062 80467 8 rooms

CO WATERFORD

DUNGARVAN
Map 1 C2

Dungarvan Golf Club Knocknagranagh
☎ 058 41605 & 43310   📠 058 44113
e-mail: dungarvangc@eircom.net
web: www.dungarvangolfclub.com

A championship-standard course beside Dungarvan Bay, with lakes and hazards placed to challenge all levels of golfer. The greens are considered to be among the best in Ireland.

18 Holes, 6204mtrs, Par 72, SSS 73. Club membership 800.
Visitors Mon-Sun & BHs. Booking required Thu, weekends & BHs. Handicap certificate. Dress code. **Societies** booking required. **Green Fees** €20 weekdays (€30 weekends off peak, €35 peak) **Course Designer** Moss Fives **Prof** David Hayes **Facilities** ⊕ ⫩ 🍴 🛒 **Leisure** Sky sports, snooker **Location** off N25
Hotel ★★★ 68% HL Lawlors, DUNGARVAN ☎ 058 41122 📠 058 41000 89 en suite

Gold Coast Golf & Leisure Ballinacourty
☎ 058 44055   📠 058 44055
e-mail: goldcoastgolf@cablesurf.com
web: www.goldcoastclub.com

Parkland beside the Atlantic Ocean with unrivalled views of Dungarvan Bay. The mature tree-lined fairways of the old course are tastefully integrated with the long and challenging newer holes to create a superb course.

18 Holes, 6171mtrs, Par 72, SSS 72, Course record 70. Club membership 600.
Visitors Mon-Sun & BHs. Booking required. **Societies** booking required. **Green Fees** €20 per 18 holes (€30 weekends & BHs) **Course Designer** Maurice Fives **Facilities** ⊕ ⫩ 🍴 🛒 **Leisure** hard tennis courts, heated indoor swimming pool, sauna, gymnasium **Conf** facs **Location** 3km N of town off N25
Hotel ★★★ 68% HL Lawlors, DUNGARVAN ☎ 058 41122 📠 058 41000 89 en suite

West Waterford Golf & Country Club
☎ 058 43216 & 41475   📠 058 44343
e-mail: info@westwaterfordgolf.com
web: www.westwaterfordgolf.com

Designed by Eddie Hackett, the course is on 150 acres of rolling parkland by the Brickey River with a backdrop of the Comeragh Mountains, Knockmealdowns and Drum Hills. The first nine holes are laid out on a large plateau featuring a stream which comes into play at the 3rd and 4th holes. The river at the southern boundary affects several later holes.

18 Holes, 6137mtrs, Par 72, SSS 72. Club membership 603.
Visitors Mon-Sun & BHs. Booking required weekends & BHs. Dress code. **Societies** welcome. **Green Fees** not confirmed **Course Designer** Eddie Hackett **Facilities** ⊕ ⫩ 🍴 🛒 **Leisure** hard tennis courts **Conf** Corporate Hospitality Days **Location** 5km W of town off N25
Hotel ★★★ 68% HL Lawlors, DUNGARVAN ☎ 058 41122 📠 058 41000 89 en suite

DUNMORE EAST
Map 1 C2

Dunmore East Golf Club
☎ 051 383151   📠 051 383151
web: www.dunmoreeastgolfclub.ie

18 Holes, 6070mtrs, Par 72, SSS 69, Course record 65.
Course Designer W H Jones **Location** into Dunmore East, first left, left at Strand Inn, right
Telephone for further details
Hotel ★★★ 77% HL Majestic, TRAMORE ☎ 051 381761 📠 051 381766 60 en suite

LISMORE
Map 1 C2

Lismore Golf Club Ballyin
☎ 058 54026   📠 058 53338
e-mail: lismoregolf@eircom.net
web: www.lismoregolf.org

Picturesque, tree-dotted, sloping, nine-hole parkland course on the banks of the Blackwater River.

9 Holes, 5300mtrs, Par 69, SSS 67. Club membership 400.
Visitors Mon-Sun & BHs. Booking required weekends. Dress code. **Societies** booking required. **Green Fees** €20 per 18 holes 🍴 **Course Designer** Eddie Hackett **Prof** T. W. Murphy **Facilities** 🛒 🍴 **Location** 1.6km W of town on R666
Hotel ★★★ 68% HL Lawlors, DUNGARVAN ☎ 058 41122 📠 058 41000 89 en suite

TRAMORE
Map 1 C2

Tramore Golf Club Newtown Hill
☎ 051 386170   📠 051 390961
web: www.tramoregolfclub.com

18 Holes, 6060mtrs, Par 72, SSS 72, Course record 66.
Course Designer Capt H C Tippet **Location** 0.8km W of town on R675 coast road
Telephone for further details
Hotel ★★★ 77% HL Majestic, TRAMORE ☎ 051 381761 📠 051 381766 60 en suite

WATERFORD
Map 1 C2

Faithlegg Golf Club
☎ 051 380000 & 086 3840215   📠 051 382010
web: www.faithlegg.com

18 Holes, 6629yds, Par 72, SSS 72, Course record 69.
Course Designer Patrick Merrigan **Location** 9km E of town off R684 towards Cheekpoint
Telephone for further details
Hotel ★★★ 79% HL Tower, The Mall, WATERFORD ☎ 051 875801 & 862300 📠 051 870129 136 en suite

Waterford Castle Golf Club The Island, Ballinakill
☎ 051 871633 🖹 051 879316
e-mail: golf@waterfordcastle.com
web: www.waterfordcastle.com/golf

A unique 130-hectare island course in the River Suir and accessed by private ferry. The course has four water features on the 2nd, 3rd, 4th and 16th holes with a Swilken Bridge on the 3rd hole. Two of the more challenging holes are the par 4s at the 9th and 12th, the 9th being a 379-metre uphill, dog-leg right. The 417-metre 12th is a fine test of accuracy and distance. The views from the course are superb.

18 Holes, 6231mtrs, Par 72, SSS 71, Course record 66. Club membership 770.

Visitors Mon-Sat & BHs. Booking required. Dress code. **Societies** booking required. **Green Fees** Winter 25- 35, Summer 35- 55 **Course Designer** Des Smyth **Prof** James Funnell **Facilities** ⊕ ⦿ 🍴 ⛾ 🏌 🛒 ⚐ ◇ ⚒ 🏧 ⚒ ♟ **Leisure** hard tennis courts **Conf** facs Corporate Hospitality Days **Location** 3km E of town via private ferry **Hotel** ★★★★ HL Waterford Castle, The Island, WATERFORD ☎ 051 878203 🖹 051 879316 19 en suite

Waterford Golf Club Newrath
☎ 051 876748 🖹 051 853405
e-mail: info@waterfordgolfclub.com
web: www.waterfordgolfclub.com

One of the finest inland courses in Ireland. This is exemplified by the spectacular closing stretch, in particular the downhill 18th with its elevated tee, a wonderful viewpoint and a narrow gorse lined fairway demanding a very accurate tee shot.

18 Holes, 5722mtrs, Par 71, SSS 70, Course record 64. Club membership 1102.

Visitors Mon, Wed-Sat & BHs. Booking required. Dress code. **Societies** booking required. **Green Fees** €35 per round (€45 Sat & BHs) **Course Designer** W Park/J Braid **Prof** Harry Ewing **Facilities** ⊕ ⦿ 🍴 ⛾ 🏌 🛒 ⚐ ⚒ 🏧 ♟ **Conf** facs Corporate Hospitality Days **Location** 1.6km N of town on N77 **Hotel** ★★★ 79% HL Tower, The Mall, WATERFORD ☎ 051 875801 & 862300 🖹 051 870129 136 en suite

CO WESTMEATH

ATHLONE   Map 1 C4

Glasson Country House Hotel & Golf Club Glasson
☎ 090 6485120 🖹 090 6485444
e-mail: info@glassongolf.ie
web: www.glassongolfhotel.ie

Opened in 1993, the course has a reputation for being one of the most challenging and scenic courses in Ireland. Designed by Christy O'Connor Jnr it is reputedly his best yet. Surrounded on three sides by Lough Ree the views from everywhere on the course are breathtaking.

18 Holes, 6251mtrs, Par 73, SSS 76, Course record 63. Club membership 220.

Visitors Booking required. **Societies** booking required. **Green Fees** €40-€65 **Course Designer** Christy O'Connor Jnr **Facilities** ⊕ ⦿ 🍴 ⛾ 🏌 🛒 ⚐ ◇ ⚒ 🏧 ⚒ ♟ **Leisure** fishing, sauna, gymnasium, chipping green, steam room **Conf** facs Corporate Hospitality Days **Location** M6 exit 10. 10km N of town on N55

MOATE   Map 1 C4

Mount Temple Golf Course, Mount Temple Village
☎ 090 6481841
e-mail: mounttemple@eircom.net
web: www.mounttemplegolfclub.com

A traditionally built, championship course with unique links-type greens and natural undulating fairways. A challenge for all levels of golfers and all year golfing available. A modern golf academy and driving range attached.

18 Holes, 5927metres, Par 72, SSS 72, Course record 67. Club membership 250.

Visitors Mon-Sun & BHs. Booking required weekends & BHs. Dress code **Societies** booking required. **Green Fees** €25 per round, (€30 weekends & BHs) **Course Designer** Michael Dolan **Prof** Mel Flanagan **Facilities** ⊕ ⦿ 🍴 ⛾ 🏌 🛒 ⚐ ◇ ⚒ 🏧 ⚒ ♟ **Conf** facs Corporate Hospitality Days **Location** M6 junct 6/7, 5km NW of town to Mount Temple **Hotel** ★★★ 75% HL Bloomfield House Hotel, Leisure Club & Spa, Belvedere, MULLINGAR ☎ 044 93440894 🖹 044 9343767 111 en suite

MULLINGAR   Map 1 C4

Mullingar Golf Club
☎ 044 9348366 🖹 044 9341499
e-mail: mullingargolfclub@hotmail.com
web: www.mullingargolfclub.com

The wide rolling fairways between mature trees provide parkland golf at its very best. The course, designed by the great James Braid, offers a tough challenge. It has been the venue of the Irish Professional Championship. One advantage of the layout is that the clubhouse is never far away. It is also the host to the Annual Mullingar Scratch Trophy.

18 Holes, 6111mtrs, Par 72, SSS 72, Course record 65. Club membership 1000.

Visitors Mon, Tue, Thu-Sat except BHs. Booking required Sat. Handicap certificate. Dress code. **Societies** booking required. **Green Fees** 40 per 18 holes (45 Sat) **Course Designer** James Braid **Prof** John Burns **Facilities** ⊕ ⦿ 🍴 ⛾ 🏌 🛒 ⚐ ⚒ 🏧 ♟ **Leisure** snooker table **Conf** facs Corporate Hospitality Days **Location** 5km S of town on N52 **Hotel** ★★★★ 80% HL Mullingar Park, Dublin Road, MULLINGAR ☎ 044 9344446 & 9337500 🖹 044 9335937 95 en suite

CO WEXFORD

ENNISCORTHY   Map 1 D3

Enniscorthy Golf Club Knockmarshall
☎ 053 9233191 🖹 053 9237367
e-mail: info@enniscorthygc.ie
web: www.enniscorthygc.ie

A pleasant course suitable for all levels of ability.

18 Holes, 6115mtrs, Par 72, SSS 72. Club membership 900.

Visitors Mon-Sun & BHs. Booking required. Handicap certifcate. Dress code **Societies** booking required. **Green Fees** €25-€30 per round (€35 Fri-Sun & BHs) **Course Designer** Eddie Hackett **Prof** Stephen Fitzpatrick **Facilities** ⊕ ⦿ 🍴 ⛾ 🏌 🛒 ⚐ 🏧 ⚒ ♟ **Leisure** sauna **Conf** Corporate Hospitality Days **Location** 1.6km W of town on N30

IRELAND

GOREY
Map 1 D3

Courtown Golf Club Kiltennel
☎ 055 25166 🖨 055 25553
web: www.courtowngolfclub.com
18 Holes, 5898mtrs, Par 71, SSS 71, Course record 65.
Course Designer Harris & Associates **Location** 5km SE of town off R742
Telephone for further details
Hotel ★★★★ 76% HL Ashdown Park Hotel, The Coach Road, GOREY TOWN ☎ 053 9480500 🖨 053 9480777 79 en suite

ROSSLARE
Map 1 D2

Rosslare Golf Club Rosslare Strand
☎ 053 9132203 🖨 053 9132263
e-mail: office@rosslaregolf.com
web: www.rosslaregolf.com
This traditional links course is within minutes of the ferry terminal at Rosslare. Many of the greens are sunken and are always in beautiful condition, but the semi-blind approaches are among features of this course which provide a healthy challenge. Celebrated 100 years of golf in 2005.
Old Course: 18 Holes, 6205mtrs, Par 72, SSS 73.
Burrow: 12 Holes, 3917metres, Par 46.
Club membership 1500.
Visitors Mon-Sun & BHs. Booking required. Dress code.
Societies booking required. **Green Fees** not confirmed **Course Designer** Hawtree/Taylor **Prof** Johnny Young **Facilities** ⓣ 🍴 ⓘ 🍺 ☕ 🍽 🏌 🛍 ⚙ 🛒 ⚙ 🏌 **Leisure** sauna **Conf** Corporate Hospitality Days **Location** N of Rosslare village
Hotel ★★★★ HL Kelly's Resort Hotel & Spa, ROSSLARE
☎ 053 9132114 🖨 053 9132222 118 en suite

St Helen's Bay Golf & Country Club St Helens
☎ 053 9133234 🖨 053 9133803
web: www.sthelensbay.com
27 Holes, 5894mtrs, Par 72, SSS 72, Course record 69.
Course Designer Philip Walton **Location** SE of Rosslare Harbour off N25
Telephone for further details
Hotel ★★★★ HL Kelly's Resort Hotel & Spa, ROSSLARE
☎ 053 9132114 🖨 053 9132222 118 en suite

WEXFORD
Map 1 D3

Wexford Golf Club Mulgannon
☎ 053 42238 🖨 053 42243
web: www.wexfordgolfclub.ie
18 Holes, 5950mtrs, Par 71, SSS 70.
Location
Telephone for further details
Hotel ★★★★ FH Killiane Castle, Drinagh, WEXFORD
☎ 053 9158885 🖨 053 9158885 8 rooms

CO WICKLOW

ARKLOW
Map 1 D3

Arklow Golf Club Abbeylands
☎ 0402 32492 🖨 0402 91604
e-mail: arklowgolflinks@eircom.net
web: www.arklowgolflinks.com
Scenic links course.
18 Holes, 6505mtrs, Par 69, SSS 71, Course record 64.
Club membership 1000.
Visitors Mon-Sat & BHs. Booking required. Handicap certificate. Dress code. **Societies** Booking required. **Green Fees** not confirmed **Course Designer** Hawtree & Taylor **Facilities** ⓣ 🍴 🍺 ☕ 🍽 🏌 ⚙ **Location** 0.8km E of town centre
Hotel ★★★ CHH Marlfield House Hotel, GOREY ☎ 053 9421124
🖨 053 9421572 19 en suite

BALTINGLASS
Map 1 D3

Baltinglass Golf Club Dublin Rd
☎ 059 6481350 🖨 059 6481842
web: www.baltinglassgc.com
18 Holes, 5912mtrs, Par 71, SSS 71, Course record 68.
Course Designer Eddie Connaughton **Location** 500mtrs N of village
Telephone for further details
Hotel ★★★ 78% HL Seven Oaks, Athy Road, CARLOW
☎ 059 9131308 🖨 059 9132155 89 en suite

BLAINROE
Map 1 D3

Blainroe Golf Club
☎ 0404 68168 🖨 0404 69369
web: www.blainroe.com
With sea views from all 18 holes, this enjoyable and challenging parkland course is always well maintained and offers an interesting variety of holes with the 14th played over the sea from a cliff promontory, probably being the feature. The modern clubhouse overlooks a private beach.
18 Holes, 6140mtrs, Par 72, SSS 73, Course record 68.
Club membership 1300.
Visitors Mon-Sat & BHs. Booking required. Dress code
Societies booking required. **Green Fees** €40 (€50 Sat & BHs) **Course Designer** Fred Hawtree **Prof** John McDonald **Facilities** ⓣ 🍴 🍺 ☕ 🍽 🏌 🏨 ⚙ 🛒 ⚙ **Leisure** private beach **Conf** Corporate Hospitality Days **Location** 5km SE of Wicklow on R750 coast road
Hotel ★★★★ FH Kilpatrick House, Redcross, WICKLOW
☎ 0404 47137 & 087 6358325 🖨 0404 47866 4 rooms (3 en suite)

BLESSINGTON
Map 1 D3

Tulfarris Hotel & Golf Resort
☎ 045 867609 🖨 045 867601
e-mail: proshop@tulfarris.com
web: www.tulfarris.com
Designed by Paddy Merrigan, this course is on the Blessington lakeshore with the Wicklow Mountains as a backdrop. The use of the natural landscape is evident throughout the whole course, the variety of trees guarding fairways and green approaches.
continued

IRELAND

Save on Hotels. Book at **theAA.com/hotel**

CO WICKLOW

18 Holes, 7165yds, Par 72. Club membership 255.
Visitors Mon-Sun & BHs. Dress code. **Societies** booking required.
Green Fees €30 per round (€40 weekends) **Course Designer** Patrick
Merrigan **Facilities** ⊕ ⵙ◎ ⵗ ⯅ 🖥 📠 ⵙ ◇ ⵗ
ⵗ ⵗ **Leisure** hard tennis courts, fishing, gymnasium **Conf** facs
Corporate Hospitality Days **Location** 3.5km from village off N81
Hotel ★★★ 79% HL Maudlins House, Dublin Road, NAAS
☎ 045 896999 📠 045 906411 25 en suite

BRAY
Map 1 D4

Bray Golf Club Greystones Rd
☎ 01 2763200 📠 01 2763262
e-mail: info@braygolfclub.com
web: www.braygolfclub.com

A USGA standard parkland course of nearly 81 hectares, combining
stunning scenery with a classic layout. The 11th par 4 signature hole
provides a fine view of the coastline.

18 Holes, 5645mtrs, Par 71, SSS 71, Course record 66.
Club membership 790.

Visitors Mon, Thu-Sat except BHs. Booking required. Dress code.
Societies booking required. **Green Fees** not confirmed **Course
Designer** Smyth/Brannigan **Prof** Ciaran Carroll **Facilities** ⊕ ⵙ◎
⯅ ⵗ ⵗ ⯅ 🖥 ⵗ ⵗ 📠 ⵗ ⵗ **Conf** facs Corporate
Hospitality Days **Location** near town off R761
Hotel ★★★ 73% HL Royal Hotel & Leisure Centre, Main Street,
BRAY ☎ 01 2862935 & 2724900 📠 01 2867373 130 en suite

Old Conna Golf Club Ferndale Rd
☎ 01 2826055 & 2826766 📠 01 2825611
18 Holes, 5989mtrs, Par 72, SSS 72, Course record 68.
Course Designer Eddie Hackett **Location** 3.5km from town centre
Telephone for further details
Hotel ★★★ 73% HL Royal Hotel & Leisure Centre, Main Street,
BRAY ☎ 01 2862935 & 2724900 📠 01 2867373 130 en suite

Woodbrook Golf Club Dublin Rd
☎ 01 2824799 📠 01 2821950
web: www.woodbrook.ie
18 Holes, 6017mtrs, Par 72, SSS 71, Course record 65.
Course Designer Peter McEvoy **Location** on N11
Telephone for further details
Hotel ★★★ 73% HL Royal Hotel & Leisure Centre, Main Street,
BRAY ☎ 01 2862935 & 2724900 📠 01 2867373 130 en suite

BRITTAS BAY
Map 1 D3

The European Club
☎ 0404 47415 📠 0404 47449
web: www.theeuropeanclub.com
20 Holes, 6737mtrs, Par 71, SSS 73, Course record 67.
Course Designer Pat Ruddy **Location** 1.6km from Brittas Bay
Telephone for further details
Hotel ★★★★ FH Kilpatrick House, Redcross, WICKLOW
☎ 0404 47137 & 087 6358325 📠 0404 47866 4 rooms (3 en
suite)

DELGANY
Map 1 D3

Delgany Golf Club
☎ 01 2874536 📠 01 2873977
e-mail: delganygolf@eircom.net
web: www.delganygolfclub.com

Undulating parkland amid beautiful scenery. Recently remodelled with
sand-based greens and tees to USGA specifications.

18 Holes, 5473mtrs, Par 69, SSS 68, Course record 62.
Club membership 1200.

Visitors Mon-Sun & BHs. Booking required. Handicap certificate. Dress
code. **Societies** booking required. **Green Fees** not confirmed **Course
Designer** H Vardon **Prof** Gavin Kavanagh **Facilities** ⊕ ⵙ◎ ⯅
⯅ ⵗ ⯅ 🖥 ⵗ ⵗ ⵗ ⵗ **Conf** Corporate Hospitality Days
Location 1.2km from village off N11
Hotel ★★★★ 77% HL Glenview, Glen O' the Downs, DELGANY
☎ 01 2873399 📠 01 2877511 70 en suite

Glen of the Downs Golf Club Coolnaskeagh
☎ 01 2876240 📠 01 2870063
web: www.glenofthedowns.com
18 Holes, 5468mtrs, Par 71, SSS 70, Course record 68.
Course Designer Peter McEvoy **Location** off N11 southbound at
Glenview exit, 4m from Bray
Telephone for further details
Hotel ★★★★ 77% HL Glenview, Glen O' the Downs, DELGANY
☎ 01 2873399 📠 01 2877511 70 en suite

DUNLAVIN
Map 1 D3

Rathsallagh House Golf & Country Club
☎ 045 403316 📠 045 403295
e-mail: golf@rathsallagh.com
web: www.rathsallagh.com

Designed by Peter McEvoy and Christy O'Connor Jnr, this is a
spectacular course which will test the professionals without
intimidating the club golfer. Set in 525 acres of lush parkland with
thousands of mature trees, natural water hazards and gently rolling
landscape. The greens are of high quality, in design, construction and
condition.

18 Holes, 6483mtrs, Par 72, SSS 72, Course record 67.
Club membership 460.

Visitors Mon-Sun & BHs. Booking required. Dress code.
Societies booking required. **Green Fees** €45 per round (€55 weekends
& BHs) **Course Designer** McEvoy/O'Connor **Prof** Brendan McDaid
Facilities ⊕ ⵙ◎ ⯅ ⵗ ⵗ ⯅ 🖥 ⵗ ◇ ⵗ 📠 ⵗ ⵗ
Leisure hard tennis courts, private jacuzzi/steam room, croquet lawn,
walled garden **Conf** facs Corporate Hospitality Days **Location** SW of
village off N9
Hotel ★★★★ FH Tynte House, DUNLAVIN ☎ 045 401561
📠 045 401586 7 rooms

IRELAND

GREYSTONES   Map 1 D3

Charlesland Golf Club
☎ 01 2874350 & 2878200   📠 01 2874360
e-mail: teetimes@charlesland.com
web: www.charlesland.com

Championship length course with a double dog-leg at the 9th and
18th. Water hazards on seven holes. Signature hole is the par 3 13th
which at 229 metres from the championship tee makes it one of the
longest par 3's in Ireland.

18 Holes, 6169mtrs, Par 72, SSS 72, Course record 68.
Club membership 680.

Visitors Mon-Sun & BHs. Booking required. Dress code.
Societies booking required. **Green Fees** €35 per 18 holes Mon-Thu
(€40 Fri & Sun, €50 Sat) **Course Designer** Eddie Hackett **Prof** James
Nash **Facilities** 🕐 🍴 🍺 ⬜ 🍽 ⛳ 🏨 ⛳ ◇ ✦ 🚜 ✦
✦ **Conf** facs Corporate Hospitality Days **Location** 1.6km S of town
on R762
Hotel ★★★★ 77% HL Glenview, Glen O' the Downs, DELGANY
☎ 01 2873399 📠 01 2877511 70 en suite

NEWTOWN MOUNT KENNEDY   Map 1 D3

Druids Glen Golf Club see page 469
☎ 01 2870847 📠 01 2873699
e-mail: reservations@druidsglenresort.ie
web: www.druidsglenresort.com

Kilcoole Golf Club
☎ 01 2872066 📠 01 2010497
web: www.kilcoolegolfclub.com

9 Holes, 5506mtrs, Par 70, SSS 69, Course record 66.
Location S of village on R761
Telephone for further details
Hotel ★★★★ 77% HL Glenview, Glen O' the Downs, DELGANY
☎ 01 2873399 📠 01 2877511 70 en suite

RATHDRUM   Map 1 D3

Glenmalure Golf Course Greenane
☎ 0404 46679 📠 0404 46783
web: www.glenmalure-golf.ie

18 Holes, 4846metres, Par 71, SSS 67, Course record 71.
Course Designer P Suttle **Location** 3km W of town
Telephone for further details

ROUNDWOOD   Map 1 D3

Roundwood Golf Club Newtown
☎ 01 2818488 & 2802555 📠 01 2843642
web: www.roundwoodgolf.com

18 Holes, 6113mtrs, Par 72, SSS 72, Course record 70.
Location 4km NE of village on R765
Telephone for further details
Hotel ★★★ 71% HL The Glendalough, GLENDALOUGH
☎ 0404 45135 📠 0404 45142 44 en suite

SHILLELAGH   Map 1 D3

Coollattin Golf Course Coollattin
☎ 053 9429125 📠 053 9429930
web: www.coollattingolfclub.com

18 Holes, 5622mtrs, Par 70, SSS 68, Course record 70.
Course Designer Peter McEvoy **Location** off R749
Telephone for further details
Hotel ★★★ CHH Marlfield House Hotel, GOREY ☎ 053 9421124
📠 053 9421572 19 en suite

WICKLOW   Map 1 D3

Wicklow Golf Course Dunbur Rd
☎ 0404 67379 📠 0404 64756
e-mail: info@wicklowgolfclub.ie
web: www.wicklowgolfclub.ie

Situated on the cliffs overlooking Wicklow Bay, this course provides
a challenging test of golf, each hole having individual features.
Spectacular views of the coastline from every hole.

18 Holes, 5437mtrs, Par 71, SSS 70. Club membership 700.
Visitors Mon-Sun & BHs. Booking advisable. Dress code.
Societies booking advisable. **Green Fees** €30 Mon-Thu, €35 Fri-Sun &
BHs. Winter rate from €20 **Course Designer** Craddock & Ruddy **Prof** E
McLoughlin **Facilities** 🕐 🍴 🍺 ⬜ 🍽 ⛳ 🏨 ⛳ ✦ 🚜
✦ **Conf** Corporate Hospitality Days **Location** SE of town centre
Hotel ★★★★ FH Kilpatrick House, Redcross, WICKLOW
☎ 0404 47137 & 087 6358325 📠 0404 47866 4 rooms (3 en suite)

WOODENBRIDGE   Map 1 D3

Woodenbridge Golf Club Woodenbridge, Arklow
☎ 0402 35202 📠 0402 35754
e-mail: reception@woodenbridge.ie
web: www.woodenbridge.ie

A level parkland course with undulating fairways and greens,
traversed by two lovely meandering rivers.

18 Holes, 5787metres, Par 71, SSS 70.
Club membership 1200.

Visitors Mon-Fri, Sun & BH. Booking required. **Societies** welcome
Green Fees €55 per 18 holes (€65 Sun & BHs) **Course
Designer** Patrick Merrigan **Facilities** 🕐 🍴 🍺 ⬜ 🍽 ⛳ 🏨
✦ **Conf** Corporate Hospitality Days **Location** N of village

DRUIDS GLEN GOLF CLUB

CO WICKLOW - NEWTOWN MOUNT KENNEDY - MAP 1 D3

Druids Glen Golf Resort is home to two championship courses, Druids Glen and Druids Heath. Druids Glen held the Irish Open an unprecedented four occasions from 1996-1999, the quality of the tournament reflected in its winners with Colin Montgomerie being a two time champion and the tournament was also the scene for Sergio Garcia's maiden tour victory in 1999. Druids Glen also played host to the inaugural 'Seve Trophy' in 2002. The stunning parkland layout which is known as 'the Augusta of Europe' features tree-lined holes which demand driving accuracy while the back nine sees numerous approach shots over water testing the nerve of the most experienced player. In contrast Druids Heath is a heathland course with strong links influences. It is set on rolling countryside overlooking the Irish Sea with the Wicklow Mountains as its backdrop and provides stunning panoramic views as well as being a stern test of golf.

☎ 01 2870847   🖷 01 2873699
e-mail: reservations@druidsglenresort.ie   **web:** www.druidsglenresort.com
Druids Glen: 18 Holes, 5998metres, Par 71, SSS 73, Course record 62.
Druids Heath: 18 Holes, 6062mtrs, Par 71, SSS 74, Course record 71. Club membership 219.
Visitors Mon-Sun & BHs. Booking required. Dress code. **Societies** booking required. **Green Fees** Druids Glen from €55 (weekends €70), Druids Heath from €35 (€45) **Course Designer** Tom Craddock/Pat Ruddy **Prof** George Henry **Facilities** 🛈 🍴 🛒 🖵 🍴 🏌 🏠 🛐 ◇ 🏌 🏌 🏌 🏌 **Leisure** heated indoor swimming pool, sauna, gymnasium **Conf** facs Corporate Hospitality Days **Location** S of village on R761
Hotel ★★★★ 77% HL Glenview, Glen O' the Downs, DELGANY ☎ 01 2873399 🖷 01 2877511 70 en suite

KEY TO ATLAS

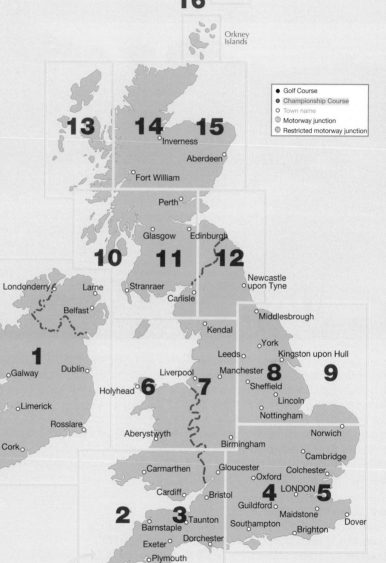

Shetland Islands

16

Orkney Islands

- ● Golf Course
- ● Championship Course
- ○ Town name
- Ⓜ Motorway junction
- Ⓡ Restricted motorway junction

13 **14** **15**

Inverness

Aberdeen

Fort William

Perth

Glasgow Edinburgh

10 **11** **12**

Newcastle upon Tyne

Londonderry Larne

Belfast

Stranraer

Carlisle

Kendal

Middlesbrough

York

Leeds Kingston upon Hull

1

Galway Dublin

Liverpool Manchester **8** **9**

Holyhead **6** **7** Sheffield

Limerick

Lincoln

Rosslare

Nottingham

Aberystwyth Norwich

Cork

Birmingham

Cambridge

Carmarthen Gloucester Colchester

Cardiff Oxford

Bristol **4** LONDON **5**

2 **3** Taunton Guildford

Barnstaple Southampton Maidstone Dover

Dorchester Brighton

Exeter

Plymouth

Penzance

Isles of Scilly

Channel Islands **16**

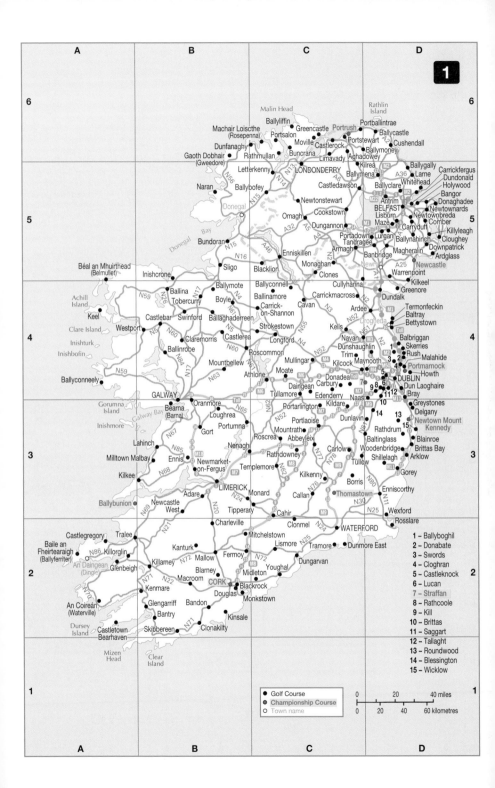

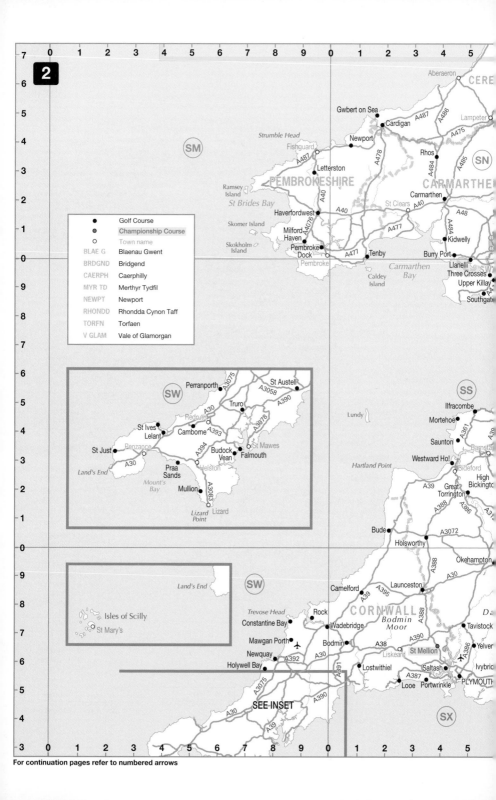

2

●		Golf Course
●		Championship Course
○		Town name
BLAE G		Blaenau Gwent
BRDGND		Bridgend
CAERPH		Caerphilly
MYR TD		Merthyr Tydfil
NEWPT		Newport
RHONDD		Rhondda Cynon Taff
TORFN		Torfaen
V GLAM		Vale of Glamorgan

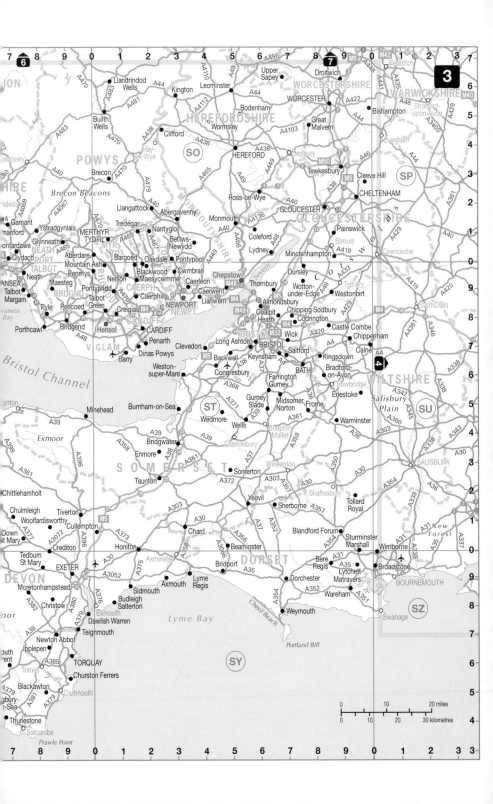

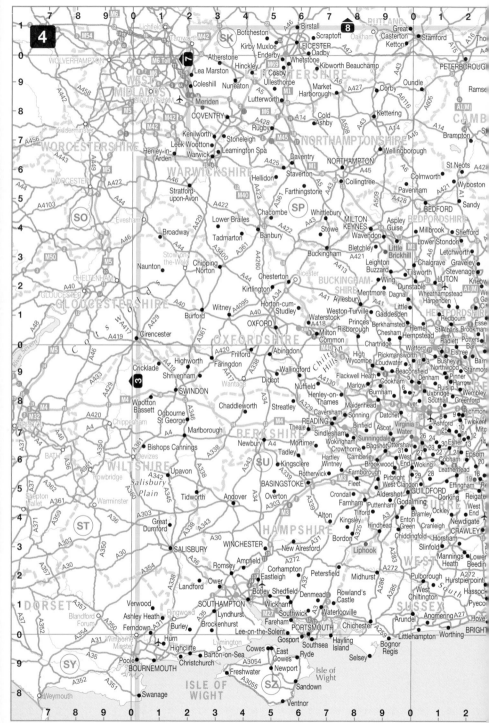

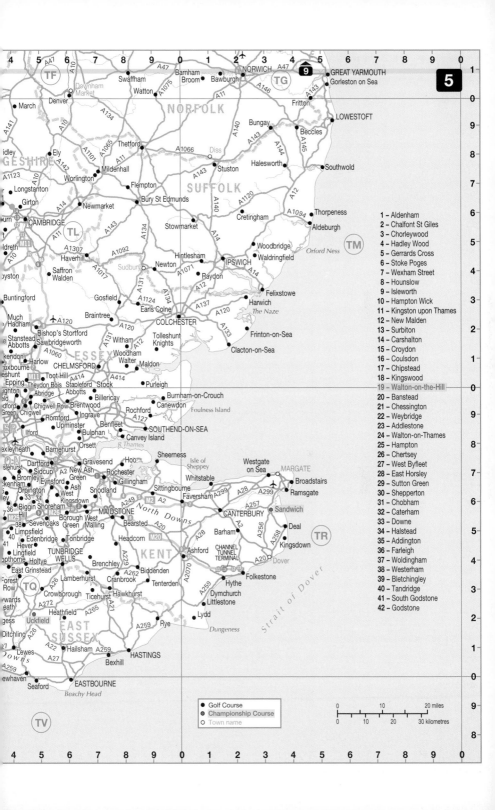

5

1 – Aldenham
2 – Chalfont St Giles
3 – Chorleywood
4 – Hadley Wood
5 – Gerrards Cross
6 – Stoke Poges
7 – Wexham Street
8 – Hounslow
9 – Isleworth
10 – Hampton Wick
11 – Kingston upon Thames
12 – New Malden
13 – Surbiton
14 – Carshalton
15 – Croydon
16 – Coulsdon
17 – Chipstead
18 – Kingswood
19 – Walton-on-the-Hill
20 – Banstead
21 – Chessington
22 – Weybridge
23 – Addlestone
24 – Walton-on-Thames
25 – Hampton
26 – Chertsey
27 – West Byfleet
28 – East Horsley
29 – Sutton Green
30 – Shepperton
31 – Chobham
32 – Caterham
33 – Downe
34 – Halstead
35 – Addington
36 – Farleigh
37 – Woldingham
38 – Westerham
39 – Bletchingley
40 – Tandridge
41 – South Godstone
42 – Godstone

● Golf Course
● Championship Course
○ Town name

| 0 | | 10 | | 20 miles |
| 0 | 10 | 20 | 30 kilometres |

A595

Point of Ayre

A10

Seascale

Isle of Man

Ramsey

Maughold Head

ISLE OF MAN

A3

A3

Peel

A4

A1

A2

Silecro

Port Erin

A3

A5

DOUGLAS

Port St Mary

Castletown

Dreswick Point

SC

*Irish
Sea*

Carmel Head

Amlwch

Great Ormes Head

Holyhead

Anglesey

A5025

Llandudno

Colwyn Bay

Rhyl

Presta

Holy Island

Brynteg

Beaumaris

Conwy

Abergele

Rhuddlan

Whitf

Rhosneigr

A55

Bangor

Penmaenmawr

A55

Bodelwyddan

St Asa

ISLE OF ANGLESEY

A4080

Llanfairfechan

Denbigh

A525

Caernarfon

A5

A470

A543

Ruthi

*Caernarfon
Bay*

A4085

A4086

CONWY

DENBIG

SH

Betws-y-Coed

A5

A4

Morfa Nefyn

A499

A487

A498

Blaenau Ffestiniog

A470

Lleyn Peninsula

A497

Porthmadog

Ffestiniog

A4212

A494

Bala

Criccieth

Pwllheli

Harlech

A470

Abersoch

GWYNEDD

A496

A470

Bardsey Island

Dolgellau

A458

A470

Golf Course
Championship Course
Town name
FLINTS **Flintshire**

A487

POWYS

A493

Machynlleth

A470

Aberdyfi

A470

Cardigan Bay

Borth

A487

A44

Newt

A483

0   10   20 miles
0   10   20   30 kilometres

Llanidloes

SN

Aberystwyth

CEREDIGION

A470

Rhayader

For continuation pages refer to numbered arrows

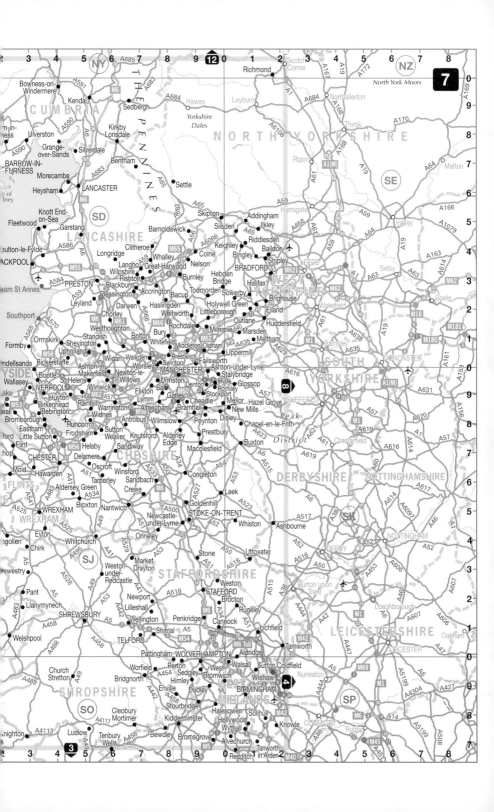

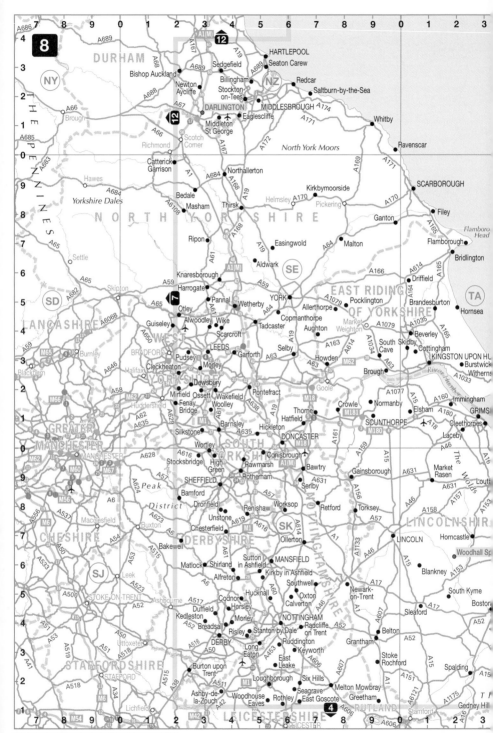

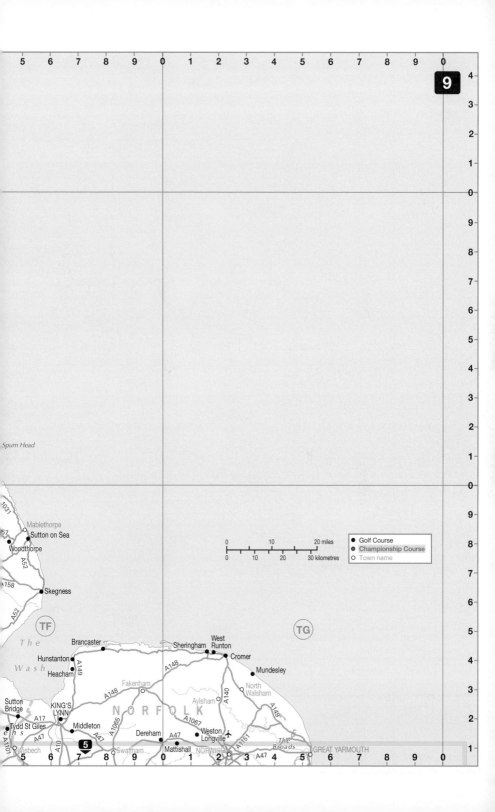

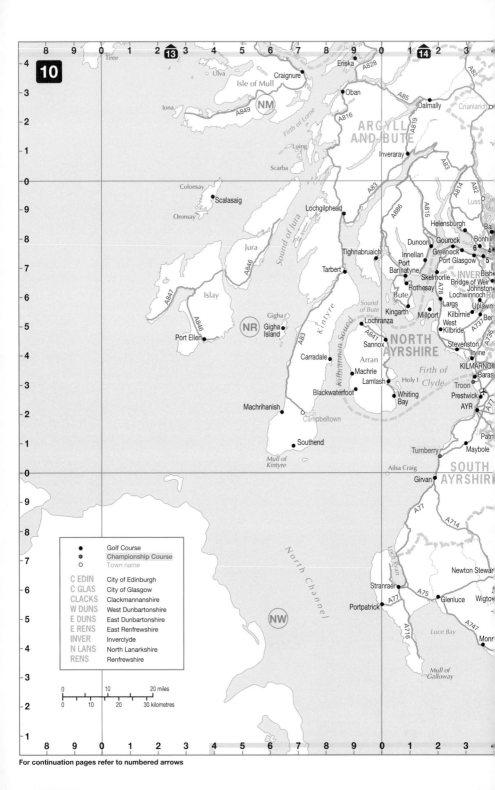

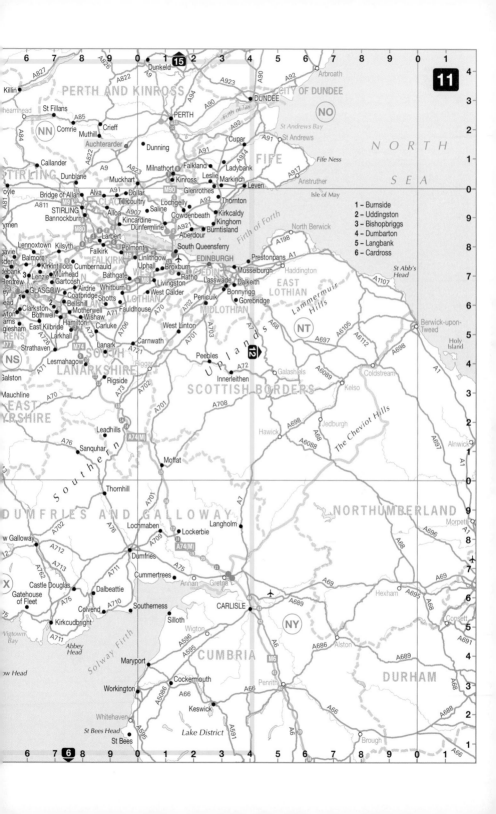

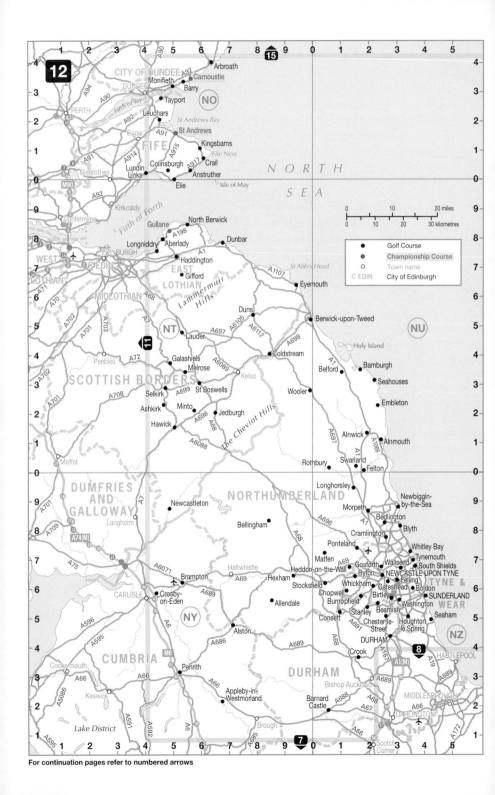

For continuation pages refer to numbered arrows

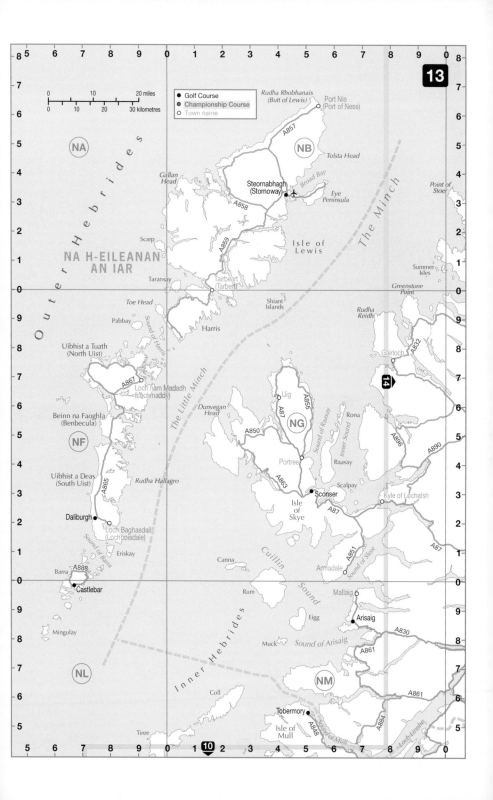

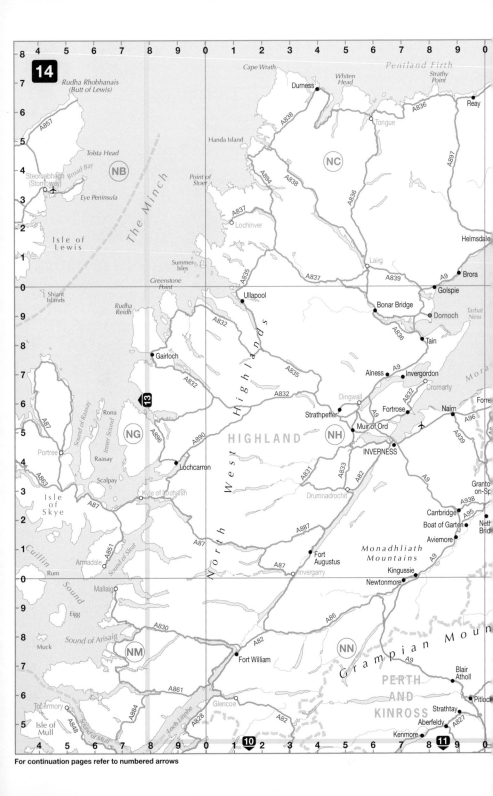

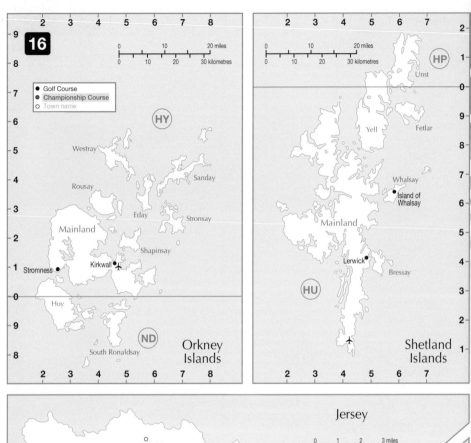

16

Golf Course
Championship Course
Town name

0   10   20 miles
0   10   20   30 kilometres

HY

Westray

Rousay

Sanday

Eday

Stronsay

Mainland

Shapinsay

Stromness

Kirkwall

Hoy

ND

South Ronaldsay

Orkney Islands

0   10   20 miles
0   10   20   30 kilometres

HP

Unst

Yell

Fetlar

Whalsay

Island of Whalsay

Mainland

Lerwick

Bressay

HU

Shetland Islands

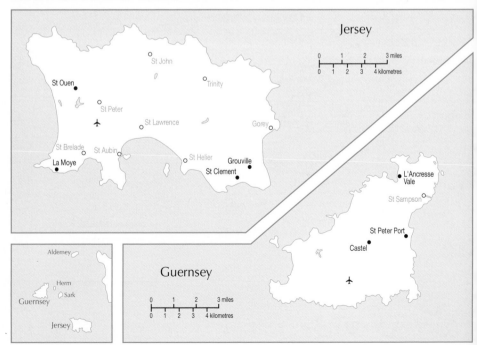

Jersey

St John

St Ouen

Trinity

St Peter

St Lawrence

Gorey

St Brelade

St Aubin

St Helier

Grouville

La Moye

St Clement

0   1   2   3 miles
0   1   2   3   4 kilometres

L'Ancresse Vale

St Sampson

St Peter Port

Castel

Alderney

Herm

Guernsey

Sark

Jersey

Guernsey

0   1   2   3 miles
0   1   2   3   4 kilometres

Driving Ranges

CUMBRIA

BRAMPTON
Brampton — 54
CARLISLE
Carlisle — 54
CROSBY-ON-EDEN
Eden — 55
KENDAL
Carus Green Golf Course & Driving Range — 55
PENRITH
Penrith — 56

DERBYSHIRE

BREADSALL
Breadsall Priory, A Marriott Hotel & Country Club — 58
CHESTERFIELD
Grassmoor Golf Centre — 59
HORSLEY
Horsley Lodge — 61
LONG EATON
Trent Lock Golf Centre — 61
MORLEY
Morley Hayes — 62
NEW MILLS
New Mills — 62
STANTON BY DALE
Erewash Valley — 62

DEVON

BLACKAWTON
Dartmouth Golf & Country Club — 63
CULLOMPTON
Padbrook Park — 64
HOLSWORTHY
Holsworthy — 66
ILFRACOMBE
Ilfracombe — 66
IPPLEPEN
Dainton Park — 66
NEWTON ABBOT
Hele Park Golf Centre — 67
OKEHAMPTON
Ashbury Golf Hotel — 68
SAUNTON
Saunton — 68

DORSET

BERE REGIS
The Dorset Golf & Country Club — 71
BOURNEMOUTH
Playgolf Bournemouth — 72
Solent Meads Golf Centre — 72
BRIDPORT
Bridport & West Dorset — 72
FERNDOWN
Dudsbury — 73

Ferndown Forest — 73
Ferndown — 74
LYME REGIS
Lyme Regis — 74
POOLE
Parkstone — 74
SHERBORNE
Sherborne — 75
STURMINSTER MARSHALL
Sturminster Marshall — 75
VERWOOD
Crane Valley — 75
WEYMOUTH
Weymouth — 76
WIMBORNE
Canford Magna — 76

CO DURHAM

CHESTER-LE-STREET
Roseberry Grange — 77
DARLINGTON
Headlam Hall Hotel — 78
Rockcliffe Hall — 79
Stressholme — 78
DURHAM
Ramside Hall — 80
MIDDLETON ST GEORGE
Dinsdale Spa — 80
SEDGEFIELD
Knotty Hill Golf Centre — 81

ESSEX

ABRIDGE
Abridge Golf and Country Club — 82
BILLERICAY
Stock Brook Golf & Country Club — 82
BRAINTREE
Braintree — 82
BRENTWOOD
Warley Park — 83
CHELMSFORD
Channels — 84
Regiment Way Golf Centre — 84
COLCHESTER
Lexden Wood — 85
Stoke by Nayland — 85
EARLS COLNE
Essex Golf & Country Club — 86
EPPING
Blakes — 86
The Epping — 86
Nazeing — 86
HARLOW
North Weald — 87
MALDON
Forrester Park — 88
SAFFRON WALDEN
Saffron Walden — 88
STOCK
Crondon Park — 89

TOLLESHUNT KNIGHTS
Five Lakes Hotel, Golf, Country Club & Spa — 89
TOOT HILL
Toot Hill — 89
WOODHAM WALTER
Warren — 90

GLOUCESTERSHIRE

ALMONDSBURY
Bristol — 90
CHELTENHAM
Lilley Brook — 90
CIRENCESTER
Cirencester — 91
South Cerney — 91
COALPIT HEATH
The Kendleshire — 91
CODRINGTON
The Players — 92
GLOUCESTER
Brickhampton Court Golf Complex — 92
Ramada Gloucester — 92
Rodway Hill — 94
MINCHINHAMPTON
Minchinhampton (New Course) — 94
WESTONBIRT
Westonbirt — 95
WICK
Tracy Park Golf & Country Club — 96

GREATER LONDON

ADDINGTON
Addington Court Golf Centre — 96
The Addington — 96
BARNET
The Shire London — 97
BIGGIN HILL
Cherry Lodge — 98
CARSHALTON
Oaks Sports Centre — 98
CHESSINGTON
Chessington Golf Centre — 98
COULSDON
Woodcote Park — 99
CROYDON
Selsdon Park Hotel — 99
DOWNE
West Kent — 99
HADLEY WOOD
Hadley Wood — 100
HAMPTON WICK
Hampton Court Palace — 101
HOUNSLOW
Airlinks — 101
NORTHWOOD
Sandy Lodge — 102
RICHMOND (UPON THAMES)
Royal Mid-Surrey — 103

ROMFORD	
Maylands	103
Risebridge Golf Centre	104
RUISLIP	
Ruislip	104

GREATER MANCHESTER

ALTRINCHAM	
Dunham Forest Golf & Country Club	106
BOLTON	
Regent Park	108
BURY	
Lowes Park	108
MIDDLETON	
The Manchester	111
OLDHAM	
Crompton & Royton	112
ROCHDALE	
Castle Hawk	112

HAMPSHIRE

ALDERSHOT	
ALTON	
Worldham	116
ANDOVER	
Hampshire	117
BARTON-ON-SEA	
Barton-on-Sea	117
BASINGSTOKE	
Dummer	117
Weybrook Park	117
BOTLEY	
Macdonald Botley Park Hotel, Golf & Spa	118
BROCKENHURST	
Brokenhurst Manor	118
EASTLEIGH	
East Horton Golf Centre	119
KINGSCLERE	
Sandford Springs	120
LEE-ON-THE-SOLENT	
Lee-on-the-Solent	120
LIPHOOK	
Liphook	122
Old Thorns Golf & Country Estate	121
NEW ALRESFORD	
Alresford	122
OVERTON	
Test Valley	122
PORTSMOUTH	
Great Salterns Public Course	123
SHEDFIELD	
Meon Valley, A Marriott Hotel & Country Club	124
TADLEY	
Bishopswood	124
WICKHAM	
Wickham Park	125

WINCHESTER	
Hockley	125
South Winchester	125

HEREFORDSHIRE

KINGTON	
Kington	126
ROSS-ON-WYE	
South Herefordshire	126

HERTFORDSHIRE

BISHOP'S STORTFORD	
Bishop's Stortford	127
Great Hadham Golf & Country Club	127
BUSHEY	
Bushey Golf & Country Club	128
ELSTREE	
Elstree Golf and Country Club	129
HARPENDEN	
Harpenden	129
LETCHWORTH	
Letchworth	130
LITTLE GADDESDEN	
Ashridge	130
REDBOURN	
Redbourn	131
RICKMANSWORTH	
The Grove	131
Moor Park	131
ROYSTON	
Heydon Grange Golf & Country Club	132
ST ALBANS	
Verulam	132
WARE	
Hanbury Manor, A Marriott Hotel & Country Club	133
Whitehill Golf	134
WATFORD	
West Herts	134
WELWYN GARDEN CITY	
Mill Green	134

KENT

ADDINGTON	
West Malling	135
ASH	
The London	135
ASHFORD	
Homelands Golf Centre	136
BARHAM	
Broome Park	136
BIDDENDEN	
Chart Hills	136
CANTERBURY	
Canterbury	137
DARTFORD	
Birchwood Park Golf Centre	137

DEAL	
Royal Cinque Ports	138
EDENBRIDGE	
Sweetwoods Park	138
HEVER	
Hever Castle	139
HOO	
Deangate Ridge	140
LITTLESTONE	
Littlestone	141
Littlestone Warren	141
MAIDSTONE	
Tudor Park, A Marriott Hotel & Country Club	142
NEW ASH GREEN	
Redlibbets	142
RAMSGATE	
Stonelees Golf Centre	142
ROCHESTER	
Rochester & Cobham Park	142
SANDWICH	
Royal St George's	143
SITTINGBOURNE	
The Oast Golf Centre	145
SNODLAND	
Oastpark	145
TENTERDEN	
London Beach Country Hotel	145
TONBRIDGE	
Poult Wood Golf Centre	146
WEST KINGSDOWN	
Woodlands Manor	146
WEST MALLING	
Kings Hill	146
WESTERHAM	
Westerham	147

LANCASHIRE

CLITHEROE	
Clitheroe	150
GARSTANG	
Best Western Garstang Country Hotel & Golf Centre	150
HEYSHAM	
Heysham	152
LEYLAND	
Leyland	152
LONGRIDGE	
Longridge	152
LYTHAM ST ANNES	
Royal Lytham & St Annes	153
ORMSKIRK	
Hurlston Hall Golf & Country Club	155
PLEASINGTON	
Pleasington	155
PRESTON	
Preston	156

LEICESTERSHIRE

BOTCHESTON
Forest Hill | 158
COSBY
Cosby | 158
EAST GOSCOTE
Beedles Lake Golf Centre | 158
KIBWORTH BEAUCHAMP
Kibworth | 159
KIRBY MUXLOE
Kirby Muxloe | 159
LEICESTER
Humberstone Heights | 159
The Leicestershire | 159
LUTTERWORTH
Kilworth Springs | 160
MELTON MOWBRAY
Melton Mowbray | 160
Stapleford Park | 160
SEAGRAVE
Park Hill | 161
SIX HILLS
Six Hills | 161
WHETSTONE
Whetstone | 162

LINCOLNSHIRE

BELTON
De Vere Belton Woods Hotel | 162
BOSTON
Boston | 163
Boston West Golf Centre | 163
CLEETHORPES
Tetney | 163
GAINSBOROUGH
Gainsborough | 164
GRANTHAM
Sudbrook Moor | 164
GRIMSBY
Waltham Windmill | 165
LACEBY
Manor | 165
LINCOLN
Canwick Park | 165
LOUTH
Kenwick Park | 166
SCUNTHORPE
Forest Pines Hotel & Golf Resort | 167
Grange Park | 167
SPALDING
Spalding | 168
TORKSEY
Millfield Golf Complex | 170
WOODHALL SPA
The National Golf Centre | 169

LONDON

E4 CHINGFORD
West Essex | 171
N14 SOUTHGATE
Trent Park | 172
N21 WINCHMORE HILL
Bush Hill Park | 172
NW7 MILL HILL
Mill Hill | 173
SE28 WOOLWICH
Thamesview Golf Centre | 173
SW19 WIMBLEDON
Royal Wimbledon | 174

MERSEYSIDE

BLUNDELLSANDS
West Lancashire | 175
FORMBY
Formby | 176
Formby Hall Resort & Spa | 176
Formby Ladies | 176
HOYLAKE
Royal Liverpool | 177
ST HELENS
Sherdley Park | 180
SOUTHPORT
Royal Birkdale | 181
Southport & Ainsdale | 180

NORFOLK

BARNHAM BROOM
Barnham Broom Hotel, Golf &
  Spa | 182
BAWBURGH
Bawburgh | 182
BRANCASTER
Royal West Norfolk | 182
FRITTON
Caldecott Hall Golf & Leisure | 183
HEACHAM
Heacham Manor Golf Club &
  Hotel | 184
HUNSTANTON
Hunstanton | 184
Searles Leisure Resort | 185
KING'S LYNN
Eagles Golf Centre | 185
MIDDLETON
Middleton Hall | 186
MUNDESLEY
Mundesley | 186
NORWICH
Wensum Valley Hotel, Golf &
  Country Club | 187
THETFORD
Feltwell | 188
WATTON
Richmond Park | 188

NORTHAMPTONSHIRE

CHACOMBE
Cherwell Edge | 189
COLD ASHBY
Cold Ashby | 189
FARTHINGSTONE
Farthingstone Hotel | 190
HELLIDON
Hellidon Lakes Golf & Spa Hotel | 190
KETTERING
Pytchley Golf Lodge | 190
NORTHAMPTON
Brampton Heath Golf Centre | 191
Delapre Golf Centre | 191
Northamptonshire County | 192
WHITTLEBURY
Whittlebury Park Golf & Country
  Club | 193

NORTHUMBERLAND

BERWICK-UPON-TWEED
Berwick-upon-Tweed (Goswick) | 194
FELTON
Burgham Park Golf & Leisure
  Club | 195
HEDDON-ON-THE-WALL
Close House Hotel & Golf | 195
LONGHORSLEY
Macdonald Linden Hall, Golf &
  Country Club | 196
MATFEN
Matfen Hall Country House Hotel | 196
PONTELAND
Ponteland | 197
ROTHBURY
Rothbury | 197

NOTTINGHAMSHIRE

CALVERTON
Ramsdale Park Golf Centre | 198
Springwater | 198
KIRKBY IN ASHFIELD
Notts (Hollinwell) | 198
NEWARK-ON-TRENT
Newark | 199
NOTTINGHAM
Edwalton Municipal | 199
OLLERTON
Rufford Park Golf & Country Club | 200
OXTON
Oakmere Park | 200
RADCLIFFE ON TRENT
Cotgrave Place | 201
WORKSOP
Bondhay | 202
College Pines | 202

OXFORDSHIRE

ABINGDON
Drayton Park | 202
CHESTERTON
Bicester Golf & Country Club | 203
CHIPPING NORTON
Wychwood | 204
DIDCOT
Hadden Hill | 204
FARINGDON
Carswell Golf & Country Club | 204
HENLEY-ON-THAMES
Henley | 205
KIRTLINGTON
Kirtlington | 206
MILTON COMMON
The Oxfordshire | 206
OXFORD
Hinksey Heights | 206
TADMARTON
Tadmarton Heath | 207
WATERSTOCK
Waterstock | 208

RUTLAND

GREAT CASTERTON
Rutland County | 208
GREETHAM
Greetham Valley Hotel, Golf & Conference Centre | 208
KETTON

SHROPSHIRE

BRIDGNORTH
OSWESTRY
Mile End | 210
WESTON-UNDER-REDCASTLE
Hawkstone Park Hotel & Golf Centre | 211

SOMERSET

BATH
Bath | 212
BRIDGWATER
Cannington | 212
BURNHAM-ON-SEA
Burnham & Berrow | 213
CHARD
Windwhistle | 213
CONGRESBURY
Mendip Spring | 213
FARRINGTON GURNEY
Farrington Golf & Country Club | 214
FROME
Frome | 214
Orchardleigh | 214
GURNEY SLADE
Mendip | 214

LONG ASHTON
Long Ashton | 214
Woodspring Golf & Country Club | 215
SALTFORD
Saltford | 215
SOMERTON
Wheathill | 215
TAUNTON
Oake Manor | 216
Taunton Vale | 216
WELLS
Wells (Somerset) | 216
WESTON-SUPER-MARE
Weston-Super-Mare | 217
YEOVIL
Yeovil | 217

STAFFORDSHIRE

BURTON UPON TRENT
Belmont Driving Range | 217
Branston Golf & Country Club | 218
The Craythorne | 218
ENVILLE
Enville | 218
NEWCASTLE-UNDER-LYME
Jack Barkers Keele Golf Centre | 219
PATTINGHAM
Patshull Park Hotel Golf & Country Club | 220
PENKRIDGE
The Chase | 220
PERTON
Perton Park | 220
RUGELEY
St Thomas's Priory | 221
STOKE-ON-TRENT
Trentham | 221
STONE
Barlaston | 222
Izaak Walton | 222

SUFFOLK

CRETINGHAM
Cretingham | 224
HALESWORTH
Halesworth | 225
IPSWICH
Fynn Valley | 226
MILDENHALL
West Suffolk Golf Centre | 226
STOWMARKET
Stowmarket | 227
STUSTON
Diss | 227
WOODBRIDGE
Best Western Ufford Park Hotel Golf & Spa | 228
Seckford | 228
Woodbridge | 228

SURREY

BRAMLEY
Bramley | 230
CAMBERLEY
Pine Ridge | 230
CATERHAM
Surrey National | 231
CRANLEIGH
Wildwood Golf & Country Club | 232
DORKING
Betchworth Park | 232
ENTON GREEN
West Surrey | 232
EPSOM
Horton Park | 233
GODALMING
Broadwater Park | 234
GUILDFORD
Guildford | 234
Rokers | 234
HINDHEAD
The Hindhead | 235
KINGSWOOD
Kingswood Golf and Country House | 235
Surrey Downs | 235
LEATHERHEAD
Pachesham Park Golf Complex | 235
LINGFIELD
Lingfield Park | 236
NEWDIGATE
Rusper | 236
OCKLEY
Gatton Manor Hotel & | 236
OTTERSHAW
Foxhills Club and Resort | 236
PUTTENHAM
Puttenham | 238
SOUTH GODSTONE
Horne Park | 238
TILFORD
Hankley Common | 240
VIRGINIA WATER
Wentworth | 239
WALTON-ON-THAMES
Burhill | 240
WEST BYFLEET
West Byfleet | 240
WEST CLANDON
Clandon Regis | 242
WEST END
Windlemere | 242
WOKING
Hoebridge Golf Centre | 242
WOLDINGHAM
Woldingham | 243

SUSSEX, EAST

SUSSEX, WEST

TYNE & WEAR

WARWICKSHIRE

WEST MIDLANDS

WIGHT, ISLE OF

WILTSHIRE

WORCESTERSHIRE

YORKSHIRE, EAST RIDING OF

HOWDEN	
Boothferry	280
RAYWELL	
Hessle	281
SKIDBY	
Skidby Lakes	282

YORKSHIRE, NORTH

ALDWARK	
COPMANTHORPE	
Pike Hills	283
EASINGWOLD	
Easingwold	283
HARROGATE	
Rudding Park Hotel, Spa & Golf	284
MALTON	
Malton & Norton	285
PANNAL	
Pannal	286
REDCAR	
Cleveland	286
RIPON	
Ripon City	286
SALTBURN-BY-THE-SEA	
Hunley Hotel &	287
SELBY	
Selby	288
YORK	
Forest of Galtres	289
Forest Park	289
Swallow Hall	289
York	289

YORKSHIRE, SOUTH

BARNSLEY	
Sandhill	290
BAWTRY	
Bawtry	290
HATFIELD	
Kings Wood	291
RAWMARSH	
Wath	291
SHEFFIELD	
Concord Park	292
Rother Valley Golf Centre	293
SILKSTONE	
Silkstone	293

YORKSHIRE, WEST

BRIGHOUSE	
Willow Valley Golf	296
GUISELEY	
Bradford (Hawksworth)	297
HUDDERSFIELD	
Bradley Park	297
Huddersfield	298
LEEDS	
Cookridge Hall	299
De Vere Oulton Hall	299

Moor Allerton	300
Moortown	300
OTLEY	
Otley	301
PONTEFRACT	
Mid Yorkshire	302
SCARCROFT	
Scarcroft	303
WETHERBY	
Wetherby	304
WOOLLEY	
Woolley Park	305

CHANNEL ISLANDS

GUERNSEY

L'ANCRESSE VALE	
Royal Guernsey	305
CASTEL	
La Grande Mare Hotel Golf & Country Club	305
ST PETER PORT	
St Pierre Park	305

JERSEY

GROUVILLE	
ST CLEMENT	
St Clements Golf & Sports Centre	306
ST OUEN	
Les Mielles Golf & Country Club	306

ISLE OF MAN

CASTLETOWN	290
DOUGLAS	
Mount Murray Hotel & Country Club	307

SCOTLAND

CITY OF ABERDEEN

ABERDEEN	
Murcar Links	310

ABERDEENSHIRE

BANCHORY	
Inchmarlo Resort &	312
BANFF	
Duff House Royal	312
CRUDEN BAY	
Cruden Bay	312
FRASERBURGH	
Fraserburgh	313
NEWBURGH	
Newburgh on Ythan	314

NEWMACHAR	
Newmachar	314
OLDMELDRUM	
Old Meldrum	314

ANGUS

ARBROATH	
Arbroath	316
BARRY	
Panmure	316
CARNOUSTIE	
Carnoustie Golf Links	317
EDZELL	
Edzell	316

ARGYLL & BUTE

ERISKA	
Isle of Eriska Hotel, Spa & Island	319

DUMFRIES & GALLOWAY

CUMMERTREES	
Powfoot	322
DUMFRIES	
Dumfriesshire Golf Centre	322
WIGTOWN	

CITY OF DUNDEE

DUNDEE	
Ballumbie Castle	325

EAST LOTHIAN

DUNBAR	
Dunbar	329
GIFFORD	
Castle Park	329
GULLANE	
Gullane	330
NORTH BERWICK	
Whitekirk Golf & Country Club	332
PRESTONPANS	
Royal Musselburgh	332

CITY OF EDINBURGH

EDINBURGH	
Bruntsfield Links Golfing Society	334
Marriott Dalmahoy Hotel Golf & Country Club	335
Swanston New	337

FALKIRK

FALKIRK	
Falkirk	338

FIFE

COLINSBURGH
Charleton 339
CRAIL
Crail Golfing Society 339
DUNFERMLINE
Forrester Park 340
LEUCHARS
Drumoig Hotel 342
ST ANDREWS
The Duke's 343
Fairmont St Andrews 344
St Andrews Links 345
SALINE
Saline 344

CITY OF GLASGOW

GLASGOW
Cowglen 346

HIGHLAND

ALNESS
Alness 347
AVIEMORE
Spey Valley 347
INVERNESS
Loch Ness 351
NAIRN
The Nairn 352
THURSO
Thurso 353

MIDLOTHIAN

LASSWADE
Kings Acre 355

MORAY

BALLINDALLOCH
Ballindalloch Castle 355
BUCKIE
Strathlene Buckie 355
ELGIN
Elgin 356
FORRES
Forres 356

NORTH AYRSHIRE

GREAT CUMBRAE ISLAND (MILLPORT)
Millport 357

PERTH & KINROSS

ALYTH
The Alyth Golf Club 1894 361
Strathmore Golf Centre 361

AUCHTERARDER
Gleneagles Hotel 363
BLAIRGOWRIE
Blairgowrie 362
MILNATHORT
Milnathort 365
PERTH
Murrayshall House Hotel 366

SCOTTISH BORDERS

KELSO
The Roxburghe Hotel 369
PEEBLES
Macdonald Cardrona Hotel 370

SOUTH AYRSHIRE

TROON
Royal Troon 371
TURNBERRY
Turnberry Resort 373

SOUTH LANARKSHIRE

HAMILTON
Hamilton 375
Strathclyde Park 375

STIRLING

BANNOCKBURN
Brucefields Family Golf Centre 377
CALLANDER
Callander 377

WEST LOTHIAN

LIVINGSTON
Pumpherston 379
WHITBURN
Polkemmet Country Park 380

SCOTTISH ISLANDS

BARRA, ISLE OF

CASTLEBAY
Barra 381

SOUTH UIST

DALIBURGH
Askernish 383

WALES

BRIDGEND

BRIDGEND
Southerndown 387
PORTHCAWL
Royal Porthcawl 388
PYLE
Pyle & Kenfig 388

CAERPHILLY

BARGOED
OAKDALE
Oakdale 389

CARDIFF

CARDIFF
Radyr 390

CARMARTHENSHIRE

AMMANFORD
Glynhir 391
CARMARTHEN
Carmarthen 391
KIDWELLY
Glyn Abbey 392

CEREDIGION

ABERYSTWYTH
Aberystwyth 392
LLANRHYSTUD
Penrhos Golf & Country Club 393

CONWY

ABERGELE
Abergele 393
LLANDUDNO
North Wales 394

DENBIGHSHIRE

BODELWYDDAN
Kinmel Park Golf Course &
  Driving Range 395
RHUDDLAN
Rhuddlan 395

GWYNEDD

CAERNARFON
Royal Town of Caernarfon 398
PORTHMADOG
Porthmadog 400

MONMOUTHSHIRE

ABERGAVENNY
Wernddu Golf Centre 402
BETTWS NEWYDD
Alice Springs 402
CHEPSTOW
St Pierre, A Marriott Hotel &
Country Club 401

NEWPORT

CAERLEON
Caerleon 404
NEWPORT
Celtic Manor Resort 405
Parc 404

PEMBROKESHIRE

NEWPORT (PEMBROKESHIRE)
Newport Links 406
TENBY
Tenby 406

POWYS

BRECON
Cradoc 407

SWANSEA

SOUTHGATE
Pennard 409
SWANSEA
Clyne 409
UPPER KILLAY
Fairwood Park 410

TORFAEN

CWMBRAN
Green Meadow Golf & Country
Club 410

VALE OF GLAMORGAN

BARRY
St Andrews Major 411
HENSOL
Vale Resort 413
ST NICHOLAS
Cottrell Park Golf Resort 412

WREXHAM

CHIRK
Chirk 414
EYTON
Plassey Oaks Golf Complex 414
WREXHAM
Clays Golf Centre 414

NORTHERN IRELAND

CO ANTRIM

BALLYCLARE
Greenacres 416
BALLYMENA
Galgorm Castle 417
PORTRUSH
Royal Portrush 419

CO ARMAGH

TANDRAGEE
Tandragee 420

BELFAST

BELFAST
Mount Ober Golf & Country Club 421

CO DOWN

BANBRIDGE
Banbridge 422
BANGOR
Blackwood Golf Centre 422
HOLYWOOD
Holywood 424

CO FERMANAGH

ENNISKILLEN
Ashwoods Golf Centre 426
Castle Hume 426

CO LONDONDERRY

LONDONDERRY
Foyle International Golf Centre 428

REPUBLIC OF IRELAND

CO CAVAN

BALLYCONNELL
Slieve Russell Hotel Golf &
Country Club 430
CAVAN
County Cavan 431

CO CLARE

NEWMARKET-ON-FERGUS
Dromoland Castle Golf & Country
Club 432

CO CORK

BANDON
Bandon 432
CASTLETOWNBERE (CASTLETOWN
BEARHAVEN)
Berehaven 434
CORK
Cork 434
Fota Island Resort 433
DOUGLAS
Douglas 435
KANTURK
Kanturk 435
KINSALE
Old Head Golf Links 435
MIDLETON
East Cork 436

CO DONEGAL

BALLYLIFFIN
Ballyliffin 437
GWEEDORE
Gweedore 438
NARIN (NARAN)
Narin & Portnoo 438
ROSEPENNA
Rosapenna 439

CO DUBLIN

BALLYBOGHILL
Hollywood Lakes 439
CASTLEKNOCK
Elm Green 439
DUBLIN
Howth 441
Rathfarnham 442
The Royal Dublin 442
St Margaret's Golf & Country
Club 442
PORTMARNOCK
Portmarnock 443

CO GALWAY

BALLYCONNEELY
Connemara Championship Links 445
ORANMORE
Galway Bay Golf Resort 446

CO KERRY

BALLYBUNION
Ballybunion 449
KILLARNEY
Killarney Golf & Fishing Club 448
WATERVILLE (AN COIREÁN)
Waterville House & Golf Links 450

CO KILDARE

CARBURY
Highfield Golf & Country Club 450
KILDARE
The Curragh 450
STRAFFAN
The K Club 451

CO KILKENNY

KILKENNY
Kilkenny 452
THOMASTOWN
Mount Juliet Hotel 453

CO LAOIS

KILLENARD
The Heritage Golf & Spa Resort 455
PORTLAOISE
The Heath 454

CO LEITRIM

CARRICK-ON-SHANNON
Carrick-on-Shannon 454

CO LIMERICK

LIMERICK
Limerick County Golf & Country
    Club 456

NEWCASTLE WEST
Newcastle West 456

CO LONGFORD

LONGFORD
County Longford 456

CO LOUTH

BALTRAY
County Louth 457
TERMONFECKIN
Seapoint 457

CO MAYO

BALLINROBE
Ballinrobe 457
WESTPORT
Westport 458

CO MONAGHAN

CARRICKMACROSS
Mannan Castle 460
MONAGHAN
Rossmore 460

CO WATERFORD

DUNGARVAN
Gold Coast Golf & Leisure 464
LISMORE
Lismore 464

WATERFORD
Waterford Castle 465
Waterford 465

CO WESTMEATH

ATHLONE
Glasson Country House Hotel 465
MOATE
Mount Temple 465
MULLINGAR
Mullingar 465

CO WEXFORD

ENNISCORTHY
Enniscorthy 465
ROSSLARE
Rosslare 466

CO WICKLOW

BLESSINGTON
Tulfarris Hotel & Golf Resort 466
BRAY
Bray 467
DUNLAVIN
Rathsallagh House Golf &
    Country Club 467
GREYSTONES
Charlesland 468
NEWTOWN MOUNT KENNEDY
Druids Glen 469

Location Index

Y

Golf Course Index